Lecture Notes in Artificial Intelligence   3452

Edited by J. G. Carbonell and J. Siekmann

Subseries of Lecture Notes in Computer Science

Franz Baader   Andrei Voronkov (Eds.)

Logic for Programming, Artificial Intelligence, and Reasoning

11th International Conference, LPAR 2004
Montevideo, Uruguay, March 14-18, 2005
Proceedings

 Springer

Series Editors

Jaime G. Carbonell, Carnegie Mellon University, Pittsburgh, PA, USA
Jörg Siekmann, University of Saarland, Saarbrücken, Germany

Volume Editors

Franz Baader
TU Dresden
Theoretical Computer Science
01062 Dresden, Germany
E-mail: baader@tcs.inf.tu-dresden.de

Andrei Voronkov
University of Manchester
Department of Computer Science
Oxford Rd, Manchester M13 9PL, UK
E-mail: voronkov@cs.man.ac.uk

Library of Congress Control Number: 2005921519

CR Subject Classification (1998): I.2.3, I.2, F.4.1, F.3, D.2.4, D.1.6

ISSN 0302-9743
ISBN 3-540-25236-3 Springer Berlin Heidelberg New York

This work is subject to copyright. All rights are reserved, whether the whole or part of the material is concerned, specifically the rights of translation, reprinting, re-use of illustrations, recitation, broadcasting, reproduction on microfilms or in any other way, and storage in data banks. Duplication of this publication or parts thereof is permitted only under the provisions of the German Copyright Law of September 9, 1965, in its current version, and permission for use must always be obtained from Springer. Violations are liable to prosecution under the German Copyright Law.

Springer is a part of Springer Science+Business Media

springeronline.com

© Springer-Verlag Berlin Heidelberg 2005
Printed in Germany

Typesetting: Camera-ready by author, data conversion by Markus Richter, Heidelberg
Printed on acid-free paper   SPIN: 11403487   06/3142   5 4 3 2 1 0

Preface

This volume contains the papers presented at the 11th International Conference on Logic for Programming, Artificial Intelligence, and Reasoning (LPAR), held from March 14 to 18, 2005, in Montevideo, Uruguay, together with the 5th International Workshop on the Implementation of Logics (organized by Stephan Schulz and Boris Konev) and the Workshop on Analytic Proof Systems (organized by Matthias Baaz).

The call for papers attracted 77 paper submissions, each of which was reviewed by at least three expert reviewers. The final decisions on the papers were taken during an electronic Program Committee meeting held on the Internet. The Internet-based submission, reviewing, and discussion software EasyChair, provided by the second PC co-chair, supported each stage of the reviewing process. But the most important work was, of course, done by the 34 PC members and their external reviewers, who provided high-quality reviews. After intense discussions to resolve conflicts among the reviewers, the Program Committee decided to accept 33 papers.

The conference program also included 4 invited talks, by Jürgen Giesl, Alexander Leitsch, Helmut Seidl, and Igor Walukiewicz, which are documented by short or extended abstracts in these proceedings. In addition, Martín Abadi held a tutorial on Reasoning About Security Protocols, and Ian Horrocks on Description Logic Reasoning.

Apart from the authors, invited speakers, tutorialists, Program Committee members, and external reviewers, we would like to thank the other people and organizations that made this LPAR a success: the Local Arrangements Chair, Alberto Pardo, and all the other people involved in the local organization; the Chair for Automata Theory at TU Dresden, the Kurt Gödel Society, and the European Union (in the Information Society Technologies programme of the European Commission, Future and Emerging Technologies under the IST-2001-33123 CoLogNET project), which provided partial funding for our invited speakers; and the Centro Latinoamericano de Estudios en Informatica (CLEI), which provided scholarships for several Latin American participants of the conference.

January 2005

Franz Baader
Andrei Voronkov

Conference Organization

Program Chairs

Franz Baader (Technische Universität Dresden, Germany)
Andrei Voronkov (University of Manchester, UK)

Program Committee

Matthias Baaz (Technische Universität Wien)
David Basin (ETH Zurich)
Philippe Besnard (CNRS, Toulouse)
Thomas Eiter (Technische Universität Wien)
Javier Esparza (Universität Stuttgart)
Marcelo Finger (Universidade de Sao Paulo)
Rajeev Gore (Australian National University)
Georg Gottlob (Technische Universität Wien)
Erich Grädel (RWTH Aachen)
Martin Grohe (Humboldt Universität Berlin)
Miki Hermann (Ecole Polytechnique)
Deepak Kapur (University of New Mexico)
Hélène Kirchner (LORIA)
Dexter Kozen (Cornell University)
Orna Kupferman (Hebrew University)
Dietrich Kuske (Technische Universität Dresden)
Maurizio Lenzerini (Università di Roma)
Leonid Libkin (University of Toronto)
Christopher Lynch (Clarkson University)
Dale Miller (INRIA)
Ilkka Niemelä (Helsinki University of Technology)
Tobias Nipkow (Technische Universität München)
Luke Ong (Oxford University)
Alberto Pardo (Universidad de la Republica, Montevideo)
David Pym (University of Bath)
Wolfgang Reif (Universität Augsburg)
Ulrike Sattler (Technische Universität Dresden)
Wolfgang Thomas (RWTH Aachen)
Cesare Tinelli (University of Iowa)
Ralf Treinen (ENS Cachan)
Toby Walsh (University College Cork)
Frank Wolter (University of Liverpool)

Local Organization

Alberto Pardo (Universidad de la Republica, Montevideo)

External Reviewers

Marcelo Arenas
Steffen van Bakel
Michael Balser
Clark Barrett
Stefan Berghofer
Gustavo Betarte
Sabine Broda
Marco Cadoli
Agata Ciabattoni
Jeremy Dawson
Francesco M. Donini
Gilles Dowek
Marcelo Falappa
Michael Fink
Holger Grandy
Dominik Haneberg
Duncan Hull
Steffen Hölldobler
Tomi Janhunen
Tom Kelsey
Boris Konev
Gerhard Lakemeyer
Markus Lohrey
Carlos Luna
Michael Maher
Stephan Merz
Thomas Meyer
Cesar Munoz
Linh Anh Nguyen
Hans de Nivelle
Emilia Oikarinen
Frank Ortmeier
Nicolas Peltier
Silvio Ranise
Antoine Reilles
Andrea Schalk
Tobias Scheffer
Manfred Schmidt-Schauss
Philippe Schnoebelen
Paula Severi
Simon Baeumler
Philippe Balbiani
Pablo Barcelo
Peter Baumgartner
Dietmar Berwanger
Ana Bove
Kai Bruennler
Amine Chaieb
Veronique Cortier
Stéphanie Delaune
Francesco Donini
Roy Dyckhoff
Maribel Fernandez
Jean Goubault-Larrecq
Tim Griffin
Keijo Heljanko
Ullrich Hustadt
Giovambattista Ianni
Lukasz Kaiser
Felix Klaedtke
Oliver Kutz
Thomas Linke
Dominique Longin
Carsten Lutz
Marc Meister
George Metcalfe
Aart Middeldorp
Ralf Möller
Robert Nieuwenhuis
Michael Norrish
Albert Oliveras
Maurice Pagnucco
Norbert Preining
Horst Reichel
Mark Reynolds
Torsten Schaub
Roman Schindlauer
Jonathan Schmitt
Nicole Schweikardt
Luis Sierra

Gregor Snelting
Kurt Stenzel
Tommi Syrjänen
Hans Tompits
Mateu Villaret
Martin Wildmoser
Stefan Woltran

Viorica Sofronie-Stokkermans
Georg Struth
Alwen Tiu
Laurent Vigneron
Pascal Weil
Burkhart Wolff
Hantao Zhang

Conferences Preceding LPAR-11

RCLP 1990, Irkutsk, Soviet Union
RCLP 1991, Leningrad, Soviet Union, aboard the ship "Michail Lomonosov"
LPAR 1992, St. Petersburg, Russia, aboard the ship "Michail Lomonosov"
LPAR 1993, St. Petersburg, Russia
LPAR 1994, Kiev, Ukraine, aboard the ship "Marshal Koshevoi"
LPAR 1999, Tbilisi, Republic of Georgia
LPAR 2000, Réunion Island, France
LPAR 2001, Havana, Cuba
LPAR 2002, Tbilisi, Republic of Georgia
LPAR 2003, Almaty, Kazakhstan

Table of Contents

CERES in Many-Valued Logics
Matthias Baaz and Alexander Leitsch 1

A Decomposition Rule for Decision Procedures by Resolution-Based Calculi
Ullrich Hustadt, Boris Motik, and Ulrike Sattler 21

Abstract DPLL and Abstract DPLL Modulo Theories
Robert Nieuwenhuis, Albert Oliveras, and Cesare Tinelli 36

Combining Lists with Non-stably Infinite Theories
Pascal Fontaine, Silvio Ranise, and Calogero G. Zarba 51

Abstract Model Generation for Preprocessing Clause Sets
Miyuki Koshimura, Mayumi Umeda, and Ryuzo Hasegawa 67

Flat and One-Variable Clauses: Complexity of Verifying Cryptographic Protocols with Single Blind Copying
Helmut Seidl and Kumar Neeraj Verma 79

Applications of General Exact Satisfiability in Propositional Logic Modelling
Vilhelm Dahllöf 95

BCiC: A System for Code Authenticationand Verification
Nathan Whitehead and Martín Abadi 110

Ordered Resolution with Selection for $\mathcal{H}(@)$
Carlos Areces and Daniel Gorín 125

On a Semantic Subsumption Test
Jerzy Marcinkowski, Jan Otop, and Grzegorz Stelmaszek 142

Suitable Graphs for Answer Set Programming
Thomas Linke and Vladimir Sarsakov 154

Weighted Answer Sets and Applications in Intelligence Analysis
Davy Van Nieuwenborgh, Stijn Heymans, and Dirk Vermeir 169

How to Fix It: Using Fixpoints in Different Contexts
Igor Walukiewicz 184

Reasoning About Systems with Transition Fairness
Benjamin Aminof, Thomas Ball, and Orna Kupferman 194

Entanglement – A Measure for the Complexity of Directed Graphs
with Applications to Logic and Games
Dietmar Berwanger and Erich Grädel 209

How the Location of * Influences Complexity in Kleene Algebra
with Tests
Chris Hardin 224

The Equational Theory of $\langle \mathbb{N}, 0, 1, +, \times, \uparrow \rangle$ Is Decidable, but Not
Finitely Axiomatisable
Roberto Di Cosmo and Thomas Dufour 240

A Trichotomy in the Complexity of Propositional Circumscription
Gustav Nordh 257

Exploiting Fixable, Removable, and Implied Values in Constraint
Satisfaction Problems
Lucas Bordeaux, Marco Cadoli, and Toni Mancini 270

Evaluating QBFs via Symbolic Skolemization
Marco Benedetti 285

The Dependency Pair Framework: Combining Techniques for
Automated Termination Proofs
Jürgen Giesl, René Thiemann, and Peter Schneider-Kamp 301

Automated Termination Analysis for Incompletely Defined Programs
Christoph Walther and Stephan Schweitzer 332

Automatic Certification of Heap Consumption
*Lennart Beringer, Martin Hofmann, Alberto Momigliano, and
Olha Shkaravska* 347

A Formalization of Off-Line Guessing for Security Protocol Analysis
Paul Hankes Drielsma, Sebastian Mödersheim, and Luca Viganò 363

Abstraction-Carrying Code
Elvira Albert, Germán Puebla, and Manuel Hermenegildo 380

A Verification Environment for Sequential Imperative Programs in
Isabelle/HOL
Norbert Schirmer 398

Can a Higher-Order and a First-Order Theorem Prover Cooperate?
*Christoph Benzmüller, Volker Sorge, Mateja Jamnik, and
Manfred Kerber* 415

A Generic Framework for Interprocedural Analyses of Numerical
Properties
Markus Müller-Olm and Helmut Seidl 432

Second-Order Matching via Explicit Substitutions
  *Flávio L.C. de Moura, Fairouz Kamareddine, and
  Mauricio Ayala-Rincón* 433

Knowledge-Based Synthesis of Distributed Systems Using Event
Structures
  *Mark Bickford, Robert C. Constable, Joseph Y. Halpern, and
  Sabina Petride* 449

The Inverse Method for the Logic of Bunched Implications
  *Kevin Donnelly, Tyler Gibson, Neel Krishnaswami, Stephen Magill,
  and Sungwoo Park* 466

Cut-Elimination: Experiments with CERES
  *Matthias Baaz, Stefan Hetzl, Alexander Leitsch, Clemens Richter,
  and Hendrik Spohr* 481

Uniform Rules and Dialogue Games for Fuzzy Logics
  Agata Ciabattoni, Christian G. Fermüller, and George Metcalfe 496

Nonmonotonic Description Logic Programs: Implementation and
Experiments
  *Thomas Eiter, Giovambattista Ianni, Roman Schindlauer, and
  Hans Tompits* 511

Implementing Efficient Resource Management for Linear Logic
Programming
  Pablo López and Jeff Polakow 528

Layered Clausal Resolution in the Multi-modal Logic of Beliefs and
Goals
  Jamshid Bagherzadeh and S. Arun-Kumar 544

Author Index 561

CERES in Many Valued Logics*

Matthias Baaz[1] and Alexander Leitsch[2]

[1] Institut für Computermathematik (E-118),
TU-Vienna, Wiedner Hauptstraße 8-10,
1040 Vienna, Austria
baaz@logic.at

[2] Institut für Computersprachen (E-185),
TU-Vienna, Favoritenstraße 9,
1040 Vienna, Austria
leitsch@logic.at

Abstract. CERES is a method for cut-elimination in classical logic which is based on resolution. In this paper we extend CERES to CERES-m, a resolution-based method of cut-elimination in Gentzen calculi for arbitrary finitely-valued logics. Like in the classical case the core of the method is the construction of a resolution proof in finitely-valued logics. Compared to Gentzen-type cut-elimination methods the advantage of CERES-m is a twofold one: 1. it is easier to define and 2. it is computationally superior and thus more appropriate for implementations and experiments.

1 Introduction

The core of classical cut-elimination methods in the style of Gentzen [8] consists of the permutation of inferences and of the reduction of cuts to cuts on the immediate subformulas of the cut formula. If we switch from two- valued to many-valued logic, the reduction steps become intrinsically tedious and opaque [3] in contrast to the extension of CERES to the many-valued case, which is straightforward.

We introduce CERES-m for correct (possible partial) calculi for m-valued first order logics based on m-valued connectives, distributive quantifiers [7] and arbitrary atomic initial sequents closed under substitution. We do not touch the completeness issue of these calculi, instead we derive clause terms from the proof representing the formulas which are ancestor formulas of the cut formulas; the evaluation of these clause terms guarantees the existence of a resolution refutation as core of a proof with atomic cuts only. This resolution refutation is extended to a proof of the original end-sequent by adjoining cut-free parts of the original proof. Therefore, it is sufficient to refute the suitably assembled components of the initial sequents using a m-valued theorem prover [2].

---

* supported by the Austrian Science Fund (FWF) proj. no P16264-N05

2 Definitions and Notation

Definition 1 (language). *The alphabet Σ consists of an infinite supply of variables, of infinite sets of n-ary function symbols and predicate symbols er σ contains a set W of truth symbols denoting the truth values of the logic, a finite number of connectives $\circ_1, \ldots, \circ_m$ of arity $n_1, \ldots, n_m$, and a finite number of quantifiers $Q_1, \ldots, Q_k$.*

Definition 2 (formula). *An atomic formula is an expression of the form $P(t_1, \ldots, t_n)$ where P is an n-ary predicate symbol in Σ and $t_1, \ldots, t_n$ are terms over Σ. Atomic formulas are formulas.*

If $\circ$ is an n-ary connective and $A_1, \ldots, A_n$ are formulas then $\circ(A_1, \ldots, A_n)$ is a formula.

If Q is quantifier in Σ and x is a variable then $(Qx)A$ is a formula.

Definition 3 (signed formula). *Let $w \in W$ and A be a formula. Then $w\colon A$ is called a signed formula.*

Definition 4 (sequent). *A sequent is a finite sequence of signed formulas. The number of signed formulas occurring in a sequent S is called the* length *of S and is denoted by $l(S)$. $\hat{S}$ is called the* unsigned version *of S if every signed formula $w\colon A$ in S is replaced by A. The length of unsigned versions is defined in the same way. A sequent S is called* atomic *if $\hat{S}$ is a sequence of atomic formulas.*

Remark 1. Note that the classical sequent $(\forall x)P(x) \vdash Q(a)$ can be written as $\mathbf{f}\colon (\forall x)P(x), \mathbf{t}\colon Q(a)$.

m-valued sequents are sometimes written as m-sided sequents. We refrain from this notation, because it denotes a preferred order of truth values, which even in the two-valued case might induce unjustified conclusions.

Definition 5 (axiom set). *A set $\mathcal{A}$ of atomic sequents is called an axiom set if $\mathcal{A}$ is closed under substitution.*

The calculus we are defining below is capable of formalizing any finitely valued logic. Concerning the quantifiers we assume them to be of distributive type [7]. Distribution quantifiers are functions from the non-empty sets of truth-values to the set of truth values, where the domain represents the situation in the structure, i.e. the truth values actually taken.

Definition 6. *Let $A(x)$ be a formula with free variable x. The* distribution *$Distr(A(x))$ of $A(x)$ is the set of all truth values in W to which $A(x)$ evaluates (for arbitrary assignments of domain elements to x).*

Definition 7. *Let q be a mapping $2^W \to W$. In interpreting the formula $(Qx)A(x)$ via q we first compute $Distr(A(x))$ and then $q(Distr(A(x)))$, which is the truth value of $(Qx)A(x)$ under the interpretation.*

In the calculus defined below the distinction between quantifier introductions with (strong) and without eigenvariable conditions (weak) are vital.

Definition 8. *A strong quantifier is a triple (V, w, w') (for $V \subseteq W$) s.t. $(Qx)A(x)$ evaluates to w if $Distr(A(x)) \subseteq V$ and to w' otherwise. A weak quantifier is a triple (u, w, w') s.t. $(Qx)A(x)$ evaluates to w if $u \in Distr(A(x))$, and to w' otherwise.*

Remark 2. Strong and weak quantifiers are dual w.r.t. to set complementation. In fact to any strong quantifier there corresponds a weak one and vice versa. Like in classical logic we may speak about weak and strong occurrences of quantifiers in sequents and formulas.

Note that strong and weak quantifiers define merely a subclass of distribution quantifiers. Nevertheless the following property holds:

Proposition 1. *Any distributive quantifier can be expressed by strong and weak quantifiers and many valued associative, commutative and idempotent connectives (which are variants of conjunction and disjunction).*

Definition 9 (LM-type calculi). *We define an LM-type calculus $\mathbf{K}$. The initial sequents are (arbitrary) atomic sequents of an axiom set $\mathcal{A}$. In the rules of $\mathbf{K}$ we always mark the auxiliary formulas (i.e. the formulas in the premiss(es) used for the inference) and the principal (i.e. the inferred) formula using different marking symbols. Thus, in our definition, classical $\wedge$-introduction to the right takes the form*

$$\frac{\Gamma, \mathbf{t}\colon A^+ \quad \Gamma, \mathbf{t}\colon B^+}{\Gamma, \mathbf{t}\colon A \wedge B^*}$$

If $\Pi \vdash \Gamma, \Delta$ is a sequent then $\Pi \vdash \Gamma, \Delta^+$ indicates that all signed formulas in Δ are auxiliary formulas of the defined inference. $\Gamma \vdash \Delta, w\colon A^*$ indicates that $A\colon w^*$ is the principal formula (i.e. the inferred formula) of the inference.

Auxiliary formulas and the principal formula of an inference are always supposed to be rightmost. Therefore we usually avoid markings as the status of the formulas is clear from the notation.

logical rules:

Let $\circ$ be an n-nary connective. For any $w \in W$ we have an introduction rule $\circ\colon w$ of the form

$$\frac{\Gamma, \Delta_1^+ \quad \ldots \quad \Gamma, \Delta_m^+}{\Gamma, w\colon \circ(\pi(\hat{\Delta}_1, \ldots, \hat{\Delta}_m, \hat{\Delta}))^*} \circ\colon w$$

where $l(\Delta_1, \ldots, \Delta_m, \Delta) = n$ (the Δ_i are sequences of signed formulas which are all auxiliary signed formulas of the inference) and $\pi(S)$ denotes a permutation of a sequent S.

Note that, for simplicity, we chose the additive version of all logical introduction rules.

In the introduction rules for quantifiers we distinguish strong *and* weak *introduction rules. Any strong quantifier rule $Q\colon w$ (for a strong quantifier (V, w, w')) is of the form*

$$\frac{\Gamma, u_1\colon A(\alpha)^+, \ldots, u_m\colon A(\alpha)^+}{\Gamma, w\colon (Qx)A(x)^*} \; Q\colon w$$

where α is an eigenvariable not occurring in Γ, and $V = \{u_1, \ldots, u_m\}$.

Any weak quantifier rule (for a weak quantifier (u, w, w')) is of the form

$$\frac{\Gamma, u\colon A(t)^+}{\Gamma, w\colon (Qx)A(x)^*} \; Q\colon w$$

where t is a term containing no variables which are bound in $A(x)$. We say that t is eliminated *by $Q\colon w$.*

We need define a special n-ary connective for every strong quantifier in order to carry out skolemization. Indeed if we skip the introduction of a strong quantifier the m (possibly $m > 1$) auxiliary formulas must be contracted into a single one after the removal of the strong quantifier (see definition of skolemization below). Thus for every rule

$$\frac{\Gamma, u_1\colon A(\alpha_1)^+, \ldots, u_m\colon A(\alpha_m)^+}{\Gamma, w\colon (Qx)A(x)^*} \; Q\colon w$$

we define a propositional rule

$$\frac{\Gamma, u_1\colon A(t)^+, \ldots, u_m\colon A(t)^+}{\Gamma, w\colon A(t)^*} \; c_Q\colon w$$

This new operator c_Q can be eliminated by the de-skolemization procedure afterwards.

structural rules:

The structural rule of weakening is defined like in **LK** *(but we need only one weakening rule and may add more then one formula).*

$$\frac{\Gamma}{\Gamma, \Delta} \; w$$

for sequents Γ and Δ.

To put the auxiliary formulas on the right positions we need permutation rules of the form

$$\frac{F_1, \ldots, F_n}{F_{\pi(1)}, \ldots, F_{\pi(n)}} \; \pi$$

where π is a permutation of $\{1, \ldots, n\}$ and the F_i are signed formulas.

Instead of the usual contraction rules we define an n-contraction rule for any $n \geq 2$ and $F_1 = \ldots = F_n = F$:

$$\frac{\Gamma, F_1, \ldots, F_n}{\Gamma, F} \; c \cdot n$$

In contrast to **LK** *we do not have a single cut rule, but instead rules* $cut_{ww'}$ *for any* $w, w' \in W$ *with* $w \neq w'$. *Any such rule is of the form*

$$\frac{\Gamma, w\colon A \quad \Gamma', w'\colon A}{\Gamma, \Gamma'} \; cut_{ww'}$$

Definition 10 (proof). *A proof of a sequent S from an axiom set $\mathcal{A}$ is a directed labelled tree. The root is labelled by S, the leaves are labelled by elements of $\mathcal{A}$. The edges are defined according to the inference rules (in an n-ary rule the children of a node are labelled by the antecedents, the parent node is labelled by the consequent). Let N be a node in the proof ϕ then we write $\phi.N$ for the corresponding subproof ending in N. For the number of nodes in ϕ we write $\|\phi\|$.*

Definition 11. *Let* **K** *be an LM-type calculus. We define $\mathcal{P}[\mathbf{K}]$ as the set of all* **K**-*proofs. $\mathcal{P}^i[\mathbf{K}]$ is the subset of $\mathcal{P}[\mathbf{K}]$ consisting of all proofs with cut-complexity $\leq i$ ($\mathcal{P}^0[\mathbf{K}]$ is the set of proofs with at most atomic cuts). $\mathcal{P}^\emptyset[\mathbf{K}]$ is the subset of all cut-free proofs.*

Example 1. We define $W = \{0, u, 1\}$ and the connectives as in the 3-valued Kleene logic, but introduce a new quantifier D ("D" for determined) which gives true iff all truth values are in $\{0, 1\}$. We only define the rules for $\vee$ and for D, as no other operators occur in the proof below.

$$\frac{0\colon A, 1\colon A \quad 0\colon B, 1\colon B \quad 1\colon A, 1\colon B}{1\colon A \vee B} \; \vee\colon 1$$

$$\frac{u\colon A, u\colon B}{u\colon A \vee B} \; \vee\colon u \quad \frac{0\colon A, 0\colon B}{0\colon A \vee B} \; \vee\colon 0$$

$$\frac{0\colon A(\alpha), 1\colon A(\alpha)}{1\colon (Dx)A(x)} \; D\colon 1 \quad \frac{u\colon A(t)}{0\colon (Dx)A(x)} \; D\colon 0$$

where α is an eigenvariable and t is a term containig no variables bound in $A(x)$. Note that $D\colon 1$ is a strong, and $D\colon 0$ a weak quantifier introduction. The formula $u\colon (Dx)A(x)$ can only be introduced via weakening.

For the notation of proofs we frequently abbreviate sequences of structural rules bei $*$; thus $\pi^* + \vee\colon u$ means that $\vee\colon u$ is performed and permutations before and/or afterwards. This makes the proofs more legible and allows to focus on the logically relevant inferences. As in the definition of LM-type calculi we mark the auxiliary formulas of logical inferences and cut by $+$, the principle ones by $*$.

Let ϕ be the following proof

$$\frac{\phi_1 \quad \phi_2}{0\colon (Dx)((P(x) \lor Q(x)) \lor R(x)), 1\colon (Dx)P(x)}\ cut$$

where $\phi_1 =$

$$\dfrac{\dfrac{\dfrac{\dfrac{\begin{array}{c}(\psi')\\ 0\colon P(\alpha) \lor Q(\alpha),\ u\colon P(\alpha) \lor Q(\alpha),\ 1\colon P(\alpha) \lor Q(\alpha)\end{array}}{0\colon P(\alpha) \lor Q(\alpha),\ u\colon P(\alpha) \lor Q(\alpha),\ u\colon R(\alpha)^*,\ 1\colon P(\alpha) \lor Q(\alpha)}\ \pi^* + w}{0\colon A(\alpha) \lor Q(\alpha),\ u\colon (P(\alpha) \lor Q(\alpha)) \lor R(\alpha)^{+*},\ 1\colon P(\alpha) \lor Q(\alpha)}\ \lor\colon u}{0\colon (Dx)((P(x) \lor Q(x)) \lor R(x))^*,\ 0\colon P(\alpha) \lor Q(\alpha)^+,\ 1\colon P(\alpha) \lor Q(\alpha)^+}\ \pi^* + D\colon 0}{0\colon (Dx)((P(x) \lor Q(x)) \lor R(x)),\ 1\colon (Dx)(P(x) \lor Q(x))^*}\ D\colon 1$$

and $\phi_2 =$

$$\dfrac{\dfrac{\dfrac{\dfrac{0\colon P(\beta),\ u\colon P(\beta),\ 1\colon P(\beta)}{0\colon P(\beta),\ 1\colon P(\beta),\ u\colon P(\beta)^+,\ u\colon Q(\beta)^{*+}}\ \pi^* + w}{0\colon P(\beta),\ u\colon P(\beta) \lor Q(\beta)^{*+},\ 1\colon P(\beta)}\ \pi^* + \lor\colon u}{0\colon (Dx)(P(x) \lor Q(x))^*,\ 0\colon P(\beta)^+,\ 1\colon P(\beta)^+}\ \pi^* + D\colon 0}{0\colon (Dx)(P(x) \lor Q(x)),\ 1\colon (Dx)P(x)^*}\ D\colon 1$$

we have to define ψ' as our axiom set must be atomic. We set

$$\psi' = \psi(A, B)\{A \leftarrow P(\alpha), A \leftarrow Q(\alpha)\}$$

and define
$\psi(A, B) =$

$$\dfrac{\dfrac{\dfrac{S, 0\colon A, 1\colon A \quad S, 0\colon B, 1\colon B \quad S, 1\colon A, 1\colon B}{0\colon A,\ u\colon A, u\colon B,\ 1\colon A \lor B}\ \lor\colon 1 \qquad \dfrac{T, 0\colon A, 1\colon A \quad T, 0\colon B, 1\colon B \quad T, 1\colon A, 1\colon B}{0\colon B,\ u\colon A, u\colon B,\ 1\colon A \lor B}}{0\colon A \lor B,\ u\colon A, u\colon B,\ 1\colon A \lor B}\ \lor\colon 0}{0\colon A \lor B,\ u\colon A \lor B,\ 1\colon A \lor B}\ \pi^* + \lor\colon u$$

For $S = 0\colon A,\ u\colon A, u\colon B$ and $T = 0\colon B,\ u\colon A, u\colon B$. It is easy to see that the end sequent is valid as the axioms contain $0\colon A,\ u\colon A, 1\colon A$ and $0\colon B,\ u\colon B, 1\colon B$ as subsequents.

Definition 12 (W-clause). *A W-clause is an atomic sequent (where W is the set of truth symbols). The empty sequent is called empty clause and is denoted by $\Box$.*

Let S be an W-clause. S' is called a renamed variant of S if $S' = S\eta$ for a variable permutation η.

Definition 13 (W-resolution). *We define a resolution calculus R_W which only depends on the set W (but not on the logical rules of $\mathbf{K}$). R_W operates on W-clauses; its rules are:*

1. $res_{ww'}$ for all $w, w' \in W$ and $w \neq w'$,
2. w-factoring for $w \in W$,
3. permutations.

Let $S: \Gamma, w: A$ and $S': \Gamma', w': A'$ (where $w \neq w'$) be two W-clauses and $S'': \Gamma'', w': A''$ be a variant of S' s.t. S and S' are variable disjoint. Assume that $\{A, B'\}$ are unifiable by a most general unifier σ. Then the rule $res_{ww'}$ on S, S' generates a resolvent R for
$$R = \Gamma\sigma, \Gamma''\sigma.$$
Let $S: \Gamma, w: A_1, \ldots, w: A_m$ be a clause and σ be a most general unifier of $\{A_1, \ldots, A_m\}$. Then the clause
$$S': \Gamma\sigma, w: A_1\sigma$$
is called a w-factor of S.

A W-resolution proof of a clause S from a set of clauses $\mathcal{S}$ is a directed labelled tree s.t. the root is labelled by S and the leaves are labelled by elements of $\mathcal{S}$. The edges correspond the applications of w-factoring (unary), permutation (unary) and $res_{ww'}$ (binary).

It is proved in [1] that W-resolution is complete. For the LM-type calculus we only require soundness w.r.t. the underlying logic. So from now on we assume that **K** is sound.

Note that we did not define clauses as sets of signed literals; therefore we need the permutation rule in order to "prepare" the clauses for resolution and factoring.

Definition 14 (ground projection). Let γ be a W-resolution proof and $\{x_1, \ldots, x_n\}$ be the variables occurring in the indexed clauses of γ. Then, for all ground terms $t_1, \ldots, t_n$, $\gamma\{x_1 \leftarrow t_1, \ldots, x_1 \leftarrow t_n\}$ is called a ground projection of γ.

Remark 3. Ground projections of resolution proofs are ordinary proofs in **K**; indeed factoring becomes n-contraction and resolution becomes cut.

Definition 15 (ancestor relation). Let
$$\frac{S_1: \Gamma, \Delta_1^+ \quad \ldots \quad S_m: \Gamma, \Delta_m^+}{S: \Gamma, w: A^*} \, x$$
be a an inference in a proof ϕ; let μ be the occurrence of the principal signed formula $w: A$ in S and ν_{ij} be the occurrence of the j-th auxiliary formula in S_i. Then all ν_{ij} are ancestors of μ.

The ancestor relation in ϕ is defined as the reflexive and transitive closure of the above relation.

By $S(N, \Omega)$ ($\bar{S}(N, \Omega)$) we denote the subsequent of S at the node N of ϕ consisting of all formulas which are (not) ancestors of a formula occurrence in Ω.

Example 2. Let $\psi(A, B)$ as in Example 1:

$$\frac{\dfrac{S, 0: A, 1: A \quad S, 0: B, 1: B \quad S, 1: A, 1: B}{0: A^\dagger, u: A, u: B, 1: A \vee B} \vee :1 \quad \dfrac{T, 0: A, 1: A \quad T, 0: B, 1: B \quad T, 1: A, 1: B}{0: B^\dagger, u: A, u: B, 1: A \vee B}}{\dfrac{0: A \vee B^\dagger, u: A, u: B, 1: A \vee B}{0: A \vee B^\dagger, u: A \vee B, 1: A \vee B} \pi^* + \vee : u} \vee :0$$

Let N_0 be the root of $\psi(A, B)$ and μ be the occurrence of the first formula $(0: A \vee B)$ in N. The formula occurrences which are ancestors of μ are labelled with †. The marking is not visible in S and T where the ancestors occur. In the antecedent N_1, N_2 of the binary inference $\vee: 0$ we have $S(N_1, \{\mu\}) = 0: A$ and $S(N_2, \{\mu\}) = 0: B$.

3 Skolemization

As CERES-m (like CERES [6] and [5]) augments a ground resolution proof with cut-free parts of the original proof related only to the end-sequent, eigenvariable conditions in these proof parts might be violated. To get rid of this problem, the endsequent of the proof and the formulas, which are ancestors of the end-sequent have to be skolemized, i.e eigenvariables have to be replaced by suitable Skolem terms. To obtain a skolemization of the end-sequent, we have to represent (analyze) distributive quantifiers in terms of strong quantifiers (covering exclusively eigenvariables) and weak quantifiers (covering exclusively terms). This was the main motivation for the choice of our definition of quantifiers in Definition 9. The strong quantifiers are replaced by Skolem functions depending on the weakly quantified variables determined by the scope. Note that distributive quantifiers are in general mixed, i.e. they are neither weak nor strong, even in the two-valued case.

3.1 Skolemization of Proofs

Definition 16 (skolemization). *Let $\Delta: \Gamma, w: A$ be a sequent and $(Qx)B$ be a subformula of A at the position λ where Qx is a maximal strong quantifier in $w: A$. Let $y_1, \ldots, y_m$ be free variables occurring in $(Qx)B$, then we define*

$$sk(\Delta) = \Gamma, w: A[B\{x \to f(y_1, \ldots, y_m)\}]_\lambda$$

where f is a function symbol not occurring in Δ.

If $w: A$ contains no strong quantifier then we define $sk(\Delta) = \Delta$.

A sequent S is in Skolem form if there exists no permutation S' of S s.t. $sk(S') \neq S'$. S' is called a Skolem form of S if S' is in Skolem form and can be obtained from S by permutations and the operator sk.

The skolemization of proofs can be defined in a way quite similar to the classical case (see [4]).

Definition 17 (skolemization of K-proofs). *Let* **K** *be an* LM-*type calculus. We define a transformation of proofs which maps a proof ϕ of S from $\mathcal{A}$ into a proof $sk(\phi)$ of S' from $\mathcal{A}'$ where S' is the Skolem form of S and $\mathcal{A}'$ is an instance of $\mathcal{A}$.*

Locate an uppermost logical inference which introduces a signed formula $w\colon A$ which is not an ancestor of a cut and contains a strong quantifier.

(a) The formula is introduced by a strong quantifier inference:

$$\frac{\begin{matrix}\psi[\alpha]\\ S'\colon \Gamma, u_1\colon A(\alpha)^+, \ldots, u_m\colon A(\alpha)^+\end{matrix}}{S\colon \Gamma, w\colon (Qx)A(x)^*}\ Q\colon w$$

in ϕ and N', N be the nodes in ϕ labelled by S', S. Let P be the path from the root to N', locate all weak quantifier inferences ξ_i (i=1,...,n) on P and all terms t_i eliminated by ξ_i. Then we delete the inference node N and replace the derivation ψ of N' by

$$\frac{\begin{matrix}\psi[f(t_1,\ldots,t_n)]\\ S'\colon \Gamma, u_1\colon A(f(t_1,\ldots,t_n))^+, \ldots, u_m\colon A(f(t_1,\ldots,t_n))^+\end{matrix}}{S_0\colon \Gamma, w\colon A(f(t_1,\ldots,t_n))^*}\ c_Q : w$$

where f is a function symbol not occurring in ϕ and c_Q is the connective corresponding to Q. The sequents on P are adapted according to the inferences on P.

(b) The formula is inferred by a propositional inference or by weakening (within the principal formula $w\colon A$) then we replace $w\colon A$ by the Skolem form of $w\colon A$ where the Skolem function symbol does not occur in ϕ.

Let ϕ' be the proof after such a skolemization step. We iterate the procedure until no occurrence of a strong quantifier is an ancestor of an occurrence in the end sequent. The resulting proof is called $sk(\phi)$. Note that $sk(\phi)$ is a proof from the same *axiom set $\mathcal{A}$ as $\mathcal{A}$ is closed under substitution.*

Definition 18. *A proof ϕ is called* skolemized *if $sk(\phi) = \phi$.*

Note that skolemized proofs may contain strong quantifiers, but these are ancestors of cut, in the end-sequent there are none.

Example 3. Let ϕ be the proof from Example 1:

$$\frac{\phi_1 \quad \phi_2}{0\colon (Dx)((P(x) \vee Q(x)) \vee R(x)), 1\colon (Dx)P(x)}\ cut$$

where ϕ_1 =

$$\cfrac{\cfrac{\cfrac{\cfrac{\begin{matrix}(\psi')\\ 0\colon P(\alpha) \vee Q(\alpha),\ u\colon P(\alpha) \vee Q(\alpha),\ 1\colon P(\alpha) \vee Q(\alpha)\end{matrix}}{0\colon P(\alpha) \vee Q(\alpha),\ u\colon P(\alpha) \vee Q(\alpha),\ u\colon R(\alpha)^*,\ 1\colon P(\alpha) \vee Q(\alpha)}\ \pi^* + w}{0\colon A(\alpha) \vee Q(\alpha),\ u\colon (P(\alpha) \vee Q(\alpha)) \vee R(\alpha)^{+*},\ 1\colon P(\alpha) \vee Q(\alpha)}\ \vee\colon u}{0\colon (Dx)((P(x) \vee Q(x)) \vee R(x))^*,\ 0\colon P(\alpha) \vee Q(\alpha)^+,\ 1\colon P(\alpha) \vee Q(\alpha)^+}\ \pi^* + D\colon 0}{0\colon (Dx)((P(x) \vee Q(x)) \vee R(x)),\ 1\colon (Dx)(P(x) \vee Q(x))^*}\ D\colon 1$$

and $\phi_2 =$

$$
\cfrac{
  \cfrac{
    \cfrac{
      \cfrac{
        \cfrac{0\colon P(\beta),\ u\colon P(\beta),\ 1\colon P(\beta)}{0\colon P(\beta),\ 1\colon P(\beta),\ u\colon P(\beta)^+,\ u\colon Q(\beta)^{*+}} \pi^* + w
      }{0\colon P(\beta),\ u\colon P(\beta)\vee Q(\beta)^{*+},\ 1\colon P(\beta)} \pi^* + \vee\colon u
    }{0\colon (Dx)(P(x)\vee Q(x))^*,\ 0\colon P(\beta)^+,\ 1\colon P(\beta)^+} \pi^* + D\colon 0
  }{0\colon (Dx)(P(x)\vee Q(x)),\ 1\colon (Dx)P(x)^*} D\colon 1
$$

The proof is not skolemized as the endsequent contains a strong quantifier occurrence in the formula $1\colon (Dx)P(x)$. This formula comes from the proof ϕ_2. Thus we must skolemize ϕ_2 and adapt the end sequent of ϕ. It is easy to verify that $sk(\phi_2) =$

$$
\cfrac{
  \cfrac{
    \cfrac{
      \cfrac{
        \cfrac{0\colon P(c),\ u\colon P(c),\ 1\colon P(c)}{0\colon P(c),\ 1\colon P(c),\ u\colon P(c)^+,\ u\colon Q(c)^{*+}} \pi^* + w
      }{0\colon P(c),\ u\colon P(c)\vee Q(c)^{*+},\ 1\colon P(c)} \pi^* + \vee\colon u
    }{0\colon (Dx)(P(x)\vee Q(x))^*,\ 0\colon P(c)^+,\ 1\colon P(c)^+} \pi^* + D\colon 0
  }{0\colon (Dx)(P(x)\vee Q(x)),\ 1\colon P(c)^*} c_{D-1}
$$

Then $sk(\phi) =$

$$
\cfrac{\phi_1 \quad sk(\phi_2)}{0\colon (Dx)((P(x)\vee Q(x))\vee R(x)),\ 1\colon P(c)}\ \mathrm{cut}
$$

Note that ϕ_1 cannot be skolemized as the strong quantifiers in ϕ_1 are ancestors of the cut in ϕ.

3.2 De-Skolemization of Proofs

Skolem functions can be replaced by the original structure of (strong and weak) quantifiers by the following straightforward algorithm at most exponential in the maximal size of the original proof and of the CERES-m proof of the Skolemized end sequent: Order the Skolem terms (terms, whose outermost function symbol is a Skolem function) by inclusion. The size of the proof resulting from CERES-m together with the number of inferences in the original proof limits the number of relevant Skolem terms. Always replace a maximal Skolem term by a fresh variable, and determine the formula F in the proof, for which the corresponding strong quantifier should be introduced. In re-introducing the quantifier we eliminate the newly introduced connectives c_Q. As the eigenvariable condition might be violated at the lowest possible position, where the quantifier can be introduced (because e.g. the quantified formula has to become part of a larger formula by an inference) suppress all inferences on F such that F occurs as side formula besides the original end-sequent. Then perform all inferences on F. This at most triples the size of the proof (a copy of the proof together with suitable contractions might be necessary).

3.3 Re-introduction of Distributive Quantifiers

The distributive quantifiers are by now represented by a combination of strong quantifiers, weak quantifiers and connectives. A simple permutation of inferences in the proof leads to the immediate derivation in several steps of the representation of the distributive quantifier from the premises of the distributive quantifier inference. The replacement of the representation by the distributive quantifier is then simple.

4 CERES-m

As in the classical case (see [5] and [6]) we restrict cut-elimination to skolemized proofs. After cut-elimination the obtained proof can be re-skolemized, i.e. it can be transformed into a derivation of the original (unskolemized) end-sequent.

Definition 19. *Let* **K** *be an LM-type calculus. We define* $\mathcal{SK}[\mathbf{K}]$ *be the set of all skolemized proofs in* **K**. $\mathcal{SK}^0[\mathbf{K}]$ *is the set of all cut-free proofs in* $\mathcal{SK}[\mathbf{K}]$ *and, for all* $i \geq 0$, $\mathcal{SK}^i[\mathbf{K}]$ *is the subset of* $\mathcal{SK}[\mathbf{K}]$ *containing all proofs with cut-formulas of formula complexity* $\leq i$.

Our goal is to transform a derivation in $\mathcal{SK}[\mathbf{K}]$ into a derivation in $\mathcal{SK}^0[\mathbf{K}]$ (i.e. we reduce all cuts to atomic ones). The first step in the corresponding procedure consists in the definition of a clause term corresponding to the subderivations of an **K**-proof ending in a cut. In particular we focus on derivations of the cut formulas themselves, i.e. on the derivation of formulas having no successors in the end-sequent. Below we will see that this analysis of proofs, first introduced in [5], is quite general and can easily be generalized to LM-type calculi.

Definition 20 (clause term). *The signature of clause terms consists of that of W-clauses and the operators* $\oplus^n$ *and* $\otimes^n$ *for* $n \geq 2$.

- *(Finite) sets of W-clauses are clause terms.*
- *If* $X_1, \ldots, X_n$ *are clause terms then* $\oplus^n(X_1, \ldots, X_n)$ *is a clause term.*
- *If* $X_1, \ldots, X_n$ *are clause terms then* $\otimes^n(X_1, \ldots, X_n)$ *is a clause term.*

Clause terms denote sets of W-clauses; the following definition gives the precise semantics.

Definition 21. *We define a mapping* $|\ |$ *from clause terms to sets of W-clauses in the following way:*

$$|\mathcal{S}| = \mathcal{C} \text{ for sets of W-clauses } \mathcal{S},$$
$$|\oplus^n(X_1, \ldots, X_n)| = \bigcup_{i=1}^{n} |X_i|,$$
$$|\otimes^n(X_1, \ldots, X_n)| = merge(|X_1|, \ldots, |X_n|),$$

where

$$merge(\mathcal{S}_1,\ldots,\mathcal{S}_n) = \{S_1\ldots S_n \mid S_1 \in \mathcal{S}_1,\ldots S_n \in \mathcal{S}_n\}.$$

We define clause terms to be equivalent if the corresponding sets of clauses are equal, i.e. $X \sim Y$ *iff* $|X| = |Y|$.

Definition 22 (characteristic term). *Let* **K** *be an LM-type calculus,* ϕ *be a proof of* S *and let* Ω *be the set of all occurrences of cut formulas in* ϕ. *We define the* characteristic (clause) term $\Theta(\phi)$ *inductively:*

Let N *be the occurrence of an initial sequent* S' *in* ϕ. *Then* $\Theta(\phi)/N = \{S(N,\Omega)\}$ *(see Definition 15).*

Let us assume that the clause terms $\Theta(\phi)/N$ *are already constructed for all nodes* N *in* ϕ *with* $\text{depth}(N) \leq k$. *Now let* N *be a node with* $\text{depth}(\nu) = k+1$. *We distinguish the following cases:*

(a) N *is the consequent of* M, *i.e. a unary rule applied to* M *gives* N. *Here we simply define*

$$\Theta(\varphi)/N = \Theta(\varphi)/M.$$

(b) N *is the consequent of* $M_1,\ldots,M_n$, *for* $n \geq 2$, *i.e. an n-ary rule* x *applied to* $M_1,\ldots,M_n$ *gives* N.

(b1) *The auxiliary formulas of* x *are ancestors of* Ω, *i.e. the formulas occur in* $S(M_i,\Omega)$ *for all* $i = 1,\ldots,n$. *Then*

$$\Theta(\phi)/N = \oplus^n(\Theta(\varphi)/M_1,\ldots,\Theta(\varphi)/M_n).$$

(b2) *The auxiliary formulas of* x *are not ancestors of* Ω. *In this case we define*

$$\Theta(\phi)/N = \otimes^n(\Theta(\varphi)/M_1,\ldots,\Theta(\varphi)/M_n).$$

Note that, in an n-ary inference, either all auxiliary formulas are ancestors of Ω *or none of them.*

Finally the characteristic term $\Theta(\phi)$ *of* ϕ *is defined as* $\Theta(\phi)/N_0$ *where* N_0 *is the root node of* ϕ.

Definition 23 (characteristic clause set). *Let* ϕ *be proof in an LM-type calculus* **K** *and* $\Theta(\phi)$ *be the characteristic term of* ϕ. *Then* $\text{CL}(\phi)$, *defined as* $\text{CL}(\phi) = |\Theta(\phi)|$, *is called the* characteristic clause set *of* ϕ.

Remark 4. If ϕ *is a cut-free proof then there are no occurrences of cut formulas in* ϕ *and* $\text{CL}(\phi) = \{\Box\}$.

Example 4. Let ϕ' be the skolemized proof defined in Example 3. It is easy to verify that the characteristic clause set $\mathrm{CL}(\phi')$ is

$$\{u\colon P(c),$$
$$0\colon P(\alpha),\ 0\colon P(\alpha),\ 1\colon P(\alpha)$$
$$0\colon P(\alpha),\ 0\colon Q(\alpha),\ 1\colon Q(\alpha)$$
$$0\colon P(\alpha),\ 1\colon P(\alpha),\ 1\colon Q(\alpha)$$
$$0\colon Q(\alpha),\ 0\colon P(\alpha),\ 1\colon P(\alpha)$$
$$0\colon Q(\alpha),\ 0\colon Q(\alpha),\ 1\colon Q(\alpha)$$
$$0\colon Q(\alpha),\ 1\colon P(\alpha),\ 1\colon Q(\alpha)\}.$$

The set $\mathrm{CL}(\phi')$ can be refuted via W-resolution for $W = \{0, u, 1\}$. A W-resolution refutation is ($0f$ stands for 0-factoring) $\gamma =$

$$\cfrac{\cfrac{\cfrac{0\colon P(\alpha),\ 0\colon P(\alpha),\ 1\colon P(\alpha) \quad u\colon P(c)}{0\colon P(c),\ 0\colon P(c)}\ res_{1u}}{0\colon P(c)}\ 0f \qquad u\colon P(c)}{\Box}\ res_{0u}$$

A ground projection of γ (even the only one) is $\gamma' = \gamma\{\alpha \leftarrow c\} =$

$$\cfrac{\cfrac{\cfrac{0\colon P(c),\ 0\colon P(c),\ 1\colon P(c) \quad u\colon P(c)}{0\colon P(c),\ 0\colon P(c)}\ cut_{1u}}{0\colon P(c)}\ c \qquad u\colon P(c)}{\Box}\ cut_{0u}$$

Obviously γ' is a proof in **K**.

In Example 4 we have seen that the characteristic clause set of a proof is refutable by W-resolution. This is a general principle and the most significant property of cut-elimination by resolution.

Definition 24. *From now on we write Ω for the set of all occurrences of cut-formulas in ϕ. So, for any node N in ϕ $S(N, \Omega)$ is the subsequent of S containing the ancestors of a cut. $\bar{S}(N, \Omega)$ denotes the subsequent of S containing all non-ancestors of a cut.*

Remark 5. Note that for any sequent S occurring at a node N of ϕ, S is a permutation variant of $S(N, \Omega), \bar{S}(N, \Omega)$.

Theorem 1. *Let ϕ be a proof in an LM-calculus **K**. Then there exists a W-resolution refutation of $\mathrm{CL}(\phi)$.*

Proof. According to Definition 22 we have to show that

(∗) for all nodes N in ϕ there exists a proof of $S(N, \Omega)$ from $\mathcal{S}_N$, where $\mathcal{S}_N$ is defined as $|\Theta(\phi)/N|$ (i.e. the set of clauses corresponding to N, see Definition 22). If N_0 is the root node of ϕ labelled by S then, clearly, no ancestor of a cut exists in S and so $S(N_0, \Omega) = \Box$. But by definition $\mathcal{S}_{N_0} = \mathrm{CL}(\phi)$. So we obtain a proof of $\Box$ from $\mathrm{CL}(\phi)$ in $\mathbf{K}$. By the completeness of W-resolution there exists a W-resolution refutation of $\mathrm{CL}(\phi)$.

It remains to prove (∗):

Let N be a leaf node in ϕ. Then by definition of $\mathrm{CL}(\phi)$ $\mathcal{S}_N = \{S(N, \Omega)\}$. So $S(N, \Omega)$ itself is the required proof of $S(N, \Omega)$ from $\mathcal{S}_N$.

(IH):

Now assume inductively that for all nodes N of depth $\leq n$ in ϕ there exists a proof ψ_N of $S(N, \Omega)$ from $\mathcal{S}_N$.

So let N be a node of depth $n+1$ in ϕ. We distinguish the following cases:

(a) N is the consequent of M, i.e. N is the result of a unary inference in ϕ. That means $\phi.N =$

$$\frac{\phi.M}{S(N)} \; x$$

By (IH) there exists a proof ψ_M of $S(M, \Omega)$ from $\mathcal{S}_M$. By Definition 22 $\mathcal{S}_N = \mathcal{S}_M$. If the auxiliary formula of the last inference is in $S(M, \Omega)$ we define $\psi_N =$

$$\frac{\psi_M}{S'} \; x$$

Obviously S' is just $S(N, \Omega)$.

If the auxiliary formula of the last inference in $\phi.N$ is not in $S(M, \Omega)$ we simply drop the inference and define $\psi_N = \psi.M$. As the ancestors of cut did not change ψ_N is just a proof of $S(N, \Omega)$ from $\mathcal{S}_N$.

(b) N is the consequent of an n-ary inference for $n \geq 2$, i.e. $\phi.N =$

$$\frac{\phi.M_1 \quad \ldots \quad \phi.M_n}{S(N)} \; x$$

By (IH) there exist proofs ψ_{M_i} of $S(M_i, \Omega)$ from $\mathcal{S}_{M_i}$.

(b1) The auxiliary formulas of the last inference in $\phi.N$ are in $S(M_i, \Omega)$, i.e. the inference yields an ancestor of a cut. Then, by Definition 22

$$\mathcal{S}_N = \mathcal{S}_{M_1} \cup \ldots \cup \mathcal{S}_{M_n}.$$

Then clearly the proof ψ_N:

$$\frac{\psi_{M_1} \quad \ldots \quad \psi_{M_n}}{S'} \; x$$

is a proof of S' from $\mathcal{S}_N$ and $S' = S(N, \Omega)$.

(b2) The auxiliary formulas of the last inference in $\phi.N$ are not in $S(M_i, \Omega)$, i.e. the principal formula of the inference is not an ancestor of a cut. Then, by Definition 22

$$\mathcal{S}_N = merge(\mathcal{S}_{M_1}, \ldots, \mathcal{S}_{M_n}).$$

We write $\mathcal{S}_i$ for $\mathcal{S}_{M_i}$ and ψ_i for ψ_{M_i}, Γ_i for $S(M_i, \Omega)$ and define

$$\mathcal{D}_i = merge(\mathcal{S}_1, \ldots, \mathcal{S}_i),$$
$$\Delta_i = \Gamma_1, \ldots, \Gamma_i,$$

for $i = 1, \ldots, n$. Our aim is to define a proof ψ_N of $S(N, \Omega)$ from $\mathcal{S}_N$ where $\mathcal{S}_N = \mathcal{D}_n$.

We proceed inductively and define proofs χ_i of Δ_i from $\mathcal{D}_i$. Note that for $i = n$ we obtain a proof χ_n of $S(M_1, \Omega), \ldots, S(M_n, \Omega)$ from $\mathcal{S}_N$, and $S(N, \Omega) = S(M_1, \Omega), \ldots, S(M_n, \Omega)$. This is just what we want.

For $i = 1$ we define $\chi_1 = \psi_1$.

Assume that $i < n$ and we already have a proof χ_i of Δ_i from $\mathcal{D}_i$. For every $D \in \mathcal{S}_{i+1}$ we define a proof $\chi_i[D]$:

Replace all axioms C in χ_i by the derivation

$$\frac{C, D}{D, C} \pi$$

and simulate χ_i on the extended axioms (the clause D remains passive). The result is a proof $\chi'[D]$ of the sequent

$$D, \ldots, D, \Delta_i.$$

Note that the propagation of D through the proof is possible as no eigenvariable conditions can be violated, as we assume the original proof to be regular (if not then we may transform the ψ_i into proofs with mutually disjoint sets of eigenvariables). Then we define $\chi_i[D]$ as

$$\frac{\chi'[D]}{\Delta_i, D} c^* + \pi$$

Next we replace every axiom D in the derivation ψ_{i+1} by the proof $\chi_i[D]$ and (again) simulate ψ_{i+1} on the end-sequents of the $\chi_i[D]$ where the Δ_i remain passive. Again we can be sure that no eigenvariable condition is violated and we obtain a proof ρ of

$$\Delta_i, \ldots, \Delta_i, \Gamma_{i+1}.$$

from the clause set $merge(\mathcal{D}_i, \mathcal{S}_{i+1})$ which is $\mathcal{D}_{i+1}$. Finally we define $\chi_{i+1} =$

$$\frac{\rho}{\Delta_i, \Gamma_{i+1}} \pi^* + c^*$$

Indeed, χ_{i+1} is a proof of Δ_{i+1} from $\mathcal{D}_{i+1}$. ◇

Like in the classical case ([6]) we define projections of the proof ϕ relative to clauses C in $\mathrm{CL}(\phi)$. The basic idea is the following: we drop all inferences which infer ancestors of a cut formula; the result is a cut-free proof of the end sequent extended by the clause C. Of course we do not obtain cut-elimination itself, but instead a cut free proof of the end sequent extended by a clause. These cut-free proofs are eventually inserted into a resolution proof, which eventually gives a proof with atomic cuts only.

Lemma 1. *Let ϕ be a deduction in $\mathcal{SK}[\mathbf{K}]$ of a sequent S. Let C be a clause in $\mathrm{CL}(\phi)$. Then there exists a deduction $\phi[C]$ of C, S s.t. $\phi[C]$ is cut-free (in particular $\phi(C) \in \mathcal{SK}^{\emptyset}[\mathbf{K}]$) and $\|\phi[C]\| \leq 2 * \|\phi\|$.*

Proof. Let $\mathcal{S}_N$ be $|\Theta(\phi)/N|$ (like in the proof of Theorem 1). We prove that

($\star$) for every node N in ϕ and for every $C \in \mathcal{S}_N$ there exists a proof $T(\phi, N, C)$ of $C, \bar{S}(N, \Omega)$ s.t.
$$\|T(\phi, N, C)\| \leq 2\|\phi.N\|.$$

Indeed, it is sufficient to prove ($\star$): for the root node N_0 we have $S = \bar{S}(N_0, \Omega)$ (no signed formula of the end sequent is an ancestor of Ω), $\phi.N_0 = \phi$ and $\mathrm{CL}(\phi) = \mathcal{S}_{N_0}$; so at the end we just define $\phi[C] = T(\phi, N_0, C)$ for every $C \in \mathrm{CL}(\phi)$.

We prove $\star$ by induction on the depth of a node N in ϕ.

(IB) N is a leaf in ϕ.

Then, by definition of $\mathcal{S}_N$ we have $\mathcal{S} = \{S(N, \Omega)\}$ and $C \colon S(N, \Omega)$ is the only clause in $\mathcal{S}_N$. Let $\Gamma = \bar{S}(N, \Omega)$. Then $S(N)$ (the sequent labelling the node N) is a permutation variant of C, Γ and we define $T(\phi, N, C) =$

$$\frac{S(N)}{C, \Gamma} \pi$$

If no permutation is necessary we just define $T(\phi, N, C) = S(N)$. In both cases

$$\|T(\phi, N, C)\| \leq 2 = 2\|\phi.N\|.$$

(IH) Assume ($\star$) holds for all nodes of depth $\leq k$.

Let N be a node of depth $k + 1$. We distinguish the following cases:

(1) N is inferred from M via a unary inference x. By Definition of the clause term we have $\mathcal{S}_N = \mathcal{S}_M$. So any clause in $\mathcal{S}_N$ is already in $\mathcal{S}_M$.
 (1a) The auxiliary formula of x is an ancestor of Ω. Then clearly $\bar{S}(N, \Omega) = \bar{S}(M, \Omega)$ and we define $T(\phi, N, C) = T(\phi, M, C)$. Clearly

$$\|T(\phi, N, C)\| = \|T(\phi, M, C)\| \leq_{(IH)} 2\|\phi.M\| < 2\|\phi.N\|.$$

(1b) The auxiliary formula of x is not an ancestor of Ω. Let $\Gamma = \bar{S}(M,\Omega), \Gamma' = \bar{S}(N,\Omega)$; thus the auxiliary formula of x is in Γ. By (IH) there exists a proof $\psi: T(\phi, M, C)$ of C, Γ and $\|\psi\| \leq 2\|\phi.M\|$. We define $T(\phi, N, C) =$

$$\frac{(\psi)}{C, \Gamma} \; x$$
$$\overline{C, \Gamma'}$$

Note that x cannot be a strong quantifier inference as the proof ϕ is skolemized and there are no strong quantifiers in the end sequent. Thus $T(\phi, N, C)$ is well-defined. Moreover

$$\|T(\phi, N, C)\| = \|T(\phi, M, C)\| + 1 \leq_{(IH)} 2\|\phi.M\| + 1 < 2\|\phi.N\|.$$

(2) N is inferred from $M_1, \ldots, M_n$ via the inference x for $n \geq 2$. By (IH) there are proofs $T(\phi, M_i, C_i)$ for $i = 1, \ldots, n$ and $C_i \in \mathcal{S}_{M_i}$. Let $\bar{S}(M_i, \Omega) = \Gamma_i$ and $\bar{S}(N, \Omega) = \Gamma'_1, \ldots, \Gamma'_n$. We abbreviate $T(\phi, M_i, C_i)$ by ψ_i.

(2a) The auxiliary formulas of x are in $\Gamma_1, \ldots, \Gamma_n$. Let C be a clause in $\mathcal{S}_N$. Then, by definition of the characteristic clause set, $C = C_1, \ldots, C_n$ for $C_i \in \mathcal{S}_{M_i}$ ($\mathcal{S}_N$ is defined by merge). We define $T(\phi, N, C)$ as

$$\frac{(\psi_1) \quad\quad (\psi_n)}{C_1, \Gamma_1 \quad \ldots \quad C_n, \Gamma_n} \; x$$
$$\overline{C_1, \ldots, C_n, \Gamma'_1, \ldots, \Gamma'_n}$$

By definition of $\| \; \|$ we have

$$\|\phi.N\| = 1 + \sum_{i=1}^{n} \|\phi.M_i\|,$$

$$\|\psi_i\| \leq 2\|\phi.M_i\| \text{ by (IH)}$$

Therefore

$$\|T(\phi, N, C)\| = 1 + \sum_{i=1}^{n} \|\psi_i\| \leq 1 + 2\sum_{i=1}^{n} \|\phi.M_i\| < 2\|\phi.N\|.$$

(2b) The auxiliary formulas of x are not in $\Gamma_1, \ldots, \Gamma_n$. Let C by a clause in $\mathcal{S}_N$. Then x operates on ancestors of cuts and $\mathcal{S}_N = \bigcup_{i=1}^{n} \mathcal{S}_{M_i}$, thus $C \in \mathcal{S}_{M_i}$ for some $i \in \{1, \ldots, n\}$. Moreover $\Gamma'_i = \Gamma_i$ for $i = 1, \ldots, n$. We define $T(\phi, N, C)$ as

$$\frac{\dfrac{(\psi_i)}{C, \Gamma_i}}{\dfrac{C, \Gamma_i, \Gamma_1, \ldots, \Gamma_{i-1}, \Gamma_{i+1}, \ldots, \Gamma_n}{C, \Gamma_1, \ldots, \Gamma_n} \; \pi} \; w$$

Then

$$\|T(\phi, N, C)\| \leq \|\psi_i\| + 2 < 2\|\phi.N\|.$$

Example 5. Let ϕ' be the proof from Example 3. We have computed the set $\mathrm{CL}(\phi')$ in example 4. We select the clause $C\colon 0\colon P(\alpha),\ 0\colon P(\alpha),\ 1\colon P(\alpha)$ and compute the projection $\phi'[C]$:

$$
\cfrac{\cfrac{\cfrac{\cfrac{\cfrac{\cfrac{0\colon P(\alpha),\ u\colon P(\alpha),\ u\colon Q(\alpha),\ 0\colon P(\alpha),\ 1\colon P(\alpha)}{0\colon P(\alpha),\ 0\colon P(\alpha), 1\colon P(\alpha),\ u\colon P(\alpha),\ u\colon Q(\alpha)}\ \pi}{0\colon P(\alpha),\ 0\colon P(\alpha), 1\colon P(\alpha),\ u\colon P(\alpha)\lor Q(\alpha)}\ \lor\colon u}{0\colon P(\alpha),\ 0\colon P(\alpha), 1\colon P(\alpha),\ u\colon P(\alpha)\lor Q(\alpha),\ u\colon R(\alpha)}\ w}{0\colon P(\alpha),\ 0\colon P(\alpha), 1\colon P(\alpha),\ u\colon (P(\alpha)\lor Q(\alpha))\lor R(\alpha)}\ \lor\colon u}{0\colon P(\alpha),\ 0\colon P(\alpha), 1\colon P(\alpha),\ 0\colon (Dx)((P(x)\lor Q(x))\lor R(x))}\ D\colon 0}{0\colon P(\alpha),\ 0\colon P(\alpha), 1\colon P(\alpha),\ 0\colon (Dx)((P(x)\lor Q(x))\lor R(x)),\ 1\colon P(c)}\ w
$$

Let ϕ be a proof of S s.t. $\phi\in\mathcal{SK}[\mathbf{K}]$ and let γ be a W-resolution refutation of $\mathrm{CL}(\phi)$. We define a ground projection γ' of γ which is a $\mathbf{K}$-proof of $\square$ from instances of $\mathrm{CL}(\phi)$. This proof γ' can be transformed into a proof $\gamma'[\phi]$ of S from the axiom set $\mathcal{A}$ s.t. $\gamma'[\phi]\in\mathcal{SK}^0[\mathbf{K}]$ ($\gamma'[\phi]$ is a proof with atomic cuts). Indeed, γ' is the skeleton of the proof of S with atomic cuts and the real core of the end result; $\gamma'[\phi]$ can be considered as an application of γ' to (the projections of) ϕ.

Theorem 2. *Let ϕ be a proof of S from $\mathcal{A}$ in $\mathcal{SK}[\mathbf{K}]$ and let γ' be a ground projection of a W-refutation of $\mathrm{CL}(\phi)$. Then there exists a proof $\gamma'[\phi]$ of S with $\gamma'[\phi]\in\mathcal{SK}^0[\mathbf{K}]$ and*

$$\|\gamma'[\phi]\| \leq \|\gamma'\|(2*\|\phi\| + l(S) + 2).$$

Proof. We construct $\gamma'[\phi]$:

(1) Replace every axiom C in γ' by the projection $\phi[C]$. Then instead of C we obtain the proof $\phi[C]$ of C, S. For every occurrence of an axiom C in γ we obtain a proof of length $\leq 2*\|\phi\|$ (by Lemma 1).
(2) Apply the permutation rule to all end sequents of the $\phi[C]$ and infer S, C. The result is a proof $\psi[C]$ with $\|\psi[C]\| \leq 2*\|\phi\| + 1$.
(3) Simulate γ' on the extended sequents S, C, where the left part S remains passive (note that, according to our definition, inferences take place on the right). The result is a proof χ of a sequent $S,\ldots, S$ from $\mathcal{A}$ s.t.

$$\|\chi\| \leq \|\gamma'\| * (2*\|\phi\| + 1) + \|\gamma\|.$$

Note that χ is indeed a $\mathbf{K}$-proof as all inferences in γ' are also inferences of $\mathbf{K}$.

(4) Apply one permutation and contractions to the end sequent of χ for obtaining the end sequent S. The resulting proof is $\gamma'[\phi]$, the proof we are searching for. As the number of occurrences of S in the end sequent is $\leq \|\gamma'\|$ the additional number of inferences is $\leq 1 + l(S)*\|\gamma'\|$. By putting things together we obtain

$$\|\gamma'[\phi]\| \leq \|\gamma'\|(2*\|\phi\| + l(S) + 2).$$

◇

Looking at the estimation in Theorem 2 we see that the main source of complexity is the length of the W-resolution proof γ'. Indeed, γ (and thus γ') can be considered as the characteristic part of $\gamma'[\phi]$ representing the essence of cut-elimination. To sum up the procedure CERES-m for cut-elimination in any LM-type logic **K** cab be defined as:

Definition 25 (CERES-m).

> input: $\phi \in \mathcal{P}[\mathbf{K}]$.
> construct a Skolem form ϕ' of ϕ.
> compute $\mathrm{CL}(\phi')$.
> construct a W-refutation γ of $\mathrm{CL}(\phi')$.
> compute a ground projection γ' of γ.
> compute $\gamma'[\phi']$ ($\gamma'[\phi'] \in \mathcal{SK}^0[\mathbf{K}]$).
> reskolemize $\gamma'[\phi']$ to ϕ'' ($\phi'' \in \mathcal{P}^0[\mathbf{K}]$).

Example 6. The proof ϕ from Example 1 has been skolemized to a proof ϕ' in Example 3. In Example 4 we have computed the characteristic clause set $\mathrm{CL}(\phi')$ and gave a refutation γ of $\mathrm{CL}(\phi')$ and a ground projection $\gamma': \gamma\{\alpha \leftarrow c\}$. Recall γ':

$$\frac{\dfrac{\dfrac{0\colon P(c),\ 0\colon P(c),\ 1\colon P(c) \quad u\colon P(c)}{0\colon P(c),\ 0\colon P(c)}\,cut_{1u}}{0\colon P(c)}\,c \qquad u\colon P(c)}{\Box}\,cut_{0u}$$

and the instances $C_1' = u\colon P(c)$ and $C_2' = 0\colon P(c),\ 0\colon P(c),\ 1\colon P(c)$ of two signed clauses in $\mathrm{CL}(\phi')$ which defined the axioms of γ'. We obtain $\gamma'[\phi']$ by substituting the axioms C_1', C_2' by the projections $\phi[C_1'], \phi[C_2']$ ($\phi[C_2']$ is an instance of the projection computed in Example 5). The end sequent of ϕ' is

$$S\colon\ 0\colon (Dx)((P(x) \vee Q(x)) \vee R(x)),\ 1\colon P(c)$$

So we obtain $\gamma'[\phi'] =$

$$\frac{\dfrac{\dfrac{\dfrac{(\phi'[C_2'])}{0\colon P(c),\ 0\colon P(c),\ 1\colon P(c),\ S}\,\pi \quad \dfrac{(\phi[C_1'])}{u\colon P(c),\ S}\,\pi}{\dfrac{S,\ 0\colon P(c),\ 0\colon P(c),\ 1\colon P(c) \quad S,\ u\colon P(c)}{S,\ S,\ 0\colon P(c),\ 0\colon P(c)}}\,cut_{1u}}{\dfrac{S,\ S,\ 0\colon P(c)}{}\,c \qquad \dfrac{(\phi[C_1'])}{\dfrac{u\colon P(c),\ S}{S,\ u\colon P(c)}\,\pi}}{\dfrac{S,\ S,\ S}{S}\,c^*}\,cut_{0u}$$

5 Conclusion

Besides establishing a feasible cut-elimination method for many-valued first order logics the main aim of this paper is to demonstrate the stability of CERES w.r.t. cut elimination problems beyond classical first order logic. The authors are convinced, that this stability of CERES will it enable to incorporate intrinsic non-classical logics such as intuitionistic logic and possibly to extend CERES to the second order case, where inductive methods of cut-elimination fail by Gödel's Second Incompleteness Theorem.

References

1. M. Baaz, C. Fermüller: Resolution-Based Theorem Proving for Many-Valued Logics, *Journal of Symbolic Computation*, **19**(4), pp. 353-391, 1995.
2. M. Baaz, C. Fermüller, G. Salzer: Automated Deduction for Many-Valued Logics, in: Handbook of Automated Reasoning 2, eds. J. A. Robinson, A. Voronkov, Elsevier and MIT Press, pp. 1356-1402, 2001.
3. M. Baaz, C. Fermüller, R. Zach: Elimination of Cuts in First-order Finite-valued Logics, *J. Inform. Process. Cybernet. (EIK)*, **29**(6) , pp. 333-355, 1994.
4. M. Baaz, A. Leitsch: Cut normal forms and proof complexity, *Annals of Pure and Applied Logic*, **97**, pp. 127-177, 1999.
5. M. Baaz, A. Leitsch: Cut-Elimination and Redundancy-Elimination by Resolution, *Journal of Symbolic Computation*, **29**, pp. 149-176, 2000.
6. M. Baaz, A. Leitsch: Towards a Clausal Analysis of Cut-Elimination, *Journal of Symbolic Computation*, to appear.
7. W. A. Carnielli: Systematization of Finite Many-Valued Logics through the Method of Tableaux, *Journal of Symbolic Logic*, **52**(2), pp. 473-493, 1987.
8. G. Gentzen: Untersuchungen über das logische Schließen, *Mathematische Zeitschrift* **39**, pp. 405–431, 1934–1935.

A Decomposition Rule for Decision Procedures by Resolution-Based Calculi

Ullrich Hustadt[1], Boris Motik[2], and Ulrike Sattler[3]

[1] Department of Computer Science, University of Liverpool
Liverpool, UK
U.Hustadt@csc.liv.ac.uk
[2] FZI Research Center for Information Technologies at the University of Karlsruhe
Karlsruhe, Germany
motik@fzi.de
[3] Department of Computer Science, University of Manchester
Manchester, UK
sattler@cs.man.ac.uk

Abstract. Resolution-based calculi are among the most widely used calculi for theorem proving in first-order logic. Numerous refinements of resolution are nowadays available, such as e.g. *basic superposition*, a calculus highly optimized for theorem proving with equality. However, even such an advanced calculus does not restrict inferences enough to obtain decision procedures for complex logics, such as $\mathcal{SHIQ}$. In this paper, we present a new *decomposition* inference rule, which can be combined with any resolution-based calculus compatible with the standard notion of redundancy. We combine decomposition with basic superposition to obtain three new decision procedures: (*i*) for the description logic $\mathcal{SHIQ}$, (*ii*) for the description logic $\mathcal{ALCHIQ}b$, and (*iii*) for answering conjunctive queries over $\mathcal{SHIQ}$ knowledge bases. The first two procedures are worst-case optimal and, based on the vast experience in building efficient theorem provers, we expect them to be suitable for practical usage.

1 Introduction

Resolution-based calculi are nowadays among the most widely used calculi for theorem proving in first-order logic. The reasons for that are twofold. On the theoretical side, the initial resolution calculus was significantly refined to obtain various efficient calculi without losing soundness or completeness (e.g. [2,15]). On the practical side, implementation techniques for efficient theorem provers have been devised and applied in practice (an overview is given in [21]).

Because of its popularity, resolution is often used as a framework for deciding various fragments of first-order logic. The fundamental principles for deciding a first-order fragment $\mathcal{L}$ by resolution are known from [12]. First, one selects a sound and complete resolution calculus $\mathcal{C}$. Next, one identifies the set of clauses $\mathcal{N}_\mathcal{L}$ such that for a finite signature, $\mathcal{N}_\mathcal{L}$ is finite and each formula $\varphi \in \mathcal{L}$, when translated into clauses, produces clauses from $\mathcal{N}_\mathcal{L}$. Finally, one demonstrates *closure* of $\mathcal{N}_\mathcal{L}$ under $\mathcal{C}$, namely, that applying an inference of $\mathcal{C}$ to clauses from $\mathcal{N}_\mathcal{L}$ produces a clause in $\mathcal{N}_\mathcal{L}$. This is sufficient to obtain a refutation decision procedure for $\mathcal{L}$ since, in the worst case, $\mathcal{C}$ will derive all clauses of $\mathcal{N}_\mathcal{L}$. An overview of decision procedures derived by these principles is given in [8].

The calculus $\mathcal{C}$ should be chosen to restrict inferences as much as possible without losing completeness. Namely, an unoptimized calculus usually performs unnecessary inferences which hinder closure of $\mathcal{N}_\mathcal{L}$ under $\mathcal{C}$. Consider the decision procedure for $\mathcal{SHIQ}^-$ description logic we presented in [11]. This logic provides so-called *number restrictions*, which are translated into first-order logic using counting quantifiers. We translate counting quantifiers into (in)equalities, and decide $\mathcal{SHIQ}^-$ by saturation under *basic superposition* [3,14]. The prominent feature of basic superposition is the *basicness* restriction, by which superposition into terms introduced by unification can be omitted without compromising completeness. This restriction is crucial to obtain closure under inferences.

Interestingly, this approach does not yield a decision procedure for the slightly more expressive DL $\mathcal{SHIQ}$ [9] ($\mathcal{SHIQ}^-$ allows number restrictions only on roles without subroles). Namely, basic superposition alone is not restrictive enough to limit the term depth in conclusions. Therefore, we present *decomposition*, a new inference rule which can be used to transform certain conclusions. We show that decomposition is sound and complete when combined with basic superposition, which is interesting because of a non-standard approach to lifting used in basic superposition; however, the rule can be combined with any saturation calculus compatible with the standard notion of redundancy [2].

Decomposition indeed solves the motivating problem since it allows us to establish the closure under inferences for $\mathcal{SHIQ}$, and even yields an optimal decision procedure[4]. Furthermore, decomposition proves to be versatile and useful for other decidable fragments of first-order logic: we extend the basic superposition algorithm to handle $\mathcal{ALCHIQ}b$, a description logic providing *safe* Boolean role expressions. As for $\mathcal{SHIQ}$, this algorithm is optimal. Finally, we derive a decision procedure for answering conjunctive queries over $\mathcal{SHIQ}$ knowledge bases. Based on the vast experience in building efficient theorem provers, we believe that these algorithms are suitable for practice.

All results in this paper have been summarized in a technical report [10].

2 Preliminaries

Description Logics. Given a set of role names N_R, a $\mathcal{SHIQ}$ *role* is either some $R \in N_R$ or an *inverse role* R^- for some $R \in N_R$. A $\mathcal{SHIQ}$ RBox $KB_\mathcal{R}$ is a finite set of role inclusion axioms $R \sqsubseteq S$ and transitivity axioms $\mathsf{Trans}(R)$, for R and S $\mathcal{SHIQ}$ roles. As usual, for $R \in N_R$, we set $\mathsf{Inv}(R) = R^-$ and $\mathsf{Inv}(R^-) = R$, and we assume that, if $R \sqsubseteq S \in KB_\mathcal{R}$ ($\mathsf{Trans}(R) \in KB_\mathcal{R}$), then $\mathsf{Inv}(R) \sqsubseteq \mathsf{Inv}(S) \in KB_\mathcal{R}$ ($\mathsf{Trans}(\mathsf{Inv}(R)) \in KB_\mathcal{R}$) as well. A role R is *simple* if for each role $S \sqsubseteq^* R$, $\mathsf{Trans}(S) \notin KB_\mathcal{R}$ ($\sqsubseteq^*$ is the reflexive-transitive closure of $\sqsubseteq$).

---

[4] Optimal under the assumption that numbers in number restrictions are coded in unary.

Given a set of concept names N_C, $\mathcal{SHIQ}$ concepts are inductively defined as follows: each $A \in N_C$ is a $\mathcal{SHIQ}$ concept and, if C is a $\mathcal{SHIQ}$ concept, R a role, S a simple role, and n an integer, then $\neg C$, $C_1 \sqcap C_2$, $\forall R.C$, and $\leq n\, S.C$ are also $\mathcal{SHIQ}$ concepts. As usual, we use $C_1 \sqcup C_2$, $\exists R.C$, $\geq n\, S.C$ as abbreviations for $\neg(\neg C_1 \sqcap \neg C_2)$, $\neg \forall R.\neg C$, and $\neg(\leq (n-1)\, S.C)$. A TBox $KB_\mathcal{T}$ is a finite set of concept inclusion axioms $C \sqsubseteq D$. An ABox $KB_\mathcal{A}$ is a finite set of axioms $C(a)$, $R(a,b)$, and (in)equalities $a \approx b$ and $a \not\approx b$. A $\mathcal{SHIQ}$ knowledge base KB is a triple $(KB_\mathcal{R}, KB_\mathcal{T}, KB_\mathcal{A})$. The semantics of KB is given by translating it into first-order logic by the operator π from Table 1. The main inference problem is checking KB satisfiability, i.e. determining if a first-order model of $\pi(KB)$ exists.

The logic $\mathcal{SHIQ}^-$ is obtained from $\mathcal{SHIQ}$ by restricting roles in number restrictions $\leq n\, S.C$ and $\geq n\, S.C$ to *very* simple roles; a role S is *very simple* in $KB_\mathcal{R}$ if there is no role S' with $S' \sqsubseteq S \in KB_\mathcal{R}$. The restriction $\mathcal{ALCHIQ}$ of $\mathcal{SHIQ}$ is obtained by disallowing transitivity axioms Trans(R) in RBoxes.

Considering complexity, we must decide how to measure the *size* of concepts and knowledge bases. Here, we simply use their length, and assume *unary coding of numbers*, i.e. $|\leq n\, R.C| = n + 1 + |C|$.

Basic Superposition. We assume the standard notions of first-order clauses with equality: all existential quantifiers have been eliminated using Skolemization; all remaining variables are universally quantified; we only consider the equality predicate, i.e. all non-equational literals A are encoded as $A \approx \top$ in a multi-sorted setting; and we treat $\approx$ as having built-in symmetry. Moreover, we assume the reader to be familiar with standard resolution [2].

Basic superposition [3,14] is an optimized version of superposition which prohibits superposition into terms introduced by unification in previously performed inferences. Its inferences rules are formalized by distinguishing two parts of a clause: (i) the *skeleton* clause C and (ii) the *substitution* σ representing the cumulative effects of all unifications. Such a representation of a clause $C\sigma$ is called a *closure*, and is written as $C \cdot \sigma$. A closure can conveniently be represented by *marking* the terms in $C\sigma$ occurring at variable positions of C with [ ]. Any position at or beneath a marked position is called a *substitution position*.

The calculus requires two parameters. The first is an *admissible* ordering on terms $\succ$, i.e. a *reduction ordering* total on ground terms. If $\succ$ is total on non-ground terms (as is the case in this paper), it can be extended to literals by associating, with each literal $L = s \circ t$, $\circ \in \{\approx, \not\approx\}$, a complexity measure $c_L = (\max(s,t), p_L, \min(s,t))$, where p_L is 1 if $\circ$ is $\approx$, and 0 otherwise. Now $L_1 \succ L_2$ iff $c_{L_1} \succ c_{L_2}$, where c_{L_i} are compared lexicographically, with $1 \succ 0$. The second parameter of the calculus is a *selection function* which selects an arbitrary set of negative literals in each clause.

The basic superposition calculus is a refutation procedure. If a set of closures N is *saturated up to redundancy* (meaning that all inferences from premises in N are redundant in N), then N is unsatisfiable if and only if it contains the empty closure. A literal $L \cdot \sigma$ is (strictly) maximal w.r.t. a closure $C \cdot \sigma$ if no $L' \in C$ exists, such that $L'\sigma \succ L\sigma$ ($L'\sigma \succeq L\sigma$). A literal $L \cdot \sigma$ is *(strictly) eligible for superposition* in $(C \vee L) \cdot \sigma$ if there are no selected literals in $(C \vee L) \cdot \sigma$ and $L \cdot \sigma$

Table 1. Semantics of $\mathcal{SHIQ}$ by Mapping to FOL

Concepts to FOL: $\pi_y(A, X) = A(X)$	$\pi_y(C \sqcap D, X) = \pi_y(C, X) \wedge \pi_y(D, X)$
$\pi_y(\neg C, X) = \neg \pi_y(C, X)$	$\pi_y(\forall R.C, X) = \forall y : R(X, y) \rightarrow \pi_x(C, y)$
$\pi_y(\leq n\, S.C, X) = \forall y_1, \ldots, y_{n+1} :$	$\bigwedge S(X, y_i) \wedge \bigwedge \pi_x(C, y_i) \rightarrow \bigvee y_i \approx y_j$

Axioms to FOL:	$\pi(C \sqsubseteq D) = \forall x : \pi_y(C, x) \rightarrow \pi_y(D, x)$
	$\pi(R \sqsubseteq S) = \forall x, y : R(x, y) \rightarrow S(x, y)$
	$\pi(\mathsf{Trans}(R)) = \forall x, y, z : R(x, y) \wedge R(y, z) \rightarrow R(x, z)$

KB to FOL:	$\pi(R) = \forall x, y : R(x, y) \leftrightarrow R^-(y, x)$
	$\pi(KB_\mathcal{R}) = \bigwedge_{\alpha \in KB_\mathcal{R}} \pi(\alpha) \wedge \bigwedge_{R \in N_R} \pi(R)$
	$\pi(KB_\mathcal{T}) = \bigwedge_{\alpha \in KB_\mathcal{T}} \pi(\alpha)$
	$\pi(KB_\mathcal{A}) = \bigwedge_{C(a) \in KB_\mathcal{A}} \pi_y(C, a) \wedge \bigwedge_{R(a,b) \in KB_\mathcal{A}} R(a, b) \wedge$
	$\qquad \bigwedge_{a \approx b \in KB_\mathcal{A}} a \approx b \wedge \bigwedge_{a \not\approx b \in KB_\mathcal{A}} a \not\approx b$
	$\pi(KB) = \pi(KB_\mathcal{R}) \wedge \pi(KB_\mathcal{T}) \wedge \pi(KB_\mathcal{A})$

X is a meta variable and is substituted by the actual variable.
π_x is defined as π_y by substituting $x_{(i)}$ for all $y_{(i)}$, respectively, and π_y for π_x.

Table 2. Inference Rules of the $\mathcal{BS}$ Calculus

Positive superposition: $$\frac{(C \vee s \approx t) \cdot \rho \quad (D \vee w \approx v) \cdot \rho}{(C \vee D \vee w[t]_p \approx v) \cdot \theta}$$	(i) $\sigma = \mathsf{MGU}(s\rho, w\rho\|_p)$ and $\theta = \rho\sigma$, (ii) $t\theta \not\succeq s\theta$ and $v\theta \not\succeq w\theta$, (iii) $(s \approx t) \cdot \theta$ is strictly eligible for superposition, (iv) $(w \approx v) \cdot \theta$ is strictly eligible for superposition, (v) $s\theta \approx t\theta \not\succeq w\theta \approx v\theta$, (vi) $w\|_p$ is not a variable.
Negative superposition: $$\frac{(C \vee s \approx t) \cdot \rho \quad (D \vee w \not\approx v) \cdot \rho}{(C \vee D \vee w[t]_p \not\approx v) \cdot \theta}$$	(i) $\sigma = \mathsf{MGU}(s\rho, w\rho\|_p)$ and $\theta = \rho\sigma$, (ii) $t\theta \not\succeq s\theta$ and $v\theta \not\succeq w\theta$, (iii) $(s \approx t) \cdot \theta$ is strictly eligible for superposition, (iv) $(w \not\approx v) \cdot \theta$ is eligible for resolution, (v) $w\|_p$ is not a variable.
Reflexivity resolution: $$\frac{(C \vee s \not\approx t) \cdot \rho}{C \cdot \theta}$$	(i) $\sigma = \mathsf{MGU}(s\rho, t\rho)$ and $\theta = \rho\sigma$, (ii) $(s \not\approx t) \cdot \theta$ is eligible for resolution.
Equality factoring: $$\frac{(C \vee s \approx t \vee s' \approx t') \cdot \rho}{(C \vee t \not\approx t' \vee s' \approx t') \cdot \theta}$$	(i) $\sigma = \mathsf{MGU}(s\rho, s'\rho)$ and $\theta = \rho\sigma$, (ii) $t\theta \not\succeq s\theta$ and $t'\theta \not\succeq s'\theta$, (iii) $(s \approx t) \cdot \theta$ is eligible for superposition.
Ordered Hyperresolution: $$\frac{E_1 \ldots E_n \quad E}{(C_1 \vee \ldots \vee C_n \vee D) \cdot \theta}$$	(i) E_i are of the form $(C_i \vee A_i) \cdot \rho$, for $1 \leq i \leq n$, (ii) E is of the form $(D \vee \neg B_1 \vee \ldots \vee \neg B_n) \cdot \rho$, (iii) σ is the most general substitution such that $A_i\theta = B_i\theta$ for $1 \leq i \leq n$, and $\theta = \rho\sigma$, (iv) $A_i \cdot \theta$ is strictly eligible for superposition, (v) $\neg B_i \cdot \theta$ are selected, or nothing is selected, $i = 1$ and $\neg B_1 \cdot \theta$ is maximal w.r.t. $D \cdot \theta$.

is (strictly) maximal w.r.t. $C \cdot \sigma$; $L \cdot \sigma$ is *eligible for resolution* in $(C \vee L) \cdot \sigma$ if it is selected in $(C \vee L) \cdot \sigma$ or there are no selected literals in $(C \vee L) \cdot \sigma$ and $L \cdot \sigma$ is maximal w.r.t. $C \cdot \sigma$. We denote basic superposition with $\mathcal{BS}$ and present its inference rules in Table 2. The ordered hyperresolution rule is a macro inference, combining negative superposition and reflexivity resolution. The closure E is called the *main premise*, and the closures E_i are called the *side premises*. An overview of the completeness proof and compatible redundancy elimination rules are given in [10].

3 Motivation

To motivate the need for decomposition, we give an overview of our procedure for deciding satisfiability of a $\mathcal{SHIQ}^-$ knowledge base KB using $\mathcal{BS}$ from [11] and highlight the problems related to deciding full $\mathcal{SHIQ}$. We assume that KB has an *extensionally reduced* ABox, where all concepts occurring in ABox assertions are atomic. This is without loss of generality, since each axiom $C(a)$, where C is complex, can be replaced with axioms $A_C(a)$ and $A_C \sqsubseteq C$, for A_C a new concept; this transformation is obviously polynomial.

3.1 Deciding $\mathcal{SHIQ}^-$ by $\mathcal{BS}$

Eliminating Transitivity. A minor problem in deciding satisfiability of KB are the transitivity axioms, which, in their clausal form, do not contain so-called *covering* literals (i.e. literals containing all variables of a clause). Such clauses are known to be difficult to handle, so we preprocess KB into an equisatisfiable $\mathcal{ALCHIQ}^-$ knowledge base $\Omega(KB)$. Roughly speaking, we replace each transitivity axiom $\text{Trans}(S)$ with axioms $\forall R.C \sqsubseteq \forall S.(\forall S.C)$, for each R with $S \sqsubseteq^* R$ and C a concept occurring in KB. This transformation is polynomial.

Preprocessing. We next translate $\Omega(KB)$ into a first-order formula $\pi(KB)$ according to Table 1. Assuming unary coding of numbers, $\pi(KB)$ can be computed in polynomial time. To transform $\pi(KB)$ into a set of closures $\Xi(KB)$, we apply the well-known *structural transformation* [16]. Roughly speaking, the structural transformation introduces a new name for each non-atomic subformula of $\pi(KB)$. It is well-known that $\pi(KB)$ and $\Xi(KB)$ are equisatisfiable, and that $\Xi(KB)$ can be computed in polynomial time.

For any KB, all closures from $\Xi(KB)$ are of types from Table 3; we call them $\mathcal{ALCHIQ}^-$-closures. We use the following notation: for a term t, with $\mathbf{P}(t)$ we denote a disjunction of the form $(\neg)P_1(t) \vee \ldots \vee (\neg)P_n(t)$, and with $\mathbf{P}(\mathbf{f}(x))$ we denote a disjunction of the form $\mathbf{P_1}(f_1(x)) \vee \ldots \vee \mathbf{P_m}(f_m(x))$ (notice that this allows each $\mathbf{P_i}(f_i(x))$ to contain positive and negative literals). With $\langle t \rangle$ we denote that the term t may, but need not be marked. In all closure types, some of the disjuncts may be empty. Furthermore, for each function symbol f occurring in $\Xi(KB)$, there is exactly one closure of type 3 containing $f(x)$ unmarked; this closure is called the R^f-*generator*, the disjunction $\mathbf{P^f}(x)$ is called the f-*support*, and R is called the *designated role* for f and is denoted as $\text{role}(f)$.

Parameters for $\mathcal{BS}$. We use $\mathcal{BS}_{DL}$ to denote the $\mathcal{BS}$ calculus parameterized as follows. We use a standard *lexicographic path ordering* [7,1] (LPO) for comparing terms. LPOs are based on a precedence $>_P$ over function, constant, and predicate symbols. If the precedence is total, LPO is admissible for basic superposition. To decide $\mathcal{ALCHIQ}^-$, we can use any precedence such that $f >_P c >_P p >_P \top$, for any function symbol f, constant c, and predicate symbol p. We select all negative binary literals in a closure. On $\mathcal{ALCHIQ}^-$-closures $\mathcal{BS}_{DL}$ compares only terms with at most one variable, and LPOs are total for such terms. Hence, literals in $\mathcal{ALCHIQ}^-$-closures can be compared as explained in Section 2.

Table 3. Types of $\mathcal{ALCHIQ}^-$-closures

1	$\neg R(x,y) \vee \mathsf{Inv}(R)(y,x)$
2	$\neg R(x,y) \vee S(x,y)$
3	$\mathbf{P^f}(x) \vee R(x, \langle f(x) \rangle)$
4	$\mathbf{P^f}(x) \vee R([f(x)], x)$
5	$\mathbf{P_1}(x) \vee \mathbf{P_2}(\langle \mathbf{f}(x) \rangle) \vee \langle f_i(x) \rangle \approx/\not\approx \langle f_j(x) \rangle$
6	$\mathbf{P_1}(x) \vee \mathbf{P_2}([g(x)]) \vee \mathbf{P_3}(\langle \mathbf{f}([g(x)]) \rangle) \vee \langle t_i \rangle \approx/\not\approx \langle t_j \rangle$
	where t_i and t_j are either of the form $f([g(x)])$ or of the form x
7	$\mathbf{P_1}(x) \vee \neg R(x, y_i) \vee \mathbf{P_2}(\mathbf{y}) \vee y_i \approx y_j$
8	$R(\langle \mathbf{a} \rangle, \langle \mathbf{b} \rangle) \vee \mathbf{P}(\langle \mathbf{t} \rangle) \vee \langle t_i \rangle \approx/\not\approx \langle t_j \rangle$
	where t, t_i and t_j are either some constant b or a functional term $f_i([a])$

Conditions:

(i): In any term $f(t)$, the inner term t occurs marked.
(ii): In all positive equality literals with at least one function symbol, both sides are marked.
(iii): Any closure containing a term $f(t)$ contains $\mathbf{P^f}(t)$ as well.
(iv): In a literal $[f_i(t)] \approx [f_j(t)]$, $\mathsf{role}(f_i) = \mathsf{role}(f_j)$.
(v): In a literal $[f(g(x))] \approx x$, $\mathsf{role}(f) = \mathsf{Inv}(\mathsf{role}(g))$.
(vi): For each $[f_i(a)] \approx [b]$ a *witness* closure of the form $R(\langle a \rangle, \langle b \rangle) \vee D$ exists, with $\mathsf{role}(f_i) = R$, D does not contain functional terms or negative binary literals, and is contained in this closure.

Closure of $\mathcal{ALCHIQ}^-$-closures under Inferences. The following lemma is central to our work, since it implies, together with a bound on the number of $\mathcal{ALCHIQ}^-$-closures, termination of $\mathcal{BS}_{DL}$. The proof is by examining all inferences of $\mathcal{BS}_{DL}$ for all possible types of $\mathcal{ALCHIQ}^-$-closures.

Lemma 1. *Let $\Xi(KB) = N_0, \ldots, N_i \cup \{C\}$ be a $\mathcal{BS}_{DL}$-derivation, where C is the conclusion derived from premises in N_i. Then C is either an $\mathcal{ALCHIQ}^-$-closure or it is redundant in N_i.*

Termination and Complexity Analysis. Let $|KB|$ denote the size of KB with numbers coded in unary. It is straightforward to see that, given a knowledge base KB, the size of a set of non-redundant $\mathcal{ALCHIQ}^-$-closures over the vocabulary from $\Xi(KB)$ is exponentially bounded in $|KB|$: let r be the number of role names, a the number of atomic concept names, c the number of constants, f the number of Skolem function symbols occurring in $\Xi(KB)$, and v the maximal number of variables in a closure. Obviously, r, a, and c are linear in $|KB|$ and, for unary coding of numbers, f and v are also linear in $|KB|$. Thus we have at most $(f+1)^2(v+c)$ terms of depth at most 2, which, together with the possible marking, yields at most $t = 2(f+1)^2(v+c)$ terms in a closure. This yields at most $at + rt^2$ atoms, which, together with the equality literals, and allowing each atom to occur negatively, gives at most $\ell = 2(at + (r+1)t^2)$ literals in a closure. Each closure can contain an arbitrary subset of these literals, so the total number of closures is bounded by 2^ℓ. Thus we obtain an exponential bound on the size of the set of closures that $\mathcal{BS}_{DL}$ can derive. Each inference step can be carried out in exponential time, so, since $\mathcal{BS}_{DL}$ is a sound and complete refutation procedure [3], we have the following result:

Theorem 1 ([11]). *For an $\mathcal{ALCHIQ}^-$ knowledge base KB, saturating $\Xi(KB)$ by $\mathcal{BS}_{DL}$ with eager application of redundancy elimination rules decides satisfiability of KB and runs in time exponential in $|KB|$, for unary coding of numbers.*

3.2 Removing the Restriction to Very Simple Roles

For a $\mathcal{SHIQ}$ knowledge base KB containing number restrictions on roles which are not very simple, the saturation of $\Xi(KB)$ may contain closures whose structure corresponds to Table 3, but for which conditions $(iii) - (vi)$ do not hold; we call such closures $\mathcal{ALCHIQ}$-closures. Let KB be the knowledge base containing axioms $(1) - (9)$:

$$R \sqsubseteq T \Rightarrow \neg R(x,y) \vee T(x,y) \quad (1)$$
$$S \sqsubseteq T \Rightarrow \neg S(x,y) \vee T(x,y) \quad (2)$$
$$C \sqsubseteq \exists R.T \Rightarrow \neg C(x) \vee R(x, f(x)) \quad (3)$$
$$\top \sqsubseteq \exists S^-.T \Rightarrow S^-(x, g(x)) \quad (4)$$
$$\top \sqsubseteq \leq 1T \Rightarrow \neg T(x, y_1) \vee \neg T(x, y_2) \vee y_1 \approx y_2 \quad (5)$$
$$\exists S.T \sqsubseteq D \Rightarrow \neg S(x,y) \vee D(x) \quad (6)$$
$$\exists R.T \sqsubseteq \neg D \Rightarrow \neg R(x,y) \vee \neg D(x) \quad (7)$$
$$\top \sqsubseteq C \Rightarrow C(x) \quad (8)$$
$$\neg S^-(x,y) \vee S(y,x) \quad (9)$$

$$S([g(x)], x) \quad (10)$$
$$\neg C(x) \vee T(x, [f(x)]) \quad (11)$$
$$T([g(x)], x) \quad (12)$$
$$\neg C([g(x)]) \vee [f(g(x))] \approx x \quad (13)$$
$$\neg C([g(x)]) \vee R([g(x)], x) \quad (14)$$
$$D([g(x)]) \quad (15)$$
$$\neg D([g(x)]) \vee \neg C([g(x)]) \quad (16)$$
$$\neg C([g(x)]) \quad (17)$$
$$\square \quad (18)$$

Consider a saturation of $\Xi(KB)$ by $\mathcal{BS}_{DL}$ producing closures $(10) - (13)$. For (13), Condition (v) is not satisfied: $\mathsf{role}(f) = R \neq \mathsf{Inv}(\mathsf{role}(g)) = \mathsf{Inv}(S^-) = S$. This is because in (5), a number restriction was stated on a role that is not very simple. Now (13) can be superposed into (3), resulting in (14), which is obviously not an $\mathcal{ALCHIQ}$-closure.

If KB were an $\mathcal{ALCHIQ}^-$ knowledge base, Condition (v) would hold, so we would be able to assume that a closure $R([g(x)], x)$ exists. This closure would subsume (14), so we would simply throw (14) away and continue saturation.

Since Condition (v) does not hold, a subsuming closure does not exist, so in order not to lose completeness, we must keep (14) and perform further inferences with it. This might cause termination problems: in general, (14) might be resolved with some closure of type 6 of the form $C([g(h(x))])$, producing a closure of the form $R([g(h(x))], [h(x)])$. The term depth in the binary literal is now two, and it may be used to derive closures with ever deeper terms. Thus, the set of derivable closures becomes infinite, and we cannot conclude that the saturation necessarily terminates.

A careful analysis reveals that various refinements of the ordering and the selection function will not help. Furthermore, the inference deriving (14) is necessary. Namely, KB is unsatisfiable, and the empty closure is derived through steps $(15) - (18)$, which require (14).

4 Transformation by Decomposition

To solve the problems outlined in Subsection 3.2, we introduce *decomposition*, a transformation that can be applied to the conclusions of some $\mathcal{BS}$ inferences. It is a general technique not limited to description logics. In the following, for $\mathbf{x}$ a vector of distinct variables $x_1, \ldots, x_n$, and $\mathbf{t}$ a vector of (not necessarily distinct) terms $t_1, \ldots, t_n$, let $\{\mathbf{x} \mapsto \mathbf{t}\}$ denote the substitution $\{x_1 \mapsto t_1, \ldots, x_n \mapsto t_n\}$, and let $Q([\mathbf{t}])$ denote $Q([t_1], \ldots, [t_n])$.

Definition 1. *Let $C \cdot \rho$ be a closure and N a set of closures. A decomposition of $C \cdot \rho$ w.r.t. N is a pair of closures $C_1 \cdot \rho \vee Q([\mathbf{t}])$ and $C_2 \cdot \theta \vee \neg Q(\mathbf{x})$ where $\mathbf{t}$ is a vector of n terms, $\mathbf{x}$ is a vector of n distinct variables, $n \geq 0$, satisfying these conditions: (i) $C = C_1 \cup C_2$, (ii) $\rho = \theta\{\mathbf{x} \mapsto \mathbf{t}\}$, (iii) $\mathbf{x}$ is exactly the set of free variables of $C_2\theta$, and (iv) if $C_2 \cdot \theta \vee \neg Q'(\mathbf{x}) \in N$, then $Q = Q'$, otherwise Q is a new predicate not occurring in N. The closure $C_2 \cdot \theta$ is called the fixed part, the closure $C_1 \cdot \rho$ is called the variable part and the predicate Q is called the definition predicate. An application of decomposition is often written as $C \cdot \rho \rightsquigarrow C_1 \cdot \rho \vee Q([\mathbf{t}]), C_2 \cdot \theta \vee \neg Q(\mathbf{x})$.*

Let ξ be a $\mathcal{BS}$ inference with a most general unifier σ on a literal $L_m \cdot \eta$ from a main premise $D_m \cdot \eta$ and with a side premise $D_s \cdot \eta$. The conclusion of ξ is eligible for decomposition if, for each ground substitution τ such that $\xi\tau$ satisfies the constraints of $\mathcal{BS}$, we have $\neg Q(\mathbf{t})\tau \prec L_m \eta \sigma \tau$. With $\mathcal{BS}^+$ we denote the $\mathcal{BS}$ calculus where decomposition can be applied to conclusions of eligible inferences.

The definition of eligibility is defined to cover the most general case. In the following, we use a simpler test: ξ is eligible for decomposition if $\neg Q(\mathbf{t}) \prec L_m \eta \sigma$, or a literal $L \in D_s$ exists such that $\neg Q(\mathbf{t}) \prec L\eta\sigma$. The latter is a sufficient approximation, since $L\eta\sigma\tau \prec L_m\eta\sigma\tau$ for each τ as in Definition 1.

E.g., consider superposition from $[f(g(x))] \approx [h(g(x))]$ into $C(x) \vee R(x, f(x))$ resulting in $D = C([g(x)]) \vee R([g(x)], [h(g(x))])$. The conclusion is not an $\mathcal{ALCHIQ}$-closure, so keeping it might lead to non-termination. D can be decomposed into $C([g(x)]) \vee Q_{R,f}([g(x)])$ and $\neg Q_{R,f}(x) \vee R(x, [h(x)])$, which are both $\mathcal{ALCHIQ}$-closures. The inference is eligible for decomposition if we ensure that $\neg Q_{R,f}(g(x)) \prec R(g(x), h(g(x)))$ (e.g. by using $R >_P Q_{R,f}$ in LPO).

The soundness and completeness proofs for $\mathcal{BS}^+$ are given in [10]; here we present the intuition behind these results. As shown by Lemma 2, decomposition is sound: it merely introduces a new name for $C_2 \cdot \theta$. Any model of $C \cdot \rho$ can be extended to a model of $C_1 \cdot \rho \vee Q([\mathbf{t}])$ and $C_2 \cdot \theta \vee \neg Q(\mathbf{x})$ by adjusting the interpretation of Q.

Lemma 2. *Let $N_0, \ldots, N_i$ be a $\mathcal{BS}^+$-derivation, and let I_0 be a model of N_0. Then for $i > 1$, N_i has a model I_i such that, if the inference deriving N_i from N_{i-1} involves a decomposition step as specified in Definition 1 introducing a new predicate Q, then $I_i = I_{i-1} \cup \{Q(\mathbf{s}) \mid \mathbf{s}$ is a vector of ground terms such that $C_2\theta\{\mathbf{x} \mapsto \mathbf{s}\}$ is true in $I_{i-1}\}$; otherwise $I_i = I_{i-1}$.*

The notion of *variable irreducibility* is a central concept in the completeness proof of basic superposition. Roughly speaking, a closure $C \cdot \rho\tau$ is a *variable* *irreducible ground instance* of $C \cdot \rho$ w.r.t. a ground and convergent rewrite system R if substitution positions in $C \cdot \rho\tau$ are not reducible by rewrite rules in R. We use this to prove completeness, by showing that decomposition is compatible with the usual notion of redundancy for $\mathcal{BS}$ [3,14], as shown by Lemma 3. We do so in two steps. First, the eligibility criterion ensures that (*) ground instances of $C_1 \cdot \rho \vee Q([\mathbf{t}])$ and $C_2 \cdot \theta \vee \neg Q(\mathbf{x})$ are smaller than the corresponding ground instances of $D_m \cdot \eta$. Second, (**) for each variable irreducible ground instance $C \cdot \rho\tau$ of $C \cdot \rho$, there are variable irreducible ground instances E_1 and E_2 of $C_1 \cdot \rho \vee Q([\mathbf{t}])$ and $C_2 \cdot \theta \vee \neg Q(\mathbf{x})$, respectively, such that $\{E_1, E_2\} \models C \cdot \rho\tau$. Property (**) holds since the terms $\mathbf{t}$ are extracted from the substitution part of $C \cdot \rho$. Effectively, (**) means that decomposition does not lose "relevant" variable irreducible ground instances of $C \cdot \rho$ which are used in the proof. Actually, closures $C_1 \cdot \rho \vee Q([\mathbf{t}])$ and $C_2 \cdot \theta \vee \neg Q(\mathbf{x})$ can have "excessive" variable irreducible ground instances without a counterpart ground instance of $C \cdot \rho$. However, this is not a problem, since decomposition is sound.

Lemma 3. *Let ξ be a $\mathcal{BS}$ inference applied to premises from a closure set N resulting in a closure $C \cdot \rho$. If $C \cdot \rho$ can be decomposed into closures $C_1 \cdot \rho \vee Q([\mathbf{t}])$ and $C_2 \cdot \theta \vee \neg Q(\mathbf{x})$ which are both redundant in N, then the inference ξ is redundant in N.*

Soundness and compatibility with the notion of redundancy imply that $\mathcal{BS}^+$ is a sound and complete calculus, as shown by Theorem 2. Note that, to obtain the saturated set N, we can use any fair saturation strategy [2]. Furthermore, the decomposition rule can be applied an infinite number of times in a saturation, and it is even allowed to introduce an infinite number of definition predicates. In the latter case, we just need to ensure that the term ordering is well-founded.

Theorem 2. *For N_0 a set of closures of the form $C \cdot \{\}$, let N be a set of closures obtained by saturating N_0 under $\mathcal{BS}^+$. Then N_0 is satisfiable if and only if N does not contain the empty closure.*

For a resolution calculus $\mathcal{C}$ other than $\mathcal{BS}$, Lemma 2 applies as well. Furthermore, if $\mathcal{C}$ is compatible with the standard notion of redundancy [2], Lemma 3 holds as well: (*) holds for $\mathcal{C}$ identically, and (**) is needed only for $\mathcal{BS}$, due to a non-standard lifting strategy. Hence, decomposition can be combined with any such calculus.

Related Work. In [17] and [6] a similar rule for splitting without backtracking was considered, and in [18] a similar separation rule was introduced to decide fluted logic. Decomposition allows replacing complex terms with simpler ones, so it is different from splitting (which does not allow component clauses to contain common variables) or separation (which links component clauses only by literals without functional terms). Furthermore, by the eligibility criterion we make decomposition compatible with the standard notion of redundancy. Thus, decomposition becomes a full-fledged inference rule and can be applied an infinite number of times in a saturation. Finally, combining decomposition with basic superposition is not trivial, due to a non-standard approach to lifting.

5 Applications of Decomposition

To show the usefulness of decomposition, in this section, we use it to extend the algorithm from Section 3 to obtain three new decision procedures.

5.1 Deciding $\mathcal{ALCHIQ}$

Definition 2. $\mathcal{BS}_{DL}^+$ *is the modification of the* $\mathcal{BS}_{DL}$ *calculus where conclusions are decomposed, whenever possible, as follows, for an arbitrary term* t:

$$D \cdot \rho \vee R([t],[f(t)]) \rightsquigarrow \quad D \cdot \rho \vee Q_{R,f}([t])$$
$$\neg Q_{R,f}(x) \vee R(x,[f(x)])$$
$$D \cdot \rho \vee R([f(t)],[t]) \rightsquigarrow \quad D \cdot \rho \vee Q_{\mathsf{Inv}(R),f}([t])$$
$$\neg Q_{\mathsf{Inv}(R),f}(x) \vee R([f(x)],x)$$

and where the precedence of the LPO is $f >_P c >_P p >_P Q_{S,f} >_P \top$, *for any function symbol* f, *constant symbol* c, *non-definition predicate* p *and definition predicate* $Q_{S,f}$.

For a (possibly inverse) role S and a function symbol f, the predicate $Q_{S,f}$ is unique. Since $R([f(x)],x)$ and $\mathsf{Inv}(R)(x,[f(x)])$ are logically equivalent by the operator π, it is safe to use $Q_{\mathsf{Inv}(R),f}$ as the definition predicate for $R([f(x)],x)$.

Inferences of $\mathcal{BS}_{DL}$, when applied to $\mathcal{ALCHIQ}$-closures, derive an $\mathcal{ALCHIQ}$-closure even if conditions $(iii) - (vi)$ are not enforced. The only exception is the superposition from a closure of type 5 or 6 into a closure of type 3, but such closures are decomposed by $\mathcal{BS}_{DL}^+$ into two $\mathcal{ALCHIQ}$-closures; the inference is eligible for decomposition since $\neg Q_{R,f}(t) \prec R(t,g(t))$ (which is the maximal literal of the closure of type 3 after unification). Furthermore, $Q_{S,f}$ is unique for a pair of S and f, so the number of definition predicates is polynomially bounded. This allows us to derive an exponential bound on the number of $\mathcal{ALCHIQ}$-closures as in Theorem 1 and thus to obtain a decision procedure.

Theorem 3. *For an $\mathcal{ALCHIQ}$ knowledge base KB, saturation of $\Xi(KB)$ by $\mathcal{BS}_{DL}^+$ decides satisfiability of KB, and runs in time exponential in $|KB|$.*

5.2 Safe Role Expressions

A prominent limitation of $\mathcal{ALCHIQ}$ is the rather restricted form of role expressions that may occur in a knowledge base. This can be overcome by allowing for *safe* Boolean role expressions in TBox and ABox axioms. The resulting logic is called $\mathcal{ALCHIQ}b$, and can be viewed as the "union" of $\mathcal{ALCHIQ}$ and $\mathcal{ALCIQ}b$ [20]. Using safe expressions, it is possible to state negative or disjunctive knowledge regarding roles. Roughly speaking, safe role expressions are built using union, disjunction, and *relativized* negation of roles. This allows for statements such as $\forall x, y : isParentOf(x,y) \rightarrow isMotherOf(x,y) \vee isFatherOf(x,y)$, but does not allow for "fully negated" statements such as: $\forall x, y : \neg isMotherOf(x,y) \rightarrow isFatherOf(x,y)$. The safety restriction is needed for the algorithm to remain in EXPTIME; namely, it is known that reasoning with non-safe role expressions is NEXPTIME-complete [13].

Definition 3. *A* role expression *is a finite expression built over the set of roles using the connectives* ⊔, ⊓ *and* ¬ *in the usual way. A role expression E is* safe *if each conjunction of the disjunctive normal form of E contains at least one non-negated atom. The description logic* $\mathcal{ALCHIQ}b$ *is obtained from* $\mathcal{ALCHIQ}$ *by allowing concepts* $\exists E.C$, $\forall E.C$, $\geq n\,E.C$ *and* $\leq n\,E.C$, *inclusion axioms* $E \sqsubseteq F$ *and ABox axioms* $E(a,b)$, *where E is a safe role expression, and F is any role expression. The semantics of* $\mathcal{ALCHIQ}b$ *is obtained by extending the operator* π *from Table 1 in the obvious way.*

We assume w.l.o.g. that all concepts in KB contain only atomic roles, since one can always replace a role expression with a new atomic role and add a corresponding role inclusion axiom. Hence, the only difference to the case of $\mathcal{ALCHIQ}$ logic is that KB contains axioms of the form $E \sqsubseteq F$, where E is a safe role expression. Such an axiom is equivalent to the first-order formula $\varphi = \forall x, y : \pi(\neg E \sqcup F)$. Assume that E is in disjunctive normal form; since it is safe, $\neg E$ is equivalent to a conjunction of disjuncts, where each disjunct contains at least one negated atom. Hence, translation of φ into first-order logic produces closures of the form $\varGamma = \neg R_1(x,y) \vee \ldots \vee \neg R_n(x,y) \vee S_1(x,y) \vee \ldots \vee S_m(x,y)$, where $n \geq 1, m \geq 0$. Computing the disjunctive normal form might introduce an exponential blow-up, so to compute $\varXi(KB)$ we use structural transformation, which runs in polynomial time, but also produces only closures of type $\varGamma$.

Next, we consider saturation of $\varXi(KB)$ using $\mathcal{BS}_{DL}^+$, and define $\mathcal{ALCHIQ}b$-closures to be of the form as specified in Table 3 where closures of type 2 are replaced with closures of the form $\varGamma$ above. Since in $\mathcal{BS}_{DL}^+$ all negative binary literals are selected and a closure of type 3 always contains at least one negative binary literal, it can participate only in a hyperresolution inference with closures of type 3 or 4. Due to the occurs-check in unification, side premises are either all of type 3 or all of type 4. Hyperresolvents can have two forms, which are decomposed, whenever possible, as follows, for $\mathbf{S}(s,t) = S_1(s,t) \vee \ldots \vee S_m(s,t)$:

$$\mathbf{P}(x) \vee \mathbf{S}(x,[f(x)]) \rightsquigarrow \begin{array}{l} \neg Q_{S_i,f}(x) \vee S_i(x,[f(x)]) \text{ for } 1 \leq i \leq m \\ \mathbf{P}(x) \vee Q_{S_1,f}(x) \vee \ldots \vee Q_{S_m,f}(x) \end{array}$$

$$\mathbf{P}(x) \vee \mathbf{S}([f(x)],x) \rightsquigarrow \begin{array}{l} \neg Q_{\mathsf{Inv}(S_i),f}(x) \vee S_i([f(x)],x) \text{ for } 1 \leq i \leq m \\ \mathbf{P}(x) \vee Q_{\mathsf{Inv}(S_1),f}(x) \vee \ldots \vee Q_{\mathsf{Inv}(S_m),f}(x) \end{array}$$

Again, we decompose a non-$\mathcal{ALCHIQ}b$-closure into several $\mathcal{ALCHIQ}b$-closures. Hence, we may establish the bound on the size of the closure set as in Subsection 5.1, to obtain the following result:

Theorem 4. *For an* $\mathcal{ALCHIQ}b$ *knowledge base* KB, *saturation of* $\varXi(KB)$ *by* $\mathcal{BS}_{DL}^+$ *decides satisfiability of* KB *in time exponential in* $|KB|$.

5.3 Conjunctive Queries over $\mathcal{SHIQ}$ Knowledge Bases

Conjunctive queries [5] are a standard formalism for relational queries. Here, we present an algorithm for answering conjunctive queries over a $\mathcal{SHIQ}$ knowledge base KB. To eliminate transitivity axioms, we encode KB into an equisatisfiable

$\mathcal{ALCHIQ}$ knowledge base $\Omega(KB)$ [11]. Unfortunately, this transformation does not preserve entailment of ground non-simple roles. Hence, in the following we prohibit the use of non-simple roles in conjunctive queries (such roles can still be used in KB), and focus on $\mathcal{ALCHIQ}$.

Definition 4. *Let KB be an $\mathcal{ALCHIQ}$ knowledge base, and let $x_1, \ldots, x_n$ and $y_1, \ldots, y_m$ be sets of distinguished and non-distinguished variables, written as $\mathbf{x}$ and $\mathbf{y}$, respectively. A conjunctive query over KB, denoted as $Q(\mathbf{x}, \mathbf{y})$, is a conjunction of DL-atoms of the form $(\neg)A(s)$ or $R(s,t)$, where s and t are individuals from KB or distinguished or non-distinguished variables. The basic inferences for conjunctive queries are:*

- Query answering. *An* answer *of a query $Q(\mathbf{x}, \mathbf{y})$ w.r.t. KB is an assignment θ of individuals to distinguished variables, such that $\pi(KB) \models \exists \mathbf{y} : Q(\mathbf{x}\theta, \mathbf{y})$.*
- Query containment. *A query $Q_2(\mathbf{x}, \mathbf{y_2})$ is* contained *in a query $Q_1(\mathbf{x}, \mathbf{y_1})$ w.r.t. KB if $\pi(KB) \models \forall \mathbf{x} : [\exists \mathbf{y_2} : Q_2(\mathbf{x}, \mathbf{y_2}) \to \exists \mathbf{y_1} : Q_1(\mathbf{x}, \mathbf{y_1})]$.*

Query containment is reducible to query answering by well-known transformations of first-order formulae: $Q_2(\mathbf{x}, \mathbf{y_1})$ is contained in $Q_1(\mathbf{x}, \mathbf{y_2})$ w.r.t. KB if and only if $\mathbf{a}$ is an answer to $Q_1(\mathbf{x}, \mathbf{y_1})$ over $KB \cup \{Q_2(\mathbf{a}, \mathbf{b})\}$, where $\mathbf{a}$ and $\mathbf{b}$ are vectors of new distinct individuals, not occurring in $Q_1(\mathbf{x}, \mathbf{y_1})$, $Q_2(\mathbf{x}, \mathbf{y_2})$ and KB. Therefore, in the rest we only consider query answering.

Let KB be an $\mathcal{ALCHIQ}$ knowledge base. Obviously, for a conjunctive query $Q(\mathbf{x}, \mathbf{y})$, the assignment θ such that $\theta \mathbf{x} = \mathbf{a}$, is an answer of the query w.r.t. KB if and only if the set of closures $\Gamma' = \Xi(KB) \cup \{\neg Q(\mathbf{a}, \mathbf{y})\}$ is unsatisfiable, where $\neg Q(\mathbf{a}, \mathbf{y})$ is the closure obtained by negating each conjunct of $Q(\mathbf{a}, \mathbf{y})$.

A conjunctive query $Q(\mathbf{a}, \mathbf{y})$ is *weakly connected* if its literals cannot be decomposed into two subsets not sharing common variables. W.l.o.g. we assume that $Q(\mathbf{a}, \mathbf{y})$ is weakly connected: if $Q(\mathbf{a}, \mathbf{y})$ can be split into n weakly connected mutually variable-disjoint subqueries $Q_1(\mathbf{a_1}, \mathbf{y_1}), \ldots, Q_n(\mathbf{a_n}, \mathbf{y_n})$, then $\pi(KB) \models \bigwedge_{1 \leq i \leq n} \exists \mathbf{y_i} : Q_i(\mathbf{a_i}, \mathbf{y_i})$ if and only if $\pi(KB) \models \exists \mathbf{y_i} : Q_i(\mathbf{a_i}, \mathbf{y_i})$ for all $1 \leq i \leq n$. The subqueries $Q_i(\mathbf{a_i}, \mathbf{y_i})$ can be computed in polynomial time, so this assumption does not increase the complexity of reasoning.

A slight problem arises if $\neg Q(\mathbf{a}, \mathbf{y})$ contains unmarked constants: assuming that $a_i \in \mathbf{a_i}$ and $a'_i \in \mathbf{a'_i}$ for $i \in \{1, 2\}$, a superposition of $a_1 \approx a'_1 \vee a_2 \approx a'_2$ into $\neg Q_1(\mathbf{a_1}, \mathbf{y_1})$ and $\neg Q_2(\mathbf{a_2}, \mathbf{y_2})$ may produce a closure $\neg Q_1(\mathbf{a'_1}, \mathbf{y_1}) \vee \neg Q_2(\mathbf{a'_2}, \mathbf{y_2})$. Such an inference produces a conclusion with more variables than each of its premises, thus leading to non-termination. To prevent this, we apply the structural transformation to $\neg Q(\mathbf{a}, \mathbf{y})$ and replace Γ' with Γ, where for each $a \in \mathbf{a}$, $\mathcal{O}_a$ is a new predicate unique for a, x_a is a new variable unique for a, and $\mathbf{x_a}$ is the vector of variables obtained from $\mathbf{a}$ by replacing each $a \in \mathbf{a}$ with x_a:

$$\Gamma = \Xi(KB) \cup \{\neg Q(\mathbf{x_a}, \mathbf{y}) \vee \bigvee_{a \in \mathbf{a}} \neg \mathcal{O}_a(x_a)\} \cup \bigcup_{a \in \mathbf{a}} \{\mathcal{O}_a(a)\}$$

The sets Γ' and Γ are obviously equisatisfiable. In the rest we write $\neg \mathcal{O}_\mathbf{a}(\mathbf{x_a})$ for $\bigvee_{a \in \mathbf{a}} \neg \mathcal{O}_a(x_a)$. We now define the calculus for deciding satisfiability of Γ:

Definition 5. $\mathcal{BS}^+_{CQ}$ *is the extension of the* $\mathcal{BS}^+_{DL}$ *calculus, where the selection function is as follows: if a closure C contains a literal* $\mathcal{O}_a(\bot_a)$, *then all such literals are selected; otherwise, all negative binary literals are selected. The precedence for LPO is* $f >_P c >_P p >_P \mathcal{O}_a >_P Q_{R,f} >_P p_{a,b} >_P \top$. *In addition to decomposition inferences from Definition 2, the following decompositions are performed whenever possible, where the t_i are of the form $f_{i,1}(\ldots f_{i,m}(x)\ldots)$.*

$$(\neg)A_1([t_1]) \vee \ldots \vee (\neg)A_n([t_n]) \rightsquigarrow \frac{Q_{(\neg)A_1,t_1}(x) \vee \ldots \vee Q_{(\neg)A_n,t_n}(x)}{\neg Q_{(\neg)A_i,t_i}(x) \vee (\neg)A_i([t_i]), \; 1 \leq i \leq n}$$

$$C \cdot \rho \vee \mathcal{O}_a(\langle b \rangle) \rightsquigarrow \frac{C \cdot \rho \vee p_{a,b}}{\neg p_{a,b} \vee \mathcal{O}_a(b)}$$

Definition 6. *The class of $\mathcal{CQ}$-closures w.r.t. a conjunctive query $Q(\mathbf{a},\mathbf{y})$ over an $\mathcal{ALCHIQ}$ knowledge base KB is the generalization of closures from Table 3 obtained as follows:*

- *Conditions (iii) – (vi) are dropped.*
- *Closure types 5 and 6 are replaced with a new type 5', which contains all closures C satisfying each of the following conditions:*
  1. *C contains only equality, unary or propositional literals.*
  2. *C contains only one variable x.*
  3. *The depth of a term in C is bounded by the number of literals of $Q(\mathbf{a},\mathbf{y})$.*
  4. *If C contains a term of the form $f(t)$, then all terms of the same depth in C are of the form $g(t)$, and all terms of smaller depth are (not necessarily proper) subterms of t.*
  5. *Only the outmost position of a term in C can be unmarked, i.e. each functional term is either of the form $[f(t)]$ or of the form $f([t])$.*
  6. *Equality and inequality literals in C can have the form $[f(t)] \circ [g(t)]$ or $[f(g(t))] \circ [t]$ for $\circ \in \{\approx, \not\approx\}$.*
- *Closure type 8 is modified to allow unary and (in)equality literals to contain unary terms whose depth is bounded by the number of literals in $Q(\mathbf{a},\mathbf{y})$; only outermost positions in a term can be unmarked; all (in)equality literals are of the form $[f(a)] \circ [b]$, $[f(t)] \circ [g(t)]$, $[f(g(t))] \circ [t]$ or $\langle a \rangle \circ \langle b \rangle$, for $\circ \in \{\approx, \not\approx\}$ and t a ground term; and a closure can contain propositional literals $(\neg)p_{a,b}$.*
- *A new* query closure *type contains closures of the form $\neg Q([\mathbf{a}],\mathbf{y}) \vee \mathbf{p}$, where $Q([\mathbf{a}],\mathbf{y})$ is weakly connected, it contains at least one binary literal and $\mathbf{p}$ is a possibly empty disjunction of propositional literals $\mathbf{p} = \bigvee (\neg) p_{a,b}$.*
- *A new* initial closure *type contains closures of the form $\neg \mathcal{O}_a(\mathbf{x_a}) \vee \neg Q(\mathbf{x_a},\mathbf{y})$.*

We show the closure of $\mathcal{CQ}$-closures under $\mathcal{BS}^+_{CQ}$ in [10]. Roughly speaking, since all literals $\neg \mathcal{O}_a(x_a)$ are selected, the only possible inference for an initial closure is hyperresolution with $\neg p_{a,b} \vee \mathcal{O}_a(b)$ or $\mathcal{O}_a(a)$, generating a query closure with marked terms. Propositional symbols $p_{a,b}$ are used to decompose closures resulting from superposition into $\mathcal{O}_a(b)$; since such literals are smallest in any closure, they cannot participate in inferences with a closure of type 5'.

Consider an inference with a closure $\neg Q([\mathbf{a}],\mathbf{y}) \vee \mathbf{p}$ such that $Q([\mathbf{a}],\mathbf{y})$ is weakly connected. Since all constants are marked, superposition into such a closure is not possible. The only possible inference is hyperresolution with side premises of type 3, 4 and 8 with a unifier σ. If $Q([\mathbf{a}],\mathbf{y})$ contains a constant or if some side premise is ground, then $Q([\mathbf{a}],\mathbf{y})\sigma$ is ground because $Q([\mathbf{a}],\mathbf{y})$ is weakly connected. Otherwise, since the query closure is weakly connected, the hyperresolution produces a closure of the form $\bigvee(\neg)A_i([t_i])$ with t_i of the form $f_{i,1}(\ldots f_{i,m}(x)\ldots)$. This closure does not satisfy condition 4 of $\mathcal{CQ}$-closures, so it is decomposed into several closures of type 5'; eligibility is ensured since $\neg Q_{(\neg)A_i,t_i}(x) \prec (\neg)A_i(t_i)$, and $(\neg)A_i(t_i)$ originates from some side premise $E_j\sigma$. All side premises contain at most one functional term of depth one, so the depth of functional terms in the conclusion is bounded by the length of the maximal path in $Q([\mathbf{a}],\mathbf{y})$, which is bounded by $|Q(\mathbf{a},\mathbf{y})|$.

To build a term of the form $f_1(\ldots f_m(x)\ldots)$, one selects a subset of at most $|Q(\mathbf{a},\mathbf{y})|$ function symbols; the number of such subsets is exponential in $|Q(\mathbf{a},\mathbf{y})|$. This gives an exponential bound on the closure length, and a doubly exponential bound on the number of $\mathcal{CQ}$-closures, leading to the following result:

Theorem 5. *For a conjunctive query $Q(\mathbf{a},\mathbf{y})$ over an $\mathcal{ALCHIQ}$ knowledge base KB, saturation of Γ by $\mathcal{BS}_{CQ}^+$ decides satisfiability of Γ in time doubly exponential in $|KB| + |Q(\mathbf{a},\mathbf{y})|$.*

Related Work. Answering conjunctive queries over the related description logic $\mathcal{SH}f$ was considered in [19]. In this approach, transitive roles can be used in the queries, but $\mathcal{SH}f$ does not provide inverse roles. Conjunctive queries were also considered in [4]. To the best of our knowledge, this is the first work that considers answering conjunctive queries over description logic knowledge bases in the framework of resolution.

6 Conclusion

We have proposed *decomposition*, a general inference rule applicable to any resolution calculus compatible with the standard notion of redundancy. This rule transforms certain conclusions of the calculus at hand, and thus can be used to turn a resolution calculus into a decision procedure.

For three decidable fragments of first-order logic, we present three decision procedures obtained by combining basic superposition with decomposition, and by choosing an appropriate term ordering and selection function. More precisely, we obtain two new decision procedures for checking satisfiability of $\mathcal{SHIQ}$ and $\mathcal{ALCHIQ}b$ knowledge bases, and a procedure for answering conjunctive queries over $\mathcal{SHIQ}$ knowledge bases. The first two procedures are worst-case optimal, and we expect them to be suitable for implementation due to the vast experience in building saturation theorem provers. An implementation of these algorithms is under way, and we hope to soon be able to confirm our expectations.

In addition, we plan to extend the algorithm for $\mathcal{ALCHIQ}b$ to support arbitrary role expressions, and to find a way to handle transitivity directly within our calculus, to avoid the reduction and to allow transitive roles in queries.

References

1. F. Baader and T. Nipkow. *Term Rewriting and All That.* Cambridge University Press, 1998.
2. L. Bachmair and H. Ganzinger. Resolution Theorem Proving. In A. Robinson and A. Voronkov, editors, *Handbook of Automated Reasoning*, pages 19–99. Elsevier Science, 2001.
3. L. Bachmair, H. Ganzinger, C. Lynch, and W. Snyder. Basic Paramodulation. *Information and Computation*, 121(2):172–192, 1995.
4. D. Calvanese, G. De Giacomo, and M. Lenzerini. On the Decidability of Query Containment under Constraints. In *Proc. PODS 1998*, pages 149–158. ACM Press, 1998.
5. A. K. Chandra and P. M. Merlin. Optimal implementation of conjunctive queries in relational data bases. In *Proc. STOC 1977*, pages 77–90. ACM Press, 1977.
6. H. de Nivelle. Splitting through new proposition symbols. In *Proc. LPAR 2001*, volume 2250 of *LNAI*, pages 172–185. Springer, 2001.
7. N. Dershowitz and D.A. Plaisted. Rewriting. In A. Robinson and A. Voronkov, editors, *Handbook of Automated Reasoning*, pages 535–610. Elsevier Science, 2001.
8. C. Fermüller, A. Leitsch, U. Hustadt, and T. Tammet. Resolution Decision Procedures. In A. Robinson and A. Voronkov, editors, *Handbook of Automated Reasoning*, pages 1791–1849. Elsevier Science, 2001.
9. I. Horrocks, U. Sattler, and S. Tobies. Practical Reasoning for Very Expressive Description Logics. *Logic Journal of the IGPL*, 8(3):239–263, 2000.
10. U. Hustadt, B. Motik, and U. Sattler. Reasoning for Description Logics around $\mathcal{SHIQ}$ in a Resolution Framework. Technical Report 3-8-04/04, FZI, Germany, 2004. http://www.fzi.de/wim/publikationen.php?id=1172.
11. U. Hustadt, B. Motik, and U. Sattler. Reducing $\mathcal{SHIQ}^-$ Description Logic to Disjunctive Datalog Programs. In *Proc. KR 2004*, pages 152–162. AAAI Press, 2004.
12. W. H. Joyner Jr. Resolution Strategies as Decision Procedures. *J. ACM*, 23(3):398–417, 1976.
13. C. Lutz and U. Sattler. The Complexity of Reasoning with Boolean Modal Logics. In *Advances in Modal Logics*, volume 3. CSLI Publications, Stanford, 2001.
14. R. Nieuwenhuis and A. Rubio. Theorem Proving with Ordering and Equality Constrained Clauses. *J. Logic and Computation*, 19(4):312–351, 1995.
15. R. Nieuwenhuis and A. Rubio. Paramodulation-Based Theorem Proving. In A. Robinson and A. Voronkov, editors, *Handbook of Automated Reasoning*, pages 371–443. Elsevier Science, 2001.
16. D. A. Plaisted and S. Greenbaum. A Structure-preserving Clause Form Transformation. *J. Symbolic Logic and Computation*, 2(3):293–304, 1986.
17. A. Riazanov and A. Voronkov. Splitting Without Backtracking. In *Proc. IJCAI 2001*, pages 611–617. Morgan Kaufmann, 2001.
18. R. A. Schmidt and U. Hustadt. A Resolution Decision Procedure for Fluted Logic. In D. McAllester, editor, *Proc. CADE 2000*, pages 433–448. Springer, 2000.
19. S. Tessaris. *Questions and answers: reasoning and querying in Description Logic.* PhD thesis, University of Manchester, UK, 2001.
20. S. Tobies. *Complexity Results and Practical Algorithms for Logics in Knowledge Representation.* PhD thesis, RWTH Aachen, Germany, 2001.
21. C. Weidenbach. Combining Superposition, Sorts and Splitting. In A. Robinson and A. Voronkov, editors, *Handbook of Automated Reasoning*, pages 1965–2013. Elsevier Science, 2001.

Abstract DPLL and Abstract DPLL Modulo Theories

Robert Nieuwenhuis[1]*, Albert Oliveras[1]*, and Cesare Tinelli[2]**

[1] Technical University of Catalonia, Barcelona
www.lsi.upc.es/~{roberto|oliveras}
[2] Dept. of Computer Science, The University of Iowa, www.cs.uiowa.edu/~tinelli

Abstract. We introduce *Abstract DPLL*, a general and simple abstract rule-based formulation of the Davis-Putnam-Logemann-Loveland (DPLL) procedure. Its properties, such as soundness, completeness or termination, immediately carry over to the modern DPLL implementations with features such as non-chronological backtracking or clause learning. This allows one to formally reason about practical DPLL algorithms in a simple way. In the second part of this paper we extend the framework to *Abstract DPLL modulo theories*. This allows us to express—and formally reason about—state-of-the-art concrete DPLL-based techniques for satisfiability modulo background theories, such as the different *lazy* approaches, or our DPLL(T) framework.

1 Introduction

Most state-of-the-art SAT solvers [MMZ+01,GN02] today are based on different variations of the Davis-Putnam-Logemann-Loveland (DPLL) procedure [DP60,DLL62], a procedure for deciding the satisfiability of propositional formulas in conjunctive normal form.

Starting essentially with the pioneering work on the GRASP [MSS99] and SATO [Zha97] systems, the spectacular improvements in the performance of DPLL-based SAT solvers achieved in the last years are due to i) better implementation techniques, such as, e.g., the *2-watched literal* approach for unit propagation, and ii) several conceptual enhancements on the original DPLL procedure aimed at reducing the amount of explored search space such as *non-chronological backtracking, conflict-driven lemma learning*, and *restarts*.

Because of their success, both the DPLL procedure and its enhancements have been recently adapted to satisfiability problems in more expressive logics than propositional logic. In particular, they have been used to build efficient solvers for the satisfiability of (certain classes of) ground first-order formulas with respect to theories such as the theory of equality, of the integer/real numbers, or of arrays [ACG00,ABC+02,BDS02,dMR02,FJOS03,GHN+04].

---
* Partially supported by Spanish Min. of Educ. and Science by the LogicTools project (TIN2004-03382, both these authors), and FPU grant AP2002-3533 (Oliveras).
** Partially supported by Grant No. 237422 from the National Science Foundation.

Altogether, it has become non-trivial to reason formally about the properties of such enhanced DPLL procedures and their extensions to satisfiability modulo theories (SMT). However, so far there have been no attempts to do so in the literature, to our knowledge at least, except for a work by Tinelli [Tin02] (one of these authors). That work describes DPLL and DPLL modulo theories at an abstract, formal level by means of a sequent-style logical calculus. This calculus consists of a few deterministic derivation rules, modelling the constraint propagation mechanism of the DPLL procedure, and one branching rule, modelling the non-deterministic guessing step of DPLL. Because of the branching rule the calculus produces *derivation trees*. As a consequence, it can explictly model neither backtracking (chronological or not) nor lemma learning—they are metalogical features for the calculus. Also, the calculus implicitly assumes the procedure to keep track of the current truth values of all clauses, which is not the case in practical implementations.

In this paper we address these limitations of Tinelli's calculus by modelling the DPLL procedure and its SMT extensions as *transitions systems*. While still as declarative in nature as the calculus in [Tin02], our transition systems can explicitly model various features of state-of-the-art DPLL-based solvers, thus bridging the gap between abstract calculi for DPLL and actual implementations.

In Section 2, using transition systems defined by means of conditional transition rules, we introduce general and simple abstract formulations of several variants of propositional DPLL, and discuss their soundness, completeness, and termination. These properties immediately carry over to modern DPLL implementations with features such as non-chronological backtracking and learning. In fact, we also explain and formalize what is done by the different implementations. For example, we explain how different systems implement our backjumping rule, how devices such as implication graphs are just one possibility for computing new lemmas, and how standard backtracking is a special case of the backjumping rule.

We also provide a general and simple termination argument for DPLL procedures that does not depend on an exhaustive enumeration of all truth assignments; instead, it cleanly expresses that a search state becomes more advanced if an additional unit is deduced, the higher up in the search tree the better—which is the very essence of the idea of backjumping.

Our transition systems allow one to formally reason about practical DPLL implementations in a simple way, which to our knowledge had not been done before. In Section 3 we extend the framework to *Abstract DPLL modulo theories*. This allows us to express—and formally reason about—most state-of-the-art DPLL-based techniques for satisfiability modulo background theories, such as various so-called *lazy* approaches [ACG00,ABC+02,BDS02,dMR02,FJOS03] and our own DPLL(T) framework [GHN+04].

2 The Abstract DPLL Procedure

The DPLL procedure works by trying to build incrementally a satisfying truth assignment for a given propositional formula F in conjunctive normal form. At each step, the current assignment M for F is augmented either by a process of *boolean constraint propagation*, which deduces deterministically from M and F the truth value of additional variables of F, or by a non-deterministic guess, or *decision*, on the truth value of one of the remaining undefined variables.

Modern implementations of DPLL use efficient constraint propagation algorithms, and sophisticated backtracking mechanisms for recovering from wrong decisions. We provide here a general abstract framework for describing both constraint propagation and backtracking in DPLL-based systems.

In this section we deal with propositional logic. Atoms are propositional symbols from a finite set P. If $p \in P$, then p is a *positive* literal and $\neg p$ is a *negative* literal. The *negation* of a literal l, written $\neg l$, denotes $\neg p$ if l is p, and p if l is $\neg p$. A *clause* is a set of literals and a *cnf* (formula) is a set of clauses. A (partial truth) *assignment* M is a set of literals such that $\{p, \neg p\} \subseteq M$ for no p. A literal l is *true* in M if $l \in M$, is *false* in M if $\neg l \in M$, and is *undefined* otherwise. M is *total* if no literal of P is undefined in M. A clause C is true in M if $C \cap M \neq \emptyset$, is false in M, denoted $M \models \neg C$, if all its literals are false in M, and is undefined otherwise. A cnf F is true in M (or satisfied by M), denoted $M \models F$, if all its clauses are true in M. In that case, M is called a *model* of F. If F has no models then it is *unsatisfiable*. We write $F \models C$ ($F \models F'$) if the clause C (cnf F') is true in all models of F. If $F \models F'$ and $F' \models F$, we say that F and F' are logically equivalent. We denote by $C \vee l$ the clause D such that $l \in D$ and $C = D \setminus \{l\}$.

2.1 The Basic DPLL Procedure

Here, a DPLL procedure will be modeled by a *transition system*: a set of *states* together with a relation, called the *transition relation*, over these states. States will be denoted by (possibly subscripted) S. We write $S \Longrightarrow S'$ to mean that the pair (S, S') is in the transition relation, and then say that S' is *reachable* from S in one *transition step*. We denote by $\Longrightarrow^*$ the reflexive-transitive closure of $\Longrightarrow$. We write $S \Longrightarrow^! S'$ if $S \Longrightarrow^* S'$ and S' is a *final* state, i.e., if $S' \Longrightarrow S''$ for no S''.

A state is either *fail* or a pair $M \parallel F$, where F is a finite set of clauses and M is a sequence of *annotated literals*. We will denote the empty sequence of literals by $\emptyset$, unit sequences by their only literal, and the concatenation of two sequences by simple juxtaposition. We will not go into a complete formalization of annotated literals; it suffices to know that some literals l will be annotated as being *decision literals*; this fact will be denoted here by writing l^d (roughly, decision literals are the ones that have been added to M by the Decide rule given below). Most of the time the sequence M will be simply seen as a set of literals, denoting an assignment, i.e., ignoring both the annotations and the fact that M is a sequence and not a set.

In what follows, the transition relation will be defined by means of (conditional) transition rules. If F is a cnf formula and C is a clause, we will sometimes write F, C in the second component of a state as a shorthand for $F \cup \{C\}$.

Definition 1. *The* Basic DPLL system *consists of the following transition rules:*

UnitPropagate :

$$M \parallel F, C \vee l \implies M\, l \parallel F, C \vee l \quad \text{if} \quad \begin{cases} M \models \neg C \\ l \text{ is undefined in } M \end{cases}$$

Decide :

$$M \parallel F \implies M\, l^d \parallel F \quad \text{if} \quad \begin{cases} l \text{ or } \neg l \text{ occurs in a clause of } F \\ l \text{ is undefined in } M \end{cases}$$

Fail :

$$M \parallel F, C \implies fail \quad \text{if} \quad \begin{cases} M \models \neg C \\ M \text{ contains no decision literals} \end{cases}$$

Backjump :

$$M\, l^d\, N \parallel F \implies M\, l' \parallel F \quad \text{if} \quad \begin{cases} \text{there is some clause } C \vee l' \text{ s.t.:} \\ \quad F \models C \vee l' \text{ and } M \models \neg C \\ l' \text{ is undefined in } M \\ l' \text{ or } \neg l' \text{ occurs in a clause of } F \end{cases}$$

Below we will show that the transition relation *terminates* when starting from $\emptyset \parallel F$, that is, there exist no infinite sequences of the form $\emptyset \parallel F \implies S_1 \implies \ldots$, and we will define a *Basic DPLL procedure* to be any procedure taking an input cnf F and computing a sequence $\emptyset \parallel F \implies^! S$.

Of course, actual DPLL implementations may use the above rules in more restrictive ways, using particular application strategies. For example, many systems will eagerly apply UnitPropagate, but this is not necessary; in fact, below we will show that *any strategy is adequate*: the final state produced by the strategy will be either *fail*, when F is unsatisfiable, or else a state of the form $M \parallel F'$ where M is a model of F. This result holds even if UnitPropagate is not applied at all. Similarly, most implementations will try to minimize the number of applications of Decide. Others may apply it only with literals l belonging to some clause that is not yet true in M (in that case the procedure can also terminate if M is a non-total model).

Example 2. In the following sequence of transitions, to improve readability we have denoted atoms by natural numbers, negation by overlining, and written decision literals in bold:

$$\begin{array}{rll}
\emptyset \parallel 1 \vee \overline{3},\ \overline{1} \vee \overline{4} \vee 5 \vee 2,\ \overline{1} \vee \overline{2} & \implies & (\text{Decide}) \\
\mathbf{3} \parallel 1 \vee \overline{3},\ \overline{1} \vee \overline{4} \vee 5 \vee 2,\ \overline{1} \vee \overline{2} & \implies & (\text{UnitPropagate}) \\
\mathbf{3}\ 1 \parallel 1 \vee \overline{3},\ \overline{1} \vee \overline{4} \vee 5 \vee 2,\ \overline{1} \vee \overline{2} & \implies & (\text{UnitPropagate}) \\
\mathbf{3}\ 1\ \overline{2} \parallel 1 \vee \overline{3},\ \overline{1} \vee \overline{4} \vee 5 \vee 2,\ \overline{1} \vee \overline{2} & \implies & (\text{Decide}) \\
\mathbf{3}\ 1\ \overline{2}\ \mathbf{4} \parallel 1 \vee \overline{3},\ \overline{1} \vee \overline{4} \vee 5 \vee 2,\ \overline{1} \vee \overline{2} & \implies & (\text{UnitPropagate}) \\
\mathbf{3}\ 1\ \overline{2}\ \mathbf{4}\ 5 \parallel 1 \vee \overline{3},\ \overline{1} \vee \overline{4} \vee 5 \vee 2,\ \overline{1} \vee \overline{2} & & \text{Final state: model found.} \quad \square
\end{array}$$

Concerning the rules Fail and Backjump, we will show below that if in some state $M \parallel F$ there is a *conflict*, i.e., a clause of F that is false in M, it is always the case that either Fail applies (if there are no decision literals in M) or Backjump applies (if there is at least one decision literal in M). In fact, in most implementations Backjump is only applied when such a conflict arises, this is why it is usually called *conflict-driven backjumping*. Note that M can be seen as a sequence $M_0 \, l_1 \, M_1 \, \ldots \, l_k \, M_k$, where the l_i are all the decision literals in M. As in actual DPLL implementations, such a state is said to be in *decision level* k, and the literals of each $l_i \, M_i$ are said to belong to decision level i.

Example 3. Another example of application of the Basic DPLL rules is:

$$
\begin{array}{rcl}
\emptyset \parallel \overline{1}\vee 2,\ \overline{3}\vee 4,\ \overline{5}\vee \overline{6},\ 6\vee \overline{5}\vee \overline{2} & \Longrightarrow & \text{(Decide)} \\
1 \parallel \overline{1}\vee 2,\ \overline{3}\vee 4,\ \overline{5}\vee \overline{6},\ 6\vee \overline{5}\vee \overline{2} & \Longrightarrow & \text{(UnitPropagate)} \\
1\ 2 \parallel \overline{1}\vee 2,\ \overline{3}\vee 4,\ \overline{5}\vee \overline{6},\ 6\vee \overline{5}\vee \overline{2} & \Longrightarrow & \text{(Decide)} \\
1\ 2\ 3 \parallel \overline{1}\vee 2,\ \overline{3}\vee 4,\ \overline{5}\vee \overline{6},\ 6\vee \overline{5}\vee \overline{2} & \Longrightarrow & \text{(UnitPropagate)} \\
1\ 2\ 3\ 4 \parallel \overline{1}\vee 2,\ \overline{3}\vee 4,\ \overline{5}\vee \overline{6},\ 6\vee \overline{5}\vee \overline{2} & \Longrightarrow & \text{(Decide)} \\
1\ 2\ 3\ 4\ 5 \parallel \overline{1}\vee 2,\ \overline{3}\vee 4,\ \overline{5}\vee \overline{6},\ 6\vee \overline{5}\vee \overline{2} & \Longrightarrow & \text{(UnitPropagate)} \\
1\ 2\ 3\ 4\ 5\ \overline{6} \parallel \overline{1}\vee 2,\ \overline{3}\vee 4,\ \overline{5}\vee \overline{6},\ 6\vee \overline{5}\vee \overline{2} & \Longrightarrow & \text{(Backjump)} \\
1\ 2\ \overline{5} \parallel \overline{1}\vee 2,\ \overline{3}\vee 4,\ \overline{5}\vee \overline{6},\ 6\vee \overline{5}\vee \overline{2} & &
\end{array}
$$

Indeed, before the application of Backjump there was a conflict: the clause $6\vee\overline{5}\vee\overline{2}$ is false in $1\ 2\ 3\ 4\ 5\ \overline{6}$. We have backjumped from decision level 3 to decision level 1, whereas standard backtracking would reverse only the last decision, and return to $1\ 2\ 3\ 4\ \overline{5}$ (decision level 2). The Backjump rule applies here because we can take $\overline{1}\vee\overline{5}$ playing the role of the *backjump clause* $C\vee l'$ in the definition of the rule. In fact, one can always take a disjunction of negated decision literals for this (see the proof of Lemma 6). But in practice one can usually find better backjump clauses by *conflict analysis*, that is, by analyzing the so called *conflict graph* (see, e.g., [MSS99] for details). □

The Backjump rule makes progress in the search by returning to a strictly lower decision level, but with the additional information given by the literal l' that is added to it. In most DPLL implementations the backjump clause $C\vee l'$ is added to the clause set as a *learned* clause (*conflict-driven clause learning*). However, in this Basic system the second component of each state (the clause set) remains unchanged; this will change in Subsection 2.3 when the learning rule is added. In fact, for some readers it may be surprising that backjumping can be done without clause learning. Such a distinction gives the system more flexibility, allowing it to model, for example, the original DPLL procedure [DLL62].

2.2 Correctness of Basic DPLL

In what follows, (possibly subscripted) F and M will always denote finite clause sets and annotated literal sequences, respectively.

Lemma 4. *If $\emptyset \parallel F \Longrightarrow^* M \parallel F$ then the following hold.*

1. *All the atoms in M are atoms of F.*
2. *M contains no literal more than once and is indeed an assignment, i.e., it contains no pair of literals of the form p and $\neg p$.*
3. *If M is of the form $M_0 \, l_1 \, M_1 \, \ldots \, l_n \, M_n$, where $l_1, \ldots, l_n$ are all the decision literals of M, then $F \cup \{l_1, \ldots, l_i\} \models M_i$ for all i in $0 \ldots n$.*

Theorem 5 (Termination). *There exist no infinite sequences of the form $\emptyset \parallel F \Longrightarrow S_1 \Longrightarrow \ldots$*

Proof. We define a well-founded strict partial ordering $\succ$ on states, and show that each rule application $M \parallel F \Longrightarrow M' \parallel F'$ is decreasing with respect to this ordering, i.e., $M \parallel F \succ M' \parallel F'$.

Let M be of the form $M_0 \, l_1 \, M_1 \, \ldots \, l_p \, M_p$, where $l_1, \ldots, l_p$ are all the decision literals of M. Similarly, let M' be $M'_0 \, l'_1 \, M'_1 \, \ldots \, l'_{p'} \, M'_{p'}$.

Let N be the number of distinct atoms (propositional variables) in F. It is not difficult to show that p, p' and the length of M and M' are always smaller than or equal to N. Define $m(M)$ to be $N - length(M)$, that is, $m(M)$ is the number of literals "missing" in M for M to be total. Now define: $M \parallel F \succ M' \parallel F'$ if

(i) there is some i with $0 \leq i \leq p, p'$ such that

$$m(M_0) = m(M'_0), \quad \ldots \quad m(M_{i-1}) = m(M'_{i-1}), \quad m(M_i) > m(M'_i) \text{ or}$$

(ii) $m(M_0) = m(M'_0), \quad \ldots \quad m(M_p) = m(M'_p)$ and $m(M) > m(M')$.

Comparing the number of missing literals in sequences is clearly a strict ordering (i.e., it is an irreflexive and transitive relation) and it is also well-founded, and hence this also holds for its lexicographic extension on tuples of sequences of bounded length. It is easy to see that all Basic DPLL rule applications are decreasing with respect to $\succ$ if *fail* is added as an additional minimal element. The rules UnitPropagate and Backjump decrease by case (i) of the definition and Decide decreases by case (ii). □

In the previous termination proof one can observe that DPLL search *progresses* (that is, it makes progress w.r.t. $\succ$) by adding a literal to the current decision level (by UnitPropagate), by adding an additional decision level (Decide) or, which is especially interesting, by what the Backjump rule does, i.e., adding an additional literal to a previous decision level, even if all the work done in later decision levels is "thrown away".

Note that it is not trivial to check whether a state is final, because of the Backjump rule. But in practice Backjump is applied only if there is a conflict. If in a state $M \parallel F$ there is no conflict, and UnitPropagate and Decide are not applicable either (i.e., there are no undefined literals in M), then one can of course stop because M is a model of F.

Lemma 6. *Assume that $\emptyset \parallel F \Longrightarrow^* M \parallel F$ and that $M \models \neg D$ for some clause D in F. Then either Fail or Backjump applies to $M \parallel F$.*

Proof. If there is no decision literal in M, it is immediate that Fail applies. Otherwise, M is of the form $M_0 \ l_1 \ M_1 \ \ldots \ l_n \ M_n$ for some $n > 0$, where $l_1, \ldots, l_n$ are all the decision literals of M. Since $M \models \neg D$, we have, due to Lemma 4-3, that $F \cup \{l_1, \ldots, l_n\} \models \neg D$. Now consider any i in $1 \ldots n$ such that $F \cup \{l_1, \ldots, l_i\} \models \neg D$, and j in $0 \ldots i-1$ such that $F \cup \{l_1, \ldots, l_j, l_i\} \models \neg D$. We will show that then backjumping to decision level j is possible.

Let C be the clause $\neg l_1 \vee \ldots \vee \neg l_j$, and note that M is of the form $M' \ l_{j+1} \ N$. Then Backjump applies to $M \parallel F$ as: $M' \ l_{j+1} \ N \parallel F \Longrightarrow M' \ \neg l_i \parallel F$ because for the clause $C \vee \neg l_i$ all three conditions of the Backjump rule hold. In fact:

(i) $F \models C \vee \neg l_i$ because $F \cup \{l_1, \ldots, l_j, l_i\} \models \neg D$ implies, being D a clause in F, that $F \models \neg l_1 \vee \ldots \vee \neg l_j \vee \neg l_i$. We also obviously have that $M' \models \neg C$.

(ii) $\neg l_i$ is undefined in M' (by Lemma 4-2) and

(iii) either l_i or $\neg l_i$ occurs in a clause of F (by Lemma 4-1). □

It is interesting to observe that the smaller the j in the previous proof the better, because one can backjump "higher up". Note also that, if we take i to be n and j to be $n-1$, the Backjump rule models standard backtracking.

Lemma 7. *If $\emptyset \parallel F \Longrightarrow^! M \parallel F$, then $M \models F$.*

Definition 8. *A Basic DPLL procedure is any procedure taking an input cnf F and computing a sequence $\emptyset \parallel F \Longrightarrow^! S$.*

Now, we can prove that our Basic DPLL system, and hence any Basic DPLL procedure, provides a decision procedure for the satisfiability of cnf formulas.

Theorem 9. *The Basic DPLL system provides a decision procedure for the satisfiability of cnf formulas F, that is:*

1. *$\emptyset \parallel F \Longrightarrow^! fail$ if, and only if, F is unsatisfiable.*
2. *$\emptyset \parallel F \Longrightarrow^! M \parallel F$ if, and only if, F is satisfiable.*
3. *If $\emptyset \parallel F \Longrightarrow^! M \parallel F$ then M is a model of F.*

Proof. For the left-to-right implication of property 1: if $\emptyset \parallel F \Longrightarrow^! fail$ then there is some state $M \parallel F$ such that $\emptyset \parallel F \Longrightarrow^* M \parallel F \Longrightarrow fail$, there is no decision literal in M and $M \models \neg C$ for some clause C in F. By the case $i = 0$ of Lemma 4-3 we have that $F \models M$, and so $F \models \neg C$. However, since C is a clause in F it follows that F is unsatisfiable. For the right-to-left implication of property 1, if $\emptyset \parallel F \not\Longrightarrow^! fail$, then by Theorem 5 there must be a state $M \parallel F$ such that $\emptyset \parallel F \Longrightarrow^! M \parallel F$. Then F is satisfiable by Lemma 7.

For property 2, if $\emptyset \parallel F \Longrightarrow^! M \parallel F$ then F is satisfiable by Lemma 7. Conversely, if $\emptyset \parallel F \not\Longrightarrow^! M \parallel F$, then by Theorem 5 again, $\emptyset \parallel F \Longrightarrow^! fail$ and hence F is unsatisfiable by property 1. Property 3 is again Lemma 7. □

The previous theorem does not just prove the desirable properties for a concrete DPLL procedure; rather, it proves the correctness of *any* procedure applying these steps, with *any* strategy. For example, the designer of a practical

DPLL implementation is free to choose her own heuristic for selecting the next decision literal in Decide, or choose the priorities between the different rules.

Note that we may have $\emptyset \parallel F \Longrightarrow^! M \parallel F$ and also $\emptyset \parallel F \Longrightarrow^! M' \parallel F$, for different M and M'.[3] Then, the formula F is satisfiable and both M and M' are models of F.

2.3 DPLL with Clause Learning

Definition 10. *The DPLL system with learning consists of the four transition rules of the Basic DPLL system, plus the following two additional rules:*

Learn :
$$M \parallel F \quad \Longrightarrow \quad M \parallel F, C \quad \text{if} \quad \begin{cases} \text{all atoms of } C \text{ occur in } F \\ F \models C \end{cases}$$

Forget :
$$M \parallel F, C \quad \Longrightarrow \quad M \parallel F \qquad \text{if} \quad \{F \models C$$

In these two rules, the clause C is said to be learned *and* forgotten, *respectively. In the following, we denote by $\Longrightarrow_L$ the transition relation defined by the DPLL system with learning.*

Example 11. (Example 3 continued). When applying Backjump, many actual DPLL implementations learn the backjump clause:

$$
\begin{array}{llll}
\ldots \quad \ldots \\
1\,2\,3\,4 \parallel \overline{1}\vee 2,\ \overline{3}\vee 4,\ \overline{5}\vee\overline{6},\ 6\vee\overline{5}\vee\overline{2} & \Longrightarrow_L & \text{(Decide)} \\
1\,2\,3\,4\,5 \parallel \overline{1}\vee 2,\ \overline{3}\vee 4,\ \overline{5}\vee\overline{6},\ 6\vee\overline{5}\vee\overline{2} & \Longrightarrow_L & \text{(UnitPropagate)} \\
1\,2\,3\,4\,5\,\overline{6} \parallel \overline{1}\vee 2,\ \overline{3}\vee 4,\ \overline{5}\vee\overline{6},\ 6\vee\overline{5}\vee\overline{2} & \Longrightarrow_L & \text{(Backjump)} \\
1\,2\,\overline{5} \parallel \overline{1}\vee 2,\ \overline{3}\vee 4,\ \overline{5}\vee\overline{6},\ 6\vee\overline{5}\vee\overline{2} & \Longrightarrow_L & \text{(Learn)} \\
1\,2\,\overline{5} \parallel \overline{1}\vee 2,\ \overline{3}\vee 4,\ \overline{5}\vee\overline{6},\ 6\vee\overline{5}\vee\overline{2},\ \overline{1}\vee\overline{5} &
\end{array}
$$

When backjumping to decision level j, the backjump clause $C \vee l'$ (in the example $\overline{1} \vee \overline{5}$) is always such that, if it had existed the last time the procedure was at level j, the literal l' could have been added by UnitPropagate. Learning such clauses hence avoids repeated work by preventing decisions such as **5**, if, after more backjumping, one reaches again a state similar to this decision level j (where "similar" roughly means that it could produce the same conflict). Indeed, reaching such similar states frequently happens in industrial problems having some regular structure. The use of Forget is to free memory by removing a clause C, once a search region presenting such similar states has been abandoned. In practice this is usually done if the activity of C (i.e., the number of times C causes some conflict or some unit propagation) has become low [MMZ+01]. □

The results given in the previous subsection for Basic DPLL smoothly extend to DPLL with learning, and again the starting point is the following.

---

[3] *Confluence*, in the sense of, e.g., rewrite systems is not needed here.

Lemma 12. *If $\emptyset \parallel F \Longrightarrow_L^* M \parallel F'$ then the following hold.*

1. *All the atoms in M and all the atoms in F' are atoms of F.*
2. *M contains no literal more than once and is indeed an assignment, i.e., it contains no pair of literals of the form p and $\neg p$.*
3. *F' is logically equivalent to F.*
4. *If M is of the form $M_0 \, l_1 \, M_1 \, \ldots \, l_n \, M_n$, where $l_1, \ldots, l_n$ are all the decision literals of M, then $F \cup \{l_1, \ldots, l_i\} \models M_i$ for all $i = 0 \ldots n$.*

Proof. It is easy to see that property 3 holds. Using this fact, the other properties can be proven similarly to the proof of Lemma 4.

Theorem 13 (Termination of $\Longrightarrow_L$). *There exist no infinite sequences of the form $\emptyset \parallel F \Longrightarrow_L S_1 \Longrightarrow_L \ldots$ if no clause C is learned infinitely many times along a sequence.*

Proof. The ordering used in Theorem 5 can also be applied here, since, by Lemma 12, atoms appearing in any state are atoms of F. Therefore an infinite sequence of the form $\emptyset \parallel F \Longrightarrow_L S_1 \Longrightarrow_L \ldots$ cannot contain any infinite subsequence of contiguous $\Longrightarrow$ steps, and must hence contain infinitely many Learn or Forget steps, which is not possible since there are only finitely many different clauses with atoms in F, and no clause C is learned infinitely many times along the sequence. □

Note that the condition that no clause C is learned infinitely many times is in fact a necessary and sufficient condition for termination. This condition is easily enforced by applying at least one rule of the Basic DPLL system between two successive applications of Learn. Since states do not increase with respect to the ordering used in Theorem 5 when Learn is applied, any strict alternation between Learn and Basic DPLL rules must be finite as well. As with the basic DPLL system, we have the following definition and theorem (with identical proof).

Definition 14. *A DPLL procedure with learning is any procedure taking an input cnf F and computing a sequence $\emptyset \parallel F \Longrightarrow_L^* S$ where S is a final state with respect to the Basic DPLL system.*

Theorem 15. *The DPLL system with learning provides a decision procedure for the satisfiability of cnf formulas F, that is:*

1. *$\emptyset \parallel F \Longrightarrow_L^! $ fail if, and only if, F is unsatisfiable.*
2. *$\emptyset \parallel F \Longrightarrow_L^* M \parallel F'$, where $M \parallel F'$ is a final state with respect to the Basic DPLL system, if, and only if, F is satisfiable.*
3. *If $\emptyset \parallel F \Longrightarrow_L^* M \parallel F'$, where $M \parallel F'$ is a final state with respect to the Basic DPLL system, then M is a model of F.*

3 Abstract DPLL Modulo Theories

This section deals with procedures for Satisfiability Modulo Theories (SMT), that is, procedures for deciding the satisfiability of ground[4] cnf formulas in the context of a background theory T. Typical theories considered in this context are EUF (equality with uninterpreted function symbols), linear arithmetic (over the integers and over the reals), some theories of arrays and of other data structures such as lists, finite sets, and so on. For each of these theories there exist efficient procedures (in practice) that decide the satisfiability, in the theory, of *conjunctions* of ground literals. To decide efficiently the satisfiability of ground *cnf* formulas, many people have recently worked on combining these decision procedures with DPLL based SAT engines. In this section we show that many of the existing combinations can be described and discussed within the Abstract DPLL framework.

In the rest of the paper we consider first-order logic without equality—of which the purely propositional case we have seen until now is a particular instance. We adopt the standard notions of first-order structure, satisfaction, entailment, etc., extended with the following. A *theory* is a satisfiable set of closed first-order formulas. A formula F is *(un)satisfiable in* a theory T, or T-*(in)consistent*, if there is a (no) model of T that satisfies F, that is, if $T \cup F$ is (un)satisfiable. If F and G are formulas, F *entails* G *in* T, written $F \models_T G$, if $T \models \neg F \vee G$. If $F \models_T G$ and $G \models_T F$, we say that F and G are T-*equivalent*. We extend the notion of (partial truth) assignment M from Section 2 to a set of ground first-order literals in the obvious way. We say that M is a T-*model* of a ground formula F if M, seen as the conjunction of its literals, is T-consistent and $M \models_T F$.

In the following we will use T to denote a background theory T such that the satisfiability in T of conjunctions of ground literals is decidable. To decide the satisfiability of ground cnf formulas we consider again the DPLL systems introduced in the previous section—with arbitrary ground atoms now used in place of propositional symbols—and add new rules for dealing with T. However, in the side conditions of the rules presented in the previous section, entailment between formulas is now replaced by entailment in T between formulas. That is, the condition $F \models C$ in Learn and Forget is now $F \models_T C$, the Backjump rule is

$$M\, l^d\, N \parallel F \implies M\, l' \parallel F \quad \text{if} \quad \begin{cases} \text{there is some clause } C \vee l' \text{ s.t.:} \\ F \models_T C \vee l' \text{ and } M \models \neg C \\ l' \text{ is undefined in } M \\ l' \text{ or } \neg l' \text{ occurs in a clause of } F \end{cases}$$

and Decide, Fail and UnitPropagate remain unchanged. We point out that the rules of the previous section can now be seen as a particular instance of the new ones if we consider T to be the empty theory.

---

[4] By *ground* we mean containing no variables—although possibly containing constants not in T.

3.1 A Simple Example: The Classical Very Lazy Approach

One way for dealing with SMT is what has been called the *lazy* approach [dMR02,ABC+02,BDS02,FJOS03]. This approach initially considers each atom occurring in a formula F to be checked for satisfiability simply as a propositional symbol, and sends the formula to a SAT solver. If the SAT solver returns a propositional model of F that is T-inconsistent, a ground clause, a *lemma*, precluding that model is added to F and the SAT solver is started again. This process is repeated until the SAT solver finds a T-consistent model or returns unsatisfiable. The main advantage of such a lazy approach is its flexibility, since it can easily combine any SAT solver with any decision procedure for conjunctions of theory literals, as long as the decision procedure is able to generate such lemmas.

The addition of these lemmas can be modelled by the following rule, which we will call Very Lazy Theory Learning:

$$M\, l\, M_1 \parallel F \implies \emptyset \parallel F,\ \neg l_1 \vee \ldots \vee \neg l_n \vee \neg l \quad \text{if} \quad \begin{cases} M\, l\, M_1 \models F \\ \{l_1, \ldots, l_n\} \subseteq M \\ l_1 \wedge \ldots \wedge l_n \models_T \neg l \end{cases}$$

Combining this rule with the four Basic DPLL rules, or with the six rules of DPLL with learning, the resulting Very Lazy DPLL system terminates if no clause is learned infinitely many times, since only finitely many such new clauses (built over input literals) exist. For this condition to be fulfilled, applying at least one rule of the Basic DPLL system between any two Learn applications does not suffice. It suffices if, in addition, no clause generated with Very Lazy Theory Learning is ever forgotten. The system is also easily proved correct as it is done in the following subsection, by observing that M, seen as the conjunction of its literals, is T-consistent for every state $M \parallel F$ that is final with respect to Basic DPLL and Very Lazy Theory Learning. However, in what follows we will focus on other more interesting—and in practice better—lazy techniques, based on tighter integrations between DPLL and theory solvers.

3.2 Less Lazy Approaches

It is clear that, as soon as a DPLL procedure reaches a state $M \parallel F$ with a (possibly non-total) T-inconsistent M, the corresponding lemma can already be added. Furthermore, it is also not necessary to restart from scratch once the lemma has been added. These ideas can be modelled by the following rule.

Definition 16. *The* Lazy Theory Learning *rule is the following:*

$$M\, l\, M_1 \parallel F \implies M\, l\, M_1 \parallel F,\ \neg l_1 \vee \ldots \vee \neg l_n \vee \neg l \quad \text{if} \quad \begin{cases} \{l_1, \ldots, l_n\} \subseteq M \\ l_1 \wedge \ldots \wedge l_n \models_T \neg l \\ \neg l_1 \vee \ldots \vee \neg l_n \vee \neg l \notin F \end{cases}$$

The Lazy Theory DPLL *system consists of this rule and the six rules of DPLL with learning. In the following, we denote by* $\implies_{LT}$ *the transition relation defined by the Lazy Theory DPLL system.*

Note that the lemma $\neg l_1 \vee \ldots \vee \neg l_n \vee \neg l$ added by an application of the Lazy Theory Learning rule is, by construction, always false in $M\,l$, making either Fail or Backjump applicable to the resulting state. In practice, one of these two rules is always applied immediately after Lazy Theory Learning. This makes the third test in the rule—introduced here to ensure termination—unnecessary.

This DPLL system is still called lazy because it does not consider any theory information until a T-inconsistent partial interpretation $M\,l$ has been reached. As we will see, this is the essential difference between these lazy approaches and the DPLL(T) approach that is described in Subsection 3.3 below.

All the results below are proved as in the previous section. However, the following key lemma is needed to show that for any state of the form $M \parallel F$ that is final with respect to Basic DPLL and Lazy Theory Learning, M is T-consistent and $M \models_T F$.

Lemma 17. *Let* $\emptyset \parallel F_0 \Longrightarrow_{LT}^* M \parallel F$. *If M is T-inconsistent then the rule Lazy Theory Learning applies to $M \parallel F$.*

Theorem 18 (Termination of $\Longrightarrow_{LT}$). *There exists no infinite sequence of the form $\emptyset \parallel F \Longrightarrow_{LT} S_1 \Longrightarrow_{LT} \ldots$ if no clause C is learned by Learn or Lazy Theory Learning infinitely many times along a sequence.*

Definition 19. *A Lazy Theory DPLL procedure for T is any procedure taking an input cnf F and computing a sequence $\emptyset \parallel F \Longrightarrow_{LT}^* S$ where S is a final state with respect to the Basic DPLL system and Lazy Theory Learning.*

Theorem 20. *The Lazy Theory DPLL system provides a decision procedure for the satisfiability in T of cnf formulas F, that is:*

1. *$\emptyset \parallel F \Longrightarrow_{LT}^! fail$ if, and only if, F is unsatisfiable in T.*

2. *$\emptyset \parallel F \Longrightarrow_{LT}^* M \parallel F'$, where $M \parallel F'$ is a final state wrt the Basic DPLL system and Lazy Theory Learning, if, and only if, F is satisfiable in T.*

3. *If $\emptyset \parallel F \Longrightarrow_{LT}^* M \parallel F'$, where $M \parallel F'$ is a final state wrt the Basic DPLL system and Lazy Theory Learning, then M is a T-model of F.*

Systems such as CVC Lite [BB04] are concrete implementations of Lazy Theory DPLL. Usually, in such implementations the Lazy Theory Learning rule is applied eagerly, that is, with an empty M_1, as soon as the current partial interpretation becomes T-inconsistent. Therefore, the soundness and completeness of the approach followed by CVC Lite is a particular instance of the previous theorem.

3.3 The DPLL(T) Approach with Eager Theory Propagation

The Lazy Theory DPLL systems we have seen are lazy in the sense that they use theory information only after a theory-inconsistent partial assignment has been generated. In this subsection we describe the DPLL(T) approach [GHN+04] with eager theory propagation, which allows the use of theory information as soon as possible. This new information reduces the search space by discovering the truth value of literals otherwise considered to be unassigned. Moreover, it does this without sacrificing modularity or flexibility: combining arbitrary theory decision procedures for conjunctions of literals with a DPLL system is as simple as for the lazy approaches such as that of CVC Lite. The key idea behind DPLL(T) is the following rule:

Definition 21. *The* **Theory Propagate** *rule is the following:*

$$M \parallel F \implies M\, l \parallel F \quad \text{if} \quad \begin{cases} M \models_T l \\ l \text{ or } \neg l \text{ occurs in a clause of } F \\ l \text{ is undefined in } M \end{cases}$$

The DPLL(T) *system with eager theory propagation consists of this rule and the six rules of DPLL with learning. We denote by* $\implies_{Edpll(T)}$ *the transition relation defined by the DPLL(T) system with eager theory propagation where* **Theory Propagate** *has priority over all the other rules.*

All results as in the previous sections apply here, including termination under the usual assumption (since **Theory Propagate** also decreases with respect to the ordering $\succ$ used in Theorem 5). The only additional ingredient needed is the following lemma.

Lemma 22. *If* $\emptyset \parallel F_0 \implies^*_{Edpll(T)} M \parallel F$ *then M is T-consistent.*

Proof. This property is true initially, and all rules preserve it, by the fact that $M \models_T l$ if, and only if, $M \cup \{\neg l\}$ is T-inconsistent: the rules only add literals to M that are undefined in M, and **Theory Propagate** adds all literals l of F that are theory consequences of M, before any literal $\neg l$ making it T-inconsistent can be added to M by any of the other rules. □

Definition 23. *A* DPLL(T) *procedure with Eager Theory Propagation for T is any procedure taking an input cnf F and computing a sequence* $\emptyset \parallel F \implies^*_{Edpll(T)} S$ *where S is a final state wrt* **Theory Propagate** *and the Basic DPLL system.*

Theorem 24. *The DPLL system with eager theory propagation provides a decision procedure for the satisfiability in T of cnf formulas F, that is:*

1. $\emptyset \parallel F \implies^!_{Edpll(T)}$ fail *if, and only if, F is unsatisfiable in T.*
2. $\emptyset \parallel F \implies^*_{Edpll(T)} M \parallel F'$, *where $M \parallel F'$ is a final state wrt the Basic DPLL system and* **Theory Propagate**, *if, and only if, F is satisfiable in T.*
3. *If* $\emptyset \parallel F \implies^*_{Edpll(T)} M \parallel F'$, *where $M \parallel F'$ is a final state wrt the Basic DPLL system and* **Theory Propagate**, *then M is a T-model of F.*

In practice, the DPLL(T) approach can be implemented, very much in the spirit of the CLP(X) scheme in constraint logic programming, by building a component DPLL(X) common to all theories, and instantiating it with solvers for different theories T to obtain different DPLL(T) procedures. At each state $M \parallel F$, the theory solver only sees the part M and communicates to the DPLL(X) engine any input literals entailed by M in the given theory. More details on an architecture for concrete DPLL(T) systems can be found in [GHN+04].

3.4 The DPLL(T) Approach with Non-exhaustive Propagation

For some theories eager Theory Propagate is expensive in an actual implementation. For example, in our experience with EUF, this is the case for detecting input literals entailed by disequations. However, using the information coming from the "cheap enough" applications of Theory Propagate is extremely useful for pruning the search space. Therefore one would like to have a combination of Theory Propagate, for the cheaper cases, and Lazy Theory Learning, for covering the incompletenesses of Theory Propagate making the equivalent of Lemma 22 hold. This is actually what is done in the DPLL(T) implementation of [GHN+04].

Definition 25. *The DPLL(T) system with non-exhaustive theory propagation consists of the* Lazy Theory Learning *and* Theory Propagate *rules and the six rules of DPLL with learning. We denote by* $\Longrightarrow_{NEdpll(T)}$ *the transition relation defined by the DPLL(T) system with eager theory propagation.*

Definition 26. *A DPLL(T) procedure with Non-Exhaustive Theory Propagation for T is any procedure taking an input cnf F and computing a sequence* $\emptyset \parallel F \Longrightarrow^*_{NEdpll(T)} S$ *where S is a final state with respect to the Basic DPLL system and* Lazy Theory Learning.

A necessary and sufficient condition for ensuring the termination of the previous system is again that no clause can be learned by Lazy Theory Learning or Learn infinitely many times. In practice, this can be achieved by the same strategy presented in Subsection 3.2. Hence, we have:

Theorem 27. *The DPLL system with non-exhaustive theory propagation provides a decision procedure for the satisfiability in T of cnf formulas F, that is:*

1. $\emptyset \parallel F \Longrightarrow^!_{NEdpll(T)}$ *fail if, and only if, F is unsatisfiable in T.*

2. $\emptyset \parallel F \Longrightarrow^*_{NEdpll(T)} M \parallel F'$, *where* $M \parallel F'$ *is a final state wrt Basic DPLL and* Lazy Theory Learning, *if, and only if, F is satisfiable in T.*

3. *If* $\emptyset \parallel F \Longrightarrow^*_{NEdpll(T)} M \parallel F'$, *where* $M \parallel F'$ *is a final state wrt Basic DPLL and* Lazy Theory Learning, *then M is a T-model of F.*

4 Conclusions

We have presented a declarative formal framework for modeling DPLL-based solvers for propositional satisfiability or for satisfiability modulo theories. We have shown that the essence of these solvers can be described simply and abstractly in terms of rule-based transition systems over states consisting of a truth assignment and a clause set.

The declarative and formal nature of our transition systems makes it easier to prove properties such as soundness, completeness or termination of DPLL-style algorithms. Furthermore, it facilitates their comparison as their differences can be more easily seen as differences in the set of their transition rules or in their rule application strategy.

The approach we presented is as flexible and declarative as the one followed in [Tin02], which first formulated basic DPLL and DPLL modulo theories abstractly, as sequent-style calculi. But it considerably improves on that work because it allows one to model more features of modern DPLL-based engines directly within the framework. This contrasts with the calculi in [Tin02] where features as backjumping and learning can be discussed only at the control level, in terms of proof procedures for the calculi.

References

ABC[+]02. G. Audemard, P. Bertoli, A. Cimatti, A. Kornilowicz, and R. Sebastiani. A SAT based approach for solving formulas over boolean and linear mathematical propositions. In *CADE-18*, LNCS 2392, pages 195–210, 2002.

ACG00. Alessandro Armando, Claudio Castellini, and Enrico Giunchiglia. SAT-based procedures for temporal reasoning. In *Procs. 5th European Conference on Planning*, LNCS 1809, pages 97–108, 2000.

BB04. Clark W. Barrett and Sergey Berezin. CVC lite: A new implementation of the cooperating validity checker. Category B. In *Procs. 16th Int. Conf. Computer Aided Verification (CAV)*, LNCS 3114, pages 515–518, 2004.

BDS02. Clark Barrett, David Dill, and Aaron Stump. Checking satisfiability of first-order formulas by incremental translation into sat. In *Procs. 14th Intl. Conf. on Computer Aided Verification (CAV)*, LNCS 2404, 2002.

DLL62. Martin Davis, George Logemann, and Donald Loveland. A machine program for theorem-proving. *Comm. of the ACM*, 5(7):394–397, 1962.

dMR02. Leonardo de Moura and Harald Rueß. Lemmas on demand for satisfiability solvers. In *Procs. 5th Int. Symp. on the Theory and Applications of Satisfiability Testing, SAT'02*, pages 244–251, 2002.

DP60. Martin Davis and Hilary Putnam. A computing procedure for quantification theory. *Journal of the ACM*, 7:201–215, 1960.

FJOS03. C. Flanagan, R. Joshi, X. Ou, and J. B. Saxe. Theorem proving using lazy proof explanation. In *Procs. 15th Int. Conf. on Computer Aided Verification (CAV)*, LNCS 2725, 2003.

GHN[+]04. H. Ganzinger, G. Hagen, R. Nieuwenhuis, A. Oliveras, and C. Tinelli. DPLL(T): Fast decision procedures. In *Procs. 16th Int. Conf. Computer Aided Verification (CAV)*, LNCS 3114, pages 175–188, 2004.

GN02. E. Goldberg and Y. Novikov. BerkMin: A fast and robust SAT-solver. In *Design, Automation, and Test in Europe (DATE '02)*, pages 142–149, 2002.

MMZ[+]01. M. Moskewicz, Conor. Madigan, Y. Zhao, L. Zhang, and S. Malik. Chaff: Engineering an Efficient SAT Solver. In *Proc. 38th Design Automation Conference (DAC'01)*, 2001.

MSS99. Joao Marques-Silva and Karem A. Sakallah. GRASP: A search algorithm for propositional satisfiability. *IEEE Trans. Comput.*, 48(5):506–521.

Tin02. Cesare Tinelli. A DPLL-based calculus for ground satisfiability modulo theories. In *Procs. 8th European Conf. on Logics in Artificial Intelligence*, LNAI 2424, pages 308–319, 2002.

Zha97. Hantao Zhang. SATO: An efficient propositional prover. In *CADE-14*, LNCS 1249, pages 272–275, 1997.

Combining Lists with Non-stably Infinite Theories

Pascal Fontaine, Silvio Ranise, and Calogero G. Zarba

LORIA and INRIA-Lorraine

Abstract. In program verification one has often to reason about lists over elements of a given nature. Thus, it becomes important to be able to combine the theory of lists with a generic theory T modeling the elements. This combination can be achieved using the Nelson-Oppen method *only if* T is stably infinite.

The goal of this paper is to relax the stable-infiniteness requirement. More specifically, we provide a new method that is able to combine the theory of lists with any theory T of the elements, regardless of whether T is stably infinite or not. The crux of our combination method is to guess an arrangement over a set of variables that is larger than the one considered by Nelson and Oppen.

Furthermore, our results entail that it is also possible to combine T with the more general theory of lists with a length function.

1 Introduction

In program verification one has often to decide the validity or satisfiability of logical formulae involving lists over elements of a given nature. For instance, these formulae may involve lists of integers or lists of booleans.

One way to reason about lists over elements of a given nature is to use the Nelson-Oppen method [12] in order to modularly combine a decision procedure for a theory modeling lists with a decision procedure for a theory modeling the elements. This solution requires that the theory of the elements be *stably infinite*. Unfortunately, this requirement is not satisfied by many interesting theories such as, for instance, the theory of booleans and the theory of integers modulo n.

In this paper, we show how to relax the stable infiniteness requirement. More specifically, let T_{list} be the two-sorted theory of lists involving a sort elem for elements, a sort list for flat lists of elements, plus the symbols nil, car, cdr, and cons. For instance, a valid formula in T_{list} is

$$x \approx \mathsf{cdr}(\mathsf{cons}(a, \mathsf{nil})) \;\rightarrow\; x \not\approx \mathsf{cons}(b, y)\,.$$

We consider the theory T_{len} that extends T_{list} with a sort int for the integers, the symbols $0, 1, +, -, <$ for reasoning over the integers, and a function symbol length whose sort is list $\rightarrow$ int. For instance, a valid formula in T_{len} is

$$x \not\approx \mathsf{cdr}(\mathsf{cons}(a, \mathsf{nil})) \;\rightarrow\; \mathsf{length}(x) > 0\,.$$

We then provide a combination method that is able to combine T_{len} with any theory T_{elem} modeling the elements, regardless of whether T_{elem} is stably infinite or not.

The core ideas of our combination method are:

- modifying the Nelson-Oppen method in such a way to guess an arrangement over an extended set of free constants, and not just the shared ones.
- appropriately computing a certain minimal cardinality k_0, so that we can ensure that the domain of the elements must have at least k_0 elements.

1.1 Related Work

The importance of reasoning about lists is corroborated by the numerous flavors of theories of lists [1,3,4,13,14,18] present in literature, as well as by the increasing number of tools [6,7,11,15,16,19] containing some capabilities for reasoning about lists.

The idea of guessing an arrangement over a larger sets of free constants was already used by Zarba in order to combine the theory of sets [24] and the theory of multisets [22] with any arbitrary theory T of the elements, regardless of whether T is stably infinite or not. This idea was also used by Fontaine and Gribomont [8] in order to combine the theory of arrays with any other non-necessarily stably infinite theory T.

The idea of computing minimal cardinalities was used by Zarba [23] in order to combine the theory of finite sets with a non-necessarily stably infinite theory T of the elements, in the presence of the cardinality operator. This idea was also exploited by Tinelli and Zarba [20], who provided a method for combining any *shiny* theory S with any non-necessarily stably infinite theory T. Examples of shiny theories include the theory of equality, the theories of partial and total orders, and the theories of lattices with maximum and minimum.

2 Many-Sorted Logic

2.1 Syntax

We fix the following infinite sets: a set **sorts** of sorts, a set **con** of constant symbols, a set **fun** of functions symbols, and a set **pred** of predicate symbols. We also fix an infinite set of variable symbols for every sort in **sorts**.

A *signature* Σ is a tuple $\langle S, C, F, P \rangle$ where $S \subseteq$ **sorts**, $C \subseteq$ **con**, $F \subseteq$ **fun**, $P \subseteq$ **pred**, all the symbols in C have sorts in S, and all the symbols in F, P have sorts constructed using the sorts in S. If $\Sigma = \langle S, C, F, P \rangle$ is a signature, we sometimes write Σ^S for S, Σ^C for C, Σ^F for F, and Σ^P for P.

If $\Sigma_1 = \langle S_1, C_1, F_1, P_1 \rangle$ and $\Sigma_2 = \langle S_2, C_2, F_2, P_2 \rangle$ are signatures, we write $\Sigma_1 \subseteq \Sigma_2$ when $S_1 \subseteq S_2$, $C_1 \subseteq C_2$, $F_1 \subseteq F_2$, and $P_1 \subseteq P_2$. If $\Sigma_1 = \langle S_1, C_1, F_1, P_1 \rangle$ and $\Sigma_2 = \langle S_2, C_2, F_2, P_2 \rangle$ are signatures, their *union* is the signature $\Sigma_1 \cup \Sigma_2 = \langle S_1 \cup S_2, C_1 \cup C_2, F_1 \cup F_2, P_1 \cup P_2 \rangle$.

Given a signature Σ and a set of variables, we assume the standard notions of Σ-term, Σ-atom, Σ-literal, Σ-formula. If φ is either a term or a formula, we denote by $vars_\sigma(\varphi)$ the set of variables of sort σ occurring in φ.

In the rest of this paper we identify a conjunction of formulae $\varphi_1 \wedge \cdots \wedge \varphi_n$ with the set $\{\varphi_1, \ldots, \varphi_n\}$. In addition, we abbreviate literals of the form $\neg(s \approx t)$ with $s \not\approx t$.

2.2 Semantics

Definition 1. If Σ is a signature, a Σ-INTERPRETATION $\mathcal{A}$ over a set of variables V is a map which interprets:[1]

- each sort $\sigma \in \Sigma^S$ as a non-empty domain A_σ;
- each variable $x \in V$ of sort σ as an element $x^{\mathcal{A}} \in A_\sigma$;
- each constant symbol $c \in \Sigma^C$ of sort σ as an element $c^{\mathcal{A}} \in A_\sigma$;
- each function symbol $f \in \Sigma^F$ of sort $\sigma_1 \times \cdots \times \sigma_n \to \tau$ as a function $f^{\mathcal{A}} : A_{\sigma_1} \times \cdots \times A_{\sigma_n} \to A_\tau$;
- each predicate symbol $p \in \Sigma^P$ of sort $\sigma_1 \times \cdots \times \sigma_n$ as a subset $P^{\mathcal{A}}$ of $A_{\sigma_1} \times \cdots \times A_{\sigma_n}$. □

A Σ-formula is *satisfiable* if it evaluates to true under some Σ-interpretation. Let $\mathcal{A}$ be an Σ-interpretation over the set of variables V, and let $\Sigma' \subseteq \Sigma$ and $V' \subseteq V$. We denote by $\mathcal{A}^{\Sigma',V'}$ the interpretation obtained from $\mathcal{A}$ by restricting it to interpret only the symbols in Σ' and variables in V'. For convenience, $\mathcal{A}^{\Sigma'}$ also denotes $\mathcal{A}^{\Sigma',V}$.

A Σ-*structure* is a Σ-interpretation over an empty set of variables.

2.3 Theories

Following Ganzinger [9], we define theories as sets of structures rather than as sets of formulas. More formally:

Definition 2. A Σ-THEORY is a pair $\langle \Sigma, \mathbf{A} \rangle$ where Σ is a signature and $\mathbf{A}$ is a set of Σ-structures. □

Definition 3. Let T be a Σ-theory, and let $\Sigma \subseteq \Omega$. An Ω-interpretation $\mathcal{A}$ is a T-INTERPRETATION if $\mathcal{A}^{\Sigma,\emptyset} \in T$. □

A formula is T-*satisfiable* if it evaluates to true under some T-interpretation.

Given a Σ-theory T, the *ground satisfiability problem* of T is the problem of deciding, for each ground Σ-formula φ, whether or not φ is T-satisfiable.

Definition 4. Let Σ be a signature, let $S \subseteq \Sigma^S$ be a nonempty set of sorts, and let T be a Σ-theory. We say that T is STABLY INFINITE with respect to S if every ground Σ-formula φ is T-satisfiable if and only if there exists a T-interpretation satisfying φ such that A_σ is infinite, for each sort $\sigma \in S$. □

---

[1] Unless otherwise specified, we use the convention that calligraphic letters denote interpretations, and that the corresponding Roman letters, appropriately subscripted, denote the domains of the interpretations.

Definition 5 (Combination of theories). Let $T_i = \langle \Sigma_i, \mathbf{A}_i \rangle$ be a theory, for $i = 1, 2$. The COMBINATION of T_1 and T_2 is the theory $comb(T_1, T_2) = \langle \Sigma, \mathbf{A} \rangle$ where $\Sigma = \Sigma_1 \cup \Sigma_2$ and $\mathbf{A} = \{\mathcal{A} \mid \mathcal{A}^{\Sigma_1} \in \mathbf{A}_1 \text{ and } \mathcal{A}^{\Sigma_2} \in \mathbf{A}_2\}$. □

2.4 The Theory of Integers

Let us fix a signature Σ_{int} containing a sort int for the integers, plus the constant symbols 0 and 1 of sort int, the function symbols $+$ and $-$ of sort int × int → int, and the predicate symbol $<$, of sort int × int.

Definition 6. The STANDARD int-STRUCTURE is the Σ_{int}-structure $\mathcal{A}$ specified by letting $A_{\mathsf{int}} = \mathbb{Z}$ and interpreting the symbols $0, 1, +, -, <$ according to their intuitive meaning over $\mathbb{Z}$. □

Definition 7. The THEORY OF INTEGERS is the pair $T_{\mathsf{int}} = \langle \Sigma_{\mathsf{int}}, \{\mathcal{A}\} \rangle$, where $\mathcal{A}$ is the standard int-structure. □

The ground satisfiability problem of T_{int} can be decided by using methods based on integer automata [21], the omega test [2,17], or appropriate extensions of the Fourier-Motzkin method [10].

2.5 Lists

Let A be a non-empty set, and assume that the special object $\bot$ does not belong to A.[2] A *list* x over A of *length* n is a map $x : \mathbb{N} \to A \cup \{\bot\}$ such that $x(i) \in A$, for $i < n$, and $x(i) = \bot$, for $i \geq n$. We write $|x| = n$ to indicate that the length of the list x is n. We denote by A^* the set of lists over A.

We denote by nil the empty list, that is, $nil(i) = \bot$, for each $i \in \mathbb{N}$. We denote by car and $cons$ the partial functions defined as follows: given a list $x \neq nil$, we let $car(x) = x(0)$, whereas $cdr(x)$ is the unique list y such that $y(n) = x(n+1)$, for each $n \in \mathbb{N}$.

Given an element $e \in A$ and a list x in A^*, we denote by $cons(e, x)$ the list y such that $y(0) = e$, and $y(n+1) = x(n)$, for each $n \in \mathbb{N}$.

2.6 The Theory of Lists

We fix a signature Σ_{list} containing a sort elem for elements and a sort list for lists of elements, plus the constant symbol $\bot_{\mathsf{elem}}$ of sort elem, the constant symbols nil and $\bot_{\mathsf{list}}$ of sort list, the function symbols car of sort list → elem, the function symbol cdr of sort list → list, and the function symbol cons of sort elem × list → list.

Definition 8. A STANDARD list-STRUCTURE $\mathcal{A}$ is a Σ_{list}-structure satisfying the following conditions:

---

[2] Using this special object $\bot$ to define lists is not fundamental but it is convenient for the following.

- $\bot \notin A_{\mathsf{elem}}$;
- $A_{\mathsf{list}} = (A_{\mathsf{elem}})^*$;
- $\mathsf{nil}^{\mathcal{A}} = nil$;
- $\mathsf{car}^{\mathcal{A}}(nil) = (\bot_{\mathsf{elem}})^{\mathcal{A}}$;
- $\mathsf{cdr}^{\mathcal{A}}(nil) = (\bot_{\mathsf{list}})^{\mathcal{A}}$;
- $\mathsf{car}^{\mathcal{A}}(x) = car(x)$, for each $x \in A_{\mathsf{list}}$ such that $x \neq nil$;
  $\mathsf{cdr}^{\mathcal{A}}(x) = cdr(x)$, for each $x \in A_{\mathsf{list}}$ such that $x \neq nil$;
- $\mathsf{cons}^{\mathcal{A}}(e, x) = cons(e, x)$, for each $e \in A_{\mathsf{elem}}$ and $x \in A_{\mathsf{list}}$. □

Note that although *car* and *cdr* are partial functions, standard list-structures interpret the symbols car and cdr as total functions. In particular, all standard list-structures ensure that the constants $\bot_{\mathsf{elem}}$ and $\bot_{\mathsf{list}}$ have the same interpretations of the terms car(nil) and cdr(nil), respectively. However $\bot_{\mathsf{elem}}$ and $\bot_{\mathsf{list}}$ may be interpreted by any element and list in the respective domain. There are thus many standard list-structures.

Definition 9. The THEORY OF LISTS is the pair $T_{\mathsf{list}} = \langle \Sigma_{\mathsf{list}}, \mathbf{A} \rangle$, where $\mathbf{A}$ is the set of all standard list-structures. □

As a by product of the results of this paper, we will see that the ground satisfiability problem of T_{list} can be decided by appropriately adapting Oppen's decision procedure for a one-sorted theory of lists without nil [14].

2.7 The Theory of Lists with a Length Function

We fix a signature Σ_{len} containing all the symbols in Σ_{int} and Σ_{list}, plus the function symbol length of sort list $\to$ int.

Definition 10. A STANDARD len-STRUCTURE $\mathcal{A}$ is a Σ_{len}-structure satisfying the following conditions:

- $\mathcal{A}^{\Sigma_{\mathsf{int}}}$ is the standard int-structure;
- $\mathcal{A}^{\Sigma_{\mathsf{list}}}$ is a standard list-structure;
- $\mathsf{length}^{\mathcal{A}}(x) = |x|$, for each $x \in A_{\mathsf{list}}$. □

Definition 11. The THEORY OF LISTS WITH A LENGTH FUNCTION is the pair $T_{\mathsf{len}} = \langle \Sigma_{\mathsf{len}}, \mathbf{A} \rangle$, where $\mathbf{A}$ is the set of all standard len-structures. □

The ground satisfiability problem of T_{len} can be decided by appropriately adapting a decision procedure for a two-sorted theory of recursively defined data structures with integer constraints [25].

3 The Combination Method

Let Σ_{elem} be a signature such that $\Sigma^S = \{\mathsf{elem}\}$, and let T_{elem} be any Σ_{elem}-theory, not necessarily stably infinite with respect to the sort elem. Assume that the ground satisfiability problem of T_{elem} is decidable. We now describe a

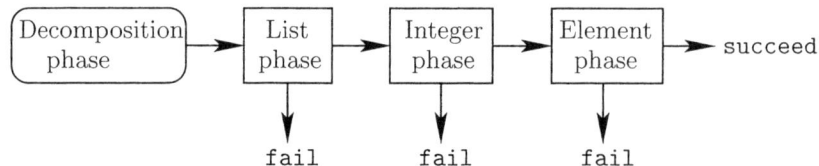

Fig. 1. The phases of our combination method

combination-based decision procedure for the ground satisfiability problem of $T = comb(T_{\mathsf{elem}}, T_{\mathsf{len}})$.

In our combination method we use as black boxes a decision procedure for the ground satisfiability problem of T_{elem} and a decision procedure for the ground satisfiability problem of T_{int}. We also use—albeit not strictly as a black box—Oppen's decision procedure for recursively defined data structures.

Without loss of generality, we restrict ourselves to conjunctions Γ of literals in *separate* form: $\Gamma = \Gamma_{\mathsf{elem}} \cup \Gamma_{\mathsf{int}} \cup \Gamma_{\mathsf{list}} \cup \Gamma_{\mathsf{length}}$ where:

(a) Γ_{elem} contains only Σ_{elem}-literals;
(b) Γ_{int} contains only Σ_{int}-literals;
(c) Γ_{list} contains only flat Σ_{list}-literals of the form

$$x \approx y, \qquad x \not\approx y, \qquad x \approx \mathsf{nil},$$
$$e \approx \bot_{\mathsf{elem}}, \qquad x \approx \bot_{\mathsf{list}}, \qquad x \approx \mathsf{cons}(e, y),$$

where e_1, e_2, e are elem-variables and x, y are list-variables;
(d) Γ_{length} contains only literals of the form $u \approx \mathsf{length}(x)$ where u is an int-variable and x is a list-variable;
(e) for each list-variable $x \in vars_{\mathsf{list}}(\Gamma)$, either $x \approx \mathsf{nil}$ or $x \not\approx \mathsf{nil}$ is in Γ_{list}.

Notice that, given a set of literals in T, it is easy to build an equisatisfiable separation verifying (a),(b),(d) the usual way [12] by introducing fresh variables. However to furthermore ensure (c) and (e), and in particular to eliminate all occurences of car and cdr, it is necessary to include disjunctions to the set of literals. For efficiency concerns, this transformation is done at the formula level; it is described in Section 5.

Our combination method consists of the four phases depicted in Figure 1, and described below.

3.1 Decomposition Phase

Let $\Gamma = \Gamma_{\mathsf{elem}} \cup \Gamma_{\mathsf{int}} \cup \Gamma_{\mathsf{list}} \cup \Gamma_{\mathsf{length}}$ be a conjunction of literals in separate form. Also let $V_{\mathsf{elem}} = vars_{\mathsf{elem}}(\Gamma_{\mathsf{list}}) \cup \{\bot_{\mathsf{elem}}\}$ and $V_{\mathsf{list}} = vars_{\mathsf{list}}(\Gamma)$. In the decomposition phase we non-deterministically guess an equivalence relation $\sim_{\mathsf{elem}}$ of V_{elem}, and we construct the following set of literals:

$$\alpha_{\mathsf{elem}} = \{e_1 \approx e_2 \mid e_1 \sim_{\mathsf{elem}} e_2\} \cup \{e_1 \not\approx e_2 \mid e_1 \not\sim_{\mathsf{elem}} e_2\}.$$

Note that our decomposition phase differs from the one of Nelson-Oppen method. In fact, in the Nelson-Oppen method one guesses an equivalence relation over the smaller set of variables $\mathit{vars}_{\mathsf{elem}}(\Gamma_{\mathsf{elem}}) \cap \mathit{vars}_{\mathsf{elem}}(\Gamma_{\mathsf{list}})$. We need to use the larger set V_{elem} because we do not have any stable infiniteness assumption over the theory T_{elem} of the elements.

3.2 List Phase

In the list phase we essentially employ Oppen's decision procedure for recursively defined data structures. By not using Oppen's procedure just as a black box, we will later be able to use the information constructed in this phase in the later phases of our method. (Cf. Section 5.)

More in detail, in the list phase we construct the least equivalence relation $\sim_{\mathsf{list}}$ of V_{list} satisfying the following conditions:

(a) if $x \approx y$ is in Γ_{list} then $x \sim_{\mathsf{list}} y$;
(b) if $x_1 \approx \mathsf{cons}(e_1, y_1)$ and $x_2 \approx \mathsf{cons}(e_2, y_2)$ are in Γ_{list}, and $e_1 \sim_{\mathsf{elem}} e_2$ and $y_1 \sim_{\mathsf{list}} y_2$ then $x_1 \sim_{\mathsf{list}} x_2$;
(c) if $x_1 \approx \mathsf{cons}(e_1, y_1)$ and $x_2 \approx \mathsf{cons}(e_2, y_2)$ are in Γ_{list}, and $x_1 \sim_{\mathsf{list}} x_2$ then $e_1 \sim_{\mathsf{elem}} e_2$ and $y_1 \sim_{\mathsf{list}} y_2$.

Furthermore, we construct the relation $\prec_{\mathsf{list}}$ of V_{list} defined by letting $x \prec_{\mathsf{list}} y$ if and only if there are list-variables $x', y' \in V_{\mathsf{list}}$ and an elem-variable $e \in V_{\mathsf{elem}}$ such that $x \sim_{\mathsf{list}} x'$, $y \sim_{\mathsf{list}} y'$, and the literal $y' \approx \mathsf{cons}(e, x')$ is in Γ_{list}.

We end our method by outputting `fail` if at least one of the following conditions does not hold:

(C1) If $x \sim_{\mathsf{list}} y$ then the literal $x \not\approx y$ is not in Γ_{list};
(C2) There are no two literals $x \approx \mathsf{nil}$ and $y \approx \mathsf{cons}(e, z)$ in Γ_{list} for which $x \sim_{\mathsf{list}} y$;
(C3) The relation $\prec_{\mathsf{list}}$ is well-founded.

If instead all conditions (C1)–(C3) hold, we proceed to the next phase.

3.3 Integer Phase

In this phase we extract integer constraints from the conjunctions Γ_{list} and Γ_{length}, as well as from the equivalence relation $\sim_{\mathsf{list}}$ constructed in the list phase.

More in detail, we generate a fresh int-variable u_x, for each list-variable x in V_{list}, and we construct the following set of literals

$$\begin{aligned}
\alpha_{\mathsf{int}} = \ & \{u_x \approx 0 \mid x \approx \mathsf{nil} \text{ is in } \Gamma_{\mathsf{list}}\} \cup \\
& \{u_x > 0 \mid x \not\approx \mathsf{nil} \text{ is in } \Gamma_{\mathsf{list}}\} \cup \\
& \{u_x = u_y + 1 \mid x \approx \mathsf{cons}(e, y) \text{ is in } \Gamma_{\mathsf{list}}\} \cup \\
& \{u \approx u_x \mid u \approx \mathsf{length}(x) \text{ is in } \Gamma_{\mathsf{length}}\} \cup \\
& \{u_x \approx u_y \mid x \sim_{\mathsf{list}} y\}.
\end{aligned}$$

Then, we check whether $\Gamma_{\mathsf{int}} \cup \alpha_{\mathsf{int}}$ is T_{int}-satisfiable. If this is not the case, we end our method by outputting `fail`; otherwise we proceed to the next phase.

3.4 Element Phase

We will prove later that when we reach this point we can already conclude that $\alpha_{\mathsf{elem}} \cup \Gamma_{\mathsf{list}} \cup \Gamma_{\mathsf{int}} \cup \Gamma_{\mathsf{length}}$ is T_{len}-satisfiable.[3] Therefore, we can effectively compute the minimal integer k_0 for which there exists a T_{len}-interpretation $\mathcal{A}$ satisfying $\alpha_{\mathsf{elem}} \cup \Gamma_{\mathsf{list}} \cup \Gamma_{\mathsf{int}} \cup \Gamma_{\mathsf{length}}$ such that $k_0 = |\mathcal{A}_{\mathsf{elem}}|$.[4]

Let $\{|\mathsf{elem}| \geq k_0\}$ denotes the set of disequalities $\{e_i \not\approx e_j \mid 1 \leq i < j \leq k_0\}$, where the e_i are fresh elem-variables. The last step of the element phase consists of checking whether $\Gamma_{\mathsf{elem}} \cup \alpha_{\mathsf{elem}} \cup \{|\mathsf{elem}| \geq k_0\}$ is T_{elem}-satisfiable. If this is not the case, we end the method by outputting `fail`; otherwise we happily output `succeed`.

4 Correctness

In this section we prove that our combination method is correct. Clearly, our method is terminating. The following proposition shows that our method is also partially correct.

Proposition 12. *Let T_{elem} be a Σ_{elem}-theory such that $\Sigma^S = \{\mathsf{elem}\}$, let $T = \mathsf{comb}(T_{\mathsf{elem}}, T_{\mathsf{len}})$, and let $\Gamma = \Gamma_{\mathsf{elem}} \cup \Gamma_{\mathsf{int}} \cup \Gamma_{\mathsf{list}} \cup \Gamma_{\mathsf{length}}$ be a conjunction of literals in separate form. Then the following are equivalent:*

1. *Γ is T-satisfiable.*
2. *There exists an equivalence relation $\sim_{\mathsf{elem}}$ of $\mathsf{vars}_{\mathsf{elem}}(\Gamma_{\mathsf{list}}) \cup \{\bot_{\mathsf{elem}}\}$ for which our method outputs* succeed. $\square$

PROOF. Remember that $V_{\mathsf{elem}} = \mathsf{vars}_{\mathsf{elem}}(\Gamma_{\mathsf{list}}) \cup \{\bot_{\mathsf{elem}}\}$ and $V_{\mathsf{list}} = \mathsf{vars}_{\mathsf{list}}(\Gamma)$.
($1 \Rightarrow 2$). Let $\mathcal{M}$ be a T-interpretation satisfying Γ. We define an equivalence relation $\sim_{\mathsf{elem}}$ over V_{elem} by letting

$$e_1 \sim_{\mathsf{elem}} e_2 \iff e_1^{\mathcal{M}} = e_2^{\mathcal{M}}, \qquad \text{for each } e_1, e_2 \in V_{\mathsf{elem}}.$$

We claim that if we guess $\sim_{\mathsf{elem}}$ as defined above, then our method outputs succeed. To see this, let $\sim_{\mathsf{list}}$ be the equivalence relation constructed in the list phase, and let $\equiv_{\mathsf{list}}$ be the equivalence relation of V_{list} defined as follows:

$$x \equiv_{\mathsf{list}} y \iff x^{\mathcal{M}} = y^{\mathcal{M}}, \qquad \text{for each } x, y \in V_{\mathsf{list}}.$$

By construction $\equiv_{\mathsf{list}}$ satisfies conditions (a)–(c) in the list phase. Therefore, we have $\sim_{\mathsf{list}} \subseteq \equiv_{\mathsf{list}}$, that is:

$$x \sim_{\mathsf{list}} y \Longrightarrow x \equiv_{\mathsf{list}} y, \qquad \text{for each } x, y \in V_{\mathsf{list}}.$$

---
[3] A T_{len}-interpretation satisfying $\alpha_{\mathsf{elem}} \cup \Gamma_{\mathsf{list}} \cup \Gamma_{\mathsf{int}} \cup \Gamma_{\mathsf{length}}$ is denoted by $\mathcal{C}$ in the second part of the proof of Proposition 12.
[4] One way of computing k_0 is to use [25] to check, for increasing k, whether there exists a T_{len}-interpretation $\mathcal{A}$ satisfying $\alpha_{\mathsf{elem}} \cup \Gamma_{\mathsf{list}} \cup \Gamma_{\mathsf{int}} \cup \Gamma_{\mathsf{length}}$ such that $|\mathcal{A}_{\mathsf{elem}}| = k$.

By using the fact that $\sim_{\mathsf{list}} \subseteq \equiv_{\mathsf{list}}$, one can verify that $\sim_{\mathsf{list}}$ satisfies all conditions (C1)–(C3) of the list phase. Therefore, our method does not output fail when executing the list phase.

Next, we claim that our method also does not output fail when executing the integer phase. To justify the claim, we need to show that $\Gamma_{\mathsf{int}} \cup \alpha_{\mathsf{int}}$ is T_{int}-satisfiable. Indeed, by again using the fact that $\sim_{\mathsf{list}} \subseteq \equiv_{\mathsf{list}}$, it is possible to verify that a T_{int}-interpretation satisfying $\Gamma_{\mathsf{int}} \cup \alpha_{\mathsf{int}}$ can be obtained by extending $\mathcal{M}$ to the variables u_x by letting

$$u_x^{\mathcal{M}} = |x^{\mathcal{M}}|, \qquad \text{for each list-variable } x \in V_{\mathsf{list}}.$$

It remains to show that our method outputs succeed when executing the element phase. To see this, let k_0 be the minimal integer computed in the element phase. By construction, $\mathcal{M}$ satisfies $\Gamma_{\mathsf{elem}} \cup \alpha_{\mathsf{elem}}$. Moreover, since $\mathcal{M}$ satisfies $\alpha_{\mathsf{elem}} \cup \Gamma_{\mathsf{list}} \cup \Gamma_{\mathsf{int}} \cup \Gamma_{\mathsf{length}}$, it must have at least k_0 elements. It follows that $\mathcal{M}$ is a T_{elem}-interpretation satisfying $\Gamma_{\mathsf{elem}} \cup \alpha_{\mathsf{elem}} \cup \{|\mathsf{elem}| \geq k_0\}$.

($2 \Rightarrow 1$). Let $\sim_{\mathsf{elem}}$ be an equivalence relation of V_{elem} for which our method outputs succeed. Denote by $\sim_{\mathsf{list}}$ and $\prec_{\mathsf{list}}$ the relations of V_{list} constructed in the list phase, and denote by k_0 the minimal integer computed in the element phase. Next, note that there exists an interpretation $\mathcal{A}$ satisfying $\Gamma_{\mathsf{elem}} \cup \alpha_{\mathsf{elem}} \cup \{|\mathsf{elem}| \geq k_0\}$ and a T_{int}-interpretation $\mathcal{B}$ satisfying $\Gamma_{\mathsf{int}} \cup \alpha_{\mathsf{int}}$.

Using $\mathcal{A}$ and $\mathcal{B}$, we define a T_{len}-interpretation $\mathcal{C}$ satisfying $\alpha_{\mathsf{elem}} \cup \Gamma_{\mathsf{int}} \cup \Gamma_{\mathsf{list}} \cup \Gamma_{\mathsf{length}}$ by first letting $\mathcal{C}_{\mathsf{elem}} = \mathcal{A}_{\mathsf{elem}} \cup X$, where X is any infinite set disjoint from $\mathcal{A}_{\mathsf{elem}}$. We also let:

$$e^{\mathcal{C}} = e^{\mathcal{A}}, \qquad \text{for all } e \in \mathit{vars}_{\mathsf{elem}}(\Gamma),$$
$$u^{\mathcal{C}} = u^{\mathcal{B}}, \qquad \text{for all } u \in \mathit{vars}_{\mathsf{int}}(\Gamma).$$

In order to define $\mathcal{C}$ over the list-variables in V_{list}, we fix an injective function $h : (V_{\mathsf{list}} / \sim_{\mathsf{list}}) \to X$. Note that h exists because V_{list} is finite and X is infinite.

Next, we proceed by induction on the well-founded relation $\prec_{\mathsf{list}}$. Thus, let $x \in V_{\mathsf{list}}$. Then:

- In the **base case**, we let $x^{\mathcal{C}}$ be the unique list of length $u_x^{\mathcal{B}}$ containing only the element $h([x]_{\sim_{\mathsf{list}}})$. In other words, $x^{\mathcal{C}}(i) = h([x]_{\sim_{\mathsf{list}}})$ for $i < u_x^{\mathcal{B}}$, and $x^{\mathcal{C}}(i) = \bot$ for $i \geq u_x^{\mathcal{B}}$.
- In the **inductive case**, fix a list-variable y such that $x \prec_{\mathsf{list}} y$. Then there exists variables x', y', e such that $x \sim_{\mathsf{list}} x'$, $y \sim_{\mathsf{list}} y'$, and the literal $x' \approx \mathsf{cons}(e, y')$ is in Γ_{list}. We let $x^{\mathcal{C}} = \mathsf{cons}(e^{\mathcal{C}}, (y')^{\mathcal{C}})$.

Note that $\mathcal{C}$ is well-defined over the list-variables. Furthermore, by construction $\mathcal{C}$ is a T_{len}-interpretation satisfying $\alpha_{\mathsf{elem}} \cup \Gamma_{\mathsf{int}} \cup \Gamma_{\mathsf{list}} \cup \Gamma_{\mathsf{length}}$.

It follows that there exists a T_{len}-interpretation $\mathcal{D}$ satisfying $\alpha_{\mathsf{elem}} \cup \Gamma_{\mathsf{int}} \cup \Gamma_{\mathsf{list}} \cup \Gamma_{\mathsf{length}}$ and such that $|D_{\mathsf{elem}}| = k_0$. But then, we can use $\mathcal{D}$ and $\mathcal{A}$ to obtain

```
1: φ := preprocess(φ)
2: φᵃ ← abs(φ)
3: while φᵃ ≠ false do
4:     Γᵃ ← pick_assign(φᵃ)
5:     Γ ← prop2fol(Γᵃ)
6:     (ρ, π) ← check_sat(Γ)
7:     if ρ = fail then
8:         φᵃ ← φᵃ ∧ ¬fol2prop(π)
9:     else
10:        return succeed
11:    end if
12: end while
```

Fig. 2. haRVey's main loop

a T-interpretation $\mathcal{M}$ satisfying Γ by letting $M_{\text{elem}} = A_{\text{elem}}$ and

$$e^{\mathcal{M}} = e^{\mathcal{A}}, \qquad \text{for all } e \in \Sigma^C_{\text{elem}} \cup vars_{\text{elem}}(\Gamma),$$
$$f^{\mathcal{M}} = f^{\mathcal{A}}, \qquad \text{for all } f \in \Sigma^F_{\text{elem}},$$
$$p^{\mathcal{M}} = p^{\mathcal{A}}, \qquad \text{for all } p \in \Sigma^P_{\text{elem}},$$
$$u^{\mathcal{M}} = u^{\mathcal{D}}, \qquad \text{for all } u \in vars_{\text{int}}(\Gamma).$$

In order to define $\mathcal{M}$ over the list-variables, fix an injective function $g : D_{\text{elem}} \to A_{\text{elem}}$. For convenience, also let $g(\bot) = \bot$. Note that g exists because $|D_{\text{elem}}| = k_0 \leq |A_{\text{elem}}|$. We let:

$$x^{\mathcal{M}}(i) = g(x^{\mathcal{D}}(i)), \qquad \text{for all } x \in vars_{\text{list}}(\Gamma) \text{ and } i \in \mathbb{N}.$$

By construction, $\mathcal{M}$ is a T-interpretation satisfying Γ. ∎

From Proposition 12 and the fact that our combination method is terminating, we obtain the following decidability result.

Theorem 13 (Decidability). *Let T_{elem} be a Σ_{elem}-theory such that the ground satisfiability problem is decidable. Then the ground satisfiability problem of the theory $comb(T_{\text{elem}}, T_{\text{len}})$ is decidable.* □

5 Using the Combination Method

In this Section, we describe how to lift the proposed combination method to efficiently (at least in practice) handle arbitrary Boolean combinations of ground literals. The method is a refinement of the main loop of **haRVey** [6] (cf. Figure 2), a prover based on a combination of Boolean solving and satisfiability checking modulo theories. The idea is to obtain a propositional abstraction φ^a of a formula φ (cf. *abs*) and to enumerate all the propositional assignments (cf. *pick_assign*).

If an assignment, refined to a conjunction of first-order literals (cf. *prop2fol*), is found satisfiable modulo the background theory (cf. *check_sat* returns with $\rho = \mathtt{fail}$), then we are entitled to conclude the satisfiability of φ. Otherwise, a new assignment is considered. For efficiency, it is crucial to reduce the number of invocations to *check_sat*. To this end, it is required that *check_sat* returns a conflict set π (which is a subset of the input set of literals) so that all the propositional assignments sharing that set can be eliminated in one shot.[5]

We now give some details of the implementation of the functionalities in Figure 2 which are peculiar to using the combination method in Section 3. In particular, we describe how to satisfy the requirements necessary for the method to work correctly (see beginning of Section 3) and, most importantly, we explain how to compute the $\sim_{\mathsf{list}}$ and $\prec_{\mathsf{list}}$ of Section 3.2.

Function preprocess. A *flat atom* is an atom of the form $p(c_1, \ldots, c_n)$, $c \approx f(c_1, \ldots, c_m)$, $c_1 \approx c_2$ or $c_1 \approx d$, where p is n-ary predicate symbol ($n \geq 0$), f is an m-ary function symbol ($m > 0$), c_i is an element of **par**, and d is a constant. A *flat literal* is either a flat atom or the negation of a flat atom of one of the two forms $\neg p(c_1, \ldots, c_n)$ or $c_1 \not\approx c_2$. A formula is said to be flattened if all its literals are flat. It is easy to get an equisatisfiable flattened formula from any ground formula by introducing fresh variables to name subterms.

The preprocessing step also removes all occurrences of car and cdr in the formula using the following equivalences

$$e \approx \mathsf{car}(x) \equiv (x \approx \mathsf{nil} \wedge e \approx \bot_{\mathsf{elem}}) \vee (x \not\approx \mathsf{nil} \wedge (\exists_{\mathsf{list}} y)(x \approx \mathsf{cons}(e, y)))$$
$$x \approx \mathsf{cdr}(y) \equiv (y \approx \mathsf{nil} \wedge x \approx \bot_{\mathsf{list}}) \vee (y \not\approx \mathsf{nil} \wedge (\exists_{\mathsf{elem}} e)(y \approx \mathsf{cons}(e, x)))$$

For instance, $\varphi[a \approx \mathsf{car}(x)]$ is equisatisfiable to $\varphi[a \approx e] \wedge e \approx \mathsf{car}(x)$. In this last formula, the atom $e \approx \mathsf{car}(x)$ has always positive polarity. In a later step, it can be replaced by $(x \approx \mathsf{nil} \wedge e \approx \bot_{\mathsf{elem}}) \vee (x \not\approx \mathsf{nil} \wedge (\exists_{\mathsf{list}} y)(x \approx \mathsf{cons}(e, y)))$ and since the polarity is positive, the existential quantifier can be Skolemized by simply introducing a fresh variable. Exhaustively applying this transformation gives a new ground formula, without car and cdr.

Finally, and still by introducing fresh variables, functions cons and length are made to appear only in unit clauses of the form $\mathsf{cons}(e, x) \approx y$ or $\mathsf{length}(x) \approx u$. For instance formula $\varphi[\mathsf{cons}(e, x) \not\approx y]$ is replaced by $\varphi[y' \not\approx y] \wedge y' \approx \mathsf{cons}(e, x)$.

Function pick_assign. The function *pick_assign* is implemented by the Boolean solver and returns a propositional assignment satisfying φ^a. It is easy to tune the solver to make *pick_assign* return a propositional assignment Γ^a such that $prop2fol(\Gamma^a)$ contains the literals representing the fact that each list variable is equal to nil or not.

---

[5] Best results are obtained in practice when this set is chosen to be minimal: an unsatisfiable set such that each subset is satisfiable.

Function check_sat. First of all, we notice that, thanks to *preprocess*, the function *pick_assign* returns a set Γ of literals which can be put in separate form satisfying conditions (a)–(e) at the beginning of Section 3 by simply partitioning the literals.

Our combination method uses decision procedures for the quantifier-free fragment of arithmetic and for the theory of acyclic lists. While we use a decision procedure for the first theory as a black box, we require the decision procedure for the theory of acyclic lists to be able to return $\sim_{\text{list}}$ and $\prec_{\text{list}}$. For this reason, we detail below how to do this.

Reasoning About Acyclic Lists

We introduce a graph structure encapsulating all constraints on the T_{list}-models of a set of equalities of the form $x \approx y$, $e \approx e'$, $x \approx \text{cons}(e, y)$, where x, y are list-variables, and e, e' are elem-variables. In fact, this structure is implicitly computed by the algorithm described in [14]. We here make it explicit, and explain how to extract relations $\sim_{\text{list}}$ and $\prec_{\text{list}}$ from it. The structure may also be used in order to guide the guessing in Section 3.1.

From now on, if not otherwise specified, nil is treated as any other variable. An equality $x \approx \text{nil}$ can thus be seen as an equality between two different list variables. Given finite sets of list and element variables, a list-graph is a tuple $\langle V_{\text{list}}, V_{\text{elem}}, s_{\text{list}}, s_{\text{elem}} \rangle$ with

- V_{list} (V_{elem}) is a partition of list (resp. element) variables. It is the set of list (resp. element) nodes. Variables in a node are *labels* for that node;
- s_{list} (s_{elem}) is a function from V_{list} to subsets of V_{list} (resp. V_{elem}). Given a list node u, $s_{\text{list}}(u)$ ($s_{\text{elem}}(u)$) is the set of list (resp. element) successors of u.

A T_{list}-interpretation $\mathcal{A}$ agrees with a list-graph if the following conditions are met:

- if x and y label the same node then $\mathcal{A} \models x \approx y$, where x and y are both element variables or both list variables;
- if y labels the list successor of x then $\mathcal{A} \models \exists e\ x \approx \text{cons}(e, y)$;
- if e labels the element successor of x then $\mathcal{A} \models \exists y\ x \approx \text{cons}(e, y)$.

Assume L is a T_{list}-satisfiable set of equalities of the form $x \approx y$, $e \approx e'$, $x \approx \text{cons}(e, y)$. Then there is a list-graph G such that, for every T_{list}-interpretation $\mathcal{A}$, $\mathcal{A}$ agrees with G if and only if $\mathcal{A}$ is a model of L. Indeed, the following graph verifies this property:

- x and y label the same node if and only if $L \models_{\text{list}} x \approx y$,[6] where x and y are both element variables or both list variables;
- y labels the list successor of x if and only if $L \models_{\text{list}} \exists e\ x \approx \text{cons}(e, y)$;
- e labels the element successor of x if and only if $L \models_{\text{list}} \exists y\ x \approx \text{cons}(e, y)$.

---

[6] $\models_{\text{list}}$ denotes logical consequence in the theory of lists. That is $L \models_{\text{list}} x \approx y$ if every T_{list}-model of L is a model of $x \approx y$.

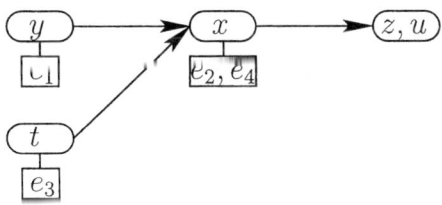

Fig. 3. example of canonical list-graph

This graph is unique. It is such that, for each $v \in V_{\mathsf{list}}$, $s_{\mathsf{list}}(v)$ and $s_{\mathsf{elem}}(v)$ are either a singleton or the empty set. In other words, every list node has at most one list successor, and one element successor. In fact, it can be showed that every node has two or zero successor, since the cdr and car functions are not explicitly used in the set of equalities. If nil labels a list-node, then this node has no list successors. It is acyclic in the sense that s_{list} is acyclic. Finally, for each $u, v \in V_{\mathsf{list}}$, if $s_{\mathsf{list}}(u) = s_{\mathsf{list}}(v)$, $s_{\mathsf{list}}(u) \neq \emptyset$, $s_{\mathsf{elem}}(u) = s_{\mathsf{elem}}(v)$, and $s_{\mathsf{elem}}(u) \neq \emptyset$, then $u = v$. In other words, two different list nodes must not have the same list and element successors.

This graph will thus be called the *canonical* list-graph for a set of equalities. For instance, the canonical list-graph for the set of equalities

$$y \approx \mathsf{cons}(e_1, x), x \approx \mathsf{cons}(e_2, z), x \approx \mathsf{cons}(e_4, u), t \approx \mathsf{cons}(e_3, x)$$

is given in Figure 3.

Given the canonical list-graph for a set of equalities, we have that $x \sim_{\mathsf{list}} y$ is true if and only if x and y both label the same list node and $\prec_{\mathsf{list}}$ *is the transitive closure of the list successor relation.*

Computing Canonical list-Graphs

To compute the canonical graph for a set of equalities, three transformations on list-graphs are necessary:

- a congruence step replaces two lists nodes u and v such that $s_{\mathsf{list}}(u) = s_{\mathsf{list}}(v)$ and $s_{\mathsf{elem}}(u) = s_{\mathsf{elem}}(v)$ by a unique node $u \cup v$.[7] The new node inherits all successors of the nodes it replaces. All list nodes which had u or v as list successor are made to have $u \cup v$ as list successor.
- a list unification step (Unify-cdr) replaces two list successors u and v of one node t by a unique node $u \cup v$. The new node inherits all successors of the nodes it replaces. All list nodes which had u or v as list successor are made to have $u \cup v$ as list successor.
- an element unification step (Unify-car) replaces two element successors u and v of one node t by a unique node $u \cup v$. All list nodes which had u or v as element successor are made to have $u \cup v$ as list successor.

---
[7] Remember u and v are disjoint sets of list variables.

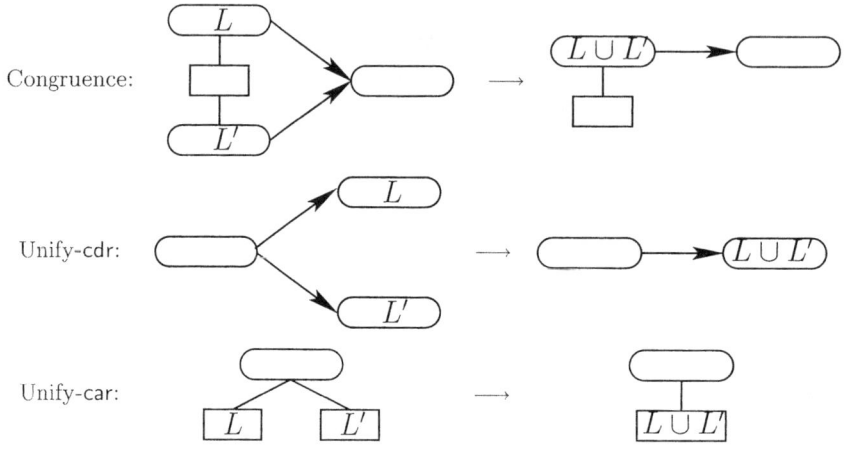

Fig. 4. Transformation steps

These transformations are depicted in Figure 4.

Let L be a set of equalities of the form $x \approx y$, $e \approx e'$, $x \approx \mathsf{cons}(e, y)$. To build the canonical graph for this set, the first operation is to compute the reflexive, symmetric and transitive closure of all equalities between variables in the set L. Second, for every equality $\mathsf{cons}(e, x) \approx y$, the nodes labeled by x and e are made list and element successors of the node labeled by y. Third, the graph is unified, beginning with nodes without parent, finishing with those without successor, using unification steps (beginning with all element unification steps). Last, the congruence rule is applied, from the nodes without successors, to the nodes without parents. In presence of nil, a postprocessing ensures that the node it labels has no successor.

If the graph happens to be cyclic, or if nil happens to have a successor, the procedure fails. In that case the initial set of equalities is unsatisfiable. A careful implementation of this procedure is linear in time [14].

The obtained graph (after a finite number of transformation steps) is indeed the canonical graph: every T_{list}-interpretation $\mathcal{A}$ agreeing with a graph G also agrees with the graph obtained from G by a transformation step. That ensures that every model of L agrees with the final graph. To show that every T_{list}-interpretation agreeing with the graph is also a model for L, it suffices to show that every equality of L is trivially satisfied by any interpretation agreeing with the graph.

There is a T_{list}-interpretation agreeing with a canonical list-graph, such that every node is assigned to a different element or list. As a consequence, satisfiability checking of a set of literals in T_{list} can be simply implemented by building the canonical list-graph for all equalities in the set, and check afterward if no inequality has both members labeling the same node.

Two final remarks are in order. First, the list-graph may be build before guessing an arrangement of the element variables, and may be used to guide this guessing. Indeed it is not necessary to consider an α_{elem} implying that two variables labeling the same node in the list-graph are different. Second, for the algorithm in Figure 2 to be efficient, it is required also that $check\_sat$ returns a small (minimal, if possible) conflict set π out of the input set of literals. For instance, the decision procedure for acyclic lists should produce small unsatisfiable subsets of the input set of literals, or be able to give the equations necessary to deduce a given equality from a satisfiable set. We believe this is possible by adapting the method developed for congruence closure in [5].

6 Conclusion

We presented a combination method that is able to combine a many-sorted theory T_{len} modeling lists of elements in the presence of the length operator with a theory T_{elem} modeling the elements.

Our method works regardless of whether the theory of the elements is stably infinite or not. We were able to relax the stable infiniteness requirement by employing the following basic ideas:

- guess an arrangement larger than the one computed by Nelson and Oppen;
- compute a certain minimal cardinality k_0, so that we can ensure that the domain of the elements must have at least k_0 elements.

Future works include implementing the proposed method in **haRVey**, and in particular, study heuristics to make it more efficient, and investigate extending the procedure for acyclic lists to compute minimal conflict sets. On the theoretical side, it remains to determine the exact complexity of the algorithm, and examine the proposed combination when some sorts (elem, list, int) are equal.

Acknowledgments

We are grateful to Christophe Ringeissen for insightful discussions on the problem of combining non-stably infinite theories. We would also like to thank the reviewers for their comments.

References

1. A. Armando, S. Ranise, and M. Rusinowitch. A rewriting approach to satisfiability procedures. *Information and Computation*, 183(2):140–164, 2003.
2. S. Berezin, V. Ganesh, and D. L. Dill. An Online Proof-Producing Decision Procedure for Mixed-Integer Linear Arithmetic. In *Proceedings of TACAS'03*, volume 2619 of *LNCS*, Warshaw, Poland, April 2003.
3. N. S. Bjørner. *Integrating Decision Procedures for Temporal Verification*. PhD thesis, Stanford University, 1998.

4. R. S. Boyer and J. S. Moore. *A Computational Logic.* ACM Monograph SERIES, 1979.
5. L. de Moura, H. Rueß, and N. Shankar. Justifying equality. In *PDPAR*, 2004.
6. D. Déharbe and S. Ranise. Light-Weight Theorem Proving for Debugging and Verifying Units of Code. In *Proc. of the International Conference on Software Engineering and Formal Methods (SEFM03)*. IEEE Computer Society Press, 2003.
7. J.-C. Filliâtre, S. Owre, H. Rueß, and N. Shankar. ICS: integrated canonizer and solver. In G. Berry, H. Comon, and A. Finkel, editors, *Computer Aided Verification (CAV)*, volume 2102 of *LNCS*, pages 246–249. Springer-Verlag, 2001.
8. P. Fontaine and P. Gribomont. Combining non-stably infinite, non-first order theories. In S. Ranise and C. Tinelli, editors, *Pragmatics of Decision Procedures in Automated Reasoning*, 2004.
9. H. Ganzinger. Shostak light. In A. Voronkov, editor, *Automated Deduction – CADE-18*, volume 2392 of *LNCS*, pages 332–346. Springer, 2002.
10. D. Kapur and X. Nie. Reasoning about Numbers in Tecton. In *Proc. 8th Inl. Symp. Methodologies for Intelligent Systems*, pages 57–70, 1994.
11. T. F. Melham. Automating Recursive Type Definitions in Higher Order Logic. In *Current Trends in Hardware Verification and Theorem Proving*, LNCS, pages 341–386. Sprigner-Verlag, 1989.
12. G. Nelson and D. C. Oppen. Simplifications by cooperating decision procedures. *ACM Trans. on Programming Languages and Systems*, 1(2):245–257, Oct. 1979.
13. G. Nelson and D. C. Oppen. Fast decision procedures based on congruence closure. *Journal of the Association for Computing Machinery*, 27(2):356–364, 1980.
14. D. C. Oppen. Reasoning about recursively defined data structures. *Journal of the ACM*, 27(3):403–411, 1980.
15. S. Owre and N. Shankar. Abstract Datatypes in PVS. Technical Report CSL-93-9R, SRI International, 1997.
16. L. C. Paulson. A fixedpoint approach to implementing (co)inductive definitions. In A. Bundy, editor, *Automated Deduction – CADE-12*, LNAI 814, pages 148–161. Springer, 1994. 12th international conference.
17. W. Pugh. The omega test: a fast integer programming algorithm for dependence analysis. *Supercomputing*, pages 4–13, 1991.
18. R. E. Shostak. Deciding combination of theories. *Journal of the Association for Computing Machinery*, 31(1):1–12, 1984.
19. A. Stump, C. W. Barrett, and D. L. Dill. CVC: a cooperating validity checker. In E. Brinksma and K. G. Larsen, editors, *Computer Aided Verification (CAV)*, volume 2404 of *LNCS*, pages 500–504. Springer, 2002.
20. C. Tinelli and C. G. Zarba. Combining non-stably infinite theories. *Journal of Automated Reasoning*, 2004. To appear.
21. P. Wolper and B. Boigelot. On the construction of automata from linear arithmetic constraints. In S. Graf and M. I. Schwartzbach, editors, *TACAS*, volume 1785 of *LNCS*, pages 1–19, Berlin, Mar. 2000. Springer-Verlag.
22. C. G. Zarba. Combining multisets with integers. In A. Voronkov, editor, *Automated Deduction – CADE-18*, volume 2392 of *LNCS*, pages 363–376. Springer, 2002.
23. C. G. Zarba. Combining sets with integers. In A. Armando, editor, *Frontiers of Combining Systems*, volume 2309 of *LNCS*, pages 103–116. Springer, 2002.
24. C. G. Zarba. Combining sets with elements. In N. Dershowitz, editor, *Verification: Theory and Practice*, volume 2772 of *LNCS*, pages 762–782. Springer, 2004.
25. T. Zhang, H. B. Sipma, and Z. Manna. Decision procedures for recursive data structures with integer constraints. In D. A. Basin and M. Rusinowitch, editors, *Automated Reasoning*, volume 3097 of *LNCS*, pages 152–167. Springer, 2004.

Abstract Model Generation for Preprocessing Clause Sets

Miyuki Koshimura, Mayumi Umeda, and Ryuzo Hasegawa

Kyushu University, 6-1 Kasuga-koen, Kasuga, Fukuoka, 816-8580 Japan
{koshi,umeda,hasegawa}@ar.is.kyushu-u.ac.jp

Abstract. Abstract model generation refers to model generation for abstract clause sets in which arguments of atoms are ignored. We give two abstract clause sets which are obtained from normal clause sets. One is for checking satisfiability of the original normal clause set. Another is used for eliminating unnecessary clauses from the original one. These abstract clause sets are propositional, i.e. decidable. Thus, we can use them for preprocessing the original one.

1 Introduction

The use of abstraction seems to be helpful in many subfields of artificial intelligence [10,7,4,3,2]. The most common use of abstraction in theorem proving has been to abstract the problem, to prove its abstracted version, and then to use the structure of the resulting proof as guides in searching for the original problem. This assumes that the structure of the abstract proof is similar to that of the original problem. The most common approach is to integrate the abstract proving into the deduction process by specifying clause selection functions that imitate the abstract proof. On the other hand, there is another approach which uses the abstract proving as a preprocessing step in the (ground) prover [8].

The benefit of preprocessing a set S of clauses can be large. In the extreme S may be solved in the preprocessing stage. In this paper, we use model generation [6,5] as a procedure for preprocessing S rather than proving S. We apply model generation to abstractions of S. We present two types of abstraction; *c-abstraction* and *d-abstraction*. In these abstractions, we abstract away all arguments from atoms. Thus, abstract clause sets are propositional.

S is satisfiable if its d-abstraction is satisfiable. In this case, we determine its satisfiability without proving S itself. If a clause in S contains an atom whose abstraction is not in the model of c-abstraction of S, the clause is unnecessary for checking unsatisfiability. Thus, the clause can be eliminated.

This c-abstraction based elimination is a kind of simplification which simplifies a set of clauses. Its effect is parallel to that of a simplification operation eliminating pure literals [15]. However, their strength is not comparable. That is, the former can eliminate more clauses than the latter does in some cases, and vice versa. We evaluate effects of abstract model generation for preprocessing with all CNF problems in the TPTP problem library.

2 Model Generation

Throughout this paper, a *clause* $\neg A_1 \vee \ldots \vee \neg A_m \vee B_1 \vee \ldots \vee B_n$ is represented in implicational form: $A_1 \wedge \ldots \wedge A_m \rightarrow B_1 \vee \ldots \vee B_n$ where A_i ($1 \leq i \leq m$) and B_j ($1 \leq j \leq n$) are atoms; the left hand side of "$\rightarrow$" is said to be the *antecedent*; and the right hand side of "$\rightarrow$" the *consequent*.

A clause is said to be *positive* if its antecedent is $true$ ($m = 0$), and *negative* if its consequent is $false$ ($n = 0$); otherwise it is *mixed* ($m \neq 0, n \neq 0$). A clause is said to be *violated* under a set M of ground atoms if with some ground substitution σ the following condition holds: $\forall i (1 \leq i \leq m) A_i \sigma \in M \wedge \forall j (1 \leq j \leq n) B_j \sigma \notin M$.

A model generation proof procedure is sketched in Fig. 1. The procedure MG takes a partial interpretation Mc (model candidate) and a set of clauses S to be proven, and builds a (sub)proof-tree of S.

A leaf labeled with $\top$ tells us that a model of S has been found as a current model candidate. If every leaf of the constructed proof-tree is labeled with $\bot$, S is unsatisfiable; otherwise S is satisfiable. In the latter case, at least one leaf is labeled with $\top$ or at least one branch grows infinitely.

---

procedure $MGTP(S) : P$; /* Input(S):Clause set, Output(P):Proof-tree of S */
  return($MG(\emptyset, S)$);

procedure $MG(Mc, S) : P$;/* Input(Mc): Model candidate */

1. (Model rejection) If a negative clause ($A_1 \wedge \ldots \wedge A_m \rightarrow false$) $\in S$ is violated under Mc with a ground substitution σ, **return**$\langle \overset{!}{\bot} \rangle$

2. (Model extension) If a positive or mixed clause ($A_1 \wedge \ldots \wedge A_m \rightarrow B_1 \vee \ldots \vee B_n$) $\in S$ is violated under Mc with a ground substitution σ,

   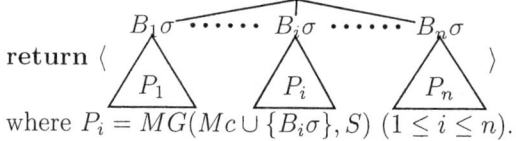

   where $P_i = MG(Mc \cup \{B_i \sigma\}, S)$ ($1 \leq i \leq n$).

3. (Model finding) If neither 1 nor 2 is applicable, **return** $\langle \overset{!}{\top} \rangle$;

Fig. 1. Model generation procedure

3 Abstract Clauses

An *abstract atom* of $P(t_1, \ldots, t_n)$ is an atom P. That is, the abstract atom abstracts away its arguments. Henceforth, we will use capital letters $A, B, A_1, B_1, \ldots$ as denoting normal atoms, and small letters $a, b, a_1, b_1, \ldots$ as denoting abstract atoms corresponding to the capital letters.

A *d-abstract clause* of $A_1 \wedge \ldots \wedge A_m \to B_1 \vee \ldots \vee B_n$ is a clause $a_1 \wedge \ldots \wedge a_m \to b_1 \vee \ldots \vee b_n$. A set of d-abstract clauses obtained from a normal clause set S by replacing normal clauses with d-abstract ones is denoted by $d\_abs(S)$.

Theorem 1. *Let S be a set of clauses. If $d\_abs(S)$ is satisfiable, then S is satisfiable.*

$d\_abs(S)$ is a set of propositional clauses, so, checking its satisfiability is decidable, while checking satisfiability of S is generally undecidable[1].

Example 1 (D-abstraction). Let $S = \{p(x) \wedge q(x) \wedge s(y) \to false,\ p(x) \wedge r(x) \to s(f(x)),\ q(x) \to r(x) \vee s(f(x)),\ p(x) \to q(x) \vee r(y),\ true \to p(a)\}$, then $d\_abs(S) = \{p \wedge q \wedge s \to false,\ p \wedge r \to s,\ q \to r \vee s,\ p \to q \vee r,\ true \to p\}$.

$d\_abs(S)$ has a model $\{p, r, s\}$ and thus is satisfiable. Therefore, we conclude S is satisfiable.

C-abstract clauses of $A_1 \wedge \ldots \wedge A_m \to B_1 \vee \ldots \vee B_n$ are n clauses $a_1 \wedge \ldots \wedge a_m \to b_1$, $a_1 \wedge \ldots \wedge a_m \to b_2$, $\cdots$, and $a_1 \wedge \ldots \wedge a_m \to b_n$. Note that there is no c-abstract clause for a negative clause $A_1 \wedge \ldots \wedge A_m \to false$.

A set of c-abstract clauses obtained from a normal clause set S by replacing normal clauses with c-abstract ones is denoted by $c\_abs(S)$. Note that negative clauses are eliminated in $c\_abs(S)$ and all clauses in $c\_abs(S)$ are Horn clauses. Therefore, we obtain a unique model of $c\_abs(S)$ with the model generation procedure.

A clause $A_1 \wedge \ldots \wedge A_m \to B_1 \vee \ldots \vee B_n$ is *relevant* to a set $\mathcal{A}$ of abstract atoms if $\forall i (1 \leq i \leq m)(a_i \in \mathcal{A})$, otherwise, *irrelevant*. If a clause $C(\in S)$ is used for model extension or rejection in the model generation procedure on S, C is relevant to the model of $c\_abs(S)$. Thus, we obtain the following lemma.

Lemma 1. *Let S be a set of clauses, P be a proof tree of S, M be a model of $c\_abs(S)$, and $C = A_1 \wedge \ldots \wedge A_m \to B_1 \vee \ldots \vee B_n \in S$ be a clause used for model extension or rejection in P. Then, $\forall i(1 \leq i \leq m) a_i \in M$ where a_i is the abstract atom of $A_i (1 \leq i \leq m)$. That is, C is relevant to M.*

Proof. Let $C^k = A_1^k \wedge \ldots \wedge A_m^k \to B_1^k \vee \ldots \vee B_n^k \in S$ be a clause used for the k-th model extension or rejection in P. We can easily show the following property by induction on k: $\forall i (1 \leq i \leq m) a_i^k \in M \wedge \forall j (1 \leq j \leq n) b_j^k \in M$ where a_i^k is the abstract atom of $A_i^k (1 \leq i \leq m)$ and b_j^k is the abstract atom of $B_j^k (1 \leq j \leq n)$. This property implies the lemma. □

The lemma says that if a clause $C(\in S)$ is irrelevant to the model of $c\_abs(S)$, then C is never used for model extensions or rejections in the model generation procedure on S. Therefore, we ignore irrelevant clauses when we apply the model generation procedure on S.

---

[1] $d\_abs(S)$ is exactly the same as the propositional abstraction proposed by Plaisted [7] and thus folklore. But, it is still interesting to see experimental data on all satisfiable problems from the TPTP library.

Theorem 2. *If the model generation determines that a set S of clauses is unsatisfiable, then it also determines that $S \setminus IR(S)$ is unsatisfiable, where $IR(S) = \{C|C \text{ is irrelevant to } M\}$ and M is a model of $c\_abs(S)$.*

The model generation is a sound and complete proof procedure [1], therefore, we obtain the corollary.

Corollary 1. *Let S be a set of clauses. Then, S is unsatisfiable iff $S \setminus IR(S)$ is unsatisfiable.*

By proving $S \setminus IR(S)$ instead of S, we can diminish its execution cost if $IR(S) \neq \emptyset$. If $S \setminus IR(S) = \emptyset$, we conclude that S is satisfiable. When $IR(S) = \emptyset$, we may decrease the number of clauses in S by applying the same consideration on the set $CON(S) = \{B_1 \wedge \ldots \wedge B_n \to A_1 \vee \ldots \vee A_m \mid (A_1 \wedge \ldots \wedge A_m \to B_1 \vee \ldots \vee B_n) \in S\}$ which is obtained from the contrapositive set of S by reversing every literal polarity. Thus, we obtain a process which eliminates unnecessary clauses in S:

(1) Let S be a set of clauses.
(2) $i = 0$, $S_0 = S$.
(3) $S_{i+1} = S_i \setminus IR(S_i)$, $i = i + 1$.
(4) If $i = 1$ or $S_i \neq S_{i-1}$, then $S_i = CON(S_i)$ and goto (3).
(5) If i is an even number, then $S_i = CON(S_i)$.

We stop the process when it reaches a fixpoint gotten as $S_i = S_{i-1}$. Then, we try to prove the final S_i instead of S.

Example 2 (C-abstraction). Let $S(= S_0)$ be a set of 6 clauses from $C1$ to $C6$:

$C1 : r(x) \to false$ $\quad C2 : v(x) \to r(x)$ $\quad C3 : s(x) \to r(x)$
$C4 : q(x) \to s(x) \vee u(x)$ $\quad C5 : p(x) \to q(x)$ $\quad C6 : true \to p(a)$

Then, c-abstraction $c\_abs(S_0)$ is a set of the following clauses:

$C2_1 : v \to r$ $\quad C3_1 : s \to r$ $\quad C4_1 : q \to s$
$C4_2 : q \to u$ $\quad C5_1 : p \to q$ $\quad C6_1 : true \to p$

We obtain the model $\{p, q, u, s, r\}$ of $c\_abs(S_0)$ with model generation. The clause $C2$ is irrelevant to this model and thus eliminated. So, $S_1 = \{C1, C3, C4, C5, C6\}$, then $S_1 = CON(S_1) = \{C1^C, C3^C, C4^C, C5^C, C6^C\}$ where

$C1^C : true \to r(x)$ $\quad C3^C : r(x) \to s(x)$ $\quad C4^C : s(x) \wedge u(x) \to q(x)$
$C5^C : q(x) \to p(x)$ $\quad C6^C : p(a) \to false$

Next, we obtain the model $\{r, s\}$ of $c\_abs(S_1)$. Therefore, $C4^C$, $C5^C$, and $C6^C$ are irrelevant to this model and thus eliminated. So, $S_2 = \{C1^C, C3^C\}$, then $S_2 = CON(S_2) = \{C1, C3\}$. We continue this process until no clause is eliminated. Finally, S_3 becomes an empty set. Thus, we conclude S is satisfiable.

4 Experimental Results

The method is implemented on top of a constraint logic programming system B-Prolog [17]. We use all 5522 CNF problems in the TPTP problem library version 2.7.0 [13,14]. We remove equality axioms using the tptp2X utility (distributed with TPTP) with option "-t rm_equality:rsftp" from each problem if any. The problems were run on a DELL computer (Mobile Intel Pentium III 650MHz CPU, 512MB memory, Linux 2.6.0).

If a problem S contains equality which is represented using the equal/2 predicate in TPTP, we simply add a positive unit clause "$true \rightarrow equal$" to $d\_abs(S)$ and $c\_abs(S)$ before preprocessing. In other words, we assume that all individuals are equal in d-abstraction and the equal/2 predicate is relevant in c-abstraction.

4.1 D-Abstraction: Checking Satisfiability

In 766 satisfiable first-order problems, 223 problems are determined as satisfiable with their d-abstract clause sets, within one second for each. Table 1 (a) shows the number of problems solved by d-abstraction for each problem domain in TPTP. The first column shows domain names, and the second column shows the number of problems solved and the number of satisfiable first-order problems in that domain. For example, there are 17 satisfiable first-order problems in the BOO domain. Among them, 4 problems are solved by d-abstraction. 45 % of 223 problems are in the SYN category and 19 % are in the NLP category. Table 1 (b) shows similar information for every problem rating[2]. The effectiveness of d-abstraction seems to be independent of the problem domains and ratings.

4.2 C-Abstraction: Eliminating Unnecessary Clauses

In 5522 CNF problems, 725 problems are reduced by c-abstraction based elimination. For the ALG, COM, FLD, GRA, HEN, HWC, KRS, LDA, RNG, ROB, SWC, and TOP categories, no problem is reduced. The average preprocessing time is 3.75 seconds for 725 problems. More than 90% problems are reduced within one second for each, while 35 problems need more than ten seconds for reducing. All these 35 problems are in the SYN category and consist of more than 1000 clauses.

Table 2 (a) shows the numbers of problems reduced with c-abstraction for each problem domain. For example, there are 83 CNF problems in the HWV category. 31 problems of them are reduced. For the NLP and SYN categories, more than half of the problems are reduced.

---

[2] In the TPTP distribution, each problem file consists of a header part and a body part. The header part contains information about problem. The rating filed is in the header part. The rating gives the difficulty of the problem. It is a real number in the range 0.0 to 1.0, where 0.0 means that the problem is easy and 1.0 means that the problem is hard.

Table 1. Numbers of problems solved by d-abstraction

(a) Domain

ALG	0/2	GRA	0/0	LCL	10/44	RNG	5/10
ANA	2/2	GRP	12/75	LDA	0/0	ROB	2/5
BOO	4/17	HAL	0/0	MGT	2/11	SET	4/12
CAT	6/10	HEN	3/3	MSC	1/2	SWC	0/1
COL	0/6	HWC	2/2	NLP	42/236	SWV	3/9
COM	0/0	HWV	6/8	NUM	4/7	SYN	100/216
FLD	0/0	KRS	2/8	PLA	2/2	TOP	1/19
GEO	0/17	LAT	8/22	PUZ	2/20		

(b) Rating

0.00	91/232	0.67	0/80
0.14	41/79	0.71	18/29
0.17	4/33	0.83	0/1
0.29	18/25	0.86	14/51
0.33	3/109	1.00	0/12
0.43	15/18		
0.50	0/41		
0.57	19/56		

Table 2. Numbers of problems reduced by c-abstraction

(a) Domain

ALG	0/15	GRA	0/1	LCL	4/527	RNG	0/104
ANA	4/21	GRP	17/791	LDA	0/23	ROB	0/38
BOO	1/133	HAL	0/0	MGT	3/78	SET	5/706
CAT	2/62	HEN	0/67	MSC	2/13	SWC	0/423
COL	13/193	HWC	0/6	NLP	156/258	SWV	5/21
COM	0/8	HWV	31/83	NUM	5/315	SYN	462/839
FLD	0/279	KRS	0/17	PLA	2/32	TOP	0/24
GEO	6/253	LAT	1/104	PUZ	6/82		

(b) Ratio(%)

0-9	87	50-59	19
10-19	6	60-69	55
20-29	32	70-79	118
30-39	17	80-89	167
40-49	108	90-99	116

Table 2 (b) shows the ratio of remaining clauses to the original ones. For example, the first row indicates that there are 87 problems less than 10 % clauses of which are remaining after reduction. There are 57 problems which are reduced to the empty sets. All such problems are determined as satisfiable without proof.

In order to measure the c-abstraction effect, we solved all 725 problems, by using three provers with a time limit of 600 seconds: DCTP 1.31 [12], Vampire 7.0 [9], and E 0.82 [11][3]. These provers attended the CADE ATP system competition CASC-J2[16]. Vampire 7.0 won the first place in the MIX and FOF divisions, DCTP 1.31 won the third place in the EPR division, and E 0.82 won the third place in the MIX division.

Table 3 (a) shows summaries of c-abstraction effects on these three provers. The "before" column shows statistics for the original clause sets, while the "after" column shows statistics for their reduced clause sets. The last row shows the average cpu time in seconds. The parenthetic number in the "after" column shows the cpu time including preprocessing. Table 3 (b) shows a detailed version of (a). We succeed in enhancing performance of the three provers: The numbers of problems solved are increased from 642 to 647 for DCTP, from 626 to 642 for Vampire, and from 650 to 661 for E.

---

[3] DCTP runs with options "-negpref -complexity -fullrewrite -alternate -resisol".
Vampire runs with options "–mode casc-j2 -p off -t 600".
E runs with options "-s –print-statistics -xAuto -tAuto –memory-limit=384 –tptp-in".

Table 3. Effect of c-abstraction

(a) Summary

ALL	DCTP 1.31		Vampire 7.0		E 0.82	
	before	after	before	after	before	after
Attempted	725					
Solved	642	647	626	642	650	661
Av. Time(s)	6.15	5.10(9.28)	11.69	7.08(8.80)	5.48	11.64(15.73)

(b) Category summary

Domain (Attempted)	DCTP 1.31		Vampire 7.0		E 0.82	
	before	after	before	after	before	after
ANA	0	1	1	1	1	1
(4)	-	0.0(0.08)	15.53	15.28(15.36)	46.61	36.98(37.06)
BOO	1	1	1	1	1	1
(1)	0.0	0.0(0.07)	150.09	0.46(0.53)	22.66	0.50(0.57)
CAT	1	1	0	0	0	0
(2)	0.0	0.0(0.08)	-	-	-	-
COL	4	4	4	4	0	0
(13)	12.69	6.61(6.73)	159.39	159.22(159.33)	-	-
GEO	1	1	1	1	1	1
(6)	0.0	0.0(0.07)	0.73	0.11(0.18)	0.86	0.48(0.55)
GRP	17	17	7	8	9	11
(17)	1.05	1.05(1.12)	3.45	3.11(3.19)	1.62	1.35(1.43)
HWV	22	25	28	28	30	29
(31)	1.50	0.08(0.17)	12.76	4.67(4.77)	2.04	10.50(10.59)
LAT	1	1	0	0	0	0
(1)	0.01	0.01(0.09)	-	-	-	-
LCL	4	4	1	4	0	4
(4)	0.00	0.00(0.08)	235.93	0.37(0.45)	-	0.85(0.93)
MGT	3	3	3	3	3	3
(3)	0.03	0.03(0.11)	11.30	11.39(11.47)	0.51	0.52(0.60)
MSC	2	2	2	2	2	2
(2)	0.01	0.0(0.07)	0.41	0.27(0.34)	0.49	0.52(0.59)
NLP	126	126	140	140	146	146
(156)	0.05	0.04(0.14)	9.96	8.56(8.66)	3.19	33.17(33.27)
NUM	5	5	2	5	2	5
(5)	0.0	0.0(0.08)	0.12	0.33(0.40)	0.49	0.60(0.67)
PLA	2	2	2	2	2	2
(2)	0.01	0.0(0.08)	0.13	0.12(0.20)	0.49	0.48(0.56)
PUZ	6	6	5	6	6	6
(6)	0.03	0.03(0.11)	0.13	0.27(0.35)	0.51	0.51(0.59)
SET	4	4	4	4	3	4
(5)	0.09	0.05(0.13)	79.62	18.24(18.31)	0.49	82.65(82.73)
SWV	5	5	4	5	4	5
(5)	0.01	0.0(0.08)	84.62	0.31(0.39)	0.62	0.57(0.65)
SYN	438	439	421	428	440	441
(462)	8.76	7.39(13.52)	9.05	6.57(8.20)	6.69	4.87(10.95)

There is a series of 10 satisfiable problems in the NLP domain which have a negative effect on E. The average proving times for these problems are increased by 440 seconds after c-abstraction. This is a major cause why the average run time of E is increased from 5.48 seconds to 11.68 seconds.

C-abstraction effects on Vampire and E seem to be stronger than that on DCTP. This is due to the fact that there exist problems which have no positive clause or no negative clause. These problems are obviously satisfiable. But, for such problems, Vampire and E sometimes consume a lot of cpu time (or reach a time limit) while DCTP immediately stops. There are 18 such cases for Vampire and 11 cases for E. These problems become empty sets by c-abstraction, so it is easy to determine them as satisfiable[4]

Table 4. Positive and negative effects of c-abstraction

Problem	Time (secs)	No. of clauses		DCTP 1.31		Vampire 7.0		E 0.82	
		original	reduced	before	after	before	after	before	after
ANA006-1	0.08	14	5	T.O.	0.00	T.O.	T.O.	T.O.	T.O.
BOO008-1	0.07	21	1	0.00	0.00	150.09	0.46	22.66	0.50
COL092-2	0.12	195	183	24.66	12.96	T.O.	T.O.	T.O.	T.O.
HWV009-1	0.10	92	66	T.O.	0.10	0.54	0.20	0.56	0.57
HWV031-1	0.10	93	67	T.O.	T.O.	T.O.	T.O.	35.22	283.71
NLP037-1	0.08	66	12	0.02	0.00	65.30	0.10	0.51	0.50
NLP186-1	0.11	108	99	T.O.	T.O.	0.25	0.26	34.69	538.11
NUM288-1	0.07	12	0	0.0	0.0	T.O.	0.44	T.O.	0.85
SET787-1	0.08	14	12	0.34	0.21	71.12	71.55	T.O.	329.16
SWV017-1	0.09	37	5	0.01	0.00	215.64	0.44	0.55	0.51
SYN597-1	0.08	28	23	5.36	5.37	30.91	209.20	3.47	T.O.
SYN599-1	0.08	29	25	89.48	89.57	209.29	162.53	42.30	5.07
SYN610-1	0.08	30	26	T.O.	T.O.	15.18	209.38	5.17	2.87
SYN624-1	0.07	35	26	0.25	0.25	4.80	61.30	111.65	0.68
SYN708-1	0.09	83	61	T.O.	T.O.	36.04	124.57	72.27	60.82
SYN742-1	0.08	31	0	0.04	0.00	169.80	0.10	0.67	0.49
SYN813-1	1.69	504	378	34.41	T.O.	13.59	9.19	10.71	2.96
SYN818-1	104.59	2621	1397	258.68	87.32	T.O.	T.O.	59.65	18.31
SYN821-1	27.53	1716	712	56.24	122.71	T.O.	26.52	T.O.	5.42
SYN822-1	33.15	1768	1138	65.15	34.17	T.O.	59.11	T.O.	71.08
SYN897-1	0.86	122	97	T.O.	4.85	2.26	1.87	1.35	1.11
SYN912-1	2.72	1780	247	61.90	0.62	T.O.	T.O.	T.O.	T.O.

Table 4 shows problems which exhibit positive or negative effect of c-abstraction on the 3 provers. The second column shows cpu times for preprocessing in seconds, the third the number of original clauses, and the fourth the number of

---

[4] Vampire regards an empty clause set as an error of the input and aborts. We treat such a case as a normal proof which tells that the set is satisfiable.

clauses remaining after preprocessing. The last 6 columns show proving time of the 3 provers. The "before" column shows the time for the original clause sets, while the "after" column shows the time for their reduced clause sets. "T.O." indicates that the problem is not solved in 600 seconds.

We succeeded in enhancing the provers' performance for several problems. For example on SYN912-1, DCTP's proving times is decreased from 61.90 seconds to 0.62 seconds after 2.72 seconds preprocessing which decreases the number of clauses from 1780 to 247. Vampire and E can prove SYN822-1 in 59.11 and 71.08 seconds respectively after preprocessing, while they cannot prove it within 600 seconds before preprocessing.

On the other hand, there are some problems which show negative effects of c-abstraction. For example on NLP186-1, E's proving time is increased from 34.69 seconds to 538.11 seconds. DCTP can not prove SYN813-1 within 600 seconds after preprocessing, while it can prove the same problem in 34.41 seconds before preprocessing. There is another type of problem which show both positive and negative effects. For example, SYN624-1 shows a negative effect on Vampire and a positive effect on E: Vampire's proving times is increased from 4.80 seconds to 61.30 seconds while E's proving time is decreased from 111.65 seconds to 0.68 seconds.

There are some satisfiable problems which are reduced to empty sets of clauses in DCTP's preprocessing phase after c-abstraction based clause elimination. In these problems, 48 problems are not reduced to empty sets without c-abstraction. This indicates that c-abstraction based clause elimination enhances the effects of other preprocessing operations.

4.3 C-Abstraction Based Elimination and Pure Literal Elimination

A pure literal is a literal in a clause that cannot be resolved against any literal in any clause. Clauses that contain pure literals can be eliminated, because such a clause cannot contribute a resolution proof. Pure literal elimination has a similar effect to c-abstraction's because c-abstraction based preprocessing eliminates clauses which contain literals irrelevant to model generation.

Pure literal elimination is sometimes stronger and sometimes weaker than c-abstraction based elimination. The strength comes from a unification operation which is necessary to the former but unnecessary to the latter. On the other hand, weakness comes from (model generation) inferences which are necessary to the latter but unnecessary to the former.

In 5522 CNF problem, 562 problems are reduced by pure literal elimination. This indicates that c-abstraction is applicable to more problems than pure literal elimination. The average elimination time is 4.49 seconds for 562 problems. More than 85% of the problems are reduced within one second for each, while 38 problems needs more than ten seconds for reducing. Pure literal elimination takes more time than c-abstraction does on average. This is caused by the task of unification.

Table 5 (a) shows the numbers of problems reduced by pure literal elimination for every problem domain. Table 5 (b) shows the ratio of remaining clauses to

Table 5. Pure literal elimination

(a) Domain

ALG	0/15	GRA	0/1	LCL	0/527	RNG	0/104
ANA	3/21	GRP	13/791	LDA	0/23	ROB	0/38
BOO	0/133	HAL	0/0	MGT	4/78	SET	2/706
CAT	1/62	HEN	0/67	MSC	0/13	SWC	0/423
COL	13/193	HWC	0/6	NLP	142/258	SWV	0/21
COM	2/8	HWV	6/83	NUM	0/315	SYN	358/839
FLD	0/279	KRS	0/17	PLA	1/32	TOP	0/24
GEO	6/253	LAT	0/104	PUZ	11/82		

(b) Ratio(%)

0-9	18	50-59	13
10-19	4	60-69	27
20-29	3	70-79	43
30-39	5	80-89	98
40-49	2	90-99	350

(c) Effect

ALL	DCTP 1.31		Vampire 7.0		E 0.82	
	before	after	before	after	before	after
Attempted	562					
Solved	509	510	485	485	507	509
Av. Time(s)	6.98	6.77(11.63)	7.10	6.70(8.25)	4.82	13.37(18.15)

the original ones. There are 350 problems which are in the ratio from 90% to 99%. This is 3 times as many as those of c-abstraction (cf. Table 2). We may say that the clause elimination effect of c-abstraction is generally stronger than that of pure literal elimination.

Table 5 (c) shows the summaries of pure literal elimination effects on the provers. A little effect can be seen on the performance of the provers. Indeed, there is no change in terms of problems solved within 600 seconds after preprocessing for Vampire. The influence of pure literal elimination upon the performance of these provers is weaker than that of c-abstraction.

There are 752 problems which are reduced by c-abstraction based elimination or pure literal elimination. They can be classified into 4 groups by the set inclusion relation as follows: (1) A is a proper subset of B, (2) A equals B, (3) A is a proper superset of B, and (4) there is no set inclusion relation between A and B, where A is a problem (i.e. a set of clauses) reduced by c-abstraction base elimination and B is a problem reduced by pure literal elimination. There are 333 problems in the first group, 182 in the second, 62 in the third, and 175 in the fourth. This indicates that pure literal elimination is different from c-abstraction. And it seems reasonable to suppose that the latter gains the ascendancy over the former with respect to clause elimination.

By the way, it is possible to apply pure literal elimination after c-abstraction. Our experiment shows that only simple problems are further reduced by pure literal elimination after c-abstraction. Thus, pure literal elimination after c-abstraction has no influence upon the performance of DCTP, Vampire, and E.

4.4 C-Abstraction Combined with D-Abstraction

Among 725 problems reduced by c-abstraction, there are 87 problems which are determined as satisfiable by d-abstraction. We don't need to prove these problems anymore. Is is natural to combine c-abstraction with d-abstraction. Table 6 shows the summary of c-abstraction effects on the remaining 638 problems. The parenthetic number in the "after" column shows the cpu time including c-abstraction and d-abstraction.

Table 6. Effect of C-abstraction on problems passed through d-abstraction

ALL	DCTP 1.31		Vampire 7.0		E 0.82	
	before	after	before	after	before	after
Attempted	638					
Solved	556	560	565	567	585	583
Av. Time(s)	7.06	5.86(10.83)	8.86	8.71(10.09)	5.97	13.10(17.87)

There is a positive effect on DCTP. The number of problems solved is increased from 556 to 560 and the average cpu time is decreased from 7.06 seconds to 5.86 seconds. For Vampire, c-abstraction barely has a positive effect. The number of problems solved is increased from 565 to 567, but the average cpu time is almost unchaged. Unfortunately, there is a negative effect on E. The number of problems solved is decreased from 585 to 583 and the average cpu time is increased from 5.97 seconds to 13.10 seconds.

5 Conclusion

Preprocessing a set of clauses has a great impact on the success of a subsequent automated reasoning system. We have introduced two abstractions of the given clause set for preprocessing it. Experimental results show that these abstractions are effective for several problems. 29% of satisfiable first-order problems in TPTP are determined as satisfiable with their d-abstract clause sets. 13% of CNF problems in TPTP are reduced with d-abstraction.

C-abstraction sometimes has positive effects and sometimes negative effects on state-of-the-art theorem provers: DCTP, Vampire, and E. As a whole, without d-abstraction, these provers profit from c-abstraction. On the other hand for the problems passed through d-abstraction, DCTP and Vampire profit from c-abstraction, but E does not. This situation may be improved if we find a combination of the provers' options that fit for c-abstraction. Furthermore, the combination of the proposed method and other preprocessing operations can enhance their abilities.

Acknowledgement

This research was partially supported by Grant-in-Aid for Scientific Research (No. A-15200002) from the Ministry of Education, Culture, Sports, Science and Technology of Japan.

References

1. François Bry and Adnan Yahya. Positive Unit Hyperresolution Tableaux and Their Application to Minimal Model Generation. *Journal of Automated Reasoning*, 25:35–82, 2000.
2. Marc Fuchs and Dirk Fuchs. Abstraction-Based Relevancy Testing for Model Elimination. In Harald Ganzinger, editor, *CADE-16*, volume 1632 of *LNAI*, pages 344–358. Springer, July 1999.
3. Fausto Giunchiglia and Toby Walsh. A theory of abstraction. *Artificial Intelligence*, 57:323–389, 1992.
4. Craig A. Knoblock, Josh D. Tenenberg, and Qiang Yang. Characterizing Abstraction Hierarchies for Planing. In *Proceedings of the Ninth National Conference on Artificial Intelligence*, pages 692–697. AAAI Press, 1991.
5. Miyuki Koshimura and Ryuzo Hasegawa. Proof Simplification for Model Generation and Its Applications. In Michel Parigot and Andrei Voronkov, editors, *LPAR2000*, volume 1955 of *LNAI*, pages 96–113. Springer, November 2000.
6. Rainer Manthey and François Bry. SATCHMO: a theorem prover implemented in Prolog. In E. Lusk and R. Overbeek, editors, *CADE-9*, volume 310 of *LNCS*, pages 415–434. Springer, May 1988.
7. David A. Plaisted. Theorem Proving with Abstraction. *Artificial Intelligence*, 16:47–108, 1981.
8. David A. Plaisted and Adnan Yahya. A relevance restriction strategy for automated deduction. *Artificial Intelligence*, 144:59–93, 2003.
9. Alexandre Riazanov and Andrei Voronkov. The design and implementation of VAMPIRE. *AI Communications*, 15(2):91–110, 2002.
10. Earl D. Sacerdoti. Planning in a Hierarchy of Abstraction Spaces. *Artificial Intelligence*, 5:115–135, 1974.
11. Stephan Schulz. E - a brainiac theorem prover. *AI Communications*, 15(2):111–126, 2002.
12. Gernot Stenz. DCTP 1.2 - System Abstract. In Uwe Egly and Christian G. Fernmuller, editors, *TABLEAUX-2002*, volume 2381 of *LNAI*, pages 335–340. Springer, 2002.
13. G. Sutcliffe and C.B. Suttner. The TPTP Problem Library: CNF Release v1.2.1. *Journal of Automated Reasoning*, 21(2):177–203, 1998.
14. G. Sutcliffe and C.B. Suttner. The TPTP Problem Library for Automated Theorem Proving. http://www.cs.miami.edu/~tptp/, 2004.
15. Geoff Sutcliffe and Stuart Melville. The Practice of Clausification in Automatic Theorem Proving. *South African Computer Journal*, 18:57–68, 1996.
16. Geoff Sutcliffe and Christian Suttner. The CADE ATP System Competition. In David Basin and Michaël Rusinowitch, editors, *IJCAR 2004*, volume 3097 of *LNAI*, pages 490–491. Springer, July 2004.
17. Neng-Fa Zhou. B-Prolog User's Manual (Version 6.6). http://www.probp.com, 2004.

Flat and One-Variable Clauses: Complexity of Verifying Cryptographic Protocols with Single Blind Copying

Helmut Seidl and Kumar Neeraj Verma

Institut für Informatik, TU München, Germany
{seidl,verma}@in.tum.de

Abstract. Cryptographic protocols with single blind copying were defined and modeled by Comon and Cortier using the new class $\mathcal{C}$ of first order clauses, which extends the Skolem class. They showed its satisfiability problem to be in 3-DEXPTIME. We improve this result by showing that satisfiability for this class is NEXPTIME-complete, using new resolution techniques. We show satisfiability to be DEXPTIME-complete if clauses are Horn, which is what is required for modeling cryptographic protocols. While translation to Horn clauses only gives a DEXPTIME upper bound for the secrecy problem for these protocols, we further show that this secrecy problem is actually DEXPTIME-complete.

1 Introduction

Several researchers have pursued modeling of cryptographic protocols using first order clauses [3,6,15] and related formalisms like tree automata and set constraints[5,11,12]. While protocol insecurity is NP-complete in case of a bounded number of sessions [14], this is helpful only for detecting some attacks. For certifying protocols, the number of sessions cannot be bounded, although we may use other safe abstractions. The approach using first order clauses is particularly useful for this class of problems. A common safe abstraction is to allow a bounded number of nonces, i.e. random numbers, to be used in infinitely many sessions. Security however still remains undecidable [5]. Hence further restrictions are necessary to obtain decidability.

In this direction, Comon and Cortier [6,8] proposed the notion of protocols with single blind copying. Intuitively this restriction means that agents are allowed to copy at most one piece of data blindly in any protocol step, a restriction satisfied by most protocols in the literature. Comon and Cortier modeled the secrecy problem for these protocols using the new class $\mathcal{C}$ of first order clauses, which extends the Skolem class, and showed satisfiability for $\mathcal{C}$ to be decidable [6] in 3-DEXPTIME [8]. The NEXPTIME lower bound is easy. We show in this paper that satisfiability of this class is in NEXPTIME, thus NEXPTIME-complete. If clauses are restricted to be Horn, which suffices for modeling of cryptographic protocols, we show that satisfiability is DEXPTIME-complete (again the lower bound is easy). While translation to clauses only gives a DEXPTIME upper bound for the secrecy problem for this class of protocols, we further show that the secrecy problem for these protocols is also DEXPTIME-complete.

For proving our upper bounds, we introduce several variants of standard ordered resolution with selection and splitting [2]. Notably we consider resolution as consisting of instantiation of clauses, and of generation of propositional implications. This is in the style of Ganzinger and Korovin [10], but we enhance this approach, and generate interesting implications to obtain optimal complexity. More precisely, while the approach of Ganzinger and Korovin [10] has a single phase of instantiation followed by propositional satisfiability checking, we generate certain interesting propositional implications, instantiate them, and iterate the process. We further show how this technique can be employed also in presence of rules for replacement of literals in clauses, which obey some ordering constraints. To deal with the notion of single blind copying we show how terms containing a single variable can be decomposed into simple terms whose unifiers are of very simple forms. As byproducts, we obtain optimal complexity for several subclasses of $\mathcal{C}$, involving so called *flat* and *one-variable* clauses.

Outline: We start in Section 2 by recalling basic notions about first order logic and resolution refinements. In Section 3 we introduce cryptographic protocols with single blind copying, discuss their modeling using the class $\mathcal{C}$ of first order clauses, and show that their secrecy problem is DEXPTIME-hard. To decide the class $\mathcal{C}$ we start with the subclass of one-variable clauses in Section 4 and show its satisfiability to be DEXPTIME-complete. Satisfiability of the fragment of $\mathcal{C}$ involving flat clauses is shown to NEXPTIME-complete in Section 5. In Section 6, the techniques from the two cases are combined with further ideas to show that satisfiability for $\mathcal{C}$ is NEXPTIME-complete. In Section 7 we adapt this proof to show that satisfiability for the Horn fragment of $\mathcal{C}$ is DEXPTIME-complete.

2 Resolution

We recall standard notions from first order logic. Fix a signature Σ of function symbols each with a given arity, and containing at least one zero-ary symbol. Let r be the maximal arity of function symbols in Σ. Fix a set $\mathbf{X} = \{\mathbf{x}_1, \mathbf{x}_2, \mathbf{x}_3, \ldots\}$ of variables. Note that $\mathbf{x}_1, \mathbf{x}_2, \ldots$ (in bold face) are the actual elements of $\mathbf{X}$, where as $x, y, z, x_1, y_1, \ldots$ are used to represent arbitrary elements of $\mathbf{X}$. The set $T_\Sigma(\mathbf{X})$ of terms built from Σ and $\mathbf{X}$ is defined as usual. T_Σ is the set of *ground terms*, i.e. those not containing any variables. Atoms A are of the form $P(t_1, \ldots, t_n)$ where P is an n-ary predicate and t_i's are terms. Literals L are either positive literals $+A$ (or simply A) or negative literals $-A$, where A is an atom. $-(-A)$ is another notation for A. $\pm$ denotes $+$ or $-$ and $\mp$ denotes the opposite sign (and similarly for notations $\pm', \mp', \ldots$). A *clause* is a finite set of literals. A *negative clause* is one which contains only negative literals. If M is any term, literal or clause then the set $\mathsf{fv}(M)$ of variables occurring in them is defined as usual. If C_1 and C_2 are clauses then $C_1 \vee C_2$ denotes $C_1 \cup C_2$. $C \vee \{L\}$ is written as $C \vee L$ (In this notation, we allow the possibility of $L \in C$). If $C_1, \ldots, C_n$ are clauses such that $\mathsf{fv}(C_i) \cap \mathsf{fv}(C_j) = \emptyset$ for $i \neq j$, and if C_i is non-empty for $i \geq 2$, then the clause $C_1 \vee \ldots \vee C_n$ is also written as $C_1 \sqcup \ldots \sqcup C_n$ to emphasize this property. *Ground literals and clauses* are ones not containing variables. A term, literal or clause is *trivial* if it contains no function symbols. A substitution is a function $\sigma : \mathbf{X} \to T_\Sigma(\mathbf{X})$. *Ground substitutions* map every variable to a ground term. We write $\sigma = \{x_1 \mapsto t_1, \ldots, x_n \mapsto t_n\}$ to say that $x_i \sigma = t_i$ for $1 \leq i \leq n$ and $x\sigma = x$ for $x \notin \{x_1, \ldots, x_n\}$. If M is a term, literal, clause, substitution or set of such objects, then the effect $M\sigma$ of applying σ to M is

Flat and One-Variable Clauses: Complexity of Verifying Cryptographic Protocols   81

defined as usual. *Renamings* are bijections $\sigma : \mathbf{X} \to \mathbf{X}$. If M is a term, literal, clause or substitution, then a renaming of M is of the form $M\sigma$ for some renaming σ, and an instance of M is of the form $M\sigma$ for some substitution σ. If M and N are terms or literals then a *unifier* of M and N is a substitution σ such that $M\sigma = N\sigma$. If such a unifier exists then there is also a *most general unifier (mgu)*, i.e. a unifier σ such that for every unifier σ' of M and N, there is some σ'' such that $\sigma' = \sigma\sigma''$. Most general unifiers are unique upto renaming: if σ_1 and σ_2 are two mgus of M and N then σ_1 is a renaming of σ_2. Hence we may use the notation $mgu(M,N)$ to denote one of them. We write $M[x_1, \ldots, x_n]$ to say that $\mathsf{fv}(M) \subseteq \{x_1, \ldots, x_n\}$. If $t_1, \ldots, t_n$ are terms then $M[t_1, \ldots, t_n]$ denotes $M\{x_1 \mapsto t_1, \ldots, x_n \mapsto t_n\}$. If N is a set of terms them $M[N] = \{M[t_1, \ldots, t_n] \mid t_1, \ldots, t_n \in N\}$. If M is a set of terms, atoms, literals or clauses them $M[N] = \bigcup_{m \in M} m[N]$. A *Herbrand interpretation* $\mathcal{H}$ is a set of ground atoms. A clause C is *satisfied* in $\mathcal{H}$ if for every ground substitution σ, either $A \in \mathcal{H}$ for some $A \in C\sigma$, or $A \notin \mathcal{H}$ for some $-A \in C\sigma$. A set S of clauses is satisfied in $\mathcal{H}$ if every clause of S is satisfied in $\mathcal{H}$. If such a $\mathcal{H}$ exists then S is *satisfiable*, and $\mathcal{H}$ is a *Herbrand model* of S. A *Horn clause* is one containing at most one positive literal. If a set of Horn clauses is satisfiable then it has a least Herbrand model wrt the subset ordering.

Resolution and its refinements are well known methods for testing satisfiability of clauses. Given a strict partial order $<$ on atoms, a literal $\pm A$ is *maximal* in a clause C if there is no literal $\pm' B \in C$ with $A < B$. *Binary ordered resolution* and *ordered factorization* wrt ordering $<$ are defined by the following two rules respectively:

$$\frac{C_1 \vee A \quad -B \vee C_2}{C_1 \sigma \vee C_2 \sigma} \qquad \frac{C_1 \vee \pm A \vee \pm B}{C_1 \sigma \vee A\sigma}$$

where $\sigma = mgu(A,B)$ in both rules, A and B are maximal in the left and right premises respectively of the first rule, and A and B are both maximal in the premise of the second rule. We rename the premises of the first rule before resolution so that they don't share variables. The ordering $<$ is *stable* if: whenever $A_1 < A_2$ then $A_1\sigma < A_2\sigma$ for all substitutions σ. We write $S \Rightarrow_< S \cup \{C\}$ to say that C is obtained by one application of the binary ordered resolution or binary factorization rule on clauses in S (the subscript denotes the ordering used).

Another resolution rule is *splitting*. This can be described using *tableaux*. A *tableau* is of the form $S_1 \mid \ldots \mid S_n$, where $n \geq 0$ and each S_i, called a *branch* of the tableau, is a set of clauses (the $\mid$ operator is associative and commutative). A tableau is *satisfiable* if at least one of its branches is satisfiable. The tableau is called *closed* if each S_i contains the empty clause, denoted $\square$. The *splitting* step on tableaux is defined by the rule: $\mathcal{T} \mid S \to_{spl} \mathcal{T} \mid (S \setminus \{C_1 \sqcup C_2\}) \cup \{C_1\} \mid (S \setminus \{C_1 \sqcup C_2\}) \cup \{C_2\}$ whenever $C_1 \sqcup C_2 \in S$ and C_1 and C_2 are non-empty. C_1 and C_2 are called *components* of the clause $C_1 \sqcup C_2$ being split. It is well known that splitting preserves satisfiability of tableaux. We may choose to apply splitting eagerly, or lazily or in some other fashion. Hence we define a *splitting strategy* to be a function f such that $\mathcal{T} \to_{spl} f(\mathcal{T})$ for all tableaux $\mathcal{T}$. The relation $\Rightarrow_<$ is extended to tableaux as expected. Ordered resolution with splitting strategy is then defined by the following rule: $\mathcal{T}_1 \Rightarrow_{<,f} f(\mathcal{T}_2)$ if $\mathcal{T}_1 \Rightarrow_< \mathcal{T}_2$. This provides us with a well known sound and complete method for testing satisfiability.

For any binary relation R, R^* will denote the reflexive transitive closure of R, and R^+ will denote the transitive closure of R.

Lemma 1 ([2]). *For any set S of clauses, for any stable ordering $<$, and for any splitting strategy f, S is unsatisfiable iff $S \Rightarrow^*_{<,f} T$ for some closed T.*

If all predicates are zero-ary then the resulting clauses are *propositional clauses*. In this case we write $S \vDash_p T$ to say that every Herbrand model of S is a Herbrand model of T. This notation will also be used when S and T are sets of first order clauses, by treating every (ground or non-ground) atom as a zero-ary predicate. For example $\{P(a), -P(a)\} \vDash_p \Box$ but $\{P(x), -P(x)\} \nvDash_p \Box$. $S \vDash_p \{C\}$ is also written as $S \vDash_p C$. If $S \vDash_p C$ then clearly $S\sigma \vDash_p C\sigma$ for all substitution σ.

3 Cryptographic Protocols

We assume that Σ contains the binary functions $\{\_\}\_$ and $\langle\_,\_\rangle$ denoting encryption and pairing. *Messages* are terms of $T_\Sigma(\mathbf{X})$. A *state* is of the form $S(M_1, \ldots, M_n)$ where S with arity n is from a finite set of *control points* and M_i are messages. It denotes an agent at control point S with messages M_i in its memory. An *initialization state* is a state not containing variables. A *protocol rule* is of the form $S_1(M_1, \ldots, M_m)$: recv$(M) \rightarrow S_2(N_1, \ldots, N_n)$: send(N). Here M_i, N_j are messages, and M and N are each either a message, or a dummy symbol ? indicating nothing is received (resp. sent). For secrecy analysis we can replace ? by some public message, i.e. one which is known to everyone including the adversary. The rule says that an agent in state $S_1(M_1, \ldots, M_m)$ can receive message M, send a message N, and then move to state $S_2(N_1, \ldots, N_n)$, thus also modifying the messages in its memory. A *protocol* is a finite set of initialization states and protocol rules. This model is in the style of [9] and [5]. The assumption of single blind copying then says that each protocol rule contains at most one variable (which may occur anywhere any number of times in that rule). For example, the public-key Needham-Schroeder protocol below

$$A \rightarrow B : \{A, N_A\}_{K_B}$$
$$B \rightarrow A : \{N_A, N_B\}_{K_B}$$
$$A \rightarrow B : \{N_B\}_{K_B}$$

is written in our notation as follows. For every pair of agents A and B in our system (finitely many of them suffice for finding all attacks against secrecy [7,6]) we have two nonces N^1_{AB} and N^2_{AB} to be used in sessions where A plays the initiator's role and B plays the responder's role. We have initialization states $\mathsf{Init}_0(A, N^1_{AB})$ and $\mathsf{Resp}_0(B, N^2_{AB})$ for all agents A and B. Corresponding to the three lines in the protocol we have rules for all agents A and B:

$\mathsf{Init}_0(A, N^1_{AB})$:recv(?) $\rightarrow$ $\mathsf{Init}_1(A, N^1_{AB})$:send($\{\langle A, N^1_{AB}\rangle\}_{K_B}$)
$\mathsf{Resp}_0(B, N^2_{AB})$:recv($\{\langle A, x\rangle\}_{K_B}$) $\rightarrow \mathsf{Resp}_1(B, x, N^2_{AB})$:send($\{\langle x, N^2_{AB}\rangle\}_{K_A}$)
$\mathsf{Init}_1(A, N^1_{AB})$:recv($\{\langle N^1_{AB}, x\rangle\}_{K_A}$)$\rightarrow$ $\mathsf{Init}_2(A, N^1_{AB}, x)$:send($\{x\}_{K_B}$)
$\mathsf{Resp}_1(B, x, N^2_{AB})$:recv($\{N^2_{AB}\}_{K_B}$) $\rightarrow \mathsf{Resp}_2(B, x, N^2_{AB})$:send(?)

Any initialization state can be created any number of times and any protocol rule can be executed any number of times. The adversary has full control over the network: all messages received by agents are actually sent by the adversary and all messages sent by agents are actually received by the adversary. The adversary can obtain new messages from messages he knows, e.g. by performing encryption and decryption. To model this using Horn clauses, we create a unary predicate reach to model reachable states, and a unary predicate known to model messages known to the adversary. The initialization state $S(M_1, \ldots, M_n)$ is then modeled by the clause reach($S(M_1, \ldots, M_n)$), where S is a new function symbol we create. The protocol rule $S_1(M_1, \ldots, M_m) : \text{recv}(M) \to S_2(N_1, \ldots, N_n) : \text{send}(N)$ is modeled by the clauses known(N) $\vee$ −reach($S_1(M_1, \ldots, M_m)$) $\vee$ −known(M) and reach($S_2(N_1, \ldots, N_n)$) $\vee$ −reach($S_1(M_1, \ldots, M_m)$) $\vee$ −known(M). Under the assumption of single blind copying it is clear that all these clauses are *one-variable clauses*, i.e. clauses containing at most one variable. We need further clauses to express adversary capabilities. The clauses known($\{\mathbf{x}_1\}_{\mathbf{x}_2}$) $\vee$ −known($\mathbf{x}_1$) $\vee$ −known($\mathbf{x}_2$) and known($\mathbf{x}_1$) $\vee$ −known($\{\mathbf{x}_1\}_{\mathbf{x}_2}$) $\vee$ −known($\mathbf{x}_2$) express the encryption and decryption abilities of the adversary. We have similar clauses for his pairing and unpairing abilities, as well as clauses known($f(\mathbf{x}_1, \ldots, \mathbf{x}_n)$) $\vee$ −known($\mathbf{x}_1$) $\vee \ldots \vee$ −known($\mathbf{x}_n$) for any function f that the adversary knows to apply. All these are clearly *flat clauses*, i.e. clauses of the form $C = \bigvee_{i=1}^{k} \pm_i P_i(f_i(x_1^i, \ldots, x_{n_i}^i)) \vee \bigvee_{j=1}^{l} \pm_j Q_j(x_j)$, where $\{x_1^i, \ldots, x_{n_i}^i\} = \text{fv}(C)$ for $1 \leq i \leq k$. Asymmetric keys, i.e. keys K such that message $\{M\}_K$ can only be decrypted with the inverse key K^{-1}, are also easily dealt with using flat and one-variable clauses. The adversary's knowledge of other data c like agent's names, public keys, etc are expressed by clauses known(c). Then the least Herbrand model of this set of clauses describes exactly the reachable states and the messages known to the adversary. Then to check whether some message M remains secret, we add the clause −known(M) and check whether the resulting set is satisfiable.

A set of clauses is in the class $\mathcal{V}_1$ if each of its members is a one-variable clause. A set of clauses is in the class $\mathcal{F}$ if each of its members is a flat clause. More generally we have the class $\mathcal{C}$ proposed by Comon and Cortier [6,8]: a set of clauses S is in the class $\mathcal{C}$ if for each $C \in S$ one of the following conditions is satisfied:
 − C is a one-variable clause
 − $C = \bigvee_{i=1}^{k} \pm_i P_i(u_i[f_i(x_1^i, \ldots, x_{n_i}^i)]) \vee \bigvee_{j=1}^{l} \pm_j Q_j(x_j)$, where for $1 \leq i \leq k$ we have $\{x_1^i, \ldots, x_{n_i}^i\} = \text{fv}(C)$ and u_i contains at most one variable.
If all clauses are Horn then we have the corresponding classes $\mathcal{V}_1 Horn$, $\mathcal{F} Horn$ and $\mathcal{C} Horn$. Clearly the classes $\mathcal{V}_1$ (resp. $\mathcal{V}_1 Horn$) and $\mathcal{F}$ (resp. $\mathcal{F} Horn$) are included in the class $\mathcal{C}$ (resp. $\mathcal{C} Horn$) since the u_i's above can be trivial. Conversely any clause set in $\mathcal{C}$ can be considered as containing just flat and one-variable clauses. This is because we can replace a clause $C \vee \pm P(u[f(x_1, \ldots, x_n)])$ by the clause $C \vee \pm Pu(f(x_1, \ldots, x_n))$ and add clauses $-Pu(x) \vee P(u[x])$ and $Pu(x) \vee -P(u[x])$ where Pu is a fresh predicate. This transformation takes polynomial time and preserves satisfiability of the clause set. Hence now we need to deal with just flat and one-variable clauses. In the rest of the paper we derive optimal complexity results for all these classes.

Still this only gives us an upper bound for the secrecy problem of protocols since the clauses could be more general than necessary. It turns out, however, that this is not the case. In order to show this we rely on a reduction of the reachability problem for *alternating pushdown systems (APDS)*. In form of Horn clauses, an *APDS* is a finite set of clauses of the form (i) $P(a)$ where a is a zero-ary symbol, (ii) $P(s[x]) \vee -Q(t[x])$ where

s and t involve only unary function symbols, and (iii) $P(x) \vee -P_1(x) \vee -P_2(x)$. Given such an APDS S, a ground atom $P(t)$ is *reachable* if $P(t)$ is in the least Herbrand model of S, i.e. if $S \cup \{-P(t)\}$ is unsatisfiable. Reachability in APDS is DEXPTIME-hard [4]. We encode this problem into secrecy of protocols, as in [9]. Let K be a (symmetric) key not known to the adversary. Encode atoms $P(t)$ as messages $\{\langle P, t \rangle\}_K$, by treating P as some data. Create an initialization state S (no message is stored in the state). Clause (i) is translated as $S : \text{recv}(?) \rightarrow S : \text{send}(\{\langle P, a \rangle\}_K)$. Clause (ii) is translated as $S : \text{recv}(\{\langle Q, t[x] \rangle\}_K) \rightarrow S : \text{send}(\{\langle P, s[x] \rangle\}_K)$. Clause (iii) is translated as $S : \text{recv}(\langle\{\langle P_1, x \rangle\}_K, \{\langle P_2, x \rangle\}_K\rangle) \rightarrow S : \text{send}(\{\langle P, x \rangle\}_K)$. The intuition is that the adversary cannot decrypt messages encrypted with K. He also cannot encrypt messages with K. He can only forward messages which are encrypted with K. However he has the ability to pair messages. This is utilized in the translation of clause (iii). Then a message $\{M\}_K$ is known to the adversary iff M is of the form $\langle P, t \rangle$ and $P(t)$ is reachable in the APDS.

Theorem 1. *Secrecy problem for cryptographic protocols with single blind copying, with bounded number of nonces but unbounded number of sessions is DEXPTIME-hard, even if no message is allowed to be stored at any control point.*

4 One Variable Clauses: Decomposition of Terms

We first show that satisfiability for the classes $\mathcal{V}_1$ and $\mathcal{V}_1 Horn$ is DEXPTIME-complete. Note that although we consider only unary predicates, this is no restriction in the case of one-variable clauses, since we can encode atoms $P(t_1, \ldots, t_n)$ as $P'(f_n(t_1 \ldots, t_n))$ for fresh P' and f_n for every P of arity n. As shown in [6,8], ordered resolution on one-variable clauses, for a suitable ordering, leads to a linear bound on the height of terms produced. This does not suffice for obtaining a DEXPTIME upper bound and we need to examine the forms of unifiers produced during resolution. We consider terms containing at most one variable (call them *one-variable terms*) to be compositions of simpler terms. A non-ground one-variable term $t[x]$ is called *reduced* if it is not of the form $u[v[x]]$ for any non-ground non-trivial one-variable terms $u[x]$ and $v[x]$. The term $f(g(x), h(g(x)))$ for example is not reduced because it can be written as $f(x, h(x))[g(x)]$. The term $f'(x, g(x), a)$ is reduced. Unifying it with the reduced term $f'(h(y), g(h(a)), y)$ produces ground unifier $\{x \mapsto h(y)[a], y \mapsto a\}$ and both $h(y)$ and a are strict subterms of the given terms. Indeed we find:

Lemma 2. *Let $s[x]$ and $t[y]$ be reduced, non-ground and non-trivial terms where $x \neq y$ and $s[x] \neq t[x]$. If s and t have a unifier σ then $x\sigma, y\sigma \in U[V]$ where U is the set of non-ground (possibly trivial) strict subterms of s and t, and V is the set of ground strict subterms of s and t.*

In case both terms (even if not reduced) have the same variable we have the following easy result:

Lemma 3. *Let σ be a unifier of two non-trivial, non-ground and distinct one-variable terms $s[x]$ and $t[x]$. Then $x\sigma$ is a ground strict subterm of s or of t.*

In the following one-variable clauses are simplified to involve only reduced terms.

Lemma 4. *Any non-ground one-variable term $t[x]$ can be uniquely written as $t[x] = t_1[t_2[\ldots[t_n[x]]\ldots]]$ where $n \geq 0$ and each $t_i[x]$ is non-trivial, non-ground and reduced. This decomposition can be computed in time polynomial in the size of t.*

Above and elsewhere, if $n = 0$ then $t_1[t_2[\ldots[t_n[x]]\ldots]]$ denotes x. Now if a clause set contains a clause $C = C' \vee \pm P(t[x])$, with $t[x]$ being non-ground, if $t[x] = t_1[\ldots[t_n[x]]\ldots]$ where each t_i is non-trivial and reduced, then we create fresh predicates $Pt_1 \ldots t_i$ for $1 \leq i \leq p-1$ and replace C by the clause $C' \vee \pm Pt_1 \ldots t_{n-1}(t_n[x])$. Also we add clauses $Pt_1 \ldots t_i(t_{i+1}[x]) \vee -Pt_1 \ldots t_{i+1}(x)$ and $-Pt_1 \ldots t_i(t_{i+1}[x]) \vee Pt_1 \ldots t_{i+1}(x)$ for $0 \leq i \leq n-2$ to our clause set. Note that the predicates $Pt_1 \ldots t_i$ are considered invariant under renaming of terms t_j. For $i = 0$, $Pt_1 \ldots t_i$ is same as P. Our transformation preserves satisfiability of the clause set. By Lemma 4 this takes polynomial time and eventually all non-ground literals in clauses are of the form $\pm P(t)$ with reduced t. Next if the clause set is of the form $S \cup \{C_1 \cup C_2\}$, where C_1 is non-empty and has only ground literals, and C_2 is non-empty and has only non-ground literals, then we do splitting to produce $S \cup \{C_1\} \mid S \cup \{C_2\}$. This process produces at most exponentially many branches each of which has polynomial size. Now it suffices to decide satisfiability of each branch in DEXPTIME. Hence now we assume that each clause is either:

(Ca) a ground clause, or

(Cb) a clause containing exactly one variable, each of whose literals is of the form $\pm P(t[x])$ where t is non-ground and reduced.

Consider a set S of clauses of type Ca and Cb. We show how to decide satisfiability of the set S. Wlog we assume that all clauses in S of type Cb contain the variable $\mathbf{x}_1$. Let Ng be the set of non-ground terms $t[\mathbf{x}_1]$ occurring as arguments in literals in S. Let Ngs be the set of non-ground subterms $t[\mathbf{x}_1]$ of terms in Ng. We assume that Ng and Ngs always contain the trivial term $\mathbf{x}_1$, otherwise we add this term to both sets. Let G be the set of ground subterms of terms occurring as arguments in literals in S. The sizes of Ng, Ngs and G are polynomial. Let $S^\dagger$ be the set of clauses of type Ca and Cb which only contain literals of the form $\pm P(t)$ for some $t \in \mathsf{Ng} \cup \mathsf{Ng}[\mathsf{Ngs}[G]]$ (observe that $G \subseteq \mathsf{Ngs}[G] \subseteq \mathsf{Ng}[\mathsf{Ngs}[G]])$. The size of $S^\dagger$ is at most exponential.

For resolution we use ordering $\prec$: $P(s) \prec Q(t)$ iff s is a strict subterm of t. We call $\prec$ the subterm ordering without causing confusion. This is clearly stable. This is the ordering that we are going to use throughout this paper. In particular this means that if a clause contains literals $\pm P(x)$ and $\pm' Q(t)$ where t is non-trivial and contains x, then we cannot choose the literal $\pm P(x)$ to resolve upon in this clause. Because of the simple form of unifiers of reduced terms we have:

Lemma 5. *Binary ordered resolution and ordered factorization, wrt the subterm ordering, on clauses in $S^\dagger$ produces clauses which are again in $S^\dagger$ (upto renaming).*

Hence to decide satisfiability of $S \subseteq S^\dagger$, we keep generating new clauses of $S^\dagger$ by doing ordered binary resolution and ordered factorization wrt the subterm ordering till no new clause can be generated, and then check whether the empty clause has been produced. Also recall that APDS consist of Horn one-variable clauses. Hence:

Theorem 2. *Satisfiability for the classes $\mathcal{V}_1$ and $\mathcal{V}_1 Horn$ is DEXPTIME-complete.*

5 Flat Clauses: Resolution Modulo Propositional Reasoning

Next we show how to decide the class $\mathcal{F}$ of flat clauses in NEXPTIME. This is well known when the maximal arity r is a constant, or when all non-trivial literals in a clause have the same *sequence* (instead of the same *set*) of variables. But we are not aware of a proof of NEXPTIME upper bound in the general case. We show how to obtain NEXPTIME upper bound in the general case, by doing resolution modulo propositional reasoning. While this constitutes an interesting result of its own, the techniques allow us to deal with the full class $\mathcal{C}$ efficiently. Also this shows that the generality of the class $\mathcal{C}$ does not cost more in terms of complexity. An ϵ-*block* is a one-variable clause which contains only trivial literals. A complex clause C is a flat clause $\bigvee_{i=1}^{k} \pm_i P_i(f_i(x_1^i, \ldots, x_{n_i}^i)) \vee \bigvee_{j=1}^{l} \pm_j Q_j(x_j)$ in which $k \geq 1$. A flat clause is either a complex clause, or an ϵ-*clause* which is defined to be a disjunction of ϵ-blocks, i.e. to be of the form $C_1[x_1] \sqcup \ldots \sqcup C_n[x_n]$ where each C_i is an ϵ-block. ϵ-clauses are difficult to deal with, hence we split them to produce ϵ-blocks. Hence define ϵ-*splitting* as the restriction of the splitting rule in which one of the components is an ϵ-block.

Recall that r is the maximal arity of symbols in Σ. Any complex clause C can be renamed to make it *good* i.e. such that $\mathrm{fv}(C) \subseteq \mathbf{X}_r = \{\mathbf{x}_1, \ldots, \mathbf{x}_r\}$. An ϵ-block C can be renamed to make it *good* i.e. of the form $C[\mathbf{x}_{r+1}]$. The choice of $\mathbf{x}_{r+1}$ is not crucial. Now notice that ordered resolution between complex clauses and ϵ-blocks only produces flat clauses, which can then be split to be left with only complex and ϵ-blocks. E.g. Resolution between $P_1(\mathbf{x}_1) \vee -P_2(\mathbf{x}_2) \vee P_3(f(\mathbf{x}_1, \mathbf{x}_2)) \vee -P_4(g(\mathbf{x}_2, \mathbf{x}_1))$ and $P_4(g(\mathbf{x}_1, \mathbf{x}_1)) \vee -P_5(h(\mathbf{x}_1)) \vee P_6(\mathbf{x}_1)$ produces $P_1(\mathbf{x}_1) \vee -P_2(\mathbf{x}_1) \vee P_3(f(\mathbf{x}_1, \mathbf{x}_1)) \vee -P_5(h(\mathbf{x}_1)) \vee P_6(\mathbf{x}_1)$. Resolution between $P_2(\mathbf{x}_{r+1})$ and $-P_2(f(\mathbf{x}_1, \mathbf{x}_2)) \vee P_3(\mathbf{x}_1) \vee P_4(\mathbf{x}_2)$ produces $P_3(\mathbf{x}_1) \vee P_4(\mathbf{x}_2)$ which can then be split. The point is that we always choose a non-trivial literal from a clause for resolution, if there is one. As there are finitely many complex clauses and ϵ-blocks this gives us a decision procedure. Note however that the number of complex clauses is doubly exponential. This is because we allow clauses of the form $P_1(f_1(\mathbf{x}_1, \mathbf{x}_1, \mathbf{x}_2)) \vee P_2(f_2(\mathbf{x}_2, \mathbf{x}_1)) \vee P_3(f_3(\mathbf{x}_2, \mathbf{x}_1, \mathbf{x}_2)) \vee \ldots$, i.e. the nontrivial terms contain arbitrary number of repetitions of variables in arbitrary order. The number of such variable sequences of r variables is exponentially many, hence the number of clauses is doubly exponential. Letting the maximal arity r to be a constant, or forcing all non-trivial literals in a clause to have the same variable sequence would have produced only exponentially many clauses. In presence of splitting, this would have given us the well-known NEXPTIME upper bound, which is also optimal. But we are not aware of a proof of NEXPTIME upper bound in the general case. To obtain NEXPTIME upper bound in the general case we introduce the technique of resolution modulo propositional reasoning.

For a clause C, define the set of its projections as $\pi(C) = C[\mathbf{X}_r]$. Essentially projection involves making certain variables in a clause equal. As we saw, resolution between two complex clauses amounts to propositional resolution between their projections. Define the set $\mathsf{U} = \{f(x_1, \ldots, x_n) \mid f \in \Sigma \text{ and each } x_i \in \mathbf{X}_r\}$ of size exponential in r. Resolution between ϵ-block C_1 and a good complex clause C_2 amounts to propositional resolution of a clause from $C[\mathsf{U}]$ with C_2. Also note that propositional resolution followed by further projection is equivalent to projection followed by propositional resolution. Each complex clause has exponentially many projections. This suggests that we can compute beforehand the exponentially many projections of complex clauses and exponentially many instantiations of ϵ-blocks. All new complex clauses generated by propositional resolution are ignored. But after several such propositional resolution steps, we may get an ϵ-clause, which should then be split and instantiated and used for obtaining further propositional resolvents. In other words we only compute such propositionally implied ϵ-clauses, do splitting and instantiation and iterate the process. This generates all resolvents upto propositional implication. The difference from the approach of Ganzinger and Korovin [10] is that they have a single phase of instantiation followed by propositional satisfiability checking. In contrast, we compute certain interesting propositional implications which are further instantiated, and iterate the process. We now formalize our approach.

For a set S of clauses, let comp(S) be the set of complex clauses in S, eps(S) be the set of ϵ-blocks in S, $\pi(S) = \bigcup_{C \in S} \pi(C)$ and $\mathsf{I}(S) = S \cup \pi(\mathsf{comp}(S)) \cup \mathsf{eps}(S)[\mathsf{U}]$. For sets S and T of complex clauses and ϵ-blocks, write $S \sqsubseteq T$ to mean that:
- if C is a complex clause in S then $\mathsf{I}(T) \vDash_p \pi(C)$, and
- every ϵ-block in S can be renamed as some $C[\mathbf{x}_{r+1}] \in T$.

For tableaux $\mathcal{T}_1$ and $\mathcal{T}_2$ involving only complex clauses and ϵ-blocks we write $\mathcal{T}_1 \sqsubseteq \mathcal{T}_2$ if $\mathcal{T}_1$ can be written as $S_1 \mid \ldots \mid S_n$ and $\mathcal{T}_2$ can be written as $T_1 \mid \ldots \mid T_n$ (note same n) such that $S_i \sqsubseteq T_i$ for $1 \leq i \leq n$. Intuitively $\mathcal{T}_2$ is a succinct representation of $\mathcal{T}_1$. Define the splitting strategy f as the one which repeatedly applies ϵ-splitting on a tableau as long as possible. The relation $\Rightarrow_{\prec, f}$ provides us a sound and complete method for testing unsatisfiability. We define the alternative procedure for testing unsatisfiability by using succinct representations of tableaux. We define ▶ by the rule: $\mathcal{T} \mid S ▶ \mathcal{T} \mid S \cup \{C_1[\mathbf{x}_{r+1}]\} \mid \ldots \mid S \cup \{C_k[\mathbf{x}_{r+1}]\}$ whenever $\mathsf{I}(S) \vDash_p C = C_1[\mathbf{x}_{i_1}] \sqcup \ldots \sqcup C_k[\mathbf{x}_{i_k}]$, C is an ϵ-clause, and $1 \leq i_1, \ldots, i_k \leq r$. Then ▶ simulates $\Rightarrow_{\prec, f}$:

Lemma 6. *If S is a set of complex clauses and ϵ-blocks, $S \sqsubseteq T$ and $S \Rightarrow_{\prec, f} \mathcal{T}$, then all clauses occurring in $\mathcal{T}$ are complex clauses or ϵ-blocks and $T ▶^* \mathcal{T}'$ for some $\mathcal{T}'$ such that $\mathcal{T} \sqsubseteq \mathcal{T}'$.*

Hence we have completeness of ▶:

Lemma 7. *If a set S of good complex clauses and ϵ-blocks is unsatisfiable then $S ▶^* \mathcal{T}$ for some closed $\mathcal{T}$.*

Proof. By Lemma 1, $S \Rightarrow^*_{\prec, f} S_1 \mid \ldots \mid S_n$ such that each $S_i \ni \square$. Since all complex clauses and ϵ-blocks in S are good, we have $S \sqsubseteq S$. Hence by Lemma 6, we have some $T_1, \ldots, T_n$ such that $S ▶^* T_1 \mid \ldots \mid T_n$ and $S_i \sqsubseteq T_i$ for $1 \leq i \leq n$. Since $\square \in S_i$ and $\square$ is an ϵ-block, hence $\square \in T_i$ for $1 \leq i \leq n$. □

Call a set S of good complex clauses and ϵ-blocks *saturated* if the following condition is satisfied: if $\mathsf{I}(S) \vDash_p B_1[\mathbf{x}_{i_1}] \sqcup \ldots \sqcup B_k[\mathbf{x}_{i_k}]$ with $1 \leq i_1, \ldots, i_k \leq r$, each B_i being an ϵ-block, then there is some $1 \leq j \leq k$ such that $B_j[\mathbf{x}_{r+1}] \in S$.

Lemma 8. *If S is a satisfiable set of good complex clauses and ϵ-blocks then $S ▶^* \mathcal{T} \mid T$ for some $\mathcal{T}$ and some saturated set T of good complex clauses and ϵ-blocks, such that $\square \notin T$.*

Proof. We construct a sequence $S = S_0 \subseteq S_1 \subseteq S_2 \subseteq \ldots$ of good complex clauses and ϵ-blocks such that S_i is satisfiable and $S_i \blacktriangleright^* S_{i+1} \mid \mathcal{T}_i$ for some $\mathcal{T}_i$ for each i. $S = S_0$ is satisfiable by assumption. Now assume we have already defined $S_0, \ldots, S_i$ and $\mathcal{T}_0, \ldots, \mathcal{T}_{i-1}$. Let $C^l = B_1^l[\mathbf{x}_{i_1^l}] \sqcup \ldots \sqcup B_k^l[\mathbf{x}_{i_{k_l}^l}]$ for $1 \leq l \leq N$ be all the possible ϵ-clauses such that $\mathsf{I}(S_i) \vDash_{\mathsf{p}} C^l$, $1 \leq i_1^l, \ldots, i_{k_l}^l \leq r$. Since S_i is satisfiable, $S_i \cup \{C^l \mid 1 \leq l \leq N\}$ is satisfiable. Since $\mathbf{x}_{i_1^l}, \ldots, \mathbf{x}_{i_{k_l}^l}$ are mutually distinct for $1 \leq l \leq N$, there are $1 \leq j_l \leq k_l$ for $1 \leq l \leq N$ such that $S_i \cup \{B_{j_l}^l[\mathbf{x}_{i_{j_l}^l}] \mid 1 \leq l \leq N\}$ is satisfiable. Let $S_{i+1} = S_i \cup \{B_{j_l}^l[\mathbf{x}_{r+1}] \mid 1 \leq l \leq N\}$. S_{i+1} is satisfiable. Also it is clear that $S_i \blacktriangleright^* S_{i+1} \mid \mathcal{T}_i$ for some $\mathcal{T}_i$. If $S_{i+1} = S_i$ then S_i is saturated, otherwise S_{i+1} has strictly more ϵ-blocks. As there are only finitely many good ϵ-blocks, eventually we will end up with a saturated set T in this way. Since T is satisfiable, $\square \notin T$. From construction it is clear that there is some $\mathcal{T}$ such that $S \blacktriangleright^* \mathcal{T} \mid T$. $\square$

Theorem 3. *Satisfiability for the class $\mathcal{F}$ is NEXPTIME-complete.*

Proof. The lower bound comes from reduction of satisfiability of positive set constraints which is NEXPTIME-complete [1]. For the upper bound let S be a finite set of flat clauses. Repeatedly apply ϵ-splitting to obtain $f(S) = S_1 \mid \ldots \mid S_m$. S is satisfiable iff some S_i is satisfiable. The number m of branches in $f(S)$ is at most exponential. Also each branch has size linear in the size of S. We non-deterministically choose some S_i and check its satisfiability in NEXPTIME.

Hence wlog we may assume that the given set S has only complex clauses and ϵ-blocks. Wlog all clauses in S are good. We non-deterministically choose a certain number of good ϵ-blocks $B_1[\mathbf{x}_{r+1}], \ldots, B_N[\mathbf{x}_{r+1}]$ and check that $T = S_1 \cup \{B_1[\mathbf{x}_{r+1}], \ldots, B_N[\mathbf{x}_{r+1}]\}$ is saturated and $\square \notin T$. By Lemma 8, if S is satisfiable then clearly there is such a set T. Conversely if there is such a set T, then whenever $T \blacktriangleright^* \mathcal{T}$, we will have $\mathcal{T} = T \mid \mathcal{T}'$ for some $\mathcal{T}'$. Hence we can never have $T \blacktriangleright^* \mathcal{T}$ where $\mathcal{T}$ is closed. Then by Lemma 7 we conclude that T is satisfiable. Hence $S \subseteq T$ is also satisfiable.

Guessing the set T requires non-deterministically choosing from among exponentially many ϵ-blocks. To check that T is saturated, for every ϵ-clause $C = B_1[\mathbf{x}_{i_1}] \sqcup \ldots \sqcup B_k[\mathbf{x}_{i_k}]$, with $1 \leq i_1, \ldots, i_k \leq r$, and $B_j[\mathbf{x}_{r+1}] \notin T$ for $1 \leq j \leq k$, we check that $\mathsf{I}(T) \nvDash_{\mathsf{p}} C$, i.e. $\mathsf{I}(T) \cup \neg C$ is propositionally satisfiable (where $\neg(L_1 \vee \ldots \vee L_n)$ denotes $\{-L_1, \ldots, -L_n\}$). This can be checked in NEXPTIME since propositional satisfiability can be checked in NPTIME. We need to do such checks for at most exponentially many possible values of C. $\square$

6 Combination: Ordered Literal Replacement

Combining flat and one-variable clauses creates additional difficulties. First observe that resolving a one variable clause $C_1 \vee \pm P(f(s_1[x], \ldots, s_n[x]))$ with a complex clause $\mp P(f(x_1, \ldots, x_n)) \vee C_2$ produces a one-variable clause. If $s_i[x] = s_j[x]$ for all $x_i = x_j$, and if C_2 contains a literal $P(x_i)$ then the resolvent contains a literal $P(s_i[x])$. The problem now is that even if $f(s_1[x], \ldots, s_n[x])$ is reduced, $s_i[x]$ may not be reduced. E.g. $f(g(h(x)), x)$ is reduced but $g(h(x))$ is not reduced. Like in Section 4 we may think of replacing this literal by simpler literals involving fresh predicates. Firstly we have to ensure that in this process we would not generate infinitely many predicates. Secondly it is not clear that mixing ordered resolution steps with replacement of literals is still complete. Correctness is easy to show since the new clause is in some sense equivalent to the old deleted clause. However deletion of clauses arbitrarily can violate completeness of the resolution procedure. The key factor which preserves completeness is that we replace literals by smaller literals wrt the given ordering $<$.

Formally a *replacement rule* is of the form $A_1 \to A_2$ where A_1 and A_2 are (not necessarily ground) atoms. The clause set *associated* with this rule is $\{A_1 \vee -A_2, -A_1 \vee A_2\}$. Intuitively such a replacement rule says that A_1 and A_2 are equivalent. The clause set $cl(\mathcal{R})$ associated with a set $\mathcal{R}$ of replacement rules is the union of the clause sets associated with the individual replacement rules in $\mathcal{R}$. Given a stable ordering $<$ on atoms, a replacement rule $A_1 \to A_2$ is *ordered* iff $A_2 < A_1$. We define the relation $\to_\mathcal{R}$ as: $S \to_\mathcal{R} (S \setminus \{\pm A_1\sigma \vee C\}) \cup \{\pm A_2\sigma \vee C\}$ whenever S is a set of clauses, $\pm A_1\sigma \vee C \in S$, $A_1 \to A_2 \in \mathcal{R}$ and σ is some substitution. Hence we replace literals in a clause by smaller literals. The relation is extended to tableaux as usual. This is reminiscent of the well-studied case of resolution with some equational theory on terms. There, however, the ordering $<$ used for resolution is compatible with the equational theory and one essentially works with the equivalence classes of terms and atoms. This is not the case here.

Next note that in the above resolution example, even if $f(s_1[x], \ldots, s_n[x])$ is nonground, some s_i may be ground. Hence the resolvent may have ground as well as non-ground literals. We avoided this in Section 4 by initial preprocessing. Now we may think of splitting these resolvents during the resolution procedure. This however will be difficult to simulate using the alternative resolution procedure on succinct representations of tableaux because we will generate doubly exponentially many one-variable clauses. To avoid this we use a variant of splitting called *splitting-with-naming* [13]. Instead of creating two branches after splitting, this rule puts both components into the same set, but with tags to simulate branches produced by ordinary splitting. Fix a finite set $\mathbb{P}$ of predicate symbols. $\mathbb{P}$-clauses are clauses whose predicates are all from $\mathbb{P}$. Introduce fresh zero-ary predicates $\overline{C}$ for $\mathbb{P}$-clauses C modulo renaming, i.e. $\overline{C_1} = \overline{C_2}$ iff $C_1\sigma = C_2$ for some renaming σ. Literals $\pm\overline{C}$ for $\mathbb{P}$-clauses C are *splitting literals*. The *splitting-with-naming* rule is defined as: $S \to_{nspl} (S \setminus \{C_1 \sqcup C_2\}) \cup \{C_1 \vee -\overline{C_2}, \overline{C_2} \vee C_2\}$ where $C_1 \sqcup C_2 \in S$, C_2 is non-empty and has only non-splitting literals, and C_1 has at least one non-splitting literal. Intuitively $\overline{C_2}$ represents the negation of C_2. We will use both splitting and splitting-with-naming according to some predefined strategy. Hence for a finite set $\mathcal{Q}$ of splitting atoms, define $\mathcal{Q}$-*splitting* as the restriction of the splitting-with-naming rule where the splitting atom produced is restricted to be from $\mathcal{Q}$. Call this restricted relation as $\to_{\mathcal{Q}-nspl}$. This is extended to tableaux as usual. Now once we have generated the clauses $C_1 \vee -\overline{C_2}$ and $\overline{C_2} \vee C_2$ we would like to keep resolving on the second part of the second clause till we are left with the clause $\overline{C_2}$ (possibly with other positive splitting literals) which would then be resolved with the first clause to produce C_1 (possibly with other positive splitting literals) and only then the literals in C_1 would be resolved upon. Such a strategy cannot be ensured by ordered resolution, hence we introduce a new rule. An ordering $<$ over non-splitting atoms is extended to the ordering $<_s$ by letting $q <_s A$ whenever q is a splitting atom and A is a non-splitting atom,

and $A <_s B$ whenever A, B are non-splitting atoms and $A < B$. We define *modified ordered binary resolution* by the following rule:
$$\frac{C_1 \vee A \quad -B \vee C_2}{C_1\sigma \vee C_2\sigma}$$
where $\sigma = mgu(A, B)$ and the following conditions are satisfied:
(1) C_1 has no negative splitting literal, and A is maximal in C_1.
(2) (a) either $B \in \mathcal{Q}$, or
   (b) C_2 has no negative splitting literal, and B is maximal in C_2.

As usual we rename the premises before resolution so that they don't share variables. This rule says that we must select a negative splitting literal to resolve upon in any clause, provided the clause has at least one such literal. If no such literal is present in the clause, then the ordering $<_s$ enforces that a positive splitting literal will not be selected as long as the clause has some non-splitting literal. We write $S \Rightarrow_{<_s} S \cup \{C\}$ to say that C is obtained by one application of the modified binary ordered resolution or the (unmodified) ordered factorization rule on clauses in S. This is extended to tableaux as usual. A *$\mathcal{Q}$-splitting-replacement strategy* is a function f such that $T(\rightarrow_{\mathcal{Q}-nspl} \cup \rightarrow_{spl} \cup \rightarrow_{\mathcal{R}})^* f(T)$ for any tableaux T. Hence we allow both normal splitting and $\mathcal{Q}$-splitting. Modified ordered resolution with $\mathcal{Q}$-splitting-replacement strategy f is defined by the relation: $S \Rightarrow_{<_s,f,\mathcal{R}} f(T)$ whenever $S \Rightarrow_{<_s} T$. This is extended to tableaux as usual. The above modified ordered binary resolution rule can be considered as an instance of *ordered resolution with selection* [2], which is known to be sound and complete even with splitting and its variants. Our manner of extending $<$ to $<_s$ is essential for completeness. We now show that soundness and completeness hold even under arbitrary ordered replacement strategies. It is not clear if such rules have been studied elsewhere. Wlog we forbid the useless case of replacement rules containing splitting symbols. The relation $<$ is *enumerable* if the set of all ground atoms can be enumerated as $A_1, A_2, \ldots$ such that if $A_i < A_j$ then $i < j$. The subterm ordering is enumerable.

Theorem 4. *Modified ordered resolution, wrt a stable and enumerable ordering, with $\mathcal{Q}$-splitting and ordered literal replacement is sound and complete for any strategy. I.e. for any set S of $\mathbb{P}$-clauses, for any strict stable and enumerable partial order $<$ on atoms, for any set $\mathcal{R}$ of ordered replacement rules, for any finite set $\mathcal{Q}$ of splitting atoms, and for any $\mathcal{Q}$-splitting-replacement strategy f, $S \cup cl(\mathcal{R})$ is unsatisfiable iff $S \Rightarrow^*_{<_s,f,\mathcal{R}} T$ for some closed T.*

For the rest of this section fix a set $\mathbb{S}$ of one-variable $\mathbb{P}$-clauses and complex $\mathbb{P}$-clauses whose satisfiability we need to decide. Let Ng be the set of non-ground terms occurring as arguments in literals in the one-variable clauses of $\mathbb{S}$. We rename all terms in Ng to contain only the variable x_{r+1}. Wlog assume $\mathsf{x}_{r+1} \in$ Ng. Let Ngs be the set of non-ground subterms of terms in Ng, and Ngr $= \{s[\mathsf{x}_{r+1}] \mid s$ is non-ground and reduced, and for some $t, s[t] \in$ Ngs$\}$. Define Ngrr $= \{s_1[\ldots[s_m]\ldots] \mid s_1[\ldots[s_n]\ldots] \in$ Ngs, $m \leq n$, and each s_i is non-trivial and reduced$\}$. Define the set of predicates $\mathbb{Q} = \{Ps \mid P \in \mathbb{P}, s \in$ Ngrr$\}$. Note that $\mathbb{P} \subseteq \mathbb{Q}$. Define the set of replacement rules $\mathcal{R} = \{Ps_1 \ldots s_{m-1}(s_m[\mathsf{x}_{r+1}]) \rightarrow Ps_1 \ldots s_m([\mathsf{x}_{r+1}]) \mid Ps_1 \ldots s_m \in \mathbb{Q}\}$. They are clearly ordered wrt $\prec$. Let G be the set of ground subterms of terms occurring as arguments in literals in $\mathbb{S}$. For the rest of this section the set of splitting atoms that we are going to use is

$Q_0 = \{\pm P(t) \mid P \in \mathbb{P}, t \in G\}$. Their purpose is to remove ground literals from a non-ground clause. All sets defined above have polynomial size. We also need the set $\text{Ngr}_1 = \{\mathbf{x}_{r+1}\} \cup \{f(s_1, \ldots, s_n) \mid \exists g(t_1, \ldots, t_m) \in \text{Ngr} \cdot \{s_1, \ldots, s_n\} = \{t_1, \ldots, t_m\}\}$ which has exponential size. These terms are produced by resolution of non-ground one-variable clauses with complex clauses, and are also reduced. In the ground case we have the set $G_1 = \{f(s_1, \ldots, s_n) \mid \exists g(t_1, \ldots, t_m) \in G \mid \{s_1, \ldots, s_n\} = \{t_1, \ldots, t_m\}\}$ of exponential size. For a set $\mathbb{P}'$ of predicates and a set U of terms, the set $\mathbb{P}'[U]$ of atoms is defined as usual. For a set V of atoms the set $-V$ and $\pm V$ of literals is defined as usual. The following types of clauses will be required during resolution:

C1 clauses $C \vee D$, where C is an ϵ-block with predicates from $\mathbb{Q}$, and $D \subseteq \pm Q_0$.
C2 clauses $C \vee D$ where C is a one-variable clause with literals from $\pm \mathbb{Q}(\text{Ngr}_1)$, C has at least one non-trivial literal, and $D \subseteq \pm Q_0$.
C3 clauses $C \vee D$ where C is a non-empty clause with literals from $\pm \mathbb{Q}(\text{Ngr}_1[\text{Ngrr}[G_1]])$, and $D \subseteq \pm Q_0$.
C4 clauses $C \vee D$ where $C = \bigvee_{i=1}^{k} \pm_i P_i(f_i(x_1^i, \ldots, x_{n_i}^i)) \vee \bigvee_{j=1}^{l} \pm_j Q_j(x_j)$ is a complex clause with each $P_i \in \mathbb{Q}$, each $Q_j \in \mathbb{P}$ and $D \subseteq \pm Q_0$.

We have already argued why we need splitting literals in the above clauses, and why we need Ngr_1 instead of Ngr in type C2. In type C3 we have Ngrr in place of the set Ngs that we had in Section 4, to take care of interactions between one-variable clauses and complex clauses. In type C4 the trivial literals involve predicates only from $\mathbb{P}$ (and not $\mathbb{Q}$). This is what ensures that we need only finitely many fresh predicates (those from $\mathbb{Q} \setminus \mathbb{P}$) because these are the literals that are involved in replacements when this clause is resolved with a one-variable clause. The Q_0-splitting steps that we use in this section consist of replacing a tableau $\mathcal{T} \mid S$ by the tableau $\mathcal{T} \mid (S \setminus \{C \vee L\}) \cup \{C \vee -\overline{L}, \overline{L} \vee L\}$, where C is non-ground, $L \in \pm \mathbb{P}(G)$ and $C \vee L \in S$. The replacement steps we are going to use are of the following kind:
(1) replacing clause $C_1[x] = C \vee \pm P(t_1[\ldots [t_n[s[x]]] \ldots])$ by clause $C_2[x] = C \vee \pm Pt_1 \ldots t_n(s[x])\}$ where $P \in \mathbb{P}$, $s[\mathbf{x}_{r+1}] \in \text{Ngr}$ is non-trivial, and $t_1[\ldots [t_n] \ldots] \in \text{Ngrr}$. We have $\{C_1[\mathbf{x}_{r+1}]\} \cup cl(\mathcal{R})[\text{Ngrr}] \models_p C_2[\mathbf{x}_{r+1}]$.
(2) replacing ground clause $C_1 = C \vee \pm P(t_1[\ldots [t_n[g]] \ldots])$ by clause $C_2 = C \vee \pm Pt_1 \ldots t_n[g]\}$ where $P \in \mathbb{P}, g \in \text{Ngrr}[G_1]$ and $t_1[\ldots [t_n] \ldots] \in \text{Ngrr}$. This replacement is done only when $t_1[\ldots [t_n[g]] \ldots] \in \text{Ngrr}[\text{Ngrr}[G_1]] \setminus \text{Ngr}_1[\text{Ngrr}[G_1]]$. We have $\{C_1\} \cup cl(\mathcal{R})[\text{Ngrr}[\text{Ngrr}[G_1]]] \models_p C_2$.
Define the Q_0-splitting-replacement strategy f as one which repeatedly applies first ϵ-splitting, then the above Q_0-splitting steps, then the above two replacement steps till no further change is possible. Then $\Rightarrow_{\prec_s, f, \mathcal{R}}$ gives us a sound and complete method for testing unsatisfiability.

As in Section 5 we now define a succinct representation of tableaux and an alternative resolution procedure for them. As we said, a literal $\overline{L} \in Q_0$ represents $-L$. Hence for a clause C we define $\underline{C}$ as the clause obtained by replacing every $\pm \overline{L}$ by the literal $\mp L$. This is extended to sets of clauses as usual. As before $\mathsf{U} = \{f(x_1, \ldots, x_n) \mid f \in \Sigma$, and each $x_i \in \mathbf{X}_r\}$. The functions eps and comp of Section 5 are now extended to return ϵ-blocks and complex clauses respectively, possibly in disjunction with splitting literals. For a set S of clauses, define $ov(S)$ as the set of clauses of type C2 in S. The function π is as before. We need to define which kinds of instantiations are to be used to generate propositional implications. For a clause C, define $\mathsf{I}_1(C) = \{C\} \cup C[\mathsf{U}] \cup C[\mathsf{U}[\mathsf{Ngrr} \cup \mathsf{Ngrr}[\mathsf{Ngrr}[\mathsf{G}_1]]]] \cup C[\mathsf{Ngr}_1] \cup C[\mathsf{Ngr}_1[\mathsf{Ngrr}[\mathsf{G}_1]]]$. These are the instantiations necessary for ϵ-blocks. Define $\mathsf{I}_2(C) = \{C\} \cup C[\mathsf{Ngrr}[\mathsf{G}_1]]$. These are necessary for one-variable clauses. Define $\mathsf{I}_3(C) = \{C\}$. Ground clauses require no instantiation. Define $\mathsf{I}_4(C) = \pi(C) \cup C[\mathsf{Ngrr} \cup [\mathsf{Ngrr}[\mathsf{Ngrr}[\mathsf{G}_1]]]]$. These are necessary for complex clauses. For a set S of clauses, define $\mathsf{I}_i(S) = \bigcup_{C \in S} \mathsf{I}_i(C)$. For a set S of clauses of type C1-C4 define $\mathsf{I}(S) = \underline{S} \cup \mathsf{I}_1(\underline{\mathsf{eps}(S)}) \cup \mathsf{I}_2(\underline{\mathsf{ov}(S)}) \cup \mathsf{I}_4(\underline{\mathsf{comp}(S)}) \cup cl(\mathcal{R})[\mathsf{Ngrr} \cup \mathsf{Ngrr}[\mathsf{Ngrr}[\mathsf{G}_1]]]$. Note that instantiations of clauses in $cl(\mathcal{R})$ are necessary for the replacement rules, as argued above. For a set T of clauses define the following properties:

(P1$_T$) C satisfies property P1$_T$ iff $C[\mathbf{x}_{r+1}] \in T$.
(P2$_T$) C satisfies property P2$_T$ iff $\mathsf{I}(T) \vDash_{\mathsf{p}} \mathsf{I}_2(\underline{C}[\mathbf{x}_{r+1}])$.
(P3$_T$) C satisfies property P3$_T$ iff $\mathsf{I}(T) \vDash_{\mathsf{p}} \mathsf{I}_3(\underline{C})$.
(P4$_T$) C satisfies property P4$_T$ iff $\mathsf{I}(T) \vDash_{\mathsf{p}} \mathsf{I}_4(\underline{C})$.

For sets of clauses S and T, define $S \sqsubseteq T$ to mean that every $C \in S$ is of type Ci and satisfies property Pi_T for some $1 \leq i \leq 4$. This is extended to tableaux as usual. The alternative resolution procedure for testing unsatisfiability by using succinct representations of tableaux is now defined by the rule: $\mathcal{T} \mid S \blacktriangleright \mathcal{T} \mid S \cup \{C_1[\mathbf{x}_{r+1}] \sqcup D\} \mid S \cup \{C_2[\mathbf{x}_{r+1}]\} \mid \ldots \mid S \cup \{C_k[\mathbf{x}_{r+1}]\}$ whenever $\mathsf{I}(S) \vDash_{\mathsf{p}} C_1[\mathbf{x}_{i_1}] \sqcup \ldots \sqcup C_k[\mathbf{x}_{i_k}] \sqcup \underline{D}$, each C_i is an ϵ-block, $1 \leq i_1, \ldots, i_k \leq r$ and $D \subseteq \pm\mathcal{Q}_0$. The simulation property now states:

Lemma 9. *If $S \sqsubseteq T$ and $S \Rightarrow_{\prec_s, f, \mathcal{R}} T$ then $T \blacktriangleright^* T'$ for some T' such that $\mathcal{T} \sqsubseteq \mathcal{T}'$.*

Hence as for flat clauses we obtain:

Theorem 5. *Satisfiability for the class $\mathcal{C}$ is NEXPTIME-complete.*

7 The Horn Case

We show that in the Horn case, the upper bound can be improved to DEXPTIME. The essential idea is that propositional satisfiability of Horn clauses is in PTIME instead of NPTIME. But now we need to eliminate the use of tableaux altogether. To this end, we replace the ϵ-splitting rule of Section 6 by splitting-with-naming. Accordingly we define the set of splitting atoms as $\mathcal{Q} = \mathcal{Q}_0 \cup \mathcal{Q}_1$ where $\mathcal{Q}_1 = \{\overline{C} \mid C$ is a non-empty negative ϵ – block with predicates from $\mathbb{P}\}$. We know that binary resolution and factorization on Horn clauses produces Horn clauses. Replacements on Horn clauses using the rules from $\mathcal{R}$ produces Horn clauses. $\mathcal{Q}_1$-splitting on Horn clauses produces Horn clauses. E.g. clause $P(\mathbf{x}_1) \vee -Q(\mathbf{x}_1) \vee -R(\mathbf{x}_2)$ produces $P(\mathbf{x}_1) \vee -Q(\mathbf{x}_1) \vee --\overline{R(\mathbf{x}_2)}$ and $-\overline{R(\mathbf{x}_2)} \vee -R(\mathbf{x}_2)$. $\mathcal{Q}_0$-splitting on $P(f(x)) \vee -Q(a)$ produces $P(f(\mathbf{x}_1)) \vee --Q(a)$ and $-Q(a) \vee -Q(a)$ which are Horn. However $\mathcal{Q}_0$-splitting on $C = -P(f(\mathbf{x}_1)) \vee Q(a)$ produces $C_1 = -P(f(\mathbf{x}_1)) \vee -\overline{Q(a)}$ and $C_2 = \overline{Q(a)} \vee Q(a)$. C_2 is not Horn. However $\underline{C_1} = C$ and $\underline{C_2} = -Q(a) \vee Q(a)$ are Horn. Finally, as $\mathcal{Q}_1$ has exponentially many atoms, we must restrict their occurrences in clauses. Accordingly, for $1 \leq i \leq 4$, define clauses of type Ci' to be of the form $C \vee E$ where C is of type Ci, $E \subseteq \pm\mathcal{Q}_1$, $\underline{C \vee E}$ is Horn and E has at most r negative literals ($\underline{C}$ is defined as before, hence it leaves atoms from $\mathcal{Q}_1$ unchanged). Now the $\mathcal{Q}$-splitting-replacement strategy f first applies $\mathcal{Q}_1$-splitting as long as possible, then applies $\mathcal{Q}_0$-splitting as long as possible and then applies the replacement steps of Section 6 as long as possible. Succinct representations are now defined as: $S \sqsubseteq T$ iff for each $C \in S$, C is of type Ci' and satisfies Pi_T for some $1 \leq i \leq 4$. The abstract resolution procedure is defined as: $T \blacktriangleright T \cup \{B_1[\mathbf{x}_{r+1}] \vee \neg q_2 \vee \ldots \vee \neg q_k \sqcup D \sqcup E\} \cup \{q_i \vee B_i[\mathbf{x}_{r+1}] \mid 2 \leq i \leq k\}$ whenever $I(T) \vdash_p \underline{C}$, $C - B_1[\mathbf{x}_{l_1}] \sqcup \ldots \sqcup B_k[\mathbf{y}_{i_k}] \sqcup D \sqcup E$, $\underline{C}$ is Horn, $1 \leq i_1, \ldots, i_h \leq r$, B_1 is an ϵ-block, B_i is a negative ϵ-block and $q_i = \overline{B_i}$ for $2 \leq i \leq k$, $D \subseteq \pm \mathcal{Q}_0$ and $E \subseteq \pm \mathcal{Q}_1$ such that if $k = 1$ then E has at most r negative literals, and if $k > 1$ then E has no negative literal.

Lemma 10. *If $S \sqsubseteq T$ and $S \Rightarrow_{\prec_s, f, \mathcal{R}} S'$ then $T \blacktriangleright^* T'$ for some T' such that $S' \sqsubseteq T'$.*

Now for deciding satisfiability of a set of flat and one-variable clauses we proceed as in the non-Horn case. But now instead of non-deterministically adding clauses, we compute a sequence $S = S_0 \blacktriangleright S_1 \blacktriangleright S_2 \ldots$ starting from the given set S, till no more clauses can be added, and then check whether $\square$ has been generated. The length of this sequence is at most exponential. Computing S_{i+1} from S_i requires at most exponential time because the number of possibilities for C in the definition of $\blacktriangleright$ above is exponential. (Note that this idea of $\mathcal{Q}_1$-splitting would not have helped in the non-Horn case because we cannot bound the number of positive splitting literals in a clause in the non-Horn case, whereas Horn clauses by definition have at most one positive literal). Also note that APDS can be encoded using flat Horn clauses. Hence:

Theorem 6. *Satisfiability for the classes $\mathcal{C}Horn$ and $\mathcal{F}Horn$ is DEXPTIME-complete.*

Together with Theorem 1, this gives us optimal complexity for protocol verification:

Theorem 7. *Secrecy of cryptographic protocols with single blind copying, with bounded number of nonces but unbounded number of sessions is DEXPTIME-complete.*

8 Conclusion

We proved DEXPTIME-hardness of secrecy for cryptographic protocols with single blind copying, and improved the upper bound from 3-DEXPTIME to DEXPTIME. We improved the 3-DEXPTIME upper bound for satisfiability for the class $\mathcal{C}$ to NEXPTIME in the general case and DEXPTIME in the Horn case, which match known lower bounds. For this we invented new resolution techniques like ordered resolution with splitting modulo propositional reasoning, ordered literal replacements and decompositions of one-variable terms. As byproducts we obtained optimum complexity for several fragments of $\mathcal{C}$ involving flat and one-variable clauses. Security for several other decidable classes of protocols with unbounded number of sessions and bounded number of nonces is in DEXPTIME, suggesting that DEXPTIME is a reasonable complexity class for this class of protocols.

References

1. A. Aiken, D. Kozen, M. Vardi, and E. Wimmers. The complexity of set constraints. In *CSL'93*, pages 1–17. Springer-Verlag LNCS 832, 1993.
2. L. Bachmair and H. Ganzinger. Resolution theorem proving. In *Handbook of Automated Reasoning*, volume I, chapter 2, pages 19–99. North-Holland, 2001.
3. B. Blanchet. An efficient cryptographic protocol verifier based on Prolog rules. In *CSFW'01*, pages 82–96. IEEE Computer Society Press, 2001.
4. A. K. Chandra, D. C. Kozen, and L. J. Stockmeyer. Alternation. *Journal of the ACM*, 28(1), 1981.
5. H. Comon and V. Cortier. Tree automata with one memory, set constraints and cryptographic protocols. *Theoretical Computer Science*, 2004. To appear.
6. H. Comon-Lundh and V. Cortier. New decidability results for fragments of first-order logic and application to cryptographic protocols. In *RTA'03*, pages 148–164. Springer-Verlag LNCS 2706, 2003.
7. H. Comon-Lundh and V. Cortier. Security properties: Two agents are sufficient. In *ESOP'03*, pages 99–113. Springer-Verlag LNCS 2618, 2003.
8. V. Cortier. *Vérification Automatique des Protocoles Cryptographiques*. PhD thesis, ENS Cachan, France, 2003.
9. N. A. Durgin, P. Lincoln, J. Mitchell, and A. Scedrov. Undecidability of bounded security protocols. In *FMSP'99*, Trento, Italy, 1999.
10. H. Ganzinger and K. Korovin. New directions in instantiation-based theorem proving. In *LICS'01*, pages 55–64. IEEE Computer Society Press, 2003.
11. J. Goubault-Larrecq, M. Roger, and K. N. Verma. Abstraction and resolution modulo AC: How to verify Diffie-Hellman-like protocols automatically. *Journal of Logic and Algebraic Programming*, 2004. To Appear. Available as Research Report LSV-04-7, LSV, ENS Cachan.
12. D. Monniaux. Abstracting cryptographic protocols with tree automata. In *SAS'99*, pages 149–163. Springer-Verlag LNCS 1694, 1999.
13. A. Riazanov and A. Voronkov. Splitting without backtracking. In *IJCAI'01*, pages 611–617, 2001.
14. M. Rusinowitch and M. Turuani. Protocol insecurity with finite number of sessions is NP-complete. In *CSFW'01*. IEEE Computer Society Press, 2001.
15. C. Weidenbach. Towards an automatic analysis of security protocols. In *CADE'99*, pages 378–382. Springer-Verlag LNAI 1632, 1999.

Applications of General Exact Satisfiability in Propositional Logic Modelling

Vilhelm Dahllöf*

Dept. of Computer and Information Science
Linköping University
SE-581 83 Linköping, Sweden
vilda@ida.liu.se

Abstract. There is a trend to study extended variants of propositional logic which have explicit means to represent cardinality constraints. That is accomplished using so-called c-atoms. We show that c-atoms can be efficiently reduced to a general form of Exact Satisfiability. The general X_iSAT problem is to find an assignment for a CNF such that exactly i literals are true in each clause for any $i \geq 1$. We show that this problem is solvable in time $O(1.4143^n)$ (where n is the number of variables) regardless of i if we allow exponential space. For polynomial space, we present an algorithm solving X_iSAT for all i strictly better than the trivial $O(2^n)$ bound. For $i = 2$, $i = 3$ and $i = 4$ we obtain upper time bounds in $O(1.5157^n)$, $O(1.6202^n)$ and $O(1.6844^n)$, respectively. We also present a dedicated X_2SAT algorithm running in polynomial space and time $O(1.4511^n)$.

1 Introduction

Propositional logic can be used to model and compute a plethora of problems. Typically one constructs a theory such that its models encode solutions to the problem of interest. Recently there has been a dramatic improvement in the performance of programs for finding models, see *e.g.* [15,18,10]. However, most of these programs are SAT-solvers, restricting their input to instances of the satisfiability problem. That raises at least two issues:

1. It forces the formulation of unnecessarily large theories even for quite simple constraints.
2. To exactly solve SAT one must deploy exponential-time algorithms where no other base than 2 is known. While several ways trying to work around this have been proposed such as incomplete solvers using randomized and/or heuristic methods, fact remains that SAT has a very difficult structure.

---

* The research is supported by CUGS – National Graduate School in Computer Science, Sweden.

As for the first issue, several extensions to the basic language have been proposed such as equality, pseudo boolean constraints and c-atoms, see *e.g.* [13,5,1]. We will return to the c-atoms later.

The second issue makes it clear that it would be desirable to find another less hard problem capable of expressing interesting theories. Such a problem would by necessity be NP-hard. However, it might have a structure allowing faster algorithms than SAT. In this paper we will focus on one such candidate.

One well-studied variant of SAT is EXACT SATISFIABILITY, X$_1$SAT (sometimes denoted just XSAT), which asks for an assignment such that exactly one literal is true in every clause. It is NP-complete, even when restricted to clauses of maximum length 3 (a problem called X$_1$3SAT or ONE-IN-THREE SAT), see [9]. It is closely related to problems such as EXACT HITTING SET and has sometimes been treated in connection with these, see [7]. Exact algorithms for X$_1$SAT and X$_1$3SAT have been presented by several authors [6,8,11,16,4,3]. The so-far best algorithms by Byskov *et al.* [3] have running times in $O(1.1003^n)$ (for X$_1$3SAT) and $O(1.1748^n)$ (for X$_1$SAT). Note that X$_1$3SAT in earlier papers usually was denoted X3SAT.

A natural extension of X$_1$SAT is the problem X$_i$SAT, asking if a formula allows an assignment to the variables such that exactly i literals are true in each clause. In the context of propositional logic modelling, X$_i$SAT is of interest when it comes to means to represent cardinality constraints. Such extensions have been studied by *e.g.* [14,5,2,19]. They accomplish the extension using so-called *cardinality atoms* (although the author of [19] does not use the name, he does use the concept). A cardinality atom is an expression $k\{a_1,\ldots,a_n\}m$, where $a_1,\ldots,a_n$ are boolean variables and the expression is *true* iff at least k and no more than m of the a_i's are true. One way to handle the cardinality atoms is by compiling (reducing) them into ordinary SAT clauses and then using SAT-solvers. Liu and Truszczyński [14] describe two possible reductions. First a method that does not introduce any new variables but increases the number of clauses exponentially. They dismiss this technique: "This approach ... is practical only if k and m are small (do not exceed, say 2). Otherwise the size ... quickly gets too large for SAT solvers to be effective." They also present a second method that does not have this problem. However, the reduction more than doubles the number of variables. Rather than compiling the c-atoms away, Liu and Truszczyński investigates the possibility of keeping them and then applying an incomplete search method. In effect, they deal with a formula having different kinds of clauses (ordinary SAT clauses as well as different kinds of c-atoms).

Note that an X$_i$SAT clause $(a_1 \lor a_2 \ldots a_n)$ is not just a special case of the c-atom $h\{a_1, a_2 \ldots a_n\}i$. If we add the new variable b into the X$_i$SAT clause, then finding a model for the modified clause $(b \lor a_1 \lor a_2 \ldots a_n)$ is tantamount to finding a satisfying assignment for the c-atom $i-1\{a_1, a_2 \ldots a_n\}i$. Repeating the procedure, we obtain a transformation that is more efficient than transforming to SAT, as this reduction introduces $i - h$ new variables. Also, we see that X$_i$SAT well captures interesting properties of c-atoms. We hope that the algorithms and tools presented here will facilitate a better utilization of the c-atoms in practice as well as enhancing our theoretical understanding of these constraints.

This paper will show that X_iSAT is solvable in time $O(1.4143^n)$, where n is the number of variables, if a space consumption in $O(1.1893^n)$ is allowed. This method is an application of a general algorithm for a special class of NP-complete problems described by Schroeppel and Shamir [17]. While of theoretical interest, showing that the running time does not necessarily depend upon i, the use of exponential space is of course highly undesirable. For practical use, in the context of c-atoms, we present a branch-and-bound algorithm with polynomial space requirements that obtains a running time considerably better than the trivial $O(2^n)$ bound.

In the following presentation we first give some preliminaries and definitions. Section 3 presents some features of the language X_iSAT. Then follows Section 4 which presents and analyzes exact algorithms for deciding X_iSAT in polynomial space. Section 5 shows how to deal with X_iSAT using exponential space. Conclusions and a brief discussion about our results and possible future research directions are given in Section 6.

2 Preliminaries

A *propositional variable* (or *variable* for short) has either the value *true* or *false*. A *literal* is a variable p or its negation $\bar{p}$. The literal p is *true* iff the corresponding variable p has the value *true* and $\bar{p}$ is *true* iff the corresponding variable p has the value *false*. A *clause* is a number of literals connected by logical or ($\vee$). The *length* of a clause x, denoted $|x|$, is the number of literals in it. We will sometimes need a sub-clause notation in this way: $(a \vee b \vee C)$, such that $C = c_0 \vee \ldots \vee c_n$ is a disjunction of one or more literals. In the following, literals will be indicated by lower-case letters and sub-clauses by upper-case letters. A *formula* is a sequence of clauses connected by logical and ($\wedge$). $Var(F)$ for a formula F denotes the set of variables of F. The *degree of c*, denoted $\delta(c)$, is the number of clauses that contain either c or $\bar{c}$. If $\delta(c) = 1$ we call c a *singleton*. If $\delta(c) \geq 3$ we say that c is *heavy*.

Substitution of a by δ in the formula F is denoted $F(a/\delta)$; the notation $F(a/\delta; b/\gamma)$ indicates repeated substitution: $F(a/\delta)(b/\gamma)$ (first a is replaced and then b). We will assume that the substitution operation also takes care of some trivial simplifications such as replacing the occurence of $a \vee \bar{a}$ in a clause with *true*. $F(B/false)$, where B is a disjunction of literals, means that every literal of B is replaced by *false*. For a given disjunction of literals $B = a \vee b \vee \bar{c} \ldots$, $\bar{B}$ is the inversion of B, i.e., $\bar{B} = \bar{a} \vee \bar{b} \vee c \ldots$.

$F = (a \vee b \vee c) \wedge (\bar{a} \vee b \vee d) \wedge (\bar{c} \vee d)$
$M = \{a, b, \bar{c}, d\}$

Fig. 1. An instance F of X_2SAT and a model M of F

The *Exact i Satisfiability Problem* (X$_i$SAT) for a formula is to find an assignment to the variables such that exactly i literals are true in each clause. Such an assignment is known as a *model*. Given a formula F, an assignment to the variables is *inconsistent* if any clause has no true literal (it is *unsatisfied*) or more than i true literals (it is *over-satisfied*). Figure 1 shows a formula in X$_2$SAT and a model for it. The languages X$_1$SAT, X$_2$SAT, X$_3$SAT *etc.* are referred to as *sublanguages* of X$_i$SAT. Note that X$_i$SAT is *not* the language $L = \{F \mid$ such that there is a truth assignment for F making the same number of literals true in every clause$\}$, but rather, $L = \bigcup_{i=1}^{\infty}$ X$_i$SAT.

In the branch-and-bound algorithm for X$_i$SAT to be presented later, the recursive decomposition will create various kinds of constraints represented as clauses, that is, when setting the variables of a clause, other clauses will be affected. For instance, the clause $(a \vee b \vee c \vee d)^{\text{X}_2\text{SAT}}$, which requires two true literals to be satisfied, will become $(a \vee b \vee c)^{\text{X}_1\text{SAT}}$ if d is set to true. When there are different types of clauses in a formula, we say that it is *mixed*. Depending on how many true literals a clause needs to be satisfied we will use notations such as $(a \vee b \vee c \vee d)^{\text{X}_2\text{SAT}}$ and the like.

For terms such as NP-completeness *etc.*, the reader is referred to [9]. The notation $p_1 \leq_m^p p_2$ means that there exists a polynomial transformation from the problem p_1 to the problem p_2.

When analyzing the running time of the algorithms, we will encounter recurrences of the form $T(n) \leq \sum_{i=1}^{k} T(n - r_i) + \text{poly}(n)$. They satisfy $T(n) \in O(\tau(r_1, \ldots, r_k)^n)$ where $\tau(r_1, \ldots, r_k)$ is the largest, real-valued root of the function

$$f(x) = 1 - \sum_{i=1}^{k} x^{-r_i} \qquad (1)$$

see [12]. Since this bound does not depend on the polynomial factor poly(n), we ignore all polynomial-time calculations. Let $R = \sum_{i=1}^{k} r_i$ and then note that due to the nature of the function $f(x) = 1 - \sum_{i=1}^{k} x^{-r_i}$, the smallest possible real-valued root (and hence the best running time) will appear when each r_i is as close to R/k as possible, *i.e.*, when the decrease of size of the instance is balanced through the branches. Say for instance that $R = 4, k = 2$. Then $\tau(1,3) = \tau(3,1) \approx 1.4656$ and $\tau(2,2) \approx 1.4142$. We will refer to this as *the balanced branching effect*. We will use the shorthand notation $\tau(r^k \ldots)$ for $\tau(\underbrace{r, r \ldots r}_{k}, \ldots)$, *e.g.*, $\tau(5^2, 3^3)$ for $\tau(5,5,3,3,3)$.

3 Properties of the X$_i$SAT Problem

The X$_i$SAT problem is obviously NP-complete since X$_1$SAT $\leq_m^p$ X$_i$SAT: any occurrence of the literal a is replaced by i occurences. The reduction gives a hint that X$_i$SAT might be harder to solve for higher i, which indeed seems to be the case for polynomial space algorithms. Surprisingly, this does not hold for the exponential space algorithm to be presented.

One property of X$_i$SAT that will prove useful in the following algorithms is given in this lemma:

Lemma 1. *A formula F, where each variable occurs at most twice, can be reduced in polynomial time to a formula F', such that $F' \in$ X$_1$SAT iff $F \in$ X$_i$SAT, the number of variables is increased only by a polynomial amount and each variable in F' occurs at most twice.*

Proof. For clarity of presentation we consider a special case, namely the clause $x = (a \vee b \vee c \vee d)^{\text{X}_2\text{SAT}}$ which we want to transfer into X$_1$SAT clauses. As any pair of the literals may be both *false*, both *true* or one *true* and one *false* in any combination, they cannot appear in the same X$_1$SAT clause. A possible solution is this reduction from x:

$(\bar{a} \vee k \vee l)^{\text{X}_1\text{SAT}}$ $(k \vee m \vee o \vee q)^{\text{X}_1\text{SAT}}$
$(\bar{b} \vee m \vee n)^{\text{X}_1\text{SAT}}$ $(l \vee n \vee p \vee r)^{\text{X}_1\text{SAT}}$
$(\bar{c} \vee o \vee p)^{\text{X}_1\text{SAT}}$
$(\bar{d} \vee q \vee r)^{\text{X}_1\text{SAT}}$

It is straightforward to verify that this construction works and is extendible to other exact constraints and clause lengths.

The following is needed in the main algorithm for X$_i$SAT:

Corollary 1. *For a formula F where each variable occurs at most twice, it is polynomial time decidable whether $F \in$ X$_i$SAT.*

The corollary follows from Lemma 1 and the fact that for a formula F where each variable occurs at most twice, one can apply polynomial-time matching techniques to see whether there is an X$_1$SAT model. These techniques were first described by Porschen *et al.* in [16] in the context of X$_1$3SAT. They can easily be extended to general X$_1$SAT formulae, see *e.g.* [4].

In [7] Drori and Peleg introduced the name *canonization* for all the various polynomial time pruning rules that can be applied to an instance of X$_1$SAT. For example, a clause $(a \vee b)^{\text{X}_1\text{SAT}} \in F$ implies that one of a and b, but not both, must be *true*, and so F can be replaced by $F(a/\bar{b})$. Some of these rules extend to X$_i$SAT, other not. We here present the ones used in this paper. It is straightforward to see that they can be performed in polynomial time and that they do not change the X$_i$SAT satisfiability when applied to a formula F.

1. Pick an X$_i$SAT clause with $i + k$ singletons. Remove k singletons.
2. Pick a clause $(a \vee b)^{\text{X}_1\text{SAT}}$, remove it and let $F := F(a/\bar{b})$
3. Pick an X$_i$SAT clause A such that $|A| = i$. Remove it and let $F := F(a_j/true)$ for all literals a_j of A.
4. Pick two clauses $(a \vee b \vee A)^{\text{X}_1\text{SAT}}$ and $(\bar{a} \vee b \vee B)^{\text{X}_1\text{SAT}}$ and let $F := F(b/false)$
5. For two X$_i$SAT clauses (A) and $(A \vee B)$ let $F := F(B/false)$

6. If there are two clauses $x = (A \vee B)^{\text{X}_2\text{SAT}}$ and $y = (A \vee \bar{B})^{\text{X}_2\text{SAT}}$, such that $|B| \bmod 2 = 1$ or $|B| > 4$, then let $F := \{\varnothing\}$
7. If there are two clauses $x = (A \vee b \vee c)^{\text{X}_2\text{SAT}}$ and $y = (A \vee \bar{b} \vee \bar{c})^{\text{X}_2\text{SAT}}$, then let $F := F(b/\bar{c})$
8. For two X_iSAT clauses $(a \vee A)$ and $(A \vee b)$, let $F := F(a/b)$
9. If there are two clauses $(a \vee A \vee b)^{\text{X}_2\text{SAT}}$ and $(\bar{a} \vee A \vee c)^{\text{X}_2\text{SAT}}$, then let $F := F(b/\bar{c})$
10. If there are two clauses $(a \vee b \vee A \vee c)^{\text{X}_2\text{SAT}}$ and $(\bar{a} \vee \bar{b} \vee A \vee d)^{\text{X}_2\text{SAT}}$, then let $F := F(c/\bar{d})$
11. If there are two clauses $(a \vee b \vee c \vee d \vee e \vee A)^{\text{X}_2\text{SAT}}$ and $(\bar{a} \vee \bar{b} \vee \bar{c} \vee \bar{d} \vee \bar{e} \vee B)^{\text{X}_2\text{SAT}}$, then let $F := \{\varnothing\}$
12. If there are two clauses $(a \vee b \vee c \vee d \vee A)^{\text{X}_2\text{SAT}}$ and $(\bar{a} \vee \bar{b} \vee \bar{c} \vee \bar{d} \vee B)^{\text{X}_2\text{SAT}}$, then let $F := F(A/false; B/false)$
13. If there are two clauses $(a \vee b \vee c \vee A)^{\text{X}_2\text{SAT}}$ and $(\bar{a} \vee \bar{b} \vee \bar{c} \vee B)^{\text{X}_2\text{SAT}}$, then let $F := F(A/false; B/false)$

Clause Length	X_1SAT	X_2SAT	X_3SAT	X_4SAT
1	*	*	*	*
2	*	*	*	*
3	$3^{n/3} < 1.45^n$	$3^{n/3} < 1.45^n$	*	*
4	$4^{n/4} < 1.42^n$	$6^{n/4} < 1.57^n$	$4^{n/4} < 1.42^n$	*
5	$5^{n/5} < 1.38^n$	$10^{n/5} < 1.59^n$	$10^{n/5} < 1.59^n$	$5^{n/5} < 1.38^n$
6	$6^{n/6} < 1.35^n$	$15^{n/6} < 1.58^n$	$20^{n/6} < 1.65^n$	$15^{n/6} < 1.58^n$
7	$7^{n/7} < 1.33^n$	$21^{n/7} < 1.55^n$	$35^{n/7} < 1.67^n$	$35^{n/7} < 1.67^n$
8	$8^{n/8} < 1.30^n$	$28^{n/8} < 1.52^n$	$56^{n/8} < 1.66^n$	$70^{n/8} < 1.71^n$
9	$9^{n/9} < 1.28^n$	$36^{n/9} < 1.49^n$	$84^{n/9} < 1.64^n$	$126^{n/9} < 1.72^n$
10	$10^{n/10} < 1.26^n$	$45^{n/10} < 1.47^n$	$120^{n/10} < 1.62^n$	$210^{n/10} < 1.71^n$

Fig. 2. Running times for D_i should it always encounter the same kind of clause; '*' indicates polynomial time

4 Polynomial Space Exact Algorithms for X_iSAT

The basic idea behind all known poly-space algorithms for X_1SAT has been DPLL branching. One way to deal with X_iSAT is to generalize the approach so that for a certain clause y, we test all $\binom{|y|}{i}$ assignments to the variables of y making i literals true. That makes $\binom{|y|}{i}$ recursive calls, in each of which $|y|$ variables are removed – when i literals are true, the rest have to be false and so $|y|$ variables are set. Of course the length of y is crucial for the running time. Short clauses (in comparison with i) are good w.r.t. the running time. However, as opposed to the ordinary SAT-problem, long clauses are also good. In Fig. 2 is an overview of the first sublanguages of X_iSAT and the first clause lengths. Each entry is calculated as $\binom{|y|}{i}^{n/|y|}$. Note that for a fixed i, this table is polynomial time computable (assuming that the longest clause length is a polynomial in i). Hence, we can easily find a clause which is the best choice, i.e., gives the fastest running time. We call such a clause *preferable*. As the formula changes during the recursive decomposition of generalized DPLL branching different clauses will become preferable. The following algorithm elaborates on this idea. For clarity of presentation we assume that a variable occurs in each clause at most once. (Laxation of this would not introduce any new worst case, however, it would introduce some uninteresting technicalities.) We also assume that in the substitution, if a (partial) assignment is made such that any clause becomes over-satisfied or too short to ever be satisfied, then the unsatisfiable formula $F = \{\varnothing\}$ is returned. The purpose of Line 2 is to limit the number of singletons in the following lines. It works by forcing a certain percentage of the variables to be heavy. The choice of 3/5 is rather arbitrary – it works well for the first sublanguages. As will become clear in the time complexity analysis it is reasonable to believe that for higher i a larger constant will give a better trade-off. Note that when F is small enough Line 2 is applicable and so the recursion ends. Line 1 will limit the number of singletons in a preferable clause when the clause is long. The benefit of this will be clear in the time complexity analysis.

Algorithm $D_i(F)$

1. If there is an X$_i$SAT clause with $i + k$ singletons then remove k of those singletons;
2. If 3/5 or less of the variables are heavy then cycle through all possible assignments to these variables. For each such partial assignment to the variables, transform the instance to an X$_1$SAT instance, using the reduction of Lemma 1, then use the matching techniques by Porschen et al. to decide whether there is a model. Answer 'Yes' if such a model is found and 'No' otherwise;
3. Pick a preferable clause y with as few singletons as possible and make $\binom{|y|}{i}$ recursive calls, each call having the form $D_i(F(a_1/true; a_2/true \ldots a_i/true; a_{i+1}/false \ldots))$.

Theorem 1. $D_i(F)$ *decides whether* $F \in$ X$_i$SAT

Proof. Line 1 is a canonical rule. Line 2 is correct by Lemma 1 and the correctness of the matching techniques. Line 3 is correct since all models for F must have i literals true in y.

We now examine D_i w.r.t. to time complexity. Let T_{D_i} indicate the running time of $D_i(F)$.

Theorem 2. *For every fixed i, T_{D_i} is in*

$$O\left(\max\left\{\max_{\substack{m \leq n \\ i \leq m}} \binom{m}{i}^{1/m}, 1.5157\right\}^n\right) \subset o(2^n)$$

Proof. Line 1 takes polynomial time to execute. As for line 2, we can safely disregard the polynomial time work spent on matching. Hence the interesting thing is the size of the recursion tree, which is $2^{3n/5} \approx 1.5157^n$. Similarly for line 3, we disregard the polynomial work done. The recursion tree of $D_i(F)$ has size at most $\binom{m}{i}^{n/m}$ and so the big-Oh expression is justified.

To justify the $o(2^n)$ inclusion, first note that $\binom{m}{i}^{n/m} = 2^{\log_2 \binom{m}{i}^{n/m}} = 2^{\frac{n}{m} \log_2 \binom{m}{i}}$. Then, remember that $\binom{m}{i}$ is the number of subsets of size i whose elements are picked from a set of size m. As the powerset has size 2^m, $\binom{m}{i}$ is always smaller than that. Hence it follows that $\log_2 \binom{m}{i} < m$ and so $2^{\frac{n}{m} \log_2 \binom{m}{i}} < 2^n$.

It is interesting to note that already the above rough analysis shows that the running time is better than any known DPLL-style algorithm for SAT. This indicates the practical usefulness of X$_i$SAT in the context of c-atoms – X$_i$SAT seems to have a more benign structure than SAT. We now try to refine the analysis to achieve a tighter upper time bound. Unfortunately, in order to do that we need to know the worst clause length for every sublanguage. Looking again at Fig. 2 one could think that the worst clause length is $2i + 1$. However, that is not always the case. Extending the table, one sees that the pattern is changed for X$_{12}$SAT where the worst clause length is 26. It is still an open problem where to find the worst clause length for a given sublanguage. However, for the first sublanguages we can perform a better analysis:

Theorem 3. *For* X$_2$SAT, X$_3$SAT *and* X$_4$SAT T_{D_i} *is in* $O(1.5157^n)$, $O(1.6214^n)$ *and* $O(1.6848^n)$, *respectively.*

Proof. Starting with X$_2$SAT, we need to take a closer look at Line 3.

Once Line 3 has been applied, the formula is likely to have become mixed, and so in the general case, y might be a clause requiring one or two true literals. If y requires one true literal we have a worst clause length of 3, where 3 branches are made, in each of which 3 variables are removed. If the algorithm always did this branching, we would have a branching tree of size $O(1.4423^n)$. If y requires two true literals, we will have a worst case when $|y| = 5$. If D_i always had to branch upon such a y, we would have a running time in $O\left(\binom{5}{2}^{n/5}\right) \subset O(1.5849^n)$. However, note that due to the previous cases and the fact that y has the smallest possible number of singletons, at most one variable of y is a singleton. (Line 1 is not strong enough to impose this, but Line 2 ensures that there are clauses with at least 4 heavy variables.) That means that in each of the 10 calls, other clauses will be affected. As y was most preferable, all clauses must have length 5, and of the 10 calls at most one call will not set a literal true in another clause (only one combination of the non-singletons will not set a literal true). Hence, for the worst case, in 9 of the recursive calls the algorithm will in the immediately following step encounter an X$_1$SAT clause of length 4 and in one recursive call encounter an X$_2$SAT clause of length 4. This means that we will have an upper time bound $O(c^n)$ where $c = \tau(9^6, 9^{9.4}) \approx 1.5149$. In this case, Line 2 will decide the overall running time of the algorithm.

Looking at Fig. 2, let us examine the other clause lengths that are possible worst case candidates.

1. Clause length 4: In this case there will be at most one singleton in the clause picked and so we get $c = \tau(7^{5\cdot 3}, 7^3) \approx 1.5113$.
2. Clause length 6: As $\frac{2\cdot 6}{5} = 2.4$ there may be two singletons in the clause we picked. Hence we get $c = \tau(11^{14\cdot 9}, 11^{2\cdot 10}) \approx 1.5055$.
3. Clause length 7: As $\frac{2\cdot 7}{5} = 2.8$ there may be two singletons in the clause we picked. Hence we get $c = \tau(13^{19\cdot 6}, 13^{2\cdot 15}) \approx 1.4657$.
4. Clause length 8: $\frac{2\cdot 8}{5} = 3.2$ but Line 2 prevents the possibility of three singletons. Hence we get $c = \tau(15^{26\cdot 7}, 15^{2\cdot 21}) \approx 1.4345$.

When it comes to X$_3$SAT and X$_4$SAT the analysis is almost identical. Here c will be $\tau(13^{33\cdot 15}, 13^{2\cdot 20})$ and $\tau(17^{123\cdot 56}, 17^{3\cdot 70})$, respectively.

The use of canonization has proved fruitful in the construction of algorithms for X$_1$SAT, and so one could hope that the use of more canonical rules would improve D_i further (in terms of proven upper time bounds). However, the problem is that while canonization helps improve many cases such as overlaps between clauses, many singletons and few occurrences of high degreed variables, yet the worst case of the algorithm still remains, namely: all clauses have the worst possible length, no pair of clauses share more than one variable and there are many heavy variables. For X$_2$SAT the author has constructed an algorithm that obtains a better upper time than D_i. The algorithm $D_2(F)$ carefully chooses variables to branch on, uses canonization, and arrives at the bad case described. Then the algorithm picks a clause that has two heavy variables a and b. It makes three recursive calls, $D_2(F(a/true; b/true))$, $D_2(F(a/\bar{b}))$ and $D_2(F(a/false; b/false))$. By a careful case analysis of how D_2 behaves in the three calls, an interesting time bound can be established. When this case is no longer applicable, it can be shown that there are sufficiently few heavy variables left and the cycling and matching technique can be used.

Algorithm $D_2(F)$

0. Canonize F and if $|Var(F)| < 10$ then perform an exhaustive search to find a model
1. Pick a clause $(a \vee b \vee A)^{\text{X}_1\text{SAT}}$ or a clause $(\bar{a} \vee \bar{b} \vee \bar{c})^{\text{X}_2\text{SAT}}$; return $D_2(F(a/\bar{b}))$ OR $D_2(F(a/false; b/false))$
2. Pick a clause $(a \vee b \vee c \vee d)^{\text{X}_2\text{SAT}}$; return $D_2(F(a/\bar{b}; c/\bar{d}))$ OR $D_2(F(a/b; c/d; b/\bar{d}))$
3. Pick two clauses $(a \vee b \vee c \vee A)^{\text{X}_2\text{SAT}}$ and $(\bar{a} \vee \bar{b} \vee c \vee B)^{\text{X}_2\text{SAT}}$ such that $Var(A) \cap Var(B) = \emptyset$; return $D_2(F(c/true; a/\bar{b}))$ OR $D_2(F(c/false))$
4. Pick two clauses $(a \vee b \vee c \vee A)^{\text{X}_2\text{SAT}}$ and $(\bar{a} \vee b \vee c \vee B)^{\text{X}_2\text{SAT}}$; return $D_2(F(b/\bar{c}; a/true))$ OR $D_2(F(b/\bar{c}; a/false))$ OR $D_2(F(b/false; c/false))$
5. Pick two clauses $(a \vee b \vee A)^{\text{X}_2\text{SAT}}$ and $(\bar{a} \vee b \vee B)^{\text{X}_2\text{SAT}}$; return $D_2(F(a/true; b/true))$ OR $D_2(F(a/false; b/true))$ OR $D_2(F(b/false))$
6. Pick two clauses $x = (A \vee B)^{\text{X}_2\text{SAT}}$ and $y = (A \vee C)^{\text{X}_2\text{SAT}}$ such that $|A| \geq 2$; return $D_2(F \cup (A)^{\text{X}_2\text{SAT}})$ OR $D_2(F \cup (A)^{\text{X}_1\text{SAT}})$ OR $D_2(F(A/false))$.

7. Pick a clause $x = (a \vee b \vee A)^{\text{X}_2\text{SAT}}$ such that a and b are heavy; return $D_2(F(a/true; b/true))$ OR $D_2(F(a/\bar{b}))$ OR $D_2(F(a/false; b/false))$.
8. Cycle through all possible assignments to the heavy variables. For each such partial assignment to the variables, transform the instance to an X_1SAT instance, using the reduction of Lemma 1, then use the matching techniques by Porschen et al. to decide whether there is a model. Answer 'Yes' if such a model is found and 'No' otherwise.

The following theorem establishes the correctness of D_2:

Theorem 4. $D_2(F)$ *will correctly decide whether* F *has an* X_2SAT *model.*

Proof. We look at the cases of D_2:

0. Correct by assumption.
1. If the clause is an X_1SAT clause both a and b cannot be *true*, so the two cases 1) one of a and b is *true*; 2) both are *false*, cover all possibilities. If the clause is $(\bar{a} \vee \bar{b} \vee \bar{c})^{\text{X}_2\text{SAT}}$, we have seen that this clause in effect is identical to $(a \vee b \vee c)^{\text{X}_1\text{SAT}}$ and so this is also correct.
2. The two cases cover all possibilities: either it holds that one of a and b and one of c and d are *true*, or it holds that both a and b are *true* and the other two *false* or vice versa.
3. When $c = true$ it holds that $a \neq b$
4. Both of b and c cannot be *true*, and so all possible cases are covered.
5. One of $b = true$ and $b = false$ holds. In the first case one of $a = true$ and $a = false$ holds.
6. Two, one or zero variables of A are *true*.
7. The second branch covers the two possibilities $a = true, b = false$ and $a = false, b = true$.
8. Correct by Lemma 1 and the correctness of the matching techniques.

The time complexity analysis consists of a number of case and sub-case analyses. Typically the analysis of a case m will establish an upper time bound U_α "for this case" which should be interpreted: if throughout the whole execution of the algorithm, α is the only case applicable, then U_α is an upper bound of the execution time. Hence one can easily see that an overall upper time bound for the algorithm is the maximum U_j established for all cases j.

Theorem 5. *Algorithm* D_2 *runs in time* $O(1.4511^n)$

Proof. We examine each of the cases:

0. Runs in polynomial time.
1. We look at the possible subcases:
    (a) We picked a clause $(a \vee b \vee c \vee d)^{\text{X}_1\text{SAT}}$: In the first branch, the call $D_2(F(a/\bar{b}))$ will make the substitution operation apply the following steps: the clause will become $(\bar{b} \vee b \vee c \vee d)^{\text{X}_1\text{SAT}}$ which will become $(true \vee c \vee d)^{\text{X}_1\text{SAT}}$ which will remove the clause and replace c and d by

$false$ and hence 3 variables are removed. The second branch will result in the following steps: $(false \lor false \lor c \lor d)^{X_1SAT}$, $(c \lor d)^{X_1SAT}$. The clause $(c \lor d)$ will then be immediately taken care of by the canonization step following. Hence, this case runs in $O(\tau(3,3)^n) \subseteq O(1.2600^n)$ time.
   (b) We picked a clause $(a \lor b \lor c)^{X_1SAT}$: In the first branch, when a is replaced by $\bar{b}$, the other literal will be put to $false$ by the substitution operation, so two variables are removed. In the other branch, when $a = b = false$, the clause $(c)^{X_1SAT}$ is created and so, three variables are removed in this branch. Hence, this case runs in time $O(\tau(3,2)^n) \subseteq O(1.3248^n)$.
   (c) We picked an X_1SAT clause longer than 4. The worst case is when the clause has length 5. This case runs in $O(\tau(4,2)^n) \subseteq O(1.2721^n)$ time.
   (d) We picked a clause $(\bar{a} \lor \bar{b} \lor \bar{c})^{X_2SAT}$. This case runs in time $O(\tau(3,2)^n) \subseteq O(1.2721^n)$.
2. We have a running time for this case in $O(\tau(2,3)^n) \subseteq O(1.2600^n)$.
3. As the formula has been canonized, $|A \cup B| \geq 3$ and so in the first branch at least 5 variables are removed (c is $true$ and $b \lor \bar{b}$ equals $true$ and so the literals of A and B are set to $false$). Hence we have a running time in $O(\tau(5,1)^n) \subseteq O(1.3248^n)$ time.
4. This case runs in $O(\tau(4,4,2)^n) \subseteq O(1.4143^n)$ time.
5. This case runs in $O(\tau(5,5,1)^n) \subseteq O(1.4511^n)$ time.
6. Doing a naive analysis like in previous cases, looking only at the direct effects we would obtain very bad figures. For example, assume $|x| = |y| = 5$ and $|A| = 2$, we would reason that in the first branch 2+3+3 variables are removed, in the second 1 variable and in the third 2 variables, giving an upper bound in $O(\tau(8,1,2)^n) \subseteq O(1.6408^n)$. However, if one broadens the perspective to the branchings that will be done immediately afterwards, we end up with better time bounds. In our example, the first branch we cannot say more about, and so we stay with 8 variables removed. In the second branch, however, we will have the two clauses $(B)^{X_1SAT}$ and $(C)^{X_1SAT}$. Following their way downward the recursion tree we see that effectively, there will be four branches and the number of variables removed are 7,6,6 and 5, respectively (the one variable removed by the explicit creation of $(A)^{X_1SAT}$ included). We may continue and reason similarly about the third branch, however, the figures we obtained are good enough: $O(\tau(8;7,6,6,5;2)^n) \subseteq O(1.4401^n)$. Note that the sign ';' is used to help the reader see how the expansion is done. We now look at the remaining cases:
   (a) For $|A| = 2$, we have already described the worst case, because if any of B and C are longer than 3 we will be able to remove more variables.
   (b) For $|A| = 3$; if $|B| = |C| = 2$ we note that the second branch can be expanded to two branches due to the explicit creation of $(A)^{X_1SAT}$ and so we get a running time in $O(\tau(4;5,4;3)) \subseteq O(1.4253^n)$. If $|B| = 2, |C| = 3$ we note that the second branch can be expanded to four branches and we get a running time in $O(\tau(5;5,6,6,7;3)^n \subseteq O(1.4276^n)$. If $|B| = |C| = 3$ we may expand each of the three branches, the first to two branches, the second to eight branches and the third to two, thereby obtaining a running time in $O(\tau(9,8;8,8,7,7,7,6,9,8;8,7)^n \subseteq$

$O(1.3993^n)$. When we look back in the complexity analysis we see that the worst case possible for any $\textsc{x}_1\textsc{sat}$ clause or any $\textsc{x}_2\textsc{sat}$ clause shorter than 5 is that in one branch 2 variables are removed and in the other 3. As this was the case for all extra branchings when $|B| = |C| = 3$ we are now done with the subcase of $|A| = 3$.

(c) For $|A| = 4$, we note that due to the canonical rules $|x| + |y| > 10$, and so the first subcase to consider is $|B| = 1, |C| = 2$. As a matter of fact, we will have only two branches, because in the third branch the formula will immediately be found unsatisfiable by the canonization. Hence this case runs in $O(\tau(3,2)^n \subseteq O(1.3248^n)$ time. If $|B| = |C| = 2$ a naive analysis show that we have a running time in $O(\tau(4,2,4)^n \subseteq O(1.4143^n)$. For $|B| = |C| = 2$ we also have the bound $O(\tau(4,2,4)^n \subseteq O(1.4143^n)$. For $|B| = 2, |C| = 3$ we get the bound $O(\tau(5;4,4;4)) \subseteq O(1.3888^n)$. If $|B| = |C| = 2$ we get a running time in $O(\tau(6;3,3;4)) \subseteq O(1.4459^n)$ and this is clearly the worst case for $|A| = 4$.

(d) For $|A| = 5$, if $|B| = 1, |C| = 2$, we get a running time in $O(\tau(3,2,5))^n \subseteq O(1.4300^n)$. $|B| = |C| = 2$ gives a bound $O(\tau(4,2,5)^n) \subseteq O(1.3803^n)$. If $|B| = 2, |C| = 3$ we get a running time in $O(\tau(5,1,5))^n \subseteq O(1.4511^n)$. For $|B| > 2, |C| = 3$ we have a bound $O(\tau(6;4,2;5)^n) \subseteq O(1.4352^n)$ (the second branch is expanded by making use of $(A)^{\textsc{x}_1\textsc{sat}}$). The other cases are better than this last one. We also see that for $|A| > 5$ we will have no case worse than the ones already analyzed.

7. We know that there are $\textsc{x}_2\textsc{sat}$ clauses $a \in y$, $a \in y'$, $b \in z$ and $b \in z'$ which, by the earlier cases, are all different from x, do not share any other variables than a and b and are at least 5 in length. That means that there is a subset of the formula looking like this ($\dot{a}$ indicates a or $\bar{a}$):

$y = (\dot{a} \lor c \lor c' \lor C)^{\textsc{x}_2\textsc{sat}}$
$y' = (\dot{a} \lor d \lor d' \lor D)^{\textsc{x}_2\textsc{sat}}$
$x = (a \lor b \lor a' \lor a'' \lor A)^{\textsc{x}_2\textsc{sat}}$
$z = (\dot{b} \lor e \lor e' \lor E)^{\textsc{x}_2\textsc{sat}}$
$z' = (\dot{b} \lor f \lor f' \lor F)^{\textsc{x}_2\textsc{sat}}$

We will examine the cases depending on $|x|$, using the same expanded view as in the previous case:

(a) If $|x| = 5$ then there are five variants depending on the actual look of $\dot{a}$ and $\dot{b}$ – none of the dotted variables is negated, one is negated, etc.

None of the dotted is negated: this case runs in $O(\tau(21, 19^4, 17^6, 15^4, 13; 3, 4; 4, 5))^n \subseteq O(1.4413^n)$ time. The first branch can be extended into 16 branches, taking care of the four $\textsc{x}_1\textsc{sat}$ clauses created by $a = b = true$. The first figure, 21, is 5 (obtained from x) $+ 4 + 4 + 4 + 4$ (obtained from the other four clauses). Note that due to the balanced branching effect, the worst case will be when $|y| = |y'| = |z| = |z'| = 6$.

One of the dotted is negated: this case runs in $O(\tau(17, 15^3, 13^3, 11; 3, 4; 8, 6, 9, 7)^n) \subseteq O(1.4138^n)$ time.

Two of the dotted are negated: this case runs in $O(\tau(13, 11, 11, 9; 3, 4; 12, 10, 10, 8, 13, 11, 11, 9)^n) \subseteq O(1.4001^n)$ time.

Three of the dotted are negated: this case runs in $O(\tau(9, 7; 3, 4; 16, 14^3, 12^7, 10, 17, 15^3, 19^3, 11)^n) \subseteq O(1.3034^n)$ time.
All of the dotted are negated: this case runs in $O(\tau(5; 3, 4; 20, 18^4, 16^6, 14^4, 12, 21, 19^4, 17^6, 15^4, 13)^n) \subseteq O(1.3920^n)$ time.

(b) For $|x| = 6$ we can of course make the same subcase analysis as above, however, by now we have seen that due to the balanced branching effect, we only need to look at the case when no dotted is negated. This case has a running time in $O(\tau(22, 20, 20^3, 18^6, 16^4, 14; 4, 4; 4, 5))^n \subseteq O(1.4396^n)$.

(c) For $|x| = 7$, in the third branch, when $a = b = false$, there will be a X$_2$SAT clause of length 5 created. We will not expand that branch and so we get a running time in $O(\tau(23, 21^4, 19^6, 17^4, 15; 5, 3; 2))^n \subseteq O(1.4400^n)$ time. Clearly, there is no need to examine the cases when $|x| > 7$ – they will all be better than this one.

8. As all clauses have at least length 5 and contains at most one heavy variable, the ratio —heavy variables— to $|Var(F)|$ is at most $2/12$. $2^{1/6} \approx 1.1225$ and the so-for worst case runs in $O(1.4511^n)$. Hence we see that this case will not be the worst case.

5 Solving X$_i$SAT in Exponential Space

From the above algorithms and properties presented, it seems reasonable that the running time of an algorithm for deciding X$_i$SAT should always depend heavily upon the actual i. However, that is not always the case. In the early 1980's, Shroeppel and Shamir found a way to solve a class of NP-complete problems in time $O(2^{n/2}) \subset O(1.4143^n)$ and space $O(2^{n/4}) \subset O(1.1893^n)$. There has been a recent interest in this kind of algorithms, for instance [20]. There are two conditions a problem must satisfy in order for the algorithm of Shroeppel and Shamir to be applicable: first, that given a solution (or rather an assignment in the solution space), the problem instances satisfied by the solution must be enumerable in polynomial time and space, and second, that a problem instance can be split in a way such that the split operation enjoys certain algebraic properties. One could think that the enumerability requirement makes the algorithm unapplicable to problems involving Boolean formulae (given an assignment one can construct an infinite set of formulae for which that is a model). However, we may consider the formula fixed and so the requirement boils down to simple evaluation. In the context of X$_i$SAT, a possible implementation of their algorithm looks like this: The X$_i$SAT instance is described by a list of variables and a list of numbers indicating for each clause how many true literals it needs to be satisfied, i.e., i. Now split the variable list in four parts and for each part, tabulate all possible assignments to the variables, and for each assignment make a list indicating for each clause how many literals became true. We now have four tables and want to scan them to see if there a four lists which can be piece-wise added so that the list $(i, i, i \ldots)$ is obtained. If these four lists are found the formula has an X$_i$SAT model. We will not go into details on how the search is done. Instead, we will restate the main theorem of Shroeppel and Shamir and then prove that the split-operation described for X$_i$SAT makes the theorem applicable.

Theorem 6. (Shamir and Shroeppel) *If a set of problems is polynomially enumerable and has a monotonic composition operator, then its instances of size n can be solved in time $T = O(2^{n/2})$ and space $S = O(2^{n/4})$.*

In the above described representation of X_iSAT the requirement of polynomially enumerability is satisfied as, for a fixed formula, simple evaluation reveals whether an assignment satisfies the formula. A composition operator $\oplus$ is *monotonic* iff

1. for all problem instances P' and P'', $|P' \oplus P''| = |P'| + |P''|$
2. for any two solutions x' to P' and x'' to P'' there is a simple concatenation $x'x''$ which is a solution to $P' \oplus P''$.
3. for every solution x to P any any represenation of x as $x'x''$, there are problems P' and P'' such that x' solves P', x'' solves P'' and $P = P' \oplus P''$.
4. $P' \oplus P''$ can be computed in polynomial time (of the lengths of P' and P'').

In our case, $\oplus$ is the concatenation of the variable lists of P' and P'' and the piece-wise addition of the list of numbers. Clearly it is monotonic.

6 Discussion and Conclusions

We have shown that c-atoms can be efficiently reduced to an NP-complete problem called X_iSAT which is novel to this paper. X_iSAT has a nice structure allowing the construction of algorithms faster than the trivial $O(2^n)$ bound. It is likely that exact model checkers that are to deal with c-atoms would benefit from working with formulae consisting of both SAT clauses as well as X_iSAT clauses.

When it comes to further improved algorithms, there are several possible directions. In the past, the algorithms for X_1SAT have benefitted greatly from new canonical rules. For instance the special resolution rule which has been so successfully applied in [3]. Unfortunately, that very rule does not extend to other sublanguages of X_iSAT. However, there are probably other rules that will prove useful. Better tools for analyzing the run time complexity of the extended DPLL-style algorithms presented in this paper would also be helpful.

Due to the low upper time bounds for X_1SAT ("low" for an NP-complete problem), no randomized algorithms have been proposed, to the best of our knowledge. However, such algorithms should be of interest for the general X_iSAT problem if deployed in incomplete model checkers.

7 Acknowledgements

We thank Magnus Wahlström and Peter Jonsson for proofreading and valuable comments.

References

1. F. Aloul, A. Ramani, I. Markov, and K. Sakallah. Pbs: a backtrack-search pseudo-boolean solver and optimizer. In *Proc. 5th Int. Symp. Theory and Applications of Satisfiability (SAT2002)*, pages 346–353, 2002.
2. B. Benhamou, L. Sais, and P. Siegel. Two proof procedures for a cardinality based language in propositional calculus. In *11th Annual Symposium on Theoretical Aspects of Computer Science (STACS1994)*, volume 775, pages 71–82, 1994.
3. J. M. Byskov, B. A. Madsen, and B. Skjernaa. New algorithms for exact satisfiability. *Theoretical Computer Science*, 2004. To appear.
4. V. Dahllöf, P. Jonsson, and R. Beigel. Algorithms for four variants of the exact satisfiability problem. *Theoretical Computer Science*, 320(2–3):373–394, 2004.
5. M. Dransfield, L. Liu, V. Marek, and M. Truszczyński. Satisfiability and computing van der Waerden numbers. *The Electronic Journal of Combinatorics*, 2004.
6. L. Drori and D. Peleg. Faster exact solutions for some NP-hard problems. In *Proc. 7th Annual European Symposium on Algorithms (ESA1999)*, pages 450–461, 1999.
7. L. Drori and D. Peleg. Faster solutions for exact hitting set and exact SAT. Technical report, Belfer Institute of Mathematics and Computer Science, 1999.
8. L. Drori and D. Peleg. Faster solutions for some NP-hard problems. *Theoretical Computer Science*, 287:473–499, 2002.
9. M. Garey and D. Johnson. *Computers and Intractability: A Guide to the Theory of NP-Completeness*. Freeman, New York, 1979.
10. E. Goldberg and Y. Novikov. Berkmin: a fast and robust sat-solver. In *Proc. Design, Automation and Test in Europe Conference and Exposition (DATE 2002)*, pages 142–149, 2002.
11. E. Hirsch and A. Kulikov. A $2^{n/6.15}$-time algorithm for X3SAT.
12. O. Kullmann. New methods for 3-SAT decision and worst-case analysis. *Theoretical Computer Science*, 223:1–72, 1999.
13. C. M. Li. Integrating equivalency reasoning into Davis-Putnam procedure. In *Proc. 17th Nat. Conf. AI (AAAI2000)*, pages 291–296, 2000.
14. L. Liu and M. Truszczyński. Local-search techniques for propositional logic extended with cardinality constraints. In *Proceedings of the 9th International Conference on Principles and Practice of Constraint Programming – CP 2003*, pages 495–509, 2003.
15. Matthew, Moskewicz, C. Madigan, Y. Zhao, L. Zhang, and S. Malik. Chaff: Engineering an efficient SAT solver. In *Proc. 38th Design Automation Conference (DAC2001)*, pages 530–535, 2001.
16. S. Porschen, B. Randerath, and E. Speckenmeyer. X3SAT is decidable in time $O(2^{n/5})$. In *Proc. 5th Int. Symp. on Theory and Appl. of SAT*, pages 231–235, 2002.
17. R. Schroeppel and A. Shamir. A $T = O(2^{n/2})$, $S = O(2^{n/4})$ algorithm for certain NP-complete problems. *SIAM Journal on Computing*, 1981.
18. J. M. Silva and K. Sakallah. Graps: A search algorithm for propositional satisfiability. *IEEE Trans. Computers*, 48(5):506–521, 1999.
19. P. Simons. *Extending and Implementing the Stable Model Semantics*. PhD thesis, Helsinki University of Technology, 2000.
20. R. Williams. A new algorithm for optimal constraint satisfaction and its implications. In *Proc 31st Int. Colloq. Automata Languages and Programming (ICALP2004)*, pages 1227–1237, 2004.

BCiC: A System for Code Authentication and Verification

Nathan Whitehead and Martín Abadi

Department of Computer Science
University of California, Santa Cruz
{nwhitehe,abadi}@cs.ucsc.edu

Abstract. We present BCiC, a system for verifying and authenticating code that combines language-based proof methods with public-key digital signatures. BCiC aims to augment the rigor of formal proofs about intrinsic properties of code by relying on authentication and trust relations. BCiC integrates the Binder security language with the Calculus of (Co)Inductive Constructions (CiC). In this respect, it is a descendant of our previous logic BLF, which was based on LF rather than CiC. This paper focuses on the architecture and implementation of BCiC. In addition to a logical inference engine, the design most notably includes a network communication module for the efficient exchange of logical facts between hosts, and a cryptography module for generating and checking signatures. The implementation cooperates with the Open Verifier, a state-of-the-art system for proof-carrying code with modular checkers.

1 Introduction

Modern software comes from a multitude of sources, and it often comes in pieces. Some applications dynamically link to libraries, some are extended with applets or plug-in modules, and others can be automatically updated. In every case, policies and mechanisms for establishing trust in new code are essential. When the new code is signed with a public-key digital signature, trust in the code may be based on trust in its signer. More generally, trust in the code may result from authenticating the source of the code. However, such trust has limits: many signers are unknown or only partly known to the consumers of code, and even reputable signers make mistakes. Therefore, evaluating the code itself and its properties is also important. It can yield fundamental safety guarantees, as in Java bytecode verification [17], and it need not burden code consumers with proofs of code properties, as research on proof-carrying code (PCC) [18] demonstrates. (With PCC, code comes accompanied by safety proofs, and consumers need only check, not generate, the proofs.) Nevertheless, formal specification and analysis of code remain difficult and often incomplete, particularly when we go beyond basic memory-safety guarantees.

In this paper we present an approach and a system for establishing trust in code that combine signatures and proofs. We define a policy language that allows references to signed assertions and supports reasoning about trust in the signers. The policy language can also express theorems about code properties, and supports reasoning about the correctness of proofs of the theorems. The final decision to run code, and what privileges to give to the code, may require both signatures from trusted parties and direct proofs of code safety. For instance, it may require a partial proof of safety with trusted, signed assertions as hypotheses.

Specifically, we introduce BCiC, a system for verifying and authenticating code that combines language-based proof methods with public-key digital signatures. BCiC aims to augment the rigor of formal proofs about intrinsic properties of code by relying on authentication and trust relations. BCiC integrates the Binder security language [10] with the Calculus of (Co)Inductive Constructions (CiC) [8]. In this respect, it is a descendant of our previous logic BLF [22], which was based on LF [13] rather than CiC. Here we go beyond our work on BLF by designing and building a concrete system. In addition to a logical inference engine, the design most notably includes a network communication module for the efficient exchange of logical facts between hosts, and a cryptography module for generating and checking signatures. The implementation cooperates with the Open Verifier [6], a state-of-the-art system for proof-carrying code with modular checkers.

After considering previous and related work in Section 2, we give a short example in Section 3 and present a high-level overview of our system in Section 4. In Section 5 we define the syntax and logical meaning of policies, and describe the implementation of the logical inference engine. In Section 6 we present two important components of the system in more detail, the cryptography module and the network module. In Section 7 we describe the integration of BCiC with the Open Verifier. We conclude with some comments on future work in Section 8.

2 Related Work and Background

Many existing systems combine reason and authority in some way. Checking the validity of an X.509 certificate involves a combination of trusting principals and reasoning about the transitivity of certification. Environments that execute network code often combine static typechecks of the code with signature checks [17, 11, 15]. These systems can verify only fixed, simple properties of the code. PCC allows more interesting properties to be checked, but existing work on PCC [18, 1, 3, 19] assumes that properties and proof rules are fixed ahead of time between the code producer and the code consumer; they also do not support signatures in their reasoning. Our previous paper [22] contains further discussion of related work, in particular of research on proof-carrying authentication [2, 4, 16]. For the sake of brevity we do not reproduce that material here; it is somewhat less relevant for the present paper.

BLF is a logic for authorizing code that combines reason and authority [22]. The logic in our new system is similar to BLF but, instead of combining Binder [10] and LF [13], it combines Binder and CiC, the Calculus of (Co)Inductive Constructions [8], used in the Coq tool [21, 5]. We switched to CiC in order to allow the use of Coq for theorem proving. We have found that inductive definitions for data structures yield significant advantages in proofs. The Coq environment also allows a high degree of organization and automation, and is thus friendly to large-scale theorem proving efforts. Our formal description in Section 5 is an updated version of our previous presentation, adapted to the new choice of logical framework.

Although the change in logical framework is significant, the primary difference between our current and previous work is that BCiC has a definite system architecture and a concrete realization whereas BLF does not. Previously we implemented BLF in an abstract way. All computation was contained in one machine and the interactions between hosts were simulated. Public-key digital signatures were considered abstract terms; no actual cryptographic algorithms were used. Similarly, logical formulas were manipulated abstractly. In our present work the implementation is concrete. Signatures and logical formulas have concrete representations as binary bit strings in a standardized format. Hosts communicate with one another over the Internet in order to share data, following the formal semantics of the import and export functions in Section 5. We have also connected our system with an actual PCC framework, the Open Verifier, as described in Section 7.

The implementation of our communication structure, in which pairs of hosts synchronize and exchange new information, is inspired by work on replicated databases and database synchronization [9, 14]. In our case, the database which is being synchronized is a set of logical statements.

3 An Example

This section motivates and introduces some components of the system through an example.

Suppose that Alice is a user who requires that every program she executes neither access memory incorrectly nor use too many resources. There may be a relatively straightforward way to prove memory safety for the programs of interest, but not one for characterizing resource usage. Moreover, excessive resource usage may not be viewed as very harmful when there is someone to blame and perhaps bill. Accordingly, Alice may want proofs for memory safety but may trust Bob on resource usage. Alice constructs a policy that includes:

```
use R in
  forallobj P:program
  mayrun(P) :- sat(safe P), economical(P)
  economical(P) :- Bob says economical(P)
end
```

The first line indicates that R applies, as an environment. This environment is a set of constructors and proof rules that define the syntax of programs and the rules employed for proving memory safety. It is specific to a particular programming language and proof methodology. For instance, R may contain the following snippet, which defines standard constructs for memory access:

```
mem : Type
sel : mem -> val -> val
upd : mem -> val -> val -> mem
```

The second line of the policy (`forallobj P:program`) is a universal quantification over all programs P. The first clause indicates that Alice believes that she may execute a program P if there is a proof that P is memory safe and she thinks that P is economical. The second clause reflects Alice's trust in Bob. In more complex examples, other clauses may provide other ways of establishing `economical(P)`. The operator `says`, from Binder, represents assertions by principals. The `sat` construct is a special logic predicate that holds when there is a CiC proof of its argument. The other predicates (`mayrun` and `economical`) are user-defined predicates.

In turn, Bob trusts Charlie to write only economical programs, and has in his policy:

```
use R in
  forallobj P:program
  economical(P) :- Charlie says mine(P)
end
```

where `mine` is another user-defined predicate.

Suppose further that Charlie supplies a program P0 that Alice wishes to execute. Charlie produces a CiC proof, Pf, of memory safety of the program. Charlie publishes his proof by asserting `proof(Pf)`, specifically by typing the command `bcicclient assert proof(Pf)`. The predicate `proof` does not have any built-in logical meaning; it simply serves for introducing the proof Pf. Similarly, Charlie asserts `mine(P0)`.

Alice, Bob, and Charlie all run BCiC servers in the background. When the servers are set up, they are given the address of an existing server. From that point, they synchronize and receive a list of all other known servers. Once connected, they occasionally choose other servers with which to synchronize. After sufficient synchronization, Alice can deduce `economical(P0)` and `Charlie says proof(Pf)`. After the logic inference engine checks the proof Pf, Alice obtains `sat(safe P0)`. Now when Alice queries `mayrun(P0)`, she receives the answer "yes" and is prepared to run P0.

4 Overview

Although our system must implement the logic presented in the next section in order to support reasoning about signatures and proofs (like the reasoning in the example), the system is much more than a bare implementation of the logic. In such a bare implementation, for instance, signed statements may simply be logical expressions—appropriate for initial experimentation but not much else. In order to be useful, signed statements must have concrete, secure digital representations. Thus, in our system, signatures employ cryptography; they are unforgeable and tamper-evident. Furthermore, our system deals with communication over an insecure network. The network module should minimize the need for manual user intervention for synchronization.

The implementation has several parts:

- The *parser* understands the syntax of the logic and can translate between textual and abstract syntax tree representations.
- The *logic interpreter* performs deductions in the logic from a set of given statements to produce a larger (but still finite) set of deduced statements.
- The *cryptography module* implements the necessary cryptographic operations, such as generating and checking signatures.

- The *network module* can communicate statements over the network.
- The *user interface* accepts textual input from the user and determines which action should be taken. The user interface is a simple command-line utility that communicates with an existing daemon over a secure local socket.
- The *supervisor* is in charge of coordinating the global behavior of the program. It loads existing databases of statements, decides when to communicate on the network, sign statements, draw inferences, and accept input from the user.
- The *policy* gives rules for deciding when code should be executed, who to trust initially about what, and so forth.
- The *database* holds all known true facts from any source.

Figure 1 shows the organization of these components in the system. Boxes represent code modules, circles represent data. The figure also shows the Open Verifier; this part is explained in Section 7.

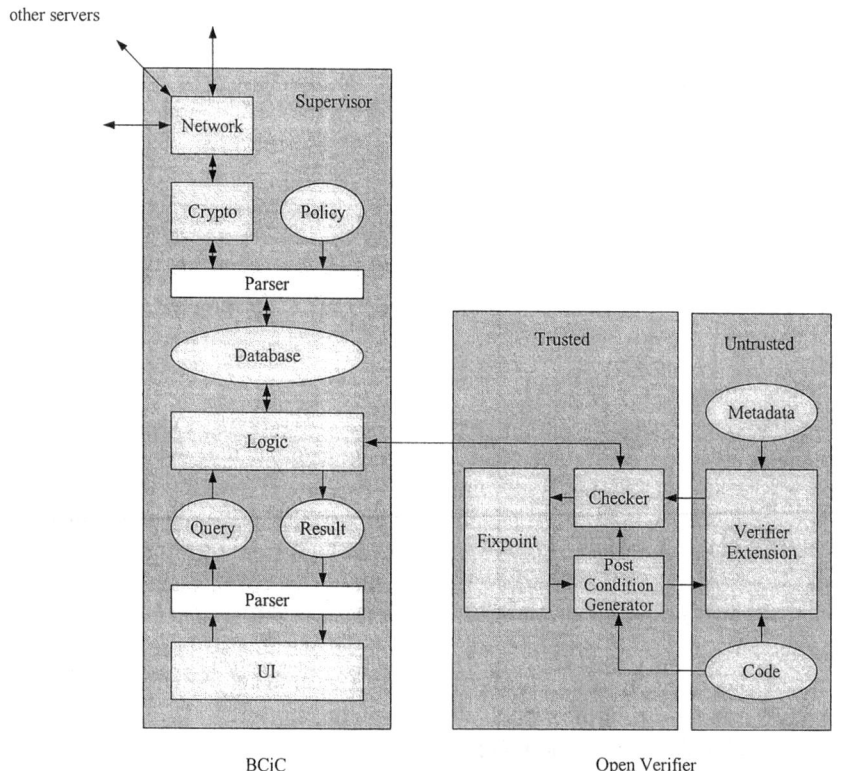

Fig. 1. System components

5 BCiC's Policy Language

This section presents the syntax and semantics of our policy language in a somewhat abbreviated fashion. Details can be found in the appendix. The interested reader is also encouraged to refer to corresponding descriptions for BLF [22] for additional explanations. What we describe here, however, should suffice for understanding the rest of this paper.

5.1 Formal Presentation of the Language

The policy language has both a user syntax (defined in Figure 2 of the appendix) and an internal syntax (in Figure 4). The user syntax allows proof rules to be stated in environments of the form `use R in ... end`. On the other hand, the internal syntax records proof rules at every point where they are employed, as extra parameters rather than with `use`. A simple annotation function translates from the user syntax into the internal syntax (Figure 3). Rulesets (type signatures) are typed according to the identifiers that they define. In this respect, BCiC is more constrained than BLF. Therefore, when one quantifies over rulesets, only rulesets with the proper definitions are considered.

The logical meaning of policies is given by proof rules (in Figure 5). These proof rules rely on the CiC typing relation (written $\vdash_{CiC}$). They also rely on conversions to normal form, as calculated by Coq. In other respects, the proof rules are a fairly ordinary logical system for standard logical constructs. We formulate them as sequent deductions [12].

The import function is used for determining the logical meaning of signed statements received over the network. It is a partial function that takes a key and a formula and returns a new formula. Our method for importing statements follows Binder. An atomic formula A signed with a key U is imported as U `says` A. It is also possible to export and import some (but not all) non-atomic formulas. A clause can be imported from U only if the head of the clause is not already quoted with `says`. If the original clause is H :- B, then the imported clause will be U `says` H :- B' where B' is the original body with every formula F without a `says` prefix replaced with U `says` F. In terms of g-formulas and d-formulas as used in the formal syntax, a g-formula G without a `says` prefix is translated to U `says` G. A g-formula of the form V `says` G remains unchanged in translation. A d-formula D without `says` gets translated to U `says` D, while d-formulas of the form V `says` D are untranslatable.

5.2 The Logic Interpreter

The logic module is responsible for managing the fact database and responding to queries. Initially the fact database contains only the facts in the local policy. After synchronizing with other hosts and exchanging signed statements, the fact database will grow. The main job of the logic interpreter is finding all possible logical deductions within the database and adding them to the database.

This method of answering queries is bottom-up evaluation. The bottom-up approach has the advantage that it is simple and clearly exhaustive. In contrast, the termination of top-down inference for Datalog (and therefore for Binder) requires tabling, which can give rise to subtle issues [20, 7]. Moreover, bottom-up evaluation immediately offers a convenient memoizing capability. Although bottom-up evaluation can require more time and space than top-down evaluation, we believe that bottom-up evaluation is practical for our application.

The basic operation of the logic interpreter is as for BLF except for term normalization. The interpreter repeatedly examines the database and systematically attempts to apply every term to every other term. If the application succeeds, then the new result is normalized and added to the database and the process repeats. Normalization is done in a module that applies the rules for CiC using code borrowed from Coq.

Although the logic interpreter always terminates on pure Datalog policies, it need not terminate on policies that make a non-trivial use of CiC. Infinite loops may happen when applying one dependent type to another results in a more complicated type. Fortunately, we have not seen this behavior in practice. Moreover, it should be possible to define a syntactic restriction that guarantees termination. We have such a restriction in BLF, and believe that we know how to port it to BCiC if it proves necessary.

6 Other System Modules

This section describes the cryptography module and the network module in more detail.

6.1 The Cryptography Module

The cryptography module is based on Xavier Leroy's library for OCaml, `cryptokit`, a library that provides cryptographic primitives. We use these primitives for generating keys, for signing, and for verifying signatures. We rely on RSA signatures with a key length of 1024 bits, and we apply SHA-1 hashing before signing. Each signed logical statement is accompanied by public-key information about the signer. Verifying that Alice signs statement X leads to an entry in the fact database, with the formula `Alice says X`. We serialize and deserialize statements using the `Marshal` standard library functions of OCaml.

When keys are not managed securely, the integrity of every signature is suspect. Therefore, following standard practices, we store secret keys in encrypted form, keyed to the hash of a passphrase supplied by the user. We use AES encryption and SHA-1 hashes for storing secret RSA keys.

6.2 The Network Module

The network module is only in charge of communicating signed statements between hosts, not determining their logical meaning. When new statements become available, the logic inference module must decide how they are to be interpreted. When the logic inference algorithm adds new unquoted conclusions (that is, formulas without `says`) to the database, the cryptography module creates new signatures and stores them in the database, and the network module communicates them to other hosts.

Network communication is done using TCP/IP connections on a specific port. Users may leave a Unix daemon running at all times waiting for connections, if they wish. When two BCiC nodes connect, they follow a protocol to decide which statements are known to one and not the other. These statements are then transmitted over the connection. Connections can be scheduled to occur automatically with randomly chosen partners at regular intervals, or can be requested manually by users. Full-time servers may run the daemon and automatically communicate with one another, while individual client machines may rather connect to the nearest server sporadically at a user's request.

The most interesting aspect of the network module is the algorithm for coordinating updates. When nodes connect, they must decide who has new statements that need to be transmitted. Simply transmitting all the statements at every connection would be tremendously inefficient. A slightly more realistic possibility is a naive protocol in which each node hashes every statement in its database and communicates the entire set of hashes to the other node. Then it is easy for each node to decide which statements it must send. If n is the total number of statements known by both sides, then the naive protocol takes $O(n)$ steps per synchronization.

The naive protocol is likely not to be efficient enough in the long run. The size of the fact databases will steadily increase over time, if nothing else because expiration and revocation are rare (and they are not even modeled explicitly in the logic, although the implementation deals with them). More specifically, we may estimate the performance of the naive protocol as follows. A large library may be composed of several hundred functions. The library provider may wish to declare some functions correct by assertion and to verify other, simpler functions. One way to do this is for the library provider to sign assertions for each of the functions separately. As new versions of library functions become available, new statements will be generated. A fairly typical Linux operating system in our lab currently uses 652 libraries and 2777 applications. If every library requires 100 statements and releases 10 major versions a year, with each version containing 10 function updates, and every application releases 10 new versions a year, then the database will initially contain 67977 statements and will increase by 92970 statements each year. After two years the naive protocol will be exchanging 5 Mb at each connection. Even if one reduces the number of statements at the expense of statement size by signing one large conjunction that contains statements for all the functions in a library release, the protocol will still be exchanging 2.7 Mb at each connection after two years.

There are many possible solutions to the synchronization problem. It is not too hard to imagine methods that record timestamps or remember which facts have already been communicated to other servers. We chose to implement a recursive divide-and-conquer protocol that does not require any extra storage outside the databases themselves. It is asymptotically efficient for small updates between large databases.

Our approach requires that every statement in every database be hashed and stored sorted by hash value. Our protocol synchronizes ranges of hash values between two databases. To synchronize two entire databases, the protocol is performed over the entire range of possible hash values. To synchronize all hash values between L and H, first both participants extract all hash values in their databases between L and H. Each list is encoded and hashed, then exchanged between the participants. A special token is used to represent the hash of the empty list. If the hash values agree, then both databases are already synchronized and the protocol terminates. If one hash is nonempty and one is empty, then the protocol terminates and the participant with the nonempty list knows they must transfer the contents of the list. If both hashes are nonempty and differ, then the range of hash values is split into two equal subranges, L to M and M to H. The protocol is then applied recursively on these two subranges. (We could also use more than two subranges, of course.) If n is the total number of statements known by both sides, and m is the maximum number of statements known by one side that are not known by the other, then an update takes $O(m \log n)$ steps.

Transmitting one large batch of data is often much faster than performing several rounds of communication to determine which parts of the data should be sent. By communicating the number of statements that were hashed at each exchange, the implementation can switch to the naive protocol when the number falls beneath a threshold. In experiments we found the optimal threshold to be approximately 1200 children for connections between computers in our lab and a laptop off campus. The network module of BCiC uses the naive protocol on databases of size 1200 or smaller, and uses the recursive protocol on larger databases.

7 Integrating BCiC with the Open Verifier

The Open Verifier [6] supports verifying untrusted code using modular verifiers. Programs are expressed in a low-level assembly language with formally specified semantics. Code producers may provide verification modules for creating proofs of code safety on demand, rather than actual proofs. Figure 1 illustrates the workings of the Open Verifier. The code, verifier extension module, and metadata on the right are untrusted and provided by the code producer. The trusted components on the left (the fixpoint module, post-condition generator, and checker) communicate with the untrusted verifier extension in order to generate a conjunction of invariants with proofs.

In this section we explain how BCiC can be connected to the Open Verifier. We focus on what we have implemented: a scheme in which the Open Verifier can call BCiC. We also discuss, more briefly, a scheme in which BCiC can call the Open Verifier.

7.1 The Open Verifier Calling BCiC

Supplementing the Open Verifier with BCiC makes verification with plug-in verifiers even more flexible. Instead of requiring that verifiers be able to prove code safety absolutely, we allow the verifiers to use assumptions that are trusted because they have been asserted by trusted authorities. This arrangement might be necessary for difficult safety properties. It also allows a verifier to prove something different than required if there is a trusted assumption that says that the property proved implies the required property. In particular, the verifier may do a "proof by typechecking": it may typecheck a program, and a trusted assumption may declare that typechecked programs are safe.

In the normal operation of the Open Verifier, the fixpoint module collects invariants that must be verified. First the fixpoint module supplies an initial invariant to the post-condition generator. The strongest post-condition is calculated and then passed to the untrusted verifier extension, which responds with weaker invariants and proofs that they are indeed weaker. These proofs are checked using Coq by the checker module. The weaker invariants are collected in the fixpoint module, which continues to calculate a fixpoint of invariants by possibly sending more invariants back to the post condition generator.

The connection between BCiC and the Open Verifier affects the communication between the post-condition generator, the untrusted verifier extension, and the checker. We have integrated BCiC so that when the Open Verifier decides that it needs justification for a weaker invariant, instead of the Open Verifier asking the extension directly, BCiC first checks its database of facts. If the statement already appears in the database, then the extension is never queried and the Open Verifier continues as if the justification were received. If the statement is not in the database, then the extension is asked for the justification as usual.

This scheme allows the BCiC database to short-circuit the interactive proof protocol at any point. Untrusted code can be asserted to be safe without any proof. In this case there must be an entry in the BCiC database that corresponds to the first query that the Open Verifier provides to the extension. In particular, this scheme handles "proofs by typechecking". When the extension can verify that the code typechecks but cannot justify the soundness of the typechecking rules, the soundness lemmas can appear in the BCiC database.

7.2 BCiC Calling the Open Verifier

Currently the Open Verifier is limited to verifying a single, generic memory-safety property. This focus is reasonable in light of current verification techniques, but allowing signatures opens the door to handling other properties. BCiC can support reasoning about those properties, calling the Open Verifier when appropriate.

For this purpose, we envision a mechanism whereby the conclusions of the Open Verifier can be used as new facts in the BCiC database. More specifically, the conclusions of the Open Verifier are represented as logical facts in BCiC, with a new predicate verified. We are currently refining our design and implementation of this scheme, and a mechanism for running programs subject to BCiC policies.

8 Conclusion

In this paper we describe BCiC, a system for reasoning about code that can combine proofs of code properties and assertions from trusted authorities. We present the underlying logic, show the architecture of the system itself, and describe our method of integration with the Open Verifier. Going from an abstract logic to an actual system requires a fair amount of work and a number of significant design choices. Although our system is still experimental, we believe that it shows one possible avenue for progress in code authentication and verification.

So far we have used BCiC for experimenting with small programs created to exercise various features of theorem provers. Perhaps the most important remaining work is to apply BCiC to large, useful programs. Clearly BCiC can handle those programs—at least in uninteresting ways—since it subsumes technologies that scale well (typechecking, public-key digital signatures). Going further, it would also be interesting to deploy the system in an environment where many users may place different amounts of trust in many programs. This deployment would allow more experimentation with policies and would test the effectiveness of the network protocol.

Acknowledgments

Thanks to George Necula for helpful discussions and allowing us access to the source code of the Open Verifier. Thanks to Katia Hayati and Bogdan Warinschi for providing feedback on early drafts of this paper. This work was supported in part by the National Science Foundation under Grants CCR-0204162 and CCR-0208800.

References

1. Andrew W. Appel. Foundational proof-carrying code. In *Proceedings of the 16th Annual Symposium on Logic in Computer Science*, pages 247–258, June 2001.
2. Andrew W. Appel and Edward W. Felten. Proof-carrying authentication. In *Proceedings of the 5th ACM Conference on Computer and Communications Security*, pages 52–62, November 1999.
3. Andrew W. Appel and Amy P. Felty. A semantic model of types and machine instructions for proof-carrying code. In *Proceedings of the 27th Annual ACM SIGPLAN-SIGACT Symposium on Principles of Programming Languages*, pages 243–253, January 2000.
4. Lujo Bauer, Michael A. Schneider, and Edward W. Felten. A general and flexible access-control system for the Web. In *Proceedings of the 11th USENIX Security Symposium 2002*, pages 93–108, 2002.
5. Yves Bertot and Pierre Castéran. *Interactive Theorem Proving and Program Development*. Springer, 2004.
6. Bor-Yuh Evan Chang, Adam Chlipala, George C. Necula, and Robert R. Schneck. The Open Verifier framework for foundational verifiers. In *Proceedings of the 2005 ACM SIGPLAN International Workshop on Types in Language Design and Implementation (TLDI)*, pages 1–12, 2005.
7. W. Chen and D. S. Warren. Tabled evaluation with delaying for general logic programs. *Journal of the ACM*, 43(1):20–74, January 1996.
8. Thierry Coquand and Gérard Huet. The calculus of constructions. *Information and Computation*, 76(2/3):95–120, 1988.
9. A. Demers, D. Greene, C. Hauser, W. Irish, J. Larson, S. Shenker, H. Sturgis, D. Swinehart, and D. Terry. Epidemic algorithms for replicated database maintenance. In *Proceedings of the Sixth Symposium on Principles of Distributed Computing*, pages 1–12, August 1987.
10. John DeTreville. Binder, a logic-based security language. In *Proceedings of the 2002 IEEE Symposium on Security and Privacy*, pages 105–113, May 2002.
11. ECMA. Standard ECMA-335: Common Language Infrastructure, December 2001. Available on-line at: http://msdn.microsoft.com/net/ecma/.
12. Jean-Yves Girard, Paul Taylor, and Yves Lafont. *Proofs and Types*. Cambridge University Press, 1990. http://nick.dcs.qmul.ac.uk/ pt/stable/Proofs+Types.html.
13. Robert Harper, Furio Honsell, and Gordon Plotkin. A framework for defining logics. *Journal of the ACM*, 40(1):143–184, 1993.
14. JoAnne Holliday, Robert C. Steinke, Divyakant Agrawal, and Amr El Abbadi. Epidemic algorithms for replicated databases. *IEEE Transactions on Knowledge Data Engineering*, 15(5):1218–1238, 2003.

15. Sebastian Lange, Brian LaMacchia, Matthew Lyons, Rudi Martin, Brian Pratt, and Greg Singleton. *.NET Framework Security*. Addison Wesley, 2002.
16. Eunyoung Lee and Andrew W. Appel. Policy-enforced linking of untrusted components. In *Proceedings of the 11th ACM SIGSOFT Symposium on Foundations of Software Engineering*, pages 371–374, September 2003.
17. T. Lindholm and F. Yellin. *The Java^{TM} Virtual Machine Specification*. Addison Wesley, 1997.
18. George C. Necula. Proof-carrying code. In *Proceedings of the 24th ACM SIGPLAN-SIGACT Symposium on Principles of Programming Languages (POPL'97)*, pages 106–119, 1997.
19. George C. Necula and Robert R. Schneck. A sound framework for untrusted verification-condition generators. In *Proceedings of the 18th Annual IEEE Symposium on Logic in Computer Science*, pages 248–260, July 2003.
20. P. Rao, K. Sagonas, T. Swift, D. S. Warren, and J. Freire. XSB: A system for efficiently computing well-founded semantics. In *Proceedings of the 4th International Conference on Logic Programming and Nonmonotonic Reasoning*, volume 1265 of *Lecture Notes in Artificial Intelligence*, pages 430–440, Berlin, July 1997. Springer.
21. The Coq Development Team. The Coq proof assistant. http://coq.inria.fr/.
22. Nathan Whitehead, Martín Abadi, and George Necula. By reason and authority: A system for authorization of proof-carrying code. In *Proceedings of the 17th IEEE Computer Security Foundations Workshop*, pages 236–250, June 2004.

Appendix

This appendix contains Figures 2 through 5. These figures provide details of the formal syntax and semantics of BCiC. Some additional background and informal explanations can be found with the formal presentation of BLF [22].

⟨var, rsvar, termvar, cicvar⟩ ::= ⟨identifier⟩

⟨policy⟩ ::= [⟨dform⟩.]⁺

⟨predicate⟩ ::= ⟨identifier⟩

⟨principal⟩ ::= ⟨key⟩ | ⟨var⟩

⟨argument⟩ ::= ⟨identifier⟩ | ⟨key⟩ | ⟨var⟩ | ⟨expr⟩
   | ⟨ruleset⟩

⟨ruleset⟩ ::= ⟨rsvar⟩ | ⟨actualruleset⟩ | ⟨rsvar⟩; ⟨ruleset⟩

⟨actualruleset⟩ ::= ruleset ([⟨identifier⟩ : ⟨lfterm⟩.]*)

⟨expr⟩ ::= ⟨termvar⟩ | ⟨cicvar⟩ | type | set | prop | ⟨expr⟩ ⟨expr⟩
   | ⟨expr⟩ → ⟨expr⟩ | {⟨cicvar⟩ : ⟨expr⟩} ⟨expr⟩
   | [⟨cicvar⟩ : ⟨expr⟩] ⟨expr⟩

⟨gform⟩ ::= ⟨atomic⟩ | ⟨gform⟩, ⟨gform⟩ | ⟨gform⟩; ⟨gform⟩
   | exists ⟨var⟩ ⟨gform⟩
   | existrules ⟨rsvar⟩ : ⟨rulesettype⟩ ⟨gform⟩
   | existsobj ⟨termvar⟩ : ⟨expr⟩ ⟨gform⟩
   | use ⟨ruleset⟩ in ⟨gform⟩ end

⟨dform⟩ ::= ⟨atomic⟩ | ⟨dform⟩, ⟨dform⟩
   | ⟨dform⟩ :- ⟨gform⟩ | forall ⟨var⟩ ⟨dform⟩
   | forallrules ⟨rsvar⟩ : ⟨rulesettype⟩ ⟨dform⟩
   | forallobj ⟨termvar⟩ : ⟨expr⟩ ⟨dform⟩
   | use ⟨ruleset⟩ in ⟨dform⟩ end

⟨atomic⟩ ::= [⟨principal⟩ says] sat(⟨expr⟩)
   | [⟨principal⟩ says] believe(⟨expr⟩)
   | [⟨principal⟩ says] ⟨predicate⟩
     ([⟨argument⟩ [, ⟨argument⟩]*])

⟨rulesettype⟩ ::= [⟨identifier⟩ [, ⟨identifier⟩]*]

Fig. 2. Syntax

$$[A, B]_R = [A]_R, [B]_R$$
$$[A; B]_R = [A]_R; [B]_R$$
$$[D \text{ :- } G]_R = [D]_R \text{ :- } [G]_R$$
$$[\texttt{forall } x \ D]_R = \texttt{forall } x \ [D]_R$$
$$[\texttt{exists } x \ G]_R = \texttt{exists } x \ [G]_R$$
$$[\texttt{forallrules } r : T \ D]_R = \texttt{forallrules } r : T \ [D]_R$$
$$[\texttt{existsrules } r : T \ G]_R = \texttt{existsrules } r : T \ [G]_R$$
$$[\texttt{forallobj } x : T \ D]_R = \texttt{forallobj}' \ R \ x : T \ [D]_R$$
$$[\texttt{existsobj } x : T \ G]_R = \texttt{existsobj}' \ R \ x : T \ [G]_R$$
$$[\texttt{use } R' \texttt{ in } A \texttt{ end}]_R = [A]_{R;R'}$$
$$[P \texttt{ says } X]_R = P \texttt{ says } [X]_R$$
$$[\texttt{sat}(T)]_R = \texttt{sat}'(R, T)$$
$$[\texttt{believe}(T)]_R = \texttt{believe}'(R, T)$$
$$[\texttt{P}(\alpha_1, \alpha_2, \ldots, \alpha_n)]_R = \texttt{P}(\alpha_1, \alpha_2, \ldots, \alpha_n)$$

Fig. 3. Annotation function

⟨gform⟩ ::= ⟨atomic⟩ | ⟨gform⟩, ⟨gform⟩ | ⟨gform⟩; ⟨gform⟩
    | exists ⟨var⟩ ⟨gform⟩
    | existsrules ⟨rsvar⟩ : ⟨rulesettype⟩ ⟨gform⟩
    | existsobj' ⟨ruleset⟩ ⟨termvar⟩ : ⟨expr⟩ ⟨gform⟩

⟨dform⟩ ::= ⟨atomic⟩ | ⟨dform⟩, ⟨dform⟩
    | ⟨dform⟩ :- ⟨gform⟩ | forall ⟨var⟩ ⟨dform⟩
    | forallrules ⟨rsvar⟩ : ⟨rulesettype⟩ ⟨dform⟩
    | forallobj' ⟨ruleset⟩ ⟨termvar⟩ : ⟨expr⟩ ⟨dform⟩

⟨atomic⟩ ::= [⟨principal⟩ says] sat'(⟨ruleset⟩, ⟨expr⟩)
    | [⟨principal⟩ says] believe'(⟨ruleset⟩, ⟨expr⟩)
    | [⟨principal⟩ says] ⟨predicate⟩
        ([⟨argument⟩ [, ⟨argument⟩]*])

$\vdots$

Fig. 4. Internal syntax

$$\frac{}{A, \Gamma \Rightarrow \Delta, A} \quad A \text{ is atomic}$$

$$\frac{\phi(\Gamma) \Rightarrow \Delta}{\Gamma \Rightarrow \Delta} \quad \frac{\Gamma \Rightarrow \phi(\Delta)}{\Gamma \Rightarrow \Delta} \quad \phi \text{ is a permutation}$$

$$\frac{\Gamma \Rightarrow \Delta}{\Gamma, D \Rightarrow \Delta} \quad \frac{\Gamma \Rightarrow \Delta}{\Gamma \Rightarrow \Delta, G} \quad \frac{\Gamma, D, D \Rightarrow \Delta}{\Gamma, D \Rightarrow \Delta} \quad \frac{\Gamma \Rightarrow \Delta, G, G}{\Gamma \Rightarrow \Delta, G}$$

$$\frac{D_1, D_2, \Gamma \Rightarrow \Delta}{(D_1, D_2), \Gamma \Rightarrow \Delta} \quad \frac{\Gamma \Rightarrow \Delta, G_1 \quad \Gamma \Rightarrow \Delta, G_2}{\Gamma \Rightarrow \Delta, (G_1, G_2)}$$

$$\frac{\Gamma \Rightarrow \Delta, G \quad D, \Gamma \Rightarrow \Delta}{D \mathbin{:\text{-}} G, \Gamma \Rightarrow \Delta} \quad \frac{\Gamma \Rightarrow \Delta, G_1, G_2}{\Gamma \Rightarrow \Delta, (G_1; G_2)}$$

$$\frac{D[A/x], \texttt{forall } x\, D, \Gamma \Rightarrow \Delta}{\texttt{forall } x\, D, \Gamma \Rightarrow \Delta} \quad \frac{\Gamma \Rightarrow \Delta, \texttt{exists } x\, G, G[A/x]}{\Gamma \Rightarrow \Delta, \texttt{exists } x\, G}$$

$$\frac{D[O/x], \texttt{forallobj}'\, R\, x:T\, D, \Gamma \Rightarrow \Delta \quad R \vdash_{CiC} O:T}{\texttt{forallobj}'\, R\, x:T\, D, \Gamma \Rightarrow \Delta}$$

$$\frac{\Gamma \Rightarrow \Delta, \texttt{existsobj}'\, R\, x:T\, G, G[O/x] \quad R \vdash_{CiC} O:T}{\Gamma \Rightarrow \Delta, \texttt{existsobj}'\, R\, x:T.\, G}$$

$$\frac{D[R/r], \texttt{forallrules}\, r\, D, \Gamma \Rightarrow \Delta}{\texttt{forallrules}\, r\, D, \Gamma \Rightarrow \Delta} \quad \frac{\Gamma \Rightarrow \Delta, \texttt{existrules}\, r\, G, G[R/r]}{\Gamma \Rightarrow \Delta, \texttt{existrules}\, r\, G}$$

$$\frac{R \vdash_{CiC} O:T}{\Gamma \Rightarrow \Delta, \texttt{sat}'(R,T)} \quad \frac{\Gamma \Rightarrow \Delta, \texttt{sat}'(R, \{x:T\}B) \quad R \vdash_{CiC} O:T}{\Gamma \Rightarrow \Delta, \texttt{sat}'(R, B[O/x])}$$

$$\frac{\Gamma \Rightarrow \Delta, \texttt{believe}'(R,T), \texttt{sat}'(R,T)}{\Gamma \Rightarrow \Delta, \texttt{believe}'(R,T)}$$

$$\frac{\Gamma \Rightarrow \Delta, \texttt{believe}'(R, \{x:T\}B) \quad R \vdash_{CiC} O:T}{\Gamma \Rightarrow \Delta, \texttt{believe}'(R, B[O/x])}$$

$$\frac{\Gamma \Rightarrow \Delta, \texttt{sat}'(R, \{x:T\}B) \quad \Gamma \Rightarrow \Delta, \texttt{sat}'(R,T)}{\Gamma \Rightarrow \Delta, \texttt{sat}'(R,B)} \quad x \text{ does not occur in } B$$

$$\frac{\Gamma \Rightarrow \Delta, \texttt{believe}'(R, \{x:T\}B) \quad \Gamma \Rightarrow \Delta, \texttt{believe}'(R,T)}{\Gamma \Rightarrow \Delta, \texttt{believe}'(R,B)} \quad x \text{ does not occur in } B$$

$$\frac{\Gamma \Rightarrow \Delta, \texttt{sat}'(R,T')}{\Gamma \Rightarrow \Delta, \texttt{sat}'(R,T)} \quad T \text{ and } T' \text{ have the same normal form in ruleset } R$$

$$\frac{\Gamma \Rightarrow \Delta, \texttt{believe}'(R,T')}{\Gamma \Rightarrow \Delta, \texttt{believe}'(R,T)} \quad T \text{ and } T' \text{ have the same normal form in ruleset } R$$

Fig. 5. Proof rules

Ordered Resolution with Selection for $\mathcal{H}(@)$

Carlos Areces[1] and Daniel Gorín[2]

[1] LORIA INRIA Lorraine
areces@loria.fr
[2] Universidad de Buenos Aires
dgorin@dc.uba.ar

Abstract. The hybrid logic $\mathcal{H}(@)$ is obtained by adding nominals and the satisfaction operator @ to the basic modal logic. The resulting logic gains expressive power without increasing the complexity of the satisfiability problem, which remains within PSpace. A resolution calculus for $\mathcal{H}(@)$ was introduced in [5], but it did not provide strategies for ordered resolution and selection functions. Additionally, the problem of termination was left open.

In this paper we address both issues. We first define proper notions of admissible orderings and selection functions and prove the refutational completeness of the obtained ordered resolution calculus using a standard "candidate model" construction [10]. Next, we refine some of the nominal-handling rules and show that the resulting calculus is sound, complete and can only generate a finite number of clauses, establishing termination. Finally, the theoretical results were tested empirically by implementing the new strategies into HyLoRes [6,18], an experimental prototype for the original calculus described in [5]. Both versions of the prover were compared and we discuss some preliminary results.

1 Introduction

Modal logics are languages which offer relatively high expressive power, but which, unlike full classical first-order logic, have a decidable satisfiability problem [12] (deciding satisfiability for the basic modal logic is PSpace-complete). Traditional modal logics, though, suffer from some important expressive limitations: 1) they can't make explicit reference to concrete elements of the domain, and 2) they can't express equality between elements. Hybrid logics [11] are a family of extensions of classical modal logics that aim to solve these limitations by the introduction of nominals and special modal operators.

Intuitively, a nominal is a *name* for an element of a model even though, from a syntactic point of view, it behaves like a proposition symbol and can be used wherever the latter is acceptable. For instance, if i and j are nominals, and p is a proposition symbol, we can write formulas such as $i \wedge p \wedge \langle r \rangle (p \wedge [r]j)$. In this paper we will consider only the basic hybrid logic $\mathcal{H}(@)$, i.e., the extension of the basic modal logic with nominals and the satisfaction operator @, that allows the evaluation of a formula at a specific element of the model.

F. Baader and A. Voronkov (Eds.): LPAR 2004, LNAI 3452, pp. 125–141, 2005.
© Springer-Verlag Berlin Heidelberg 2005

Formally, the set of formulas of $\mathcal{H}(@)$ is defined with respect to a signature $\mathcal{S} = \langle \text{PROP}, \text{NOM}, \text{REL} \rangle$, where $\text{PROP} = \{p, q, r, \ldots\}$ (the proposition symbols), $\text{NOM} = \{i, j, k, \ldots\}$ (the nominals), and $\text{REL} = \{r_1, r_2, r_3, \ldots\}$ (the relation symbols) are infinite, enumerable, pairwise disjoint sets. $\text{ATOM} = \text{PROP} \cup \text{NOM}$ is the set of atomic symbols. Given a signature $\mathcal{S}$ the set of $\mathcal{H}(@)$-formulas over $\mathcal{S}$ is defined as:

$$\mathcal{H}(@) ::= a \mid \neg \varphi \mid \varphi \wedge \varphi' \mid \langle r \rangle \varphi \mid @_n \varphi$$

where $a \in \text{ATOM}$, $n \in \text{NOM}$, $r \in \text{REL}$ and $\varphi, \varphi' \in \mathcal{H}(@)$. The remaining standard operators ($\vee$, $\rightarrow$, $[r]$, etc.) are defined in the usual way.

Definition 1 (validity). *A hybrid model is a structure $M = \langle W, \{r^M \mid r \in \text{REL}\}, V \rangle$ where W is a non-empty set (the domain of the model, whose elements are called states), $r^M \subseteq W \times W$ is a binary relation for each $r \in \text{REL}$, $V(p) \subseteq W$ for each $p \in \text{PROP}$, and $V(n) = \{w\}$ for some $w \in W$ when $n \in \text{NOM}$.*

Given a hybrid model $M = \langle W, \{r^M \mid r \in \text{REL}\}, V \rangle$ and an element $w \in W$, the satisfiability relation $M, w \models \varphi$ (read "model M satisfies the formula φ at state w") is defined as follows:

$$\begin{aligned}
M, w &\models a & &\text{iff} & &w \in V(a), \ a \in \text{ATOM} \\
M, w &\models \neg \varphi & &\text{iff} & &M, w \not\models \varphi \\
M, w &\models \varphi_1 \wedge \varphi_2 & &\text{iff} & &M, w \models \varphi_1 \text{ and } M, w \models \varphi_2 \\
M, w &\models \langle r \rangle \varphi & &\text{iff} & &\text{exists } w' \in W \text{ such that } r^M(w, w') \text{ and } M, w' \models \varphi \\
M, w &\models @_n \varphi & &\text{iff} & &M, w' \models \varphi, \text{ with } w' \in V(n).
\end{aligned}$$

The logic $\mathcal{H}(@)$ introduces, through nominals and @, a weak notion of equality reasoning. For example, the formulas

$$\begin{aligned}
&@_i i & &\text{(reflexivity)}, \\
&@_i j \leftrightarrow @_j i & &\text{(symmetry)}, \\
&(@_i j \wedge @_j k) \rightarrow @_i k & &\text{(transitivity), and} \\
&@_i j \rightarrow (\varphi \leftrightarrow \varphi(i/j)) & &\text{(substitution by identicals)}
\end{aligned}$$

are tautologies of $\mathcal{H}(@)$. This notion is not present in the basic modal logic and it can be shown that $\mathcal{H}(@)$ is strictly more expressive [2]. Nevertheless, its satisfiability problem remains within PSpace [3].

The most successful automated theorem proving implementations for modal logics are based on the tableau method and much of their outstanding performance is due to the heavy use of several heuristics and refinements [8]. However, a number of these heuristics don't work or become rather involved when the underlying logic allows some form of equality. When nominals are added, the performance of the tableaux-based theorem provers is severely affected. In this scenario, it makes sense to investigate other kinds of algorithms. In particular, we will discuss resolution, the most successful automated theorem proving method for first-order logic with equality [10,9].

In [5] a resolution based calculus for $\mathcal{H}(@)$ is proposed. The formulation of the calculus that we will present takes formulas in *negation normal form*, i.e., the negation operator can only be applied to atoms[1]. As a consequence, both $\vee$ and $[\ ]$ become primitive symbols. Let $\mathcal{S} = \langle \mathsf{PROP}, \mathsf{NOM}, \mathsf{REL} \rangle$ be a signature, we define the set $\mathcal{H}^{\mathrm{NNF}}(@)$ as follows:

$$\mathcal{H}^{\mathrm{NNF}}(@) ::= a \mid \neg a \mid \varphi \vee \varphi' \mid \varphi \wedge \varphi' \mid \langle r \rangle \varphi \mid [r]\varphi \mid @_i\varphi$$

where $a \in \mathsf{ATOM}$, $r \in \mathsf{REL}$, $i \in \mathsf{NOM}$ and $\varphi, \varphi' \in \mathcal{H}^{\mathrm{NNF}}(@)$. We will call formulas of the form $@_i\varphi$, *@-formulas*. We will consider, from now on, only formulas of $\mathcal{H}^{\mathrm{NNF}}(@)$, unless the contrary is stated.

Like the resolution calculus for first-order logic, the hybrid resolution calculus works on sets of *clauses*. A clause, in this context, is a set of arbitrary $\mathcal{H}^{\mathrm{NNF}}(@)$ @-formulas. A clause represents the disjunction of its formulas, but there's no additional restriction regarding the form of the formulas (i.e., they do not need to be literals). It is worth noting that to allow only @-formulas in a clause is not an expressivity limitation in terms of satisfiability: a formula φ is satisfiable if and only if for an arbitrary nominal i not occurring in φ, $@_i\varphi$ is satisfiable.

Given a formula $\varphi \in \mathcal{H}^{\mathrm{NNF}}(@)$, we define $ClSet(\varphi) = \{\{@_i\varphi\}\}$, for i an arbitrary nominal not occurring in φ. We can now define $ClSet^*(\varphi)$ — the saturated set of clauses for φ — as the smallest set that includes $ClSet(\varphi)$ and is saturated under the rules of the resolution calculus $\mathbf{R}[\mathcal{H}^{\mathrm{NNF}}(@)]$ given in Figure 1, where $i, j \in \mathsf{NOM}$ and $p \in \mathsf{PROP}$.

$$(\wedge) \frac{Cl \cup \{@_i(\varphi_1 \wedge \varphi_2)\}}{\begin{array}{c} Cl \cup \{@_i\varphi_1\} \\ Cl \cup \{@_i\varphi_2\} \end{array}} \qquad (\vee) \frac{Cl \cup \{@_i(\varphi_1 \vee \varphi_2)\}}{Cl \cup \{@_i\varphi_1, @_i\varphi_2\}}$$

$$(\mathrm{RES}) \frac{Cl_1 \cup \{@_ip\} \quad Cl_2 \cup \{@_i\neg p\}}{Cl_1 \cup Cl_2}$$

$$([r]) \frac{Cl_1 \cup \{@_i[r]\varphi\} \quad Cl_2 \cup \{@_i\langle r \rangle j\}}{Cl_1 \cup Cl_2 \cup \{@_j\varphi\}} \qquad (\langle r \rangle) \frac{Cl \cup \{@_i\langle r \rangle \varphi\}}{\begin{array}{c} Cl \cup \{@_i\langle r \rangle j\} \\ Cl \cup \{@_j\varphi\} \end{array}} \text{ for a new } j \in \mathsf{NOM}$$

$$(@) \frac{Cl \cup \{@_i@_j\varphi\}}{Cl \cup \{@_j\varphi\}}$$

$$(\mathrm{SYM}) \frac{Cl \cup \{@_ij\}}{Cl \cup \{@_ji\}} \qquad (\mathrm{REF}) \frac{Cl \cup \{@_i\neg i\}}{Cl} \qquad (\mathrm{PAR}) \frac{Cl_1 \cup \{@_ij\} \quad Cl_2 \cup \{\varphi(j)\}}{Cl_1 \cup Cl_2 \cup \{\varphi(j/i)\}}$$

Fig. 1. The Resolution Calculus $\mathbf{R}[\mathcal{H}^{\mathrm{NNF}}(@)]$

We can group these rules according to their role. The $(\wedge)$, $(\vee)$ and $(@)$ rules handle formula simplification. The $(\langle r \rangle)$ rule does a mild skolemization, assigning a new name (through a new nominal) to an element of the model which was

---

[1] The restriction to formulas in negation normal form simplifies the definition of admissible orderings and selections functions, but it also have effects on the calculus as we can see in Figure 1 where the (RES) rule applies only to literals.

existentially quantified (through a diamond). The (RES) rule works like the resolution rule for first-order logic, while the ([r]) rule encodes a non-trivial unification plus a resolution step. Finally, the (SYM), (REF) and (PAR) rules are the standard set of rules for equality handling in (function free) first-order logic resolution [9].

The construction of $ClSet^*(\varphi)$ is a correct and complete algorithm to decide satisfiability for $\mathcal{H}^{\text{NNF}}(@)$ (and hence for $\mathcal{H}(@)$): φ is unsatisfiable if and only if the empty clause $\{\}$ is an element of $ClSet^*(\varphi)$ [5]. However, $ClSet^*(\varphi)$ might be an infinite set because each application of the $\langle r \rangle$-rule introduces a new nominal. Thus, there are formulas whose satisfiability this algorithm can't decide in a finite number of steps. In Section 4 we show how to turn this calculus into a decision method for $\mathcal{H}(@)$.

A standard technique to regulate the generation of clauses in resolution for first-order logic is called *ordered resolution with selection functions* [10]. The general idea is to establish certain conditions under which it is safe to *chose* a literal from each clause such that rules are to be applied to a clause only to eliminate its chosen literal. The ordered resolution calculus with selection functions is refutationally complete for first-order logic when an ordering $\succ$ with certain properties is used (see [10] for further details). In the following sections we develop similar strategies for $\mathbf{R}[\mathcal{H}^{\text{NNF}}(@)]$.

2 Ordered Hybrid Resolution with Selection Functions

In the context of resolution systems, an ordering between formulas is called *admissible* when it can be used in a calculus of ordered resolution, preserving refutational completeness. In this section we propose an ordered resolution calculus for $\mathcal{H}^{\text{NNF}}(@)$.

The following definitions are standard (see, e.g. [13]). A binary relation $\succ$ is called an *ordering* if it is transitive and irreflexive; if, additionally, for any two distinct elements x and y one of $x \succ y$ or $y \succ x$ holds, $\succ$ is said to be *total*. An ordering $\succ$ is called *well-founded* when there is no infinite chain $x_1 \succ x_2 \succ x_3 \ldots$. Let $\succ$ be an ordering between formulas, and let's indicate with $\varphi[\psi]_p$ a formula φ where ψ appears at position p. We say that $\succ$ has the *subformula property* if $\varphi[\psi]_p \succ \psi$ whenever $\varphi[\psi]_p \neq \psi$, and that it is a *rewrite ordering* when $\varphi[\psi_1]_p \succ \varphi[\psi_2]_p$ iff $\psi_1 \succ \psi_2$. A well-founded rewrite ordering is called a *reduction ordering*, and if it also has the subformula property, it is called a *simplification ordering*. We will use the same symbol to denote both an ordering on formulas and its standard extension to clauses.

We can now define the notion of admissible ordering for resolution on $\mathcal{H}^{\text{NNF}}(@)$.

Definition 2 (admissible ordering). *An ordering $\succ$ over $\mathcal{H}^{\text{NNF}}(@)$ is admissible if it is a total simplification ordering satisfying the following conditions for all $\varphi, \psi \in \mathcal{H}^{\text{NNF}}(@)$ and all $i, j \in \mathsf{NOM}$:*

A1) $\varphi \succ i$ *for all* $\varphi \notin \mathsf{NOM}$
A2) if $\varphi \succ \psi$*, then* $@_i\varphi \succ @_j\psi$

A3) if $\langle r \rangle i$ is a proper subformula of φ, then $\varphi \succ \langle r \rangle j$
A4) $[\,]i \succ \langle\,\rangle j$.

Condition A1 states that nominals must be smaller than formulas other than nominals, condition A2 requires the operator @ not to affect the ordering among formulas, condition A3 introduces a very weak notion of structural complexity, while condition A4 prioritizes $[\,]$ over $\langle\,\rangle$.

It is easy to show that the conditions in Definition 2 are not too restrictive, and that there actually exists orderings satisfying them. A standard method for building simplification orderings is by using the *lexicographic path orderings* ($\succ_{lpo}$), (see [13] for a definition), which is defined given a set of operators O and an ordering $>$ on O (the precedence), over the set of well formed terms $T(O)$. When the ordering $>$ is well-founded (and total), then $\succ_{lpo}$ is a (total) simplification ordering.

In this context, since we will define an ordering based on lpo, it will be convenient to treat @, $\langle\,\rangle$ and $[\,]$ as binary operators: $@(\cdot,\cdot) : \mathcal{H}^{\text{NNF}}(@) \times \text{NOM} \to \mathcal{H}^{\text{NNF}}(@)^2$, $\langle\,\rangle(\cdot,\cdot) : \text{REL} \times \mathcal{H}^{\text{NNF}}(@) \to \mathcal{H}^{\text{NNF}}(@)$ and $[\,](\cdot,\cdot) : \text{REL} \times \mathcal{H}^{\text{NNF}}(@) \to \mathcal{H}^{\text{NNF}}(@)$ but we will keep the notation $@_n \varphi$, $\langle r \rangle \varphi$ and $[r] \varphi$.

We give the following constructive definition of an admissible ordering based on lpo over the set $O = \text{PROP} \cup \text{NOM} \cup \text{REL} \cup \{\neg, \wedge, \vee, @, \langle\,\rangle, [\,]\}$ with the obvious arities (note that $\mathcal{H}^{\text{NNF}}(@) \subset T(O)$).

Definition 3. *Given a hybrid signature* $\mathcal{S} = \langle \{p_i \mid i \in \mathbb{N}\}, \{n_i \mid i \in \mathbb{N}\}, \{r_i \mid i \in \mathbb{N}\}\rangle$, *let* O *be the set* $\mathcal{S} \cup \{\neg, \wedge, \vee, @, [\,], \langle\,\rangle\}$, *and define the precedence relation* $> \subseteq O \times O$ *as the transitive closure of the set*

$$\{(@, \neg), (\neg, \wedge), (\wedge, \vee), (\vee, [\,]), ([\,], \langle\,\rangle)\} \cup$$
$$\{(\langle\,\rangle, r_i), (r_i, p_j), (p_j, n_k) \mid i, j, k \in \mathbb{N}\} \cup$$
$$\{(r_i, r_j), (p_i, p_j), (n_i, n_j) \mid i > j\}.$$

By definition, $>$ *is total, irreflexive and well-founded. Let* $\succ_{lpo}$ *be the lpo over* $\mathcal{H}^{\text{NNF}}(@)$ *that uses* $>$ *as precedence. It follows that* $\succ_{lpo}$ *must be a total simplification ordering. Finally, define* $\succ_h$ *as*

$$\varphi \succ_h \psi \text{ iff } \begin{cases} size(\varphi) > size(\psi), \text{ or} \\ size(\varphi) = size(\psi) \text{ and } \varphi \succ_{lpo} \psi \end{cases}$$

where $size(\varphi)$ *is the number of operators in* φ.

Proposition 1. $\succ_h$ *is an admissible ordering.*

Observe that no admissible ordering can be defined using lpo alone. It suffices to note that there's no way to guarantee $\langle r' \rangle \langle r \rangle i \succ_{lpo} \langle r \rangle j$ when $r \succ_{lpo} r'$ and $j \succ_{lpo} i$, which violates A3. Unless stated otherwise, from now on we will use $\succ$ to refer to some arbitrary but fixed admissible ordering.

---
[2] The order of the parameters of this operator has been chosen to simplify Definition 3 and the proof of Proposition 1.

$$(\wedge) \; \frac{Cl \cup \{@_i(\varphi_1 \wedge \varphi_2)\}}{\begin{array}{c} Cl \cup \{@_i\varphi_1\} \\ Cl \cup \{@_i\varphi_2\} \end{array}} \qquad (\vee) \; \frac{Cl \cup \{@_i(\varphi_1 \vee \varphi_2)\}}{Cl \cup \{@_i\varphi_1, @_i\varphi_2\}}$$

$$(\text{RES}) \; \frac{Cl_1 \cup \{@_ip\} \quad Cl_2 \cup \{@_i\neg p\}}{Cl_1 \cup Cl_2}$$

$$([r]) \; \frac{Cl_1 \cup \{@_i[r]\varphi\} \quad Cl_2 \cup \{@_i\langle r\rangle j\}}{Cl_1 \cup Cl_2 \cup \{@_j\varphi\}} \qquad (\langle r \rangle) \; \frac{Cl \cup \{@_i\langle r\rangle \varphi\}}{\begin{array}{c} Cl \cup \{@_i\langle r\rangle j\} \\ Cl \cup \{@_j\varphi\} \end{array}} \; \begin{array}{l} \text{for a new } j \in \mathsf{NOM} \\ \text{and } \varphi \notin \mathsf{NOM} \end{array}$$

$$(@) \; \frac{Cl \cup \{@_i@_j\varphi\}}{Cl \cup \{@_j\varphi\}} \qquad (\text{REF}) \; \frac{Cl \cup \{@_i\neg i\}}{Cl}$$

$$(\text{SYM}) \; \frac{Cl \cup \{@_j i\}}{Cl \cup \{@_{ij}\}} \; \text{if } i \succ j \qquad (\text{PAR}) \; \frac{Cl_1 \cup \{@_j i\} \quad Cl_2 \cup \{\varphi(j)\}}{Cl_1 \cup Cl_2 \cup \{\varphi(j/i)\}} \; \begin{array}{l} \text{if } j \succ i \text{ and} \\ \varphi(j) \succ @_j i \end{array}$$

Restrictions: Assume an admissible ordering $\succ$ and a selection function S. In the following, φ and ψ are the formulas explicitly displayed in the rules. The main premise of each rule is the rightmost, the other premise (in rules with two premises) is the side premise.

- If $C = C' \cup \{\varphi\}$ is the main premise, then either $S(C) = \{\varphi\}$ or, $S(C) = \emptyset$ and $\{\varphi\} \succ C'$.
- If $D = D' \cup \{\psi\}$ is the side premise, then $\{\psi\} \succ D'$ and $S(D) = \emptyset$.

Fig. 2. The Resolution Calculus $\mathbf{R}^{\text{OS}}[\mathcal{H}^{\text{NNF}}(@)]$

Finally, in resolution for first-order logic, a selection function may chose only negative literals from a clause. As we work with clauses which can contain arbitrary @-formulas from $\mathcal{H}^{\text{NNF}}(@)$ we define "negative literals" as the complement of the set PLIT of positive literals, where PLIT ::= $@_ij \mid @_ip \mid @_i\langle r\rangle j$, for $i, j \in \mathsf{NOM}$, $p \in \mathsf{PROP}$ and $r \in \mathsf{REL}$.

Definition 4 (selection function). *A function S from clauses to clauses is a selection function if and only if, for every clause C we have $S(C) \subseteq C$, $|S(C)| \leq 1$ and $S(C) \cap \mathsf{PLIT} = \emptyset$.*

We are now ready to formulate the strategy of ordered resolution with selection functions for $\mathcal{H}^{\text{NNF}}(@)$. Figure 2 contains the rules of the calculus.

The rules of $\mathbf{R}^{\text{OS}}[\mathcal{H}^{\text{NNF}}(@)]$ differ from the ones in Figure 1 only in the addition of some restrictions, both local (in the ($\langle r \rangle$), (SYM) and (PAR) rules) and global. Notice that, as an effect of the global restrictions, there is only one formula in each clause that may be involved in an inference. We will call this formula the *distinguished formula* of the clause.

3 Refutational Completeness of $\mathbf{R}^{\text{OS}}[\mathcal{H}^{\text{NNF}}(@)]$

The standard proof of refutational completeness for first-order logic resolution is via the generation of potential Herbrand models [10]. In this section we start by showing that an appropriate notion of Herbrand model can be defined for hybrid languages containing nominals and @.

The following result was established in [20] for CPDL a version of PDL (Propositional Dynamic Logic [17]) extended with hybrid operators, but it holds for any hybrid logics containing nominals and @. For N a hybrid model, let $\text{diag}(N)$, the *diagram of N*, be the set $\text{diag}(N) = \{\varphi \mid \varphi \in \text{PLIT and } N \models \varphi\} \cup \{\neg\varphi \mid \varphi \in \text{PLIT and } N \not\models \varphi\}$, and call a model *named* if each state of its domain satisfies at least one nominal.

Theorem 1 (Scott's Isomorphism Theorem). *Let M and N be two countable, named hybrid models. Then M and N are isomorphic iff $M \models \text{diag}(N)$.*

Based on Theorem 1 we can define hybrid Herbrand models as follows:

Definition 5 (Herbrand model). *Let $\mathcal{S} = \langle \text{PROP}, \text{NOM}, \text{REL} \rangle$ be a hybrid signature. A hybrid Herbrand model for $\mathcal{H}(@)$ over $\mathcal{S}$ is any set $I \subseteq \text{PLIT}$.*

We identify a Herbrand model with a set of positive literals. This set will uniquely define certain hybrid model.

Definition 6. *Given a hybrid Herbrand model I, let $\sim_I$ be the minimum equivalence relation over NOM that extends the set $\{(i,j) \mid @_i j \in I\}$. We now define the hybrid model uniquely determined by I as $\langle W^I, \{r^I \mid r \in \text{REL}\}, V^I \rangle$ where*

$$\begin{aligned} W^I &= \text{NOM}/{\sim_I} \\ r^I &= \{([j],[k]) \mid @_j \langle r \rangle k \in I\} \\ V^I(p) &= \{[j] \mid @_j p \in I\}, p \in \text{PROP} \\ V^I(i) &= \{[i]\}, i \in \text{NOM}. \end{aligned}$$

where $\text{NOM}/{\sim_I}$ is the set consisting of equivalence classes of $\sim_I$, and $[i]$ is the equivalence class assigned to i by $\sim_I$.

From now on, we will not distinguish between a hybrid Herbrand model I and its associated model. We will say, for instance, that a formula $@_i \varphi$ is true in I whenever it is satisfied by its associated model (as we are always referring to @-formulas no explicit point of evaluation is needed).

The following theorem (easily proved using Theorem 1) shows that we can work with Herbrand models instead of arbitrary models.

Theorem 2. *Given Γ, a set of @-formulas of $\mathcal{H}(@)$ over a signature $\mathcal{S} = \langle \text{PROP}, \text{NOM}, \text{REL} \rangle$, Γ has a hybrid model if and only if it has a hybrid Herbrand model over the signature $\mathcal{S}' = \langle \text{PROP}, \text{NOM} \cup \text{NOM}', \text{REL} \rangle$, where NOM' is a numerable set disjoint from NOM.*

We are now ready to prove the refutational completeness of $\mathbf{R}^{\text{OS}}[\mathcal{H}^{\text{NNF}}(@)]$. The idea is to build a candidate Herbrand model from an arbitrary (and potentially infinite) set of clauses, such that if the least clause of the set is not true under this model, then the calculus must allow the derivation of a new clause which will also fail to be true in the model. By definition, the empty clause is the smallest clause in any admissible ordering, and it can be shown that admissible orderings ensure that any consequent of a rule is smaller than the main premise. We will, thus, prove that the process leads to either the construction of a Herbrand model for the initial formula (i.e., the initial formula was satisfiable), or to the inclusion of the empty clause in the saturated set (i.e., the initial formula was unsatisfiable).

The definition of a candidate model given below is more complex than the one in [10]. This is because the latter was used for first-order logic without equality, while in $\mathcal{H}(@)$ we have to deal with equalities of the form $@_i j$.

Definition 7 (σ_I). *Given a hybrid Herbrand interpretation I, we define the following substitution of nominals by nominals:*

$$\sigma_I = \{i \mapsto j \mid i \sim_I j \land (\forall k)(k \sim_I j \rightarrow k \succeq j)\}.$$

σ_I substitutes each nominal with the least nominal of its class, which is taken as the class representative.

Definition 8. *We define the set of* simple *formulas of $\mathcal{H}^{\text{NNF}}(@)$ over S as:*

$$\mathsf{SIMP} ::= @_i j \ (\text{with } i \succ j) \mid @_i p \mid @_i \neg a \mid @_i \langle r \rangle j \mid @_i [r] \varphi$$

where $i, j \in \mathsf{NOM}$, $p \in \mathsf{PROP}$, $a \in \mathsf{ATOM}$, $r \in \mathsf{REL}$ and $\varphi \in \mathcal{H}^{\text{NNF}}(@)$.

Let N be a fixed set of clauses. The following three definitions must be taken as a unit. They are presented separately for clarity but are mutually recursive.

Definition 9 (I_C). *Let C be a clause (not necessarily in N), we name I_C the hybrid Herbrand interpretation given by $\bigcup_{C \succ D} \varepsilon_D$.*

Definition 10 (reduced form). *Let C be a clause and φ its maximal formula. If $\varphi \in \mathsf{SIMP}$ and either a) $\varphi \in \mathsf{PLIT}$ and $\varphi = \varphi \sigma_{I_C}$, or b) $\varphi = @_i[r]\psi$ and $i = i\sigma_{I_C}$; then we say that both φ and C are in* reduced form.

Definition 11 (ε_C). *Let C be a clause (not necessarily in N). If it simultaneously holds that: a) $C \in N$, b) C is in reduced form, c) The maximal formula in C is in PLIT, d) C is false under I_C, and e) $S(C) = \emptyset$; then $\varepsilon_C = \{\varphi\}$, where φ is the maximal formula in C; otherwise, ε_C is the empty set.*

We say that C produces φ if $\varepsilon_C = \{\varphi\}$ and call it a *productive clause*. I_C is the partial interpretation of N below C. Only those clauses whose maximal formula φ is a positive literal and have no selected formulas may be productive.

Definition 12 (candidate model). *I_N, a candidate model for N, is defined as $\bigcup_{C \in N} \varepsilon_C$.*

If a clause C is false under I, we say that C is a *counterexample* of I. Analyzing all the rules of the calculus and considering separately those distinguished formulas that are not in reduced form, the following result can be proved.

Proposition 2. *Let N be a set of clauses and $C \in N$ be the minimum counterexample of I_N, with respect to an admissible ordering $\succ$. If $C \neq \{\}$, then there exists an inference using one of the rules of the calculus such that:*

1. *C is the main premise*
2. *the side premise (when present) is productive*
3. *all the consequents are smaller, with respect to $\succ$, than C and at least one of them is a counterexample of I_N.*

Proof. Using Definition 2 we can easily check that every consequent in the calculus is smaller than the main premise of its inference. The hard part of the proof is to verify that a proper side premise (when required) exists.

Let φ be the distinguished formula of C. If $\varphi \notin$ SIMP, C is trivially the premise of some unary rule and the proposition holds. Now, suppose $\varphi \in$ SIMP is not in reduced form; this means that some clause D produces $@_i j$ for an i occurring in φ. It is easy to check that, in this case, (PAR) can be applied on D and C. Finally, if φ is in reduced form, it must be of the form $@_i \neg a$ (for $a \in$ ATOM) or $@_i[r]\psi$. The first case is handled either by the (REF) or the (RES) rules, and the proof is analogous to the standard one for first-order logic.

The latter case deserves more attention. The non-trivial part of the proof is to see that a clause in N must produce some $@_i\langle r\rangle j$ such that $@_j\psi$ is false in I_N; but this follows from the fact that C is a counterexample in reduced form and that, for any $k, l \in$ NOM, if $@_k l \in I_N$, then $l = k\sigma_{I_N}$.

Refutational completeness can be easily established from Proposition 2.

Theorem 3. $\mathbf{R}^{\mathrm{OS}}[\mathcal{H}^{\mathrm{NNF}}(@)]$ *is refutationally complete.*

4 Termination of the Calculus

In this section we show how the calculus $\mathbf{R}^{\mathrm{OS}}[\mathcal{H}^{\mathrm{NNF}}(@)]$ can be turned into a decision procedure for satisfiability. We will introduce the necessary changes to ensure that for any formula $\varphi \in \mathcal{H}(@)$, $\mathit{ClSet}^*(\varphi)$ is a finite set. If this condition holds, implementing an algorithm that computes $\mathit{ClSet}^*(\varphi)$ in finite time (e.g., the "given clause algorithm" [23]) is straightforward.

The calculus $\mathbf{R}[\mathcal{H}^{\mathrm{NNF}}(@)]$ of Figure 1 can trivially generate an infinite saturated set of clauses as the ($\langle r \rangle$) rule can be applied on formulas of the form $@_i \langle r \rangle j$ for $j \in$ NOM.[3] $\mathbf{R}^{\mathrm{OS}}[\mathcal{H}^{\mathrm{NNF}}(@)]$ avoids this behavior, but an infinite number of nominals can still be introduced by interaction between the ($[r]$), ($\langle r \rangle$) and (PAR) rules. As no other symbols but nominals are introduced during resolution, and given that formulas in consequent clauses are never larger (in number of operators) than those in the antecedent, if we can control the generation of nominals we will obtain termination.

---

[3] Actually, just repetitive application of the ($\langle r \rangle$) rule to the same clause can lead to the generation of an infinite set, but this can be easily avoided by ensuring that the rule is applied only once to each $\langle r \rangle$-formula in a clause.

There are essentially two ways in which an infinite number of nominals can be introduced by the rules of $\mathbf{R}^{\text{OS}}[\mathcal{H}^{\text{NNF}}(@)]$:

Type 1. A formula of the form $@_i \langle r \rangle \varphi$ introduces a new nominal which, in turn, contributes to the derivation of a new clause containing $@_i \langle r \rangle \varphi$. All new nominals are immediate successors of i and they are actually representing the same state in the model, but the calculus cannot detect it.

Type 2. There is a formula φ and an infinite sequence of distinct nominals $n_0, n_1, n_2, \ldots$ such that, for all $i \in \mathbb{N}$, some $@_{n_i} \langle r \rangle \varphi_i$ in the saturated set introduces, by way of the ($\langle r \rangle$) rule, the nominal n_{i+1}. The calculus is exploring a cycle in the model, and cannot detect when to stop the search.

For concrete examples, try the rules of $\mathbf{R}^{\text{OS}}[\mathcal{H}^{\text{NNF}}(@)]$ over the formulas $@_i([r](i \wedge (q \vee \langle r \rangle p)) \wedge \langle r \rangle p)$ and $@_i([r](i \wedge \langle r \rangle p) \wedge \langle r \rangle p)$ using any admissible ordering where i is the least nominal.

As we see, to obtain termination we need to impose some control on the way new nominals are generated by the ($\langle r \rangle$) rule, and on how chains of nominal successors are treated. Solving problems of Type 1 is relatively easy. The next proposition provides the key to the solution.

Proposition 3. *Let* $\varphi, \psi \in \mathcal{H}^{\text{NNF}}(@)$ *be such that* $\varphi[@_i \langle r \rangle \psi]_p$, *and let* $j \in \text{NOM}$ *not occur in* φ. *Then,* φ *is satisfiable iff* $\varphi[@_i \langle r \rangle \psi / (@_i \langle r \rangle j \wedge @_j \psi)]$ *is satisfiable.*

Notice that the proposition involves *simultaneous replacement* of all subformulas $@_i \langle r \rangle \psi$ in φ by $(@_i \langle r \rangle j \wedge @_j \psi)$. The ($\langle r \rangle$) rule instead, uses *a new nominal* in each application, even when applied to the same formula $@_i \langle r \rangle \psi$.

The solution to problems of Type 1 then is to define a function *nom* assigning a unique nominal to each formula $@_i \langle r \rangle \psi$ and redefine the ($\langle r \rangle$) rule with the help of *nom*. Solving problems of Type 2 is more involved, and it is here where the (PAR) rule plays an important role. We will see that we can use, also here, the function *nom* to our advantage.

Let's start by properly defining this function. We first differentiate between nominals which appear in the input formula and nominals generated by application of the ($\langle r \rangle$) rule. Let NOM_i (the set of *initial nominals*) and NOM_c (the set of *computation nominals*) be infinite sets such that $\text{NOM}_i \cap \text{NOM}_c = \{\}$ and $\text{NOM}_i \cup \text{NOM}_c = \text{NOM}$.

We additionally assume, without loss of generality, that $\text{NOM}_c = \bigcup_{k \in \mathbb{N}} N_c^k$, where the sets N_c^k are infinite, pairwise disjoint and well-ordered by $\succ$. And we impose the additional, mild condition on $\succ$ requiring $s \succ t$ whenever $s \in \text{NOM}_c^j$, $t \in \text{NOM}_c^k$ and $j > k$. These conditions will simplify the definition of *nom* and the proof of termination. From now on we assume that NOM_c and $\succ$ comply with these requirements.

Now, let $\mathcal{H}_i^{\text{NNF}}(@)$ be the subset of $\mathcal{H}^{\text{NNF}}(@)$ where only nominals in NOM_i occur and define

$$\mathcal{H}_{@\Diamond}^{\text{NNF}}(@) = \{@_i \langle r \rangle \varphi \mid i \in \text{NOM}, r \in \text{REL}, \varphi \in \mathcal{H}_i^{\text{NNF}}(@), \varphi \notin \text{NOM}\},$$

the set of those @-formulas of $\mathcal{H}^{\text{NNF}}(@)$ that can be the distinguished formula of a premise of the ($\langle r \rangle$) rule.

$$(\wedge) \frac{Cl \cup \{@_i(\varphi_1 \wedge \varphi_2)\}}{Cl \cup \{@_i\varphi_1\} \atop Cl \cup \{@_i\varphi_2\}} \qquad (\vee) \frac{Cl \cup \{@_i(\varphi_1 \vee \varphi_2)\}}{Cl \cup \{@_i\varphi_1, @_i\varphi_2\}}$$

$$(\text{RES}) \frac{Cl_1 \cup \{@_ip\} \quad Cl_2 \cup \{@_i \neg p\}}{Cl_1 \cup Cl_2}$$

$$([r]) \frac{Cl_1 \cup \{@_i[r]\varphi\} \quad Cl_2 \cup \{@_i\langle r\rangle s\}}{Cl_1 \cup Cl_2 \cup \{@_j\varphi\}} \qquad (\langle r\rangle') \frac{Cl \cup \{@_i\langle r\rangle \varphi\}}{Cl \cup \{@_i\langle r\rangle j\} \atop Cl \cup \{@_j\varphi\}} \begin{array}{l} \varphi \notin \text{NOM and} \\ j = nom^\succ(@_i\langle r\rangle\varphi) \end{array}$$

$$(@) \frac{Cl \cup \{@_i@_j\varphi\}}{Cl \cup \{@_j\varphi\}} \qquad (\text{REF}) \frac{Cl \cup \{@_i \neg i\}}{Cl} \qquad (\text{SYM}) \frac{Cl \cup \{@_ji\}}{Cl \cup \{@_ij\}} \text{ if } i \succ j$$

$$(\text{PAR}') \frac{Cl_1 \cup \{@_ji\} \quad Cl_2 \cup \{\varphi(j)\}}{Cl_1 \cup Cl_2 \cup \{\varphi(j/i)\}} \begin{array}{l} \text{if } j \succ i,\ \varphi(j) \succ @_ji,\ \text{and whenever} \\ \varphi(j) = @_k\langle r\rangle l,\ \text{then } l \in \text{NOM}_i,\ \text{or} \\ i \in \text{NOM}_i \text{ and } l = j \end{array}$$

$$(\text{PAR-@}\Diamond) \frac{Cl_1 \cup \{@_ji\} \quad Cl_2 \cup \{@_j\langle r\rangle k\}}{Cl_1 \cup Cl_2 \cup \{@_i\langle r\rangle l\} \atop Cl_1 \cup Cl_2 \cup \{@_kl\}} \begin{array}{l} \text{if } j \succ i \text{ and } k \in \text{NOM}_c,\ \text{and for} \\ \text{some } \varphi,\ k = nom^\succ(@_j\varphi),\ \text{and} \\ l = nom^\succ(@_i\varphi) \end{array}$$

Restrictions: Assume an admissible ordering $\succ$, a proper $nom^\succ$ function and a selection function S. In the following, φ and ψ are the formulas explicitly displayed in the rules. The main premise of each rule is the rightmost, the other premise (in rules with two premises) is the side premise.

- If $C = C' \cup \{\varphi\}$ is the main premise, then either $S(C) = \{\varphi\}$ or, $S(C) = \emptyset$ and $\{\varphi\} \succ C'$.
- If $D = D' \cup \{\psi\}$ is the side premise, then $\{\psi\} \succ D'$ and $S(D) = \emptyset$.

Fig. 3. The Resolution Calculus $\mathbf{R}_T^{OS}[\mathcal{H}^{\text{NNF}}(@)]$

Definition 13 ($nom^\succ$). *Given $\succ$ an admissible ordering, let $nom^\succ : \mathcal{H}^{\text{NNF}}_{@\Diamond}(@) \to \text{NOM}_c$ be any function such that*

1. *$nom^\succ$ is injective,*
2. *$i \succ j$ iff $nom^\succ(@_i\langle r\rangle \varphi) \succ nom^\succ(@_j\langle r\rangle \varphi)$, for any $i, j \in \text{NOM}_c$, and*
3. *for all $j \in \text{NOM}_c^i$ there exists a formula $@_k\langle r\rangle\varphi$ such that $j = nom^\succ(@_k\langle r\rangle\varphi)$ and, either $i = 0$ and $k \in \text{NOM}_i$, or else $k \in \text{NOM}_c^{i-1}$*

Condition 1) is required for soundness: we can use the same nominal for each $@_i\langle r\rangle\varphi$ formula, but no two different formulas in $\mathcal{H}^{\text{NNF}}_{@\Diamond}(@)$ should use the same nominal. Condition 2) is needed to guarantee refutational completeness. Finally, condition 3) avoids cycles (like in $i = nom^\succ(@_i\langle r\rangle\psi)$) and, more important, it is required in order to obtain a terminating calculus.

It can be easily shown that Definition 13 is not too restrictive; i.e., that it can be satisfied by a concrete function. For example, let n_φ be a new nominal for each formula $\varphi \in \mathcal{H}^{\text{NNF}}_{@\Diamond}(@)$ and make $n_\varphi = nom^\succ(\varphi)$.

Figure 3 shows the calculus $\mathbf{R}_T^{\mathrm{OS}}[\mathcal{H}^{\mathrm{NNF}}(@)]$ for which we will establish refutational completeness and termination. Notice that the $(\langle r \rangle)$ rule has been replaced by $(\langle r \rangle')$ which uses the $nom^\succ$ function to always assign the same nominal to a formula in $\mathcal{H}_{@\diamond}^{\mathrm{NNF}}$. The (PAR) rule has been replaced by two rules: (PAR') and (PAR-@◊). (PAR') is just a restriction of (PAR) which does not handle certain formulas of the form $@_i\langle r \rangle j$. Such formulas are treated in a special way by the (PAR-@◊) rule. The (PAR-@◊) rule deserves some explanation. The intuition behind this rule is the following: if j and i denote the same state in the model (as indicated by the distinguished formula $@_j i$ in the side premise) then, by Proposition 3, k and l can be taken to be equal too. However, by Definition 13, $k \succ l$ and, thus, l should be preferred over k.

We now proceed to discuss soundness, refutational completeness and termination of $\mathbf{R}_T^{\mathrm{OS}}[\mathcal{H}^{\mathrm{NNF}}(@)]$, starting with soundness:

Theorem 4. *If $\varphi \in \mathcal{H}_i^{\mathrm{NNF}}(@)$ is satisfiable, then $ClSet^*(\varphi)$ (closed by the rules of $R_T^{\mathrm{OS}}[\mathcal{H}^{\mathrm{NNF}}(@)]$) is satisfiable.*

Proof. The proof is based on the fact that, for any $\succ$ and $nom^\succ$, given a model for φ, we can build another model for φ but such that certain criteria of compatibility with $nom^\succ$ also holds. In essence, for M to be "compatible" with $nom^\succ$ the following conditions should hold:

- if $M \models @_i\langle r \rangle \psi$ and $j = nom^\succ(@_i\langle r \rangle \psi)$, then $M \models @_i\langle r \rangle j$, and $M \models @_j \psi$,
- if $k = nom^\succ(@_i\langle r \rangle \psi)$, $l = nom^\succ(@_j\langle r \rangle \psi)$ and $M \models @_i j$, then $M \models @_k l$.

In order to prove completeness, one should note that, by Definition 13, the consequents of the (PAR-@◊) rule are always smaller than the main premise. Using this fact, the proof of Theorem 2 is easily adapted (handling the $(\langle r \rangle')$ rule is straightforward).

Theorem 5. $R_T^{\mathrm{OS}}[\mathcal{H}^{\mathrm{NNF}}(@)]$ *is refutationally complete.*

We finally turn to the problem of proving that $\mathbf{R}_T^{\mathrm{OS}}[\mathcal{H}^{\mathrm{NNF}}(@)]$ doesn't generate infinite saturated sets. We are ready to exactly formulate conditions under which the problems of Type 1 and 2 we discussed above cannot occur. Let $\mathrm{NOM}(\varGamma)$ be the set of all nominals occurring in $\varGamma$, we want to establish that for all $\varphi \in \mathcal{H}_{@\diamond}^{\mathrm{NNF}}(@)$:

1. every set $\mathrm{NOM}_c^i \cap \mathrm{NOM}(ClSet^*(\varphi))$ is finite, for all $i \in \mathbb{N}$, and
2. the set $\{i \mid i \in \mathbb{N} \text{ and } \mathrm{NOM}_c^i \cap \mathrm{NOM}(ClSet^*(\varphi)) \neq \{\}\}$ is finite.

In the next proposition we show that these two conditions can be guaranteed.

Proposition 4. *Let $\varphi \in \mathcal{H}_i^{\mathrm{NNF}}(@)$, then the set of nominals in $ClSet^*(\varphi)$ computed using the rules in $R_T^{\mathrm{OS}}[\mathcal{H}^{\mathrm{NNF}}(@)]$ is finite.*

Proof. For any $i \in \mathrm{NOM}$, the function $level(i)$ is defined as 0 if $i \in \mathrm{NOM}_i$ or the only $n \geq 1$ such that $i \in \mathrm{NOM}_c^{n-1}$ otherwise. Now, given $@_i \varphi \in \mathcal{H}_i^{\mathrm{NNF}}(@)$ define $d'(@_i \varphi) = level(i) + d(\varphi)$ where $d(\varphi)$ is the modal depth of φ. The proof of the proposition directly follows from these properties:

1. For every clause $\{@_i\langle r\rangle j\} \cup C \in \mathit{ClSet}^*(\varphi)$, either $level(j) = 0$ or $level(j) = level(i) + 1$.
2. For all formula ψ occurring in $\mathit{ClSet}^*(\varphi)$, if some $i \in \mathsf{NOM}_c$ occurs in ψ, then ψ is of the form: $@_i\psi'$, $@_j\langle r\rangle i$, or $@_j i$ (i does not occur in ψ' and $i \neq j$).
3. If ψ occurs in some clause in $\mathit{ClSet}^*(\varphi)$, then $d'(\psi) \leq d(\varphi)$ and, moreover, if $\psi = @_i j$, then $level(j) \leq d(\varphi)$. Therefore, for all formula ψ, if i is a nominal occurring in a formula in $\mathit{ClSet}^*(\psi)$, then $level(i) \leq d(\psi)$.
4. For all nominal i, the number of distinct formulas of the form $@_i\langle r\rangle\psi$ ($\psi \notin \mathsf{NOM}$) occurring in $\mathit{ClSet}^*(\varphi)$ is finite.
5. For all $k \in \mathbb{N}$, the set $\mathsf{NOM}_c^k \cap \mathsf{NOM}(\mathit{ClSet}^*(\varphi))$ is finite.

Termination of $\mathbf{R}_T^{\mathrm{OS}}[\mathcal{H}^{\mathrm{NNF}}(@)]$ is a direct corollary of the above proposition.

Theorem 6. $R_T^{\mathrm{OS}}[\mathcal{H}^{\mathrm{NNF}}(@)]$ *is a decision procedure for the problem of satisfiability of* $\mathcal{H}(@)$.

5 Implementation and Testing

HyLoRes 1.0 is an automated theorem prover for the logic $\mathcal{H}(@,\downarrow)$[4] (but we will only use it for formulas of $\mathcal{H}(@)$) written in Haskell, of approximately 5000 lines of code, based on the resolution calculus proposed in [5]. It must be noted that this is not a tool aiming to compete with state-of-the-art theorem provers. Automated provers such as SPASS [1], Vampire [22], RACER [16] or *SAT [15] include an important number of heuristics and optimizations with which they achieve an outstanding performance. HyLoRes implements a relatively small set of optimizations and it is still mainly a proof of concept implementation.

We have developed a new version (2.0) of HyLoRes that uses the rules of the $\mathbf{R}_T^{\mathrm{OS}}[\mathcal{H}^{\mathrm{NNF}}(@)]$ calculus presented in Figure 3. Several tests were run to compare the performance of versions 1.0 and 2.0. In this section we comment on some of the results obtained.

Nowadays, the standard test suite for basic modal logic satisfiability is the "random 3CNF$\square_m$" [21], an adaptation of the random 3CNF for propositional logic [19]. This type of test generates batches of random formulas subject to certain restriction parameters (e.g., number of propositional variables, modal depth, maximum number of clauses, etc.).

The standard definition of random 3CNF$\square_m$ generates formulas that are strictly modal (i.e., without neither nominals nor the @ operator). An extension, called random h3CNF$\square_m$ and implemented as the generator hGen, is described in [7] that suits the needs of theorem provers for hybrid logics. hGen generates formulas for sublanguages of $\mathcal{H}(@,A,\downarrow)$ ($\mathcal{H}(@)$ extended with the $\downarrow$ binder and the universal modality A).

The parameters involved in the generation of test batches were: number of propositional variables (V), number of nominals (N), maximum modal depth (D) and number of clauses (L). After fixing the values for V, N and D, a batch

---
[4] $\mathcal{H}(@,\downarrow)$ is $\mathcal{H}(@)$ extended with the $\downarrow$ binder, see [4] for details.

of 100 formulas of $\mathcal{H}(@)$ was generated for each value of L in a given range. They were then used as input for both theorem provers, with a timeout value of 40 seconds per formula. To plot the results, the median of the execution time and of the number of clauses generated were taken.

First Test. We compared the performance of both versions of the prover using simple formulas ($V = 2$, $N = 3$, $D = 1$). Figure 4 shows four graphs: the satisfiability/unsatisfiability curves together with percentage of timeouts in the first line, and the comparison of space and time resources used in the second. In all cases, the x-axis represent number of clauses produced by the random generator (notice that, the bigger the number of clauses generated the bigger the probability of the clause set to be unsatisfiable). In the first line, the y-axis shows the percentage of cases of satisfiability, unsatisfiability, and timeouts. In the second line, the y-axis is a logscale and shows median of the number of clauses generated in the left graph, and median of the execution time (in seconds) in the right graph.

The performance of HyLoRes 2.0 was clearly better than that of its predecessor. Figure 4 shows that HyLoRes 1.0 couldn't solve an important fraction of the simpler problems, while HyLoRes 2.0 solved them all. It is interesting to observe that HyLoRes 1.0 had the larger number of timeouts in the region where most of the formulas are satisfiable, while HyLoRes 2.0 is benefiting here from the restrictions on ordering and selection functions which accelerate saturation.

It is noticeable that in this test the initialization time of HyLoRes 2.0 is higher than the time needed to solve the problem itself.

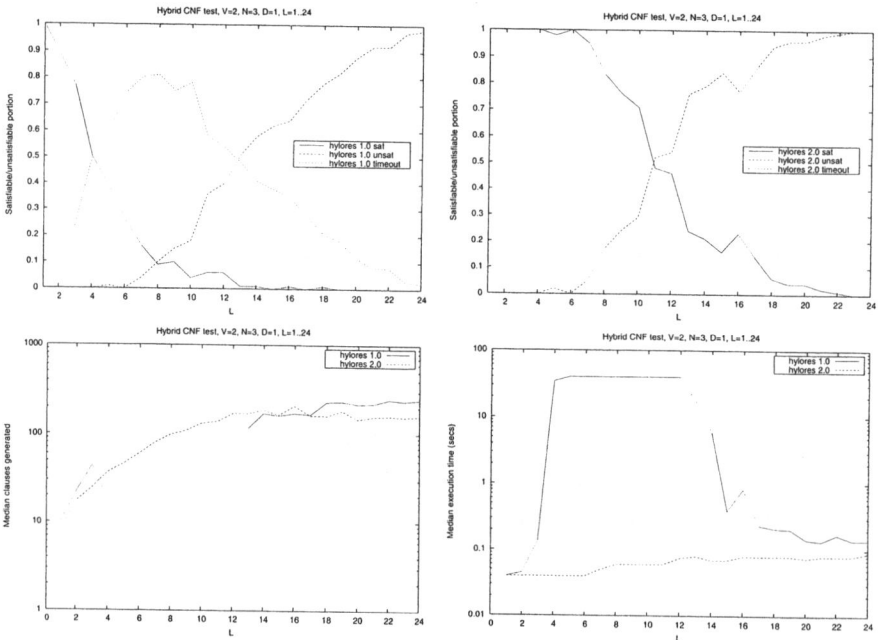

Fig. 4. h3CNF$\square_m$ and HyLoRes 1.0 and 2.0 – Simple formulas

Second Test. As one can clearly see in Figure 4, a large number of timeouts negatively affects the representativeness of the plot (see how the satisfiability/unsatisfiability percentage curves differ between the two graphs in the first line of the figure). When the modal depth of the formulas is augmented, the number of cases that HyLoRes 1.0 can solve in a reasonable time becomes too small to be relevant. Hence the more difficult tests were run only over different configurations of HyLoRes 2.0.

Figure 5 shows the results for formulas where only the strictly modal complexity was increased: $V = 8$, $N = 3$ and $D = 7$. We only show now the distribution of satisfiability, unsatisfiability and timeouts in the left graph and the cpu usage on the right graph. In this case, the number of timeouts in the harder zone is below 15%, however, the mean answer time is still below one second.

This test suggests again that the strategies of order and selection function are effective (see how times in the satisfiability section are better than the ones in the unsatisfiable region).

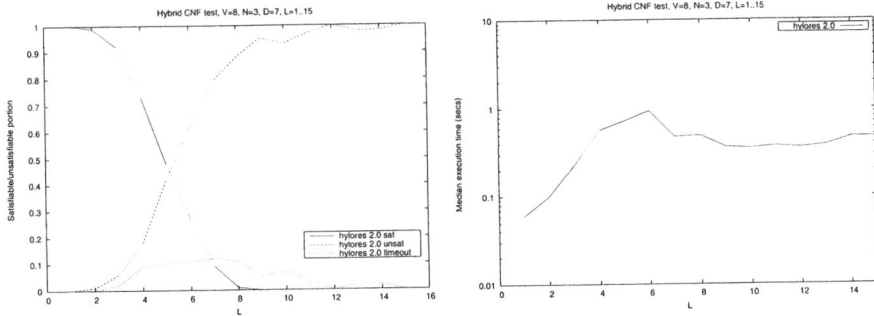

Fig. 5. h3CNF$\Box_m$ and HyLoRes 2.0 – Complex formulas, small number of nominals

Third Test. Finally, Figure 6 shows the results obtained with formulas with an increased number of nominals and a low modal depth: $V = 6$, $N = 7$, $D = 2$. A larger number of nominals means a more frequent application of paramodulation rules. This is why HyLoRes 2.0 has a larger number of timeouts here, while the median execution time in the harder zone is over 10 seconds.

This test indicate that heuristics to control paramodulation (for example those described in [9]) should be implemented in HyLoRes, as the naive paramodulation used at the moment is too expensive. It is important to observe, though, that the formulas used in the test shown in Figure 6 have twice the modal depth, three times the number of propositional variables and more than twice the number of nominals than those of Figure 4, which HyLoRes 1.0 could barely handle.

6 Conclusions and Future Work

We presented in this paper a sound, complete and terminating strategy of resolution with order and selection functions for the hybrid language $\mathcal{H}(@)$. The paper shows in addition that standard resolution techniques and notions (e.g., the can-

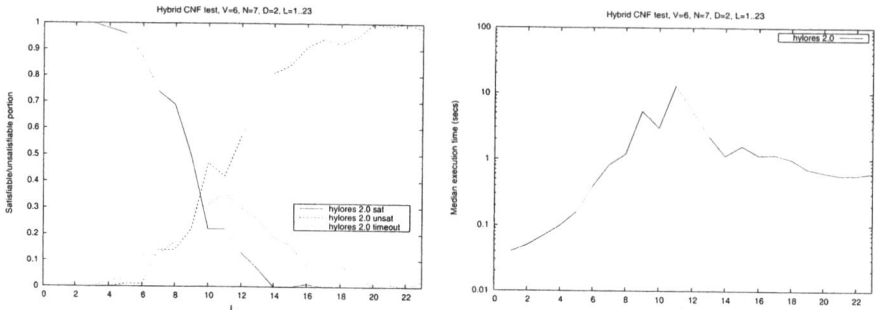

Fig. 6. h3CNF$\square_m$ and HyLoRes 2.0 – Medium formulas, larger number of nominals

didate model construction, the notion of admissible orderings, the definition of Herbrand models, etc.) which are crucial part of the actual work on resolution for classical logics can be adapted to the framework of modal logics when the hybrid operators (nominals and @) are present. Moreover, the strategy has been implemented in the HyLoRes prover and the preliminary tests show significant improvements.

We have not yet investigated the complexity of our resolution strategy. We conjecture that it is ExpTime-hard (and hence not optimal). Further refinements of the ordering and selection functions used, possibly together with the implementation of stronger resolution strategies (e.g. hyper resolution) might reduce the complexity to the optimal bound of PSpace (see, [14]), but these are topics for future research. More generally, further work on how to choose suitable parameters (which orderings and selection functions are most effective for a certain input) and the implementation of optimizations, heuristics and simplifications by rewriting remain to be done to enhance the usability of HyLoRes.

Suitable generalizations of the standard notions of redundancy [10] (e.g., backwards and forwards subsumption) should also be developed in detail. HyLoRes already implements of some basic ideas, but both theory and practice as it applies to resolution for modal-like languages, should be further developed.

We are also interested in investigated fragments of $\mathcal{H}(@)$ for which resolution might have a specially good behavior (e.g., find a suitable notion of Horn formulas) on the one hand, and on the other in developing extensions the actual framework to languages more expressive than $\mathcal{H}(@)$ (e.g., considering the addition of the $\downarrow$ binder and the universal modality A).

References

1. B. Afshordel, U. Brahm, C. Cohrs, T. Engel, E. Keen, C. Theobald, D. Topić, and C. Weidenbach. System description: SPASS Version 1.0.0. In *Automated deduction—CADE-16 (Trento, 1999)*, pages 187–201, Berlin, 1999. Springer.
2. C. Areces. *Logic Engineering. The Case of Description and Hybrid Logics*. PhD thesis, Institute for Logic, Language and Computation, University of Amsterdam, Amsterdam, The Netherlands, October 2000.

3. C. Areces, P. Blackburn, and M. Marx. A road-map on complexity for hybrid logics. In *Proc. of the 8th Annual Conference of the EACSL*, pages 307–321, 1999.
4. C. Areces, P. Blackburn, and M. Marx. Hybrid logics: Characterization, interpolation and complexity. *Journal of Symbolic Logic*, 66(3):977–1010, 2001.
5. C. Areces, H. de Nivelle, and M. de Rijke. Resolution in modal, description and hybrid logic. *Journal of Logic and Computation*, 11(5):717–736, 2001.
6. C. Areces and J. Heguiabehere. HyLoRes: A hybrid logic prover based on direct resolution. In *Advances in Modal Logic*, Toulouse, France, 2002.
7. C. Areces and J. Heguiabehere. hGen: A random CNF formula generator for Hybrid Languages. In *Proc. of Methods for Modalities 3*, Nancy, France, 2003.
8. F. Baader, D. Calvanese, D. McGuinness, D. Nardi, and P. Patel-Schneider, editors. *The Description Logic Handbook: Theory, Implementation, and Applications*. Cambridge University Press, 2003.
9. L. Bachmair and H. Ganzinger. Equational reasoning in saturation-based theorem proving. In *Automated deduction—a basis for applications, Vol. I*, pages 353–397. Kluwer, Dordrecht, 1998.
10. L. Bachmair and H. Ganzinger. Resolution theorem proving. In J. Robinson and A. Voronkov, editors, *Handbook of Automated Reasoning*, volume 1, chapter 2, pages 19–99. Elsevier, 2001.
11. P. Blackburn. Representation, reasoning, and relational structures: a hybrid logic manifesto. *Logic Journal of the IGPL*, 8(3):339–365, 2000.
12. P. Blackburn, M. de Rijke, and Y. Venema. *Modal Logic*. Cambridge University Press, 2002.
13. N. Dershowitz and J. Jouannaud. Rewrite systems. In J. van Leeuwen, editor, *Handbook of Theoretical Computer Science. Volume B: Formal Models and Sematics (B)*, pages 243–320. Elsevier and MIT Press, 1990.
14. L. Georgieva, U. Hustadt, and R. Schmidt. Computational space efficiency and minimal model generation for guarded formulae. In R. Nieuwenhuis and A. Voronkov, editors, *Proc. of the 8th LPAR 2001*, number 2250 in LNAI, pages 85–99, 2001.
15. E. Giunchiglia, A. Tacchella, and F. Giunchiglia. SAT-based decision procedures for classical modal logics. *Journal of Automated Reasoning*, 28(2):143–171, 2002.
16. V. Haarslev and R. Möller. RACER system description. In *IJCAR 2001*, number 2083 in LNAI, Siena, 2001.
17. D. Harel. Dynamic logic. In D. Gabbay and F. Guenthner, editors, *Handbook of Philosophical Logic. Vol. II*, volume 165 of *Synthese Library*, pages 497–604. D. Reidel Publishing Co., Dordrecht, 1984.
18. HyLoRes' Home Page. http://www.loria.fr/~areces/HyLoRes/, 2004.
19. D. Mitchell, B. Sleman, and H. Levesque. Hard and easy distributions of SAT problems. In *Proc. of the 10th National Conference on Artificial Intelligence*, pages 459–465, 1992.
20. S. Passy and T. Tinchev. An essay in combinatory dynamic logic. *Information and Computation*, 93(2):263–332, 1991.
21. P. Patel-Schneider and R. Sebastiani. A new general method to generate random modal formulae for testing decision procedures. *Journal of Artificial Intelligence Research*, 18:351–389, May 2003.
22. A. Riazanov and A. Voronkov. The design and implementation of VAMPIRE. *AI Communications*, 15(2):91–110, 2002. Special issue on CASC.
23. A. Voronkov. Algorithms, datastructures, and other issues in efficient automated deduction. In *IJCAR 2001*, number 2083 in LNAI, pages 13–28, Siena, 2001.

On a Semantic Subsumption Test

Jerzy Marcinkowski, Jan Otop, and Grzegorz Stelmaszek

Institute of Computer Science, University of Wrocław,
Przesmyckiego 20, 51151 Wrocław, Poland

Abstract. We observe, that subsumption of clauses (in the language of first order logic), so far understood as a syntactic notion, can also be defined by semantical means. Subsumption is NP-complete and testing subsumption takes roughly half of the running time of a typical first order resolution-based theorem prover. We also give some experimental evidence, that replacing syntactic indexing for subsumption by our semantic Monte Carlo technique can, in some situations, significantly decrease the cost of subsumption testing.

Finally, we provide some evidence that a similar semantic idea can be probably successfully used for testing for AC matching, which is another NP-complete problem whose millions of instances are being solved by theorem provers.

1 Introduction

On the level of abstraction appropriate for this paper, a clausual first order resolution/paramodulation based theorem prover can be viewed as an implementation of the following algorithm.

There are two sets of clauses, A (as *available*) and SOS (as *set of support*). A is initially empty. SOS is initially the set of clauses we want to find a contradiction in.

While SOS is nonempty, and while the empty clause has not been proved:
a. select a clause $\mathcal{D} \in SOS$ and move it to A,
b. resolve (using the available inference rules) $\mathcal{D}$ with all possible partners from A,
c. for any clause $\mathcal{C}$ inferred in the previous step, check if it is not subsumed by some clause already in $A \cup SOS$. If there is no clause subsuming $\mathcal{C}$ then add $\mathcal{C}$ to SOS,
d. demodulate $\mathcal{C}$ using existing demodulators,
e. check for backward subsumption: delete each clause in $A \cup SOS$ which is subsumed by $\mathcal{C}$.

See subsection 3.1 for the preliminaries about subsumption.

Our main interest in this paper is the subsumption testing step **c.**[1]. It takes around half of the running time of a typical theorem prover. This is not surprising, since millions of pairs of clauses need to be tested for subsumption in a

---

[1] Although, also step **e.** will be briefly addressed in Section 2.

single run, and since deciding, for two given clauses, whether one of them subsumes another is NP-hard. Complicated data structures have been developed to support subsumption tests, including discrimination trees [C93], [G86], with their most advanced version, called code trees [V95], implemented in *Vampire* [V] (see [SRV01] for a survey of term indexing). Since subsumption is a syntactic notion, it is the syntax of the clauses which is indexed in the trees.

In this paper we show some evidence, that in some cases, a simple semantical indexing technique can possibly prove more efficient in this context, than the known complicated syntactic data structures.

2 Semantic Redundancy Detection – First Idea

In our approach, as the first step of the run of the theorem prover, we fix some finite number p (in our implementation this number is between 20 and 64) of small randomly drawn structures $M_1, M_2 \ldots M_p$ over the signature of interest. Then, for each newborn clause $\mathcal{C}$ we compute what we call *profile of* $\mathcal{C}$: the tuple of numbers $P(\mathcal{C}) = \langle i_1, i_2, \ldots i_p \rangle$, where i_j is the truth value of $\mathcal{C}$ in M_j (this is not a mistake, as we are going to explain in Section 3 the truth values i_j can indeed be numbers from the set $\{1, 2, 3\}$ rather than bits). We index clauses in SOS and in A with respect to their profiles.

For two profiles $P_1 = \langle i_1, i_2, \ldots i_p \rangle$ and $P_2 \langle l_1, l_2, \ldots l_p \rangle$ we say that P_1 dominates P_2 if for each j it holds that $i_j \geq l_j$.

Now, our idea is shamefully simple: if $\mathcal{C}_1$ subsumes $\mathcal{C}_2$ then $P_{\mathcal{C}_2}$ dominates $P_{\mathcal{C}_1}$, whatever the structures $M_1, M_2 \ldots M_p$ are. So, if for some profile P in the index, and for some newborn clause $\mathcal{C}$, profile $P_{\mathcal{C}}$ does not dominate P then we get the negative answer we wanted to get: we can be sure that no clause with index entry P can subsume $\mathcal{C}$.

Testing domination is very fast. A profile is remembered as 64 bits (if i_j are numbers from the set $\{0, 1, 2\}$ then we store them using unary encoding, which takes 2 bits per number, so we can afford at most 32 profiles then). Testing whether one profile dominates another takes just two machine instructions.

If we are lucky, then we can test negative for subsumption hundreds of clauses for the cost of two machine instructions. If we are not lucky, then the profile $P_{\mathcal{C}}$ dominates P and we get the positive answer that some of the clauses with index P may subsume $\mathcal{C}$. We need to perform a full syntactic subsumption test then, for $\mathcal{C}$ and each clause $\mathcal{C}'$ in $A \cup SOS$ such that $P = P(\mathcal{C}')$.

As for each indexing technique, the performance of our method depends on two factors. The first of them is the computational overhead, the second is the selectivity of the index, or, in other words, the fraction of negative instances returned as false positives.

The computational overhead is mainly the cost of computing the profiles. It is, of course, linear with respect to the number p - the length of the profiles, and proportional to the size of the models to the power of the number of variables in the clauses. This rough calculation led us to the implementation decision of having relatively many (up to 64 of them, as we said) small (consisting of 4, or even of 2 elements) models.

What concerns selectivity, we built our first hopes on a (clearly oversimplifying) assumption that the truth values of clauses in models would be distributed uniformly and independently. Then (assuming that we use 64 profiles), if there are just two truth values, zero and one, the probability of a false positive, which is the probability that a random profile P_1 of length 64 dominates P_2, should be $(3/4)^{64}$ which is around 10^{-9}.

The more truth values the better. The probability of a false positive would go down to only $(2/3)^{64}$, which is about 10^{-12} if we had three truth values[2].

Of course the real distribution is not that beautiful. One could also fear that our harsh restrictions on the size of the models must result with bad selectivity. But the results are anyway quite optimistic: In Section 3.3 and 3.4 we show that for a very natural example profiles built of 64 models of size four, or even size two give very good selectivity. In Section 4, where our main experimental results are presented, we show that an index using a profile of 64 models of size two performs, on inputs consisting of long clauses, better than discrimination trees.

It could appear from what we wrote so far, that what our index can detect is non-implication of clauses rather than non-subsumption. This could mean that we will get a false positive result each time when $\mathcal{C}$ implies $\mathcal{D}$ but does not subsume it. As we however explain in the next section this problem can be avoided by using a logic in which implication[3] coincides with subsumption.

2.1 Backward Subsumption

One of the options in a run of a typical theorem prover is another redundancy test: detecting backward subsumption. Whereas (forward) subsumption test prevents us from adding to SOS a clause that is less general than (i.e. subsumed by) a clause already present in $A \cup SOS$, backward subsumption test removes from SOS the clauses which are subsumed by a newly added clause C. It is not a default option of theorem provers, since the number of removed redundant clauses is usually too small compared to the time that the procedure takes. In our method the main overhead is computing the profiles. This means that we can have backward subsumption almost for free.

3 On a Semantics of Subsumption

3.1 Subsumption: Preliminaries

Let Σ be a first order signature (which means that it consists of some constants, function symbols and relation symbols), and let V be a countable set of variables. We denote as $T_V(\Sigma)$ the set of all terms over Σ with variables from V.

---

[2] But with 32 models and three truth values it would be about 10^{-6}. Surprisingly we will go back to this point in the end of Section 4.3.
[3] The word *implication* always means *semantic implication* in this paper. Do not confuse it with syntactic notion of *derivability*.

A clause is a universal closure of a disjunction of literals over Σ. We often think of a clause as of the finite set of its literals, so that we can for example use the notation $\mathcal{C} \subseteq \mathcal{D}$ for clauses $\mathcal{C}$ and $\mathcal{D}$.

We say that $\mathcal{C}$ subsumes $\mathcal{D}$ if there exists a substitution σ such that $\sigma(\mathcal{C}) \subseteq \mathcal{D}$. Subsumption is a way of saying that one clause is "more general" than another but it should not be confused with implication:

Example. Consider a clause $\mathcal{C}_{1\_step} = \{\neg P(x), P(f(x))\}$ and a clause $\mathcal{C}_{2\_steps} = \{\neg P(x), P(f(f(x)))\}$. It is easy to see that $\mathcal{C}_{1\_step}$ implies $\mathcal{C}_{2\_steps}$ but does not subsume it.

So subsumption does not follow from implication. The opposite is trivially true, but despite its triviality we will state and prove the result here. This is because we will need to refer to its proof later and because we want to fix notations:

Definition 1. *Let M be a relational structure over Σ and let τ be a valuation of variables in M, i.e. a function from V to M (to keep the notations simple we do not distinguish between the structure M and its universe). By $\bar{\tau}$ we mean the canonical extension of τ to objects like terms, atomic formulas and literals (so, if L is a literal then $\bar{\tau}(L)$ is a truth value). Let $\mathcal{C}$ be a clause. Define the truth value of $\mathcal{C}$ in M, (denoted as $TV(\mathcal{C}, M)$) as: $\min_{\tau:V\to M} \max_{L\in \mathcal{C}} \bar{\tau}(L)$ We say that $\mathcal{C}$ (finitely) implies $\mathcal{D}$ if for any (finite) structure M it holds that $TV(\mathcal{C}, M) \leq TV(\mathcal{D}, M)$.*

Notice that our definition, although maybe written in a slightly bizarre way, is just the standard one. The minimum (taken over the set of possible valuations) is exactly universal quantification, while the maximum over values of literals is disjunction (of course we assume that **false** is 0 and thus is smaller than **true** which equals 1).

Observation 1 *If $\mathcal{C}$ subsumes $\mathcal{D}$ then $\mathcal{C}$ implies $\mathcal{D}$.*

Proof. Assume $\mathcal{C}$ subsumes $\mathcal{D}$. This means that there exists a substitution σ such that $\sigma(\mathcal{C}) \subseteq \mathcal{D}$. We need to show that for any valuation τ_D there exists a valuation τ_C such that $\max_{C\in\mathcal{C}} \bar{\tau}_C(C) \leq \max_{D\in\mathcal{D}} \bar{\tau}_D(D)$. Take $\tau_C = \tau_D \sigma$. Then $\max_{C\in\mathcal{C}} \bar{\tau}_C(C) = \max_{D\in\sigma(\mathcal{C})} \bar{\tau}_D(D) \leq \max_{D\in\mathcal{D}} \bar{\tau}_D(D)$. ∎

3.2 Multi-valued Logics

By a multi-valued logic we mean here any pair $\mathcal{L} = \langle L, \neg \rangle$, where L is a totally ordered set of truth values and $\neg : L \to L$ is a function. Notice that the standard notion of relational structure can be generalized to multi-valued logics: the only difference is that the interpretation of relational symbol of arity k is a function from M^k to L now, not from M^k to $\{0, 1\}$ as usually (M is the universe of the relational structure). Also Definition 1 can be applied in the context of multi-valued logics. It turns out that Observation 1 survives the generalization:

Observation 2 *If C subsumes D then C implies clause D in each multivalued logic $\mathcal{L}$.*

Proof. Reread the proof of Observation 1. ∎

3.3 Main Observation

Consider the following Strange Four-Valued Logic (S4VL). The elements of L are XT (so extremely true that even its negation remains extremely true: ¬XT=XT), T (simply true: ¬T=F), F (simply false ¬F=T) and XF (so extremely false that even its negation remains extremely false: ¬XF=XF). The total order is $XT > T > F > XF$. It turns out that implication in S4VL does not coincide with standard implication. Consider the clauses from the example from Section 3.1. We take $M = \{0, 1, 2, 3\}$ and interpret the function symbols as $f(0) = 1$, $f(1) = 2$, $f(2) = f(3) = 3$. As the interpretation of P we take $P(0) = T$, $P(2) = F$, $P(1) = P(3) = XT$. Then $TV(\mathcal{C}_{1\_step}, M) = T$ but $TV(\mathcal{C}_{2\_steps}, M) = F$, so $\mathcal{C}_{1\_step}$ does not imply $\mathcal{C}_{2\_steps}$ in S4VL. This is not just a coincidence, as we are going to show now:

Observation 3 (A semantics of subsumption) *Subsumption of clauses is finite implication in S4VL.*

Notice, that since finite implication in any logic follows from implication in the same logic, by Observation 2 we get that subsumption of clauses coincides with implication in S4VL.

Proof. Let $\mathcal{D}$ be any clause. We will construct a finite relational structure $M_\mathcal{D}$, with relational symbols interpreted as functions to {XT,T,F,XF}, such that $TV(\mathcal{C}, M_\mathcal{D}) > TV(\mathcal{D}, M_\mathcal{D})$ for each clause $\mathcal{C}$ such that $\mathcal{C}$ does not subsume $\mathcal{D}$. The construction will be a generalization of the example from the beginning of this subsection. Let d be a natural number greater than the depth of the deepest term in $\mathcal{D}$. For two terms $t, s \in T_V(\Sigma)$ let R be the equivalence relation such that sRt if and only if t and s are equal up to depth d. We define the universe of $M_\mathcal{D}$ to be the set of all equivalence classes of R. Notice that the equivalence classes of terms not deeper than d are singletons, so we can identify such terms with their classes. The interpretation of functions from Σ in $M_\mathcal{D}$ is defined in the canonical way. What remains to be defined are the functions which are the interpretations of the relation symbols from Σ. Let $P(\bar{t})$ be an atomic formula. We consider four cases:

(i) $P(\bar{t}) \in \mathcal{D}$ and $(\neg P(\bar{t})) \in \mathcal{D}$. Then interpret $P(\bar{t})$ as XF.
(ii) $P(\bar{t}) \in \mathcal{D}$ but $(\neg P(\bar{t})) \notin \mathcal{D}$. Then interpret $P(\bar{t})$ as F.
(iii) $P(\bar{t}) \notin \mathcal{D}$ but $(\neg P(\bar{t})) \in \mathcal{D}$. Then interpret $P(\bar{t})$ as T.
(iv) $P(\bar{t}) \notin \mathcal{D}$ and $(\neg P(\bar{t})) \notin \mathcal{D}$. Then interpret $P(\bar{t})$ as XT.

Let now τ_{id} be identity. Then $\min_{\tau:V \to M_\mathcal{D}} \max_{L \in \mathcal{D}} \bar{\tau}(L) \leq \max_{L \in \mathcal{D}} \bar{\tau}_{id}(L) \leq F$. On the other hand, if $\mathcal{C}$ does not subsume $\mathcal{D}$, then for any valuation τ there exists a literal $L \in \mathcal{C}$ such that $\bar{\tau}(C) \notin \mathcal{D}$. This implies that $\bar{\tau}(C) \geq T$. So $\min_{\tau:V \to M_{\mathcal{D}}} \max_{L \in \mathcal{D}} \bar{\tau}(L) \geq T$. ∎

Since in practice we never test for subsumption clauses containing both a literal and its negation (they are easily detected and deleted as tautologies), XF is unnecessary, and we just need 3 truth values for a logic in which implication of clauses coincides with subsumption[4]. If the interpretation of P is assumed to be a function with three truth values, then there are $4^4 * 3^4$ four-element models for the signature $\{P, f\}$ of our running example[5]. Among them, there are 2220 (which is 10.7%) such structures M that $TV(\mathcal{C}_{1\_step}, M) > TV(\mathcal{C}_{2\_steps}, M)$. This means that the probability that for a random sequence $M_1, M_2 \ldots M_{64}$ of four-element models $P_{\mathcal{C}_{1\_step}}$ will dominate $P_{\mathcal{C}_{2\_steps}}$ (and our semantic subsumption test will return a false positive) is $0.893^{64} < 0.001$.

Notice that S4VL is by no means the unique logic for which Observation 3 holds true. For example a logic with the same set of truth values as S4VL, and the same negation, but with the ordering $T > XT > XF > F$ would work as well.

3.4 Size of the Models

Unlike the set of truth values, the structure $M_{\mathcal{D}}$, witnessing no-subsumption cannot be kept small. In our proof it is exponential in the size of $\mathcal{D}$. It is quite unlikely that it could always be polynomial: this would mean that subsumption is in co-NP, and thus that NP=co-NP. It appears however that for most of the practical situations there are many structures which witness no-subsumption and which are of size much smaller than the upper bound following from the proof of Observation 3.

Exercise. The size of the structure $M_{\mathcal{C}_{2\_steps}}$, constructed as in the proof of Observation 3 is four. Show that among the 36 two-element models for the signature $\{P, f\}$ and logic S4VL, there are 4 structures M such that $TV(\mathcal{C}_{1\_step}, M) > TV(\mathcal{C}_{2\_steps}, M)$. The signature is too small here to allow profiles of length 64, but the frequency of "good" models is almost the same here as among the four elements models.

4 Implementation

We implemented our semantic subsumption test in the Otter theorem prover [OT]. The reason for this choice was that we found Otter sources relatively easy to understand, and thus to make changes in[6]. We realize that it is not the fastest theorem prover available, and that being able to improve Otter is not really a

---

[4] Let us leave the truth value XF to the politicians. They know how to make good use of it.
[5] We count ordered structures here.
[6] We are grateful to the authors of Otter for their copyright policy, which made our work possible.

good reason to be proud. But on the other hand, like Otter itself, our techniques also still leave a lot of room for improvement.

Compared to the original Otter we deleted the discrimination tree based subsumption test[7], and replaced it by a semantic test. We took care not to change anything else in the prover, so the proof search itself remains unchanged. In principle our versions should be able to prove the same theorems in the same way as Otter does, although not necessarily in the same time limit.

We tested four parameter choices for out implementation. The parameters are: the number of models in a profile, the size of the models, the number of possible truth values in the interpretations of the predicates, and the way in which negation is handled (see Table 1).

For each of the versions, we wanted the profile to be no longer than 64 bits, which means that the number of models multiplied by [the number of possible truth values minus one] could not be greater than 64.

Table 1. Our versions of Otter

	Number of models	Size of models	Number of truth values	Interpretation of negation
2/2 semantic Otter	64	2	2	identity
2/3 semantic Otter	32	2	3	S4VL
3/3 semantic Otter	32	3	3	identity
4/4 semantic Otter	20	4	4	identity

Concerning negation, let us remind ourselves that Observation 2 holds for any interpretation of negation. In three of our four versions we interpreted negation as the identity, in one version it was interpreted according to the rules of the logic S4VL.

We also ran some tests with a version of 2/2 semantic Otter with the classical interpretation of negation. It appears to be a little bit worse than 2/2 semantic Otter, but the tests were too few to be conclusive.

4.1 Indexing the Profiles

As we said in Section 2, our main idea is that the clauses are indexed by their profiles. In our interpretation we decided to index also the profiles themselves.

We use a tree of (maximal) depth 16 and (maximal) arity 16, where the children of a node $i_1 i_2 \ldots i_{4k}$ (nodes represent prefixes of profiles) are all the

---

[7] Because of unit deletion we could not however completely get rid of discrimination trees.

nodes of the form $i_1 i_2 \ldots i_{4k} i_{4k+1} \ldots i_{4k+4}$, where $i_j \in \{0, 1\}$. But of course we do not create a node unless there is a clause with a corresponding profile.

Now, for a given new clause $\mathcal{C}$ we want to select all the profiles P from the index, such that $P(\mathcal{C}) = j_1 j_1 \ldots j_{64}$ dominates P. In order to do so, being in the node $i_1 i_2 \ldots i_{4k}$ enter all its existing children of the form $i_1 i_2 \ldots i_{4k} i_{4k+1} \ldots i_{4k+4}$ such that $j_{4k+1} \ldots j_{4k+4}$ dominates $i_{4k+1} \ldots i_{4k+4}$.

4.2 Computing the Profiles

The most expensive operation in our approach is computing the profile of a new clause. This means computing its truth value in the given structures. Pessimistically it can take time proportional to the number of possible valuations of variables, which is k^n where n is the number of variables in the variables in the clause and k is the size of the structure. Since the clauses that we encounter can easily have more than 10 variables, the cost seems almost unaffordable. In our implementation we used a semi-naive algorithm which, in practical cases, reduces the number of valuations that need to be considered. It takes advantage of the fact that the variables rarely are "non-local" for the same subterms: to compute the set of possible values of the term $g(t_1(x_1, \ldots x_5, z), t_2(y_1, \ldots y_5, z))$ in a structure consisting of 4 elements we do not need to consider 4^{11} valuations. It is enough to compute the set of possible values of $t_1(x_1, \ldots x_5, z)$ as a function of z, and the set of possible values of $t_2(y_1, \ldots y_5, z)$ as a function of z, which requires only 4^6 valuations. The last number can usually be reduced again, if we repeat the trick inside t_1 and t_2.

There are at least 2 possible ways in which we think we could be looking for a real optimization here:

1. So far we treat terms as trees. We think we could benefit a lot from exploiting their DAG structure.

2. Each new clause $\mathcal{C}$ is a result of applying an inference rule to some clauses $\mathcal{C}_1$ and $\mathcal{C}_2$, whose profiles were computed before. The structure of $\mathcal{C}$ is to some extent similar to the structures of $\mathcal{C}_1$ and $\mathcal{C}_2$. Maybe we could gain something by remembering the partial results of the computations of $P(\mathcal{C}_1)$ and $P(\mathcal{C}_2)$.

4.3 Results of the Tests

We ran Otter and 2/2 semantic Otter against the whole TPTP library We selected our Reference Set, as the set of the 345 theorems which satisfy the two conditions:

-at least one of the two programs proves it within 300 seconds, with a memory limit of 515 megabytes,

-at least one of the two programs needs more than 5 seconds to prove it.

Then we ran the remaining 3 versions of semantic Otter on the Reference Set. The results of the tests can be found in Tables 2-5.

As one could expect, the results are quite encouraging for problems with long clauses, and very poor for short clauses. What we found surprising is the

Table 2. Otter vs. 2/2 semantic Otter (by maximal number of literals in the input clauses, run on the Reference Set)

Maximal number of literals in the input clauses	Theorems not proved by 2/2 semantic Otter	Theorems for which Otter was > 30% faster	Theorems for which they perform equally	Theorems for which Otter was > 30% slower	Theorems not proved by Otter
4 or less	77	165	4	11	5
5	3	14	1	4	1
6	0	0	0	2	1
7	0	1	0	5	1
8	0	0	0	6	11
9	1	0	0	0	1
10 to 19	0	1	0	10	6
FOF	0	0	0	3	5

sharpness of the threshold: semantic Otter rarely beats the original version for the instances with a clause with the maximal number of literals in the input equal to 5 or less, and hardly ever gets beaten for the instances with a clause with 6 or more literals. This means that a hybrid Otter, reading the input first and then, on the basis of the length of the clauses deciding if it should use the semantic tests or rather stick to the traditional way, would easily outplay all the versions of the prover.

What we did not expect was also that 2/2 semantic Otter would be the best of the semantic versions. The results in Table 4 could be altered by the fact that the definition of the Reference Set itself depended on the behavior of 2/2 semantic Otter. But the results in Table 5 constitute a hard piece of evidence: 2/2 semantic Otter is faster than its brothers. And, with its two truth values, it cannot even see the difference between non-implication and non-subsumption. We are not sure where the reasons of this superiority are. Clearly, computing the profiles should be twice cheaper in in 2/3 semantic Otter than in 2/2. So the selectivity of the 2/2 version must be better than of 2/3. Could it have anything to do with the rough calculations in footnote 2 (Section 2)?

Table 3. Otter vs. 2/2 semantic Otter (by TPTP domain, not all domains included, run on the Reference Set)

TPTP domain	Theorems not proved by 2/2 semantic Otter	Theorems for which Otter was ≥ 30% faster	Theorems for which they perform equally	Theorems for which Otter was ≥ 30% slower	Theorems not proved by Otter
BOO	3	16	0	0	1
GRP	24	65	4	7	5
LCL	45	52	0	0	0
SYN	3	14	0	1	0
CAT	0	0	0	6	1
GEO	0	0	0	8	19
HWV	0	0	0	9	1
MGT	0	0	0	3	1

5 Future Work

Develop better algorithms for computing the profiles, and for indexing. Tune the parameters (including the way negation is treated). Implement the thing in Vampire.

6 Related Idea: AC Matching and Unification

For a structure M and a term $t \in T_V(\Sigma)$ define $Var(t, M)$ as $\{\bar{\tau}(v) : \tau : V \to M\}$, that is the set of possible values of t in M. Suppose t is an instance of s. Then for each structure M it holds that $Var(t, M) \subseteq Var(s, M)$. If t and s are unifiable then, for each structure M, it holds that $Var(t, M) \cap Var(s, M) \neq \emptyset$. This leads to the idea of a semantic matching/unification test. This does not make much sense in the case of matching and unification in the free term algebra - they are easy to compute anyway. But the above observation holds true also for the AC case. AC matching, like subsumption, is NP-complete and it turns out that it is AC matching that takes most of the running time of EQP [EQP], a cousin of Otter built to prove theorems in first-order equational logic.

We built a naive implementation of the above idea in EQP. Terms were profiled by 32 random models, each of them of size 4 (the interpretations of the AC symbol were drawn to be AC functions). For the evaluation of $Var(t, M)$ we used the algorithm from Section 4.2. Of course we did not remove the original *matching* procedure from EQP. But each time EQP wants to execute this

Table 4. Theorems not proved by different versions of otter (by the maximal number of literals in the input clauses, run on the Reference Set)

Maximal number of literals in the input clauses	Theorems not proved by 2/2 semantic Otter	Theorems not proved by 2/3 semantic Otter	Theorems not proved by 3/3 semantic Otter	Theorems not proved by 4/4 semantic Otter	Theorems not proved by Otter
4 or less	77	101	93	105	5
5	3	8	6	8	1
6	0	1	0	0	1
7	0	1	0	0	1
8	0	6	2	6	11
9	1	1	1	1	1
10 to 19	0	7	2	2	6
FOF	0	2	2	2	5

Table 5. 2/2 semantic Otter vs. other semantic versions (on theorems from Reference Set proved by both compared versions)

Version of Otter	Theorems on which 2/2 semantic Otter is faster	Theorems on which 2/2 semantic Otter is slower
2/3 semantic Otter	169	12
3/3 semantic Otter	121	2
4/4 semantic Otter	187	4

procedure for some terms s and t we first check if for each of our models M_i it holds that $V_{M_i}(t, M_i) \subseteq V_{M_i}(s, M_i)$. If this is not the case we can be sure the terms do not match. Otherwise we proceed with the original EQP *matching*.

Our program was tested on Lemma 1 and Lemma 2 from the proof of the famous Robbins Conjecture [MC97]. The results we got are quite encouraging (see Table 6)

Table 6. EQP vs. semantic EQP on the lemmas of Robbins Conjecture

	EQP	semantic EQP
Lemma 1 - total time	72.67 sec	36.74 sec
Lemma 1 - matching time	56.13 sec	20.49 sec
Lemma 2 - total time	25477.20 sec	11405.72 sec
Lemma 2 - matching time	21030.06 sec	6812.41 sec

References

C93.   J. Christian; Flat terms, discrimination nets, and fast term rewriting; Journal of Automated Reasoning 10(1), 95-113 (1993)
EQP.   EQP Equational Prover; http://www-unix.mcs.anl.gov/AR/eqp/
G86.   S. Greenbaum; Input transformations and resolution implementation techniques for theorem proving in first order logic, PhD thesis, Univ. of Illinois, at Urbana Champaign, (1986)
MC97. W. McCune, "Solution of the Robbins Problem", Journal of Automated Reasoning 19(3), 263–276 (1997)
OT.   Otter: An Automated Deduction System; http://www-unix.mcs.anl.gov/AR/otter/
TPTP. The TPTP (Thousands of Problems for Theorem Provers) Problem Library for Automated Theorem Proving by Geoff Sutcliffe and Christian Suttner; http://www.cs.miami.edu/~tptp/
SRV01. R. Sekar, I.V. Ramakrishnan, A. Voronkov; Term Indexing; in Handbook of Automated Reasoning, A. Robinson and A. Voronkov eds, Elsevier/MIT Press, 2001
V95.   A. Voronkov; The anatomy of vampire: implementing bottom-up procedures with code trees; Journal of Automated Reasoning 15(2), 237–265 (1995)
V.   http://www.cs.man.ac.uk/~riazanoa/Vampire/ and http://www.prover.info/

Suitable Graphs for Answer Set Programming

Thomas Linke and Vladimir Sarsakov

Institut für Informatik, Universität Potsdam
linke@cs.uni-potsdam.de

Abstract. Often graphs are used to investigate properties of logic programs. In general, different graphs represent different kinds of information of the underlying programs. Sometimes this information is not sufficient for solving a certain problem. In this paper we define graphs which are *suitable* for computing answer sets of logic programs. Intuitively, a graph associated to a logic program is suitable for answer set semantics if its structure is sufficient to compute the answer sets of the corresponding program. We identify different classes of graphs to be suitable for different classes of programs. We also give first experimental results showing the impact of the used graph type to one particular graph based algorithm for answer set computation.

1 Introduction

Many different types of graphs are associated with a given logic program in order to investigate its properties or to compute its answer sets. Among them we find dependency graphs (DGs) [3], (defined on atoms), rule graphs (RGs) [9] (defined on rules for reduced negative normal programs) and more recently extended dependency graphs (EDG) [6,8] (defined on labeled atoms), as well as rule dependency graphs (RDGs) [12,16] (defined on rules of normal programs). In general, different graphs represent different dependencies among rules or atoms (literals) of a given program. Sometimes this information is not sufficient for solving a certain problem. In this paper we are interested in the question which graphs are suitable for computing answer sets of logic programs. Intuitively, a class of graphs is suitable for answer set semantics of a class of programs if the structure of a graph is sufficient to compute the answer sets of the corresponding program. For an example, let us take a look at the dependency graphs of the following two programs together with its answer sets:

$$P_1 = \left\{ \begin{array}{l} x \leftarrow not\ a, not\ x. \\ x \leftarrow not\ b. \\ a \leftarrow not\ b. \\ b \leftarrow not\ a. \end{array} \right\} \qquad P_2 = \left\{ \begin{array}{l} x \leftarrow not\ a, not\ b, not\ x. \\ a \leftarrow not\ b. \\ b \leftarrow not\ a. \end{array} \right\}$$

$AS(P_1) = \{\{a, x\}\}$ $\qquad AS(P_2) = \{\{a\}, \{b\}\}.$

The dependency graph [3] of a program is defined on its atoms s.t. there is a positive (negative) edge from p to q if p appears positively (negatively) in the body of a rule with head q. According to this definition both programs P_1 and P_2 have the same DG which is shown in Figure 1. On the other hand, programs P_1

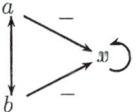

Fig. 1. The dependency graph of programs P_1 and P_2

and P_2 have different answer sets $AS(P_1)$ and $AS(P_2)$. This semantic difference between the two programs cannot be detected from the structure of the corresponding dependency graph, since it does not contain information on the rules of the two programs. Hence classical dependency graphs are not suitable for answer set computation of negative programs (programs without positive body atoms). For dealing with this problem different alternative graph representations for logic programs have been proposed [9,6,18,13,16]. However, considering normal logic programs with multiple positive atoms in the bodies of rules, same problems as the above arise in the aforementioned approaches. In this case, rule graphs for example are not able to represent information indicating which node (rule) is responsible for deriving which positive body atom of another rule (see RDG of programs P_4 and P_5 in Figure 4). Therefore the approaches in [9,6] rely on a translation of normal programs into negative ones before using there respective graph representation for characterizing answer sets, whereas [13,18] utilizes some kind of additional meta-information not present in the graph structure. In fact, so far this kind of meta-information was also used in the noMoRe system [1] to deal with arbitrary normal programs.

This paper deals with this problem. In fact, different types of graphs are defined and their suitability for answer set computation of some syntactically restricted subclasses of nested logic programs [15] is investigated. The main idea of our approach is to allow different kinds of nodes in a graph, in order to incorporate more information of the underlying logic program, than e.g. the classical dependency graph does (see above example and Figure 1). This avoids the use of negative programs or meta-information. In fact, a program consists of bodies, rules and heads, which all may appear as nodes in a corresponding graph. The first central contribution of this work is the identification of so-called *body-head-graphs* as the most compact graph representation for all classes of programs under consideration. We formalize the concept of suitability and prove that body-head-graphs are suitable for answer set computation of *normal nested logic programs (nNLPs)*, a syntactically restricted subclass of nested logic programs. To the best of our knowledge, this is the first time that graphs corresponding to those programs are introduced and utilized to characterize and compute their answer sets. Hence we generalize results from [9,6,18,13,16]. Additionally, we obtain suitable graphs for *normal logic programs (nLP)*, normal logic programs with at *most one positive body atom* (nLP_1) and *negative* programs (nLP_0).

Furthermore, we have implemented our approach in the noMoRe system. This ensures fair experimental results when comparing the different graph representations. Our first experimental results indicate that body-head-graphs are better suited for computing answer sets than the other discussed graph representations, as they lead to the most efficient graph-based computation of answer sets.

The paper is organized as follows. In the next section basic concepts for logic programming and directed graphs are introduced. Section 3 defines different new graphs associated with logic programs. Then, in Section 4, a special nonstandard graph coloring for a general class of labeled directed graphs is defined without any references to programs. In Section 5 suitability of graphs for answer sets programming is defined by relating the aforementioned graph colorings for the graphs given in Section 3 to the answer sets of the corresponding programs. Experimental results comparing the different graphs are presented in Section 6 and Section 7 concludes the paper.

2 Background

In this paper we consider a proper subclass of propositional nested logic programs [14]. Nested logic programs generalize logic programs by allowing bodies and heads of rules to contain arbitrary nested expressions. Let $\mathcal{L}$ be a propositional language. Then an *expression* is formed from propositional atoms from $\mathcal{L}$ using the operators

$$,\quad ;\quad not$$

standing for conjunction, disjunction and default negation, respectively. *Literals* are expressions of the form p (*positive* literals) or $not\ p$ (*negative* literals), where p is some propositional atom. A *rule* r has the form

$$h_1, \ldots, h_k \leftarrow B_1; \ldots; B_n \qquad (1)$$

where $h_1, \ldots, h_k$ are atoms and $B_1, \ldots, B_n$ are conjunctions of literals or $\top$ (true) or $\bot$ (false). A rule r is called a *fact* if $n = 1$ and $B_1 = \top$; r is called *normal* if $k = 1$ and $n = 1$. If rule r contains no default negation not then it is called a *basic* rule; a program is *basic* if it contains only basic rules. A *normal nested logic program* (nNLP) is a finite set of rules of the form (1). A *normal logic program* (nLP) is a finite set of normal rules. Furthermore, we consider the class of normal programs with *at most one positive body literal* (nLP_1) and the class of *negative programs* (nLP_0), which do not have any positive body literals. Notice that $nLP_0 \subset nLP_1 \subset nLP \subset nNLP$. For a rule r we define the *head* and the *body* of r as $Head(r) = \{h_1, \ldots, h_k\}$ and $Body(r) = \{B_1, \ldots, B_n\}$, respectively. For a set of rules P we define $Head(P) = \cup_{r \in P} Head(r)$ and $Body(P) = \cup_{r \in P} Body(r)$. If $B \in Body(P)$ s.t. $B = (p_1, \ldots, p_l, not\ s_1, \ldots, not\ s_m)$ then $B^+ = \{p_1, \ldots, p_l\}$ and $B^- = \{s_1, \ldots, s_m\}$ denote the positive and negative part of B, respectively. If $B = \top$ then we set $B^+ = B^- = \emptyset$. If $B = \bot$ then we set $B^+ = B^- = \bot$. Furthermore, let $Atm(P)$ denote the set of all atoms occurring in program P.

Answer sets were first defined in [15] for general nested programs. Here we adapt the definition of stable models [11] (answer sets for normal programs) to normal nested logic programs. A set of atoms X is *closed under* a basic program P iff for any $r \in P$, $Head(r) \subseteq X$ whenever there is a $B \in Body(r)$ s.t. $B^+ \subseteq X$. The smallest set of atoms which is closed under a basic program P is denoted by $Cn(P)$. The *reduct*, P^X, of a program P *relative to* a set X of atoms is defined in two steps. First, let $B \in Body(P)$ and let X be some set of atoms. Then the *reduct* B^X of B relative to X is defined as

$$B^X = \begin{cases} B^+ & \text{if } B^- \cap X = \emptyset \\ \bot & \text{otherwise.} \end{cases}$$

For a rule of the form (1) we define $r^X = h_1, \ldots, h_k \leftarrow B_1^X; \ldots; B_n^X$. Second, for a normal nested program P we define $P^X = \{r^X \mid r \in P \text{ and } Body(r^X) \neq \{\bot\}\}$. Then P^X is a basic program. We say that a set X of atoms is an *answer set* of a program P iff $Cn(P^X) = X$. For normal logic programs this definition coincides with the definition of stable models [14]. The set of all answer sets of program P is denoted by $AS(P)$.

Now let P be a normal nested logic program and let X be a set of atoms. Rule $r \in P$ is *captured wrt* X iff for each $B \in Body(r)$ we have $B^+ \cup B^- \subseteq X$. Program P is *captured* iff all of its rules are captured wrt $Head(P)$. Observe that each logic program P can be transformed to some captured program P' s.t. $AS(P) = AS(P')$. Hence, without loss of generality, we restrict ourselves to captured programs.

A *directed graph* (or *digraph*) G is a pair $G = (V, E)$ such that V is a finite set (nodes) and $E \subseteq V \times V$ is a set (arcs). For a digraph $G = (V, E)$ and a vertex $v \in V$, we define the sets of all *predecessors* and *successors* of v as $Pred(v) = \{u \mid (u, v) \in E\}$ and $Succ(v) = \{u \mid (v, u) \in E\}$, respectively. A digraph $G' = (V', E')$ is a *subgraph* of $G = (V, E)$ iff $V' \subseteq V$ and $E' \subseteq E$. A *path from* v *to* v' in $G = (V, E)$ is a sequence $P_{vv'} = (v_1, \ldots, v_n)$ of nodes of G s.t. $n > 1$, $v = v_1$, $v' = v_n$ and $(v_i, v_{i+1}) \in E$ for each $1 \leq i < n$. A graph $G = (V, E)$ is *acyclic* iff for each node v there is no path from v to v.

3 Graphs for Logic Programs

This section defines different graphs corresponding to logic programs. We need the following general concept of labeled digraphs.

Definition 1. *Let V and L and $E \subseteq V \times V$ be finite sets. A quadruple $G = (V, E, l, L)$ is a labeled digraph iff the following two conditions hold:*

1. *(V, E) is a digraph and*
2. *$l : E \to L$ is a function (labeling function).*

Labeld digraph $G = (V, E, l, L)$ is *acyclic* iff digraph (V, E) is acyclic. Let $G = (V, E, l, L)$ be a labeled digraph s.t. $L = \{l_1, \ldots, l_n\}$. Then we denote G by $(V, E_{l_1}, \ldots, E_{l_n})$ where $E_k = \{(u, v) \mid (u, v) \in E, l((u, v)) = k\}$ for each $k \in L$.

Let $\mathcal{G}_{+,*,-}$ denote the class of labeled digraphs with label set $L = \{+,*,-\}$. $G = (V, E_+, E_*, E_-)$ is a *subgraph* of $G' = (V', E'_+, E'_*, E'_-)$ iff $V \subseteq V'$ and $E_i \subseteq E'_i$ for each $i \in \{+,*,-\}$.

The arcs in $G \in \mathcal{G}_{+,*,-}$ are called *i-arcs* for each $i \in L$. For a graph $G \in \mathcal{G}_{+,*,-}$ and a node v of G define the *i-predecessors* and *i-successors* of v for each $i \in L$ as follows:
$$\text{Pred}_G^i(v) = \{v' \mid (v', v) \in E_i\} \text{ for } i \in \{+,*,-\}$$
$$\text{Succ}_G^i(v) = \{v' \mid (v, v') \in E_i\} \text{ for } i \in \{+,*,-\}.$$

As mentioned in Section 1, a program consists of bodies, rules and heads (atoms). Based on this observation we define different dependency graphs associated with a program P.

Definition 2. *Let P be a logic program.*
The BH-graph *(body-head-graph)* $BH_P = (Body(P) \cup Head(P), E_+, E_*, E_-)$ *of P is a directed graph with labeled arcs*

$$E_+ = \{(B, h) \mid r \in P, B \in Body(r), h \in Head(r)\}$$
$$E_* = \{(h, B) \mid B \in Body(P), h \in Head(P), h \in B^+\}$$
$$E_- = \{(h, B) \mid B \in Body(P), h \in Head(P), h \in B^-\}.$$

The RH-graph *(rule-head-graph)* $RH_P = (P \cup Head(P), E_+, E_*, E_-)$ *of P is a directed graph with labeled arcs*

$$E_+ = \{(r, h) \mid r \in P, h \in Head(r)\}$$
$$E_* = \{(h, r) \mid r \in P, h \in Head(P), h \in B^+, B \in Body(r)\}$$
$$E_- = \{(h, r) \mid r \in P, h \in Head(P), h \in B^-, B \in Body(r)\}.$$

The BR-graph *(body-rule-graph)* $BR_P = (Body(P) \cup P, E_+, \emptyset, E_-)$ *of P is a directed graph with labeled arcs*

$$E_+ = \{(B, r) \mid r \in P, B \in Body(r)\} \cup$$
$$\{(r, B) \mid r \in P, B \in Body(P), Head(r) \cap B^+ \neq \emptyset\}$$
$$E_- = \{(r, B) \mid r \in P, B \in Body(P), Head(r) \cap B^- \neq \emptyset\}.$$

Observe that all graphs in Definition 2 have two different kinds of nodes such as rules and heads for rule-head-graphs, bodies and rules for body-rule-graphs and bodies and heads for body-head-graphs. Oppositely many graphs found in the literature have a single kind of nodes such as the atoms or the rules of a given program. The introduction of two different kinds of nodes enables us to put more information into a graph corresponding to a logic program. For the same purpose a similar technique based on indexed copies of nodes of the classical DG was proposed in [6].

Take a look at the RH-graph of the following two normal nested programs:

$$P_2 = \begin{cases} x \leftarrow not\ a, not\ b, not\ x. \\ a \leftarrow not\ b. \\ b \leftarrow not\ a. \end{cases} \qquad P_3 = \begin{cases} x \leftarrow (not\ a, not\ x); (not\ b). \\ a \leftarrow not\ b. \\ b \leftarrow not\ a. \end{cases}$$

$AS(P_2) = \{\{a\}, \{b\}\}$ \qquad\qquad $AS(P_3) = \{\{a, x\}\}.$

Assume the rules of both programs are named r_1, r_2 and r_3, respectively. Then P_2 and P_3 have the same RH-graph shown in Figure 2. Since both programs process different answer sets the RH-graph should not be suitable for nNLP. However, the clearly different BH-graphs of P_2 and P_3 are shown in Figure 3[1].

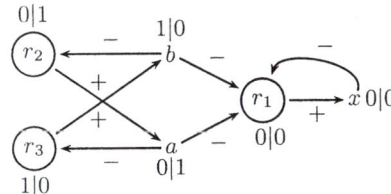

Fig. 2. RH-graph of programs P_2 and P_3

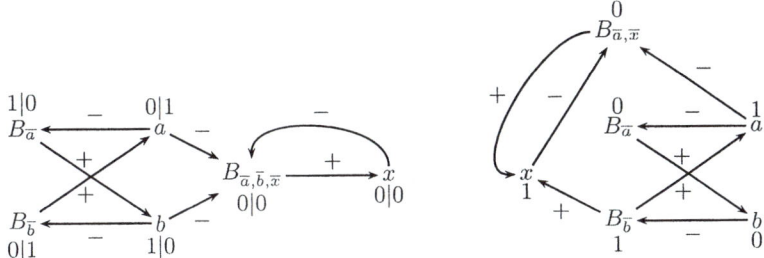

Fig. 3. BH-graphs of programs P_2 (left) and P_3 (right)

For completeness we also investigate three types of graphs where the nodes are the bodies, rules and heads, respectively.

Definition 3. *Let P be a logic program.*
The B-graph (body-graph) $B_P = (Body(P), E_+, \emptyset, E_-)$ of P is a directed graph with labeled arcs

$$E_+ = \{(B', B) \mid r' \in P, B' \in Body(r'), Head(r') \cap B^+ \neq \emptyset\}$$
$$E_- = \{(B', B) \mid r' \in P, B' \in Body(r'), Head(r') \cap B^- \neq \emptyset\}.$$

The R-graph (rule-graph) $R_P = (P, E_+, \emptyset, E_-)$ of P is a directed graph with labeled arcs

$$E_+ = \{(r', r) \mid Head(r') \cap B^+ \neq \emptyset, B \in Body(r)\}$$
$$E_- = \{(r', r) \mid Head(r') \cap B^- \neq \emptyset, B \in Body(r)\}.$$

---

[1] Observe that all graphs in the figures are depicted together with its a-colorings, which are defined in Section 3 and further investigated in Section 4.

The H-graph (head-graph) $H_P = (Head(P), E_+, \emptyset, E_-)$ of P is a directed graph with labeled arcs

$$E_+ = \{(h', h) \mid r \in P, h \in Head(r), h' \in B^+ \text{ for } B \in Body(r)\}$$
$$E_- = \{(h', h) \mid r \in P, h \in Head(r), h' \in B^- \text{ for } B \in Body(r)\}.$$

Observe, that for normal programs R_P and H_P coincide with the rule dependency graph (RDG) and the classical dependency graph (DG), respectively. However, in this paper we use a different arc labeling to obtain a uniform graph representation framework. That is, 1-arcs and 0-arcs of RDGs are renamed to $-$-arcs and $+$-arcs, respectively. Figure 4 shows the R-graph (RDG) of the following two programs:

$$P_4 = \begin{Bmatrix} r_1 : a \leftarrow not\ b. \\ r_2 : b \leftarrow not\ a. \\ r_3 : c \leftarrow a. \\ r_4 : d \leftarrow b. \\ r_5 : x \leftarrow c, d. \\ r_6 : x \leftarrow not\ x. \end{Bmatrix} \qquad P_5 = \begin{Bmatrix} r_1 : a \leftarrow not\ b. \\ r_2 : b \leftarrow not\ a. \\ r_3 : c \leftarrow a. \\ r_4 : c \leftarrow b. \\ r_5 : x \leftarrow c. \\ r_6 : x \leftarrow not\ x. \end{Bmatrix}$$

$$AS(P_4) = \emptyset \qquad\qquad AS(P_5) = \{\{a, c, x\}, \{b, c, x\}\}.$$

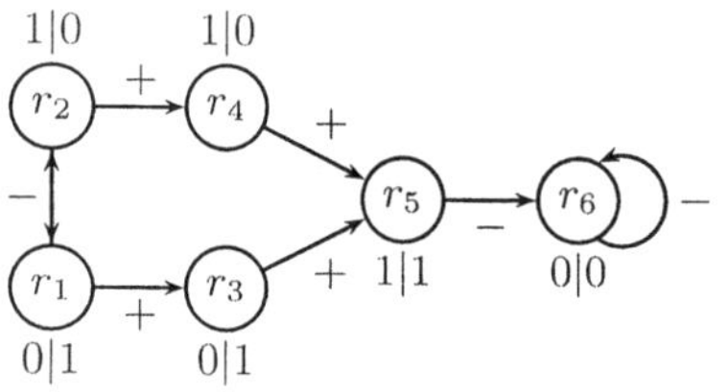

Fig. 4. R-graph of programs P_4 and P_5

According to Definition 3, in the R-graph of both programs P_4 and P_5, rules r_3 and r_4 are both $+$-predecessors of r_5. Hence R-graphs are not able to represent the information indicating which of the positive body atoms is responsible for which $+$-predecessor of node r_5. Therefore, following our intuition, R-graphs should not be suitable for normal programs, as both programs P_4 and P_5 have the same R-graph but different answer sets. On the other hand, the RH-graphs of P_4 and P_5 are different, because in the first case (P_4) r_5 has $*$-predecessors c and d, whereas in the second case (P_5) r_5 has the single $*$-predecessor c. The same holds for the BH-graph of both programs. So far we have seen that the graphs defined in this section are able to represent different information about logic programs.

Finally, we define different mappings associating the graphs from Definitions 2 and 3 to a given program.

Definition 4. *For each* $\Gamma \in \{BH, RH, BR, R, B, H\}$ *define mapping* $\Gamma : nNLP \to \mathcal{G}_{+,*,-}$ *as* $P \mapsto \Gamma_P$.

4 Graphs and A-Colorings

In this section, we define a special kind of labeled digraphs, without any reference to logic programs. For those graphs we define non-standard 2-colorings (with two colors), which reflect activation and deactivation of the nodes of a given graph. Hence, these colorings are called *a-colorings*.

The intuition behind the following definition is to give a graph-based characterization of the Cn-operator for all graphs presented in the last section.

Definition 5. *Let $G, G^v \in \mathcal{G}_{+,*,-}$ be labeled digraphs s.t. $G = (V, E_+, E_*, E_-)$, $G^v = (V^v, E_+^v, E_*^v, \emptyset)$ and G^v is a subgraph of G s.t. $v \in V^v$.*

Then G^v is a proof graph for v in G iff G^v is acyclic and for each $v' \in V^v$ the following two conditions hold:

1. $\{(v'', v') \mid v'' \in Pred_G^*(v')\} \subseteq E_*^v$
2. *if $Pred_G^+(v') \neq \emptyset$ then $\{(v'', v') \mid v'' \in Pred_G^+(v')\} \cap E_+^v \neq \emptyset$.*

According to this definition a proof graph G^v for v in G is acyclic and does not contain any $-$-arcs. That is, proof graphs do not consider negative body atoms while ensuring recursive supportedness for single nodes (e.g. rules, atoms). In this way, proof graphs form a graph-theoretical counterpart of $Cn(P^X)$ where negative body atoms are not considered by taking the reduct P^X instead of the initial program P. Furthermore, for a node v' in a proof graph G^v all $*$-predecessors and all arcs from them to v' in G are also arcs in G^v; and if there exist $+$-predecessors of v' in G then at least one of them together with its $+$-arc to v' is also in G^v. The intuition behind this definition is to separate two different (recursive) activation modes of nodes depending on its $*$- or $+$-predecessors, respectively. The idea is that, a node can be activated if all of its $*$-predecessors are active and it can be activated if some of its $+$-predecessors are active, provided that there are some $+$-predecessors. Observe, that for all graphs defined in Section 3, every node has either $*$-predecessors or $+$-predecessors (or none of them), but not both. On the other hand, $-$-arcs represent negative dependencies (blockage) between nodes and a node may have $-$-predecessors or not, no matter which other predecessors it has.

For example, a body B in a BH-graph may be activated if **all** of its $*$-predecessors (heads) are active, which means if all positive atoms in B are true then B may also be true depending only on its negative atoms. On the other hand a head h in a BH-graph is activated if **one** of its $+$-predecessors (bodies) is active, which means h is true if there exists some applicable rule r s.t. $B \in Body(r)$ and $h \in Head(r)$[2].

The concept of a proof graph is closely related to the one of a maximal support graph for R-graphs (RDGs) [12]. There are two differences. First, proof graphs are more general since they are defined for all graphs presented in Section 3, whereas maximal support graphs are only defined for rule graphs (RDGs). Second, when restricting our attention to rule-graphs (RDGs) a maximal support graph is the "union" of all proof graphs for all of its nodes (rules).

---

[2] Heads do not have $-$-predecessors.

A *coloring* of a graph $G = (V, E_+, E_*, E_-)$ is a mapping $\mathcal{C} : V \to \{1, 0\}$. We define $\mathcal{C}_1 = \{v \mid \mathcal{C}(v) = 1\}$ and $\mathcal{C}_0 = \{v \mid \mathcal{C}(v) = 0\}$. If a node is colored with 1 this node is activated and if it is colored 0 it is deactivated. A total coloring $\mathcal{C}$ is identified with $(\mathcal{C}_1, \mathcal{C}_0)$ and the pair $(G, \mathcal{C})$ is called a *colored graph*. Let $\mathbb{C}_G$ denote the set of all colorings of G.

Definition 6. *Let $\mathcal{C}$ be a total coloring of $G = (V, E_+, E_*, E_-)$ and let $v \in V$ be a node.*

Then v is blocked wrt $(G, \mathcal{C})$ iff there exists $v' \in Pred^-(v)$ s.t. $v' \in \mathcal{C}_1$.

Furthermore, v is grounded wrt $(G, \mathcal{C})$ iff there exists a proof graph G^v for v in G s.t. $V^v \setminus \{v\} \subseteq \mathcal{C}_1$.

With these concepts at hand, we define a-colorings as follows:

Definition 7. *Let $G \in \mathcal{G}_{+,*,-}$ be a labeled digraph s.t. $G = (V, E_+, E_*, E_-)$ and let $\mathcal{C}$ be a total coloring of G. Then $\mathcal{C}$ is an a-coloring of G iff for each $v \in V$ we have*

$$v \in \mathcal{C}_1 \text{ iff } v \text{ is grounded and not blocked wrt } (G, \mathcal{C}).$$

Let $ACol(G)$ denote the set of all a-colorings of G. As examples, in Figures 2, 3 and 4 we also have depicted the a-colorings of all shown graphs. If there are two a-colorings they are given right and left of |, respectively. Examples how to compute a-colorings of R-graphs (RDGs) in terms of different operators can be found in [12][3]. Furthermore, the noMoRe system can also be used for a step-by-step visualization of the computation of a-colorings for BH-, RH- and R-graphs [5]. This nicely demonstrates the different behavior of these graphs during answer set computation.

5 Suitability

In this section, we further clarify our intuition of suitable graphs for answer set programming (ASP). The idea is to relate a-colorings of graphs, which are defined independently of logic programs (see Section 3), to answer sets of the corresponding programs. If it is possible to establish a tractable one to one correspondence between the answer sets of the programs (of a given class) and the a-colorings of the corresponding graphs then the class of those graphs is suitable for the class of programs. Let $\mathcal{G}$ be a class of graphs and define $\mathbb{C}_\mathcal{G} = \bigcup_{G \in \mathcal{G}} \mathbb{C}_G$, the collection of all coloring of graphs in $\mathcal{G}$.

Definition 8. *Let $\mathcal{P}$ be a class of logic programs and let $\Gamma : \mathcal{P} \to \mathcal{G}_{+,*,-}$ be a mapping.*

Then Γ is suitable for $\mathcal{P}$ iff there exists a partial, polynomial time mapping $\varphi : \mathcal{P} \times \mathbb{C}_{\mathcal{G}_{+,*,-}} \to 2^\mathcal{L}$ s.t. for each $P \in \mathcal{P}$ we have

1. *if $\mathcal{C} \in ACol(\Gamma_P)$ then $\varphi(P, \mathcal{C}) \in AS(P)$*

---

[3] In [12] a-colorings are called *admissible colorings*, since they are defined by referring to the generating rules of answer sets.

2. if $X \in AS(P)$ then there is a unique $\mathcal{C} \in ACol(\Gamma_P)$ s.t. $\varphi(P,\mathcal{C}) = X$.

This definition requires an one to one correspondence between a-colorings and answer sets. Notice that it is important that mapping φ is computable in polynomial time, because otherwise we would always get a trivial φ by directly computing the answer sets of P without referring to the a-colorings of Γ_P. By forcing φ to be polynomial, the answer set has to be easily extractable from a given a-coloring of a corresponding graph.

We have the following main results:

Theorem 1. *Let BH, RH, BR, R, B and H the mappings from Definition 4. Then we have the following results:*

1. *BH is suitable for $nNLP$.*
2. *RH is suitable for nLP.*
3. *BR, R and B are suitable for nLP_1/nLP_0.*
4. *RH is not suitable for $nNLP$.*
5. *BR, R and B are not suitable for nLP.*
6. *H is not suitable for nLP_0.*

In fact, examples P_3, P_4 and P_1 serve as counterexamples to show the negative results 4., 5. (only for R-graphs) and 6. in Theorem 1, respectively. On the other hand, the a-colorings of the BH-graphs of P_2 and P_3 in Figure 3 correspond to the respective answer set of both programs.

Next we investigate how exactly answer sets and a-colorings are related wrt the different graphs from Section 3. Let P be a program and let $X \subseteq Atm(P)$ be a set of atoms. We define the set of generating bodies and the set of generating rules of P wrt X as

$$GB(P,X) = \{B \in Body(P) \mid B^+ \subseteq X \text{ and } B^- \cap X = \emptyset\} \text{ and}$$
$$GR(P,X) = \{r \in P \mid \text{ there is some } B \in Body(r) \text{ s.t. } B \in GB(P,X)\},$$

respectively. Furthermore, for a subset $S \subseteq P \cup Body(P) \cup Head(P)$ we define $Hs(S) = S \cap Head(P)$, $Bs(S) = S \cap Body(P)$ and $Rs(S) = S \cap P$.

Theorem 2. *Let P be a logic program, let $\Gamma \in \{BH, RH, BR, B, R, H\}$, let $\Gamma_P = (V, E_+, E_*, E_-)$ be the Γ-graph of P and let $\mathcal{C}$ be a total coloring of Γ_P. Then we have the following equivalences:*

1. *If $P \in nNLP$ then $\mathcal{C} \in ACol(BH_P)$ s.t. $X = Hs(\mathcal{C}_1)$ iff
$X \in AS(P)$ s.t. $\mathcal{C}_1 = GB(P,X) \cup X$.*
2. *If $P \in nLP$ then $\mathcal{C} \in ACol(RH_P)$ s.t. $X = Hs(\mathcal{C}_1)$ iff
$X \in AS(P)$ s.t. $\mathcal{C}_1 = GR(P,X) \cup X$.*
3. *If $P \in nLP_1$ then $\mathcal{C} \in ACol(BR_P)$ s.t. $X = Head(Rs(\mathcal{C}_1))$ iff
$X \in AS(P)$ s.t. $\mathcal{C}_1 = GB(P,X) \cup GR(P,X)$.*
4. *If $P \in nLP_1$ then $\mathcal{C} \in ACol(R_P)$ s.t. $X = Head(\mathcal{C}_1)$ iff
$X \in AS(P)$ s.t. $\mathcal{C}_1 = GR(P,X)$.*
5. *If $P \in nLP_1$ then $\mathcal{C} \in ACol(B_P)$ s.t. $X = Head(\{r \in P \mid Body(r) \cap \mathcal{C}_1 \neq \emptyset\})$
iff $X \in AS(P)$ s.t. $\mathcal{C}_1 = GB(P,X)$.*

This theorem demonstrates how an answer set can be effectively extracted from an a-coloring of a graph, provided that the graph is suitable for the underlying program class.

6 Empirical Results

Our main goal on the empirical part of this work was to do some fair experiments comparing different graphs within an uniform implementation. Hence, for experimental results, we have implemented computation of a-colorings for BH-, RH- and R-graphs in noMoRe [1][4]. This ensures, that all the results of our experiments are fully comparable, since all parts of the implementation except the underlying graph structure (which includes most of the source code as well as used algorithms for graph coloring), are the same for all tests. In fact, our new implementation generalizes the basic graph coloring procedure of noMoRe, which is formally discussed in [13], to BH- and RH-graphs.

As benchmarks we present Hamiltonian cycle (HAM) problems for two reasons. First, in [20] it is pointed out that HAM problems may be the "golden standard" of ASP benchmarking, since the problem description is not tight. That is, HAM problems cannot be solved by using a standard SAT solver on the program completion of a given program (which is possible for most of the current ASP problems). Second, our HAM encoding leads to programs in nLP$_1$ and thus provides us with a hard problem which can also be tested with R-graphs.

In Tables 1 and 2 we have summarized some results for HAM problems for complete graphs (all answer sets) and so-called *clumpy* graphs (one answer set), respectively. Table 1 gives the number of choices, nodes and edges as well as the time needed for computing all a-colorings of BH-, RH- and R-graphs for the HAM problem of complete graphs with n nodes. Table 2 gives the same results for computing one a-coloring of those graphs for the HAM problem for clumpy graphs with n clumps.

Observe that, although the HAM problem for complete graphs is trivial for humans, it is difficult for ASP solvers, especially if we want to compute multiple answer sets, since it reflects the system behavior on backtracking. Clumpy graphs were introduced in [20] as hard instances of HAM problems, since they are directed graphs with less uniform distributed edges (so called "clumps"), such that the existence of some (but few) Hamiltonian cycles is guaranteed (see [20] for details). Our results show (i) that BH-graphs provide the most compact graph representation for logic programs and (ii) that this compactness pays off in the size of the graph, in the number of choices and in the time needed. Similar effects can also be observed for other problem classes such as planning and coloring problems. The new version of noMoRe including test cases is available at http://www.cs.uni-potsdam.de/~linke/nomore.

---

[4] For results comparing a new C++ Version of noMoRe using BH-graphs with state-of-the-art ASP systems like smodels and dlv see [19,4].

Table 1. Results for computing **all** answer sets of HAM problems on complete graphs with n nodes

HAM $n =$	7			8			9		
graph	BH	RH	R	BH	RH	R	BH	RH	R
choices	1853	2676	2676	14776	21259	21259	132343	190240	190240
nodes	108	150	93	139	195	122	174	240	155
edges	279	279	1548	366	366	2394	465	465	3504
time	3.12s	6.03s	7.46s	59.73s	117.6s	138.38s	325s	683s	916s

Table 2. Results for computing **one** answer set of HAM problems on clumpy graphs with n clumps. For each n average values of five different instances are given

clumps $n =$	4			5			6		
graph	BH	RH	R	BH	RH	R	BH	RH	R
choices	35	41	60.8	73.6	86	180	8119	8567	21972
nodes	178.4	238	141	293.6	397	237	464.2	632	380
edges	423	423	1209	711	711	2300	1140	1140	3253
time	0.07s	0.12s	0.14s	0.31s	6.87s	0.96s	41.63s	67.74s	196.8s

7 Related Work and Discussion

Graphs associated with logic programs are used to detect structural properties of programs, such as stratification [2], existence of answer sets [10,6], or characterization of answer set semantics and well-founded semantics [9,6,16,18]. The usage of rule-oriented dependency graphs is common to [9,6,16,13]. In fact, the coloration of such graphs for characterizing answer sets was independently developed in [6] and [16] and further investigated in [13]. However, as the two normal logic programs P_2 and P_3 demonstrate, rule (dependency) graphs are not suitable for computing answer sets of normal logic programs.

Therefore, the approaches in [9,6] rely on translations of normal programs into negative ones before using their respective dependency graphs for characterizing answer sets. In the noMoRe system [1] and its underlying theory [18,13,17] some kind of additional (meta-)information not present in the rule graph structure is necessary for deciding which positive body atoms of a rule like $a \leftarrow b_1, \ldots, b_n$ are already suppported by other rules.

The main contribution of this work is the formal introduction of suitability for existing and newly introduced graphs associated with logic programs, to characterize situations where no additional information except the graph structure is needed. In fact, we have generalized a-colorings as given in [16,18] to all graphs introduced in this paper. Especially body-head-graphs, which are shown to be suitable for normal (nested) logic programs, handle multiple positive body atoms in normal programs in an elegant and correct way and thus avoid the above mentioned meta-information. Since none of the aforementioned graph-based approaches deals with normal nested logic programs our work generalizes all those approaches[5]. Furthermore, BH-graphs also handle disjunctions of conjunctions of literals as bodies correctly. To the best of our knowledge, this is the first time that graphs corresponding to normal nested programs are introduced and used for characterizing and computing answer sets. As a byproduct the application of transformations utilized in [17] in order to replace all rules with same head and all rules with same body by just one nested normal rule, respectively, comes for free when using BH-graphs. That is, for all considered program classes body-head-graphs give a much more compact representation than the other mentioned graphs. This also turns out in the efficiency of their implementation compared with the other graph representations (see Section 6) and the observation that the ratio of the number of distinct bodies over the number of rules is alway less than one. Hence BH-graphs should be the preferred graph representation of logic programs.

Also [7] compares different graph representations, but our approach is different in two important aspects. First, we deal with a syntactically richer class of programs and second, our concept of suitability relies on graph colorings whereas the one in [7] is defined directly wrt answer sets and uses atom renaming.

Finally, one may ask whether we do not have investigated rule-body-head-graphs in this context. The reason is that distinguishing rules and bodies does not give much more information on the underlying logic program. This is reflected in Theorem 1, where it is shown that BH-graphs are sufficient to deal with normal nested programs; another argument is that BR-graphs are even not suitable for normal logic programs and thus they are not able to represent more information than R- or B-graphs on its own.

Acknowledgements

The authors were partially supported by the German Science Foundation (DFG) under grant FOR 375/1 and SCHA 550/6, TP C and the Information Society Technologies program of the European Commission, Future and Emerging Technologies under the IST-2001-37004 WASP project.

References

1. C. Anger, K. Konczak, and T. Linke. NoMoRe: A system for non-monotonic reasoning under answer set semantics. In W. Faber T. Eiter and M. Truszczyński, editors, *Proceedings of the 6th International Conference on Logic Programming and Nonmonotonic Reasoning (LPNMR'01)*, pages 406–410. Springer, 2001.
2. K. Apt, H. Blair, and A. Walker. Towards a theory of declarative knowledge. In J. Minker, editor, *Foundations of Deductive Databases and Logic Programming*, chapter 2, pages 89–148. Morgan Kaufmann Publishers, 1987.

---

[5] Observe, that normal nested logic programs are also utilized in [21] for translating nested programs into extended ones.

3. K. R. Apt and R. N. Bol. Logic programming and negation: A survey. *Journal of Logic Programming*, 19/20:9–71, 1994.
4. Asparagus. http://asparagus.cs.uni-potsdam.de.
5. A. Bösel, T. Linke, and T. Schaub. Profiling answer set programming: The visualization component of the noMoRe system. In J. J. Alferes and J. Leite, editors, *Logics in Artificial Intelligence (JELIA04)*, volume 3229 of *Lecture Notes in Computer Science*, pages 702–705. Springer, 2004.
6. G. Brignoli, S. Costantini, O. D'Antona, and A. Provetti. Characterizing and computing stable models of logic programs: the non-stratified case. In C. Baral and H. Mohanty, editors, *Proc. of Conference on Information Technology*, pages 197–201, Bhubaneswar, India, December 1999. AAAI Press.
7. S. Costantini. Comparing different graph representations of logic programs under the answer set semantics. In T. C. Son and A. Provetti, editors, *Proc. of the AAAI Spring 2001 Symposium on: Answer Set Programming, Towards Efficient and Scalable Knowledge Representation and Reasoning*, Stanford, CA, USA, 2001. AAAI Press.
8. S. Costantini, O. D'Antona, and A. Provetti. On the equivalence and range of applicability of graph-based representations of logic programs. *Information Processing Letters*, 84(5):241–249, 2002.
9. Y. Dimopoulos and A. Torres. Graph theoretical structures in logic programs and default theories. *Theoretical Computer Science*, 170:209–244, 1996.
10. F. Fages. Consistency of clark's completion and the existence of stable models. *Journal of Methods of Logic in Computer Science*, 1:51–60, 1994.
11. M. Gelfond and V. Lifschitz. The stable model semantics for logic programming. In *Proceedings of the International Conference on Logic Programming*, pages 1070–1080. The MIT Press, 1988.
12. K. Konczak, T. Linke, and T. Schaub. Graphs and colorings for answer set programming: Abridged report. In V. Lifschitz and I. Niemelä, editors, *Proceedings of the Seventh International Conference on Logic Programming and Nonmonotonic Reasoning (LPNMR'04)*, volume 2923 of *Lecture Notes in Computer Science*, pages 127–140. Springer-Verlag Heidelberg, 2003.
13. K. Konczak, T. Linke, and T. Schaub. Graphs and colorings for answer set programming: Abridged report. In V. Lifschitz and I. Niemelä, editors, *Proceedings of the Seventh International Conference on Logic Programming and Nonmonotonic Reasoning (LPNMR'04)*, volume 2923 of *Lecture Notes in Artificial Intelligence*, pages 127–140. Springer Verlag, 2004.
14. V. Lifschitz. Answer set planning. In *Proceedings of the 1999 International Conference on Logic Programming*, pages 23–37. MIT Press, 1999.
15. V. Lifschitz, L. Tang, and H. Turner. Nested expressions in logic programs. *Annals of Mathematics and Artificial Intelligence*, 25(3-4):369–389, 1999.
16. T. Linke. Graph theoretical characterization and computation of answer sets. In B. Nebel, editor, *Proceedings of the International Joint Conference on Artificial Intelligence*, pages 641–645. Morgan Kaufmann Publishers, 2001.
17. T. Linke. Using nested logic programs for answer set programming. In M. De Voss and A. Provetti, editors, *Answer Set Programming: Advances in Theory and Implementation (ASP03)*, volume 78, pages 181–194. CEUR Workshop Proceedings, 2003.
18. T. Linke, C. Anger, and K. Konczak. More on nomore. In S. Flesca, S. Greco, N. Leone, and G. Ianni, editors, *Proceedings of the Eighth European on Logics in Artificial Intelligence (JELIA'02)*, volume 2424 of *Lecture Notes in Artificial Intelligence*, pages 468–480. Springer Verlag, 2002.

19. http://www.cs.uni-potsdam.de/nomore.
20. J. Ward and J. S. Schlipf. Answer set programming with clause learning. In V. Lifschitz and I. Niemelä, editors, *Proceedings of the Seventh International Conference on Logic Programming and Nonmonotonic Reasoning (LPNMR'04)*, volume 2923 of *Lecture Notes in Computer Science*, pages 302 – 313. Springer-Verlag Heidelberg, 2003.
21. J. You, L. Yuan, and M. Zhange. On the equivalence between answer sets and models of completion for nested logic programs. In *Proc. IJCAI03*, page to appear, 2003.

Weighted Answer Sets and Applications in Intelligence Analysis

Davy Van Nieuwenborgh*, Stijn Heymans, and Dirk Vermeir**

Dept. of Computer Science
Vrije Universiteit Brussel, VUB
Pleinlaan 2, B1050 Brussels, Belgium
{dvnieuwe,sheymans,dvermeir}@vub.ac.be

Abstract. The extended answer set semantics for simple logic programs, i.e. programs with only classical negation, allows for the defeat of rules to resolve contradictions. In addition, a partial order relation on the program's rules can be used to deduce a preference relation on its extended answer sets. In this paper, we propose a "quantitative" preference relation that associates a weight with each rule in a program. Intuitively, these weights define the "cost" of defeating a rule. An extended answer set is preferred if it minimizes the sum of the weights of its defeated rules. We characterize the expressiveness of the resulting semantics and show that it can capture negation as failure. Moreover the semantics can be conveniently extended to sequences of weight preferences, without increasing the expressiveness. We illustrate an application of the approach by showing how it can elegantly express subgraph isomorphic approximation problems, a concept often used in intelligence analysis to find specific regions of interest in a large graph of observed activities.

1 Introduction

Over the last decade a lot of research has been done on declarative programming using the answer set semantics [10,2,16], a generalization of the stable model semantics [8]. In answer set programming, one uses a logic program to modularly describe the requirements that must be fulfilled by the solutions to a particular problem, i.e. the answer sets of the program correspond to the intended solutions of the problem. One of the possible problems in answer set programming is the absence of any solutions in case of inconsistent programs. To remedy this, the authors proposed [14] the *extended answer set semantics* which allows for the *defeat* of problematic rules. E.g., the rules $a \leftarrow$, $b \leftarrow$ and $\neg a \leftarrow b$ are clearly inconsistent and have no classical answer sets, while both $\{a, b\}$ and $\{\neg a, b\}$ will be recognized as extended answer sets. Intuitively, $\neg a \leftarrow b$ is defeated by $a \leftarrow$ in $\{a, b\}$, while $\neg a \leftarrow b$ defeats $a \leftarrow$ in $\{\neg a, b\}$.

Within the context of inconsistent programs, it is natural to have some kind of preference relation that is used to prefer certain extended answer sets above others.

---

* Supported by the FWO
** This work was partially funded by the Information Society Technologies programme of the European Commission, Future and Emerging Technologies under the IST-2001-37004 WASP project

In [14], a "qualitative" preference semantics is proposed, using a preference relation on rules, to induce a partial ordering on the extended answer sets of a program.

As an alternative, this paper considers a "quantitative" preference relation for the extended answer set semantics on simple programs, i.e. programs containing only classical negation. We assign each rule in a program a (nonnegative) weight, representing the cost associated with defeating the rule. Solutions for these weighted programs, called *weighted answer sets*, are those extended answer sets that minimize the sum of the weights of defeated rules.

The resulting semantics turns out to be more expressive than classical answer set programming, even in the absence of negation as failure. We demonstrate that e.g. the membership problem is complete for the second level of the deterministic class of the polynomial hierarchy, i.e. Δ_2^P-complete. Furthermore, we show how negation as failure can be added to the formalism without increasing the complexity.

In some situations more than one actor is involved in the process of finding a solution to a particular problem. Quite often we have a sequence of decision makers, where each one sorts out the best solutions according to her preferences among the solutions that are preferred by the previous one in the sequence. Intuitively, the solutions that are still preferred by the last decision maker in the sequence are the ones that are acceptable by all parties. E.g., in a job selection procedure, the secretary will only keep the applicants that passed all the tests. Secondly, the head of the department will prefer people that have better marks on their math tests, and among those, the management of the firm will select those with a better psychological profile.

Such hierarchies of individual weight preferences are supported by *weight sequence programs*, where each rule in a program is equipped with a sequence $\langle w_i \rangle_{i=1,\ldots,n}$ of weights corresponding to the cost each decision maker associates with defeating this rule (w_i has a higher priority than w_{i+1}). Semantically, weighted answer sets for such programs will be obtained from first finding the weighted answer sets w.r.t. the weights of the first decision maker, i.e. the weights w_1, and among those finding the ones that are minimal w.r.t. the weights of the second decision maker, i.e. the weights w_2, etc. Regarding the complexity, it turns out that such sequences of weights do not result in any additional expressiveness of the formalism, nevertheless allowing to express certain problems more intuitively.

The proposed semantics has applications in several areas where quantitative preferences are useful. E.g., in the area of subgraph isomorphism algorithms [12] it is useful, in case of absence of an exact match of the pattern graph in the larger graph, to search for *subgraph isomorphic approximations* (SIA for short) of the larger graph that are minimal in some sense, i.e. searching for a "minimal" set of items to add to the larger graph such that the pattern occurs in it. We show how the solutions of such SIA problems correspond with the weighted answer sets of a weighted program that can be constructed out of the given instance graphs. Applications of SIA can be found in the area of intelligence analysis [9,4], where it is common to search for a pattern of interest in a large attributed relational graph [9] (ARG for short). An ARG is a normal graph where nodes and edges can carry additional attributes e.g. denoting relationships. In intelligence analysis, ARGs are used to model observed activity in the world under consideration. We show how the translation of the SIA problem for graphs into weighted programs can be intuitively adapted to the setting of ARGs, thus providing a useful tool for intelligence analysis

The remainder of this paper is organized as follows: Section 2 introduces weighted programs and the corresponding weighted answer set semantics, together with a characterization of the expressiveness. Additionally, we show how negation as failure can be added without increasing the complexity. Section 3 formalizes weight sequence programs and we show that these systems do not have additional expressiveness in comparison to normal weighted programs. In Section 4, we introduce the problem of subgraph isomorphic approximations in graph theory and show how weighted programs can be conveniently used to compute them. Section 5 discusses a generalization of subgraph isomorphic approximations in the area of attributed relational graphs. Finally, we conclude in Section 6. Due to space restrictions, proofs have been omitted.[1]

2 Weighted Programs

We use the following basic definitions and notation. A *literal* is an *atom* a or a negated atom $\neg a$. For a set of literals X, $\neg X$ denotes $\{\neg a \mid a \in X\}$ where $\neg\neg a = a$. X is *consistent* if $X \cap \neg X = \emptyset$. An *interpretation* I is a consistent set of literals. A *simple rule* r is of the form $a \leftarrow \beta$ with $\{a\} \cup \beta$ a finite set of literals[2]. The rule r is *satisfied* by I, denoted $I \models r$, if $a \in I$ whenever $\beta \subseteq I$, i.e. if r is *applicable* ($\beta \subseteq I$), then it must be *applied* ($a \in I$).

A countable set of simple rules is called a *simple logic program* (SLP). The *Herbrand base* $\mathcal{B}_P$ of a SLP P contains all atoms appearing in P. For a SLP P and an interpretation I we say that a rule $a \leftarrow \beta \in P$ is *defeated* w.r.t. I iff there exists an applied *competing rule* $\neg a \leftarrow \beta' \in P$. Furthermore, we use $P_I \subseteq P$ to denote the *reduct* of P w.r.t. I, i.e. $P_I = \{r \in P \mid I \models r\}$, the set of rules satisfied by I.

An interpretation I is called a model of a SLP P if $P_I = P$, i.e. I satisfies all rules in P. If there is no model J of P such that $J \subset I$, I is a minimal model or *answer set* of P. An *extended answer set* for P is any interpretation I such that I is an answer set of P_I and each unsatisfied rule in $P \setminus P_I$ is defeated.

Example 1. Consider the following SLP P about diabetes.

$hypoglycemia \leftarrow$ $\quad\quad diabetes \leftarrow$ $\quad\quad sugar \leftarrow hypoglycemia$
$\neg sugar \leftarrow diabetes$ $\quad\quad cola\_light \leftarrow \neg sugar$ $\quad\quad cola \leftarrow sugar$

Clearly, while this program has no traditional answer sets, it has, however, two extended answer sets $I = \{diabetes, hypoglycemia, sugar, cola\}$ and $J = \{diabetes, hypoglycemia, \neg sugar, cola\_light\}$.

The extended answer sets of a program are not always equally preferred. E.g., in the above example, when low on sugar ($hypoglycemia$), one would prefer drinking $cola$, rather than taking no sugar at all ($\neg sugar$). So, defeating the rule $sugar \leftarrow hypoglycemia$ is "worse" than defeating the rule $\neg sugar \leftarrow diabetes$. Therefore, we

---

[1] They are available in http://tinf2.vub.ac.be/~dvnieuwe/graphasptech.ps
[2] As usual, we assume that programs have already been grounded.

equip the rules in simple programs with a weight representing the "penalty" involved when defeating the rule. Naturally, extended answer sets that minimize the total penalty of a program are to be preferred over others.

Definition 1. *A **simple weight rule** is a rule r of the form $a \leftarrow \beta \langle w \rangle$, where $\{a\} \cup \beta$ is a finite set of literals and w is an associated weight value, i.e. a non-negative integer. We use $w(r)$ to denote the weight of r. A countable set of such simple weight rules is a **simple weight program** (SWP). The **extended answer sets** of a SWP P coincide with the extended answer sets of the SLP P' obtained from P by removing the weights from the rules.*

The program from Example 1 can be extended to a SWP containing a larger "penalty" weight for the hypoglycemia rules, i.e. the program:

$hypoglycemia \leftarrow \langle 0 \rangle$ $diabetes \leftarrow \langle 0 \rangle$ $sugar \leftarrow hypoglycemia \langle 1 \rangle$
$\neg sugar \leftarrow diabetes \langle 0 \rangle$ $cola\_light \leftarrow \neg sugar \langle 0 \rangle$ $cola \leftarrow sugar \langle 0 \rangle$

This program still has I and J as its extended answer sets, but intuitively I is better than J as it satisfies the rule with weight 1 while J does not, which we formalize in the following definition.

Definition 2. *The **penalty** of an extended answer set S w.r.t. a SWP P, is defined by $\Phi_P(S) = \sum_{r \in P \backslash P_S} w(r)$, i.e. the sum of the weights of all defeated rules in P w.r.t. S. For two extended answer sets S_1 and S_2 of P, we define $S_1 \preceq S_2$ iff $\Phi_P(S_1) \leq \Phi_P(S_2)$. A **weighted answer set** of P is an extended answer set of P that is minimal w.r.t. $\prec$ ($a \prec b$ iff $a \preceq b$ and not $b \preceq a$) among the set of all extended answer sets of P. A weighted answer set S of P with $\Phi_P(S) = 0$ is called a **proper weighted answer set**.*

Intuitively, weighted answer sets are those solutions that minimize the penalties incurred by defeating rules. For the weighted version of the program from Example 1 one obtains that $\Phi_P(I) = 0$ and $\Phi_P(J) = 1$ such that $I \prec J$, which corresponds with our intuition.

While the previous example uses only two different weight values, the following example shows that one can use the proposed semantics to represent complex relations between defeated rules.

Example 2. Consider a company that wants to hire an employee. To get hired, you have to do some tests and based on these results the company decides.

$math \leftarrow \langle 0 \rangle$ $lang \leftarrow \langle 0 \rangle$ $psych \leftarrow \langle 0 \rangle$ $prac \leftarrow \langle 0 \rangle$ $phys \leftarrow \langle 0 \rangle$
$\neg math \leftarrow \langle 0 \rangle$ $\neg lang \leftarrow \langle 0 \rangle$ $\neg psych \leftarrow \langle 0 \rangle$ $\neg prac \leftarrow \langle 0 \rangle$ $\neg phys \leftarrow \langle 0 \rangle$
$hire \leftarrow \langle 3 \rangle$ $\neg hire \leftarrow \neg math \langle 1 \rangle$ $\neg hire \leftarrow \neg lang \langle 1 \rangle$
$\neg hire \leftarrow \neg psych \langle 3 \rangle$ $\neg hire \leftarrow \neg prac \langle 2 \rangle$ $\neg hire \leftarrow \neg phys \langle 4 \rangle$

Intuitively, the rules with weight 0, i.e. no penalty involved when defeated, represent the choice between passing or not passing a certain test. Furthermore, the last five rules encode which penalty is involved when a person fails a certain test, but still gets hired. E.g., not passing the practical test is the same as failing both math and language. On the other hand, not passing the physical is considered unacceptable while failing the psychological test will be tolerated only if it is the only failed test. Finally, the rule $hire \leftarrow \langle 3 \rangle$ expresses the company's policy: defeating this rule is cheaper from the moment the penalty gets higher than 3.

Some of the program's extended answer sets are $M_1 = \{math, lang, psych, prac, phys, hire\}$, $M_2 = \{\neg math, \neg lang, psych, prac, phys, hire\}$, $M_3 = \{math, lang, psych, \neg prac, phys, hire\}$, $M_4 = \{\neg math, lang, psych, \neg prac, phys, hire\}$ and $M_5 = \{\neg math, lang, psych, \neg prac, phys, \neg hire\}$.

Computing the penalties for these extended answer sets results in $\Phi_P(M_1) = 0$, $\Phi_P(M_2) = \Phi_P(M_3) = 2$ and $\Phi_P(M_4) = \Phi_P(M_5) = 3$. These values imply the following order among the given extended answer sets: $M_1 \prec \{M_2, M_3\} \prec \{M_4, M_5\}$. It can be checked, that M_1 is the only (proper) weighted answer set of P. While M_2 has a penalty of 2 by defeating two rules with weight 1, M_3 only defeats a single rule, but with weight 2, yielding that M_2 and M_3 are incomparable, and thus equally preferred. Similarly, M_4 and M_5 only differ in the *hire* atom and are incomparable with each other, both having a penalty of 3.

Combining simple programs with weights turns out to be rather expressive.

Theorem 1. *Let P be a SWP and let l be a literal. Deciding whether there exists a weighted answer set M of P containing l is Δ_2^P-complete.*

The above result illustrates that the weighted answer set semantics is more powerful than the classical answer set semantics for (non-disjunctive) programs containing also negation as failure. Below, we provide a simple translation for such programs to SWPs. In addition, we show that extending SWPs with negation as failure does not increase their expressiveness.

In this context, an *extended literal* is a literal or a *naf-literal* of the form *not l* where l is a literal. The latter form denotes negation as failure. For a set of extended literals X, we use X^- to denote the set of ordinary literals underlying the naf-literals in X, i.e. $X^- = \{l \mid not\ l \in X\}$. For a set of ordinary literals Y, we use *not Y* to denote the set *not* $Y = \{not\ y \mid y \in Y\}$. An extended literal l is true w.r.t. an interpretation I, denoted $I \models l$, if $l \in I$ in case l is ordinary, or $a \notin I$ if $l = not\ a$ for some ordinary literal a. As usual, $I \models X$ for some set of (extended) literals l iff $\forall l \in X \cdot I \models l$.

An *extended rule* is a rule of the form $a \leftarrow \beta$ where a is a literal and β is a finite set of extended literals. An extended rule $r = a \leftarrow \beta$ is *satisfied* by I, denoted $I \models r$, if $a \in I$ whenever $I \models \beta$, i.e. if r is *applicable* ($I \models \beta$), then it must be *applied* ($a \in I$). A countable set of extended rules is called an *extended logic program* (ELP). When an ELP P does not contain classical negation, we call P a *seminegative logic program*. We adopt from SLP the notion of the reduct P_I w.r.t. an interpretation I and the notion of defeating of rules.

For an extended logic program P and an interpretation I we define the *GL-reduct*[8] for P w.r.t. I, denoted P^I, as the program consisting of those rules $a \leftarrow (\beta \setminus not\ \beta^-)$ where $a \leftarrow \beta$ is in P and $I \models not\ \beta^-$. Now, all rules in P^I are free from negation as failure, i.e. P^I is a simple program. An interpretation I is then an *answer set* of P iff I is an answer set of the GL-reduct P^I. Again, an *extended answer set* for P is any interpretation I that is an answer set of P_I and that defeats each rule in $P \setminus P_I$.

Theorem 2. *Let P be a seminegative program. The weighted version of P is defined by $N(P) = P' \cup P_n$, where $P' = \{a \leftarrow \beta'\langle 1\rangle \mid a \leftarrow \beta \in P\}$ with β' obtained from β by replacing each naf-literal not p with $\neg p$, and $P_n = \{\neg a \leftarrow \langle 0\rangle \mid a \in \mathcal{B}_P\}$. Then, M is an answer set of P iff $M \cup \neg(\mathcal{B}_P \setminus M)$ is a proper weighted answer set of $N(P)$.*

Intuitively, the rules in P_n introduce negation as failure using classical negation by allowing their defeat "for free", while defeating rules in P', corresponding to the original rules in P, is penalized.

Example 3. Consider the seminegative program $P = \{a \leftarrow \text{not } b, b \leftarrow \text{not } a\}$. The weighted version $N(P)$ consists of the rules $\{\neg a \leftarrow \langle 0\rangle, \neg b \leftarrow \langle 0\rangle, a \leftarrow \neg b\langle 1\rangle, b \leftarrow \neg a\langle 1\rangle\}$. This program has two proper weighted answer sets, i.e. $I = \{a, \neg b\}$ and $J = \{\neg a, b\}$, corresponding with the answer sets $\{a\}$ and $\{b\}$ of P.

Simple weighted programs can be extended with negation as failure, i.e. extended weighted programs (EWP), without increasing the expressiveness of the formalism. The latter is confirmed by the next theorem which reduces an EWP to an equivalent SWP. For this reduction, we define a mapping ψ translating original naf-literals by: $\psi(\text{not } a) = a_n$ and $\psi(\text{not } \neg a) = a_n^\neg$, where for each atom $a \in \mathcal{B}_P$, a_n and $a_n^\neg$ are fresh atoms. We use $\psi(X)$, X a set of naf-literals, to denote $\{\psi(x) \mid x \in X\}$.

Theorem 3. *Let P be a finite EWP. The SWP version of P, denoted $S(P)$, is defined by $S(P) = P_n \cup P' \cup P_c$, where $P_n = \{\psi(\text{not } l) \leftarrow \langle 0\rangle \mid l \in \mathcal{B}_P \cup \neg \mathcal{B}_P\}$, $P' = \{a \leftarrow \beta'\langle w\rangle \mid a \leftarrow \beta\langle w\rangle \in P\}$ where β' is obtained from β by replacing not β^- with $\psi(\text{not } \beta^-)$, and $P_c = \{\neg \psi(\text{not } l) \leftarrow l\langle \Upsilon\rangle \mid l \in \mathcal{B}_P \cup \neg \mathcal{B}_P\}$ where $\Upsilon = 1 + \sum_{r \in P} w(r)$.*

Then, M is a weighted answer set of P iff there exists a weighted answer set M' of $S(P)$ such that (a) $\Phi_{S(P)}(M') < \Upsilon$; and (b) $M = M' \cap (\mathcal{B}_P \cup \neg \mathcal{B}_P)$.

Intuitively, the rules in P_n introduce negation as failure for all literals in the Herbrand base. As defeating negation as failure should be free, the rules all get a weight of 0. In P' we adapt the original program with the corresponding weights by replacing the naf-literals by their new representation. The rules in P_c ensure the consistency of any solution by allowing the new representations of naf-literals to be defeated. To enforce the satisfaction of these rules, we give them a weight that is higher than any possible combination of weights in the original program, i.e. the sum of all weights plus 1. As a result, $S(P)$ will only yield weighted answer sets with high penalties, i.e. defeating some of the rules in P_c, iff the original program itself has no solutions, making condition (a) in Theorem 3 necessary.

E.g., the single rule program $Q = \{a \leftarrow \text{not } a\langle 0\rangle\}$ has no weighted answer sets. Its translation $S(Q) = \{a_n \leftarrow \langle 0\rangle, a_n^\neg \leftarrow \langle 0\rangle, \neg a_n \leftarrow a\langle 1\rangle, \neg a_n^\neg \leftarrow \neg a\langle 1\rangle, a \leftarrow a_n\langle 0\rangle\}$ has only one weighted answer set $I = \{a_n, a_n^\neg, a\}$ for which the penalty is $\Phi_Q(I) = 1$, yielding a value not strictly smaller than 1, corresponding to the non-existence of weighted answer sets for the original program.

Combining Theorem 3 with Theorem 1 yields that EWPs have the same complexity as SWPs, i.e. Δ_2^P-complete.

3 Weight Sequences

In [13] an intuitive semantics is presented for sequences of individual complex qualitative preferences. The idea is to apply each individual preference in the sequence in turn and to let it sort out the preferred answer sets left over by the previous preferences in the sequence. It is shown in [13] that this semantics is quite expressive as it can handle arbitrary complete problems of the polynomial hierarchy. More specifically, for a sequence of n preference relations, the semantics is Σ_{n+1}^P-complete.

It is natural to wonder if a similar semantics for sequences of individual weights will also yield a complexity blow-up depending on the length of the sequence. It turns out that this is not the case as sequences of weights remain Δ_2^P-complete.

Definition 3. *An **n-weight sequence rule** is a rule r of the form $a \leftarrow \beta \langle w_i \rangle_{i=1,\ldots,n}$, where $\{a\} \cup \beta$ is a finite set of literals and $\langle w_i \rangle_{i=1,\ldots,n}$ is a sequence of n associated weight values, i.e. a sequence of non-negative integers. We use $w_i(r)$ to denote the weight w_i of r. A countable set of n-weight sequence rules is an **n-weight sequence program** (nWSP). The **extended answer sets** of an nWSP P coincide with the extended answer sets of the SLP P' obtained from P by removing the weight sequences from the rules.*

*The **penalty** of an extended answer set S w.r.t. the weights i ($1 \leq i \leq n$) and an nWSP P, is defined by $\Phi_P^i(S) = \sum_{r \in P \setminus P_S} w_i(r)$, i.e. the sum of the weights w_i of all defeated rules in P w.r.t. S. Each of the penalties Φ_P^i induces a preference relation $\prec_i$ between the extended answer sets, as in Definition 2.*

We define the preference of extended answer sets up to a certain weight level by induction.

Definition 4. *Let P be a nWSP. An extended answer set S is preferable up to weight level $\prec_i$, $1 \leq i \leq n$, iff*

- *$i = 1$ and S is minimal w.r.t. $\prec_1$, or*
- *$i > 1$, S is preferable up to $\prec_{i-1}$, and there is no T, preferable up to $\prec_{i-1}$, such that $T \prec_i S$.*

*An extended answer set S of P is a **weighted answer set** iff it is preferable up to $\prec_n$.*

Example 4. Consider the problem of two people having to decide what to eat for dinner. After checking the available ingredients, the cook preparing the dinner decides to let his wife propose some possible combinations from which he will choose the final one. As his wife is rather hungry, she decides to choose the meal which is quickest to make, the reason for which she assigns weights corresponding with times needed to make a particular part of the meal. On the other hand, her husband is tired and wants to make a meal that is easy to prepare, yielding weights representing the difficulty to make a particular part of the meal. Further, they agree on some constraints that each meal should satisfy, e.g. with french fries they take mayonnaise, etc. The 2WSP corresponding with this problem is shown below.

Note that the rule $\neg v \leftarrow v \langle 200, 200 \rangle$ enforces the satisfaction of the common constraints, as it implies that every solution not making one of the rules with v in the head applicable, is better than any solution making one of those rules applicable.

$$french\_fries \leftarrow \langle 0,0 \rangle \qquad rice \leftarrow \langle 0,0 \rangle \qquad steak \leftarrow \langle 0,0 \rangle$$
$$\neg french\_fries \leftarrow \langle 15,1 \rangle \qquad \neg rice \leftarrow \langle 5,1 \rangle \qquad \neg steak \leftarrow \langle 10,1 \rangle$$
$$stew \leftarrow \langle 0,0 \rangle \qquad meat\_ball \leftarrow \langle 0,0 \rangle \qquad mayonnaise \leftarrow \langle 0,0 \rangle$$
$$\neg stew \leftarrow \langle 75,3 \rangle \qquad \neg meat\_ball \leftarrow \langle 20,2 \rangle \qquad \neg mayonnaise \leftarrow \langle 10,5 \rangle$$
$$tomato\_sauce \leftarrow \langle 0,0 \rangle \qquad \neg tomato\_sauce \leftarrow \langle 10,2 \rangle$$
$$v \leftarrow \neg french\_fries, \neg rice \langle 0,0 \rangle \qquad v \leftarrow \neg steak, \neg meat\_ball, \neg stew \langle 0,0 \rangle$$
$$v \leftarrow steak, \neg french\_fries \langle 0,0 \rangle \qquad v \leftarrow rice, meat\_ball, \neg tomato\_sauce \langle 0,0 \rangle$$
$$v \leftarrow french\_fries, \neg mayonnaise \langle 0,0 \rangle \qquad \neg v \leftarrow v \langle 200, 200 \rangle$$

For the extended answer sets[3] $S_1 = \{french\_fries, steak, mayonnaise\}$ and $S_2 = \{rice, meat\_ball, tomato\_sauce\}$ one can check that $\Phi_P^1(S_1) = \Phi_P^1(S_2) = 35$ and no other extended answer sets exists with a smaller penalty for Φ_P^1, yielding that both S_1 and S_2 are preferable up to weight level $\prec_1$. On the other hand, $\Phi_P^2(S_1) = 7$ and $\Phi_P^2(S_2) = 5$, making S_2 preferable up to weight level $\prec_2$, yielding that S_2 is the weighted answer set for this problem.

Finally, rearranging the weight sequence yields, in general, different solutions. E.g., if the cook first decides which meals he wants to make and afterwards his wife can choose a particular one, it can be checked that $S_3 = \{rice, stew\}$ will be the weighted answer set of the problem.

In the following theorem we show that an n-weight sequence program can be transformed into a simple weight program such that the weighted answer sets of the former coincide with the weighted answer sets of the latter.

Theorem 4. *Let P be an nWSP and let P' be the SWP defined by*

$$P' = \{a \leftarrow \beta \langle w_i \times 10^{\xi_i} \rangle \mid a \leftarrow \beta \langle w_i \rangle_{i=1,\ldots,n} \} ,$$

where $\xi_n = 0$ and $\xi_i = \sum_{j \in [i+1\ldots n]} \left(length \left(\sum_{r \in P} w_j(r) \right) \right)$ otherwise, with $length(x)$ the number of digits in x, e.g. $length(2611) = 4$.
Then, S is a weighted answer set of P iff S is a weighted answer set of P'.

Reconsider the rule $\neg stew \leftarrow \langle 75, 3 \rangle$ from Example 4. In the SWP version of this program, the rule would yield the rules $\neg stew \leftarrow \langle 3 \rangle$ and $\neg stew \leftarrow \langle 75000 \rangle$, as $\sum_{r \in P} w_2(r) = 215$, yielding that $length(215) = 3$ and $75 \times 10^3 = 75000$.

The above transformation can be performed in polynomial time, yielding the following complexity result for n-weighted sequence programs.

Corollary 1. *Let P be an nWSP. Deciding whether there exists a weighted answer set S of P containing l is Δ_2^P-complete.*

This result implies that, unlike for sequences of qualitative preferences [13], introducing sequences of weights does not yield an increase of expressiveness. Nevertheless, these sequences allow for a more intuitive expression of certain problems.

---

[3] To keep the size of the extended answer sets small, we only provide the positive literals.

4 Approximate Subgraph Isomorphisms

While approximate subgraph isomorphisms are similar to finding largest common subtrees [1], the formalisation we introduce in this section is, to the best of our knowledge, new.

A *graph* is a tuple $G = \langle N, E \rangle$, where N is a finite set of *nodes*, and $E \subseteq N \times N$ is a set of tuples representing the *edges* in the graph. We assume that graphs are directed; an undirected edge from n to m can still be represented by having both $\langle m, n \rangle$ and $\langle n, m \rangle$ in E.

Two graphs $G_1 = \langle N_1, E_1 \rangle$ and $G_2 = \langle N_2, E_2 \rangle$ are said to be *isomorphic*, denoted $G_1 \cong G_2$, if there exists a bijection $f : N_1 \to N_2$ such that $f(E_1) = E_2$, where $f(E_1)$ denotes $\{\langle f(t), f(h) \rangle \mid \langle t, h \rangle \in E\}$. On the other hand, G_2 is called a *subgraph* of G_1, denoted $G_2 \preceq G_1$, iff $N_2 \subseteq N_1$ and $E_2 \subseteq E_1$. Furthermore, G_2 is called *subgraph isomorphic* to G_1, denoted $G_2 \precsim G_1$, if there exists a subgraph $G_3 \preceq G_1$ such that $G_2 \cong G_3$.

Subgraph isomorphism itself is sometimes too strong a notion for certain applications. E.g., when a graph $G_2 = \langle N_2, E_2 \rangle$ is not subgraph isomorphic to a graph $G_1 = \langle N_1, E_1 \rangle$, it may be interesting to know what is "missing" in G_1 for G_2 to be subgraph isomorphic to it. In this context, a graph $G_3 = \langle N_3, E_3 \rangle$ is called an *extension* of G_1 w.r.t. G_2 just when $G_1 \preceq G_3$ and $N_3 = N_1$ when $|N_1| \geq |N_2|$ or $N_3 = N_1 \cup \{x_i \mid 1 \leq i \leq |N_2| - |N_1|\}$ otherwise, where the x_i are new nodes not occurring in N_1. The latter construction of N_3 is necessary to handle the cases in which the graph to search for is bigger than the graph to search in. A graph G_3 is a *subgraph isomorphic approximation* of G_1 w.r.t. G_2 iff G_3 is an extension of G_1 w.r.t. G_2 and $G_2 \precsim G_3$. We use $G_2 \precsim_{G_1} G_3$ to denote that G_2 is *approximately subgraph isomorphic* to G_3 w.r.t. G_1, i.e. G_3 is a subgraph isomorphic approximation of G_1 w.r.t. G_2. The set of all subgraph isomorphic approximations of G_1 w.r.t. G_2 is denoted by $\mathcal{A}_{G_1}(G_2)$.

Obviously, not every subgraph isomorphic approximation $G_3 \in \mathcal{A}_{G_1}(G_2)$ is equally interesting. E.g., the fully connected graph $\langle N_3, N_3 \times N_3 \rangle$ is, clearly, always a subgraph isomorphic approximation and thus in $\mathcal{A}_{G_1}(G_2)$. However, in most cases there will exist smaller extensions of G_1 in $\mathcal{A}_{G_1}(G_2)$. Therefore, we are particularly interested in elements from $\mathcal{A}_{G_1}(G_2)$ that have a minimal, in some sense, difference with the original graph G_1. Here we use $\Delta_{G_1}(G_3)$ to denote the *unidirectional edge difference* between G_1 and G_3, i.e. $\Delta_{G_1}(G_3) = E_3 \setminus E_1$.

Two minimality criteria, which are widely used in areas like diagnostic reasoning [5,6,15], are cardinal minimality and subset minimality. In the former case, we select those elements from $\mathcal{A}_{G_1}(G_2)$ that are minimal w.r.t. cardinality among the elements in $\mathcal{A}_{G_1}(G_2)$. Formally, a graph $G_3 \in \mathcal{A}_{G_1}(G_2)$ is said to be a *subgraph isomorphic c-approximation* iff there does not exist a graph $G_4 \in \mathcal{A}_{G_1}(G_2)$ such that $|\Delta_{G_1}(G_4)| < |\Delta_{G_1}(G_3)|$. The set of all c-approximations is denoted by $\mathcal{A}^c_{G_1}(G_2)$.

Example 5. Consider the three undirected graphs G_1, G_2 and G_3 represented in Figure 1. Clearly, G_1 is subgraph isomorphic to G_2, i.e. $G_1 \precsim G_2$, but not to G_3. However, adding a single (bidirectional) edge between e.g. m and r in G_3, i.e. $G_4 = \langle N_3, E_3 \cup \{\langle m, r \rangle, \langle r, m \rangle\}\rangle$, results in a subgraph isomorphic approximation of G_3 w.r.t. G_1, i.e. $G_1 \precsim_{G_3} G_4$. Obviously, G_4 is cardinal minimal yielding that $G_4 \in \mathcal{A}^c_{G_3}(G_1)$.

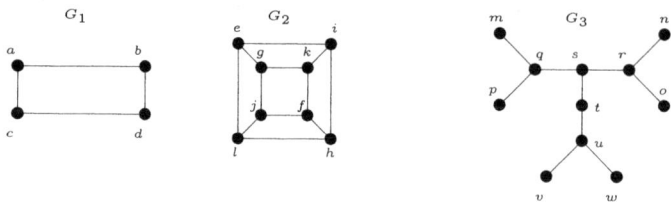

Fig. 1. The graphs G_1, G_2 and G_3 of Example 5

Subset minimal isomorphic approximations can be defined in a similar way. However, in contrast with diagnostic reasoning, subset minimality is less intuitive in this setting. E.g. adding the edges $\langle p, o \rangle$, $\langle o, w \rangle$, $\langle w, v \rangle$ and $\langle v, p \rangle$ (and their reverses) to G_3 in Example 5 yields a subset minimal isomorphic approximation w.r.t. G_1. However, if we see G_3 as an activity graph and G_1 as a pattern of interest, as is often done by intelligence agencies for detecting possible threats [4], the previously mentioned subset minimal approximation is not very useful as it forces the agency to check 4 possible relations between currently unrelated things. On the other hand, the approximations in $\mathcal{A}^c_{G_3}(G_1)$ are of much more value as they all yield one missing link to complete the pattern, implying that the agency can quickly confirm these solutions (see also the next section).

Obviously, when a graph is subgraph isomorphic to another one, the latter is the only c-approximation of itself.

Theorem 5. *Let G_1 and G_2 be graphs such that $G_2 \precsim G_1$. Then, $\mathcal{A}^c_{G_1}(G_2) = \{G_1\}$.*

Using the weighted answer set semantics, we have the means to effectively compute the c-approximations of a given graph G_1 w.r.t. a graph G_2. In what follows, we will sometimes use non-grounded rules for clarity, but grounding is performed as usual.

Intuitively, we introduce the edges of G_1 as facts of the form $edge(x, y) \leftarrow \langle 0 \rangle$, where $\langle x, y \rangle \in E_1$. For each possible edge $\langle x, y \rangle \notin E_1$, with $x, y \in N_1$, we give a choice to either include it or not in an approximation by introducing the facts $edge(x, y) \leftarrow \langle 0 \rangle$ and $\neg edge(x, y) \leftarrow \langle 1 \rangle$. The penalty involved in the latter fact is to ensure that the computed approximations are cardinal minimal, i.e. not inserting an edge (defeating the former rule) can be done freely, but inserting an edge (defeating the latter rule) has to be minimized. In case $|N_1| < |N_2|$ we also add edges to the $|N_2| - |N_1|$ new nodes.

To match G_2 with the possible approximations, we need to introduce for each node $n \in N_2$ a unique new variable name N. Searching for a match of G_2 in the approximation is done by the single rule $match \leftarrow \beta\langle 0 \rangle$, where $\beta = \{edge(X, Y) \mid \langle x, y \rangle \in E_2\} \cup \{X \neq Y \mid \langle x, y \rangle \in E_2 \wedge x \neq y\}$. Finally, we add the single rule $match \leftarrow not\ match\langle 0 \rangle$ which forces any solution to contain a match (note that this rule cannot be defeated).

Definition 5. *Let $G_1 = \langle N_1, E_1 \rangle$ and $G_2 = \langle N_2, E_2 \rangle$ be graphs. The program computing the c-approximations of G_1 w.r.t. G_2, denoted $\mathcal{L}_{G_1}(G_2)$, is defined by the rules:*

- $\{edge(x, y) \leftarrow \langle 0 \rangle \mid \langle x, y \rangle \in E_1\}$;
- $\{edge(x, y) \leftarrow \langle 0 \rangle\ ;\ \neg edge(x, y) \leftarrow \langle 1 \rangle \mid x, y \in N_1 \cup \{x_i \mid (|N_1| < |N_2|) \wedge (1 \leq i \leq |N_2| - |N_1|)\} \wedge \langle x, y \rangle \notin E_1\}$;

- $\{match \leftarrow \beta\langle 0\rangle\}$, where $\beta = \{edge(X,Y) \mid \langle x,y\rangle \in E_2\} \cup \{X \neq Y \mid \langle x,y\rangle \in E_3 \wedge x \neq y\}$; and
- $\{match \leftarrow not\ match\langle 0\rangle\}$.

If we reconsider the graphs G_1 and G_3 from Example 5, the program $\mathcal{L}_{G_3}(G_1)$ contains, besides the numerous $edge/2$ facts, the rule

$match \leftarrow edge(A,B), edge(B,D), edge(D,C), edge(C,A), edge(B,A), edge(D,B)$
$edge(C,D), edge(A,C), A \neq B, B \neq D, D \neq C, C \neq A$.

One of the possible weighted answer sets of $\mathcal{L}_{G_3}(G_1)$ is e.g. $S = \{edge(x,y) \mid \langle x,y\rangle \in E_3\} \cup \{edge(m,r), edge(r,m)\} \cup (\{\neg edge(x,y) \mid x,y \in N_3 \wedge \langle x,y\rangle \notin E_3\} \setminus \{edge(m,r), edge(r,m)\})$. Clearly, S corresponds with the extension G_4 from Example 5, which is a cardinal minimal approximation of G_3 w.r.t. G_1. This behavior is confirmed by the following theorem.

Theorem 6. *Let $G_1 = \langle N_1, E_1\rangle$ and $G_2 = \langle N_2, E_2\rangle$ be graphs. Then, $G_3 = \langle N_3, E_3\rangle \in \mathcal{A}^c_{G_1}(G_2)$ iff $M = \{edge(x,y) \mid \langle x,y\rangle \in E_3\} \cup \{\neg edge(x,y) \mid x,y \in N_3 \wedge \langle x,y\rangle \notin E_3\} \cup \{match\}$ is a weighted answer set of $\mathcal{L}_{G_1}(G_2)$.*

In the current approach no distinction is made between the edges that can be added to a graph to obtain an approximation. However, one can imagine situations in which adding one edge is more "difficult" than adding another, i.e. the cost of adding an edge may vary. E.g., for an intelligence agency, it may be easier to check a relationship between people in the home country, than between people in foreign countries, but checking 4 internal relationships may be as hard as checking 1 external relationship, resulting in a cost of 4 for edges between externals and a cost of 1 for edges between internals. Such costs represent a quantitative preference relation between edge additions.

In this case, optimal solutions are approximations that minimize the sum of all costs associated with the added edges in the approximation. It is not difficult to see that this kind of minimization can easily be computed by an adapted version of the program in Definition 5: just replace the weights 1 with the cost associated for adding the edge to an approximation. Clearly, Theorem 6 remains valid in this extension.

Similarly, we could think of an agency where possible threats are first selected, by some field agent, depending on the effort needed to check certain relationships. Afterwards, the supervisor will apply, on the proposed investigations of his field agent, another kind of quantitative preferences, e.g. using information from other departments. In case there are still a number of possible solutions left over after the supervisor, even a third individual, e.g. the director, could apply his preferences on these possibilities. Again, it is not difficult to see that this problem can be elegantly modeled by an adapted version of the program in Definition 5, this time using the n-weight sequence programs introduced in Section 3. Also in this extension, an adapted version of Theorem 6 remains valid.

5 An Application in Intelligence Analysis

Attributed relational graphs (ARGs), an extension of the abstract directed graphs defined in the previous section, are often used in e.g. intelligence analysis to understand complex, and often uncertain, situations. The nodes in such ARGs are used to describe objects in the observed world, e.g. persons, organizations, ..., while the edges are used to represent relationships between the nodes, e.g. interaction, ownership, trust, ...

In addition, ARG nodes and edges may have additional attributes that describe the details of the specific objects or relationships: e.g. the name of a person, the kind of chemical, the type of conversation. An example of such an ARG, based on an example

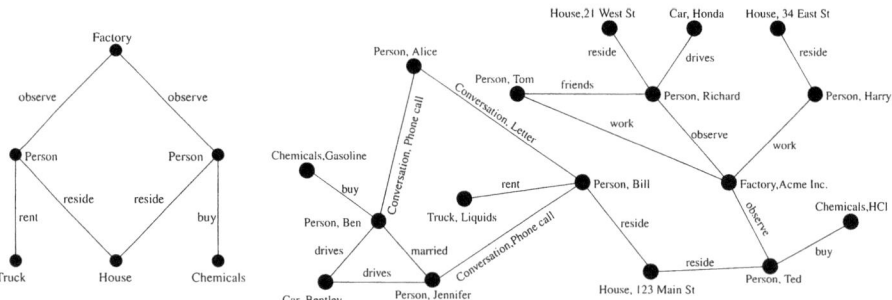

Fig. 2. The pattern graph [4]

Fig. 3. The observed activity graph [4]

from [4], can be found in Figure 3. Here, a person named Bill has rented a truck for carrying liquids and that same person resides in a house at 123 Main street together with a person called Ted. Furthermore, Ted has been observing a factory called Acme Inc. and he also bought large quantities of the chemical HCl.

Intelligence analysts normally define small abstract patterns which are believed to be indications of possible threats. An example of such a pattern, based on the same example from [4], can be found in Figure 2. Intuitively, it states that two persons residing at the same place and both observing the same factory can be dangerous if one person buys some chemical, while the other rents a truck.

Having both an ARG of observed activity and a pattern, the analysts need tools for finding specific regions in the ARG that "closely" match the defined threat pattern. Subgraph isomorphic approximations turn out to be valuable tools to accomplish this task [4]. The framework and results we developed in Section 4 can be intuitively adapted to the setting of ARGs, where the transformation into a weighted program allows an analyst to compute subgraph isomorphic approximations that are minimal in some quantitative sense. In situations where investigating missing additional relationships is equally hard, the analyst can use the cardinal minimal approximations. On the other hand, if investigating some relationship has a higher cost than investigating others, an analyst could rely upon the extension of the framework of Section 4, i.e. defining a cost with each relationship (edge) that can be added to have a subgraph isomorphic approximation and only keeping the approximations that minimize the sum of the costs. Similarly, it could be the case that the analist is not the only one in charge of making the final decision or that he has multiple equivalent possibilities. In such situations, it can be useful to apply the quantitative preferences of some other people, e.g. a supervisor or the director, to refine the number of solutions, so obtaining the most preferred solution. By using the second extension of the framework of Section 4 also this kind of reasoning with ARGs can be solved, i.e. by using weight sequence programs.

Instead of formally adapting the framework and the results, we illustrate the adaptation, and its usefulness, using the example on intelligence analysis: we will translate the ARG and pattern of Figures 3 and 2 into a weighted program and show that the solutions of the program correspond with the regions of threat in the ARG w.r.t. the given pattern.

First we translate, for convenience, the nodes of the ARG to *node*-predicates. E.g. a person named Bill forces the fact $node(person, bill) \leftarrow \langle 0 \rangle$ into the program, while the factory Acme Inc. is responsible for the fact $node(factory, acme\_inc) \leftarrow \langle 0 \rangle$. In total, we have 17 of such facts in our weighted program.

Next, we have to describe the relationships between the nodes using extended versions of the *edge/2*-predicates used in the previous section. E.g. Ted residing at the house in 123 Main street gives rise to the fact

$$edge(person, ted, reside, house, 123\_main\_street) \leftarrow \langle 0 \rangle \ ,$$

while the conversation between Jennifer and Bill can be described by the fact

$$edge(person, bill, conversation, phone, person, jennifer) \leftarrow \langle 0 \rangle \ .$$

Note that the different *edge*-facts can have different arities, which is not a problem as long as the arities, and the ordering of the arguments, are the same for the same relationship. E.g. *edge*-facts representing the conversation relationship always have six arguments: the first two correspond to a node, the third has to be "conversation", the fourth the type of conversation and the last two again correspond to a node.

Also note that ARGs are directed graphs, but certain relations are bidirectional, e.g. *friends* and *married*. For these relationships we have to explicitly add both directions using the *edge*-facts: e.g. both $edge(person, richard, friend, person, tom) \leftarrow \langle 0 \rangle$ and $edge(person, tom, friend, person, richard) \leftarrow \langle 0 \rangle$ have to be present in the weighted program. One could argue that a conversation through phone is also bidirectional, but we use a directed edge here to represent who initiated the call.

The pattern in Figure 2 can be translated into the following rule, where names starting with an uppercase letter correspond to a variable:

$$\begin{aligned} match \leftarrow \ & edge(person, NamePerson1, observe, factory, NameFactory), \\ & edge(person, NamePerson2, observe, factory, NameFactory), \\ & edge(person, NamePerson1, reside, house, AddressHouse), \\ & edge(person, NamePerson2, reside, house, AddressHouse), \\ & edge(person, NamePerson1, rent, truck, KindOfTruck), \\ & edge(person, NamePerson2, buy, chemicals, KindOfChemical) \langle 0 \rangle \end{aligned}$$

The above pattern matching rule also matches situations where only one person observes a factory and does both the renting of the truck and the buying of the chemicals. If one wants to have explicitly two different persons, we need to add the condition $NamePerson1 \neq NamePerson2$ to the rule.

Finally, we have to add rules for the edges that can eventually be added to our activity graph to obtain a subgraph isomorphic approximation. These edges will directly point out the region of interest in the activity graph as the minimization assures that only edges are added where necessary, i.e. on those places in the activity graph where the pattern (almost) matches. While we introduced all possible edges in the simulation of Section 4, doing the same in the context of ARGs may not be the best way to go. Indeed, ARGs can have multiple edges between the same nodes but with different attributes, which are not always useful to define between certain types of nodes. E.g. $edge(chemical, hcl, buys, chemical, gasoline) \leftarrow \langle 0 \rangle$ is theoretically possible, but useless in real life. Therefore, one should avoid the introduction of meaningless edges in the program, possibly by adding extra semantical constraints, e.g. typing the attributes in ARGS. Some examples of choices of edges to add are:

$$edge(person, bill, observe, factory, acme\_inc) \leftarrow \langle 0 \rangle$$
$$\neg\, edge(person, bill, observe, factory, acme\_inc) \leftarrow \langle v \rangle$$
$$edge(person, bill, buy, chemical, hcl) \leftarrow \langle 0 \rangle$$
$$\neg\, edge(person, bill, buy, chemical, hcl) \leftarrow \langle w \rangle$$
$$edge(person, alice, conversation, phone, person, ted) \leftarrow \langle 0 \rangle$$
$$\neg\, edge(person, alice, conversation, phone, person, ted) \leftarrow \langle z \rangle$$

In the above rules for possible edges to add, the rules with a positive occurrences of the *edge*-predicate always have a weight of 0, as not adding an edge, i.e. defeating the rule, can be done for free. On the other hand, the negative occurrences have a weight corresponding to the cost associated with adding the edge. In case we use cardinal minimality, the costs (e.g. v, w and z) will all be 1, while in case of total cost minimality we could define $v = 4$, $w = 2$ and $z = 1$ yielding that it is twice as hard to check if someone observed a factory than checking if he bought some chemical, which in turn is twice as hard than checking if he made a phone call.

For simplicity, we only consider cardinal minimality (and no sequences) in what follows, i.e. we take all the weights of the rules with negative occurrence of an *edge*-predicate to be 1. If we consider the weighted program obtained in the way we described above, we will have two weighted answer sets S and T. Both will contain all the edges from the original activity graph together with the fact $match$. Additionally, S will contain the fact $edge(person, bill, observe, factory, acme\_inc)$ together with all negated versions of the other *edge*-predicates we added to the program Similarly, T will contain the fact $edge(person, ted, rent, truck, liquids)$ together with all negated versions, except the one occurring positively. Clearly, both S and T correspond with the only cardinal minimal subgraph isomorphic approximations of the problem.

As said before, we can add the condition $NamePerson1 \neq NamePerson2$ to the pattern rule in our program if we explicitly want two different persons. When we consider the weighted program obtained in that way, S will be the single weighted answer set of the program, corresponding to the single subgraph isomorphic approximation of the problem.

6 Conclusions and Directions for Further Research

We presented a simple and intuitive quantitative preferential semantics based on the extended answer set semantics, characterized its expressiveness and illustrated its usefulness using an application in the area of intelligence analysis. Possible topics for further research include the efficient implementation of the semantics, e.g. using existing answer set solvers such as dlv [7] or smodels [11]. Furthermore, the relationships between the present proposal and other weighted semantics such as weak constraints [3] need to be investigated.

References

1. Tatsuya Akutsu and Magnús M. Halldórsson. On the approximation of largest common subtrees and largest common point sets. *Theoretical Comp. Science*, 233(1-2):33–50, 2000.
2. Chitta Baral. *Knowledge Representation, Reasoning and Declarative Problem Solving*. Cambridge Press, 2003.
3. Francesco Buccafurri, Nicola Leone, and Pasquale Rullo. Strong and weak constraints in disjunctive datalog. In *Proceedings of the 4th International Conference on Logic Programming (LPNMR '97)*, pages 2–17, 1997.
4. Thayne Coffman, Seth Greenblatt, and Sherry Marcus. Graph-based technologies for intelligence analysis. *Communications of the ACM*, 47(3):45–47, 2004.
5. L. Console and P. Torasso. A spectrum of logical definitions of model-based diagnosis. *Computational Intelligence*, 7(3):133–141, 1991.
6. Thomas Eiter, Wolfgang Faber, Nicola Leone, and Gerald Pfeifer. The diagnosis frontend of the dlv system. *AI Communications*, 12(1-2):99–111, 1999.
7. Thomas Eiter, Wolfgang Faber, Nicola Leone, and Gerald Pfeifer. Declarative problem-solving using the dlv system. *Logic-Based Artificial Intelligence*, pages 79–103, 2000.
8. Michael Gelfond and Vladimir Lifschitz. The stable model semantics for logic programming. In *Logic Programming, Proceedings of the Fifth International Conference and Symposium*, pages 1070–1080. MIT Press, 1988.
9. R.J. Heuer. Psychology of intelligence analysis. Center for the Study of Intelligence, Central Intelligence Agency, 2001.
10. Vladimir Lifschitz. Answer set programming and plan generation. *Journal of Artificial Intelligence*, 138(1-2):39–54, 2002.
11. Syrjänen T. and Niemelä I. The smodels system. In *Proceedings of the 6th International Conference on Logic Programming and Nonmonotonic Reasoning*, volume 2173 of *Lecture Notes in Computer Science*, pages 434–438, Vienna, Austria, September 2001. Springer.
12. J.R. Ullman. An algorithm for subgraph isomorphism. *J. of the ACM*, 23(1):31–42, 1976.
13. Davy Van Nieuwenborgh, Stijn Heymans, and Dirk Vermeir. On programs with linearly ordered multiple preferences. In *Proc. of 20th Intl. Conference on Logic Programming (ICLP 2004)*, volume 3132 of *Lecture Notes in Computer Science*, pages 180–194. Springer, 2004.
14. Davy Van Nieuwenborgh and Dirk Vermeir. Preferred answer sets for ordered logic programs. In *European Conference on Logics in Artificial Intelligence, JELIA 2002*, volume 2424 of *Lecture Notes in Artificial Intelligence*, pages 432–443, 2002.
15. Davy Van Nieuwenborgh and Dirk Vermeir. Ordered diagnosis. In *Proceedings of the 10th International Conference on Logic for Programming, Artificial Intelligence, and Reasoning (LPAR2003)*, volume 2850 of *LNAI*, pages 244–258. Springer, 2003.
16. Marina De Vos and Dirk Vermeir. Logic programming agents playing games. In *Research and Development in Intelligent Systems XIX (ES2002)*, BCS Conference Series, pages 323–336. Springer-Verlag, 2002.

How to Fix It:
Using Fixpoints in Different Contexts*

Igor Walukiewicz

LaBRI, Université Bordeaux-1
351, Cours de la Libération
F-33 405, Talence cedex, France

Abstract. In this note we discuss the expressive power of μ-calculi. We concentrate on those that are extensions of propositional modal logics with a fixpoint operator. The objective is to try to match the expressive power of monadic second-order logic. We consider different kinds of models: from trees and transition systems up to traces and timed systems.

1 Introduction

Regular languages are a very interesting class because they have many closure properties and many equivalent characterizations. Just to give an example, regular languages of finite words are characterized by finite automata and also by monadic second-order logic (MSOL). The logical characterization testifies the nice closure properties of the class. The automata characterization permits, among others, the development of an important set of tools used in verification. Regular languages can also be characterized by the μ-calculus. It is a logical characterization, but its good algorithmic properties bring it close to the automata characterization. Indeed, the connections between the μ-calculus and alternating automata are so strong that one can almost say that they are the same modulo the vocabulary used to describe them.

It is easy to interpret MSOL over different domains: trees, traces, graphs, real-time sequences. This way we obtain immediately an expressibility yardstick in all these different settings. We can then hope to adapt other characterizations of regular languages to other domains so that they match expressiveness of MSOL. If successful one gets a similar set of powerful tools as the one for regular languages of finite words.

The goal of this note is to put together three attempts [6,11,7] to match the power of MSOL over three different domains. The presented characterizations will be either in terms of fixpoint logic or in terms of alternating automata. We will begin with the equivalence of the μ-calculus and MSOL on infinite binary trees. We will show how this equivalence generalizes nicely to all transition systems. Next, we will proceed to trace models that are the simplest among so called non-interleaving models for concurrency. Unlike words, which are linear

---
* Work supported by the ACI Sécurité Informatique VERSYDIS.

orders on events, traces are partial orders on events. The intuition is that if two events are not ordered then they have happened concurrently. Once again, after defining a μ-calculus appropriately we are able to get the equivalence with MSOL and automata over traces. Finally, we will discuss the real-time setting. The situation here is more delicate because both the standard automata model as well as MSOL are undecidable. We will present a recent result which gives a decidable fixpoint calculus but with yet unknown expressive power.

2   The μ-Calculus over Transition Systems

In this section we recall the definition of the μ-calculus and discuss the expressive power of the logic over trees and transitions systems. The μ-calculus is an extension of the modal logic K with fixpoint operators. This addition gives a logic with very interesting expressive power. While modal logic K is less expressive than first-order logic, the μ-calculus expresses a good fragment of the properties definable in monadic second-order logic.

Formulas of the μ-calculus over the sets $Prop = \{p_1, p_2, \ldots\}$ of *propositional constants*, $Act = \{a, b, \ldots\}$ of *actions*, and $Var = \{X, Y, \ldots\}$ of *variables*, are defined by the following grammar:

$$F := Prop \mid \neg Prop \mid Var \mid F \vee F \mid F \wedge F \mid$$
$$\langle Act \rangle F \mid [Act] F \mid \mu Var.F \mid \nu Var.F$$

Note that we allow negations only before propositional constants. This is not a problem as we will be interested in *sentences*, i.e., formulas where all variables are bound by μ or ν. Negation of a sentence is defined by de Morgan laws and the duality between the least and the greatest fixed points (cf. [3,10]). In the following $\alpha, \beta, \ldots$ will denote formulas of the logic.

Formulas are interpreted in *transition systems* which are tuples of the form $\mathcal{M} = \langle S, \{R_a\}_{a \in Act}, \rho \rangle$, where: S is a nonempty set of *states*, $R_a \subseteq S \times S$ is a binary relation interpreting the action a, and $\rho : Prop \to \mathcal{P}(S)$ is a function assigning to each propositional constant a set of states where this constant holds.

For a given transition system $\mathcal{M}$ and an *assignment* $V : Var \to \mathcal{P}(S)$, the set of states in which a formula φ is true, denoted $\| \varphi \|_V^{\mathcal{M}}$, is defined inductively as follows:

$$\| p \|_V^{\mathcal{M}} = \rho(p) \qquad \| \neg p \|_V^{\mathcal{M}} = S - \rho(p)$$
$$\| X \|_V^{\mathcal{M}} = V(X)$$
$$\| \langle a \rangle \alpha \|_V^{\mathcal{M}} = \{s : \exists s'. R_a(s, s') \wedge s' \in \| \alpha \|_V^{\mathcal{M}}\}$$
$$\| \mu X.\alpha(X) \|_V^{\mathcal{M}} = \bigcap \{S' \subseteq S : \| \alpha \|_{V[S'/X]}^{\mathcal{M}} \subseteq S'\}$$
$$\| \nu X.\alpha(X) \|_V^{\mathcal{M}} = \bigcup \{S' \subseteq S : S' \subseteq \| \alpha \|_{V[S'/X]}^{\mathcal{M}}\}$$

We have omitted here the obvious clauses for boolean operators and for $[a]\alpha$ formula. We will omit V in the notation if α is a sentence and will sometimes write $\mathcal{M}, s \models \alpha$ instead of $s \in \| \alpha \|^{\mathcal{M}}$.

The question we are interested in is what kind of properties are expressible in the logic. For this we introduce the notion of a *pointed transition system* which is a pair $(\mathcal{M}, s)$ consisting of a transition system and its state. A μ-calculus sentence defines a class of pointed transition systems $(\mathcal{M}, s)$ such that $\mathcal{M}, s \vDash \alpha$.

To answer the question about the expressive power we will first consider a restricted class of graphs, namely deterministic trees. For this class we get a perfect match with other well known formalism: monadic second-order logic.

Monadic second-order logic (MSOL) is an extension of first-order logic with quantification over sets of elements. The signature of the logic consists of one binary relation R_a for each $a \in Act$ and a monadic relation P_p for each $p \in Prop$. Let $Var_1 = \{x, y, \dots\}$ and $Var_2 = \{X, Y, \dots\}$ be the sets first and second order variables, respectively. The syntax of MSOL is given by the usual rules for the first-order logic together with the following:

- if $X \in Var_2$, $y \in Var_1$ and α is a formula then $X(y)$ and $\exists X.\alpha$ are formulas.

Given a transition system $\mathcal{M} = \langle S, \{R_a\}_{a \in Act}, \rho \rangle$, the semantic of a formula is defined as in the first-order logic. Because we have both first and second-order variables, the valuation V should assign to a variable either an element or a set of elements respectively. The two new constructs are interpreted by:

- $M, V \vDash X(y)$ iff $V(y) \in V(X)$,
- $M, V \vDash \exists X.\alpha$ iff there is $S' \subseteq S$ such that $M, V[S'/X] \vDash \alpha$.

A pointed transition system $(\mathcal{M}, s)$ can be considered as a transition system with one more proposition P_{start} that is true only in s. With this convention we can talk about a class of pointed transition systems defined by a MSOL formula.

A *deterministic tree* is a transition system whose underlying edge labeled graph is a tree and such that for each node and for each relation R_a there is at most one outgoing transition on R_a from the node. Such a tree can be also considered as a pointed transition system where the chosen state is the root of the tree. Observe that for every deterministic tree $\mathcal{M}$ and a state s the truth of a μ-calculus formula in s depends only on the subtree rooted in s. Thus for definability it does not make much sense to consider pointed structures with other distinguished states than the root.

Theorem 1 ([8]). *A set of deterministic trees is definable by a MSOL sentence iff it is definable by a μ-calculus sentence.*

The restriction to deterministic trees is necessary because over graphs MSOL can say much more than the μ-calculus about structural properties of graphs. It can say for example that there is a cycle in a transition system; this explains why we need to restrict to trees. It can also say that the number successors of a node is bigger than some threshold; this explains the condition of determinism.

Consider a standard definition of bisimulation between pointed transition systems (where it is required that bisimilar states should satisfy the same propositions). The two structural properties mentioned above are not invariant under bisimulation while all μ-calculus definable properties are. Given this, the following theorem says that over transition systems the μ-calculus has the best possible expressive power.

Definition 1. *A property is* invariant under bisimulation *iff for arbitrary two pointed transition systems either both have the property, or both do not have it.*

Theorem 2 ([6]). *A property of transition systems is definable in the μ-calculus iff it is definable in MSOL and it is invariant under bisimulation.*

3 Traces

A trace is a partial order with some particular properties. It can be used to represent an execution of the system where we do not want to put some artificial order on actions that appear concurrently. A trace can be represented by a transition system so it makes sense to talk about monadic second-order logic and the μ-calculus properties of traces. Due to the particularity of the setting it is not reasonable to consider bisimulation invariant properties of traces. Thus the theorem from the previous section looses its appeal. We will see that the μ-calculus is weaker than MSOL over traces. One can obtain the equivalence by giving to the μ-calculus access to some information about the concurrency in the system.

A *trace alphabet* is a pair (Σ, D) where Σ is a finite set of actions and $D \subseteq \Sigma \times \Sigma$ is a reflexive and symmetric *dependence relation*.

A Σ-labeled graph is $\langle S, R, \lambda \rangle$ where S is the set of vertices, R defines the edges and $\lambda : S \to \Sigma$ is a labeling function.

Definition 2. *A* trace *or a* dependence graph *over a trace alphabet (Σ, D) is a Σ-labeled graph $\langle E, R, \lambda \rangle$ satisfying the following conditions:*

(T1) $\forall e, e' \in E.\ (\lambda(e), \lambda(e')) \in D \Leftrightarrow (R(e, e') \vee R(e', e) \vee e = e')$.
(T2) the transitive closure R^* of R is a partial order and
$\{e' : R^*(e', e)\}$ *is finite for every e.*

The nodes of a dependence graph are called events. *An a-event is an event $e \in E$ which is labeled by a, i.e., $\lambda(e) = a$. We say that e is* before e' *iff $R^*(e, e')$ holds. In this case we also say that e' is* after e.

The first condition of the definition of dependence graphs says that the events are related only if they are labeled by dependent letters. The second says that there cannot be neither circular dependencies nor infinite descending chains. So the past of each event (i.e. the set of events that appear before it) is finite. The traces we consider here are sometimes called real traces [5]. From the definition it follows that they are either finite or countably infinite.

Definition 3. *A* transition system representation *of a trace $G = \langle E, R, \lambda \rangle$ is a transition system $\mathcal{M}(G) = \langle E, R_H, \rho \rangle$ over the set of propositions $\{P_a : a \in \Sigma\}$ where (i) the function ρ is defined by $\rho(P_a) = \{e : \lambda(e) = a\}$; and (ii) R_H is the smallest relation needed to determine R, i.e., $R_H^* = R^*$ and if $R_H(e, e')$ then there is no e'' different from e and e' such that $R_H(e, e'')$ and $R_H(e'', e')$ hold.*

The dependence graph representation has too many transitions to be interesting for the logic as the μ-calculus. Working with this representation would be similar to considering transitive closure of relations and not relations themselves. The transition system representation we have defined uses Hasse diagram of the trace (which exists and is unique in this setting). To be consistent with the definitions from the previous section we also need to change the labeling function. In traces this function assigns a label to each node, in transition systems it assigns a set of nodes to each label. Observe that a representation of a trace is a transition system with a singleton action alphabet.

Thanks to the above definition we can use formalisms of transition systems to talk about traces. In particular we will talk about μ-calculus or MSOL definable sets of traces considered as pointed transition systems. In principle there can be more than one minimal element in a trace and this can pose a problem with definition of a pointed transition system. Because of this we assume a relatively harmless proviso that every trace has the least event. Thus a transition system $\mathcal{M}(G)$ can be considered as pointed transition system $(\mathcal{M}(G), e)$ where e is the least event of G.

It turns out that the class of MSOL definable trace languages have very similar characterizations as in the case of infinite words. The following theorem summarizing many results on traces can be found in [4].

Theorem 3. *Fix a given trace alphabet. For a set L of traces the following are equivalent:*

- *L is definable by a MSOL formula.*
- *L is definable by a c-regular expression.*
- *L is recognizable by an asynchronous automaton.*
- *The set of linearizations of traces in L is a recognizable language of finite and infinite words.*

We will not need asynchronous automata or c-regular expressions, so we will not define them here. If linearizations are concerned, let us just say that a linearization of a trace is an infinite word which corresponds to some linear order of type ω extending the partial order of the trace.

We next show that the μ-calculus over traces cannot even express some first-order definable properties. This example motivates the search for extensions of the μ-calculus that can capture the power of MSOL over traces.

Proposition 1. *No μ-calculus sentence can distinguish between the transition system representations of the two traces presented in Figure 1. In the left graph the dots stand for the sequence $(dc)^\omega$ and in the right graph for $(cd)^\omega$. In this example the trace alphabet $(\{\bot, a, b, c, d\}, D)$ where D is the smallest symmetric and reflexive relation containing the pairs $\{(a,c), (b,d), (c,d)\} \cup \{\bot\} \times \{a,b,c,d\}$.*

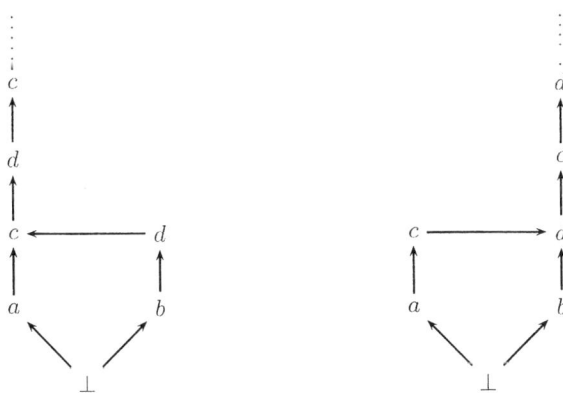

Fig. 1. Indistinguishable traces

Proof. The two pointed transition systems are bisimilar. Proposition follows from the fact that no μ-calculus formula can distinguish between two bisimilar pointed transition systems. □

The two traces from the proposition are distinguishable by a first-order formula because in the left trace first d comes before first c and it is the opposite in the right trace.

The above example implies that one needs to add something to the μ-calculus in order to be able to say more about the structure of a trace. One of the possible extensions is that with concurrency information.

Definition 4. *Let $\mathcal{M}(G) = \langle E, R, \rho \rangle$ be a transition system representation of a trace G. Relation $co \subseteq E \times E$, called the* concurrency relation, *is defined by: $co(e, e')$ iff neither $R^*(e, e')$ nor $R^*(e', e)$ hold.*

Definition 5. *Let $\mathcal{M}(G) = \langle E, R, \rho \rangle$ be a transition system representation of a trace G. We define an enriched representation $\mathcal{M}_{co}(G) = \langle E, R, \rho_{co} \rangle$ by adding new propositions co_a for $a \in Act$ and setting $\rho_{co}(co_a) = \{e : \exists e' \in \lambda(p_a).\ co(e, e')\}$. (Naturally ρ and ρ_{co} coincide on all other propositions.)*

Intuitively a co_a proposition holds in an event if there is a concurrent event labeled by a. This way a μ-calculus formula can get some information about what happens in parallel to the current event. Observe that co relation is definable in MSOL. The following theorem says that $\mathcal{M}_{co}$ representations are reach enough to get the equivalence between the μ-calculus and MSOL.

Theorem 4 ([11]). *For every MSOL formula φ there is a μ-calculus formula α_φ such that for every trace G $\mathcal{M}(G) \models \varphi$ iff $\mathcal{M}_{co}(G) \models \alpha_\varphi$.*

4 Real-Time Languages

By a *timed word* over Σ we mean a finite sequence

$$w = (a_1, t_1)(a_2, t_2)\ldots(a_n, t_n)$$

of pairs from $\Sigma \times \mathbb{R}_+$. Each t_i describes the amount of time that passed between reading a_{i-1} and a_i, i.e., a_1 was read at time t_1, a_2 was read at time t_1+t_2, and so on. Note that we consider only finite timed words.

The presence of a dense domain makes a big difference and adoption of the tools described in previous sections proceeds with some difficulties. The standard automata model for real-time setting [1] is not closed under complement. First-order logic with monadic predicates and $+1$ relation is undecidable over real line. So it the MSOL theory of the real line (without $+1$ predicate) [9]. These negative results indicate that some extra care is need to obtain decidable formalisms with good expressive power.

Actually, it is quite difficult to get a formalism with a reasonable expressive power and closed under boolean operations. One such formalism is event-clock automata [2]. These are a special variant of timed automata where the reset operation on clocks is restricted. Here, we would like to present a different approach. It is well known that the μ-calculus over transition systems is equivalent to alternating automata and that there are very direct translations between the two formalism. Thus we would like to find an alternating automata model for timed-words. The first attempt would be to generalize the standard notion of timed automata [1] by introducing alternation. This is bound to fail as the universality problem for timed automata is undecidable and, in consequence, we would get a model with undecidable emptiness problem.

A solution is to restrict to automata with one clock [7]. With one clock alternating automata can still recognize languages not recognizable by nondeterministic automata with many clocks and moreover they have decidable emptiness problem. Below we define alternating timed automata in full generality and then state the results for the one-clock version.

For a given finite set $\mathcal{C}$ of *clock variables* (or *clocks* in short), consider the set $\Phi(\mathcal{C})$ of clock constraints σ defined by

$$\sigma \quad ::= \quad x < c \mid x \leq c \mid \sigma_1 \wedge \sigma_2 \mid \neg \sigma,$$

where c stands for an arbitrary nonnegative integer constant, and $x \in \mathcal{C}$. For instance, note that tt (always true), or $x = c$, can be defined as abbreviations. Each constraint σ denotes a subset $[\sigma]$ of $(\mathbb{R}_+)^\mathcal{C}$, in a natural way, where $\mathbb{R}_+$ stands for the set of nonnegative reals.

Transition relation of a timed automaton [1] is usually defined by a finite set of rules δ of the form

$$\delta \subseteq Q \times \Sigma \times \Phi(\mathcal{C}) \times Q \times \mathcal{P}(\mathcal{C}),$$

where Q is a set of *locations* (control states) and Σ is an input alphabet. A rule $\langle q, a, \sigma, q', r \rangle \in \delta$ means, roughly, that when in a location q, if the next input letter is a and the constraint σ is satisfied by the current valuation of clock variables then the next location can be q' and the clocks in r should be reset to 0. Our definition below uses an easy observation, that the relation δ can be suitably rearranged into a finite partial function

$$Q \times \Sigma \times \Phi(\mathcal{C}) \xrightarrow{\cdot} \mathcal{P}(Q \times \mathcal{P}(\mathcal{C})).$$

The definition below comes naturally when one thinks of an element of the codomain as a disjunction of a finite number of pairs (q, r). Let $\mathcal{B}^+(X)$ denote the set of all positive boolean formulas over the set X of propositions, i.e., the set generated by:
$$\phi ::= X \mid \phi_1 \wedge \phi_2 \mid \phi_1 \vee \phi_2.$$

Definition 6 (Alternating timed automaton). *An alternating timed automaton is a tuple $\mathcal{A} = (Q, q_0, \Sigma, \mathcal{C}, F, \delta)$ where: Q is a finite set of locations, Σ is a finite input alphabet, $\mathcal{C}$ is a finite set of clock variables, and $\delta : Q \times \Sigma \times \Phi(\mathcal{C}) \to \mathcal{B}^+(Q \times \mathcal{P}(\mathcal{C}))$ is a finite partial function. Moreover $q_0 \in Q$ is an initial state and $F \subseteq Q$ is a set of accepting states. We also put an additional restriction:*

(Partition) *For every q and a, the set $\{[\sigma] : \delta(q, a, \sigma)$ is defined$\}$ gives a (finite) partition of $(\mathbb{R}_+)^\mathcal{C}$.*

The (Partition) condition does not limit the expressive power of automata. We impose it because it permits to give a nice symmetric semantic for the automata as explained below. We will often write rules of the automaton in a form: $q, a, \sigma \mapsto b$.

To define an execution of an automaton, we will need two operations on valuations $\mathbf{v} \in (\mathbb{R}_+)^\mathcal{C}$. A valuation $\mathbf{v}+t$, for $t \in \mathbb{R}_+$, is obtained from $\mathbf{v}$ by augmenting value of each clock by t. A valuation $\mathbf{v}[r := 0]$, for $r \subseteq \mathcal{C}$, is obtained by reseting values of all clocks in r to zero.

In order to define acceptance, for an alternating timed automaton $\mathcal{A}$ and a timed word $w = (a_1, t_1)(a_2, t_2)\ldots(a_n, t_n)$, we define the *acceptance game* $G_{\mathcal{A}, w}$ between two players Adam and Eve. Intuitively, the objective of Eve is to accept w, while the aim of Adam is the opposite. A play starts at the initial configuration $(q_0, \mathbf{v}_0)$, where $\mathbf{v}_0 : \mathcal{C} \to \mathbb{R}_+$ is a valuation assigning 0 to each clock variable. It consists of n phases. The $(k+1)$-th phase starts in $(q_k, \mathbf{v}_k)$, ends in some configuration $(q_{k+1}, \mathbf{v}_{k+1})$ and proceeds as follows. Let $\overline{\mathbf{v}} := \mathbf{v}_k + t_{k+1}$. Let σ be the unique constraint such that $\overline{\mathbf{v}}$ satisfies σ and $b = \delta(q_k, a_{k+1}, \sigma)$ is defined. Now, the outcome of the phase is determined by the formula b. There are three cases:

- $b = b_1 \wedge b_2$: Adam chooses one of subformulas b_1, b_2 and the play continues with b replaced by the chosen subformula;
- $b = b_1 \vee b_2$: dually, Eve chooses one of subformulas;
- $b = (q, r) \in Q \times \mathcal{P}(\mathcal{C})$: the phase ends with the result $(q_{k+1}, \mathbf{v}_{k+1}) := (q, \overline{\mathbf{v}}[r := 0])$. A new phase is starting from this configuration if $k+1 < n$.

The winner is Eve if q_n is accepting ($q_n \in F$), otherwise Adam wins.

Definition 7 (Acceptance). *The automaton $\mathcal{A}$ accepts w iff Eve has a winning strategy in the game $G_{\mathcal{A}, w}$. By $L(\mathcal{A})$ we denote the language of all timed words w accepted by $\mathcal{A}$.*

To show the power of alternation we give an example of an automaton for a language not recognizable by standard (i.e. nondeterministic) timed automata (cf. [1]).

Example 1. Consider a language consisting of timed words w over a singleton alphabet $\{a\}$ that contain no pair of letters such that one of them is precisely one time unit later than the other. The alternating automaton for this language has three states q_0, q_1, q_2. State q_0 is initial. The automaton has a single clock x and the following transition rules:

$$q_0, a, tt \mapsto (q_0, \emptyset) \wedge (q_1, \{x\}) \qquad q_1, a, x \neq 1 \mapsto (q_1, \emptyset)$$
$$q_1, a, x=1 \mapsto (q_2, \emptyset) \qquad q_2, a, tt \mapsto (q_2, \emptyset)$$

States q_0 and q_1 are accepting. Clearly, Adam has a strategy to reach q_2 iff the word is not in the language, i.e., some letter is one time unit after some other.

As one expects, we have the following:

Proposition 2. *The class of languages accepted by alternating timed automata is effectively closed under all boolean operations: union, intersection and complementation. These operations to do not increase the number of clocks of the automaton.*

The closure under conjunction and disjunction is straightforward since we permit positive boolean expressions as values of the transition function. Due to the condition (Partition) the automaton for the complement is obtained by exchanging conjunctions with disjunctions in all transitions and exchanging accepting states with non-accepting states.

An alternating timed automaton $\mathcal{A}$ is called *purely existential* if no conjunction appears in the transition rues δ. It is obvious that every purely-existential automaton is a standard nondeterministic timed automaton. The converse requires a proof because of the (Partition) condition.

Proposition 3. *Every standard nondeterministic automaton is equivalent to a purely-existential automaton.*

The automaton from Example 1 uses only one clock. This shows that one clock alternating automata can recognize some languages not recognizable by nondeterministic automata with many clocks. The converse is also true. It is enough to consider the language consisting of the words containing an appearance of a letter b at times t_1, t_2, for some $0 < t_1 < t_2 < 1$, and such that there is no b at time between t_1 and t_2 while there is precisely one b between $t_1 + 1$ and $t_2 + 1$.

Theorem 5 ([7]). *The emptiness problem is decidable for one-clock alternating timed automata.*

Thanks to this theorem we have a decidable formalism of timed-words that is closed under boolean operations. One can think of developing a variant of the

μ-calculus which would correspond to these automata. It should not be too difficult given that the translation between alternating automata and the μ-calculus works in many other settings. The main obstacles in this line of development are rather negative complexity results. The complexity of the emptiness problem for one-clock alternating automata is not primitively recursive [7]. Moreover, if we consider infinite words and alternating Büchi timed automata with one clock then the problem becomes undecidable.

References

1. R. Alur and D.L. Dill. A theory of timed automata. *Theoretical Computer Science*, 126:183–235, 1994.
2. R. Alur, L. Fix, and T. Henzinger. Event-clock automata: A determinizable class of timed automata. *Theoretical Computer Science*, 204, 1997.
3. Andreé Arnold and Damian Niwiński. *The Rudiments of the Mu-Calculus*, volume 146 of *Studies in Logic*. North-Holand, 2001.
4. Werner Ebinger. Logical definability of trace languages. In Volker Diekert and Grzegorz Rozenberg, editors, *The Book of Traces*, pages 382–390. World Scientific, 1995.
5. Paul Gastin and Antoine Petit. Infninite traces. In V. Diekert and G. Rozenberg, editors, *The Book of Traces*. World Scientific, 1995.
6. David Janin and Igor Walukiewicz. On the expressive completeness of the propositional mu-calculus with respect to monadic second order logic. In *CONCUR'96*, volume 1119 of *Lecture Notes in Computer Science*, pages 263–277, 1996.
7. Slawomir Lasota and Igor Walukiewicz. Alternating timed automata. In *FOSSACS'05*, Lecture Notes in Computer Science, 2005. To appear.
8. Damian Niwiński. Fixed points vs. infinite generation. In *LICS '88*, pages 402–409, 1988.
9. Saharon Shelah. The monadic second order theory of order. *Annals of Mathematics*, 102:379–419, 1975.
10. Colin Stirling. *Modal and Temporal Properties of Processes*. Texts in Computer Science. Springer, 2001.
11. Igor Walukiewicz. Local logics for traces. *Journal of Automata, Languages and Combinatorics*, 7(2):259–290, 2002.

Reasoning About Systems with Transition Fairness

Benjamin Aminof[1], Thomas Ball[2], and Orna Kupferman[1]

[1] Hebrew University, School of Engineering and Computer Science, Jerusalem 91904, Israel
{benj,orna}@cs.huji.ac.il
[2] Microsoft Research, One Microsoft way, Redmond, WA 98052, USA
tball@microsoft.com

Abstract. Formal verification methods model systems by Kripke structures. In order to model live behaviors of systems, Kripke structures are augmented with *fairness conditions*. Such conditions partition the computations of the systems into fair computations, with respect to which verification proceeds, and unfair computations, which are ignored. Reasoning about Kripke structures augmented with fairness is typically harder than reasoning about non-fair Kripke structures. We consider the *transition fairness* condition, where a computation π is fair iff each transition that is enabled in π infinitely often is also taken in π infinitely often. Transition fairness is a natural and useful fairness condition. We show that reasoning about Kripke structures augmented with transition fairness is not harder than reasoning about non-fair Kripke structures. We demonstrate it for fair CTL and LTL model checking, and the problem of calculating the dominators and postdominators.

1 Introduction

In *formal verification*, we check that a system is correct with respect to a desired behavior by checking that a mathematical model of the system satisfies a formal specification of the behavior. In *model checking*, we model the system by a *Kripke structure*, whose states correspond to configurations of the system, and we specify the desired behavior by means of a *temporal-logic* formula. The model-checking problem is then to decide, given a Kripke structure K and a temporal-logic formula ψ, whether K satisfies ψ [CE81,QS81]. Symbolic methods, abstraction, compositional methods, and many more heuristics have made model checking a successful verification methodology, used in industrial design of both hardware and software [CGP99].

Kripke structures describe only the *safe* behaviors of systems. In order to model *live* behaviors, we have to augment Kripke structures with *fairness conditions*. Such conditions partition the set of infinite paths of a Kripke structure K (and thus also the set of infinite computations of the system that K models) into fair and unfair computations [Fra86,MP92]. For example, when the Kripke structure models a concurrent system, we may wish to restrict attention only to computations in which the scheduler enables each process to proceed infinitely many times.

The model-checking problem can be adjusted to the fair setting: in the *linear-time* approach, specifications describe the desired behavior of all the computations of the system, and thus refer to the language induced by the Kripke structure. Then, fair model checking amounts to verifying that all the fair computations satisfy the desired behavior. In the *branching-time* approach, specifications may contain the path quantifiers A (for all paths) and E (exists a path) and thus refer to the tree obtained by unwinding the Kripke structure. Then, in fair model checking, path quantification ranges over fair paths only [CES86]. The transition to the fair setting involves a computational price. The exact complexity of the fair model-checking problem depends on the specification formalism and the specific fairness condition that is used.

We consider the fairness condition in which a computation π is fair iff each transition that is enabled in π infinitely often is also taken in π infinitely often. That is, for every transition $\langle w, w' \rangle$ in the Kripke structure, if the path π visits the state w infinitely many times, then π should also have infinitely many visits to w that are immediately followed by a visit to w'. We refer to this type of fairness as *transition fairness*. The transition fairness condition is related to the classical *strong-fairness* condition [MP92] (*Streett* fairness)[3], and is a very natural one in reasoning about concurrent systems [LPS81,KPSZ02].

In order to see why transition fairness is so natural and useful, let us consider the possible sources for nondeterminism in a Kripke structure. We distinguish between *external* and *internal* nondeterminism [Hoa85]. External nondeterminism is caused by the interaction of the system with its environment, and the fact that different inputs are expected in each state of the system. Then, transition fairness requires that in every state of the interaction that is visited infinitely often, the environment provides each input infinitely often. Internal nondeterminism is caused by abstraction. In the case of a concurrent composition between processes, we usually abstract the scheduler. Then, transition fairness restricts attention to a scheduling policy in which for each process, if a process is enabled in a state infinitely often, then it is also scheduled to proceed infinitely often. In case we abstract other factors of the system, like information that is irrelevant for the specification, transition fairness is less natural and restricts attention to computations that are fair with respect to the abstracted information. For an extensive study of transition fairness, further motivation for it, and related definitions of fairness, see [QS83].

Reasoning about systems augmented with the strong-fairness condition is not easy, and is related to the emptiness problem for nondeterministic Streett automata. While the latter problem is PTIME-complete [EL87,KV98a], no linear solutions are known, for both the enumerative and symbolic approaches. The best enumerative algorithm makes use of a lock-step search, used in dynamic graph algorithms, and is at most quadratic in the size of the automaton [HT96]. The best symbolic algorithm is based on the improved algorithm for detecting strongly connected components and requires $O(n(k + \log n))$ symbolic steps, for an automaton of size n and a strong-fairness condition with k pairs

---

[3] The Streett fairness condition consists of a set of pairs $\langle L_i, U_i \rangle$, with L_i and U_i being a subset of the state space. A path π is fair if for all pairs, if the set L_i is visited infinitely often, then so is U_i. By having a pair $\langle \{w\}, \{w'\} \rangle$ for each transition $\langle w, w' \rangle$ in the Kripke structure, we can encode transition fairness with the Streett fairness condition (a technical issue is the fact w' may be reached via a different transition. This can be easily solved by adding an internal state to each transition). In Section 2.2 we discuss other related fairness conditions.

[KPR98,BGS00][4]. The complexity of model checking a specification φ with respect to a Kripke structure K augmented with a strong-fairness condition with k pairs is then the complexity of checking emptiness for an automaton of size $|K|2^{|\varphi|}$, in the case of LTL[5], and $|\varphi|$ repeated checks for an automaton of size $|K|$, in the case of CTL.

We study the problem of reasoning about systems augmented with the transition fairness condition, and show that this special case of the strong-fairness condition is considerably simpler. We consider the CTL and LTL model-checking problems, as well as the related problem of finding *dominators* and *postdominators* [C+91] in directed graphs.

For model checking, we show that fair CTL model checking can be reduced to non-fair CTL model checking. To do so, we introduce a function f with the following properties. Given a CTL formula φ, the function f maps φ to another CTL formula $f(\varphi)$ such that for every Kripke structure K and state w in it, w satisfies φ fairly iff w satisfies $f(\varphi)$ non-fairly. The size of $f(\varphi)$ is linear in the size of φ. The complexity of the algorithm that follows then coincides with the one for non-fair CTL model checking. Since the function f is simple, it is easy to implement it on top of both enumerative and symbolic CTL model-checking tools. We note that another reduction of fair model checking to unfair model checking by a transformation of the specification is described in [QS83]. The logic studied there contains operators corresponding to CTL's EF ("potential reachability") and AF ("inevitable reachability") and the transformation results in formulas that are not CTL formulas.

In order to handle LTL model checking, we introduce a function g that maps LTL formulas θ of some specific forms to a CTL formula $g(\theta)$ such that a fair Kripke structure K has a path that fairly satisfies θ iff K fairly satisfies $g(\theta)$, which in turn can be reduced to checking whether K satisfies $f(g(\theta))$. The forms of θ we handle are these that correspond to the Büchi, Rabin, and Streett acceptance conditions for automata on infinite words. In the automata-theoretic approach to LTL model checking [VW94], we translate an LTL formula ψ into an automaton $\mathcal{A}_{\neg\psi}$ that accepts exactly all the computations that violate ψ. Model checking is then reduced to checking the emptiness of the product of K with $\mathcal{A}_{\neg\psi}$. When K is augmented with a fairness condition, checking the emptiness of the product of K with $\mathcal{A}_{\neg\psi}$ corresponds to checking whether the product contains a path whose projection on the states of K is fair, and which satisfies a formula θ induced by the acceptance condition of $\mathcal{A}_{\neg\psi}$, and is therefore of one of the forms above. Our algorithm can therefore handle many LTL model-checking instances. On the other hand, we show that taking the product of K with $\mathcal{A}_{\neg\psi}$ does not preserve transition fairness, thus our algorithm does not handle all LTL model-checking instances.

The problem of finding the *postdominators* (or, dually, the *dominators*) of a given state in the Kripke structure has application in the area of program analysis and compiler optimizations [C+91]. In this application area, the control-flow graph of a program is the Kripke structure, where states correspond to basic blocks in the program and transitions correspond to control-flow transitions between basic blocks in the program. Domina-

---
[4] We note that while it is possible to detect SCC also in linearly many symbolic steps [GPP03], it is not known whether the technique there can be applied for an efficient nonemptiness check of Streett automata.

[5] See [LH00] for the case the system is modeled by a petri net.

tors form the basis of an intermediate representation known as static single assignment form [C+91], widely used in optimizing compilers. Computation of postdominators is required for the computation of control dependences in the program dependence graph [FOW87], a data structure used for the automatic parallelization of programs as well as program slicing.

For a state w of a Kripke structure, the set of postdominators of w, denoted $pd(w)$, is the set of states s such that all paths from w eventually reach s. Dually, the set of dominators of w, denoted $dom(w)$, is the set of states s such that all paths to w pass through s. The definition of $pd(w)$ and its applications are of interest mainly in Kripke structures augmented with fairness. Indeed, it makes sense to require s to be reachable only along fair paths, in particular, paths that eventually reach a halting or an error state, or paths that are fair with respect to our transition fairness condition. That is, the definition of $pd(w)$ as used in compiler optimizations generally assumes that loops eventually terminate.

It is easy to show that if x postdominates w and $x \neq w$ then $pd(x) \subset pd(w)$. This means that the postdomination relation can be represented as a tree, where x is the parent of w in the tree iff $pd(w) = \{w\} \cup pd(x)$ (in this case, x is called the "immediate postdominator" of w). There are several efficient algorithms for calculating dominator and postdominator trees [LT79,BKAW98]. Once the tree has been computed, the set $pd(x)$ can be enumerated in time proportional to $|pd(x)|$, for all states x. However, the above techniques maintain an explicit representation of the Kripke structure as a directed graph and explicitly represent the postdominator tree. We use the technique we developed for fair CTL model checking in order to describe a symbolic algorithm that efficiently computes an ROBDD of pairs $\langle w, s \rangle$ such that $s \in pd(w)$. Such a representation is useful because in the application domain of program analysis it often is necessary to enumerate $pd(w)$ for many w without knowing in advance which w will be queried.

Due to lack of space, this version does not contain all the proofs. For the full version, see [ABK04].

2 Preliminaries

2.1 Temporal Logics

We describe the desired behavior of systems by temporal-logic formulas. The logic *LTL* is a linear temporal logic. Formulas of LTL describe computations and are constructed from a set AP of atomic propositions using the usual Boolean operators and the temporal operators X ("next") and U ("until"). Formally, given a set AP, an LTL formula is one of the following:

- **true**, **false**, or p, for $p \in AP$.
- $\neg \psi_1, \psi_1 \vee \psi_2, X\psi_1$, or $\psi_1 U \psi_2$, where ψ_1 and ψ_2 are LTL formulas.

We also use the abbreviations $\wedge, \rightarrow$, and $\leftrightarrow$, interpreted in the usual way, $F\psi = \textbf{true}U\psi$ ("eventually"), $G\psi = \neg F \neg \psi$ ("always"), and $\psi_1 W \psi_2 = \psi_1 U \psi_2 \vee G \psi_1$ ("weak until").

The logic *CTL* is a branching temporal logic. In CTL, we precede each temporal operator by a path quantifier, either E ("for some path") or A ("for all paths"). Thus, a CTL formula is either:

- true, false, or p, for $p \in AP$.
- $\neg\varphi_1$ or $\varphi_1 \vee \varphi_2$, where φ_1 and φ_2 are CTL formulas.
- $EX\varphi_1$ or $AX\varphi_1$, where φ_1 is a CTL formula.
- $E\varphi_1 U \varphi_2$ or $A\varphi_1 U \varphi_2$, where φ_1 and φ_2 are CTL formulas.

Note that the G and F abbreviations used in LTL can be used also in CTL, i.e., $AF\varphi_1 = \mathbf{A\,true}U\varphi_1$, and so can the W abbreviation. Thus, while $E\varphi_1 W \varphi_2 = E(\varphi_1 U \varphi_2 \vee G\varphi_1)$ is not a CTL formula, it is equivalent to the CTL formula $E\varphi_1 U \varphi_2 \vee EG\varphi_1$. Similarly, $A\varphi_1 W \varphi_2$ is equivalent to the CTL formula $\neg E(\neg\varphi_2)U(\neg\varphi_1 \wedge \neg\varphi_2)$. Accordingly, we refer to EW and AW as legal CTL modalities. The *size* $|\varphi|$ of an LTL or a CTL formula φ is the number of its subformulas. Note that φ can be represented by a DAG with $|\varphi|$ vertices.

We define the semantics of temporal-logic formulas with respect to *Kripke structures*, with which we model systems. A Kripke structure $K = \langle AP, W, R, W_0, L \rangle$ consists of a set AP of atomic propositions, a set W of states, a set $W_0 \subseteq W$ of initial states, a transition relation $R \subseteq W \times W$ that is total in its first element (i.e., for each $w \in W$ there exists at least one w' with $R(w, w')$), and a labeling function $L : W \to 2^{AP}$, which maps each state to the set of atomic propositions true in this state. When $R(w, w')$, we say that w' is a *successor* of w. A *path* in K represents a *computation* of the system modeled by the Kripke structure and is a (possibly finite) sequence of states $\pi = w_0, w_1, \ldots$, such that for all $i \geq 0$, we have $R(w_i, w_{i+1})$. The path π is *initial* if $w_0 \in W_0$. We use π^i to denote the suffix $w_i, w_{i+1}, \ldots$ of π, and we use $\pi[i]$ to denote the i'th state in π. The set of states that π visits is denoted by $visit(\pi)$, and the set of states that π visits infinitely often is denoted by $inf(\pi)$. Formally, $visit(\pi) = \{w : w = w_j \text{ for some } j\}$, and $inf(\pi) = \{w : w = w_j \text{ for infinitely many } j\}$. Note that $inf(\pi) \subseteq visit(\pi)$.

Recall that LTL is a linear temporal logic, thus its formulas are interpreted over paths of the Kripke structure. We use $K, \pi \models \psi$ to indicate that the LTL formula ψ holds along the path π of K. On the other hand, CTL is a branching temporal logic and its formulas are interpreted over states of the Kripke structure. We use $K, w \models \varphi$ to indicate that the CTL formula φ holds in the state w of K. When K is clear from the context, we simply write $\pi \models \psi$ or $w \models \varphi$. For the definition of the relation $\models$ see [Eme90]. We say that a Kripke structure K satisfies an LTL formula ψ, denoted $K \models \psi$, if all the initial paths of K satisfy ψ. Likewise, K satisfies a CTL formula φ, denoted $K \models \varphi$, if all the initial states of K satisfy φ.

A Kripke structure $K = \langle AP, W, R, W_0, L \rangle$ induces a directed graph $G_K = \langle W, R \rangle$. Notations and definitions from graph theory are then applied to Kripke structures in a straightforward way. A state w is *reachable* from a state v iff there is a finite (possibly empty) path $w_0, w_1, \ldots, w_n$ such that $v = w_0$ and $w = w_n$ and for every $0 \leq i < n$, we have $R(w_i, w_{i+1})$. A *strongly connected component* (SCC, for short) is a subset C of W such that every state in C is reachable from every other state in C, via states in C. A *maximal strongly connected component* (MSCC, for short) is an SCC C that is maximal in the sense that we cannot add states to it and still have an SCC. Note that the MSCCs partition W.

Given two MSCC's C and C' we say that $C \leq C'$ if there are states $v \in C'$ and $w \in C$ such that w is reachable from v. The relation $\leq$ defined above constitutes a partial ordering of the set of MSCCs of K. A MSCC C is called a *bottom MSCC* if for every MSCC C', we have that either C and C' are not comparable or $C \leq C'$. Note that all the bottom MSCCs in a Kripke structure are not trivial (i.e., they contain at least one edge) since R is total in its first element.

It is not hard to see that for every state $v \in W$ there is at least one bottom MSCC C such that for every state $w \in C$, we have that w is reachable from v. Observe that since there are no trivial bottom MSCCs we can assume that every w above is reachable from v using a non-empty path.

2.2 Fairness

A *fairness condition* on a Kripke structure K partitions the paths of K into *fair* and *unfair* paths. The Büchi, Rabin, and Streett acceptance conditions for word automata (for a survey on word automata see [Tho90]) can also be viewed as fairness conditions on Kripke structures. For example, a path π of K is fair with respect to a Büchi condition $\alpha \subseteq W$ iff π visits states in α infinitely often. In this paper we consider *transition fairness*, defined as follows:

- A path π is fair with respect to the transition fairness condition iff all the transitions that are enabled along π infinitely often are also taken along π infinitely often. Formally, a transition $\langle v, w \rangle \in R$ is *enabled* in position i along π, if $\pi[i] = v$. It is *taken*, if in addition $\pi[i+1] = w$. Thus, equivalently, a path π is fair with respect to the transition fairness condition iff for all $v \in W$, if $v \in inf(\pi)$ and $R(v,w)$ then $\pi[i] = v$ and $\pi[i+1] = w$ for infinitely many i's.

A *fair Kripke structure* $\mathcal{K} = \langle K, \alpha \rangle$ consists of a Kripke structure K and a fairness condition α for K (note that in the case of transition fairness, there is no need to specify a specific α, thus α is some flag indicating the type of fairness). The semantics of LTL and CTL is adjusted to fair Kripke structures by letting path quantification range over fair paths only. For example, an LTL formula ψ is *fairly satisfied* in $\mathcal{K}$, denoted $\mathcal{K} \models_F \psi$, if all the fair initial paths of K satisfy ψ. For CTL, we use $\mathcal{K}, w \models_F \varphi$ to indicate that a CTL formula φ is fairly satisfied in the state w of the fair Kripke structure $\mathcal{K}$, and use $\mathcal{K} \models_F \varphi$ to indicate that φ is fairly satisfied in all the initial states of K. For details, see [CGP99].

Note that the transition fairness condition is related to the *successor* fairness condition, where a path π is fair iff all the successors of a state in π that is visited infinitely often are also visited infinitely often. That is, π is fair iff for all $v \in W$, if $v \in inf(\pi)$ and $R(v, w)$ then $w \in inf(\pi)$. Successor fairness is a special case of the Streett fairness condition, and, like transition fairness, is used in order to ignore paths that get stuck in a MSCC that is not a bottom MSCC (for an application in the probabilistic setting see [Var85]). Transition fairness is stronger than successor fairness in the sense that for every Kripke structure K, if a path π of K is fair with respect to the transition fairness condition, then π is also fair with respect to the successor fairness condition. The opposite is not necessarily true, as π may satisfy the successor fairness condition and not satisfy the transition fairness condition. However, it is not hard to see that given a Kripke structure with a successor fairness condition one can obtain, by inserting a new state in the middle of every transition, a corresponding Kripke structure for which each transition-fair path induces a corresponding successor-fair path in the original structure. The "stretching" effect the new states have on the paths can be easily overcome). Our results are thus also valid for the successor fairness condition.

In the rest of this paper we study the model-checking problem and the problem of finding dominators and postdominators for Kripke structures augmented with the transition fairness condition. For simplicity, we will only use the terms "fair path" or "fair Kripke structure", without repeating the type of fairness.

2.3 Observations on Fair Paths

Recall that if a fair path π visits a state v infinitely often, then it also visits all the successors of v infinitely often. Such a fair behavior cascades from every successor to its own successors. As we formally state below, this guarantees that a fair path eventually gets trapped in some bottom MSCC, where it traverses all the states of the MSCC infinitely often. Formally, we have the following:

Lemma 1. *Let* $\mathcal{K} = \langle K, \alpha \rangle$, *with* $K = \langle AP, W, R, W_0, L \rangle$, *be a fair Kripke structure. If π is a fair path in $\mathcal{K}$ then there exists a bottom MSCC C in K, and an index i, such that $inf(\pi) = visit(\pi^i) = C$.*

Lemma 2. *Let* $\mathcal{K} = \langle K, \alpha \rangle$, *with* $K = \langle AP, W, R, W_0, L \rangle$, *be a fair Kripke structure. Every (possibly empty) finite path $w_0, w_1, \ldots, w_k$ in $\mathcal{K}$ can be extended to an infinite fair path $w_0, w_1, \ldots, w_k, \ldots$.*

3 Fair Model Checking

In this section we reduce fair model checking to non-fair CTL model checking, and analyze the complexity of the algorithm that follows. We start with CTL, and then proceed to fragments of LTL.

3.1 Fair CTL Model Checking

Our fair CTL model-checking algorithm is based on a function f that maps each CTL formula φ to another CTL formula $f(\varphi)$ such that for every fair Kripke structure $\mathcal{K} = \langle K, \alpha \rangle$ and state w in it, we have that $\mathcal{K}, w$ satisfies φ fairly iff K, w satisfies $f(\varphi)$ non-fairly. The function f is independent of K and the size of $f(\varphi)$ is linear in the size of φ (recall that we assume a DAG representation of CTL formulas. Thus, a sub-formula that appears more than once is represented by a single node, and is evaluated only once). Formally, we have the following:

Theorem 1. *There is a function $f :$ CTL formulas $\to$ CTL formulas such that for every CTL formula φ, the following hold.*

(1) $|f(\varphi)| = O(|\varphi|)$.
(2) *For every fair Kripke structure $\mathcal{K} = \langle K, \alpha \rangle$, with $K = \langle AP, W, R, W_0, L \rangle$, and state $w \in W$, we have $\mathcal{K}, w \models_F \varphi$ iff $K, w \models f(\varphi)$.*

Proof: We define f by induction on the structure of φ as follows.

- $f(\mathbf{true}) = \mathbf{true}$ and $f(\mathbf{false}) = \mathbf{false}$.
- $f(p) = p$ for $p \in AP$.
- $f(\neg \varphi_1) = \neg f(\varphi_1)$.
- $f(\varphi_1 \vee \varphi_2) = f(\varphi_1) \vee f(\varphi_2)$.
- $f(EX\varphi_1) = EXf(\varphi_1)$.
- $f(AX\varphi_1) = AXf(\varphi_1)$.
- $f(E\varphi_1 U \varphi_2) = Ef(\varphi_1)Uf(\varphi_2)$.
- $f(A\varphi_1 U \varphi_2) = A(f(\varphi_1) \wedge EFf(\varphi_2))Wf(\varphi_2)$.

It is easy to see that $|f(\varphi)| = O(|\varphi|)$. We prove Claim (2) in detail. The proof proceeds by an induction on the structure of φ. The induction base, where $\varphi = \mathbf{true}$, $\varphi = \mathbf{false}$, or $\varphi = p$, for $p \in AP$ is trivial. For the induction step, assume that Claim (2) holds for φ_1 and φ_2. That is, for every fair Kripke structure $\mathcal{K}$, and every state $w \in W$, we have that $\mathcal{K}, w \models_F \varphi_1$ iff $K, w \models f(\varphi_1)$, and similarly for φ_2.

The cases where φ is of the form $\neg \varphi_1$, $\varphi_1 \vee \varphi_2$, $EX\varphi_1$, $AX\varphi_1$, or $E\varphi_1 U \varphi_2$ are relatively easy, and are described in [ABK04]. Intuitively, the cases $EX\varphi_1$, $AX\varphi_1$, and $E\varphi_1 U \varphi_2$ all follow from the fact that their truth value is established by a finite prefix of a path which by Lemma 2 can always be extended to a fair path. Here we consider the more interesting case, where $\varphi = A\varphi_1 U \varphi_2$.

As an intuition, consider the special case where $\varphi = AFp$. Note that $f(AFp) = A(EFp)Wp$. Thus, we have to prove that all the fair paths that start at some state w eventually reach a state labeled p iff all (possibly unfair) paths that start at w either eventually reach p or always visit states from which a state labeled p is reachable. The 'if' direction is true since, by Lemma 1, every fair path has a tail for which all reachable states are actually visited. The 'only if' direction is true since, by Lemma 2, every state is the initial state of some fair path.

Assume first that $\mathcal{K}, w \models_F A\varphi_1 U \varphi_2$. Consider a (possibly unfair) path π starting at w. We show that either (case 1) there is $k \geq 0$ such that $\pi[k] \models f(\varphi_2)$ and all $0 \leq i < k$ are such that $\pi[i] \models f(\varphi_1) \wedge EFf(\varphi_2)$, or (case 2) all $i \geq 0$ are such that $\pi[i] \models f(\varphi_1) \wedge EFf(\varphi_2)$. It follows that $K, w \models A(f(\varphi_1) \wedge EFf(\varphi_2))Wf(\varphi_2)$.

We distinguish between two cases, which actually correspond to the two cases above. If there is a state along π that fairly satisfies φ_2, we prove that case 1 above holds: let $k \geq 0$ be the minimal index for which $\pi[k] \models_F \varphi_2$. By Lemma 2, the path $\pi[0], \ldots, \pi[k]$ can be extended to a fair path. Since $\mathcal{K}, w \models_F A\varphi_1 U \varphi_2$, our choice of k guarantees that $\pi[k] \models_F \varphi_2$ and $\pi[i] \models_F \varphi_1$ for all $0 \leq i < k$. By the induction hypothesis, $\pi[k] \models f(\varphi_2)$ and $\pi[i] \models f(\varphi_1)$ for all $0 \leq i < k$. Moreover, since $\pi[k] \models f(\varphi_2)$, then for all $0 \leq i < k$, we have that $\pi[i] \models EFf(\varphi_2)$. Thus, case 1 holds for π.

In the other case, that is, if no state along π fairly satisfies φ_2, we prove that case 2 above holds. Consider an index $i \geq 0$. By Lemma 2, the path $\pi[0], \ldots, \pi[i]$ can be extended to a fair path π_i. Since $\mathcal{K}, w \models_F A\varphi_1 U \varphi_2$, there is an index k such that $\pi_i[k] \models_F \varphi_2$ and $\pi_i[j] \models_F \varphi_1$ for all $0 \leq j < k$. Since $\pi[j] \not\models_F \varphi_2$ for all $j \leq i$, it must be that $k > i$. By the induction hypothesis, $\pi_i[j] \models f(\varphi_1)$ for all $0 \leq j < k$. Moreover, since $\pi_i[k] \models f(\varphi_2)$, then for all $0 \leq j < k$, we have that $\pi_i[j] \models EFf(\varphi_2)$. Recall that $k > i$. Thus, in particular, $\pi_i[i] = \pi[i] \models f(\varphi_1) \wedge EFf(\varphi_2)$, and case 2 holds for π.

Assume now that $K, w \models A(f(\varphi_1) \wedge EFf(\varphi_2))Wf(\varphi_2)$. Let π be a fair path that starts at w. We first prove that there must be an index $k \geq 0$ such that $K, \pi[k] \models f(\varphi_2)$. since π is fair, By Lemma 1, there is a bottom MSCC $C \subseteq K$, and an index i, such that $visit(\pi^i) = C$. Assume by way of contradiction that no k as above exists. Then for all $j \geq 0$, we have that $K, \pi[j] \models (f(\varphi_1) \wedge EFf(\varphi_2))$. Since C is at the bottom, all states reachable from states in C are also in C. Hence, as $\pi[i] \in C$ and $K, \pi[i] \models EFf(\varphi_2)$, there is a state $v \in C$ such that $v \models f(\varphi_2)$. Since, however, $C = visit(\pi^i)$, there must be $k \geq 0$ such that $v = \pi[k]$, and we reach a contradiction. So, let k be the minimal index for which $K, \pi[k] \models f(\varphi_2)$. Then, by assumption, $K, \pi[i] \models f(\varphi_1)$ for all $0 \leq i \leq k$. Thus, by the induction hypothesis, $K, \pi \models \varphi_1 U \varphi_2$, and we are done. □

For the sake of completeness, we state here the result of applying the function f on abbreviated CTL operators.

- $f(EF\varphi_1) = EFf(\varphi_1)$.
- $f(AF\varphi_1) = A(EFf(\varphi_1))Wf(\varphi_1)$.
- $f(EG\varphi_1) = Ef(\varphi_1)UAGf(\varphi_1)$.
- $f(AG\varphi_1) = AGf(\varphi_1)$.
- $f(E\varphi_1 W \varphi_2) = Ef(\varphi_1)U(f(\varphi_2) \vee AGf(\varphi_1))$.
- $f(A\varphi_1 W \varphi_2) = Af(\varphi_1)Wf(\varphi_2)$.

Since f involves a linear blow-up and reduces fair CTL model checking to non-fair CTL model checking, the improved complexity for fair CTL model checking follows from the known complexity of the non-fair case [CES86,BCM+92]:

Corollary 1. *The fair CTL model-checking problem $\mathcal{K} \models \varphi$ for $\mathcal{K}$ augmented with transition fairness can be solved in time linear in $|\mathcal{K}|$ and $|\varphi|$, or using at most $|\mathcal{K}||\varphi|$ symbolic steps.*

Interestingly, the function f maps *universal CTL* (ACTL, for short) formulas (that is, formulas that do not use the existential path quantifier, and whose satisfaction is preserved under simulation [GL94]) to CTL formulas that do use the existential path quantifier. As we now show, the use of the existential path quantifier is essential. We prove it already for the ACTL formula AFp.

Theorem 2. *There is no ACTL formula φ such that for all fair Kripke structures $\mathcal{K} = \langle K, \alpha \rangle$, we have $\mathcal{K} \models_F AFp$ iff $K \models \varphi$.*

Proof: Consider the two Kripke structures K and K' appearing in Figure 1 below. Note that K' is obtained from K by eliminating the state w_2 and the transitions to and from it. Since a path that consistently avoids w_2 in K is not fair, $K \models_F AFp$. On the other hand, since the single path of K' is fair and never reaches a state labeled p, we have that $K' \not\models AFp$. Accordingly, the formula φ we seek should be such that $K \models \varphi$ and $K' \not\models \varphi$. Since, however, K' is simulated by K, and satisfaction of ACTL formulas is preserved under simulation [GL94], no such φ exists. □

In Section 5 we discuss the theoretical aspects of Theorem 2, and its relation to the open problem about the expressive power of the linear fragments of CTL and ACTL.

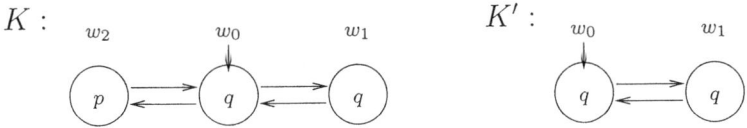

Fig. 1. While K simulates K', only K fairly satisfies AFp

3.2 Beyond CTL

The correctness of the function f follows from the observations on fair paths studied in Section 2.3. In this section we use these observations in the context of LTL model checking. We show that for many common LTL formulas, fair model checking can be reduced to fair CTL model checking, which in turn can be reduced to non-fair CTL model checking[6]. The LTL formulas we consider are those that specify acceptance by Büchi, Rabin, and Streett automata. Formally, we have the following.

Theorem 3. *Let $l_1, u_1, l_2, u_2, \ldots, l_k, u_k$ be atomic propositions, for some $k \geq 1$. Consider the following three forms of LTL formulas:*

1. *(Büchi)* $\theta = GFl_1$.
2. *(Rabin)* $\theta = \bigvee_{1 \leq i \leq k}(GFl_i \wedge FGu_i)$.
3. *(Streett)* $\theta = \bigwedge_{1 \leq i \leq k}(GFu_i \vee FGl_i)$.

There is a partial mapping $g : LTL\ formulas \to CTL\ formulas$ such that for every LTL formula θ of one of the three forms above, the following hold.

(1) $|g(\theta)| = O(|\theta|)$.
(2) *For every fair Kripke structure $\mathcal{K} = \langle K, \alpha \rangle$, with $K = \langle AP, W, R, W_0, L \rangle$, and every state $w \in W$, there is a fair path π in $\mathcal{K}$, starting at w, such that $K, \pi \models \theta$ iff $K, w \models_F g(\theta)$.*

Proof: We define g as follows.

1. $g(GFl_1) = EGEFl_1$.
2. $g(\bigvee_{1 \leq i \leq k}(GFl_i \wedge FGu_i)) = EF(\bigvee_{1 \leq i \leq k}(AGEFl_i \wedge AGu_i))$.
3. $g(\bigwedge_{1 \leq i \leq k}(GFu_i \vee FGl_i)) = EF(\bigwedge_{1 \leq i \leq k}(AGEFu_i \vee AGl_i))$.

It is easy to see that $|g(\theta)| = O(|\theta|)$. The proof of the correctness of g is given in [ABK04]. □

One immediate application of Theorem 3 is fair LTL model checking of formulas of the form $\neg \theta$, for θ of one of the three forms above (note that Theorem 3 follows the existential approach, where one looks for a path that violates the property). A more

---
[6] We note that, unlike other reductions of LTL to CTL model checking [KV98b,BRS99], our method here makes use of the fact that the LTL formulas should hold only in the fair paths of the Kripke structure.

ambitious application is to use the function g in order to fairly model check all LTL formulas: let ψ be an LTL formula. In the automata-theoretic approach to LTL model checking [VW94], we check whether all the paths of a Kripke structure K satisfy ψ by checking whether the product of K with an automaton $\mathcal{A}_{\neg\psi}$ that accepts all the words that violate ψ does not contain a *bad path* — a path whose projection on the states of $\mathcal{A}_{\neg\psi}$ is an accepting run of $\mathcal{A}_{\neg\psi}$. Indeed, the projection of such a path on the states of K is a path of K that is accepted by $\mathcal{A}_{\neg\psi}$, and thus violates ψ. The search for a bad path is reduced to checking whether there is a path in the product that satisfies an LTL formula θ induced by the acceptance condition of $\mathcal{A}_{\neg\psi}$. Thus, assuming $\mathcal{A}_{\neg\psi}$ is a Büchi, Rabin, or Streett automaton, θ is of one of the forms handled in Theorem 3. When the Kripke structure K is augmented with a fairness condition, ψ is violated iff the product contains a path whose projection on the states of $\mathcal{A}_{\neg\psi}$ is an accepting run of $\mathcal{A}_{\neg\psi}$, and whose projection on the states of K is a fair path of K. A detection of such a path can be done as described above by augmenting the product with a fairness condition. Then, the path that satisfies θ should be a fair path. To conclude, fair LTL model checking can be reduced to checking whether the product of K and $\mathcal{A}_{\neg\psi}$ has a fair path that satisfies an LTL formula of a specific form.

Unfortunately, the fact that K is augmented with the transition fairness condition does not imply that fair paths in the product correspond to fair paths in K, and vice versa. Technically, the product of K with $\mathcal{A}_{\neg\psi}$ may have non-fair paths whose projection on the states of K is a fair path of K. Below we show that the problem exists already for deterministic Büchi automata, implying that determinization, or a restriction to the Büchi acceptance condition do not solve this problem. (See [ABK04] for the proof.)

Theorem 4. *There is a fair Kripke structure $\mathcal{K} = \langle K, \alpha \rangle$ and a deterministic Büchi automaton $\mathcal{A}$ with a set F of accepting states such that there exists a fair path in $\mathcal{K}$ that is accepted by $\mathcal{A}$, yet the product of $\mathcal{K}$ and $\mathcal{A}$ has no fair path that visits infinitely many states whose projection on the states of $\mathcal{A}$ is in F.*

Reducing fair LTL model checking to fair CTL model checking, we are able to use Corollary 1, and obtain similar complexity results for LTL:

Corollary 2. *The fair LTL model-checking problem $\mathcal{K} \models_F \neg\theta$ for $\mathcal{K}$ augmented with transition fairness and θ of one of the forms handled in Theorem 3 can be solved in time linear in $|\mathcal{K}|$ and $|\theta|$, or using at most $|\mathcal{K}||\theta|$ symbolic steps. Moreover, if ψ is an LTL formula and $\mathcal{K} \models_F \psi$ iff the product of $\mathcal{K}$ with $\mathcal{A}_{\neg\psi}$ fairly satisfies $\neg\theta$, then the LTL model-checking problem $\mathcal{K} \models_F \psi$ can be solved in time linear in $|\mathcal{K}|$ and $\mathcal{A}_{\neg\psi}$, or using at most $|\mathcal{K}||\mathcal{A}_{\neg\psi}|$ symbolic steps.*

We note that the automaton $\mathcal{A}_{\neg\psi}$ may be exponential in $|\psi|$ [VW94]. Moreover, sometimes we can achieve the desired property of the product having the transition fairness condition by applying to $\mathcal{A}_{\neg\psi}$ transformations that blow-up its state space further. Nevertheless, since K is typically much larger than ψ and the exponential blow up, as well as additional blow ups, do rarely appear in practice, the technique still pays off, as the algorithm that follows is linear in $|K|$, rather than quadratic in $|K|$, if one keeps the fairness condition (recall that the traditional algorithm for fair LTL model checking is quadratic in $|K|$).

4 Computation of Postdominators and Dominators

In this section we use the technique developed in Section 3 in order to describe an efficient and symbolic algorithm for calculating the dominators and post-dominators of states in a Kripke structure augmented with transition fairness.

For a state w of a Kripke structure K, the set of postdominators of w, denoted $pd(w)$, is the set of states s such that all paths from w eventually reach s. Dually, the set of dominators of w, denoted $dom(w)$, is the set of states s such that all paths to w pass through s. Let K^{rev} be the Kripke structure derived from K by reversing the direction of transitions. That is, K^{rev} is identical to K, only that its transition relation R^{rev} is such that for all states w and w', we have that $R^{rev}(w,w')$ iff $R(w',w)$. It is not hard hard to see that $dom(w)$ is the set of states s such that all paths from w eventually reach s in K^{rev}. Thus, a state s is in $pd(w)$ in K iff s is in $dom(w)$ in K^{rev}. We study here the computation of postdominators. By the above, our results can be applied also for the computation of dominators.

As discussed in Section 1, the calculation of $pd(w)$ is not an easy problem. On the other hand, it is not hard to calculate, given s, all the states w for which $s \in pd(w)$. Indeed, w has to (fairly) satisfy AFs. Let $pd^{-1}(s)$ be the set of all states w such that s is in $pd(w)$. That is, $pd^{-1}(s) = \{w : s \in pd(w)\}$. The definition of pd^{-1} still leaves open the problem of calculating pd effectively. In many applications, however, the goal is to calculate all pairs $\langle s, w \rangle$ such that $s \in pd(w)$. Then, the fact that we consider pd^{-1} is not a disadvantage. Indeed, instead of calculating $pd(w)$ for all w, we can calculate $pd^{-1}(s)$ for all s. On the other hand, such an approach requires linearly many calculations of pd^{-1} – one calculation for each $s \in W$. So, even if calculation of pd^{-1} is reduced to a single fair CTL model-checking query, and even when such a query is reduced, as described in Section 3, to a non-fair model-checking query, and is calculated symbolically, we have to apply it linearly many times. The whole procedure is therefore not truly symbolic[7].

We describe a truly symbolic algorithm for this task. Consider a Kripke structure $K = \langle AP, W, R, W_0, L \rangle$. Let $PD = \{\langle s, w \rangle : s \in pd(w)\}$, and let $x_1, \ldots, x_n$ be n variables used for encoding the state space of K. We assume that K is given symbolically. In particular, we are given an ROBDD f_R over $x_1, \ldots, x_n, x'_1, \ldots, x'_n$ that describes the transition relation R. We generate an ROBDD f_{pd} over $x_1, \ldots, x_n, x'_1, \ldots, x'_n$ such that $f_{pd}(x_1, \ldots, x_n, x'_1, \ldots, x'_n) = \mathbf{true}$ iff the states s and w encoded by $x_1, \ldots, x_n$ and $x'_1, \ldots, x'_n$, respectively, are such that $\langle s, w \rangle \in PD$.

To explain our algorithm, we first describe it for a Kripke structure K with no fairness. Then, $PD = \{\langle s, w \rangle : w \models AFs\}$. Consider the operator (on a set $P \subseteq W \times W$) $PairAX(P) = \{\langle v, w \rangle : \text{for all successors } u \text{ of } w, \text{ we have} \langle v, u \rangle \in P\}$. Thus, for each pair $\langle v, w \rangle$ in P, the operator $PairAX(P)$ applies the AX operator (universal preimage) to w, leaving v unchanged. Note that $PairAX$ can be implemented symbolically: given an ROBDD for P and the ROBDD f_R, the construction of an ROBDD for $PairAX(P)$ is similar to the construction of an ROBDD for $AX(S)$, given an ROBDD for a set S of states [BCM+92]. Now, let $P_0 = \{\langle w, w \rangle : w \in W\}$, and $P_{i+1} = P_i \cup PairAX(P_i)$, for all $i \geq 0$. Intuitively, P_i contains all pairs $\langle s, w \rangle$

---

[7] For a similar challenge, in the context of *coverage in model checking*, see [CKV01].

such that all the paths from w reach s within at most i transitions. It follows that the fixed-point of the above sequence is the set PD. In other words, we can describe PD by means of the fixed-point expression $\mu y.P_0 \vee PairAX(y)$, and calculate it symbolically.

When K is augmented by a transition fairness condition, $PD = \{\langle s,w\rangle : w \models_F AFs\}$. Equivalently, by Theorem 1, $PD = \{\langle s,w\rangle : w \models A(EFs)Ws\}$. Recall that $A\varphi_1 W \varphi_2 = \neg E(\neg \varphi_2)U(\neg\varphi_1 \wedge \neg\varphi_2)$. Accordingly, $A(EFs)Ws = \neg E(\neg s)U(AG\neg s)$. Consider the operator $PairEX(P) = \{\langle v,w\rangle :$ there is a successor u of w for which$\langle v,u\rangle \in P\}$. Like $PairAX$, the operator $PairEX$ is "the pair version" of the operator EX, and it can be implemented symbolically. Finally, let $P_0 = \{\langle w,s\rangle : w \neq s\}$. Using P_0, $PairAX$, and $PairEX$, we can describe the set PD by means of the (alternation free) fixed-point expression $\neg \mu y.\nu z.(P_0 \wedge AXz) \vee (P_0 \wedge PairEX(y))$, and calculate it symbolically.

We note that, in the context of postdominators and dominators, K is often augmented with a fairness condition that restricts attention to paths that visit some designated states. In particular, in $pd(w)$ we care for paths that start at w and eventually reach a halting or error states, and in $dom(w)$ we care for paths that start at some initial state and eventually reach w. Our idea above applies also in these cases. Then, instead of using the technique in Section 3, removal of fairness is easier. To see this, consider the problem of calculating $pd^{-1}(s)$ in a Kripke structure in which the fairness condition restricts attention to paths that eventually visit a state labeled end. Note that then, $w \models_F AFs$ iff $w \models \varphi$, for the CTL* formula $\varphi = A(Fend \to Fs)$. As proved in [EH86], φ has an equivalent CTL formula, and PD can be calculated using the operator $PairAX$.

5 Discussion

We studied reasoning about systems augmented with the transition fairness condition. We showed that while fairness usually makes reasoning harder, this is not the case for transition fairness.

The key to our results is the ability to translate a specification φ to a CTL formula φ' of size linear in the size of φ such that φ is satisfied fairly iff φ' is satisfied non-fairly. The formula φ' may contain the existential path quantifier E, even if φ imposes only universal requirements (that is, φ is in LTL or ACTL). For example, if $\varphi = AFp$, then $\varphi' = A(EFp)Wp$, and we showed that the use of the existential path quantifier in φ' is required – no φ' in ACTL can do the job. These observations are of interest with respect to the relative expressive power of the linear fragments of CTL and ACTL. Consider an LTL formula ψ. Assume that ψ has an equivalent CTL formula. Can we then guarantee that ψ also has an equivalent ACTL formula? This seems very likely, as ψ imposes only linear, and hence universal, requirements. The question, however, is open, and the characterization in [Mai00], of LTL $\cap$ ACTL, may not apply for LTL $\cap$ CTL. The fact that the existential path quantifier is essential in the domain of the function f implies that, in the context of transition fairness, the answer to the question is negative: there are formulas in LTL $\cap$ ACTL that have a non-fair equivalence in CTL, but no non-fair equivalence in ACTL.

Another issue that is still open is extending the technique described in Section 3.2 to full LTL. As explained there, a straightforward application of the automata-theoretic approach does not work, as the transition fairness condition of the Kripke structure induces a different type of fairness condition in the product. We are searching for properties of the specification automaton, possibly properties relating the Kripke structure and the specification automaton, with which the technique can be applied in all LTL model-checking instances. We note that even when the transition to an automaton with such a property involves an additional exponential blow-up, the technique pays off, as it reduces the LTL model-checking task to an evaluation of a single fixed-point on the product, rather than a nested fixed-point, in the case a reduction to CTL model checking is impossible.

References

ABK04. B. Aminof, T. Ball, and O. Kupferman. Reasoning about systems with transition fairness. Technical Report MSR-TR-2004-89, September 2004.

BCM+92. J.R. Burch, E.M. Clarke, K.L. McMillan, D.L. Dill, and L.J. Hwang. Symbolic model checking: 10^{20} states and beyond. *I&C*, 98(2):142–170, June 1992.

BGS00. R. Bloem, H.N. Gabow, and F. Somenzi. An algorithm for strongly connected component analysis in $n \log n$ symbolic steps. In *Formal Methods in Computer Aided Design*, LNCS 1954, pages 37–54, 2000.

BKAW98. A.L. Buchsbaum, H. Kaplan, A.Rogers, and J.R. Westbrook. A new, simpler linear-time dominators algorithm. *ACM TOPLAS.*, 20(6):1265–1296, 1998.

BRS99. R. Bloem, K. Ravi, and F. Somenzi. Efficient decision procedures for model checking of linear time logic properties. In *Proc. 11th CAV*, LNCS 1633, pages 222-235, 1999.

CE81. E.M. Clarke and E.A. Emerson. Design and synthesis of synchronization skeletons using branching time temporal logic. In *Proc. Workshop on Logic of Programs*, LNCS 131, pages 52–71, 1981.

CES86. E.M. Clarke, E.A. Emerson, and A.P. Sistla. Automatic verification of finite-state concurrent systems using temporal logic specifications. *ACM Transactions on Programming Languages and Systems*, 8(2):244–263, January 1986.

C+91. Ron Cytron, Jeanne Ferrante, Barry K. Rosen, Mark N. Wegman, and F. Kenneth Zadeck. Efficiently computing static single assignment form and the control dependence graph. *ACM Trans. Program. Lang. Syst.*, 13(4):451–490, 1991.

CGP99. E.M. Clarke, O. Grumberg, and D. Peled. *Model Checking*. MIT Press, 1999.

CKV01. H. Chockler, O. Kupferman, and M.Y. Vardi. Coverage metrics for temporal logic model checking. In *7th TACAS*, LNCS 2031, pages 528 – 542, 2001.

EH86. E.A. Emerson and J.Y. Halpern. 'Sometimes' and 'not never' revisited: on branching versus linear time. *Journal of the ACM*, 33(1):151–178, 1986.

EL87. E.A. Emerson and C.-L. Lei. Modalities for model checking: branching time logic strikes back. *Science of Computer Programming*, 8:275–306, 1987.

Eme90. E.A. Emerson. Temporal and modal logic. In J. Van Leeuwen, editor, *Handbook of Theoretical Computer Science*, volume B, chapter 16, pages 997–1072. Elsevier, MIT Press, 1990.

FOW87. J. Ferrante, K. Ottenstein, and J. Warren. The program dependence graph and its use in optimization. *ACM Trans. Program. Lang. Syst.*, 9(3):319–349, 1987.

Fra86. N. Francez. Fairness. Springer-Verlag, New York, 1986.

GL94. O. Grumberg and D.E. Long. Model checking and modular verification. *ACM Trans. on Programming Languages and Systems*, 16(3):843–871, 1994.

GPP03. R. Gentilini, C. Piazza, and A. Policriti. Computing strongly connected components in a linear number of symbolic steps. In *14th ACM-SIAM Symposium on Discrete Algorithms*, pages 573–582, Baltimore, Maryland, 2003.

Hoa85. C.A.R. Hoare. *Communicating Sequential Processes*. Prentice-Hall, 1985.

HT96. M. Henzinger and J.A. Telle. Faster algorithms for the nonemptiness of Streett automata and for communication protocol pruning. In *Proc. 5th Scandinavian Workshop on Algorithm Theory*, LNCS 1097, pages 10–20, 1996.

KG96. O. Kupferman and O. Grumberg. Buy one, get one free!!! *Journal of Logic and Computation*, 6(4):523–539, 1996.

KPR98. Y. Kesten, A. Pnueli, and L. Raviv. Algorithmic verification of linear temporal logic specifications. In *Proc. 25th ICALP*, LNCS 1443, pages 1–16, 1998.

KPSZ02. Y. Kesten, A. Pnueli, E. Shahar, and L. Zuck. Network invariant in action. In *Proc. 13th CONCUR*, LNCS 2421, pages 101–115, 2002.

KV98a. O. Kupferman and M.Y. Vardi. Verification of fair transition systems. *Chicago Journal of Theoretical Computer Science*, 1998(2), March 1998.

KV98b. O. Kupferman and M.Y. Vardi. Relating linear and branching model checking. In *Proc PROCOMET*, pages 304 - 326, Chapman & Hall, 1998.

LH00. Timo Latvala and Keijo Heljanko. Coping with strong fairness. *Fundamenta Informaticae*, 43(1–4):175–193, 2000.

LPS81. D. Lehman, A. Pnueli, and J. Stavi. Impartiality, justice, and fairness – the ethics of concurrent termination. In *Proc. 8th ICALP*, LNCS 115, pages 264–277, 1981.

LT79. T. Lengauer and R.E. Tarjan. A fast algorithm for finding dominators in a flowgraph. *ACM Trans. Prog. Lang. and Sys.*, 1(1):121–141, 1979.

Mai00. M. Maidl. *Using Model Checking for System Verification*. PhD thesis, Ludwig-Maximilians-Universität München, 2000.

MP92. Z. Manna and A. Pnueli. *The Temporal Logic of Reactive and Concurrent Systems: Specification*. Springer-Verlag, Berlin, January 1992.

QS81. J.P. Queille and J. Sifakis. Specification and verification of concurrent systems in Cesar. In *Proc. 5th International Symp. on Programming*, LNCS 137, pages 337–351, 1981.

QS83. J.P. Queille and J. Sifakis. Fairness and related properties in transition systems - A temporal logic to deal with fairness. In *Acta Informatica* 19:195-220, 1983.

Tho90. W. Thomas. Automata on infinite objects. *Handbook of Theoretical Computer Science*, pages 165–191, 1990.

Var85. M.Y. Vardi. Automatic verification of probabilistic concurrent finite-state programs. In *Proc. 26th FOCS*, pages 327–338, October 1985.

VW94. M.Y. Vardi and P. Wolper. Reasoning about infinite computations. *Information and Computation*, 115(1):1–37, November 1994.

Entanglement – A Measure for the Complexity of Directed Graphs with Applications to Logic and Games[*]

Dietmar Berwanger and Erich Grädel

Mathematische Grundlagen der Informatik, RWTH Aachen

Abstract. We propose a new parameter for the complexity of finite directed graphs which measures to what extent the cycles of the graph are intertwined. This measure, called entanglement, is defined by way of a game that is somewhat similar in spirit to the robber and cops games used to describe tree width, directed tree width, and hypertree width. Nevertheless, on many classes of graphs, there are significant differences between entanglement and the various incarnations of tree width.

Entanglement is intimately connected to the computational and descriptive complexity of the modal μ-calculus. On the one hand, the number of fixed point variables needed to describe a finite graph up to bisimulation is captured by its entanglement. This plays a crucial role in the proof that the variable hierarchy of the μ-calculus is strict.

In addition to this, we prove that parity games of bounded entanglement can be solved in polynomial time. Specifically, we establish that the complexity of solving a parity game can be parametrised in terms of the minimal entanglement of a subgame induced by a winning strategy.

1 Entanglement: How to Catch a Thief

Let $\mathcal{G} = (V, E)$ be a finite directed graph. The *entanglement* of $\mathcal{G}$, denoted $\mathrm{ent}(\mathcal{G})$, measures to what extent the cycles of $\mathcal{G}$ are entangled. We define the entanglement by way of a game, played by a thief against k detectives on $\mathcal{G}$ according to the following rules. Initially the thief selects an arbitrary position v_0 of $\mathcal{G}$ and the detectives are outside the graph. In any move the detectives may either stay where they are, or place one of them on the current position v of the thief. The thief, in turn, has to move to a successor $w \in vE$ that is not occupied by a detective. If no such position exists, the thief is caught and the detectives have won. Note that the thief sees the move of the detectives before she decides on her own move, and that she has to leave her current position no matter whether the detectives stay where they are or not. The entanglement of $\mathcal{G}$ is the minimal number $k \in \mathbb{N}$ such that k detectives have a strategy to catch the thief on $\mathcal{G}$.

---

[*] This research has been partially supported by the European Community Research Training Network "Games and Automata for Synthesis and Validation" (GAMES).

The entanglement is an interesting measure on *directed* graphs. To deal with undirected graphs, we view undirected edges $\{u,v\}$ as pairs (u,v) and (v,u) of directed edges. In the following a graph is always meant to be directed.

To get a feeling for this measure we collect a few simple observations concerning the entanglement of certain familiar graphs. The proofs are simple and left to the reader.

Proposition 1. *Let $\mathcal{G}$ be any finite directed graph.*

(1) $\text{ent}(\mathcal{G}) = 0$ *if, and only if, $\mathcal{G}$ is acyclic.*
(2) *If $\mathcal{G}$ is the graph of a unary function, then $\text{ent}(\mathcal{G}) = 1$.*
(3) *If $\mathcal{G}$ an undirected tree, then $\text{ent}(\mathcal{G}) \le 2$.*
(4) *If $\mathcal{G}$ is the fully connected directed graph with n nodes, then $\text{ent}(\mathcal{G}) = n$.*

Let C_n denote the directed cycle with n nodes. Given two graphs $\mathcal{G} = (V, E)$ and $\mathcal{G}' = (V', E')$ their asynchronous product is the graph $\mathcal{G} \times \mathcal{G}' = (V \times V', F)$ where $F = \{(uu', vv') : [(u,v) \in E \wedge u' = v'] \vee [u = v \wedge (u'v') \in E']\}$.

Note, that $T_{mn} := C_m \times C_n$ is the $(m \times n)$-torus or, to put it differently, the graph obtained from the directed $(m+1) \times (n+1)$-grid by identifying the left and right border and the upper and lower border.

Proposition 2. (1) *For every n, $\text{ent}(T_{nn}) = n$.*
(2) *For every $m \ne n$, $\text{ent}(T_{mn}) = \min(m,n) + 1$.*

Proof. On T_{nn}, n detectives can catch the thief by placing themselves on a diagonal, thus blocking every row and every column of the torus. On the other side, it is obvious that the thief can escape against $n-1$ detectives.

On T_{mn} with $m < n$, m detectives are needed to block every row, and an additional detective forces the thief to leave any row after at most n moves, so that she finally must run into a detective. Again, it is obvious that the thief escapes if there are less than $m+1$ detectives. □

The following proposition characterises the graphs with entanglement one.

Proposition 3. *The entanglement of a directed graph is one, if and only if, the graph is not acyclic, and in every strongly connected component, there is a node whose removal makes the component acyclic.*

Proof. On any graph with this property, one detective catches the thief by placing himself on the critical node in the current strongly connected component when the thief passes there. The thief will have to return to this node or leave the current component. Eventually she will be caught in a terminal component.

Conversely if there is a strongly connected component without such a critical node, then the thief may always proceed from her current position towards an unguarded cycle and thus escape forever. □

Corollary 1. *For $k = 0$ and $k = 1$, the problem whether a given graph has entanglement k is* NLOGSPACE-*complete.*

To compute upper bounds on the entanglement of certain interesting graphs, we can use the following sufficient criterion for the existence of a winning strategy for k detectives. For any $k \in \mathbb{N}$, let $[k] := \{0, \ldots, k-1\}$.

Lemma 1. *Let $\mathcal{G} = (V, E)$ be a finite directed graph such that, for some $k \in \mathbb{N}$, there exists a partial labelling $i : V \to [k]$ under which every strongly connected subgraph $\mathcal{C} \subseteq \mathcal{G}$ contains a vertex v whose label is unique in $\mathcal{C}$, that is, $i(v) \neq i(w)$ for all $w \in \mathcal{C}$. Then $\operatorname{ent}(\mathcal{G}) \leq k$.*

Proof. We may interpret the labelling i as a memoryless strategy for the detectives, indicating at every position v occurring in a play, that detective $i(v)$ shall be posted there, or that no detective shall move if $i(v)$ is undefined. Towards a contradiction, suppose that although the detectives move according to strategy i, the thief can escape, that is, she succeeds to form an infinite path without meeting any detective. Let $\mathcal{C}$ be the set of positions visited infinitely often by this path. Clearly, $\mathcal{C}$ induces in $\mathcal{G}$ a strongly connected subgraph. Let $v \in \mathcal{C}$ be a node whose label $i(v)$ is unique in $\mathcal{C}$. According to the strategy described by i, detective $i(v)$ remains at v once the play has stabilised in $\mathcal{C}$. But since the thief visits every position in $\mathcal{C}$ infinitely often, she is caught at v. □

Proposition 4. *For every n, the undirected $(n \times n)$-grid has entanglement at most $3n$.*

Proof. Consider the labelling $i : [n] \times [n] \to [3n]$ obtained by first assigning the values $0, \ldots, n$ to the horizontal median of the grid, i.e., $i(\lfloor \frac{n}{2} \rfloor, j) := j$ for all $j \in [n]$. For the two $\frac{n}{2} \times n$ grids obtained when removing the positions already labelled, we proceed independently and assign the values $n, \ldots, n + \frac{n}{2}$ to their vertical medians, and so on, in step k applying the procedure to the still unlabelled domain consisting of 2^k many $\frac{n}{2^k} \times \frac{n}{2^k}$ disconnected grids. It is easy to verify that the labelling obtained this way satisfies the criterion of Lemma 1. □

2 Entanglement Versus Tree Width

The definition of entanglement is reminiscent of robber and cops games introduced by Seymour and Thomas in [10] for characterising tree width, and Johnson, Robertson, Seymour, and Thomas [6] for directed tree width. However, entanglement is a quite different, and for some purposes more accurate, measure than tree width and directed tree width.

This becomes apparent on trees with back-edges which also play an important role in our analysis of the variable hierarchy of the modal μ-calculus. It is easy to see that the directed tree width of any tree with back-edges is one. However, we will see that the entanglement of trees with back-edges can be arbitrarily large.

We now discuss the relationship between (undirected) tree width and entanglement. First, we observe that acyclic graphs (that have entanglement 0) can of course have arbitrary tree width. On the other hand we prove that the entanglement of a graph can be bounded by its tree width times the logarithm of its size.

Proposition 5. *For any finite undirected graph $\mathcal{G}$ of tree width k, we have that* $\operatorname{ent}(\mathcal{G}) \leq (k+1) \cdot \log |\mathcal{G}|$.

Proof. By definition, every graph $\mathcal{G} = (V, E)$ of tree width k can be decomposed as a tree $\mathcal{T}$ labelled with subsets of at most $k+1$ elements of V, called *blocks*, such that (1) every edge $\{u, v\} \in E$ is included in some block and (2) for any element $v \in V$ the set of blocks containing v is connected.

In every subtree $\mathcal{S}$ of such a decomposition tree, there exists a node s, we may call it the *centre* of $\mathcal{S}$, which balances $\mathcal{S}$ in the sense that the subtree rooted at s and its complement carry almost the same number of vertices (differences up to k are admissible). Consider now the following memoryless detective strategy. First, all vertices in the centre s of the decomposition tree receive indices $0, \ldots, k$. Then, we repeat the process independently for the two subtrees (i.e., the one rooted in s and its complement) and assign to the vertices in their respective centres indices from $k+1, \ldots, 2k+2$. The process ends when all vertices of $\mathcal{G}$ are labelled. In this way, at most $(k+1) \log |V|$ detective indices are assigned. Since the blocks of a tree decomposition separate the graph, every strongly connected subgraph of $\mathcal{G}$ will contain at least one unique label. This shows that the constructed labelling indeed represents a memoryless strategy for at most $(k+1) \log |V|$ detectives. □

However, bounded tree width does not imply bounded entanglement.

Proposition 6. *There exist graphs with tree width two that have arbitrarily large entanglement.*

Proof. Let $\mathcal{T}_k^\downarrow$ be the full binary tree of depth k with edges oriented downwards, and let $\mathcal{T}_k^\uparrow$ be the same tree with edges oriented upwards. Every node $v^\downarrow \in \mathcal{T}_k^\downarrow$ has a *double* $v^\uparrow \in \mathcal{T}_k^\uparrow$, and vice versa. The graph $G(2, k)$ is constructed by taking the union $\mathcal{T}_k^\downarrow \cup \mathcal{T}_k^\uparrow$, adding edges from each leaf to its double (in both directions), and adding the edges $(u^\uparrow, v^\downarrow)$ for each edge $(u^\uparrow, v^\uparrow)$ of $\mathcal{T}_k^\uparrow$. It is easy to see that $G(2, k)$ has tree width 2.

We claim that $\operatorname{ent}(G(2, k)) > k$. To prove this we describe a strategy by which the thief escapes against k detectives. We call a path in $G(2, k)$ *free* if all nodes on the path and all their doubles are unguarded by the detectives. We say that a node is *blocked* if both the node and its double are guarded. The thief moves according to the following strategy: *at a leaf $w^\uparrow$, she selects an ancestor $u^\downarrow$ of $w^\downarrow$ from which there is a free path to a leaf $v^\downarrow$. She goes to $v^\downarrow$ by moving upwards through $\mathcal{T}_k^\uparrow$, stepping over to $u^\downarrow$ and moving downwards through $\mathcal{T}_k^\downarrow$. Finally she steps over to $v^\uparrow$.*

With this strategy, the thief is never below a blocked node. A leaf has (including itself) $k+1$ ancestors in $\mathcal{T}_k^\downarrow$, so there is always an ancestor with a free path to a leaf. Thus, the thief can maintain this strategy and escape forever. □

3 Trees with Back-Edges and Partial Unravellings

Let $\mathcal{T} = (V, E)$ be a directed tree. We write $\preceq_E$ for the associated partial order on $\mathcal{T}$. Note that $\preceq_E$ is just the reflexive transitive closure of E.

Definition 1. A directed graph $\mathcal{T} = (V, F)$ is a *tree with back-edges* if there is a partition $F = E \cup B$ of the edges into tree-edges and back-edges such that (V, E) is indeed a directed tree, and whenever $(u, v) \in B$, then $v \preceq_E u$.

The following observation shows that, up to the choice of the root, the decomposition into tree-edges and back-edges is unique.

Lemma 2. *Let $\mathcal{T} = (V, F)$ be a tree with back-edges and $v \in V$. Then there exists at most one decomposition $F = E \cup B$ into tree-edges and back-edges such that (V, E) is a tree with root v.*

Definition 2. Let $\mathcal{T} = (V, F)$ be a tree with back-edges, with decomposition $F = E \cup B$ into tree-edges and back-edges. The *feedback* of a node v of $\mathcal{T}$ is the number of ancestors of v that are reachable by a back-edge from a descendant of v. The feedback of $\mathcal{T}$, denoted $\mathrm{fb}(\mathcal{T})$ is the maximal feedback of nodes on $\mathcal{G}$. More formally,

$$\mathrm{fb}(\mathcal{T}) = \max_{v \in V} |\{u \in V : \exists w (u \preceq_E v \preceq_E w \wedge (w, u) \in B)\}|.$$

We call a back edge (w, u), and likewise its target u, *active* at a node v in $\mathcal{T}$, if $u \preceq_E v \preceq_E w$.

Note that the feedback of $\mathcal{T}$ may depend on how the edges are decomposed into tree-edges and back-edges, i.e. on the choice of the root. Consider, for instance the following graph C_3^+ (the cycle C_3 with an additional self-loop on one of its nodes). Clearly, for every choice of the root, C_3^+ is a tree with two back-edges. If the node with the self-loop is taken as the root, then the feedback is 1, otherwise it is 2.

Lemma 3. *Let $\mathcal{T} = (V, E, B)$ be a tree with back-edges of feedback k. Then there exists a partial labelling $i : V \mapsto \{0, \ldots, k-1\}$ assigning to every target u of a back edge an index $i(u)$ in such a way that no two nodes u, u' that are active at the same node v have the same index.*

Proof. The values of this labelling are set while traversing the tree in breadth-first order. Notice that every node u with an incoming back-edge is active at itself. As $\mathcal{T}$ has feedback k, there can be at most $k - 1$ other nodes active at u. All of these are ancestors of u, hence their index is already defined. There is at least one index which we can assign to u so that no conflict with the other currently active nodes arises.

Lemma 4. *The entanglement of a tree with back-edges is at most its feedback:* $\mathrm{ent}(\mathcal{T}) \leq \mathrm{fb}(\mathcal{T})$.

Proof. Suppose that $\mathrm{fb}(\mathcal{T}) = k$. By Lemma 3 there is a labelling i of the targets of the back-edges in $\mathcal{T}$ by numbers $0, \ldots, k - 1$ assigning different values to any two nodes u, u' that are active at the same node v. This labelling induces the following strategy for the k detectives: at every node v reached by the thief, send detective number $i(v)$ to that position or, if the value is undefined, do nothing. By induction over the stages of the play, we can now show that this strategy maintains the following invariant: at every node v occurring in a play on $\mathcal{T}$, all active nodes $u \neq v$ are occupied and, if the current node is itself active, a detective is on the way. To see this, let us trace the evolution of the set $Z \subseteq T$ of nodes occupied by a detective. In the beginning of the play, Z is empty. A node v can be included into Z if it is visited by the thief and active with regard to itself. At this point, our strategy appoints detective $i(v)$ to move to v. Since, by construction of the labelling, the designated detective $i(v)$ must come from a currently inactive position and, hence, all currently active positions except v remain in Z. But if every node which becomes active is added to Z and no active node is ever given up, the thief can never move along a back edge, so that after a finite number of steps she reaches a leaf of the tree and loses. But this means that we have a winning strategy for k detectives, hence $\mathrm{ent}(\mathcal{T}) \leq k$. □

Note however, that the entanglement of a tree with back-edges can be much smaller than its feedback. A simple example are paths with back-edges: let $P_n = (\{0, \ldots, n-1\}, E_n, B_n)$ be the path with n nodes and all possible back-edges, i.e., $E_n = \{(i, i+1) : i < n-1\}$ and $B_n = \{(i,j) : i \geq j\}$. Obviously, $\mathrm{fb}(P_n) = n$, but two detectives suffice to catch the thief on P_n.

It is well-known that every graph $\mathcal{G}$ can be unravelled from any node v to a tree $\mathcal{T}_{G,v}$ whose nodes are the paths in $\mathcal{G}$ from v. Clearly $\mathcal{T}_{G,v}$ is infinite unless $\mathcal{G}$ is finite and no cycle in $\mathcal{G}$ is reachable from v. A *finite unravelling* of a (finite) graph $\mathcal{G}$ is defined in a similar way, but rather than an infinite tree, it produces a finite tree with back-edges. To construct a finite unravelling we proceed as in the usual unravelling process with the following modification: whenever we have a path $v_0 v_1 \ldots v_n$ in $\mathcal{G}$ with corresponding node $\bar{v} = v_0 v_1 \ldots v_n$ in the unravelling, and a successor w of v_n that coincides with v_i (for any $i \leq n$), then we may, instead of creating the new node $\bar{v}w$ (with a tree-edge from $\bar{v}$ to $\bar{v}w$) put a back-edge from $\bar{v}$ to its ancestor $v_0 \ldots v_i$. Clearly this process is nondeterministic. In this way, any finite graph can be unravelled, in many different ways, to a finite tree with back-edges.

Observe that different finite unravellings of a graph may have different feedback and different entanglement. Clearly the entanglement of a graph is bounded by the entanglement of its finite unravellings. Indeed a winning strategy for k detectives on a finite unravelling of $\mathcal{G}$ immediately translates to a winning strategy on $\mathcal{G}$.

Proposition 7. *The entanglement of a graph is the minimal feedback (and the minimal entanglement) of its finite unravellings:*

$$\mathrm{ent}(\mathcal{G}) = \min\{\mathrm{fb}(\mathcal{T}) : \mathcal{T} \text{ is a finite unravelling of } \mathcal{G}\}$$
$$= \min\{\mathrm{ent}(\mathcal{T}) : \mathcal{T} \text{ is a finite unravelling of } \mathcal{G}\}.$$

Proof. For any finite unravelling $\mathcal{T}$ of a graph $\mathcal{G}$, we have $\mathrm{ent}(\mathcal{G}) \leq \mathrm{ent}(\mathcal{T}) \leq \mathrm{fb}(\mathcal{T})$. It remains to show that for any graph $\mathcal{G}$ there exists some finite unravelling $\mathcal{T}$ with $\mathrm{fb}(\mathcal{T}) \leq \mathrm{ent}(\mathcal{G})$.

To prove this, we view winning strategies for the detectives as descriptions of finite unravellings. A strategy for k detectives tells us, for any finite path πv of the thief whether a detective should be posted at the current node v, and if so, which one. Such a strategy can be represented by a partial function g mapping finite paths in $\mathcal{G}$ to $\{0, \ldots, k-1\}$. On the other hand, during the process of unravelling a graph to a (finite) tree with back edges, we need to decide, for every successor v of the current node, whether to create a new copy of v or to return to a previously visited one, if any is available. To put this notion on a formal ground, we define an *unravelling function* for a rooted graph $\mathcal{G}, v_0$ as a partial function ρ between finite paths from v_0 through $\mathcal{G}$, mapping any path $v_0, \ldots, v_{r-1}, v_r$ in its domain to a strict prefix $v_0, v_1, \cdots, v_{j-1}$ such that $v_{j-1} = v_r$. Such a function gives rise to an unravelling of $\mathcal{G}$ in the following way: we start at the root and follow finite paths through $\mathcal{G}$. Whenever the current path π can be prolonged by a position v and the value of ρ at πv is undefined, a fresh copy of v corresponding to πw is created as a successor of π. In particular, this always happens if v was not yet visited. Otherwise, if $\rho(\pi v)$ is defined, then the current path π is bent back to its prefix $\rho(\pi)$ which also corresponds to a copy of v. Formally, the unravelling of $\mathcal{G}$ *driven* by ρ is the tree with back edges $\mathcal{T}$ defined as follows:

- the domain of $\mathcal{T}$ is the smallest set T which contains v_0 and for each path $\pi \in T$, it also contains all prolongations πv in $\mathcal{G}$ at which ρ is undefined;
- the tree-edge partition is

$$E^{\mathcal{T}} := \{ (v_0, \ldots, v_{r-1},\ v_0, \ldots, v_{r-1}, v_r) \in T \times T \mid (v_{r-1}, v_r) \in E^{\mathcal{G}} \};$$

- for all paths $\pi := v_0, \ldots, v_{r-1} \in T$ where $\rho(\pi v)$ is defined, the back-relation $B^{\mathcal{T}}$ contains the pair $(\pi, \rho(\pi v))$ if $(v_{r-1}, v) \in E^{\mathcal{G}}$.

We are now ready to prove that every winning strategy g for the k detectives on $\mathcal{G}, v_0$ corresponds to an unravelling function ρ for $\mathcal{G}, v_0$ that controls a finite unravelling with feedback k.

Note that the strategy g gives rise to a k-tuple $(g_0, \ldots, g_{k-1})$ of functions mapping every initial segment π of a possible play according to g to a k-tuple $(g_0(\pi), \ldots, g_{k-1}(\pi))$ where each $g_i(\pi)$ is a prefix of π recording the state of the play (i.e., the current path of the thief) at the last move of detective i.

Now, for every path π and possible prolongation by v, we check whether, after playing π, there is any detective posted at v. If this is the case, i.e, when, for some i, the end node of $g_i(\pi)$ is v, we set $\rho(\pi v) := \pi_i$. Otherwise we leave the value of ρ undefined at π, v. It is not hard to check that, if g is a winning strategy for the detectives, the associated unravelling is finite and has feedback k. □

4 Descriptive Complexity

The modal μ-calculus L_μ introduced by Kozen [8] is a highly expressive formalism which extends basic modal logic with monadic variables and binds them to extremal fixed points of definable operators.

Syntax. For a set ACT of actions, a set PROP of atomic propositions, and a set VAR of monadic variables, the formulae of L_μ are defined by the grammar

$$\varphi ::= \text{false} \mid \text{true} \mid p \mid \neg p \mid X \mid \varphi \vee \varphi \mid \varphi \wedge \varphi \mid \langle a \rangle \varphi \mid [a]\varphi \mid \mu X.\varphi \mid \nu X.\varphi$$

where $p \in \text{PROP}$, $a \in \text{ACT}$, and $X \in \text{VAR}$. An L_μ-formula in which no universal modality $[a]\varphi$ occurs is called *existential*.

The number of variables occurring in a formula provides a relevant measure of its conceptual complexity. For any $k \in \mathbb{N}$, the *k-variable fragment* $L_\mu[k]$ of the μ-calculus is the set of formulae $\psi \in L_\mu$ that contain at most k distinct variables.

Semantics. Formulae of L_μ are interpreted on transition systems, or Kripke structures. Formally, a transition system $\mathcal{K} = (V, (E_a)_{a \in \text{ACT}}, (V_p)_{p \in \text{PROP}})$ is a coloured graph with edges labelled by action and vertices labelled by atomic propositions. Given a sentence ψ and a structure $\mathcal{K}$ with state v, we write $\mathcal{K}, v \models \psi$ to denote that ψ holds in $\mathcal{K}$ at state v. The set of states $v \in K$ such that $\mathcal{K}, v \models \psi$ is denoted by $[\![\psi]\!]^\mathcal{K}$.

Here, we only define $[\![\psi]\!]^\mathcal{K}$ for fixed-point formulae ψ. Towards this, note that a formula $\psi(X)$ with a monadic variable X defines on every transition structure $\mathcal{K}$ (providing interpretations for all free variables other than X occurring in ψ) an operator $\psi^\mathcal{K} : \mathcal{P}(K) \to \mathcal{P}(K)$ assigning to every set $X \subseteq K$ the set $\psi^\mathcal{K}(X) := [\![\psi]\!]^{\mathcal{K}, X} = \{v \in K : (\mathcal{K}, X), v \models \psi\}$. As X occurs only positively in ψ, the operator $\psi^\mathcal{K}$ is *monotone* for every $\mathcal{K}$, and therefore, by a well-known theorem due to Knaster and Tarski, has a least fixed point $\text{lfp}(\psi^\mathcal{K})$ and a greatest fixed point $\text{gfp}(\psi^\mathcal{K})$. Now we put

$$[\![\mu X.\psi]\!]^\mathcal{K} := \text{lfp}(\psi^\mathcal{K}) \text{ and } [\![\nu X.\psi]\!]^\mathcal{K} := \text{gfp}(\psi^\mathcal{K}).$$

As a modal logic, the μ-calculus distinguishes between transitions structures only up to behavioural equivalence, captured by the notion of bisimulation.

Definition 3. A *bisimulation* between two transition structures $\mathcal{K}$ and $\mathcal{K}'$ is a simulation Z from $\mathcal{K}$ to $\mathcal{K}'$ so that the inverse relation Z^{-1} is a simulation from $\mathcal{K}'$ to $\mathcal{K}$. Two transition structures $\mathcal{K}, u$ and $\mathcal{K}', u'$ are *bisimilar*, denoted $\mathcal{K}, u \sim \mathcal{K}', u'$, if there is a bisimulation Z between them, with $(u, u') \in Z$.

An important model-theoretic feature of modal logics is the *tree model property* meaning that every satisfiable formula is satisfiable in a tree. This is a straightforward consequence of bisimulation invariance, since $\mathcal{K}, u$ is bisimilar to its *infinite unravelling*, i.e., a tree whose nodes correspond to the finite paths in $\mathcal{K}, u$. Every such path π inherits the atomic propositions of its last node v; for every node w reachable from v in $\mathcal{K}$ via an a transition, π is connected to its prolongation by w via an a-transition. Notice that in terms of our notion of unravelling defined in the proof of Proposition 7, the infinite unravelling of a system is just the unravelling driven by a function defined nowhere.

The entanglement of a transition system $\mathcal{K} = (V, (E_a)_{a \in \text{ACT}}, (V_p)_{p \in \text{PROP}})$ is the entanglement of the underlying graph (V, E) where $E = \bigcup_{a \in \text{ACT}} E_a$. We now show that every transition structure of entanglement k can be described, up to bisimulation, in the μ-calculus using only k fixed-point variables.

Proposition 8. Let $\mathcal{K}$ be a finite transition system with $\text{ent}(\mathcal{K}) = k$. For any node v of $\mathcal{K}$, there is a formula $\psi_v \in L_\mu[k]$ such that

$$\mathcal{K}', v' \models \psi_v \iff \mathcal{K}', v' \sim \mathcal{K}, v.$$

Proof. According to Proposition 7, the system $\mathcal{K}$ can be unravelled from any node v_0 to a finite tree $\mathcal{T}$ with back-edges, with root v_0 and feedback k. Clearly $\mathcal{T}, v_0 \sim \mathcal{K}, v_0$. Hence, it is sufficient to prove the proposition for $\mathcal{T}, v_0$. For every action $a \in \text{ACT}$, the transitions in $\mathcal{T}$ are partitioned into tree-edges and back-edges $E_a \cup B_a$.

Let $i : \mathcal{T} \mapsto \{0, \ldots, k-1\}$ be the partial labelling of $\mathcal{T}$ defined in Lemma 3. At hand with this labelling, we construct a sequence of formulae $(\psi_v)_{v \in \mathcal{T}}$ over fixed-point variables $X_0, \ldots, X_{k-1}$ while traversing the nodes of $\mathcal{T}$ in reverse breadth-first order.

The atomic type of any node v is described by the formula

$$\alpha_v := \bigwedge_{\substack{p \in \text{PROP} \\ v \in V_p}} p \wedge \bigwedge_{\substack{p \in \text{PROP} \\ v \notin V_p}} \neg p.$$

To describe the relationship of v with its successors, let

$$\varphi_v := \alpha_v \wedge \bigwedge_{a \in \text{ACT}} \left(\bigwedge_{(v,w) \in E_a} \langle a \rangle \psi_w \wedge \bigwedge_{(v,w) \in B_a} \langle a \rangle X_{i(w)} \right.$$
$$\left. \wedge [a] \left(\bigvee_{(v,w) \in E_a} \psi_w \vee \bigvee_{(v,w) \in B_a} X_{i(w)} \right) \right).$$

If v has an incoming back-edge, we set $\psi_v := \nu X_{i(v)} . \varphi_v$, if this is not the case we set $\psi_v := \varphi_v$. Note that since we proceed from the leaves of $\mathcal{T}$ to the root, this process is well-defined, and that in ψ_v the variables $X_{i(u)}$ occur free, for any node $u \neq v$ that is active at v. In particular the formula ψ_{v_0}, corresponding to the root of $\mathcal{T}$, is closed.

It remains to prove that $\mathcal{K}', v' \models \psi_{v_0} \iff \mathcal{K}', v' \sim \mathcal{T}, v_0$. We first show that $\mathcal{T}, v_0 \models \psi_{v_0}$, and hence $\mathcal{K}', v' \models \psi_{v_0}$ for any $\mathcal{K}', v' \sim \mathcal{T}, v_0$. To see this we prove that Verifier has a winning strategy for the associated model checking game.

Note that, since ψ_{v_0} has only greatest fixed points, any infinite play of the model checking game is won by Verifier. It thus suffices to show that from any position of form (v, φ_v), Verifier has a strategy to make sure that the play proceeds to a next position of form (w, φ_w), unless Falsifier moves to position (v, α_v) and then loses in the next move. But by the construction of the formula, it is obvious that Verifier can play so that any position at which she has to move has one of the following three types:

(1) $(v, \langle a \rangle \psi_w)$, where $(v, w) \in E_a$. In this case, Verifier moves to position (w, ψ_w).
(2) $(v, \langle a \rangle X_{i(w)})$, where $(v, w) \in B_a$. In this case Verifier moves to $(w, X_{i(w)})$.
(3) $(w, \bigvee_{(v,w) \in E_a} \psi_w \vee \bigvee_{(v,w) \in B_a} X_{i(w)})$ where $w \in vE_a \cup vB_a$. In this case, Verifier selects the appropriate disjunct and moves to either (w, ψ_w) or $(w, X_{i(w)})$.

In all cases the play will proceed to (w, φ_w). Hence, Falsifier can force a play to be finite only by moving to a position (v, α_v). Otherwise the resulting play is infinite and thus also won by Verifier.

For the converse, suppose that $\mathcal{K}', v' \not\sim \mathcal{T}, v_0$. Since $\mathcal{T}$ is finite, the non-bisimilarity it witnessed by a finite stage. That is, there is a basic modal formula separating $\mathcal{K}', v'$ from $\mathcal{T}, v_0$, and Falsifier can force the model checking game for ψ_{v_0} on $\mathcal{K}', v'$ in finitely many moves to a position of form (w', α_w) such that w and w' have distinct atomic types. This proves that $\mathcal{K}', v' \not\models \psi_{v_0}$. □

As the entanglement of a transition system regards only the underlying graph, one can easily find examples of high entanglement that can be described with very few variables. For instance, in a transition structure over a strongly connected finite graph with no atomic propositions and only a single action a, all states are bisimilar, and can be described by $\nu X.(\langle a \rangle X \wedge [a]X)$, regardless of the entanglement of the underlying graph. Nevertheless, the following theorem establishes a strong relationship between the notion of entanglement and the descriptive complexity of L_μ.

Theorem 4 ([2]). *Every strongly connected graph of entanglement k can be labelled in such a way that no μ-calculus formula with less than k variables can describe the resulting transition structure, up to simulation.*

This theorem, which generalises a result of [3], provides the witnesses for the expressive strictness of the μ-calculus variable hierarchy proved in [4].

5 Computational Complexity

An intriguing open problem related to the μ-calculus regards the computational complexity of its evaluation problem: Given a formula ψ and a finite transition structure $\mathcal{K}, v$, decide whether ψ holds in $\mathcal{K}, v$. Equivalently, this problem can be phrased in terms of *parity games*, the natural evaluation games for L_μ [11].

Parity games are path-forming games played between two players on labelled graphs $\mathcal{G} = (V, V_0, E, \Omega)$ equipped with a *priority* labelling $\Omega : V \to \mathbb{N}$. All plays start from a given initial node v_0. At every node $v \in V_0$, the first player, called Player 0, can move to a successor $w \in vE$; at positions $v \in V_1 := V \setminus V_0$, his opponent Player 1 moves. Once a player gets stuck, he loses. If the play goes on infinitely, the winner is determined by looking at the sequence $\Omega(v_0), \Omega(v_1), \ldots$ of priorities seen during the play. In case the least priority appearing infinitely often in this sequence is even, Player 0 wins the play, otherwise Player 1 wins.

A *memoryless strategy* for Player i in a parity game $\mathcal{G}$ is a function σ that indicates a successor $\sigma(v) \in vE$ for every position $v \in V_i$. A strategy for a player is *winning*, if he wins every play starting in which he moves according to this strategy. The Memoryless Determinacy Theorem of Emerson and Jutla states that parity games are always determined with memoryless strategies.

Theorem 5 (Memoryless Determinacy, [5]). *In any parity game, one of the players has a memoryless winning strategy.*

Any memoryless strategy σ induces a subgraph $\mathcal{G}_\sigma$ of the original game graph. If σ is a winning strategy for a player, he wins every play on $\mathcal{G}_\sigma$. Since these subgames are small objects and it can be checked efficiently whether a player wins every play on a given graph, the winner of a finite parity game can be determined in NP $\cap$ co-NP. In general, the best known deterministic algorithms to decide the winner of a parity game have running times that are polynomial with respect to the size of the game graph, but exponential with respect to the number of different priorities occurring in the game [7]. However, for game graphs of bounded tree width, Obdrzalek has showed in [9], that the problem can be solved in polynomial time with respect to the the size of the graph, independently of the number of priorities.

In the remainder of this paper we will show that the entanglement of a parity game graph is a pivotal parameter for its computational complexity. To maintain the relationship between games and algorithms conceptually close, we base our analysis on alternating machines (for a comprehensive introduction, see e.g. [1]).

5.1 Alternating Cycle Detection

Many algorithmic issues in graph theory are related to the problem of cycle detection, typically, to determine whether a given graph contains a cycle satisfying certain properties. When alternation comes into play, that is, when we consider paths formed interactively, the questions become particularly interesting but often rather complex, too. In this framework, we will study the entanglement of a graph as a measure of how much memory is needed to determine whether a path formed on-the-fly enters a cycle.

As a basis for later development, let us first consider a procedure for deciding whether k detectives are sufficient to capture the thief on a given graph. The following algorithm represents a straightforward implementation of the game as an alternating algorithm, where the role of the thief is played by the existential player while the detectives are controlled by the universal player.

```
procedure Entanglement(G, v₀, k)
input graph G = (V, E), initial position v₀, candidate k ≤ |V|
// accept iff ent(G, v₀) ≤ k
v := v₀, (dᵢ)ᵢ∈[k] := ⊥;
do
   existentially guess  i ∈ [k] ∪ {pass}    // appoint detective i or pass
   if i ≠ pass then  dᵢ := v                // guard current node
   if vE \ {dᵢ : i ∈ [k]} = ∅ then  accept
   else universally choose  v ∈ vE;
repeat
```

Since this algorithm requires space only to store the current positions of the thief and the k detectives, it runs in alternating space $O((k+1)\log|V|)$ which corresponds to deterministic polynomial time.

Lemma 5. *The problem of deciding, for a fixed parameter k, whether a given graph $\mathcal{G}$ has $\mathrm{ent}(\mathcal{G}) \leq k$ can be solved in polynomial time.*

Notice that if we regard k as part of the input, the algorithm gives an EXPTIME upper bound for deciding the entanglement of a graph.

5.2 Parity Games

Similar to the thief and detective game, the dynamics of a parity game consists in forming a path through a graph. However, while in the former game the detectives can influence the forming process only indirectly, by obstructing ways of return, in a parity game both players determine directly how the path is prolonged in their turn. Besides this dynamic aspect, also the objectives of players are quite different at a first sight. While the detectives aim at turning the play back to a guarded position, each player of a parity game tries to achieve that the least priority seen infinitely often on the path is of a certain parity.

The key insight which brings the two games to a common ground is the Memoryless Determinacy Theorem for parity games: whichever player has a winning strategy in a given game $\mathcal{G} = (V, V_0, E, \Omega)$, also has a memoryless one. This means, that either player may commit, for each reachable position $v \in V$ which he controls, to precisely one successor $\sigma(v) \in vE$ and henceforth follow this commitment in every play of $\mathcal{G}$ without risking any chance to win. It follows that, whenever a play returns to a previously visited position v, the winner can be established by looking at the least priority seen since the first occurrence of v. Therefore can view parity games on finite game graphs as path forming games of finite duration where the objective is to reach a cycle with minimal priority of a certain parity.

We obtain an immediate method to determine the winner of a parity game by simulating the players' moves while maintaining the history of visited positions in order to detect whether a cycle has been reached. To store the full history, an implementation of this method requires space $O(|V|\log|V|)$ in the worst case; since the procedure uses alternation to simulate the single game moves, this situates us in $\text{ASPACE}(O(|V|\log|V|))$, or $\text{DTIME}(|V|^{O(|V|)})$.

What makes this approach highly impractical is its extensive representation of the play's history. In fact, the power of alternation is limited to the formation of the path, while the history is surveyed in a deterministic way. We can significantly improve this by interleaving thief and detective games with parity games in such a way that the formation of cycles in history is surveyed interactively.

Intuitively, we may think of a parity game as an affair between three agents, Player 0 and 1, and a referee who wishes to establish which of the two indeed wins the game. In our initial approach, the referee memorises the entire history of the game. But as we have seen, the occurrence of a cycle in a path-forming game on $\mathcal{G}$ can be detected by storing at most $\text{ent}(\mathcal{G})$ many positions. Hence, if we could provide the referee with the power of sufficiently many detectives, this would reduce the space requirement. The crux of the matter is how to fit such a three-player setting into the two-player model of alternating computation.

Our proposal to overcome this difficulty is to let one of the players act as a referee who challenges the other player in the parity game, but in the same time controls the detectives in an overlying thief and detective game which regards the interactively formed path as if it would be formed by the thief alone.

Formally, this leads to a new game. For a game graph $\mathcal{G} = (V, V_0, E, \Omega)$, a player $i \in \{0,1\}$, and a number k, the *superdetective* game $\mathcal{G}[i,k]$ is played between the Superdetective controlling k detectives and the positions of V_i, and the Challenger in hold of the positions in V_{1-i}. Starting from an initial position position v_0, in any move the Superdetective may place one of the k detectives on the current position v, or leave them in place. If the current position v belongs to V_{1-i}, Challenger has to move to some position $w \in vE$, otherwise the Superdetective moves. (If a player gets stuck, he immediately loses.) The play ends if a position w occupied by a detective is reached and the Superdetective wins if, and only if, the least priority seen since the detective was placed there is even, for $i = 0$ respectively odd, for $i = 1$.

The following lemma states that parity games can be reduced to Superdetective games with an appropriate number of detectives.

Lemma 6. (1) *If Player i has a winning strategy for the parity game $\mathcal{G}$, then the Superdetective wins the superdetective game $\mathcal{G}[i,k]$ with $k = \text{ent}(\mathcal{G})$.*
(2) *If for some $k \in \mathbb{N}$, the Superdetective wins the game $\mathcal{G}[i,k]$, then Player i has a winning strategy for the parity game $\mathcal{G}$.*

Proof. Let σ be a memoryless winning strategy of Player i for the game $\mathcal{G}$ and let $\mathcal{G}_\sigma$ be the subgame of $\mathcal{G}$ induced by this strategy. Then, the least priority seen on any cycle of $\mathcal{G}_\sigma$ is favourable to Player i. This remains true for any cycle formed in $\mathcal{G}[i,k]$ where Player i acting as a Superdetective follows the same strategy σ. On the other hand, obviously $\text{ent}(\mathcal{G}_\sigma) \leq \text{ent}(\mathcal{G}) = k$, which means that the Superdetective also has a strategy to place the k detectives so that every path through $\mathcal{G}_\sigma$ will finally meet a guarded position v and hence form a cycle, witnessing that he wins. This proves (1).

For (2) assume that Player $1-i$ has a memoryless winning strategy τ in the parity game $\mathcal{G}$. But then he could follow this strategy when acting as a Challenger in the $\mathcal{G}[i,k]$, so that the play would actually remain in $\mathcal{G}_\tau$ where no cycle is favourable to Player i. Hence, regardless of the number of detectives, the Superdetective cannot win $\mathcal{G}[i,k]$. □

Note that computing the winner of a superdetective game $\mathcal{G}[i,k]$ requires alternating space $(2k+1)\log|V|$. Indeed, one just plays the game recording the current position of the thief, and the current position of each detective along with the minimal priority that has been seen since he was last posted.

procedure Superdetective($\mathcal{G}, v_0, j, k$)
input parity game $\mathcal{G} = (V, V_0, E, \Omega)$, initial position $v_0 \in V$, player j, k detectives
// accept iff Superdetective has a winning strategy in $\mathcal{G}[j,k]$ with k detectives
$v := v_0$ // current position
$(d_i)_{i \in [k]} := \bot$ // positions guarded by detectives
$(h_i)_{i \in [k]} := \bot$ // most significant priorities

```
    repeat
        if j = 0 then
            existentially guess  i ∈ [k] ∪ {pass}   // appoint detective i or pass
        else
            universally choose  i ∈ [k] ∪ {pass}    // other player's detective
        if i ≠ pass then
            d_i := v; h_i := Ω(v)                   // guard current node
            v := Move(G, v)                         // simulate a game step
            forall i ∈ [k] do                       // update history
                h_i := min(h_i, Ω(v))
        repeat
    until ( v = d_i for some i )                    // cycle detected
    if (j = 0 and h_i is even) or (j = 1 and h_i is odd) then accept
    else reject
```

We are now ready to prove that parity games of bounded entanglement can be solved in polynomial time. In fact, we establish a more specific result, taking into account the minimal entanglement of subgames induced by a winning strategy.

Theorem 6. *The winner of a parity game $G = (V, V_0, E, \Omega)$ can be determined in* ASPACE($\mathcal{O}(k \log |V|)$), *where k is the minimum entanglement of a subgame G_σ induced by a memoryless winning strategy σ in G.* □

Proof. We first describe the procedure informally, by way of a game. Given a parity game $G = (V, V_0, E, \Omega)$ and an initial position v_0, each player i selects a number k_i and claims that he has a winning strategy from v_0 such that ent(G_σ) $\leq k_i$. The smaller of the two numbers k_0, k_1 is then chosen to verify that Superdetective wins the game $G[i, k_i]$. If this is the case the procedure accepts the claim of Player i, otherwise Player $(1 - i)$ is declared the winner.

Here is a more formal description of the procedure:

```
procedure SolveParity(G, v)
input parity game G = (V, V_0, E, Ω), initial position v ∈ V
// accept iff Player 0 wins the game
existentially guess  k_0 ≤ |V|
universally choose  k_1 ≤ |V|
if k_0 ≤ k_1 then
    if Superdetective(G, v, 0, k_0) then accept
    else reject
else
    if Superdetective(G, v, 1, k_1) then reject
    else accept
```

We claim that Player 0 has a winning strategy in a parity game G, v if, and only if, the alternating procedure ParitySolve(G, v) accepts.

To see this, assume that Player 0 has a memoryless winning strategy σ from v. Then, the guess $k_0 := $ ent(G_σ) leads to acceptance. Indeed, for $k_1 \geq k_0$, Player 0 wins the superdetective game $G[0, k_0]$ by using the strategy σ as a parity player together with the detective strategy for G_σ. On the other hand, for $k_1 < k_0$, the procedure accepts as well, since Player 1 cannot win the superdetective game $\mathcal{G}[1, k_1]$ without having a winning strategy for the parity game. The converse follows by symmetric arguments exchanging the roles of the two players. □

Corollary 2. *Parity games of bounded entanglement can be solved in polynomial time.*

References

[1] J. L. BALCAZAR, J. DIAZ, AND J. GABARRO, *Structural complexity 2*, Springer-Verlag, 1988.
[2] D. BERWANGER, *Games and Logical Expressiveness*, Ph. D. Thesis, RWTH Aachen (2005).
[3] D. BERWANGER, E. GRÄDEL, AND G. LENZI, *On the variable hierarchy of the modal mu-calculus*, in Computer Science Logic, CSL 2002, J. Bradfield, ed., vol. 2471 of LNCS, Springer-Verlag, 2002, pp. 352–366.
[4] D. BERWANGER AND G. LENZI, *The variable hierarchy of the μ-calculus is strict*, in STACS 2005, Proceedings of the 22nd Symposium on Theoretical Aspects of Computer Science, LNCS, Springer-Verlag, 2005.
[5] A. EMERSON AND C. JUTLA, *Tree automata, mu-calculus and determinacy*, in Proc. 32nd IEEE Symp. on Foundations of Computer Science, 1991, pp. 368–377.
[6] T. JOHNSON, N. ROBERTSON, P. D. SEYMOUR, AND R. THOMAS, *Directed tree-width*, J. Comb. Theory Ser. B, 82 (2001), pp. 138–154.
[7] M. JURDZIŃSKI, *Small progress measures for solving parity games*, in STACS 2000, 17th Annual Symposium on Theoretical Aspects of Computer Science, Proceedings, vol. 1770 of Lecture Notes in Computer Science, Springer, 2000, pp. 290–301.
[8] D. KOZEN, *Results on the propositional μ-calculus*, Theoretical Computer Science, 27 (1983), pp. 333–354.
[9] J. OBDRZALEK, *Fast mu-calculus model checking when tree-width is bounded*, in CAV'03, vol. 2725 of LNCS, Springer-Verlag, 2003, pp. 80–92.
[10] P. D. SEYMOUR AND R. THOMAS, *Graph searching and a min-max theorem for tree-width*, J. Comb. Theory Ser. B, 58 (1993), pp. 22–33.
[11] C. STIRLING, *Bisimulation, modal logic and model checking games*, Logic Journal of the IGPL, 7 (1999), pp. 103–124.

How the Location of * Influences Complexity in Kleene Algebra with Tests

Chris Hardin

Department of Mathematics
Cornell University
Ithaca, New York 14853-4201, USA
hardin@math.cornell.edu

Abstract. The universal Horn theory of relational Kleene algebra with tests is of practical interest, particularly for program semantics, where Horn formulas can be used to verify correctness of programs or compiler optimizations. Unfortunately, this theory is known to be Π_1^1-complete. However, many formulas arising in practice fall into fragments of the theory that are of lower complexity. In this paper, we see that the location of occurrences of the Kleene asterate operator * within a formula has a great impact on complexity. Using syntactic criteria based on the location of *, we give a fragment of the theory that is Σ_1^0-complete, and a slightly larger fragment that is Π_2^0-complete. We show that the same results hold over *-continuous Kleene algebras with tests. The techniques exhibit a relationship between first-order logic and the Horn theories of relational and *-continuous Kleene algebra, even though the theories are not first-order axiomatizable.

1 Introduction

The universal Horn theories of *-continuous and relational Kleene algebras (with tests) are of great interest, particularly for program semantics. Unfortunately, these Horn theories are are Π_1^1-complete [8,5], making them difficult to work with in full generality. However, under various restrictions on the formulas, the complexity is often much lower. For example, when the hypotheses are restricted to the form $s = 0$, the theory (in both cases) is *PSPACE*-complete [2,3,10,6]. See [8,6] for further examples. In this paper, we investigate how the location of * in a Horn formula affects complexity.

For the rest of the introduction, we find it convenient to be non-rigorous and use many terms without defining them, in the hopes of quickly and abstractly sketching the material that will be presented and some intuition behind it. The rest of the paper is more self-contained—barely even requiring the introduction, although it does assume a familiarity with first-order logic—and more responsible about proof.

The *-continuity axiom, stated succinctly as $xy^*z = \sup_{n\in\omega} xy^n z$, can equivalently be expressed by

$$xy^n z \leq xy^* z \quad \text{(for each } n \in \omega\text{)} \tag{1}$$

F. Baader and A. Voronkov (Eds.): LPAR 2004, LNAI 3452, pp. 224–239, 2005.
© Springer-Verlag Berlin Heidelberg 2005

and the infinitary Horn formula

$$\bigwedge_{n \in \omega} xy^n z \leq w \rightarrow xy^* z \leq w . \qquad (2)$$

Informally, (1), by bounding xy^*z from below, describes the bigness of y^*, while (2), by bounding xy^*z from above, describes the smallness of y^*. The bigness condition (1) is first-order, while the smallness condition (2) is not. By appropriately restricting where $*$ may appear in a Horn formula, we can make the validity of the Horn formula (over $*$-continuous Kleene algebras) depend only on the bigness of $*$, while the smallness is irrelevant; first-order logic will then be adequate for determining the validity of such formulas, which will pull the complexity down to Σ_1^0 ("There exists a proof..."). Specifically, the restriction will be that in the hypotheses, $*$ may only appear on the left-hand side of inequalities $s_i \leq t_i$, and in the conclusion, $*$ may only appear on the right hand side of an inequality $s \leq t$; such formulas are called *simple*.

Since everything but (2) in the definition of $*$-continuous Kleene algebra is first-order, while the Horn theory is Π_1^1-complete, it must be the smallness condition (2) that admits Π_1^1-hardness. How does this happen? Here are two intuitions, closely related to each other:

1. First-order logical consequence comes down to the well-foundedness of finitely branching trees, which (with suitable effectiveness conditions on the trees) is Σ_1^0. (One can think of these trees as proof trees; one can also think of these trees as systematic attempts to construct a counterexample, in which infinite paths yield counterexamples, while well-foundedness constitutes a proof. The distinction is only superficial.)
   We could extend first-order logic to incorporate (2) by adding the infinitary inference rule
   $$\frac{xy^n z \leq w \quad (\text{for each } n \in \omega)}{xy^* z \leq w} .$$
   However, our proof trees will no longer be finitely branching, and the problem of well-foundedness of (recursive) infinitely branching trees is Π_1^1-complete. Loosely, what has happened here is that well-foundedness can no longer be expressed as "There exists n such that there are no nodes of depth n," which was adequate for finitely branching trees; instead, well-foundedness must now be expressed as "All paths eventually hit a leaf node," and quantifying over paths is second-order.

2. Given a set A of first-order formulas (in the language of Kleene algebra), let $\mathsf{Th}(A) = \{\varphi \mid A \models \varphi\}$. This is a *closure operator* in the standard sense: $A \subseteq \mathsf{Th}(A)$, $\mathsf{Th}(\mathsf{Th}(A)) = \mathsf{Th}(A)$, $A \subseteq B \Rightarrow \mathsf{Th}(A) \subseteq \mathsf{Th}(B)$; A is *closed* if $A = \mathsf{Th}(A)$. There are two ways to build $\mathsf{Th}(A)$ from A: from below, and from above. To build $\mathsf{Th}(A)$ from below, we start with A, and iterate the process of throwing in axioms and applying inference rules; after countably many iterations, we will have $\mathsf{Th}(A)$, and this lets us express $\varphi \in \mathsf{Th}(A)$ with the Σ_1^0 formula "There exists a stage in this iterative process at which φ appears." To build $\mathsf{Th}(A)$ from above, we take the intersection of all closed

sets containing A;[1] this lets us express $\varphi \in \mathsf{Th}(A)$ by "For all closed sets C containing A, $\varphi \in C$," which is Π_1^1.

Suppose that we extend our notion of logical consequence to incorporate (2), and let Th' denote closure under this notion. We can build $\mathsf{Th}'(A)$ from below and above as before, but when building from below, we must iterate transfinitely (since we will have an infinitary inference rule for (2)); in particular, we cannot express $\varphi \in \mathsf{Th}'(A)$ with a Σ_1^0 formula. We must resort to the Π_1^1 definition involving intersections of closed sets.

In both instances, incorporating (2) results in a loss of compactness, breaking whatever Σ_1^0 definition of logical consequence we had.

If we only incorporate (2) in a restricted way, we can end up with a complexity between Σ_1^0 and Π_1^1. A *semisimple* Horn formula will be like a simple Horn formula, except that $*$ may appear anywhere in the conclusion. The validity of such formulas will rely on (2), but only slightly, in that (2) is only used to convert a semisimple Horn formula into an infinite conjuction of simple Horn formulas; the question of validity of such conjunctions is Π_2^0.

These will be our main results: when we restrict to simple Horn formulas, the Horn theories of $*$-continuous and relational Kleene algebras are Σ_1^0-complete; when we restrict to semisimple Horn formulas, the Horn theories are Π_2^0-complete.

2 Preliminaries

2.1 Kleene Algebra

Definition 1. *An* idempotent semiring *is a structure* $(S, +, \cdot, 0, 1)$ *satisfying*

$$
\begin{aligned}
x + x &= x \quad \text{(idempotence)} & 1 \cdot x &= x \cdot 1 = x \\
x + 0 &= x & x \cdot (y \cdot z) &= (x \cdot y) \cdot z \\
x + y &= y + x & x \cdot (y + z) &= x \cdot y + x \cdot z \\
x + (y + z) &= (x + y) + z & (y + z) \cdot x &= y \cdot x + z \cdot x \\
0 \cdot x &= x \cdot 0 = 0
\end{aligned}
$$

(In other words, $(S, +, 0)$ is an upper semilattice with bottom element 0, $(S, \cdot, 1)$ is a monoid, 0 is an annihilator for $\cdot$, and $\cdot$ distributes over $+$ on the right and left.) We let IS *denote the class of all idempotent semirings.*

We often drop $\cdot$, writing xy for $x \cdot y$. The upper semilattice structure induces a natural partial order on any idempotent semiring: $x \leq y \Leftrightarrow x + y = y$.

$+$ and $\cdot$ enjoy the following form of monotonicity: if $x \leq x'$ and $y \leq y'$, then $x + y \leq x' + y'$, and $xy \leq x'y'$. (For $+$, this is trivial. For $\cdot$, suppose $x \leq x'$ and $y \leq y'$. Then $x + x' = x'$, so we have $xy + x'y = (x + x')y = x'y$, so $xy \leq x'y$. We similarly have $x'y \leq x'y'$, so $xy \leq x'y'$.)

---

[1] This might seem circular because our definition of closed was in terms of Th, but it is easy to show that a set is closed iff it contains all axioms and is closed under applications of inference rules.

The names of the several classes of algebras we consider will serve as convenient abbreviations for the type of algebra they contain. For example, "Every IS extends..." would mean "Every idempotent semiring extends...". We use the notation Ax(IS) to denote the idempotent semiring axioms.

Definition 2. *A* Kleene algebra *is a structure* $(K, +, \cdot, {}^*, 0, 1)$ *such that* $(K, +, \cdot, 0, 1)$ *forms an idempotent semiring, and which satisfies*

$$1 + xx^* \leq x^* \tag{3}$$
$$1 + x^*x \leq x^* \tag{4}$$
$$p + qx \leq x \rightarrow q^*p \leq x \tag{5}$$
$$p + xq \leq x \rightarrow pq^* \leq x \tag{6}$$

(The order of precedence among the operators is $* > \cdot > +$, *so that* $p + qr^* = p + (q \cdot (r^*))$.*) We let* KA *denote the class of all Kleene algebras.*

Given a set Σ of constant symbols, let RExp_Σ be the set of Kleene algebra terms over Σ. We call the elements of RExp_Σ regular expressions, and the elements of Σ atomic program symbols. An interpretation is a homomorphism $I : \mathsf{RExp}_\Sigma \to K$, where K is a Kleene algebra. I is determined uniquely by its values on Σ.

Equation (3) implies that q^*p is a solution to the inequality $p + qx \leq x$, and (5) implies that it is the least solution; (4) and (6) say that pq^* is the least solution to $p + xq \leq x$.

We use $\models$ to denote ordinary Tarskian satisfaction. However, since we have constant symbols from Σ not in the signatures of the underlying algebras, we will pair each algebra with an interpretation when speaking about satisfaction. For example, given a Kleene algebra K, interpretation $I : \mathsf{RExp}_\Sigma \to K$, and formula φ whose atomic program symbols are among Σ, we will write $K, I \models \varphi$ to indicate that K satisfies φ when the symbols in Σ are evaluated according to I. $K \models \varphi$ means that $K, I \models \varphi$ for every interpretation $I : \mathsf{RExp}_\Sigma \to K$. We also use $\models$ in two other standard ways: for a class $\mathbf{C}$ of algebras, $\mathbf{C} \models \varphi$ means that $K \models \varphi$ for each $K \in \mathbf{C}$; for a set Φ of formulas, $\Phi \models \varphi$ means that $K \models \varphi$ for each algebra K satisfying every formula in Φ.

Definition 3. *For an arbitrary monoid* M, *its powerset* 2^M *forms a Kleene algebra as follows.*

$$0 = \emptyset$$
$$1 = \{1^M\} \quad \text{(where } 1^M \text{ is the identity element of } M)$$
$$A + B = A \cup B$$
$$A \cdot B = \{xy \mid x \in A, y \in B\}$$
$$A^* = \bigcup_{k \in \omega} A^k$$

We let REG M denote the smallest subalgebra of 2^M containing the singletons $\{x\}$, $x \in M$. (The elements of REG M are the regular subsets of M.) 2^M and its subalgebras are known as language algebras.

Of particular interest is the case $M = \Sigma^*$, the monoid of all strings over alphabet Σ, under concatenation (the empty string is the identity). We define the canonical interpretation $R : \mathsf{RExp}_\Sigma \to \mathsf{REG}\ \Sigma^*$ by letting $R(p) = \{p\}$ (and extending R homomorphically to the rest of RExp_Σ).

Relational Kleene algebras are also of interest.

Definition 4. *For an arbitrary set X, the set $2^{X \times X}$ of all binary relations on X forms a Kleene algebra $\mathcal{R}(X)$ as follows.*

$$0 = \varnothing$$
$$1 = \iota_X = \{(x,x) \mid x \in X\}$$
$$R + S = R \cup S$$
$$R \cdot S = R \circ S \quad \text{(the relational composition of } R \text{ with } S\text{)}$$
$$R^* = \bigcup_{k \in \omega} R^k \quad \text{(the reflexive transitive closure of } R\text{)}$$

A Kleene algebra K is relational *if it is a subalgebra of $\mathcal{R}(X)$ for some X; X is called the* base *of K. We let RKA denote the class of all relational Kleene algebras.*

The definitions of $*$ in 2^M and $\mathcal{R}(X)$ exemplify the most common intuition about the meaning of $*$, which is that $y^* = \sup_{n \in \omega} y^n$, or informally, $y^* = 1 + y + y^2 + \cdots$. (More generally, if we require that multiplication distributes over this supremum, we have $xy^*z = x1z + xyz + xy^2z + \cdots = \sup_{n \in \omega} xy^n z$.) However, this property of $*$ does not follow from the KA $*$-axioms, and must be postulated separately.

Definition 5. *A Kleene algebra K is $*$-continuous if it satisfies*

$$xy^*z = \sup_{k \in \omega} xy^k z$$

for all $x, y, z \in K$. We let KA^* denote the class of all $*$-continuous Kleene algebras.

As in the introduction, this is equivalent to the bigness condition (1) and the smallness condition (2). Because first-order logic cannot be extended to accommodate formulas such as (2) without breaking compactness, it is not surprising that compactness is well suited for violating $*$-continuity, as shown by the proof of the following proposition.

Proposition 6. *There is a Kleene algebra that is not $*$-continuous.*

Proof. Let $\Phi = \mathsf{Ax}(\mathsf{KA}) \cup \{1 < x,\ 1 + a < x,\ 1 + a + a^2 < x, \ldots\} \cup \{x < a^*\}$. Φ is finitely satisfiable, so it is satisfiable. Any model of Φ is a Kleene algebra, and x will witness that a^* is not the least upper bound for $\{a^n \mid n \in \omega\}$. □

The following lemma is a useful generalization of $*$-continuity.

Lemma 7. *Suppose $K \in \mathsf{KA}^*$, $I : \mathsf{RExp}_\Sigma \to K$ is an interpretation, and $t \in \mathsf{RExp}_\Sigma$. Then*
$$I(t) = \sup_{\sigma \in R(t)} I(\sigma) \ .$$

Proof. By induction on structure of t. For details, see [9, Lemma 7.1, pp. 246–248]. □

Since relational composition distributes over arbitrary union, it is immediate from the definition of $*$ in $\mathcal{R}(X)$ that relational Kleene algebras are $*$-continuous, so $\mathsf{RKA} \subseteq \mathsf{KA}^*$.

Lemma 8. *For any monoid M, 2^M and its subalgebras are isomorphic to relational Kleene algebras. In particular, $\mathsf{REG}\ M$ is isomorphic to a relational Kleene algebra.*

Proof. Define $\varphi : 2^M \to \mathcal{R}(M)$ by
$$\varphi(A) = \{(x, xy) \mid x \in M,\ y \in A\} \ .$$

It is straightforward to show that φ is an injective homomorphism. So, 2^M (or any subalgebra of 2^M) is isomorphic to its image under φ. □

Definition 9. *A universal Horn formula is a formula of the form*
$$s_1 = t_1 \wedge \cdots \wedge s_k = t_k \to s = t \ ,$$

where s_i, t_i, s, t are terms in the appropriate language. The set of universal Horn formulas valid over a class $\mathbf{C}$ of algebras is the universal Horn theory of $\mathbf{C}$, which we denote by $\mathcal{H}\mathbf{C}$.

Note that, because any inequality $x \leq y$ is in fact an equation $x + y = y$, inequalities are allowed in Horn formulas.

Despite the lack of quantifiers in our presentation, universal Horn formulas are in fact universal statements, at least when speaking of their validity. (For example, $K \models p \leq 1 \to p^2 = p \iff K \models \forall x(x \leq 1 \to x^2 = x)$.) The missing quantifier is hiding in our definition of $K \models \varphi$. We will often drop the word "universal".

Horn formulas are very important in universal algebra—second only to equations, as formulas go—but take on particular importance in Kleene algebra: the hypotheses of a Horn formula are used to capture (or partially capture) the intended semantics of the atomic program symbols when reasoning about programs. (For example, if p is intended to mean "let x := 1" and q is intended to mean "let y := 1", we might wish to reason under hypotheses such as $pq = qp$, $p^2 = p$, and $q^2 = q$.)

Proposition 10. $\mathcal{H}\mathsf{KA} \subsetneq \mathcal{H}\mathsf{KA}^* \subsetneq \mathcal{H}\mathsf{RKA}$

Despite the above proposition, there are many special cases in which these Horn theories coincide. The following lemma, which will be useful for other reasons, is one such example.

Lemma 11. *Suppose $M = \Sigma^*/E$ is a finitely presented monoid (where Σ is the set of generators, and $E = \{\sigma_1 = \tau_1, \ldots, \sigma_n = \tau_n\}$ is a set of equations, with $\sigma_i, \tau_i \in \Sigma^*$). Let $J : \Sigma^* \to M$ be the interpretation mapping each element of Σ^* to its equivalence class in M. The following are equivalent for any $\sigma, \tau \in \Sigma^*$.*

(i) $M, J \models \sigma = \tau$
(ii) $E \to \sigma = \tau$ *is valid in all monoids.*
(iii) $\mathsf{KA} \models E \to \sigma = \tau$
(iv) $\mathsf{KA}^* \models E \to \sigma = \tau$
(v) $\mathsf{RKA} \models E \to \sigma = \tau$
(vi) $\mathsf{KA} \models E \to \sigma \leq \tau$
(vii) $\mathsf{KA}^* \models E \to \sigma \leq \tau$
(viii) $\mathsf{RKA} \models E \to \sigma \leq \tau$

Lemma 12. *$\mathcal{H}\mathsf{RKA}$, $\mathcal{H}\mathsf{KA}^*$, and $\mathcal{H}\mathsf{KA}$, restricted to formulas containing only monoid equations (that is, equations whose terms are built from atomic program symbols, 1, and $\cdot$), are each Σ_1^0-complete.*

Proof. The word problem for finitely presented monoids, known to be Σ_1^0-complete, is exactly the same as determining the validity (over all monoids) of Horn formulas consisting of monoid equations. By Lemma 11, this is equivalent to determining the validity of such Horn formulas in KA, KA*, or RKA. □

2.2 Kleene Algebra with Tests

Definition 13. *A* Kleene algebra with tests *is a two-sorted structure $(K, B, +, \cdot, ^*, ^-, 0, 1)$, where $(K, +, \cdot, ^*, 0, 1)$ is a Kleene algebra, and $(B, +, \cdot, ^-, 0, 1)$ is a Boolean subalgebra. The elements of B are called* tests. *We let* KAT *denote the class of all Kleene algebras with tests; we let* KAT* *denote the subclass of all *-continuous Kleene algebras with tests.*

Now, instead of just having atomic program symbols, we must also have symbols to use for tests. For a finite set P of atomic program symbols and a finite set B of atomic test symbols, $\mathsf{RExp}_{\mathsf{P},\mathsf{B}}$ is the set of KAT terms over P and B; negation can only be applied to Boolean terms, which are terms built from $0, 1, +, \cdot, ^-$, and atomic test symbols. An interpretation $I : \mathsf{RExp}_{\mathsf{P},\mathsf{B}} \to K$ must map each atomic test to a test in K (and it follows by induction that it will map all Boolean terms to tests).

$\mathcal{R}(X)$ forms a Kleene algebra with tests by keeping the previously defined Kleene algebra structure, and letting $B = \{r \in \mathcal{R}(X) \mid r \leq 1\}$, $\bar{b} = \iota_X - b$. A Kleene algebra with tests K is relational if it is a subalgebra of $\mathcal{R}(X)$ for some X. We let RKAT denote the class of all relational Kleene algebras with tests.

Every Kleene algebra induces a Kleene algebra with tests by letting $B = \{0,1\}$, the two-element Boolean algebra; conversely, every Kleene algebra with tests induces a Kleene algebra by taking its reduct to the signature of Kleene algebra (i.e., taking its image under the map $(K, B, +, \cdot, {}^*, \bar{\ }, 0, 1) \mapsto (K, +, \cdot, {}^*, 0, 1)$). With this in mind, it is easy to see that for any formula φ in the language of Kleene algebra, $\mathsf{KAT} \models \varphi \Leftrightarrow \mathsf{KA} \models \varphi$, $\mathsf{KAT}^* \models \varphi \Leftrightarrow \mathsf{KA}^* \models \varphi$, and $\mathsf{RKAT} \models \varphi \Leftrightarrow \mathsf{RKA} \models \varphi$.

Definition 14. *Let* $\mathsf{Atoms_B}$ *denote the atoms of the free Boolean algebra on generators* B, *which we can treat as elements of* $\mathsf{RExp_{P,B}}$ *in a canonical way by ordering* B *and writing elements of* $\mathsf{Atoms_B}$ *as conjunctions in which exactly one of b and $\bar{b}$ appears for each $b \in \mathsf{B}$, in order. For example, if* $\mathsf{B} = \{a, b\}$, *then* $\mathsf{Atoms_B} = \{ab, a\bar{b}, \bar{a}b, \bar{a}\bar{b}\}$. *We use letters* $\alpha, \beta, \gamma, \delta$ *to denote elements of* $\mathsf{Atoms_B}$.

A guarded string *over* P *and* B *is an element of* $\mathsf{RExp_{P,B}}$ *of the form*

$$\alpha_0 p_1 \alpha_1 \cdots p_k \alpha_k ,$$

where $k \geq 0$, $\alpha_i \in \mathsf{Atoms_B}$, $p_i \in \mathsf{P}$. *Let* $\mathsf{GS_{P,B}}$ *(or simply* GS*) denote the set of all guarded strings on* P *and* B.

We define a partial binary operation $\diamond$ *on* GS *by*

$$\alpha \sigma \beta \diamond \gamma \tau \delta = \begin{cases} \alpha \sigma \beta \tau \delta & \text{if } \beta = \gamma; \\ \text{undefined} & \text{otherwise.} \end{cases}$$

The powerset 2^{GS} *of* GS *forms a Kleene algebra with tests as follows. The tests are the subsets of* $\mathsf{Atoms_B}$, *and*

$$0 = \varnothing$$
$$1 = \mathsf{Atoms_B}$$
$$A + B = A \cup B$$
$$A \cdot B = \{\sigma \diamond \tau \mid \sigma \in A, \tau \in B, \text{ and } \sigma \diamond \tau \text{ is defined}\}$$
$$A^* = \bigcup_{k \in \omega} A^k$$
$$\overline{A} = \mathsf{Atoms_B} - A$$

The canonical interpretation $G : \mathsf{RExp_{P,B}} \to 2^{\mathsf{GS}}$ *is defined by*

$$G(p) = \{\alpha p \beta \mid \alpha, \beta \in \mathsf{Atoms_B}\} \quad \text{for } p \in \mathsf{P} ,$$
$$G(b) = \{\alpha \mid \alpha \leq b\}^2 \quad \text{for } b \in \mathsf{B} ,$$

extended homomorphically. Let $\mathsf{REG\ GS}$ *denote the elements of* 2^{GS} *which are* $G(s)$ *for some* $s \in \mathsf{RExp_{P,B}}$.

---

[2] The partial order here is the natural partial order on the free Boolean algebra on generators B. In this case, $\alpha \leq b$ iff b appears positively in α.

REG GS is also called the *guarded string model*, and is the free KAT on generators P, B in the sense that $G(s) = G(t)$ iff $\mathsf{KAT} \models s = t$ [10]. The guarded string model can be treated in more generality as a special case of a *trace model* [6], which we do not define here.

Lemma 15. *Let* $K \in \mathsf{KAT}^*$, $I : \mathsf{RExp}_{\mathsf{P},\mathsf{B}} \to K$ *an interpretation, and* $p, q, r \in \mathsf{RExp}_{\mathsf{P},\mathsf{B}}$. *Then*
$$I(pqr) = \sup_{\sigma \in G(q)} I(p\sigma r) .$$
In particular, $I(q) = \sup_{\sigma \in G(q)} I(\sigma)$.

Proof. See [10]. □

2.3 Complete Idempotent Semirings

A *-continuous Kleene algebra can be thought of as an idempotent semiring where certain suprema are guaranteed to exist ($\sup_n q^n = q^*$), with multiplication distributing over these suprema ($pq^*r = \sup_n pq^n r$). If we strengthen this to require arbitrary suprema to exist, with multiplication distributing over these arbitrary suprema, we get the notion of *complete idempotent semiring*.[3]

The algebras we consider in this section will all have a Boolean subalgebra (that is, they will be "with tests"), but all the results still hold without tests.

Definition 16. *An* idempotent semiring with tests *is a two-sorted structure* $(S, B, +, \cdot, \bar{}, 0, 1)$, *where* $(S, +, \cdot, 0, 1)$ *is an idempotent semiring, and* $(B, +, \cdot, \bar{}, 0, 1)$ *is a Boolean subalgebra. The elements of* B *are called* tests. *We let* IST *denote the class of all idempotent semirings with tests.*

For a finite set P *of atomic programs and a finite set* B *of atomic tests,* $\mathsf{RExp}^0_{\mathsf{P},\mathsf{B}}$ *is the set of* IST *terms over* P *and* B, *i.e., the *-free terms in* $\mathsf{RExp}_{\mathsf{P},\mathsf{B}}$.

An $S \in \mathsf{IST}$ *is* complete *if the partial order on* S *induced by* $+$ *is complete*[4] *(We do not require the supremum of an arbitrary set of tests to be a test.)*

$\mathsf{RExp}^0_{\mathsf{P},\mathsf{B}}$ *is the set of* IST *terms over* P *and* B; *this coincides with the *-free terms of* $\mathsf{RExp}_{\mathsf{P},\mathsf{B}}$, *and we have* $\mathsf{RExp}^0_{\mathsf{P},\mathsf{B}} \subseteq \mathsf{RExp}_{\mathsf{P},\mathsf{B}}$.

A complete IST forms a *-continuous Kleene algebra with tests by defining $x^* = \sup_{n \in \omega} x^n$.

Lemma 17. *Given a monoid* $(S, \cdot, 1)$ *with a complete partial order* $\leq$ *such that* $\cdot$ *distributes over arbitrary suprema,* S *forms a complete idempotent semiring by defining* $0 = \sup \varnothing$ *and* $x + y = \sup\{x, y\}$. *If* S *has a Boolean subalgebra (with* $0, 1, +, \cdot$ *coinciding with the operations on* S), *then* S *forms a complete* IST.

---
[3] Complete idempotent semirings are often referred to as S-algebras [4].
[4] Here, a partial order $(P, \leq)$ is complete if every subset of P has a supremum, as in [1]. In particular, we require $\varnothing$ and P to have suprema; this is in contrast to other existing notions of complete partial order.

Proof. Trivial, except perhaps for the requirement that 0 is an annihilator for $\cdot$, which follows from distributivity and the definition of 0:

$$0 \cdot x = (\sup \varnothing) \cdot x = \sup(\varnothing \cdot x) = \sup \varnothing = 0 \ .$$

$x \cdot 0 = 0$ is similar. □

Theorem 18. *Every* IST *extends to a complete* IST.

Proof. We use ideal completion, where an ideal I is a nonempty subset of the semiring which is closed downward and closed under $+$. The details are given in a full version of this paper.

(Note that if a given $S \in$ IST happens to be a Kleene algebra, this construction will not typically respect $*$. However, if S is a $*$-continuous Kleene algebra, one can strengthen the notion of ideal to require $pq^*r \in I$ whenever $pq^n r \in I$ for all n, and using ideal completion with this notion of ideal will preserve $*$. For details of this see [7].) □

Corollary 19. $\mathcal{H}$KAT, $\mathcal{H}$KAT*, *and* $\mathcal{H}$IST, *restricted to $*$-free formulas, coincide.*

Proof. KAT$^* \subseteq$ KAT $\subseteq$ IST, so any Horn formula valid over IST is valid over KAT and KAT*. If a Horn formula is valid over KAT*, then it must be valid over IST, since every IST extends to a complete IST, which is a $*$-continuous Kleene algebra, and validity of Horn formulas is preserved in subalgebras. □

3 Simple and Semisimple Horn Formulas

Definition 20. *A Horn formula φ of* KAT *is semisimple if it is of the form*

$$s_1 \leq t_1 \wedge \cdots \wedge s_n \leq t_n \to s \leq t$$

where $t_1, \ldots, t_n$ are $*$-free (i.e., have no occurrence of $*$). We say that φ is simple if, in addition, s is $*$-free.

The coercion of a Horn formula $E \to s \leq t$ is the formula $E \wedge p \leq s \wedge t \leq p' \to p \leq p'$ where p and p' are fresh atomic program symbols. $E \to s \leq t$ is coerced if s and t are atomic program symbols (in particular, the coercion of a formula is coerced).

Lemma 21. *A Horn formula $E \to s \leq t$ is valid over any particular $K \in$* KAT *iff its coercion is. (If the formula is $*$-free, then validity is also preserved in any* IST.*)*

Note that the coercion of any simple Horn formula is simple, so when working with simple Horn formulas, we will often assume without loss of generality that they are coerced.

Note that there are many Horn formulas which are not simple, but are equivalent to simple formulas or conjunctions thereof. For example, $p \leq 1 \to p^2 = p$ is not simple, but is equivalent to

$$(p \leq 1 \to p^2 \leq p) \wedge (p \leq 1 \to p \leq p^2) \ .$$

A more subtle example is $q^* = 1 \to q \leq 1$. If we expand $q^* = 1$ to $q^* \leq 1 \wedge 1 \leq q^*$, we still do not have a simple formula; however, the latter hypothesis is a KA tautology, so it can be dropped, leaving us with the simple formula

$$q^* \leq 1 \to q \leq 1 \ .$$

Our goal is the following four theorems.

Theorem 22. $\mathcal{H}\mathsf{KAT}^*$, *restricted to simple Horn formulas, is Σ_1^0-complete.*

Theorem 23. $\mathcal{H}\mathsf{RKAT}$, *restricted to simple Horn formulas, is Σ_1^0-complete.*

Theorem 24. $\mathcal{H}\mathsf{KAT}^*$, *restricted to semisimple Horn formulas, is Π_2^0-complete.*

Theorem 25. $\mathcal{H}\mathsf{RKAT}$, *restricted to semisimple Horn formulas, is Π_2^0-complete.*

(In each case, the lower bound will not require tests, so the results also apply to $\mathcal{H}\mathsf{KA}^*$ and $\mathcal{H}\mathsf{RKA}$.)

In [8] and [5], the reduction used to show that $\mathcal{H}\mathsf{KA}^*$ and $\mathcal{H}\mathsf{RKA}$ are Π_1^1-complete uses formulas that are equivalent to simple formulas except for a single occurrence of $*$ on the right-hand side of one hypothesis. (Furthermore, they have no occurrence of 0, 1, or $+$, and only the one occurrence of $*$.) Semisimple formulas are as general as possible without allowing $*$ on the right-hand side of a hypothesis, which in turn allows for Π_1^1-completeness, so if we wish to find any larger fragments of $\mathcal{H}\mathsf{KA}^*$ or $\mathcal{H}\mathsf{RKA}$ that are not Π_1^1-complete, the criteria will have to be more discriminating than simply where $*$ occurs.

3.1 Simple and Semisimple Formulas in KAT*

In KAT, first-order logic can handle $*$ well, because its axiomatization is first order. The $*$-continuity axiom ($xy^*z = \sup_{n \in \omega} xy^n z$) is not first order, though, and the fact that $\mathcal{H}\mathsf{KAT}^*$ is Π_1^1-complete shows that there is no hope of finding a first-order substitute. As we will see in this section, the notion of simple formula captures the portion of $\mathcal{H}\mathsf{KAT}^*$ that first-order logic can (indirectly) handle anyway.

The $*$-continuity axiom, when the definition of supremum is unravelled, becomes

$$xy^*z \leq w \Leftrightarrow \bigwedge_{n \in \omega} xy^n z \leq w \ ,$$

or, using Lemma 15 (and abusing notation),

$$s \leq t \Leftrightarrow \bigwedge_{\sigma \in G(s)} \sigma \leq t \ .$$

Our basic tactic will be to replace any hypothesis $s \leq t$, where t is $*$-free, with the infinite set of $*$-free hypotheses $\sigma \leq t$, $\sigma \in G(s)$, which first order logic can better digest.

Fix a simple Horn formula φ of the form

$$s_1 \leq t_1 \wedge \cdots \wedge s_n \leq t_n \to s \leq t ,$$

and assume without loss of generality that φ is coerced, so that $s_1, \ldots, s_n$ are the only terms that may contain $*$. Let

$$\Gamma_\varphi = \{\sigma \leq t_i \mid \sigma \in G(s_i),\ 1 \leq i \leq n\} .$$

Lemma 26. *For φ as above, the following are equivalent.*

(i) $\mathsf{KAT} \models \varphi$
(ii) $\mathsf{KAT}^* \models \varphi$
(iii) $\mathsf{Ax}(\mathsf{IST}) \cup \Gamma_\varphi \models s \leq t$ *($\mathsf{Ax}(\mathsf{IST})$ denotes the IST axioms.)*

Proof. (i)$\Rightarrow$(ii) is immediate, since $\mathsf{KAT}^* \subseteq \mathsf{KAT}$.

Suppose (ii) holds. Let $S \in \mathsf{IST}$, and let $I : \mathsf{RExp}^0_{\mathsf{P},\mathsf{B}} \to S$ be any interpretation such that $S, I \models \Gamma_\varphi$; we must show $S, I \models s \leq t$. By Theorem 18, S extends to a complete semiring S'. I extends uniquely to an interpretation $I' : \mathsf{RExp}_{\mathsf{P},\mathsf{B}} \to S'$. For any $\sigma \in G(s_i)$, $1 \leq i \leq n$, we have $I'(\sigma) = I(\sigma) \leq I(t_i) = I'(t_i)$, so by Lemma 15, $I'(s_i) = \sup_{\sigma \in G(s_i)} I'(\sigma) \leq I'(t_i)$. So, since $S', I' \models \varphi$ by assumption, and we have just shown that S', I' satisfies each hypothesis of φ, we must have $S', I' \models s \leq t$. Then $I(s) = I'(s) \leq I'(t) = I(t)$, so $S, I \models s \leq t$, giving us (iii).

Now suppose (iii) holds. Take any $K \in \mathsf{KAT}$ and interpretation $I : \mathsf{RExp}_{\mathsf{P},\mathsf{B}} \to K$. Suppose $I(s_i) \leq I(t_i)$ for $1 \leq i \leq n$. Then for any $\sigma \in G(s_i)$, $1 \leq i \leq n$, we have $I(\sigma) \leq I(s_i) \leq I(t_i)$, so $K, I \models \Gamma_\varphi$. We also have $K, I \models \mathsf{Ax}(\mathsf{IST})$, so by (iii), $K, I \models s \leq t$. Therefore, $K, I \models \varphi$, giving us (i). □

Proof (of Theorem 22). The upper bound follows from Lemma 26, since the Horn theory of KAT is Σ^0_1. (The entire theory of KAT is Σ^0_1 since it is finitely axiomatized.)

The lower bound is by Lemma 12. (Although Horn formulas consisting of monoid equations are not technically simple, each hypothesis can be replaced by a pair of inequalities, and Lemma 11 shows that we can, in this case, replace the conclusion with an inequality.) □

Proof (of Theorem 24). Essentially, $*$-continuity lets us treat a semisimple formula $E \to s \leq t$ as the infinite conjunction $\bigwedge_{\sigma \in G(s)} E \to \sigma \leq t$. The details are given in a full version of this paper. □

Theorem 27. *Let $s_1 \leq t_1 \wedge \cdots \wedge s_n \leq t_n \to s \leq t$ be any simple Horn formula. The following are equivalent.*

(i) $\mathsf{KAT}^* \models s_1 \leq t_1 \wedge \cdots \wedge s_n \leq t_n \to s \leq t$

(ii) *There exist finite sets $T \subseteq G(t)$ and $S_i \subseteq G(s_i)$, $1 \leq i \leq n$, such that*

$$\mathsf{KAT}^* \models (\Sigma S_1) \leq t_1 \wedge \cdots \wedge (\Sigma S_n) \leq t_n \to s \leq (\Sigma T) \ .$$

(iii) *There exist finite sets $T \subseteq G(t)$ and $S_i \subseteq G(s_i)$, $1 \leq i \leq n$, such that*

$$\mathsf{IST} \models (\Sigma S_1) \leq t_1 \wedge \cdots \wedge (\Sigma S_n) \leq t_n \to s \leq (\Sigma T) \ .$$

(Here, ΣS denotes the sum of the elements of S.)

3.2 Simple and Semisimple Formulas in RKAT

The ideas of Section 3.1 also work for relational algebras, but we must use first-order logic differently.

Fix finite $\mathsf{P} = \{p_1, \ldots, p_m\}$, $\mathsf{B} = \{b_1, \ldots, b_\ell\}$. Let $\mathcal{L}_{\mathsf{P},\mathsf{B}}$ be the first-order language with binary predicate symbols $P_1, \ldots, P_m, B_1, \ldots, B_\ell$ (in addition to equality) and no function or constant symbols. Let β be the formula

$$\bigwedge_{i=1}^{\ell} \forall x, y [B_i(x,y) \to x = y] \ ,$$

which will ensure that interpretations of the B_i make suitable Boolean elements in a relational algebra, by making them subsets of the identity relation.

For any $\mathcal{L}_{\mathsf{P},\mathsf{B}}$-structure $\mathcal{A}$ modeling β (or simply, "for any $\mathcal{A} \models \beta$"), $|\mathcal{A}|$ will denote the universe of $\mathcal{A}$, while $P_1^{\mathcal{A}}, \ldots, P_m^{\mathcal{A}}, B_1^{\mathcal{A}}, \ldots, B_\ell^{\mathcal{A}}$ will denote the interpretations of $P_1, \ldots, P_m, B_1, \ldots, B_\ell$ in $\mathcal{A}$, and we define the interpretation $I^{\mathcal{A}} : \mathsf{RExp}_{\mathsf{P},\mathsf{B}} \to \mathcal{R}(|\mathcal{A}|)$ by $I^{\mathcal{A}}(p_i) = P_i^{\mathcal{A}}$, $I^{\mathcal{A}}(b_i) = B_i^{\mathcal{A}}$.

For each $t \in \mathsf{RExp}_{\mathsf{P},\mathsf{B}}^0$, we define the formula $\theta_t(x,y)$ of $\mathcal{L}_{\mathsf{P},\mathsf{B}}$ by induction on t as follows.

$$\begin{aligned}
\theta_0(x,y) &\Leftrightarrow \mathsf{false} & \theta_{\overline{t}}(x,y) &\Leftrightarrow x = y \wedge \neg \theta_t(x,y) \\
\theta_1(x,y) &\Leftrightarrow x = y & \theta_{s+t}(x,y) &\Leftrightarrow \theta_s(x,y) \vee \theta_t(x,y) \\
\theta_{p_i}(x,y) &\Leftrightarrow P_i(x,y) & \theta_{st}(x,y) &\Leftrightarrow \exists z [\theta_s(x,z) \wedge \theta_t(z,y)] \\
\theta_{b_i}(x,y) &\Leftrightarrow B_i(x,y) & &
\end{aligned}$$

(Given a formula $\varphi(x,y)$, when we write $\varphi(x,z)$, the usual convention applies: if the variable z already occurs in $\varphi(x,y)$, it is renamed as necessary before substituting z for y to get $\varphi(x,z)$, to avoid variable capture.)

Lemma 28. *Take any $\mathcal{A} \models \beta$. Then for all $a, a' \in |\mathcal{A}|$ and $t \in \mathsf{RExp}_{\mathsf{P},\mathsf{B}}^0$,*

$$(a, a') \in I^{\mathcal{A}}(t) \Leftrightarrow \mathcal{A} \models \theta_t(a, a') \ .$$

Proof. Straightforward induction on t. □

Now, for any inequality $s \leq t$ for $s, t \in \mathsf{RExp}_{\mathsf{P},\mathsf{B}}^0$, we define the sentence $\theta_{s \leq t}$ by

$$\theta_{s \leq t} \Leftrightarrow \forall x, y [\theta_s(x,y) \to \theta_t(x,y)] \ .$$

Lemma 29. *Take any* $\mathcal{A} \models \beta$. *Then for all* $s, t \in \mathsf{RExp}_{\mathsf{P},\mathsf{B}}^0$,

$$\mathcal{R}(|\mathcal{A}|), I^{\mathcal{A}} \models s \leq t \Leftrightarrow \mathcal{A} \models \theta_{s \leq t} .$$

As we did in Section 3.1, fix a simple Horn formula φ of the form

$$s_1 \leq t_1 \wedge \cdots \wedge s_n \leq l_n \rightarrow s \leq l ,$$

assuming without loss of generality that s and t are $*$-free, and let $\Gamma_\varphi = \{\sigma \leq t_i \mid \sigma \in G(s_i),\ 1 \leq i \leq n\}$. Let

$$\widehat{\Gamma}_\varphi = \{\theta_{u \leq v} \mid u \leq v \text{ appears in } \Gamma_\varphi\} .$$

Lemma 30. *The following are equivalent.*

(i) $\mathsf{RKAT} \models \varphi$
(ii) $\{\beta\} \cup \widehat{\Gamma}_\varphi \models \theta_{s \leq t}$

Proof. Suppose (i) holds. Suppose $\mathcal{A} \models \{\beta\} \cup \widehat{\Gamma}_\varphi$. Then by Lemma 29, $\mathcal{R}(|\mathcal{A}|), I^{\mathcal{A}} \models u \leq v$ for all $u \leq v$ appearing in Γ_φ; that is, $\mathcal{R}(|\mathcal{A}|), I^{\mathcal{A}} \models \sigma \leq t_i$ for all $\sigma \in G(s_i)$, $1 \leq i \leq n$. $\mathcal{R}(|\mathcal{A}|)$ is $*$-continuous, so by Lemma 15, $\mathcal{R}(|\mathcal{A}|), I^{\mathcal{A}} \models s_i \leq t_i$, $1 \leq i \leq n$. So, applying (i), $\mathcal{R}(|\mathcal{A}|), I^{\mathcal{A}} \models s \leq t$. Applying Lemma 29 again, we have $\mathcal{A} \models \theta_{s \leq t}$, giving us (ii).

Now suppose (ii) holds. Take any $K \in \mathsf{RKAT}$. Let X be the base of K. Suppose $I : \mathsf{RExp}_{\mathsf{P},\mathsf{B}} \to K$ is an interpretation such that $K, I \models s_i \leq t_n$, $1 \leq i \leq n$. Define the $\mathcal{L}_{\mathsf{P},\mathsf{B}}$-structure $\mathcal{A}$ by $|\mathcal{A}| = X$, $P_i^{\mathcal{A}} = I(p_i)$, $B_i^{\mathcal{A}} = I(b_i)$. Then $I = I^{\mathcal{A}}$, so from $K, I \models s_i \leq t_i$, $1 \leq i \leq n$, we get $\mathcal{R}(|\mathcal{A}|), I^{\mathcal{A}} \models s_i \leq t_i$, $1 \leq i \leq n$. It follows that $\mathcal{R}(|\mathcal{A}|), I^{\mathcal{A}} \models \sigma \leq t_i$ for all $\sigma \in G(s_i)$, $1 \leq i \leq n$; that is, $\mathcal{R}(|\mathcal{A}|), I^{\mathcal{A}} \models \Gamma_\varphi$. Thus, by Lemma 29, $\mathcal{A} \models \widehat{\Gamma}_\varphi$. Since each $I(b_i)$ is a subset of the identity relation, we have $\mathcal{A} \models \beta$. So, applying (ii), $\mathcal{A} \models \theta_{s \leq t}$. Applying Lemma 29 again, we have $\mathcal{R}(|\mathcal{A}|), I^{\mathcal{A}} \models s \leq t$. This gives us $K, I \models s \leq t$ (since $I = I^{\mathcal{A}}$). We now have (i), as desired. □

Proof (of Theorem 23). The upper bound comes from Lemma 30, since the predicate $\{\beta\} \cup \widehat{\Gamma}_\varphi \models \theta_{s \leq t}$ is Σ_0^1 in φ. (The set $\{\beta\} \cup \widehat{\Gamma}_\varphi$ is uniformly computable in φ, so we can effectively enumerate its logical consequences.) The lower bound comes from Lemma 12. □

Lemma 31. *Let E be a finite set of monoid equations over Σ. Then for any $s \in \mathsf{RExp}_\Sigma$ and $\tau \in \Sigma^*$, the following are equivalent.*

(i) $\mathsf{KA}^* \models E \to s \leq \tau$
(ii) $\mathsf{RKA} \models E \to s \leq \tau$

Proof (of Theorem 25). The upper bound is by the same argument as in the proof of Theorem 24. The lower bound, also as in the proof of Theorem 24, is from the reduction in [8]; we can use the same reduction because the formulas in the reduction are of the form that Lemma 31 applies to. □

Theorem 32. *Let $s_1 \leq t_1 \wedge \cdots \wedge s_n \leq t_n \to s \leq t$ be any simple Horn formula. The following are equivalent.*

(i) $\mathsf{RKAT} \models s_1 \leq t_1 \wedge \cdots \wedge s_n \leq t_n \to s \leq t$
(ii) *There exist finite sets $T \subseteq G(t)$ and $S_i \subseteq G(s_i)$, $1 \leq i \leq n$, such that*

$$\mathsf{RKAT} \models (\Sigma S_1) \leq t_1 \wedge \cdots \wedge (\Sigma S_n) \leq t_n \to s \leq (\Sigma T) \ .$$

(iii) *There exist finite sets $T \subseteq G(t)$ and $S_i \subseteq G(s_i)$, $1 \leq i \leq n$, such that*

$$\beta \models \theta_{(\Sigma S_1) \leq t_1} \wedge \cdots \wedge \theta_{(\Sigma S_n) \leq t_n} \to \theta_{s \leq (\Sigma T)} \ .$$

Proof. Similar to Theorem 27. □

4 Bigness and Smallness of ∗

In the introduction, we stated that the validity of simple Horn formulas depends only on the bigness of ∗. We now make that precise.

Definition 33. *A ∗-algebra is an algebra over the signature of KAT satisfying the IST axioms (in other words, the result of dropping the ∗ axioms from KAT). A big-∗-algebra is a ∗-algebra satisfying the bigness condition (1) from the introduction. A small-∗-algebra is a ∗-algebra satisfying the smallness condition (2). We let BIG^* and SMALL^* denote the classes of big-∗- and small-∗-algebras, respectively.*

Clearly, $\mathsf{BIG}^* \cap \mathsf{SMALL}^* = \mathsf{KAT}^*$. We also have $\mathsf{KAT} \subseteq \mathsf{BIG}^*$, $\mathsf{KAT} \not\subseteq \mathsf{SMALL}^*$.

Theorem 34. *For any simple Horn formula φ, the following are equivalent.*

(i) $\mathsf{KAT}^* \models \varphi$
(ii) $\mathsf{BIG}^* \models \varphi$
(iii) $\mathsf{KAT} \models \varphi$

If we reverse the inequalities in the definition of simple formula, we get formulas whose validity (in KAT^*) depends only on the smallness of ∗.

Definition 35. *A Horn formula φ of KAT is cosimple if it is of the form*

$$s_1 \leq t_1 \wedge \cdots \wedge s_n \leq t_n \to s \leq t$$

where $s_1, \ldots, s_n$ and t are ∗-free.

Theorem 36. *For any cosimple Horn formula φ, the following are equivalent.*

(i) $\mathsf{KAT}^* \models \varphi$
(ii) $\mathsf{SMALL}^* \models \varphi$

(Note the absence of the case $\mathsf{KAT} \models \varphi$.)

Acknowledgments

I am grateful to Dexter Kozen for his comments on various drafts of this article.

References

1. Stanley Burris and H. P. Sankappanavar. *A Course in Universal Algebra*. Springer-Verlag, New York, 1981. (Also available online:
   http://www.thoralf.uwaterloo.ca/htdocs/ualg.html)
2. Ernie Cohen. Hypotheses in Kleene Algebra. Unpublished.
3. Ernie Cohen, Dexter Kozen, and Frederick Smith. The complexity of Kleene algebra with tests. Technical Report 96-1598, Computer Science Department, Cornell University, July 1996.
4. J. H. Conway. *Regular Algebra and Finite Machines*. Chapman and Hall, London, 1971.
5. Chris Hardin and Dexter Kozen. On the Complexity of the Horn Theory of REL. Technical Report 2003-1896, Computer Science Department, Cornell University, May 2003.
6. Chris Hardin and Dexter Kozen. On the Elimination of Hypotheses in Kleene Algebra with Tests. Technical Report 2002-1879, Computer Science Department, Cornell University, October 2002.
7. Dexter Kozen. On Kleene algebras and closed semirings. In Rovan, editor, *Proc. Math. Found. Comput. Sci.*, volume 452 of *Lect. Notes in Comput. Sci.*, pages 26–47. Springer, 1990.
8. Dexter Kozen. On the Complexity of Reasoning in Kleene Algebra. *Information and Computation* 179, 152-162, 2002.
9. Dexter Kozen. *The Design and Analysis of Algorithms*. Springer-Verlag, New York, 1991.
10. Dexter Kozen and Frederick Smith. Kleene algebra with tests: completeness and decidability. Proc. 10th Int. Workshop on Computer Science Logic (CSL'96), ed. D. van Dalen and M. Bezem, Utrecht, The Netherlands, Springer-Verlag Lecture Notes in Computer Science Volume 1258, September 1996, 244–259.

The Equational Theory of $\langle \mathbb{N}, 0, 1, +, \times, \uparrow \rangle$ Is Decidable, but Not Finitely Axiomatisable

Roberto Di Cosmo and Thomas Dufour

PPS Laboratory (http://www.pps.jussieu.fr)
Université Paris 7
France
{dicosmo,dufour}@pps.jussieu.fr

Abstract. In 1969, Tarski asked whether the arithmetic identities taught in high school are complete for showing all arithmetic equations valid for the natural numbers. We know the answer to this question for various subsystems obtained by restricting in different ways the language of arithmetic expressions, yet, up to now we knew nothing of the original system that Tarski considered when he started all this research, namely the theory of integers under sum, product, exponentiation with two constants for zero and one.
This paper closes this long standing open problem, by providing an elementary proof, relying on previous work of R. Gurevič, of the fact that Tarski's original system is decidable, yet not finitely aximatisable.
We also show some consequences of this result for the theory of isomorphisms of types.

1 Introduction

Over forty years ago, Tarski asked whether the arithmetic identities taught in high school are complete for showing all arithmetic equations valid for the natural numbers. The answer to this question has occupied many prestigious mathematicians over half a century, that gave the answer for various subsystems, the most intriguing one being the one involving a constant for the number one and the operations of product and exponentiation, for which a complete equational theory exists and also characterizes isomorphism in the typed lambda calculus and in Cartesian Closed Categories, thus exposing interesting connections between number theory, category theory, lambda calculus and type theory.

Yet, up to now we knew nothing of the original system that Tarski considered when he started all this research, namely the equational theory of natural numbers under sum, product, exponentiation and with the two constants for zero and one.

We provide here an elementary proof, relying on previous work of R. Gurevič, of the fact that the equational theory of the arithmetical system with constants 0 and 1 is decidable, but not finitely axiomatisable. By "elementary", we do not mean "simple", but we do want to stress the fact that we proceed by a set of transformations of derivations and formal systems that are well in the tradition of logic and theoretical computer science.

As a first consequence of this result, we can conclude that the theory of isomorphisms of types for bicartesian closed categories is undecidable, a question left open in [BDCF02].

The paper is organized as follows: subsection 1.1 gives a rather comprehensive overview of Tarski's High School Algebra Problem, and subsection 1.2 pinpoints its interest in computer science; section 2 provides a few basic definitions and notations; section 3 provides a proof that the equational theory of $\langle \mathbb{N}, 0, 1, +, \times, \uparrow \rangle$ can be reduced to the equational theory of $\langle \mathbb{N}, 1, +, \times, \uparrow \rangle$, modulo the equations and the conditional equation involving zero that we are taught in high school (figure 2), which in turn gives a decision procedure for the system; section 4 shows that the theory of $\langle \mathbb{N}, 0, 1, +, \times, \uparrow \rangle$ is not finitely axiomatisable, and section 5 concludes.

1.1 Tarski's High School Algebra Problem

In 1969, Tarski [DT69] asked if the equational theory $\mathcal{E}$ of the usual arithmetic identities of figure 1 that are taught in high school are complete for the standard model $\langle \mathbb{N}, 1, +, \times, \uparrow \rangle$ of positive natural numbers; i.e., if they are enough to prove all the arithmetic identities (he considered zero fundamental too, but, probably due to the presence of one conditional equation, he left for further investigation the case of the other equations of figure 2, that we are also taught in high school).

$(\mathcal{E}_1)\ 1 \times x = x \quad (\mathcal{E}_2)\ x \times y = y \times x \quad (\mathcal{E}_3)\ (x \times y) \times z = x \times (y \times z)$

$(\mathcal{E}_4)\ x^1 = x \qquad\qquad\qquad (\mathcal{E}_5)\ 1^x = 1$

$(\mathcal{E}_6)\ x^{y \times z} = (x^y)^z \qquad\quad (\mathcal{E}_7)\ (x \times y)^z = x^z \times y^z$

$(\mathcal{E}_8)\ x + y = y + x \qquad\qquad (\mathcal{E}_9)\ (x + y) + z = x + (y + z)$

$(\mathcal{E}_{10})\ x \times (y + z) = x \times y + x \times z \qquad (\mathcal{E}_{11})\ x^{(y+z)} = x^y \times x^z$

Fig. 1. Equations without zero

$(\mathcal{Z}_1)\ 0 \times x = 0 \quad (\mathcal{Z}_2)\ 0 + x = x \quad (\mathcal{Z}_3)\ x^0 = 1$

$(\mathcal{Z}_4)\ 0^x = 0 \quad (x > 0)$

Fig. 2. Equations and conditional equation for zero

He conjectured that they were[1], but was not able to prove the result. Martin [Mar72] showed that the identity $(\mathcal{E}_6)$ is complete for the standard model $\langle \mathbb{N}, \uparrow \rangle$ of positive nat-

---

[1] Actually, he conjectured something stronger, namely that $\mathcal{E}$ is complete for $\langle \mathbb{N}, Ack(n, \_, \_) \rangle$, the natural numbers equipped with a family of generalised binary operators $Ack(n, \_, \_)$ that

ural numbers with exponentiation, and that the identities ($\mathcal{E}_2$), ($\mathcal{E}_3$), ($\mathcal{E}_6$), and ($\mathcal{E}_7$) are complete for the standard model $\langle \mathbb{N}, \times, \uparrow \rangle$ of positive natural numbers with multiplication and exponentiation. Further, he exhibited the identity

$$(x^u + x^u)^v \times (y^v + y^v)^u = (x^v + x^v)^u \times (y^u + y^u)^v$$

that in the language without the constant 1 is not provable in $\mathcal{E}$.[2] The question was not completely settled by this counterexample, because it is was only a counterexample in the language without a constant for 1, that Tarski clearly considered necessary in his paper, as well as the constant for 0, even if he did not explicitly mention it in his conjecture. In the presence of a constant 1, the following new equations come into play, and allow us to easily prove Martin's equality.

$$1a = a \quad a^1 = a \quad 1^a = 1$$

This problem attracted the interest of many other mathematicians, like Leon Henkin, who focused on the equalities valid in $\langle \mathbb{N}, 0, + \rangle$, and showed the completeness of the usual known axioms (commutativity, associativity of the sum and the zero axiom), and gives a very nice presentation of the topic in [Hen77].

Wilkie [Wil81] was the first to establish Tarski's conjecture in the negative. Indeed, by a proof-theoretic analysis, he showed that the identity

$$(A^x + B^x)^y \times (C^y + D^y)^x = (A^y + B^y)^x \times (C^x + D^x)^y$$

where $A = 1+x$, $B = 1+x+x^2$, $C = 1+x^3$, $D = 1+x^2+x^4$ is not provable in $\mathcal{E}$.

Gurevič later gave an argument by an ad hoc counter-model [Gur85] and, more importantly, showed that there is no finite axiomatisation for the valid equations in the standard model $\langle \mathbb{N}, 1, +, \times, \uparrow \rangle$ of positive natural numbers with one, multiplication, exponentiation, and addition [Gur90]. He did this by producing an infinite family of equations such that for every sound finite set of axioms one of the equations can be shown not to follow. Gurevič's identities, which generalize Wilkie's identities, are the following

$$\left(A^x + B_n^x\right)^{2^x} \times \left(C_n^{2^x} + D_n^{2^x}\right)^x = \left(A^{2^x} + B_n^{2^x}\right)^x \times \left(C_n^x + D_n^x\right)^{2^x}$$

where
$$A = 1 + x$$
$$B_n = 1 + x + \cdots + x^{n-1} = \sum_{i=0}^{n-1} x^i$$
$$C_n = 1 + x^n$$
$$D_n = 1 + x^2 + \cdots + x^{2(n-1)} = \sum_{i=0}^{n-1} x^{2i}$$
$$n \geq 3 \quad \text{is odd}$$

---

extend the usual sum $+$, product $\times$ and exponentiation $\uparrow$ operators. In Tarski's definition, $Ack(0, \_, \_)$ is the sum, $Ack(1, \_, \_)$ is multiplication, $Ack(2, \_, \_)$ is exponentiation (for the other cases see for example [Rog88]).

[2] He also showed that there are no nontrivial equations for $\langle \mathbb{N}, Ack(n, \_, \_) \rangle$ if $n > 2$.

Nonetheless, equality in all these structures, even if not finitely axiomatisable, was shown to be decidable [Mac81,Gur85].[3]

As often happens in number theory, these last results use far more complex tools than simple arithmetic reasoning, as in the case of [HR84], where Nevanlinna theory is used to identify a subclass of numerical expressions for which the usual axioms for $+$, $\times$, $\uparrow$ and 1 are complete.

1.2 Connections with Type Isomorphisms and Applications in Library Search

Two types A and B in a given language are called *isomorphic* if there exist conversion functions $f : A \to B$ and $g : B \to A$ which are mutual inverses [DC95].

From a practical perspective, type isomorphisms are used as a basis for library search tools of various kind, and one is interested in knowing whether type isomorphisms in the presence of sums are finitely axiomatisable, and whether an efficient decision procedure exists, to incorporate it in library search tools like those described in [Rit90,DC95].

There is a connection between the characterization of type isomorphisms in typed lambda calculi and Tarski's high school algebra problem: for types built out of type constructors chosen amongst the unit, product, and arrow, two types are isomorphic if and only if their associated arithmetic expressions (obtained by interpreting the unit by the number one, product by multiplication, and arrow by exponentiation) are equal in the standard model of natural numbers. In this case, type isomorphism (and numerical equality) is finitely axiomatisable and decidable; hence so is the equational theory of isomorphisms in cartesian closed categories. Zibin, Gil and Considine [ZGC03] provide very efficient $O(n \log n)$ decision procedures for this system. In the same vein, Soloviev [Sol93], gave a complete axiomatisation of isomorphisms in symmetric monoidal closed categories, and Dosen and Petric [DP97] provided the arithmetic structure that exactly corresponds to these isomorphisms.

Balat, Fiore and the first author investigated the question as to whether such correspondence was limited to the case of the well-behaved unit, product, and arrow type constructors and, in particular, if it could be extended to more problematic types involving the empty type and the sum type constructor [BDCF02,BDCF04], with the following fundamental result:

> Gurevič's identities are indeed type isomorphisms, and one can then show that the theory of type isomorphisms in the presence of the product, arrow, and sum type constructors, and the unit type is not finitely axiomatisable.

Since nothing was known for arithmetic equality in the presence of zero, one could not conclude the non finite axiomatisability of type isomorphisms in the presence of the empty type: it could be the case that, with the zero added, the Gurevič's identities collapse into a finite set of equations.

---

[3] For the interested reader, here is how the decision procedure works: from the size of the equation that has to be verified, it is possible to derive an upper bound; if the two sides coincide for all values of the variables up to this upper bound, then they coincide everywhere.

Worse than that: even if every isomorphism does produce a numerical equality[4], when the zero constant is added, there is a numerical equality which is not an isomorphism, hence type isomorphism and arithmetic equality no longer coincide in the presence of zero.

With the results of this paper, we can conclude that the family of Gurevič's identities does not collapse in the presence of zero, and hence, even with the empty set, type isomorphisms are not finitely axiomatisable.

2 Definitions and Notations

Definition 1. *The terms in $\langle \mathbb{N}, 0, 1, +, \times, \uparrow \rangle$ are $t ::= x \mid 0 \mid 1 \mid t + t \mid t \times t \mid t^t$, and the terms in $\langle \mathbb{N}, 1, +, \times, \uparrow \rangle$ are $\bar{t} ::= x \mid 1 \mid \bar{t} + \bar{t} \mid \bar{t} \times \bar{t} \mid \bar{t}^{\bar{t}}$, where x is a metavariable denoting a countably infinite set of variables $\mathcal{V} = \{x, y, z, \dots\}$. We will use the letters $t, s, u, \dots$ for the terms of $\langle \mathbb{N}, 0, 1, +, \times, \uparrow \rangle$.*

Definition 2. *Let t be a term of $\langle \mathbb{N}, 0, 1, +, \times, \uparrow \rangle$, we write $\mathrm{Var}(t)$ for the set of its variables.*

Definition 3 (Context). *A context – written $\Gamma, \Delta, \dots$ – is a formula of the propositional logic with the operators $\neg, \vee, \wedge$, in which the atomic formulas are the "$x = 0$", for $x \in \mathcal{V}$. We also include $\top$ (true), and $\bot$ (false).*

Definition 4 (Exhaustive context). *Given $A, B \subset \mathcal{V}$ two finite sets, we let $[A, B]$ be the following context:*

$$[A, B] = \bigwedge_{x \in A} x = 0 \wedge \bigwedge_{x \in B \setminus A} \neg x = 0$$

*A context Γ will be said to be **exhaustive for** t (a term) if there exist two finite sets A and $B \supset \mathrm{Var}(t)$ such that Γ is equivalent – as a logical proposition – to $[A, B]$.*

Definition 5 (Syntactically positive terms). *A term t in $\langle \mathbb{N}, 0, 1, +, \times, \uparrow \rangle$ is said to be **syntactically positive in context** Γ when Γ is exhaustive for t and $\forall x \in \mathrm{Var}(t)$, $\Gamma \Rightarrow \neg x = 0$.*

Definition 6. *Let φ be a valuation ($\varphi : \mathcal{V} \to \mathbb{N}$). We write $[\![t]\!]_\varphi$ the interpretation of t relative to this valuation.*

Definition 7. *Let Γ be a context and φ a valuation, we write $[\![\Gamma]\!]_\varphi$ the logical value defined as follows:*

$$[\![x = 0]\!]_\varphi = \begin{cases} \top & \text{if } \varphi(x) = 0 \\ \bot & \text{if } \varphi(x) \neq 0 \end{cases}$$

$[\![\Gamma \wedge \Delta]\!]_\varphi = [\![\Gamma]\!]_\varphi \wedge [\![\Delta]\!]_\varphi, \quad [\![\Gamma \vee \Delta]\!]_\varphi = [\![\Gamma]\!]_\varphi \vee [\![\Delta]\!]_\varphi, \quad [\![\neg \Gamma]\!]_\varphi = \neg [\![\Gamma]\!]_\varphi.$

*A valuation φ will be said to **satisfy** a context Γ if $[\![\Gamma]\!]_\varphi = \top$.*

---

[4] A type isomorphism can be turned into a bijection of finite sets, and hence into an equation between cardinalities, expressed using the arithmetic languages; hence all isomorphisms are arithmetical equalities.

3 $\langle \mathbb{N}, 0, 1, +, \times, \uparrow \rangle$ as an Extension of $\langle \mathbb{N}, 1, +, \times, \uparrow \rangle$

Introduction In this section we create a formal system (called *ZP*) that produces "conditional equations" of terms in $\langle \mathbb{N}, 0, 1, +, \times, \uparrow \rangle$. That system starts with the equalities in $\langle \mathbb{N}, 1, +, \times, \uparrow \rangle$ and builds on them. The semantics of this system will be proved to relate to equality in $\langle \mathbb{N}, 0, 1, +, \times, \uparrow \rangle$ in a fashion that allows us to deduce, first the relationship between equality in $\langle \mathbb{N}, 0, 1, +, \times, \uparrow \rangle$ and in $\langle \mathbb{N}, 1, +, \times, \uparrow \rangle$, second that equality in $\langle \mathbb{N}, 0, 1, +, \times, \uparrow \rangle$ is decidable.

Definition 8 (The *ZP* formal system). *We define a formal system, which we will call ZP. It contains two statements: "$\Gamma \vdash t \doteq s$" and "$\Gamma \vdash t$ positive", which are inferred as described in figure 3.*

Remark Informally, these statements mean: "If Γ holds, then t and s are equal (respectively: t is positive)". Proving this is actually the point of proposition 2.

Proposition 1. *Let t be a term, and Γ a context which is exhaustive for t. There are a term t' and a derivation that proves $\Gamma \vdash t \doteq t'$, where one of the following conditions holds:*

1. *$t' = 0$*
2. *t' is syntactically positive in context Γ.*

PROOF: The proof is essentially a reduction by induction on t and can be seen in appendix A.1. □

Lemma 1 *Let t be a term which is syntactically positive term in context Γ. There exists a derivation of the statement $\Gamma \vdash t$ positive.*

PROOF: With the fact that being syntactically positive extends to sub-terms, plus rules N0, N1, N3-N5, we have an obvious proof by structural induction. □

Proposition 2 (Semantics of the statements of *ZP*). *The following statements hold:*

$$\Gamma \vdash t \doteq s \Leftrightarrow \forall \varphi \text{ satisfying } \Gamma \; [\![t]\!]_\varphi = [\![s]\!]_\varphi \tag{1}$$

$$\Gamma \vdash t \text{ positive} \Leftrightarrow \forall \varphi \text{ satisfying } \Gamma \; [\![t]\!]_\varphi \neq 0 \tag{2}$$

PROOF: The left-to-right implications in (1) and (2) will be proved simultaneously by structural induction on the derivation of the statement. This is shown in appendix A.2.

In order to prove the right-to-left implication in (1), we will begin by stating that it is enough to prove it under the following stronger hypotheses:
For all $A \subset B = \text{Var}(t + s)$,

$$\forall \psi \text{ satisfying } [A, B] \; [\![t]\!]_\psi = [\![s]\!]_\psi \Rightarrow [A, B] \vdash t \doteq s$$

This is supported by the four quite simple facts about contexts and valuations that can be found in appendix A.3.

$$\boxed{\text{E0}} \frac{}{\Gamma \vdash t \doteq s} \quad \text{If condition (†) holds}$$

(†) : t and s are syntactically positive in context Γ, and $t = s$ in $\langle \mathbb{N}, 1, +, \times, \uparrow \rangle$.[5]

$$\boxed{\text{E1}} \frac{}{x = 0 \vdash x \doteq 0}$$

$$\boxed{\text{E2}} \frac{}{\top \vdash t + 0 \doteq t} \qquad \boxed{\text{E2'}} \frac{}{\top \vdash 0 + t \doteq t}$$

$$\boxed{\text{E3}} \frac{}{\top \vdash t \times 0 \doteq 0} \qquad \boxed{\text{E3'}} \frac{}{\top \vdash 0 \times t \doteq 0}$$

$$\boxed{\text{E4}} \frac{}{\top \vdash t^0 \doteq 1} \qquad \boxed{\text{E5}} \frac{\Gamma \vdash t \text{ positive}}{\Gamma \vdash 0^t \doteq 0}$$

$$\boxed{\text{E6}} \frac{\Gamma \vdash t \doteq s}{\Delta \vdash t \doteq s} \quad \text{If } \Delta \Rightarrow \Gamma$$

$$\boxed{\text{E7}} \frac{\Gamma \vdash t \doteq s \quad \Delta \vdash t \doteq s}{\Gamma \vee \Delta \vdash t \doteq s}$$

....

$$\boxed{\text{N0}} \frac{}{\neg x = 0 \vdash x \text{ positive}} \qquad \boxed{\text{N1}} \frac{}{\top \vdash 1 \text{ positive}}$$

$$\boxed{\text{N2}} \frac{\Gamma \vdash t \text{ positive} \quad \Gamma \vdash t \doteq s}{\Gamma \vdash s \text{ positive}} \qquad \boxed{\text{N3}} \frac{\Gamma \vdash t \text{ positive}}{\Gamma \vdash t + s \text{ positive}}$$

$$\boxed{\text{N4}} \frac{\Gamma \vdash t \text{ positive} \quad \Gamma \vdash s \text{ positive}}{\Gamma \vdash t \times s \text{ positive}} \qquad \boxed{\text{N5}} \frac{\Gamma \vdash t \text{ positive} \quad \Gamma \vdash s \text{ positive}}{\Gamma \vdash t^s \text{ positive}}$$

$$\boxed{\text{N6}} \frac{\Gamma \vdash t \text{ positive}}{\Delta \vdash t \text{ positive}} \quad \text{If } \Delta \Rightarrow \Gamma$$

$$\boxed{\text{N7}} \frac{\Gamma \vdash t \text{ positive} \quad \Delta \vdash t \text{ positive}}{\Gamma \vee \Delta \vdash t \text{ positive}}$$

....

$$\boxed{\text{REFL}} \frac{}{\top \vdash t \doteq t} \qquad \boxed{\text{SYM}} \frac{\Gamma \vdash t \doteq s}{\Gamma \vdash s \doteq t} \qquad \boxed{\text{TRANS}} \frac{\Gamma \vdash t \doteq s \quad \Gamma \vdash s \doteq u}{\Gamma \vdash t \doteq u}$$

$$\boxed{\text{CONT}} \frac{\Gamma \vdash t \doteq s}{\Gamma \vdash C[t] \doteq C[s]} \quad C[\cdot] \text{ denotes a context with only one placeholder}[6]$$

Fig. 3. Rules of inference of the statements "$\Gamma \vdash t \doteq s$" and "$\Gamma \vdash t$ positive" (*ZP*)

Let us now prove this restricted property:$[A, B]$ is exhaustive for t and s so proposition 1 stipulates that there exist some terms t' and s', which are both 0 or syntactically

---

[5] Since t and s are syntactically positive, they contain no 0, so it is meaningful to ask whether they are equal as terms of $\langle \mathbb{N}, 1, +, \times, \uparrow \rangle$.

[6] Here "context" has its usual meaning with terms of a first-order language. Such a context is a term of the language with an extra 0-ary symbol $[\cdot]$ called placeholder, which can be seen as a

positive in context $[A, B]$, such that $[A, B] \vdash t \doteq t'$ and $[A, B] \vdash s \doteq s'$. Then let ψ be a valuation that satisfies $[A, B]$ we have $\|t\|_\psi = \|t'\|_\psi$ and $\|s\|_\psi = \|s'\|_\psi$, so $[\![t']\!]_\psi = [\![s']\!]_\psi$.

With what we proved earlier in this proposition (namely the left-to-right implications), we can state that either:

- $t' = 0$ and $s' = 0$, and $[A, B] \vdash t' \doteq s'$ is derived with REFL, or
- t' and s' are both syntactically positive. Let φ be a valuation with values in $\mathbb{N} \setminus \{0\}$, there exists a valuation ψ satisfying $[A, B]$ such that $[\![t']\!]_\psi = [\![t']\!]_\varphi$, and $[\![s']\!]_\psi = [\![s']\!]_\varphi$[7]. Hence t' is equal to s' in $\langle \mathbb{N}, 1, +, \times, \uparrow \rangle$, and we have a derivation of $[A, B] \vdash t' \doteq s'$ with rule E0.

Finally, to prove the right-to-left implication in (2), let us notice that it also suffices, reasoning like we just did, to prove this when Γ is exhaustive for t. In that case, proposition 1 implies that there is a term t' such that $\Gamma \vdash t \doteq t'$ and t' is syntactically positive in context Γ[8], so lemma 1 gives us a derivation of $\Gamma \vdash t'$ positive, and with rule N2 a derivation of $\Gamma \vdash t$ positive. □

Corollary 2 *Equality in $\langle \mathbb{N}, 0, 1, +, \times, \uparrow \rangle$ is decidable.*

PROOF: It is a known fact that equality in $\langle \mathbb{N}, 1, +, \times, \uparrow \rangle$ is decidable.

Let t and s be two terms of $\langle \mathbb{N}, 0, 1, +, \times, \uparrow \rangle$. Let also $\mathcal{C}$ be the following set of contexts:

$$\mathcal{C} = \{[X, \mathrm{Var}(t + s)] \mid X \subseteq \mathrm{Var}(t + s)\}$$

We contend that $\top \vdash t \doteq s$ if and only if $\forall \Gamma \in \mathcal{C}\; \Gamma \vdash t \doteq s$. This is a direct consequence of proposition 2.

By using proposition 1, we get two new terms t' and s' such that $\Gamma \vdash t \doteq s$ is equivalent to $\Gamma \vdash t' \doteq s'$. Since these new terms are either 0 or syntactically positive in context Γ, the new equality is either obviously true or false, or an equality in $\langle \mathbb{N}, 1, +, \times, \uparrow \rangle$. We have reduced deciding an equality in $\langle \mathbb{N}, 0, 1, +, \times, \uparrow \rangle$ to deciding a finite number of equalities in $\langle \mathbb{N}, 1, +, \times, \uparrow \rangle$, therefore equality in $\langle \mathbb{N}, 0, 1, +, \times, \uparrow \rangle$ is decidable. □

Conclusion Eventually, we have displayed a formal system whose derivations prove the equalities of $\langle \mathbb{N}, 0, 1, +, \times, \uparrow \rangle$, which are represented by the statement $\top \vdash t \doteq s$. This statement calls upon equality in $\langle \mathbb{N}, 1, +, \times, \uparrow \rangle$ plus rules depicting the equations: $t + 0 = t, t \times 0 = 0, t^0 = 1$ and $0^t = 0$ if $t \neq 0$.

---

special variable, and $C[t]$ stands for $C[\psi[\cdot]]$ (usual substitution). For example if $C = x + [\cdot]$ and $t = x^{1+x}$, $C[t] = x + x^{1+x}$.

[7] This is due to the fact that the variables in A can no longer occur in t' or s', since these terms are syntactically positive in context$[A, B]$.

[8] Obviously t' cannot be 0, because of (1).

4 Axioms of Equality in $\langle \mathbb{N}, 0, 1, +, \times, \uparrow \rangle$

Introduction Throughout this section (until just before theorem 7, actually) we will make the assumption that equality in $\langle \mathbb{N}, 0, 1, +, \times, \uparrow \rangle$ has a finite system of axioms, our goal being to prove the contrary.

We first need to modify the formal system ZP, replacing the equality imported from $\langle \mathbb{N}, 1, +, \times, \uparrow \rangle$ (which appeared in rule E0) with a finite set of axioms. We call ZP_{ax} this new system, which is equivalent to ZP under our finite axioms hypothesis.

We will then use our previous results, along with a few new notations, to prove that the axioms of equality in $\langle \mathbb{N}, 0, 1, +, \times, \uparrow \rangle$, once reasonably "projected" to $\langle \mathbb{N}, 1, +, \times, \uparrow \rangle$, form a finite system of axioms for equality in $\langle \mathbb{N}, 1, +, \times, \uparrow \rangle$, which is known to be impossible.

In order to realize this projection, we will evolve the system ZP_{ax} gradually, so that the derivations in ZP_{ax} will come to be transformed (also gradually) into derivations in $\langle \mathbb{N}, 1, +, \times, \uparrow \rangle$.

Definition 9 (The ZP_{ax} formal system). *The formal system we call ZP_{ax} includes the same rules as ZP, except that:*

– *A finite set of axioms $\mathcal{A}_1, \ldots, \mathcal{A}_n$ is added. These axioms are:*

$$\boxed{\mathcal{A}_i} \; \frac{}{\top \vdash l_i \doteq r_i}$$

– *Rule E0 is withdrawn.*

Definition 10 (Partial evaluation in a given context). *Given a context Γ, we define a partial function $\Gamma(t)$ for the terms t for which Γ is exhaustive.*

It is defined by structural induction on the term t, as shown in figure 4.

Proposition 3. *Let Γ be a context and t a term such that $\Gamma(t)$ is defined. We contend the following properties hold:*

1. *$\Gamma(t)$ is either 0, or a syntactically positive term (in context Γ);*
2. *If t is syntactically positive in context Γ then $\Gamma(t) = t$;*
3. *If $\Gamma(t) \neq 0$ then $\Gamma \vdash t$ positive can be derived in ZP;*
4. *$\Gamma \vdash \Gamma(t) \doteq t$ can be derived in ZP without E0;*
5. *The converse of 3. holds.*

PROOF:

1. This is trivially proved by structural induction.
2. Idem, recalling that being syntactically positive extends to sub-terms.
3. If $\Gamma(t) \neq 0$ then $\Gamma(t)$ is syntactically positive in context Γ, so that the statement $\Gamma \vdash t$ positive can be derived thanks to lemma 1.
4. This goes by structural induction on t. Let us examine further a single case. Suppose that $t = s + u$, with $\Gamma(s) \neq 0$ and $\Gamma(u) = 0$. By induction there is a derivation D of $\Gamma \vdash \Gamma(s) \doteq s$, and a derivation D' of $\Gamma \vdash 0 \doteq u$. We build the following derivation:

$$\Gamma(0) = 0 \quad \Gamma(1) = 1 \quad \Gamma(x) = \begin{cases} 0 \text{ if } \Gamma \Rightarrow x = 0 \\ x \text{ if } \Gamma \Rightarrow \neg x = 0 \end{cases}$$

$$\Gamma(t+s) = \begin{cases} \Gamma(t) & \text{if } \Gamma(s) = 0 \\ \Gamma(s) & \text{if } \Gamma(t) = 0 \\ \Gamma(t) + \Gamma(s) & \text{otherwise} \end{cases}$$

$$\Gamma(t \times s) = \begin{cases} 0 & \text{if } \Gamma(t) = 0 \text{ or } \Gamma(s) = 0 \\ \Gamma(t) \times \Gamma(s) & \text{otherwise} \end{cases}$$

$$\Gamma(t^s) = \begin{cases} 1 & \text{if } \Gamma(s) = 0 \\ 0 & \text{if } \Gamma(t) = 0 \text{ and } \Gamma(s) \neq 0 \\ \Gamma(t)^{\Gamma(s)} & \text{otherwise} \end{cases}$$

Fig. 4. Partial evaulation of terms in a context Γ

$$\dfrac{\dfrac{(D)}{\Gamma \vdash \Gamma(s) \doteq s}}{\Gamma \vdash \Gamma(s) + 0 \doteq s + 0} \quad \dfrac{(D')}{\Gamma \vdash 0 \doteq u}$$
$$\dfrac{\Gamma \vdash \Gamma(s) + 0 \doteq s + u}{\Gamma \vdash \Gamma(s) \doteq s + u}$$

The last step is actually a contraction of E2 and TRANS, written so for improved readability. Since $\Gamma(t) = \Gamma(s)$, this is the derivation we wanted. Other cases are similarly treated (let us notice, although, that when $t = s^u$ with $\Gamma(s) = 0$ and $\Gamma(u) \neq 0$, we need to summon point 3. to get a derivation of $\Gamma \vdash u$ positive).

5. This is a consequence of point 4. and proposition 2. □

Remark This shows that partial evaluation is actually an implementation of the existential result in proposition 1.

Definition 11 (The ZP_{ax}^+ formal system). *The formal system called ZP_{ax}^+ is the system ZP_{ax} to which we add the following new axioms $A_1^+, \ldots, A_n^+$:*

$$\boxed{A_i^+} \dfrac{}{\Gamma_{A_i} \vdash \Gamma_{A_i}(l_i) \doteq \Gamma_{A_i}(r_i)} \quad \text{where } \Gamma_{A_i} = [\varnothing, \text{Var}(l_i + r_i)]$$

Remark The "axioms" A_i^+ can actually be derived in the system ZP_{ax}, as proposition 3 implies that $\Gamma_{A_i} \vdash \Gamma_{A_i}(l_i) \doteq l_i$ can be derived in ZP_{ax} (mutatis mutandis r_i).

Definition 12 (Local equality statements). *The statement $\Gamma \vdash t \doteq s$ is said to be local if Γ is exhaustive for $t + s$.*

Definition 13. *We define two particular sets of rules:*

$$G_0 = \{E1, E2, E2', E3, E3', E4, \text{REFL}\}$$

$$G = G_0 \cup \{A_1, \ldots, A_n\}$$

Definition 14 ("L" property). *A derivation D in ZP_{ax} will be said to have the property "L" (or to be an **L**-derivation), if the following properties hold:*

L1 *The conclusion of D is $\Delta \vdash t \doteq s$, and this statement is local.*
L2 *Any statement $\Gamma \vdash t' \doteq s'$ occurring in D has one of the following qualities:*
  - *$\Gamma = \top$ or $\Gamma = (x = 0)$ and this statement follows immediately a rule in G, or*
  - *$\Gamma = \Delta$ (as in **L1**), and this statement is local.*
L3 *No rule E7 occurs in D.*
L4 *Rule E6 only occurs in D where it follows immediately a rule $R \in G$.*

*Conditions **L2** to **L4** are lifted for any part of the derivation "above" an occurrence of rule E5.*

Remark The caution of this last sentence is justified by the possibility of equality statements to appear above an E5, because of rule N2. Practically, in the following proofs by structural induction on derivations, we will never use induction hypotheses when said derivation ends with an E5.

Definition 15 ("EL" property). *Let $G' = G_0 \cup \{\mathcal{A}_1^+, \ldots, \mathcal{A}_n^+\}$. A derivation in ZP_{ax}^+ will be said to have the property "**EL**" (or to be an **EL**-derivation) if it has the properties **L1** to **L4**, where G is replaced with G' in **L2** and **L4**, and the following two extra properties:*

EL1 *No original axiom $\mathcal{A}_i$ occurs in D.*
EL2 *For any statement $\Gamma \vdash t \doteq s$ in D such that $\Gamma(t)$ and $\Gamma(s)$ are defined, $\Gamma(t) = t$ and $\Gamma(s) = s$.*

We now contend that certain derivations (namely those made in contexts where all variables are positive) can be transformed into **L**-derivations, and then into **EL**-derivations, which is the topic of the three next lemmas.

The first of this three lemmas is a plain technicality pertaining to **L**-derivations.

Lemma 3 *Let D be an **L**-derivation of $\Delta \vdash t \doteq s$. Let also A and B be two finite sets of variables that do not occur in Δ. There exists an **L**-derivation of $\Delta \wedge [A, B] \vdash t \doteq s$.*

PROOF: This is actually quite obvious. All that is needed is to replace Δ with $\Delta \wedge [A, B]$ everywhere[9]. It will also be necessary to insert an N6 between the premise and conclusion of any E5. Also, in the (supposedly rare) situation where $\Delta = \top$, it will be necessary to insert an E6 after any rule $R \in G$. □

Lemma 4 *Let D be a derivation of $\Gamma \vdash t \doteq s$ in ZP_{ax} and Δ a context that is exhaustive for t and s, and such that $\Delta \Rightarrow \Gamma$ holds.*

*There exists a context $\Delta' = [\varnothing, A]$ (where the variables in A do not occur in Δ) and an **L**-derivation of $\Delta \wedge \Delta' \vdash t \doteq s$.*

---
[9] Again, this need not apply to any part of the derivation above an E5.

Remark Since no hypothesis but finiteness is made about A we can safely ignore the case $\Delta = \top$, thanks to lemma 3.

PROOF: We proceed by structural induction on D, and distinguish cases according to the last rule used in this derivation. See appendix A.4. □

Lemma 5 *If $[\varnothing, \mathrm{Var}(t+s)] \vdash t \doteq s$ can be derived in ZP_{ax}, and if no 0 appears in either t or s, there exists a finite set of variables A (whose elements do not occur in $t+s$) and an **EL**-derivation of $\Delta' \vdash \Delta'(t) \doteq \Delta'(s)$ in ZP_{ax}^+, where $\Delta' = [\varnothing, \mathrm{Var}(t+s)] \wedge [\varnothing, A]$.*

PROOF: Proposition 4 yields us an **L**-derivation, call it D, of the statement $\Delta' \vdash t \doteq s$. The **EL**-derivation will be built by structural induction from D. Again we distinguish cases according to the last rule used in D, keeping in mind some structural properties about **L**-derivations. This is done in appendix A.5. □

We will now introduce a last evolution of our formal system before actually going to equality in $\langle \mathbb{N}, 1, +, \times, \uparrow \rangle$.

Definition 16 (The P_{ax} formal system). *P_{ax} is a sub-system of ZP_{ax}^+ which includes the following rules:*

- the axioms $\mathcal{A}_1^+, \ldots, \mathcal{A}_n^+$,
- REFL, SYM, TRANS, CONT,
- E6.

Remarque Clearly any statement which can be derived in P_{ax} can also be derived in ZP_{ax}.

Corollary 6 *With the same hypotheses and notations as in lemma 5, there is a derivation of $[\varnothing, \mathrm{Var}(t+s)] \wedge [\varnothing, A] \vdash t \doteq s$ in P_{ax}. Moreover, no 0 occurs in the terms of this derivation at all.*

PROOF: Clearly the **EL**-derivation granted by lemma 5 is actually a derivation in P_{ax}. The terms of its conclusion have no zeros, and we will prove that if a rule in an **EL**-derivation has no 0 in its conclusion, it can have none in its premise(s).

$\mathcal{A}_i^+$, **REFL** Those rules have no premises.
SYM, CONT, E6 The terms in the premise are the same as (or subterms of) those in the conclusion.
TRANS A new term can appear in the premise, but since it is partially evaluated it is either syntactically positive or 0. But since it is derived to be equal to the terms of the conclusion, and since these are syntactically positive, the "new" term must also be syntactically positive. □

Theorem 7. *The equational therory of $\langle \mathbb{N}, 0, 1, +, \times, \uparrow \rangle$ cannot derive from a finite set of axioms.*

PROOF: As we said before, we reason *ad absurdum*. Let us then assume that such a finite set of axioms $\{\mathcal{A}_i\}_{i \in \{1,\ldots,n\}}$ exists.

Let us also consider Th the equational theory of $\langle \mathbb{N}, 1, +, \times, \uparrow \rangle$ with the axioms $\{\mathcal{A}_i^+\}_{i \in \{1,\ldots,n\}}$ (as defined previously). Since these axioms are true in ZP_{ax} (which is by hypothesis equivalent to ZP), they are true in $\langle \mathbb{N}, 1, +, \times, \uparrow \rangle$ (see proposition 2). So Th only proves equalities that are true in $\langle \mathbb{N}, 1, +, \times, \uparrow \rangle$.

Let now t and s be two terms that are equal in $\langle \mathbb{N}, 1, +, \times, \uparrow \rangle$. They support the hypotheses of lemma 5, since $[\varnothing, \text{Var}(t+s)] \vdash t \doteq s$ can be derived in ZP (using E0), thus in ZP_{ax}.

Corollary 6 then yields a derivation of $\Delta \vdash t \doteq s$ in P_{ax}, which contains no 0 in its terms.

If contexts are removed from this derivation, the E6 rules can be stripped as well (they become empty transitions), and we get a derivation in a formal system with $\{\mathcal{A}_i^+\}_{i \in \{1,\ldots,n\}}$ as axioms, and the usual transitivity, symmetry, reflexivity and context rules, which is equivalent to Th

Therefore any equality in $\langle \mathbb{N}, 1, +, \times, \uparrow \rangle$ can be derived in Th. Since it is known that equality in $\langle \mathbb{N}, 1, +, \times, \uparrow \rangle$ cannot derive from any finite set of axioms, we have a contradiction. □

5 Conclusions

We have proved that $\langle \mathbb{N}, 0, 1, +, \times, \uparrow \rangle$ has a decidable, but not finitely axiomatisable, equational theory, and clearly shown that the only difference between $\langle \mathbb{N}, 0, 1, +, \times, \uparrow \rangle$ and $\langle \mathbb{N}, 1, +, \times, \uparrow \rangle$ is given by the system $\mathcal{Z}$ in figure 2.

As a consequence, the family of Gurevič's equalities does not collapse, and we also obtain the following additional result

Theorem 8. *The theory of type isomorphisms in Bi-Cartesian Closed Categories is not finitely axiomatisable*

that closes the long standing open problem of the finite axiomatisability of type isomorphisms for the lambda calculus with sums and the empty types [DC95].

By using the decidability result for $\langle \mathbb{N}, 0, 1, +, \times, \uparrow \rangle$ and the fact that all isomorphisms are equalities, we can reject all non-isomorphisms that are also non-arithmetical identities, but, due to the fact that some arithmetic identities are not isomorphisms of BiCCCs, it is left open whether such isomorphisms are indeed decidable.

Acknowledgements The first author would like to thank Claude Kirchner, Vincent Balat and Christophe Calves for interesting discussions on these subjects.

References

BDCF02. Vincent Balat, Roberto Di Cosmo, and Marcelo Fiore. Remarks on isomorphisms in typed lambda calculi with empty and sum type. In *LICS*. IEEE, July 2002.

BDCF04. Vincent Balat, Roberto Di Cosmo, and Marcelo Fiore. Extensional normalisation and type-directed partial evaluation for typed lamda calculus with sums. In *31st Ann. ACM Symp. on Principles of Programming Languages (POPL)*, pages 64–76. ACM, 2004.

DC95. Roberto Di Cosmo. *Isomorphisms of types: from λ-calculus to information retrieval and language design*. Birkhauser, 1995.

DP97. Kosta Dosen and Zoran Petric. Isomorphic objects in symmetric monoidal closed categories. *Mathematical Structures in Computer Science*, 7(6):639–662, 1997.

DT69. J. Doner and Alfred Tarski. An extended arithmetic of ordinal numbers. *Fundamenta Mathematica*, 65:95–127, 1969.

Gur85. R. Gurevič. Equational theory of positive numbers with exponentiation. *Proceedings of the American Mathematical Society*, 94(1):135–141, 1985.

Gur90. R. Gurevič. Equational theory of positive numbers with exponentiation is not finitely axiomatizable. *Annals of Pure and Applied Logic*, 49:1–30, 1990.

Hen77. Leon Henkin. The logic of equality. *American Mathematical Monthly*, 84:597–612, October 1977.

HR84. C. W. Henson and L. A. Rubel. Some applications of Nevanlinna theory to mathematical logic: Identities of exponential functions. *Trans. Am. Math. Soc.*, 282(1):1–32, March 1984.

Mac81. A. Macintyre. The laws of exponentiation. In C. Berline, K. McAloon, and J.-P. Ressayre, editors, *Model Theory and Arithmetic*, volume 890 of *Lecture Notes in Mathematics*, pages 185–197. Springer-Verlag, 1981.

Mar72. Charles F. Martin. Axiomatic bases for equational theories of natural numbers. *Notices of the Am. Math. Soc.*, 19(7):778, 1972.

Rit90. Mikael Rittri. *Searching program libraries by type and proving compiler correctness by bisimulation*. PhD thesis, University of Göteborg, Göteborg, Sweden, 1990.

Rog88. Hartley Rogers, Jr. *Theory of Recursive Functions and Effective Computability*. The MIT Press, Cambridge, Massachusetts; London, England, second edition, 1988.

Sol93. Sergei V. Soloviev. A complete axiom system for isomorphism of types in closed categories. In A. Voronkov, editor, *Logic Programming and Automated Reasoning, 4th International Conference*, volume 698 of *Lecture Notes in Artificial Intelligence (subseries of LNCS)*, pages 360–371, St. Petersburg, Russia, 1993. Springer-Verlag.

Wil81. A. J. Wilkie. On exponentiation — A solution to Tarski's high school algebra problem. Math. Inst. Oxford University (preprint), 1981.

ZGC03. Yoav Zibin, Joseph (Yossi) Gil, and Jeffrey Considine. Efficient algorithms for isomorphisms of simple types. In *Proceedings of the 30th ACM SIGPLAN-SIGACT symposium on Principles of programming languages*, pages 160–171. ACM Press, 2003.

A Appendix

A.1 Proof of Proposition 1

Let $H(t) = \#_0(t) + 2 \times \sum_{x/\Gamma \Rightarrow x=0} \#_x(t)$, where $\#_s(t)$ is the number of times s occurs in t. We proceed by induction in lexicographical order on $(S(t), H(t))$ where $S(t)$ is the size of t^{10}.

If $H(t) = 0$ or $t = 0$, taking $t' = t$ is OK.

Otherwise, i.e. if $t \neq 0$ and $H(t) > 0$, t matches one of the following patterns:

---

[10] This is the size in the usual meaning: the number of nodes in the syntax tree of t.

1. $C[0 \times s]$ or $C[s \times 0]$,
2. $C[0 + s]$ or $C[s + 0]$,
3. $C[s^0]$,
4. $C[x]$ where $\Gamma \Rightarrow x = 0$,
5. $C[0^s]$ where s is syntactically positive.

($C[\cdot]$ denotes a context with only one placeholder.)

1. The induction hypothesis yields a derivation D of $\Gamma \vdash C[0] \doteq t'$ where t' is 0 or syntactically positive, hence the following derivation:

$$\cfrac{\cfrac{\cfrac{\overline{\top \vdash s \times 0 \doteq 0}}{\Gamma \vdash s \times 0 \doteq 0}}{\Gamma \vdash t \doteq C[0]} \quad \cfrac{(D)}{\Gamma \vdash C[0] \doteq t'}}{\Gamma \vdash t \doteq t'}$$

   We proceed similarly when $t = C[0 \times s]$, using the rule E3' instead of E3.

2. The induction hypothesis again yields a derivation D of $\Gamma \vdash C[s] \doteq t'$ where t' is 0 or syntactically positive, and we build the following derivation.

$$\cfrac{\cfrac{\cfrac{\overline{\top \vdash s + 0 \doteq s}}{\Gamma \vdash s + 0 \doteq s}}{\Gamma \vdash t \doteq C[s]} \quad \cfrac{(D)}{\Gamma \vdash C[s] \doteq t'}}{\Gamma \vdash t \doteq t'}$$

   We proceed similarly when $t = C[0 + s]$, using the rule E2' instead of E2.

3. By induction there is a derivation D of $\Gamma \vdash C[1] \doteq t'$ with a suitable t', and we derive:

$$\cfrac{\cfrac{\cfrac{\overline{\top \vdash s^0 \doteq 1}}{\Gamma \vdash s^0 \doteq 1}}{\Gamma \vdash t \doteq C[1]} \quad \cfrac{(D)}{\Gamma \vdash C[1] \doteq t'}}{\Gamma \vdash t \doteq t'}$$

4. By induction there is a derivation D of $\Gamma \vdash C[0] \doteq t'$ with a suitable t', and we derive:

$$\cfrac{\cfrac{\cfrac{\overline{x = 0 \vdash x \doteq 0}}{\Gamma \vdash x \doteq 0}}{\Gamma \vdash t \doteq C[0]} \quad \cfrac{(D)}{\Gamma \vdash C[0] \doteq t'}}{\Gamma \vdash t \doteq t'}$$

5. By induction there is a derivation D of $\Gamma \vdash C[0] \doteq t'$ with a suitable t', and we derive:

$$\cfrac{\cfrac{\cfrac{(D')}{\Gamma \vdash s \text{ positive}}}{\cfrac{\Gamma \vdash 0^s \doteq 0}{\Gamma \vdash t \doteq C[0]}} \quad \cfrac{(D)}{\Gamma \vdash C[0] \doteq t'}}{\Gamma \vdash t \doteq t'}$$

   Here, we will need the lemma 1 pertaining to the relationship between the "$\Gamma \vdash t$ positive" statement and being syntactically positive, in order to provide the derivation D'.

A.2 Proof of Proposition 2 (1)

Depending on the last rule used in this derivation, we have:

REFL, E1 to E4 These are trivial cases.
SYM, TRANS, CONT, E5 These are also obvious, using the induction hypothesis.
E0 Thanks to the (↑) condition, $\forall \psi$ such that $\forall x\ \psi(x) \neq 0$, $[\![t]\!]_\varphi = [\![o]\!]_\psi$.
  Let ψ be a valuation satisfying Γ; since t and s are syntactically positive in context Γ, necessarily $\forall x \in \text{Var}(t+s)\ \psi(x) \neq 0$, and there exists a valuation φ as above such that $[\![t]\!]_\varphi = [\![t]\!]_\psi$, and $[\![s]\!]_\varphi = [\![s]\!]_\psi$. Thus $[\![t]\!]_\psi = [\![s]\!]_\psi$ holds.
E6 By induction : $\forall \varphi$ satisfying Γ, $[\![t]\!]_\varphi = [\![s]\!]_\varphi$. Since $\Delta \Rightarrow \Gamma$ it is clear that any valuation φ satisfying Δ also satisfies Γ, hence $\forall \varphi$ satisfying Δ, $[\![t]\!]_\varphi = [\![s]\!]_\varphi$.
E7 As well as with E6, any valuation φ satisfying $\Gamma \vee \Delta$ satisfies either Γ or Δ.
N0 and N1 Are also trivial cases.
N2 to N5 The induction hypothesis obviously allows to conclude.
N6 This case is treated like E6.
N7 Like E7.

A.3 Proof of Proposition 2 (2)

We let Γ be such that $\forall \varphi$ satisfying Γ, $[\![t]\!]_\varphi = [\![s]\!]_\varphi$.

Fact 1 Γ has a logically equivalent form that is written

$$([A_1, B] \wedge \Delta_1) \vee \cdots \vee ([A_n, B] \wedge \Delta_n)$$

where

- $B = \text{Var}(t+s)$,
- $\forall i\ A_i \subset B$,
- $\forall i\ \Delta_i$ is a $\wedge$-formula in which no variable in $\text{Var}(t+s)$ appears.

To draft a proof, let us say that one needs to put Γ in a normal disjunctive form, call it Γ', which is in turn equivalent to $\Gamma' \wedge \bigwedge_{x \in \text{Var}(t+s)}(x = 0 \vee \neg x = 0)$. What remains to be done is distributing this expression, taking out the antilogic conjunctive clauses, and grouping the atoms in each clause.

Fact 2 $\forall \psi$ satisfying $[A_i, B]$, there is a φ satisfying $[A_i, B] \wedge \Delta_i$ (thus satisfying Γ), such that $[\![t]\!]_\psi = [\![t]\!]_\varphi$, and $[\![s]\!]_\psi = [\![s]\!]_\varphi$.
  All that is needed is to "change the values of ψ so that it satisfies Δ_i", which can assuredly be done without modifying the value of $\psi(x)$ for any $x \in \text{Var}(t+s)$.

Fact 3 $(\forall \varphi$ satisfying $\Gamma\ [\![t]\!]_\varphi = [\![s]\!]_\varphi) \Rightarrow \forall i\ (\forall \psi$ satisfying $[A_i, B]\ [\![t]\!]_\psi = [\![s]\!]_\psi)$
  This is obvious thanks to fact 2.

Fact 4 $(\forall i\ [A_i, B] \vdash t \doteq s) \Rightarrow \Gamma \vdash t \doteq s$.
  One needs only use rules E6 (to bring in the Δ_is) and E7.

A.4 Proof of Lemma 4

R ∈ G Follow with an E6, with Δ as new context.
E5 Insert an N6 with Δ as new context between the premise and conclusion of this E5.
E6 D has the following form :

$$\frac{\dfrac{(D')}{\Gamma' \vdash t \doteq s}}{\Gamma \vdash t \doteq s}$$

where $\Gamma \Rightarrow \Gamma'$. Thus $\Delta \Rightarrow \Gamma'$ and the induction hypothesis applies to the derivation of $\Gamma' \vdash t \doteq s$, yielding the wanted **L**-derivation.
E7 D has the following form :

$$\frac{\dfrac{(D')}{\Gamma' \vdash t \doteq s} \quad \dfrac{(D'')}{\Gamma'' \vdash t \doteq s}}{\Gamma' \vee \Gamma'' \vdash t \doteq s}$$

Since Δ is exhaustive for t and s, it is a $\wedge$-formula and either $\Delta \Rightarrow \Gamma'$ or $\Delta \Rightarrow \Gamma''$ holds. If for example , $\Delta \Rightarrow \Gamma'$ holds, the induction hypothesis can be applied to the derivation of $\Gamma' \vdash t \doteq s$, yielding the wanted **L**-derivation.
SYM, CONT Trivial.
TRANS By induction hypothesis we have **L**-derivations of $\Delta \wedge \Delta_0 \vdash t \doteq s$ and $\Delta \wedge \Delta_1 \vdash s \doteq u$. By letting $\Delta' = \Delta_0 \wedge \Delta_1$, and summoning lemma 3 we get **L**-derivations of $\Delta \wedge \Delta' \vdash t \doteq s$ and $\Delta \wedge \Delta' \vdash s \doteq u$. All that is left is to apply TRANS again.

A.5 Proof of Lemma 5

$\mathcal{A}_i$ **followed by E6** Use $\mathcal{A}_i^+$, then E6.
R ∈ G_0 followed by E6 For any rule in G_0, when its conclusion is written $\Gamma \vdash l \doteq r$ we have $\Delta' \Rightarrow \Gamma$ (see **L2**, **L4**), and $\Delta'(l) = \Delta'(r)$ (checking this is easy). The **EL**-derivation we want is a suitable use of REFL followed by E6.
E5 Idem.
SYM Immediate induction step.
CONT In this case, the **L**-derivation (D) looks like this:

$$\frac{\dfrac{(D')}{\Delta' \vdash t \doteq s}}{\Delta' \vdash C[t] \doteq C[s]}$$

By induction we have an **EL**-derivation of $\Delta' \vdash \Delta'(t) \doteq \Delta'(s)$, and one of two things happens:
- Either $\Delta'(t) = \Delta'(s) = 0$, and $\Delta'(C[t]) = \Delta'(C[s])$ – both are $\Delta'(C[0])$, which can be derived by REFL + E6.
- Or $\Delta'(t)$ and $\Delta'(s)$ are syntactically positive in context Δ', and $\Delta'(C[t]) = \Delta'(C[\cdot])[\Delta'(t)]$ (*mutatis mutandis s*). So we just have to apply CONT again, with context $\Delta'(C[\cdot])$, to get the desired **EL**-derivation.

TRANS As SYM, relying on **L2** to summon the induction hypothesis.

Properties **L1** to **L4** are clearly preserved, **EL0** clearly holds, and **EL1** as well since $\Gamma(\Gamma(t)) = \Gamma(t)$ whenever $\Gamma(t)$ is defined.

A Trichotomy in the Complexity of Propositional Circumscription

Gustav Nordh*

Department of Computer and Information Science
Linköpings Universitet
S-581 83 Linköping, Sweden
gusno@ida.liu.se

Abstract. Circumscription is one of the most important and well studied formalisms in the realm of nonmonotonic reasoning. The inference problem for propositional circumscription has been extensively studied from the viewpoint of computational complexity. We prove that there exists a trichotomy for the complexity of the inference problem in propositional variable circumscription. More specifically we prove that every restricted case of the problem is either Π_2^P-complete, coNP-complete, or in P.

1 Introduction

Circumscription, introduced by McCarthy [13], is perhaps the most well developed and extensively studied formalism in nonmonotonic reasoning. The key intuition behind circumscription is that by focusing on minimal models of formulas we achieve some degree of common sense, because minimal models have as few "exceptions" as possible.

Propositional circumscription is the basic case of circumscription in which satisfying truth assignments of propositional formulas are partially ordered according to the coordinatewise partial order $\leq$ on Boolean vectors, which extends the order $0 \leq 1$ on $\{0, 1\}$. In propositional variable circumscription only a certain subset of the variables in formulas are subject to minimization, others must maintain a fixed value or are subject to no restrictions at all. Given a propositional formula T and a partition of the variables in T into three (possibly empty) disjoint subsets $(P; Z; Q)$ where P is the set of variables we want to minimize, Z is the set of variables allowed to vary and Q is the set of variables that must maintain a fixed value, we define the partial order on satisfying models as follows. Let α, β be two models of T, then $\alpha \leq_{(P;Z)} \beta$ if α and β assign the same value to the variables in Q and for every variable p in P, $\alpha(p) \leq \beta(p)$ (moreover if there exists a variable p in P such that $\alpha(p) \neq \beta(p)$, we write $\alpha <_{(P;Z)} \beta$). A minimal model of a formula T is a satisfying model α such that there exists no satisfying model β where $\beta <_{(P;Z)} \alpha$.

---

* Supported by the *National Graduate School in Computer Science* (CUGS), Sweden.

We will from now on call the restricted form of propositional circumscription where all variables are subject to minimization (that is $Q = Z = \emptyset$) for basic circumscription, and the more general propositional variable circumscription for propositional circumscription.

Every logical formalism gives rise to the fundamental problem of inference. In the case of propositional circumscription the inference problem can be formulated as follows.

- **Inference:** Given two propositional Boolean formulas T and T' and a partition of the variables in T into three disjoint (possibly empty) subsets $(P; Z; Q)$, is T' true in every minimal model of T.

The formulas T and T' are assumed to be given in conjunctive normal form. It is easy to realize that the inference problem is equivalent (under polynomial-time conjunctive reductions) to the case where T' is a single clause, since T' can be inferred from T under propositional circumscription if and only if each clause of T' can be so inferred. Moreover we follow the approach in [10,11,14] where the clauses of T are allowed to be arbitrary logical relations (sometimes called generalized clauses). This approach was first used by Schaefer to classify the complexity of the satisfiability problem in propositional logic and is sometimes referred to as Schaefer's framework [18].

Circumscription in propositional logic is very well studied from the computational complexity perspective [2,4,7,8,10,11,14]. The inference problem for propositional circumscription has been proved to be Π_2^P-complete [8]. This result displays a dramatic increase in the computational complexity compared to the case of ordinary propositional logic, where the inference problem is coNP-complete [3]. This negative result raise the problem of identifying restricted cases in which the inference problem for propositional circumscription have computational complexity lower than the general case.

The most natural way to study such restrictions is to study restrictions on the formulas representing knowledge bases, denoted T in above. This is also the approach followed in most of the previous research in the area. Hence in the case of restrictions of the inference problem, we only restrict the formula T while T' are subject to no restrictions. The ultimate goal of this line of research is to determine the complexity of every restricted special case of the problem. The first result of this type was proved by Schaefer [18], who succeeded in obtaining a complete classification of the satisfiability problem in propositional logic. He proved that every special case of the satisfiability problem in propositional logic either is tractable or NP-complete (note that this implies that the inference problem in propositional logic is either tractable or coNP-complete). Recall the result due to Ladner [12] that if $P \neq NP$, then there exist decision problems in NP that are neither tractable nor NP-complete. Hence the existence of dichotomy theorems like Schaefer's can not be taken for granted.

Some partial results are known for the complexity of the inference problem. More specifically, both in the general case and in the case where $Q = Z = \emptyset$, it has been proved that every special case of the problem is either Π_2^P-complete or lies in coNP [10,14].

Until now we have lacked a clear picture of the complexity of the inference problem in propositional circumscription, i.e., no complete classification of special cases of the problem with a complexity in coNP as coNP-complete or in P is known. Some cases are known to be coNP-complete, but to the best of our knowledge only one case of the inference problem (where Q and Z need not be empty) is known to be in P [?].

We prove that there exists a trichotomy theorem for the complexity of the inference problem, i.e., for every special case of the problem it is either in P, coNP-complete, or Π_2^P-complete. Moreover we discover two new tractable cases. These results are obtained by the use of techniques from universal algebra. These techniques were first applied to the propositional circumscription problem in [14] where dichotomies for the model checking and inference problem for propositional circumscription in 3-valued logic were proved.

Although basic circumscription (where $Q = Z = \emptyset$) is a restricted case of the problem we study, our trichotomy does not imply a trichotomy for basic circumscription. This is because our hardness results do not in general carry over to the restricted case where $Q = Z = \emptyset$. Hence the existence of a trichotomy for the inference problem in basic propositional circumscription is still open.

The paper is organized as follows. In Section 2 we give the necessary background on Constraint Satisfaction Problems (CSPs) and the algebraic techniques that we will use throughout this paper. In Section 3 we prove our trichotomy theorem for the complexity of circumscription in propositional logic and finally in Section 4 we give some conclusions.

2 Preliminaries

In this section we introduce the notation and basic results on CSPs and the algebraic techniques that we will use in the rest of this paper.

2.1 Constraint Satisfaction Problems

The set of all n-tuples of elements from $\{0,1\}$ is denoted by $\{0,1\}^n$. Any subset of $\{0,1\}^n$ is called an n-ary relation on $\{0,1\}$. The set of all finitary relations over $\{0,1\}$ is denoted by BR.

Definition 1. *A constraint language over $\{0,1\}$ is an arbitrary set $\Gamma \subseteq BR$.*

Constraint languages are the way in which we specify restrictions on our problems. For example in the case of the inference problem for propositional circumscription over the constraint language Γ, we demand that all the relations in the knowledge base are present in Γ.

Definition 2. *The Boolean constraint satisfaction problem (or the generalized satisfiability problem as Schaefer called it) over the constraint language $\Gamma \subseteq BR$, denoted $\text{CSP}(\Gamma)$, is defined to be the decision problem with instance (V, C), where*

- *V is a set of variables, and*

- C is a set of constraints $\{C_1, \ldots, C_q\}$, in which each constraint C_i is a pair (s_i, ϱ_i) with s_i a list of variables of length m_i, called the constraint scope, and ϱ_i an m_i-ary relation over the set $\{0,1\}$, belonging to Γ, called the constraint relation.

The question is whether there exists a solution to (V, C), that is, a function from V to $\{0, 1\}$ such that, for each constraint in C, the image of the constraint scope is a member of the constraint relation.

Example 1. Let NAE be the following ternary relation on $\{0, 1\}$:

$$NAE = \{0,1\}^3 \setminus \{(0,0,0), (1,1,1)\}.$$

It is easy to see that the well known NP-complete problem NOT-ALL-EQUAL 3-SAT can be expressed as CSP($\{NAE\}$).

Next we consider operations on $\{0, 1\}$. Any operation on $\{0, 1\}$ can be extended in a standard way to an operation on tuples over $\{0, 1\}$, as follows.

Definition 3. *Let f be a k-ary operation on $\{0, 1\}$ and let R be an n-ary relation over $\{0, 1\}$. For any collection of k tuples, $t_1, t_2, \ldots, t_k \in R$, the n-tuple $f(t_1, t_2, \ldots, t_k)$ is defined as follows: $f(t_1, t_2, \ldots, t_k) = (f(t_1[1], t_2[1], \ldots, t_k[1]), f(t_1[2], t_2[2], \ldots, t_k[2]), \ldots, f(t_1[n], t_2[n], \ldots, t_k[n]))$, where $t_j[i]$ is the i-th component in tuple t_j.*

A technique that has shown to be useful in determining the computational complexity of CSP(Γ) is that of investigating whether Γ is closed under certain families of operations [9].

Definition 4. *Let $\varrho_i \in \Gamma$. If f is an operation such that for all $t_1, t_2, \ldots, t_k \in \varrho_i$ $f(t_1, t_2, \ldots, t_k) \in \varrho_i$, then ϱ_i is closed under f. If all constraint relations in Γ are closed under f then Γ is closed under f. An operation f such that Γ is closed under f is called a polymorphism of Γ. The set of all polymorphisms of Γ is denoted Pol(Γ). Given a set of operations F, the set of all relations that is closed under all the operations in F is denoted Inv(F).*

Definition 5. *For any set $\Gamma \subseteq BR$ the set $\langle \Gamma \rangle$ consists of all relations that can be expressed using relations from $\Gamma \cup \{=\}$ ($=$ is the equality relation on $\{0, 1\}$), conjunction, and existential quantification.*

Intuitively, constraints using relations from $\langle \Gamma \rangle$ are exactly those which can be simulated by constraints using relations from Γ. The sets of relations of the form $\langle \Gamma \rangle$ are referred to as relational clones, or co-clones. An alternative characterization of relational clones is given in the following theorem.

Theorem 1 ([17]). *For every set $\Gamma \subseteq BR$, $\langle \Gamma \rangle = Inv(Pol(\Gamma))$.*

The first dichotomy theorem for a broad class of decision problems was Schaefer's dichotomy theorem for the complexity of the satisfiability problem in propositional logic [18]. Schaefer's result has later been given a much shorter and simplified proof using the algebraic techniques that we will later apply to the inference problem for propositional circumscription. Schaefer's result can be formulated in algebraic terms as follows.

Theorem 2 ([9]). *Let $\Gamma \subset BR$ be a constraint language. CSP(Γ) is NP-complete if Pol(Γ) only contains essentially unary operations, and tractable otherwise. Note that an operation f is essentially unary if and only if $f(d_1, \ldots, d_n) = g(d_i)$ for some non constant unary operation g, and any $d_1, \ldots, d_n \in \{0, 1\}$.*

As we will see later, constraint languages containing the relations $\{(0)\}$ and $\{(1)\}$ will be of particular importance to us.

Definition 6. *Given a constraint language Γ, the idempotent constraint language corresponding to Γ is $\Gamma \cup \{\{(0)\}, \{(1)\}\}$ which is denoted by Γ^{id}.*

2.2 Propositional Circumscription

In this section we make some formal definitions and recall some of the results from [14]. Note that the focus of [14] is on propositional circumscription in many-valued logics, and as a consequence the clause to be inferred is allowed to be a general constraint. Since we only consider circumscription in Boolean logic in this paper, this generalization is no longer necessary and in order to comply with the definitions of the problem in [2,10] we require that the clause to be inferred is an ordinary clause. The results from [14] still holds.

First we introduce the minimal constraint inference problem. It should be clear that this problem is equivalent to the inference problem for propositional circumscription.

Definition 7. *The minimal constraint inference problem over the constraint language $\Gamma \subseteq BR$, denoted MIN-INF-CSP(Γ), is defined to be the decision problem with instance (V, P, Z, Q, C, ψ), where $(P; Z; Q)$ is a partition of V into disjoint (possibly empty) subsets and*

- *V is a set of variables,*
- *P represents the variables to minimize,*
- *Z represents the variables that vary,*
- *Q represents the variables that are fixed,*
- *C is a set of constraints $\{C_1, \ldots, C_q\}$ in which each constraint C_i is a pair (s_i, ϱ_i) with s_i a list of variables of length m_i, called the constraint scope, and ϱ_i an m_i-ary relation over the set $\{0, 1\}$, belonging to Γ, called the constraint relation, and*
- *ψ is a clause such that the set of variables in ψ is a subset of V.*

The question is whether each minimal model α of (V, P, Z, Q, C) is also a model of ψ.

The size of a problem instance of MIN-INF-CSP(Γ) is the length of the encoding of all tuples in all the constraints in C.

We define formally what we mean when we say that a certain special case of a problem is tractable or complete for certain complexity class.

Definition 8. *The problem* MIN-INF-CSP(Γ) *is called tractable if for any finite* $\Gamma' \subseteq \Gamma$ *the problem* MIN-INF-CSP(Γ') *is solvable in polynomial time. The problem* MIN-INF-CSP(Γ) *is called C-complete (for a complexity class C) if* MIN-INF-CSP(Γ') *is C-hard for a certain finite* $\Gamma' \subseteq \Gamma$, *and* MIN-INF-CSP$(\Gamma) \in C$.

The following theorem forms the basis of the algebraic approach to determine the complexity of the inference problem for circumscription in propositional logic. It states that when investigating the complexity of MIN-INF-CSP(Γ) it is sufficient to consider constraint languages that are relational clones.

Theorem 3 ([14]). MIN-INF-CSP(Γ) *is in P (coNP-complete, Π_2^P-complete) if and only if* MIN-INF-CSP$(\langle\Gamma\rangle)$ *is in P (coNP-complete, Π_2^P-complete).*

Proof. Since $\Gamma \subseteq \langle\Gamma\rangle$, any instance of MIN-INF-CSP(Γ) is also an instance of MIN-INF-CSP$(\langle\Gamma\rangle)$. So MIN-INF-CSP$(\langle\Gamma\rangle)$ is at least as hard as MIN-INF-CSP(Γ).

To prove the converse, i.e., that MIN-INF-CSP(Γ) is at least as hard as MIN-INF-CSP$(\langle\Gamma\rangle)$, take a finite set $\Gamma_0 \subseteq \langle\Gamma\rangle$ and an instance $S = (V, P, Z, Q, C, \psi)$ of MIN-INF-CSP(Γ_0). We transform S into an equivalent instance $S' = (V', P', Z', Q', C', \psi')$ of MIN-INF-CSP(Γ_1), where Γ_1 is a finite subset of Γ.

For every constraint $C = ((v_1, \ldots, v_m), \varrho)$ in S, ϱ can be represented on the form $\varrho(v_1, \ldots, v_m) =$

$$\exists v_{m+1}, \ldots, \exists v_n\, \varrho_1(v_{11}, \ldots, v_{1n_1}) \wedge \ldots \wedge \varrho_k(v_{k1}, \ldots, v_{kn_k})$$

where $\varrho_1, \ldots, \varrho_k \in \Gamma \cup \{=\}$, $v_{m+1}, \ldots, v_n$ are new variables not previously present in S, and $v_{11}, \ldots, v_{1n_1}, v_{21}, \ldots, v_{kn_k} \in \{v_1, \ldots, v_n\}$. Replace the constraint C with the constraints $((v_{11}, \ldots, v_{1n_1}), \varrho_1), \ldots, ((v_{k1}, \ldots, v_{kn_k}), \varrho_k)$. Add $v_{m+1}, \ldots, v_n$ to V and Z. If we repeat the same reduction for every constraint in C it results in an equivalent instance $S'' = (V'', P, Z'', Q, C''', \psi)$ of MIN-INF-CSP$(\Gamma_1 \cup \{=\})$.

For each equality constraint $((v_i, v_j), =)$ in S'' we do the following:

- If both v_i and v_j are in P (Z'', Q) we remove v_i from P (Z'', Q) and V'', replace all occurrences of v_i in C''' and ψ by v_j.
- If v_j is in Q and v_i is in P we remove v_i from P and V'', replace all occurrences of v_i in C''' and ψ by v_j. The case where v_j is in P and v_i is in Q is handled in the same way.
- The case that remains is when one of v_i and v_j is in Z'', assume without loss of generality that v_i is in Z''. We remove v_i from Z'' and V'', replace all occurrences of v_i in C''' and ψ by v_j.

Finally remove $((v_i, v_j), =)$ from C'''.

The resulting instance $S' = (V', P', Z', Q', C', \psi')$ of MIN-INF-CSP(Γ_1) is equivalent to S and has been obtained in polynomial time. Hence MIN-INF-CSP(Γ) is in P (coNP-complete, Π_2^P-complete) if and only if MIN-INF-CSP$(\langle\Gamma\rangle)$ is in P (coNP-complete, Π_2^P-complete). $\square$

The following theorem reduces the set of constraint languages that need to be considered even further.

Theorem 4 ([14]). MIN-INF-CSP(Γ) *is in P (coNP-complete, Π_2^P-complete) if and only if* MIN-INF-CSP(Γ^{id}) *is in P (coNP-complete, Π_2^P-complete).*

Proof. Since $\Gamma \subseteq \Gamma^{id}$, any instance of MIN-INF-CSP(Γ) is an instance of MIN-INF-CSP(Γ^{id}). So MIN-INF-CSP(Γ^{id}) is at least as hard as MIN-INF-CSP(Γ).

To prove the converse, i.e., that MIN-INF-CSP(Γ) is at least as hard as MIN-INF-CSP(Γ^{id}), take a finite set $\Gamma_0 \subseteq \Gamma^{id}$) and an instance $S = (V, P, Z, Q, D, \leq, C, \psi)$ of MIN-INF-CSP(Γ_0). We transform S into an equivalent instance $S' = (V', P', Z', Q', D, \leq, C', \psi')$ of MIN-INF-CSP(Γ_1), where Γ_1 is a finite subset of Γ.

For all variables x occurring in a constraint in S of the type $((x), (0))$ or $((x), (1))$ we do as follows. Remove x from P and Z, add x to Q and remove the constraint. Update ψ as follows. If x occurs in the form $((x), (0))$, then add x to the clause ψ. If x occurs in the form $((x), (1))$, then add $\neg x$ to ψ.

The idea behind the reduction is as follows. If $((x), (0))$ is a constraint in C, we remove it and modify ψ to make sure that every minimal model α of $C \setminus \{((x), (0))\}$ such that $\alpha(x) = 1$, is a model of ψ, and in the case where $\alpha(x) = 0$ we make sure that α is a model of the modified ψ if and only if α was a model of the original ψ. The case where $((x), (1))$ is a constraint in C is handled in the same way. It should be clear that S and S' are equivalent. □

We conclude this section by stating the dichotomy for the complexity of the inference problem in propositional circumscription that was proved in [14].

Theorem 5 ([14]). *Let $\Gamma \subseteq BR$ be a constraint language.* MIN-INF-CSP(Γ) *is Π_2^P-complete if $Pol(\Gamma^{id})$ only contains essentially unary operations, and it is in coNP otherwise.*

3 Trichotomy Theorem for the Inference Problem

In this section we prove our trichotomy theorem for the complexity of the inference problem in propositional circumscription. In the light of Theorem 5, what remains to be proved is that every problem MIN-INF-CSP(Γ) in coNP is either coNP-hard or in P. Some important cases like Horn clauses [2] and affine clauses [7] are already known to be coNP-complete. But to the best of our knowledge the only case known to be in P is when the knowledge base only consists of clauses containing at most one positive and negative literal (i.e., clauses that are both Horn and dual-Horn) [2]. Our main results is the discovery of two new tractable classes of knowledge bases (width-2 affine and clauses only containing negative literals) and a proof that for all other classes of knowledge bases the problem is coNP-hard.

We prove this by further exploiting the results obtained in [14], e.g., Theorem 3 that states that to determine the complexity of MIN-INF-CSP(Γ) it is sufficient to consider constraint languages that are relational clones.

Emil Post [16] classified all Boolean clones/relational clones and proved that they form a lattice under set inclusion. Our proofs rely heavily on Post's lattice of Boolean clones/relational clones. An excellent introduction to Post's classification of Boolean clones can be found in the recent survey article [1], for a more complete account, see [15,17].

See Figure 1 for the lattice of Boolean relational clones. Note that the names for the relational clones in Figure 1 do not agree with Post's names. Post also considered other classes of Boolean functions/relations, so called iterative classes, and this leads to some confusion and inconsistencies if we would use Post's names. The terminology used in Figure 1 was developed by Klaus Wagner in an attempt to construct a consistent scheme of names for clones/relational clones, and was subsequently used in [1].

Now we introduce some relational clones that will be of particular importance to us.

- **Relational Clone IR_2:** For $a \in \{0,1\}$, a Boolean function f is called a-reproducing if $f(a,\ldots,a) = a$. The clones R_a contain all a-reproducing Boolean functions. The clone R_2 contains all functions that are both 0-reproducing and 1-reproducing. Hence $Inv(R_2) = IR_2$ is the relational clone consisting of all relations closed under all functions that are both 0-reproducing and 1-reproducing. Note that functions satisfying $f(a,\ldots,a) = a$ for all a in its domain are usually called idempotent.
- **Relational Clone ID_1:** ID_1 is the relational clone consisting of all relations closed under the affine operation $f(x,y,z) = x \oplus y \oplus z$ and the ternary majority operation $g(x,y,z) = xy \vee yz \vee xz$. It is proved in [5] (Lemma 4.11) that any relation in ID_1 can be represented as a linear equation on at most two variables over the two element field $GF(2)$. Constraint languages $\Gamma \subseteq ID_1$ are usually called width-2 affine in the literature.
- **Relational Clone IS_1:** S_1 is the clone consisting of all 1-separating functions (see [1] for the definition of 1-separating functions). It is proved in [6] (Lemma 39) that $Inv(S_1) = IS_1$ is the relational clone consisting only of relations of the form $\{0,1\}^n \setminus (1,1,\ldots,1)$. That is, IS_1 consists of all relations corresponding to clauses where all literals are negative. Note that [6] uses Post's original names for the Boolean clones and that S_1 is F_8^∞ in Post's notation.

As we have seen in Theorem 4 relational clones of the form $\langle \Gamma^{id} \rangle$ are of particular importance to us (remember that MIN-INF-CSP(Γ) is of the same complexity as MIN-INF-CSP(Γ^{id})). We call relational clones of this form for idempotent relational clones. It can be deduced that a relational clone Γ is idempotent if and only if $IR_2 \subseteq \Gamma$. Hence we have the following lemma.

Lemma 1. *Let Γ_1 be a Boolean relational clone and Γ_2 the relational clone that is the least upper bound of IR_2 and Γ_1 in Post's lattice of relational clones. Then the following holds, MIN-INF-CSP(Γ_1) is in P (coNP-complete, Π_2^P-complete) if and only if MIN-INF-CSP(Γ_2) is in P (coNP-complete, Π_2^P-complete).*

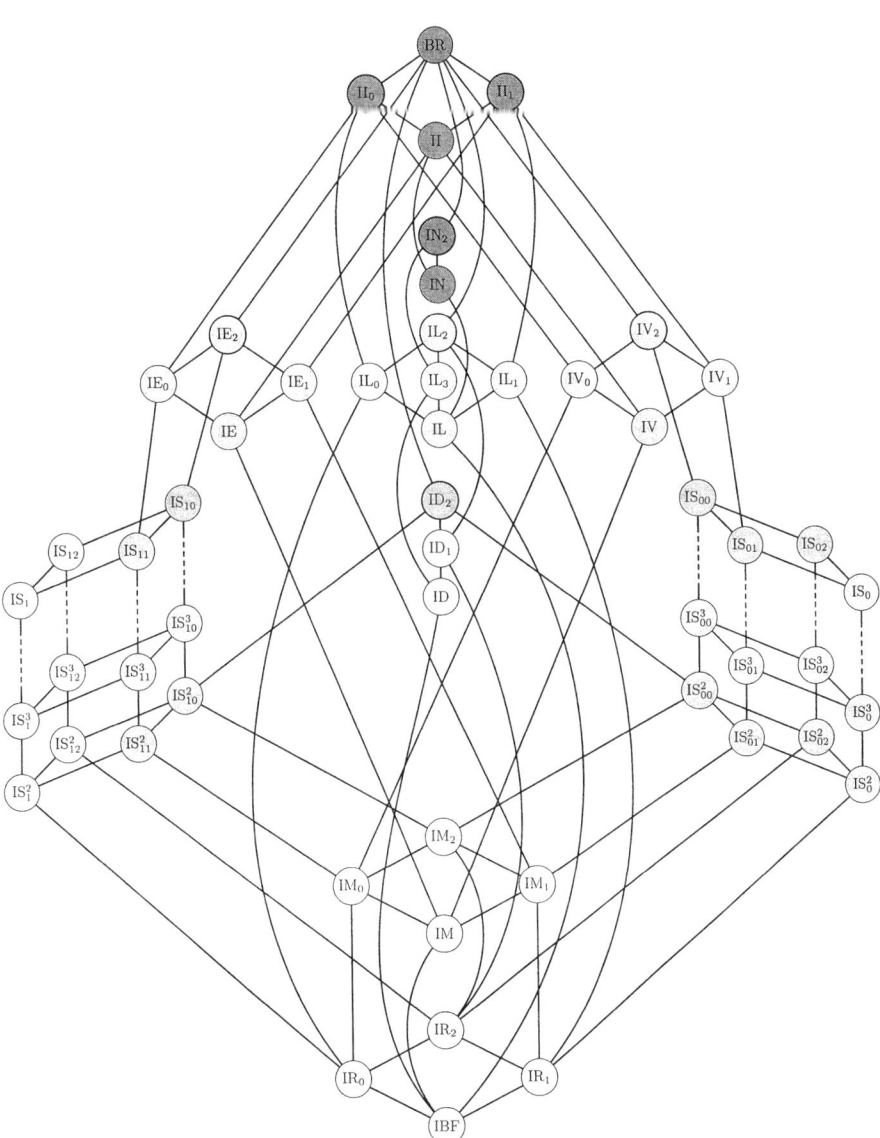

Fig. 1. Lattice (under set inclusion) of all Boolean relational clones (co-clones) and their complexity for the inference problem in propositional circumscription. White means in P, light grey means coNP-complete, and dark grey means Π_2^P-complete

Proof. Remember that IR_2 is the relational clone consisting of all relations that are closed under all functions that are both 0-reproducing and 1-reproducing. Thus, $\{\{(0)\}, \{(1)\}\} \subseteq IR_2$. If F is a set of Boolean functions containing a non a-reproducing function f, then $\{\{(0)\}, \{(1)\}\} \not\subseteq Inv(F)$. Hence, given a relational clone Γ, then $\{\{(0)\}, \{(1)\}\} \subseteq \Gamma$ if and only if $IR_2 \subseteq \Gamma$.

Thus it follows that the least upper bound of IR_2 and Γ_1 in the lattice of relational clones is $\langle \Gamma_1^{id} \rangle = \Gamma_2$. Now by Theorem 4 we get that MIN-INF-CSP(Γ_1) is in P (coNP-complete, Π_2^P-complete) if and only if MIN-INF-CSP(Γ_2) is in P (coNP-complete, Π_2^P-complete). □

Next we prove our two new tractable cases of MIN-INF-CSP(Γ). First out is the width-2 affine case.

Lemma 2. MIN-INF-CSP(ID_1) *is in P.*

Proof. Remember that the set of constraints that can be expressed by ID_1 can be represented as a system of linear equations over $GF(2)$ where each equation contains at most two variables. Hence each constraint is equivalent to an equation of the following form, $x = c$, $x = y$ or $x = -y$, where $c = 0$ or 1.

Now consider an instance $S = (V, P, Z, Q, C, \psi)$ of MIN-INF-CSP(Γ), where $\Gamma \subseteq ID_1$. We begin by reducing $S = (V, P, Z, Q, C, \psi)$ into an equivalent instance $S' = (V', P', Z', Q', C', \psi')$ such that C' has some special properties. Note that by the symmetry of equations the cases where the roles of x and y are reversed are handled in the same way.

- For all equations of the form $x = c$ we do as follows. If $x = 1$ ($x = 0$) is an equation in C and x ($\neg x$) is a literal in ψ, then every minimal model of C is also a model of ψ and we are done. Otherwise, replace all occurrences of x in C by 1 (0). Remove x from V, P, Z, Q, and remove $\neg x$ (x) from ψ. Finally remove $x = c$ from C.
- For all equations of the form $x = y$ ($x = -y$) where $x \in Q$ and y is present in another equation we do as follows. Replace all occurrences of y in all other equations and ψ by x ($-x$) and remove y from V, P, Z, and Q. Finally remove $x = y$ ($x = -y$) from C.
- For all equations of the form $x = y$ ($x = -y$) where $y \in Z$ and y is present in another equation we do as follows. Replace all occurrences of y in all other equations and ψ by x ($-x$) and remove y from Z and V. Finally remove $x = y$ ($x = -y$) from C.
- For all equations of the form $x = y$ ($x = -y$) where $x \in P$, $y \in P$, and y is present in another equation we do as follows. Replace all occurrences of y in all other equations and ψ by x ($-x$) and remove y from P and V. Finally remove $x = y$ ($x = -y$) from C.

We repeat the above process until no more equations can be removed. It can be realized that in the resulting system of equations C', no variable in Z' occurs in more than one equation, no variable in Q' occurs in an equation together with a variable that occurs in another equation. Moreover, no variable in P' occurs in an equation together with a variable from $P' \cup Z'$ that occurs in another equation.

Now, if ψ' is a tautology, then of course ψ' is true in every minimal model of C', and we are done. So we assume that ψ' is not a tautology. Since ψ' is a clause it is easy to find the (single) assignment of the variables (in ψ') that does not satisfy ψ'. Note that, since C' is affine it is easy to decide whether a partial solution can be extended to a total solution, and it is clear that ψ' can be inferred from C' under circumscription if and only if this assignment cannot be extended to a minimal solution to C'. So the question that remains is whether this partial solution (that can be extended to a total solution) can be extended to a minimal solution to C' or not.

Consider the equations of the form $x = y$ or $x = -y$ where neither x nor y is in Q and x is present in ψ'. Then an assignment to x can be extended to a minimal solution to C' if and only if

- x is assigned to 0 in all equations $x = y$ where $x \in P'$ and $y \in P' \cup Z'$ and all equations $x = -y$ where $x \in P'$ and $y \in Z'$, and
- x is assigned to 0 (1) in all equations $x = y$ ($x = -y$) where $x \in Z'$ and $y \in P'$.

□

Now on to the case of clauses where all literals are negative.

Lemma 3. MIN-INF-CSP(IS_1) *is in P.*

Proof. We recall that IS_1 consists of all relations corresponding to clauses where all literals are negative. That is, relations of the form $\{0,1\}^n \setminus (1,1,\ldots,1)$.

Now consider an instance $S = (V, P, Z, Q, C, \psi)$ of MIN-INF-CSP(Γ), where $\Gamma \subseteq IS_1$. The cases where ψ is a tautology is trivial, so we assume that ψ is not a tautology. Since ψ is a clause it is easy to find the (single) assignment of the variables that does not satisfy ψ. It is clear that ψ can be inferred from C under circumscription if and only if this assignment cannot be extended to a minimal solution to C. Note that since C consists of Horn clauses (with only negative literals) it is easy to decide whether a partial solution can be extended to a total solution, and it should be clear that such a partial solution can be extended to a minimal solution if and only if all variables in P that are assigned by this partial solution are assigned the value 0. Hence MIN-INF-CSP(IS_1) is in P. □

Next we give the complexity of MIN-INF-CSP(Γ) for 8 particular relational clones.

Theorem 6. MIN-INF-CSP(Γ) *is coNP-complete when:* 1. $\Gamma = IS_{11}^2$; 2. $\Gamma = IS_0^2$; 3. $\Gamma = IL$; 4. $\Gamma = IV$; or 5. $\Gamma = IE$. MIN-INF-CSP(Γ) *is in P when:* 6. $\Gamma = IS_{12}$; 7. $\Gamma = ID_1$; or 8. $\Gamma = IM_2$.

Proof. 1. The least upper bound of IS_{11}^2 and IR_2 is IS_{10}^2. IS_{10}^2 contains all Horn clauses with at most 2 variables and it is proved in [2] that MIN-INF-CSP(IS_{10}^2) is coNP-complete, hence by Lemma 1 it follows that MIN-INF-CSP(IS_{11}^2) is coNP-complete.

2. IS_0^2 contains clauses of the form $(x \vee y)$, that is clauses only consisting of two positive literals. It is proved in [2] that MIN-INF-CSP(IS_0^2) is coNP-complete.
3. The least upper bound of IL and IR_2 is IL_2, the set of affine clauses. It is proved in [7] that MIN-INF-CSP(IL_2) is coNP-complete, hence by Lemma 1 it follows that MIN-INF-CSP(IL) is coNP-complete.
4. The least upper bound of IV and IR_2 is IV_2, the set of dual-Horn clauses. By Case 2. and Lemma 1 it follows that MIN-INF-CSP(IV) is coNP-complete.
5. The least upper bound of IE and IR_2 is IE_2, the set of Horn clauses. By Case 1. and Lemma 1 it follows that MIN-INF-CSP(IE) is coNP-complete.
6. It is proved in Lemma 3 that MIN-INF-CSP(IS_1) is in P. The least upper bound of IS_1 and IR_2 is IS_{12}, hence by Lemma 1 it follows that MIN-INF-CSP(IS_{12}) is in P.
7. This is proved in Lemma 2.
8. IM_2 consists of all clauses that are both Horn and dual Horn. It is proved in [2] that MIN-INF-CSP(IM_2) is in P.

□

The previous theorem together with the structure of Post's lattice of relational clones and the results proved in [14] yields a trichotomy for the complexity of MIN-INF-CSP(Γ). The results are summarized in terms of the relational clones in Figure 1. A perhaps more intelligible summary is given in the conclusions below.

4 Conclusions

Only one tractable case of the inference problem for propositional circumscription (where Q and Z need not to be empty) is known, namely when the knowledge base only consists of clauses that are both Horn and dual-Horn [2]. We have found two new tractable classes of knowledge bases (width-2 affine clauses, and Horn clauses only containing negative literals) for the inference problem in propositional circumscription. We have proved that the inference problem is coNP-hard for all other classes of knowledge bases. This together with the results in [14] gives us the following trichotomy for the complexity of the inference problem in propositional circumscription:

- **P:** Horn and dual-Horn, width-2 affine, negative Horn;
- **coNP-complete:** Horn, dual-Horn, affine, bijunctive, (and not Horn and dual-Horn, width-2 affine, or negative Horn);
- Π_2^P**-complete:** All that are not Horn, dual-Horn, affine, or bijunctive.

In closing we note that the problem of establishing a trichotomy (as conjectured in [10]) for the complexity of the inference problem for propositional circumscription in the restricted case where all variables must be minimized ($Q = Z = \emptyset$) is still open.

Acknowledgments

The author thanks Steffen Reith for providing the visualization of Post's lattice in Figure 1.

References

1. E. Böhler, N. Creignou, S. Reith, and H. Vollmer. Playing with boolean blocks, part I: Post's lattice with applications to complexity theory. *ACM SIGACT-Newsletter*, 34(4):38–52, 2003.
2. M. Cadoli and M. Lenzerini. The complexity of closed world reasoning and circumscription. *Journal of Computer and System Sciences*, pages 255–301, 1994.
3. S. Cook. The complexity of theorem proving procedures. In *Proceedings of the 3rd ACM Symposium on Theory of Computing*, pages 151–158, 1971.
4. S. Coste-Marquis and P. Marquis. Complexity results for propositional closed world reasoning and circumscription from tractable knoledge bases. In *Proceedings of the 16th International Joint Conference on Artificial Intelligence*, pages 24–29, 1999.
5. N. Creignou, S. Khanna, and M. Sudan. *Complexity classifications of boolean constraint satisfaction problems*. SIAM, Philadelphia, 2001.
6. V. Dalmau. *Computational Complexity of Problems over Generalized Formulas*. PhD thesis, Department LSI, Universitat Politècnica de Catalanya, Barcelona, 2000.
7. A. Durand and M. Hermann. The inference problem for propositional circumscription of affine formulas is coNP-complete. In *Proceedings of the 20th Annual Symposium on Theoretical Aspects of Computer Science*, pages 451–462, 2003.
8. T. Eiter and G. Gottlob. Propositional circumscription and extended closed-world reasoning are Π_2^P-complete. *Theoretical Computer Science*, 114:231–245, 1993.
9. P. Jeavons, D. Cohen, and M. Gyssens. Closure properties of constraints. *Journal of the ACM*, 44:527–548, 1997.
10. L. Kirousis and P. Kolaitis. A dichotomy in the complexity of propositional circumscription. In *Proceedings of the 16th Annual IEEE Symposium on Logic in Computer Science*, pages 71–80, 2001.
11. L. Kirousis and P. Kolaitis. The complexity of minimal satisfiability problems. *Information and Computation*, 187(1):20–39, 2003.
12. R. Ladner. On the structure of polynomial time reducibility. *Journal of the ACM*, 22:155–171, 1975.
13. J. McCarthy. Circumscription - a form of nonmonotonic reasoning. *Artificial Intelligence*, 13:27–39, 1980.
14. G. Nordh and P. Jonsson. An algebraic approach to the complexity of propositional circumscription. In *Proceedings of the 19th Annual IEEE Symposium on Logic in Computer Science*, pages 367–376, 2004.
15. N. Pippenger. *Theories of Computability*. Cambridge University Press, Cambridge, 1997.
16. E. Post. The two-valued iterative systems of mathematical logic. *Annals of Mathematical Studies*, 5:1–122, 1941.
17. R. Pöschel and L. Kaluznin. *Funktionen- und Relationenalgebren*. DVW, Berlin, 1979.
18. T.J. Schaefer. The complexity of satisfiability problems. In *Proceedings of the 10th ACM Symposium on Theory of Computing*, pages 216–226, 1978.

Exploiting Fixable, Removable, and Implied Values in Constraint Satisfaction Problems

Lucas Bordeaux, Marco Cadoli, and Toni Mancini

Dipartimento di Informatica e Sistemistica
Università di Roma "La Sapienza"
Via Salaria 113, I-00198 Roma, Italy
{bordeaux|cadoli|tmancini}@dis.uniroma1.it

Abstract. Complete algorithms for constraint solving typically exploit properties like (in)consistency or interchangeability, which they detect by means of incomplete yet effective algorithms and use to reduce the search space. In this paper, we study a wide range of properties which includes most of the ones used by existing CSP algorithms as well as some which have not yet been considered in the literature, and we investigate their use in CSP solving. We clarify the relationships between these notions and characterise the complexity of the problem of checking them. Following the CSP approach, we then determine a number of relaxations (for instance *local* versions) which provide sufficient conditions whose detection is tractable. This work is a first step towards a comprehensive framework for CSP properties, and it also shows that new notions still remain to be exploited.

1 Introduction

Many Constraint Satisfaction Problems (CSPs) which arise in the modelling of real-life problems exhibit "structural" properties that distinguish them from random instances. Detecting such properties has been widely recognised to be an effective way for improving the solving process. To this end, several of them have already been identified, and different techniques have been developed in order to exploit them, with the goal of reducing the search space to be explored. Good examples are value substitutability and interchangeability [11], more general forms of symmetries [6,12], and functional dependencies among variables [18,1].

Unfortunately, checking whether such properties hold, is (or is thought to be) often computationally hard. As an example, let us consider interchangeability. Value a is said to be interchangeable with value b for variable x if every solution which assigns a to x remains a solution if x is changed to b, and vice versa [11]. The problem of checking interchangeability is coNP-complete (*cf.* Proposition 2). Analogously, detecting some other forms of symmetry reduces to the graph automorphism problem [5] (for which there are no polynomial time algorithms, even if there is evidence that it is not NP-complete [16]).

To this end, in order to allow general algorithms to exploit such properties efficiently, different approaches can be followed. First of all, syntactic restrictions on the constraint languages can be enforced, in order to allow for the efficient verification of the properties of interest. Alternatively, "local" versions of such properties can be defined, that can be used to infer their global counterparts, and such that they can be verified in polynomial time. As an instance of this "local reasoning" approach, instead of checking whether a value is *fully* interchangeable for a variable, Freuder [11] proposes to check whether that value is *neighbourhood*, or *k-interchangeable*. This task involves considering only subsets of the constraints of bounded size, and hence can be performed in polynomial time. Neighbourhood and k-interchangeability are sufficient (but not necessary) conditions for full interchangeability, and have been proven to be highly effective in practice (*cf.*, *e.g.*, [4,3]). Moreover, in some cases, the existence of some properties can also derive from intrinsic characteristics of the problem, or even from an explicit promise [9], *cf.* forthcoming Example 1.

In this paper we give a formal characterisation of several properties of CSPs which can be exploited in order to save search. Some of them are well-known, while some others are, to the best of our knowledge, original. All the presented definitions are then collected in a unified framework, and hierarchically classified in order to highlight the semantical connections that hold among them. Afterwards, we present a formal discussion of their computational properties, and show how some of them can be practically exploited by the solving engine in order to save search.

In general, all these properties can be detected either statically, during a preprocessing stage of the input CSP (*cf. e.g.*, [2]), dynamically, during search (since they may arise at any time), or explicitly "promised" by an external entity.

Example 1 (Factoring [17,23]). This problem is a simplified version of one of the most important problems in public-key cryptography. Given a (large) positive integer Z, which is known to be the product of two *prime* numbers (different from 1), it amounts to find its factors X and Y.

An intuitive formulation of this problem as a CSP, in order to deal with arbitrarily large numbers, amounts to encode the combinatorial circuit of integer multiplication, and is as follows: assuming the input integer Z having n digits (in base b) $z_1, \ldots, z_n$, we consider $2n$ variables $x_1, \ldots, x_n$ and $y_1, \ldots, y_n$ one for each digit (in base b) of the two factors, X and Y (with x_1 and y_1 being the least significant ones). The domain for all these variables is $[0, b-1]$. In order to maintain information about the carries, $n+1$ additional variables $c_1, \ldots, c_{n+1}$ must be considered, with domain $[0..(b-1)^2 n/b]$.

As for the constraints (cf. Fig. 1 for the intuition), they are the following:

1. Constraints on factors:
   (a) Factors must be different from 1, or, equivalently, $X \neq Z$ and $Y \neq Z$ must hold;
   (b) For every digit $i \in [1,n]$: $z_i = c_i + \sum_{j,k \in [1,n]: j+k=i+1}(x_j * y_k \mod b)$;

2. Constraints on carries:
   (a) Carry on the least significant digit is 0: $c_1 = 0$;
   (b) Carries on other digits: $\forall i \in [2, n+1]$, $c_i = c_{i-1} + \sum_{j,k \in [1,n]: j+k=i} \frac{x_j * y_k}{b}$;
   (c) Carry on the most significant digit is 0: $c_{n+1} = 0$; □

$$\begin{array}{rrrrrrr}
 & & 7 & 8 & 7 & * \\
 & & 7 & 9 & 7 & = \\
\hline
0 & 6 & 13 & 18 & 12 & 4 & 0 \\
 & & 49 & 56 & 49 & & \\
 & 63 & 72 & 63 & - & & \\
49 & 56 & 49 & - & - & & \\
\hline
6 & 2 & 7 & 2 & 3 & 9 &
\end{array}
\qquad
\begin{array}{ccccccc}
 & & & & x_3 & x_2 & x_1 \quad * \\
 & & & & y_3 & y_2 & y_1 \quad = \\
\hline
c_7 & c_6 & c_5 & c_4 & c_3 & c_2 & c_1 \\
 & & & & x_3y_1 & x_2y_1 & x_1y_1 \\
 & & & x_3y_2 & x_2y_2 & x_1y_2 & - \\
 & & x_3y_3 & x_2y_3 & x_1y_3 & - & - \\
\hline
z_6 & z_5 & z_4 & z_3 & z_2 & z_1
\end{array}$$

Fig. 1. Factoring instance 627239, $n = 6$, $b = 10$

It is worth noting that, when a guess on the two factors X and Y (i.e., on variables $x_1, \ldots, x_n$ and $y_1, \ldots, y_n$) has been made, values for variables $c_1, \ldots, c_{n+1}$ are completely determined, since they follow from the semantics of the multiplication. Functional dependencies arise very often, e.g.,, in all problems for which an intermediate state has to be maintained, and their detection and exploitation has been recognized to be of great importance from an efficiency point of view, since it can lead to significant reductions of the search space (cf., e.g., [13,1,2]).

The presence of functional dependencies among variables of a CSP highlights an interesting problem, i.e., that of *computing* the values of dependent variables when a choice of the defining ones has been made. It is worth noting that this problem, always present as a subproblem of a CSP with dependencies, has exactly one solution. Hence, the knowledge of such a *promise* can be useful to the solver. It is worth noting that there are also problems which intrinsically exhibit promises. This is the case of, e.g., Factoring, where we additionally add the symmetry-breaking constraint forcing $x_1, \ldots, x_n$ to be lexicographically less than or equal to $y_1, \ldots, y_n$. This new formulation is guaranteed to have exactly one solution.

In what follows, we investigate the relations that hold among different concepts. In particular, we reconsider the notions of *inconsistency*, *substitutability* and *interchangeability*, and propose the concepts of *fixable*, *removable*, and *implied* value for a given variable, and those of *determined*, *dependent*, and *irrelevant* variable. These properties make it possible to transform a problem into a simpler one. Depending on the case, this transformation is guaranteed to preserve all solutions of the problem, or to preserve at least one if one exists.

In order to give the intuition of some of the properties we are going to define, let us reconsider the Factoring problem.

Example 2 (Factoring, Example 1 continued). Let us consider an instance such that Z is given in binary notation (*i.e.*, $b = 2$) and with the least significant digit, $z_1 = 1$. This implies that the last digit of both factors X and Y must be 1. Hence, we can say that value 1 is *implied* for variables x_1 and y_1, and that 0 is *removable* for them and, more precisely *inconsistent*. Moreover, for this problem, which, if the symmetry is broken, has a unique solution, we also know that all variables $x_1, \ldots, x_n$ and $y_1, \ldots, y_n$ are *determined* (*cf.* forthcoming Definition 1), regardless of the instance, and because of the functional dependence already discussed in Example 1, we have that variables encoding carries, i.e., c_i ($i \in [1,n]$), are *dependent* on $\{x_1, \ldots x_n, y_1, \ldots, y_n\}$. □

Unfortunately, solving problem instances with unique solutions is likely to remain intractable (cf., e.g., [22]). But this does not exclude, of course, the possibility to find good heuristics for instances with such a promise, or to look for other properties that are implied by the existence of unique solutions, that can be exploited in order to improve the search process. In particular, determined and implied values play an important role in this and other classes of problems. As the previous example shows, such problems arise frequently in practice, either as subproblems of other CSPs, as in presence of functional dependencies, or because of intrinsic characteristics of the problem at hand. In general, if a problem has a unique solution, all variables have a determined value.

Another central role is played by the removability property, that characterises precisely the case when a value can be safely removed from the domain of a variable, while preserving satisfiability. This property is of course weaker than inconsistency, (since some solutions may be lost), but can be safely used in place of it when we are interested in finding only a solution of the input CSP, if one exists, and not all of them.

Unfortunately, detecting the proposed properties is computationally hard in general. In particular, we show that these tasks are all coNP-complete. This holds also for Freuder's substitutability and interchangeability (this result is, to the best of our knowledge, original). Hence, in order to be able to practically make the relevant checks during preprocessing and search, we show how some of the proposed properties can be verified efficiently along two lines: by imposing restrictions on the constraint language, and by exploiting locality, *i.e.*, by checking them for single constraints.

The outline of the paper is as follows: after recalling some preliminaries, in Section 2 we formally define all the properties we are interested in, and discuss the semantical connections that hold among them. Then, in Section 3 we present the intractability results of checking such properties. Hence, in Section 4 we show some tractability results, investigating the two aforementioned approaches in order to be able to efficiently make the required reasoning: imposing restrictions on the constraint languages, and exploring locality. Finally, in Section 5 we draw conclusions and address future work.

2 A Hierarchy of Properties

2.1 Preliminaries

Let $\mathbb{D}$ be a finite set of size at least 2. A V-tuple t, where V represents a finite set of variables, is a mapping which associates a value $t_x \in \mathbb{D}$ to every $x \in V$. A V-*relation* is a set of V-tuples. A *Constraint Satisfaction Problem* (CSP) is a triple $\langle X, D, C \rangle$ where:

- X is a finite set of variables,
- D associates to every variable $x \in V$ a domain $D_x \subseteq \mathbb{D}$ and
- C is a finite set of constraints, each of which is a V-relation for some $V \subseteq X$.

Given a V-tuple t and a subset $U \subseteq V$ of its variables, we denote by $t|_U$ the *restriction* of t to U, which has the same value as t on the variables of U and is undefined elsewhere. The explicit assignment of the value of a V-tuple t on a variable $x \in V$ to value a is written $t[x := a]$. The relational operators of *selection*, *projection* and *complement* will be useful: given a V-relation c, a subset U of V and a value $a \in D_x$, we denote by $\sigma_{x=a}(c)$ (resp. $\sigma_{x \neq a}(c)$) the V-relation which contains the tuples of c whose value on x is a (resp. is different from a), by $\pi_U(c)$ the set of restrictions to U of tuples of c (i.e., the set of U-tuples $\{t \mid \exists t' \in c\ (t = t'|_U)\}$) and by $\bar{c}$ the set of V-tuples $\{t \mid t \notin c\}$.

An X-tuple t *satisfies* a V-relation $c \in C$ if $t|_V \in c$. We denote by $Sol(c)$ the set of X-tuples which satisfy c. The set $\bigcap_{c \in C} Sol(c)$ of X-tuples which satisfy all the constraints is called the *solution space*, and denoted $Sol(C)$. The set of X-tuples t such that $t_x \in D_x$ for all variables x is called the *search space* and noted S_D, or simply S if the domain is implicit from the context. Note that $\sigma_{x=a}(S)$ denotes the search space obtained by fixing D_x to $\{a\}$ if $a \in D_x$ and is empty otherwise. For the sake of simplicity, the sets X and C will be considered as globally defined and shall therefore be omitted from the parameters of most definitions; only the search space will be explicitly mentioned.

2.2 Definitions

Definition 1. *The following properties are defined for a search space S, variables x and y, values a and b, and for a set of variables V:*

$$\text{fixable}(S, x, a) \equiv \forall t \in S\ (t \in Sol(C) \to t[x := a] \in Sol(C))$$

$$\text{substitutable}(S, x, a, b) \equiv \forall t \in S\ \begin{pmatrix} t_x = a \land t \in Sol(C) \to \\ t[x := b] \in Sol(C) \end{pmatrix}$$

$$\text{interchangeable}(S, x, a, b) \equiv \begin{array}{l} \text{substitutable}(S, x, a, b) \land \\ \text{substitutable}(S, x, b, a) \end{array}$$

$$\text{removable}(S, x, a) \equiv \forall t \in S\ \begin{pmatrix} t_x = a \land t \in Sol(C) \to \\ \exists b \neq a\ (t[x := b] \in Sol(C)) \end{pmatrix}$$

$$\text{inconsistent}(S, x, a) \equiv \forall t \in S\ (t \in Sol(C) \to t_x \neq a)$$

$$\text{implied}(S, x, a) \equiv \forall t \in S\ (t \in Sol(C) \to t_x = a)$$

$$\text{determined}(S, x) \equiv \forall t \in S\ \begin{pmatrix} t \in Sol(C) \to \\ \forall b \neq t_x\ (t[x := b] \notin Sol(C)) \end{pmatrix}$$

$$\text{dependent}(S, V, y) \equiv \forall t, t' \in S\ \left(\begin{pmatrix} t \in Sol(C) \land \\ t' \in Sol(C) \land \\ \forall x \in V\ (t_x = t'_x) \end{pmatrix} \to t_y = t'_y \right)$$

$$\text{irrelevant}(S, x) \equiv \forall t \in S\ \begin{pmatrix} t \in Sol(C) \to \\ \forall a \in D_x\ (t[x := a] \in Sol(C)) \end{pmatrix}$$

In the few cases where an ambiguity arises on the considered set of constraints, we will indicate it using subscript (e.g., irrelevant$_C(S,x)$) Note that all the definitions but the last three ones are *value*-oriented, in that they are properties of particular values of the domain. On the contrary, dependency, irrelevance and determinacy are *variable-oriented* properties which do not directly express results on particular values of the domains but have important relations with the value-oriented notions.

The notion of consistency was proposed in [21,19] and is one of the best-studied notions in CSP. Substitutability and interchangeability were introduced in [11]. Implied values, which are known as *backbones* in the literature, were seemingly first explicitly studied in [20]. To the best of our knowledge, the notion of removable and fixable values have on the contrary not been considered. Determined, irrelevant and dependent variables have been studied in a number of contexts but we are aware of little work concerning their application in the context of CSP. The following example illustrates some of the properties.

Example 3. Consider a CSP modeling the colouring problem for the graph below. Let $c1\ldots c4$ denote the variables involved, and Σ denote the search space in which all four variables have domain $\{R,G,B\}$. We have:

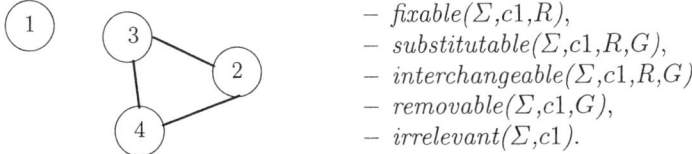

- *fixable(Σ,c1,R)*,
- *substitutable(Σ,c1,R,G)*,
- *interchangeable(Σ,c1,R,G)*,
- *removable(Σ,c1,G)*,
- *irrelevant(Σ,c1)*.

Example 4. Consider a CSP over boolean variables a, b, and c, whose constraints are written below. Denoting as Ξ the search space in which all variables range over $\{true, false\}$. We have:

$$a \quad \wedge$$
$$a \rightarrow b \quad \wedge$$
$$(c \vee d) \leftrightarrow e$$

- *inconsistent(Ξ,b,false)*,
- *implied(Ξ,b,true)*,
- *determined(Ξ,b)*,
- *dependent(Ξ,\{c,d\},e)*.

2.3 Semantical Relations

The notions presented in Definition 1 are semantically connected, and we clarify here the main relationships that exist between them.

Proposition 1. *The relations shown in Figure 2 hold between the properties defined in Definition 1.*

Proof. (sketch)

dependence-determinacy: *we have dependent($S, \{x_1, \ldots, x_i\}, y$) iff any solution t has a value on y which is given by a function f of the values it assigns to $x_1 \ldots x_i$, iff in any search space $\sigma_{x_1=a_1\ldots x_i=a_i}(S)$ (where all these variables receive a fixed value), all solutions assign the same value $f(a_1, \ldots, a_n)$ to y.*

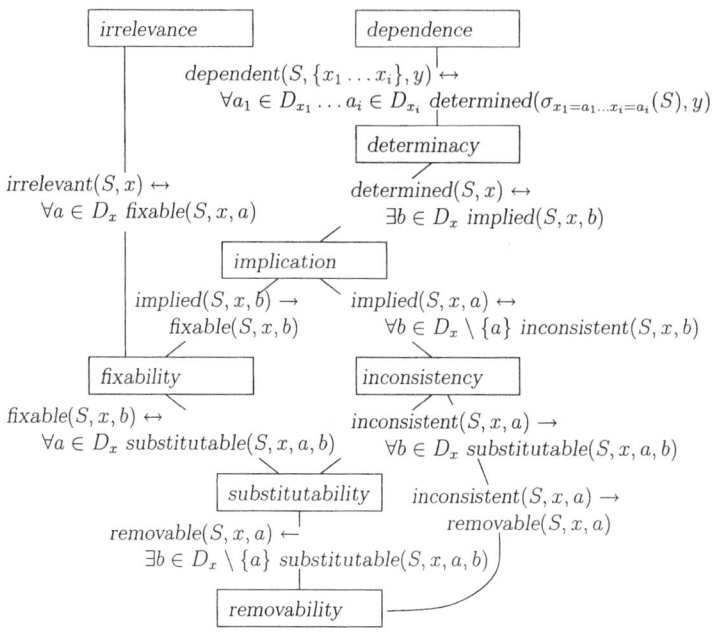

Fig. 2. Relations between the properties

irrelevance-fixability: $t \in Sol(C) \to \forall a \in D_x(t[x := a] \in Sol(C))$ rewrites to $\forall a \in D_x(t \in Sol(C) \to t[x := a] \in Sol(C))$.

determinacy-implication: *if we have* $implied(S, x, b)$ *for some* b, *then for any* t *and any* $a \neq b$ *we have* $t[x := a] \notin Sol(C)$. *If we have* $determined(S, x)$ *and* $t \in Sol(C)$, *then* $implied(S, x, t_x)$ *(no* t' *with* $t'_x \neq t_x$ *is in* $Sol(C)$*)*.

implication-fixability: $implied(S, x, b)$ *means that every* $t \in Sol(C)$ *has* $t_x = b$. *Hence for every* $t \in Sol(C)$, *we have* $t[x := b] = t \in Sol(C)$.

implication-inconsistency: $implied(S, x, a)$ *holds iff* $\forall t \ (t_x \neq a \to t \notin Sol(C))$, *i.e., iff* $\forall t \ \forall b \in D_x \setminus \{a\} \ (t_x = b \to t \notin Sol(C))$. *This rewrites to* $\forall b \in D_x \setminus \{a\}$ $inconsistent(S, x, b)$.

fixability-substitutability: *Let* $D_x = \{a_1, .., a_d\}$. *We have* $\bigwedge_{i \in 1..d} substitutable(S, x, a_i, b)$ *iff* $\forall t \ ((t_x = a_1 \vee \cdots \vee t_x = a_d) \wedge t \in Sol(C) \to t[x := b] \in Sol(C))$, *which rewrites to* $fixable(S, x, v)$.

inconsistency-substitutability: *suppose we have* $inconsistent(S, x, a)$. *No solution* t *with* $t_x = a$ *exists, hence the implication* $t_x = a \wedge t \in Sol(C) \to \ldots$ *is always valid.*

inconsistency-removability: *same argument as for inconsistency-substitutability.*

substitutability-removability: *suppose we have* $substitutable(S, x, a, b)$ *for some value* b. *This can be written* $\exists b \ \forall t \ (t_x = a \wedge t \in Sol(C) \to t[x := b] \in Sol(C))$, *which implies that* $\forall t \ \exists b(t_x = a \wedge t \in Sol(C) \to t[x := b] \in Sol(C))$. *The latter rewrites to* $\forall t \ (t_x = a \wedge t \in Sol(C) \to \exists b \ t[x := b] \in Sol(C))$.

Note also that determined values are strongly related to problems with a unique solution: if a problem has a unique solution, then all its variables have an implied value (*cf.* Example 1).

2.4 Exploiting Properties in Constraint Solving

An important reason why the aforementioned properties are interesting is that, when detected, they allow us to reduce the search space by removing values. Two key notions here are inconsistency and removability:

- Suppressing a value a from the domain of a variable x preserves all solutions (*i.e.*, $\sigma_{x \neq a}(S) \cap Sol(C) = S \cap Sol(C)$) iff a is inconsistent for variable x.
- Suppressing a value a from the domain of variable x preserves the *satisfiability* of the problem (*i.e.*, $\sigma_{x \neq a}(S) \cap Sol(C) = \emptyset \leftrightarrow S \cap Sol(C) = \emptyset$) iff value a is removable from the domain of x.
- Instantiating a value a from the domain of variable x preserves the *satisfiability* of the problem (*i.e.*, $\sigma_{x=a}(S) \cap Sol(C) = \emptyset \leftrightarrow S \cap Sol(C) = \emptyset$) if value a is fixable for x.

The removability property is therefore weaker than the inconsistency one, and this shows an interesting benefit: in cases where we do not want to find all solutions of a problem but we simply want to find one, removability is the ideal property to use.

Some of these definitions can be used to construct *solution-preserving* mappings, *i.e.*, mappings which transform solutions into solutions.

Definition 2 (solution-preserving transformation). *A* solution-preserving transformation *is a total mapping τ from S to S such that*

$$\forall t \in S \ (t \in Sol(C) \rightarrow \tau(t) \in Sol(C))$$

To understand the connection between solution-preserving transformations and the aforementioned properties, consider the following mappings:

$$\tau_1(t) = t[x := a]$$

$$\tau_2(t) = \begin{cases} t[x := b] & \text{if } t_x = a \\ t & \text{otherwise} \end{cases}$$

$$\tau_3(t) = \begin{cases} t[x := b] & \text{if } t_x = a \\ t[x := a] & \text{if } t_x = b \\ t & \text{otherwise} \end{cases}$$

Checking whether value a is fixable for variable x, whether value a is substitutable to value b for variable x, and whether values a and b are interchangeable for value x amounts to checking whether mappings τ_1, τ_2 and τ_3 (respectively) are solution-preserving.

3 Intractability Results

In this section, we show that the problem of checking whether properties defined in Definition 1 hold is intractable. From now on, we assume that the input is given as a set of constraints C over a set of variables X. We also assume that the problem of checking whether $t \in Sol(C)$ is polynomial in the size of the representation of the input. Additionally, we assume that the size of D is fixed. Such properties hold for propositional logic and for CSPs, in the sense of [8].

We note that the problem of checking each property of Definition 1 is in coNP, because it can be done by guessing all tuples in S in non-deterministic polynomial time, and making the relevant tests in polynomial time (as for interchangeability, we note that the logical and of two properties in coNP is still in coNP). In the rest of this section, proofs are therefore restricted to the coNP-hardness part.

Proposition 2 (coNP-completeness of properties of Definition 1). *Given a CSP, the following tasks are coNP-complete:*

- *Checking whether value a is fixable, removable, inconsistent, implied, determined for variable x;*
- *Checking whether value a is substitutable to, or interchangeable with b for variable x;*
- *Checking whether variable y is dependent on variables in V;*
- *Checking whether variable x is irrelevant.*

Proof. For the sake of simplicity, we give the proofs for fixability and substitutability. The other proofs can be given in a similar way, by using also Proposition 1. To prove that checking fixability and substitutability are hard for coNP, we reduce a coNP-complete problem, i.e., that of checking that an arbitrary CSP is unsatisfiable, to fixability and substitutability. In particular, the proofs hold even if the domains are binary, in which case the CSP can be written as a propositional formula, e.g., in CNF.

Fixability. Let us consider an arbitrary propositional formula ϕ in CNF, over variables X, and a variable $x \notin X$. Let ψ be defined as $\phi \wedge \neg x$. We have that ψ is unsatisfiable if and only if ϕ is unsatisfiable.

We now show that ϕ is unsatisfiable if and only if value true is fixable for x in formula ψ. Let us first assume that ϕ is unsatisfiable. It follows that true is fixable for x in ψ, because ψ has no models.

As for the other direction, by Definition 1, if true is fixable for x in ψ, then, every model of ψ remains a model if x is assigned to true. However, since, by construction, models of ψ never assign true to x, it follows that true is fixable for x in ψ only if no solutions to ψ exist, hence, only if ϕ is unsatisfiable.

Substitutability. Let us consider an arbitrary propositional formula ϕ in CNF, over variables X, and a variable $x \notin X$. Let ψ be the defined as $\phi \wedge x$. We have that ψ is unsatisfiable if and only if ϕ is unsatisfiable.

We now show that ϕ is unsatisfiable if and only if value true is substitutable to false for x in ψ. Let us first assume that ϕ is unsatisfiable. It follows that true is substitutable to false for x in ψ, because ψ has no models.

As for the other direction, by Definition 1, if true is substitutable to false for x in ψ, then, every model of ψ with x assigned to true remains a model if x is assigned to false. However, since, by construction, models of ψ never assign false to $\bot$, it follows that true is substitutable to false for x in ψ only if no solutions to ϕ exist.

It is worth noting that the intractability of checking the above properties hold also for binary CSPs (*i.e.*, CSPs in which all constraints relate at most two variables). As an example, the following result holds.

Corollary 1 (coNP-completeness of fixability for binary constraints). *Given a CSP with only binary constraints, checking whether a value a is fixable for a variable x is coNP-complete.*

Proof. Let $\Phi = \langle X, D, C \rangle$ be a binary CSP. Consider an arbitrary variable $y \notin X$ and let a and b be arbitrary values. Let Ψ denote the CSP $\langle X', D', C' \rangle$ with $X' = X \cup \{y\}$, $D'_x = D_x$ forall $x \in X$, $D'_y = \{a, b\}$, and $C' = C \cup \{y \neq a\}$. Ψ is binary and, by using the same arguments of the proof of Proposition 2, it follows that Φ is unsatisfiable if and only if value a for variable y is fixable for Ψ. From the observation that a CSP encoding of the graph 3-colourability problem can be made using only binary constraints, the thesis follows, since checking unsatisfiability of this problem (which is coNP-hard) can be reduced into checking fixability in a binary CSP.

4 Tractability Results

Since detecting any of the properties we are interested in in the paper is a computationally hard problem, a natural question is to determine special cases where this can be done efficiently. We investigate two approaches: we exhibit syntactical restrictions which make the problem tractable, and we study *local* relaxations of these definitions which are polynomial-time checkable, and which therefore provide incomplete algorithms for detecting the property.

4.1 Tractability for Restricted Constraint Languages

A number of syntactical restrictions to the constraint satisfaction problem are known which make it tractable. For instance, in the case of boolean constraints, *i.e.*, propositional formulae, the satisfiability problem becomes tractable if the instance is expressed using only Horn clauses, only dual Horn clauses (*i.e.*, clauses with at most one negative literal), only clauses of size at most 2, or only affine constraints (*i.e.*, constraints built using XOR) [24]. It is natural to wonder if all the properties identified in Definition 1 are also easy to determine for these classes of formulae. This is indeed the case for most of them, and we give a more general condition under which tractable classes for the consistency property are also tractable for other properties of our framework. We note that a recent paper [15] gives a complete characterization of tractable cases for a related property.

We say that a language is *closed under instantiation* (*resp. under complementation*) if whenever a constraint c is expressible in the language, the relation $\pi_{X \setminus \{x\}}(\sigma_{x=a}(c))$ (*resp.* the complementation $\bar{c}$) is also representable by a conjunction of constraints of this language. For instance, taking a Horn clause, a dual Horn clause, a 2CNF clause or an affine constraint, we can express the relation obtained by instantiating a variable to a value or by complementing the constraint as a conjunction of constraints of the same type.

Proposition 3. *If the satisfiability problem for the language is tractable and if the language is closed under complementation and instantiation, then checking any property among fixability, substitutability, interchangeability, inconsistency, determinacy or irrelevance is tractable.*

Proof. We start by the substitutability property and note that value a is substitutable by b for variable x if

$$\pi_{X\setminus\{x\}}(\sigma_{x=a}(Sol(C))) \subseteq \pi_{X\setminus\{x\}}(\sigma_{x=b}(Sol(C)))$$

This inclusion holds iff $t_x = a \wedge t \in Sol(C) \to t[x := b] \in Sol(C)$. This inclusion is false, i.e., we do not have substitutability if the set

$$\pi_{X\setminus\{x\}}(\sigma_{x=a}(Sol(C))) \cap \overline{\pi_{X\setminus\{x\}}(\sigma_{x=b}(Sol(C)))} \quad (1)$$

is non empty. Since $\sigma_{x=a}(Sol(C)) = \sigma_{x=a}(\bigcap_{c \in C} Sol(c)) = \bigcap_{c \in C}(\sigma_{x=a}(Sol(c)))$, we have:

$$\pi_{X\setminus\{x\}}(\sigma_{x=b}(Sol(C))) = \pi_{X\setminus\{x\}}\left(\bigcap_{c \in C}(\sigma_{x=b}(Sol(c)))\right)$$

Although the projection of an intersection of relations is not equal to the intersection of their projections in general, the latter rewrites to:

$$\bigcap_{c \in C} \pi_{X\setminus\{x\}}(\sigma_{x=b}(Sol(c)))$$

This is due to the fact that we select on x before eliminating it by projection. We only prove the inclusion which does not hold in general: suppose we have $t \in \bigcap_{c \in C} \pi_{X\setminus\{x\}}(\sigma_{x=b}(Sol(c)))$. This means that $\forall c \in C$, there exists a tuple t^c such that $t^c|_{X\setminus\{x\}} = t$ and $t^c \in \sigma_{x=b}(Sol(c))$. It follows that $t^c_x = b$ and that we have indeed a unique t with $t_x = b$ and $t^c|_{X\setminus\{x\}} = t$ which is such that $\forall c \in C$ ($t \in \sigma_{x=b}(Sol(c))$), i.e., $t \in \pi_{X\setminus\{x\}}(\bigcap_{c \in C}(\sigma_{x=b}(Sol(c))))$.

Equation (1) is therefore equivalent to:

$$\pi_{X\setminus\{x\}}(\sigma_{x=a}(Sol(c))) \cap \bigcup_{c \in C} \overline{\pi_{X\setminus\{x\}}(\sigma_{x=b}(Sol(c)))}$$

A solution exists (and we therefore do not have substitutability) if one of the sets

$$\pi_{X\setminus\{x\}}(\sigma_{x=a}(Sol(c))) \cap \overline{\pi_{X\setminus\{x\}}(\sigma_{x=b}(Sol(c)))}$$

obtained for every $c \in C$ has a solution. If the language is closed under instantiation and complement, we can express the new constraint $\overline{\pi_{X\setminus\{x\}}(\sigma_{x=a}(Sol(c)))}$ as a constraint c' of the language. Each of the sets has a solution iff the CSP $\langle X, D, \{\sigma_{x=a}(c) \mid c \in C\} \cup \{c'\}\rangle$ is satisfiable. We have reduced the substitutability testing problem to solving m instances of a constraint satisfaction problem whose constraints are all in the original language, which is tractable.

The result for the fixability, interchangeability and irrelevance properties follows directly. Consistency of value a for variable x can directly be expressed as the satisfiability of $\pi_{X\setminus\{x\}}(\sigma_{x=a}(Sol(C)))$, which can be expressed in the language since we assume closure under instantiation, and the proofs for the implication and determinacy properties follow from this result.

A slightly different closure property is needed for the removability of value a for variable x since it is expressed as $\pi_{X\setminus\{x\}}(Sol(C)) \subseteq \pi_{X\setminus\{x\}}(\sigma_{x\neq a}(Sol(C)))$.

Nevertheless, since on boolean domains a value v is *removable* if v is substitutable by $\neg v$, and from the remarks on the closure properties of Schaefer's classes, and the previous proposition, we obtain that:

Corollary 2. *Testing fixability, substitutability, interchangeability, inconsistency, determinacy, irrelevance and removability is tractable for a boolean CSP where constraints are either Horn clauses, dual Horn clauses, clauses of size at most two or affine constraints.*

4.2 Tractability Through Locality

An important class of incomplete criteria to determine in polynomial time whether a complex property holds are those based on *local* reasoning. This approach has proved extremely successful for consistency [19] and interchangeability [11] properties. We propose in this section a systematic investigation of whether a local approach can be used for value-based properties.

Verifying a property $P(C)$ of a set of constraints C *locally* means that we verify the property on a well-chosen number of sub-problems. We must ensure that this approach is sound for the considered property:

Definition 3 (soundness of local reasoning). *We say that local reasoning on a property P is sound if, for all subsets of constraints $C_1 \subseteq C, \ldots, C_k \subseteq C$ such that $\bigcup_{i \in 1..k} C_i = C$, we have*

$$\left(\bigwedge_{i \in 1..k} P(C_i)\right) \rightarrow P(C)$$

Note that if a property P satisfies this requirement, its negation satisfies a stronger soundness property: $\left(\bigvee_{i \in 1..k} \neg P(C_i)\right) \rightarrow \neg P(C)$. A typical choice of granularity is to simply consider that each C_i contains one of the constraints of C as is done, for instance, for arc-consistency. On the other extreme, if we take a unique $C_1 = C$, we have a global checking. Between these two extremes, a wide range of intermediate levels can be defined [10,11].

Reasoning locally is typically tractable if we focus on a moderate number of subsets of C, and under the condition that we can bound the complexity of reasoning on each of these subsets. A typical assumption in CSP is that we can bound the arity of the constraints, and that every constraint is for instance binary. In this case, the cost of determining any property of the constraint is polynomial (here again we are indeed polynomial *in the domain size*, we therefore assume that the input is represented in a way polynomial in the domain size, for instance with the domains listed explicitly); and if we choose to reason locally by considering each constraint separately, or by taking groups of constraints of bounded size, then local checking is tractable.

Proposition 4. *Local reasoning is sound for the properties of substitutability, interchangeability, fixability, inconsistency and implication.*

Proof. The result is well-known for consistency [19], substitutability and interchangeability [11]. Fixability of variable x to value b can be expressed as

$$\forall a \neq b \; (\text{substitutable}_C(S, x, a, b))$$

Therefore, if we have $\bigwedge_{i \in 1..k} \text{fixable}_{C_i}(S, x, b)$ (which is equivalent to $\bigwedge_i \bigwedge_{a \neq b} \text{substitutable}_{C_i}(S, x, a, b)$ and to $\bigwedge_{a \neq b} \bigwedge_i \text{substitutable}_{C_i}(S, x, a, b)$), then we have $\bigwedge_{a \neq b} \text{substitutable}_C(S, x, a, b)$, which means $\text{fixable}_C(S, x, b)$. The implication property satisfies the following, stronger property (which implies that local reasoning is sound):

$$\left(\bigvee_{i \in 1...m} \text{implied}_{C_i}(S, x, a) \right) \rightarrow \text{implied}_C(S, x, a)$$

In effect, if a value a is implied for variable x in any C_i, then all tuples t with $t_x \neq a$ violate the constraints of C_i and do a fortiori not belong to $Sol(C)$.

There is only one property, namely removability, for which the local approach is unfortunately not sound:

Proposition 5. *Local reasoning is **not** sound for the removability property.*

Proof. Take $C = C_1 \wedge C_2$, where C_1 is defined as $x \leq y$ and C_2 as $x \geq y$. Suppose the domain has values $\{1, 2, 3\}$. Value 2 for x is removable from both constraints considered independently since, in both cases, we can change the value of any solution which assigns 2 to x to another value. Still, value 2 is not removable from their conjunction.

Note that removing values which are shown to be removable only locally can even make a satisfiable problem unsatisfiable: if furthermore we add the constraints C_3, defined as $x \neq 1$ and C_4, defined as $x \neq 3$, then value 2 for x is removable in each constraint, while the only (global) solution actually has value 2 on x.

This proposition raises an interesting issue: does there exist new (*i.e.*, other than the special cases of substitutable and inconsistent values) properties for which local reasoning is sound and which imply removability?

We end this section by noting that the local version of the fixability property is indeed a generalisation for arbitrary domains of the *pure literal rule* [7] which is well-known in the case of boolean constraints in conjunctive normal form. The pure literal rule exploits the cases where no constraint (clause) of the problem has a positive (*resp.* negative) occurrence of some variable x. In this case, assigning value 0 (*resp.* 1) to x preserves the satisfiability of the problem: if a solution t with $t_x = 1$ exists, then $t[x := 0]$ will also be a solution since no clause constrains x to have value 1. It is clear that the pure literal rule is a rule to detect fixability based on a reasoning local to each clause (a variable x is fixable to, say, 1 in a clause iff this clause does not contain the literal $\neg x$, and the pure literal rule checks that this condition holds for every constraint).

5 Conclusions and Perspectives

In this paper we focused on structural properties of CSPs that can be exploited by the solver in order to simplify search. Starting from the well-known notions of inconsistency and substitutability, we propose *removability* as a property which subsumes both of them, as well as several new others, *e.g.*, fixability, which are particularly interesting if we want to find just a solution of the input CSP, and not to compute all of them. By classifying these properties in a unified hierarchy, we investigated the semantical connections among them, and provided a first step towards a comprehensive framework. Note that our central definitions are *value-based* and that more general definitions inspired from the *tuple-based* notion of substitutability proposed in [14] could be considered in future work.

Then, we tackled the questions related to their automated detection and of their exploitation by the solving engine for simplifying problems. In particular, we showed how detecting all the proposed properties is generally intractable, but, for many of them, it becomes polynomial-time in two cases: by restricting the constraint languages, and by exploiting locality. Moreover, we discussed how in some cases such properties may arise from explicit promises made by users. This is the case of problems with properties such as functional dependencies and unique solutions.

Two of the perspectives raised by our work concern the new properties which have emerged from it. We have identified the removability property as an ideal characterisation of the values which can be removed while preserving satisfiability. Unfortunately, negative results (coNP-completeness of the detection of this property and impossibility of local reasoning) make it impossible to directly use the removability property in practice. This justifies the use of weaker notions (like inconsistency or substitutability) which imply the removability property, yet can be checked by tractable means (of course at the price of losing completeness). An interesting problem is to determine new cases where removability-checking is tractable. Lastly, the benefits of fixability have long been known in the boolean case, since this property has been used in the form of the pure literal rule in many SAT solvers. Its generalisation to CSPs has not yet been considered, and will be the subject of future work. Another issue we intend to explore is the application of the properties of Definition 1 to problems not in NP, *e.g.*, to model checking of formulae of temporal logic or quantified boolean formulae.

Acknowledgements. Work partially supported by project ASTRO funded by the Italian Ministry for Research under the FIRB framework (funds for basic research), and by a COFIN/PRIN project. We thank the reviewers for their careful reading which helped us improving the paper.

References

1. M. Cadoli and T. Mancini. Exploiting functional dependencies in declarative problem specifications. In *9th Euro. Conf. on Logic in Artificial Intelligence (JELIA)*, pages 628–640. Springer, 2004.
2. M. Cadoli and T. Mancini. Using a theorem prover for reasoning on constraint problems. In *3rd Int. CP Workshop on Modelling and Reformulating CSPs*, 2004.

3. B. Choueiry, A. Lal, and E. C. Freuder. Interchangeability and dynamic bundling for non-binary finite CSPs. In *Int. Workshop on Constraint Solving and Constraint Logic Programming (CSCLP)*, page To appear. Springer, 2004.
4. B. Choueiry and G. Noubir. On the computation of local interchangeability in discrete constraint satisfaction problems. In *Nat. (US) Conf. on Artificial Intelligence (AAAI)*, pages 326–333. AAAI, 1998.
5. J. M. Crawford. A theoretical analysis of reasoning by symmetry in first-order logic (extended abstract). In *AAAI Workshop on Tractable Reasoning*, 1992.
6. J. M. Crawford, M. L. Ginsberg, E. M. Luks, and A. Roy. Symmetry-breaking predicates for search problems. In *Int. Conf. on Principles of Knowledge Representation and Reasoning (KR)*, pages 148–159. Morgan Kaufmann, 1996.
7. M. Davis and H. Putnam. A computing procedure for quantification theory. *J. of the ACM*, 7(3):201–215, 1960.
8. R. Dechter. Constraint networks (survey). In *Encyclopedia of Artificial Intelligence, 2nd edition*, pages 276–285. 1992.
9. S. Even, A. Selman, and Y. Yacobi. The complexity of promise problems with applications to public-key cryptography. *Information and Control*, 61(2):159–173, 1984.
10. E. C. Freuder. Synthesizing constraint expressions. *Comm. of the ACM*, 21(11):958–966, 1978.
11. E. C. Freuder. Eliminating interchangeable values in constraint satisfaction problems. In *Nat. (US) Conf. on Artificial Intelligence (AAAI)*, pages 227–233. AAAI Press, 1991.
12. I. P. Gent and B. M. Smith. Symmetry breaking in constraint programming. In *Euro. Conf. on Artificial Intelligence (ECAI)*, pages 599–603. IOS Press, 2000.
13. E. Giunchiglia, A. Massarotto, and R. Sebastiani. Act, and the rest will follow: Exploiting determinism in planning as satisfiability. In *Nat. (US) Conf. on Artificial Intelligence (AAAI)*, pages 948–953. AAAI, 1998.
14. P. Jeavons, D. A. Cohen, and M. C. Cooper. A substitution operation for constraints. In *Int. Conf. on Principles and Practice of Constraint Programming (CP)*, pages 1–9. Springer, 1994.
15. P. Jonsson and A. Krokhin. Recognizing frozen variables in constraint satisfaction problems. *Theoretical Computer Science (TCS)*, 329(1-3):93–113, 2004.
16. J. Köbler, U. Schöning, and J. Torán. *The graph isomorphism problem: its computational complexity*. Birkhauser, 1993.
17. A. Lenstra and H. W. Lenstra. Algorithms in number theory. In J. van Leeuwen, editor, *The Handbook of Theoretical Computer Science, vol. 1: Algorithms and Complexity*. MIT Press, 1990.
18. C. M. Li. Integrating equivalency reasoning into Davis-Putnam procedure. In *Nat. (US) Conf. on Artificial Intelligence (AAAI)*, pages 291–296. AAAI press, 2000.
19. A.K. Mackworth. Consistency in networks of relations. *Artificial Intelligence*, 8:99–118, 1977.
20. R. Monasson, R. Zecchina, S. Kirkpatrick, B. Selman, and L. Troyansky. Determining computational complexity from characteristic 'phase transitions'. *Nature*, 400:133–137, 1999.
21. U. Montanari. Networks of constraints: Fundamental properties and applications to picture processing. *Information Science*, 7(2):85–132, 1974.
22. Ch. H. Papadimitriou. *Computational Complexity*. Addison Wesley, 1994.
23. T. Pyhälä. Factoring benchmarks for SAT solvers. Technical report, Helsinki university of technology, 2004.
24. T. J. Schaefer. The complexity of satisfiability problems. In *ACM Symp. on Theory of Computing (STOC)*, pages 216–226. ACM, 1978.

Evaluating QBFs via Symbolic Skolemization

Marco Benedetti[§]

Istituto per la Ricerca Scientifica e Tecnologica (IRST)
Via Sommarive 18, 38055 Povo, Trento, Italy
benedetti@itc.it

Abstract. We describe a novel decision procedure for Quantified Boolean Formulas (QBFs) which aims to unleash the hidden potential of quantified reasoning in applications. The Skolem theorem acts like a glue holding several ingredients together: BDD-based representations for boolean functions, search-based QBF decision procedure, and compilation-to-SAT techniques, among the others. To leverage all these techniques at once we show how to evaluate QBFs by symbolically reasoning on a compact representation for the propositional expansion of the skolemized problem. We also report about a first implementation of the procedure, which yields very interesting experimental results.

1 Introduction

Unquestionably, the most effective tools for solving a large class of industrial-scale problems (such as computer-aided design of integrated circuits [19], Planning [17], Model Checking for dynamic systems [5], Scheduling, Operations Research, and Cryptography, to name a few) are SAT solvers, which are search-based reasoning engines designed to decide the existence of models for propositional instances (PROP).

One step ahead of PROP, we encounter the more expressive language of quantified boolean formulas (QBFs), which adds the valuable possibility to quantify (universally or existentially) over the truth value of variables. Many of the problems mentioned above feature a far more handily QBF formulation, which is also (possibly) exponentially more succinct than the propositional one. For sure, by sticking to PROP we avoid worsening the decision complexity from NP to PSPACE. But, we also loose the expressive power of quantification, which not only provide a natural way to state relevant facts or rules, but could also be exploited during the solving process. At least in principle.

What really matters to applications is the capability of a reasoning engine to solve those problems that arise in practice. Hence, we ask: Is the balance between the above pros and cons favorable to QBF? Do quantified decision procedures add substantial value to the reasoning capabilities of purely propositional SAT solvers? The answer is: *not yet*. QBF is a promising formalism, but substantial improvements in decision procedures are expected before its potential can be unleashed to applications [1, 21, 4].

The observations above motivates this paper, in which we describe a new solving paradigm that captures the added value of quantified reasoning. A twofold novelty is introduced. On the one hand, we reinterpret the Skolem theorem to reassess quantified reasoning as a quantifier-free, propositional reasoning over a purposely designed

---

[§] This work was supported by PAT (*Provincia Autonoma di Trento*, Italy), grant n. 3248/2003.

symbolic representation. We show how this allows to mix (1) the inference power of quantified reasoning, (2) the strength of many well known SAT techniques, and (3) the classical search-based decision procedures for QBF. On the other hand, several powerful techniques for automated reasoning are arranged within a coherent framework in a way that is advantageous and instrumental in realizing the just mentioned approach.

The essential component of our construction traces back to the Twenties (the Skolem theorem [31]). Following the timeline, we capitalize on the seminal contributions to propositional theorem proving from the Sixties (DPLL algorithms [9, 10]). Then, a compact formalism from the Eighties to reason on boolean functions [6] is employed. Effective quantified reasoning comes from the Nineties [7, 18]. In the same years, techniques to translate real-world problems into SAT arised [17, 19, 5] which are adapted to our case. Finally, symbolic representations for propositional problems gained attention in the last few years [8, 25, 28], and are largely useful here. These techniques are exercised together thanks to a symbolic representation for the propositional expansion of skolemized QBF instances, also resorting to SAT-based reasoning when it pays back.

In the rest of this paper we introduce some preliminaries (Section 2), present symbolic skolemization (Section 3), discuss symbolic reasoning strategies (Section 4), analyze experimental results (Section 5), and give our concluding remarks (Section 6).

2 Preliminaries

We consider quantified boolean formulas in *prenex conjunctive normal form*[1], such as

$$f = \forall a \exists b \forall c \exists d. \; (\neg a \lor c \lor d) \land (\neg b \lor \neg d) \land (a \lor b \lor \neg d) \land (\neg a \lor b) \tag{1}$$

where "$\forall a \exists b \forall c \exists d$" is called *prefix* and is followed by a conjunctive normal form (CNF) *matrix*, i.e. a propositional formula made up by conjuncting clauses, each clause being a disjunction of literals (a variable or a negated variable). More in general, we consider formulas $Q_1 V_1 Q_2 V_2 \ldots Q_n V_n. \mathcal{M}$ where $Q_i \in \{\forall, \exists\}$, $Q_i \neq Q_{i+1}$, and the matrix $\mathcal{M}$ has variables $var(\mathcal{M}) = \cup_{i=1}^n V_i$ ($V_i \cap V_j = \emptyset$ for $i \neq j$). Variables $v \in V_i$ are said to be existentially (universally) quantified if $Q_i = \exists$ ($Q_i = \forall$). The set of existentially (universally) quantified variables in a QBF f is denoted by $var_\exists(f)$ ($var_\forall(f)$). The universal depth $\delta(v)$ of an existential variable $v \in V_i$ is the number of universal variables dominating v: $\delta(v) = \sum_{Q_j = \forall, j < i} |V_j|$. For clauses, it is $\delta(\Gamma) = max_{v \in var_\exists(\Gamma)} \delta(v)$.

We use lowercase (uppercase) roman letters for propositional variables (clauses), and greek letters for values in the boolean space $\mathfrak{B} = \{0, 1\}$ and vectors in $\mathfrak{B}^n$. For example: $\Psi = \langle \psi_1, \ldots, \psi_n \rangle \in \mathcal{I} \subseteq \mathfrak{B}^n$. The complement of $\mathcal{I} \subseteq \mathfrak{B}^n$ is denoted by $\overline{\mathcal{I}}$.

Double negation on literals is disallowed: $\neg\neg l$ is rewritten as l. We use exclusive-or to build literals out of variables: $\varphi \otimes v$ means v when $\varphi = 0$, and $\neg v$ when $\varphi = 1$. Given a literal $l = \varphi \otimes v$, we pose $var(l) = v$. An *assignment* is a consistent set of literals (i.e. a set S such that $\nexists l \in S | \neg l \in S$). We denote by $C * l$ the result of applying the assignment $\{l\}$ to the clause C. C is unchanged if $var(l) \notin var(C)$, is *subsumed* if $l \in C$, and *resolves* to $C \setminus \{\neg l\}$ if $\neg l \in C$. This notion is extended to sets of clauses and literals: $f * A$ is the formula resulting from applying A to each clause in f.

---

[1] This choice causes no loss of generality and is shared by all the available encodings of real-world problems [15]. However, it might be responsible for an increase in proof complexity.

Finally, *forall reduction* is a model preserving transformation for QBFs that consists in removing from each clause C all the universal literals $\pi \otimes v \leftarrow C$ with $v \in V_i$ such that $var_\exists(C) \cap V_j = \emptyset$ for every $j > i$. We always consider forall-reduced formulas.

3 Symbolic Propositional Skolemization for QBFs

We leverage the Skolem theorem to map any QBF instance onto a satisfiability equivalent SAT instance featuring a very compact symbolic representation. We interleave the development of the general method with the presentation of a running example.

3.1 Propositional Skolemization

The Skolem theorem [31] shows how to transform any given *First Order Logic* (FOL) statement f into a *skolemized* formula $Sk(f)$ that has two properties: (1) $Sk(f)$ contains no existential quantifier, and (2) $Sk(f)$ is satisfiable iff f is satisfiable (see [12] for a survey). Existential quantifiers are eliminated by replacing the variables they bind with *Skolem functions* whose definition domains are appositely chosen to preserve satisfiability. We empoly an *outer* form of skolemization [26], in which the function introduced for $e \in var_\exists(f)$ depends on all the universal variables that have e in their scope (for prenex formulas: all the universal variables to the left of e in the prefix).

Functions have no direct representation in $PROP$, but their *definability* can be captured at the expense of a possibly exponential blowup in the size of the instance.

We adopt a three-step *propositional skolemization* for a QBF instance f.

1. Translation of f into a satisfiability equivalent FOL instance $FOL(f)$.
2. Application of the Skolem theorem to $FOL(f)$ to obtain a (satisfiability preserving) FOL instance $Sk(FOL(f))$ with no existential quantifier.
3. Translation of $Sk(FOL(f))$ into an equivalent SAT instance $Prop(Sk(FOL(f)))$.

The first step is a slight rephrase of the problem, but it allows us to plainly capture the intuition behind propositional skolemization. Skolem funtions leverage the existence of two semantics levels in FOL, namely the level of *predicates* and the level of *terms*. Skolem functions are terms that are substituted for other terms (the existential variables) as arguments of predicates. QBF and $PROP$ lack the formal mechanisms necessary to cope with those two levels. They just feature the predicate level, though this is obfuscated by their variable-oriented syntax. To uncover such level, we introduce a FOL unary predicate $\mathbf{p}$ defined over the boolean space $\mathfrak{B}$, and interpreted as $\mathbf{p}(1) = TRUE$, $\mathbf{p}(0) = FALSE$, and restrict the domain of interpretation of every variable to be the boolean space as well. This immediately allows us to rewrite every QBF as a satisfiability equivalent FOL formula. For example, by rewriting the QBF (1) we obtain

$$f' = FOL(f) = \forall a \exists b \forall c \exists d. \ (\neg \mathbf{p}(a) \lor \mathbf{p}(c) \lor \mathbf{p}(d)) \land (\neg \mathbf{p}(b) \lor \neg \mathbf{p}(d)) \\ \land (\mathbf{p}(a) \lor \mathbf{p}(b) \lor \neg \mathbf{p}(d)) \land (\neg \mathbf{p}(a) \lor \mathbf{p}(b))$$

In the second step we eliminate existential quantifiers by substituting to each existential variable v a Skolem function s^v depending on the proper subset of dominating universal quantifiers. We obtain a satisfiability-equivalent purely universal formula.

$$Sk(f') = \forall a \forall c. \ (\neg \mathbf{p}(a) \lor \mathbf{p}(c) \lor \mathbf{p}(s^d(a,c))) \land (\neg \mathbf{p}(s^b(a)) \lor \neg \mathbf{p}(s^d(a,c))) \\ \land (\mathbf{p}(a) \lor \mathbf{p}(s^b(a)) \lor \neg \mathbf{p}(s^d(a,c))) \land (\neg \mathbf{p}(a) \lor \mathbf{p}(s^b(a))) \quad (2)$$

From a FOL point of view, existential quantifiers are simply disappeared. The dute we pay for this simplification is the loss of logical equivalence. From a higher-level point of view, we can predicate over the interpretation of terms and explicitly state what the Skolem theorem implicitly says when it reduces the satisfiability of $FOL(f)$ to the satisfiability of $Sk(FOL(f))$, i.e. that each *inner* existential FOL quantification over v has been substituted by an *outer* higher-order existential quantification over s^v (over the existence of a proper interpretation for the Skolem terms). Informally:

$$\forall a \exists b \forall c \exists d.\ f(a,b,c,d) \quad \overset{SAT}{\Longleftrightarrow} \quad [\exists s^b \exists s^d] \forall a \forall c.\ f(a, s^b(a), c, s^d(a,c))$$

In the third step (translation to $PROP$), the actual work is done. It amounts to *flatten* the two semantics levels introduced above onto one single propositional level. This transformation is made easy by the constructive property that for every formula $Sk(FOL(f))$ with $f \in QBF$ both the predicate-level and the term-level interpretations map boolean spaces onto boolean values. We join their definition spaces and interpretation functions, and give an inductive translation procedure from $Sk(FOL(f))$ to $PROP$.

The only non-trivial piece of work consists of building a CNF propositional representation for every (possibly negated) Skolem term. As a constructive consequence of steps 1-2, every Skolem function $s(a_1, a_2, \ldots, a_n)$ we manage is a relation over $\mathfrak{B}^{n+1}$ that maps $\mathfrak{B}^n$ onto $\mathfrak{B}$. Each one is completely specified by 2^n boolean parameters giving the truth value of the function on each point of its domain, so 2^{2^n} different Skolem n-ary functions exist. Let us denote by s_Ψ the boolean parameter that represents the truth value of a boolean n-ary function s evaluated in $\Psi = \langle \psi_i, \psi_2, \ldots, \psi_n \rangle \in \mathfrak{B}^n$. We directly obtain a CNF propositional version for $s(a_1, a_2, \ldots, a_n)$ as follows:

$$Prop(\varphi \otimes s(a_1, \ldots, a_n)) \doteq \bigwedge_{\Psi \in \mathfrak{B}^n} (\varphi \otimes s_\Psi) \vee \neg(\psi_1 \otimes a_1) \vee \neg(\psi_2 \otimes a_2) \vee \cdots \vee \neg(\psi_n \otimes a_n)$$

For example, the Skolem terms $\neg s^b(a)$ and $s^d(a,c)$ are translated as $Prop(\neg s^b(a)) = (\neg s_0^b \vee a) \wedge (\neg s_1^b \vee \neg a)$, and $Prop(s^d(a,c)) = (s_{11}^d \vee \neg a \vee \neg c) \wedge (s_{10}^d \vee \neg a \vee c) \wedge (s_{01}^d \vee a \vee \neg c) \wedge (s_{00}^d \vee a \vee c)$. So, $Prop(s^d(a,c))$ may be seen as a function mapping a point $\langle \alpha, \gamma \rangle \in \mathfrak{B}^2$ onto the proper value $s_{\alpha\gamma}^d = s^d(\alpha, \gamma)$, and the same for $Prop(\neg s^b(a))$.

The next step extends the translation from terms to predicates. Let us first consider a clause containing only one existentially quantified variable e with polarity φ:

$$\forall u_1 \forall u_2 \cdots \forall u_n \exists e.\ (\pi_1 \otimes u_{i_1}) \vee (\pi_2 \otimes u_{i_2}) \vee \cdots \vee (\pi_r \otimes u_{i_r}) \vee (\varphi \otimes e)$$

where $u_1, u_2, \ldots, u_n$ are all the universal variables dominating e, while a subset $u_{i_1}, u_{i_2}, \ldots, u_{i_r}$, $r \leq n$ of such variables appears in the clause with polarities $\pi_1, \pi_2, \ldots, \pi_r$. By substituting for e the expansion $Prop(\varphi \otimes s(u_1, \ldots, u_n))$ of the Skolem function $s : \mathfrak{B}^n \to \mathfrak{B}$ defined by the 2^n parameters $\{s_{0\ldots00}, s_{0\ldots01}, \cdots, s_{1\ldots11}\}$, we obtain:

$$\exists s_{0\ldots00} \exists s_{0\ldots01} \cdots \exists s_{1\ldots11}$$
$$\forall u_1 \forall u_2 \cdots \forall u_n$$
$$(\pi_1 \otimes u_{i_1}) \vee (\pi_2 \otimes u_{i_2}) \vee \cdots \vee (\pi_r \otimes u_{i_r}) \vee$$
$$\vee \left(\bigwedge_{\Psi \in \mathfrak{B}^n} (\varphi \otimes s_\Psi) \vee \neg(\psi_1 \otimes u_1) \vee \cdots \vee \neg(\psi_n \otimes u_n) \right)$$

As a consequence of the semantics flattening we have performed, the "meta" existential quantifier over an n-ary Skolem function has been transformed into a set of 2^n outer existential quantifiers. In the worst case, we have to distribute the disjunction over all the clauses in the last term, thus obtaining 2^n clauses. Fortunately, some (many) of those clauses are trivially satisfied by complementary literals. In particular, whenever $\psi_{i_j} = \pi_j$ for at least one $j \subset [1, \ldots, r]$, the clause is satisfied, so that we get only $2^{n-r} = 2^{\delta(e)-r}$ clauses. Moreover, skolemized clauses no longer contain existential variables dominated by universal variables, hence all the universal literals are *forall reducible*. As a result of these two properties, we obtain the set of unit clauses:

$$\exists s_{0\ldots00}\exists s_{0\ldots01}\cdots\exists s_{1\ldots11}. \bigwedge_{\Psi \in \mathcal{I}} \varphi \otimes e_{\Psi}, \text{ where } \mathcal{I} = \{\Psi \in \mathfrak{B}^n | \forall j. \psi_{i_j} \neq \pi_j\}$$

In the general case we have clauses containing m existential variables $\{e_1, e_2, \ldots, e_m\}$ with $\delta(e_1) \leq \delta(e_2) \leq \ldots \leq \delta(e_m)$ and polarities $\varphi_1, \ldots, \varphi_m$, where each e_i is dominated by a set $\cup_{j=0}^{i} U_j$ of universal variables. Each clause also contains a possibly empty subset of universal literals $\{\pi_k \otimes u_k, k = i_{j-1}+1, \ldots, i_j\} \subseteq U_j$ for each $j = 1, \ldots, m$, with $i_0 = 0$. The general shape for the clause is

$$\forall U_1 \exists e_1 \cdots \forall U_m \exists e_m. \quad (\pi_1 \otimes u_{i_1}) \vee \cdots \vee (\pi_{j_1} \otimes u_{i_{j_1}}) \vee (\varphi_1 \otimes e_1) \vee$$
$$(\pi_{j_1+1} \otimes u_{i_{j_1+1}}) \vee \cdots \vee (\pi_{j_2} \otimes u_{i_{j_2}}) \vee (\varphi_2 \otimes e_2) \vee \quad (3)$$
$$\vdots$$
$$(\pi_{j_{m-1}+1} \otimes u_{i_{j_{m-1}+1}}) \vee \cdots \vee (\pi_{j_m} \otimes u_{i_{j_m}}) \vee (\varphi_m \otimes e_m)$$

By (a) propositionally skolemizing all the existential variables in such clause, and (b) applying forall reduction to all the variables in $\cup_{j=0}^{m} U_j$, we obtain:

$$\exists S_1 \cdots \exists S_m. \bigwedge_{\substack{\Psi \in \mathfrak{B}^{\delta_m} \\ \forall j. \psi_{i_j} \neq \pi_j}} (\varphi_1 \otimes s_{\Psi|\delta_1}^{(1)}) \vee (\varphi_2 \otimes s_{\Psi|\delta_2}^{(2)}) \vee \cdots \vee (\varphi_m \otimes s_{\Psi|\delta_m}^{(m)}) \quad (4)$$

where $\Psi|_k$ denotes the k-bit long prefix of Ψ, $\delta_i = \delta(e_i)$, the boolean parameter $s_{\Psi'}^{(i)}$ represents the truth value over $\Psi' = \Psi|_{\delta_i} \in \mathfrak{B}^{\delta_i}$ of the Skolem function $s^{(i)}$ introduced for e_i, and $S_i = \{s_{\Psi}^{(i)} | \Psi \in \mathfrak{B}^{\delta_i}\}$. The abstraction operator "$|$" generalizes to sets as $\mathcal{I}|_k \doteq \{\langle \psi_1 \ldots, \psi_k \rangle | \exists \langle \psi_1, \ldots, \psi_k, \ldots, \psi_n \rangle \in \mathcal{I}\}$ with $\mathcal{I} \subseteq \mathfrak{B}^n$ and $k \leq n$.

We denote by $PropSk(\cdot)$ the function that applied to a generic QBF clause represented by Expression (3) yields the result of our three-step translation, i.e. the set of clauses represented by Expression (4). The cardinality of this clause set is $2^{\delta(e_m)-j_m}$.

To translate an entire formula, we observe that Skolem terms are introduced once per variable. So, the propositional skolemization of any formula is obtained by joining together the skolem clauses obtained out of each QBF clause, always re-using the same parameters on the same existential variable. The overall procedure defines a satisfiability-preserving mapping $PropSk : QBF \longrightarrow PROP$ between the original QBF space and a purely propositional space. For a QBF f with $var_\exists(f) = \{e_1, \ldots, e_m\}$, the $PROP$ instance is defined over the set of fresh variables $\{s_{\Psi}^{(i)}, i = 1, \ldots, m, \Psi \in \mathfrak{B}^{\delta(e_i)}\}$.

As an example, by propositionally skolemizing (1) we obtain

$$\exists s_0^b \exists s_1^b \exists s_{00}^d \exists s_{01}^d \exists s_{10}^d \exists s_{11}^d. \; (s_{01}^d) \wedge (\neg s_0^b \vee \neg s_{00}^d) \wedge (\neg s_0^b \vee \neg s_{01}^d) \wedge (\neg s_1^b \vee \neg s_{10}^d) \\ \wedge (\neg s_1^b \vee \neg s_{11}^d) \wedge (s_1^b \vee \neg s_{10}^d) \wedge (s_1^b \vee \neg s_{11}^d) \wedge (s_0^b) \quad (5)$$

If (and only if) we find a model for (5) we are entitled to conclude that (2) is satisfiable, so that (1) evaluates to $TRUE$. Not only we are ensured that a proper interpretation for the Skolem functions s^b and s^d do exist to satisfy the formula, but we have explicitily *computed* such an interpretation. Every model for (5) gives us the desired truth value of acceptable skolem functions over each point of their domains.

3.2 Symbolic Representation

The term "symbolic representation" has a broad AI-related sense, but it has been used with a much more specific meaning in the realm of model checking (MC). According to MC's usage of the word, a symbolic representation is one that allows to shift from *explicit* MC techniques—where each state of a system to be checked is individually represented and manipulated—to *symbolic* MC approaches—where data structures are employed that allow to compactly and implicitly represent (possibly huge) sets of states, and also to reason about them as a whole. We adopt MC's viewpoint here, as we are interested in symbolically representing and manipulating sets of clauses.

This interest originates in the observation that $PropSk(f)$ may be exponentially larger than f. Without some powerful tool for compactly representing and managing propositional skolemizations, not only it may be unfeasible to solve the resulting SAT instances, but they might not even fit into the memory of any real machine.

Related approaches exist in the literature (see Section 6), but we have to manage a very special case here, and we want to profit from its structure. In particular, we are only interested in representing clause-sets coming from propositional skolemization of QBF formulas, with a representation that is closed under the operations we define in the next section. Our representation employs one single *symbolic clause* to compactly represent the whole clause set described by the Expression (4) w.r.t. the QBF clause C described in Expression (3). We need to memorize three pieces of information:

1. The list $\Gamma = [\varphi_1 \otimes e_1, \ldots, \varphi_m \otimes e_m]$ of existential literals in the originating clause.
2. The set of indexes $\mathcal{I} = \{\Psi \in \mathfrak{B}^{\delta(e_m)} \mid \forall j. \psi_{i_j} \neq \pi_j\}$.
3. The list $[\delta(e_1), \ldots, \delta(e_m)]$ of the universal depths of each existential literal.

The information in Item 3 is not related to a single clause. Rather, it is an attribute of the formula as a whole that only depends on the prefix, and that needs to be represented once per formula. By contrast, the couple $\langle \Gamma, \mathcal{I} \rangle$ actually defines a symbolic clause $Symb(C)$ which we compactly denote by writing $\Gamma_\mathcal{I}$. The $Symb(\cdot)$ transformation is readily extended to QBF instances as $Symb : QBF \longrightarrow PROP_{SYMB}$, where $PROP_{SYMB}$ denotes the space of symbolic propositional instances. It is

$$Symb(\forall U_1 \exists e_1 \cdots \forall U_m \exists e_m.M) \doteq \exists [e_1]_{\delta_1} \cdots \exists [e_m]_{\delta_m}. \bigwedge_{C \in M} Symb(C) \qquad (6)$$

where $\exists [e_1]_{\delta_1} \cdots \exists [e_m]_{\delta_m}$ is a *symbolic prefix* mentioning a *symbolic variable* $[e_i]_{\delta_i}$ for each original existential variable e_i at universal depth $\delta_i = \delta(e_i)$.

For example, the symbolic representation of the QBF formula (1) is:

$$\mathcal{F} = \exists [b]_1 \exists [d]_2. \, [d]_{\{10\}} \wedge [\neg b, \neg d]_{\{00,01,10,11\}} \wedge [b, \neg d]_{\{00,01\}} \wedge [b]_{\{1\}} \qquad (7)$$

Each symbolic clause is made up of *symbolic literals*, that we represent as symbolic unit clauses. For example, the clause $[b, \neg d]_{\{00,01\}}$, under the prefix $\exists [b]_1 \exists [d]_2$, is made up by the symbolic literals $[b]_{\{0\}}$ and $[\neg d]_{\{00,01\}}$. A symbolic literal $[\varphi \otimes e]_\mathcal{I}$ belongs to a symbolic clause $\Gamma_\mathcal{J}$, written $[\varphi \otimes e]_\mathcal{I} \in \Gamma_\mathcal{J}$, when $\varphi \otimes e \in \Gamma$ and $\mathcal{I} \subseteq \mathcal{J}|_{\delta(e)}$. As opposite to symbolic objects, the standard propositional elements are called *ground* objects. For example, the ground literals $\neg d_{00}$ and $\neg d_{01}$ belong to the symbolic literal $[\neg d]_{\{00,01\}}$, while the ground clauses $b_0 \vee \neg d_{01}$ and $b_0 \vee \neg d_{00}$ belongs to $[b, \neg d]_{\{00,01\}}$.

Symbolic formulas have both a *symbolic size* and a *ground size*. The symbolic size of $\mathcal{F}$ is the number of symbolic clauses (or literals) in the formula. The ground size is the number of clauses (or literals) in $Prop(\mathcal{F})$. So, the symbolic size (number of clauses) for a symbolic formula $\mathcal{F}$ is $|\mathcal{F}|_{symb} = \sum_{\Gamma_\mathcal{I} \in \mathcal{F}} |\Gamma|$, while its ground size is $|\mathcal{F}|_{ground} = \sum_{\Gamma_\mathcal{I} \in \mathcal{F}} |\mathcal{I}|$. For example, the formula (7) has symbolic size equal to 4 and ground size equal to 8. The ground size is always greater than the symbolic size, as each symbolic clause represents at least one ground clause.

Symbolic formulas exhibit three appealing properties: (1) they preserve the satisfiability of the originating QBF instance, (2) they are compactly representable, and (3) they can be efficiently manipulated to perform deductions. We here consider the first two properties, and delay the discussion on the third one until the next section.

Semantics for Symbolic Formulas. We define an evaluation mechanism for symbolic formulas based on the standard evaluation of their propositional expansion. According to Expression (4), we can re-gain the ground meaning of $\Gamma_\mathcal{I} = [\varphi_1 \otimes e_1, \ldots, \varphi_m \otimes e_m]_\mathcal{I}$ under the relevant prefix $\mathcal{P} = \exists [e_1]_{\delta_1} \cdots \exists [e_m]_{\delta_m}$ through a function $Prop$ defined as

$$Prop(\mathcal{P}, \Gamma_\mathcal{I}) \doteq \bigwedge_{\Psi \in \mathcal{I}} \varphi_1 \otimes s^{(1)}_{\Psi|\delta_1} \vee \ldots \vee \varphi_m \otimes s^{(m)}_{\Psi|\delta_m} \qquad (8)$$

This function is extended to a symbolic formula $\mathcal{F}$ with matrix $\mathcal{M}$ and prefix $\mathcal{P}$ by posing $Prop(\mathcal{F}) \doteq \bigwedge_{\Gamma_\mathcal{I} \in \mathcal{M}} Prop(\mathcal{P}, \Gamma_\mathcal{I})$. In particular, a consistent set of symbolic literals $\{[e_1]_{\mathcal{I}_1}, \ldots, [e_k]_{\mathcal{I}_k}\}$ is a model for $\mathcal{F} = \mathcal{P}. \mathcal{M} = Symb(f), f \in QBF$ iff the ground assignment $\cup_{j=1,\ldots,k} Prop(\mathcal{P}, [e_j]_{\mathcal{I}_j})$ is a model for $Prop(Symb(f))$. By construction, it is $Prop(Symb(f)) = PropSk(f)$, hence the QBF f evaluates to $TRUE$ iff $Symb(f)$ is satisfiable. For example, the $Prop$ function applied to (7) yields (5).

Compact Representation. The (possible) exponential blowup in every symbolic clause $\Gamma_\mathcal{I}$ has been purposely confined to the cardinality of $\mathcal{I}$. We pursue compactness for its symbolic representation, notwithstanding its ground size, by employing a second layer of abstraction, consisting in the compact representation of $\mathcal{I}$ by means of *reduced ordered binary decision diagrams* (BDDs) defined over the set of variables $var_\forall(f)$.

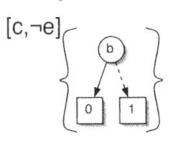
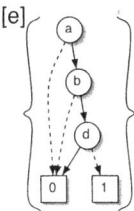

According to the semantics of BDDs, an entire set $\mathcal{I} = \{\Psi \in \mathfrak{B}^{\delta(e_m)} \mid \forall j.\psi_{i_j} \neq \pi_j\}$ is represented by a single linear-sized BDD (in m) requiring one internal node for each universal variable in the originating clause. The whole symbolic representation has a linear size w.r.t. the number of literals in the originating QBF clause. The picture aside depicts our representation of the skolemized version of $\forall a \forall b \exists c \forall d \exists e. (b \vee c \vee \neg e) \wedge (\neg a \vee \neg b \vee d \vee e)$. As an additional source of compactness, we notice that BDDs are semantically canonical representations, so they share *at least* all the representations for QBF clauses with the same universal literals. As we produce only one symbolic clause out of each QBF clause, the representation of $Symb(f)$ enlarges at most linearly with $|f|$. However, this *only holds for the initial representation*. The symbolic size may increase as a consequence of the symbolic inferences described in the next section.

4 Reasoning on Propositional Skolemizations

The evaluation of the original QBF instance has been restated as a satisfiability test on the symbolically represented existential instance $Symb(f)$. The peculiar structure of $Symb(f)$ allows to attack the SAT problem from three different perspectives, each one featuring specific strengths. We describe such methods in the subsequent three sections. Far from being mutually exclusive, those three strategies can be used in a synergic way, so that each one contributes at its best towards the common goal (see Section 4.3).

4.1 Ground Reasoning

The original QBF f can be evaluated by explicitly constructing $Prop(Symb(f))$ and solving it via state-of-the-art SAT solvers (they are very efficient on QBF-derived instances). We resort to this option only when the ground instance is affordable[2], which is not the case for many real-world problems. Yet, the reduced problems generated as described in Section 4.2, 4.3 are eventually small enough to be solved this way.

Altought theoretically straightforward, the computation of $Prop(Symb(f))$ deserves a lot of attention on the practical side, due to the (possibly) large number of (possibly) huge SAT instances generated out of each QBF formula. Groundization is made up of two steps: (1) generation of the *ground space* and (2) generation of the ground clauses. The latter step is executed according to Expression (8). The former constructs a mapping between the *structured* namespace of symbolic literals and a *flat*, SAT-solver friendly namespace for ground literals. It amounts to associate a unique positive integer to each ground variable that belongs to at least one clause in the current symbolic formula (and to them only). To prevent the SAT solver from suffering unnecessarily large data structures, the set of variable codes generated for the formula as a whole should be composed of all and only the integers in the interval $[1, n]$, for some sufficiently large n. In essence, we need a partial, efficiently invertible function $V_{map} : D_\exists \times D_\forall \to [1, n]$ where $D_\exists = var_\exists(f)$, $D_\forall = \mathfrak{B}^{|var_\forall(f)|}$, and n just suffices to allow bijection.

4.2 Symbolic Reasoning

We define some *symbolic inference rules* over $PROP_{SYMB}$ to directly manipulate $Symb(f)$ while preserving the satisfiability of $Prop(Symb(f))$. As opposed to ground reasoning, the emphasis is on designing symbolic versions of the standard inference rules that work without expanding symbolic objects to ground objects. In essence, it is a matter of defining how the basic steps (subsumption, resolution, assignment, substitution) can be performed at a purely symbolic level on sets of ground clauses at once.

Complete refutation strategies—such as those based on SL, linear, or directional resolution—could be employed in principle. However, efficient and easy-to-implement forms of incomplete reasoning exist that capture many inferences relevant to QBF-derived instances. Even if the rules adopted are not refutationally complete, the computation of their deductive closure *normalizes* the instance. So, a satisfiability-equivalent, symbolic output formula with a (much) smaller ground size than the original one is generated, and other complete methods can safely work on such simplified version.

---

[2] By *affordable* we mean that the instance can be decided without running out of memory. Affordability thus depends on the SAT engine employed and on the available amount of memory.

The central step towards symbolic reasoning amounts to extend the star operator. Formerly absent empty clause sets $\Gamma_\emptyset$ may result, which are eliminated from the formula.

$$\Gamma_{\mathcal{I}} * [l]_{\mathcal{J}} = \begin{cases} \Gamma_{\mathcal{I}\cap\overline{\mathcal{J}}} & \text{when } l \in \Gamma \\ \Gamma_{\mathcal{I}\cap\overline{\mathcal{J}}} \wedge \Gamma'_{(\mathcal{I}\cap\mathcal{J})|_{\delta(\Gamma')}} & \text{with } \Gamma' = \Gamma \setminus \{\neg l\}, \text{when } \neg l \in \Gamma \\ \Gamma_{\mathcal{I}} & \text{otherwise} \end{cases} \tag{9}$$

The efficiency of symbolic reasoning thus stems from the structured nature of the representation, which takes universal reasoning apart form existential reasoning. BDD operations conveniently deal with the former, list-based representations with the latter.

We now exemplify four (incomplete) symbolic rules that are highly effective on average and can be implemented rather efficiently. In particular, notice that it is easy to symbolically extract both pure literals and unit clauses. Let us consider the formula

$$\begin{aligned} \exists a\forall b\exists c\forall de\exists fgh\forall i\exists l.\ &(\neg c\vee a) \wedge (\neg a\vee\neg g) \wedge (\neg e \vee h) \wedge (c \vee \neg e \vee g\vee\neg h) \\ &\wedge(\neg b\vee d\vee\neg f\vee l) \wedge (\neg e\vee f\vee g) \wedge (i\vee\neg c\vee\neg h\vee d\vee\neg l) \end{aligned} \tag{10}$$

and its symbolic matrix $\mathcal{M}$ (under the prefix $\exists[a]_0\exists[c]_1\exists[f]_3\exists[g]_3\exists[h]_3\exists[l]_4$):

$$\begin{aligned} &[\neg c, a]_{\{0,1\}} \wedge [\neg a, \neg g]_{\{0,1\}^3} \wedge [h]_{\{001,011,101,111\}} \wedge [c, g, \neg h]_{\{001,011,101,111\}} \wedge \\ &[\neg f, l]_{\{1000,1001,1010,1011\}} \wedge [g, f]_{\{001,011,101,111\}} \wedge [\neg c, \neg h, \neg l]_{\{0000,1000,0010,1010\}} \end{aligned}$$

The simplest rule is the *symbolic unit clause propagation* (SUCP). It builds on top of the observation that each symbolic unit clause $[\gamma]_{\mathcal{I}}$ in the formula represents a set $\{\gamma_i | i \in \mathcal{I}\}$ of ground literals. All of them need to be assigned to avoid contradictions. These assignments are performed all-at-once by the star operator. The only unit clause in our symbolic formula is $[h]_{\{001,011,101,111\}}$. By assigning this literal we obtain

$$\begin{aligned} &[\neg c, a]_{\{0,1\}} \wedge [\neg a, \neg g]_{\{0,1\}^3} \wedge [c, g]_{\{001,011,101,111\}} \wedge [\neg f, l]_{\{1000,1001,1010,1011\}} \\ &\wedge[g, f]_{\{001,011,101,111\}} \wedge [\neg c, \neg l]_{\{0000,1000\}} \wedge [\neg c, \neg h, \neg l]_{\{0010,1010\}} \end{aligned}$$

The next rule we apply is the *symbolic pure literal elimination* (SPLE). It does what we would expect from the standard rule, but performs its job in a purely symbolic manner, by (a) constructing a complete symbolic representation of the set of every pure ground literal, and (b) applying the resulting symbolic literals to the formula. The pure literals on v are $[v]_{\mathcal{I}^+\setminus(\mathcal{I}^+\cap\mathcal{I}^-)}$ and $[\neg v]_{\mathcal{I}^-\setminus(\mathcal{I}^+\cap\mathcal{I}^-)}$, where $\mathcal{I}^+ = \cup_{[v]_{\mathcal{I}}\in\mathcal{M}}\mathcal{I}$ and $\mathcal{I}^- = \cup_{[\neg v]_{\mathcal{I}}\in\mathcal{M}}\mathcal{I}$. The pure literals in our example are $[f]_{\{001,011,111\}}$, $[\neg f]_{\{100\}}$, $[\neg g]_{\{000,010,100,110\}}$, $[\neg h]_{\{000,100\}}$, $[l]_{\{1001,1011\}}$, and $[\neg l]_{\{0000,0010\}}$, so we obtain

$$\begin{aligned} &[\neg c, a]_{\{0,1\}} \wedge [\neg a, \neg g]_{\{001,011,101,111\}} \wedge [c, g]_{\{001,011,101,111\}} \\ &\wedge[\neg f, l]_{\{1010\}} \wedge [g, f]_{\{101\}} \wedge [\neg c, \neg l]_{\{1010\}} \end{aligned}$$

The next two rules only consider the subset of *binary* symbolic clauses, employing a graph-based approach similar to the one used to simplify standard propositional instances with many binary clauses [2]. We build a *symbolic implication graph* (SIG), which has two nodes labeled by $[a]_{\delta(a)}$ and $[\neg a]_{\delta(a)}$ for each existential variable a in the original QBF, and a couple of arcs $[\neg a]_{\delta(a)} \xrightarrow{\mathcal{I}} [b]_{\delta(b)}$ and $[\neg b]_{\delta(b)} \xrightarrow{\mathcal{I}} [a]_{\delta(a)}$ for each binary symbolic clause $[a, b]_{\mathcal{I}}$. So, unlike standard implication graphs, SIGs feature labeled arcs. The arcs originating from $[a, b]_{\mathcal{I}}$ are labeled by $\mathcal{I}$. Each symbolic arc $a \xrightarrow{\mathcal{I}} b$ represents a set of ground arcs $\{a_{\Psi|_{\delta(a)}} \longrightarrow b_{\Psi|_{\delta(b)}}, \Psi \in \mathcal{I}\}$ in the corresponding ground graph. The two rules we apply are as follows.

1. *Symbolic Hyper Binary Resolution* (SHBR). It enumerates all the resolution chains of symbolic binary clauses (via a depth-first, non-redundant traversal of the SIG), looking for *failed* literals, i.e. for literals $[a]_\mathcal{I}$ such that each $\neg a_\Psi \in [\neg a]_\mathcal{I}$ can be derived (via a finite number of resolution steps only involving binary clauses) as a consequence of the hypothesis a_Ψ. Each ground literal in $[a]_\mathcal{I}$ generates a contradiction, so we force the opposite symbolic assignment, shifting our attention onto $\mathcal{F} * [\neg a]_\mathcal{I}$. A literal $[a]_\mathcal{I}$ is failed if we encounter the following (portion of a) resolution path: $[a] \xrightarrow{\mathcal{I}_1} [a_1] \xrightarrow{\mathcal{I}_2} [a_2] \cdots \xrightarrow{\mathcal{I}_n} \neg[a]$, with $\mathcal{I} = (\cap_{j=1,\ldots,n} \mathcal{I}_j)|_{\delta(a)} \neq \emptyset$.

2. *Symbolic Equivalence Reasoning* (SER). It aims at identifying symbolic equivalences $[a] \xleftrightarrow{\mathcal{I}} [b]$, meaning that for all $\Psi \in \mathcal{I}$, $a_{\Psi|\delta(a)} \leftrightarrow b_{\Psi|\delta(b)}$ is a consequence of $Prop(\mathcal{F})$. It is easy to rewrite the substitution rule to apply all such equivalences at once, producing at most two symbolic clauses out of each clause involved in. To reduce the ground size of the formula we substitute $[a]$ for $[b]$ if $\delta(a) \leq \delta(b)$, and vice-versa. SER is performed by extracting all the strongly connected components (SCCs) from the SIG, temporarily discarding arc labels. Then, for each SCC we enumerate all its non-intersecting loops $[a] \xrightarrow{\mathcal{I}_1} [a_1] \xrightarrow{\mathcal{I}_2} [a_2] \cdots \xrightarrow{\mathcal{I}_n} [a]$ (let us suppose without loose of generality that $\delta(a) \leq \delta(a_i), i = 1, \ldots, n-1$), and apply the substitutions $[a] \xleftrightarrow{\mathcal{I}} [a_i], i = 1, \ldots, n-1$, with $\mathcal{I} = (\cap_{j=1,\ldots,n} \mathcal{I}_j)|_{\delta(a)}$.

In our example, all the remaining symbolic clauses are binary. Notice that for the class of QBF instances with at most two existential literals per clause, the symbolic binary rules inherit completeness from their standard counterpart.

In the figure aside a fragment of the sample SIG is depicted. By SER we obtain $[c] \xleftrightarrow{\mathcal{I}} [\neg g]$ with $\mathcal{I} = \{\{001, 011, 101, 111\}\}\delta(c) < \delta(g)$, hence: $[a, \neg c]_{\{0,1\}} \wedge [\neg a, c]_{\{0,1\}} \wedge [\neg f, l]_{\{1010\}} \wedge [\neg c, f]_{\{101\}} \wedge [\neg c, \neg l]_{\{1010\}}$.

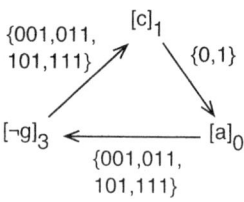

Then, the failed literal $[c]_{\{1\}}$ can be deduced from $[c] \xrightarrow{\{101\}} [f] \xrightarrow{\{1010\}} [l] \xrightarrow{\{1010\}} [\neg c]$, so $[a, \neg c]_{\{0\}} \wedge [\neg a, c]_{\{0\}} \wedge [\neg a]_{\{1\}} \wedge [\neg f, l]_{\{1010\}}$ remains. By assigning the pure literal $[l]_{1010}$ and the unit clause $[\neg a]_{\{1\}}$ we have $[a, \neg c]_{\{0\}} \wedge [\neg a, c]_{\{0\}}$, hence the empty formula by SER on $[c] \xleftrightarrow{\{0\}} [a]$.

Applied until fixpoint, the above set of rules $\mathcal{R} = \{$SUCP,SPLE,SHBR,SER$\}$ defines a satisfiability preserving trasformation $Norm_\mathcal{R} : PROP_{SYMB} \to PROP_{SYMB}$.

4.3 Branching Reasoning

In addition to symbolic and SAT reasoning, our representation fits well into search-based branching decision procedures. As far as QBFs are concerned, branching procedures extend the DPLL-approach [9] to the quantified case [7]. They look for models following the left-to-right order of the variables in the prefix during a depth-first visit of the semantic evaluation tree of the formula. Existential variables generate *or* nodes that disjunctively split the branch, universal quantifiers are associated to *and* nodes that split branches conjunctively. Each node n is labeled by the cofactored matrix $M * \Delta$ where Δ is the assignment on the path to n, while the root is labeled by the original matrix M.

A model, if one exists, is a subtree with all the leaves labeled by ⊤, extracted by choosing only one child for each existential node, and both children for conjunctive nodes. For example, the formula $\exists a \forall b \exists c.(a \vee b \vee c) \wedge (b \vee \neg c) \wedge (a \vee \neg b \vee \neg c) \wedge (\neg a \vee b)$ is decided to be false by visiting the tree reported aside and failing to extract any model. Inspired by the above strategy, we build an evaluation procedure that mixes ground, symbolic, and branching reasoning. We just need to define the following projection operator.

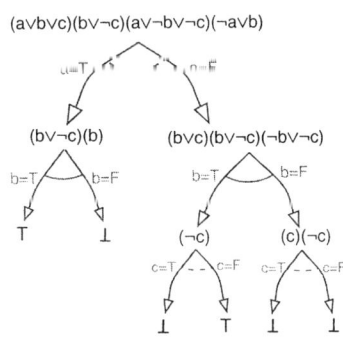

$$\Gamma_{\mathcal{I}\downarrow_\alpha} \doteq \Gamma_{\mathcal{I}'} \text{ with } \alpha \in \mathfrak{B} \text{ and } \mathcal{I}' = \{\langle \psi_2, \ldots, \psi_{\delta(\Gamma)} \rangle | \langle \alpha, \psi_2, \ldots, \psi_{\delta(\Gamma)} \rangle \in \mathcal{I}\}$$

Projection is used for universal branching and is readily extended to formulas:

$$(\exists [e_1]_{\delta_1} \cdots \exists [e_m]_{\delta_m}.\mathcal{M}) \downarrow_\alpha = \exists [e_1]_{\delta_1 - 1} \cdots \exists [e_m]_{\delta_m - 1}.(\mathcal{M} \downarrow_\alpha) \quad (11)$$

where $\mathcal{M} \downarrow_\alpha = \wedge_{\Gamma_\mathcal{I} \in \mathcal{M}} \Gamma_{\mathcal{I} \downarrow_\alpha}$. Existential branching is done according to Expression (9). The resulting decision procedure is reported below.

As far as splitting over existential variables is concerned, the purely existential nature of $Prop(\mathcal{F})$ makes the whole procedure more similar to search-based SAT solvers than to QBF decision procedures. By contrast, when the split is performed over universal variables, something conceptually different happens: the instance is partitioned into two completely disjoint existential sub-instances, according to (11).

The two base-cases do not deal with trivial sub-formulas. Well in advance, either symbolic reasoning (whenever the current sub-instance falls within its deductive power) or ground reasoning act as powerful look-ahead tools. The usual enhancements to branching procedures (backjumping, learning, heuristics, etc.) also apply.

Function symbEval (*symbolic formula* $\mathcal{F}$)

begin

$\mathcal{F}' \leftarrow Norm_\mathcal{R}(\mathcal{F})$;

if $\mathcal{F}' = \emptyset$ **then**
| **return** TRUE;
else if $\perp \in \mathcal{F}'$ **then**
| **return** FALSE;
else
   if ($|\mathcal{F}'|_{ground}$ *is affordable*) **then**
   | **return** SAT($prop(\mathcal{F}')$);
   else
     Let $\mathcal{F}'$ be $\exists [e_1]_{\delta_1} \cdots \exists [e_m]_{\delta_m}.\mathcal{M}$;
     if ($\delta_1 > 0$) **then**
     | **return** symbEval ($\exists [e_1]_{\delta_1 - 1} \cdots \exists [e_m]_{\delta_m - 1}.\mathcal{M}\downarrow_0$) *and*
       symbEval ($\exists [e_1]_{\delta_1 - 1} \cdots \exists [e_m]_{\delta_m - 1}.\mathcal{M}\downarrow_1$);
     else
     | **return** symbEval ($\exists [e_2]_{\delta_2} \cdots \exists [e_m]_{\delta_m}.\mathcal{M} * [e_1]$) *or*
       symbEval ($\exists [e_2]_{\delta_2} \cdots \exists [e_m]_{\delta_m}.\mathcal{M} * [\neg e_1]$);

end

5 Implementation and Experimentation

We present a first implementation of our decision procedure and a preliminary experimental evaluation. The interested reader may find further details and a wider experimentation in [3]. The resulting solver—called sKizzo—is a 60k-line piece of object-oriented C code managing ROBDDs through the CUDD package [32], version 2.4.0, and performing SAT solving using zChaff [24], version 2004.5.13.

We focus on a subset of the non-random families of instances collected in the QBFLIB's archive [15]. Among the others, we consider (1) Rintanen's benchmarks [29], the first and best-known collection of QBF problems, made up of 47 instances divided into 5 families, obtained by encoding planning problems, (2) Ayari's benchmarks [1], made up of 72 instances divided into 5 families, obtained from real-world verification

Table 1. The effect of symbolic reasoning over the size of instances

Instance	Symbolic size (clauses)			Ground size (clauses)			Symb. time
	Before	After	Diff.	Before	After	Diff.	
Adder2-2-c	234	193	-18%	$1.0 \cdot 10^6$	$5.4 \cdot 10^5$	-46.0%	100%
Adder2-6-s	3,315	2,236	-33%	$1.8 \cdot 10^{12}$	$1.0 \cdot 10^6$	-99.9%	23%
Adder2-8-s	6,060	4,070	-33%	$1.0 \cdot 10^{16}$	$2.2 \cdot 10^7$	-99.9%	14%
BLOCKS3i.5.4	2,640	2,814	+7%	$4.0 \cdot 10^4$	$3.0 \cdot 10^4$	-25.0%	100%
BLOCKS3ii.5.2	1,886	2,095	+11%	$2.9 \cdot 10^4$	$2.1 \cdot 10^4$	-28.0%	100%
BLOCKS3iii.5	1,226	1,614	+32%	$1.9 \cdot 10^4$	$1.3 \cdot 10^4$	-32.0%	100%
CHAIN12v.13	486	0	-100%	$1.8 \cdot 10^6$	0	-100.0%	100%
CHAIN17v.18	861	0	-100%	$1.1 \cdot 10^8$	0	-100.0%	100%
CHAIN23v.24	1,443	0	-100%	$1.2 \cdot 10^{10}$	0	-100.0%	100%
cnt08	1,237	0	-100%	$6.1 \cdot 10^4$	0	-100.0%	100%
cnt08re	1,309	1,240	-5%	$6.5 \cdot 10^4$	$1.1 \cdot 10^4$	-83.0%	<1%
cnt12	2,505	0	-100%	$1.3 \cdot 10^6$	0	-100.0%	100%
cnt12re	2,733	2,820	+3%	$1.5 \cdot 10^6$	$2.6 \cdot 10^5$	-83.0%	<1%
flipflop-9-c	74,066	71,691	-3%	$9.4 \cdot 10^{12}$	$9.2 \cdot 10^{12}$	-2.0%	100%
flipflop-10-c	128,245	124,844	-3%	$1.3 \cdot 10^{14}$	$1.3 \cdot 10^{14}$	-1.0%	100%
flipflop-11-c	210,674	205,995	-2%	$1.7 \cdot 10^{15}$	$1.7 \cdot 10^{15}$	-1.0%	100%
impl04	32	0	-100%	$1.4 \cdot 10^2$	0	-100%	100%
impl12	96	0	-100%	$3.7 \cdot 10^4$	0	-100%	100%
impl20	160	0	-100%	$9.4 \cdot 10^6$	0	-100%	100%
k-branch-n-9	12,923	20,608	+59%	$2.1 \cdot 10^{18}$	$1.6 \cdot 10^{18}$	-23.8%	3%
k-branch-p-13	28,676	78,006	+172%	$3.7 \cdot 10^{24}$	$2.9 \cdot 10^{24}$	-21.6%	100%
k-d4-n-16	5,133	5,535	+8%	$4.2 \cdot 10^{22}$	$2.4 \cdot 10^{22}$	-42.9%	2%
k-d4-p-16	2,959	5,044	+70%	$4.7 \cdot 10^{17}$	$3.1 \cdot 10^{17}$	-34.0%	100%
mutex-4-s	362	0	-100%	$1.9 \cdot 10^7$	0	-100%	100%
mutex-8-s	834	367	-56%	$2.9 \cdot 10^{12}$	$3.5 \cdot 10^4$	-99.9%	70%
TOILET10.1.iv.20	3,466	3,326	-4%	$2.1 \cdot 10^4$	$7.4 \cdot 10^3$	-64.8%	55%
TOILET16.1.iv.32	10,495	8,175	-22%	$5.6 \cdot 10^4$	$8.6 \cdot 10^3$	-84.6%	72%
toilet-a-08-01.11	3,109	1,069	-66%	$6.0 \cdot 10^4$	$2.7 \cdot 10^4$	-55.0%	3%
toilet-c-10-01.14	1,974	1,874	-5%	$7.5 \cdot 10^3$	$4.0 \cdot 10^3$	-46.6%	1%
toilet-g-20-01.2	460	0	-100%	$1.1 \cdot 10^3$	0	-100.0%	100%
tree-exa2-40	51	1	-100%	$5.6 \cdot 10^{14}$	1	-100%	100%
tree-exa10-30	58	0	-100%	58	0	-100%	100%

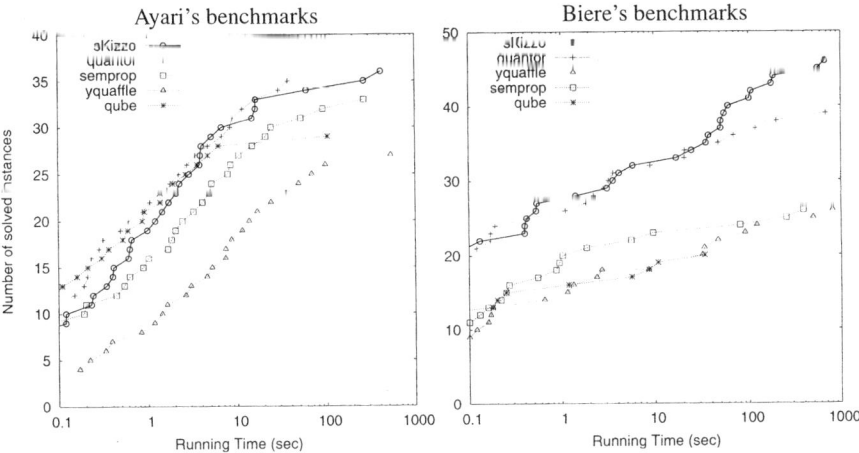

Fig. 1. Comparison with other solvers over two groups of families

problems on circuits and protocol descriptions (these instances are quite challenging for modern solvers, and some of them have never been solved), and (3) Biere's benchmarks [4], made up of 64 instances divided into 4 families, where the n-th instance in each family refers to model checking problem on a n-bit counter. The verification is easy for BDD-based symbolic MC and very difficult for SAT-based bounded MC, as it captures the worst-case scenario in which the number of steps necessary to falsify the property equals the diameter of the system. QBF reasoning has been shown not to outperform SAT-based reasoning (Bounded Model Checking) on these benchmarks.

Table 1 measures the relative importance of symbolic reasoning w.r.t. all the other reasoning strategies. It puts side by side the symbolic/ground size of a few instances before and after $Norm_\mathcal{R}$ is applied for the first time. The last column gives the amount of time spent in (the first application of) symbolic reasoning. When this percentage is equal to 100%, the instance is just symbolically solved. As expected, the ground size of instances is always reduced, whilst the symbolic size of some of them is increased as an effect of symbolic reasoning. The reduction ratio for the ground size is quite family-dependent, though not sensibly instance-depending. Most of the simpler families are completely solved by symbolic reasoning. Conversely, for more complex instances symbolic reasoning does not suffices. Quite often, the number of ground clauses before symbolic reasoning is intractable (state-of-the-art solvers can afford millions clauses, not billions). Some of them stays unaffordable even after $Norm_\mathcal{R}$, but many undergo a strong reduction of the ground size. Several problems exist that—thought not strongly reduced during the first call to $Norm_\mathcal{R}$—are hardly simplified during the recursive calls (not shown in the table). The overall effect of symbolic reasoning is quite incisive.

Figure 1 compares sKizzo with publically available state-of-the-art solvers, among which we find the three top-rated solvers according to most of the results presented in [20] (see also Section 6). The number of solved instances in two groups of families is plotted against the (non-cumulative) time taken to solve such instances. The overall performance is quite impressive, especially if we take into consideration that sKizzo is just a first non-optimized implementation.

6 Related Work and Discussion

Most QBF solvers leverage revised versions of search-based techniques developed in the SAT framework, ranging from the extension of resolution-based reasoning [18] to the employment of lookback techniques [23], encountering along the way a key contribution by Cadoli, Giovanardi and Schaerf [7] in which the original extension of DPLL to QBF is presented. Up to a certain point, these extensions have been successful. In the solver evaluation reported in [21], all the competitive solvers (such as QSAT [30], QSOLVE [11], QUAFFLE [34], QuBE [15], SEMPROP [22]) are search-based.

A few alternative algorithms for QBF are emerging [20]. Some of them reverse the order in which quantifiers are considered (such as Quantor [4]), others employ some compact representation for the problem (such as ZQSAT [14] and QMRES/QBDD [28]). Many restate the very goal of the solver: it is no longer a matter of *searching for a solution*, rather an attempt to directly *solve the instance* (this distinction traces back to [9, 10]). Resolution-based solving techniques have also received renewed attention, especially when used in conjunction with compressed representation for clauses [8, 13, 25]. In the SAT framework, these so-called *symbolic* approaches show a certain strength on specific classes of instances, but seem to be not competitive in general [27]. In the QBF scenario, both the idea of *compressed/symbolic* representations, and the shift from *searching* to *solving* are more promising [28, 4, 14].

The foundational work of Skolem [31] has had the widest possible application. We here just cite a recent work by Jackson [16]. Forms of reasoning about binary subformulas are regarded as an effective pre-processing step in the propositional framework [2]. The interest in binary decision diagrams as a tool for manipulating boolean functions traces back to the seminal work by Bryant [6]. Their usage in SAT/QBF satisfiability algorithms have been explored at least in [33, 8, 25, 13, 27, 28, 14].

Several features distinguish our approach from previous ones. For example, it: (1) largely abstracts over variable ordering and number of alternations in the prefix; (2) explicitly leverages skolemization; (3) profits from the peculiar structure of QBF-derived instances to symbolically represent them; (4) advantageously integrates search-based and solving decision strategies in QBF reasoning; (5) repeatedly engages a SAT solver as an oracle; (6) employs a hybrid PROP/QBF branching style. For further differences and an in-depth comparison, see [3].

7 Conclusions and Future Work

Our work is motivated by the outstanding potential of QBF in applications. Advances in decision procedures for this formalism are ardently expected, and quantified reasoners worhty of inheriting the amazing success of SAT solvers are a looming possibility. In this respect, we firstly succeed to efficiently retain both the expressive power of quantification and the strength of the purely propositional reasoning. Our preliminary experimental evaluation yields remarkable results. Large room for improvements exist as

(1) our implementation is just a first, non-optimized prototype, and (2) several effective QBF and SAT reasoning techniques (q resolution, subsumption control, backjumping, etc.) have been left out of the first implementation to focus on the main topic.

To further investigate our guideline, we are (1) strengthening the symbolic machinery by adding new rules, (2) conceiving a symbolic *model verifier*, and (3) designing the integration with an industrial-scale model checker.

Acknowledgements

I thank Gigina Aiello and Paolo Traverso for supporting my research efforts, and Sara Bernardini for the many days she has spent on listening to my early ideas on symbolic skolemization. I'm grateful to Marco Cadoli for discussing this work with me. Finally, Amedeo Cesta deserves a special thought for his indefatigable encouragement.

References

1. A. Ayari and D. Basin. Bounded Model Construction for Monadic Second-order Logics. In *Proc. of CAV'00*, 2000.
2. F. Bacchus and J. Winter. Effective Preprocessing with Hyper-Resolution and Equality Reduction. In *Proc. of SAT'03*, 2003.
3. M. Benedetti. sKizzo: a QBF Decision Procedure based on Propositional Skolemization and Symbolic Reasoning, Tech.Rep. 04-11-03, ITC-irst, available at sra.itc.it/people/benedetti/sKizzo, 2004.
4. A. Biere. Resolve and Expand. In *Proc. of SAT'04*, pages 238–246, 2004.
5. A. Biere, A. Cimatti, E. M. Clarke, M. Fujita, and Y. Zhu. Symbolic Model Checking without BDDs. In *Proc. of Design Automation Conference*, volume 1579, pages 193–207, 1999.
6. R. E. Bryant. Graph-based algorithms for Boolean function manipulation. *IEEE Transaction on Computing*, C-35(8):677–691, 1986.
7. Marco Cadoli, Andrea Giovanardi, and Marco Schaerf. An algorithm to evaluate quantified boolean formulae. In *Proceedings of the fifteenth national/tenth conference on Artificial intelligence/Innovative applications of artificial intelligence*, pages 262–267. American Association for Artificial Intelligence, 1998.
8. P. Chatalic and L. Simon. Multi-Resolution on compressed sets of clauses. In *Proceedings of the Twelfth International Conference on Tools with Artificial Intelligence (ICTAI'00)*, 2000.
9. M. Davis, G. Logemann, and D. Loveland. A machine program for theorem proving. *Journal of the ACM*, 5:394–397, 1962.
10. M. Davis and H. Putnam. A computing procedure for quantification theory. *Journal of the ACM*, 7, 1960.
11. R. Feldmann, B. Monien, and S. Schamberger. A Distributed Algorithm to Evaluate Quantified Boolean Formulas. In *Proceedings of the AAAI National Conference on Artificial Intelligence*, pages 285–290, 2000.
12. M. Fitting. *First-Order Logic and Automated Theorem Proving*. Springer Verlag, 1996.
13. J. Franco, M. Kouril, J. Schlipf, J. Ward, S. Weaver, M. Dransfield, and W. Vanfleet. SBSAT: a state-based, BDD-based satisfiability solver. In *Proceedings of SAT'03*, 2003.
14. M. GhasemZadeh, V. Klotz, and C. Meinel. ZQSAT: A QSAT Solver based on Zero-suppressed Binary Decision Diagrams, available at http://www.informatik.uni-trier.de/TI/bdd-research/zqsat/zqsat.html, 2004.

15. E. Giunchiglia, M. Narizzano, and A. Tacchella. QuBE: A system for deciding Quantified Boolean Formulas Satisfiability. In *Proc. of the International Joint Conference on Automated Reasoning (IJCAR'2001)*, 2001.
16. Daniel Jackson. Automating first-order relational logic. In *Proceedings of the 8th ACM SIGSOFT international symposium on Foundations of software engineering*, pages 130–139. ACM Press, 2000.
17. H. Kautz and B. Selman. Planning as satisfiability. In *Proc. of ECAI 1992*, pages 359–363.
18. H. Kleine-Buning, M. Karpinski, and A. Flogel. Resolution for quantified Boolean formulas. *Information and Computation*, 117(1):12–18, 1995.
19. T. Larrabee. Test pattern generation using boolean satisfiability. In *IEEE Transaction on Computer-aided Design*, pages 4–15, 1992.
20. D. Le Berre, M. Narizzano, L. Simon, and A. Tacchella. Second QBF solvers evaluation, avaliable on-line at www.qbflib.org, 2004.
21. D. Le Berre, L. Simon, and A. Tacchella. Challenges in the QBF arena: the SAT'03 evaluation of QBF solvers, avaliable on-line at www.qbflib.org, 2003.
22. R. Letz. Advances in Decision Procedures for Quantified Boolean Formulas. In *Proceedings of the First International Workshop on Quantified Boolean Formulae (QBF'01)*, pages 55–64, 2001.
23. R. Letz. Lemma and model caching in decision procedures for quantified boolean formulas. In *Proc. of the Int. Conf. on Automated Reasoning with Analytic Tableaux and Related Methods*, pages 160–175. Springer-Verlag, 2002.
24. M. W. Moskewicz, C. F. Madigan, Y. Zhao, L. Zhang, and S. Malik. Chaff: Engineering an Efficient SAT Solver. In *proceedings of the 38th Design Automation Conference*, 2001.
25. D. B. Motter and I. L. Markov. A compressed, breadth-first search for satisfiability. *LNCS*, 2409:29–42, 2002.
26. A. Nonnengart and C. Weidenbach. Computing Small Clause Normal Forms. In Alan Robinson and Andrei Voronkov, editors, *Handbook of Automated Reasoning*, chapter 6, pages 335 – 367. Elsevier, Amsterdam, Netherlands, 2001.
27. G. Pan and M.Y. Vardi. Search vs. Symbolic Techniques in Satisfiability Solving. In *Proceedings of SAT 2004*, 2004.
28. G. Pan and M.Y. Vardi. Symbolic Decision Procedures for QBF. In *Proceedings of the Tenth International Conference on Principles and Practice of Constraint Programming (CP04)*, 2004.
29. J. Rintanen. Construction Conditional Plans by a Theorem-prover. *Journal of A. I. Research*, pages 323–352, 1999.
30. J. Rintanen. Partial implicit unfolding in the davis-putnam procedure for quantified boolean formulae. In *Proceedings of the International Conference on Logic for Programming, Artificial Intelligence and Reasoning (LPAR'01)*, 2001.
31. T. Skolem. Logico-combinatorial investigations in the satisfiability or provability of mathematical propositions: a simplified proof of a theorem by L. Löwenheim and generalizations of the theorem. In *From Frege to Gödel. A Source Book in Mathematical Logic, 1879-1931*, pages 252–263. Harvard University Press, Cambridge, 1967 (1920).
32. Fabio Somenzi. Colorado University Binary Decision Diagrams, vlsi.colorado.edu/ fabio/CUDD, 1995.
33. T. E. Uribe and M. E. Stickel. Ordered binary decision diagrams and the Davis-Putnam procedure. In J. P. Jouannaud, editor, *1st International Conference on Constraints in Computational Logics*, volume 845, pages 34–49, 1994.
34. L. Zhang and S. Malik. Towards Symmetric Treatment of Conflicts And Satisfaction in Quantified Boolean Satisfiability Solver. In *Proc. of CP'02*, 2002.

The Dependency Pair Framework: Combining Techniques for Automated Termination Proofs

Jürgen Giesl, René Thiemann, and Peter Schneider-Kamp

LuFG Informatik II, RWTH Aachen, Ahornstr. 55, 52074 Aachen, Germany
{giesl|thiemann|psk}@informatik.rwth-aachen.de

Abstract. The dependency pair approach is one of the most powerful techniques for automated termination proofs of term rewrite systems. Up to now, it was regarded as one of several possible methods to prove termination. In this paper, we show that dependency pairs can instead be used as a general concept to integrate arbitrary techniques for termination analysis. In this way, the benefits of different techniques can be combined and their modularity and power are increased significantly. We refer to this new concept as the "dependency pair *framework*" to distinguish it from the old "dependency pair *approach*". Moreover, this framework facilitates the development of new methods for termination analysis. To demonstrate this, we present several new techniques within the dependency pair framework which simplify termination problems considerably. We implemented the dependency pair framework in our termination prover AProVE and evaluated it on large collections of examples.

1 Introduction

Termination of term rewrite systems (TRSs) has been studied for decades and several methods were developed to prove termination of TRSs automatically (one of the most powerful techniques is the *dependency pair approach* [1,6,7]). Up to now, all these methods were seen as separate approaches on their own.

In contrast, this paper shows that dependency pairs are suitable as a general framework to integrate arbitrary techniques for termination proofs. In this way, the benefits of all available methods can be combined and the classical dependency pair *approach* is just a special case of this new dependency pair *framework*. By combining termination techniques within the dependency pair framework (instead of trying to apply them on a TRS directly, one after another), the flexibility, modularity, and power of these techniques are increased significantly.

We introduce the dependency pair framework in Sect. 2. Here, each technique for termination proofs is seen as a *dependency pair processor* that transforms a *dependency pair problem* into a set of new (and hopefully, simpler) ones. Sect. 3 shows how to formulate the components of the classical dependency pair approach as processors. This increases their applicability substantially and it demonstrates that the dependency pair approach is indeed a special case of the dependency pair framework. In Sect. 4 we introduce new processors which simplify dependency pair problems significantly and which are only possible due to the new formulation of the dependency pair framework. This demonstrates that the dependency pair framework is particularly well suitable as a basis for future developments in automated termination proving. In Sect. 5 we discuss how to integrate other (existing) methods for automated termination proofs into the dependency pair framework by formulating them as processors as well.

Finally, to construct an automatic termination prover using the dependency pair framework, a main problem is to develop strategies to decide which processors should be applied to a given DP problem. Suitable heuristics and our implementation in the termination prover AProVE are discussed in Sect. 6.

2 The Dependency Pair Framework

We extend the *dependency pair approach* to a framework for the combination of arbitrary termination techniques. The reader is referred to [2] for the basics of term rewriting and to [1,7] for further details on the dependency pair approach.

We restrict ourselves to finite signatures $\mathcal{F}$ and TRSs. $\mathcal{T}(\mathcal{F}, \mathcal{V})$ denotes the set of terms over $\mathcal{F}$ and the infinite set of variables $\mathcal{V}$. A *TRS over* $\mathcal{F}$ is a set of rules $l \to r$ where l and r are from $\mathcal{T}(\mathcal{F}, \mathcal{V})$, $\mathcal{V}(r) \subseteq \mathcal{V}(l)$, and $l \notin \mathcal{V}$. To handle different evaluation strategies (like innermost or full rewriting) in a uniform way, we introduce the new notion of $\mathcal{Q}$-*restricted rewriting*. In $\mathcal{Q}$-restricted rewriting, one may only perform a rewrite step if the proper subterms of the redex are not reducible w.r.t. $\mathcal{Q}$ (i.e., if they are $\mathcal{Q}$-*normal forms*). This notion is particularly useful when defining techniques for innermost termination proofs later on.

Definition 1 ($\mathcal{Q}$-restricted Rewriting). *Let $\mathcal{R}$ and $\mathcal{Q}$ be TRSs. We define the $\mathcal{Q}$-restricted rewrite relation as $s \xrightarrow{\mathcal{Q}}_{\mathcal{R},p} t$ iff p is a position of s, $s|_p = l\sigma$ for some rule $l \to r \in \mathcal{R}$ and some substitution σ, $t = s[r\sigma]_p$, and all proper subterms of the redex $s|_p$ are in $\mathcal{Q}$-normal form. Moreover, $s \xrightarrow{\mathcal{Q}}_{\mathcal{R}} t$ means that $s \xrightarrow{\mathcal{Q}}_{\mathcal{R},p} t$ for some position p. A TRS $\mathcal{R}$ is $\mathcal{Q}$-terminating iff $\xrightarrow{\mathcal{Q}}_{\mathcal{R}}$ is well founded.*[1]

Example 1. Consider $\mathcal{R} = \{\mathsf{f}(\mathsf{a}) \to \mathsf{f}(\mathsf{a}), \mathsf{a} \to \mathsf{b}\}$. If $\mathcal{Q}$ contains the rule $\mathsf{a} \to \mathsf{b}$, then the step from $\mathsf{f}(\mathsf{a})$ to $\mathsf{f}(\mathsf{a})$ is no longer possible with $\xrightarrow{\mathcal{Q}}_{\mathcal{R}}$ since the proper subterm a of the redex $\mathsf{f}(\mathsf{a})$ is not a $\mathcal{Q}$-normal form. Thus, $\mathcal{R}$ is $\mathcal{Q}$-terminating.

$\mathcal{Q}$-restricted rewriting subsumes both innermost and ordinary rewriting. Ordinary rewriting is $\mathcal{Q}$-restricted rewriting for $\mathcal{Q} = \varnothing$ and innermost rewriting is $\mathcal{Q}$-restricted rewriting with $\mathcal{Q} = \mathcal{R}$ ($\to_{\mathcal{R}} = \xrightarrow{\varnothing}_{\mathcal{R}}$ and $\xrightarrow{i}_{\mathcal{R}} = \xrightarrow{\mathcal{R}}_{\mathcal{R}}$). The following lemma shows that $\xrightarrow{\mathcal{Q}}_{\mathcal{R}}$ is "increasing" if $\mathcal{R}$ is "increasing" and $\mathcal{Q}$ is "decreasing".

Lemma 1 (Monotonicity of $\xrightarrow{\mathcal{Q}}_{\mathcal{R}}$). $\mathcal{R}' \subseteq \mathcal{R}$ *and* $\mathcal{Q}' \supseteq \mathcal{Q}$ *implies* $\xrightarrow{\mathcal{Q}'}_{\mathcal{R}'} \subseteq \xrightarrow{\mathcal{Q}}_{\mathcal{R}}$.

Proof. Obvious. □

This lemma already indicates why $\mathcal{Q}$-restricted rewriting is better suitable for termination analysis than innermost rewriting. There exist several techniques which can simplify termination proofs by removing rules from the TRS $\mathcal{R}$. For full rewriting and also for $\mathcal{Q}$-restricted rewriting, removal of rules is always advantageous, since it can never introduce non-termination (termination of $\xrightarrow{\mathcal{Q}}_{\mathcal{R}}$

---

[1] Since the right-hand sides of $\mathcal{Q}$'s rules are not needed to define $\mathcal{Q}$-restricted rewriting, Def. 1 could also be formulated if $\mathcal{Q}$ is a set of *terms* instead of *rules*.

implies termination of $\to_{\mathcal{R}'}^{\mathcal{Q}}$ if $\mathcal{R}' \subseteq \mathcal{R}$). But for innermost rewriting, this is not true. For instance, by removing the rule $\mathsf{a} \to \mathsf{b}$ from the innermost terminating TRS $\mathcal{R}$ of Ex. 1, we result in a TRS $\mathcal{R}'$ that is not innermost terminating (hence, $\xrightarrow{i}_{\mathcal{R}'} \not\subseteq \xrightarrow{i}_{\mathcal{R}}$). Here, $\mathcal{Q}$-restricted rewriting has the advantage that the rules $\mathcal{Q}$ which restrict the set of possible redexes are separated from the rules $\mathcal{R}$ used for rewriting and thus, $\mathcal{R}$ and $\mathcal{Q}$ can be changed independently.

Now we present a termination criterion for $\mathcal{Q}$-restricted rewriting based on dependency pairs. For a TRS $\mathcal{R}$ over $\mathcal{F}$, the *defined symbols* are $\mathcal{D} = \{root(l) \mid l \to r \in \mathcal{R}\}$ and the *constructors* are $\mathcal{C} = \mathcal{F} \setminus \mathcal{D}$. For every $f \in \mathcal{D}$ we extend the signature $\mathcal{F}$ by a fresh *tuple symbol* $f^\sharp$, where $f^\sharp$ has the same arity as f and we often write F for $f^\sharp$. If $t = g(t_1, \ldots, t_m)$ with $g \in \mathcal{D}$, we let $t^\sharp$ denote $g^\sharp(t_1, \ldots, t_m)$.

Definition 2 (Dependency Pair). *The set of dependency pairs for a TRS $\mathcal{R}$ is $DP(\mathcal{R}) = \{l^\sharp \to t^\sharp \mid l \to r \in \mathcal{R}, root(t) \in \mathcal{D}, t \text{ is a subterm of } r\}$.*[2]

Example 2. The following TRS computes subtraction and division, cf. [1, Ex. 2].

$$\mathsf{minus}(x, 0) \to x \quad (1) \qquad \mathsf{div}(0, \mathsf{s}(y)) \to 0 \quad (4)$$
$$\mathsf{minus}(0, \mathsf{s}(y)) \to 0 \quad (2) \qquad \mathsf{div}(\mathsf{s}(x), \mathsf{s}(y)) \to \mathsf{s}(\mathsf{div}(\mathsf{minus}(x,y), \mathsf{s}(y))) \quad (5)$$
$$\mathsf{minus}(\mathsf{s}(x), \mathsf{s}(y)) \to \mathsf{minus}(x, y) \quad (3)$$

Here, the defined symbols are minus and div and the symbols 0 and s are constructors. We obtain the following dependency pairs:

$$\mathsf{MINUS}(\mathsf{s}(x), \mathsf{s}(y)) \to \mathsf{MINUS}(x, y) \quad (6) \qquad \mathsf{DIV}(\mathsf{s}(x), \mathsf{s}(y)) \to \mathsf{MINUS}(x, y) \quad (7)$$
$$\mathsf{DIV}(\mathsf{s}(x), \mathsf{s}(y)) \to \mathsf{DIV}(\mathsf{minus}(x, y), \mathsf{s}(y)) \quad (8)$$

To verify $\mathcal{Q}$-termination, we use the notion of *chains*. Intuitively, a dependency pair corresponds to a function call and a chain represents a possible sequence of calls that can occur in a reduction. For termination, we try to prove that there are no infinite chains. We always assume that different occurrences of dependency pairs are variable disjoint and consider substitutions whose domains may be infinite. In the following definition, $\mathcal{P}$ is usually a set of dependency pairs.

Definition 3 (Chain). *Let $\mathcal{P}, \mathcal{Q}, \mathcal{R}$ be TRSs. A (possibly infinite) sequence of pairs $s_1 \to t_1, s_2 \to t_2, \ldots$ from $\mathcal{P}$ is a $(\mathcal{P}, \mathcal{Q}, \mathcal{R})$-chain iff there is a substitution σ such that $t_i\sigma \xrightarrow{\mathcal{Q}}_{\mathcal{R}}^* s_{i+1}\sigma$ for all i and all $s_i\sigma$ are in $\mathcal{Q}$-normal form. A chain is minimal iff there is a σ as above where all $t_i\sigma$ are terminating w.r.t. $\xrightarrow{\mathcal{Q}}_{\mathcal{R}}$.*

Example 3. If $\mathcal{Q} \subseteq \mathcal{R}$, then the TRS of Ex. 2 has the following chain which consists of two occurrences of the dependency pair (8).

$$\mathsf{DIV}(\mathsf{s}(x_1), \mathsf{s}(y_1)) \to \mathsf{DIV}(\mathsf{minus}(x_1, y_1), \mathsf{s}(y_1)),$$
$$\mathsf{DIV}(\mathsf{s}(x_2), \mathsf{s}(y_2)) \to \mathsf{DIV}(\mathsf{minus}(x_2, y_2), \mathsf{s}(y_2))$$

The reason is that $\mathsf{DIV}(\mathsf{minus}(x_1, y_1), \mathsf{s}(y_1))\sigma \xrightarrow{\mathcal{Q}}_{\mathcal{R}}^* \mathsf{DIV}(\mathsf{s}(x_2), \mathsf{s}(y_2))\sigma$ holds for some substitution σ (e.g., $\sigma(x_1) = \mathsf{s}(0)$ and $\sigma(x_2) = \sigma(y_i) = 0$ for $i \in \{1, 2\}$) such that all instantiated left-hand sides $\mathsf{DIV}(\mathsf{s}(x_i), \mathsf{s}(y_i))\sigma$ are in $\mathcal{Q}$-normal form. Moreover, the chain is minimal, since all instantiated right-hand sides of the dependency pairs are terminating w.r.t. $\xrightarrow{\mathcal{Q}}_{\mathcal{R}}$.

---

[2] It even suffices only to regard dependency pairs where t is no proper subterm of l [4].

As mentioned above, termination corresponds to absence of infinite chains. Here, it suffices to consider minimal chains, since minimal non-terminating terms (whose proper subterms are terminating) correspond to infinite minimal chains. The following termination criterion is immediately obtained from [1, Thm. 6].

Theorem 1 (Termination Criterion). *These three properties are equivalent:*

- $\mathcal{R}$ *is* $\mathcal{Q}$-*terminating*
- *there is no infinite* $(DP(\mathcal{R}), \mathcal{Q}, \mathcal{R})$-*chain*
- *there is no infinite* minimal $(DP(\mathcal{R}), \mathcal{Q}, \mathcal{R})$-*chain*

With this criterion, we can now state the dependency pair framework. The basic idea of this framework is to examine a set of dependency pairs $\mathcal{P}$ together with the TRSs $\mathcal{Q}$ and $\mathcal{R}$ and to prove absence of (minimal) infinite $(\mathcal{P}, \mathcal{Q}, \mathcal{R})$-chains instead of examining the relation $\xrightarrow{\mathcal{Q}}_{\mathcal{R}}$ directly. The advantages of this approach will become clear in the sequel. For example, it will be possible to decompose this so-called *dependency pair problem* into several independent sub-problems. These problems can then be solved separately using different techniques, which leads to a very modular approach to termination proving.

More precisely, a dependency pair problem ("DP problem", for short) consists of three TRSs $\mathcal{P}$, $\mathcal{Q}$, and $\mathcal{R}$ (where initially, $\mathcal{P} = DP(\mathcal{R})$) and a flag $f \in \{\mathbf{m}, \mathbf{a}\}$ which stands for "<u>m</u>inimal" or "<u>a</u>rbitrary". Initially, we have $f = \mathbf{m}$. Our goal is to show that there is no infinite minimal $(\mathcal{P}, \mathcal{Q}, \mathcal{R})$-chain if $f = \mathbf{m}$ and that there is no infinite (possibly non-minimal) $(\mathcal{P}, \mathcal{Q}, \mathcal{R})$-chain if $f = \mathbf{a}$. If this is possible, then we call the problem *finite*.

A DP problem $(\mathcal{P}, \mathcal{Q}, \mathcal{R}, f)$ that is not finite is called *infinite*. But in addition, $(\mathcal{P}, \mathcal{Q}, \mathcal{R}, f)$ is already *infinite* whenever $\mathcal{R}$ is not $\mathcal{Q}$-terminating. So in particular, the existence of any (possibly non-minimal) infinite $(\mathcal{P}, \mathcal{Q}, \mathcal{R})$-chain suffices to conclude that $(\mathcal{P}, \mathcal{Q}, \mathcal{R}, f)$ is infinite, even if $f = \mathbf{m}$. While the initial DP problem $(DP(\mathcal{R}), \mathcal{Q}, \mathcal{R}, \mathbf{m})$ is either finite or infinite, other DP problems $(\mathcal{P}, \mathcal{Q}, \mathcal{R}, f)$ which can occur in termination proofs can be both finite and infinite. For example, the DP problem $(\mathcal{P}, \mathcal{Q}, \mathcal{R}, \mathbf{m})$ with $\mathcal{P} = \{\mathsf{A} \to \mathsf{B}\}$, $\mathcal{Q} = \varnothing$ and $\mathcal{R} = \{\mathsf{a} \to \mathsf{a}, \mathsf{a} \to \mathsf{b}, \mathsf{b} \to \mathsf{c}\}$ is finite since there is no infinite minimal $(\mathcal{P}, \mathcal{Q}, \mathcal{R})$-chain, but also infinite since $\mathcal{R}$ is not $(\mathcal{Q}$-$)$terminating.

Such DP problems do not cause difficulties. If one detects an infinite problem during a termination proof, one can always abort the proof, since termination has been disproved (provided that all proof steps were "complete", i.e., that they preserved the termination behavior). If the problem is both finite and infinite, then even if one only considers it as being finite, the proof is still correct, since then there exists another resulting DP problem which is infinite and not finite. The reason is that by Thm. 1, non-termination implies that there is an infinite (minimal) chain. Indeed, when proving termination of the TRS $\mathcal{R}$ above one also obtains a DP problem with the infinite minimal chain $\mathsf{A} \to \mathsf{A}, \mathsf{A} \to \mathsf{A}, \ldots$

Termination techniques should now operate on DP problems instead of TRSs. They should transform a DP problem into a new set of problems which then have to be solved instead. Alternatively, they can also return the answer "no". We refer to such techniques as *dependency pair processors* ("DP processors").

Definition 1 (DP Problems and Processors). *A DP problem $(\mathcal{P}, \mathcal{Q}, \mathcal{R}, f)$ consists of three TRSs $\mathcal{P}, \mathcal{Q}, \mathcal{R}$ and a flag $f \in \{\mathbf{m}, \mathbf{a}\}$. A DP problem $(\mathcal{P}, \mathcal{Q}, \mathcal{R}, \mathbf{m})$ is finite iff there is no infinite minimal $(\mathcal{P}, \mathcal{Q}, \mathcal{R})$-chain and $(\mathcal{P}, \mathcal{Q}, \mathcal{R}, \mathbf{a})$ is finite iff there is no infinite $(\mathcal{P}, \mathcal{Q}, \mathcal{R})$-chain. A DP problem $(\mathcal{P}, \mathcal{Q}, \mathcal{R}, f)$ is infinite iff it is not finite or if $\mathcal{R}$ is not $\mathcal{Q}$-terminating.*

A DP processor is a function Proc which takes a DP problem as input and returns either a set of DP problems or the result "no". A DP processor Proc is sound if for all DP problems d, d is finite whenever $Proc(d)$ is not "no" and all DP problems in $Proc(d)$ are finite. A DP processor Proc is complete if for all DP problems d, d is infinite whenever $Proc(d)$ is "no" or when $Proc(d)$ contains an infinite DP problem.

Thus, soundness is required in order to use a DP processor *Proc* to prove termination (in particular, to conclude that d is finite if $Proc(d) = \varnothing$). Completeness is needed in order to use *Proc* to prove non-termination (in particular, to conclude that d is infinite if $Proc(d) = $ no). Even if one is only interested in proving termination, completeness is still advantageous, since it ensures that one does not transform non-infinite DP problems into infinite ones (i.e., applying the processor does not "harm"). The reason for the above non-symmetric definition of "finite" and "infinite" is that in this way there are more finite resp. infinite DP problems and therefore, it becomes easier to detect (in)finiteness of a problem.[3]

The following corollary introduces the dependency pair framework ("DP framework", for short). The idea is to start with the initial DP problem where $\mathcal{P} = DP(\mathcal{R})$ and $f = \mathbf{m}$. Then this problem is transformed repeatedly by sound DP processors. If the final processors return empty sets of DP problems, then termination is proved. If one of the processors returns "no" and all processors used before were complete, then one has proved that the original TRS is not terminating. The proof of Cor. 1 is immediate from Def. 4 and Thm. 1.

Corollary 1 (Dependency Pair Framework). *Let $\mathcal{R}$ and $\mathcal{Q}$ be TRSs. We construct a tree whose nodes are labelled with DP problems or "yes" or "no" and whose root is labelled with $(DP(\mathcal{R}), \mathcal{Q}, \mathcal{R}, \mathbf{m})$. For every inner node labelled with d, there is a sound DP processor Proc satisfying one of the following conditions:*

- *$Proc(d) = $ no and the node has just one child, labelled with "no"*
- *$Proc(d) = \varnothing$ and the node has just one child, labelled with "yes"*
- *$Proc(d) \neq $ no, $Proc(d) \neq \varnothing$, and the children of the node are labelled with the DP problems in $Proc(d)$*

If all leaves of the tree are labelled with "yes", then $\mathcal{R}$ is $\mathcal{Q}$-terminating. Otherwise, if there is a leaf labelled with "no" and if all processors used on the path from the root to this leaf are complete, then $\mathcal{R}$ is not $\mathcal{Q}$-terminating.

---
[3] That a DP problem $(\mathcal{P}, \mathcal{Q}, \mathcal{R}, \mathbf{m})$ is already "finite" if there are no infinite *minimal* chains will be required for the soundness of many processors (cf. Thm. 3, Thm. 6, Thm. 8, and Thm. 10) and that a DP problem is already "infinite" if $\mathcal{R}$ is not $\mathcal{Q}$-terminating will be required for the completeness of most processors for dependency pair transformations (cf. Ex. 11 in Sect. 3.3).

Example 4. If d_0 is the initial problem $(DP(\mathcal{R}), \mathcal{Q}, \mathcal{R}, \mathbf{m})$, $Proc_0$, $Proc_1$, $Proc_2$ are sound DP processors, and $Proc_0(d_0) = \{d_1, d_2\}$, $Proc_1(d_1) = \varnothing$, $Proc_2(d_2) = \varnothing$, then one could obtain the first tree below and conclude termination.

But if $Proc_1(d_1) = \{d_3, d_4, d_5\}$ and $Proc_2(d_2) =$ no, one could get the second tree. If both $Proc_0$ and $Proc_2$ are complete, then one could conclude non-termination.

In the remainder of the paper, we present several sound DP processors which can be used for termination proofs within the DP framework. Of course, it is desirable to find DP processors which transform a DP problem $(\mathcal{P}, \mathcal{Q}, \mathcal{R}, f)$ into a set of "simpler" problems and whose application can never "harm". Therefore, we are particularly interested in processors which decrease $\mathcal{P}$ and $\mathcal{R}$ and which increase $\mathcal{Q}$. As stated by Lemma 1, decreasing the set of rules $\mathcal{R}$ and increasing $\mathcal{Q}$ leads to a more restricted rewrite relation and thus, it can never transform a non-infinite DP problem into an infinite one. In other words, any DP processor which removes rules from $\mathcal{P}$ and $\mathcal{R}$ and which adds rules to $\mathcal{Q}$ is complete.

Lemma 2 (Completeness of DP Processors). *Let Proc be a DP processor where for all DP problems $(\mathcal{P}, \mathcal{Q}, \mathcal{R}, f)$ and all $(\mathcal{P}', \mathcal{Q}', \mathcal{R}', f') \in Proc((\mathcal{P}, \mathcal{Q}, \mathcal{R}, f))$ we have $\mathcal{P}' \subseteq \mathcal{P}$, $\mathcal{R}' \subseteq \mathcal{R}$, and $\mathcal{Q}' \supseteq \mathcal{Q}$. Then Proc is complete.*

Proof. Let some $(\mathcal{P}', \mathcal{Q}', \mathcal{R}', f') \in Proc((\mathcal{P}, \mathcal{Q}, \mathcal{R}, f))$ be infinite and suppose that $(\mathcal{P}, \mathcal{Q}, \mathcal{R}, f)$ is not infinite. Thus, $\mathcal{R}$ is $\mathcal{Q}$-terminating and $(\mathcal{P}, \mathcal{Q}, \mathcal{R}, f)$ is finite. Due to $\mathcal{Q}$-termination of $\mathcal{R}$, every $(\mathcal{P}, \mathcal{Q}, \mathcal{R})$-chain is minimal and thus, there is no infinite $(\mathcal{P}, \mathcal{Q}, \mathcal{R})$-chain, even if $f = \mathbf{m}$.

Note that $\mathcal{Q}'$-termination of $\mathcal{R}'$ follows from $\mathcal{Q}$-termination of $\mathcal{R}$ by Lemma 1. So if $(\mathcal{P}', \mathcal{Q}', \mathcal{R}', f')$ is infinite, there must be an infinite $(\mathcal{P}', \mathcal{Q}', \mathcal{R}')$-chain. But then this is also an infinite $(\mathcal{P}, \mathcal{Q}, \mathcal{R})$-chain which contradicts the observation above. The reason is that $t_i\sigma \xrightarrow{\mathcal{Q}'}{}^*_{\mathcal{R}'} s_{i+1}\sigma$ implies $t_i\sigma \xrightarrow{\mathcal{Q}}{}^*_{\mathcal{R}} s_{i+1}\sigma$ by Lemma 1 and if $s_i\sigma$ is a $\mathcal{Q}'$-normal form then it is also a $\mathcal{Q}$-normal form. □

3   DP Processors from the Dependency Pair Approach

In the classical dependency pair approach, finiteness of a DP problem was shown by first modularizing the proof using the *dependency graph* (cf. Sect. 3.1.) Afterwards, a set of inequalities was generated and one tried to find certain orders satisfying these inequalities (cf. Sect. 3.2). Moreover, before constructing the dependency graph, it was possible to transform dependency pairs (cf. Sect. 3.3). In this section, we develop DP processors which perform these three tasks. Thus, the whole dependency pair approach is now presented as a set of processors working on DP problems. Each step of the dependency pair approach is formulated as a DP processor on its own. In this way, flexibility is increased substantially: now these DP processors may be applied repeatedly and in any order, whereas their order of application was fixed in the original dependency pair approach.

All processors in this section only modify the set of pairs $\mathcal{P}$ in a DP problem $(\mathcal{P}, \mathcal{Q}, \mathcal{R}, f)$. Processors which also modify the sets $\mathcal{Q}$ and $\mathcal{R}$ will be discussed in Sect. 4 and processors which also modify f will be shown in Sect. 5.

3.1 A DP Processor Based on the Dependency Graph

We now present a processor to decompose a DP problem into several separate sub-problems. To this end, one tries to determine which pairs can follow each other in chains by constructing a so-called *dependency graph*.

Definition 5 (Dependency Graph). *Let $(\mathcal{P}, \mathcal{Q}, \mathcal{R}, f)$ be a DP problem. The nodes of the $(\mathcal{P}, \mathcal{Q}, \mathcal{R})$-dependency graph are the pairs of $\mathcal{P}$ and there is an arc from $s \to t$ to $u \to v$ iff $s \to t, u \to v$ is a $(\mathcal{P}, \mathcal{Q}, \mathcal{R})$-chain.*

Example 5. We regard the TRS for subtraction and division from Ex. 2 again. Here we obtain the following $(\mathcal{P}, \mathcal{Q}, \mathcal{R})$-dependency graph for all $\mathcal{Q} \subseteq \mathcal{R}$.

```
┌──────────────────────────────────────────────┐  ┌──────────────────────────────────────┐
│ DIV(s(x), s(y)) → DIV(minus(x, y), s(y)) (8) │  │ MINUS(s(x), s(y)) → MINUS(x, y) (6)  │
└──────────────────────────────────────────────┘  └──────────────────────────────────────┘
                      ┌───────────────────────────────────────────┐
                      │ DIV(s(x), s(y)) → MINUS(x, y) (7)         │
                      └───────────────────────────────────────────┘
```

Obviously, every infinite chain corresponds to a cycle in the dependency graph. Since this graph is in general not computable, for automation one constructs an *estimated* graph. To this end, one has to approximate whether two pairs $s \to t, u \to v$ form a $(\mathcal{P}, \mathcal{Q}, \mathcal{R})$-chain. In this case, one draws an arc from $s \to t$ to $u \to v$. As long as the approximation is sound (i.e., as long as it is an over-approximation), the resulting graph contains the real dependency graph and thus, every infinite chain also corresponds to a cycle in the estimated graph.

In the classical dependency pair approach, several such approximations were developed (e.g., [1,11]) and for example, all of them would be able to compute the graph given in Ex. 5. However, instead of $(\mathcal{P}, \mathcal{Q}, \mathcal{R})$-chains, here one only considered chains where $\mathcal{Q} = \varnothing$ (for full termination) or where $\mathcal{Q} = \mathcal{R}$ (for innermost termination). The latter were called "*innermost* chains". By Lemma 1, every $(\mathcal{P}, \mathcal{Q}, \mathcal{R})$-chain is also a $(\mathcal{P}, \varnothing, \mathcal{R})$-chain (i.e., an ordinary chain in the classical dependency pair approach) and if $\mathcal{Q} \supseteq \mathcal{R}$, it is also an innermost chain. Thus, all existing methods to (over-)approximate chains in the dependency pair approach can also be used to approximate $(\mathcal{P}, \mathcal{Q}, \mathcal{R})$-chains for any $\mathcal{Q}$. Moreover, if $\mathcal{Q} \supseteq \mathcal{R}$, then all approximations for innermost chains can be applied as well. Hence, one can still use the existing estimation techniques for (innermost) dependency graphs in order to estimate $(\mathcal{P}, \mathcal{Q}, \mathcal{R})$-dependency graphs.

Now it is sufficient to prove absence of infinite (minimal) chains for maximal cycles (so-called *strongly connected components*, SCCs) of the dependency graph. Here, a subset $\mathcal{P}'$ of dependency pairs is called a *cycle* iff for all pairs $s \to t$ and $u \to v$ in $\mathcal{P}'$, there is a path from $s \to t$ to $u \to v$ traversing only pairs from $\mathcal{P}'$. A cycle $\mathcal{P}'$ is called an *SCC* if $\mathcal{P}'$ is not a proper subset of any other cycle.

Theorem 2 (DP Processor Based on the Dependency Graph). *The following DP Processor Proc is sound and complete. For a DP problem $(\mathcal{P}, \mathcal{Q}, \mathcal{R}, f)$ Proc returns $\{(\mathcal{P}_1, \mathcal{Q}, \mathcal{R}, f), \ldots, (\mathcal{P}_n, \mathcal{Q}, \mathcal{R}, f)\}$, where $\mathcal{P}_1, \ldots, \mathcal{P}_n$ are the SCCs of the (estimated) $(\mathcal{P}, \mathcal{Q}, \mathcal{R})$-dependency graph.*

Proof. Completeness follows from Lemma 2, since $\mathcal{P}_i \subseteq \mathcal{P}$ for all i. Proc is sound since after a finite number of pairs in the beginning, any infinite (minimal) $(\mathcal{P}, \mathcal{Q}, \mathcal{R})$-chain only contains pairs from some SCC. Hence, there would also be an infinite (minimal) $(\mathcal{P}_i, \mathcal{Q}, \mathcal{R})$-chain for some $\mathcal{P}_i$. □

Example 6. To prove $\mathcal{Q}$-termination of the TRS $\mathcal{R}$ for subtraction and division from Ex. 2, we start with the initial DP problem $(\mathcal{P}, \mathcal{Q}, \mathcal{R}, \mathbf{m})$, where $\mathcal{P}$ is the set of dependency pairs $\{(6), (7), (8)\}$. As shown in Ex. 5, the SCCs of the dependency graph consist of (6) and (8), respectively. Hence, the above DP processor transforms the initial DP problem into the two new problems $(\{(6)\}, \mathcal{Q}, \mathcal{R}, \mathbf{m})$ and $(\{(8)\}, \mathcal{Q}, \mathcal{R}, \mathbf{m})$. These two problems can now be solved independently. In other words, we can now prove termination of minus and div separately.

In contrast to the classical dependency pair approach, now the dependency graph can be (re-)computed at any time during the termination proof. This leads to very modular proofs, since one may always decompose DP problems into subproblems which can be solved independently, e.g., by different DP processors.

3.2 A DP Processor Based on Orders

Classical techniques for automated termination proofs try to find a *reduction order* $\succ$, i.e., an order which is well-founded, monotonic, and stable (closed under contexts and substitutions), such that $l \succ r$ holds for all rules $l \to r$ of the TRS. In practice, one mainly uses *simplification orders*, where a term is always greater than its proper subterms [3,19]. Examples for such orders are the *lexicographic* or *recursive path order* [3,14], the *Knuth-Bendix order* [15], and (most) *polynomial orders* [17]. However, the power of this approach is limited, since termination of many important TRSs cannot be proved with simplification orders. For instance, simplification orders fail on the TRS of Ex. 2, since the left-hand side of Rule (5) is embedded in its right-hand side if y is instantiated with $\mathsf{s}(x)$.

The dependency pair approach was introduced to overcome the limitations of classical simplification orders. For any TRS, it generates a set of inequality constraints and if there exists a well-founded order satisfying the constraints, then termination is proved. Hence, one can use existing techniques to search for suitable orders and it turns out that in this way, classical simplification orders can prove termination of numerous TRSs where they would have failed otherwise.

We now formalize this idea in the context of the DP framework. To remove pairs from $\mathcal{P}$ in a DP problem $(\mathcal{P}, \mathcal{Q}, \mathcal{R}, f)$, one can generate constraints which should be satisfied by a *reduction pair* [16] $(\succsim, \succ)$ where $\succsim$ is reflexive, transitive, monotonic, and stable and $\succ$ is a stable well-founded order compatible with $\succsim$ (i.e., $\succsim \circ \succ \subseteq \succ$ and $\succ \circ \succsim \subseteq \succ$). But $\succ$ does not have to be monotonic. The constraints require that at least one pair in $\mathcal{P}$ is strictly decreasing (w.r.t. $\succ$) and all remaining pairs in $\mathcal{P}$ and all rules in $\mathcal{R}$ are weakly decreasing (w.r.t. $\succsim$).

Requiring $l \succsim r$ for all rules $l \to r \in \mathcal{R}$ ensures that in chains $s_1 \to t_1, s_2 \to t_2, \ldots$ with $t_i \sigma \overset{Q}{\hookrightarrow}_\mathcal{R}^* s_{i+1}\sigma$, we have $t_i \sigma \succsim s_{i+1}\sigma$. Hence, the existence of such a reduction pair implies that there is no chain which contains the strictly decreasing pairs of $\mathcal{P}$ infinitely often. Thus, all of these pairs can be deleted from $\mathcal{P}$.

If the $\mathcal{Q}$-restricted rewrite relation is contained in the innermost rewrite relation (i.e., if $\mathcal{Q} \supseteq \mathcal{R}$), this approach can be improved. Now a weak decrease $l \succsim r$ is not required for all rules but only for the *usable rules*. For any term t, all function symbols occurring in t are "usable". Moreover, if some symbol f is usable and there is a rule $f(\ldots) \to r$ in $\mathcal{R}$ whose right-hand side r contains a symbol g, then g is usable as well. Let $\mathcal{US}(t,\mathcal{R})$ denote the set of *usable symbols* and we define the *usable rules* $\mathcal{U}(t,\mathcal{R})$ as the set of those rules $f(\ldots) \to \ldots$ from $\mathcal{R}$ where $f \in \mathcal{US}(t,\mathcal{R})$. Analogously, for a TRS $\mathcal{P}$, the usable symbols and rules are defined as $\mathcal{US}(\mathcal{P},\mathcal{R}) = \bigcup_{s \to t \in \mathcal{P}} \mathcal{US}(t,\mathcal{R})$ and $\mathcal{U}(\mathcal{P},\mathcal{R}) = \bigcup_{s \to t \in \mathcal{P}} \mathcal{U}(t,\mathcal{R})$. Further refinements to reduce the set of usable rules can be found in [8,12,21].

Example 7. Let $\mathcal{R}$ be the TRS of Ex. 2. For the problem $(\{\mathsf{MINUS}(\mathsf{s}(x),\mathsf{s}(y)) \to \mathsf{MINUS}(x,y)\}, \mathcal{Q}, \mathcal{R}, \mathbf{m})$ one would now have to find a reduction pair $(\succsim, \succ)$ such that $\mathsf{MINUS}(\mathsf{s}(x),\mathsf{s}(y)) \succ \mathsf{MINUS}(x,y)$ and $l \succsim r$ for all rules. But if one only wants to prove innermost termination (or $\mathcal{Q}$-termination for $\mathcal{Q} \supseteq \mathcal{R}$), it suffices to require $l \succsim r$ just for the usable rules. Since the only usable symbol of the dependency pair's right-hand side $\mathsf{MINUS}(x,y)$ is MINUS, there are no usable rules. So for this DP problem, one only has to find a stable well-founded order $\succ$ satisfying $\mathsf{MINUS}(\mathsf{s}(x),\mathsf{s}(y)) \succ \mathsf{MINUS}(x,y)$. This can easily be done with any of the existing classical reduction orders. Thus, the dependency pair can be deleted and the resulting DP problem $(\emptyset, \mathcal{Q}, \mathcal{R}, \mathbf{m})$ is transformed into the empty set by the dependency graph processor of Thm. 2.

In [21], we recently extended previous results of [8,23] and showed that if one only has to prove absence of *minimal* chains (i.e., if $f = \mathbf{m}$), then usable rules can also be used for proving full instead of just innermost termination, provided that $\succsim$ is $\mathcal{C}_\varepsilon$-*compatible* (i.e., $\mathsf{c}(x,y) \succsim x$ and $\mathsf{c}(x,y) \succsim y$ for a fresh function symbol c). This holds for virtually all relations $\succsim$ generated automatically by standard techniques. Then, to prove $\mathcal{Q}$-termination (for arbitrary $\mathcal{Q}$) it is enough to require $l \succsim r$ just for the usable rules. In this way, the DP problem for minus can be solved as in Ex. 7 for arbitrary $\mathcal{Q}$.

To generate reduction pairs $(\succsim, \succ)$ automatically, one often uses classical (monotonic) simplification orders. However, $\succ$ does not have to be monotonic. To benefit from this possibility and to build non-monotonic orders from simplification orders, one may pre-process the constraints first and delete certain function symbols and arguments by an *argument filtering* π [1]. For example, if π_1 eliminates the second argument of the function symbol minus, then for any term t, $\pi_1(t)$ results from replacing all subterms $\mathsf{minus}(t_1, t_2)$ by $\mathsf{minus}(t_1)$. Moreover, one can also use argument filterings which collapse function symbols to one of their arguments (i.e., one could also define an argument filtering π_2 with $\pi_2(\mathsf{minus}(t_1, t_2)) = t_1$). Now instead of a reduction pair $(\succsim, \succ)$, one may use the reduction pair $(\succsim_\pi, \succ_\pi)$ with $s \succsim_\pi t$ iff $\pi(s) \succsim \pi(t)$ and $s \succ_\pi t$ iff $\pi(s) \succ \pi(t)$. Techniques to search for argument filterings efficiently were developed in [8,11].

Example 8. Regard the other DP problem ({DIV(s(x), s(y)) → DIV(minus(x, y), s(y))}, $\mathcal{Q}, \mathcal{R}, \mathbf{m}$) resulting from the TRS $\mathcal{R}$ of Ex. 2. The usable rules of the term DIV(minus(x, y), s(y)) are just the minus-rules. Thus, if we use $\mathcal{C}_\varepsilon$-compatible relations $\succsim$, it suffices to find a reduction pair $(\succsim, \succ)$ and an argument filtering π such that DIV(s(x), s(y)) $\succ_\pi$ DIV(minus(x, y), s(y)) and $l \succsim_\pi r$ for all minus-rules.

If we apply the argument filtering π_1 above, the constraint from the dependency pair becomes DIV(s(x), s(y)) $\succ$ DIV(minus(x), s(y)) and if we use the argument filtering π_2, it becomes DIV(s(x), s(y)) $\succ$ DIV(x, s(y)). In both cases, all resulting constraints can easily be satisfied (e.g., by the lexicographic path order). Thus, the dependency pair can be deleted from this DP problem as well and in this way, termination of the TRS in Ex. 2 can easily be shown automatically.

For any TRS $\mathcal{P}$ and any relation $\succ$, let $\mathcal{P}_\succ = \{s \to t \in \mathcal{P} \mid s \succ t\}$, i.e., $\mathcal{P}_\succ$ contains those rules of $\mathcal{P}$ which decrease w.r.t. $\succ$. Now we can define a DP processor which deletes all pairs from $\mathcal{P}$ which are strictly decreasing w.r.t. a reduction pair and an argument filtering (i.e., all pairs of $\mathcal{P}_{\succ_\pi}$). The reason is that they cannot occur infinitely many times in a chain.

Theorem 3 (DP Processor Based on Reduction Pairs). *Let $(\succsim, \succ)$ be a reduction pair and π be an argument filtering. Then the following DP processor Proc is sound and complete. For a DP problem $(\mathcal{P}, \mathcal{Q}, \mathcal{R}, f)$, Proc returns*

- $\{(\mathcal{P} \setminus \mathcal{P}_{\succ_\pi}, \mathcal{Q}, \mathcal{R}, f)\}$, *if*
  - $\mathcal{P}_{\succ_\pi} \cup \mathcal{P}_{\succsim_\pi} = \mathcal{P}$ *and*
  - $\mathcal{R}_{\succsim_\pi} \supseteq \mathcal{U}(\mathcal{P}, \mathcal{R})$ *and*
  - $\mathcal{Q} \supseteq \mathcal{R}$ *or* $\mathcal{R}_{\succsim_\pi} = \mathcal{R}$ *or* ($\succsim$ *is $\mathcal{C}_\varepsilon$-compatible and $f = \mathbf{m}$*)
- $\{(\mathcal{P}, \mathcal{Q}, \mathcal{R}, f)\}$, *otherwise*

Proof. Completeness follows from Lemma 2. If $\succsim$ is $\mathcal{C}_\varepsilon$-compatible, soundness is proved as in [21, Thm. 22]. (The extension from ordinary to $\mathcal{Q}$-restricted rewriting is completely straightforward.) The case $\mathcal{R}_{\succsim_\pi} = \mathcal{R}$ is the classical dependency pair approach for termination and its soundness is proved in [7, Thm. 3.5] and [1, Thm. 11]. Finally, for the case $\mathcal{Q} \supseteq \mathcal{R}$ recall that the $\mathcal{Q}$-restricted rewrite relation is contained in the innermost rewrite relation and thus, every $(\mathcal{P}, \mathcal{Q}, \mathcal{R})$-chain is an innermost chain. Hence, then the soundness follows from the corresponding result of [7, Thm. 5.6] for innermost termination. □

Whenever a processor modifies a DP problem, it is usually advantageous to apply the dependency graph processor of Thm. 2 afterwards. The reason is that in this way one can split the DP problem into new subproblems and probably also remove further rules of $\mathcal{P}$. This is a generalization of a strategy which was originally suggested within the classical dependency pair approach in [11]. Here, SCCs of the dependency graph were re-computed whenever some dependency pairs were strictly oriented and therefore removed. In the DP framework, this would now correspond to a repeated alternating application of the processors in Thm. 2 and in Thm. 3. However, by formalizing termination techniques as DP processors, many additional strategies can now easily be formulated as well, cf. Sect. 6.

3.3 DP Processors Based on Dependency Pair Transformations

As shown in [1,6,8], to increase the power of the dependency pair approach, a dependency pair may be transformed by *rewriting*, *narrowing*, or *instantiation*. We now adapt these transformations to the DP framework. Given a DP problem $(\mathcal{P}, \mathcal{Q}, \mathcal{R}, f)$, they replace one of the pairs $s \to t$ in $\mathcal{P}$ by several new ones (i.e., the result is of the form $(\mathcal{P}', \mathcal{Q}, \mathcal{R}, f)$). In contrast to the previous processors, we usually do not have $\mathcal{P}' \subseteq \mathcal{P}$, but $\mathcal{P}'$ is obtained by replacing $s \to t$ with new pairs resulting from rewriting, narrowing, or instantiating $s \to t$.

Compared to the original versions of these transformations in the dependency pair approach, they are now improved and modularized considerably. The reason is that now these transformations can be applied at any time during the proof and the conditions for their applicability only have to take the pairs and rules in the current DP problem into account. In this way, these conditions are much more often satisfied than in the original dependency pair approach, where such transformations were only permitted in the very beginning.

In the dependency pair approach, there were two variants of the narrowing and the instantiation transformation (for termination and for innermost termination, respectively), cf. [8]. The DP processors for narrowing and instantiation are immediately obtained from the original transformations, by applying the variants for termination if $\mathcal{Q} = \varnothing$ and by applying the variants for innermost termination if $\mathcal{Q} \supseteq \mathcal{R}$.[4] The soundness and completeness results for these transformations directly carry over from the classical dependency pair approach to their versions in the DP framework: instantiation is sound and complete and narrowing is sound. Completeness of narrowing holds as well in the termination case (i.e., if $\mathcal{Q} = \varnothing$), but not if $\mathcal{Q} \supseteq \mathcal{R}$, cf. [1, Ex. 43]. The proofs for these results are completely analogous to the ones in the dependency pair approach (i.e., to [1, Thm. 27 and 42] for narrowing and to [6, Thm. 20] for instantiation).

While adapting narrowing and instantiation to the DP framework is straightforward, the adaption of the *rewriting* transformation is more problematic. In the classical dependency pair approach, rewriting is only applicable for innermost termination proofs (i.e., if $\mathcal{Q} = \mathcal{R}$). The problem is that the original proofs for its soundness and completeness [6, Thm. 14, 15, 18, 19] do not extend to the case where $\mathcal{Q} \supseteq \mathcal{R}$.[5] However, such an extension is urgently required in the DP framework, since in Sect. 4 we will introduce new powerful DP processors which reduce the set of rules $\mathcal{R}$ in a DP problem. Thus, even if one starts with an innermost termination problem $(\mathcal{P}, \mathcal{Q}, \mathcal{R}, f)$ where $\mathcal{Q} = \mathcal{R}$, after application of some

---

[4] Of course, when applying the transformations for $\mathcal{Q} \supseteq \mathcal{R}$ instead of "normal forms" in [8] one always has to regard "$\mathcal{Q}$-normal forms".

[5] In contrast to the narrowing and instantiation transformations which perform *all* possible narrowings or instantiations, here one may replace $s \to t$ by *any* pair resulting from rewriting t. The soundness proof relies on the result that weak innermost termination and non-overlappingness imply confluence and termination [10] and the completeness proof relies on the result that innermost termination implies normalization. Obviously, these results do not extend to $\mathcal{Q} \supseteq \mathcal{R}$, i.e., in general $\mathcal{Q}$-termination and non-overlappingness do not imply confluence, termination, or normalization.

DP processors one might result in a problem $(\mathcal{P}', \mathcal{Q}', \mathcal{R}', f')$ where $\mathcal{Q}' \supseteq \mathcal{R}'$. Now it would be desirable if one could still apply the rewriting transformation (this will be demonstrated in Ex. 14). Therefore, we now present a new proof to show that the rewriting transformation is sound for any $\mathcal{Q} \supseteq \mathcal{R}$ in the DP framework. Moreover, if for all subterms q below the position where the rewriting took place we have $\mathcal{U}(q, \mathcal{Q}) \subseteq \mathcal{R}$, then it is also complete. So q's usable rules w.r.t. $\mathcal{Q}$ also have to be contained in $\mathcal{R}$. In the special case of innermost termination where $\mathcal{Q} = \mathcal{R}$, this completeness condition is always fulfilled (i.e., our results encompass the completeness result for innermost termination from [6, Thm. 19]).[6]

For the proof, we need the following sufficient criterion for confluence of the $\mathcal{Q}$-restricted rewrite relation. It states that if there are no critical pairs on the root level, then we even have the *diamond property* (i.e., if $t \xrightarrow{\mathcal{Q}}_\mathcal{R} t_1$ and $t \xrightarrow{\mathcal{Q}}_\mathcal{R} t_2$, then $t_1 = t_2$ or there exists a t' such that $t_1 \xrightarrow{\mathcal{Q}}_\mathcal{R} t'$ and $t_2 \xrightarrow{\mathcal{Q}}_\mathcal{R} t'$).

Lemma 3 (Confluence of $\xrightarrow{\mathcal{Q}}_\mathcal{R}$). *Let $\mathcal{Q} \supseteq \mathcal{R}$ and let $\mathcal{R}$ be non-overlaying (i.e., left-hand sides of different $\mathcal{R}$-rules do not unify after variable renaming). Then $\xrightarrow{\mathcal{Q}}_\mathcal{R}$ has the diamond property and hence, it is confluent.*

Proof. Let $t \xrightarrow{\mathcal{Q}}_{\mathcal{R},p_1} t_1$ and $t \xrightarrow{\mathcal{Q}}_{\mathcal{R},p_2} t_2$. Since $t|_{p_1}$ and $t|_{p_2}$ are no $\mathcal{R}$-normal forms and thus no $\mathcal{Q}$-normal forms (by $\mathcal{Q} \supseteq \mathcal{R}$), p_2 cannot be strictly above p_1 and p_1 cannot be strictly above p_2. If $p_1 = p_2$, then $t_1 = t_2$, as we used the same rule in both reductions since $\mathcal{R}$ is non-overlaying. Otherwise, p_1 and p_2 are not above each other, and thus, t_1 and t_2 can obviously be joined in one step. □

Now we introduce the rewriting processor. It states that in a DP problem $(\mathcal{P}, \mathcal{Q}, \mathcal{R}, f)$ with $\mathcal{Q} \supseteq \mathcal{R}$, any $s \to t \in \mathcal{P}$ can be replaced by $s \to t'$ if t rewrites to t' at some position p. The only applicability condition is that the usable rules for the redex $t|_p$ must be non-overlapping (i.e., they must not have critical pairs).

Theorem 4 (Rewriting Processor). *Let Proc be a processor which transforms a DP problem $(\mathcal{P} \cup \{s \to t\}, \mathcal{Q}, \mathcal{R}, f)$ either into $\{(\mathcal{P} \cup \{s \to t'\}, \mathcal{Q}, \mathcal{R}, f)\}$ or into $\{(\mathcal{P} \cup \{s \to t\}, \mathcal{Q}, \mathcal{R}, f)\}$ again. In the first case, the following two conditions must be satisfied:*

- $t \to_{\mathcal{R}, p} t'$ *and* $\mathcal{U}(t|_p, \mathcal{R})$ *is non-overlapping*
- $\mathcal{Q} \supseteq \mathcal{R}$

Proc is sound, and it is complete if $\mathcal{U}(q, \mathcal{Q}) \subseteq \mathcal{R}$ for all proper subterms q of $t|_p$.

Proof. Let $t = t[l\mu]_p \to_\mathcal{R} t[r\mu]_p = t'$ for some $l \to r \in \mathcal{R}$ and a substitution μ.

We first prove the soundness and only consider the case where $f = \mathbf{m}$. The case $f = \mathbf{a}$ is analogous. Let $s \to t, u \to v$ be a minimal $(\mathcal{P}, \mathcal{Q}, \mathcal{R})$-chain. Thus, $t\sigma \xrightarrow{\mathcal{Q}}{}^*_\mathcal{R} u\sigma$, both $s\sigma$ and $u\sigma$ are in $\mathcal{Q}$-normal form, and $t\sigma$ and $v\sigma$ are terminating w.r.t. $\xrightarrow{\mathcal{Q}}_\mathcal{R}$. We want to show that $t'\sigma \xrightarrow{\mathcal{Q}}{}^*_\mathcal{R} u\sigma$ and that $t'\sigma$ is also terminating w.r.t. $\xrightarrow{\mathcal{Q}}_\mathcal{R}$. Then we can exchange all occurrences of $s \to t$ in chains by $s \to t'$.

---

[6] A similar completeness result also holds for narrowing: if $\mathcal{Q} \supseteq \mathcal{R}$, then the narrowing processor is still complete if for all narrowed subterms, the usable rules w.r.t. $\mathcal{R}$ are non-overlapping and for all subterms q below those positions that were narrowed we have $\mathcal{U}(q, \mathcal{Q}) \subseteq \mathcal{R}$. Again, the latter condition is always satisfied if $\mathcal{Q} = \mathcal{R}$. Thus, this encompasses the completeness result of [6, Thm. 17] for innermost termination.

We consider the reduction $t\sigma = t\sigma[l\mu\sigma]_p \xrightarrow{\mathcal{Q}}{}^*_{\mathcal{R}} u\sigma$. As $u\sigma$ is in $\mathcal{Q}$-normal form and as $\xrightarrow{\mathcal{Q}}_{\mathcal{R}}$-reductions cannot take place above $\mathcal{Q}$-redexes, w.l.o.g. we first reduce $l\mu\sigma$ to some $\mathcal{Q}$-normal form w. Thus, $t\sigma = t\sigma[l\mu\sigma]_p \xrightarrow{\mathcal{Q}}{}^*_{\mathcal{R}} t\sigma[w]_p \xrightarrow{\mathcal{Q}}{}^*_{\mathcal{R}} u\sigma$ where $l\mu\sigma \xrightarrow{\mathcal{Q}}{}^*_{\mathcal{R}} w$. Since σ instantiates all variables by normal forms w.r.t. $\mathcal{Q} \supseteq \mathcal{R}$, the only rules applicable to $t|_p\sigma = l\mu\sigma$ or its reducts are from $\mathcal{U}(t|_p, \mathcal{R})$. For readability, we abbreviate $\mathcal{U}(t|_p, \mathcal{R})$ by $\mathcal{U}$. Hence, $l\mu\sigma \xrightarrow{\mathcal{Q}}{}^*_{\mathcal{U}} w$. As w is a $\mathcal{Q}$-normal form, w.l.o.g. one first reduces all terms $x\mu\sigma$ with $x \in \mathcal{V}(l)$ to $\mathcal{Q}$-normal forms. As $\mathcal{U}$ is non-overlapping and $\mathcal{Q} \supseteq \mathcal{R} \supseteq \mathcal{U}$, by Lemma 3 these normal forms are unique. Thus, $l\mu\sigma \xrightarrow{\mathcal{Q}}{}^*_{\mathcal{U}} l\delta \xrightarrow{\mathcal{Q}}{}^*_{\mathcal{U}} w$ for some $\mathcal{Q}$-normal substitution δ (i.e., $\delta(x)$ is in $\mathcal{Q}$-normal form for all $x \in \mathcal{V}$) and for all $x \in \mathcal{V}(l)$ we have $x\mu\sigma \xrightarrow{\mathcal{Q}}{}^*_{\mathcal{U}} x\delta$. Note that $l\delta$ is not yet a $\mathcal{Q}$-normal form as $l \to r \in \mathcal{R} \subseteq \mathcal{Q}$. Thus, we need at least one more step to get from $l\delta$ to w. As δ is a $\mathcal{Q}$-normal substitution, the reduction is above δ and as $\mathcal{U}$ is non-overlapping, the only possible reduction is $l\delta \xrightarrow{\mathcal{Q}}_{\mathcal{U}} r\delta \xrightarrow{\mathcal{Q}}{}^*_{\mathcal{U}} w$. This finally proves $t'\sigma = t\sigma[r\mu\sigma]_p \xrightarrow{\mathcal{Q}}{}^*_{\mathcal{R}} t\sigma[r\delta]_p \xrightarrow{\mathcal{Q}}{}^*_{\mathcal{R}} t\sigma[w]_p \xrightarrow{\mathcal{Q}}{}^*_{\mathcal{R}} u\sigma$.

Now minimality (i.e., termination of $t'\sigma$ w.r.t. $\xrightarrow{\mathcal{Q}}_{\mathcal{R}}$), can be proved in an analogous way. As before, w.l.o.g. any infinite $\xrightarrow{\mathcal{Q}}_{\mathcal{R}}$-reduction of $t'\sigma = t\sigma[r\mu\sigma]_p$ first reduces all redexes in $x\mu\sigma$ for $x \in \mathcal{V}(r)$. These reductions either lead to non-termination or they end in some $\xrightarrow{\mathcal{Q}}_{\mathcal{R}}$-normal forms. Since $x \in \mathcal{V}(r) \subseteq \mathcal{V}(l)$, all $x\mu$ are contained in $t|_p$. As σ instantiates variables by normal forms w.r.t. $\mathcal{Q} \supseteq \mathcal{R}$, again the only rules applicable to subterms of $t|_p\sigma$ (like $x\mu\sigma$) are from $\mathcal{U}$. As $\xrightarrow{\mathcal{Q}}_{\mathcal{U}}$ is confluent by Lemma 3, the reduction must begin with $r\mu\sigma \xrightarrow{\mathcal{Q}}{}^*_{\mathcal{R}} r\delta$. Hence, whenever $t'\sigma$ is non-terminating w.r.t. $\xrightarrow{\mathcal{Q}}_{\mathcal{R}}$ then so is $t\sigma[r\delta]_p$. But this would contradict the termination of t w.r.t. $\xrightarrow{\mathcal{Q}}_{\mathcal{R}}$ as we know that $t \xrightarrow{\mathcal{Q}}{}^*_{\mathcal{R}} t\sigma[r\delta]_p$.

The completeness of the rewriting processor is obvious if $\mathcal{R}$ is not $\mathcal{Q}$-terminating. Otherwise, we show that if there is a reduction $t'\sigma \xrightarrow{\mathcal{Q}}{}^*_{\mathcal{R}} u\sigma$ such that $s\sigma$ and $u\sigma$ are in $\mathcal{Q}$-normal form, then $t\sigma \xrightarrow{\mathcal{Q}}{}^*_{\mathcal{R}} u\sigma$ also holds. We use the same way of reasoning as for the soundness proof. So if $t'\sigma = t\sigma[r\mu\sigma]_p \xrightarrow{\mathcal{Q}}{}^*_{\mathcal{R}} u\sigma$, we may assume that we first reduce $r\mu\sigma$ to some $\mathcal{Q}$-normal form w which is again done with $\xrightarrow{\mathcal{Q}}_{\mathcal{U}}$ reductions. By the confluence of $\xrightarrow{\mathcal{Q}}_{\mathcal{U}}$ (Lemma 3), we have $r\mu\sigma \xrightarrow{\mathcal{Q}}{}^*_{\mathcal{U}} r\delta \xrightarrow{\mathcal{Q}}{}^*_{\mathcal{U}} w$ for some $\mathcal{Q}$-normal substitution δ. In the same way as before we obtain $t'\sigma = t\sigma[r\mu\sigma]_p \xrightarrow{\mathcal{Q}}{}^*_{\mathcal{R}} t\sigma[r\delta]_p \xrightarrow{\mathcal{Q}}{}^*_{\mathcal{R}} t\sigma[w]_p \xrightarrow{\mathcal{Q}}{}^*_{\mathcal{R}} u\sigma$. It remains to show that $l\mu\sigma \xrightarrow{\mathcal{Q}}{}^*_{\mathcal{R}} r\delta$, as this implies $t\sigma = t\sigma[l\mu\sigma]_p \xrightarrow{\mathcal{Q}}{}^*_{\mathcal{R}} t\sigma[r\delta]_p \xrightarrow{\mathcal{Q}}{}^*_{\mathcal{R}} t\sigma[w]_p \xrightarrow{\mathcal{Q}}{}^*_{\mathcal{R}} u\sigma$.

We know that $x\mu\sigma \xrightarrow{\mathcal{Q}}{}^*_{\mathcal{R}} x\delta$ for all $x \in \mathcal{V}(r)$, where $x\delta$ is in $\mathcal{Q}$-normal form. By $\mathcal{Q} \supseteq \mathcal{R}$, $x\delta$ is in normal form w.r.t. $\xrightarrow{\mathcal{Q}}_{\mathcal{R}}$, too. As $\mathcal{R}$ is $\mathcal{Q}$-terminating, we can extend δ such that $x\delta$ is a normal form of $x\mu\sigma$ w.r.t. $\xrightarrow{\mathcal{Q}}_{\mathcal{R}}$ for every variable $x \in \mathcal{V}(l) \setminus \mathcal{V}(r)$. Then we have $l\mu\sigma \xrightarrow{\mathcal{Q}}{}^*_{\mathcal{R}} l\delta$. To prove the desired result $l\delta \xrightarrow{\mathcal{Q}}_{\mathcal{R}} r\delta$, we show that $l\delta$ does not contain $\mathcal{Q}$-redexes as proper subterms.

First suppose that $l\delta$ contains a $\mathcal{Q}$-redex at a position o of l where $l|_o \notin \mathcal{V}$. If a rule $l' \to r' \in \mathcal{Q}$ can be applied to $l|_o\delta$ at root position, then we have $l' \to r' \in \mathcal{U}(l|_o, \mathcal{Q}) \subseteq \mathcal{U}(l|_o\mu, \mathcal{Q}) \subseteq \mathcal{R}$, by the prerequisite of the theorem. Since root(l') occurs in $l|_o$ and hence in l, we also have $l' \to r' \in \mathcal{U}(t|_p, \mathcal{R})$. But then $l' \to r'$ and $l \to r$ are two rules from $\mathcal{U}(t|_p, \mathcal{R})$ which form a critical pair. This contradicts the requirement that $\mathcal{U}(t|_p, \mathcal{R})$ is non-overlapping.

Now we show that $x\delta$ cannot contain a $\mathcal{Q}$-redex for $x \in \mathcal{V}(l)$. Note that if $x\delta$ is not a $\mathcal{Q}$-normal form, it is also not a normal form w.r.t. $\xrightarrow{\mathcal{Q}}_{\mathcal{Q}}$. Thus, there is a term w' such that $x\mu\sigma \xrightarrow{Q}{}^*_Q x\delta \xrightarrow{Q}_Q w'$. We now show that Q-reductions starting from $x\mu\sigma$ can only use rules from $\mathcal{R}$. Then we also have $x\mu\sigma \xrightarrow{Q}{}^*_{\mathcal{R}} x\delta \xrightarrow{Q}_{\mathcal{R}} w'$. But this contradicts the fact that $x\delta$ is in normal form w.r.t. $\xrightarrow{Q}_{\mathcal{R}}$.

Any Q-reduction starting from $x\mu\sigma$ only uses rules from $\mathcal{U}(x\mu, Q)$, since σ is a Q-normal substitution. As $x\mu$ is a subterm of $t|_p$, by the prerequisite of the theorem we have $\mathcal{U}(x\mu, Q) \subseteq \mathcal{R}$. Thus, any Q-reduction starting from $x\mu\sigma$ can indeed only use rules from $\mathcal{R}$. □

Example 9. We replace the minus-rule (3) of Ex. 2 by the following rules:

$$\text{minus}(\text{s}(x), \text{s}(y)) \to \text{minus}(\text{p}(\text{s}(x)), \text{p}(\text{s}(y))) \quad (9)$$
$$\text{minus}(x, \text{plus}(y, z)) \to \text{minus}(\text{minus}(x, y), z) \quad (10)$$
$$\text{p}(\text{s}(x)) \to x \quad (11)$$
$$\text{plus}(0, y) \to y \quad (12)$$
$$\text{plus}(\text{s}(x), y) \to \text{s}(\text{plus}(x, y)) \quad (13)$$

Now (innermost) termination cannot be shown by the previous processors (if one uses reduction pairs based on (quasi-)simplification orders in Thm. 3).[7] The reason is that the dependency pair $\text{MINUS}(\text{s}(x), \text{s}(y)) \to \text{MINUS}(\text{p}(\text{s}(x)), \text{p}(\text{s}(y)))$ from Rule (9) is not strictly decreasing w.r.t. any classical reduction order.

However, by the rewrite processor, the right-hand side of this dependency pair can be rewritten twice to obtain $\text{MINUS}(\text{s}(x), \text{s}(y)) \to \text{MINUS}(x, y)$. The processor is applicable, since the only usable rule of the redexes $\text{p}(\text{s}(x))$ and $\text{p}(\text{s}(y))$ is (11) which is non-overlapping (although the whole TRS is overlapping). Afterwards, innermost termination can easily be shown. However, since rewriting is only possible for $Q \supseteq \mathcal{R}$, this step is not permitted if one wants to prove termination (where $Q = \varnothing$). Note that this TRSs does not belong to those classes of TRSs where it is known that innermost termination implies termination. (A well-known such class are locally confluent overlay systems [10], but due to Rule (10) this system is neither locally confluent nor an overlay system.) In Sect. 4, we will introduce new DP processors to simplify DP problems and it will turn out that then the termination of this example is very easy to prove, cf. Ex. 14 and 15.[8]

The following examples show why straightforward extensions of the rewriting processor would destroy soundness or completeness, respectively.

Example 10. Since non-overlayingness already implies confluence of the Q-restricted rewrite relation by Lemma 3, a natural question is whether the rewrite

---

[7] Here, $\succsim$ is a *quasi-simplification order* if $s \succsim t$ for all subterms t of s. However, a proof with Thm. 3 using the very recently developed negative polynomial orders of [13] would be possible. An example where negative polynomials fail as well is Ex. 16.
[8] Alternatively, termination can also be proved using the *narrowing* transformation. Then the right-hand side $\text{MINUS}(\text{p}(\text{s}(x)), \text{p}(\text{s}(y)))$ would be replaced by its narrowings $\text{MINUS}(x, \text{p}(\text{s}(y)))$ and $\text{MINUS}(\text{p}(\text{s}(x)), y)$. However, narrowing is only permitted for right-hand sides of dependency pairs which do not unify with left-hand sides. Thus, narrowing would no longer be possible if one adds the rule $\text{minus}(\text{p}(x), y) \to \text{p}(\text{minus}(x, y))$, since $\text{MINUS}(\text{p}(\text{s}(x)), \text{p}(\text{s}(y)))$ unifies with the left-hand side of the new dependency pair $\text{MINUS}(\text{p}(x), y) \to \text{MINUS}(x, y)$. In contrast, the termination proof with the new DP processors in Ex. 14 and 15 would still work.

processor in Thm. 4 would already be sound if the usable rules $\mathcal{U}(t|_p, \mathcal{R})$ are just non-overlaying instead of non-overlapping. This is refuted by the following counterexample. Let $\mathcal{R} = \mathcal{Q} = \{f(c) \to d, f(h(x)) \to a, h(b) \to c, g(d, x) \to g(f(h(x)), x)\}$. Then $\mathcal{R}$ is not innermost terminating (i.e., not $\mathcal{Q}$-terminating):

$$g(d, b) \xrightarrow{i}_\mathcal{R} g(f(h(b)), b) \xrightarrow{i}_\mathcal{R} g(f(c), b) \xrightarrow{i}_\mathcal{R} g(d, b) \xrightarrow{i}_\mathcal{R} \ldots$$

The dependency graph has only one SCC $\{G(d, x) \to G(f(h(x)), x)\}$. Since $\mathcal{R}$ is non-overlaying and $G(f(h(x)), x) \to_\mathcal{R} G(a, x)$, rewriting would transform the dependency pair of the SCC into the new pair $G(d, x) \to G(a, x)$. Now the dependency graph processor would delete this pair, since it is obviously not on any cycle of the (new) dependency graph. Thus, we could falsely "prove" termination.

The problem is that although the dependency pair was rewritten by a $\mathcal{Q}$-restricted step, it is no longer $\mathcal{Q}$-restricted if one instantiates x with b. So to guarantee that any reduction from $G(f(h(x)), x)\sigma$ to an instantiated left-hand side of a dependency pair is also possible from $G(a, x)\sigma$, one needs non-overlappingness and not just confluence of $\mathcal{U}(t|_p, \mathcal{R})$'s $\mathcal{Q}$-restricted rewrite relation.

Example 11. This processor shows why we defined a DP problem $(\mathcal{P}, \mathcal{Q}, \mathcal{R}, f)$ to be "infinite" if it is not finite *or if $\mathcal{R}$ is not $\mathcal{Q}$-terminating*, cf. Def. 4. The reason is that if "infinite" would be defined as "not finite", then the rewriting processor would be incomplete, i.e., it could transform DP problems that are not infinite into problems with infinite chains, even if $\mathcal{Q} = \mathcal{R}$. Let $\mathcal{P} = \{F(x, x) \to F(b, g(a(x), x))\}$ and $\mathcal{Q} = \mathcal{R} = \{g(x, y) \to y, a(b) \to a(b)\}$. Obviously, $\mathcal{R}$ is not $\mathcal{Q}$-terminating. But there is no infinite $(\mathcal{P}, \mathcal{Q}, \mathcal{R})$-chain as $F(b, g(a(x_1), x_1))\sigma \xrightarrow{\mathcal{Q}}_\mathcal{R}^* F(x_2, x_2)\sigma$ implies $\sigma(x_2) = b$. Thus $F(b, g(a(x_2), x_2))\sigma = F(b, g(a(b), b))$ can only be reduced by $\xrightarrow{\mathcal{Q}}_\mathcal{R}$ to itself, but it does not unify with $F(x_3, x_3)$.

However, the rewriting processor could rewrite the right-hand side $F(b, g(a(x), x))$ of the dependency pair to $F(b, x)$. This results in $\mathcal{P}' = \{F(x, x) \to F(b, x)\}$. Now there is clearly an infinite (minimal) $(\mathcal{P}', \mathcal{Q}, \mathcal{R})$-chain.

Example 12. Finally, we also show that the condition $\mathcal{U}(q, \mathcal{Q}) \subseteq \mathcal{R}$ for all proper subterms q of $t|_p$ is required for completeness. We again let $\mathcal{P} = \{F(x, x) \to F(b, g(a(x), x))\}$. Moreover, $\mathcal{R} = \{g(x, y) \to y\}$ and $\mathcal{Q} = \mathcal{R} \cup \{a(b) \to a(b)\}$. Now $\mathcal{R}$ is $\mathcal{Q}$-terminating. As in Ex. 11, there is no infinite $(\mathcal{P}, \mathcal{Q}, \mathcal{R})$-chain. But the rewriting processor would replace $\mathcal{P}$ by $\mathcal{P}' = \{F(x, x) \to F(b, x)\}$ and there is again a minimal infinite $(\mathcal{P}', \mathcal{Q}, \mathcal{R})$-chain. Note however, that the redex $g(a(x), x)$ of the reduction has a proper subterm $a(x)$ whose usable rules w.r.t. $\mathcal{Q}$ are not contained in $\mathcal{R}$. So the condition for completeness in Thm. 4 is violated.

4 New Dependency Pair Processors

Now we introduce new processors which improve the power of termination analysis considerably. The techniques of the classical dependency pair approach from Sect. 3 only modify the pairs $\mathcal{P}$ in a DP problem $(\mathcal{P}, \mathcal{Q}, \mathcal{R}, f)$. In contrast, we now present techniques to decrease the underlying set of rules $\mathcal{R}$ (Sect. 4.1 and 4.2) or to increase the set $\mathcal{Q}$ that restricts possible redexes (Sect. 4.3).

4.1 DP Processors Based on Usable Rules

The first processor shows that in a DP problem $(\mathcal{P}, \mathcal{Q}, \mathcal{R}, f)$ one can remove all non-usable rules from $\mathcal{R}$ if $\mathcal{Q} \supseteq \mathcal{R}$ (i.e., if $\xrightarrow{\mathcal{Q}}_{\mathcal{R}} \subseteq \xrightarrow{i}_{\mathcal{R}}$).

Example 13. After applying the dependency graph processor, the TRS $\mathcal{R}$ for division from Ex. 2 results in the problems ($\{\mathsf{MINUS}(\mathsf{s}(x), \mathsf{s}(y)) \to \mathsf{MINUS}(x,y)\}$, $\mathcal{Q}, \mathcal{R}, \mathbf{m}$) and ($\{\mathsf{DIV}(\mathsf{s}(x), \mathsf{s}(y)) \to \mathsf{DIV}(\mathsf{minus}(x,y), \mathsf{s}(y))\}, \mathcal{Q}, \mathcal{R}, \mathbf{m}$), cf. Ex. 5.

When proving innermost termination (or if $\mathcal{Q} \supseteq \mathcal{R}$), one can replace $\mathcal{R}$ by the usable rules of $\mathsf{MINUS}(x,y)$ and $\mathsf{DIV}(\mathsf{minus}(x,y), \mathsf{s}(y))$, respectively. So the problems become ($\{\mathsf{MINUS}(\mathsf{s}(x), \mathsf{s}(y)) \to \mathsf{MINUS}(x,y)\}, \mathcal{Q}, \varnothing, \mathbf{m}$) and ($\{\mathsf{DIV}(\mathsf{s}(x), \mathsf{s}(y)) \to \mathsf{DIV}(\mathsf{minus}(x,y), \mathsf{s}(y))\}, \mathcal{Q}, \mathcal{R}', \mathbf{m}$), where $\mathcal{R}'$ are the minus-rules.

A similar restriction to the usable rules was already possible with the DP processor based on reduction pairs in Thm. 3. However, with that processor one immediately had to find a reduction pair which orients the usable rules $\mathcal{U}(\mathcal{P}, \mathcal{R})$ and the pairs in $\mathcal{P}$, and afterwards one remained with a DP problem $(\mathcal{P} \setminus \mathcal{P}_{\succ_\pi}, \mathcal{Q}, \mathcal{R}, f)$ which still contains the full set of rules $\mathcal{R}$. In contrast, this new processor requires no orientation with reduction pairs and it has the advantage that subsequent DP processors can benefit from the removal of non-usable rules. Therefore whenever $\mathcal{Q} \supseteq \mathcal{R}$, this processor should be applied first.

Theorem 5 (DP Processor Based on Usable Rules). *The following DP processor Proc is sound and complete. For a DP problem $(\mathcal{P}, \mathcal{Q}, \mathcal{R}, f)$, Proc returns $\{(\mathcal{P}, \mathcal{Q}, \mathcal{U}(\mathcal{P}, \mathcal{R}), f)\}$ if $\mathcal{Q} \supseteq \mathcal{R}$ and $\{(\mathcal{P}, \mathcal{Q}, \mathcal{R}, f)\}$ otherwise.*

Proof. Completeness follows from Lemma 2. For soundness, let $s_1 \to t_1, s_2 \to t_2, \ldots$ be an infinite $(\mathcal{P}, \mathcal{Q}, \mathcal{R})$-chain. Thus there is a σ such that $t_i \sigma \xrightarrow{\mathcal{Q}}^*_{\mathcal{R}} s_{i+1}\sigma$, $s_i\sigma$ is in $\mathcal{Q}$-normal form, and if the chain is minimal then $t_i\sigma$ is terminating w.r.t. $\xrightarrow{\mathcal{Q}}_{\mathcal{R}}$ for all i. By Lemma 1 then $t_i\sigma$ also terminates w.r.t. $\xrightarrow{\mathcal{Q}}_{\mathcal{U}(\mathcal{P}, \mathcal{R})}$.

Since σ instantiates all variables by normal forms w.r.t. $\mathcal{Q} \supseteq \mathcal{R}$, the only rules applicable to $t_i\sigma$ or its reducts are from $\mathcal{U}(\mathcal{P}, \mathcal{R})$. Hence, $t_i\sigma \xrightarrow{\mathcal{Q}}^*_{\mathcal{U}(\mathcal{P}, \mathcal{R})} s_{i+1}\sigma$. So $s_1 \to t_1, s_2 \to t_2, \ldots$ is also an infinite (minimal) $(\mathcal{P}, \mathcal{Q}, \mathcal{U}(\mathcal{P}, \mathcal{R}))$-chain. □

Note that completeness of this processor is due to our new notions of "$\mathcal{Q}$-restricted rewriting" and of "$(\mathcal{P}, \mathcal{Q}, \mathcal{R})$-chains", which use two different TRSs $\mathcal{Q}$ and $\mathcal{R}$ to restrict potential redexes and to determine possible rewrite steps, respectively. In other words, this processor would be incomplete in the original dependency pair approach, where one regarded innermost termination and "innermost chains". As an example let $\mathcal{P} = \{\mathsf{F}(\mathsf{a}, x) \to \mathsf{F}(x,x)\}$ and $\mathcal{R} = \{\mathsf{f}(\mathsf{a}, x) \to \mathsf{f}(x,x), \mathsf{a} \to \mathsf{b}\}$. Now there is no infinite innermost chain (i.e., no infinite $(\mathcal{P}, \mathcal{R}, \mathcal{R})$-chain), since the left-hand side of the dependency pair in $\mathcal{P}$ is not in $\mathcal{R}$-normal form. As there are no usable rules, this processor would replace $\mathcal{R}$ by the empty set. In the DP framework, one would obtain the DP problem $(\mathcal{P}, \mathcal{R}, \varnothing, f)$ which still has no infinite chain, but in the classical dependency pair approach, the second component of this DP problem would be disregarded. Since there is an infinite (minimal) innermost chain of $\mathcal{P}$'s dependency pair if the underlying TRS is empty, then this processor would be incomplete.

A similar processor can also be defined in the general case (for arbitrary $\mathcal{Q}$). Thus, this processor is also suitable for full (instead of just innermost) termination proofs. In contrast to Thm. 5, in order to apply this processor one has to satisfy a set of constraints and one can only use it if one tries to prove absence of *minimal* chains. On the other hand, this processor does not only delete non-usable rules, but it also removes all rules from $\mathcal{P}$ and $\mathcal{R}$ that contain non-usable symbols on their left-hand sides. To this end, for any TRS $\mathcal{P}$ and any subset $\mathcal{F}'$ of the signature we define $\mathcal{P}_{\neg\mathcal{F}'}$ as the set of those rules of $\mathcal{P}$ which contain symbols on left-hand sides that are not in $\mathcal{F}'$, i.e., $\mathcal{P}_{\neg\mathcal{F}'} = \{s \to t \in \mathcal{P} \mid s \notin \mathcal{T}(\mathcal{F}', \mathcal{V})\}$.

As in Thm. 3, to apply this processor, all pairs in $\mathcal{P}$ and all their usable rules have to be (weakly) decreasing. But in contrast to Thm. 3, none of the pairs in $\mathcal{P}$ has to be strictly decreasing. On the other hand, now we require monotonicity and $\mathcal{C}_\varepsilon$-compatibility of the order $\succ$ and one may not use argument filterings.

Theorem 6 (DP Processor Based on Usable Rules and Reduction Pairs). *Let $(\succsim, \succ)$ be a reduction pair where $\succ$ is monotonic and $\mathcal{C}_\varepsilon$-compatible. The following DP processor Proc is sound and complete. For a DP problem $(\mathcal{P}, \mathcal{Q}, \mathcal{R}, f)$, Proc returns*

- $\{\,(\mathcal{P} \setminus \mathcal{P}_{\neg\mathcal{US}(\mathcal{P}, \mathcal{R})},\ \mathcal{Q},\ \mathcal{U}(\mathcal{P}, \mathcal{R}) \setminus \mathcal{R}_{\neg\mathcal{US}(\mathcal{P}, \mathcal{R})}, f)\,\}$, *if*

  - $\mathcal{P}_{\succsim} = \mathcal{P}$ *and*
  - $\mathcal{R}_{\succsim} \supseteq \mathcal{U}(\mathcal{P}, \mathcal{R})$ *and*
  - $f = \mathbf{m}$

- $\{\,(\mathcal{P}, \mathcal{Q}, \mathcal{R}, f)\,\}$, *otherwise*

Proof. Completeness follows by Lemma 2. For soundness, let $s_1 \to t_1, s_2 \to t_2, \ldots$ be an infinite minimal $(\mathcal{P}, \mathcal{Q}, \mathcal{R})$-chain. So there is a substitution σ and rules $\{l_{i,1} \to r_{i,1}, \ldots, l_{i,m_i} \to r_{i,m_i}\} \subseteq \mathcal{R}$ with $m_i \geq 0$ where $t_i\sigma = v_{i,0} \xrightarrow{\mathcal{Q}}_{\{l_{i,1} \to r_{i,1}\}} v_{i,1} \xrightarrow{\mathcal{Q}}_{\{l_{i,2} \to r_{i,2}\}} \cdots \xrightarrow{\mathcal{Q}}_{\{l_{i,m_i} \to r_{i,m_i}\}} v_{i,m_i} = s_{i+1}\sigma$, $s_i\sigma$ is in $\mathcal{Q}$-normal form, and the term $t_i\sigma$ is terminating w.r.t. $\to_{\mathcal{R}}$ for all i. We now show that this chain ends in an infinite minimal $(\mathcal{P} \setminus \mathcal{P}_{\neg\mathcal{US}(\mathcal{P},\mathcal{R})}, \mathcal{Q}, \mathcal{U}(\mathcal{P}, \mathcal{R}) \setminus \mathcal{R}_{\neg\mathcal{US}(\mathcal{P},\mathcal{R})})$-chain.

By [21, Lemma 16], there exists a mapping $\mathcal{I} : \mathcal{T}(\mathcal{F}, \mathcal{V}) \to \mathcal{T}(\mathcal{F} \cup \{\mathsf{c}\}, \mathcal{V})$ such that[9] we have $t_i \mathcal{I}(\sigma) = \mathcal{I}(t_i\sigma) = \mathcal{I}(v_{i,0}) \xrightarrow{+}_{\mathcal{C}_\varepsilon \cup (\mathcal{U}(\mathcal{P},\mathcal{R}) \cap \{l_{i,1} \to r_{i,1}\})} \mathcal{I}(v_{i,1}) \xrightarrow{+}_{\mathcal{C}_\varepsilon \cup (\mathcal{U}(\mathcal{P},\mathcal{R}) \cap \{l_{i,2} \to r_{i,2}\})} \cdots \xrightarrow{+}_{\mathcal{C}_\varepsilon \cup (\mathcal{U}(\mathcal{P},\mathcal{R}) \cap \{l_{i,m_i} \to r_{i,m_i}\})} \mathcal{I}(v_{i,m_i}) = \mathcal{I}(s_{i+1}\sigma) \xrightarrow{*}_{\mathcal{C}_\varepsilon} s_{i+1}\mathcal{I}(\sigma)$. Here, "$\to_{\mathcal{C}_\varepsilon \cup (\mathcal{U}(\mathcal{P},\mathcal{R}) \cap \{l_{i,j} \to r_{i,j}\})}$" denotes a reduction with $\mathcal{C}_\varepsilon \cup \{l_{i,j} \to r_{i,j}\}$, where the rule $l_{i,j} \to r_{i,j}$ may only be used if it is contained in $\mathcal{U}(\mathcal{P}, \mathcal{R})$. Moreover, $\mathcal{I}(\sigma)$ is the substitution with $\mathcal{I}(\sigma)(x) = \mathcal{I}(\sigma(x))$ for all $x \in \mathcal{V}$.

As $\mathcal{P} \cup \mathcal{U}(\mathcal{P}, \mathcal{R}) \subseteq \succsim$ and $\succ$ is $\mathcal{C}_\varepsilon$-compatible, the reduction $s_1\mathcal{I}(\sigma) \to_{\mathcal{P}} t_1\mathcal{I}(\sigma) \xrightarrow{*}_{\mathcal{C}_\varepsilon \cup \mathcal{U}(\mathcal{P},\mathcal{R})} s_2\mathcal{I}(\sigma) \to_{\mathcal{P}} t_2\mathcal{I}(\sigma) \xrightarrow{*}_{\mathcal{C}_\varepsilon \cup \mathcal{U}(\mathcal{P},\mathcal{R})} \cdots$ only has finitely many $\to_{\mathcal{C}_\varepsilon}$-steps. So there is an n where for all $i \geq n$ we have $t_i \mathcal{I}(\sigma) = \mathcal{I}(t_i\sigma) = \mathcal{I}(v_{i,0}) \xrightarrow{+}_{\{l_{i,1} \to r_{i,1}\}} \mathcal{I}(v_{i,1}) \xrightarrow{+}_{\{l_{i,2} \to r_{i,2}\}} \cdots \xrightarrow{+}_{\{l_{i,m_i} \to r_{i,m_i}\}} \mathcal{I}(v_{i,m_i}) = \mathcal{I}(s_{i+1}\sigma) = s_{i+1}\mathcal{I}(\sigma)$.

---

[9] As in the proof of Thm. 3, the lemma and the mapping $\mathcal{I}$ have to be adapted to $\mathcal{Q}$-restricted instead of full rewriting, which however is completely straightforward.

Due to the definition of $\mathcal{I}$ [21, Def. 14], for any term $s \in \mathcal{T}(\mathcal{F}, \mathcal{V})$ one proves by structural induction that symbols from $\mathcal{F} \setminus \mathcal{US}(\mathcal{P}, \mathcal{R})$ only occur below c-symbols in $\mathcal{I}(s)$. So since $s_i \mathcal{I}(\sigma) = \mathcal{I}(s_i \sigma)$ for $i > n$, symbols from $\mathcal{F} \setminus \mathcal{US}(\mathcal{P}, \mathcal{R})$ only occur below c in $s_i \mathcal{I}(\sigma)$. As s_i does not contain c, we have $s_i \in \mathcal{T}(\mathcal{US}(\mathcal{P}, \mathcal{R}), \mathcal{V})$. Thus, $s_i \to t_i \in \mathcal{P} \setminus \mathcal{P}_{\neg \mathcal{US}(\mathcal{P},\mathcal{R})}$ for all $i \geq n$.

Inspection of the proof of [21, Lemma 16] reveals that the reductions from $\mathcal{I}(t_i \sigma)$ to $\mathcal{I}(s_{i+1}\sigma)$ never take place below any c-symbol. Hence by the observation above, in the redexes of this reduction, symbols from $\mathcal{F} \setminus \mathcal{US}(\mathcal{P}, \mathcal{R})$ only occur below c-symbols. Thus the rules $l_{i,1} \to r_{i,1}, \ldots, l_{i,m_i} \to r_{i,m_i}$ used for the reductions are from $\mathcal{U}(\mathcal{P}, \mathcal{R}) \setminus \mathcal{R}_{\neg \mathcal{US}(\mathcal{P},\mathcal{R})}$.

Hence, even if one uses the *original* substitution σ instead of $\mathcal{I}(\sigma)$, all rules $l_{i,j} \to r_{i,j}$ used in the reduction from $t_i \sigma$ to $s_{i+1} \sigma$ are from $\mathcal{U}(\mathcal{P}, \mathcal{R}) \setminus \mathcal{R}_{\neg \mathcal{US}(\mathcal{P},\mathcal{R})}$. Since these reductions were performed with $\mathcal{Q}$-restricted rewriting, the tail $s_{n+1} \to t_{n+1}, s_{n+2} \to t_{n+2}, \ldots$ of the chain is an infinite $(\mathcal{P} \setminus \mathcal{P}_{\neg \mathcal{US}(\mathcal{P},\mathcal{R})}, \mathcal{Q}, \mathcal{U}(\mathcal{P}, \mathcal{R}) \setminus \mathcal{R}_{\neg \mathcal{US}(\mathcal{P},\mathcal{R})})$-chain. The chain is also minimal: since all $t_i \sigma$ are terminating w.r.t. $\xrightarrow{\mathcal{Q}}_{\mathcal{R}}$, they are also terminating w.r.t. $\xrightarrow{\mathcal{Q}}_{\mathcal{U}(\mathcal{P},\mathcal{R}) \setminus \mathcal{R}_{\neg \mathcal{US}(\mathcal{P},\mathcal{R})}}$ by Lemma 1. □

Example 14. We regard the termination proof of the TRS $\mathcal{R}$ from Ex. 9, i.e.

minus(x, 0) → x	(1)	p(s(x)) → x	(11)
minus(0, s(y)) → 0	(2)	plus(0, y) → y	(12)
minus(s(x), s(y)) → minus(p(s(x)), p(s(y)))	(9)	plus(s(x), y) → s(plus(x, y))	(13)
minus(x, plus(y, z)) → minus(minus(x, y), z)	(10)		

together with the rules (4) and (5) for division. By the dependency graph processor (Thm. 2) we get two DP problems corresponding to the termination of div and plus (which can easily be solved) and the problem $(\{(14), (15), (16)\}, \emptyset, \mathcal{R}, \mathsf{m})$ with the following dependency pairs:

$$\mathsf{MINUS}(\mathsf{s}(x), \mathsf{s}(y)) \to \mathsf{MINUS}(\mathsf{p}(\mathsf{s}(x)), \mathsf{p}(\mathsf{s}(y))) \qquad (14)$$

$$\mathsf{MINUS}(x, \mathsf{plus}(y, z)) \to \mathsf{MINUS}(\mathsf{minus}(x, y), z) \qquad (15)$$

$$\mathsf{MINUS}(x, \mathsf{plus}(y, z)) \to \mathsf{MINUS}(x, y) \qquad (16)$$

As discussed in Ex. 9, this problem cannot be solved by the previous processors if one uses reduction pairs based on (quasi-)simplification orders.

We now show how the processor of Thm. 6 simplifies this DP problem. An efficient approach to mechanize this processor is to use reduction pairs $(\succsim, \succ)$ based on linear polynomial interpretations $\mathcal{P}ol$ with coefficients from $\{0, 1\}$. Due to the monotonicity of $\succ$, for an n-ary function symbol $f \in \mathcal{F}$, we either have $\mathcal{P}ol(f(t_1, \ldots, t_n)) = \mathcal{P}ol(t_1) + \ldots + \mathcal{P}ol(t_n)$ or $\mathcal{P}ol(f(t_1, \ldots, t_n)) = \mathcal{P}ol(t_1) + \ldots + \mathcal{P}ol(t_n) + 1$. Since there are just two possible interpretations for each function symbol, the search space is small and our experiments show that with these orders, the processor of Thm. 6 is already very successful.

Here, we use the polynomial interpretation $\mathcal{P}ol$ with $\mathcal{P}ol(f(t_1, \ldots, t_n)) = \mathcal{P}ol(t_1) + \ldots + \mathcal{P}ol(t_n)$ for every function symbol $f \in \mathcal{F}$ (i.e., $\mathcal{P}ol(f) = 0$ for constants f). With this reduction pair, the conditions of Thm. 6 are satisfied whenever $\mathcal{P}$ and $\mathcal{U}(\mathcal{P}, \mathcal{R})$ are non-duplicating. Therefore, we can now remove the dependency pairs (15) and (16) and the rule (10) which contain the non-usable symbol plus on their left hand sides. Moreover, we can delete all non-usable rules (i.e., all rules except the ones for p and minus). So the DP problem $(\{(14),(15),(16)\},\varnothing,\mathcal{R},\mathbf{m})$ is transformed to $(\{(14)\},\varnothing,\{(1),(2),(9),(11)\},\mathbf{m})$.

The only defined usable symbol in (14) is p. Hence, if we apply the processor again with the same reduction pair as above, we can remove the non-usable minus-rules. Thus, we obtain the DP problem $(\{(14)\},\varnothing,\{(11)\},\mathbf{m})$. To solve such DP problems, we will introduce another processor in the next section.

Obviously, the processor of Thm. 6 can also be applied for innermost termination proofs in the same way. Then we would obtain the resulting DP problem $(\{(14)\},\mathcal{R},\{(11)\},\mathbf{m})$ instead, i.e., then the second component would be the original TRS. Note that since the processor of Thm. 6 removes rules from the third component of the DP problem, the resulting problem is not a real "innermost termination problem" anymore. In other words, now the second component $\mathcal{R}$ is a proper superset of the third component $\{(11)\}$. Due to our extension of the rewriting transformation to this case in Thm. 4, we can still apply the rewriting processor and replace the dependency pair (14) by $\mathsf{MINUS}(\mathsf{s}(x),\mathsf{s}(y)) \to \mathsf{MINUS}(x,y)$ as in Ex. 9. Afterwards, the proof can be completed immediately. But if we would only have the classical rewrite transformation from the dependency pair approach, this step would not be possible.

4.2 A DP Processor Based on Removal of Rules

Now we introduce a processor to remove further rules from $\mathcal{R}$. As in Thm. 3, for a DP problem $(\mathcal{P},\mathcal{Q},\mathcal{R},f)$, all rules in $\mathcal{P}$ and $\mathcal{R}$ are oriented with a reduction pair $(\succsim,\succ)$. The processor in Thm. 3 was used to remove pairs from $\mathcal{P}$ which could be oriented with $\succ$. In contrast, the present processor removes rules from both $\mathcal{P}$ and $\mathcal{R}$ if they can be oriented with $\succ$. On the other hand, here we are again restricted to monotonic orders $\succ$ and we may not use argument filterings.

Theorem 7 (DP Processor Based on Rule Removal). *Let $(\succsim,\succ)$ be a reduction pair where $\succ$ is monotonic. The following DP processor Proc is sound and complete. For a DP problem $(\mathcal{P},\mathcal{Q},\mathcal{R},f)$, Proc returns*

- $\{(\mathcal{P} \setminus \mathcal{P}_\succ, \mathcal{Q}, \mathcal{R} \setminus \mathcal{R}_\succ, f)\}$, *if*
  - $\mathcal{P}_\succ \cup \mathcal{P}_\succsim = \mathcal{P}$ *and*
  - $\mathcal{R}_\succ \cup \mathcal{R}_\succsim = \mathcal{R}$
- $\{(\mathcal{P},\mathcal{Q},\mathcal{R},f)\}$, *otherwise*

Proof. Completeness follows by Lemma 2. For soundness, let $s_1 \to t_1, s_2 \to t_2, \ldots$ be an infinite $(\mathcal{P},\mathcal{Q},\mathcal{R})$-chain. So there is a σ with $t_i\sigma \xrightarrow{\mathcal{Q}}{}_\mathcal{R}^* s_{i+1}\sigma$ and if the chain is minimal, then $t_i\sigma$ is terminating w.r.t. $\xrightarrow{\mathcal{Q}}_\mathcal{R}$ for all i.

As in the proof of [21, Thm. 23], one can show that in the reductions $t_i\sigma \xrightarrow{\mathcal{Q}}{}_\mathcal{R}^* s_{i+1}\sigma$, $\mathcal{R}_\succ$-rules are only applied for finitely many i and that $s_i \to t_i \in \mathcal{P}_\succ$ only holds for finitely many i as well. So $s_i \to t_i \in \mathcal{P} \setminus \mathcal{P}_\succ$ and $t_i\sigma \xrightarrow{\mathcal{Q}}{}_{\mathcal{R}\setminus\mathcal{R}_\succ}^* s_{i+1}\sigma$ for all $i \geq n$ for some $n \in \mathbb{N}$. Moreover, if all $t_i\sigma$ are terminating w.r.t. $\xrightarrow{\mathcal{Q}}_\mathcal{R}$, then by Lemma 1 they are terminating w.r.t. $\xrightarrow{\mathcal{Q}}_{\mathcal{R}\setminus\mathcal{R}_\succ}$ as well. Thus, $s_n \to t_n, s_{n+1} \to t_{n+1}, \ldots$ is an infinite (minimal) $(\mathcal{P} \setminus \mathcal{P}_\succ, \mathcal{Q}, \mathcal{R} \setminus \mathcal{R}_\succ)$-chain. □

Example 15. We continue the termination proof of Ex. 14. To finish the proof, we only have to solve the problem $(\{(14)\}, \varnothing, \{(11)\}, \mathbf{m})$, i.e., $(\{\mathsf{MINUS}(\mathsf{s}(x), \mathsf{s}(y)) \to \mathsf{MINUS}(\mathsf{p}(\mathsf{s}(x)), \mathsf{p}(\mathsf{s}(y)))\}, \varnothing, \{\mathsf{p}(\mathsf{s}(x)) \to x\}, \mathbf{m})$. With the DP processor of Thm. 7 this can easily be done, whereas it is difficult with the previous processors. As with Thm. 6, for efficiency it is often enough to restrict oneself to linear polynomial interpretations with coefficients from $\{0, 1\}$. We use the reduction pair based on the interpretation $\mathcal{P}ol$ with $\mathcal{P}ol(\mathsf{s}(t)) = \mathcal{P}ol(t) + 1$ and $\mathcal{P}ol(f(t_1, \ldots, t_n)) = \mathcal{P}ol(t_1) + \ldots + \mathcal{P}ol(t_n)$ for every other symbol $f \in \mathcal{F}$. In general, this reduction pair satisfies $l \succsim r$ whenever a rule $l \to r$ is non-duplicating and the number of s-symbols in l is greater than or equal to the number of s-symbols in r. By Thm. 7, those rules where l contains more s-symbols than r can be removed. So in our example, the rule (11) (i.e., $\mathsf{p}(\mathsf{s}(x)) \to x$) can be deleted. The resulting DP problem is $(\{\mathsf{MINUS}(\mathsf{s}(x), \mathsf{s}(y)) \to \mathsf{MINUS}(\mathsf{p}(\mathsf{s}(x)), \mathsf{p}(\mathsf{s}(y)))\}, \varnothing, \varnothing, \mathbf{m})$.

Note that now p is not a defined symbol anymore. Therefore, the dependency pair $\mathsf{MINUS}(\mathsf{s}(x), \mathsf{s}(y)) \to \mathsf{MINUS}(\mathsf{p}(\mathsf{s}(x)), \mathsf{p}(\mathsf{s}(y)))$ is no longer on a cycle of the dependency graph (since now terms starting with p cannot reduce to terms starting with s anymore). This can be detected by all existing estimations of dependency graphs (e.g., [1,11]). Hence by the the dependency graph processor of Thm. 2, we obtain the empty set of DP problems, i.e., the termination proof is completed. This demonstrates an advantage of the DP framework, since now it is possible to apply techniques like the dependency graph repeatedly at any point during the termination proof. In contrast, in the classical dependency pair approach this technique was only applied at the beginning.

Note that similar to Thm. 5, in the classical dependency pair approach the processor of Thm. 7 would not be complete for innermost termination. This is shown by the example $\mathcal{P} = \{\mathsf{F}(\mathsf{a}) \to \mathsf{F}(\mathsf{a})\}$ and $\mathcal{Q} = \mathcal{R} = \{\mathsf{a} \to \mathsf{b}\}$. There is no infinite innermost chain, but if one uses an order where $\mathsf{a} \succ \mathsf{b}$, one can replace $\mathcal{R}$ by the empty set. Obviously, now one obtains an infinite innermost chain (i.e., an infinite $(\mathcal{P}, \varnothing, \varnothing, f)$-chain), but there is no infinite $(\mathcal{P}, \mathcal{R}, \varnothing, f)$-chain.

In [21, Thm. 23] we presented a first method within the dependency pair approach to remove rules of the TRS $\mathcal{R}$ that are not relevant for termination. The processors in Thm. 6 and 7 are significant improvements of this earlier technique: there one could only eliminate strictly decreasing (usable) rules as in Thm. 7, but it was impossible to remove non-usable rules and rules with non-usable symbols in their left-hand sides as in Thm. 6. This removal of non-usable rules is often crucial, since these rules often block the application of other important processors, as will be shown in the next section (cf. Ex. 16).

4.3 A DP Processor to Switch to Innermost Termination

The following processor replaces a DP problem $(\mathcal{P}, \mathcal{Q}, \mathcal{R}, \mathbf{m})$ with $\mathcal{Q} \subset \mathcal{R}$ by $(\mathcal{P}, \mathcal{R}, \mathcal{R}, \mathbf{m})$, i.e., under certain conditions it suffices to prove innermost instead of full termination. Proving innermost termination is significantly simpler: the dependency graph is smaller (Sect. 3.1), there are less restrictions when applying reduction pairs (Sect. 3.2), more dependency pair transformations are applicable (Sect. 3.3), one may directly remove all non-usable rules (Sect. 4.1), etc.

So while the previous processors modified the first and third components $\mathcal{P}$ and $\mathcal{R}$ in a DP problem $(\mathcal{P}, \mathcal{Q}, \mathcal{R}, f)$, this processor modifies the second component $\mathcal{Q}$. As shown in Lemma 2, while for $\mathcal{P}$ and $\mathcal{R}$ it is advantageous to remove rules, for $\mathcal{Q}$ it is advantageous to add rules.

In the classical dependency pair approach, a switch from termination to innermost termination was only possible if the *whole* TRS belongs to a class where innermost termination implies termination. An example for such a class are locally confluent overlay systems [10] or in particular, non-overlapping TRSs.

Instead, the following processor only requires local confluence for the rules $\mathcal{R}$ of the current DP problem. After applying the processors of Sect. 4.1 and 4.2, $\mathcal{R}$ is usually just a small subset of the whole TRS. Moreover, $\mathcal{R}$ does not have to be an overlay system. One only requires that $\mathcal{R}$ may not overlap with the pairs in $\mathcal{P}$. But the rules $\mathcal{R}$ themselves may have arbitrary critical pairs. This clearly extends the known classes where innermost termination implies termination.

Theorem 8 (DP Processor for Modular Non-Overlap Check). *The following processor is sound and complete. For a problem $(\mathcal{P}, \mathcal{Q}, \mathcal{R}, f)$, Proc returns*

- $\{(\mathcal{P}, \mathcal{R}, \mathcal{R}, f)\}$, *if*

    - *for all $s \to t \in \mathcal{P}$, non-variable subterms of s do not unify with left-hand sides of rules from $\mathcal{R}$ (after variable renaming) and*
    - $\xrightarrow{\mathcal{Q}}_\mathcal{R}$ *is locally confluent and*
    - $\mathcal{Q} \subseteq \mathcal{R}$ *and*
    - $f = \mathbf{m}$

- $\{(\mathcal{P}, \mathcal{Q}, \mathcal{R}, f)\}$, *otherwise*

Proof. Completeness follows from Lemma 2. For soundness, we prove that under the conditions of the first case in Thm. 8, every minimal $(\mathcal{P}, \mathcal{Q}, \mathcal{R})$-chain $s_1 \to t_1, s_2 \to t_2, \ldots$ also results in a minimal $(\mathcal{P}, \mathcal{R}, \mathcal{R})$-chain. There is a substitution σ such that we have the following conditions for all i:

(a) $t_i \sigma \xrightarrow{\mathcal{Q}}{}^*_\mathcal{R} s_{i+1}\sigma$
(b) $s_i\sigma$ is in $\mathcal{Q}$-normal form
(c) $t_i\sigma$ is terminating w.r.t. $\xrightarrow{\mathcal{Q}}_\mathcal{R}$

By (a) and (c), $\sigma(x)$ is terminating w.r.t. $\xrightarrow{\mathcal{Q}}_\mathcal{R}$ for all $x \in \mathcal{V}(s_2) \cup \mathcal{V}(s_3) \cup \ldots$ Since $\xrightarrow{\mathcal{Q}}_\mathcal{R}$ is locally confluent, every $\sigma(x)$ has a unique normal form $\sigma(x){\downarrow}$ w.r.t. $\xrightarrow{\mathcal{Q}}_\mathcal{R}$ by Newman's lemma. Let σ' be a substitution with $\sigma'(x) = \sigma(x){\downarrow}$ for all $x \in \mathcal{V}(s_2) \cup \mathcal{V}(s_3) \cup \ldots$ and $\sigma'(x) = \sigma(x)$ otherwise. For all $i > 1$ we obtain:

(i) For all terms t we have $t\sigma \xrightarrow{\mathcal{Q}}{}^*_\mathcal{R} t\sigma'$.
(ii) If non-variable subterms of s_i do not unify with left-hand sides of rules from $\mathcal{R}$, then $s_i\sigma'$ is a normal form w.r.t. $\xrightarrow{\mathcal{Q}}_\mathcal{R}$.
(iii) A term is an $\mathcal{R}$-normal form iff it is a normal form w.r.t. $\xrightarrow{\mathcal{Q}}_\mathcal{R}$.

The observations (i) and (ii) are obvious. For (iii), the "only if" direction follows from $\xrightarrow{\mathcal{Q}}_\mathcal{R} \subseteq \to_\mathcal{R}$ (by Lemma 1). For the "if" direction, let t be a normal form w.r.t. $\xrightarrow{\mathcal{Q}}_{\mathcal{R}}$ and assume that t contains $\mathcal{R}$-redexes. Let t' be an "innermost" $\mathcal{R}$-redex, i.e., all proper subterms of t' are in $\mathcal{R}$-normal form. Since $\mathcal{Q} \subseteq \mathcal{R}$, they are also in $\mathcal{Q}$-normal form. But then t' is also a redex w.r.t. $\xrightarrow{\mathcal{Q}}_{\mathcal{R}}$. This contradicts the assumption that t is a normal form w.r.t. $\xrightarrow{\mathcal{Q}}_{\mathcal{R}}$.

Now we show that $s_2 \to t_2, s_3 \to t_3, \ldots$ is also a minimal $(\mathcal{P}, \mathcal{R}, \mathcal{R})$-chain. To this end, we use the substitution σ' instead of σ. For all $i > 1$ we have to prove:

(a') $t_i\sigma' \xrightarrow{\mathcal{R}}^*_{\mathcal{R}} s_{i+1}\sigma'$
(b') $s_i\sigma'$ is in normal form w.r.t. $\mathcal{R}$
(c') $t_i\sigma'$ is terminating w.r.t. $\xrightarrow{\mathcal{R}}_{\mathcal{R}}$

For (a'), note that $t_i\sigma \xrightarrow{\mathcal{Q}}^*_{\mathcal{R}} s_{i+1}\sigma \xrightarrow{\mathcal{Q}}^*_{\mathcal{R}} s_{i+1}\sigma'$ by (a) and (i), where $s_{i+1}\sigma'$ is a normal form w.r.t. $\xrightarrow{\mathcal{Q}}_{\mathcal{R}}$ by (ii). Moreover, since $t_i\sigma$ is terminating w.r.t. $\xrightarrow{\mathcal{Q}}_{\mathcal{R}}$ and since $\xrightarrow{\mathcal{Q}}_{\mathcal{R}}$ is locally confluent, $s_{i+1}\sigma'$ is the *unique* normal form of $t_i\sigma$ w.r.t. $\xrightarrow{\mathcal{Q}}_{\mathcal{R}}$ by Newman's lemma. Since $t_i\sigma \xrightarrow{\mathcal{Q}}^*_{\mathcal{R}} t_i\sigma'$ by (i), $t_i\sigma'$ is terminating w.r.t. $\xrightarrow{\mathcal{Q}}_{\mathcal{R}}$ by (c) and since $\xrightarrow{\mathcal{R}}_{\mathcal{R}} \subseteq \xrightarrow{\mathcal{Q}}_{\mathcal{R}}$ by Lemma 1, $t_i\sigma'$ is also terminating w.r.t. $\xrightarrow{\mathcal{R}}_{\mathcal{R}}$. Let w be a normal form of $t_i\sigma'$ w.r.t. $\xrightarrow{\mathcal{R}}_{\mathcal{R}}$. As $t_i\sigma \xrightarrow{\mathcal{Q}}^*_{\mathcal{R}} w$ and as w is also a normal form w.r.t. $\xrightarrow{\mathcal{Q}}_{\mathcal{R}}$ by (iii), w must be the unique normal form $s_{i+1}\sigma'$. Hence, $t_i\sigma' \xrightarrow{\mathcal{R}}^*_{\mathcal{R}} s_{i+1}\sigma'$.

For (b'), $s_i\sigma'$ is a normal form w.r.t. $\xrightarrow{\mathcal{Q}}_{\mathcal{R}}$ by (ii). Thus, (iii) implies that it is also a normal form w.r.t. $\mathcal{R}$.

For (c'), we have $t_i\sigma \xrightarrow{\mathcal{Q}}^*_{\mathcal{R}} t_i\sigma'$ by (i). Thus, $t_i\sigma'$ is terminating w.r.t. $\xrightarrow{\mathcal{Q}}_{\mathcal{R}}$ by (c). Hence, $t_i\sigma'$ is also terminating w.r.t. $\xrightarrow{\mathcal{R}}_{\mathcal{R}}$ since $\xrightarrow{\mathcal{R}}_{\mathcal{R}} \subseteq \xrightarrow{\mathcal{Q}}_{\mathcal{R}}$ by Lemma 1. □

To apply this processor to a DP problem $(\mathcal{P}, \mathcal{Q}, \mathcal{R}, \mathbf{m})$, one only has to check that $\mathcal{R}$ does not overlap with $\mathcal{P}$ and one has to prove local confluence of $\xrightarrow{\mathcal{Q}}_{\mathcal{R}}$. In practice, Thm. 8 is usually applied for $\mathcal{Q} = \emptyset$ (i.e., to switch from full to innermost termination). Then local confluence is equivalent to joinability of critical pairs and, for example, it suffices if $\mathcal{R}$ is non-overlapping. With such syntactic sufficient conditions for its applicability, Thm. 8 can easily be automated.

Example 16. $\mathcal{R}$ results from replacing the plus-rules (12) and (13) in Ex. 14 by

$$\text{plus}(0, y) \to y \quad (17) \qquad \text{plus}(\text{s}(x), y) \to \text{s}(\text{plus}(y, \text{minus}(\text{s}(x), \text{s}(0)))) \quad (18)$$

and by adding the rule $\text{div}(\text{plus}(x, y), z) \to \text{plus}(\text{div}(x, z), \text{div}(y, z))$.

To prove termination, now the dependency graph processor of Thm. 2 results in three DP problems (corresponding to the termination of div, minus, and plus). While the DP problems for div and minus can be solved as before, the DP problem $(\{(19)\}, \emptyset, \mathcal{R}, \mathbf{m})$ for plus cannot be handled with the existing processors if one uses base orders based on (quasi-)simplification orders or on (possibly negative) polynomial interpretations. In contrast, innermost termination of the TRS is easy to show. Here, (19) is the following dependency pair from Rule (18).

$$\text{PLUS}(\text{s}(x), y) \to \text{PLUS}(y, \text{minus}(\text{s}(x), \text{s}(0))) \quad (19)$$

Since $\mathcal{R}$ is non-duplicating, we can apply the usable rule processor of Thm. 6 with the same polynomial interpretation as in Ex. 14 (i.e., $Pol(f(t_1, \ldots, t_n)) = Pol(t_1) + \ldots + Pol(t_n)$ for all $f \in \mathcal{F}$) and replace $\mathcal{R}$ by the usable rules, i.e., by the p- and minus-rules. Moreover, Rule (10) can also be deleted, since it contains the non-usable symbol plus on its left-hand side. Thus, the DP problem is transformed into ($\{(19)\}$, $\varnothing$, $\{(1),(2),(9),(11)\}$, m). The TRS $\{(1),(2),(9),(11)\}$ is non-overlapping and thus, locally confluent. Moreover, no non-variable subterm of the left-hand side of (19) unifies with a left-hand side of these rules after variable renaming. Hence, we can apply the new DP processor of Thm. 8 to switch to an innermost termination problem.[10] To this end, we enlarge the second component of the DP problem from the empty set to $\{(1),(2),(9),(11)\}$. So now we have to solve the problem ($\{(19)\}$, $\{(1),(2),(9),(11)\}$, $\{(1),(2),(9),(11)\}$, m).

Note that the whole TRS $\mathcal{R}$ is overlapping and not locally confluent. Thus, it does not belong to a known class where innermost termination implies termination. Hence, this switch would not have been possible with existing results.

Since we now have an innermost termination problem, we may use the rewriting processor of Thm. 4 repeatedly to transform the pair (19) to $\mathsf{PLUS}(\mathsf{s}(x),y)$ $\to \mathsf{PLUS}(y,x)$. Then the usable rule processor of Thm. 5 allows us to delete all rules, since they are not usable anymore. Hence, we obtain the problem ($\{(19)\}$, $\varnothing, \varnothing$, m). By Thm. 3, now it suffices to solve the constraint $\mathsf{PLUS}(\mathsf{s}(x),y) \succ \mathsf{PLUS}(y,x)$ which is trivial by polynomial orders or recursive path orders.

By using Thm. 8 instead of removing rules as in Thm. 7, one also obtains an alternative proof for the DP problem of minus. As seen in Ex. 14, after removing all non-usable rules, one obtains the DP problem ($\{\mathsf{MINUS}(\mathsf{s}(x),\mathsf{s}(y)) \to \mathsf{MINUS}(\mathsf{p}(\mathsf{s}(s)),\mathsf{p}(\mathsf{s}(y)))\}, \varnothing, \{\mathsf{p}(\mathsf{s}(x)) \to x\}$, m). Since the rule is locally confluent and does not overlap with the remaining dependency pair, now one can use Thm. 8 to switch to the innermost case and easily solve the DP problem.

Ex. 15 already showed the advantages of re-computing the dependency graph later during the termination proof. Now we have demonstrated that it can also be beneficial to use dependency pair transformations after some other processors have been applied (like the usable rule processor of Thm. 6 and the processor for the modular non-overlap check of Thm. 8). In contrast, in the classical dependency pair approach, transformations could only be used in the very beginning of a proof, but not after deleting rules, pairs, etc. This demonstrates an advantage of the new modular DP framework.

Note that by Thm. 8, the observation that innermost termination implies termination for locally confluent overlay systems is obtained as a corollary. While the original proof for this important result of Gramlich [10] is not at all trivial, the proof of Thm. 8 is quite simple. While there already exists another easy proof [18], in this way we get an alternative simple proof for this crucial result.

---

[10] Deleting all non-usable rules with Thm. 6 is often needed to enable an application of the modular non-overlap check from Thm. 8 afterwards. In this example, the non-usable rules are not locally confluent due to the new additional div-rule and there is no other processor which can remove these rules (if one uses reduction pairs based on (quasi-)simplification orders). Therefore, if one would replace the new processor of Thm. 6 with our previous related technique in [21, Thm. 23], then one cannot switch to an innermost termination problem with Thm. 8 anymore and thus, the termination proof would fail.

Corollary 2 (Thm. 3.23. in [10]). *Let $\mathcal{R}$ be a locally confluent overlay system. If $\mathcal{R}$ is innermost terminating, then it is terminating.*

Proof. $\mathcal{R}$ terminates if the DP problem $(DP(\mathcal{R}), \varnothing, \mathcal{R}, \mathbf{m})$ is finite by Thm. 1. For overlay systems, no non-variable subterms of left-hand sides from $DP(\mathcal{R})$ unify with variable-renamed left-hand sides from $\mathcal{R}$. Thus by Thm. 8, it is sufficient if the DP problem $(DP(\mathcal{R}), \mathcal{R}, \mathcal{R}, \mathbf{m})$ is finite. This follows from innermost termination (i.e., $\mathcal{R}$-termination) of $\mathcal{R}$ by Thm. 1. □

However, Thm. 8 improves Gramlich's result significantly. Even if $\mathcal{R}$ is not a locally confluent overlay system, by representing the termination task as a DP problem, one may first apply other processors to obtain sub-problems $(\mathcal{P}', \varnothing, \mathcal{R}', \mathbf{m})$ where $\mathcal{R}'$ is indeed locally confluent and does not overlap with $\mathcal{P}'$. For these sub-problems, one can now switch to the innermost case, whereas Gramlich's result would not be applicable. As demonstrated in Ex. 16, this switch can be crucial for the termination proof.

5 DP Processors from Other Techniques

Now we show how to integrate existing termination techniques in the DP framework. In this way, these techniques can benefit from other DP processors which were applied before. This increases their applicability and power considerably.

Definition 6 (Termination Technique). *A termination technique TT maps TRSs to TRSs such that termination of $TT(\mathcal{R})$ implies termination of $\mathcal{R}$.*

Note that the above definition captures both transformational techniques (which transform a TRS $\mathcal{R}$ into a new TRS $\mathcal{R}'$ whose termination is sufficient for termination of $\mathcal{R}$) and traditional techniques which simply give a "yes" or "no" answer when trying to prove termination. For those techniques, we would define $TT(\mathcal{R}) = \varnothing$ if termination of $\mathcal{R}$ can be proved and $TT(\mathcal{R}) = \mathcal{R}$, otherwise.

Now at any point during the termination proof, instead of solving a DP problem $(\mathcal{P}, \mathcal{Q}, \mathcal{R}, f)$ one can use a termination technique and verify termination of $TT(\mathcal{P} \cup \mathcal{R})$. To this end, one should of course use the DP framework again. Hence, we now define a processor to integrate arbitrary termination techniques.

Theorem 9 (DP Processor for Termination Techniques). *Let TT be a termination technique and let Proc be a DP processor with $\mathit{Proc}((\mathcal{P}, \mathcal{Q}, \mathcal{R}, f)) = \{(DP(\mathcal{R}'), \varnothing, \mathcal{R}', \mathbf{m})\}$ where $TT(\mathcal{P} \cup \mathcal{R}) = \mathcal{R}'$. Then Proc is sound.*

Proof. Obvious from Thm. 1. □

It is easy to show that if $\mathcal{P}$'s rules have tuple symbols on their root positions,[11] if $\mathcal{Q} = \varnothing$, and if TT is "complete" (i.e., $TT(\mathcal{P} \cup \mathcal{R})$ terminates iff $\mathcal{P} \cup \mathcal{R}$ terminates), then the above processor is also complete.

---

[11] More precisely, one requires $\mathrm{root}(s), \mathrm{root}(t) \in \mathcal{F}'$ for all $s \to t \in \mathcal{P}$ and some $\mathcal{F}' \subseteq \mathcal{F}$, while $\mathcal{F}'$-symbols do not occur anywhere else in $\mathcal{P}$ and they also do not occur in $\mathcal{R}$.

Of course, if a termination technique TT is capable of handling $\mathcal{Q}$-restricted rewriting, then one could easily take this into account. Now TT would be applied to *pairs* $(\mathcal{Q}, \mathcal{R})$ and return a pair $(\mathcal{Q}', \mathcal{R}')$ such that $\mathcal{Q}'$-termination of $\mathcal{R}'$ is sufficient for $\mathcal{Q}$-termination of $\mathcal{R}$. Hence, a DP problem $(\mathcal{P}, \mathcal{Q}, \mathcal{R}, f)$ may now be transformed into $(DP(\mathcal{R}'), \mathcal{Q}', \mathcal{R}', \mathbf{m})$ where $TT(\mathcal{Q}, \mathcal{P} \cup \mathcal{R}) = (\mathcal{Q}', \mathcal{R}')$.

To improve the applicability of termination techniques, one may pre-process a DP problem $(\mathcal{P}, \mathcal{Q}, \mathcal{R}, f)$ before. The reason is that there exist powerful termination techniques which can only be applied to subclasses of TRSs. For example, the *RFC matchbounds* technique of [5] or the method of *string reversal* only operate on *string rewrite systems* (SRSs), i.e., on TRSs where all occurring function symbols have arity 1. To make such techniques applicable, one may perform a pre-processing step which transforms a DP problem with non-unary symbols into a problem on SRSs.

Note that the processors of the previous sections never change the flag f when transforming a DP problem $(\mathcal{P}, \mathcal{Q}, \mathcal{R}, f)$. Thus, when starting with the initial DP problem $(DP(\mathcal{R}), \mathcal{Q}, \mathcal{R}, \mathbf{m})$, all resulting problems have the flag $f = \mathbf{m}$. However, for the pre-processing mentioned above, we will also introduce processors which modify the flag by changing it to $\mathbf{a}$. In other words, while for the original DP problem it was sufficient to prove absence of *minimal* chains, for the problems resulting from these processors one has to prove absence of *all arbitrary* chains.

Applying such processors usually has the disadvantage that afterwards, many other processors are no longer applicable, since they only work on DP problems with $f = \mathbf{m}$, i.e., on problems where one only examines minimal chains. However, if one re-builds the dependency pairs afterwards as in Thm. 9, then any DP problem is changed back again into a problem with the flag $f = \mathbf{m}$. For this reason, if one has obtained a DP problem with the flag $\mathbf{a}$, it can even be useful to apply Thm. 9 with the "empty" termination technique where $TT(\mathcal{P} \cup \mathcal{R}) = \mathcal{P} \cup \mathcal{R}$, since afterwards it is again sufficient to regard only *minimal* chains.

We now introduce two processors which are very useful as pre-processing steps before applying termination techniques. The first processor $Proc_\mathcal{U}$ removes all non-usable rules from a reduction pair (without checking any further conditions as in Thm. 6). This corresponds to the usable rule processor of Thm. 5, but in contrast to Thm. 5 the new processor is applicable for arbitrary $\mathcal{Q}$, not just for $\mathcal{Q} \supseteq \mathcal{R}$. However, one now has to add $\mathcal{C}_\varepsilon = \{\mathsf{c}(x,y) \to x, \mathsf{c}(x,y) \to y\}$ to the usable rules. Moreover, we introduce a processor which allows us to apply argument filterings to the rules and pairs in a DP problem. Here, we define $\pi(\mathcal{R}) = \{\pi(l) \to \pi(r) \mid l \to r \in \mathcal{R}\}$ for any TRS $\mathcal{R}$.

Theorem 10 (Pre-Processing DP Processors). *The following DP processors $Proc_\mathcal{U}$ and $Proc_\pi$ are sound.*

- *For a DP problem $(\mathcal{P}, \mathcal{Q}, \mathcal{R}, f)$, $Proc_\mathcal{U}$ returns*

    - $\{(\mathcal{P}, \varnothing, \mathcal{U}(\mathcal{P}, \mathcal{R}) \cup \mathcal{C}_\varepsilon, \mathbf{a})\}$, *if $f = \mathbf{m}$*
    - $\{(\mathcal{P}, \mathcal{Q}, \mathcal{R}, f)\}$, *otherwise*

- Let π be an argument filtering. For a DP problem $(\mathcal{P}, \mathcal{Q}, \mathcal{R}, f)$, $Proc_\pi$ returns
  - $\{(\pi(\mathcal{P}), \varnothing, \pi(\mathcal{R}), \mathbf{a})\}$, if $\pi(\mathcal{P})$ and $\pi(\mathcal{R})$ are TRSs
  - $\{(\mathcal{P}, \mathcal{Q}, \mathcal{R}, f)\}$, otherwise

Proof. $Proc_\mathcal{U}$ is sound since every minimal $(\mathcal{P}, \mathcal{Q}, \mathcal{R})$-chain is a (not necessarily minimal) $(\mathcal{P}, \varnothing, \mathcal{U}(\mathcal{P}, \mathcal{R}) \cup \mathcal{C}_\varepsilon)$-chain, cf. [21, Thm. 17].[12]

We now show soundness of $Proc_\pi$: If $s_1 \to t_1, s_2 \to t_2, \ldots$ is an infinite $(\mathcal{P}, \mathcal{Q}, \mathcal{R})$-chain, then there is a substitution σ with $t_i\sigma \to_\mathcal{R}^* s_{i+1}\sigma$ for all i. Hence, $\pi(t_i)\sigma_\pi \to_{\pi(\mathcal{R})}^* \pi(s_{i+1})\sigma_\pi$ for the substitution σ_π with $\sigma_\pi(x) = \pi(\sigma(x))$ for all $x \in \mathcal{V}$. So $\pi(s_1) \to \pi(t_1), \pi(s_2) \to \pi(t_2), \ldots$ is an infinite $(\pi(\mathcal{P}), \varnothing, \pi(\mathcal{R}))$-chain. □

The following example shows that the processors are incomplete, even if $\mathcal{Q} = \varnothing$.

Example 17. Let $\mathcal{R} = \{f(a, b, x) \to f(x, x, x)\}$ [22]. $\mathcal{R}$ is terminating and thus, the resulting DP problem $(\{F(a, b, x) \to F(x, x, x)\}, \varnothing, \mathcal{R}, \mathbf{m})$ is not infinite. However, by the processor $Proc_\mathcal{U}$ we obtain the infinite DP problem $(\{F(a, b, x) \to F(x, x, x)\}, \varnothing, \mathcal{C}_\varepsilon, \mathbf{a})$, since now the instantiated right-hand side of the dependency pair reduces to the instantiated left-hand side if x is substituted by $c(a, b)$.

Incompleteness of $Proc_\pi$ is shown by $(\{F(a) \to F(b)\}, \varnothing, \varnothing, f)$ which is not infinite, but the filtering $\pi(F(x)) = F$ produces the infinite problem $(\{F \to F\}, \varnothing, \varnothing, \mathbf{a})$.

Now we demonstrate why the argument filtering processor $Proc_\pi$ has to set the flag f to $\mathbf{a}$, i.e., we show why one has to prove absence of *arbitrary* (possibly non-minimal) chains after the filtering. For the processor $Proc_\mathcal{U}$ it is currently open whether changing f to $\mathbf{a}$ is really needed for soundness. In other words, it is not known whether a processor which transforms $(\mathcal{P}, \mathcal{Q}, \mathcal{R}, \mathbf{m})$ into $\{(\mathcal{P}, \varnothing, \mathcal{U}(\mathcal{P}, \mathcal{R}) \cup \mathcal{C}_\varepsilon, \mathbf{m})\}$ would be sound.

Example 18. An argument filtering processor which replaces $(\mathcal{P}, \mathcal{Q}, \mathcal{R}, \mathbf{m})$ by $\{(\pi(\mathcal{P}), \varnothing, \pi(\mathcal{R}), \mathbf{m})\}$ is not sound, even if $\mathcal{Q} = \varnothing$ and if π does not modify the function symbols of $\mathcal{R}$: The DP problem $(\mathcal{P}, \varnothing, \mathcal{R}, \mathbf{m})$ with $\mathcal{P} = \{F(g(s(a))) \to F(g(s(a)))\}$ and $\mathcal{R} = \{g(a) \to g(a)\}$ has an infinite minimal chain, but if one filters $\mathcal{P}$ with $\pi(s(x)) = x$, then there is no infinite *minimal* chain anymore. The reason is that then the filtered right-hand side $F(g(a))$ of the pair in $\pi(\mathcal{P})$ is no longer terminating w.r.t. $\mathcal{R}$.

However, it is easy to show that if $\mathcal{P}$'s rules have tuple symbols on their root positions (as in Footnote 11) and if the filtering π only modifies these tuple symbols, then one could define $Proc_\pi((\mathcal{P}, \mathcal{Q}, \mathcal{R}, f)) = \{(\pi(\mathcal{P}), \mathcal{Q}, \mathcal{R}, f)\}$ if $\pi(\mathcal{P})$ is a TRS. In other words, then both the TRS $\mathcal{Q}$ and the flag f could remain unchanged and the resulting processor $Proc_\pi$ would still be sound. (This observation can also be extended to more general forms of $\mathcal{P}$.)

The next example shows that replacing $\mathcal{Q}$ by $\varnothing$ after the filtering is needed for the soundness of $Proc_\pi$, even if π does not modify any symbols of $\mathcal{Q}$.

---

[12] The extension from ordinary to $\mathcal{Q}$-restricted rewriting is again straightforward.

Example 19. Consider the problem $(\mathcal{P}, \mathcal{Q}, \mathcal{R}, \mathbf{m})$ with $\mathcal{P} = \{\mathsf{F}(x) \to \mathsf{F}(\mathsf{g}(\mathsf{s}(x)))\}$, $\mathcal{Q} = \{\mathsf{g}(\mathsf{g}(x)) \to x\}$, and $\mathcal{R} = \varnothing$. Clearly, there is a (minimal) infinite $(\mathcal{P}, \mathcal{Q}, \mathcal{R})$-chain as $\mathsf{F}(x) \to \mathsf{F}(\mathsf{g}(\mathsf{s}(x))), \mathsf{F}(\mathsf{g}(\mathsf{s}(x))) \to \mathsf{F}(\mathsf{g}(\mathsf{s}(\mathsf{g}(\mathsf{s}(x))))), \ldots$, are instantiations of the pair in $\mathcal{P}$ which are in $\mathcal{Q}$-normal form. However, if one uses the argument filtering with $\pi(\mathsf{s}(x)) = x$, we would replace $\mathcal{P}$ by $\pi(\mathcal{P}) = \{\mathsf{F}(x) \to \mathsf{F}(\mathsf{g}(x))\}$ whereas $\mathcal{Q}$ would remain unchanged. Now there is no infinite $(\pi(\mathcal{P}), \mathcal{Q}, \mathcal{R})$-chain anymore, since terms of the form $\mathsf{F}(\mathsf{g}(\mathsf{g}(\ldots)))$ are not in $\mathcal{Q}$-normal form.

As a larger last example, we now demonstrate the benefits of Thm. 10 for the integration of *string reversal* into the DP framework. As mentioned before, string reversal is a transformational termination technique which is only applicable to SRSs. The *reversal* t^{-1} of a term t with only unary symbols is obtained by reversing the order of its function symbols (e.g., the reversal of $f(g(h(x)))$ is $h(g(f(x))))$. For a TRS $\mathcal{R}$, its reversal is $\mathcal{R}^{-1} = \{l^{-1} \to r^{-1} \mid l \to r \in \mathcal{R}\}$. It is well known that an SRS $\mathcal{R}$ is terminating iff $\mathcal{R}^{-1}$ is terminating. Thus, we can use the termination technique TT_{REV} with $TT_{REV}(\mathcal{R}) = \mathcal{R}^{-1}$ if $\mathcal{R}$ is an SRS and $TT_{REV}(\mathcal{R}) = \mathcal{R}$, otherwise.

Example 20. The TRS $\mathcal{R}$ contains the following rules together with the plus-rules (12) and (13) from Ex. 9. Here, $\mathsf{mult}(x, y, z)$ computes $x * y + z$.

$$\mathsf{times}(x, y) \to \mathsf{mult}(x, y, 0) \quad (20)$$
$$\mathsf{mult}(0, y, z) \to z \quad (21)$$
$$\mathsf{mult}(\mathsf{s}(x), y, z) \to \mathsf{mult}(\mathsf{p}(\mathsf{s}(x)), y, \mathsf{plus}(y, z)) \quad (22)$$
$$\mathsf{times}(\mathsf{plus}(x, y), z) \to \mathsf{plus}(\mathsf{times}(x, z), \mathsf{times}(y, z)) \quad (23)$$
$$\mathsf{p}(\mathsf{s}(0)) \to 0 \quad (24)$$
$$\mathsf{p}(\mathsf{s}(\mathsf{s}(x))) \to \mathsf{s}(\mathsf{p}(\mathsf{s}(x))) \quad (25)$$

By the processor based on the dependency graph of Thm. 2, we obtain four DP problems corresponding to the termination of p, plus, times, and mult. The first three are easy to handle, but the problem $(\{\mathsf{MULT}(\mathsf{s}(x), y, z) \to \mathsf{MULT}(\mathsf{p}(\mathsf{s}(x)), y, \mathsf{plus}(y, z))\}, \varnothing, \mathcal{R}, \mathbf{m})$ cannot be solved by the processors of the previous sections if one uses reduction pairs based on (quasi-)simplification orders.

However, by applying the new processors of this section, we can transform this DP problem into an SRS and apply the termination technique "string reversal". Afterwards, it can easily be solved. We first apply the processor $Proc_\mathcal{U}$ of Thm. 10 to remove the non-usable rules for times and mult which results in $(\{\mathsf{MULT}(\mathsf{s}(x), y, z) \to \mathsf{MULT}(\mathsf{p}(\mathsf{s}(x)), y, \mathsf{plus}(y, z))\}, \varnothing, \{(12), (13), (24), (25)\} \cup \mathcal{C}_\varepsilon,$ **a**). Next we eliminate the second and third argument of MULT by the argument filtering processor $Proc_\pi$ of Thm. 10 and replace the dependency pair by $\mathsf{MULT}(\mathsf{s}(x)) \to \mathsf{MULT}(\mathsf{p}(\mathsf{s}(x)))$. Now the processor for removal of rules from Thm. 7 is used with a polynomial interpretation where $\mathcal{P}ol(\mathsf{c}(x, y)) = x + y + 1$, $\mathcal{P}ol(\mathsf{plus}(x, y)) = 2x + y + 1$, $\mathcal{P}ol(\mathsf{p}(x)) = x$, and $\mathcal{P}ol(\mathsf{s}(x)) = x + 1$. Then the rules (12), (13), and (24) are strictly decreasing and can be removed, i.e., we result in $(\{\mathsf{MULT}(\mathsf{s}(x)) \to \mathsf{MULT}(\mathsf{p}(\mathsf{s}(x)))\}, \varnothing, \{\mathsf{p}(\mathsf{s}(\mathsf{s}(x))) \to \mathsf{s}(\mathsf{p}(\mathsf{s}(x)))\}, \mathbf{a})$.

Note that we have obtained a DP problem containing only symbols of arity 1. Therefore, we can apply the termination technique TT_{REV} and try to prove termination of the reversed TRS $\mathcal{R}' = \{\mathsf{s}(\mathsf{MULT}(x)) \to \mathsf{s}(\mathsf{p}(\mathsf{MULT}(x))), \mathsf{s}(\mathsf{s}(\mathsf{p}(x))) \to \mathsf{s}(\mathsf{p}(\mathsf{s}(x)))\}$. The resulting DP problem $(DP(\mathcal{R}'), \varnothing, \mathcal{R}', \mathbf{m})$ is easy to solve:

the dependency graph processor yields $(\{S(s(p(x))) \to S(x)\}, \emptyset, \mathcal{R}', \mathbf{m})$ and by the usable rule processor we can delete all rules of $\mathcal{R}'$ and also the remaining pair $S(s(p(x))) \to S(x)$ which contains the non-usable symbol p on the left-hand side.

To summarize, the advantage of integrating termination techniques like string reversal into the DP framework is that they can solve certain parts of the termination proof, whereas different techniques are used for other parts (e.g., because these parts do not correspond to an SRS). Moreover, as shown in the above example, since one can modify DP problems by argument filterings, one can also apply SRS-termination techniques for DP problems which originally contained non-unary function symbols. So in general, the applicability, modularity, and power of existing termination techniques is increased significantly by the integration into the DP framework. While Thm. 9 shows how to integrate arbitrary techniques, certain termination techniques may also be adapted in order to operate on DP problems directly instead of TRSs. Then instead of integrating them with Thm. 9, they could be directly used as processors in the DP framework.

6 Strategies for the Dependency Pair Framework

The DP framework allows us to combine DP processors in a completely modular and flexible way. A system for termination proofs with the DP framework tries to prove $\mathcal{Q}$-termination of $\mathcal{R}$ for two TRSs $\mathcal{Q}$ and $\mathcal{R}$. It starts with the initial DP problem $(DP(\mathcal{R}), \mathcal{Q}, \mathcal{R}, \mathbf{m})$ and then constructs a tree as in Cor. 1. As long as there is a DP problem d left, it chooses a DP processor $Proc$ and computes $Proc(d)$. If $Proc(d) = \mathsf{no}$, the proof is stopped. Then the system returns "no" if $Proc$ and all processors used on the path from the initial DP problem to d are complete and otherwise it returns "maybe". If $Proc(d) \neq \mathsf{no}$, then d is replaced by $Proc(d)$ and the procedure continues. As soon as there are no DP problems left anymore, the system returns "yes". To avoid non-termination of the system, it can also abort the proof after some time limit and return "maybe". This algorithm and a large number of DP processors (including those presented in this paper) have been implemented in our automated termination tool AProVE [9] which can be obtained from http://www-i2.informatik.rwth-aachen.de/AProVE.

To obtain a powerful system for termination proofs, a main challenge is to develop strategies to decide which DP processor should be applied to a DP problem d. A general heuristic is to apply fast processors first and to use more powerful slower processors later on in order to handle those problems which cannot already be solved by fast processors. The strategy of AProVE is to select the first DP processor $Proc$ from the following list which satisfies $Proc(d) \neq \{d\}$.

1. DP processor based on the dependency graph (Thm. 2)
2. DP processor based on usable rules (Thm. 5)
3. DP processor for modular non-overlap check (Thm. 8)
4. Narrowing, rewriting, and instantiation processors in "safe" cases [8] where they "simplify" the DP problem (Thm. 4)
5. DP processor based on usable rules and reduction pairs (Thm. 6)

6. DP processor based on rule removal (Thm. 7)
7. DP processor based on red. pairs: linear polynomials over $\{0,1\}$ (Thm. 3)
8. DP processor for non-termination analysis[13]
9. Narrowing, rewriting, and instantiation (up to a certain limit) (Thm. 4)
10. DP processor based on red. pairs: linear polynomials over $\{0,1,2\}$ (Thm. 3)
11. DP processor based on reduction pairs: lexicographic path orders (Thm. 3)
12. DP processor based on reduction pairs: non-linear polynomials (Thm. 3)
13. DP processor based on string reversal (Thm. 9)

Of course, one can also use different strategies for different forms of TRSs. For example, if the underlying TRS is an SRS, AProVE uses a slightly different strategy, which also includes DP processors based on other techniques like RFC matchbounds [5] and semantic labelling [24], cf. Sect. 5.

Due to the DP framework (with the above strategies), AProVE was the most powerful system at the competition of termination tools at the *7th International Workshop on Termination* (WST '04). Here, the tools were tested on 936 examples from the *termination problem data base* (TPDB) [20], a collection of termination problems from several sources and different areas of computer science. This demonstrates that the DP framework is indeed very well suited for automation and for application in practice.

7 Conclusion and Future Work

We introduced the dependency pair framework for termination proofs (Sect. 2) which generalizes the classical dependency pair approach into a general basis for automated termination proofs. We first showed how to formulate the existing components of the dependency pair approach as DP processors within this framework (Sect. 3). Now these components can be applied at any time during the termination proof and their applicability conditions only concern the current DP problem, not the whole TRSs. Afterwards, we developed several new DP processors to simplify termination problems (Sect. 4) and we showed how to integrate arbitrary existing termination techniques into the DP framework (Sect. 5). For all processors, we also investigated their completeness which allows us to use them also when proving non-termination. As demonstrated in Sect. 6, this framework is indeed suitable for automation in practice. For future work, we see two main directions of research:

While there already exist several powerful DP processors, these processors are not yet sufficient to handle all termination problems occurring in practice. Therefore, one important topic for further work is the improvement of the existing DP processors and the development of new DP processors which are particularly fast or particularly powerful for certain classes of DP problems.

---

[13] A simple sound and complete DP processor *Proc* for non-termination analysis is the following: $Proc((\mathcal{P}, \mathcal{Q}, \mathcal{R}, f)) = $ no if $\mathcal{P}$ contains a rule of the form $s \to s$ where s is in $\mathcal{Q}$-normal form. Otherwise, $Proc((\mathcal{P}, \mathcal{Q}, \mathcal{R}, f)) = (\mathcal{P}, \mathcal{Q}, \mathcal{R}, f)$. Obviously, this processor can be improved to detect more cases of non-termination.

The other important line of research is the development of new strategies to decide which DP processor should be applied next on a particular DP problem. We have presented such a strategy in Sect. 6, but depending on the area of application, other strategies can be advantageous.

To summarize, in this paper we have shown that the combination of techniques for termination proofs within the dependency pair framework leads to a very modular, flexible, and powerful approach. Therefore, we think that this framework is particularly suitable as a basis for future research on automated termination proving.

References

1. T. Arts and J. Giesl. Termination of term rewriting using dependency pairs. *Theoretical Computer Science*, 236:133–178, 2000.
2. F. Baader and T. Nipkow. *Term Rewriting and All That*. Cambridge University Press, 1998.
3. N. Dershowitz. Termination of rewriting. *J. Symb. Computation*, 3:69–116, 1987.
4. N. Dershowitz. Termination by abstraction. In *Proc. ICLP '04*, LNCS 3132, pages 1–18, 2004.
5. A. Geser, D. Hofbauer, and J. Waldmann. Match-bounded string rewriting systems. In *Proc. MFCS '03*, LNCS 2747, pages 449–459, 2003.
6. J. Giesl and T. Arts. Verification of Erlang processes by dependency pairs. *Appl. Algebra in Engineering, Communication and Computing*, 12(1,2):39–72, 2001.
7. J. Giesl, T. Arts, and E. Ohlebusch. Modular termination proofs for rewriting using dependency pairs. *Journal of Symbolic Computation*, 34(1):21–58, 2002.
8. J. Giesl, R. Thiemann, P. Schneider-Kamp, and S. Falke. Improving dependency pairs. In *Proc. LPAR '03*, LNAI 2850, pages 165–179, 2003.
9. J. Giesl, R. Thiemann, P. Schneider-Kamp, and S. Falke. Automated termination proofs with AProVE. In *Proc. RTA '04*, LNCS 3091, pages 210–220, 2004.
10. B. Gramlich. Abstract relations between restricted termination and confluence properties of rewrite systems. *Fundamenta Informaticae*, 24:3–23, 1995.
11. N. Hirokawa and A. Middeldorp. Automating the dependency pair method. In *Proc. CADE '03*, LNAI 2741, pages 32–46, 2003. Full version to appear in *Information and Computation*.
12. N. Hirokawa and A. Middeldorp. Dependency pairs revisited. In *Proc. RTA '04*, LNCS 3091, pages 249–268, 2004.
13. N. Hirokawa and A. Middeldorp. Polynomial interpretations with negative coefficients. In *Proc. AISC '04*, LNAI 3249, pages 185–198, 2004.
14. S. Kamin and J. J. Lévy. Two generalizations of the recursive path ordering. Unpublished Manuscript, University of Illinois, IL, USA, 1980.
15. D. Knuth and P. Bendix. Simple word problems in universal algebras. In J. Leech, editor, *Computational Problems in Abstract Algebra*, pages 263–297, 1970.
16. K. Kusakari, M. Nakamura, and Y. Toyama. Argument filtering transformation. In *Proc. PPDP '99*, LNCS 1702, pages 48–62, 1999.
17. D. Lankford. On proving term rewriting systems are Noetherian. Technical Report MTP-3, Louisiana Technical University, Ruston, LA, USA, 1979.
18. Aart Middeldorp. A simple proof to a result of Bernhard Gramlich. Presented at the 5th Japanese Term Rewriting Meeting, Tsukuba, 1994. Available from http://informatik.uibk.ac.at/users/ami/research/papers/bg.pdf.

19. J. Steinbach. Simplification orderings: History of results. *Fundamenta Informaticae*, 24:47–87, 1995.
20. Termination Problem Data Base (TPDB). Available from http://www.lri.fr/~marche/wst2004-competition/tpdb.html.
21. R. Thiemann, J. Giesl, and P. Schneider-Kamp. Improved modular termination proofs using dependency pairs. In *Proc. IJCAR '04*, LNAI 3097, pages 75–90, 2004.
22. Y. Toyama. Counterexamples to the termination for the direct sum of term rewriting systems. *Information Processing Letters*, 25:141–143, 1987.
23. X. Urbain. Modular and incremental automated termination proofs. *Journal of Automated Reasoning*, 32(4): 315–355, 2004.
24. H. Zantema. Termination of term rewriting by semantic labelling. *Fundamenta Informaticae*, 24:89–105, 1995.

Automated Termination Analysis for Incompletely Defined Programs

Christoph Walther and Stephan Schweitzer

Fachgebiet Programmiermethodik
Technische Universität Darmstadt
www.informatik.tu-darmstadt.de/pm/
{chr.walther,schweitz}@informatik.tu-darmstadt.de

Abstract. Incompletely defined programs provide an elegant and easy way to write and to reason about programs which may halt with a run time error by throwing an exception or printing an error message, e.g. when attempting to divide by zero. Due to the presence of stuck computations, which arise when calling incompletely defined procedures with invalid arguments, we cannot use the method of argument bounded algorithms for proving termination by machine. We analyze the problem and present a solution to improve this termination analysis method so that it works for incompletely defined programs as well. Our technique of proving the termination of incompletely defined programs maintains performance as well as simplicity of the original method and proved successful by an implementation in the verification tool √eriFun.

1 Introduction

A central problem in the development of correct software is to verify that algorithms terminate. A non-terminating algorithm results in looping computations, hence machine resources are wasted if a given input is not in the domain of the function computed by the algorithm. Also manpower is wasted with the debugging of those algorithms, and the frustration caused by non-terminating programs is a common experience of programmers and computer scientists.

Termination analysis is concerned with the synthesis and verification of *termination hypotheses*, i.e. proof obligations the truth of which entail the termination of the algorithm under consideration. In this paper, we are concerned with functional programs where several proposals exist for proving termination, e.g. [1],[2],[3],[4],[5],[6],[7],[8],[9],[10].

In the √eriFun system [11],[12],[13], a semi-automated verifier for functional programs, the method of *argument bounded algorithms* [10] is used and proved successful for verifying the termination of procedures by machine. Recently, √eriFun was upgraded to work for *incompletely defined* programs as well [14]. Those programs compute *partially determined* functions, i.e. functions which may yield (defined but) "unknown" results for some of their input arguments. However, unsound inferences will result if our termination proof procedure is

```
structure bool   <=  true, false
structure nat    <=  0, succ(pred:nat)
structure list   <=  empty, add(hd:nat,tl:list)
function minus(x,y:nat):nat <=    function remainder(x,y:nat):nat <=
if y=0                            if y=0
  then x                            then * || 0
  else if x=0                       else if y>x
    then * || 0                       then x
    else minus(pred(x),pred(y))       else remainder(minus(x,y),y)
  fi                              fi
fi                                fi
```

Fig. 1. Data structures, incompletely and completely defined procedures

applied to incompletely defined procedures, because the method requires that only *totally determined* functions are computed by the procedures of a program. We therefore use *domain procedures* [14] to modify the method so that it can be soundly applied to prove the termination of incompletely defined programs too.

2 Completely Defined Programs

Syntax We use a programming language in which data structures are defined in the spirit of (free) algebraic data types. A data structure s is defined by stipulating the *constructors* of the data structure as well as a *selector* for each argument position of a constructor. The set of all *constructor ground terms* built with the constructors of s then defines the elements of the data structure s.

For example, truth values are represented by the set $\mathcal{T}(\{true, false\}) = \{true, false\}$ and the set of natural numbers is represented by the set $\mathcal{T}(\{0, succ\}) = \{0, succ(0), succ(succ(0)), \ldots\}$, both given by data structures bool and nat of Fig. 1.[1] Likewise, the data structure list of Fig. 1 represents the set of linear lists of natural numbers, with e.g. $add(succ(0), add(0, empty)) \in \mathcal{T}(\{0, succ, empty, add\})$. The *selectors* act as inverses to their constructors, since e.g. $hd(add(n, k)) = n$ and $tl(add(n, k)) = k$ is demanded. Each definition of a data structure s implicitly introduces an equality symbol $=_s : s \times s \to bool$ (where $s \neq bool$) and a function symbol $if_s : bool \times s \times s \to s$ for conditionals.

A procedure, which operates on these data structures, is defined by giving the procedure name, say f, the formal parameters and the result type in the *procedure head*. The *procedure body* is given as a first-order term over the set of formal parameters, the function symbols already introduced by some data structures and other procedures plus the function symbol f to allow recursive definitions, cf. Fig. 1 where "* ||" in the procedure bodies should be ignored.

A finite list P of data structure and procedure definitions—always beginning with the data structure definitions of bool and nat as given in Fig. 1—is called

---

[1] $\mathcal{T}(\Sigma, \mathcal{V})_s$ is the set of *terms* of type s, $\mathcal{T}(\Sigma)_s = \mathcal{T}(\Sigma, \emptyset)_s$, and $\mathcal{CL}(\Sigma, \mathcal{V})$ is the set of *clauses* over a signature Σ for function symbols and a set $\mathcal{V}$ of variable symbols.

a *completely defined functional program*. $\Sigma(P)$ is the set of all function symbols introduced by the data structures and procedures of P, and $\Sigma(P)^c \subset \Sigma(P)$ is the set of all constructor function symbols given by the data structures of P.

Semantics and Termination Given a (completely defined functional) program P, an interpreter $eval_P$ for P evaluates terms of $\mathcal{T}(\Sigma(P))$ to "values", i.e. terms of $\mathcal{T}(\Sigma(P)^c)$. The interpreter computes calls $f(t_1, \ldots, t_n)$ of a procedure function $f(x_1{:}s_1, \ldots, x_n{:}s_n){:}s\ \texttt{<=}\ R_f$ call-by-value, i.e. by replacing each formal parameter x_i in the procedure body R_f by the computation t'_i of the actual parameter t_i, and then continuing with the computation of the instantiated procedure body obtained. The interpreter also respects the definitions of the data structures by computing, for instance, *false* for $0{=}succ(t)$ and q for $pred(succ(t))$, provided $eval_P(t) = q$ for some $q \in \mathcal{T}(\Sigma(P)^c)$. For selectors $sel : s \to s'$ applied to constructors $cons$ to which they do not belong, so-called *witness terms* $\omega_{sel}[x] \in \mathcal{T}(\Sigma(P), \{x\})_{s'}$ with $x \in V_s$ are assigned in P to sel, and we define $eval_P(sel(cons(q_1, \ldots, q_n))) := eval_P(\omega_{sel}[cons(q_1, \ldots, q_n)])$. Hence e.g. $eval_P(tl(empty)) = empty$ and $eval_P(hd(empty)) = 0$ if $\omega_{tl}[x] := x$ and $\omega_{hd}[x] := 0$ for the selectors of data structure list, cf. Fig. 1. By these definitions, our programming language is provided with an *eager* semantics.

Since P may contain non-terminating procedures, $eval_P$ is a *partial* mapping only, i.e. $eval_P : \mathcal{T}(\Sigma(P)) \mapsto \mathcal{T}(\Sigma(P)^c)$, and we define [14]:

Definition 1. (Termination) *A procedure* function $f(x_1{:}s_1, \ldots, x_n{:}s_n){:}s\ \texttt{<=}$ … *of a completely defined program P terminates in P iff* $eval_P(f(q_1, \ldots, q_n))$ $\in \mathcal{T}(\Sigma(P)^c)$ *for all* $q_i \in \mathcal{T}(\Sigma(P)^c)_{s_i}$. *$P$ terminates iff (i) each procedure of P terminates in P and (ii)* $eval_P(\omega_{sel}[q]) \in \mathcal{T}(\Sigma(P)^c)$ *for each selector $sel : s \to s'$ and for all* $q \in \mathcal{T}(\Sigma(P)^c)_s$.

3 Incompletely Defined Programs

Motivation Incompletely defined programs provide an elegant and easy way to specify and to verify statements about (recursive) *partial* functions with *decidable* domain [14]. Incompletely defined programs compute *partially determined* functions, also called *loosely specified* or *underspecified* functions in the literature.

A *total* function is called *partially determined* iff the result of a function application is *indetermined* for some arguments, called *stuck arguments*. *Partial* functions $\phi : M \mapsto N$ with domain dom_ϕ can be represented by *partially determined* but *total* functions $\widehat{\phi} : M \to N$ by stipulating $\widehat{\phi}(m) := \phi(m)$ for each $m \in dom_\phi$ but demanding $\widehat{\phi}(m) \in N$ for each $m \in M \setminus dom_\phi$ only, being silent about which $n \in N$ exactly is assigned to $\widehat{\phi}(m)$. The elements of $M \setminus dom_\phi$ are the *stuck arguments* of $\widehat{\phi}$, and $\widehat{\phi}(m)$ is *indetermined* iff m is a stuck argument. Examples of partially determined functions are *quotient* and *remainder* with stuck arguments of form $(m, 0)$, list processing functions, like *head, last* and *minimum* with the empty list as stuck argument, and so on. If dom_ϕ is *decidable* and the completion $\widehat{\phi}$ of ϕ is *recursive*, $\widehat{\phi}$ can be computed by an incompletely defined procedure $\wp_{\widehat{\phi}}$ so that properties of ϕ can be verified by reasoning about $\wp_{\widehat{\phi}}$, using some verifier based on a logic of total functions.

An incompletely defined program is obtained by giving an incomplete case analysis in a procedure or using a specific symbol, say *, to denote an indetermined result. Such programs can be implemented by causing a *runtime error* or throwing an *exception* when called with a stuck argument, e.g. upon the attempt to divide by zero. When focussing on functional programs—as we do here—the interpreter of the programming language responds by returning a ground term $r \notin \mathcal{T}(\Sigma(P)^c)$ when called with a stuck argument, and we call such a result r a *stuck computation*.

Syntax A data structure s is incompletely defined by not stipulating witness terms for the selectors of s. For defining a procedure f incompletely, we allow the use of a wildcard * to stipulate the result when calling f with a stuck argument. E.g., procedure minus of Fig. 1 is incompletely defined if "|| 0" is ignored in the procedure body, and the value of $minus(n, m)$ is only determined if $n \geq m$. Also procedure remainder of Fig. 1 is incompletely defined when ignoring "|| 0", and the value of $remainder(n, m)$ is determined iff $m \neq 0$.

Formally, we assume a constant symbol $*_s \notin \Sigma(P)$ for each data structure s in a functional program P, and we demand upon the extension of P by a new procedure function $f(x_1:s_1,\ldots,x_n:s_n):s$ <= R_f, that $R_f \in \mathcal{T}(\Sigma(P) \cup \{f, *_s\}, \{x_1, \ldots, x_n\})$ be *-*correct*, i.e. $R_f = *$ or * is only used as a (direct) argument in the *alternatives* of an *if*-conditional.

Termination and Semantics For defining the termination and in turn the semantics of an incompletely defined program P, the notion of a *fair completion* P' of P is needed [14]: $\widehat{P}$ is the set of all fair completions of P, where each $P' \in \widehat{P}$ is a completely defined program containing each data structure s which is given in P plus the witness terms for the selectors of s. P' also contains a procedure function $f(x_1:s_1,\ldots,x_n:s_n):s$ <= R'_f for each procedure function $f(x_1:s_1,\ldots,x_n:s_n):s$ <= R_f in P. The procedure body R'_f is obtained from R_f by replacing each occurrence of * in R_f by some term from $\mathcal{T}(\Sigma(P'), \{x_1, \ldots, x_n\})$, where it does not matter whether different occurrences of * are replaced by the same or by different terms. In addition, the *fairness requirement* demands that the termination of procedure f in P' not be spoiled *just because* procedure f is completed by a non-terminating result in a *-case or a non-terminating witness term is assigned to a selector.

For example, a fair completion of a program containing the incompletely defined procedure minus of Fig. 1 may contain the completely defined procedure minus. Also the occurrence of * in procedure minus may be replaced by $succ(y)$ or 13 or $minus(x, pred(y))$ etc. in a fair completion P' of P. But we may not replace * by $minus(x, y)$ or by $loop(y)$, where function loop(x:nat):nat <= succ(loop(x)) is a procedure of P', as this violates the fairness requirement.

Definition 2. (Termination) *A procedure* function $f(x_1:s_1,\ldots,x_n:s_n):s$ <= R_f *of an incompletely defined program P terminates in P iff for each $P' \in \widehat{P}$ procedure* function $f(x_1:s_1,\ldots,x_n:s_n):s$ <= R'_f *of P' terminates in P'. P terminates iff each procedure of P terminates in P.*

Definition 3. (Standard Model $\mathcal{M}_P$, Theory Th_P) Let P be an incompletely defined and terminating program. Then a standard model $\mathcal{M}_P$ of P is a $\Sigma(P)$-algebra $\mathcal{M}_P = (\mathcal{T}(\Sigma(P)^c), \phi)$ such that some $P' \in \widehat{P}$ exists with $\phi_f(q_1, \ldots, q_n) = eval_{P'}(f(q_1, \ldots, q_n))$ for all $f \in \Sigma(P)_{s_1,\ldots,s_n,s}$ and all $q_i \in \mathcal{T}(\Sigma(P)^c)_{s_i}$. The theory Th_P of P is defined as $\{\varphi \in \mathcal{F}(\Sigma(P), \mathcal{V}) \mid \mathcal{M}_P \vDash \varphi$ for each standard model $\mathcal{M}_P$ of $P\}$. A verification system for P is sound iff $\varphi \in Th_P$ for each $\varphi \in \mathcal{F}(\Sigma(P), \mathcal{V})$ verified by the system.[2]

By Definition 3, incompletely defined procedures (and selectors) are understood as *loose specifications* of total functions. The standard models for incompletely defined (and terminating) programs differ only in the interpretation of functions applied to stuck arguments, but coincide for all other function applications. So Th_P is *incomplete*, i.e. neither $\varphi \in Th_P$ nor $\neg\varphi \in Th_P$ for some $\varphi \in \mathcal{F}(\Sigma(P), \mathcal{V})$, whereas Th_P is complete for completely defined programs P.

Verification When we formulate proof obligations of form "$\varphi \in Th_P$" for incompletely defined programs P in the following, we assume the availability of some "sound verification system for P" to compute a proof for φ. We can do so as *(i)* several verifiers for functional programs exist, see e.g. [15],[16],[17] for references, and *(ii)* (most) logics used for the verification of terminating and completely defined programs can be applied without profound modifications to verify terminating but incompletely defined programs as well, see [14].

Computation To implement our programming language, we also have to define an interpreter $eval_P$ for *incompletely* defined programs P. As the formal definition of $eval_P$ does not matter here, we refer to [14] for details. For the purpose of this paper, it is enough to know that for each $t \in \mathcal{T}(\Sigma(P))$

$$eval_P(t) \in \mathcal{T}(\Sigma(P)^c) \iff \left(eval_P(t) = eval_{P'}(t) \text{ for each } P' \in \widehat{P}\right). \quad (1)$$

4 Termination Analysis with Argument Bounded Algorithms

Argument bounded algorithms are the key concept for the automated termination analysis proposed in [10]. The method has been implemented and proved successful in verification tools, [18],[19],[20],[21],[12], and provided the base for further developments of termination analysis [22],[23],[24],[3],[4],[25],[26],[27],[9] as well. Termination analysis with argument bounded algorithms is based on the syntactic estimation $\geqslant_{\Gamma,C}$ of terms, where selector and procedure calls are estimated above by some argument(s) of the call.

A total and totally determined function $\phi : \mathcal{T}(\Sigma(P)^c)_{s_1} \times \ldots \times \mathcal{T}(\Sigma(P)^c)_{s_n} \to \mathcal{T}(\Sigma(P)^c)_{s_p}$ is called *p-bounded* iff $p \in \{1, \ldots, n\}$ and $q_p \geqslant_\# \phi(q_1, \ldots, q_n)$ for all $q_i \in \mathcal{T}(\Sigma(P)^c)_{s_i}$.[3] A function ϕ is called *argument bounded* iff it is p-bounded for

---
[2] $\mathcal{F}(\Sigma, \mathcal{V})$ is the set of *closed formulas* over Σ and $\mathcal{V}$.
[3] $>_\#$ is the *size order* comparing constructor ground terms $q \in \mathcal{T}(\Sigma(P)^c)_s$ by the number $\#_s(q)$ of *reflexive s-constructors* in q, and $q \geqslant_\# r$ abbreviates $q >_\# r$ or $q =_\# r$. A function symbol $h : s_1 \times \ldots \times s_n \to s$ is *reflexive* iff $s = s_i$ for some i.

```
function half(x:nat):nat <=
if x=0
  then 0
  else if pred(x)=0 then * else succ(half(pred(pred(x)))) fi
fi

function log(x:nat):nat <=
if x=0
  then *
  else if pred(x)=0
          then 0
          else if even(x) then succ(log(half(x))) else * fi
       fi
fi
```

Fig. 2. Incompletely defined procedures (cont.)

some $p \in \{1,\ldots,n\}$. Each p-bounded function ϕ is associated with a so-called (total and totally determined) *p-difference function* $\delta_\phi^p : \mathcal{T}(\Sigma(P)^c)_{s_1} \times \ldots \times \mathcal{T}(\Sigma(P)^c)_{s_n} \to \{true, false\}$ which satisfies $\delta_\phi^p(q_1,\ldots,q_n) \Leftrightarrow q_p >_\# \phi(q_1,\ldots,q_n)$ for all $q_i \in \mathcal{T}(\Sigma(P)^c)_{s_i}$.

Given a family $\Gamma = (\Gamma_p)_{p\in\mathbb{N}}$ of sets of p-bounded function symbols $g \in \Sigma(P)$ which denote p-bounded functions ϕ, and the function symbols Δ_g^p denoting their p-difference functions δ_ϕ^p, inequalities can be proved by the *estimation calculus* [10] (called *E-calculus* for short). The formulas of the *E*-calculus are called *estimation pairs* $\langle \Delta, E \rangle$, where $\Delta \in \mathcal{CL}(\Sigma(P), \mathcal{V})$, consisting mainly of atoms of form $\Delta_g^p(\ldots)$, and E is a finite set of expressions of form $r \succcurlyeq t$ with $r, t \in \mathcal{T}(\Sigma(P), \mathcal{V})_s$. The *E*-calculus is decidable and is sound in the sense that

$$
\begin{aligned}
&(i) \ [\forall x_1{:}s_1,\ldots,x_n{:}s_n. \bigwedge C \to r \geqslant_\# t] \in Th_P \text{ , and} \\
&(ii) \ [\forall x_1{:}s_1,\ldots,x_n{:}s_n. \bigwedge C \to (\bigvee \Delta \leftrightarrow r >_\# t)] \in Th_P
\end{aligned}
\qquad (2)
$$

hold if $\vdash_{\Gamma,C} \langle \Delta, r \succcurlyeq t \rangle$, i.e. if $\langle \Delta, \{r \succcurlyeq t\} \rangle$ is a *theorem* of the *E*-calculus, where $C \in \mathcal{CL}(\Sigma(P), \mathcal{V})$ and $x_i \in \mathcal{V}_{s_i}$ are the variables in C, r and t.

The *E*-calculus is used *(i)* to generate *termination hypotheses* for completely defined procedures, *(ii)* to *test* whether a (terminating and completely defined) procedure `function` $g(x_1{:}s_1,\ldots,x_n{:}s_n){:}s_p$ `<=` R_g computes a p-bounded function ϕ, and (if so) *(iii)* to *synthesize* a p-difference procedure `function` $\Delta_g^p(x_1{:}s_1,\ldots,x_n{:}s_n){:}bool$ `<=` $R_{\Delta_g^p}$ which computes the p-difference function δ_ϕ^p for ϕ.

5 Incompletely Defined Argument Bounded Procedures

Consider the completely defined and 1-bounded procedure `minus` from Fig. 1, and assume that the incompletely defined procedure `half` of Fig. 2 is fairly completed by stipulating $half(1) := 0$ or $half(1) := 1$. Then `half` is 1-bounded too, and the following estimation proof can be obtained:

$$x \geqslant_\Gamma \mathtt{pred(x)} \geqslant_\Gamma \mathtt{half(pred(x))} \geqslant_\Gamma \mathtt{minus(half(pred(x)),succ(y))} \qquad (3)$$

Here $\geqslant_\Gamma$ abbreviates $\geqslant_{\Gamma,\emptyset}$, where $\geqslant_{\Gamma,C}$ is the *syntactic estimation relation* defined by $r \geqslant_{\Gamma,C} t$ iff $\vdash_{\Gamma,C} \langle \Delta, r \succcurlyeq t \rangle$ for some $\Delta \in \mathcal{CL}(\Sigma(P), \mathcal{V})$. However, in an incompletely defined program, where minus and half are given as in Figs. 1 and 2, the result of a function applied to a stuck argument is not determined. Therefore pred, half and minus fail to be argument bounded, hence an estimation proof like (3) cannot be obtained. This problem does not exist for completely defined programs, as we may stipulate any result we like for a function applied to a "don't-care" argument. Hence we may in particular use results which do not spoil the 1-boundedness of the above functions, and may define e.g. $pred(0) := minus(0, n) := half(1) := 0$.

Since the function computed by an incompletely defined procedure fails to be argument bounded for stuck arguments, the notion of argument boundedness as given in [10] has to be generalized:

Definition 4. (p-Boundedness) *Let P be an incompletely defined program. Then each reflexive selector of a data structure in P is 1-bounded. A procedure function $f(x_1{:}s_1, \ldots, x_n{:}s_n){:}s \mathrel{<=} R_f$ of P is p-bounded iff*
  1. $p \in \{1, \ldots, n\}$ with $s_p = s$,
  2. $\Sigma(r) \cap \{*, f\} = \emptyset$ for some result term r in the procedure body R_f, and
  3. $x_p \geqslant^{\oplus}_{\Gamma, C_r} r$ for each result term $r \neq *$ appearing under clause C_r in R_f.[4]

$\Gamma := \bigcup_{p \in \mathbb{N}} \Gamma_p$ *is the set of argument bounded function symbols in P, where each Γ_p is the set of p-bounded function symbols in P. Γ_p is defined as the smallest subset of $\Sigma(P)$ satisfying* (i) *$rsel \in \Gamma_1$ for each reflexive selector rsel of a data structure in P and* (ii) *$f \in \Gamma_p$ for each p-bounded procedure f in P.*

Requirement (3) of Definition 4 allows to ignore indetermined result terms when testing for argument boundedness and is the only relevant modification of the original definition. Requirement (2) is only an optimization, as procedures computing indetermined results only cannot contribute to the termination analysis.

For example, all reflexive selectors of the data structures given in Fig. 1 as well as the incompletely defined procedures minus, remainder, half and log of Figs. 1 and 2 now are 1-bounded, and remainder is 2-bounded too.

6 Domain Procedures

Having generalized the notion of argument boundedness by Definition 4, estimation proofs now can be obtained for incompletely defined programs too. However, such an estimation proof may be unsound, because the functions involved fail to be argument bounded for stuck arguments.

For instance, the estimation proof (3) is unsound, because a standard model exists which assigns 1 to $pred(0)$ and 2 to $half(1)$ as well as to $minus(0,1)$. Hence $0 \not\geq pred(0)$, $2 \geq 1 \not\geq half(1)$ and $3 \geq 2 \geq 1 \not\geq minus(1,2)$.

---
[4] We write $\vdash^{\oplus}_{\Gamma, C_r} \langle \ldots \rangle$ to denote the existence of an estimation proof which already may use the Argument Estimation rule (5) of Definition 5 for each recursive call $f(t_1, \ldots, t_n)$ in r. See [10] for a justification.

As a remedy, we have to exclude the applications of reflexive selectors and argument bounded procedures to stuck arguments in an estimation proof. To this effect, we use *domain procedures* which have been developed in [14] for reasoning about stuck computations explicitly: Domain procedures are given for non-procedure function symbols $\neq$ "*if*" by stipulating function $\nabla_=(x{:}s, y{:}s){:}bool <=$ *true*, function $\nabla_{sel}(x{:}s){:}bool <=$?$cons(x)$ and function $\nabla_{cons}(x_1{:}s_1, \ldots, x_n{:}s_n){:}bool <=$ *true* for the selectors sel_i and constructors $cons$ of a data structure definition structure $s <= \ldots, cons(sel_1{:}s_1, \ldots, sel_n{:}s_n), \ldots$, where ?$cons(x)$ abbreviates $x = cons(sel_1(x), \ldots, sel_n(x))$. For a procedure function $f(x_1{:}s_1, \ldots, x_n{:}s_n){:}s <= \ldots$, a domain procedure function $\nabla_f(x_1{:}s_1, \ldots, x_n{:}s_n){:}bool <= \ldots$ can be uniformly synthesized.

As proved in [14], *(i)* each domain procedure ∇_f terminates iff its "mother" procedure f terminates, *(ii)* computes a totally determined function, and *(iii)* equivalently characterizes whether the computation of a call of procedure f results in a stuck computation, i.e. for all $q_i \in \mathcal{T}(\Sigma(P)^c)_{s_i}$

$$eval_P(f(q_1, \ldots, q_n)) \in \mathcal{T}(\Sigma(P)^c) \text{ iff } eval_P(\nabla_f(q_1, \ldots, q_n)) = true.$$

Since domain procedures are tail recursive and compute a truth value, the optimization techniques developed in [10] for *difference procedures* apply to domain procedures as well: Having generated a domain procedure ∇_f, the body of ∇_f is *simplified* in a first optimization step, and then it is tried to *eliminate recursive calls* in the simplified procedure body. Recursion elimination is particularly important, because proofs are more easily obtained if the procedures "called" in a statement have no unnecessary recursive calls.

Example 1.
(i) function ∇_{minus}(x,y:nat):nat <=
   if y=0
     then true
       else if x=0 then false else ∇_{minus}(pred(x),pred(y)) fi
   fi

is computed as the optimized domain procedure for the incompletely defined procedure minus from Fig. 1, and we find $\nabla_{\text{minus}}(n, m) = true$ iff $n \geq m$.

(ii) function $\nabla_{\text{remainder}}$(x:nat, y:nat):bool <=
   if y=0 then false else true fi

is computed as the optimized domain procedure for the incompletely defined procedure remainder from Fig. 1, and $\nabla_{\text{remainder}}(n, m) = true$ iff $m \neq 0$.

(iii) function ∇_{half}(x:nat):nat <=
   if x=0
     then true
       else if pred(x)=0 then false else ∇_{half}(pred(pred(x))) fi
   fi

is computed as the optimized domain procedure for procedure half from Fig. 2, and we find $\nabla_{\text{half}}(n) = true$ iff n is *even*.

(iv) ```
function ∇_log(x:nat):nat <=
   if x=0
   then false
   else if pred(x)=0
        then true
        else if even(x) then ∇_log(half(x)) else false fi
        fi
   fi
```

is computed as the optimized domain procedure for procedure log from Fig. 2, and we find $\nabla_{\log}(n) = \textit{true}$ iff $n = 2^k$ for some $k \in \mathbb{N}$. □

To optimize domain procedure $\nabla_{\texttt{remainder}}$, recursion elimination is required, where the generated recursion elimination formulas are trivial to verify. All domain procedures of Example 1 are optimal because all recursive calls which survived recursion elimination are required.

From now on we assume that each incompletely defined program $P$ contains a domain procedure function $\nabla_f$ for each function symbol $f \in \Sigma(P)$ with $f \neq \texttt{if}$ and $f \neq \nabla_g$, where $g$ is any function symbol in $\Sigma(P)$.[5]

## 7 Estimation Proofs in Incompletely Defined Programs

Domain procedures provide the necessary prerequisite to exclude the applications of reflexive selectors and argument bounded procedures to stuck arguments in an estimation proof. For example, to guarantee soundness of the estimation proof (3) we only have to demand

$$\nabla_{\texttt{pred}}(x) \wedge \nabla_{\texttt{half}}(\texttt{pred}(x)) \wedge \nabla_{\texttt{minus}}(\texttt{half}(\texttt{pred}(x)), \texttt{succ}(y)) . \quad (4)$$

Requirement (4) expresses $x \neq 0$, $x-1$ is $even$ and $(x-1)/2 \geq 1 + y$, thus excluding the unsound estimations from Section 6. In the general case, we scan an estimation proof

$$t_1 \geqslant_{\Gamma,C} t_2 \geqslant_{\Gamma,C} \ldots \geqslant_{\Gamma,C} t_{n-1} \geqslant_{\Gamma,C} t_n \quad (5)$$

step by step and create a procedure call $\nabla_f(r_1, \ldots, r_m)$ for each estimation step $t_i \geqslant_{\Gamma,C} t_{i+1}$ with $t_{i+1} = f(r_1, \ldots, r_m)$ and $f \in \Gamma$, where $1 \leq i \leq n - 1$. These procedure calls are collected in a set $\nabla \in \mathcal{CL}(\Sigma(P), \mathcal{V})$, called the *determination clause* of the estimation proof (5).

To this effect, the estimation calculus from [10] is refined:

**Definition 5.** (pE-Calculus) *Let $P$ be an incompletely defined program, let $\Gamma$ be a family of argument bounded function symbols in $P$, and let $C \in \mathcal{CL}(\Sigma(P), \mathcal{V})$, called the* context clause. *Assume further that* ircons, $\text{ircons}_1$ *and* $\text{ircons}_2$ *are (not necessarily different) irreflexive constructors, and that* rcons, $\text{rcons}_1, \ldots,$ $\text{rcons}_n$ *are (not necessarily different) reflexive constructors of some data structures in $P$. Then the partial estimation calculus (pE-calculus) is given by:*

---
[5] This means that we do not need domain procedures of domain procedures.
```

1. **Language** Estimation triples, *i.e.* expressions of form $\langle \nabla, \Delta, E \rangle$ where $\nabla, \Delta \subset \mathcal{CL}(\Sigma(P), \mathcal{V})$ and $E \subseteq \{r \succcurlyeq t \mid r, t \in \mathcal{T}(\Sigma(P), \mathcal{V})_s\}$ with $|E| < \infty$.

2. **Inference Rules** (Estimation Rules) [6]

   Identity

   (1) $\dfrac{\langle \nabla, \Delta, E \uplus \{t \succcurlyeq t\} \rangle}{\langle \nabla, \Delta, E \rangle}$

   Equivalence

   (2) $\dfrac{\langle \nabla, \Delta, E \uplus \{r \succcurlyeq t\} \rangle}{\langle \nabla, \Delta, E \rangle}$, if $C \vdash ?ircons_2(r)$ and $C \vdash ?ircons_1(t)$

   Strong Estimation

   (3) $\dfrac{\langle \nabla, \Delta, E \uplus \{r \succcurlyeq t\} \rangle}{\langle \nabla, \Delta \cup \{true\}, E \rangle}$, if $C \vdash ?rcons(r)$ and $C \vdash ?ircons(t)$

   Strong Embedding

   (4) $\dfrac{\langle \nabla, \Delta, E \uplus \{r \succcurlyeq t\} \rangle}{\langle \nabla, \Delta \cup \{true\}, E \cup \{SEL_k(r) \succcurlyeq t\} \rangle}$, if $\begin{cases} C \vdash ?rcons(r), \text{ and} \\ k \text{ is a reflexive argument} \\ \text{position of } rcons \end{cases}$

   Argument Estimation

   (5) $\dfrac{\langle \nabla, \Delta, E \uplus \{r \succcurlyeq f(t_1, \ldots, t_n)\} \rangle}{\langle \nabla \cup \{\nabla_f(t_1, \ldots, t_n)\}, \Delta \cup \{\Delta_f^p(t_1, \ldots, t_n)\}, E \cup \{r \succcurlyeq t_p\} \rangle}$, if $f \in \Gamma_p$

   Weak Embedding

   (6) $\dfrac{\langle \nabla, \Delta, E \uplus \{r \succcurlyeq t\} \rangle}{\langle \nabla, \Delta, E \cup \bigcup_{i=1}^{h} \{SEL_{j_i}(r) \succcurlyeq SEL_{j_i}(t)\} \rangle}$, if $\begin{cases} C \vdash ?rcons(r), \\ C \vdash ?rcons(t), \text{ and} \\ j_1, \ldots, j_h \text{ are all} \\ \text{reflexive argument} \\ \text{positions of } rcons, \end{cases}$

   Minimum

   (7) $\dfrac{\langle \nabla, \Delta, E \uplus \{r \succcurlyeq t\} \rangle}{\langle \nabla, \Delta \cup \bigcup_{i=1}^{k} \{?rcons_i(r)\}, E \rangle}$, if $\begin{cases} C \vdash ?ircons(t), \text{ and} \\ rcons_1, \ldots, rcons_k \text{ are all} \\ \text{reflexive constructors of } s \end{cases}$

3. **Deduction** A deduction of $\langle \nabla_n, \Delta_n, E_n \rangle$ from $\langle \nabla_1, \Delta_1, E_1 \rangle$ is a finite sequence $\langle \nabla_1, \Delta_1, E_1 \rangle, \ldots, \langle \nabla_n, \Delta_n, E_n \rangle$ of estimation triples such that $n \geq 1$ and $\langle \nabla_i, \Delta_i, E_i \rangle \Rightarrow_{\Gamma,C} \langle \nabla_{i+1}, \Delta_{i+1}, E_{i+1} \rangle$, *i.e.* $\langle \nabla_{i+1}, \Delta_{i+1}, E_{i+1} \rangle$ results from $\langle \nabla_i, \Delta_i, E_i \rangle$ by an application of some estimation rule for each $i < n$.
   $r \succcurlyeq_{\Gamma,C} t$ abbreviates $\vdash_{\Gamma,C} \langle \nabla, \Delta, r \succcurlyeq t \rangle$ for some $\nabla, \Delta \in \mathcal{CL}(\Sigma(P), \mathcal{V})$, where $\vdash_{\Gamma,C} \langle \nabla, \Delta, r \succcurlyeq t \rangle$ denotes the existence of an estimation proof for $r \succcurlyeq t$ with determination clause ∇ and difference equivalent Δ, given by

   $$\vdash_{\Gamma,C} \langle \nabla, \Delta, r \succcurlyeq t \rangle \iff \langle \emptyset, \emptyset, \{r \succcurlyeq t\} \rangle \Rightarrow_{\Gamma,C}^{+} \langle \nabla, \Delta, \emptyset \rangle \ .$$

---

[6] We write $C \vdash ?cons_i(r)$ iff (i) $r = cons_i(\ldots)$ or (ii) $?cons_i(r) \in C$ or (iii) $\{\neg ?cons_j(r) \mid j \in \{1, \ldots, n\} \setminus \{i\}\} \subset C$ for a data structure s with constructors $cons_1, \ldots, cons_n$. $SEL_k(r)$ stands for r_k if $r = rcons(\ldots, r_k, \ldots)$, and abbreviates $sel_k(r)$ otherwise.

Theorem 1. (Soundness of the pE-calculus) *Let P be an incompletely defined and terminating program, and let $\vdash_{\Gamma,C} \langle \nabla, \Delta, r \succcurlyeq t \rangle$ where $x_1, \ldots, x_n$ with $x_i \in \mathcal{V}_{s_i}$ are all variable symbols in C, r and t. Then*

1. $[\forall x_1 : s_1, \ldots, x_n : s_n . \bigwedge \nabla \rightarrow (\bigwedge C \rightarrow r \geqslant_{\#} t)] \in Th_P$, *and*
2. $[\forall x_1 : s_1, \ldots, x_n : s_n . \bigwedge \nabla \rightarrow (\bigwedge C \rightarrow (\bigvee \Delta \leftrightarrow r >_{\#} t))] \in Th_P.$[7]

By Theorem 1, the soundness of a *pE*-deduction is relativized by the domain clause ∇ inferred. This means that the soundness statements of (2) in Section 4 hold for incompletely defined programs only if each literal of ∇ is true, i.e. if the *absence of stuck computations* is guaranteed. E.g., we now may obtain the *pE*-deduction $\langle \emptyset, \emptyset, \{\texttt{x} \succcurlyeq \texttt{minus(half(pred(x)),succ(y))}\} \rangle \Rightarrow_{\Gamma}^{+} \langle \{\nabla_{\texttt{pred}}(\texttt{x}), \nabla_{\texttt{half}}(\texttt{pred(x)}), \nabla_{\texttt{minus}}(\texttt{half(pred(x)), succ(y)})\}, \{\Delta_{\texttt{minus}}^1(\texttt{half(pred(x)), succ(y)}), \Delta_{\texttt{half}}^1(\texttt{pred(x)}), \Delta_{\texttt{pred}}^1(\texttt{x})\}, \emptyset \rangle$.

A proof procedure for the *pE*-calculus is easily obtained, because the set of theorems of the *pE*-calculus is decidable:

Theorem 2. (Decidability of pE-deductions) *Let P be an incompletely defined program, let $\mathbb{E} = \{r \succcurlyeq t \mid r, t \in \mathcal{T}(\Sigma(P), \mathcal{V})_s\}$, and let $M = \{\langle \nabla, \Delta, E \rangle \mid \nabla, \Delta \in \mathcal{CL}(\Sigma(P), \mathcal{V})$ and $E \subset \mathbb{E}$ with $|E| < \infty\}$. Then*

1. $\{\langle \nabla, \Delta, \{r \succcurlyeq t\} \rangle \in M \mid \vdash_{\Gamma, C} \langle \nabla, \Delta, r \succcurlyeq t \rangle\}$ *is decidable, and*
2. $r \geqslant_{\Gamma, C} t$ *is decidable.*

8 Synthesis of Difference Procedures

The *pE*-calculus is used similarly to the *E*-calculus in [10] to recognize *p*-boundedness of a procedure $\texttt{function } f(x_1:s_1, \ldots, x_n:s_n):s <= R_f$ and to synthesize a *p*-difference procedure $\texttt{function } \Delta_f^p(x_1:s_1, \ldots, x_n:s_n):bool <= R_{\Delta_f^p}$ for procedure f. But we have to modify the synthesis process slightly to cope with the *-symbol which may occur in the procedure bodies R_f.

We define * as the result term of $R_{\Delta_f^p}$ under a clause C whenever * appears as the result term under this clause in R_f. Consequently, a *p*-difference procedure Δ_f^p is incompletely defined iff its "mother" procedure f is.

Definition 6. (*p*-Difference Procedures) *Let P be an incompletely defined program. Then each reflexive selector $sel \in \{sel_1, \ldots, sel_n\}$ of a data structure definition $\texttt{structure } s <= \ldots, cons(sel_1:s_1, \ldots, sel_n:s_n), \ldots$ in P is associated with the 1-difference procedure*

$\quad\quad\texttt{function } \Delta_{sel}^1(x:s):bool <= \texttt{if } ?cons(x) \texttt{ then true else } * \texttt{ fi }.$

Each p-bounded procedure $\texttt{function } f(x_1:s_1, \ldots, x_n:s_n):s <= R_f$ of P is associated with some p-difference procedure

$\quad\quad\quad\texttt{function } \Delta_f^p(x_1:s_1, \ldots, x_n:s_n):bool <= R_{\Delta_f^p}$

---

[7] We refer to [28] for omitted proofs.

such that $R_{\Delta_f^p}$ is obtained from R_f by keeping each result term r with $r = *$ and by replacing each result term r with $r \neq_\#$ which appears under some clause C_r in R_f by OR(Δ_r), where $\vdash_{\Gamma,C_r}^{\oplus} \langle \nabla_r, \Delta_r, x_p \succcurlyeq r \rangle$.[8]

Theorem 3. *Let P be an incompletely defined program, let $f \in \Sigma(P)_{s_1,\ldots,s_n,s}$ be p-bounded, and let* function Δ_f^p *denote a p-difference procedure of f. Then for all $q_i \in \mathcal{T}(\Sigma(P)^c)_{s_i}$ and for all $P' \in \widehat{P}$*
1. $eval_{P'}(f(q_1,\ldots,q_n)) \in \mathcal{T}(\Sigma(P)^c) \Leftrightarrow eval_{P'}(\Delta_f^p(q_1,\ldots,q_n)) \in \{true, false\}$,
2. $eval_P(\nabla_f(q_1,\ldots,q_n)) = true \implies eval_P(\Delta_f^p(q_1,\ldots,q_n)) \in \{true, false\}$,
3. P terminates $\implies [\forall x_1 : s_1, \ldots, x_n : s_n. \nabla_f(x_1, \ldots, x_n) \to x_p \succcurlyeq_\# f(x_1, \ldots, x_n) \land (\Delta_f^p(x_1, \ldots, x_n) \leftrightarrow x_p >_\# f(x_1, \ldots, x_n))] \in Th_P$.

By Theorem 3(1), a difference procedure terminates iff its "mother" procedure terminates. By Theorem 3(2), $\nabla_f(q_1,\ldots,q_n)$ entails that computation of $\Delta_f^p(q_1,\ldots,q_n)$ does not get stuck. We therefore abandon with generating a domain procedure $\nabla_{\Delta_f^p}$ for a difference procedure Δ_f^p but use the domain procedure ∇_f of its "mother" procedure f instead. Finally by Theorem 3(3), a p-bounded procedure f computes a p-bounded function and a p-difference procedure is *sound*, i.e. it represents an *equivalent* requirement for a procedure call $f(q_1,\ldots,q_n)$ being *strictly* bounded above by its pth argument q_p, provided the computation of $f(q_1,\ldots,q_n)$ does not get stuck.

After their synthesis, the difference procedures are optimized by simplification and recursion elimination as defined in [10].

Example 2.
(i) function $\Delta_{\texttt{minus}}^1$(x,y:nat):bool <=
    if y=0 then false else if x=0 then * else true fi fi

is computed as the optimized 1-difference procedure for the incompletely defined procedure minus of Fig. 1. Hence $\Delta_{\texttt{minus}}^1(n,m) = true$ iff $m \neq 0 \neq n$ and $\Delta_{\texttt{minus}}^1(n,m) = false$ iff $m = 0$.

(ii) function $\Delta_{\texttt{remainder}}^1$(x:nat, y:nat):bool <=
     if y=0 then * else if y>x then false else true fi fi

is computed as the optimized 1-difference procedure for the incompletely defined procedure remainder of Fig. 1. Hence $\Delta_{\texttt{remainder}}^1(n,m) = true$ iff $n \geq m \neq 0$ and $\Delta_{\texttt{remainder}}^1(n,m) = false$ iff $n < m$. Since remainder is 2-bounded too, we also obtain the optimized 2-difference procedure

    function $\Delta_{\texttt{remainder}}^2$(x:nat, y:nat):bool <=
    if y=0 then * else true fi

and $\Delta_{\texttt{remainder}}^2(n,m) = true$ iff $m \neq 0$ and $\Delta_{\texttt{remainder}}^2(n,m) \neq false$.

(iii) function $\Delta_{\texttt{half}}^1$(x:nat):bool <=
      if x=0 then false else if pred(x)=0 then * else true fi fi

is computed as the optimized 1-difference procedure for procedure half of Fig. 2, hence $\Delta_{\texttt{half}}^1(n) = true$ iff $n \geq 2$ and $\Delta_{\texttt{half}}^1(n) = false$ iff $n = 0$.

---
[8] OR(C) denotes the disjunction of the elements in C represented by *if*-conditionals.

(iv) function $\Delta^1_{\log}$(x:nat):bool <=
    if x=0
      then *
      else if pred(x)=0 then true
                        else if even(x) then true else * fi fi fi

is computed as the optimized 1-difference procedure for procedure log of Fig. 2, and $\Delta^1_{\log}(n) = true$ iff $n = 1$ or $n \neq 0$ is even and $\Delta^1_{\log}(n) \neq false$. □

9 Generating Termination Hypotheses

Using the pE-calculus of Definition 5, we adjust the synthesis of termination hypotheses as defined in [10] to work also for incompletely defined procedures:

Definition 7. (Termination Hypotheses) Let function $f(x_1{:}s_1,\ldots,x_n{:}s_n){:}s$ <= R_f be a procedure of an incompletely defined program P, let $f(t_1,\ldots,t_n)$ be a recursive call which appears under some clause C in R_f, and let $\emptyset \neq \mathcal{P} \subset \{1,\ldots,n\}$ such that $\vdash_{\Gamma,C} \langle \nabla_i, \Delta_i, x_i \succcurlyeq t_i \rangle$ for each $i \in \mathcal{P}$. Then a termination hypothesis $\tau^{\mathcal{P}}_f$ of procedure f is defined as

$$\tau^{\mathcal{P}}_f = [\forall x_1{:}s_1,\ldots,x_n{:}s_n. \bigwedge C \to \bigwedge_{i \in \mathcal{P}} (\bigwedge \nabla_i) \wedge \bigvee_{i \in \mathcal{P}} (\bigvee \Delta_i)] \ . \quad (6)$$

Theorem 4. Let $P = P_0 \oplus \langle \texttt{function } f(x_1{:}s_1,\ldots,x_n{:}s_n){:}s \texttt{ <= } R_f \rangle$ be an incompletely defined program such that P_0 terminates. Then procedure f terminates in P if some non-empty $\mathcal{P} \subset \{1,\ldots,n\}$ exists such that $\tau^{\mathcal{P}}_f \in Th_{P_0}$ for each termination hypothesis $\tau^{\mathcal{P}}_f$.

Example 3. (i) We compute $\tau^{\{1\}}_{\texttt{minus}} = \tau^{\{2\}}_{\texttt{minus}} = [\forall x, y{:}nat.\ y \neq 0 \wedge x \neq 0 \to true \wedge true]$ for the incompletely defined procedure minus of Fig. 1.
(ii) We compute $\tau^{\{2\}}_{\texttt{remainder}} = [\forall x, y{:}nat.\ y \neq 0 \wedge y \not\succcurlyeq x \to false]$ and $\tau^{\{1\}}_{\texttt{remainder}} = [\forall x, y{:}nat.\ y \neq 0 \wedge y \not\succcurlyeq x \to \nabla_{\texttt{minus}}(x, y) \wedge \Delta^1_{\texttt{minus}}(x, y)]$ for the incompletely defined procedure remainder of Fig. 1.
(iii) We compute $\tau^{\{1\}}_{\texttt{half}} = [\forall x{:}nat.\ x \neq 0 \wedge pred(x) \neq 0 \to true \wedge true]$ for procedure half of Fig. 2.
(iv) We compute $\tau^{\{1\}}_{\texttt{log}} = [\forall x{:}nat.\ x \neq 0 \wedge pred(x) \neq 0 \wedge even(x) \to \nabla_{\texttt{half}}(x) \wedge \Delta^1_{\texttt{half}}(x)]$ for procedure log of Fig. 2. □

10 Summary and Conclusion

Our termination proof procedure for incompletely defined programs is implemented in the √eriFun system in the following way:

Upon definition of a data structure s, the domain procedures ∇_{sel} are generated for each selector sel of s, each *reflexive* selector sel' of s is inserted into Γ_1 and the 1-difference procedures $\Delta^1_{sel'}$ for sel' are generated, cf. Sections 6 and 8.

Upon definition of a procedure f, the pE-calculus is called to compute the termination hypotheses for procedure f, cf. Definition 7. Then the system tries to verify all termination hypotheses and if successful computes the domain procedure ∇_f and optimizes it, cf. Section 6. Next the pE-calculus is called again to test whether procedure f is p-bounded for some argument position p, cf. Definition 4. For each such p passing the test, the system computes the p-difference procedure Δ_f^p and optimizes it, cf. Section 8. Finally, f is inserted into Γ_p to be available for subsequent termination proofs, i.e. for proving the termination of procedures g which use procedure f in recursive g-calls.

Argument bounded algorithms proved as a useful concept to verify the termination of functional procedures by machine, easing the burden of a system user significantly as termination functions need to be supplied less frequently when defining procedures. Incompletely defined programs provide an elegant and easy way to write and to reason about programs which may halt with a run time error. Our proposal unifies the benefits of both approaches without sacrificing performance or simplicity, neither when proving termination nor when reasoning about programs.

Our method of proving the termination of incompletely defined programs automatically has proved successful in √eriFun [12],[13], a semi-automated verifier for functional programs. The √eriFun system is available from the web [11].

Acknowledgement We are grateful to Markus Aderhold and Andreas Schlosser for useful comments as well as to Jürgen Giesl for thorough and fruitful discussions and for constructive criticism on a draft of this paper.

References

1. Boyer, R.S., Moore, J.S.: A Computational Logic. Acad. Press, NY (1979)
2. Giesl, J.: Termination Analysis for Functional Programs using Term Orderings. In: Proc. of the 2nd Intern. Static Analysis Symposium (SAS-95). Volume 983 of Lecture Notes in Artifical Intelligence., Glasgow, Springer (1995) 154–171
3. Giesl, J.: Termination of Nested and Mutually Recursive Algorithms. Journal of Automated Reasoning **19** (1997) 1–29
4. Giesl, J., Walther, C., Brauburger, J.: Termination Analysis for Functional Programs. In Bibel, W., Schmitt, P., eds.: Automated Deduction - A Basis for Applications. Volume 3. Kluwer Acad. Publ., Dordrecht (1998) 135–164
5. Kamareddine, F., Monin, F.: An extension of an automated termination method of recursive functions. Intern. J. of Found. of Comp. Sc. **13** (2002) 361–386
6. Manoury, P., Simonot, M.: Automatizing Termination Proofs of Recursively Defined Functions. Theoretical Computer Science **135** (1994) 319–343
7. Monin, F., Simonot, M.: An Ordinal Measure based Procedure for Termination of Functions. Theoretical Computer Science **254** (2001) 63–94
8. Nielson, F., Nielson, H.R.: Termination Analysis based on Operational Semantics. Technical report, Aarhus University, Denmark (1995)
9. Sengler, C.: Termination of Algorithms over Non−Freely Generated Data Types. In McRobbie, M.A., Slaney, J.K., eds.: Proc. of the 13th Inter. Conf. on Automated Deduction (CADE-13). Volume 1104 of Lecture Notes in Artifical Intelligence., New Brunswick, NJ, Springer (1996) 121–136

10. Walther, C.: On Proving the Termination of Algorithms by Machine. Artificial Intelligence **71** (1994) 101–157
11. http://www.verifun.de.
12. Walther, C., Schweitzer, S.: About √eriFun. In Baader, F., ed.: Proc. of the 19th Inter. Conf. on Automated Deduction (CADE-19). Volume 2741 of Lecture Notes in Artifical Intelligence., Miami Beach, Springer (2003) 322–327
13. Walther, C., Schweitzer, S.: Verification in the Classroom. Journal of Automated Reasoning - Special Issue on Automated Reasoning and Theorem Proving in Education **32** (2004) 35–73
14. Walther, C., Schweitzer, S.: Reasoning about Incompletely Defined Programs. Technical Report VFR 04/02, Programmiermethodik, Technische Universität Darmstadt (2004)
15. Bundy, A.: The Automation of Proof by Mathematical Induction. In Robinson, A., Voronkov, A., eds.: Handbook of Automated Reasoning. Volume I. Elsevier (2001) 845–911
16. Comon, H.: Inductionless Induction. In Robinson, A., Voronkov, A., eds.: Handb. of Autom. Reasoning. Volume I. Elsevier (2001) 913–962
17. Walther, C.: Mathematical Induction. In Gabbay, D., Hogger, C., Robinson, J., eds.: Handbook of Logic in Artificial Intelligence and Logic Programming. Volume 2. Oxford University Press, Oxford (1994) 127–228
18. Autexier, S., Hutter, D., Langenstein, B., Mantel, H., Rock, G., Schairer, A., Stephan, W., Vogt, R., Wolpers, A.: VSE: Formal Methods Meet Industrial Needs. Intern. J. on Software Tools for Technology Transfer **3** (2000) 66–77
19. Autexier, S., Hutter, D., Mantel, H., Schairer, A.: inka 5.0 - A Logic Voyager. In Ganzinger, H., ed.: Proc. 16th Inter. Conf. on Autom. Deduction (CADE-16). Volume 1632 of Lect. Notes in Artif. Intell., Trento, Springer (1999) 207–211
20. Hutter, D., Langenstein, B., Sengler, C., Siekmann, J., Stephan, W., Wolpers, A.: Verification Support Environment (VSE). High Integrity Syst. **1** (1996) 523–530
21. Hutter, D., Sengler, C.: INKA: The Next Generation. In McRobbie, M., J.Slaney, eds.: Proc. 13th Inter. Conf. on Autom. Deduction (CADE-13). Volume 1104 of Lect. Notes in Artif. Intell., New Brunswick, Springer (1996) 288–292
22. Brauburger, J.: Automatic Termination Analysis for Partial Functions using Polynomial Orderings. In: Proc. of the 4th Intern. Static Analysis Symposium (SAS-97). Volume 1302 of Lect. Notes in Artif. Intell., Paris, Springer (1997) 330–344
23. Brauburger, J., Giesl, J.: Approximating the Domains of Functional and Imperative Programs. Science of Computer Programming **35** (1999) 113–136
24. Giesl, J.: Automated Termination Proofs with Measure Functions. In: Proc. of the 19th Annual German Conf. on Artifical Intelligence (KI-95). Volume 981 of Lecture Notes in Artifical Intelligence., Bielefeld, Springer (1995) 149–160
25. Gow, J., Bundy, A., Green, I.: Extensions to the Estimation Calculus. In Ganzinger, H., McAllester, D.A., Voronkov, A., eds.: Proc. of the 6th Inter. Conf. on Logic Progr. and Autom. Reasoning (LPAR-6). Volume 1705 of Lect. Notes in Artif. Intelligence., Tbilisi, Georgia, Springer (1999) 258–272
26. Hutter, D.: Using Rippling to Prove the Termination of Algorithms. Technical Report RR 97-03, DFKI, Saarbrücken (1997)
27. McAllester, D., Arkoudas, K.: Walther Recursion. In McRobbie, M.A., Slaney, J.K., eds.: Proc. of the 13th Inter. Conf. on Autom. Deduction. Volume 1104 of Lect. Notes in Artif. Intell., New Brunswick, NJ, Springer (1996) 643–657
28. Walther, C., Schweitzer, S.: Automated Termination Analysis for Incompletely Defined Programs. Technical Report VFR 04/03, Programmiermethodik, Technische Universität Darmstadt (2004)

Automatic Certification of Heap Consumption

Lennart Beringer[1], Martin Hofmann[2], Alberto Momigliano[1], and Olha Shkaravska[2]

[1] Laboratory for Foundations of Computer Science, The University of Edinburgh,
Mayfield Road, Edinburgh EH9 3JZ; {lenb,amomigl1}@inf.ed.ac.uk
[2] Institut für Informatik, Ludwig-Maximilians-Universität München, Oettingenstraße 67,
80538 München; {mhofmann,shkaravska}@tcs.ifi.uni-muenchen.de

Abstract. We present a program logic for verifying the heap consumption of low-level programs. The proof rules employ a uniform assertion format and have been derived from a general purpose program logic [1]. In a proof-carrying code scenario, the inference of invariants is delegated to the code provider, who employs a certifying compiler that generates a certificate from program annotations and analysis. The granularity of the proof rules matches that of the linear type system presented in [6], which enables us to perform verification by replaying typing derivations in a theorem prover, given the specifications of individual methods. The resulting verification conditions are of limited complexity, and are automatically discharged. We also outline a proof system that relaxes the linearity restrictions and relates to the type system of usage aspects presented in [2].

1 Introduction

Validating the resource consumption of a program obtained from an unknown or untrustworthy code producer is an important task of any security architecture targeting devices with limited resources. The Mobile Resource Guarantees (MRG) project [17] is developing Proof-Carrying Code (PCC) technology [14] to endow mobile code with certificates of bounded resource consumption that can be validated automatically. These certificates are generated by a compiler which, in addition to translating high-level programs into machine code, derives formal proofs based on programmer annotations and program analysis. The foundation of the validation process is a program logic that is sufficiently powerful to formulate expressive certificates. As the logic and the certificate checker are trusted components from the point of view of the program recipient, soundness of the logic with respect to an operational model of the target architecture is crucial, and should ideally be present in a machine-checkable form. In [1], we presented our general-purpose logic, including proofs of soundness and completeness, the latter relative to the ambient logic HOL. The development is completely backed up by an implementation in Isabelle/HOL, building upon, and extending, earlier work on formalised program logics by Kleymann, Nipkow and others [8, 15]. In this paper, we use this logic to justify more specialised logics for the resource *heap consumption*. We develop proof rules that allow the code producer to certify the heap consumption of a low-level program in such a way that the recipient can validate the memory behaviour prior to execution. Judgements in these heap logics arise from the base logic by restricting assertions to syntactically uniform representations and formally deriving proof rules in the theorem prover. The assertion formats are motivated by, and closely related to, typing judgements used in a certifying compiler for inferring the memory requirements of programs at source level.

Our approach to deriving proof rules for restricted assertion formats from the base logic achieves several goals: firstly, soundness of the heap logics with respect to the operational model is obtained from the soundness of the base logic. Secondly, a method for certificate generation is achieved: the type systems infers invariants (in our case: method specifications) for the low-level code based on the strategy used for compiling high-level programs. Thirdly, a strategy is obtained that allows the program recipient to verify the validity of a proof automatically: the proof rules are set up in such a way that methods can be proved in a largely syntax-directed way, with side conditions that are of low complexity. The granularity of proof rules matches that of the type systems: sequences of low-level instructions that originate from a high-level language construct are combined in a single proof rule. Thus, the consumer-side verification can follow a validation tactic that essentially replays typing judgements, where the compiler-generated invariants eliminate the need to perform complex proof search.

In the main part of this paper, we outline this certification strategy for an (affinely) linear assertion format that interprets the type system of Hofmann and Jost [6]. Continuing our work on formalisation, the derivation of the proof system from the base logic has been implemented in Isabelle/HOL, as has the verification tactic at recipient side. However, in order to demonstrate that our approach is more widely applicable, we also outline an extension that considers assertions corresponding to the more powerful type system of [2]. Here, the linearity requirements are relaxed by distinguishing between three usage disciplines a program may obey with respect to a data structure. While the formalisation of the corresponding proof system for derived assertions in a theorem prover is under way, the syntax-directedness and the computational simplicity of the side conditions again make an automatic verification by the recipient appear feasible.

2 Components of the MRG Architecture

In this section we summarise MRG's PCC architecture. We start by introducing our representation of low-level code, the Grail language, and the program logic that forms the foundation of the certification. We then move to the high-level language, Camelot, and discuss the compilation of programs into Grail, with particular emphasis on memory management. Finally, we outline the static analysis of memory consumption that will be the basis of the proof rules in the following section. For details, see [1, 4, 6, 12].

Syntax and Semantics of Grail The target of MRG's compilation, and the language to which certificates refer, is a restricted form of Java bytecode, Grail [4]. This language retains the object and method structure of bytecode, but represents method bodies as sets of mutually tail-recursive first-order functions. The syntax comprises instructions for object creation and manipulation, method invocation and primitive operations such as integer arithmetic, as well as let-bindings to combine program fragments. The main characteristic of Grail is its dual identity: its (impure) call-by-value functional semantics coincides with an imperative interpretation of the expansion of Grail programs into the Java Virtual Machine Language, provided that some mild syntactic conditions are met. In particular, we require that actual arguments in function calls coincide syntactically with the formal parameters of the function definitions. In [4] we showed that this discipline, together with Administrative-Normal-Form (ANF)-style normalisation of let-expressions, allows function calls to be interpreted as immediate jump instructions, and admits the definition of a code transformation that is the exact reversal of the expansion of Grail expressions into JVML. The formal syntax of expressions

$e \in expr ::=$ null $\mid$ int $i \mid$ var $x \mid$ prim $op\ x\ x \mid$ new $C\ [\overline{t_i := x_i}] \mid x.t \mid x.t{:=}x \mid$
$\qquad C.t \mid C.t{:=}x \mid$ let $x=e$ in $e \mid e\ ;\ e \mid$ if x then e else $e \mid$ call $f \mid C.M(\overline{a})$

$a \in args ::=$ var $x \mid$ null $\mid i$

is defined over mutually disjoint sets of method names, class names, function names (i.e. labels of basic blocks), (static) field names and variables, ranged over by M, C, f, t, and x, respectively. In the grammar, i ranges over integers and op denotes a primitive operation of type $\mathcal{V} \Rightarrow \mathcal{V} \Rightarrow \mathcal{V}$ such as an arithmetic or a comparison operator. Here $\mathcal{V}$ is the semantic category of values (ranged over by v), comprising integers, references r, and the special symbol $\bot$, which stands for the absence of a value. Heap references are either null or of the form Ref l where $l \in L$ is a location.

Expressions represent basic blocks and are built from operators, constants, and previously computed values (names). They correspond to primitive sequences of bytecode instructions which may, as a side effect, alter the heap. For example, $x.t$ and $x.t{:=}y$ represent (non-static) field access instructions, while $C.t$ and $C.t{:=}y$ denote their static counterparts. The binding let $x=e_1$ in e_2 is used if the evaluation of e_1 returns an integer or reference value on top of the JVM stack while $e_1\ ;\ e_2$ represents non-binding composition, used for example if e_1 is a field update. Object creation includes the initialisation of the object fields according to the argument list. Function calls follow the Grail calling convention (i.e. correspond to immediate jumps) and do not carry arguments. The instruction $C.M(\overline{a})$ represents static method invocation. While formal parameters of method invocations are variables, actual arguments can be variables, integer constants or null. Although a formal type and class system may be imposed on Grail programs, our program logic abstracts from these restrictions. We assume that all method declarations employ distinct names for identifying inner basic blocks.

A program is represented by a table *Ftable* mapping each function identifier to an expression and a list of formal arguments, and a table *Mtable* associating method parameters and the name of the initial basic block to class names and method identifiers. The formal basis of the program logic is an operational semantics that is expressed as a big-step evaluation relation $E \vdash h, e \Downarrow h', v$. For expression e, such a judgement relates an (initial) variable environment $E \in \mathcal{E}$ and an initial heap $h \in \mathcal{H}$ to a final heap $h' \in \mathcal{H}$ and the result value $v \in \mathcal{V}$. Heaps are finite maps from locations and field names to values, while environments are modelled as total maps from variable names to values. The rules for defining the operational semantics are omitted, but are available in [1].

The Core Program Logic In our program logic [1], judgements take the form $G \triangleright e : P$ where e is a Grail expression, G a context used for storing verification assumptions for recursive methods and functions, and P an assertion. Deviating from both Hoare-style and VDM-style logic [7], we combine pre- and post-conditions into single assertions: P is a predicate (in the meta-logic HOL) over the semantic components, and relates the initial and final heaps, the initial environment, and the result value: $P : \mathcal{E} \to \mathcal{H} \to \mathcal{H} \to \mathcal{V} \to \mathcal{B}$, where $\mathcal{B}$ is the set of booleans. For example, the rule for program composition

$$\frac{G \triangleright e_1 : P_1 \quad G \triangleright e_2 : P_2}{G \triangleright \text{let } x = e_1 \text{ in } e_2 : \lambda E\, h\, h'\, v.\ \exists h_1\, w.\ (P_1\, E\, h\, h_1\, w) \wedge w \neq \bot \wedge (P_2\, (E\langle x := w\rangle))\, h_1\, h'\, v)} \text{ VLET}$$

existentially abstracts the intermediate heap and models the binding of x to the result of evaluating e_1 by interpreting P_2 in the extended environment $E\langle x := w\rangle$. Satisfaction of a specification P by program e is denoted by $\models e : P$ and asserts that $E \vdash h, e \Downarrow h', v$ implies $P\, E\, h\, h'\, v$. In [1] we proved the soundness and (relative) completeness of the program logic with respect to this (partial) interpretation, i.e. the statement $\varnothing \triangleright e : P \iff \models e : P$. Associations between methods and their specifications are collected in a method specification table *MST*. In order to allow the usage of a proof rule for method invocation that includes parameter adaptation, each method specification additionally also abstracts over a list of actual arguments.

Compilation of Camelot Programs The high-level language Camelot is a first-order functional language with ML-style polymorphism and algebraic datatypes [12]. The following example code introduces a data type of integer lists and functions that implement the insertion sort algorithm.

```
type L = !Nil | Cons of int * L
let ins a l = match l with Nil -> Cons(a,Nil)
                         | Cons(x,t)@_ -> if a < x
                                          then Cons(a,Cons(x,t))
                                          else Cons(x, ins a t)
let sort l = match l with Nil -> Nil
                        | Cons(a,t)@_ -> ins a (sort t)
```

The compiler translates a program into Grail following a whole-program compilation approach with phases such as monomorphisation and let-normalisation. The resulting code contains a class InsSort comprising one (static) method for each Camelot function. For example, the code for insertion sort yields methods InsSort.ins and InsSort.sort whose (slightly pretty-printed) Grail representations are shown next:

---

method InsSort.ins(int a, D l) = call f
f: let b = prim *isNull* l l in
  if b then let l = null in D.make(a, l)
    else let v_3 = l.HD in let v_2 = l.TL in D.free(l) ; let b = prim *less* a v_3 in
      if b then let l = D.make(v_3, v_2) in D.make(a, l)
        else let l = InsSort.ins(a, v_2) in D.make(v_3, l)
method InsSort.sort(D l) = call g
g: let b = prim *isNull* l l in
  if b then null
    else let v_3 = l.HD in let v_2 = l.TL in D.free(l) ;
      let l = InsSort.sort(v_2) in InsSort.ins(v_3, l)

Furthermore, a class D is defined that declares sufficiently many fields for representing values of all declared types (in our case: HD and TL), plus some internal fields (TAG, FLIST, NEXT). The latter are used for discriminating between the various datatype constructors (TAG, only used for datatypes with more than one non-nullary constructor), and for implementing a freelist, i.e. a (non-cyclic) list of D-objects whose initial member is pointed to by the static field FLIST, and whose elements are linked via field NEXT. The declaration of D also contains methods for performing the operations typical of a freelist: objects can be inserted into the freelist using the method free, while the method make allocates a fresh object (method alloc) and initialises its application fields according to its method parameters (method fill). The code for these memory management methods is shown next:

method D.free(D nd)	= let f=D.FLIST in nd.NEXT:=f ; D.FLIST:=nd
method D.alloc()	= let f=D.FLIST in let b=prim $isNull\ f\ f$ in
	if b then new D []
	else let $t=f$.NEXT in D.FLIST:=t ; f
method D.fill(D x, int v, D w)	= x.HD:=v ; x.TL:=w ; x
method D.make(int v, D w)	= let x=D.alloc() in D.fill(x,v,w)

Notice that of all methods, alloc is the only one that contains the instruction new. Fresh memory can thus only be allocated through the memory management interface, and this operation is only performed if the freelist is empty. This discipline is at the heart of our verification: the interpretation of assertions in the derived program logic ensures that all requests from the freelist can be served without executing new.

Two further aspects of the compilation are worth mentioning, as they concern programmer annotations in the source program. In each datatype declaration, (at most) one constructor (like Nil in our example code) can be equipped with the annotation !, thus instructing the compiler to use a heap-free representation. The effect is visible in the compiler output: conditionals corresponding to match statements w.r.t. this constructor discriminate over the condition *isNull* instead of inspecting the content of the field TAG. The second programmer annotation, @_, indicates that the corresponding (branch of the) pattern match may be implemented destructively, i.e. the memory cell inhabited by the value against which the match is performed is returned to the freelist after the components have been accessed. The compiler output reflects this by calling method free after de-constructing the cons-cells in methods ins and sort. The compiler verifies that both annotations are used safely: a constructor annotated with ! must not have arguments, and pattern matching using @_ is only admitted if the data structure may indeed be destroyed, i.e. it is not used in the continuation of the program.

Inference of Heap Space Consumption In order to analyse the memory requirements of functional programs, Hofmann and Jost [6] introduced a type system that solves the following problem. Given a program e of type, say, bool list → bool list, calculate a (linear) function f such that computing $e(L)$ for some input list L will not require more than $f(|L|)$ additional heap cells, provided that a freelist is available for storing temporarily unused cells. In the context of the Camelot compilation, the result of such an analysis can be used to ensure that the evaluation of $e(L)$ will not perform a call to new, by wrapping the evaluation with code that allocates a freelist of the sufficient length $f(|L|)$ prior to calling e.

The analysis of [6] is formulated using an extended notion of types such that different portions of the input can contribute a different amount to memory consumption. For each (non-heapfree) datatype constructor, a numeric annotation indicates the amount of heap that is required for a single build operation using that constructor. For example, L(5) indicates the type of an integer list where each occurrence of Cons requires five free memory cells to be available – constructing the list, say, [97;634;42] thus requires fifteen additional cells to be available. Judgements in the type system are of the form $\Gamma, n \vdash e : T, m$ where T is the (extended) type of e with respect to the context Γ (which maps free variables of e to extended types), while n and m represent constants that describe memory requirements that are independent of the size of the data structures. The typing rules are defined in such a way that m and the numeric annotations in T are expressed relative to the size of the *output* data structure, while n and the annotations in Γ refer to the size of the *input* data structures. For example, evaluating a program e with typing $x : \text{L}(5), 4 \vdash e : \text{L}(2), 7$ in an environment where x is bound to the list [97;634;42] requires no more than $4 + (5*3)$ cells to be available in the freelist, and leaves a freelist of length (at least) $7 + 2*|M|$ where M is the output list.

We present next some of the typing rules, which are motivated by this understanding. The rule for constructing a list node, CONS, requires the initial freelist to contain at least as many elements as the final freelist does, plus one cell for representing the value itself, plus the additional k cells specified in the desired return type. In order to construct lists with homogeneous memory behaviour, the type associated to the tail t in the context must also be L(k).

$$\frac{n \geq 1 + k + m}{\Gamma, h : \text{int}, t : \text{L}(k), n \vdash \text{Cons}(h,t) : \text{L}(k), m} \text{ CONS}$$

$$\frac{\Gamma, n \vdash e_1 : A, m \quad \Gamma, h : \text{int}, t : \text{L}(k), n+1+k \vdash e_2 : A, m}{\Gamma, x : \text{L}(k), n \vdash \text{match } x \text{ with Nil} \Rightarrow e_1 \mid \text{Cons}(h,t)@\_ \Rightarrow e_2 : A, m} \text{ DM}$$

$$\frac{\Gamma, n \vdash e_1 : A, m \quad \Gamma, h : \text{int}, t : \text{L}(k), n+k \vdash e_2 : A, m}{\Gamma, x : \text{L}(k), n \vdash \text{match } x \text{ with Nil} \Rightarrow e_1 \mid \text{Cons}(h,t) \Rightarrow e_2 : A, m} \text{ M}$$

$$\frac{\Gamma_1, n \vdash e_1 : A, k \quad \Gamma_2, x : A, k \vdash e_2 : B, m}{\Gamma_1, \Gamma_2, n \vdash \text{let } x = e_1 \text{ in } e_2 : B, m} \text{ LET} \qquad \frac{\Gamma, x : A_1, y : A_2, n \vdash e : A, m}{\Gamma, z : A_1 \oplus A_2, n \vdash e[z/x, z/y] : A, m} \text{ SHARE}$$

The effect of a pattern match on the freelist depends on whether the match is performed destructively or not. In both cases, the branch executed in the case of an empty list has exactly the same memory behaviour as the composite expression. In the case of a non-empty list, the freelist available for the continuation grows at least by the amount k "stored in" the list node that is taken apart. In case of a destructive match, the cell inhabited by this node becomes available as well, which explains the additional $+1$ in rule DM that is not present in the rule for a non-destructive match, M. The rule for program composition, LET, reflects the above-mentioned interpretation of typing judgements, in particular the fact that the result type and the right-hand-side annotation m of a judgement refer to the size of the result of the computation, as the typing of the composite statement may be obtained compositionally from the typing of the sub-terms, glued together by the freelist constant k, and the type A, that occur in both hypothesis. Finally, the rule SHARE allows us to split resources between different variables representing the same data structure – operation $\oplus$ recursively descends through the type structure and adds the annotations in the leafs. As this contraction results in the data structure being aliased the soundness of this rule relies on the semantic condition of *benign sharing*: whenever a cell l is returned to the freelist during a destructive pattern match, the program continuation will not access l through any aliasing access path. Various static approximations to this conditions can be considered. Of these, imposing a *linear* typing discipline (i.e. considering the type system without rule SHARE, and interpreting the context split in rule LET to be a disjoint partitioning) is rather restrictive, but only moderately complex to implement, and is therefore chosen in the formal interpretation of assertions in the next section. However, as many programs cannot be typed under such a discipline, it is desirable to have alternative means at hand. The generalisation of our assertion format in Sect. 6 is a step in that direction, as it corresponds to the more permissive type system of usage aspects presented in [2].

The inference process for the type system consists of two stages. First, a skeleton type derivation is constructed where the numerical annotations $n, k, m, \ldots$ are interpreted as (rational) variables, constrained by side conditions such as the one in rule CONS. These side conditions are collected, and in a second step handed over to a linear programming solver. Any feasible solution to the linear program corresponds to a possible typing derivation. This inference process has been implemented for the language considered in [6] and for Camelot, and scales well even to programs where skeleton derivations contain thousands of variables or constraints.

In the context of certificate generation, the solution inferred by the analysis (if existing) is presented as a signature that contains one (extended) typing for each Camelot function. In the case of our example program, one such signature is

$$\{\texttt{ins} : 1, \texttt{int} \times L(0) \to L(0), 0, \texttt{sort} : 0, L(0) \to L(0), 0.\}$$

For both functions, this signature asserts that the heap consumption does not depend on the size of the input: ins consumes one heap cell, while sort executes in-place: the cell that is required in the call to ins has previously been gained in the pattern match.

3 Format and Interpretation of Assertions

In this section we introduce a class of assertions that interpret judgements of the high-level type system in the program logic. These assertions have a uniform syntactic form, and their interpretation expands to a predicate over the semantic components (environment, pre-heap, post-heap and return value), as is required of specifications by the core logic. This syntactic form,

$$[\![U, n, \Gamma \blacktriangleright T, m]\!]$$

comprises components similar to the type system:

$n, m \in \mathbb{N}$ represent the numerical results from the analysis. In the interpretation these numbers will relate to the initial and final length of the freelist, respectively.

Γ is the typing context, a partial map from program variables to extended types.
U (a finite set of program variables) is used to enforce the linear typing discipline.
T indicates the type of an expression e that satisfies the assertion.

In this paper, we only consider the data type of integer list. In the grammar

$$T \in \mathbf{T} ::= \mathbf{1} \mid \mathbf{I} \mid \mathbf{L}(k)$$

the constructors represent respectively the unit (void) type, the integer type, and the type of lists where each occurrence of the Cons constructor is equipped with $k \in \mathbb{N}$ additional free heap cells and the Nil constructor does not reserve any space. In [3] we consider additional types, for representing e.g. integer trees.

The interpretation of assertions, and the proof rules that will be presented in the following section, are formulated in such a way that the set U is inferred during the verification condition generation, and coincides with the free variables of e. Thus, the restricted context $\Gamma|_U$ amounts to the minimal context in which an expression e may be typed.

Before giving the semantic definition of an assertion, we introduce some auxiliary predicates. Given a value v of type T and a heap h, the predicate $v, h \models_T R, n$ computes the region R inhabited by v, and the number n of free heap cells associated with it according to the numerical annotations in T.

$$\frac{}{\bot, h \models_\mathbf{1} \varnothing, 0} \text{REGU} \qquad \frac{}{i, h \models_\mathbf{I} \varnothing, 0} \text{REGI} \qquad \frac{LIST(n, r, R, h)}{r, h \models_{\mathbf{L}(k)} R, k * n} \text{REGL}$$

In rule REGU, we abuse the earlier notation slightly and let the symbol $\bot$ also denote the canonical value of type $\mathbf{1}$. In rule REGL, the list predicate $LIST(n, r, R, h)$ is satisfied if reference r in heap h points to a (cycle-free) linked list of length n, whose cells inhabit exactly locations R.

$$\frac{}{LIST(0, \text{null}, \varnothing, h)} \text{NIL} \qquad \frac{h(l).\text{HD} = i \quad h(l).\text{TL} = r \quad LIST(n, r, R, h)}{LIST(n+1, \text{Ref } l, R \uplus l, h)} \text{CONS}$$

The definition directly reflects the layout of data values implemented by the Camelot compiler – the disjoint sum notation $\uplus$ indicates the implicit side condition $\{l\} \cap R = \varnothing$.

Next, we define a predicate $\Gamma, U \models_h^E R, n$ that computes the amount n of free heap associated to the variables in $\Gamma|_U$ and the heap region R inhabited by the corresponding data structures.

$$\frac{}{\Gamma, \varnothing \models_h^E \varnothing, 0} \text{HEAPE} \qquad \frac{E\langle x \rangle, h \models_{\Gamma(x)} R_1, n \quad \Gamma, U \models_h^E R_2, m}{\Gamma, U \uplus x \models_h^E R_1 \uplus R_2, n+m} \text{HEAPV}$$

Rule HEAPV, in combination with the above definition of the datatype representation predicates, enforces a strict separation both between and within data structures. We will relax some of these separation conditions in Sect. 6.

A further auxiliary predicate, $\mathit{freelist}(h, F, N)$, is defined by $FL(N, h\langle \text{D.FLIST}\rangle, F, h)$ and expresses the fact that in heap h, the static field D.FLIST points to a (non-cyclic) list of length N, where the cells collectively inhabit locations F and are linked via field NEXT. The predicate $FL(\_,\_,\_,\_)$ is defined analogously to the predicate $LIST(\_,\_,\_,\_)$.

Finally, the predicate $footprint(R,h,h') \equiv \forall l \in dom\, h \setminus R.\ h(l) = h'(l)$ bounds the set of locations on which two heaps may differ.

The interpretation $[\![U,n,\Gamma \blacktriangleright T,m]\!]$ is now defined by

$$[\![U,n,\Gamma \blacktriangleright T,m]\!] \equiv \forall q F R.$$

$$\begin{pmatrix} \exists N K\ freelist(h,F,N) \wedge \\ \Gamma, U \models_h^E R, K \wedge \\ R \cap F = \emptyset \wedge \\ n + K + q \leq N \end{pmatrix} \longrightarrow \begin{pmatrix} \exists Q S M H.\ v, h' \models_T Q, S \wedge freelist(h', H, M) \wedge \\ Q \cap H = \emptyset \wedge (Q \cup H) \subseteq (R \cup F) \wedge \\ footprint(F \cup R, h, h') \wedge \\ m + S + q \leq M \wedge dom\, h = dom\, h' \end{pmatrix}$$

where the free variables E, h, h' and v are implicitly abstracted over. A judgement $G \rhd e : [\![U,n,\Gamma \blacktriangleright T,m]\!]$ thus asserts that, whenever

- the initial heap h contains a freelist of length N, inhabiting locations F,
- the region R inhabited by the data structures $\Gamma|_U$ is disjoint from F, and
- the length N of the freelist is at least the amount K of heap owned by $\Gamma|_U$, plus the additionally required size n and some constant q,

and the evaluation of e terminates, then there are M and S and regions Q and G s. t.

- the result v (according to the type T) inhabits region Q (in the final heap h') and contributes S cells to the (final) freelist,
- the final heap contains a freelist of length M inhabiting region G,
- the result and the final freelist do not overlap,
- both G and Q are contained in the initial freelist region F, extended by the locations reachable (in the initial heap) by the variables in $\Gamma|_U$,
- locations that are neither part of the freelist nor reachable from variables from $\Gamma|_U$ remain unchanged, i.e. $F \cup R$ is an approximation of the locations touched,
- the final length M of the freelist is at least the amount S contributed by the result, plus the analysis number m and the constant q, and
- no new objects have been allocated.

Thus, data structures represented by variables in $\Gamma|_U$ are potentially destroyed. Corresponding locations may have been recycled during the evaluation of e, may have been inserted into the freelist, or have become unreachable. In contrast, locations not reachable from variables in $\Gamma|_U$ remain unchanged.

4 Proof Rules

Having introduced the assertion format, we can derive proof rules for various Grail phrases by unfolding the interpretation. The design of the proof rules was guided by the aim of minimising the complexity of verification conditions that arise from side conditions, and to mirror the high-level typing rules. Indeed, the granularity of the proof rules corresponds to that of the typing system: match statements and constructor applications are verified as single entities, i.e. only the soundness proof of the rules inspects the constituent instructions of the corresponding methods.

We first present the rules for basic syntactic constructs of Grail. There are no proof rules for object creation and (virtual or static) field access instructions, since these operations are only performed inside the memory management methods. The rules for function calls and method invocations are the rules of the base logic.

$$\frac{m \leq n}{G \triangleright \mathtt{null} : [\![\emptyset, n, \Gamma \blacktriangleright \mathbf{L}(k), m]\!]} \text{ NULL} \qquad \frac{m \leq n}{G \triangleright \mathtt{int}\, i : [\![\emptyset, n, \Gamma \blacktriangleright \mathbf{I}, m]\!]} \text{ INT}$$

$$\frac{m \leq n \quad \Gamma(x) = T}{G \triangleright \mathtt{var}\, x : [\![\{x\}, n, \Gamma \blacktriangleright T, m]\!]} \text{ VAR} \qquad \frac{\{x,y\} \subseteq \mathrm{dom}\,\Gamma \quad m \leq n}{G \triangleright \mathtt{prim}\, op\, x\, y : [\![\{x,y\}, n, \Gamma \blacktriangleright \mathbf{I}, m]\!]} \text{ PRIM}$$

$$\frac{G \triangleright e_1 : [\![U_1, n, \Gamma \blacktriangleright \mathbf{1}, m]\!] \quad G \triangleright e_2 : [\![U_2, m, \Gamma \blacktriangleright T, k]\!]}{G \triangleright e_1 ; e_2 : [\![U_1 \uplus U_2, n, \Gamma \blacktriangleright T, k]\!]} \text{ COMP}$$

$$\frac{G \triangleright e_1 : [\![U_1, n, \Gamma \blacktriangleright S, l]\!] \quad G \triangleright e_2 : [\![U_2, l, (\Gamma, x:S) \blacktriangleright T, m]\!] \quad S \neq \mathbf{1}}{G \triangleright \mathtt{let}\, x = e_1 \mathtt{\ in\ } e_2 : [\![U_1 \uplus (U_2 \setminus \{x\}), n, \Gamma \blacktriangleright T, m]\!]} \text{ LET}$$

$$\frac{G \triangleright e_1 : [\![U_1, n, \Gamma \blacktriangleright T, m]\!] \quad G \triangleright e_2 : [\![U_2, n, \Gamma \blacktriangleright T, m]\!]}{G \triangleright \mathtt{if}\, b \mathtt{\ then\ } e_1 \mathtt{\ else\ } e_2 : [\![U_1 \cup U_2, n, \Gamma \blacktriangleright T, m]\!]} \text{ IF}$$

$$\frac{(G \cup \{(\mathtt{call}\, f, P)\}) \triangleright Ftable\, f : P}{G \triangleright \mathtt{call}\, f : P} \text{ CALL}$$

$$\frac{(G \cup \{(C.M(\overline{a}), P)\}) \triangleright Mtable\, C\, M : \lambda\, E\, h\, h'\, v.\, \forall\, E'.\, E = frame\, (params\, C\, M)\, \overline{a}\, E' \longrightarrow P\, E'\, h\, h'\, v}{G \triangleright C.M(\overline{a}) : P} \text{ INVS}$$

Next, we present the rules for non-destructive and destructive match operations, and for constructor Cons. Treating the freelist management operations atomically reflects the fact that the states at intermediate program points of these composite statements do not satisfy formulae of the restricted form – they contain dangling pointers and incompletely built data structures. In rule DMATCH, the additional side condition $x \neq t$ is needed to avoid the insertion of t into the freelist by instruction D.free(x).

$$\frac{\Gamma(x) = \mathbf{L}(k) \quad h \notin \{x,t\} \quad G \triangleright e : [\![U, n+k, (\Gamma, h:\mathbf{I}, t:\mathbf{L}(k)) \blacktriangleright T, m]\!]}{G \triangleright \mathtt{let}\, h = x.\mathtt{HD} \mathtt{\ in\ let\ } t = x.\mathtt{TL} \mathtt{\ in\ } e : [\![(U \setminus \{h,t\}) \uplus x, n, \Gamma \blacktriangleright T, m]\!]} \text{ MATCH}$$

$$\frac{\begin{array}{c}\Gamma(x) = \mathbf{L}(k) \quad h \notin \{x,t\} \quad x \neq t \\ G \triangleright e : [\![U, n+k+1, (\Gamma, h:\mathbf{I}, t:\mathbf{L}(k)) \blacktriangleright T, m]\!]\end{array}}{\begin{array}{c}G \triangleright \mathtt{let}\, h = x.\mathtt{HD} \mathtt{\ in\ let\ } t = x.\mathtt{TL} \mathtt{\ in\ } \mathtt{D.free}(x) ; e : \\ [\![(U \setminus \{h,t\}) \uplus x, n, \Gamma \blacktriangleright T, m]\!]\end{array}} \text{ DMATCH}$$

$$\frac{\Gamma(y) = \mathbf{L}(k) \quad \Gamma(x) = \mathbf{I}}{G \triangleright \mathtt{D.make}(x,y) : [\![\{x,y\}, m+k+1, \Gamma \blacktriangleright \mathbf{L}(k), m]\!]} \text{ MAKE}$$

Finally, we give some structural rules. We will comment on their role in verification condition generation in the next section.

$$\frac{G \rhd e : [\![U, n, \Gamma \blacktriangleright T, m]\!] \quad n \leq n' \quad m' \leq m}{G \rhd e : [\![U, n', \Gamma \blacktriangleright T, m']\!]} \text{ RELAX}$$

$$\frac{G \rhd e : [\![V, n, \Gamma \blacktriangleright T, m]\!] \quad V \subseteq U}{G \rhd e : [\![U, n, \Gamma \blacktriangleright T, m]\!]} \text{ GEN} \qquad \frac{G \rhd e : [\![U, n, \Gamma \blacktriangleright T, m]\!]}{G \rhd e : [\![U, n+k, \Gamma \blacktriangleright T, m+k]\!]} \text{ SHIFT}$$

$$\frac{G \rhd e : [\![U, n, \Gamma \blacktriangleright T, m]\!] \quad \forall x \in U. \, \Delta(x) - \Gamma(x)}{G \rhd e : [\![U, n, \Delta \blacktriangleright T, m]\!]} \text{ CTXT}$$

Theorem 1. *All proof rules presented in this section are derivable in HOL from the core logic.*

The proof rules enforce benign sharing in a way that corresponds to linearity in the type system. The rules COMP and LET combine the U-sets using the disjoint union operator $\uplus$. From the point of view of surrounding code, linearity is also observed in the rules MATCH and DMATCH, despite variable x occurring repeatedly in the program text.

5 Verification

We now return to our example program, insertion sort, and outline the verification process. As was remarked earlier, compiling the Camelot code for insertion sort results in two class declarations: the class D with fields for the representation of data types and the (pre-verified) memory management methods, plus a class InsSort containing the application methods ins and sort. In addition, the compiler generates a certificate that contains the result of the program analysis in a form that can be automatically verified. The certificate contains the method specification table, the definition of a proof context G, and calls to a predefined Isabelle tactic. Before describing the global verification strategy, we first outline how this tactic verifies an individual method body.

For verifying that method body *Mtable C M* satisfies a specification of the restricted form, i.e. that $G \rhd \textit{Mtable C M} : [\![U, n, \Gamma \blacktriangleright T, m]\!]$ holds, we have implemented an Isabelle tactic ($\approx$ 150 lines of ML) that starts by applying the GEN rule, then applies the syntax-directed and memory management proof rules discharging the side conditions locally, and finally verifies that the initial side condition of GEN, $V \subseteq U$, holds for the inferred set V. The tactic maintains a stack of open goals that ensures that only ground conditions arise. Inspecting the proof rules shows that apart from numerical comparisons, set inclusions, and context look-ups, no advanced simplification nor decision procedures are required. The tactic is applied with a specification table *MST* that contains entries representing the result of the type analysis. Assertions are formulated from the perspective of the method body, i.e. the chosen variable names are the formal parameters. Method invocations are verified using a variation of INVS that incorporates the effect of rules SHIFT and CTXT, and a notion of variable renaming for assertions that is needed to handle the passing from actual arguments to formal parameters. In our example program, the specification table contains two entries that correspond to

$$\textit{Ins\_Spec} \equiv [\![\{a,l\}, 1, [a : \mathbf{I}, l : \mathbf{L}(0)] \blacktriangleright \mathbf{L}(0), 0]\!]$$
$$\textit{Sort\_Spec} \equiv [\![\{l\}, 0, [l : \mathbf{L}(0)] \blacktriangleright \mathbf{L}(0), 0]\!]$$

Note that we have made no effort to employ efficient data structures and we rely on naive representation of contexts and sets as provided by Isabelle/HOL. However, we have implemented a technique that allows us to verify each function body only once, based on compiler-generated merge point information. For some details see [3].

Global verification is based on the rule

$$\frac{goodContext\ MST\ G \quad finite(G) \quad (C.M(\overline{a}), MST\ M\ \overline{a}) \in G}{\varnothing \triangleright C.M(\overline{b}) : MST\ M\ \overline{b}}\ \text{VADAPTS}$$

which derives $\varnothing \triangleright C.M(\overline{b}) : B$ (notice the empty context), provided the existence of a context G that fulfils property *goodContext* and contains an entry $(C.M(\overline{a}), A)$ where A and B arise by instantiating the method specification table entry for M with the method arguments $\overline{a}$ and $\overline{b}$, respectively. The generated certificate contains the definition of such a context G, consisting of one entry $(C.M(\overline{a}), MST\ M\ \overline{a})$ for each method invocation occurring in the program. In our example program, the context G is given by

$$G \equiv \left\{ \begin{array}{l} (\mathsf{InsSort.ins}(a, v_2),\ MST\ \mathsf{ins}\ [a, v_2]),\ (\mathsf{InsSort.ins}(v_3, l),\ MST\ \mathsf{ins}\ [v_3, l]), \\ (\mathsf{InsSort.sort}(v_2),\ MST\ \mathsf{sort}\ [v_2]) \end{array} \right\}.$$

The definition of *goodContext* (see [1] for details) requires each such entry to satisfy $G \triangleright Mtable\ C\ M : \varphi(MST\ M)$, where φ models the passing of method arguments to the formal parameters. As the result of applying φ is of the form $[\![U, n, \Gamma \blacktriangleright T, m]\!]$, discharging the condition of the *goodContext* predicate may be performed by the tactic discussed above. Our verification script verifies first each method body individually, before combining the resulting local correctness statements. We thus obtain correctness of the sort method for arbitrary method arguments

Theorem 2. *We have* $\varnothing \triangleright \mathsf{InsSort.sort}(x) : MST\ \mathsf{sort}\ [x]$

for arbitrary x using a strategy that verifies each method body only once, despite the existence of two entries for ins in G.

6 Usage Aspects

As we pointed out earlier, the interpretation of assertions $[\![U, n, \Gamma \blacktriangleright T, n]\!]$ corresponds to a linear type system at the Camelot level. Although guaranteeing benign sharing, this discipline is overly restrictive, as may be illustrated by the expression `Cons(length(x), x)`, where x is used as an argument for `length`, but also in the surrounding code. Motivated by similar examples involving nontrivial sharing of heap cells, Aspinall and Hofmann [2] introduced a less restrictive type system that distinguishes three different usages a program can make of a variable. These *aspects* are ordered in increasing order of permissiveness:

1. modifying use, e.g. l in sort l, or the destroyed parameter in in-place list append;
2. non-modifying use, but shared with result, e.g. the second argument in append;
3. non-modifying use, and not shared with result, e.g. l in `length l`.

Based on aspects we can allow duplication of variables in certain cases while preserving benign sharing. For instance the nonlinear expression `let x = $e_1(y^3)$ in $e_2(x^i, y^1)$` will be allowed, where variables are annotated with their relative usage aspects. In the remainder of this section, we outline an assertion format for the type system of [2], suitably adapted to the setting of Camelot compilation. To increase readability we omit numerical annotations as they have the same format and meaning as in the linear system.

Usage Aspects for the Source Language We define a notion of usage-aspect aware contexts Γ in which variables are decorated with their usage aspects; for instance $x^i : A$ if $x : A$ is used with aspect $i \in \{1, 2, 3\}$. If $x^i : A \in \Gamma$, we write $\Gamma(x) = A$ and $\Gamma[x] = i$. The "committed to i" context Δ^i is the same as Δ, but each declaration $x^2 : A$ is replaced with $x^i : A$. If we have two contexts Δ_1, Δ_2 which only differ on usage aspects, we define the context $\Delta = \Delta_1 \wedge \Delta_2$, to have the same domain and typing, but such that $\Delta[x] = min(\Delta_1[x], \Delta_2[x])$. Some of the typing rules are:

$$\frac{\Gamma, x^i : A \vdash e : B \quad j \leq i}{\Gamma, x^j : A \vdash e : B} \text{LDROP} \qquad \frac{\Gamma \vdash e_1 : B \quad \Gamma \vdash e_2 : B}{\Gamma, x^3 : I \vdash \text{if } x \text{ then } e_1 \text{ else } e_2 : B} \text{LIF}$$

$$\frac{}{x^2 : A \vdash x : A} \text{LVAR} \qquad \frac{\Gamma, \Delta_1 \vdash e_1 : A \quad \Theta, \Delta_2, x^i : A \vdash e_2 : B \quad \Phi(i)}{\Gamma^i, \Theta, \Delta_1^i \wedge \Delta_2 \vdash \text{let } x = e_1 \text{ in } e_2 : B} \text{LLET}$$

The LVAR rule has default aspect 2, although variables can be raised (not shown here) if heap-free or weakened (LDROP) to a more destructive usage. The most complex rule is LLET: first, the context is split into parts according to variables specific to e_1 (or e_2), that is Γ (or Θ), and common variables, possibly used with different aspects Δ_1, Δ_2. A variable whose region overlaps with the result of e_1 (i.e. of a variable that is of aspect 2 in Γ, Δ_1) inherits the aspect of x in e_2 - this is why Γ^i and Δ_1^i appear in the succedent. Additionally, for a variable occurring in both contexts, the resulting usage aspect should not supersede its aspects in the two antecedents. The additional side condition $\Phi(i)$ prevents any common variable from being modified in e_1 or e_2 before being referenced in e_2: namely, $\Delta_1[z] = 1$ is never allowed, $\Delta_1[z] = 3$ is always allowed, $\Delta_1[z] = 2$ is only allowed, provided neither $i = 1$ nor $\Delta_2[z] = 1$. Further, we exclude $\Delta_1[z] = \Delta_2[z] = 2$. For more details, please see [2].

Derived Assertions for Usage Aspects In preparation of the definition of derived assertions, we extend the previous auxiliary judgements by a (boolean) *separation* flag p; the relation $v, h \models_{L(A)} R, p$ means that v points to a well formed list occupying a region R in a heap h. If the separation flag p is set to false then the regions occupied by elements of the list are allowed to overlap (internal sharing). Otherwise, these regions must be located in separated parts of the heap.

This definition is generalised to a relation over environments, heaps, contexts and regions in the following way:

$$\frac{E\langle x \rangle, h \models_{\Gamma(x)} R_1, \text{true} \quad \Gamma, U \models^E_{h,1} R_2}{\Gamma, U \uplus x \models^E_{h,1} R_1 \uplus R_2} \qquad \frac{E\langle x \rangle, h \models_{\Gamma(x)} R_1, \text{true} \quad \Gamma, U \models^E_{h,2} R_2, \text{true}}{\Gamma, U \uplus x \models^E_{h,2} R_1 \uplus R_2, \text{true}}$$

$$\frac{E\langle x \rangle, h \models_{\Gamma(x)} R_1, \text{false} \quad \Gamma, U \models^E_{h,2} R_2, \text{false}}{\Gamma, U \uplus x \models^E_{h,2} R_1 \cup R_2, \text{false}} \qquad \frac{E\langle x \rangle, h \models_{\Gamma(x)} R_1, \text{false} \quad \Gamma, U \models^E_{h,3} R_2}{\Gamma, U \uplus x \models^E_{h,3} R_1 \cup R_2}$$

The interpretation of aspect-aware assertions mirrors the correctness theorem in [2], extended with a freelist, but not including any reasoning about the freelist's length:

$[\![U_1, U_2, U_3, \Gamma \blacktriangleright T]\!] \equiv \forall F R_1 R_2 R_3$

$$\begin{pmatrix} U_1 \uplus U_2 \uplus U_3 \subseteq \text{dom}\,\Gamma \wedge \\ \text{freelist}(h,F) \wedge \\ \Gamma, U_1 \models^E_{h,1} R_1 \wedge \\ \Gamma, U_2 \models^E_{h,2} R_2, \text{false} \wedge \\ \Gamma, U_3 \models^E_{h,3} R_3 \wedge \\ R_1 \cap (R_2 \cup R_3) = \emptyset \wedge \\ F \cap (R_1 \cup R_2 \cup R_3) = \emptyset \end{pmatrix} \longrightarrow \begin{pmatrix} \exists Q H.\ v, h' \models_T Q, \text{false} \wedge \\ \text{freelist}(h',H) \wedge Q \cap H = \emptyset \wedge \\ \text{footprint}(F \cup R_1, h, h') \wedge \\ Q \subseteq (F \cup R_1 \cup R_2) \wedge \\ H \subseteq (F \cup R_1) \wedge \\ \text{dom}\,h = \text{dom}\,h' \wedge \\ \Gamma, U_2 \models^E_{h,2} R_2, \text{true} \longrightarrow v, h' \models_T Q, \text{true} \end{pmatrix}$$

A judgement $G \triangleright e : [\![U_1, U_2, U_3, \Gamma \blacktriangleright T]\!]$ thus asserts that, whenever

- variables in U_i point in the initial heap h to sets of locations R_i according to their type in Γ and usage aspect i, with internal sharing allowed when $i \geq 2$,
- the heap regions associated with variables of aspect 1 do not overlap with heap regions related to other aspects, i.e. $R_1 \cap (R_2 \cup R_3) = \emptyset$,
- the initial heap contains a freelist inhabiting region F, which does not overlap with any region pointed to by a variable in $U_1 \cup U_2 \cup U_3$,

and the evaluation of e terminates, then there exist regions Q and H such that:

- in h', result v according to type T inhabits region Q, possibly with internal sharing,
- the final heap contains a freelist in region H, not overlapping with Q,
- data structures pointed to by variables outside U_1 and F remain unchanged,
- the result region consists of locations from the initial freelist F, locations from R_1 (corresponding to destroyed data substructures, whose space has been recycled) and from R_2, which may overlap with the result region Q,
- the final freelist region consists of locations of the initial freelist and R_1,
- no new objects are allocated,
- if region R_2 does not contain any shared (sub)structures, then neither does Q.

For example, in-place list append admits a typing that corresponds to the assertion $\triangleright \text{append}(l_1, l_2) : [\![\{l_1\}, \{l_2\}, \emptyset, (l_1 : \mathbf{L}(A), l_2 : \mathbf{L}(A)) \blacktriangleright \mathbf{L}(A)]\!]$ where $l_1(l_2)$ is the destroyed (aliased) argument.

Proof Rules for Usage Aspects We now introduce some of the derived rules.

$$\frac{\Gamma(x) = T}{G \triangleright \text{var } x : [\![\emptyset, \{x\}, \emptyset, \Gamma \blacktriangleright T]\!]} \text{ DUVAR} \qquad \frac{G \triangleright e : [\![U_1, U_2 \uplus x, U_3, \Gamma \blacktriangleright T]\!]}{G \triangleright e : [\![U_1 \uplus x, U_2, U_3, \Gamma \blacktriangleright T]\!]} \text{ DUDROP21}$$

$$\frac{G \triangleright e_1 : [\![U_1, U_2, U_3, \Gamma \blacktriangleright T]\!] \quad G \triangleright e_1 : [\![U_1, U_2, U_3, \Gamma \blacktriangleright T]\!]}{G \triangleright \text{if } x \text{ then } e_1 \text{ else } e_2 : [\![U_1, U_2, U_3 \uplus x, (\Gamma, x : \mathbf{I}) \blacktriangleright T]\!]} \text{ DUIF}$$

$$\frac{G \triangleright e_1 : [\![U_{11}, U_{12}, U_{13}, \Gamma \blacktriangleright S]\!] \quad x \in U_{2i}}{G \triangleright e_2 : [\![U_{21}, U_{22}, U_{23}, (\Gamma, x : S) \blacktriangleright T]\!] \quad \Psi(i)} \text{ DULET}}{G \triangleright \text{let } x = e_1 \text{ in } e_2 : [\![U_1, U_2, U_3, \Gamma \blacktriangleright T]\!]}$$

These rules are direct counterparts of the typing rules. In particular, in the DULET rule the real work is done by the side condition $\Psi'(i)$, which statically approximates benign sharing. For instance, for $i = 2$ the side condition $\Psi(2)$ specialises to the conjunction of static assumptions $U_1 = U_{11} \cup U_{21}$, $U_2 = (U_{12} \setminus U_{21}) \cup (U_{22} \setminus \{x\})$, $U_3 = (U_{13} \setminus (U_{21} \cup U_{22})) \cup (U_{23} \setminus (U_{11} \cup U_{12}))$, $U_{11} \cap (U_{21} \cup U_{22} \cup U_{23}) = \varnothing$, $U_{12} \cap (U_{21} \cup U_{22} \cup U_{23}) \subseteq U_{23}$.

7 Conclusion and Related Work

In this paper, we have described a logic for derived assertions that allows the results of [6]'s analysis to be verified in Grail's bytecode logic. Although we have presented the logic for a specific datatype, our approach applies to algebraic datatypes in general. Because the MRG project aims to verify the consumption of a variety of resources, we have employed a general purpose logic as the basis of our formalisation. Our work is thus best compared to other work on mechanical or at least formal verification of pointer programs using variants of traditional (general purpose) Hoare logic. Historically, some of the first formal verification of pointer programs in [11] (and later [10]) used a model where the store is incorporated in the assertion logic. More recent is the verification of several algorithms, including list manipulating programs and the Schorr-Waite graph-marking algorithm, by Bornat [5] using the Jape system. This approach employs a Hoare logic for a while-language with components that are semantically modelled as pointer-indexed arrays. Separation conditions are expressed as predicates on (object) pointers. Mehta and Nipkow [13] employ the same semantic model of the heap for reasoning about pointer programs in higher-order logics. This effort extends earlier work by Nipkow et al. [15] on formalised proofs in HOL of soundness and (relative) completeness of program logics.

Proving heap-related properties has also been the topic of Separation Logic [16]. Indeed, the primitives of Separation Logic appear well suited to express the mutual separation of data structures, and their separation from the freelist more succinctly. An Isabelle/HOL implementation is presented in [18], although the author reports proofs (typically in-place reversal) to be slightly more complicated than in [13]. Furthermore, little support for automation is currently available, both for proof search and for generating invariants. Finally, properties such as heap preservation in our predicate *footprint* are more intensional than is usually the case in (Hoare-style) Separation Logic. Differently from Hoare-style logics in general, the style of our logic allows us to relate pre and post states without the use of auxiliary variables.

The contribution of the present paper is the translation of typing assertions to statements in the base logic and the formulation of derived rules which allow for automatic construction of proofs. We have indicated how the linearity restrictions may be overcome by considering the more generous sharing and separation systems induced by usage aspects. This could be pushed further toward Konečný's [9] system for layered sharing. Comparing the verification of the example programs with the verification of similar programs in the core bytecode logic demonstrates the general benefit of a proof system of derived assertions, concerning both the proof complexity and automation. Indeed, while verification in the bytecode logic appears to depend on the machinery of a general purpose theorem prover and manual intervention, a logic of derived assertions may be implementable in a stand alone prover with access to fairly straightforward simplification capabilities.

Acknowledgements This research was supported by the MRG project (IST-2001-33149) which is funded by the EC under the FET proactive initiative on Global Computing. We would like to thank all our colleagues and in particular David Aspinall for this role in implementing the certificate generation tactic.

References

1. D. Aspinall, L. Beringer, M. Hofmann, H.-W. Loidl, and A. Momigliano. A program logic for resource verification. In K. Slind, A. Bunker, and G. C. Gopalakrishnan, editors, *Proceedings of TPHOLs'04*, volume 3223 of *LNCS*, pages 34–49. Springer, Sept. 2004.
2. D. Aspinall and M. Hofmann. Another type system for in-place update. In D. L. Métayer, editor, *Proceedings of ESOP'02*, volume 2305 of *LNCS*, pages 36–52. Springer, Apr. 2002.
3. L. Beringer, M. Hofmann, A. Momigliano, and O. Shkaravska. Towards certificate generation for linear heap consumption. In *Proceedings of LRPP'04*, July 2004.
4. L. Beringer, K. MacKenzie, and I. Stark. Grail: a Functional Form for Imperative Mobile Code. In *Proceedings FGC'03*, volume 85(1) of *Electronic Notes in Theoretical Computer Science*. Elsevier, June 2003.
5. R. Bornat. Proving Pointer Programs in Hoare Logic. In R. Backhouse and J. Nuno Oliveira, editors, *Proceedings of MPC'00*, volume 1837 of *LNCS*, pages 102–126, July 2000.
6. M. Hofmann and S. Jost. Static prediction of heap space usage for first-order functional programs. In *Proceedings of POPL'03*, pages 185–197. ACM Press, Jan. 2003.
7. C. Jones. *Systematic Software Development Using VDM*. Prentice Hall, 1990.
8. T. Kleymann. *Hoare Logic and VDM: Machine-Checked Soundness and Completeness Proofs*. PhD thesis, LFCS, University of Edinburgh, 1999.
9. M. Konečný. Functional in-place update with layered datatype sharing. In M. Hofmann, editor, *Proceedings of TLCA'03*, volume 2701 of *LNCS*, pages 195–210. Springer, June 2003.
10. K. R. M. Leino. *Toward Reliable Modular Programs*. PhD thesis, California Institute of Technology, 1995. Available as Technical Report Caltech-CS-TR-95-03.
11. D. C. Luckham and N. Suzuki. Verification of array, record, and pointer operations in Pascal. *ACM Transactions on Programming Languages and Systems*, 1(2):226–244, Oct. 1979.
12. K. MacKenzie and N. Wolverson. Camelot and Grail: Resource-aware Functional Programming on the JVM. In S. Gilmore, editor, *Proceedings of TFP'03*, pages 29–46. intellect, 2003.
13. F. Mehta and T. Nipkow. Proving pointer programs in higher-order logic. In F. Baader, editor, *Proceedings of CADE-19*, volume 2741 of *LNCS/LNAI*, pages 121–135. Springer, Aug. 2003.
14. G. C. Necula. Proof-carrying code. In *Proceedings of POPL'97*, pages 106–119. ACM Press, 1997.
15. T. Nipkow. Hoare Logics for Recursive Procedures and Unbounded Nondeterminism. In J. Bradfield, editor, *Proceedings of CSL'02*, volume 2471 of *LNCS*, pages 103–119, Sept. 2002.
16. J. Reynolds. Separation Logic: A Logic for Shared Mutable Data Structures. In *Proceedings of LICS'02*. IEEE Computer Society, July 2002.
17. D. Sannella and M. Hofmann. Mobile Resource Guarantees. EU Project IST-2001-33149, 2002–2004. http://groups/inf.ed.ac.uk/mrg/.
18. T. Weber. Towards mechanized program verification with separation logic. In J. Marcinkowski and A. Tarlecki, editors, *Proceedings of CSL'04*, volume 3210 of *LNCS*, pages 250–264. Springer, Sept. 2004.

A Formalization of Off-Line Guessing for Security Protocol Analysis[*]

Paul Hankes Drielsma, Sebastian Mödersheim, and Luca Viganò

Information Security Group, ETH Zurich, CH-8092 Zurich, Switzerland
http://www.infsec.ethz.ch/~[drielsma|moedersheim|vigano]

Abstract. Guessing, or dictionary, attacks arise when an intruder exploits the fact that certain data like passwords may have low entropy, i.e. stem from a small set of values. In the case of off-line guessing, in particular, the intruder may employ guessed values to analyze the messages he has observed. Previous attempts at formalizing off-line guessing consist of extending a Dolev-Yao-style intruder model with inference rules to capture the additional capabilities of the intruder concerning guessable messages. While it is easy to convince oneself that the proposed rules are correct, in the sense that an intruder can actually perform such "guessing steps", it is difficult to see whether such a system of inference rules is complete in the sense that it captures all the kinds of attacks that we would intuitively call "guessing attacks". Moreover, the proposed systems are specialized to particular sets of cryptographic primitives and intruder capabilities. As a consequence, these systems are helpful to discover some off-line guessing attacks but are not fully appropriate for formalizing what off-line guessing precisely means and verifying that a given protocol is not vulnerable to such guessing attacks.

In this paper, we give a formalization of off-line guessing by defining a deduction system that is uniform and general in that it is independent of the overall protocol model and of the details of the considered intruder model, i.e. cryptographic primitives, algebraic properties, and intruder capabilities.

1 Introduction

Motivation. A serious vulnerability of security protocols lies in the simple fact that users tend to choose poor passwords, that is, passwords that are easy to remember and accordingly easy to guess (English words, for instance). This can give rise to *guessing* (or *dictionary*) *attacks* in which an intruder is able to guess a password or some other guessable data, and then somehow verify that his guess is correct [15,19].

One usually distinguishes between *on-line* and *off-line* guessing. One speaks of on-line guessing when the intruder employs guesses when interacting with

---

[*] This work was partially supported by the FET Open Project IST-2001-39252 and the BBW Project 02.0431, "AVISPA: Automated Validation of Internet Security Protocols and Applications".

other agents, e.g. trying to log into a system using a guessed password. One speaks of off-line guessing when the intruder (who is not necessarily passive) employs guesses when analyzing observed messages, e.g. when trying to decrypt a message that is encrypted with a guessable password.

A number of approaches have been proposed to perform formal protocol analysis in the presence of on-line guessing, e.g. [9]. In this paper, we focus on off-line guessing. Several protocols, like the ones of the EKE family [7,8], have been devised in an attempt to provide resilience to off-line guessing attacks. The idea behind these protocols is that, even if the intruder guesses the password correctly, he has no means of verifying whether his guess is correct or not.

In order to prove formally that such a protocol is correct, or detect attacks on it, it is necessary to have a precise definition of off-line guessing and of the potential vulnerabilities of protocols to such guessing attacks. A number of approaches, e.g. [10,11,12,13,17], have been proposed to formally analyze protocols under the assumption that the intruder can perform off-line guessing.

The motivation underlying our work is based on the observation that these approaches suffer from two problems. First, all these different approaches are based on extending a Dolev-Yao-style intruder [14] with sets of inference rules to capture the additional capabilities of the intruder in the context of guessable messages. While it is usually easy to convince oneself that the proposed rules are correct, in the sense that an intruder can actually perform such "guessing steps", it is difficult to see whether such a system of inference rules is complete in the sense that it captures all the kinds of attacks that we would intuitively call "guessing attacks". Second, the proposed deduction systems are specialized to particular intruder capabilities and to particular sets of cryptographic primitives and operators (and, in some cases, e.g. [12,17], they are even restricted to considering single guesses).

As a consequence, these systems are helpful to discover some off-line guessing attacks, but are not fully appropriate for formalizing what off-line guessing precisely means and proving that a particular protocol is not vulnerable to such guessing attacks.

Contributions. We propose, however, that there is a fairly simple intuition underlying off-line guessing, which captures a generic class of off-line guessing attacks without restriction to a particular intruder model or a set of cryptographic operations and their associated properties. In this paper, we overcome the above problems by precisely formulating this intuition to give a formalization of off-line guessing. More specifically, we define a deduction system that is uniform and general in that it is independent of the details of the considered intruder model, i.e. cryptographic primitives, algebraic properties, and intruder capabilities. In particular, our formalization works at the level of messages and is thus independent of the technical and conceptual details of the overall protocol model (which could be formalized, for example, by multiset rewriting, strand spaces, or process calculi). Moreover, our approach allows us to consider multiple guesses simultaneously.

Our formalization is based on the idea of explicitly representing the intermediate states of the computation of off-line guessing attacks. We call these intermediate computation states *maps*. Intuitively, a map is the result of the intruder constructing a message from his knowledge and inserting, in place of an unknown value, every value from the dictionary he uses to perform the attack; it thus maps candidate values for guessable data to the concrete message that would result in the respective cases.

Organization. In Section 2 we discuss the intuitions underlying our approach to off-line guessing, and in Section 3 we give a deduction system that captures these intuitions. As a concrete example, in Section 4 we consider Microsoft's Challenge/Response Authentication Protocol, version 2 (MS-CHAPv2). We draw conclusions and discuss related and future work in Section 5.

2 Context and Intuitions

The Dolev-Yao intruder model has proved to be an appropriate abstraction in the formal analysis of security protocols, as it idealizes the behavior and properties of cryptographic operations. However, when considering off-line guessing, this model suffers from several problems — even though guessing has nothing to do with "breaking" cryptography. In this section, we illustrate the intuitions behind our formalization of off-line guessing. To that end, we first describe the shortcomings of the Dolev-Yao model, in particular with respect to guessing, and then argue how it can be appropriately modified to faithfully model a "semi-ideal world" in which cryptography is still perfect but passwords are guessable. This will lead us to introducing the notion of maps, which explicitly represent the intermediate computation steps of an intruder during off-line guessing.

2.1 Problems with the Standard Dolev-Yao Intruder Model

Most approaches to the formal analysis of security protocols abstract away from the details of real cryptography and instead use a term-algebra of messages in the style of the Dolev-Yao intruder model [14], where concrete data like agent names, nonces, or keys are represented by constants, and cryptographic operations like different kinds of encryption are represented by function symbols. Inherent in the models considered in such approaches are several (closely related) simplifying assumptions:

- Cryptography is perfect, i.e. there is no way to decrypt messages without knowing the proper key.
- Syntactically different terms represent different messages. This assumption is often relaxed by defining algebraic properties, e.g. $(a^b)^c = (a^c)^b$, which induce an equivalence relation on the terms, and one then considers the quotient algebra in which syntactically different terms represent the same value if and only if they are equivalent.

– It is not defined what happens when someone attempts to decrypt an encrypted message using a wrong key, i.e. by explicitly modeling that in this case one obtains a string of random bits.
– The intruder always implicitly knows the format or structure of messages being exchanged in a protocol, even if he cannot decrypt them.

The Dolev-Yao intruder model, which incorporates these simplifying assumptions, has proved to be extremely successful in security protocol analysis. However, these assumptions also have many subtle implications. Firstly, when an agent creates a "fresh" nonce, this is usually modeled by picking a fresh constant symbol, which is then "by definition" different from anything that was seen before. One thus abstracts away the small chance that an agent accidentally "generates" a nonce that was used before (maybe by a different agent). Secondly, the cryptographic operations behave like injective functions, for instance $\{\!|m|\!\}_k \neq \{\!|m'|\!\}_{k'}$ if $k \neq k'$ or $m \neq m'$. This abstracts away the small probability that different operations may lead to the same result, e.g. that encrypting different plain-texts with the same key may produce the same bit-string. This leads, for instance, to the unrealistic consequence that all hash-functions are perfect, e.g. never produce the same hash-value for different messages.

These assumptions have unrealistic and counter-intuitive consequences, but still they often provide an appropriate abstraction level for analysis: "collisions" like the ones described above usually cannot be systematically exploited by an intruder, at least not if we assume a reasonable behavior of the cryptographic operations. For example, it should be computationally difficult (though, of course, not impossible) to produce different messages with the same hash-value. The Dolev-Yao model can thus indeed be effectively used to abstract away the possibility that the intruder exploits properties of real cryptography. However, when we consider guessing attacks, we can observe further clashes with the assumptions of the idealized Dolev-Yao model: the intruder may observe a message that is encrypted with a password, and if this password is poorly chosen, it may appear in a dictionary that the intruder possesses; so, roughly speaking, he "knows" the password. However, if we assume that the password is simply part of the intruder knowledge, then, according to the Dolev-Yao model, the intruder can decrypt everything encrypted with that password. This is, however, not the case in reality: although the intruder possesses a dictionary that contains the password, he does not know which entry in the dictionary it is, and it might be impossible to identify the right entry. In other words, not distinguishing between guessable and known messages in the Dolev-Yao model is like assuming that the intruder "always guesses correctly".

2.2 Rule-Based Extensions of the Dolev-Yao Intruder Model

Despite all these difficulties, it is still attractive to use a model in the style of Dolev and Yao in order to abstract from the details of real cryptography, not only for "standard" protocol analysis but also when considering a guessing intruder. In this way, several approaches, e.g. [10,12,13,17], propose extensions of a Dolev-Yao-style model for off-line guessing, where the guessable messages (i.e. those that occur in the intruder's dictionary) are not part of the initial intruder knowledge, but off-line guessing is modeled by additional rules that describe the intruder's ability to make a guess and verify it. An example of such a rule is:

- If the intruder knows a message m and its symmetric encryption $\{\!|m|\!\}_{pw}$ with a password pw, and pw is guessable,
- then he can verify his guess and thus obtain pw (and add it to his knowledge).

It is easy to convince oneself that such a rule is correct with respect to one's intuition: the intruder can generate, for every pw' in his dictionary, the term $\{\!|m|\!\}_{pw'}$ and compare each result with the original message $\{\!|m|\!\}_{pw}$. Assuming that there are no collisions, there is only one entry in his dictionary, namely pw, such that the constructed message is identical with the original one.

However, it is unclear how we can ever be sure that a given set of such rules is complete, i.e. that all the ways to find out messages by guessing are covered by the rule set. To see how hard it is to find a complete set of rules, consider the following rule, which captures another aspect of guessing:

- If the intruder knows the symmetric encryption $\{\!|\langle m_1, m_2 \rangle|\!\}_{pw}$ with a guessable password pw of a composed message $\langle m_1, m_2 \rangle$ and he knows the first component m_1,
- then he can obtain pw (and thus also m_2).

This is the case because the intruder can attempt to decrypt the given message with every entry in his dictionary as the decryption key, and — again abstracting from collisions — only for one entry of the dictionary, the decrypted message begins with m_1, which he can check as he knows m_1. This identifies the right entry pw in his dictionary and he obtains the second component m_2.

2.3 An Explicit Model of Off-line Guessing

Obviously, one can find many such rules, and even when one arrives at a set of rules that seem to cover one's intuition completely, it is unclear how to prove their completeness, as there is no formal definition of the underlying concept that should be captured by these rules. Also, when extending the model with new cryptographic operators, e.g. exponentiation, one would have to appropriately extend the set of rules for off-line guessing as well.

However, we propose that there is a simple intuition behind the two rules above and similar ones, which is based on operations the intruder can perform on every entry in his dictionary so that he can uniquely determine one particular entry of the dictionary (which then represents the "correct" guess). Our idea to formalize off-line guessing attacks is to formalize this intuition by making explicit the intermediate states of such a computation, which we express via *maps*. Roughly speaking, a map relates each entry of the dictionary (or n-tuples thereof) to the outcome of a sequence of operations under this guess (or these guesses).

v	$\{\!\|m\|\!\}_v$
d_1	$\{\!\|m\|\!\}_{d_1}$
d_2	$\{\!\|m\|\!\}_{d_2}$
⋮	⋮
d_n	$\{\!\|m\|\!\}_{d_n}$

v_1	v_2	$\{\!\|v_2\|\!\}_{v_1}$
d_1	d_1	$\{\!\|d_1\|\!\}_{d_1}$
d_1	d_2	$\{\!\|d_2\|\!\}_{d_1}$
⋮	⋮	⋮
d_n	d_n	$\{\!\|d_n\|\!\}_{d_n}$

v	$\pi_1(\{\!|\{\!\|m_1,m_2\|\!\}_{pw}\!|\!\}_v)$
d_1	$\pi_1(\{\!|\{\!\|m_1,m_2\|\!\}_{pw}\!|\!\}_{d_1})$
d_2	$\pi_1(\{\!|\{\!\|m_1,m_2\|\!\}_{pw}\!|\!\}_{d_2})$
⋮	⋮
d_n	$\pi_1(\{\!|\{\!\|m_1,m_2\|\!\}_{pw}\!|\!\}_{d_n})$

Fig. 1. Three examples of maps

Fig. 1 shows three examples of maps, where the intruder's dictionary contains the entries $\{d_1,\ldots,d_n\}$. The first is the map for the example $\{\!|m|\!\}_{pw}$ covered above, where pw appears in the dictionary, i.e. $d_c = pw$ for the "correct" entry $c \in \{1,\ldots,n\}$: the intruder encrypts the known message m with each of the d_i. Only one of the entries $\{\!|m|\!\}_{d_i}$ corresponds to the original message $\{\!|m|\!\}_{pw}$, and this entry reveals the correct password $pw = d_c$. The second example demonstrates that the concept of maps can be easily extended to multiple guesses: if the intruder knows a term $\{\!|pw'|\!\}_{pw}$ which consists of a guessable message encrypted with a guessable key-term, then the intruder can simply build every encryption of an entry in his dictionary with an entry in his dictionary.

Before we turn to the third example displayed in Fig. 1, we need to consider in more detail one of the simplifying assumptions mentioned above: what happens when encrypted messages are decrypted with a wrong key.

2.4 Decryption with a Wrong Key

In a Dolev-Yao intruder model without guessing, it is not necessary to consider what happens when decrypting messages with a wrong key; this is because the intruder knows whether he knows a particular key. Under the perfect cryptography assumption, he will thus not even attempt to decrypt messages for which he does not know the proper key. Also, we can assume that the intruder will send to honest agents only messages that they can receive, i.e. messages that are encrypted with the keys that the honest agents will use for decryption, since the intruder will not gain anything from a situation where an agent reads some random bits after decryption of incoming messages. When considering guesses, however, it is important to model what happens if the intruder decrypts messages with a wrong key, for instance because he might simply try out every entry of his dictionary as the decryption key.

It has become standard in Dolev-Yao-style intruder models to have explicit rules for decryption of messages, i.e. of the form

- If the intruder knows $\{\!|m|\!\}_k$ and k,
- then he can obtain m by decryption.

Since these rules require that the intruder knows the key k, they are not really appropriate when considering guessed keys. Rather, we want to turn to the original form of the Dolev-Yao model where the intruder can perform encryption and decryption operations using as keys any composition of messages he knows, and we add algebraic equations which, for instance, express that symmetric encryption and decryption with the same key cancel each other out, i.e.

$$\{\!|\{\!|m|\!\}_k|\!\}_k = m \ .$$

Note that, for the sake of simplicity, we have assumed here that symmetric encryption and decryption are in fact the same procedure (as is, for instance, the case for exclusive-or); this is not a restriction but may introduce unrealistic attacks in general.

The reason why we turn to this more complicated model with cancellation equations is that the term $\{\!|\{\!|m|\!\}_k|\!\}_{k'}$ is equal to the term m if and only if $k = k'$ (assuming that there are no other algebraic properties for the operation $\{\!|\cdot|\!\}$). This is exactly what we want, as the intruder can now attempt the decryption with several keys, which results in the original message m only in the case that he used the right key. In all other cases, he obtains a term of the form $\{\!|\{\!|m|\!\}_k|\!\}_{k'}$, which represents some random bits he obtained after decryption, but which he is not a priori able to distinguish from the "real" message m.[1]

We can now return to the third example of Fig. 1, where the intruder tries to find out the guessable password pw of the message $\{\!|\langle m_1, m_2\rangle|\!\}_{pw}$ where he knows the message m_1. Here, we denote with π_1 and π_2 the projections to the first and second component of a pair, i.e. we have the cancellation rules $\pi_1(\langle m_1, m_2\rangle) = m_1$ and $\pi_2(\langle m_1, m_2\rangle) = m_2$. The intruder builds a map in two steps: first he encrypts the given message $\{\!|\langle m_1, m_2\rangle|\!\}_{pw}$ with every entry of the dictionary, and then he builds the projection to the first component. Only for the correct guess, i.e. the entry c with $d_c = pw$, the resulting message has the property

$$\pi_1(\{\!|\{\!|\langle m_1, m_2\rangle|\!\}_{pw}|\!\}_{d_c}) = \pi_1(\langle m_1, m_2\rangle) = m_1 \ ,$$

and thus there is exactly one entry in this map that equals m_1, while all other entries are "irreducible" terms in the sense that they are not equal to any simpler term. Note that the intruder could not verify the correct entry the way we showed, if he did not initially know the message m_1 (and there is no other way to verify the guess).

To summarize, we have so far described a model where the intruder can compose maps by applying operations on every term in a dictionary and on messages that he knows for sure, and compare the outcome of each entry in the map with other messages he knows. Only in the case that there is a single entry in the map that he can distinguish from the other ones is the guessing successful in the sense that he can identify the correct value(s) of the guess(es). Observe that this model is independent from the concrete set of operators and algebraic equations considered (we have only used them for concrete examples) and we can

---

[1] Note that in the case that symmetric encryption and decryption are the same algorithm as in our example, the intruder might even construct the term $\{\!|\{\!|\{\!|m|\!\}_k|\!\}_{k'}|\!\}_{k'}$ by re-encrypting the term with the same key he used for decryption and, modulo the cancellation, obtain the term he started with, i.e. $\{\!|m|\!\}_k$.

thus entirely avoid specifying a large set of rules to capture all circumstances in which an intruder can guess certain messages. In fact, we have only two "rules": firstly, the intruder can arbitrarily compose messages and maps that he already knows to form new maps, and secondly, he can check if there is a particular entry in a map. In fact, as we will explain in the next section, we do not need to distinguish between messages and maps any more, as we can regard any message as a special case of a map with only one entry.

Before we introduce our formalization of off-line guessing, let us conclude this section with some remarks. First, observe that the above discussion does not contain any notion of the probability that a guessing attack is successful. Furthermore, it does not depend on the size of the dictionary, and ignores the case that a password might be guessable (in the sense that it stems from a small set of values), but is not contained in the concrete dictionary of the intruder. The reason why these technical details can be ignored is that one might consider a protocol as vulnerable if there is the mere possibility to mount an attack. In fact, although the vulnerability of a protocol to off-line guessing attacks can be modeled by expressing explicitly the probability of the intruder guessing correctly, in our model we are only concerned with expressing whether this vulnerability exists or not. Hence, a protocol that is vulnerable to off-line guessing according to our model might still be "safe" in practice if the users choose good passwords that cannot be easily guessed so that the attack becomes infeasible. Finally, one may wonder what consequences would arise if we consider an intruder with several dictionaries (instead of just one). It is, however, not difficult to see that this cannot affect our notion of a guessing attack as one could consider the union of all such dictionaries as *the* intruder's dictionary.

3 A Formal Model for Off-line Guessing

We now introduce our formalization of off-line guessing: we give a Dolev-Yao-style deduction system that attempts to capture the intuitions behind off-line guessing in a uniform and general way. As we remarked above, our formalization works at the level of messages and is thus independent of the overall protocol model and of the details of the considered intruder model, i.e. cryptographic primitives, algebraic properties, and intruder capabilities. Moreover, it allows us to consider multiple guesses simultaneously.

Definition 1. *An* intruder model $\mathcal{I} = (\Sigma, \mathcal{O}, \approx, \mathcal{D})$ *consists of a finite set* Σ *of operators where* $\Sigma_0 \subseteq \Sigma$ *is a set of constants (i.e. symbols of arity 0), a subset* $\mathcal{O} \subseteq \Sigma$ *of these operators, called the* intruder-accessible *operators, a congruence relation* $\approx \; \subseteq T_\Sigma^2$ *on terms (usually defined through a set of equations), and a finite dictionary* $\mathcal{D} \subseteq \Sigma_0$, *where* $\mathcal{D} \cap \mathcal{O} = \emptyset$ *and* $d_1 \not\approx d_2$ *for any pair of constants* $d_1, d_2 \in \mathcal{D}$ *with* $d_1 \neq d_2$.[2] *Also, let V be a set of variables disjoint from symbols in* Σ.

---

[2] For convenient modeling of fresh data, the signature Σ may contain infinitely many constants, as long as the dictionary $\mathcal{D}$ is finite, without affecting the results presented here. We assume, however, a finite signature for simplicity.

We assume that the reader is familiar with standard concepts like terms and substitutions (see, for instance, [3]). Given a substitution σ and a term t, we denote the application of σ to t by writing $t\sigma$, the domain of σ by writing $\mathrm{dom}(\sigma)$, and the variables of t by writing $\mathrm{vars}(t)$. In this paper, we consider only substitutions of variables with guesses (i.e. elements of the dictionary $\mathcal{D}$).

Example 1. As a running example, we will consider the intruder model

$$\mathcal{I}_e = (\Sigma_e, \mathcal{O}_e, \approx_e, \mathcal{D}_e),$$

where the signature Σ_e consists of a set of constants Σ_{0e} and the following operators: asymmetric encryption $\{\cdot\}.$, the inverse key of an asymmetric key-pair $\cdot^{-1}$, symmetric encryption $\{\!|\cdot|\!\}.$, function application $\cdot(\cdot)$, and pairing $\langle\cdot,\cdot\rangle$, as well as the two corresponding projections $\pi_1(\cdot)$ and $\pi_2(\cdot)$. All operators besides Σ_{0e} and $\cdot^{-1}$ are accessible to the intruder, i.e. $\mathcal{O}_e = \Sigma_e \setminus (\Sigma_{0e} \cup \{\cdot^{-1}\})$. Equivalence on terms is equality in the quotient algebra $\mathcal{T}_{\Sigma_e}/\approx_e$ for the following equations:

$$\{\{m\}_k\}_{k^{-1}} \approx_e m, \qquad \{\!|\{\!|m|\!\}_k|\!\}_k \approx_e m, \qquad (k^{-1})^{-1} \approx_e k,$$
$$\pi_1(\langle m_1, m_2\rangle) \approx_e m_1, \qquad \pi_2(\langle m_1, m_2\rangle) \approx_e m_2.$$

The dictionary $\mathcal{D}_e$ consists of a set of constants $\mathcal{D}_e = \{d_1, \ldots, d_n\}$. □

Our formalization is based on the notion of *maps* introduced in the previous section, as illustrated in Fig. 1. As we remarked above, a map is the result of the intruder constructing a message from his knowledge and inserting, in place of an unknown value, every value from the dictionary he uses to perform the attack. The main characteristic of a map is that it is uniform and complete, in the sense that exactly the same sequence of operations is performed for the various values of the guesses, and that all possible guesses in the dictionary are considered. In order to formally define what we mean by "the same sequence of operations" of a map, we introduce the notion of a *pattern term*:

Definition 2. *Let $\mathcal{I} = (\Sigma, \mathcal{O}, \approx, \mathcal{D})$ be an intruder model. A pattern term (or, simply, pattern) P is simply an element of $\mathcal{T}_\Sigma(V)$. We say that a set M is a map iff there is a pattern term P such that*

$$M = \{(\sigma, P\sigma) \mid \mathrm{dom}(\sigma) = \mathrm{vars}(P) \land \forall v \in \mathrm{vars}(P).\ v\sigma \in \mathcal{D}\}.$$

Note that this formal definition represents exactly the way we described maps informally in the previous section, namely as tables of guesses and the corresponding outcomes. For instance, each of the three maps displayed in Fig. 1 is represented by the term on top of the right-most column, i.e. $\{\!|m|\!\}_v$, $\{\!|v_2|\!\}_{v_1}$, and $\pi_1(\{\!|\{\!|\langle m_1, m_2\rangle|\!\}_{pw}|\!\}_v)$, respectively.

Note also that it follows straightforwardly from the definition that there is a bijection between maps and patterns, modulo equivalence of patterns and renaming of variables. Hence, a map is uniquely represented by a pattern that is parameterized over a set of data to be guessed, and the intruder's computation of the outcome of this pattern for every possible combination of candidate values for the guesses.

Given this bijection, in the following we will identify maps and their corresponding patterns. In particular, for a map M and the corresponding pattern P, we will identify entries of M and substitutions of variables with guesses in P, as well as look-up in M and the term resulting from the application of a substitution of variables with guesses in P.

Maps are expressive constructs: we can view all messages as maps with just one entry, represented by a ground term (so the only substitution possible is the identity). Also, the dictionary itself is a map, which is represented by a variable v. This expressiveness allows us to consider a formal model where the intruder knowledge consists only of maps.

We now define an entailment relation over maps, which tells us when the intruder can derive a map from a set of maps. In particular, given that we identify maps with corresponding patterns, we define the entailment over patterns for simplicity. This entailment relation yields a deduction system. Given that "normal" messages are a special case of maps, we can see this system as an extension of (a system for) the standard Dolev-Yao intruder. We therefore call this system the *guessing Dolev-Yao intruder* and denote the relation by $\cdot \in \mathcal{GDY}_\mathcal{I}(\cdot)$.

Definition 3. *Let* $\mathcal{I} = (\Sigma, \mathcal{O}, \approx, \mathcal{D})$ *be an intruder model. The entailment relation* $P \in \mathcal{GDY}_\mathcal{I}(\mathcal{P})$, *which expresses that the set of patterns* $\mathcal{P}$ *entails the pattern* P, *is the smallest relation closed under the following rules:*

$$\frac{}{P \in \mathcal{GDY}_\mathcal{I}(\mathcal{P})} \text{ AX}P \text{ (for } P \in \mathcal{P}), \qquad \frac{}{v \in \mathcal{GDY}_\mathcal{I}(\mathcal{P})} \text{ AX}v \text{ (for } v \in V),$$

$$\frac{P_1 \in \mathcal{GDY}_\mathcal{I}(\mathcal{P}) \quad \cdots \quad P_n \in \mathcal{GDY}_\mathcal{I}(\mathcal{P})}{op(P_1, \ldots, P_n) \in \mathcal{GDY}_\mathcal{I}(\mathcal{P})} \text{ OP (for } op \in \mathcal{O} \text{ with arity } n),$$

$$\frac{P_1 \in \mathcal{GDY}_\mathcal{I}(\mathcal{P}) \quad P_2 \in \mathcal{GDY}_\mathcal{I}(\mathcal{P})}{v\sigma \in \mathcal{GDY}_\mathcal{I}(\mathcal{P})} \text{ VER},$$

where the rule VER *has the following side conditions:*

- $v \in \text{vars}(P_1) \cup \text{vars}(P_2)$,
- $\Theta = \{\sigma \mid \text{dom}(\sigma) = \text{vars}(P_1) \cup \text{vars}(P_2) \wedge \forall v \in \text{dom}(\sigma). \, v\sigma \in \mathcal{D}\}$,
- $\sigma \in \Theta$,
- $P_1 \sigma \approx P_2 \sigma$,
- $\forall \sigma' \in \Theta. \, \text{different}_{P_1,P_2}(\sigma, \sigma') \implies P_1 \sigma' \not\approx P_2 \sigma'$, *where* $\text{different}_{P_1,P_2}(\sigma, \sigma')$ *stands for:* $P_1 \sigma \not\approx P_1 \sigma' \vee P_2 \sigma \not\approx P_2 \sigma'$,
- $\forall P' \in \mathcal{T}_\Sigma(V). \, P' \approx P_1 \implies \text{vars}(P') \supseteq \text{vars}(P_1)$ *and* $\forall P' \in \mathcal{T}_\Sigma(V). \, P' \approx P_2 \implies \text{vars}(P') \supseteq \text{vars}(P_2)$.

The first two axiomatic rules are straightforward: a set of patterns $\mathcal{P}$ entails all patterns that are contained within it, and for any guessable value, a set of patterns $\mathcal{P}$ entails a pattern representing an unverified guess of that value that has the whole of dictionary $\mathcal{D}$ as candidates. (Recall that we consider only substitutions of variables with guesses in $\mathcal{D}$.) The rule OP expresses how patterns can be combined. Given n patterns entailed by $\mathcal{P}$, the rule states that they can be combined using an n-ary operator $op \in \mathcal{O}$ yielding a pattern that is the application of op on the constituent patterns.

As explained in the previous section, the standard Dolev-Yao intruder system includes both synthesis rules for composing messages and analysis rules for decomposing them; see, for example, [4,5,6]. Examples of the latter type are decryption and the projection of a paired message into its two components. Using the equational theory, however, one can express analysis steps of the intruder as composition using decryption operators (and cancellation of encryption and decryption with corresponding keys).

We now turn our attention to the verification of guesses, rule VER. In general, verifying a guess requires that the intruder can construct two maps that correspond on exactly one entry (we discuss below how we formalize different substitutions, representing different entries, modulo the algebraic properties). Thus, there is one uniquely determined substitution of dictionary entries for the variables in the two corresponding patterns which yields the same message. This substitution corresponds to the correct guesses, and after verifying his guesses, the intruder learns these correct values for the guesses in the classical sense. Note that this simple definition avoids any notion of "different ways to construct the same message" as is often required in other formal approaches to guessing. Rather, the definition implicitly prevents that the intruder can "cheat himself": suppose he tries to verify something by taking two copies of the same map (which is not forbidden); then either the maps do not contain any variables (so there is nothing guessable to obtain) or the two maps correspond on all substitutions.

To illustrate this further, let us consider the case where the intruder has derived two patterns P_1 and P_2, and Θ is the set of all substitutions for the variables of P_1 and P_2 with entries of the dictionary. If there is one substitution $\sigma \in \Theta$ on which the two patterns yield the same message, $P_1 \sigma \approx P_2 \sigma$, and the patterns differ for all different substitutions, then the intruder has indeed verified the correct value for any of the data that he has guessed in the two patterns/maps. Thus, for any variable $v \in \text{vars}(P_1) \cup \text{vars}(P_2)$ in the two patterns, he can derive the correct value $v\sigma$.

Recall that we identify entries of a map and substitutions of variables with guesses in the corresponding pattern. The notion of different substitutions σ and σ' (in the sense that they represent different entries) is not simply $\sigma \neq \sigma'$ for the following reason. A map may contain several different entries that yield the same value. Consider, for instance, an intruder model that extends our running example $\mathcal{I}_e$ with an operator $\oplus$ representing exclusive-or, which has, among other properties, the property of being commutative. Assume further that the intruder knows the message $P_1 = pw_1 \oplus pw_2$ for two guessable but unknown passwords pw_1 and pw_2. To find out the passwords, the intruder constructs the map $P_2 = v_1 \oplus v_2$. The problem now is that for the two different entries

$\sigma = [v_1 \mapsto pw_1, v_2 \mapsto pw_2]$ and $\sigma' = [v_1 \mapsto pw_2, v_2 \mapsto pw_1]$ we have $P_2\sigma \approx P_2\sigma'$ due to the algebraic properties, and thus there are several entries on which the two maps P_1 and P_2 correspond. Therefore, our notion of different entries is relative to two maps that we want to compare, and we thus consider those pairs of substitutions σ and σ' as being different entries relative to the maps P_1 and P_2 if they indeed make a difference in at least one of the maps, i.e. if $P_1\sigma \not\approx P_1\sigma'$ or if $P_2\sigma \not\approx P_2\sigma'$.

Finally, note that the last pair of side conditions of the rule VER ensures that for the verification the intruder uses only maps P_1 and P_2 that are not equivalent to some map P' that comprises fewer variables. For instance, for our example intruder model, the rule VER cannot be applied to the map $\{\!|\{\!|m|\!\}_v|\!\}_v$ as this map is equivalent by $\approx_e$ to the map m. In other words, this condition expresses that we don't consider maps with redundant variables, i.e. those on which the outcome does not depend.

The formal model presented here only allows for derivations that are indeed possible according to the intuition given in the previous section. On the other hand, all operations the intruder could perform according to this intuition have a counter-part in the formal model, since composition and decomposition of messages with guesses is described by respective operations on maps/patterns, and verification of guesses is described by the comparison of maps/patterns. But, of course, one can only informally justify that a formal model captures the intuition underlying it.

Example 2. We illustrate with the examples from the previous section, using our paradigmatic intruder model $\mathcal{I}_e = (\Sigma_e, \mathcal{O}_e, \approx_e, \mathcal{D}_e)$. In the first example, the intruder knowledge consists of a set of patterns $\mathcal{P}$ that contains the messages $\{\!|m|\!\}_{pw}$ and m, and $pw \in \mathcal{D}_e$ is guessable. The intruder first constructs the map $\{\!|m|\!\}_v$ by encrypting m with every entry of the dictionary, and then compares it with the original message $\{\!|m|\!\}_{pw}$ to verify his guess of pw. This comparison is possible since there is exactly one entry in the dictionary that equals pw and no other substitution for v that can make $\{\!|m|\!\}_{pw}$ and $\{\!|m|\!\}_v$ equal:

$$\cfrac{\cfrac{}{\{\!|m|\!\}_{pw} \in \mathcal{GDY}_{\mathcal{I}_e}(\mathcal{P})} \text{AXP} \quad \cfrac{\cfrac{}{v \in \mathcal{GDY}_{\mathcal{I}_e}(\mathcal{P})} \text{AX}v \quad \cfrac{}{m \in \mathcal{GDY}_{\mathcal{I}_e}(\mathcal{P})} \text{AXP}}{\{\!|m|\!\}_v \in \mathcal{GDY}_{\mathcal{I}_e}(\mathcal{P})} \text{OP}}{pw \in \mathcal{GDY}_{\mathcal{I}_e}(\mathcal{P})} \text{VER}$$

In the second example, the intruder knowledge $\mathcal{P}$ contains $\{\!|m_2|\!\}_{m_1}$, but neither m_1 nor m_2. Further, both m_1 and m_2 are guessable, i.e. $m_1, m_2 \in \mathcal{D}_e$. The intruder first encrypts every entry of the dictionary with every entry of the dictionary to obtain the pattern $\{\!|v_2|\!\}_{v_1}$, which he can then compare to $\{\!|m_2|\!\}_{m_1}$. Since again only the substitution with the correct guesses can make the two terms equal, he obtains both m_1 and m_2 by this comparison. Simplifying the presentation, we have joined the derivation of the two messages into one tree:

1. $A \rightarrow S : A$
2. $S \rightarrow A : Ns$
3. $A \rightarrow S : Na, H(Pw, Na, Ns, A)$
4. $S \rightarrow A : H(Pw, Na)$

Fig. 2. The MS-CHAPv2 Protocol

$$\dfrac{\dfrac{}{\{\!|m_2|\!\}_{m_1} \in \mathcal{GDY}_{\mathcal{I}_e}(\mathcal{P})}\text{AX}P \qquad \dfrac{\dfrac{}{v_1 \in \mathcal{GDY}_{\mathcal{I}_e}(\mathcal{P})}\text{AX}v \quad \dfrac{}{v_2 \in \mathcal{GDY}_{\mathcal{I}_e}(\mathcal{P})}\text{AX}v}{\{\!|v_2|\!\}_{v_1} \in \mathcal{GDY}_{\mathcal{I}_e}(\mathcal{P})}\text{OP}}{m_1, m_2 \in \mathcal{GDY}_{\mathcal{I}_e}(\mathcal{P})}\text{VER}$$

In the third example, the intruder knowledge $\mathcal{P}$ contains the messages m_1 and $\{\!|\langle m_1, m_2\rangle|\!\}_{pw}$, and pw is guessable. The intruder tries to decrypt this message with every entry in his dictionary, obtaining the pattern $\{\!|\{\!|\langle m_1, m_2\rangle|\!\}_{pw}|\!\}_v$, and then builds the projection to the first component for every entry, which yields the pattern $\pi_1(\{\!|\{\!|\langle m_1, m_2\rangle|\!\}_{pw}|\!\}_v)$. He compares this pattern with the known message m_1 and only for the right guess $v = pw$ the pattern yields this value, so he obtains pw:

$$\dfrac{\dfrac{}{\{\!|m_2|\!\}_{m_1} \in \mathcal{GDY}_{\mathcal{I}_e}(\mathcal{P})}\text{AX}P \qquad \dfrac{\dfrac{}{v_1 \in \mathcal{GDY}_{\mathcal{I}_e}(\mathcal{P})}\text{AX}v \quad \dfrac{}{v_2 \in \mathcal{GDY}_{\mathcal{I}_e}(\mathcal{P})}\text{AX}v}{\{\!|v_2|\!\}_{v_1} \in \mathcal{GDY}_{\mathcal{I}_e}(\mathcal{P})}\text{OP}}{m_1, m_2 \in \mathcal{GDY}_{\mathcal{I}_e}(\mathcal{P})}\text{VER}$$

□

4 A Concrete Example: The MS-CHAPv2 Protocol

As a concrete example, we consider an entire protocol, namely Microsoft's Challenge/Response Authentication Protocol, version 2 (MS-CHAPv2 [21]). MS-CHAPv2 is the authentication mechanism for the Point-to-Point Tunneling Protocol (PPTP [16]), which itself is used to secure PPP connections over TCP/IP. It is well known that this protocol is vulnerable to off-line guessing attacks [20], and we illustrate how one can easily detect this vulnerability using our approach.

Fig. 2 shows an abstracted version of the MS-CHAPv2 Protocol in the Alice& Bob-style notation that is standard in the literature. Note that, for simplicity, we refrain here from explicitly displaying the pairing operator and simply use commas. The protocol should achieve mutual authentication between a client A and server S based on an initially shared password Pw, which we of course assume to be guessable.

As an illustrative case, let us consider the situation in which the intruder has observed a single run of the protocol between two honest agents a (playing in

$$\frac{\overline{h(\langle pw, na\rangle) \in \mathcal{GDY}_{\mathcal{I}_e}(\mathcal{P})} \;\text{AXP} \quad \overset{\Pi}{h(\langle v, na\rangle) \in \mathcal{GDY}_{\mathcal{I}_e}(\mathcal{P})}}{pw \in \mathcal{GDY}_{\mathcal{I}_e}(\mathcal{P})} \;\text{VER}$$

where Π is

$$\frac{\overline{h \in \mathcal{GDY}_{\mathcal{I}_e}(\mathcal{P})} \;\text{AXP} \quad \frac{\overline{v \in \mathcal{GDY}_{\mathcal{I}_e}(\mathcal{P})} \;\text{AX}v \quad \overline{na \in \mathcal{GDY}_{\mathcal{I}_e}(\mathcal{P})} \;\text{AXP}}{\langle v, na\rangle \in \mathcal{GDY}_{\mathcal{I}_e}(\mathcal{P})} \;\text{OP}}{h(\langle v, na\rangle) \in \mathcal{GDY}_{\mathcal{I}_e}(\mathcal{P})} \;\text{OP}$$

Fig. 3. An example derivation using the deduction system of Section 3

the role A) and s (playing in the role S). Then the intruder has the following knowledge (assuming that he knows the hash-function h):

$$\mathcal{P} = \{a, s, h, na, ns, h(pw, na, ns, a), h(pw, na)\} \; .$$

Note that we have used lower-case letters to distinguish the concrete data of a protocol run from the protocol variables. Fig. 3 shows that, from this knowledge, the intruder can indeed derive pw, if it is guessable.

He simply generates a map for the hash-value of the message under all values of his dictionary in place of pw, and compares the outcome with the observed message. Note that a similar attack would have already been possible after observing only the first three messages of the protocol, since the intruder can similarly build the hash-value of message three under all guesses for the password. Note also that, as we remarked above, in our model we only investigate whether a protocol is vulnerable to off-line guessing or not. Hence, if the users choose good passwords that cannot be easily guessed, it might be infeasible to exploit in practice the vulnerability of the MS-CHAPv2 Protocol that we have just described.

To conclude the section, observe that all examples we have given in this paper are examples of the intruder successfully attacking a protocol by off-line guessing. However, even though we lack space to go into the details, we observe that we can also use our formalization as the basis to prove the absence of vulnerabilities of a protocol even under off-line guessing, both in model-checking approaches (where we usually bound the number of sessions considered) or in theorem-proving ones (where we can inductively show the correctness for all situations).

5 Related Work and Concluding Remarks

We have given a formalization of off-line guessing (in the context of the idealized Dolev-Yao intruder model) which is based on the notion of using maps to explicitly represent the intermediate computation steps of an intruder during guessing. Our formalization is general and uniform in the sense that it is independent of the overall protocol model and of the details of the considered intruder model, i.e. cryptographic primitives, algebraic properties, and intruder capabilities. Moreover, it allows us to consider multiple guesses simultaneously.

Several other approaches have similarly considered extensions of the Dolev-Yao model with additional intruder capabilities to model a notion of off-line guessing, starting with the work of [17], which inspired [10,12] and was extended in [18]. These first approaches are somewhat limited (for instance [12,17] consider only single guesses) and are thus helpful to find protocol attacks, but are not fully appropriate for providing a definition of off-line guessing and verifying that a protocol is invulnerable to such guessing attacks.

The more advanced approach of [13] presents a theory of off-line guessing that overcomes such limitations and also includes an analysis of its complexity and a basis for an efficient implementation using a symbolic intruder model. Like previous approaches, it is, however, specialized to the standard Dolev-Yao intruder under a free term algebra, and it is based on involved syntactic concepts like normalized intruder derivations to ensure that the guessing extension is not "too powerful" (in the sense that the intruder could derive almost everything that is guessable). The approach of [11] is the closest to ours as it also employs cancellation equations rather than explicit decryption rules. Moreover, like our approach, it is not specialized to a particular intruder model, although it is based on an explicit formalization of protocols using the applied pi calculus of [2] where security properties are defined using a notion of indistinguishability of processes. In [1], the authors show that the intruder deduction problem in this formalism is undecidable unless one imposes strong restrictions on the considered equational theory, and we believe that similar properties hold also for our formalization. It is however not easy, at least in our opinion, to estimate whether the approaches of [11,13], as well as the previous ones, indeed faithfully formalize the notion of off-line guessing, as it is not completely clear what notion they capture. In essence, these works formally define derivation systems but give little intuition about how their respective systems relate to a common-sense understanding of off-line guessing.

We believe that one of the major contributions of our work is that it describes and formalizes such a common-sense intuition of off-line guessing in a precise way and thus provides an appropriate bridge between the intuitions and a formal model of them. A detailed investigation of our intuition led us to the notion of maps on which our formalization is based. In fact, one might say that maps provide a semantical basis for our rules as they make explicit the intermediate computations of an intruder during an off-line guessing attack. We therefore believe that our formalization is not only uniform and more general, but also conceptually simpler and easier to understand than previous approaches. Note, however, that our approach is based on algebraic equations, and is thus more difficult to implement within a protocol analysis tool than the less expressive approaches. In this paper, we have placed the emphasis on the theoretical foundations underlying our model of guessing, but we are currently working on how our deduction system can be deployed in practice by integrating it into the symbolic *lazy intruder* model that underlies our protocol model-checker OFMC [4,5,6].

We conclude by highlighting an open problem that our approach does not address (and that is not mentioned in other works on off-line guessing): when the intruder has verified a guess, for instance, of a password pw belonging to an agent A, then the guessed value is added to his "classical" knowledge. He can then use it, for example, to decrypt other messages. While this is exactly what one might expect, a problem arises when another agent, say B, accidentally has the same guessable password (in theory, there might be several such agents). In this case, in verifying his guess of A's password pw, the intruder has — quite inadvertently — also learned B's password. This problem arises if the intruder did not initially know that there was any correlation between the two passwords. This issue can easily be resolved in the case of passwords, as we can simply model the passwords of different agents by different constants. However, it is not clear how to proceed for other guessable data, like protocol key-words. This problem is related with the question of how much the intruder knows about the format of messages — and the relation of several constants in them. We leave a closer investigation of these issues for future work.

Acknowledgments. We thank Penny Anderson and David Basin for many inspiring discussions, and the anonymous referees for their helpful comments.

References

1. M. Abadi and V. Cortier. Deciding knowledge in security protocols under equational theories. In *Proc. ICALP'04*, LNCS 3142. Springer, 2004.
2. M. Abadi and C. Fournet. Mobile values, new names, and secure communication. In *Proc. POPL'01*. ACM Press, 2004.
3. F. Baader and T. Nipkow. *Term Rewriting and All That*. Cambridge U. Pr., 1998.
4. D. Basin, S. Mödersheim, and L. Viganò. An On-The-Fly Model-Checker for Security Protocol Analysis. In *Proc. ESORICS'03*, LNCS 2808. Springer, 2003.
5. D. Basin, S. Mödersheim, and L. Viganò. Constraint Differentiation: A New Reduction Technique for Constraint-Based Analysis of Security Protocols. In *Proc. CCS'03*. ACM Press, 2003.
6. D. Basin, S. Mödersheim, and L. Viganò. OFMC: A Symbolic Model-Checker for Security Protocols. *International Journal of Information Security*. 2004.
7. M. Bellare, D. Pointcheval, and P. Rogaway. Authenticated key exchange secure against dictionary attacks. In *Proc. EUROCRYPT'00*, LNCS 1807. Springer, 2000.
8. S. M. Bellovin and M. Merritt. Encrypted key exchange: Password-based protocols secure against dictionary attacks. In *Proc. IEEE Symposium on Security and Privacy 1992*. IEEE Computer Society Press, 1992.
9. E. Bresson, O. Chevassut, and D. Pointcheval. Security proofs for an efficient password-based key exchange. In *Proc. CCS'03*. ACM Press, 2003.
10. E. Cohen. Proving cryptographic protocols safe from guessing attacks. In *Proc. Foundations of Computer Security'02*. 2002.
11. R. Corin, J. Doumen, and S. Etalle. Analysing password protocol security against off-line dictionary attacks. In *Proc. WISP'04*. Electronic Notes in Theoretical Computer Science, 2004.

12. R. Corin, S. Malladi, J. Alves-Foss, and S. Etalle. Guess what? Here is a new tool that finds some new guessing attacks (extended abstract.) In *Proc. WITS'03*, Dip. Scienze dell'Informazione, Università di Bologna, Italy, 2003.
13. S. Delaune and F. Jacquemard. A theory of guessing attacks and its complexity. Research Report LSV-04-1, Lab. Specification and Verification, ENS de Cachan, France, 2004.
14. D. Dolev and A. Yao. On the Security of Public-Key Protocols. *IEEE Transactions on Information Theory*, 2(29), 1983.
15. L. Gong, T. M. A. Lomas, R. M. Needham, and J. H. Saltzer. Protecting poorly chosen secrets from guessing attacks. *IEEE Journal on Selected Areas in Communications*, 11(5):648–656, 1993.
16. K. Hamzeh, G. Pall, W. Verthein, J. Taarud, W. Little, and G. Zorn. RFC 2637: Point-to-Point Tunneling Protocol, July 1999. Status: Informational.
17. G. Lowe. Analysing Protocols Subject to Guessing Attacks. In *Proc. WITS 2002*.
18. G. Lowe. Analysing Protocols Subject to Guessing Attacks. *Journal of Computer Security*, 12(1), 2004.
19. R. Morris and K. Thompson. Password security: A case history. *Communications of the ACM*, 22(11):594, 1979.
20. B. Schneier, Mudge, and D. Wagner. Cryptanalysis of Microsoft's PPTP authentication extensions (MS-CHAPv2). In *Proc. CQRE'99*, LNCS 1740, Springer, 1999.
21. G. Zorn. RFC 2759: Microsoft PPP CHAP Extensions, Version 2, Jan. 2000. Status: Informational.

Abstraction-Carrying Code

Elvira Albert[1], Germán Puebla[2], and Manuel Hermenegildo[2,3]

[1] DSIP, Universidad Complutense Madrid
[2] Facultad de Informática, Technical University of Madrid
[3] Depts. of Comp. Sci. and El. and Comp. Eng., U. of New Mexico

Abstract. *Proof-Carrying Code* (PCC) is a general approach to mobile code safety in which programs are augmented with a certificate (or proof). The practical uptake of PCC greatly depends on the existence of a variety of enabling technologies which allow both to prove programs correct and to replace a costly verification process by an efficient checking procedure on the consumer side. In this work we propose *Abstraction-Carrying Code* (ACC), a novel approach which uses abstract interpretation as enabling technology. We argue that the large body of applications of abstract interpretation to program verification is amenable to the overall PCC scheme. In particular, we rely on an expressive class of safety policies which can be defined over different abstract domains. We use an *abstraction* (or abstract model) of the program computed by standard static analyzers as a certificate. The validity of the abstraction on the consumer side is checked in a single-pass by a very efficient and specialized abstract-interpreter. We believe that ACC brings the expressiveness, flexibility and automation which is inherent in abstract interpretation techniques to the area of mobile code safety. We have implemented and benchmarked ACC within the `Ciao` system preprocessor. The experimental results show that the checking phase is indeed faster than the proof generation phase, and that the sizes of certificates are reasonable.

1 Introduction

One of the most important challenges which computing research faces today is the development of security techniques for verifying that the execution of a program (possibly) supplied by an untrusted source is *safe*, i.e., it meets certain properties according to a predefined *safety policy*. Proof-Carrying Code (PCC) [15] is an enabling technology for mobile code safety which proposes to associate safety information in the form of a *certificate* to programs. The certificate (or proof) is created at compile time, and packaged along with the untrusted code. The consumer who receives or downloads the code+certificate package can then run a *checker* which by a straightforward inspection of the code and the certificate, can verify the validity of the certificate and thus compliance with the safety policy. The key benefit of this "certificate-based" approach to mobile code safety is that the consumer's task is reduced from the level of proving to the level of checking. Indeed the (proof) checker performs a task that should be much simpler, efficient, and automatic than generating the original certificate.

The practical uptake of PCC greatly depends on the existence of a variety of enabling technologies which allow:

1. defining *expressive safety policies* covering a wide range of properties,
2. solving the problem of how to *automatically generate the certificates* (i.e., automatically proving the programs correct), and
3. replacing a costly verification process by an efficient checking procedure on the consumer side.

The main approaches applied up to now are based on theorem proving and type analysis. For instance, in PCC the certificate is originally a proof in first-order logic of certain *verification conditions* and the checking process involves ensuring that the certificate is indeed a valid first-order proof. In Typed Assembly Languages [13], the certificate is a type annotation of the assembly language program and the checking process involves a form of type checking. Each of the different approaches possess their own set of stronger and weaker points. Depending on the particular safety property and the available computing resources in the consumer, some approaches are more suitable than others. In some cases the priority is to reduce the size of the certificate as much as possible in order to fit in small devices or to cope with scarce network access (as in, e.g., Oracle-based PCC [17] or Tactic-based PCC [1]), whereas in other cases the priority is to reduce the checking time (as in, e.g., standard PCC [15] or lightweight bytecode verification [11]). As a result of all this, a successful certificate infrastructure should have a wide set of enabling technologies available for the different requirements.

In this work we propose *Abstraction-Carrying Code* (ACC), a novel approach which uses *abstract interpretation* [5] as enabling technology to handle the above practical (and difficult) challenges. Abstract interpretation is now a well established technique which has allowed the development of very sophisticated global static program analyses that are at the same time automatic, provably correct, and practical. The basic idea of abstract interpretation is to infer information on programs by interpreting ("running") them using abstract values rather than concrete ones, thus obtaining safe approximations of the behavior of the program. The technique allows inferring much richer information than, for example, traditional types. This includes data structure shape (with pointer sharing), bounds on data structure sizes, and other operational variable instantiation properties, as well as procedure-level properties such as determinacy, termination, non-failure, and bounds on resource consumption (time or space cost). Our proposal, ACC, opens the door to the applicability of the above domains as enabling technology for PCC. In particular, ACC has the following three fundamental elements:

1. An expressive class of safety policies based on "abstract"—i.e. symbolic— properties over different abstract domains. Our framework is parametric w.r.t. the abstract domain(s) of interest, which gives us generality and expressiveness.

2. A fixpoint static analyzer is used to automatically infer an abstract model (or simply *abstraction*) about the mobile code which can then be used to prove that the code is safe w.r.t. the given policy in a straightforward way. We identify the particular *subset* of the analysis results which is sufficient for this purpose.
3. A simple, easy-to-trust (analysis) checker verifies the validity of the information on the mobile code. It is indeed a specialized abstract interpreter whose key characteristic is that it does not need to iterate in order to reach a fixpoint (in contrast to standard analyzers).

While ACC is a general approach, for concreteness we develop herein an incarnation of it in the context of (Constraint) Logic Programming, (C)LP, because this paradigm offers a good number of advantages, an important one being the maturity and sophistication of the analysis tools available for it. Also for concreteness, we build on the algorithms of (and report on an implementation on) CiaoPP [8], the abstract interpretation-based preprocessor of the Ciao multi-paradigm (Constraint) Logic Programming system. CiaoPP uses modular, incremental abstract interpretation as a fundamental tool to obtain information about programs. The semantic approximations thus produced have been applied to perform high- and low-level optimizations during program compilation, including transformations such as multiple abstract specialization, parallelization, resource usage control, and program verification. We report on our extension of the framework to incorporate ACC and on how this instantiation of ACC already shows promising results.

2 An Assertion Language to Specify the Safety Policy

The purpose of a *safety policy* is to specify precisely the conditions under which the execution of a program is considered safe. We propose the use of (a subset of) the high-level *assertion* language [18] available in CiaoPP to define an expressive class of safety policies in the context of *constraint logic programs*.

2.1 Preliminaries and Notation

We assume familiarity with constraint logic programming [10] (CLP) and the concepts of abstract interpretation [5] which underlie most analyses in CLP. The remaining of this section introduces some notation and recalls preliminary concepts on these topics.

Terms are constructed from variables (e.g., X), functors (e.g., f) and predicates (e.g., p). We denote by $\{X_1 \mapsto t_1, \ldots, X_n \mapsto t_n\}$ the *substitution* σ with $\sigma(X_i) = t_i$ for all $i = 1, \ldots, n$ (with $X_i \neq X_j$ if $i \neq j$) and $\sigma(X) = X$ for any other variable X, where t_i are terms. A *renaming* is a substitution ρ for which there exists the inverse ρ^{-1} such that $\rho\rho^{-1} \equiv \rho^{-1}\rho \equiv id$. We say that a renaming ρ is a *renaming substitution* of term t_1 w.r.t. term t_2 if $t_2 = \rho(t_1)$.

A *constraint* is essentially a conjunction of expressions built from predefined predicates. An *atom* has the form $p(t_1, \ldots, t_n)$ where p is a predicate symbol and the t_i are terms. A *literal* is either an atom or a constraint. A *goal* is a finite sequence of literals. A *rule* is of the form $H \leftarrow B$ where H, the *head*, is an atom and B, the *body*, is a possibly empty finite sequence of literals. A *CLP program*, or *program*, is a finite set of rules.

Example 1. The main predicate, create_streams/2, of the following CLP program receives a list of numbers which correspond to certain file names, and returns in the second argument the list of file handlers (*streams*) associated to the (opened) files:

```
create_streams([],[]).
create_streams([N|NL],[F|FL]):-
      number_codes(N,ChInN), app("/tmp/",ChInN,Fname),
      safe_open(Fname,write,F), create_streams(NL,FL).

safe_open(Fname,Mode,Stream):-
      atom_codes(File,Fname), open(File,Mode,Stream).
```

The call number_codes(N,ChInN) receives the number N and returns in ChInN the list of the ASCII codes of the characters comprising a representation of N. Then, it uses the well-known list concatenation predicate app/3. The call atom_codes(File,Fname) receives in Fname a list of ASCII codes and returns the atom File made up of the corresponding characters. Also, a call such as open(File,Mode,Stream) opens the file named File and returns in Stream the stream associated with the file. The argument Mode can have any of the values: read, write, or append.[4]

A distinguishing feature of our approach is that a class of safety policies can be defined for the different *abstract domains* available in the system. In particular, safety properties are expressed as *substitutions* in the context of an abstract domain (D_α) which is simpler than the selected *concrete domain* (D). An abstract value is a finite representation of a, possibly infinite, set of actual values in the concrete domain. Our approach relies on the abstract interpretation theory [5], where the set of all possible abstract semantic values which represents D_α is usually a complete lattice or cpo which is ascending chain finite. However, for this study, abstract interpretation is restricted to complete lattices over sets, both for the concrete $\langle 2^D, \subseteq \rangle$ and abstract $\langle D_\alpha, \sqsubseteq \rangle$ domains. Abstract values and sets of concrete values are related via a pair of monotonic mappings $\langle \alpha, \gamma \rangle$: *abstraction* $\alpha : 2^D \to D_\alpha$, and *concretization* $\gamma : D_\alpha \to 2^D$, such that $\forall x \in 2^D : \gamma(\alpha(x)) \supseteq x$ and $\forall y \in D_\alpha : \alpha(\gamma(y)) = y$. In general $\sqsubseteq$ is induced by $\subseteq$ and α. Similarly, the operations of *least upper bound* ($\sqcup$) and *greatest lower bound* ($\sqcap$) mimic those of 2^D in a precise sense. In this framework an *abstract property* is defined as an abstract substitution which allows us to express properties, in terms of an abstract domain, that the execution of a program must satisfy. The description domain we use in our examples is the following *regular type* domain [6].

---

[4] Predicates number_codes/2, atom_codes/2, and open/3 are ISO-standard Prolog predicates, and thus they are available in CiaoPP.

Example 2 (regular type domain). We refer to the *regular type* domain as *eterms*, since it is the name it has in CiaoPP. Abstract substitutions in *eterms* [21], over a set of variables V, assign a *regular type* to each variable in V. We use in our examples term as the most general type (i.e., term $\equiv \top$ corresponds to all possible terms). We also allow parametric types such as list(T) which denotes lists whose elements are all of type T. Type list is clearly equivalent to list(term). Also, list(T) $\sqsubseteq$ list $\sqsubseteq$ term for any type T. The least general substitution $\bot$ assigns the empty set of values to each variable.[5]

Apart from predefined types, in the *eterms* domain, one can have user-defined regular types declared by means of *Regular Unary Logic* programs [7]. For instance, in the context of mobile code, it is a safety issue whether the code tries to access files which are not related to the application in the machine consuming the code. A very simple safety policy can be to enforce that the mobile code only accesses temporary files. In a UNIX system this can be controlled (under some assumptions) by ensuring that the file resides in the directory /tmp/. The following regular type safe_name defines this notion of safety:[6]

```
:- regtype  safe_name/1.
safe_name("/tmp/"||L) :- list(L,alphanum_code).

:- regtype  alphanum_code/1.
alphanum_code(X):- member(X,"abcdefghijklmnopqrstuvwxyz").
alphanum_code(X):- member(X,"ABCDEFGHIJKLMNOPQRSTUVWXYZ").
alphanum_code(X):- member(X,"0123456789").
```

The abstract property made up of substitution $\{X \mapsto \text{safe\_name}\}$ expresses that X is bound to a string which starts by the prefix "/tmp/" followed by a list of alpha-numerical characters. In the following, we write simply safe_name(X) to represent it.

2.2 The Safety Policy

Assertions are syntactic objects which allow expressing a wide variety of high-level properties of (in our case CLP-) programs. Examples are assertions which state information on *entry points* to a program module, assertions which describe properties of built-ins, assertions which provide some type declarations, cost bounds, etc. The original assertion language [18] available in CiaoPP is composed of several assertion schemes. Among them, we simply consider the two following schemes for the purpose of this paper, which intuitively correspond to the traditional pre- and postcondition on procedures.

---

[5] Let us note that certain abstract domains assign a different meaning to $\bot$. In these cases, a distinguished symbol (i.e., an extra $\bot$) can always be added to represent unreachable points.

[6] The regtype declarations are used to define new regular types in CiaoPP.

$calls(B, \{\lambda^1_{Pre}; \ldots ; \lambda^n_{Pre}\})$: They express properties which should hold in *any* call to a given predicate similarly to the traditional precondition. B is a *predicate descriptor*, i.e., it has a predicate symbol as main functor and all arguments are distinct free variables, and λ^i_{Pre}, $i = 1, \ldots, n$, are abstract properties about execution states. The resulting assertion should be interpreted as "in all activations of B *at least* one property λ^i_{Pre} should hold in the calling state."

$success(B, [\lambda_{Pre},]\lambda_{Post})$: This assertion schema is used to describe a *postcondition* which must hold on all success states for a given predicate. B is a predicate descriptor, and λ_{Pre} and λ_{Post} are abstract properties about execution states. λ_{Pre} is optional and must be evaluated w.r.t. the store at the calling state to the predicate while condition λ_{Post} is evaluated at the success state. If the optional λ_{Pre} is present, then λ_{Post} is only required to hold in those success states which correspond to call states satisfying λ_{Pre}. Note that several success assertions with different λ_{Pre} may be given.

Therefore, abstract properties λ_{Pre} and λ_{Post} in assertions allow us to express conditions, in terms of an *abstract domain*, that the execution of a program must satisfy. Each condition is an abstract substitution corresponding to the variables in some atom. In existing approaches, safety policies usually correspond to some variants of type safety (which may also control the correct access of memory or array bounds [16]). In our system, the (co-)existence of several domains allows expressing a wider range of properties using the assertion language. They include a wide class of safety policies based on modes, types, non-failure, termination, determinacy, non-suspension, non-floundering, cost bounds, and their combinations.

In the CiaoPP preprocessor, the assertion language allows us to define the safety policy for the run-time system in the presence of foreign functions, built-ins, etc. In general, it is the task of the compiler designer to define the safety policies associated to the predefined system predicates. In addition to these assertions, the user can optionally provide further assertions manually for user-defined predicates.

Example 3. The following assertion for predicate safe_open:
    calls(safe_open(Fname,_,_), {safe_name(Fname)})
provides a simple way to guarantee that all calls to open are safe. It can be read as "the calling conventions for predicate safe_open require that the first argument be a safe_name". Meanwhile the following assertion for open is predefined in our system:
    success(open(X,Y,Z), ⊤, {constant(X),io_mode(Y),stream(Z)})
It requires, upon success, the first variable to be of type constant, the second a proper io_mode and the last one of type stream.

In contrast to traditional approaches, assertions are not compulsory for every predicate. Thus, the user can decide how much effort to put into writing assertions: the more of them there are, the more complete the partial correctness of the program is described and more possibilities to detect problems. Indeed, pre- and post-conditions are frequently provided by programmers since they are often easy to write and very useful for generating program documentation. Nevertheless, the analysis algorithm is able to obtain safe approximations of the program behavior even if no assertions are given. This is not always the case in other approaches such as classical program verification, in which loop invariants are actually required. Such invariants are hard to find and existing automated techniques are generally not sufficient to infer them, so that often they have to be provided by hand.

3 Certifying Programs by Static Analysis

Fig. 1 presents an overview of ACC as performed in the CiaoPP system. This section introduces the *certification* process (sketched to the left of the figure) carried out by the producer, i.e., the generation of a certificate to attest the adherence of the program to the safety policy. The whole certification method is based on the following idea: *an abstraction of the program computed by abstract interpretation-based analyzers can play the role of certificate for attesting program safety.* Our certification process is carried out in the following phases. We start from an initial program P. Firstly, the Safety Policy is defined by means of a set of assertions AS in the context of an abstract domain D_α, as introduced in Sect. 2, among a repertoire of Domains available in the system. Secondly, a standard Analyzer is run, which returns an *abstraction* of P's execution in terms of the abstract domain D_α. Let us note that the analyzer is domain–independent. This allows plugging in different abstract Domains provided suitable interfacing functions are defined. From the user point of view, it is sufficient to specify the particular abstract domain desired during the generation of the safety assertions. Then, a verification condition generator, VCGen extracts, from the initial assertions and the abstraction, a *Verification Condition* (VC) which can be proved only if the execution of the code does not violate the safety policy. If VC can be proved (marked as OK in Fig. 1), then the certificate (i.e., the abstraction) is sent together with the program P to the code consumer. Sections 3.1 and 3.2 give further details on the Abstraction and the VCGen process, respectively.

3.1 Using Analysis Results as Certificates

A key idea in our certification process is that the certificate is automatically generated by an abstract interpretation-based analyzer (or simply static analyzer). In particular, the *goal dependent* (a.k.a. goal oriented) analyzer of [9], which is the one implemented in the CiaoPP system, plays the role of Analyzer. This analysis algorithm (we simply write *Analysis* for short in the following) receives as input, in addition to the program P and the abstract domain D_α, a set of *calling patterns CP*. A calling pattern is a description of the calling modes (or entries) into the program. For simplicity, we assume that P comes enhanced with its entries CP. In particular, a set of calling patterns Q consists of a set of pairs of the form $\langle A : CP \rangle$ where A is a predicate descriptor and CP is an

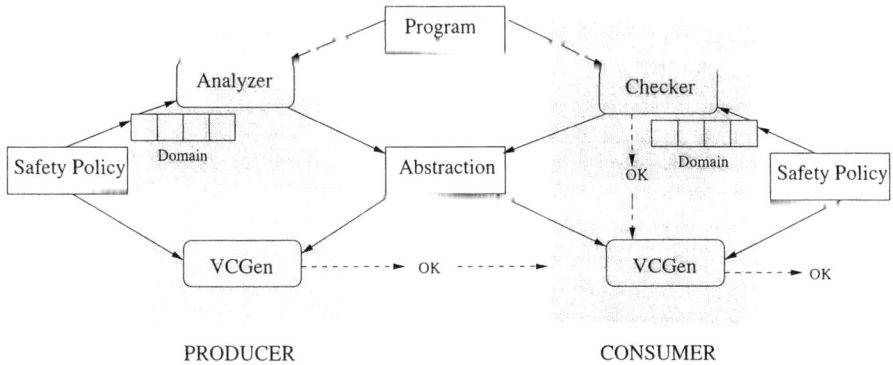

Fig. 1. Abstraction-Carrying Code in CiaoPP

abstract substitution (i.e., a condition of the run-time bindings) of A expressed as $CP \in D_\alpha$. In principle, calling patterns are only required for exported predicates. The analysis algorithm is able to generate them automatically for the remaining internal predicates. Nevertheless, they can still be automatically generated by assuming $\top$ (i.e., no initial data) for all exported predicates (although the idea is to improve this information in the initial calling patterns).

In order to compute $Analysis(P, Q, D_\alpha)$, traditional (goal dependent) abstract interpreters for (C)LP programs construct an *and–or graph* (or analysis graph) which corresponds to (or approximates) the abstract semantics of the program [2]. The graph has two sorts of nodes: *or–nodes* and *and–nodes*. Or-nodes correspond to literals whilst and–nodes to rules. Both kinds of nodes are interleaved in the graph and connected as follows. An or–node has arcs to those and–nodes which correspond to the rules whose head unifies with the literal it represents. An and–node for a rule $H :- B_1, \ldots, B_n$ has n arcs to the or-nodes which corresponds to the literals B_i in the body of the rule. Due to space limitations, and given that it is now well understood, we do not describe here algorithm $Analysis(P, Q, D_\alpha)$ (details can be found in, e.g., [9]). Nevertheless, the checking algorithm of Sect. 4 illustrates how an and–or graph is traversed.

The analysis graph computed by CiaoPP's analyzer represents an *abstract model* (or abstraction) of the program. It is represented by means of two data structures in the output: the *answer table* and the *arc dependency table*. The following definition introduces the notion of analysis table (similar definitions can be found, e.g., in [2,9]). Informally, it says that its entries are of the form $\langle A : CP \mapsto AP \rangle$ which should be interpreted as "the answer pattern for calls to A satisfying precondition (or call substitution), CP, accomplishes postcondition (or success substitution), AP."

Definition 1 (AT – analysis answer table). *Let P be a program. Let Q be a set of calling patterns expressed in the abstract domain D_α. We define an analysis answer table, AT, as the set of entries $\langle A_j : CP_j \mapsto AP_j \rangle$, $\forall j = 1..n$*

computed by $Analysis(P,Q,D_\alpha)$ [9] where, in each entry, A_j is an atom and CP_j and AP_j are, respectively, the abstract call and success substitutions.

Intuitively, the answer table contains the answer patterns for all literals in the or–nodes of the graph while the arc dependency table keeps detailed information about dependencies among or–nodes in the graph. A central idea in this work is that, for certifying program safety, it suffices to send the information stored in the analysis answer table. In contrast to the original generic algorithm [9], a simple analysis checker can be designed for validating the answer table without requiring the use of the arc dependency table at all (as we show in Sect. 4). The theory of abstract interpretation guarantees that the answer table is a safe approximation of the runtime behavior (see [2,9] for details).

Example 4. Take the calling pattern $\langle \texttt{create\_streams}(\texttt{X},\texttt{Y}), \{\texttt{list}(\texttt{X},\texttt{num})\}\rangle$, which indicates that calls to create_streams are performed with a list of numbers in the first argument. The answer table computed by CiaoPP contains (among others) these entries:

$\langle \texttt{create\_streams}(\texttt{A},\texttt{B}) : \{\texttt{list}(\texttt{A},\texttt{num})\} \mapsto \{\texttt{list}(\texttt{A},\texttt{num}), \texttt{list}(\texttt{B},\texttt{stream})\}\rangle$
$\langle \texttt{safe\_open}(\texttt{A},\texttt{B},\texttt{C}) : \{\texttt{sf}(\texttt{A}), \texttt{B}=\texttt{write}\} \mapsto \{\texttt{sf}(\texttt{A}), \texttt{B}=\texttt{write}, \texttt{stream}(\texttt{B})\}\rangle$

The first entry should be interpreted as: all calls to predicate create_streams provide as input a list of numbers in the first argument and, upon success, they yield lists of numbers and streams, respectively, in each of its two arguments. In the second entry, it is interesting to note that CiaoPP creates the auxiliary type:

sf("/tmp/"||A):-list(A,numcodes).

to represent lists of numbers starting by the prefix "/tmp/". We use the notation B = write to denote that the system generates a new type for B whose only element is constant write.

In order to increase accuracy, analyzers are usually *multivariant* on calls (see, e.g., [9]). Indeed, though not visible in this example, CiaoPP incorporates a multivariant analysis, i.e., more than one triple $\langle A : CP_1 \mapsto AP_1\rangle, \ldots, \langle A : CP_n \mapsto AP_n\rangle$ $n > 1$ with $CP_i \neq AP_i$ for some i,j may be computed for the same predicate descriptor A.

It is important to note that our approach would work directly in other programming paradigms, such as imperative or functional programming (the latter already covered in our current system), as long as a static analyzer/checker is available. Note that the fundamental components of the approach (fixpoint semantics and abstract interpretation) have both been widely applied also in these paradigms.

3.2 The Verification Condition

In the next step, the verification condition generator (VCGen in Fig. 1) extracts, from the initial assertions and answer table, a *Verification Condition* (VC) which can be proved only if the execution of the code does not violate the safety policy.

Definition 2 (VC – verification condition). *Let AT be an analysis answer table computed for a program P and a set of calling patterns Q in the abstract domain D_α. Let S be an assertion. Then, the verification condition, $VC(S, AT)$, for S w.r.t. AT is defined as follows:*

$$VC(S, AT) ::= \begin{cases} \bigwedge_{(A:CP \mapsto AP) \in AT} (\rho(CP) \sqsubseteq \lambda^1_{Prec} \vee \ldots \vee \rho(CP) \sqsubseteq \lambda^n_{Prec}) \\ \qquad \textit{if } S = calls(B, \{\lambda^1_{Prec}; \ldots; \lambda^n_{Prec}\}) \\ \bigwedge_{(A:CP \mapsto AP) \in AT} \rho(CP) \sqcap \lambda_{Prec} = \bot \vee \rho(AP) \sqsubseteq \lambda_{Post} \\ \qquad \textit{if } S = success(B, \lambda_{Prec}, \lambda_{Post}) \end{cases}$$

where ρ is a variable renaming substitution of A w.r.t. B.

If AS is a finite set of assertions, then its verification condition, $V(AS, AT)$, is the conjunction of the verification conditions of the elements of AS.

Roughly speaking, the VC generated according to Def. 2 is a conjunction of boolean expressions (possibly containing disjunctions) whose validity ensures the consistency of a set of assertions w.r.t. the answer table computed by *Analysis*. It distinguishes two different cases depending on the kind of assertion. For *calls* assertions, the VC requires that at least one precondition λ^i_{Prec} be a safe approximation of all existing abstract calling patterns for the atom B. In the case of *success* assertions, there are two cases for them to hold. The first one indicates that the precondition is never satisfied and, thus, the assertion trivially holds (and the postcondition does not need to be tested). The second corresponds to the case in which the success substitutions computed by analysis for the predicate are more particular than the one required by the assertion.

Example 5. Consider the entry for predicate safe_open in the answer table of Ex. 4 and the *calls* assertion of Ex. 3 for the same predicate. According to Def. 2, the VC is: B = write, sf(X) $\sqsubseteq$ safe_name(X) whose validity can be easily proved in our system since sf $\sqsubseteq$ safe_name. This allows CiaoPP to infer that calls to open performed within this program satisfy the simple safety policy discussed in Ex. 1. The complete example includes further assertions for the different predicates and its corresponding VCs. We do not include them here due to space limitations.

Therefore, upon creating the answer table and generating the VC, the validity of the whole boolean condition is checked by resolving each conjunct separately. Note that each conjunct consists of comparisons of pairs of abstract substitutions, which simply return either true or false but do not compute any substitution. This validation may yield three different possible status: i) the VC is indeed checked and the AT is considered a valid abstraction (marked as OK), ii) it is disproved, and thus the certificate is not valid and the code is definitely not safe to run (we should obviously correct the program before continuing the process); iii) it cannot be proved nor disproved. The latter case happens because some properties are undecidable and the analyzer performs approximations in order to always terminate. Therefore, it may not be able to infer precise enough information to verify the conditions. The user can then provide a more refined description of initial calling patterns or choose a different, finer-grained, domain. Although, it is not shown in the picture, in both the ii) and iii) cases, the certification process needs to be restarted until achieving a VC which meets i).

The following theorem states the soundness of the VC. Intuitively, it amounts to saying that if the VC holds, then the execution of the program will preserve all safety assertions. Following the notation of [15], we write $\triangleright VC$ when VC is valid.

Theorem 1 (Soundness of the Verification Condition). *Let AT be an analysis answer table for a program P and a set of calling patterns Q in an abstract domain D_α (as defined in Def. 1). Let AS be a set of assertions. Let $VC(AS, AT)$ be the verification condition for AS w.r.t. AT (generated as stated in Def. 2). If $\triangleright VC(AS, AT)$, then P satisfies all assertions in AS for all computations described by Q.*

This result derives from the fact that the static analysis algorithm of [9] computes a safe approximation of the stores reached during computation.

4 Checking Safety in the Consumer

The checking process performed by the consumer is illustrated in the right hand side of Fig. 1. Initially, the supplier sends the program P together with the certificate to the consumer. To retain the safety guarantees, the consumer can provide a new set of assertions which specify the Safety Policy required by this particular consumer. It should be noted that ACC is very flexible in that it allows different implementations on the way the safety policy is provided. Clearly, the same assertions AS used by the producer can be sent to the consumer. But, more interestingly, the consumer can decide to impose a weaker safety condition which can still be proved with the submitted abstraction. Also, the imposed safety condition can be stronger and it may not be proved if it is not implied by the current abstraction (which means that the code would be rejected). From the provided assertions, the consumer must generate again a trustworthy VC and use the incoming certificate to efficiently check that the VC holds. Thus, in the *validation* process, a code consumer not only checks the validity of the answer table but it also (re-)generates a trustworthy VC. The re-generation of VC (and its corresponding validation) is identical to the process already discussed in the previous section. Therefore, this section describes only the former part of the validation process, i.e., algorithm check.

Although global analysis is now routinely used as a practical tool, it is still unacceptable to run the whole *Analysis* to validate the certificate since it involves considerable cost. One of the main reasons is that the analysis algorithm is an iterative process which often computes answers (repeatedly) for the same call due to possible updates introduced by further computations. At each iteration, the algorithm has to manipulate rather complex data structures—which involve performing updates, lookups, etc.—until the fixpoint is reached. The whole validation process is centered around the following observation: *the checking algorithm can be defined as a very simplified "one-pass" analyzer*. The computation of the *Analysis* algorithm can be understood as: $Analysis = fixpoint(analysis\_step)$. I.e., a process which repeatedly performs a traversal of the analysis graph (denoted by $analysis\_step$) until the computed information does not change. The idea is that the simple, non-iterative, $analysis\_step$ process can play the role of abstract interpretation-based checker (or simply analysis checker). In other words, check $\equiv analysis\_step$. Intuitively, since the certification process already provides the fixpoint result as certificate, an additional analysis pass over it cannot change the result. Thus, as long as the answer table is valid, one single execution of $analysis\_step$ validates the certificate.

The next definition presents our *abstract interpretation-based checking* algorithm. It receives as an additional input a Certificate (which is the analysis fixpoint). In a single traversal, it constructs a program analysis graph by using the information in Certificate. The algorithm is devised as a graph traversal procedure which places entries in a *local* answer table, AT, as new nodes in the program analysis graph are encountered. Thus, it handles two distinct answer tables: the local AT + the incoming Certificate. The final goal of the checking is to reconstruct the analysis graph and compare the results with the information stored in Certificate. As long as Certificate is valid, both results coincide and, thus, the certificate is guaranteed to be valid w.r.t. the program.

Definition 3 (Analysis Checker). *Let P be a normalized[7] program and Q be a set of calling patterns in the abstract domain D_α. Let Certificate be a safety certificate as defined in Def. 1. The validation of Certificate is performed by the procedure check depicted in Figure 2. The algorithm uses a local answer table, AT, to compute the results (initially it does not contain any entry). Procedure check is defined in terms of five abstract operations [9] on the description domain D_α of interest:*

- Arestrict(CP, V) *performs the abstract restriction of a description CP to the set of variables in the set V, denoted $vars(V)$;*
- Aextend(CP, V) *extends the description CP to the variables in the set V;*
- Aadd(C, CP) *performs the abstract operation of conjoining the actual constraint C with the description CP;*
- Aconj(CP_1, CP_2) *performs the abstract conjunction of two descriptions;*
- Alub(CP_1, CP_2) *performs the abstract disjunction of two descriptions.*

Following the presentation of *Analysis* [9], we assume that the program P and the answer table are global parameters throughout the algorithm. The checking algorithm proceeds as follows. For each calling pattern in the set Q, the procedure process_node inspects all rules defining the considered atom. For

---

[7] For clarity of presentation, in the algorithm we assume that all rule heads are normalized, i.e., H is of the form $p(X_1, ..., X_n)$ where $X_1, ..., X_n$ are distinct free variables.

```
check(Q, Certificate)
   foreach A : CP ∈ Q
      process_node(A : CP, Certificate)
   return Valid

process_node(A : CP, Certificate)
   if (∃ a renaming σ s.t. σ(A : CP ↦ AP) in Certificate)
   then add (A : CP ↦ AP) to AT
   else return Error
   foreach rule $A_k \leftarrow B_{k,1}, \ldots, B_{k,n_k}$ in P
      $W := vars(A_k, B_{k,1}, \ldots, B_{k,n_k})$
      $CP_b :=$ Aextend$(CP, vars(B_{k,1}, \ldots, B_{k,n_k}))$
      $CPR_b :=$ Arestrict$(CP_b, B_{k,1})$
      foreach $B_{k,i}$ in the rule body $i = 1, \ldots, n_k$
         $CP_a :=$ process_arc$(B_{k,i} : CPR_b, CP_b, W,$ Certificate$)$
         if $(i <> n_k)$ then $CPR_a :=$ Arestrict$(CP_a, var(B_{k,i+1}))$
         $CP_b := CP_a$
         $CPR_b := CPR_a$
      $AP_1 :=$ Arestrict$(CP_a, vars(A_k))$
      $AP_2 :=$ Alub$(AP_1, \sigma^{-1}(AP))$
      if $AP <> AP_2$ then return Error

process_arc$(B_{k,i} : CPR_b, CP_b, W,$ Certificate$)$
   if $B_{k,i}$ is a constraint then $CP_a :=$ Aadd $(B_{k,i}, CP_b)$
   elseif ($\nexists$ a renaming σ s.t. $σ(B_{k,i} : CPR_b ↦ AP')$ in AT)
   then process_node $(B_{k,i} : CPR_b,$ Certificate$)$
   $AP_1 :=$ Aextend $(\rho^{-1}(AP), W)$ where ρ is a renaming s.t.
                              $\rho(B_{k,i} : CPR_b ↦ AP)$ in AT
   $CP_a :=$ Aconj $(CP_b, AP_1)$
   return $CP_a$
```

Fig. 2. Abstract Interpretation-based Checking in CiaoPP

each rule, it performs a left-to-right traversal of the atoms in the rule body. The processing of each atom $B_{k,i}$ in the rule body is handled by process_arc. We refer by CP_b to the description of the program point immediately *before* the atom $B_{k,i}$ and by CP_a to the description *after* processing the atom. Initially, the description CP_b takes the value of the initial description CP for the calling pattern $A : CP$ (extended to all the variables in the rule).[8] We use variables CPR_x to denote that description CP_x has been restricted, with $x \in \{a, b\}$. The procedure process_arc is aimed at computing the resulting description CP_a after processing a given atom $B_{k,i}$. It distinguishes two different cases:

– Constraints are simply abstractly added to the current description.

---

[8] Further insights on the operations on abstract substitutions (like extensions, restrictions, disjunctions etc.) can be found in [2].

- If $B_{k,i}$ is an atom, then it inspects whether it has been processed before:
  • If the atom already has an entry in the answer table, we do not need to recompute it. Indeed, this could risk the termination of the algorithm.
  • Otherwise, we process it by executing procedure process_node. On return, and in the absence of errors, this processing will have placed an answer for $B_{k,i}$ in the answer table (and possibly for other related atoms as well).

Either way, there will be an answer for the atom at this point. This answer is *conjoined*[8] with the description CP_b from the program point immediately before $B_{k,i}$ in order to obtain the description for the program point after it.

The computed result is used to process the next literal in the rule when $B_{k,i}$ is not the last literal. Otherwise, the computed result constitutes indeed the computed answer for the rule. The answer is *combined*[8] with the corresponding answer supplied by the certification process in Certificate. If Certificate is valid, the comparison should hold; otherwise the process prompts an error and the program is not safe to run.

The following theorem ensures that algorithm check is able to validate safety certificates which are stored in a valid analysis answer table.

Theorem 2 (partial correctness). *Let P be a program, let Q be a set of calling patterns in an abstract domain D_α. Let* Certificate *be a safety certificate for P and Q as stated in Def. 1. Then,* check(Q, Certificate) *terminates and validates* Certificate *in P.*

The theorem can be demonstrated by showing that check is a simplified version of *Analysis* [9] in two main aspects. Regarding the efficiency, our point to justify an efficient behavior of check for validating an answer table is that it performs a single graph traversal. Indeed, for a regular type domain, [4] demonstrates that directional type-checking for logic programs is fixed-parameter linear. The next section reports experimental evidence of efficiency issues.

5 Experimental Results

In this section we show some experimental results aimed at studying two crucial points for the practicality of our proposal: the checking time as compared to the analysis time, and the size of certificates. We have implemented the checker as a simplification of the generic abstract interpretation system of CiaoPP. It should be noted that this is an efficient, highly optimized, state-of-the-art analysis system and which is part of a working compiler. Both the analysis and checker are parametric w.r.t. the abstract domain. In these experiments they both use the same implementation of the domain-dependent functions of the *sharing+freeness* domain [14]. We have selected this domain because the information it infers is very useful for reasoning about instantiation errors, which is a crucial aspect for the safety of logic programs. The whole system is implemented in Ciao 1.11#200 [3] with compilation to bytecode. All of our experiments have

Table 1. Checking Time and Certificate Size

Bench	Analysis			Checking			Speedup		Source	Byte Code		Certificate	
	P_A	An	T_A	P_C	Ch	T_C	A/C	T_A/T_C	Source	ByteC	B/S	Cert	C/S
aiakl	2	87	89	2	71	72	1.2	1.2	1555	3805	2.4	3090	2.0
ann	22	452	474	18	254	272	1.8	1.7	12745	43884	3.4	24475	1.9
bid	4	56	60	4	35	38	1.6	1.6	4945	10376	2.1	5939	1.2
boyer	9	143	151	7	85	92	1.7	1.6	11010	32522	3.0	12300	1.1
browse	3	14	17	3	12	15	1.2	1.2	2589	8467	3.3	1661	0.6
deriv	2	86	88	1	19	20	4.6	4.4	957	4221	4.4	288	0.3
grammar	2	10	12	2	9	11	1.1	1.1	1598	3182	2.0	1259	0.8
hanoiapp	2	25	26	2	16	18	1.5	1.5	1172	2264	1.9	2325	2.0
mmatrix	1	13	14	1	10	11	1.3	1.3	557	1053	1.9	880	1.6
occur	2	16	18	2	10	12	1.7	1.6	1367	6903	5.0	1098	0.8
progeom	2	13	15	2	9	11	1.5	1.4	1619	3570	2.2	2148	1.3
read	9	792	801	8	488	497	1.6	1.6	11843	24619	2.1	25359	2.1
qplan	13	1411	1424	11	962	973	1.5	1.5	9983	33472	3.4	20509	2.1
qsortapp	1	20	21	1	12	14	1.6	1.5	664	1176	1.8	2355	3.5
query	5	11	15	4	9	12	1.2	1.3	2090	8833	4.2	531	0.3
rdtok	8	141	149	6	43	49	3.3	3.1	13704	15354	1.1	6533	0.5
serialize	2	40	42	2	17	19	2.3	2.2	987	3801	3.9	1779	1.8
warplan	8	173	181	7	108	115	1.6	1.6	5203	23971	4.6	15305	2.9
witt	16	196	212	14	72	86	2.7	2.5	17681	41760	2.4	19131	1.1
zebra	3	94	97	3	90	92	1.1	1.0	2284	5396	2.4	4058	1.8
Overall							1.63	1.61		1		2.66		1.44

been performed on a Pentium 4 at 2.4GHz and 512MB RAM running GNU Linux RH9.0. The Linux kernel used is 2.4.25, customized with the *hrtime* patch to provide improved precision and resolution in time measurements.

Execution times are given in milliseconds and measure *runtime*. They are computed as the arithmetic mean of five runs. A relatively wide range of programs has been used as benchmarks. They are the same ones used in [9], where they are described in some detail. For each benchmark, the columns for Analysis are the following: P_A is the time required by the *preprocessing phase*, in which program clauses are processed and stored in the format required by the analyzer. The *analysis* time proper is shown in column An. The actual time needed for analysis –the sum of these two times– is shown in column T_A. Similarly, in the case of checking, three columns are shown. The preprocessing phase, P_C, includes asserting the certificate in addition to asserting the program to be analyzed. As the figures show, the overhead required for asserting the certificate is negligible. Column Ch is the time for executing the checking algorithm. Finally, T_C is the total time for checking. The columns under Speedup compare analysis and checking times. As can be seen in columns A/C and T_A/T_C, the checking algorithm is faster than the analysis algorithm in all cases. The actual speedup ranges from almost none, as in the case of zebra, to over four times faster in the case of deriv. The last row summarizes the results for the different benchmarks using a weighted mean, which places more importance on those benchmarks with relatively larger analysis times. We use as weight for each program its actual analysis time. We believe that this weighted mean is more informative than the arithmetic mean, as, for example, doubling the speed in which a large and complex program is analyzed (checked) is more relevant than achieving this for small, simple programs. Overall, the speedup is 1.63 in just analysis time, or 1.61 if we also take into account the preprocessing time. We believe that the achieved speedup is significant taking into account that CiaoPP's analyzer for this domain is highly optimized and converges very efficiently. However, it is to be expected that, for other domains and implementations, the relative gains will be higher.

The second part of the table studies the size of the certificates, coded in compact (*fastread*) format, for the different benchmarks and compares it to the size of the source code for the same program and to the size of the corresponding bytecode. To make this comparison fair, we subtract 4180 bytes from the size of the bytecode for each program: the size of the bytecode for an empty program in this version of Ciao (minimal top-level drivers and exception handlers for any executable). The results show the size of the certificate to be quite reasonable. It ranges from 0.3 times the size of the source code (for deriv) to 3.5 (in the case of qsortapp). Overall, it is 1.44 times the size of the source code. We consider this acceptable since in general Prolog programs are quite compact (up to 10 times more compact than equivalent imperative programs). In fact, the size of source plus certificate is smaller (1+1.44) than that of the bytecode (2.66).

6 Discussion and Related Work

The main contribution of this work is to introduce, implement, and (preliminarily) benchmark *abstraction-carrying code* (ACC) as a novel enabling technology for PCC, which is based throughout on the use of abstract interpretation techniques. We argue that ACC is highly flexible due to the parametricity on the abstract domain inherited from the analysis engines used in (C)LP. Our approach differs from existing approaches to PCC in several aspects. In our case, the certificate is computed automatically on the producer side by an *abstract interpretation-based analyzer* and the certificate takes the form of a particular *subset* of the analysis results. The burden on the consumer side is reduced by using a simple one-*traversal* checker, which is a very simplified and efficient abstract interpreter which does not need to compute a fixpoint.

A type-level dataflow analysis of Java virtual machine bytecode is also the basis of most existing verifiers [12,11], and some are loosely based on abstract interpretation. These analyses allow proving that the program is correct w.r.t. type-related correctness conditions. In [19] a proposal is presented to split the type-based bytecode verification of the KVM (an embedded variant of the JVM) in two phases, where the producer first computes the certificate by means of a type-based dataflow analyzer and then the consumer simply checks that the types provided in the code certificate are valid. As in our case, the second phase can be done in a single, linear pass over the bytecode. However, these approaches are designed limited to types, whereas our approach is inherently parametric and thus supports a very rich set of domains, and combinations of several of them. Let us note that the checker is part of the trusted computing base and, hence, the code consumer has to trust also the domain operations. Other approaches to PCC use logic-based verification methods as enabling technology, an example is [22] which formalises a simple assembly language with procedures and presents a safety policy for arithmetic overflow in Isabelle/HOL. The coexistence of several abstract domains in our framework is somewhat related to the notion of *models* to capture the security-relevant properties of code, as addressed in the work on Model-Carrying Code (MCC) [20].

Another difference between our work and other related work is that the instance that we have described is actually defined at the source-level, whereas in existing PCC frameworks the code supplier typically packages the certificate with the *object* code rather than with the *source* code (both are untrusted). Actually, both approaches are of interest from our point of view (and, in fact, our approach can also be applied to bytecode). Open-source code is becoming much more relevant these days (in fact, Ciao and CiaoPP are themselves GNU-licensed and available in source code). As a result, it is now realistic to expect that a relatively large amount of untrusted source code is available to the consumer. The advantages of open-source with respect to safety are important since it allows inspecting the code and applying powerful techniques for program analysis and validation which allow inferring information which may be difficult to observe in low-level, compiled code.

Acknowledgments

This work was funded in part by the Information Society Technologies programme of the European Commission, Future and Emerging Technologies under the IST-2001-38059 *ASAP* project and by the Spanish Ministry of Science and Education under the MCYT TIC 2002-0055 *CUBICO* project. Part of this work was performed during a research stay of Elvira Albert and Germán Puebla at UNM supported by respective grants from the Secretaría de Estado de Educación y Universidades, Spanish Ministry of Science and Education. Manuel Hermenegildo is also supported by the Prince of Asturias Chair in Information Science and Technology at UNM.

References

1. D. Aspinall, S. Gilmore, M. Hofmann, D. Sannella, and I. Stark. Mobile resource guarantees for smart devices. In G. Barthe, L. Burdy, M. Huisman, J.-L. Lanet, and T. Muntean, editors, *Proceedings of CASSIS'04*, LNCS. Springer, 2004.
2. M. Bruynooghe. A Practical Framework for the Abstract Interpretation of Logic Programs. *Journal of Logic Programming*, 10:91–124, 1991.

3. F. Bueno, D. Cabeza, M. Carro, M. Hermenegildo, P. López-García, and G. Puebla. The Ciao System. Reference Manual (v1.10), May 2004. Technical University of Madrid (UPM). Available at http://clip.dia.fi.upm.es/Software/Ciao.
4. W. Charatonik. Directional Type Checking for Logic Programs: Beyond Discriminative Types. In *Proc. of ESOP 2000*, pages 72–87. LNCS 1782, 2000.
5. P. Cousot and R. Cousot. Abstract Interpretation: a Unified Lattice Model for Static Analysis of Programs by Construction or Approximation of Fixpoints. In *Proc. of POPL'77*, pages 238–252, 1977.
6. P.W. Dart and J. Zobel. A Regular Type Language for Logic Programs. In *Types in Logic Programming*, pages 157–187. MIT Press, 1992.
7. T. Früwirth, E. Shapiro, M.Y. Vardi, and E. Yardeni. Logic programs as types for logic programs. In *Proc. LICS'91*, pages 300–309, 1991.
8. M. Hermenegildo, G. Puebla, F. Bueno, and P. López-García. Program Development Using Abstract Interpretation (and The Ciao System Preprocessor). In *Proc. of SAS'03*, pages 127–152. Springer LNCS 2694, 2003.
9. M. Hermenegildo, G. Puebla, K. Marriott, and P. Stuckey. Incremental Analysis of Constraint Logic Programs. *ACM TOPLAS*, 22(2):187–223, March 2000.
10. J. Jaffar and M.J. Maher. Constraint Logic Programming: A Survey. *Journal of Logic Programming*, 19/20:503–581, 1994.
11. Xavier Leroy. Java bytecode verification: algorithms and formalizations. *Journal of Automated Reasoning*, 30(3-4):235–269, 2003.
12. T. Lindholm and F. Yellin. *The Java Virtual Machine Specification*. Addison-Wesley, 1997.
13. G. Morrisett, D. Walker, K. Crary, and N. Glew. From system F to typed assembly language. *ACM TOPLAS*, 21(3):527–568, 1999.
14. K. Muthukumar and M. Hermenegildo. Combined Determination of Sharing and Freeness of Program Variables Through Abstract Interpretation. In *1991 International Conference on Logic Programming*, pages 49–63. MIT Press, June 1991.
15. G. Necula. Proof-Carrying Code. In *Proc. of POPL'97*, pages 106–119. ACM Press, 1997.
16. G. Necula and P. Lee. The Design and Implementation of a Certifying Compiler. In *Proc. of PLDI'98*. ACM Press, 1998.
17. G.C. Necula and S.P. Rahul. Oracle-based checking of untrusted software. In *Proceedings of POPL'01*, pages 142–154. ACM Press, 2001.
18. G. Puebla, F. Bueno, and M. Hermenegildo. An Assertion Language for Constraint Logic Programs. In *Analysis and Visualization Tools for Constraint Programming*, pages 23–61. Springer LNCS 1870, 2000.
19. K. Rose, E. Rose. Lightweight bytecode verification. In *OOPSALA Workshop on Formal Underpinnings of Java*, 1998.
20. R. Sekar, V.N. Venkatakrishnan, S. Basu, S. Bhatkar, and D. DuVarney. Model-carrying code: A practical approach for safe execution of untrusted applications. In *Proc. of SOSP'03*, pages 15–28. ACM, 2003.
21. C. Vaucheret and F. Bueno. More precise yet efficient type inference for logic programs. In *Proc. of SAS'02*, pages 102–116. Springer LNCS 2477, 2002.
22. M. Wildmoser and T. Nipkow. Certifying Machine Code Safety: Shallow Versus Deep Embedding. In *TPHOLs*, number 3223 in LNCS. Springer, 2004.

A Verification Environment for Sequential Imperative Programs in Isabelle/HOL*

Norbert Schirmer

Technische Universität München, Institut für Informatik
http://www4.in.tum.de/~schirmer

Abstract. We develop a general language model for sequential imperative programs together with a Hoare logic. We instantiate the framework with common programming language constructs and integrate it into Isabelle/HOL, to gain a usable and sound verification environment.

1 Introduction

The main goal of this work is to develop a suitable programming language model and proof calculus, to support program verification in the interactive theorem prover Isabelle/HOL. The model should be lightweight so that program verification can be carried out on the abstraction level of the programming language. The design of a framework for program verification in an expressive logic like HOL is driven by two main goals. On the one hand we want to derive the proof calculus in HOL, so that we can guarantee soundness of the calculus with respect to the programming language semantics. On the other hand we want to apply the proof calculus to verify programs.

The main contribution of this work is to present a programming language model that operates on a polymorphic state space, but still can handle local and global variables throughout procedure calls. By this we can achieve both desired goals. We can once and for all develop a sound proof calculus as well as later on tailor the state space to fit to the current program verification task. Moreover the model is expressive enough to handle abrupt termination, side-effecting expressions, runtime faults and dynamic procedure calls. Finally we instantiate the framework with a state space representation that allows us to match programming language typing with logical typing. So type inference will take care of basic type safety issues, which simplifies the assertions and proof obligations. Parts of the frame condition for procedure specifications can be naturally expressed in this state space representation and can already be handled during verification condition generation.

---

* This work was partially funded by the German Federal Ministry of Education, Science, Research and Technology (BMBF) in the framework of the Verisoft project (http://www.verisoft.de) under grant 01 IS C38. The responsibility for this article lies with the author.

Related Work The tradition of embedding a programming language in HOL goes back to the work of Gordon [12], where a while language with variables ranging over natural numbers is introduced. A polymorphic state space was already used by Wright et. al. [21] in their machnisation of refinement concepts, by Harrison in his formalisation of Dijkstra [5] and by Prensa to verify parallel programs [18]. Still procedures were not present. Homeier [6] introduces procedures, but the variables are again limited to numbers. Later on detailed semantics for Java [16,7] and C [15] were embedded in a theorem prover. But verification of even simple programs suffers from the complex models.

The Why tool [4] implements a program logics for annotated functional programs (with references) and produces verification conditions for an external theorem prover. It can handle uninterpreted parts of annotations that are only meaningful to the external theorem prover. With this approach it is possible to map imperative languages like C to the tool by representing the heap in reference variables. Although the Why tool and the work we present in this paper both provide comparable verification environments for imperative programs the theoretical foundations to achieve this are quite different: Filliâtre builds up a sophisticated type theory incorporating an effect analysis on the input language, whereas the framework of Hoare logics and the simple type system of HOL is sufficient for our needs. Moreover our entire development, the calculus together with its soundness and completeness proof, is carried out in Isabelle/HOL, in contrast to the pen and paper proofs of Filliâtre [3].

The rest of the paper is structured as follows. We start with a brief introduction to Isabelle/HOL in Section 2; in Section 3 we introduce the programming language model and the Hoare logics; Section 4 describes the integration into Isabelle and shows how we deal with various language constructs; Section 5 concludes.

2 Preliminary Notes on Isabelle/HOL

Isabelle is a generic logical framework which allows one to encode different object logics. In this article we are only concerned with Isabelle/HOL [14], an encoding of higher order logic augmented with facilities for defining data types, records, inductive sets as well as primitive and total general recursive functions.

The syntax of Isabelle is reminiscent of ML, so we will not go into detail here. There are the usual type constructors $T_1 \times T_2$ for product and $T_1 \Rightarrow T_2$ for function space. The syntax $[\![P;\ Q]\!] \implies R$ should be read as an inference rule with the two premises P and Q and the conclusion R. Logically it is just a shorthand for $P \implies Q \implies R$. There are actually two implications $\longrightarrow$ and $\implies$. The two mean the same thing except that $\longrightarrow$ is HOL's "real" implication, whereas $\implies$ comes from Isabelle's meta-logic and expresses inference rules. Thus $\implies$ cannot appear inside a HOL formula. For the purpose of this paper the two may be identified. Similarly, we use $\bigwedge$ for the universal quantifier in the meta logic.

To emulate partial functions the polymorphic option type is frequently used: **datatype** $'a\ option = None \mid Some\ 'a$. Here $'a$ is a type variable, *None* stands for the undefined value and *Some x* for a defined value x. A partial function from type T_1 to type T_2 can be modelled as $T_1 \Rightarrow (T_2\ option)$. The domain of such a partial function f is *dom f*.

There is also a destructor for the constructor *Some*, the function *the*:: $'a\ option \Rightarrow 'a$. It is defined by the sole equation *the* $(Some\ x) = x$ and is total in the sense that *the None* is a legal, but indefinite value.

Appending two lists is written as xs @ ys and "consing" as $x \mathbin{\#} xs$.

3 Programming Language Model

3.1 Abstract Syntax

The basic model of the programming language is quite general. We want to be able to represent a sequential imperative programming language with mutually recursive procedures, local and global variables and heap. Abrupt termination like break, continue, return or exceptions should also be expressible in the model. Moreover we support a dynamic procedure call, which allows us to represent procedure pointers or dynamic method invocation.

We only fix the statements of the programming language. Expressions are ordinary HOL-expressions, therefore they do not have any side effects. Nevertheless we want to be able to express faults during expression evaluation, like division by *0* or dereferencing a *Null* pointer. We introduce *guards* in the language, which check for those runtime faults.

The state space of the programming language and also the representation of procedure names is polymorphic. The canonical type variable for the state space is $'s$ and for procedure names $'p$. The programming language is defined by a **datatype** $('s,'p)\ com$ with the following constructors:

Skip: Do nothing
Basic f: Basic commands like assignment; f is a state-update: $'s \Rightarrow 's$
Seq $c_1\ c_2$: Sequential composition, also written as $c_1;c_2$
Cond b $c_1\ c_2$: Conditional statement
Guard g c: Guarded command, also written as $g \mapsto c$
While b c: Loop
Call p: Static procedure call, $p::'p$
Throw: Initiate abrupt termination
Catch $c_1\ c_2$: Handle abrupt termination of c_1 with c_2
DynCom c: Dynamic (state dependant) command: $c::'s \Rightarrow ('s,'p)\ com$

The procedure call above is parameterless. In 4.4 we implement a call with parameters: *call init p return result*.

The dynamic command *DynCom* allows to abstract a statement over the state. It is fairy general, and we implement side-effecting expressions (4.3) and

real "dynamic" statements, like pointers to procedures or dynamic method invocation with it. We model the latter with:
 $dynCall\ init\ p\ return\ result \equiv DynCom\ (\lambda s.\ call\ init\ (p\ s)\ return\ result)$

3.2 State Space Representation

Although the semantics is defined for polymorphic state spaces we introduce the state space representation which we will use later on to give some illustrative examples. We represent the state space as a **record** in Isabelle/HOL. This idea goes back to Wenzel [23]. A simple state space with three variables B, N and M can be modelled with the following record definition:

record $vars = B::bool\ N::int\ M::int$

Records of type $vars$ have three fields, named B, N and M of type $bool$ resp. int. An example instance of such a record is $(\!|B = True,\ N = 42,\ M = 3|\!)$. For each field there is a *selector* function of the same name, e.g. $N\ (\!|B = True,\ N = 42,\ M = 3|\!) = 42$. The *update* operation is functional. For example, $v(\!|N := 0|\!)$ is a record where component N is 0 and whose B and M component are copied from v. Selections of updated components can be simplified automatically e.g. $N\ (r(\!|N := 43|\!)) = 43$. The representation of the state space as record has the advantage that the typing of variables can be expressed by means of typing in the logic. Therefore basic type safety requirements are already ensured by type inference.

3.3 Hoare Logics

We have defined two Hoare logic judgements, for partial correctness of the general form $\Gamma,\Theta \vdash P\ c\ Q,A$ and $\Gamma,\Theta \vdash_t P\ c\ Q,A$ for total correctness. P is the precondtion and Q and A are the postconditions for normal and abrupt termination. If we start in a state satisfying P, execution of command c will end up in a state satisfying Q in case of normal termination and in a state satisfying A in case of abrupt termination. Total correctness additionally guarantees termination of the program. Γ is the procedure environment, which maps procedure names to their bodies, and Θ is a set of Hoare quadruples that we may assume. Θ is used to handle recursive procedures as we will see later on. We have proven soundness and completeness of the Hoare logics with respect to an operational semantics [20]. But this paper will focus on the application of the logic.

The assertions P, Q and A are represented as set of states: $'s\ set$. This means we do not introduce a special assertion language, but can use ordinary HOL sets to describe the states.

The Hoare logic is defined inductively. The rules are syntax directed, and most of them are defined in a weakest precondition style. This makes it easy to automate rule application in a verification condition generator. Handling abrupt termination is surprisingly simple. The postcondition for abrupt termination is left unmodified by most of the rules. Only if we actually encounter a *Throw* it has to be a consequence of the precondition. This means that the proof rules do not complicate the verification of programs where abrupt termination is not present. The approach to split up the postcondition for normal and abrupt termination is also followed by [4,8].

The rules for the basic language constructs are standard:

$$\Gamma,\Theta \vdash Q\ Skip\ Q,A \qquad \Gamma,\Theta \vdash \{s.\ f\ s \in Q\}\ Basic\ f\ Q,A$$

$$\frac{\Gamma,\Theta \vdash P\ c_1\ R,A \qquad \Gamma,\Theta \vdash R\ c_2\ Q,A}{\Gamma,\Theta \vdash P\ Seq\ c_1\ c_2\ Q,A} \qquad \frac{\Gamma,\Theta \vdash (P \cap b)\ c_1\ Q,A \qquad \Gamma,\Theta \vdash (P \cap -b)\ c_2\ Q,A}{\Gamma,\Theta \vdash P\ Cond\ b\ c_1\ c_2\ Q,A}$$

$$\frac{\Gamma,\Theta \vdash P\ c\ Q,A}{\Gamma,\Theta \vdash (g \cap P)\ Guard\ g\ c\ Q,A} \qquad \frac{\Gamma,\Theta \vdash (P \cap b)\ c\ P,A}{\Gamma,\Theta \vdash P\ While\ b\ c\ (P \cap -b),A}$$

The command *Basic f* applies the function f to the current state. An example of a basic operation may be an assignment N = 2. This can be represented as *Basic* $(\lambda s.\ s(\!|N:=2|\!))$ in our language model. We can also represent field assignment or memory allocation as basic commands.

To model runtime faults that may occur during expression evaluation (like division by zero), we use the guarded command. In order to prove a guarded command we have to ensure that the guard holds.

The remaining rules will be described in the following section. Most of rules for total correctness are structurally equivalent to their partial correctness counterparts. We will only focus on those interesting rules with an impact on termination, namely loops and recursion. The basic idea is to justify termination by a well-founded relation on the state-space.

4 Verification Environment

Our main tool is a verification condition generator that is implemented as tactic called *vcg*. The Hoare logic rules are defined in a weakest precondition style, so that we can almost take them as they are. We derive variants of the Hoare rules where all assertions in the conclusions are plain variables so that they are applicable to every context. We get the following format: $\frac{P \subseteq WP\ \ldots}{\Gamma,\Theta \vdash P\ c\ Q,A}$. The ... may be recursive Hoare quadruples or side-conditions which somehow lead to the weakest precondition *WP*. If we recursively apply rules of this format until the program c is completely processed, then we have calculated the weakest precondition *WP* and are left with the verification condition $P \subseteq WP$. The set inclusion is then transformed to an implication. Finally we split the state records so that the record representation will not show up in the resulting verification condition. This leads to quite comprehensible proof obligations that closely resemble the specifications. Moreover we supply some concrete syntax for programs. The mapping to the abstract syntax should be obvious. As a shorthand an empty set Θ can be omitted and writing a Hoare triple instead of the quadruples is an abbreviation for an empty postcondition for abrupt termination.

A Verification Environment for Sequential Imperative Programs   403

If we refer to components (variables) of the state-space of the program we always mark these with ´ (in assertions and also in the program itself). Assertions are ordinary Isabelle/HOL sets. As we usually want to refer to the state-space in the assertions, we provide special brackets ⦃...⦄ for them. Internally, an assertion of the from ⦃´I ≤ 3⦄ gets expanded to {s. I s ≤ 3} in ordinary set comprehension notation of Isabelle.

Although our assertions work semantically on the state-space, stepping through verification condition generation "feels" like the expected syntactic substitutions of traditional Hoare logic. This is achieved by simplification of the record updates in the assertions calculated by the Hoare rules.

lemma
Γ⊢ ⦃´M = a ∧ ´N = b⦄ ´I := ´M; ´M := ´N; ´N := ´I ⦃´M = b ∧ ´N = a⦄
apply *vcg-step*
  1. Γ⊢ ⦃´M = a ∧ ´N = b⦄ ´I := ´M; ´M := ´N ⦃´M = b ∧ ´I = a⦄
apply *vcg-step*
  1. Γ⊢ ⦃´M = a ∧ ´N = b⦄ ´I := ´M ⦃´N = b ∧ ´I = a⦄
apply *vcg-step*
  1. ⦃´M = a ∧ ´N = b⦄ ⊆ ⦃´N = b ∧ ´M = a⦄
apply *vcg-step*
  1. ⋀M N. N = N ∧ M = M

4.1 Loops

To verify a loop, the user annotates an invariant. For total correctness the user also supplies the variant, which in our case is a well-founded relation on the state-space, which decreases by evaluation of the loop body. Formally this is expressed by first fixing the pre-state with the rsingleton set {τ}. In the postcondition for normal termination of the loop body we end up in a state s and have to show that this state is "smaller than" τ according to the relation: (s, τ) ∈ r. Since abrupt termination will exit the loop immediately we do not have to take any care in this case.

$$\frac{wf\ r \qquad \forall \tau.\ \Gamma,\Theta\vdash_t (\{\tau\} \cap P \cap b)\ c\ (\{s.\ (s, \tau) \in r\} \cap P), A}{\Gamma,\Theta\vdash_t P\ While\ b\ c\ (P \cap -b), A}$$

We make use of the infrastructure for well-founded recursion that is already present in Isabelle/HOL [14]. The following example calculates multiplication by iterated addition. The distance of the loop variable M to a decreases in every iteration. This is expressed by the measure function a − ´M on the state-space.

lemma Γ⊢$_t$ ⦃´M = 0 ∧ ´S = 0⦄
WHILE ´M ≠ a **INV**⦃´S = ´M ∗ b ∧ ´M ≤ a⦄ **VAR** *MEASURE* a − ´M
DO ´S := ´S + b; ´M := ´M + 1 **OD**
⦃´S = a ∗ b⦄
apply *vcg*

1. $\bigwedge M\ S.\ [\![M = 0;\ S = 0]\!] \Longrightarrow S = M * b \wedge M \leq a$
2. $\bigwedge M\ S.\ [\![S = M * b;\ M \leq a;\ M \neq a]\!]$
   $\Longrightarrow a - (M + 1) < a - M \wedge S + b = (M + 1) * b \wedge M + 1 \leq a$
3. $\bigwedge M\ S.\ [\![S = M * b;\ M \leq a;\ \neg\ M \neq a]\!] \Longrightarrow S = a * b$

The verification condition generator gives us three proof obligations, stemming from the path from the precondition to the invariant, from the invariant together with the loop condition through the loop body to the invariant, and finally from the invariant together with the negated loop condition to the postcondition. The variant annotation results in the proof obligation $a - (M + 1) < a - M$ after verification condition generation.

4.2 Abrupt Termination

In case of a *Throw* the abrupt postcondition has to stem from the precondition. The rule for *Catch* is dual to sequential composition. Only if the first statement terminates abruptly the second statement is executed. Thinking of exceptions the first statement forms the protected **try** part, whereas the second statement is the exception handler. Thus the precondition R for the second statement is the postcondition for abrupt termination of the first statement.

$$\Gamma,\Theta \vdash A\ Throw\ Q,A \qquad \frac{\Gamma,\Theta \vdash P\ c_1\ Q,R \quad \Gamma,\Theta \vdash R\ c_2\ Q,A}{\Gamma,\Theta \vdash P\ Catch\ c_1\ c_2\ Q,A}$$

We can implement breaking out of a loop by a **THROW** inside the loop body and enclosing the loop into a **TRY**–**CATCH** block.

lemma $\Gamma \vdash \{\!|\ I \leq 3\ |\!\}$
TRY WHILE *True* **INV** $\{\!|\ I \leq 10\ |\!\}$
   DO IF $I < 10$ **THEN** $I := I + 1$ **ELSE THROW FI OD**
CATCH SKIP YRT
$\{\!|\ I = 10\ |\!\},\{\}$
apply *vcg*

1. $\bigwedge I.\ I \leq 3 \Longrightarrow I \leq 10$
2. $\bigwedge I.\ [\![I \leq 10;\ True]\!]$
   $\Longrightarrow (I < 10 \longrightarrow I + 1 \leq 10) \wedge (\neg\ I < 10 \longrightarrow I = 10)$
3. $\bigwedge I.\ [\![I \leq 10;\ \neg\ True]\!] \Longrightarrow I = 10$

The first subgoal stems from the path from the precondition to the invariant. The second one from the loop body. We can assume the invariant and the loop condition and have to show that the invariant is preserved when we execute the **THEN** branch, and that the **ELSE** branch will imply the assertion for abrupt termination, which will be $\{\!|\ I = 10\ |\!\}$ according to the rule for *Catch* and *Skip*. The third subgoal expresses that normal termination of the while loop has to imply the postcondition. But the loop will never terminate normally and so the third subgoal will trivially hold.

To model a continue we can use the same idea and put a **TRY−CATCH** around the loop body. Or for return we can put the procedure body into a **TRY−CATCH**. To distinguish the kind of abrupt termination we can add a ghost variable Abr to the state-space and store this information before the **THROW**. For example break can be translated to $'Abr :=$ $''Break''$; **THROW**. The matching **CATCH** will peek for this variable to decide whether it is responsible or not: **IF** $'Abr = ''Break''$ **THEN SKIP ELSE THROW FI**. This idea can immediately be extended to exceptions. We just have to make sure to use a global variable to store the kind of exception, so that it will properly pass procedure boundaries.

4.3 Expressions with Side Effects

Expressions in our language model are ordinary HOL expressions (functions over the state-space) and though do not have side effects. The trivial approach is to reduce side-effecting expressions to statements and expressions without side effects. A program transformation step introduces temporary variables to store the result of subexpressions. For example we can get rid of the increment expression in r = m++ + n by first saving the initial value of m in a temporary variable: tmp = m; m = m + 1; r = tmp + n. But in our state-space model this approach is somehow annoying since the temporary variables directly affect the shape of the state record. The essence of the temporary variables is to fix the value of an expression at a certain program state, so that we can later on refer to this value. Since our dynamic command $DynCom$ allows to abstract over the state-space we already have the means to refer to certain program states. In contrast to Oheimb [16] we do not have to invent a special kind of postcondition that explicitely depends on the result value of an expression. Similar to the state monad in functional programming [22] we introduce the command $bind\ e\ c$, which binds the value of expression e (of type $'s \Rightarrow 'v$) at the current program state and feeds it into the following command c (of type $'v \Rightarrow ('s,'p)\ com$): $bind\ e\ c \equiv DynCom\ (\lambda s.\ c\ (e\ s))$. The Hoare rule for $bind$ is the following:

$$\frac{P \subseteq \{s.\ s \in P'\ s\} \qquad \forall s.\ \Gamma,\Theta \vdash (P'\ s)\ c\ (e\ s)\ Q,A}{\Gamma,\Theta \vdash P\ bind\ e\ c\ Q,A}$$

The initial state is s. The intuitive reading of the rule is backwards in the style of the weakest precondition calculation. The postcondition we want to reach is Q or A. Since statement c depends on the initial state s via expression e, the intermediate assertion P' depends on s, too. The actual precondition P describes a subset of the states of $P'\ s$.

In the following example the notation $e \gg m.\ c$ is syntax for $bind\ e\ (\lambda m.\ c)$, whereas the second $\gg$ is just a syntactic variant of sequential composition to indicate the scope of the bound variable m.

lemma
$\Gamma \vdash \{True\} \; `M \gg m. \; `M := `M + 1 \gg `R := m + `N \; \{`R = `M + `N - 1\}$
apply *vcg*
1. $\bigwedge M \; N. \; True \implies M + N = M + 1 + N - 1$

M and N are the initial values of the variables. So in the postcondition $`R$ gets substituted by $M + N$ and $`M$ by $M + 1$.

4.4 Procedures

To introduce a new procedure we provide the command **procedures**.

procedures $Fac \; (N|R) =$
IF $`N = 0$ **THEN** $`R := 1$
ELSE $`R := $ **CALL** $Fac(`N - 1); \; `R := `N * `R$ **FI**

Fac-*spec*: $\forall n. \; \Gamma \vdash \{`N = n\} \; `R := $ **PROC** $Fac(`N) \; \{`R = fac \; n\}$

A procedure is given by its signature followed by its body and some named specifications. The parameters in front of the pipe | are value parameters and behind the pipe are result parameters. Value parameters model call by value semantics. The value of a result parameter at the end of the procedure is passed back to the caller. Most common programming languages do not have the concept of a result parameter. But our language is a model for sequential programs rather than a "real" programming language. We represent **return** e as an assignment of e to the result variable. In order to capture the abrupt termination stemming from a **return** we can use the techniques described in 4.2.

To call a procedure we write $`M := $ **CALL** $Fac(`T)$. This translates to the internal form *call init "Fac" return result* with the proper *init*, *return* and *result* functions. Starting in an initial state s first the *init* function is applied, in order to pass the parameters. Then we execute the procedure body according to the environment Γ. Upon normal termination of the body in a state t, we first exit the procedure according to the function *return s t* and then continue execution with *result s t*. In case of an abrupt termination the final state is given by *return s t*. The function *return* passes back the global variables (and heap components) and restores the local variables of the caller, and *result* additionally assigns results to the scope of the caller. The *return/result* functions get both the initial state s before the procedure call and the final state t after execution of the body. If the body terminates abruptly we only apply the *return* function, thus the global state will be propagated to the caller but no result will be assigned. This is the expected semantics of an exception. We use the dynamic command to capture the states s and t in the definition of the procedure call with parameters:

call init p return result $\equiv$
DynCom
   ($\lambda s.$ **TRY** *Basic init*; *Call p* **CATCH** *Basic (return s)*; **THROW YRT**;
        DynCom ($\lambda t.$ *Basic (return s)*; *result s t*))

Back to our example $'M := \textbf{CALL}\ Fac('I)$. The *init* function copies the actual parameter I to the formal parameter N: $init\ s = s(\!|N := I\ s|\!)$. The *return* function updates the global variables of the initial state with their values in the final state. The global variables are all grouped together in a single record field: $return\ s\ t = s(\!|globals := globals\ t|\!)$. The *result* function is not just a state update function like *return*, but yields a complete command, like the second argument in the *bind* command. This allows us to use the same technique as described for side-effecting expressions to model nested procedure calls. In our example the *result* statement is an assignment that copies the formal result parameter R to M: $result\ s\ t = Basic\ (\lambda u.\ u(\!|M := R\ t|\!))$. Here s is the initial state (before parameter passing), t the final state of the procedure body, and u the state after the *return* from the procedure. In the example the initial state s is not used. But if we assign the result of the procedure to a complex left expression and implement a left to right evaluation strategy like in C we can consider s. For example consider a pointer manipulating function call: p->next = rev(q). The left value of p->next is the address where the result is assigned to. It is evaluated *before* the procedure call, according to the left to right evaluation strategy. We can refer to the initial state s to properly implement this semantics.

Procedure specifications are ordinary Hoare quadruples. We use the parameterless call for the specification; $'R := \textbf{PROC}\ Fac('N)$ is syntactic sugar for *Call "Fac"*. This emphasises that the specification describes the internal behaviour of the procedure, whereas parameter passing corresponds to the procedure call. The precondition of the factorial specification fixes the current value $'N$ to the logical variable n. Universal quantification of n enables us to adapt the specification to an actual parameter. Besides providing convenient syntax, the command *procedures* also defines a constant for the procedure body (named *Fac-body*) and creates two *locales*. The purpose of locales is to set up logical contexts to support modular reasoning [1]. One locale is named like the specification, in our case *Fac-spec*. This locale contains the procedure specification. The second locale is named *Fac-impl* and contains the assumption $\Gamma\ "Fac" = Some\ Fac\text{-}body$, which expresses that the procedure is defined in the current environment. The purpose of these locales is to give us easy means to setup the context in which we will prove programs correct.

Procedure Call By including the locale *Fac-spec*, the following lemma assumes that the specification of the factorial holds. The *vcg* will use this specification to handle the procedure call. The lemma also illustrates locality of I.

lemma includes *Fac-spec* **shows**
$\Gamma \vdash \{'M = 3 \wedge 'I = 2\}\ 'R := \textbf{CALL}\ Fac\ ('M)\ \{'R = 6 \wedge 'I = 2\}$
apply *vcg*

1. $\bigwedge I\ M.\ [\![M = 3;\ I = 2]\!] \Longrightarrow fac\ M = 6 \wedge I = 2$

If the verification condition generator encounters a procedure call, like $\Gamma,\Theta \vdash P$ *call ini p ret res* Q,A, it does not look inside the procedure body, but instead uses a specification $\forall Z.\ \Gamma,\Theta \vdash (P'\ Z)\ Call\ p\ (Q'\ Z),(A'\ Z)$ of the procedure. It adapts the specification to the actual calling context by a variant of the consequence rule, which also takes parameter and result passing into account. In the factorial example n plays the role of the auxiliary variable Z. It transports state information from the pre- to the postcondition. A detailed discussion of consequence rules and auxiliary variables can be found in [9,13].

$$\frac{\begin{array}{c} P \subseteq \{s.\ \exists Z.\ ini\ s \in P'\ Z \wedge (\forall t \in Q'\ Z.\ ret\ s\ t \in R\ s\ t) \wedge (\forall t \in A'\ Z.\ ret\ s\ t \in A)\} \\ \forall s\ t.\ \Gamma,\Theta \vdash (R\ s\ t)\ res\ s\ t\ Q,A \qquad \forall Z.\ \Gamma,\Theta \vdash (P'\ Z)\ Call\ p\ (Q'\ Z),(A'\ Z) \end{array}}{\Gamma,\Theta \vdash P\ call\ ini\ p\ ret\ res\ Q,A}$$

The idea of this rule is to adapt the specification of *Call p* to *call ini p ret res*. Figure 1 shows the sequence of intermediate states for normal termination. We

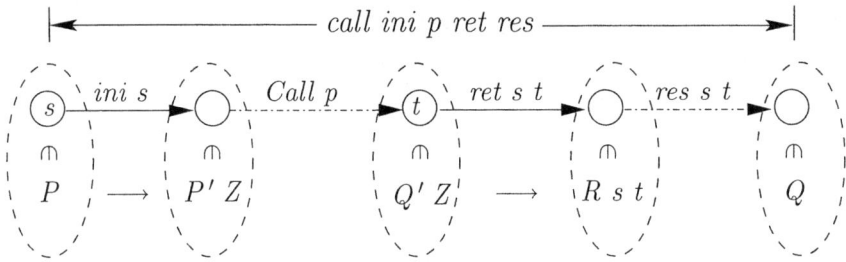

Fig. 1. Procedure call and specification

start in state s for which the precondition P holds. To be able to make use of the procedure specification we have to find a suitable instance of the auxiliary variable Z so that the precondition of the specification holds: $ini\ s \in P'\ Z$. Let t be the state immediately after execution of the procedure body, before returning to the caller and passing results. We know from the specification that the postcondition will hold: $t \in Q'\ Z$. From this we have to conclude that leaving the procedure according to the function ret will lead to a state in $R\ s\ t$. From this state execution of $res\ s\ t$ ends up in a state in Q. For abrupt termination the analogous idea applies, but without the intermediate assertion $R\ s\ t$, since execution of $res\ s\ t$ is skipped. Simplifying the record updates and selections of the side-condition yields the natural proof obligation we have seen before.

The rule for dynamic procedure call is a slight generalisation of the static procedure call. Since the selected procedure depends on the state, we have the liberty to select a suitable specification dependent on the state.

$$\frac{\begin{array}{c} P \subseteq \{s.\ \exists Z.\ ini\ s \in P'\ s\ Z \wedge \\ (\forall t \in Q'\ s\ Z.\ ret\ s\ t \in R\ s\ t) \wedge (\forall t \in A'\ s\ Z.\ ret\ s\ t \in A)\} \\ \forall s\ t.\ \Gamma,\Theta \vdash (R\ s\ t)\ res\ s\ t\ Q,A \\ \forall s \in P.\ \forall Z.\ \Gamma,\Theta \vdash (P'\ s\ Z)\ Call\ (p\ s)\ (Q'\ s\ Z),(A'\ s\ Z) \end{array}}{\Gamma,\Theta \vdash P\ dynCall\ ini\ p\ ret\ res\ Q,A}$$

A Verification Environment for Sequential Imperative Programs   409

Procedure Implementation — Partial Correctness To verify the procedure body we use the rule for recursive procedures. We extend the context with the procedure specification. In this extended context the specification will hold by the assumption rule. We then verify the procedure body by using *vcg*, which will use the assumption to handle the recursive call.

lemma includes *Fac-impl* shows
$\forall n.\ \Gamma \vdash \{\!| \mathcal{N} = n |\!\}\ \mathcal{R} := \mathbf{PROC}\ Fac(\mathcal{N})\ \{\!| \mathcal{R} = fac\ n |\!\}$
apply (*hoare-rule ProcRec1*)

1. $\forall n.\ \Gamma, (\bigcup_n \{(\{\!| \mathcal{N} = n |\!\},\ \mathcal{R} := \mathbf{PROC}\ Fac(\mathcal{N}),\ \{\!| \mathcal{R} = fac\ n |\!\},\ \{\})\})$
   $\vdash \{\!| \mathcal{N} = n |\!\}$
   IF $\mathcal{N} = 0$ **THEN** $\mathcal{R} := 1$
   ELSE CALL $Fac(\mathcal{N} - 1);\ \mathcal{R} := \mathcal{N} * \mathcal{R}$ **FI**
   $\{\!| \mathcal{R} = fac\ n |\!\}$

apply *vcg*

1. $\bigwedge N.\ (N = 0 \longrightarrow 1 = fac\ N) \land (N \neq 0 \longrightarrow N * fac\ (N - 1) = fac\ N)$

The rule *ProcRec1* is a specialised version of the general rule for recursion, tailored for one recursive procedure. The method *hoare-rule* applies a single rule and solves canonical side-conditions. Moreover it expands the procedure body.

Let us now have a look at the general recursion rule. The Hoare logic can deal with (mutually) recursive procedures. We prove that the procedure bodies respect their specification, under the assumption that recursive calls to the procedures will meet their specifications. To model this assumption the context Θ comes in. If a procedure specification is in this context, we can immediately derive this specification within the Hoare logic.

$$\frac{(P,\ c,\ Q,\ A) \in \Theta}{\Gamma, \Theta \vdash P\ c\ Q, A}$$

To handle a set $\mathcal{P}$ of mutually recursive procedures we enrich the context by all the procedure specifications, while we prove their bodies.

$$\frac{\Theta' = \Theta \cup (\bigcup_{p \in \mathcal{P}} \bigcup_Z \{(P\ p\ Z,\ Call\ p,\ Q\ p\ Z,\ A\ p\ Z)\})}{\forall p \in \mathcal{P}.\ \forall Z.\ \Gamma, \Theta' \vdash (P\ p\ Z)\ \text{the}\ (\Gamma\ p)\ (Q\ p\ Z), (A\ p\ Z) \quad \mathcal{P} \subseteq dom\ \Gamma}{\forall p \in \mathcal{P}.\ \forall Z.\ \Gamma, \Theta \vdash (P\ p\ Z)\ Call\ p\ (Q\ p\ Z), (A\ p\ Z)}$$

Since we deal with the set $\mathcal{P}$ of procedures we also have to give the pre- and postconditions for all these procedures. We use the functions P, Q and A, which map procedure names to the desired entities. Z plays the role of an auxiliary (or logical) variable. It usually fixes (parts of) the pre state, so that we can refer to it in the post state. In the Hoare rule for procedure specifications, which we have described before, we had the freedom to pick a particular Z so that $s \in P$ $\longrightarrow$ *init* $s \in P'\ Z$ holds. Since we have the freedom there, we now have to prove the procedure bodies for all possible Z. Finally, with $\mathcal{P} \subseteq dom\ \Gamma$, we make sure that the calculation will not get stuck.

Procedure Implementation — Total Correctness For total correctness the
user supplies a well-founded relation. For the factorial the input parameter N
decreases in the recursive call. This is expressed by the measure function $\lambda(s,p)$.
^sN. The relation can depend on both the state-space s and the procedure name
p. The latter is useful to handle mutual recursion. The prefix superscript in ^sN
is a shorthand for record selection $N\ s$ and is used to refer to state components
of a named state.

lemma includes *Fac-impl* **shows**
$\forall n.\ \Gamma \vdash_t \{\!|\ N = n\ |\!\}\ \mathcal{R} := \textbf{PROC}\ Fac(\mathcal{N})\ \{\!|\ \mathcal{R} = fac\ n\ |\!\}$
apply (*hoare-rule ProcRec1$_t$* [**where** *r=measure* $(\lambda(s,p).\ ^sN)$])

1. $\forall \tau\ n.\ \Gamma,(\bigcup n\ \{(\{\!|\ N = n\ |\!\} \cap \{\!|\ N < {}^\tau N\ |\!\},\ \mathcal{R} := \textbf{PROC}\ Fac(\mathcal{N}),$
   $\{\!|\ \mathcal{R} = fac\ n\ |\!\},\ \{\})\})$
   $\vdash_t (\{\tau\} \cap \{\!|\ N = n\ |\!\})$
   IF $\mathcal{N} = 0$ **THEN** $\mathcal{R} := 1$
   ELSE CALL $Fac(\mathcal{N} - 1);\ \mathcal{R} := \mathcal{N} * \mathcal{R}$ **FI**
   $\{\!|\ \mathcal{R} = fac\ n\ |\!\}$

We may only assume the specification for "smaller" states $\{\!|\ N < {}^\tau N\ |\!\}$, where
state τ gets fixed in the precondition.

apply *vcg*

1. $\bigwedge N.\ (N = 0 \longrightarrow 1 = fac\ N)\ \wedge$
   $(N \neq 0 \longrightarrow N - 1 < N \wedge N * fac\ (N-1) = fac\ N)$

The measure function results in the proof obligation $N - 1 < N$.

In contrast to partial correctness we only assume "smaller" recursive procedure calls correct while verifying the procedure bodies. Here "smaller" again is in the sense of a well-founded relation r. We fix the pre-state of the procedure p with the singleton set $\{\tau\}$. For every call to a procedure q in a state s which is "smaller" than the initial call of p in state τ according to the relation $(((s,q),(\tau,p)) \in r)$, we can safely assume the specification of q while verifying the body of p.

$$\frac{\Theta' = \lambda \tau\ p.\ \Theta \cup (\bigcup_{q \in \mathcal{P}} \bigcup_Z \{(P\ q\ Z \cap \{s.\ ((s,q),\tau,p) \in r\}, Call\ q, Q\ q\ Z, A\ q\ Z)\})}{\forall p \in \mathcal{P}.\ \forall Z.\ \Gamma, \Theta \vdash_t (P\ p\ Z)\ Call\ p\ (Q\ p\ Z),(A\ p\ Z)} \quad \begin{array}{c} \forall p \in \mathcal{P}.\ \forall \tau\ Z.\ \Gamma,\Theta'\ \tau\ p \vdash_t (\{\tau\} \cap P\ p\ Z)\ the\ (\Gamma\ p)\ (Q\ p\ Z),(A\ p\ Z) \\ wf\ r \quad \mathcal{P} \subseteq dom\ \Gamma \end{array}$$

4.5 Heap

The heap can contain structured values like **structs** in C or records in Pascal.
Our model of the heap follows Burstall [2]. We have one heap variable f of type
$ref \Rightarrow value$ for each component f of type *value* of the **struct**. References *ref*
are isomorphic to the natural numbers and contain *Null*.

A typical structure to represent a linked list in the heap is struct list {int cont; list *next}. The structure contains two components, cont and next. So we will also get two heap variables, $cont$ of type $ref \Rightarrow int$ and $next$ of type $ref \Rightarrow ref$ in our state-space record:

record $heap =$
$\quad next :: ref \Rightarrow ref$
$\quad cont :: ref \Rightarrow int$

record $state =$
$\quad globals :: heap$
$\quad p :: ref$
$\quad q :: ref$
$\quad r :: ref$

We follow the approach of [10], and abstract the pointer structure in the heap to HOL lists of references. Then we can specify further properties on the level of HOL lists, rather than on the heap:

$List\ x\ h\ [] = (x = Null)$
$List\ x\ h\ (p\ \#\ ps) = (x = p \land x \neq Null \land List\ (h\ x)\ h\ ps)$

The list of references is obtained from the heap h by starting with the reference x, following the references in h up to $Null$. With a generalised predicate that describes a path in the heap, Mehta and Nipkow [11] show how this idea can canonically be extended to cyclic lists.

We define in place list reversal. The list pointed to by p in the beginning is Ps. In the end q points to the reversed list $rev\ Ps$. The notation $r \rightarrow f$ mimics the field selection syntax of C and is translated to ordinary function application for field lookup and function update for field assignment.

procedures $Rev(p|q) =$
$'q := Null;$
WHILE $'p \neq Null$
DO $'r := 'p;\ 'p := 'p \rightarrow 'next;\ 'r \rightarrow 'next := 'q;\ 'q := 'r$ **OD**

Rev-spec:
$\quad \forall \sigma\ Ps.\ \Gamma \vdash \{\!|\sigma.\ List\ 'p\ 'next\ Ps|\!\}\ 'q := \mathbf{PROC}\ Rev('p)$
$\qquad \{\!|List\ 'q\ 'next\ (rev\ Ps) \land (\forall p.\ p \notin set\ Ps \longrightarrow ('next\ p = {}^{\sigma}next\ p))|\!\}$
Rev-modifies:
$\quad \forall \sigma.\ \Gamma \vdash \{\sigma\}\ 'q := \mathbf{PROC}\ Rev('p)\ \{t.\ t\ may\text{-}only\text{-}modify\text{-}globals\ \sigma\ in\ [next]\}$

We give two specifications this time. The first one captures the functional behaviour and additionally expresses that all parts of the $next$-heap not contained in Ps, will stay the same (σ denotes the pre-state). Fixing a state is part of the assertion syntax: $\{\!|\sigma.\ ...|\!\}$ translates to $\{s.\ s=\sigma\ ...\}$ and ${}^{\sigma}next$ to $next\ \sigma$. The second specification is a modifies-clause that lists all the state components that may be changed by the procedure. Therefore we know that the $cont$ parts will remain unchanged. Thus the main specification can focus on the relevant parts of the state-space. The assertion $t\ may\text{-}only\text{-}modify\text{-}globals\ \sigma\ in\ [next]$ abbreviates the following relation between the final state t and the initial state σ: $\exists next.$ $globals\ t = (globals\ \sigma)(\!|next:=next|\!)$. This modifies-clause can be exploited during verification condition generation. We derive that we can reduce the $result$ function in the call to Rev, which copies the global components $next$ and $cont$

back, to one that only copies *next* back. So *cont* will actually behave like a local variable in the resulting proof obligation. This is an effective way to express separation of different pointer structures in the heap and can be handled completely automatically during verification condition generation. For example, reversing a list will only modify the *next*-heap but not some *left*- and *right*-heaps of a tree structure. Moreover the modifies-clause itself can be verified automatically. The following example illustrates the effect of the modifies-clause.

lemma includes *Rev-spec* + *Rev-modifies* **shows**
$\Gamma \vdash \{\!|\,'cont{=}c \land List\ 'p\ 'next\ Ps\,|\!\}\ 'p := \mathbf{CALL}\ Rev('p)$
 $\{\!|\,'cont{=}c \land List\ 'p\ 'next\ (rev\ Ps)\,|\!\}$
apply *vcg*

1. $\bigwedge next\ cont\ p.\ List\ p\ next\ Ps \Longrightarrow$
    $\forall nexta\ q.$
      $List\ q\ nexta\ (rev\ Ps) \land (\forall p.\ p \notin set\ Ps \longrightarrow nexta\ p = next\ p) \longrightarrow$
      $cont = cont \land List\ q\ nexta\ (rev\ Ps)$

The impact of the modifies-clause shows up in the verification condition. The *cont*-heap results in the same variable before and after the procedure call (*cont* = *cont*), whereas the *next*-heap is described by *next* in the beginning and by *nexta* in the end. The specification of *Rev* relates both *next*-heap states.

Memory Management To model allocation and deallocation we need some bookkeeping of allocated references. This can be achieved by an auxiliary ghost variable *alloc* in the state-space. A good candidate is a list of allocated references. A list is per se finite, so that we can always get a new reference. By the length of the list we can also handle space limitations. Allocation of memory means to append a new reference to the allocation list. Deallocation of memory means to remove a reference from the allocation list. To guard against dangling pointers we can regard the allocation list: $\{\!|\,'p{\neq}Null \land 'p \in set\ 'alloc\,|\!\} \mapsto 'p{\rightarrow}'cont := 2$.

The use of guards is a flexible mechanism to adapt the model to the kind of language we are looking at. If it is type safe like Java and there is no explicit deallocation by the user, we can remove some guards. If the **new** instruction of the programming language does not initialise the allocated memory we can add another ghost variable to watch for initialised memory through guards.

5 Conclusion

We have presented a flexible, sound and complete Hoare calculus for sequential imperative programs with mutually recursive procedures and dynamic procedure call. We have elaborated how to model various kinds of abrupt termination like **break**, **continue**, **return** and exceptions, how to deal with side-effecting expressions, global variables, heap and memory management issues. The polymorphic state space of the programming language allows us to choose the adequate representation for the current verification task. Depending on the context we can for example decide, whether it is preferable to model certain variables as unbounded integers in HOL or as bit-vectors, without changing the program representation or logics. Guards make it possible to customise the runtime faults we are interested in. Using records as state space representation gives us a natural way to express typing of program variables and yields comprehensible verification conditions. Moreover in combination with the modifies-clause we can lift separation of heap components, which are directly expressible in the split heap model, to the level of procedures, without having to introduce a new logic like separation logic [19]. Crucial parts of the frame problem can then already be handled during verification condition generation. The calculus is developed, verified and integrated in the theorem prover Isabelle and the resulting verification environment seamless fits into the infrastructure of Isabelle/HOL.

This work is part of the Verisoft project, a long-term research project aiming at the pervasive verification of computer systems (hard- and software). We translate a subset of C to the verification environment and have started to verify parts of an operating system, a compiler and an email client. We also verify the translation into the verification environment. Moreover we validated the feasibility of our approach by verifying algorithms for binary decision diagrams, involving a high degree of side effects due to sharing in the pointer structure [17]. Applying the verification condition generator to the annotated programs results in quite sizable proof obligations. But since they closely resemble the control flow the connection to the input program is not lost. To prove them, we used the structured proof language of Isar [24] that allows us to focus and keep track of the various different aspects, so that we can conduct the proof in a sensible order. Moreover it turned out that the Isar proofs are quite robust with regard to the iterative adaptation of the invariants resulting from failed proof attempts. The already established lines of reasoning remained stable, while adding new aspects to, or strengthening parts of the invariant. Altogether we gained confidence that our approach is practically useful.

References

1. C. Ballarin. Locales and locale expressions in Isabelle/Isar. In S. Berardi, M. Coppo, and F. Damiani, editors, *Types for Proofs and Programs: International Workshop, TYPES 2003, Torino, Italy, April 30–May 4, 2003, Selected Papers*, number 3085 in LNCS, pages 34–50. Springer, 2004.
2. R. Burstall. Some techniques for proving correctness of programs which alter data structures. In B. Meltzer and D. Michie, editors, *Machine Intelligence 7*, pages 23–50. Edinburgh University Press, 1972.
3. J.-C. Filliâtre. Verification of Non-Functional Programs using Interpretations in Type Theory. *Journal of Functional Programming*, 13(4):709–745, July 2003.
4. J.-C. Filliâtre. Why: a multi-language multi-prover verification tool. Research Report 1366, LRI, Université Paris Sud, March 2003.

5. J. Harrison. Formalizing Dijkstra. In J. Grundy and M. Newey, editors, *Theorem Proving in Higher Order Logics: 11th International Conference, TPHOLs'98*, volume 1497 of *LNCS*, pages 171–188, Canberra, Australia, 1998. Springer.
6. P. V. Homeier. *Trustworthy Tools for Trustworthy Programs: A Mechanically Verified Verification Condition Generator for the Total Correctness of Procedures*. PhD thesis, Department of Computer Science, University of California, Los Angeles, 1995.
7. M. Huisman. *Java program verification in higher order logic with PVS and Isabelle*. PhD thesis, University of Nijmegen, 2000.
8. B. Jacobs. Weakest precondition reasoning for Java programs with JML annotations. *Journal of Logic and Algebraic Programming*, 58:61–88, 2004.
9. T. Kleymann. Hoare Logic and auxiliary variables. *Formal Aspects of Computing*, 11(5):541–566, 1999.
10. F. Mehta and T. Nipkow. Proving pointer programs in higher-order logic. In F. Baader, editor, *Automated Deduction — CADE-19*, volume 2741 of *LNCS*, pages 121–135. Springer, 2003.
11. F. Mehta and T. Nipkow. Proving pointer programs in higher-order logic. *Information and Computation*, 2005. To appear.
12. M.J.C. Gordon. Mechanizing programming logics in higher-order logic. In G.M. Birtwistle and P.A. Subrahmanyam, editors, *Current Trends in Hardware Verification and Automatic Theorem Proving (Proceedings of the Workshop on Hardware Verification)*, pages 387–439, Banff, Canada, 1988. Springer, Berlin.
13. T. Nipkow. Hoare logics in Isabelle/HOL. In H. Schwichtenberg and R. Steinbrüggen, editors, *Proof and System-Reliability*, pages 341–367. Kluwer, 2002.
14. T. Nipkow, L. Paulson, and M. Wenzel. *Isabelle/HOL — A Proof Assistant for Higher-Order Logic*, volume 2283 of *LNCS*. Springer, 2002.
15. M. Norrish. *C formalised in HOL*. PhD thesis, University of Cambridge, 1998.
16. D. v. Oheimb. *Analyzing Java in Isabelle/HOL: Formalization, Type Safety and Hoare Logic*. PhD thesis, Technische Universität München, 2001.
17. V. Ortner. Verification of BDD Algorithms. Master's thesis, Technische Universität München, 2004. http://www.veronika.langlotz.info/.
18. L. Prensa Nieto. *Verification of Parallel Programs with the Owicki-Gries and Rely-Guarantee Methods in Isabelle/HOL*. PhD thesis, Technische Universität München, 2002.
19. J. C. Reynolds. Separation logic: A logic for shared mutable data structures. In *Proc. 17th IEEE Symposium on Logic in Computer Science (LICS 2002)*, pages 55–74, 2002.
20. N. Schirmer. A Verification Environment for Sequential Imperative Programs in Isabelle/HOL. In G. Klein, editor, *Proc. NICTA Workshop on OS Verification 2004*, 2004. ID: 0401005T-1, http://www4.in.tum.de/~schirmer.
21. J. von Wright, J. Hekanaho, P. Luostarinen, and T. Långbacka. Mechanizing some advanced refinement concepts. *Formal Methods in System Design*, 3:49–81, 1993.
22. P. Wadler. The essence of functional programming. In *Proc. 19th ACM Symp. Principles of Programming Languages*, 1992.
23. M. Wenzel. Miscellaneous Isabelle/Isar examples for higher order logic. Isabelle/Isar proof document, 2001.
24. M. Wenzel. *Isabelle/Isar — A Versatile Environment for Human-Readable Formal Proof Documents*. PhD thesis, Institut für Informatik, Technische Universität München, 2002.
   http://tumb1.biblio.tu-muenchen.de/publ/diss/in/2002/wenzel.html.

Can a Higher-Order and a First-Order Theorem Prover Cooperate?*

Christoph Benzmüller[1], Volker Sorge[2], Mateja Jamnik[3], and Manfred Kerber[2]

[1] Fachbereich Informatik, Universität des Saarlandes
66041 Saarbrücken, Germany (www.ags.uni-sb.de/~chris)
[2] School of Computer Science, The University of Birmingham
Birmingham B15 2TT, England, UK (www.cs.bham.ac.uk/~{vxs|mmk})
[3] University of Cambridge Computer Laboratory
Cambridge CB3 0FD, England, UK (www.cl.cam.ac.uk/~mj201)

Abstract. State-of-the-art first-order automated theorem proving systems have reached considerable strength over recent years. However, in many areas of mathematics they are still a long way from reliably proving theorems that would be considered relatively simple by humans. For example, when reasoning about sets, relations, or functions, first-order systems still exhibit serious weaknesses. While it has been shown in the past that higher-order reasoning systems can solve problems of this kind automatically, the complexity inherent in their calculi and their inefficiency in dealing with large numbers of clauses prevent these systems from solving a whole range of problems.

We present a solution to this challenge by combining a higher-order and a first-order automated theorem prover, both based on the resolution principle, in a flexible and distributed environment. By this we can exploit concise problem formulations without forgoing efficient reasoning on first-order subproblems. We demonstrate the effectiveness of our approach on a set of problems still considered non-trivial for many first-order theorem provers.

1 Introduction

When dealing with problems containing higher-order concepts, such as sets, functions, or relations, today's state-of-the-art first-order automated theorem provers (ATPs) still exhibit weaknesses on problems considered relatively simple by humans (cf. [14]). One reason is that the problem formulations use an encoding in a first-order set theory, which makes it particularly challenging when trying to prove theorems from first principles, that is, basic axioms. Therefore, to aid ATPs in finding proofs, problems are often enriched by hand-picked additional lemmata, or axioms of the selected set theory are dropped leaving the theory incomplete. This has recently motivated extensions of state-of-the-art first-order

---
* This work was supported by EPSRC grant GR/M22031 and DFG-SFB 378 (first author), EU Marie-Curie-Fellowship HPMF-CT-2002-01701 (second author), and EPSRC Advanced Research Fellowship GR/R76783 (third author).

calculi and systems, as for example presented in [14] for the SATURATE system. The extended SATURATE system can solve some problems from the SET domain in the TPTP [24] which VAMPIRE [21] and E-SETHEO's [23] cannot solve.

While it has already been shown in [6,2] that many problems of this nature can be easily proved from first principles using a concise higher-order representation and the higher-order resolution ATP LEO, the combinatorial explosion inherent in LEO's calculus prevents the prover from solving a whole range of possible problems with one universal strategy. Often higher-order problems require only relatively few but essential steps of higher-order reasoning, while the overwhelming part of the reasoning is first-order or even propositional level. This suggests that LEO's performance could be improved when combining it with a first-order ATP to search efficiently for a possible refutation in the subset of those clauses that are essentially first-order.

The advantages of such a combination — further discussed in Sec. 2 — are not only that many problems can still be efficiently shown from first principles in a general purpose approach, but also that problems can be expressed in a very concise way. For instance, we present 45 problems from the SET domain of the TPTP-v3.0.1, together with their entire formalisation in less than two pages in this paper, which is difficult to achieve within a framework that does not provide λ-abstraction. We use this problem set, which is an extension of the problems considered in [14], in Sec. 4 to show the effectiveness of our approach. While many of the considered problems can be proved by LEO alone with some strategy, the combination of LEO with the first-order ATP BLIKSEM [11] is not only able to show more problems, but also needs only a single strategy to solve them. Several of our problems are considered very challenging by the first-order community and five of them (of which LEO can solve four) have a TPTP rating of 1.00, saying that they cannot be solved by any TPTP prover to date.

Technically, the combination — described in more detail in Sec. 3 — has been realised in the concurrent reasoning system OANTS [22,8] which enables the cooperation of hybrid reasoning systems to construct a common proof object. In our past experiments, OANTS has been successfully employed to check the validity of set equations using higher-order and first-order ATPs, model generation, and computer algebra [5]. While this already enabled a cooperation between LEO and a first-order ATP, the proposed solution could not be classified as a general purpose approach. A major shortcoming was that all communication of partial results had to be conducted via the common proof object, which was very inefficient for hard examples. Thus, the solved examples from set theory were considered too trivial, albeit they were often similar to those still considered challenging in the TPTP in the first-order context. In this paper we now present a novel approach to the cooperation between LEO and BLIKSEM inside OANTS by decentralising communication. This leads not only to a higher overall efficiency — Sec. 4 details our results — but also to a general purpose approach based on a single strategy in LEO.

2 Why Linking Higher-Order and First-Order?

Existing higher-order ATPs generally exhibit deficits in efficiently reasoning with first-order problems for several reasons. Unlike in the case of first-order provers, for which sophisticated calculi and strategies, as well as advanced implementation techniques, such as term indexing [19], have been developed, fully mechanisable higher-order calculi are still at a comparably early stage of development. Some problems are much harder in higher-order, for instance, unification is undecidable, strong constraining term- and literal-orderings are not available, extensionality reasoning and set variable instantiation has to be addressed. Nevertheless, for some mathematical problem domains, such as naive set theory, for instance, automated higher-order reasoning performs very well.

We motivate the need for linking higher-order and first-order ATPs with some examples from Table 1. It contains a range of challenging problems taken from the TPTP, against which we will evaluate our system in Sec. 4. The problems are given by the identifiers used in the SET domain of the TPTP, and are formalised in a variant of Church's simply typed λ-calculus with prefix polymorphism. In classical type theory terms and all their sub-terms are typed. Polymorphism allows the introduction of type variables such that statements can be made for all types. For instance, in problem SET014+4 the universally quantified variable $X_{o\alpha}$ denotes a mapping from objects of type α to objects of type o. We use Church's notation $o\alpha$, which stands for the functional type $\alpha \to o$. The reader is referred to [1] for a more detailed introduction. In the remainder, o will denote the type of truth values, and small Greek letters will denote arbitrary types. Thus, $X_{o\alpha}$ (resp. its η-longform $\lambda y_\alpha . Xy$) is actually a characteristic function denoting the set of elements of type α, for which the predicate associated with X holds. As further notational convention, we use capital letter variables to denote sets, functions, or relations, while lower case letters denote individuals. Types are usually only given in the first occurrence of a variable and omitted if inferable from the context.

The problems in Table 1 employ defined concepts that are specified in a knowledge base of hierarchical theories that LEO has access to. All concepts necessary for defining our problems in Table 1 are given in Table 2. Concepts are defined in terms of λ-expressions and they may contain other, already specified concepts. For presentation purposes, we use customary mathematical symbols $\cup, \cap$, etc., for some concepts like *union, intersection*, etc., and we also use infix notation. For instance, the definition of union on sets can be easily read in its more common mathematical representation $A \cup B := \{x | x \in A \lor x \in B\}$. Before proving a problem, LEO always expands — recursively, if necessary — all occurring concepts. This straightforward expansion to first principles is realised by an automated preprocess in our current approach.

SET171+3 We first discuss example SET171+3 to contrast our formalisation to a standard first-order one. After recursively expanding the input problem, that is, completely reducing it to first principles, LEO turns it into a negated unit clause. Since this initial clause is not in normal form, LEO first normalises it with explicit

Table 1. Problems from TPTP for the evaluation of OANTS

SET	Problem Formalisation
014+4	$\forall X_{o\alpha}, Y_{o\alpha}, A_{o\alpha} \bullet [[X \subseteq A \land Y \subseteq A] \Rightarrow (X \cup Y) \subseteq A]$
017+1	$\forall x_\alpha, y_\alpha, z_\alpha \bullet [UnOrderedPair(x,y) = UnOrderedPair(x,z) \Rightarrow y = z]$
066+1	$\forall x_\alpha, y_\alpha \bullet [UnOrderedPair(x,y) = UnOrderedPair(y,x)]$
067+1	$\forall x_\alpha, y_\alpha \bullet [UnOrderedPair(x,x) \subseteq UnOrderedPair(x,y)]$
076+1	$\forall x_\alpha, y_\alpha \forall Z_{o\alpha} \bullet x \in Z \land y \in Z \Rightarrow UnOrderedPair(x,y) \subseteq Z$
086+1	$\forall x_\alpha \bullet \exists y_\alpha \bullet [y \in Singleton(x)]$
096+1	$\forall X_{o\alpha}, y_\alpha \bullet [X \subseteq Singleton(y) \Rightarrow [X = \emptyset \lor X = Singleton(y)]]$
143+3	$\forall X_{o\alpha}, Y_{o\alpha}, Z_{o\alpha} \bullet [(X \cap Y) \cap Z = X \cap (Y \cap Z)]$
171+3	$\forall X_{o\alpha}, Y_{o\alpha}, Z_{o\alpha} \bullet [X \cup (Y \cap Z) = (X \cup Y) \cap (X \cup Z)]$
580+3	$\forall X_{o\alpha}, Y_{o\alpha}, u_\alpha \bullet [u \in ExclUnion(X,Y) \Leftrightarrow [u \in X \Leftrightarrow u \notin Y]]$
601+3	$\forall \bullet X_{o\alpha}, Y_{o\alpha}, Z_{o\alpha} [(X \cap Y) \cup ((Y \cap Z) \cup (Z \cap X)) = (X \cup Y) \cap ((Y \cup Z) \cup (Z \cup X))]$
606+3	$\forall X_{o\alpha}, Y_{o\alpha} \bullet [X \setminus (X \cap Y) = X \setminus Y]$
607+3	$\forall X_{o\alpha}, Y_{o\alpha} \bullet [X \cup (Y \setminus X) = X \cup Y]$
609+3	$\forall X_{o\alpha}, Y_{o\alpha}, Z_{o\alpha} \bullet [X \setminus (Y \setminus Z) = (X \setminus Y) \cup (X \cap Z)]$
611+3	$\forall X_{o\alpha}, Y_{o\alpha} \bullet [X \cap Y = \emptyset \Leftrightarrow X \setminus Y = X]$
612+3	$\forall X_{o\alpha}, Y_{o\alpha}, Z_{o\alpha} \bullet [X \setminus (Y \cup Z) = (X \setminus Y) \cap (X \setminus Z)]$
614+3	$\forall X_{o\alpha}, Y_{o\alpha}, Z_{o\alpha} \bullet [(X \setminus Y) \setminus Z = X \setminus (Y \cup Z)]$
615+3	$\forall X_{o\alpha}, Y_{o\alpha}, Z_{o\alpha} \bullet [(X \cup Y) \setminus Z = (X \setminus Z) \cup (Y \setminus Z)]$
623+3	$\forall X_{o\alpha}, Y_{o\alpha}, Z_{o\alpha} \bullet [ExclUnion(ExclUnion(X,Y), Z) = ExclUnion(X, ExclUnion(Y,Z))]$
624+3	$\forall X_{o\alpha}, Y_{o\alpha}, Z_{o\alpha} \bullet [Meets(X, (Y \cup Z)) \Leftrightarrow [Meets(X,Y) \lor Meets(X,Z)]]$
630+3	$\forall X_{o\alpha}, Y_{o\alpha} \bullet [Misses(X \cap Y, ExclUnion(X,Y))]$
640+3	$\forall R_{o\beta\alpha}, Q_{o\beta\alpha} \bullet [Subrel(R,Q) \Rightarrow Subrel(R, (\lambda u_\alpha \bullet \top) \times (\lambda v_\beta \bullet \top))]$
646+3	$\forall x_\alpha, y_\beta \bullet [Subrel(Pair(x,y), (\lambda u_\alpha \bullet \top) \times (\lambda v_\beta \bullet \top))]$
647+3	$\forall R_{o\beta\alpha}, X_{o\alpha} \bullet [(RDom(R) \subseteq X) \Rightarrow Subrel(R, X \times RCodom(R))]$
648+3	$\forall R_{o\beta\alpha}, Y_{o\beta} \bullet [(RCodom(R) \subseteq Y) \Rightarrow Subrel(R, RDom(R) \times Y)]$
649+3	$\forall R_{o\beta\alpha}, X_{o\alpha}, Y_{o\beta} \bullet [[RDom(R) \subseteq X \land RCodom(R) \subseteq Y] \Rightarrow Subrel(R, X \times Y)]$
651+3	$\forall R_{o\beta\alpha} \bullet [RDom(R) \subseteq A_{o\alpha} \Rightarrow Subrel(R, A \times (\lambda v_\beta \bullet \top))]$
657+3	$\forall R_{o\beta\alpha} \bullet [Field(R) \subseteq ((\lambda u_\alpha \bullet \top) \cup (\lambda v_\beta \bullet \top))]$
669+3	$\forall R_{o\alpha\alpha} \bullet [Subrel(Id(\lambda u_\alpha \bullet \top), R) \Rightarrow [(\lambda u_\alpha \bullet \top) \subseteq RDom(R) \land (\lambda u_\alpha \bullet \top) = RCodom(R)]]$
670+3	$\forall Z_{o\alpha}, R_{o\beta\alpha}, X_{o\alpha}Y_{o\beta} \bullet [IsRelOn(R,X,Y) \Rightarrow IsRelOn(RestrictRDom(R,Z), Z, Y)]$
671+3	$\forall Z_{o\alpha}, R_{o\beta\alpha}, X_{o\alpha}, Y_{o\beta} \bullet [[IsRelOn(R,X,Y) \land X \subseteq Z] \Rightarrow RestrictRDom(R,Z) = R]$
672+3	$\forall Z_{o\beta}, R_{o\beta\alpha}, X_{o\alpha}Y_{o\beta} \bullet [IsRelOn(R,X,Y) \Rightarrow IsRelOn(RestrictRCodom(R,Z), X, Z)]$
673+3	$\forall Z_{o\beta}, R_{o\beta\alpha}, X_{o\alpha}, Y_{o\beta} \bullet [[IsRelOn(R,X,Y) \land Y \subseteq Z] \Rightarrow RestrictRCodom(R,Z) = R]$
680+3	$\forall R_{o\beta\alpha}, X_{o\alpha}, Y_{o\beta} \bullet [IsRelOn(R,X,Y) \Rightarrow$ $[\forall u_\alpha \bullet u \in X \Rightarrow [u \in RDom(R) \Leftrightarrow \exists v_\beta \bullet v \in Y \land R(u,v)]]]$
683+3	$\forall R_{o\beta\alpha}, X_{o\alpha}, Y_{o\beta} \bullet [IsRelOn(R,X,Y) \Rightarrow$ $[\forall v_\beta \bullet v \in Y \Rightarrow [v \in RCodom(R) \Rightarrow \exists u_\alpha \bullet u \in X \land u \in RDom(R)]]]$
684+3	$\forall P_{o\beta\alpha}, R_{o\gamma\beta}, x_\alpha, z_\gamma \bullet [RelComp(P,R)xz \Leftrightarrow \exists y_\beta \bullet Pxy \land Ryz]$
686+3	$\forall Z_{o\alpha}, R_{o\gamma\beta}, x_\alpha \bullet [x \in InverseImageR(R,Z) \Leftrightarrow \exists y_\alpha \bullet Rxy \land x \in Z]$
716+4	$\forall F_{\beta\alpha}, G_{\gamma\beta} \bullet [[Inj(F) \land Inj(G)] \Rightarrow Inj(G \circ F)]$
724+4	$\forall F_{\beta\alpha}, G_{\gamma\beta}, H_{\gamma\beta} \bullet [[F \circ G = H \land Surj(F)] \Rightarrow G = H]$
741+4	$\forall F_{\beta\alpha}, G_{\gamma\beta}, H_{\alpha\gamma} \bullet [[Inj((F \circ G) \circ H) \land Surj((G \circ H) \circ F) \land Surj((H \circ F) \circ G)] \Rightarrow Bij(H)]$
747+4	$\forall F_{\beta\alpha}, G_{\gamma\beta}, \lhd^1_{o\alpha\alpha}, \lhd^2_{o\beta\beta}, \lhd^3_{o\gamma\gamma} \bullet [[IncreasingF(F, \lhd^1, \lhd^2) \land DecreasingF(G, \lhd^2, \lhd^3)] \Rightarrow$ $DecreasingF(F \circ G, \lhd^1, \lhd^3)]$
752+4	$\forall X_{o\alpha}, Y_{o\alpha}, F_{\beta\alpha} \bullet [ImageF(F, X \cup Y) = ImageF(F,X) \cup ImageF(F,Y)]$
753+4	$\forall X_{o\alpha}, Y_{o\alpha}, F_{\beta\alpha} \bullet [ImageF(F, X \cap Y) \subseteq ImageF(F,X) \cap ImageF(F,Y)]$
764+4	$\forall F_{\beta\alpha} \bullet [InverseImageF(F, \emptyset) = \emptyset]$
770+4	$\forall R_{o\beta\alpha}, Q_{o\beta\alpha} \bullet [[EquivRel(R) \land EquivRel(Q)] \Rightarrow$ $[EquivClasses(R) = EquivClasses(Q) \lor Disjoint(EquivClasses(R), EquivClasses(Q))]]$

clause normalisation rules to reach some proper initial clauses. In our concrete case, this normalisation process leads to the following unit clause consisting of a (syntactically not solvable) unification constraint (here $B_{o\alpha}, C_{o\alpha}, D_{o\alpha}$ are Skolem constants and Bx is obtained from expansion of $x \in B$):

$$[(\lambda x_\alpha \bullet Bx \lor (Cx \land Dx)) =^? (\lambda x_\alpha \bullet (Bx \lor Cx) \land (Bx \lor Dx))]$$

Note that negated primitive equations are generally automatically converted by LEO into unification constraints. This is why $[(\lambda x_\alpha \bullet Bx \lor (Cx \land Dx)) =^?$

Table 2. Defined concepts occurring in problems from Table 1

Defined Notions in Theory Typed Set
$\_\in\_ := \lambda x_\alpha, A_{o\alpha}\textbf{.}[Ax]$
$\emptyset := [\lambda x_\alpha\textbf{.}\bot]$
$\_\subseteq\_ := \lambda A_{o\alpha}, B_{o\alpha}\textbf{.}[\forall x_\alpha\textbf{.}x \in A \Rightarrow x \in B]$
$\_\cup\_ := \lambda A_{o\alpha}, B_{o\alpha}\textbf{.}[\lambda x_\alpha\textbf{.}x \in A \vee x \in B]$
$\_\cap\_ := \lambda A_{o\alpha}, B_{o\alpha}\textbf{.}[\lambda x_\alpha\textbf{.}x \in A \wedge x \in B]$
$\overline{\_} := \lambda A_{o\alpha}\textbf{.}[\lambda x_\alpha\textbf{.}x \notin A]$
$\_\backslash\_ := \lambda A_{o\alpha}, B_{o\alpha}\textbf{.}[\lambda x_\alpha\textbf{.}x \in A \wedge x \notin B]$
$ExclUnion(\_,\_) := \lambda A_{o\alpha}, B_{o\alpha}\textbf{.}[(A\backslash B) \cup (B\backslash A)]$
$Disjoint(\_,\_) := \lambda A_{o\alpha}, B_{o\alpha}\textbf{.}[A \cap B = \emptyset]$
$Meets(\_,\_) := \lambda A_{o\alpha}, B_{o\alpha}\textbf{.}[\exists x_\alpha\textbf{.}x \in A \wedge x \in B]$
$Misses(\_,\_) := \lambda A_{o\alpha}, B_{o\alpha}\textbf{.}[\neg \exists x_\alpha\textbf{.}x \in A \wedge x \in B]$
Defined Notions in Theory Relation
$UnOrderedPair(\_,\_) := \lambda x_\alpha, y_\alpha\textbf{.}[\lambda u_\alpha\textbf{.}u = x \vee u = y]$
$Singleton(\_) := \lambda x_\alpha\textbf{.}[\lambda u_\alpha\textbf{.}u = x]$
$Pair(\_,\_) := \lambda x_\alpha, y_\beta\textbf{.}[\lambda u_\alpha, v_\beta\textbf{.}u = x \wedge v = y]$
$\_\times\_ := \lambda A_{o\alpha}, B_{o\beta}\textbf{.}[\lambda u_\alpha, v_\beta\textbf{.}u \in A \wedge v \in B]$
$RDom(\_) := \lambda R_{o\beta\alpha}\textbf{.}[\lambda x_\alpha\textbf{.}\exists y_\beta\textbf{.}Rxy]$
$RCodom(\_) := \lambda R_{o\beta\alpha}\textbf{.}[\lambda y_\beta\textbf{.}\exists x_\alpha\textbf{.}Rxy]$
$Subrel(\_,\_) := \lambda R_{o\beta\alpha}, Q_{o\beta\alpha}\textbf{.}[\forall x_\alpha\textbf{.}\forall y_\alpha\textbf{.}Rxy \Rightarrow Qxy]$
$Id(\_) := \lambda A_{o\alpha}\textbf{.}[\lambda x_\alpha, y_\alpha\textbf{.}x \in A \wedge x = y]$
$Field(\_) := \lambda R_{o\beta\alpha}\textbf{.}[RDom(B) \cup RCodom(R)]$
$IsRelOn(\_,\_,\_) := \lambda R_{o\beta\alpha}, A_{o\alpha}\lambda B_{o\beta}\textbf{.}[\forall x_\alpha, y_\beta\textbf{.}Rxy \Rightarrow (x \in A \wedge x \in B)]$
$RestrictRCodom(\_,\_) := \lambda R_{o\beta\alpha}, A_{o\alpha}\textbf{.}[\lambda x_\alpha, y_\beta\textbf{.}x \in A \wedge Rxy]$
$RelComp(\_,\_) := \lambda R_{o\beta\alpha}, Q_{o\gamma\beta}\textbf{.}[\lambda x_\alpha, z_\gamma\textbf{.}\exists y_\beta\textbf{.}Rxy \wedge Ryz]$
$InverseImageR(\_,\_) := \lambda R_{o\beta\alpha}, B_{o\beta}\textbf{.}[\lambda x_\alpha\textbf{.}\exists y_\beta\textbf{.}y \in B \wedge Rxy]$
$Reflexive(\_) := \lambda R_{o\beta\alpha}\textbf{.}[\forall x_\alpha\textbf{.}Rxx]$
$Symmetric(\_) := \lambda R_{o\beta\alpha}\textbf{.}[\forall x_\alpha\textbf{.}\forall y_\alpha\textbf{.}Rxy \Rightarrow Ryx]$
$Transitive(\_) := \lambda R_{o\beta\alpha}\textbf{.}[\forall x_\alpha\textbf{.}\forall y_\alpha\textbf{.}\forall z_\alpha\textbf{.}Rxy \wedge Ryz \Rightarrow Rxz]$
$EquivRel(\_) := \lambda R_{o\beta\alpha}\textbf{.}[Reflexive(R) \wedge Symmetric(R) \wedge Transitive(R)]$
$EquivClasses(\_) := \lambda R_{o\alpha\alpha}\textbf{.}[\lambda A_{o\alpha}\textbf{.}\exists u_\alpha\textbf{.}u \in A \wedge \forall v_\alpha\textbf{.}v \in A \Leftrightarrow Ruv]$
Defined Notions in Theory Function
$Inj(\_) := \lambda F_{\beta\alpha}\textbf{.}[\forall x_\alpha, y_\beta\textbf{.}F(x) = F(y) \Rightarrow x = y]$
$Surj(\_) := \lambda F_{\beta\alpha}\textbf{.}[\forall y_\beta\textbf{.}\exists x_\alpha\textbf{.}y = F(x)]$
$Bij(\_) := \lambda F_{\beta\alpha}\textbf{.}Surj(F) \wedge Inj(F)$
$ImageF(\_,\_) := \lambda F_{\beta\alpha}, A_{o\alpha}\textbf{.}[\lambda y_\beta\textbf{.}\exists x_\alpha\textbf{.}x \in A \wedge y = F(x)]$
$InverseImageF(\_,\_) := \lambda F_{\beta\alpha}, B_{o\beta}\textbf{.}[\lambda x_\alpha\textbf{.}\exists y_\beta\textbf{.}y \in B \wedge y = F(x)]$
$\_\circ\_ := \lambda F_{\beta\alpha}, G_{\gamma\beta}\textbf{.}[\lambda x_\alpha\textbf{.}G(F(x))]$
$IncreasingF(\_,\_,\_) := \lambda F_{\beta\alpha}, \triangleleft^1_{o\alpha\alpha}, \triangleleft^2_{o\beta\beta}\textbf{.}[\forall x_\alpha, y_\alpha\textbf{.}x \triangleleft^1 y \Rightarrow F(x) \triangleleft^2 F(y)]$
$DecreasingF(\_,\_,\_) := \lambda F_{\beta\alpha}, \triangleleft^1_{o\alpha\alpha}, \triangleleft^2_{o\beta\beta}\textbf{.}[\forall x_\alpha, y_\alpha\textbf{.}x \triangleleft^1 y \Rightarrow F(y) \triangleleft^2 F(x)]$

$(\lambda x_\alpha\textbf{.}(Bx \vee Cx) \wedge (Bx \vee Dx))]$ is generated, and not $[(\lambda x_\alpha\textbf{.}Bx \vee (Cx \wedge Dx)) = (\lambda x_\alpha\textbf{.}(Bx \vee Cx) \wedge (Bx \vee Dx))]^F$. Observe, that we write $[.]^T$ and $[.]^F$ for positive and negative literals, respectively. LEO then applies its goal directed functional and Boolean extensionality rules which replace this unification constraint by the negative literal (where x is a Skolem constant):

$$[(Bx \vee (Cx \wedge Dx)) \Leftrightarrow ((Bx \vee Cx) \wedge (Bx \vee Dx))]^F$$

This unit clause is again not normal; normalisation, factorisation and subsumption yield the following set of clauses:

$[Bx]^F \qquad [Bx]^T \vee [Cx]^T \qquad [Bx]^T \vee [Dx]^T \qquad [Cx]^F \vee [Dx]^F$

This set is essentially of propositional logic character and trivially refutable. LEO needs 0.56 seconds for solving the problem and generates a total of 36 clauses.

Let us consider now this same example SET171+3 in its first-order formulation from the TPTP (see Table 3). We can observe that the assumptions provide

Table 3. TPTP problem SET171+3 — distributivity of $\cup$ over $\cap$

Assumptions: $\forall B, C, x.[x \in (B \cup C) \Leftrightarrow x \in B \vee x \in C]$	(1)
$\forall B, C, x.[x \in (B \cap C) \Leftrightarrow x \in B \wedge x \in C]$	(2)
$\forall B, C.[B = C \Leftrightarrow B \subseteq C \wedge C \subseteq B]$	(3)
$\forall B, C.[B \cup C = C \cup B]$	(4)
$\forall B, C.[B \cap C = C \cap B]$	(5)
$\forall B, C.[B \subseteq C \Leftrightarrow \forall x. x \in B \Rightarrow x \in C]$	(6)
$\forall B, C.[B = C \Leftrightarrow \forall x. x \in B \Leftrightarrow x \in C]$	(7)
Proof Goal: $\forall B, C, D.[B \cup (C \cap D) = (B \cup C) \cap (B \cup D)]$	(8)

only a partial axiomatisation of naive set theory. On the other hand, the specification introduces lemmata that are useful for solving the problem. In particular, assumption (7) is trivially derivable from (3) with (6). Obviously, clausal normalisation of this first-order problem description yields a much larger and more difficult set of clauses. Furthermore, definitions of concepts are not directly expanded as in LEO. It is therefore not surprising that most first-order ATPs still fail to prove this problem. In fact, very few TPTP provers were successful in proving SET171+3. Amongst them are MUSCADET 2.4. [20], VAMPIRE 7.0, and SATURATE. The natural deduction system MUSCADET uses special inference rules for sets and needs 0.2 seconds to prove this problem. VAMPIRE needs 108 seconds. The SATURATE system [14] (which extends VAMPIRE with Boolean extensionality rules that are a one-to-one correspondence to LEO's rules for Extensional Higher-Order Paramodulation [3]) can solve the problem in 2.9 seconds while generating 159 clauses. The significance of such comparisons is clearly limited since different systems are optimised to a different degree. One noted difference between the experiments with first-order provers listed above, and the experiments with LEO and LEO-BLIKSEM is that first-order systems often use a case tailored problem representation (e.g., by avoiding some base axioms of the addressed theory), while LEO and LEO-BLIKSEM have a harder task of dealing with a general (not specifically tailored) representation.

For the experiments with LEO and the cooperation of LEO with the first-order theorem prover BLIKSEM, λ-abstraction as well as the extensionality treatment inherent in LEO's calculus [4] is used. This enables a theoretically[4] Henkin-complete proof system for set theory. In the above example SET171+3, LEO generally uses the application of functional extensionality to push extensional unification constraints down to base type level, and then eventually applies Boolean extensionality to generate clauses from them. These are typically much simpler and often even *propositional-like* or *first-order-like* (FO-like, for short), that is, they do not contain any 'real' higher-order subterms (such as a λ-abstraction or

---
[4] For pragmatic reasons, such as efficiency, most of LEO's tactics are incomplete. LEO's philosophy is to rely on a theoretically complete calculus, but to practically provide a set of complimentary strategies so that these cover a broad range of theorems.

embedded equations), and are therefore suitable for treatment by a first-order ATP or even a propositional logic decision procedure.

SET624+3 Sometimes, extensionality treatment is not required and the originally higher-order problem is immediately reduced to only FO-like clauses. For example, after expanding the definitions, problem SET624+3 yields the following clause (where $B_{o\alpha}, C_{o\alpha}, D_{o\alpha}$ are again Skolem constants):

$$[(\exists x_\alpha \bullet (Bx \land (Cx \lor Dx)) \Leftrightarrow ((\exists x_\alpha \bullet Bx \land Cx) \lor (\exists x_\alpha \bullet Bx \land Dx))]^F$$

Normalisation results in 26 FO-like clauses, which present a hard problem for LEO: it needs approx. 35 seconds (see Sec. 4) to find a refutation, whereas first-order ATPs only need a fraction of a second.

SET646+3 Sometimes, problems are immediately refuted after the initial clause normalisation. For example, after definition expansion in problem SET646+3 we get the following clause (where $B_{o\alpha}, C_{o\alpha}, x_\alpha$ are again Skolem constants):

$$[Ax \Rightarrow (\forall y_\beta \bullet By \Rightarrow (\forall u_\alpha \forall v_\beta \bullet (u = x \land v = y) \Rightarrow ((\neg \bot) \land (\neg \bot))))]^F$$

Normalisation in LEO immediately generates a basic refutation (i.e., a clause $[\bot]^T \lor [\bot]^T$) without even starting proof search.

SET611+3 The examples discussed so far all essentially apply extensionality treatment and normalisation to the input problem in order to immediately generate a set of inconsistent FO-like clauses. Problem SET611+3 is more complicated as it requires several reasoning steps in LEO before the initially consistent set of available FO-like clauses grows into an inconsistent one. After definition expansion, LEO is first given the input clause:

$$[\forall A_{o\alpha}, B_{o\alpha} \bullet (\lambda x_\alpha \bullet (Ax \land Bx)) = (\lambda x_\alpha \bullet \bot)) \Leftrightarrow (\lambda x_\alpha \bullet (Ax \land \neg Bx)) = (\lambda x_\alpha \bullet Ax)]^F$$

which it normalises into:

$$[(\lambda x_\alpha \bullet (Ax \land Bx)) =^? (\lambda x_\alpha \bullet \bot)] \lor [(\lambda x_\alpha \bullet (Ax \land \neg Bx)) =^? (\lambda x_\alpha \bullet Ax)] \quad (9)$$
$$[(\lambda x_\alpha \bullet (Ax \land Bx)) = (\lambda x_\alpha \bullet \bot)]^T \lor [(\lambda x_\alpha \bullet (Ax \land \neg Bx)) = (\lambda x_\alpha \bullet Ax)]^T \quad (10)$$

As mentioned before, the unification constraint (9) corresponds to:

$$[(\lambda x_\alpha \bullet (Ax \land Bx)) = (\lambda x_\alpha \bullet \bot)]^F \lor [(\lambda x_\alpha \bullet (Ax \land \neg Bx)) = (\lambda x_\alpha \bullet Ax)]^F \quad (11)$$

LEO has to apply to each of these clauses and to each of their literals appropriate extensionality rules. Thus, several rounds of LEO's set-of-support-based reasoning procedure are required, so that all necessary extensionality reasoning steps are performed, and sufficiently many FO-like clauses are generated which can be refuted by BLIKSEM.

In summary, each of the examples discussed in this section exposes a motivation for our higher-order/first-order cooperative approach to theorem proving. In particular, they show that:

- Higher-order formulations allow for a concise problem representation which often allows easier and faster proof search than first-order formulations.
 - Higher-order problems can often be reduced to a set of first-order clauses that can be more efficiently handled by a first-order ATP.
 - Some problems are trivially refutable after clause normalisation.
 - Some problems require in-depth higher-order reasoning before a refutable first-order clause set can be extracted.

3 Higher-Order/First-Order Cooperation via OANTS

The cooperation between higher-oder and first-order reasoners, which we investigate in this paper, is realised in the concurrent hierarchical blackboard architecture OANTS [7]. We first describe in Sec. 3.1 the existing OANTS architecture. In order to overcome some of its problems, in particular efficiency problems, we devised within OANTS a new and improved cooperation method for the higher-order ATP LEO and first-order provers (in particular, BLIKSEM) – we describe this in Sec. 3.2. We address the question of how to generate the necessary clauses in Sec. 3.3, and discuss soundness and completeness of our implementation of the higher-order/first-order cooperation in Sec. 3.4.

3.1 OANTS

OANTS was originally conceived to support interactive theorem proving but was later extended to a fully automated proving system [22,8]. Its basic idea is to compose a *central proof object* by generating, in each proof situation, a ranked list of potentially applicable inference steps. In this process, all inference rules, such as calculus rules or tactics, are uniformly viewed with respect to three sets: premises, conclusions, and additional parameters. The elements of these three sets are called *arguments* of the inference rule and they usually depend on each other. An inference rule is applicable if at least some of its arguments can be instantiated with respect to the given proof context. The task of the OANTS architecture is now to determine the applicability of inference rules by computing instantiations for their arguments.

The architecture consists of two layers. On the lower layer, possible instantiations of the arguments of individual inference rules are computed. In particular, each inference rule is associated with its own blackboard and concurrent processes, one for each argument of the inference rule. The role of every process is to compute possible instantiations for its designated argument of the inference rule, and to record these on the blackboard. The computations are carried out with respect to the given proof context and by exploiting information already present on the blackboard, that is, argument instantiations computed by other processes. On the upper layer, the information from the lower layer is used for computing and heuristically ranking the inference rules that are applicable in the current proof state. The most promising rule is then applied to the central proof object and the data on the blackboards is cleared for the next round of computations.

OANTS employs resource reasoning to guide search.[5] This enables the controlled integration (e.g., by specifying time-outs) of full-fledged external reasoning systems such as automated theorem provers, computer algebra systems, or model generators into the architecture. The use of the external systems is modelled by inference rules, usually one for each system. Their corresponding computations are encapsulated in one of the independent processes in the architecture. For example, an inference rule modelling the application of an ATP has its conclusion argument set to be an open goal. A process can then place an open goal on the blackboard, where it is picked up by a process that applies the prover to it. Any computed proof or partial-proof from the external system is again written to the blackboard from where it is subsequently inserted into the proof object when the inference rule is applied. While this setup enables proof construction by a collaborative effort of diverse reasoning systems, the cooperation can only be achieved via the central proof object. This means that all partial results have to be translated back and forth between the syntaxes of the integrated systems and the language of the proof object. Since there are many types of integrated systems, the language of the proof object — a higher-order language even richer than LEO's, together with a natural deduction calculus — is expressive but also cumbersome. This leads not only to a large communication overhead, but also means that complex proof objects have to be created (large clause sets need to be transformed into large single formulae to represent them in the proof object; the support for this in OANTS to date is inefficient), even if the reasoning of all systems involved is clause-based. Consequently, the cooperation between external systems is typically rather inefficient [5].

3.2 Cooperation via a Single Inference Rule

In order to overcome the problem of the communication bottleneck described above, we devised a new method for the cooperation between a higher-order and a first-order theorem prover within OANTS. Rather than modelling each theorem prover as a separate inference rule (and hence needing to translate the communication via the language of the central proof object), we model the cooperation between a higher-order (concretely, LEO) and a first-order theorem prover (in our case study BLIKSEM) in OANTS as a single inference rule. The cooperation between these two theorem provers is carried out directly and not via the central proof object. This avoids translating clause sets into single formulae and back. While in our previous approach the cooperation between LEO and an FO-ATP was modelled at the upper layer of the OANTS architecture, our new approach presented in this paper models their cooperation by exploiting the lower layer of the OANTS blackboard architecture. This is not an ad hoc solution,

---

[5] OANTS provides facilities to define and modify the processes at run-time. But notice that we do not use these advanced features in the case study presented in this paper.

but rather, it demonstrates OANTS's flexibility in modelling the integration of cooperative reasoning systems.

Concretely, the single inference rule modelling the cooperation between LEO and a first-order theorem prover needs four arguments to be applicable: (1) an open proof goal, (2) a partial LEO proof, (3) a set of FO-like clauses in the partial proof, (4) a first-order refutation proof for the set of FO-like clauses. Each of these arguments is computed, that is, its instantiation is found, by an independent process. The first process finds open goals in the central proof object and posts them on the blackboard associated with the new rule. The second process starts an instance of the LEO theorem prover for each new open goal on the blackboard. Each LEO instance maintains its own set of FO-like clauses. The third process monitors these clauses, and as soon as it detects a change in this set, that is, if new FO-like clauses are added by LEO, it writes the entire set of clauses to the blackboard. Once FO-like clauses are posted, the fourth process first translates each of the clauses directly into a corresponding one in the format of the first-order theorem prover, and then starts the first-order theorem prover on them. Note that writing FO-like clauses on the blackboard is by far not as time consuming as generating higher-order proof objects. As soon as either LEO or the first-order prover finds a refutation, the second process reports LEO's proof or partial proof to the blackboard, that is, it instantiates argument (2). Once all four arguments of our inference rule are instantiated, the rule can be applied and the open proof goal can be closed in the central proof object. That is, the open goal can be proved by the cooperation between LEO and a first-order theorem prover. When computing applicability of the inference rule, the second and the fourth process concurrently spawn processes running LEO or a first-order prover on a different set of FO-like clauses. Thus, when actually applying the inference rule, all these instances of provers working on the same open subgoal are stopped.

The cooperation can be carried out between any first-order theorem prover and LEO instantiated with any strategy, thus resulting in different instantiations of the inference rule discussed above. While several first-order provers are integrated in OANTS and could be used, BLIKSEM was sufficient for the case study reported in this paper (see Sec. 4). In most cases, more than one BLIKSEM process was necessary. But as the problems were always concerned with only one subgoal, only one LEO process had to be started.

Our approach to the cooperation between a higher-order and a first-order theorem prover has many advantages. The main one is that the communication is restricted to the transmission of clauses, and thus it avoids intermediate translation into the language of the central proof object. This significantly reduces the communication overhead and makes effective proving of more involved theorems feasible. A disadvantage of this approach is that we cannot easily translate and integrate the two proof objects produced by LEO and BLIKSEM into the central proof object maintained by OANTS, as is possible when applying only one prover per open subgoal. Providing such translation remains future work. The repercussions will be discussed in more detail in Sec. 3.4.

3.3 Extracting FO-Like Clauses from LEO

Crucial to a successful cooperation between LEO and a first-order ATP is obviously the generation of FO-like clauses. LEO always maintains a heap of FO-like clauses. In the current LEO system this heap remains rather small since LEO's standard calculus intrinsically avoids primitive equality and instead provides a rule that replaces occurrences of primitive equality with their corresponding Leibniz definitions which are higher-order. The Leibniz principle defines equality as follows $=_{o\alpha\alpha} := \lambda x_\alpha. \lambda y_\alpha. [\forall P_{o\alpha}. Px \Rightarrow Py]$. LEO also provides a rule which replaces syntactically non-unifiable unification constraints between terms of non-Boolean base type by their respective representations that use Leibniz equality. While the clauses resulting from these rules are still refutable in LEO, they are not refutable by BLIKSEM without adding set theory axioms. We illustrate the effect by the following simple example, where a_ι, b_ι, and $f_{\iota\iota}$ are constants:

$$a = b \Rightarrow f(a) = f(b)$$

Depending on whether we work with primitive equality or Leibniz equality this problem is reduced to the clause sets in either (12) or (13) respectively (in the latter $\mathbf{P}_{o\iota}$ is a new free variable, and $Q_{o\iota}$ is a new Skolem constant):

$$[a = b]^T \qquad [f(a) =^? f(b)] \qquad (12)$$
$$[\mathbf{P}a]^F \vee [\mathbf{P}b]^T \qquad [Q(f(a))]^T \qquad [Q(f(b))]^F \qquad (13)$$

While the former is obviously refutable in BLIKSEM, the latter is not. LEO, however, still finds a refutation for the latter and generates the crucial substitution $\mathbf{P} \leftarrow \lambda x_\alpha. Q(f(x))$ by higher-order pre-unification.

To circumvent this problem, we adapted the relevant rules in LEO. Instead of immediately constructing Leibniz representation of clauses, an intermediate representation containing primitive equality is generated and dumped on the heap of FO-like clauses. As a consequence, additional useful FO-like clauses are accumulated and the heap can become quite large, in particular, since we do not apply any subsumption to the set of FO-like clauses (this is generally done more efficiently by a first-order ATP anyway). Recent research has shown that Leibniz equality is generally very bad for automating higher-order proof search. Thus, future work in LEO includes providing support for full primitive equality and avoiding Leibniz equations.

3.4 Soundness and Completeness of the Cooperation

Clearly, soundness and completeness properties depend on the corresponding properties of the systems involved, in our case, of LEO and BLIKSEM.

Soundness: The general philosophy of OANTS is to ensure the correctness of proofs by the generation of explicit proof objects, which can be checked independently from the proof generation. In particular, reasoning steps of ATPs have to be translated into OANTS's natural deduction calculus via the TRAMP proof transformation system [17] to be machine-checkable. Since the cooperative proof result of LEO-BLIKSEM cannot yet be directly inserted into the centralised proof object, the generation of a machine-checkable proof object is not yet supported. One possible solution is to insert BLIKSEM proofs into LEO proofs at the right places. Then, the modified LEO proofs can be inserted into the centralised proof object, and hence, explicit proof objects can be generated by OANTS. In principle, there is no problem with this, however, it is not yet implemented.

While there are many advantages in guaranteeing correctness of proofs by checking them, it is worth noting that the combination of LEO and BLIKSEM is sound under the assumption that the two systems are sound. Namely, to prove a theorem it is sufficient to show that a subset of clauses generated in the proof is inconsistent. If LEO generates an inconsistent set of clauses, then it does so correctly by assumption, be it a FO-like set or not. Assuming that the translation from FO-like clauses to truly first-order clauses preserves consistency/inconsistency, then a set of clauses that is given to BLIKSEM is inconsistent only if LEO generated an inconsistent set of clauses in the first place. By the assumption that BLIKSEM is sound follows that BLIKSEM will only generate the empty clause when the original clause set was inconsistent.

Thus, soundness of our cooperative approach critically relies only on the soundness of the selected transformational mapping from FO-like clauses to proper first-order clauses. We use the mapping from TRAMP, which has been previously shown to be sound and is based on [16]. Essentially, it injectively maps expressions such as $P(f(a))$ to expressions such as $@^1_{\text{pred}}(P, @^1_{\text{fun}}(f, a))$, where the @ are new first-order operators describing function and predicate application for particular types and arities. The injectivity of the mapping guarantees soundness, since it allows each proof step to be mapped back from first-order to higher-order. Hence, our higher-order/first-order cooperative approach between LEO and BLIKSEM is sound.

Completeness: Completeness (in the sense of Henkin completeness) can in principle be achieved in higher-order systems, but practically, the strategies used are typically not complete for efficiency reasons. Let us assume that we use a complete strategy in LEO. All that our procedure does is pass FO-like clauses to BLIKSEM. Hence, no proofs can be lost in this process. That is, completeness follows trivially from the completeness of LEO.

The more interesting question is whether particular cooperation strategies will be complete as well. For instance, in LEO we may want to give higher preference to real higher-order steps which guarantee the generation of first-order clauses.

4 Experiments and Results

We conducted several experiments to evaluate our hybrid reasoning approach. In particular, we concentrated on problems given in Table 1. We investigated several LEO strategies in order to compare LEO's individual performance with the performance of the LEO-BLIKSEM cooperation. Our example set differs from the one in [14] in that it contains some additional problems, and it also omits an entry for problem SET108+1. This problem addresses the universal class and can therefore not be formalised in type theory in the same concise way as the other examples, but only in a way very similar to the one given in TPTP.

Table 4 presents the results of our experiments. All timings given in the table are in seconds. The first column contains the TPTP identifier of the problem. The second column relates some of the problems to their counterparts in the Journal of Formalized Mathematics (JFM; see mizar.org/JFM) where they originally stem from. This eases the comparison with the results in [6,2], where the problems from the JFM article *Boolean Properties of Sets* were already solved: the problems are named with prefix 'B:'. Prefix 'RS1:' stands for the JFM article *Relations Defined on Sets*. The third column lists the TPTP (v3.0.1 as of 20 January 2005, see http://www.tptp.org) difficulty rating of the problem, which indicates how hard the problem is for first-order ATPs (difficulty rating 1.00 indicates that no TPTP prover can solve the problem).

The fourth, fifth and sixth columns list whether SATURATE, MUSCADET (v2.4) and E-SETHEO (csp04), respectively, can (+) or cannot (−) solve a problem. The seventh column lists the timing results for VAMPIRE (v7). The results for SATURATE are taken from [14] (a '?' in Table 4 indicates that the result was not listed in [14] and is thus unavailable). The results for MUSCADET and E-SETHEO are taken from the on-line version of the solutions provided with the TPTP. Since the listed results were obtained from different experiments on different platforms, their run-time comparison would be unfair, and was thus not carried out. The timings for VAMPIRE, on the other hand, are based on private communication with A. Voronkov and they were obtained on a computer with a very similar specification as we used for the LEO-BLIKSEM timings. Note, that the results for VAMPIRE and E-SETHEO reported in [14] differ for some of the problems to the ones in TPTP. This is probably due to different versions of the systems tested, for instance, the TPTP uses VAMPIRE version 7, while the results reported in [14] are based on version 5. The results in columns four through to seven show that some problems are still very hard for first-order ATPs, as well as for the special purpose theorem prover MUSCADET. Column eight and nine in Table 4 list the results for LEO alone and LEO-BLIKSEM, respectively. Each of these two columns is further divided into sub-columns to allow for a detailed comparison.

All our experiments (for the values of LEO and LEO-BLIKSEM) were conducted on a 2.4 GHz Xenon machine with 1GB of memory and an overall time limit of 100 seconds. For our experiments with LEO alone in column eight in Table 4 we tested four different strategies. Mainly, they differ in their treatment of equality and extensionality. This ranges from immediate expansion of primitive equality with Leibniz equality and limited extensionality reasoning, STANDARD (ST), to immediate expansion of primitive equality and moderate extensionality reasoning, EXT, to delayed expansion of primitive equality and moderate extensionality reasoning, EXT-INPUT (EI), and finally to delayed expansion of primitive equality and advanced recursive extensionality reasoning,

Table 4. Experimental data for the benchmark problems given in Table 1

TPTP-Problem	Mizar Problem	Diffi-culty	Satu-rate	Mus cadet	E-Se-theo	Vamp-ire 7	LEO			LEO-BLIKSEM				
							Strat.	Cl.	Time	Cl.	Time	FOcl	FOtm	GnCl
SET014+4		.67	+	+	+	.01	ST	41	.16	34	6.76	19	.01	7
SET017+1		.56	−	−	+	.03	EXT	3906	57.52	25	8.54	16	.01	74
SET066+1		1.00	?	−	−	−	−	−	−	26	6.80	20	10	56
SET067+1		.56	+	+	+	.04	ST	6	.02	13	.32	16	.01	12
SET076+1		.67	+	−	+	.00	−	−	−	10	.47	18	.01	35
SET086+1		.22	+	−	+	.04	ST	4	.01	4	.01	N/A	N/A	N/A
SET096+1		.56	+	−	+	.03	−	−	−	27	7.99	14	.01	25
SET143+3	B:67	.67	+	+	+	68.71	EIR	37	.38	33	7.93	18	.01	19
SET171+3	B:71	.67	+	+	−	108.31	EIR	36	.56	25	4.75	19	.01	20
SET580+3	B:23	.44	+	+	+	14.71	EIR	25	.19	6	2.73	8	.01	13
SET601+3	B:72	.22	+	+	+	168.40	EIR	145	2.20	55	4.96	8	.01	13
SET606+3	B:77	.78	+	−	+	62.02	EIR	21	.33	17	10.8	15	.01	5
SET607+3	B:79	.67	+	+	+	65.57	EIR	22	.31	17	7.79	15	.01	6
SET609+3	B:81	.89	+	+	−	161.78	EIR	37	.60	26	6.50	19	10	17
SET611+3	B:84	.44	+	−	+	60.20	EIR	996	12.69	72	32.14	38	.01	101
SET612+3	B:85	.89	+	−	−	113.33	EIR	41	.54	18	3.95	6	.01	7
SET614+3	B:88	.67	+	+	−	157.88	EIR	38	.46	19	4.34	16	.01	17
SET615+3	B:89	.67	+	+	−	109.01	EIR	38	.57	17	3.59	6	.01	9
SET623+3	B:99	1.00	?	−	−	−	EXT	43	8.84	23	9.54	10	.01	14
SET624+3	B:100	.67	+	−	+	.04	ST	4942	34.71	54	9.61	46	.01	212
SET630+3	B:112	.44	+	−	+	60.39	EIR	11	.07	6	.08	8	10	4
SET640+3	RS1:2	.22	+	−	+	70.41	EIR	2	.01	2	.01	N/A	N/A	N/A
SET646+3	RS1:8	.56	+	−	+	59.63	EIR	2	.01	2	.01	N/A	N/A	N/A
SET647+3	RS1:9	.56	+	−	+	64.21	EIR	26	.15	13	.30	13	.01	15
SET648+3	RS1:10	.56	+	−	+	64.22	EIR	26	.15	14	.30	13	.01	16
SET649+3	RS1:11	.33	−	−	+	63.77	EIR	45	.30	29	5.49	12	.01	16
SET651+3	RS1:13	.44	−	−	+	63.88	EIR	20	.10	11	.16	10	10	11
SET657+3	RS1:19	.67	+	−	+	1.44	EIR	2	.01	2	.01	N/A	N/A	N/A
SET669+3	RS1:19	.22	−	−	+	.34	EI	35	.22	35	.23	N/A	N/A	N/A
SET670+3	RS1:33	1.00	?	−	−	−	EXT	15	.17	17	.36	16	.01	6
SET671+3	RS1:34	.78	−	−	+	218.02	EIR	78	.64	7	2.71	10	.01	14
SET672+3	RS1:35	1.00	?	−	−	−	EXT	27	.4	30	.70	21	.01	11
SET673+3	RS1:36	.78	−	−	+	47.86	EIR	78	.65	14	5.66	14	.01	16
SET680+3	RS1:47	.33	+	−	+	.07	ST	185	.88	29	4.61	18	.01	24
SET683+3	RS1:50	.22	+	−	+	.06	ST	46	.20	35	8.90	18	10	24
SET684+3	RS1:51	.78	−	−	+	.33	ST	275	2.45	46	5.95	26	.01	47
SET686+3	RS1:53	.56	−	−	+	.11	ST	274	2.36	46	5.37	26	.01	46
SET716+4		.89	+	+	−	−	ST	39	.45	18	3.81	18	.01	118
SET724+4		.89	+	+	−	−	EXT	154	2.75	18	7.21	15	10	23
SET741+4		1.00	?	−	−	−	−	−	−	−	−	−	−	−
SET747+4		.89	−	+	−	−	ST	34	.46	25	1.11	18	10	10
SET752+4		.89	?	+	−	−	−	−	−	50	6.60	48	.01	4363
SET753+4		.89	?	+	−	−	−	−	−	15	3.07	12	10	19
SET764+4		.56	+	+	+	.02	EI	9	.05	8	.04	N/A	N/A	N/A
SET770+4		.89	+	+	−	−	−	−	−	−	−	−	−	−

EXT-INPUT-RECURSIVE (EIR). Column eight in Table 4 presents the fastest strategy for a respective problem (Strat.), the number of clauses generated by LEO (Cl.), and the total runtime (Time). While occasionally there were more than one LEO strategy that could solve a problem, it should be noted that none of the strategies was successful for all the problems solved by LEO.

In contrast to the experiments with LEO alone, we used only the EXT-INPUT strategy for our experiments with the LEO-BLIKSEM cooperation. Column nine in Table 4 presents the number of clauses generated by LEO (Cl.) together with the time (Time), and in addition, the number of first-order clauses sent to BLIKSEM (FOcl), the time used by BLIKSEM (FOtm), and the number of clauses generated by BLIKSEM (GnCl). Note, that we give the data only for the first instance that BLIKSEM actually succeeded in solving the problem. This time also includes the time needed to write and process input and output files over the network. While LEO and instances of BLIKSEM were running in separate threads (each run of BLIKSEM was given a 50 second time limit), the figures given in the 'Timo' column reflect the overall time needed for a successful proof. That is, it contains the time needed by all concurrent processes: LEO's own process as well as those processes administering the various instances of BLIKSEM. Since all these processes ran on a single processor, there is potential to ameliorate the overall runtimes by using real multiprocessing.

Note also, that the number of clauses in LEO's search space is typically low since subsumption is enabled. Subsumption, however, was not enabled for the accumulation of FO-like clauses in LEO's bag of FO-like clauses. This is why there are usually more clauses in this bag (which is sent to BLIKSEM) than there are available in LEO's search space. Finally, observe that for some problems a refutation was found after LEO's clausal normalisation, and therefore BLIKSEM was not applicable (N/A).

While LEO itself can solve a majority of the considered problems with some strategy, the LEO-BLIKSEM cooperation can solve more problems and, moreover, needs only a single LEO strategy. We can also observe that for many problems that appear to be relatively hard for LEO alone (e.g., SET017+1, SET611+3, SET624+3), the LEO-BLIKSEM cooperation solves them not only more quickly, but also sometimes reduces the problems to relatively small higher-order preprocessing steps with subsequent easy first-order proofs, as for instance, in the case of SET017+1.

From a mathematical viewpoint the investigated problems are trivial and, hence, they should ideally be reliably and very efficiently solvable within a proof assistant. This has been achieved for the examples in Table 4 (except for SET741+4 and SET770+4) by our hybrid approach. While some of the proof attempts now require slightly more time than when using LEO alone with a specialised strategy, they are, in most cases, still faster than when proving with a first-order system.

5 Related Work and Conclusion

Related to our approach is the TECHS system [12], which realises a cooperation between a set of heterogeneous first-order theorem provers. Similarly to our approach, partial results in TECHS are exchanged between the different theorem provers in form of clauses. The main difference to the work of Denzinger *et al.* (and other related architectures like [13]) is that our system bridges between higher-order and first-order automated theorem proving. Also, unlike in TECHS, we provide a declarative specification framework for modelling external systems as cooperating, concurrent processes that can be (re-)configured at run-time. Related is also the work of Hurd [15] which realises a generic interface between HOL and first-order theorem provers. It is similar to the solution previously achieved by TRAMP [17] in OMEGA, which serves as a basis for the sound integration of ATPs into OANTS. Both approaches pass essentially first-order clauses to first-order theorem provers and then translate their results back into HOL resp. OMEGA. Some further related work on the cooperation of Isabelle with VAMPIRE is presented in [18]. The main difference of our work to the related systems is that while our system calls first-order provers from within higher-order proof search, this is not the case for [15,17,18].

One of the motivations for our work is to show that the cooperation of higher-order and first-order automated theorem provers can be very successful and effective. The results of our case study provide evidence for this: our non-optimised system outperforms related work on state-of-the-art first-order theorem provers and their ad hoc extensions such as SATURATE [14] on 45 mathematical problems chosen from the TPTP SET category. Among them are four problems which cannot be solved by any TPTP system to date. In contrast to the first-order situation, these problems can in fact be proved in our approach reliably from first principles, that is, without avoiding relevant base axioms of the underlying set theory, and moreover, without the need to provide *relevant* lemmata and definitions by hand.

The results of our case study motivate further research in the automation of higher-order theorem proving and the experimentation with different higher-order to first-order transformation mappings (such as the ones used by Hurd) that support our hybrid reasoning approach. They also provide further evidence for the usefulness of the OANTS approach as described in [8,5] for flexibly modelling the cooperation of reasoning systems.

Our results also motivate the need for a higher-order extension of the TPTP library in which alternative higher-order problem formalisations are linked with their first-order counterparts so that first-order theorem provers could also be evaluated against higher-order systems (and vice versa).

Future work is to investigate how far our approach scales up to more complex problems and more advanced mathematical theories. In less trivial settings as discussed in this paper, we will face the problem of selecting and adding relevant lemmata to avoid immediate reduction to first principles and to appropriately instantiate set variables. Relevant related work for this setting is Bishop's approach to *selectively expand definitions* as presented in [9] and Brown's PhD thesis on *set comprehension in Church's type theory* [10].

Acknowledgements For advice and help we thank Chad Brown, Andreas Meier, Andrei Voronkov, and Claus-Peter Wirth.

References

1. P. Andrews. *An Introduction to mathematical logic and Type Theory: To Truth through Proof.* Number 27 in Applied Logic Series. Kluwer, 2002.
2. C. Benzmüller. *Equality and Extensionality in Higher-Order Theorem Proving.* PhD thesis, Universität des Saarlandes, Germany, 1999.
3. C. Benzmüller. Extensional higher-order paramodulation and RUE-resolution. *Proc. of CADE-16, LNAI* 1632, p. 399–413. Springer, 1999.

4. C. Benzmüller. Comparing approaches to resolution based higher-order theorem proving. *Synthese*, 133(1-2):203–235, 2002.
5. C. Benzmüller, M. Jamnik, M. Kerber, and V. Sorge. Experiments with an Agent-Oriented Reasoning System. *Proc. of KI 2001*, *LNAI* 2174, p.409–424. Springer, 2001.
6. C. Benzmüller and M. Kohlhase. LEO – a higher-order theorem prover. *Proc. of CADE-15*, *LNAI* 1421. Springer, 1998.
7. C. Benzmüller and V. Sorge. A Blackboard Architecture for Guiding Interactive Proofs. *Proc. of AIMSA'98*, *LNAI* 1480, p. 102–114. Springer, 1998.
8. C. Benzmüller and V. Sorge. OANTS – An open approach at combining Interactive and Automated Theorem Proving. *Proc. of Calculemus-2000*. AK Peters, 2001.
9. M. Bishop and P. Andrews. Selectively instantiating definitions. *Proc. of CADE-15*, *LNAI* 1421. Springer, 1998.
10. C. E. Brown. *Set Comprehension in Church's Type Theory*. PhD thesis, Dept. of Mathematical Sciences, Carnegie Mellon University, USA, 2004.
11. H. de Nivelle. *The Bliksem Theorem Prover, Version 1.12*. Max-Planck-Institut, Saarbrücken, Germany, 1999.
http://www.mpi-sb.mpg.de/~bliksem/manual.ps.
12. J. Denzinger and D. Fuchs. Cooperation of Heterogeneous Provers. *Proc. IJCAI-16*, p. 10–15. Morgan Kaufmann, 1999.
13. M. Fisher and A. Ireland. Multi-agent proof-planning. CADE-15 Workshop "Using AI methods in Deduction", 1998.
14. H. Ganzinger and J. Stuber. Superposition with equivalence reasoning and delayed clause normal form transformation. *Proc. of CADE-19*, *LNAI* 2741. Springer, 2003.
15. J. Hurd. An LCF-style interface between HOL and first-order logic. *Automated Deduction — CADE-18*, *LNAI* 2392, p. 134–138. Springer, 2002.
16. M. Kerber. *On the Representation of Mathematical Concepts and their Translation into First Order Logic*. PhD thesis, Universität Kaiserslautern, Germany, 1992.
17. A. Meier. TRAMP: Transformation of Machine-Found Proofs into Natural Deduction Proofs at the Assertion Level. *Proc. of CADE-17*, *LNAI* 1831. Springer, 2000.
18. J. Meng and L. C. Paulson. Experiments on supporting interactive proof using resolution. *Proc. of IJCAR 2004*, *LNCS* 3097, p. 372–384. Springer, 2004.
19. R. Nieuwenhuis, Th. Hillenbrand, A. Riazanov, and A. Voronkov. On the evaluation of indexing techniques for theorem proving. *Proc. of IJCAR-01*, *LNAI* 2083, p. 257–271. Springer, 2001.
20. D. Pastre. Muscadet2.3 : A knowledge-based theorem prover based on natural deduction. *Proc. of IJCAR-01*, *LNAI* 2083, p. 685–689. Springer, 2001.
21. A. Riazanov and A. Voronkov. Vampire 1.1 (system description). *Proc. of IJCAR-01*, *LNAI* 2083, p. 376–380. Springer, 2001.
22. V. Sorge. *OANTS: A Blackboard Architecture for the Integration of Reasoning Techniques into Proof Planning*. PhD thesis, Universität des Saarlandes, Germany, 2001.
23. G. Stenz and A. Wolf. E-SETHEO: An Automated[3] Theorem Prover – System Abstract. *Proc. of the TABLEAUX'2000*, *LNAI* 1847, p. 436–440. Springer, 2000.
24. G. Sutcliffe and C. Suttner. The TPTP Problem Library: CNF Release v1.2.1. *Journal of Automated Reasoning*, 21(2):177–203, 1998.

A Generic Framework for Interprocedural Analyses of Numerical Properties

Markus Müller-Olm[1] and Helmut Seidl[2]

[1] Universität Dortmund, Fachbereich Informatik, LS 5
Baroper Str. 301, 44221 Dortmund, Germany
markus.mueller-olm@cs.uni-dortmund.de
[2] TU München, Institut für Informatik, I2
80333 München, Germany
seidl@in.tum.de

Abstract. Relations among program variables like $1 + 3 \cdot \mathbf{x}_1 + 5 \cdot \mathbf{x}_2 \equiv 0\ [224]$ have been called *linear congruence relations*. Such a relation is *valid* at a program point iff it is satisfied by all reaching program states. Knowledge about non-trivial valid congruence relations is crucial for various aggressive program transformations. It can also form the backbone of a program correctness proof.

In his seminal paper [1], Philippe Granger presents an intraprocedural analysis which is able to infer linear congruence relations between integer variables. For affine programs, i.e., programs where all assignments are affine expressions and branching is non-deterministic, Granger's analysis is *complete*, i.e., infers *all* valid congruence relations between variables. No upper bound, though, has been proven for Granger's algorithm. Here, we present a variation of Granger's analysis which runs in polynomial time. Moreover, we provide an interprocedural extension of this algorithm. The polynomial algorithm as well as its interprocedural extension are obtained by means of multiple instances of a general framework for constructing interprocedural analyses of numerical properties. This framework can be used for different numerical domains such as fields or modular rings and thus also covers the interprocedural analyses of [2,3] where valid affine relations are inferred.

We also indicate how the base technique can be extended to deal with equality guards in the interprocedural setting.

References

1. P. Granger. Static Analysis of Linear Congruence Equalities among Variables of a Program. In *Int. Joint Conf. on Theory and Practice of Software Development (TAPSOFT)*, pages 169–192. LNCS 493, Springer-Verlag, 1991.
2. M. Müller-Olm and H. Seidl. Precise Interprocedural Analysis through Linear Algebra. In *31st ACM Symp. on Principles of Programming Languages (POPL)*, pages 330–341, 2004.
3. M. Müller-Olm and H. Seidl. Analysis of Modular Arithmetic. In *European Symposium on Programming (ESOP)*. Springer Verlag, 2005. To appear.

Second-Order Matching via Explicit Substitutions*

Flávio L.C. de Moura**[1], Fairouz Kamareddine[2], and
Mauricio Ayala-Rincón***[1]

[1] Departamento de Matemática, Universidade de Brasília, Brasília D.F., Brasil.
`flavio@mat.unb.br,ayala@mat.unb.br`
[2] School of Mathematical and Computer Sciences, Heriot-Watt University,
Edinburgh, Scotland. `fairouz@macs.hw.ac.uk`

Abstract. Matching is a basic operation extensively used in computation. Second-order matching, in particular, provides an adequate environment for expressing program transformations and pattern recognition for automated deduction. The past few years have established the benefit of using explicit substitutions for theorem proving and higher-order unification. In this paper, we will make use of explicit substitutions to facilitate matching: we develop a second-order matching algorithm via the $\lambda\sigma$-style of explicit substitutions. We introduce a convenient notation for matching in the $\lambda\sigma$-calculus. This notation keeps the matching equations separated from the incremental graftings. We characterise an important class of second-order matching problems which is essential to prove termination of the algorithm. In addition, we illustrate how the algorithm works through some examples.

Keywords: Higher-Order Unification, Second-Order Matching, Explicit Substitutions.

1 Introduction

Matching is an important mechanism extensively used in automated deduction and programming languages. For instance, second-order matching has been used in program transformation [HL78,Vis04] and theorem proving [dlTC87,dlTC88].

First-order matching, as well as first-order unification, is decidable and unitary, i.e., when a unifier exists it is unique in the sense that the most general unifier (mgu) exists [Rob65]. Second-order matching is still decidable [Hue76], but the solutions are not necessarily unique and the notion of an mgu no longer exists. In fact, the second-order matching problem[1] $\lambda x.(X\ a) \ll^? \lambda x.(c(b\ a))$, where a, b and c are constants and X is a meta-variable, has two solutions given by $X/\lambda y.(c(b\ a))$ and $X/\lambda y.(c(b\ y))$ and, none of them is an instance of the

---
* Work supported by funds from CNPq(CT-INFO) 50.6598/04-7 and PRONEX.
** Corresponding author. Supported by Brazilian CAPES Foundation.
*** Partially supported by Brazilian CNPq Council.
[1] The type information is omitted to simplify the presentation of the example.

other, and hence there is no mgu. Third and fourth order matching are decidable [Dow94,Pad00], but for higher orders, it remains unknown (for almost thirty years) whether this problem is decidable [Hue76]. In [Loa03], the undecidability of fifth-order β-matching is given, but the proof does not deal with the general case that includes η-conversion.

In [DHK00], Dowek, Hardin and Kirchner gave a general method for higher-order unification for the $\lambda\sigma$-calculus of explicit substitutions. In that paper they prove that the unification problem P has a solution in the simply typed λ-calculus if and only if the translation of this problem in the language of the $\lambda\sigma$-calculus, written P_F has a solution. However, this general unification method, which has been proved adaptable for other explicit substitutions calculi [ARK01], does not decide second-order matching in the $\lambda\sigma$-calculus as we show by a non-terminating counter-example. In addition, [Bur89] shows that matching may behave differently from unification depending on the considered equational theory and, therefore it is of interest to study matching via explicit substitutions.

In this paper we develop a second-order matching algorithm that decides a special subset of $\lambda\sigma$-terms. The contributions of this work are as follows:

1. We characterise an important subset of second-order $\lambda\sigma$-terms which the general method of Dowek, Hardin and Kirchner can decide. This subset contains all the $\lambda\sigma$-terms that can appear in a second-order matching problem derived from another matching problem originated in the simply typed λ-calculus.

2. Since the notation used by Dowek, Hardin and Kirchner is not adequate for matching because it may introduce flexible-flexible equations whose right-hand sides need to be instantiated, we present an adequate notation for dealing with matching in the $\lambda\sigma$-calculus. This notation keeps graftings (first-order substitutions) separated from the matching equations to be unified. This separation will be important during the matching because no variable, which can be instantiated, is included in the right-hand side of a matching equation and, therefore each matching rule will necessarily generate another matching problem.

3. We present a second-order matching algorithm that decides the subset of $\lambda\sigma$-terms characterised in item 1.

Using the $\lambda\sigma$-style of explicit substitutions has the well known advantage of reducing higher-order unification problems into equivalent first-order equational unification problems, and in this way, the variable instantiation mechanism of the λ-calculus is implemented by first-order substitution (grafting). Advantages of this HOU approach include, among others: being closer to implementations which is inherent to explicit substitutions; avoidance of functional encoding of scoping constraints by separating substitutions from reductions and substitutions from unification variables; conceiving HOU as equational unification modulo $\beta\eta$-conversion, which allows for natural mixing of higher order specifications with equational ones as explained in [DHK00]. Nevertheless, since higher-order unification is undecidable [Gol81], it is important to study decidable subproblems over specific λ-terms as well as of its extensions, such as the $\lambda\sigma$-calculus. In this way, this work is worthwhile because the presented algorithm decides the subset of second-order $\lambda\sigma$-terms characterised in item 1.

In the next section we give a brief presentation of the simply typed version of the λ- and $\lambda\sigma$-calculi. In section 3 we start with the characterisation of a subset of $\lambda\sigma$-terms. Afterwards, we define an adequate notation for dealing with matching problems and then, we present a second-order matching algorithm for the $\lambda\sigma$-calculus. Finally, we conclude and give directions for future work.

2 Background

We start this section with a brief presentation of the simply typed λ- and $\lambda\sigma$-calculus and some basic definitions used throughout the paper. The notation used in this presentation uses de Bruijn indexes [dB72] instead of variables with names. This is because de Bruijn's notation is more adequate for implementations of the λ-calculus since α-conversion is no longer needed.

We define types and simply typed λ-terms in de Bruijn notation as usual:

types $\quad A ::= K \mid A \to B$, where K is an atomic type.
contexts $\Gamma ::= nil \mid A.\Gamma$
terms $\quad a ::= \underline{n} \mid X \mid (a\ a) \mid \lambda_A.a$, where $n \in \mathbb{N} = \{1, 2, \ldots\}$
$\quad\quad\quad$ and $X \in \mathcal{X}$, the set of meta-variables.

The set of λ-terms built with this grammar is usually denoted by $\Lambda_{dB}(\mathcal{X})$ and the typing rules are as follows:

(var) $\dfrac{}{A.\Gamma \vdash \underline{1} : A}$ $\qquad$ (var n) $\dfrac{\Gamma \vdash \underline{n} : B}{A.\Gamma \vdash \underline{n+1} : B}$

(app) $\dfrac{\Gamma \vdash a : A \to B \quad \Gamma \vdash b : A}{\Gamma \vdash (a\ b) : B}$ $\qquad$ (lambda) $\dfrac{A.\Gamma \vdash a : B}{\Gamma \vdash \lambda_A.a : A \to B}$

The type judgement $\Gamma \vdash a : A$ can also be written as a_A^Γ.

To each meta-variable X we associate a unique type A and a unique context Γ. We assume that for each type there exists an infinite set of meta-variables with that type. We add the following typing rule for meta-variables:

(Metavar) $\quad \Gamma \vdash X : A$, $\qquad$ where Γ is any context.

β- and η-contraction are defined as usual and $=_{\beta\eta}$ denotes $\beta\eta$-conversion.

Definition 1 (Order of types and terms). *The order of a term is the order of its type and the order of a type A, written as $|A|$, is defined by:*

1. *If A is atomic then $|A| = 1$;*
2. *If $A = B \to C$ then $|A| = max\{1 + |B|, |C|\}$.*

Unification problems deal with *unification equations* which are defined by:

Definition 2 (Unification equation). *A unification equation is an equation of the form $a =^? b$ where a and b are λ-terms of the same type which are well-typed under the same context. The order of a unification equation is the highest order of the meta-variables occurring in it. A unification equation is called* *flexible-flexible* or *rigid-rigid* if the left and right-hand sides of the equation are both flexible or rigid terms, respectively. If one term is rigid and the other is flexible (independently of the order) the equation is called *flexible-rigid*. A unification equation is called trivial if it has the form $a =^? a$.

Example 1. Let $\Gamma = A.A \to A.A \to B.B.nil$ and X and Y meta-variables such that $\Gamma \vdash X : A \to A$ and $\Gamma \vdash Y : (A \to A) \to B$. The unification equation $(\underline{3}(\underline{2}(X\underline{1}))) =^? \underline{4}$ has order 2 (since X has order 2), while $Y X =^? \underline{4}$ has order 3.

Definition 3 (Unifier). *A* unifier *for a given unification equation, say $a =^? b$, is a substitution σ such that $a\sigma =_{\beta\eta} b\sigma$.*

Definition 4 (Unification problem). *A* unification problem *is a finite set of unification equations. The* order *of a unification problem is given by the highest order amongst its unification equations. A solution of a unification problem P is a substitution which is a unifier for all equations in P. In other words, a solution for P is a substitution σ such that $P\sigma$ is the trivial unification problem (i.e., formed only by trivial equations).*

Definition 5 (Matching equation[2]). *A higher-order* matching equation *is an equation of the form $a \ll^? b$, where a and b are λ-terms of the same type which are well typed under the same context and, such that the right hand side does not contain meta-variables.*

Definition 6 (Matcher). *A* matcher *for a given matching equation, say $a \ll^? b$, is a substitution σ such that $a\sigma =_{\beta\eta} b$.*

This definition corresponds to the notion of "filtering", which becomes from the assumption that the term to be matched have disjoint variable sets or they can be renamed as usual in rewriting systems and pattern matching. The alternative notion of "semi-unification" ($\exists \sigma, a\sigma =_{\beta\eta} b\sigma =_{\beta\eta} b$) is not treated here [Bur89].

Definition 7 (Matching problem). *A higher-order* matching problem *is a finite set of matching equations. The order of a matching problem is given by the highest order of its meta-variables.*

The $\lambda\sigma$-calculus of explicit substitutions extends the λ-calculus with explicit operators to simulate the substitution (meta-)operation of the λ-calculus.

The syntax of the typed $\lambda\sigma$-calculus is given by

Types	$A ::= K \mid A \to B$	
Contexts	$\Gamma ::= nil \mid A.\Gamma$	
Terms	$a ::= \underline{1} \mid X \mid (a\ b) \mid \lambda_A.a \mid a[s]$	where $X \in \mathcal{X}$
Substitutions	$s ::= id \mid \uparrow \mid a.s \mid s \circ s$	

The set of $\lambda\sigma$-terms is written as $\Lambda_{\lambda\sigma}(\mathcal{X})$.

---

[2] Adapted from [Dow01]

The $\lambda\sigma$-typing rules are given by:

(var) $\quad A.\Gamma \vdash \underline{1} : A$

(app) $\quad \dfrac{\Gamma \vdash a : A \to B \quad \Gamma \vdash b : A}{\Gamma \vdash (a\,b) : B}$

(id) $\quad \Gamma \vdash id \triangleright \Gamma$

(cons) $\quad \dfrac{\Gamma \vdash a : A \quad \Gamma \vdash s \triangleright \Gamma'}{\Gamma \vdash a.s \triangleright A.\Gamma'}$

(lambda) $\quad \dfrac{A.\Gamma \vdash a : B}{\Gamma \vdash \lambda_A.a : A \to B}$

(clos) $\quad \dfrac{\Gamma \vdash s \triangleright \Gamma' \quad \Gamma' \vdash a : A}{\Gamma \vdash a[s] : A}$

(shift) $\quad A.\Gamma \vdash \uparrow \triangleright \Gamma$

(comp) $\quad \dfrac{\Gamma \vdash s'' \triangleright \Gamma'' \quad \Gamma'' \vdash s' \triangleright \Gamma'}{\Gamma \vdash s' \circ s'' \triangleright \Gamma'}$

In addition, to each meta-variable X we associate a unique type T_X and a unique context Γ_X. We assume that for each pair (Γ, A) there is an infinite set of meta-variables X such that $\Gamma_X = \Gamma$ and $T_X = A$. We add the following type rule for meta-variables:

$$\text{(Metavar)} \quad \Gamma_X \vdash X : T_X$$

We use the $\lambda\sigma$-rules and the unification rules (named **Dec-λ**, **Dec-App**, **Dec-Fail**, **Exp-λ**, **Exp-App**, **Normalise** and **Replace**) for the $\lambda\sigma$-calculus as presented in [DHK00].

3 Second-Order Matching via Explicit Substitutions

The language of the $\lambda\sigma$-calculus is a non-trivial extension of the language of the λ-calculus, and hence, the decidability of second-order matching arises naturally in the $\lambda\sigma$-calculus. An obvious step to solve second-order matching problems in the $\lambda\sigma$-calculus would be to adapt the higher-order procedure for the $\lambda\sigma$-calculus of [DHK00] to solve second-order matching problems. As we will see in the next section, the procedure given in [DHK00] does not terminate for all second-order matching problems in the $\lambda\sigma$-calculus. Nevertheless, we characterise a sub-set of $\lambda\sigma$-terms for which we can decide second-order matching problems.

3.1 An Important Class of $\lambda\sigma$-Terms

In this section we characterise an important class of $\lambda\sigma$-terms, and in the next section, we design a second-order matching algorithm that decides this class. The necessity to define this class is due to the fact that the unification method [DHK00] does not terminate for all second-order matching problems written in the $\lambda\sigma$-style. Hence this method does not decide second-order matching in the $\lambda\sigma$-calculus. The counter-example is the following:

$$X_A^{A \to A.\Gamma}[(\lambda_A.\underline{1}_A^{A.\Gamma})_{A \to A}^{\Gamma}.id_\Gamma^{\Gamma}]_A^{\Gamma} =_{\lambda\sigma}^{?} b_A^{\Gamma}$$

where b is a given closed term, i.e. a term without occurrences of meta-variables, and Γ is a given context.

We can build the following derivation:

$X_A^{A \to A.\Gamma}[(\lambda_A.\underline{1}_A^{A.\Gamma})_{A \to A}^{\Gamma}.id_\Gamma^{\Gamma}]_A^{\Gamma} =_{\lambda\sigma}^{?} b_A^{\Gamma} \to^{\textbf{Exp-App}}$

$X_A^{A \to A.\Gamma}[(\lambda_A.\underline{1}_A^{A.\Gamma})_{A \to A}^{\Gamma}.id_{\Gamma}^{\Gamma}] =_{\lambda\sigma}^{?} b_A^{\Gamma} \wedge$
$X_A^{A \to A.\Gamma} =_{\lambda\sigma}^{?} (\underline{1}_{A \to A}^{A \to A.\Gamma} Y_A^{A \to A.\Gamma})_A^{A \to A.\Gamma} \quad \to \textbf{Replace}$
$(\underline{1}_{A \to A}^{A \to A.\Gamma} Y_A^{A \to A.\Gamma})_A^{A \to A.\Gamma}[(\lambda_A.\underline{1}_A^{A.\Gamma})_{A \to A}^{\Gamma}.id_{\Gamma}^{\Gamma}] =_{\lambda\sigma}^{?} b_A^{\Gamma} \wedge$
$X_A^{A \to A.\Gamma} =_{\lambda\sigma}^{?} (\underline{1}_{A \to A}^{A \to A.\Gamma} Y_A^{A \to A.\Gamma})_A^{A \to A.\Gamma} \quad \to \textbf{Normalise}$
$Y_A^{A \to A.\Gamma}[(\lambda_A.\underline{1}_A^{A.\Gamma})_{A \to A}^{\Gamma}.id_{\Gamma}^{\Gamma}] =_{\lambda\sigma}^{?} b_A^{\Gamma} \wedge$
$X_A^{A \to A.\Gamma} =_{\lambda\sigma}^{?} (\underline{1}_{A \to A}^{A \to A.\Gamma} Y_A^{A \to A.\Gamma})_A^{A \to A.\Gamma}$

At this point we can repeat the strategy **Exp-App**, **Replace** and **Normalise** since the last problem generated (see the last two lines) is composed by two flexible-rigid equations, the first of which is equivalent to the original problem up to renaming of meta-variables.

The class of $\lambda\sigma$-matching problems that we are going to characterise is strongly based on second-order matching problems that are generated in the simply typed λ-calculus. Let M be a matching problem in the simply typed λ-calculus. In order to solve M in the $\lambda\sigma$-calculus, we need first to rewrite M in the $\lambda\sigma$-language. This translation is given by the following *precooking* function:

Definition 8 (Precooking [DHK00]). *Let $a \in \Lambda_{dB}(\mathcal{X})$ such that $\Gamma \vdash a : A$. To every meta-variable X of type B in the term a, we associate the type B and the context Γ in the $\lambda\sigma$-calculus. The* precooking *of a from $\Lambda_{dB}(\mathcal{X})$ to the set $\Lambda_{\lambda\sigma}(\mathcal{X})$ of $\lambda\sigma$-terms is given by $a_F = F(a, 0)$, where $F(a, n)$ is defined by:*

1. $F((\lambda_B.a), n) = \lambda_B(F(a, n+1))$.
2. $F(\underline{k}, n) = \underline{1}[\uparrow^{k-1}]$.
3. $F((a\ b), n) = (F(a, n)\ F(b, n))$.
4. $F(X, n) = X[\uparrow^n]$.

Notice that $F(\underline{1}, n)$ and $F(X, 0)$ are resp. $\underline{1}$ and X since $\uparrow^0 = id$. The precooking translation is a function that takes a term from the simply typed λ-calculus and returns an equivalent term in the language of the simply typed $\lambda\sigma$-calculus. This translation is essential to avoid variable capture since the HOU procedure in the $\lambda\sigma$-calculus uses first-order substitution (grafting).

There are two important points that should be emphasised during the precooking translation: first, the unique context associated to each meta-variable in the simply typed λ-calculus in de Bruijn notation is the same unique context associated to the translated meta-variable in the $\lambda\sigma$-calculus, i.e., if $\Gamma \vdash X : A$ then $\Gamma \vdash X_F : A$; second, only meta-variables have their structure changed (in order to avoid variable capture when performing graftings) which means that $\lambda\sigma$-terms without occurrences of meta-variables are always in the image of the precooking translation. This last remark will be particularly important for matching. Although the precooking translation replaces the de Bruijn index $\underline{n}$ by its codification $\underline{1}[\uparrow^{n-1}]$, here, we avoid using this codification for clarity. To give a better intuition of what happens during the precooking translation, consider a (general) simply typed λ-term a. Suppose that a contains a meta-variable X

which is under the scope of n abstractors:
$$\lambda_{A_1}\ldots\lambda_{A_n}\cdots (\ X_B^{A_1,\ldots,A_n.\Delta}\ )\ \ldots$$
After the precooking translation we get:
$$\lambda_{A_1}\ldots\lambda_{A_n}\cdots (\ X_B^{\Delta}[(\uparrow^n)_{\Delta}^{A_1,\ldots,A_n.\Delta}]_B^{A_1,\ldots,A_n.\Delta}\ )\ \ldots$$
which is a shorthand for the simultaneous substitution:
$$\lambda_{A_1}\ldots\lambda_{A_n}\cdots (\ X_B^{\Delta}[(\underline{n+1}.\underline{n+2}.\cdots)_{\Delta}^{A_1,\ldots,A_n.\Delta}]_B^{A_1,\ldots,A_n.\Delta}\ )\ \ldots$$

Since in $\lambda\sigma$ one uses grafting, the precooking translation is the correct way to 'protect' the meta-variables and to avoid possible variable capture. The substitution $\uparrow^n$ applied to the meta-variable X, i.e., $X[\uparrow^n]$ means, on one hand, that every free de Bruijn index occurring in the term to be substituted by X must be updated by n and, on the other hand, that the first n terms of any substitution applied to $X[\uparrow^n]$ will be ignored. That is, $X[\uparrow^n][s]$ will be reduced to $X[s_{>n}]$, for any substitution s, where $s_{>n}$ represents the elements in the list s which are in positions greater than n. This means that the redexes related to the abstractors appearing in the initial problem cannot introduce terms in the substitution list applied to meta-variables. Hence, terms to be included in this list should be arguments of β-redexes generated by new abstractors which are created only by the rule **Exp-λ**.

Definition 9 (Unification Path/Matching Path). *Let P be a unification (resp. matching) problem. We say that P' is in the unification (resp. matching) path of P if $P \to^* P'$, where the relation $\to^*$ means $n \geq 0$ applications of any unification (resp. matching) rules.*

The next proposition characterises second-order problems in the language of the $\lambda\sigma$-calculus that can be decided by the method given by [DHK00].

Proposition 1 (Characterisation of a special subclass of $\lambda\sigma$-terms). *Let P_A^Γ be a second-order unification problem which is in the image of the precooking translation. Then every flexible term occurring in $P_A'^\Gamma$ which is in the unification path of P_A^Γ using the unification rules of [DHK00], and of the form $X[s]$, with X of atomic type and s in σ-normal form, is such that every element in the list s with functional type is a de Bruijn index.*

Proof. The proof is by induction on the size of the derivation that generated the term that contains $X[s]$ as sub-term. Without loss of generality we may assume that P_A^Γ is in $\lambda\sigma$-normal form (otherwise we can apply one step of **Normalise**). We use IH for the induction hypothesis.

If the considered equation belongs to P_A^Γ then by the definition of precooking, the substitution s is of the form $\uparrow^n$, for some $n \geq 0$ and, hence the proposition holds since every term in the substitution $\uparrow^n$ is a de Bruijn index.

Now suppose that the proposition holds for $P_A'^\Gamma$ which by hypothesis is in the unification path of P_A^Γ. Let $P_A''^\Gamma$ be such that $P_A'^\Gamma \to^r P_A''^\Gamma$ and r is any unification rule as given in [DHK00] except **Dec-Fail** since it does not generate a new unification problem. We have the following cases:

- If r is **Dec-λ** or **Replace** then $X[s]$ was already in P'^{Γ}_A since these rules do not change the structure of substitutions. The proposition follows by IH.
- If r is **Dec-App** then either $X[s]$ corresponds to one of the arguments a_i of $\underline{n}\ a_1 \ldots a_p$ or the equation was already in P'^{Γ}_A. In both cases, s satisfies the proposition by IH.
- If r is **Exp-λ** then either $X[s]$ is a sub-term of the new equation or it was already in P'^{Γ}_A. In the former case, the sole new meta-variable that is introduced has the form Y, that should be seen as $Y[id]$ and then the proposition holds. In the latter case the proposition holds by IH.
- If r is **Exp-App** then either $X[s]$ is a sub-term of one of the terms occurring among the new equations or it was already in P'^{Γ}_A. In the former case, all the new meta-variables $H_1, \ldots, H_k$ have the form $H_i[id]$ and then the proposition holds. In the latter case the proposition holds by IH.
- If r is **Normalise** then there are two cases that we need to consider:
  1. The application of **Normalise** is preceded by an application of **Exp-λ**: In this case, the newly introduced λ's will generate new β-redexes and the steps are as follows. The selected equation before the application of **Exp-λ** had a sub-term of the form:

  $$X^{\Delta}_{B_1 \to \cdots \to B_k \to B}[(\uparrow^n)^{A_1.\cdots.A_n.\Delta}_{\Delta}]^{A_1.\cdots.A_n.\Delta}_{B_1 \to \cdots \to B_k \to B}$$

  where $B_1, \ldots, B_k$ and B are atomic types since X is second order. After an application of **Exp-λ** followed by **Replace** we have:

  $$(\lambda_{B_1} \cdots \lambda_{B_k}.Y^{B_1.\cdots.B_k.\Delta}_B)^{\Delta}_B[(\uparrow^n)^{A_1.\cdots.A_n.\Delta}_{\Delta}]^{A_1.\cdots.A_n.\Delta}_B$$

  The normalisation step consists in pushing the substitution inside the new λ's and then performing β-reductions. After pushing the substitution inside these new abstractors we have a sub-term of the form:
  $\lambda_{B_1} \cdots \lambda_{B_k}.Y^{B_1.\cdots.B_k.\Delta}_B[\underline{1}^{B_1.\cdots.B_k.A_1.\cdots.A_n.\Delta}_{B_1} \cdots \underline{k}^{B_1.\cdots.B_k.A_1.\cdots.A_n.\Delta}_{B_k}.$
  $(\uparrow^{k+n})^{B_1.\cdots.B_k.A_1.\cdots.A_n.\Delta}_{\Delta}]^{B_1.\cdots.B_k.A_1.\cdots.A_n.\Delta}_B$

  The β-reductions that can be performed now will replace arbitrary elements by the first k de Bruijn indexes in the above substitution list, but since all of these λ's have atomic type the proposition holds. The other terms in the substitution list remain unchanged.
  2. **Normalise** was not preceded by an application of **Exp-λ**: Then, an application of **Normalise** is a consequence of an application of **Exp-App** since the rules **Dec-λ**, **Dec-App**, **Dec-Fail** and **Replace**, do not change the structure of the current terms which, by IH are in normal form. Applications of **Exp-App** do not introduce new abstractions and hence the rule $Beta^3$ does not apply. Application of Abs introduces a new de Bruijn index in the substitution list, and hence the proposition still holds. None of the others $\lambda\sigma$-rules introduce new terms in the substitution lists of the current unification problem and the proposition holds by IH. □

---

[3] See the $\lambda\sigma$-rules in [DHK00] or [ACCL91]

In other words, the substitution s in Proposition 1, has the form $a_1 \cdots a_p . \uparrow^n$ ($a_p \neq \underline{n}$), such that all the elements $a_1, \ldots, a_p$ are of atomic type, and the other part of the substitution, i.e., $\uparrow^n$ which is a short hand for $\underline{n+1}.\underline{n+2}.\cdots$, is formed by an infinite number of different de Bruijn indexes and is the only part which may have elements of functional type. This result is illustrated as:

$$X[\ \underbrace{a_1. \cdots . a_p}_{\substack{\text{atomic}\\\text{types}}} . \underbrace{\underline{n+1}.\underline{n+2}. \cdots}_{\substack{\text{at most}\\2^{nd}\text{-order types}}}\ ]$$

In section 3.3 we present a second-order matching algorithm for $\lambda\sigma$-problems whose terms belong to the class characterised by Proposition 1. Although this class forms a proper subset of all $\lambda\sigma$-terms, this restriction is not important since this class includes all $\lambda\sigma$-terms that occur in a second-order matching problem which is in the matching path of another matching problem that is in the image of the precooking translation. Thus, this class includes all the terms that can be generated by the unification procedure from a second-order matching problem originated in the simply typed λ-calculus (after the precooking translation).

3.2 The Unification by Transformation Notation

Matching problems are characterised by the fact that terms in the right-hand side of equations cannot be instantiated. Therefore, the first difficulty to use the general rules of [DHK00] is related to applications of the rule **Exp-λ** because it introduces a flexible-flexible equation whose right-hand side needs to be instantiated. As an example, let $a \ll^?_{\lambda\sigma} b$ be a second-order matching problem such that the term a has an occurrence of the meta-variable X of type $A \to A$. An application of a rule like **Exp-λ** would generate a new problem of the form $a <^?_{\lambda\sigma} b \land X \ll^?_{\lambda\sigma} \lambda_A.Y$, and of course the meta-variable Y needs to be instantiated. To solve this problem we use a notation based on the so called "unification by transformation" approach [Nip93]. According to this approach, a matching problem will be represented by a pair of the form $\langle \sigma, M \rangle$, where σ is a grafting, and M is a matching problem. The advantage of this notation is that we can define matching rules that do not introduce terms that need to be instantiated in the right-hand side of matching equations because graftings and matching equations are kept in different places. For the above example, an application of a rule with the same behaviour of **Exp-λ** should generate from the matching problem $\langle \{\}, a \ll^?_{\lambda\sigma} b \rangle$ the equivalent matching problem $\langle \{X \mapsto \lambda_A.Y\}, \{a \ll^?_{\lambda\sigma} b\}\rangle$.

This notation is independent of the matching rules and, hence we can characterise solved forms without knowing explicitly the matching rules.

Definition 10 (Solved form). *A solved form is a pair of the form $\langle \theta, M \rangle$, where the first element of the pair is a grafting and the second element is either the empty set or a finite set of trivial matching equations, i.e., equations of the form $a \ll^?_{\lambda\sigma} a$.*

Now we are ready to define the matching rules.

3.3 The Second-Order Matching Algorithm

The second-order matching rules are given in Table 1. The rules **Dec-$_m$-λ**, **Dec-$_m$-App**, **Dec-$_m$-Fail** and **Normalise$_m$** correspond respectively to **Dec-λ**, **Dec-App**, **Dec-Fail** and **Normalise** of [DHK00] written in the unification by transformation notation. The rule **Exp$_m$-λ** is the matching version of **Exp-λ**. The difference between them, in addition to the notation, is that **Exp$_m$-λ** always replaces a meta-variable of functional type by an abstraction whose body is a fresh meta-variable of atomic type and also applies the generated grafting to the current matching problem. This sole step corresponds to several applications of **Exp-λ** and **Replace**. Note that, if no replacement is done, the rule **Exp-λ** can be applied *ad infinitum*. To avoid such infinite reductions, [DHK00] defined fair strategies. The definition of **Exp$_m$-λ** avoids the necessity of defining any strategy because the rules in Table 1 cannot be applied to a given second-order matching problem forever. In fact, for a given equation each rule can be applied only once. The rules **Imit** and **Proj** generate grafting for flexible-rigid equations when the head of the flexible term is a meta-variable of atomic type. The main difference between **Imit** and **Proj** is that the latter does not introduce fresh meta-variables. In addition, while **Proj** may generate several different graftings, for **Imit** we have at most one grafting. Moreover, in the rule **Imit**, the head of the term which replaces X is a de Bruijn index of at most third order. This is because the newly introduced meta-variables have at most second-order.

To prove that the rules of Table 1 always terminate for second-order matching problems whose terms belong to the class characterised by Proposition 1, we need to define an adequate measure. We start by giving the length of a $\lambda\sigma$-term:

Definition 11 (Length of a $\lambda\sigma$-term). *Let $a \in \Lambda_{\lambda\sigma}(\mathcal{X})$. We inductively define $|a|$, the length of a, by:*

- *if $a = X$ or $a = \underline{1}$ then $|a| = 1$*
- *if $a = (b\ c)$ then $|a| = |b| + |c|$*
- *if $a = \lambda.b$ then $|a| = 1 + |b|$*
- *if $a = b[s]$ then $|a| = |b| + ||s||$, where the size of a substitution s, written as $||s||$, is inductively defined as:*
  - *if $s = \uparrow$ or $s = id$ then $||s|| = 0$*
  - *if $s = c.d$ then $||s|| = |c| + ||d||$*
  - *if $s = u \circ v$ then $||s|| = ||u|| + ||v||$*

Definition 12. *Let $M = \{a_1 \ll^?_{\lambda\sigma} b_1, \ldots, a_n \ll^?_{\lambda\sigma} b_n\}$ be a matching problem. Define $\mu(M) = (\xi, \xi', \xi'')$ in the following way:*

- $\xi = \Sigma_{i=1}^{n} |b_i|$
- $\xi' =$ *the number of meta-variables occurring in M*
- $\xi'' =$ *the sum of the order of the type of all meta-variables occurring in M.*

Now denote by $<$ the usual lexicographic order over triples.

Table 1. Second-Order Matching Rules

$\mathbf{Dec}_m\text{-}\lambda$	$\dfrac{\langle \sigma, P \cup \{\lambda_A.a \ll^?_{\lambda_\sigma} \lambda_A.b\}\rangle}{\langle \sigma, P \cup \{a \ll^?_{\lambda_\sigma} b\}\rangle}$
$\mathbf{Dec}_m\text{-}\mathbf{App}$	$\dfrac{\langle \sigma, P \cup \{(\underline{\mathtt{n}}\ a_1 \ldots a_p) \ll^?_{\lambda_\sigma} (\underline{\mathtt{n}}\ b_1 \ldots b_p)\}\rangle}{\langle \sigma, P \cup \{a_1 \ll^?_{\lambda_\sigma} b_1, \ldots, a_p \ll^?_{\lambda_\sigma} b_p\}\rangle}$
$\mathbf{Dec}_m\text{-}\mathbf{Fail}$	$\dfrac{\langle \sigma, P \cup \{(\underline{\mathtt{n}}\ a_1 \ldots a_p) \ll^?_{\lambda_\sigma} (\underline{\mathtt{m}}\ h_1 \ldots h_q)\}\rangle}{Fail}$, if $\mathtt{m} \neq \mathtt{n}$.
$\mathbf{Exp}_m\text{-}\lambda$	$\dfrac{\langle \sigma, P\rangle}{\exists Y : (A_1, \cdots, A_k.\Gamma \vdash Y : B), \langle \sigma', P\{X \mapsto \lambda_{A_1} \ldots \lambda_{A_k}.Y\}\rangle}$ if $(\Gamma \vdash X : A_1 \to \cdots \to A_k \to B) \in TVar(P)$, $Y \notin TVar(P)$, and X is not a solved variable. where $\sigma' = \sigma\{X \mapsto \lambda_{A_1} \ldots \lambda_{A_k}.Y\}$
$\mathbf{Imit}$	$\dfrac{\langle \sigma, P \cup \{X[a_1, \cdots, a_p.\uparrow^n] \ll^?_{\lambda_\sigma} (\underline{\mathtt{m}}\ b_1 \ldots b_q)\}\rangle}{\langle \sigma', P\sigma' \cup \{(\underline{\mathtt{m-n+p}}\ H_1 \ldots H_q)[a_1\sigma', \cdots, a_p\sigma'.\uparrow^n] \ll^?_{\lambda_\sigma} (\underline{\mathtt{m}}\ b_1 \ldots b_q)\}\rangle}$ if X has atomic type and $m > n$. where $\sigma' = \sigma\{X \mapsto (\underline{\mathtt{m-n+p}}\ H_1 \ldots H_q)\}$, $H_1, \ldots, H_q$ are meta variables with appropriate type and with contexts $\Gamma_{H_i} = \Gamma_X (\forall 1 \leq i \leq q)$, and $\underline{\mathtt{m-n+p}}$ is at most third order.
$\mathbf{Proj}$	$\dfrac{\langle \sigma, P \cup \{X[a_1, \cdots, a_p.\uparrow^n] \ll^?_{\lambda_\sigma} (\underline{\mathtt{m}}\ b_1 \ldots b_q)\}\rangle}{\langle \sigma\{X \mapsto \underline{\mathtt{j}}\}, \{P\{X \mapsto \underline{\mathtt{j}}\} \cup \{a_j\{X \mapsto \underline{\mathtt{j}}\} \ll^?_{\lambda_\sigma} (\underline{\mathtt{m}}\ b_1 \ldots b_q)\}\rangle}$ if X has atomic type, and the j-th element $(1 \leq j \leq p)$ of the list $a_1, \cdots, a_p$ has the same type of X.
$\mathbf{Normalise}_m$	$\dfrac{\langle \sigma, P \cup \{a \ll^?_{\lambda_\sigma} b\}\rangle}{\langle \sigma', P \cup \{a' \ll^?_{\lambda_\sigma} b'\}\rangle}$ if a or b is not in **Eta**-long form. where a' (resp. b') is the **Eta**-long form of a (resp. b), and σ' is obtained from σ by normalising all its terms. if a (resp. b) is not a solved variable and a (resp. b) otherwise.

Proposition 2. *Applications of the rules of Table 1 to second-order matching problems whose terms belong to the class characterised by Proposition 1 always terminate.*

Proof. It is enough to show that $\mu(M)$ decreases after the application of any of the rules in Table 1. We write $M \to^r M'$ to denote one step reduction by one application of rule r. Application of $\mathbf{Dec}_m\text{-}\lambda$ decreases the size of both sides of the selected equation (see definition 11), therefore $\mu(M') < \mu(M)$. Application of $\mathbf{Dec}_m\text{-}\mathbf{App}$ replaces one equation by a finite number of new equations formed by sub-terms of the previous problem, therefore ξ decreases and we have that $\mu(M') < \mu(M)$. Application of $\mathbf{Dec}_m\text{-}\mathbf{Fail}$ always stops. Application of $\mathbf{Exp}_m\text{-}\lambda$ replaces a meta-variable of functional type by a metavariable of atomic type, therefore ξ'' decreases and the first two components of the current triple remain unchanged, therefore $\mu(M') < \mu(M)$. Application of $\mathbf{Imit}$ introduces $q \geq 0$ fresh meta-variables to the new matching problem, where q is the number of arguments of the head $\underline{\mathtt{m}}$ of the rigid term in the current equation. If $q = 0$

then no new meta-variable is introduced and, hence ξ' decreases. Otherwise, the new equation $(\underline{\mathtt{m-n+p}}\ H_1 \ldots H_q)[a_1\sigma'.\cdots.a_p\sigma'.\uparrow^n] \ll^?_{\lambda\sigma} (\underline{\mathtt{m}}\ b_1 \ldots b_q)$, which is rigid-rigid must be followed by an application of $\mathbf{Dec}_m\text{-}\mathbf{App}$ which decreases $\mu(M)$. Application of $\mathbf{Proj}$ decreases ξ' since it does not introduce new meta-variables. Application of $\mathbf{Normalise}_m$ cannot be applied successively because the $\lambda\sigma$-calculus is weakly terminating. In this case, even if it is not the case that $\mu(M) < \mu(M')$ and M' is not trivial, one of the other rules must apply. Therefore the reduction terminates. □

Since we are dealing with matching problems, we have that the image of the graftings corresponding to solved forms are $\lambda\sigma$-terms that are always in the image of the precooking translation. In fact, note that the grafting of a solvable matching problem is always of the form $\{X_1 \mapsto a_1, \ldots, X_k \mapsto a_k\}$, where $a_1, \ldots, a_k$ are closed $\lambda\sigma$-terms, i.e., terms without any occurrences of meta-variables. This fact is formalised by the following proposition:

Proposition 3. *Every solved form of a second-order matching problem, obtained by application of the rules in Table 1, is in the image of the precooking translation.*

Proof. Every closed term is in the image of the precooking translation since we only need to rewrite the $\lambda\sigma$-codification of de Bruijn indexes, say $\underline{1}[\uparrow^n]$ $(n \geq 0)$, into the usual form $\underline{\mathtt{n}}$. Recall that, for clarity, in all the examples and even in the rules, we write $\underline{\mathtt{n}}$ instead of $\underline{1}[\uparrow^n]$, although this is not the notation used internally by the $\lambda\sigma$-calculus. □

According to Proposition 3, the solved forms are translated back to the simply typed λ-calculus by rewriting the codification of de Bruijn indexes used by the $\lambda\sigma$-calculus by the corresponding de Bruijn index in the λ-calculus. The whole matching process can be represented by the following scheme:

$$M \xrightarrow{\text{Precooking}} M_F \xrightarrow{\text{Matching Algorithm}} M'_F \xrightarrow{\text{Precooking}^{-1}} M'$$

Example 2. Let M be the second-order matching problem given by the equation $\Gamma \vdash \lambda_A.(X\ \underline{3}) \ll^? \lambda_A.(\underline{2}(\underline{43})) : A \to B$, whose context is given by $\Gamma = A \to B.A.A \to A.nil$, where A and B are atomic types and $\Gamma \vdash X : A \to B$. After the precooking translation, we have $\lambda_A.(X[\uparrow]\ \underline{3}) \ll^?_{\lambda\sigma} \lambda_A.(\underline{2}(\underline{43}))$. The algorithm generates the following reduction:

$$\langle \{\}, \{\lambda_A.(X[\uparrow]\ \underline{3}) \ll^?_{\lambda\sigma} \lambda_A.(\underline{2}(\underline{4}\ \underline{3}))\}\rangle$$

$$\Big\downarrow \mathbf{Dec}_m\text{-}\lambda$$

$$\langle \{\}, \{(X[\uparrow]\ \underline{3}) \ll^?_{\lambda\sigma} (\underline{2}(\underline{4}\ \underline{3}))\}\rangle$$

$$\Big\downarrow \mathbf{Exp}_m\ \lambda$$

$$\langle \{X \mapsto \lambda_A.Y\}, \{((\lambda_A.Y)[\uparrow]\ \underline{3}) \ll^?_{\lambda\sigma} (\underline{2}(\underline{4}\ \underline{3}))\}\rangle$$

$$\Big\downarrow \mathbf{Normalise}_m$$

$$\langle \{X \mapsto \lambda_A.Y\}, \{Y[\underline{3}.\uparrow] \ll^?_{\lambda\sigma} (\underline{2}(\underline{4}\ \underline{3}))\}\rangle$$

$$\Big\downarrow \mathbf{Imit}$$

$$\langle \{Y \mapsto (\underline{2}H_1), X \mapsto (\lambda_A.(\underline{2}H_1))\}, \{(\underline{2}H_1)[\underline{3}.\uparrow] \ll^?_{\lambda\sigma} (\underline{2}(\underline{4}\ \underline{3}))\}\rangle$$

$$\Big\downarrow \mathbf{Normalise}_m$$

$$\langle \{Y \mapsto (\underline{2}H_1), X \mapsto (\lambda_A.(\underline{2}H_1))\}, \{H_1[\underline{3}.\uparrow] =^?_{\lambda\sigma} (\underline{4}\ \underline{3})\}\rangle$$

$$\overset{\mathbf{Imit}}{\swarrow} \quad \overset{\mathbf{Proj}}{\searrow}$$
$$\quad T \quad\quad\quad\quad T'$$

where T' is given by:

$$\langle \{H_1 \mapsto \underline{1}, Y \mapsto (\underline{2}\ \underline{1}), X \mapsto \lambda_A.(\underline{2}\ \underline{1})\}, \{\underline{3} \ll^?_{\lambda\sigma} (\underline{4}\ \underline{3})\}\rangle$$

$$\Big\downarrow \mathbf{Dec}_m-\mathbf{Fail}$$

$$Fail$$

and T is given by:

$$\langle \{H_1 \mapsto (\underline{4}H_2), Y \mapsto (\underline{2}(\underline{4}H_2)), X \mapsto \lambda_A.(\underline{2}(\underline{4}H_2))\}, \{(\underline{4}H_2)[\underline{3}.\uparrow] \ll^?_{\lambda\sigma} (\underline{4}\ \underline{3})\}\rangle$$

$$\Big\downarrow \mathbf{Normalise}_m$$

$$\langle \{H_1 \mapsto (\underline{4}H_2), Y \mapsto (\underline{2}(\underline{4}H_2)), X \mapsto \lambda_A.(\underline{2}(\underline{4}H_2))\}, \{(\underline{4}H_2[\underline{3}.\uparrow]) \ll^?_{\lambda\sigma} (\underline{4}\ \underline{3})\}\rangle$$

$$\Big\downarrow \mathbf{Dec}_m\text{-}\mathbf{App}$$

$$\langle \{H_1 \mapsto (\underline{4}H_2), Y \mapsto (\underline{2}(\underline{4}H_2)), X \mapsto \lambda_A.(\underline{2}(\underline{4}H_2))\}, \{H_2[\underline{3}.\uparrow] \ll^?_{\lambda\sigma} \underline{3}\}\rangle$$

$$\overset{\mathbf{Imit}}{\swarrow} \quad \overset{\mathbf{Proj}}{\searrow}$$
$$\quad T'' \quad\quad\quad T'''$$

where T''' and T'''' are, respectively, given by:

$$\langle\{H_2 \mapsto \underline{3}, H_1 \mapsto (\underline{4}\ \underline{3}), Y \mapsto (\underline{2}(\underline{4}\ \underline{3})), X \mapsto \lambda_A.(\underline{2}(\underline{4}\ \underline{3}))\}, \{\underline{3} \ll^?_{\lambda\sigma} \underline{3}\}\rangle$$

and

$$\langle\{H_2 \mapsto \underline{1}, H_1 \mapsto (\underline{4}\ \underline{1}), Y \mapsto (\underline{2}(\underline{4}\ \underline{1})), X \mapsto \lambda_A.(\underline{2}(\underline{4}\ \underline{1}))\}, \{\underline{3} \ll^?_{\lambda\sigma} \underline{3}\}\rangle$$

To prove completeness and correctness of the matching rules of Table 1, we need to consider only the rules **Exp$_m$-λ**, **Imit** and **Proj** because for all the other rules the proof is the same as in [DHK00]. As usual, let us call $\mathcal{U}_{\lambda\sigma}(M)$ the set of all $\lambda\sigma$-unifiers (or matchers) of M.

Proposition 4 (Correctness). *Let $S = \{\mathbf{Exp}_m\text{-}\lambda, \mathbf{Imit}, \mathbf{Proj}\}$. The rules in S are correct, i.e., if $M \to^r M'$ then $\mathcal{U}_{\lambda\sigma}(M') \subseteq \mathcal{U}_{\lambda\sigma}(M)$, where $r \in S$.*

Proof. 1. **Exp$_m$-λ**: Suppose that γ is a matcher of $P\{X \mapsto \lambda_{A_1}\ldots\lambda_{A_k}.Y\}$. This means that the $\lambda\sigma$-normal form of $P\{X \mapsto \lambda_{A_1}\ldots\lambda_{A_k}.Y\}\gamma$ is the trivial problem, i.e, $\gamma \in \mathcal{U}_{\lambda\sigma}(P\{X \mapsto \lambda_{A_1}\ldots\lambda_{A_k}.Y\})$ and $\{X \mapsto \lambda_{A_1}\ldots\lambda_{A_k}.Y\}\gamma \in \mathcal{U}_{\lambda\sigma}(P)$ which shows that $\mathcal{U}_{\lambda\sigma}(P\{X \mapsto \lambda_{A_1}\ldots\lambda_{A_k}.Y\}) \subseteq \mathcal{U}_{\lambda\sigma}(P)$.

2. **Imit**: Let γ be a matcher of $P\sigma' \cup \{(\underline{\mathtt{m}-\mathtt{n}+\mathtt{p}}\ H_1\ldots H_q)[a_1\sigma'.\cdots.a_p\sigma'.\uparrow^n] \ll^?_{\lambda\sigma} (\underline{\mathtt{m}}\ b_1\ldots b_q)\}$, where $\sigma' = \sigma\{X \mapsto \underline{\mathtt{m}-\mathtt{n}+\mathtt{p}}\ H_1\ldots H_q\}$. This means that the $\lambda\sigma$-normal form of

$$P\sigma'\gamma \cup \{(\underline{\mathtt{m}-\mathtt{n}+\mathtt{p}}\ H_1\ldots H_q)[a_1\sigma'.\cdots.a_p\sigma'.\uparrow^n]\gamma \ll^?_{\lambda\sigma} (\underline{\mathtt{m}}\ b_1\ldots b_q)\}$$

is the trivial problem. Therefore, $\sigma'\gamma \in \mathcal{U}_{\lambda\sigma}(P \cup \{X[a_1.\cdots.a_p.\uparrow^n] \ll^?_{\lambda\sigma} (\underline{\mathtt{m}}\ b_1\ldots b_q)\})$, and hence $\mathcal{U}_{\lambda\sigma}(P\sigma' \cup \{(\underline{\mathtt{m}-\mathtt{n}+\mathtt{p}}\ H_1\ldots H_q)[a_1\sigma'.\cdots.a_p\sigma'.\uparrow^n] \ll^?_{\lambda\sigma} (\underline{\mathtt{m}}\ b_1\ldots b_q)\}) \subseteq \mathcal{U}_{\lambda\sigma}(P \cup \{X[a_1.\cdots.a_p.\uparrow^n] \ll^?_{\lambda\sigma} (\underline{\mathtt{m}}\ b_1\ldots b_q)\})$.

3. **Proj**: Let γ be a matcher of $P\{X \mapsto \underline{\mathtt{j}}\} \cup \{a_j\{X \mapsto \underline{\mathtt{j}}\} \ll^?_{\lambda\sigma} (\underline{\mathtt{m}}\ b_1\ldots b_q)\}$, i.e., the $\lambda\sigma$-normal form of $P\{X \mapsto \underline{\mathtt{j}}\}\gamma \cup \{a_j\{X \mapsto \underline{\mathtt{j}}\}\gamma \ll^?_{\lambda\sigma} (\underline{\mathtt{m}}\ b_1\ldots b_q)\}$ is the trivial problem. Hence, $\{X \mapsto \underline{\mathtt{j}}\}\gamma$ is a matcher of $P \cup \{X[a_1.\cdots.a_p.\uparrow^n] \ll^?_{\lambda\sigma} (\underline{\mathtt{m}}\ b_1\ldots b_q)\}$, i.e., $\{X \mapsto \underline{\mathtt{j}}\}\gamma \in \mathcal{U}_{\lambda\sigma}(P \cup \{X[a_1.\cdots.a_p.\uparrow^n] \ll^?_{\lambda\sigma} (\underline{\mathtt{m}}\ b_1\ldots b_q)\})$, and since $\{X \mapsto \underline{\mathtt{j}}\}\gamma \in \mathcal{U}_{\lambda\sigma}(P\{X \mapsto \underline{\mathtt{j}}\} \cup \{a_j \ll^?_{\lambda\sigma} (\underline{\mathtt{m}}\ b_1\ldots b_q)\})$, we have that $\mathcal{U}_{\lambda\sigma}(P\{X \mapsto \underline{\mathtt{j}}\} \cup \{a_j \ll^?_{\lambda\sigma} (\underline{\mathtt{m}}\ b_1\ldots b_q)\}) \subseteq \mathcal{U}_{\lambda\sigma}(P \cup \{X[a_1.\cdots.a_p.\uparrow^n] \ll^?_{\lambda\sigma} (\underline{\mathtt{m}}\ b_1\ldots b_q)\})$. □

Proposition 5 (Completeness). *Let $S = \{\mathbf{Exp}_m\text{-}\lambda, \mathbf{Imit}, \mathbf{Proj}\}$. The rules in S are complete, i.e., if $M \to^r M'$ then $\mathcal{U}_{\lambda\sigma}(M) \subseteq \mathcal{U}_{\lambda\sigma}(M')$, where $r \in S$.*

Proof. 1. **Exp$_m$-λ**: Let θ be a $\lambda\sigma$-unifier of $\langle\sigma, P\rangle$ and $X \in Tvar(P)$ such that $\Gamma \vdash X : A_1 \to \ldots \to A_k \to B$. Thus $X\theta = a : A_1 \to \ldots \to A_k \to B$ and we can assume that a is of the form $\lambda_{A_1}\ldots\lambda_{A_k}.b$ with $b : B$. Define θ' such that for all $Z \in Dom(\theta)$, $\theta'(Z) = \theta(Z)$ and $Y\theta = b$ for a new variable $Y \notin Dom(\theta)$ of type B. Then θ' is a $\lambda\sigma$-unifier of $\langle\{X \mapsto \lambda_{A_1}\ldots\lambda_{A_k}.Y\}, P\rangle$. Consequently θ is a $\lambda\sigma$-unifier of $\exists(Y : A_1.\cdots.A_k.\Gamma \vdash B), \langle\{X \mapsto \lambda_{A_1}\ldots\lambda_{A_k}.Y\}, P\rangle$.

2. **Imit** and **Proj**: Let γ be a matcher of $P \cup \{X[a_1.\cdots.a_p.\uparrow^n] \ll^?_{\lambda\sigma} \underline{\mathtt{m}}\ b_1\ldots b_q\}$, where X has atomic type and $m > n$. Let $X \mapsto \underline{\mathtt{k}}\ c_1\ldots c_r \in \gamma$. Then, we have $P\{X \mapsto \underline{\mathtt{k}}\ c_1\ldots c_r\} \cup \{(\underline{\mathtt{k}}\ c_1\ldots c_r)[a_1.\cdots.a_p.\uparrow^n] \ll^?_{\lambda\sigma} \underline{\mathtt{m}}\ b_1\ldots b_q\} \to^*_{\lambda\sigma}$

$P\{X \mapsto \underline{k}\ c_1 \ldots c_r\} \cup \{\underline{k}[a_1.\cdots.a_p.\uparrow^n]c_1[a_1.\cdots.a_p.\uparrow^n]\ldots c_r[a_1.\cdots.a_p.\uparrow^n]$
$\ll^?_{\lambda\sigma} \underline{\underline{m}}\ b_1 \ldots b_q\}$.
Now we have two options: $k \leq p$ or $k > p$. In the first case, the previous problem reduces to $P\{X \mapsto \underline{k}\ c_1 \ldots c_r\} \cup \{a_k\ c_1[a_1.\cdots.a_p.\uparrow^n]\ldots c_r[a_1.\cdots.a_p.\uparrow^n]$
$\ll^?_{\lambda\sigma} \underline{\underline{m}}\ b_1 \ldots b_q\}$ and γ is certainly a unifier of it. If $k > p$ then the problem reduces to $P\{X \mapsto \underline{k}\ a_1 \ldots a_p\} \cup \{\underline{k}\quad\underline{p} \mid \underline{n}\ a_1[a_1.\cdots.a_p.\uparrow^n]\ldots c_r[a_1.\cdots.a_p.\uparrow^n]$
$\ll^?_{\lambda\sigma} \underline{\underline{m}}\ b_1 \ldots b_q\}$ and it has a solution if and only if $k - p + n = m$ and thus $k = m - n + p$ at the condition that $k > p \Leftrightarrow m - n + p > p \Leftrightarrow m > n$, which gives the condition asserted in the rule **Imit**. □

4 Conclusions and Future Work

We presented a second-order matching algorithm that decides an important subset of $\lambda\sigma$-terms. This subset is important because it contains all the second-order $\lambda\sigma$-terms that can occur in a second-order matching problem which is originated from a matching problem in the simply typed λ-calculus. The algorithm uses an adequate notation for dealing with matching problems since it keeps graftings and matching equations as different entities. This separation is important to avoid the possible introduction of flexible terms that need to be instantiated in the right-hand side of a matching equation.

The study of the possible adaptation of this method to other calculi of explicit substitutions, such as the λs_e-calculus (for which HOU was already adapted [ARK01]) and the suspension calculus, can be helpful to identify advantages and disadvantages of these calculi in practical applications [AMK05]. Moreover, this work can be extended for matching via explicit substitutions using a richer type theory, such as dependent types [Ree03,Muñ01].

There exist different definitions of matching in the literature such as "filtering" and "semi-unification", and in certain cases, matching cannot be seen as a sub-case of higher-order unification[Bur89,Dow01]. As future work, we intend to study how these definitions are related in a higher-order framework and, how they interfere with explicit substitutions environments. In addition, another interesting problem concerns to the existence of a second-order matching algorithm that decides the whole $\lambda\sigma$-calculus and not a sub-class of it, as well as possible extensions of the current algorithm to matching problems of higher orders.

Acknowledgments. We would like to thank Claude Kirchner for the comments that motivated this work and the referees for their suggestions and constructive criticisms.

References

ACCL91. M. Abadi, L. Cardelli, P.-L. Curien, and J.-J. Lévy. Explicit Substitutions. *J. of Func. Programming*, 1(4):375–416, 1991.

ARK01. M. Ayala-Rincón and F. Kamareddine. Unification via the λs_e-Style of Explicit Substitution. *The Logical J. of the IGPL*, 9(4):489–523, 2001.

AMK05. M. Ayala-Rincón, F.L.C. de Moura and F. Kamareddine. Comparing and Implementing Calculi of Explicit Substitutions with Eta-Reduction. R. de Queiroz, B. Poizat and S. Artemov Eds. To appear in Special Issue of *Annals of Pure and Applied Logic* - WoLLIC 2002 selected papers, 2005.

Bur89. H.J. Burckert. Matching - A Special Case of Unification? *Journal of Symbolic Computation*, 8:523–536, 1989.

dB72. N.G. de Bruijn. Lambda-Calculus Notation with Nameless Dummies, a Tool for Automatic Formula Manipulation, with Application to the Church-Rosser Theorem. *Indag. Mat.*, 34(5):381–392, 1972.

DHK00. G. Dowek, T. Hardin, and C. Kirchner. Higher-order unification via explicit substitutions. *Information and Computation*, 157:183–235, 2000.

dlTC87. T. B. de la Tour and R. Caferra. Proof analogy in interactive theorem proving: A method to express and use it via second order pattern matching. In *Proceedings of AAAI 87*, pages 95–99. Morgan Kaufmann, 1987.

dlTC88. T. B. de la Tour and R. Caferra. A formal approach to some usually informal techniques used in mathematical reasoning. In P. Gianni, editor, *Proc. of the Int. Symposium on Symbolic and Algebraic Computation*, LNCS 358, pages 402–406. Springer Verlag, 1988.

Dow94. G. Dowek. Third order matching is decidable. *Annals of Pure and Applied Logic*, 69:135–155, 1994.

Dow01. G. Dowek. Higher-Order Unification and Matching. In A. Robinson and A. Voronkov, editors, *Handbook of Automated Reasoning*, volume II, chapter 16, pages 1009–1062. MIT press and Elsevier, 2001.

Gol81. W. Goldfarb. The Undecidability of the Second-Order Unification Problem. *TCS*, 13(2):225–230, 1981.

HL78. G. Huet and B. Lang. Proving and applying program transformations expressed with second order patterns. *Acta Informatica*, 11:31–55, 1978.

Hue76. G. Huet. *Résolution d'équations dans les langages d'ordre 1,2,...,ω*. PhD thesis, University Paris-7, 1976.

Loa03. R. Loader. Higher order β matching is undecidable. *Logic Journal of the IGPL*, 11(1):51–68, 2003.

Muñ01. C. Muñoz. Proof-term synthesis on dependent-type systems via explicit substitutions. *Theoretical Computer Science*, 266:407–440, 2001.

Nip93. T. Nipkow. Functional unification of higher-order patterns. In *Proc. 8th IEEE Symp. Logic in Computer Science*, pages 64–74, 1993.

Pad00. V. Padovani. Decidability of fourth-order matching. *Mathematical Structures in Computer Science*, 10(3):361–372, 2000.

Ree03. J. Reed. Extending higher-order unification to support proof irrelevance. In *TPHOLs*, pages 238–252. Springer Verlag, 2003.

Rob65. J. A. Robinson. A Machine-oriented Logic Based on the Resolution Principle. *Journal of the ACM*, 12(1):23–41, January 1965.

Vis04. E. Visser. A survey of strategies in rule-based program transformation systems. *Journal of Symbolic Computation*, 2004. Accepted for publication.

Knowledge-Based Synthesis of Distributed Systems Using Event Structures

Mark Bickford[*], Robert C. Constable[**], and Joseph Y. Halpern[***], and Sabina Petride[***]

Department of Computer Science
Cornell University
Ithaca, NY 14853
{markb,rc,halpern,petride}@cs.cornell.edu

Abstract. To produce a program guaranteed to satisfy a given specification one can synthesize it from a formal constructive proof that a computation satisfying that specification exists. This process is particularly effective if the specifications are written in a high-level language that makes it easy for designers to specify their goals. We consider a high-level specification language that results from adding *knowledge* to a fragment of Nuprl specifically tailored for specifying distributed protocols, called *event theory*. We then show how high-level *knowledge-based programs* can be synthesized from the knowledge-based specifications using a proof development system such as Nuprl. Methods of Halpern and Zuck [15] then apply to convert these knowledge-based protocols to ordinary protocols. These methods can be expressed as heuristic transformation tactics in Nuprl.

1 Introduction

Errors in software are extremely costly and disruptive. NIST (the National Institute of Standards and Technology) estimates the cost of software errors to the US economy at $59.5 billion per year. One approach to minimizing errors is to synthesize programs from specifications. Synthesis methods have produced highly reliable moderate-sized programs in cases where the computing task can be precisely specified. One of the most elegant synthesis methods is the use of so-called *correct-by-construction* program synthesis [4,9]. Here programs are constructed from *proofs* that the specifications are satisfiable. That is, a constructive proof that a specification is satisfiable gives a program that satisfies the specification. This method has been successfully used by several research groups and

---

[*] Supported in part by AF-AFOSR F49620-02-1-0170.
[**] Supported in part by ONR N00014-02-1-0455 and NSF 0208535.
[***] Supported in part by NSF under grant CCR-0208535, by ONR under grant N00014-02-1-0455, by the DoD Multidisciplinary University Research Initiative (MURI) program administered by the ONR under grants N00014-01-1-0795 and N00014-04-1-0725, and by AFOSR under grant F49620-02-1-0101.

companies to construct large complex *sequential* programs, but it has not yet been used to create substantial realistic distributed programs.

The Cornell Nuprl proof development system was among the first tools used to create correct-by-construction functional and sequential programs [9]. Nuprl has also been used extensively to optimize distributed protocols, and to specify them in the language of I/O Automata [6]. Recent work by two of the authors [5] has resulted in the definition of a fragment of the higher-order logic used by Nuprl tailored to specifying distributed protocols, called *event theory*, and the extension of Nuprl methods to synthesize distributed protocols from specifications written in event theory [5]. Event logic is a specification language closely related to I/O automata. As has long been recognized [13], designers typically think of specifications at a high level, which often involves knowledge-based statements. For example, the goal of a program might be to guarantee that a certain process knows certain information. It has been argued that a useful way of capturing these high-level knowledge-based specifications is by using high-level *knowledge-based programs* [13,14]. Knowledge-based programs are an attempt to capture the intuition that what an agent does depends on what it knows. For example, a knowledge-based program may say that process 1 should stop sending a bit to process 2 once process 1 knows that process 2 knows the bit. Such knowledge-based programs and specifications can be given precise semantics [13,14]. They have already met with some degree of success, having been used both to help in the design of new protocols and to clarify the understanding of existing protocols [10,15,21].

In this paper, we add knowledge operators to event theory raising its level of abstraction and show by example that knowledge-based programs can be synthesized from constructive proofs that specifications in event theory with knowledge operators are satisfiable. Our example uses the *sequence-transmission problem*, where a sender must transmit a sequence of bits to a receiver in such a way that the receiver eventually knows arbitrarily long prefixes of the sequence. Halpern and Zuck [15] provide two knowledge-based programs for the sequence-transmission, prove them correct, and show that many standard programs for the problem in the literature can be viewed as implementations of their high-level knowledge-based program. Here we show that these two knowledge-based programs can be synthesized from the specifications of the problem, expressed in event theory augmented by knowledge. We can then translate the arguments of Halpern and Zuck to Nuprl, to show that the knowledge-based programs can be transformed to the standard programs in the literature.

Engelhardt, van den Meyden, and Moses [11,12] have also provided techniques for synthesizing knowledge-based programs from knowledge-based specifications, by successive refinement. We see their work as complementary to ours. Since our work is based on Nuprl, we are able to take advantage of the huge library of tactics provided by Nuprl to be able to generate proofs. The expressive power of Nuprl also allows us to express all the high-level concepts of interest (both epistemic and temporal) easily. Engelhardt, van den Meyden, and Moses do not have a theorem-proving engine for their language. However, they do provide useful refinement rules that can easily be captured as tactics in Nuprl.

2 Synthesizing Programs from Constructive Proofs

2.1 Nuprl: A Brief Overview

Much current work on formal verification using theorem proving, including Nuprl, is based on type theory (see [8] for a recent overview). A type can be thought of as a set with structure that facilitates its use as a data type in computation; this structure also supports constructive reasoning. The set of types is closed under constructors such as $\times$ and $\to$, so that if A and B are types, so are $A \times B$ and $A \to B$, where, intuitively, $A \to B$ represents the computable functions from A into B. *Constructive* type theory, upon which Nuprl is based, was developed to provide a foundation for constructive mathematics. The key feature of constructive mathematics is that "there exists" is interpreted as "we can construct (a proof of)". A consequence of this approach is that the law of excluded middle does not hold.

Definition 1. *A program in Nuprl is an object of some type Pgm. A program semantics is a function S of type $Pgm \to Sem$ assigning to each program Pg of type Pgm a meaning of type Sem. A specification is a predicate X on Sem.*

We take $Pg \models X$ to be an abbreviation of $X(S(Pg))$, and $Sat(X)$ to be an abbreviation for $\exists Pg\,(Pg \models X)$. Thus, the fact that a specification is satisfiable is expressible in Nuprl. The key point for the purposes of this paper is that from a constructive proof of $Sat(X)$, we can extract a program that satisfies X.

Constructive type logic is highly undecidable, so we cannot hope to construct a proof completely automatically. However, experience has shown that, by having a large library of lemmas and proof tactics, it is possible to "almost" automate quite a few proofs, so that with a few hints from the programmer, correctness can be proved. In any case, for an instance of this general constructive framework to be useful in practice, the parameters *Pgm*, *Sem*, and S must be chosen so that (a) programs are concrete enough to be compiled, and (b) specifications are naturally expressed as predicates over *Sem*, and (c) there is a small set of *rules* for producing proofs of satisfiability.

To use this general framework for synthesis of *distributed, asynchronous* algorithms, we choose the programs in *Pgm* to be *distributed message automata*. Message automata are closely related to *IO-Automata* [17] and are roughly equivalent to *UNITY* programs [7] (but with message-passing rather than shared-variable communication). We describe distributed message automata in Section 2.3. As we shall see, they satisfy criterion (a) above.

The semantics of a program is the *system*, or set of *runs*, consistent with it. Typical specifications in the literature are predicates on runs. We can view a specification as a predicate on systems by saying that a system satisfies a specification exactly if all the runs in the system satisfy it. To satisfy criterion (b) above, we choose a formal definition of runs that builds in the fundamental order structure and provides the operators for appropriately abstract specifications. To do this we formalize runs as structures that we call *event structures*, much in the spirit of Lamport's [16] model of events in distributed systems. Event structures are explained in more detail in the next section.

2.2 Event Structures

Consider a set AG of processes or *agents*; associated with each agent in AG is a set of *local variables*. Agent i's local state at a point in time is defined as the values of its local variables at that time. There are no shared variables. Information is communicated by message passing. Sending a message on some link l is understood as enqueuing the message on l, while receiving corresponds to dequeuing the message. Communication is asynchronous and point-to-point: for each link l there is a unique agent $source(l)$ that can send messages on l, and a unique agent $destination(l)$ that can receive message on l.

Following Lamport [16], changes in the local state of an agent are modeled as *events*. Intuitively, when an event "happens", an agent either receives a message or chooses some values (perhaps nondeterministically). As a result of receiving the message or the (nondeterministic) choice, the values of some of the agent's local variables change. Formally, events are elements of a type E. There is a one-to-one function *agent* such that for any event e, $agent(e)$ is the agent whose local state changes during event e. The values of state variables before and after e happens are described by binary functions *when* and *after*, typically written using infix notation: if $agent(e) = i$ and x is one of i's variables, then $(x\ when\ e)$ describes the value of x before e, and $(x\ after\ e)$ describes its value after e.[1] To each event we associate a *value* and a *kind*. If the event happens as a result of a receiving a message on some link l, then the event has kind $rcv(l)$, and its value is the corresponding message. Any other event has kind $local(a)$, where a is the label of the event, and its value is the set of values (nondeterministically) chosen by the agent. The label of an event is just a syntactic identifier that makes it easier to do proofs and state conditions. Note that, unlike Lamport [16], we do not have events of kind *send*. We model the sending of a message on a link l by changing the value of the local variable that describes the message enqueued on l. This variable can be changed during any event; that is, any event can involve sending a message. This way of modeling events has proved to be convenient.

For each $i \in AG$, the set of events e such that $agent(e) = i$ is totally ordered. Intuitively, this set of events is the agent i's *history*. If $first(e)$ holds, then e is the first event in the history associated with $agent(e)$; if not, then e has a predecessor $pred(e)$.

Every receive event e has a corresponding *send event*, denoted $send(e)$; this is the event where the message received at e was enqueued. Following Lamport

---

[1] State variables are typed, but to simplify our discussion we suppress all type declarations.

[16], we can define a *causal order* on events as the transitive closure of the sender-receiver and predecessor relations. Thus, $\to$ is the least relation on events such that $e \to e'$ if

- e' is a receive event and e is the corresponding send event, or
- $agent(e) = agent(e)'$ and e precedes e' in the total order associated with $agent(e)$, or
- for some event e'' we have $e \to e''$ and $e'' \to e'$.

Intuitively, if $e \to e'$, then e is guaranteed to happen before e'. We write $e \geq e'$ if $e = e'$ or $e \to e'$.

Formally, an *event structure* consist of a collection of events satisfying some natural properties: only finitely many messages can be sent when an event happens; the predecessor function is one to one; the causal order is well-founded; $pred(e)$ is associated with the same agent as e; if e has kind $rcv(l)$, then the agent associated with $send(e)$ is $source(l)$; and, finally, the local variables of agent $agent(e)$ do not change between $pred(e)$ and e; that is, $(x$ after $pred(e)) = (x$ when $e)$. The type (set) of event structures is definable in Nuprl.

2.3 Distributed Message Automata

A *message automaton* is a nondeterministic state machine associated with some agent i; it specifies when i can take actions and which actions it can take. The actions in programs are essentially events in event structures. We view a *receive* action as being out of the control of the agent; all other actions have associated preconditions. At each point in time i nondeterministically decides which actions to perform, among those whose precondition is satisfied.

Message automata are built from a small set of basic clauses. With each basic clause cl in an automaton we associate a formula ϕ_{cl} in the language of event structures. The event structures consistent with cl are the ones satisfying ϕ_{cl}. If we prove a specification X is satisfiable using a set $\{\phi_{cl} \mid cl \in C\}$ of assumptions, then the set C of the clauses used in the proof is a *program* satisfying X. This is how we extract a program satisfying a specification from a proof that the specification is satisfiable.

A basic clause does one of the following:

1. defines the initial value of one state variable;
2. defines the effect of one kind of event on one state variable;
3. defines the precondition for one kind of local event;
4. lists all the kinds of events that can change the value of one particular state variable.

For convenience, we represent each of the basic clauses as a simple program in a programming language. We give some examples here:

- A basic clause of the second type that says the message $f(s, v)$ is sent by i on link l when a local event e such that $kind(e) = local(a)$ and $value(e) = v$

occurs and i's local state is s, where f is some function (recall that, in our framework, sending a message on link l amounts to changing the value of a local variable that encodes messages enqueued on l) is represented by the program

$$a(v) \text{ sends } f(state, v) \text{ on } l.^2$$

- A basic clause of the third type that says that an event a with value v and kind $local(a)$ occurs only if precondition P holds is represented by the program

$$a(v) \text{ only if } P(state, v).$$

- The program representing an instance of the last clause that says that all the events that result in sending a message on a link l are on the list L is

only events in L send on l.

The programs representing instances of the first three clauses can be easily compiled into JAVA. The last clause is called a *frame condition*; it corresponds to a promise *not* to add code.

A finite set C of basic clauses is *feasible* if there is an event structure (a run) consistent with all the clauses in C (i.e., satisfying all the clauses ϕ_{cl} such that $cl \in C$). Every basic clause is feasible. A *distributed message automaton* is a collection of message automata, one for each agent in the system. A frame condition and an effect clause may be *incompatible*; that is, they may not be simultaneously satisfiable. We can form more complicated programs from simpler programs by composition. The composition $A \oplus B$ of two programs A and B is just the union of the clauses from A and B. The rules restrict composition of message automata to automata whose clauses are pairwise compatible. The set (type) of distributed message automata is the smallest set of feasible clauses containing the four basic clauses and closed under $\oplus$. By adding the appropriate constants and functions to Nuprl, we can ensure that each program is a term in the language.

The semantics of a distributed message automaton is the set of event structures that are consistent with it. In terms of the language used in Section 2.1, an event structure is a run, and a set of event structures is a system. As we show in the full paper, the semantics can formally be defined in Nuprl as a relation $Consistent(Pg, es)$ between a program (i.e., message automaton) Pg and event structure es. The set of event structures consistent with Pg is denoted $Sys(Pg)$. The fact that $Consistent$ is definable in Nuprl is critical: it means that we can talk about whether an event structure is consistent with a program in Nuprl.

Recall that a specification is a predicate on systems, i.e., on the meaning of programs. Many specifications that arise in practice are of a special type called *run-based* specifications [13]. A run-based specification is given as a predicate on runs (i.e., event structures). We can view a predicate P on runs as a predicate

---

[2] Here the notation $a(v)$ is just a compact way of saying that the value of an event of kind $local(a)$ is v, and does not refer to function application.

on systems by taking P to hold of a system if it holds of every run of the system. If P is a run-based specification, then $\Gamma_y \models P$ exactly if

$$\forall es.(Consistent(Pg, es) \Rightarrow P(es)) \land \exists es.Consistent(Pg, es).$$

Bickford and Constable [5] derived from the formal semantics of distributed message automata a set of seven useful Nuprl axioms for proving the satisfiability of a run-based specification There are four base axioms, one for each basic clause, an additional axiom for the combination of precondition and initialization clauses, a composition axiom, and a refinement axiom. We now briefly discuss these axioms.

The refinement axiom says that if P refines Q (that is, if $P(es)$ implies $Q(es)$ for all event structures es) and A satisfies P, then A also satisfies Q:

$$A \models P \Rightarrow \forall es.(P(es) \Rightarrow Q(es)) \Rightarrow A \models Q.$$

The composition axiom says that if two programs A and B are *compatible* (that is, their clauses are pairwise compatible), denoted $A||B$, then $A \oplus B$ combines the constraints of A and B:

$$(A \models P \land B \models Q \land A||B) \Rightarrow A \oplus B \models P \land Q.$$

The axiom for each basic clause cl is just the corresponding formula ϕ_{cl}. We give two examples of the axioms here; see [5] for the others.

The axiom corresponding to the basic clause "agent i initializes x to 5" is $\forall e@i.first(e) \Rightarrow (x\ when\ e) = 5$, where $\forall e@i.P$ is an abbreviation of the formula $\forall e.agent(e) = i \Rightarrow P$. For the axiom corresponding to the precondition clause, let $state(e)$ be the state associated with event e; that is, the values of all the local variables in event e. Similarly, let $state(after(e))$ be the values of the variables after e. (This, of course, is just $state(e')$ where e' is the successor of e in the history, if there is a successor.) The intended meaning of the precondition clause $a(v)$ **only if** $P(state, v)$ in a program for agent i is that, infinitely often, agent i checks whether there is a some value v such that $P(state(e), v)$ holds; if so then, infinitely often, i chooses such a value v and an event of kind $local(a)$ and value v occurs. Moreover, an event of kind $local(a)$ occurs only when its value satisfies the precondition. Finally, the clause rules out finite event sequences where an event of kind $local(a)$ could be performed after the last event, but is not. The axiom ϕ_{cl} for this clause is the conjunction of two formulas. The first is

$$\forall e@i[\exists e' \geq e(kind(e') = local(a)) \lor \forall v'(\neg P(state(after(e)), v'))],$$

which says that either infinitely often an event of kind $local(a)$ occurs, or infinitely often P is false, or the sequence is finite and P is false after the last event. The second conjunct gives the obvious safety condition, namely, that P is a precondition for an event of kind $local(a)$: $\forall e@i.kind(e) = local(a) \Rightarrow P(state(e), val(e))$.

2.4 Example

As an example of a parameterized specification that we use later, consider the following predicate $Fair(P, f, l)$ on event structures, where P is a precondition, f is a partial function (defined on states where P holds), and l is a link. $Fair(P, f, l)$ is a conjunction of a safety condition and a liveness condition. The safety condition asserts that the value of every receive event on link l is given by f of the state of the sender and that state satisfies the precondition P. The liveness condition says that, infinitely often, either a receive event on l occurs or else the precondition P fails. In the specification, we abbreviate $P(state(e), val(e))$ by $P@e$; we similarly use $f@e$. The specification is

$Fair(P, f, l) \equiv$
$\forall e'.kind(e') = rcv(l) \Rightarrow P@send(e') \land val(e') = f@send(e')$
$\land \forall e@source(l).\exists e' \geq e.kind(e') = rcv(l) \lor \forall v'.\neg(P(state(after(send(e'))), v'))$.

This specification is satisfied by the following program $Fair\text{-}Pg(P, f, l)$ for agent $source(l)$, which combines three basic clauses:

$a(v)$ only if $P(state, v)$ ⊕ $a(v)$ sends $f(state, v)$ on l ⊕
only events in $\{local(a)\}$ send on l.

Lemma 1. *$Fair\text{-}Pg(P, f, l)$ satisfies the specification $Fair(P, f, l)$. Moreover, this can be proved using the seven axioms.*

3 Adding Knowledge to Nuprl

3.1 Consistent Cut Semantics for Knowledge

To reason about knowledge in event structures we use a standard first-order modal logic of knowledge and time. Assume that there are n processes. Consider a first-order logic of knowledge and time, where formulas are formed by starting with a set Φ of functions symbols, predicate symbols, and constant symbols of various arities. We form atomic predicates and terms as usual in first-order logic, and close under conjunction, negation, universal quantification, the temporal operator $\square$, and the operators K_i, $i = 1, \ldots, n$, one for each process i.

Typically semantics for knowledge are given with respect to a pair (r, m) consisting of a run r and a time m, assumed to be the time on some external global clock (that none of the processes necessarily knows about) [13]. In event structures, there is no external notion of time. Fortunately, Panangaden and Taylor [18] give a variant of the standard definition with respect to what they call *asynchronous runs*, which are essentially identical to event structures. Thus, we just apply their definition in our framework.

The truth of formulas is defined relative to a triple (Sys, E, c), consisting of a system Sys (i.e., a set of event structures), and event structure E in Sys, and a *consistent cut* c of E, where a *consistent cut* c in E is a set of events in E closed under the causality relation. That is, if e' is an event in c and e is an event in E that precedes e' (i.e., $e \to e'$), then e must also be in c.

Define the equivalence relations $\sim_i$, $i = 1, \ldots, n$, on consistent cuts by taking $c \sim_i c'$ if i's history is the same in c and c'. Intuitively, $c \sim_i c'$ if process i cannot tell c and c' apart, given its information. Given two consistent cuts c and c', we say that $c \preceq c'$ if, for each process i, process i's history in c is a prefix of process i's history in c'.

Given a nonempty set of objects D and a system Sys, an interpretation function π associates to each cut c and symbol s in Φ its interpretation, denoted $\pi(c, s)$, which is a predicate or function on D of the right arity. To extend this interpretation to terms, we start with a valuation V, which associates with each variable an element of D. For each variable x, we define $\pi(c, x) = V(x)$. We then define $\pi(c, f(t_1, \ldots, t_k))$ by induction on the structure of terms, taking

$$\pi(c, f(t_1, \ldots, t_k)) = \pi(c, f)(\pi(c, t_1), \ldots, \pi(c, t_k)).$$

Using V and π, we define what it means for a formula ϕ to be true at the consistent cut c in event structure E in system Sys, denoted $(Sys, E, c, \pi, V) \models \phi$, by induction on the structure of ϕ, in the usual way. For example

- $(Sys, E, c, \pi, V) \models K_i \varphi$ iff $\forall E' \in Sys$, and c' cut of E' such that $c' \sim_i c$, we have $(Sys, E', c', \pi, V) \models \varphi$
- $(Sys, E, c, \pi, V) \models \Box \varphi$ iff for all cuts c' of E such that $c \preceq c'$, we have $(Sys, E, c', \pi, V) \models \varphi$.

As usual, we take $\Diamond \phi$ to be an abbreviation of $\neg \Box \neg \phi$, so that $\Diamond \phi$ is true at (E, c) if there is some cut c' extending c where ϕ is true. Similarly we write $\Diamondminus \varphi$ if there was a time in past when φ was true, or φ holds at cut c. The complete definition of $\models$ is given in the appendix.

The satisfaction relation $\models$ can be expressed as a formula in Nuprl. More precisely, there is a translation T (which we define in the appendix) such that for all tuples (Sys, E, c), domains D, interpretations π, valuations V, and formulas φ, $T(Sys, E, c, D, \pi, V\varphi)$ is true iff $(Sys, E, c, V, \pi) \models \varphi$. There is a subtlety though. First-order epistemic logic assumes the principle of excluded middle; Nuprl is a constructive type theory that does not. To prove that T has the desired properties, we need to assume the law of the excluded middle. We remark that this assumption is necessary only for the purpose of this translation and not for the proofs we present in Section 4.

3.2 Knowledge-Based Programs and Specifications

In this section, we show how we can extend the notions of program and specification presented in Section 2 to knowledge-based programs and specifications. This allows us to employ the large body of tactics and libraries already developed in Nuprl to synthesize knowledge-based programs from knowledge-based specifications.

We have identified programs with distributed message automata, where a distributed message automaton is characterized by a set of clauses. We take a *knowledge-based message automaton* to be a function that associates to each system (i.e. set of event structures) a message automaton; intuitively, a knowledge-based message automaton allows preconditions on actions to depend on the knowledge of processes about the whole system. For the purposes of this paper, we take knowledge-based programs (hereafter abbreviated *kb programs*) to be knowledge-based message automata. Note that each standard program Pg corresponds to the kb program that associates to each system the program Pg.

What should the semantics of a kb program be? As discussed in Section 2, in the case of standard programs, a program semantics is a function S that associates with every program Pg of type Pgm the system $S(Pg)$ consisting of all the runs consistent with Pg. As we have seen, the truth of a knowledge test in a kb program depends on the whole system. Once we have a system, we can determine the truth of the knowledge tests. A kb program then reduces to a standard program. Thus, a kb program has type $Pgm^{kb} = Sem \to Pgm$. Note that composing the semantic function S with a knowledge-based program yields a function from systems to systems. A system Sys is said to *represent* a kb program Pg^{kb} if it is a fixed point of this function: Sys represents the kb program Pg^{kb} if $S(Pg^{kb} \, Sys) = Sys$. Following Fagin et al. [13,14], we take the semantics of a kb program Pg^{kb} to be the set of systems that represent Pg^{kb}.

Definition 2. *A kb program semantics S^{kb} is a function of type $Pgm^{kb} \to \mathcal{P}(Sem)$, where $\mathcal{P}(Sem)$ is the type whose elements are sets of systems.*

As observed by Fagin et al. [13,14], it is possible to construct kb programs that are represented by no systems, exactly one system, or more than one system. It is also possible to construct sufficient conditions (which are often satisfied in practice) that guarantee that a kb program is represented by exactly one system. Note that, in particular, standard programs, when viewed as kb programs, are represented by a unique system; indeed, $S^{kb}(Pg) = \{S(Pg)\}$. Thus, we can view S^{kb} as extending S.

We next consider knowledge-based specifications (hereafter abbreviated *kb specifications*). Recall that a (standard) specification is a predicate on runs. Following [13,14], we take a kb specification to be a predicate on systems.

Definition 3. *A kb specification is an object of type $Sem \to \mathcal{P}$. A kb program Pg^{kb} satisfies a kb specification X^{kb}, written $Pg^{kb} \models X^{kb}$, if all the systems representing Pg^{kb} satisfy X and $S^{kb}(Pg^{kb}) \neq \emptyset$; i.e., $\forall Sys \in S^{kb}(Pg^{kb}).\ X^{kb}(Sys) \land S^{kb}(Pg^{kb}) \neq \emptyset$.*

3.3 Example

Recall that in Section 2 a specification $Fair(P, f, l)$ was defined that requires that, infinitely often, either a precondition P fails at the state of the source of some link or a message is received on the link; the message is constructed by applying the function f at the source of the link. The specification is satisfied by a standard program $Fair\text{-}Pg(P,f,l)$. $Fair(P,f,l)$ can be generalized to a kb specification $Fair^{kb}(P^{kb}, f^{kb}, l)$ where, instead of using a precondition P and function f, we use a *kb predicate* P^{kb} and a *kb function* f^{kb}, both of which take a system as an extra argument (in addition to the other arguments of P and f). $Fair^{kb}(P^{kb}, f^{kb}, l)$ asserts that, in every run of the system, infinitely often either the kb precondition fails or a receive event with the value given by f^{kb} occurs on link l:

$Fair^{kb}(P^{kb}, f^{kb}, l) \equiv$
$\forall e'.kind(e') = rcv(l) \Rightarrow P^{kb}@send(e') \wedge val(e') = f^{kb}@send(e')$
$\wedge \forall e@source(l).\exists e' \geq e.kind(e') = rcv(l) \vee \forall v'.\neg(P^{kb}(state(after(e')), v')$

$Fair^{kb}(P^{kb}, f^{kb}, l)$ is satisfied by a kb program $Fair\text{-}Pg^{kb}(P^{kb}, f^{kb}, l)$:

$a(v)$ only if $P^{kb}(state, v) \oplus$
$a(v)$ sends $f^{kb}(state, v)$ on $l \oplus$
only events in $\{local(a)\}$ send on l

$Fair\text{-}Pg^{kb}(P^{kb}, f^{kb}, l)$ associates to each system Sys the program $Fair\text{-}Pg(P^{kb}(Sys), f^{kb}(Sys), l)$; in system Sys, a process following $Fair\text{-}Pg^{kb}(P^{kb}, f^{kb}, l)$ sends a message with value determined by $f^{kb}(Sys)$ exactly when $P^{kb}(Sys)$ is true.

Lemma 2. *$Fair\text{-}Pg^{kb}(P^{kb}, f^{kb}, l)$ satisfies the specification $Fair^{kb}(P^{kb}, f^{kb}, l)$.*

4 The Sequence Transmission Problem

In this section, we illustrate how programs can be extracted from knowledge-based specifications using the Nuprl system. We do the extraction in two stages. In the first stage, we use Nuprl to prove that the specification is satisfiable. The proof proceeds by refinement: at each step, a rule or tactic (i.e. sequence of rules invoked under a single name) is applied, and new subgoals are generated; when there are no more subgoals to be proved, the proof is complete. The proof is automated, in the sense that subgoals are generated by the system upon tactic invocation. From the proof, we can extract a knowledge-based program Pg^{kb} that satisfies the specification. In the second stage, we find standard programs that implement Pg^{kb}.

We illustrate this methodology by applying it to one of the problems that has received considerable attention in the context of knowledge-based programming, *the sequence transmission problem* (stp). The stp involves a sender S that has an input tape with a (possibly infinite) sequence $X = X[0], X[1], \ldots$ of bits, and wants to transmit X to a receiver R; R must write this sequence on an output tape Y. A solution to the problem must satisfy two conditions:

1. (safety): at all times, the sequence Y of bits written by R is a prefix of X, and
2. (liveness): every bit $X[k]$ is eventually written by R on the output tape.

Halpern and Zuck [15] define two kb programs that solve this problem, and show that a number of standard programs in the literature, like Stenning's algorithm [20], the alternating bit protocol [3], and Aho, Ullman and Yannakakis's [1] algorithms are all particular instances of these programs. Sanders [19] derives a number of kb and standard programs for the same problem, with a focus on the more practical aspects of program development. Our method uses ideas from both of these earlier works.

If messages cannot be lost, duplicated, reordered, or corrupted, then S could simply send the bits in X to R in order. However, we are interested in solutions to the stp in contexts where communication is not reliable. Without some constraints, the stp is unsolvable; following [15], we assume (a) that all corruptions are detectable and (b) a weak fairness condition: all messages sent infinitely often are eventually received.

The safety and liveness conditions above are run-based specifications. As argued by Fagin et al. in [13], it is often better to think in terms of knowledge-based specifications for this problem. The real goal of the stp is to get the receiver to know the bits. Writing $K_R(X[i])$ as an abbreviation for $K_R(X[i] = 0)$ $\vee$ $K_R(X[i] = 1)$, we really want a knowledge-based condition of the form

$$\varphi^{kb} \stackrel{def}{\equiv} \forall i \, \Diamond K_R(X[i]).$$

One way to achieve this condition is by requiring that the receiver makes progress: for each i, if for all $j < i$ there was a time when R knew $X[j]$, then eventually R knows $X[i]$.

Intuitively, the sender is responsible for R's progress. But how can S ensure that R learns the ith bit? For any finite number n, it is possible that a message sent n times is not received. Fortunately, the fairness condition ensures that if $X[i]$ is sent an unbounded number of times, R will receive it. Thus, S can ensure that R learns the ith bit if, infinitely often, either S sends $X[i]$ or S knows that R knew $X[i]$ at some time in the past. This is similar in spirit to the specification $Fair^{kb}(P^{kb}, f^{kb}, l)$ described in Example 3.3. In this case, l is the communication link from S to R, f^{kb} encodes the least bit that S does not know that R knew at some point in the past, i.e., the pair $(i, X[i])$ for the least index i such that $\neg K_S \Diamond K_R X[i]$ holds. P^{kb} is instantiated with a test on S's knowledge such that whenever P^{kb} fails, $\forall i \, \Diamond K_R X[i]$ holds. Thus, we take $P^{kb} \equiv \exists i \, \neg K_S(\Diamond K_R X[i])$ Note that, unless at some point S knows that R knows the whole sequence, P^{kb} will be true. (Indeed, in many settings, we can just take P^{kb} to be the formula true.) We abbreviate this specification as $Fair^{kb}(P_S^{kb}, f_S^{kb}, l_{SR})$.

How does the sender learn which bits the receiver knows? One possibility is for S to receive from R a request to send $X[i]$. This can be taken by S to be a signal that R knows all the preceding bits. R's program for sending this request to S can again be viewed as an instance of the specification $Fair^{kb}(P^{kb}, f^{kb}, l)$, this time for l the communication link from R to S, and f^{kb} returning the least index i such that R never knew $X[i]$. We take P^{kb} to be $\exists i \, \neg \Diamond K_R X[i]$ (again, in many contexts, we can take it to be simply true) and abbreviate this specification as $Fair^{kb}(P_R^{kb}, f_R^{kb}, l_{RS})$.

Up to this point we have only used our intuition to guess a plausible refinement for our initial specification φ^{kb}. We can now use the system to verify this intuition. That is, we prove that the satisfiability of φ^{kb} follows from the satisfiability of each of $Fair^{kb}(P_R^{kb}, f_R^{kb}, l_{RS})$ and $Fair^{kb}(P_S^{kb}, f_S^{kb}, l_{SR})$ separately:

Goal: $\models \varphi^{kb}$
Subgoal 1: $\models Fair^{kb}(P_R^{kb}, f_R^{kb}, l_{RS})$
Subgoal 2: $\models Fair^{kb}(P_S^{kb}, f_S^{kb}, l_{SR})$
Subgoal 3: $(\models Fair^{kb}(P_R^{kb}, f_R^{kb}, l_{RS})) \wedge (\models Fair^{kb}(P_S^{kb}, f_S^{kb}, l_{SR})) \Rightarrow (\models \varphi^{kb})$

The proof is carried out in Nuprl in two steps. Using Lemma 2, we can prove that there exist kb programs, $Fair\text{-}Pg^{kb}(P_R^{kb}, f_R^{kb}, l_{RS})$ and $Fair\text{-}Pg^{kb}(P_S^{kb}, f_S^{kb}, l_{SR})$, respectively, that satisfy both fairness specifications; i.e.,

$$Fair\text{-}Pg^{kb}(P_R^{kb}, f_R^{kb}, l_{RS}) \models Fair^{kb}(P_R^{kb}, f_R^{kb}, l_{RS})$$

$$Fair\text{-}Pg^{kb}(P_S^{kb}, f_S^{kb}, l_{SR}) \models Fair^{kb}(P_S^{kb}, f_S^{kb}, l_{SR}).$$

Finally we have to check that the combination of the two programs satisfies the conjunction of the specifications satisfied by each program separately. This means that we have to inspect the frame conditions for both programs, i.e. the conditions that allow only R to send messages of the form i to S, and only S to send pairs $\langle i, X[i] \rangle$ to R. Since messages sent by the programs go on separate links, the frame conditions are easily seen to be compatible with the effect clauses. Thus, we can prove

$$Fair\text{-}Pg^{kb}(P_R^{kb}, f_R^{kb}, l_{RS}) \oplus Fair\text{-}Pg^{kb}(P_S^{kb}, f_S^{kb}, l_{SR}) \models \varphi^{kb}.$$

Using the program notation of Fagin et al. [13], $Fair\text{-}Pg^{kb}(P_S^{kb}, f_S^{kb}, l_{SR})$ consists of the following collection of statements (one for each i):

if $K_S(\Diamond K_R X[0] \wedge \ldots \wedge \Diamond K_R X[i-1]) \wedge \neg K_S(\Diamond K_R X[i])$
then $\text{send}_{l_{SR}}(\langle i, X[i]\rangle)$ else skip.

Similarly, $Fair\text{-}Pg^{kb}(P_R^{kb}, f_R^{kb}, l_{RS})$ consists of the following collection of statements:

if $\Diamond K_R X[0] \wedge \ldots \ldots \wedge \Diamond K_R X[i-1] \wedge \neg \Diamond K_R X[i]$ then $\text{send}_{l_{RS}}(i)$ else skip.

Notice that whenever S sends a message $\langle i, X[i]\rangle$, i is the minimum index for which $\neg K_S(\Diamond K_R X[i])$; similarly, R always sends the minimum i for which $\neg \Diamond K_R X[i]$. We can make this explicit by letting S and R have local variables, say i and j, to keep track of these minimum indices. The variables i and j are initially set to 0; S increments i from the current value v to $v+1$ whenever he learns that $\Diamond K_R X[v]$ holds, and similarly, R increments j from v to $v+1$ whenever he learns $X[v]$. The knowledge test in the sender program can then be rewritten as $\neg K_S(\Diamond K_R X[v])$, for v the current value of i, and the knowledge test for the receiver becomes $\neg \diamondsuit K_R X[j]$; thus the derived program is essentially one of the knowledge-based programs considered by Halpern and Zuck [15].

This is not surprising, since our derivation followed much the same reasoning as that of Halpern and Zuck. However, note that we did not first give a kb program and then verify that it satisfied the specification. Rather, we derived the kb programs for the sender and receiver from the proof that the specification was satisfiable. And, while Nuprl required "hints" from us in terms of what to prove, the key ingredients of the proof, namely, the specification $Fair(P, f, l)$ and the proof that $Fair\text{-}Pg(P, f, l)$ realizes it, were already in the system, having been used in other contexts. Thus, this suggests that we may be able to apply similar techniques to derive programs satisfying other specifications in communication systems with only weak fairness guarantees.

This takes care of the first stage of the synthesis process. We now want to find a standard program that implements the knowledge-based program. As discussed by Halpern and Zuck [15], the exact standard program that we use depends on the underlying assumptions about the communications systems. Here we sketch an approach to finding the standard program.

The first step is to identify the exact properties of knowledge that are needed for the proof. We can inspect the proof and identify which properties of the knowledge operators K_S and K_R seem to be used. We replace $\diamondsuit(K_R(X[i] = v))$ by an abstract predicate $Q(X[i] = v)$ and $K_S(\diamondsuit K_R(X[i] = v))$ by $P(X[i] = v)$. As before, we abbreviate $P(X[i] = 0) \vee P(X[i] = 1)$ as $P(X[i])$, and $Q(X[i])$ for $Q(X[i] = 0) \vee Q(X[i] = 1)$. We add as hypotheses all the identified properties, now as properties of Q and P, and check whether the former proof still applies. If not, we add whatever additional properties are needed. Note that we can use Nuprl to automate these checks.

This approach enables us to prove that the specification is satisfiable in a more general setting. The specification is now written in terms of P and Q, and denoted $\tilde{\varphi}^{kb}$. $Fair^{kb}(P_R^{kb}, f_R^{kb}, l_{RS})$ is replaced by $Fair^{kb}(\tilde{Q}, \tilde{f_R}, l_{RS})$ with $\tilde{Q} \stackrel{def}{=} \exists i \, \neg Q(X[i])$, and similarly, $Fair^{kb}(P_S^{kb}, f_S^{kb}, l_{SR})$ becomes $Fair^{kb}(\tilde{P}, \tilde{f_S}, l_{SR})$ with $\tilde{P} \stackrel{def}{=} \exists i \, \neg P(X[i])$. Whenever $\tilde{Q}$ and $\tilde{P}$ hold, $\tilde{f_R}$ and $\tilde{f_S}$ return the minimum index i such that $\neg Q(X[i])$ and $\neg P(X[i])$, respectively.

The new theorem states that, under suitable hypotheses about P and Q, $\tilde{\varphi}^{kb}$ is satisfiable since both $Fair^{kb}(\tilde{Q}, \tilde{f_R}, l_{RS})$ and $Fair^{kb}(\tilde{P}, \tilde{f_S}, l_{SR})$ are satisfiable. One hypothesis we require is that P and Q must be *sound* tests, that is, $P(X[k] = v)$ and $Q(X[k] = v)$ both imply $X[k] = v$; this is clearly true of knowledge predicates. We must also assume that after R receives a message of the form $\langle i, v \rangle$, $Q(X[i] = v)$ holds; similarly, after S receives some message i, $\forall j < i \, P(X[j])$ holds. The extracted program is

$$Fair\text{-}Pg^{kb}(\tilde{Q}, \tilde{f_R}, l_{RS}) \oplus Fair\text{-}Pg^{kb}(\tilde{P}, \tilde{f_S}, l_{SR}),$$

where $Fair\text{-}Pg^{kb}(\tilde{P}, \tilde{f_S}, l_{SR})$, written using Fagin et al. notation, consists of the statements

if $P(X[0]) \wedge \ldots P(X[i-1]) \wedge \neg P(X[i])$ then $\text{send}_{l_{SR}}(\langle i, X[i] \rangle)$ else skip;

similarly, $Fair\text{-}Pg^{kb}(\tilde{Q}, \tilde{f_R}, l_{RS})$ consists of the statements

if $Q(X[0]) \wedge \ldots Q(X[i-1]) \wedge \neg Q(X[i])$ then $\mathtt{send}_{l_{RS}}(i)$ else skip.

Clearly, this is a generalization of the first kb-program for the stp. Furthermore, it is clear that other predicates P and Q satisfy these hypotheses. For example, suppose that S has a state variable i_S such that $P(X[0]) \wedge \ldots P(X[i_s - 1]) \wedge \neg P(X[i_S])$ holds at the current state of S; similarly, R has a state variable i_R such that $Q(X[0]) \wedge \ldots \wedge Q(X[i_R - 1]) \wedge \neg Q(X[i_R])$ holds. We can then simply define $P'(X[k]) \stackrel{def}{\equiv} i_S > k$ and $Q'(X[k]) \stackrel{def}{\equiv} i_R > k$; the resulting program is exactly Stenning's [20] protocol.

The key point here is that by replacing the knowledge tests by weaker predicates that imply them and do not explicitly mention knowledge, we can derive standard programs that implement the knowledge-based program. We believe that other standard implementations of the knowledge-based program can be derived in a similar way, although we have not yet concluded the derivation. We hope to report on this shortly. [3]

References

1. A. V. Aho, J. D. Ullman, A. D. Wyner, and M. Yannakakis. Bounds on the size and transmission rate of communication protocols. *Computers and Mathematics with Applications*, 8(3):205–214, 1982. This is a later version of [2].
2. A. V. Aho, J. D. Ullman, and M. Yannakakis. Modeling communication protocols by automata. In *Proc. 20th IEEE Symp. on Foundations of Computer Science*, pages 267–273. 1979.
3. K. A. Bartlett, R. A. Scantlebury, and P. T. Wilkinson. A note on reliable full-duplex transmission over half-duplex links. *Communications of the ACM*, 12:260–261, 1969.
4. J. L. Bates and Robert L. Constable. Proofs as programs. *ACM Transactions on Programming Languages and Systems*, 7(1):53–71, 1985.
5. Mark Bickford and Robert L. Constable. A logic of events. Technical Report TR2003-1893, Cornell University, 2003.
6. Mark Bickford, Christoph Kreitz, Robbert van Renesse, and Xiaoming Liu. Proving hybrid protocols correct. In Richard Boulton and Paul Jackson, editors, 14th *International Conference on Theorem Proving in Higher Order Logics*, volume 2152 of *Lecture Notes in Computer Science*, pages 105–120, Edinburgh, Scotland, September 2001. Springer-Verlag.
7. K. M. Chandy and J. Misra. *Parallel Program Design: A Foundation*. Addison-Wesley, Reading, Mass., 1988.
8. Robert L. Constable. Naïve computational type theory. In H. Schwichtenberg and R. Steinbrüggen, editors, *Proof and System-Reliability, Proceedings of International Summer School Marktoberdorf, July 24 to August 5, 2001*, volume 62 of *NATO Science Series III*, pages 213–260, Amsterdam, 2002. Kluwer Academic Publishers.

---

[3] Extracts from the event system library can be seen at http://www.cs.cornell.edu/Info/People/sfa/Nuprl/EventSystems/.

9. Robert L. Constable et al. *Implementing Mathematics with the Nuprl Proof Development System.* Prentice-Hall, NJ, 1986.
10. C. Dwork and Y. Moses. Knowledge and common knowledge in a Byzantine environment: crash failures. *Information and Computation*, 88(2):156–186, 1990.
11. K. Engelhardt, R. van der Meyden, and Y. Moses. A program refinement framework supporting reasoning about knowledge and time. In J. Tiuryn, editor, *Proc. Foundations of Software Science and Computation Structures (FOSSACS 2000)*, pages 114–129. Springer-Verlag, Berlin/New York, 1998.
12. K. Engelhardt, R. van der Meyden, and Y. Moses. A refinement theory that supports reasoning about knowledge and time for synchronous agents. In *Proc. Int. Conf. on Logic for Programming, Artificial Intelligence, and Reasoning*, pages 125–141. Springer-Verlag, Berlin/New York, 2001.
13. R. Fagin, J. Y. Halpern, Y. Moses, and M. Y. Vardi. *Reasoning about Knowledge.* MIT Press, Cambridge, Mass., 1995.
14. R. Fagin, J. Y. Halpern, Y. Moses, and M. Y. Vardi. Knowledge-based programs. *Distributed Computing*, 10(4):199–225, 1997.
15. J. Y. Halpern and L. D. Zuck. A little knowledge goes a long way: knowledge-based derivations and correctness proofs for a family of protocols. *Journal of the ACM*, 39(3):449–478, 1992.
16. L. Lamport. Time, clocks, and the ordering of events in a distributed system. *Communications of the ACM*, 21(7):558–565, 1978.
17. Nancy Lynch and Mark Tuttle. An introduction to Input/Output automata. *Centrum voor Wiskunde en Informatica*, 2(3):219–246, September 1989.
18. P. Panangaden and S. Taylor. Concurrent common knowledge: defining agreement for asynchronous systems. *Distributed Computing*, 6(2):73–93, 1992.
19. B. Sanders. A predicate transformer approach to knowledge and knowledge-based protocols. In *Proc. 10th ACM Symp. on Principles of Distributed Computing*, pages 217–230, 1991. A revised report appears as ETH Informatik Technical Report 181, 1992.
20. M. V. Stenning. A data transfer protocol. *Comput. Networks*, 1:99–110, 1976.
21. F. Stulp and R. Verbrugge. A knowledge-based algorithm for the Internet protocol (TCP). *Bulletin of Economic Research*, 54(1):69–94, 2002.

A Translating $\models$ into Nuprl

Using valuation V and interpretation π, the fact that formula ϕ is true at the consistent cut c in event structure E in system Sys is denoted $(Sys, E, c, \pi, V) \models \phi$ and defined by induction on the structure of ϕ as follows:

- if P is a predicate symbol in Φ of some arity k, and $t_1, \ldots, t_k$ are terms, then $(Sys, E, c, \pi, V) \models P(t_1, \ldots, t_k)$ iff $\pi(c, P)(\pi(c, t_1), \ldots, \pi(c, t_k))$
- $(Sys, E, c, \pi, V) \models \neg\varphi$ iff $(Sys, E, c, \pi, V) \not\models \varphi$
- $(Sys, E, c, \pi, V) \models \varphi_1 \wedge \varphi_2$ iff $(Sys, E, c, \pi, V) \models \varphi_1$ and $(Sys, E, c, \pi, V) \models \varphi_2$
- $(Sys, E, c, \pi, V) \models \forall x.\varphi$ iff, for all $d \in D$, $(Sys, E, c, \pi, V[x/d]) \models \varphi$, where $V[x/d]$ is the valuation that agrees with V on all variables except possible x, and $V[x/d](x) = d$
- $(Sys, E, c, \pi, V) \models K_i\varphi$ iff for all $E' \in Sys$ and cuts c' of E' such that $c' \sim_i c$, $(Sys, E', c', \pi, V) \models \varphi$

- $(Sys, E, c, \pi, V) \models \Box\varphi$ iff for all cuts c' of E such that $c \preceq c'$, we have $(Sys, E, c', \pi, V) \models \varphi$
- $(Sys, E, c, \pi, V) \models \Diamond\varphi$ iff there exists a cut c' of E such that $c \preceq c'$ and $(Sys, E, c', \pi, V) \models \varphi$
- $(Sys, E, c, \pi, V) \models \Diamond\!\!\!-\varphi$ iff there exists a cut c' of E such that $c' \preceq c$ and $(Sys, E, c', \pi, V) \models \varphi$.

We can now define the translation T by induction on the structure of formulas:

- if P is a predicate symbol in Φ of some arity k, and $t_1, \ldots, t_k$ are terms, then
  $T(Sys, E, c, D, \pi, V, P(t_1, \ldots, t_k)) = \pi(c, P)(\pi(c, t_1), \ldots, \pi(c, t_k))$
- $T(Sys, E, c, D, \pi, V, \neg\varphi) = \neg(T(Sys, E, c, D, \pi, V, \varphi))$
- $T(Sys, E, c, D, \pi, V, \varphi_1 \wedge \varphi_2)) = (T(Sys, E, c, D, \pi, V, \varphi_1)) \wedge (T(Sys, E, c, D, \pi, V, \varphi_2))$
- $T(Sys, E, c, D, \pi, V, (\forall x.\varphi)) = \forall x.(T(Sys, E, c, D, \pi, V, (\varphi(V\ x))))$
- $T(Sys, E, c, D, \pi, V, K_i\varphi) = \forall E'.E' \in Sys \Rightarrow \forall c'.c' \sim_i c \Rightarrow (T(Sys, E', c', D, \pi, V, \varphi))$
- $T(Sys, E, c, D, \pi, V, \Box\varphi) = \forall c'.c \preceq c' \Rightarrow (T(Sys, E, c', D, \pi, V, \varphi))$

From this definition it follows that, assuming the principle of excluded middle, $T(Sys, E, c, D, \pi, V\varphi)$ is provable iff $(Sys, E, c, V, \pi) \models \varphi$.

Proposition 1. *Assuming the principle of excluded middle, for all tuples (Sys, E, c), domains D, interpretations π, valuations V, and formulas φ, $T(Sys, E, c, D, \pi, V, \varphi)$ is provable iff $(Sys, E, c, V, \pi) \models \varphi$.*

The Inverse Method for the Logic of Bunched Implications

Kevin Donnelly[1], Tyler Gibson[2], Neel Krishnaswami[3], Stephen Magill[3], and Sungwoo Park[3]

[1] Department of Computer Science, Boston University, 111 Cummington Street, Boston MA 02215, USA,
kevind@bu.edu
[2] Department of Philosophy, Carnegie Mellon University, 5000 Forbes Avenue, Pittsburgh PA 15213, USA,
tylerg@andrew.cmu.edu
[3] Computer Science Department, Carnegie Mellon University, 5000 Forbes Avenue, Pittsburgh PA 15213, USA,
{neelk,smagill,gla}@cs.cmu.edu

Abstract. The inverse method, due to Maslov, is a forward theorem proving method for cut-free sequent calculi that relies on the subformula property. The Logic of Bunched Implications (**BI**), due to Pym and O'Hearn, is a logic which freely combines the familiar connectives of intuitionistic logic with multiplicative linear conjunction and its adjoint implication. We present the first formulation of an inverse method for propositional **BI** without units. We adapt the sequent calculus for **BI** into a forward calculus. The soundness and completeness of the calculus are proved, and a canonical form for bunches is given.

1 Introduction

1.1 The Logic of Bunched Implications

The study of substructural logics, beginning with linear logic [10], has shown the usefulness of restricting the structural rules of weakening, contraction, commutativity and associativity. These logics have shown promise in modeling a variety of situations, including reasoning about computations. For example, using the resource interpretation of linear logic, we can reason about availability and use of resources that cannot be regenerated. The example of linear logic also shows the usefulness of making available controlled uses of the eliminated structural rules (which in linear logic comes in the form of the ! and ? modalities).

The Logic of Bunched Implications (**BI**) [13,15] comes from freely combining the additive conjunction of intuitionistic logic with the multiplicative conjunction of linear logic. It is important to note that while the rules for introducing and eliminating multiplicatives are the same as those of linear logic, the use-once resource semantics of the multiplicative connectives no longer holds in **BI** because of the possibility of nested additives. In the presence of two context forming operations, there naturally arises two different implications with the following adjoint relationships.

$$A * B \vdash C \iff A \vdash B \mathbin{-\!*} C \text{ and } A \wedge B \vdash C \iff A \vdash B \supset C$$

The free combination of these conjunctions and implications leads to a logic with tree structured contexts, and a calculus in which the multiplicative conjunction distributes over the additive conjunction, but the inverse, factoring multiplicatives out of additives, does not hold. This leads to a lack of a structural canonical form, which presents a challenge to the standard formulation of the inverse method.

1.2 The Inverse Method

The inverse method [7,14] is a saturation based theorem proving technique for sequent calculi which is related to resolution [4]. First proposed by Maslov [12], the inverse method starts from a collection of axioms in a database and works forward by applying rules to the sequents in the database and adding the results of these rules back into the database until the goal sequent has been derived.

Proof search in the inverse method is of a very different character than tableau search, which must deal with disjunctive non-determinism in searching backward through the proof tree. In the inverse method we are concerned with conjunctive non-determinism, as we work forward our information grows monotonically. So the main challenge of inverse method search is to derive as few 'redundant' sequents as possible while still retaining completeness. The key property that the inverse method uses to limit conjunctive non-determinism is that in all inference rules, each of the formulas of the premises are subformulas of some formula in the conclusion. This implies that even if we restrict ourselves to only apply rules when the conclusion of the rule contains only subformulas of the goal sequent, we will still have a complete search strategy. In addition, this lets us disprove a theorem by exhausting this search space. This makes it also important to restrict rules like weakening, which would otherwise always be applicable in the forward direction. This is dealt with in the intuitionistic inverse method by eliminating weakening and changing the completeness theorem [7], a similar fix works for **BI**.

As an example of the inverse method in **IL**, consider the (intuitionistically true) goal proposition $((p \supset q) \vee (p \supset r)) \supset (p \supset (q \vee r))$. We begin by enumerating signed subformulas to find possible initial sequents. The subformulas are:

$$
\begin{array}{ll}
+ \ ((p \supset q) \vee (p \supset r)) \supset (p \supset (q \vee r))) & \quad - p \\
- \ ((p \supset q) \vee (p \supset r)) & \quad - q \\
+ \ (p \supset (q \vee r))) & \quad + p \\
- \ (p \supset q) & \quad - r \\
- \ (p \supset r) & \quad + q \\
+ \ (q \vee r) & \quad + r
\end{array}
$$

Each pair of a positive proposition p and its negative indicates a possible use of the axiom $p \vdash p$ in the proof of the goal. So we begin with a database including, $p \vdash p$, $q \vdash q$ and $r \vdash r$. We work forward from these axioms by applying rules of the intuitionistic forward calculus whenever the conclusion contains only the signed subformulas above. When we reach a sequent that can be weakened to the goal sequent, we are done. Theorem proving proceeds as follows (some sequents irrelevent to the final proof are not shown):

1. $p \vdash p$	init
2. $q \vdash q$	init
3. $r \vdash r$	init
4. $q \vdash q \vee r$	$\vee R_1$ 2
5. $r \vdash q \vee r$	$\vee R_2$ 3
6. $p \supset q, p \vdash q$	$\supset L$ 2
7. $p \supset r, p \vdash r$	$\supset L$ 3
8. $p \supset q, p \vdash q \vee r$	$\vee R_1$ 6
9. $p \supset r, p \vdash q \vee r$	$\vee R_2$ 7
10. $(p \supset q) \vee (p \supset r), p \vdash q \vee r$	$\vee L$ 8 9
11. $(p \supset q) \vee (p \supset r) \vdash p \supset (q \vee r)$	$\supset R$ 10
12. $\vdash ((p \supset q) \vee (p \supset r)) \supset (p \supset (q \vee r))$	$\supset R$ 11

One distinct advantage of inverse method theorem proving in **BI** is that the resource distribution problem for multiplicative connectives disappears in the forward direction. If we read a rule like

$$\frac{\Gamma \vdash \varphi \quad \Delta \vdash \psi}{\Gamma, \Delta \vdash \varphi * \psi} *R$$

in the reverse direction as in tableau proof-search, it is not obvious how to split the resources in the context between Γ and Δ, so this must be calculated during proof search. This can be handled in both linear logic and **BI** by using Boolean constraint methods as in [11]. However, in the forward direction the distribution problem simply disappears.

Unfortunately reading the rules in the forward direction introduces a new resource problem for the units. In particular, the for the rule

$$\frac{\Gamma(\emptyset_a) \vdash \varphi}{\Gamma(\top) \vdash \varphi} \top L$$

and similarly for IL, the rule is always applicable in the forward direction and it is not clear how many times it must be used. The solution for the similar problem in linear logic is given in [6]. It is not clear if a similar fix would work for **BI**, so we omit units from our inverse method.

In our paper we formulate a forward sequent calculus for propositional **BI** without units, which is suitable for inverse method theorem proving. We prove the soundness and completeness of our method relative to the sequent calculus rules given in [15, Ch. 6]. We describe a canonical form for bunches suitable for use in an implementation, and describe our SML implementation of our inverse method. The main contribution of our paper is in defining for the first time an inverse method for **BI**. In particular, we overcome the lack of a structural canonical form.

2 Propositional BI Without Units

In this section we present a sequent calculus for the propositional fragment of **BI** without propositional units ($\bot, I$, and $\top$). We leave out the units because their inclusion in the inverse method is quite involved, see [6] for the challenges presented by units in the inverse method for linear logic. Similar issues apply to units in **BI**.

Firstly, we have two types of connectives:

$$\begin{array}{ll} \text{Additives} & \wedge \supset \vee \\ \text{Multiplicatives} & * \mathbin{-\!*} \end{array}$$

The additive connectives are the same as those of intuitionistic logic and the multiplicatives come from intuitionistic linear logic. The contexts of **BI**, referred to as bunches, are trees where the leaves are formulas or empty bunches and the inner nodes are multiplicative (,) or additive (;) context forming operations. Note that while we leave out the propositional constants for units ($\bot, I$, and $\top$), contextual units (empty bunches) may still appear in bunches.

$$\begin{array}{rlll} \text{Bunches} \quad \Gamma ::= & \varphi & \text{propositional assumption} \\ & \mid & \varnothing_m & \text{multiplicative unit} \\ & \mid & \Gamma, \Gamma & \text{multiplicative combination} \\ & \mid & \varnothing_a & \text{additive unit} \\ & \mid & \Gamma; \Gamma & \text{additive combination} \end{array}$$

In the following we write $\Gamma(\Delta)$ to mean a bunch in which Δ is a subbunch and $\Gamma(\Delta')$ to mean the replacement of Δ by Δ' in $\Gamma(\Delta)$. The following equivalence on bunches is used to convert between isomorphic bunches.

Definition 1 (Coherent Equivalence). $\equiv$ *is the least equivalence relation on bunches satisfying:*

1. *Commutative monoid equations for $\varnothing_a$ and ;*
2. *Commutative monoid equations for $\varnothing_m$ and ,*
3. *Congruence: if $\Delta \equiv \Delta'$ then $\Gamma(\Delta) \equiv \Gamma(\Delta')$*

In section 3.3 we give a canonical form for bunches which uses n-ary operations, however all rules are given in terms of the simple binary formulation.

Judgments are of the form $\Gamma \vdash \varphi$ where Γ is a bunch and φ is a formula. The sequent calculus rules for propositional **BI** without units are given in Figure 1. The cut-rule is admissible in this system [15, Ch. 6].

Identity and Structure

$$\frac{\Gamma \vdash \varphi}{\Gamma' \vdash \varphi} \, (\Gamma \equiv \Gamma') \, E \qquad \frac{}{\varphi \vdash \varphi} \, INIT$$

$$\frac{\Gamma(\Delta) \vdash \varphi}{\Gamma(\Delta; \Delta') \vdash \varphi} \, W \qquad \frac{\Gamma(\Delta; \Delta) \vdash \varphi}{\Gamma(\Delta) \vdash \varphi} \, C$$

Additives

$$\frac{\Gamma \vdash \varphi \quad \Delta(\Delta'; \psi) \vdash \chi}{\Delta(\Delta'; \Gamma; \varphi \supset \psi) \vdash \chi} \supset L \qquad \frac{\Gamma; \varphi \vdash \psi}{\Gamma \vdash \varphi \supset \psi} \supset R$$

$$\frac{\Gamma(\varphi; \psi) \vdash \chi}{\Gamma(\varphi \wedge \psi) \vdash \chi} \wedge L \qquad \frac{\Gamma \vdash \varphi \quad \Delta \vdash \psi}{\Gamma; \Delta \vdash \varphi \wedge \psi} \wedge R$$

$$\frac{\Gamma \vdash \varphi_i}{\Gamma \vdash \varphi_1 \vee \varphi_2} \, (i=1,2) \vee R_i \qquad \frac{\Gamma(\varphi) \vdash \chi \quad \Gamma(\psi) \vdash \chi}{\Gamma(\varphi \vee \psi) \vdash \chi} \vee L$$

Multiplicatives

$$\frac{\Gamma(\varphi, \psi) \vdash \chi}{\Gamma(\varphi * \psi) \vdash \chi} *L \qquad \frac{\Gamma \vdash \varphi \quad \Delta \vdash \psi}{\Gamma, \Delta \vdash \varphi * \psi} *R$$

$$\frac{\Gamma \vdash \varphi \quad \Delta(\Delta', \psi) \vdash \chi}{\Delta(\Delta', \Gamma, \varphi \twoheadrightarrow \psi) \vdash \chi} \twoheadrightarrow L \qquad \frac{\Gamma, \varphi \vdash \psi}{\Gamma \vdash \varphi \twoheadrightarrow \psi} \twoheadrightarrow R$$

Fig. 1. Sequent calculus rules for core propositional **BI**

3 An Inverse Method for BI

3.1 The Calculus

Following the general method for producing a weakening-free forward calculus from a backward sequent calculus [7], we adapt the sequent calculus for **BI** into a calculus suitable for the inverse method. The rules for our forward sequent calculus for **BI** are as given in Figure 2.

We annotate the rules in the new system with superscript I to differentiate them from the old rules, the judgment of our new system has the form $\Gamma \vdash^I \varphi$.

The first step in generating a forward sequent calculus is to eliminate the weakening rule (or reformulate the rules so weakening is not built into them, if there is no explicit weakening rule). Since our starting point is a sequent calculus with an explicit weakening rule, we remove it. In order to state the completeness theorem for the weakening-free system we need the following.

Identity and Structure

$$\frac{\Gamma(\Delta_1;\Delta_2) \vdash^I \varphi \quad (\Delta \in \text{lubs}_\sqsubseteq (\Delta_1)(\Delta_2)) \neq \Delta_1;\Delta_2}{\Gamma(\Delta) \vdash^I \varphi} \, C^I$$

$$\frac{\Gamma \vdash^I \varphi}{\Gamma' \vdash^I \varphi} \, (\Gamma \equiv \Gamma') \, D^I \qquad \varphi \vdash^I \varphi \, INIT^I$$

Additives

$$\frac{\Gamma \vdash^I \varphi \quad \Delta(\Delta';\psi) \vdash^I \chi}{\Delta(\Delta';\Gamma;\varphi \supset \psi) \vdash^I \chi} \supset L^I \qquad \frac{\Gamma;\varphi \vdash^I \psi}{\Gamma \vdash^I \varphi \supset \psi} \supset R_1^I$$

$$\frac{\Gamma \vdash^I \varphi \quad \Delta \vdash^I \psi}{\Gamma;\Delta \vdash^I \varphi \wedge \psi} \wedge R^I \qquad \frac{\Gamma \vdash^I \psi}{\Gamma \vdash^I \varphi \supset \psi} \supset R_2^I$$

$$\frac{\Gamma(\varphi_i) \vdash^I \chi}{\Gamma(\varphi_1 \wedge \varphi_2) \vdash^I \chi} \, (i=1,2) \, \wedge L_i^I \qquad \frac{\Gamma \vdash^I \varphi_i}{\Gamma \vdash^I \varphi_1 \vee \varphi_2} \, (i=1,2) \, \vee R_i^I$$

$$\frac{\Gamma(\varphi) \vdash^I \chi \quad \Delta(\psi) \vdash^I \chi \quad \Sigma(p) \in \text{lubs}_\sqsubseteq (\Gamma(p))(\Delta(p))}{\Sigma(\varphi \vee \psi) \vdash^I \chi} \vee L^I$$
for new parameter p, not appreaing in Γ, Δ or Σ

Multiplicatives

$$\frac{\Gamma(\varphi,\psi) \vdash^I \chi}{\Gamma(\varphi * \psi) \vdash^I \chi} *L^I \qquad \frac{\Gamma \vdash^I \varphi \quad \Delta \vdash^I \psi}{\Gamma,\Delta \vdash^I \varphi * \psi} *R^I$$

$$\frac{\Gamma \vdash^I \varphi \quad \Delta(\Delta',\psi) \vdash^I \chi}{\Delta(\Delta',\Gamma,\varphi \mathbin{-\!*} \psi) \vdash^I \chi} \mathbin{-\!*} L^I \qquad \frac{\Gamma,\varphi \vdash^I \psi}{\Gamma \vdash^I \varphi \mathbin{-\!*} \psi} \mathbin{-\!*} R^I$$

Fig. 2. Forward sequent calculus rules for core propositional **BI**

Definition 2 (Bunch Ordering). $\sqsubseteq$ *is the transitive, reflexive (with respect to $\equiv$) closure of $\Gamma(\Delta) \sqsubseteq \Gamma(\Delta;\Delta')$*

Note that this is equivalent to saying $\Delta \sqsubseteq \Delta'$ iff there is some derivation of $\Delta' \vdash \varphi$ from $\Delta \vdash \varphi$ using only rules W or E.

We next have to examine each of the rules to make sure they are still complete without weakening. One rule which obviously must be changed is $\supset R$ because the original system with weakening can derive $\varphi \vdash \psi \supset \varphi$ only because we first weaken ψ into the context, then use the $\supset R$ rule. To fix this we split the rule in two: $\supset R_1^I$ which is the same as the old rule and $\supset R_2^I$ which builds in the weakening step. We also split rule $\wedge L$ into $\wedge L_1^I$ and $\wedge L_2^I$ which build in weakening, the weakening-free original rule $\wedge L^I$ is then derivable from $\wedge L_1^I$, $\wedge L_2^I$ and C^I.

More interesting complications arise with rules C and $\vee L$. In the intuitionistic inverse method we simply remove C and build contraction into the rules by unioning the contexts that would otherwise be additively combined. It is fine to union together additively combined sequents in our **BI** inverse method, but this does not remove the need for rule C. The problem is that we may be able to use rule C only after weakening two additively joined subbunches to be the same. An example is the derivation:

$$\dfrac{\dfrac{\dfrac{(\varphi,\psi);(\varphi,\chi) \vdash \eta}{(\varphi,(\psi;\chi));(\varphi,\chi) \vdash \eta} W}{\dfrac{(\varphi,(\psi;\chi));(\varphi,(\psi;\chi)) \vdash \eta}{\varphi,(\psi;\chi) \vdash \eta} C} W$$

In fact we cannot eliminate rule C, because each pair of bunches does not have a unique least upper bound with respect to $\sqsubseteq$. For example the bunches (φ, ψ) and (φ, χ) have the minimal upper bounds $\varphi, (\psi; \chi)$ and $(\varphi, \psi); (\varphi, \chi)$ and neither can be obtained from the other using just weakening and equivalence. However each pair of bunches does have a finite minimal upper bound set, defined as follows.

Definition 3 (Minimal upper bound set). *S is a minimal upper bound set for Δ and Γ iff the following hold:*

$$\forall \Sigma \in S. \ \Delta \sqsubseteq \Sigma \wedge \Gamma \sqsubseteq \Sigma, \text{ and}$$

$$\forall \Sigma. \ (\Delta \sqsubseteq \Sigma \wedge \Gamma \sqsubseteq \Sigma) \Rightarrow (\exists \Sigma' \in S. \ (\Sigma' \sqsubseteq \Sigma))$$

We write $\text{lubs}_\sqsubseteq (\Delta) (\Gamma)$ for the minimal set of upper bounds of Δ and Γ. We write it in curried notation to avoid the confusion of overloading ",'' to separate arguments as well as multiplicatively join bunches. Given the minimal upper bound set, we build weakening into the contraction rule (C^I) by replacing two additively joined bunches with a common upper bound.

Rule $\vee L$ is affected in a similar way to rule C because the rule

$$\dfrac{\Gamma(\varphi) \vdash \chi \quad \Gamma(\psi) \vdash \chi}{\Gamma(\varphi \vee \psi) \vdash \chi} \vee L$$

requires that a single bunch with two different formulas plugged in prove a particular formula. However, in the inverse method we will generally have $\Delta(\varphi) \vdash \chi$ and $\Delta'(\psi) \vdash \chi$ in the database, and if $\Delta(\varphi) \sqsubseteq \Gamma(\varphi)$ and $\Delta'(\psi) \sqsubseteq \Gamma(\psi)$ we want to be able to apply the rule. So we make a new $\vee L^I$ which uses the minimal upper bound set to achieve this.

In order to state the new $\vee L^I$ we need to either extend the definition of bunches to allow for parameters or we can just think of this parameter as a new, unique atomic proposition. The reason that we need a parameter is easy to see if we think of $\Delta(-)$ and $\Delta'(-)$ as two bunches with holes, and we want to find a common upper bound with only a single hole, $\Gamma(-)$. The parameters are just place holders for the holes.

We first prove the soundness of our calculus by a fairly straightforward induction on the derivations.

Theorem 1 (Soundness). *If $\Gamma \vdash^I \varphi$ then $\Gamma \vdash \varphi$.*

Proof (By structural induction).

case : Derivation is $\dfrac{}{\varphi \vdash^I \varphi} INIT^I$
We immediately have $\varphi \vdash \varphi$ by rule INIT.

case : Last rule is $\dfrac{\Gamma \vdash^I \varphi \quad \Delta(\Delta'; \psi) \vdash^I \chi}{\Delta(\Delta'; \Gamma; \varphi \supset \psi) \vdash^I \chi} \supset L^I$
By IH, have $\Gamma \vdash \varphi$ and $\Delta(\Delta'; \psi) \vdash \chi$.
We can use rule $\supset L$ to get $\Delta(\Delta'; \Gamma; \varphi \supset \psi) \vdash \chi$.

case : Last rule is $\dfrac{\Gamma; \varphi \vdash^I \psi}{\Gamma \vdash^I \varphi \supset \psi} \supset R_1^I$
By IH, have $\Gamma; \varphi \vdash \psi$.
By rule $\supset R$, we have $\Gamma \vdash \varphi \supset \psi$.

case : Last rule is $\dfrac{\Gamma \vdash^I \psi}{\Gamma \vdash^I \varphi \supset \psi} \supset R_2^I$
By IH, have $\Gamma \vdash \psi$.
by rule W, we have $\Gamma; \varphi \vdash \psi$.
by rule $\supset R$, we have $\Gamma \vdash \varphi \supset \psi$.

case : Last rule is $\dfrac{\Gamma(\Delta_1; \Delta_2) \vdash^I \varphi \quad (\Delta \in \mathit{lubs}_\sqsubseteq (\Delta_1)(\Delta_2)) \neq \Delta_1; \Delta_2}{\Gamma(\Delta) \vdash^I \varphi} C^I$
By IH, we have $\Gamma(\Delta_1; \Delta_2) \vdash \varphi$
Since $\Delta_1 \sqsubseteq \Delta$ we can derive $\Gamma(\Delta; \Delta_2) \vdash \varphi$
Similarly, we can derive $\Gamma(\Delta; \Delta) \vdash \varphi$ then use rule C to get $\Gamma(\Delta) \vdash \varphi$.

case : Last rule is $\dfrac{\Gamma(\varphi) \vdash^I \chi \quad \Delta(\psi) \vdash^I \chi \quad \Sigma(p) \in \mathit{lubs}_\sqsubseteq (\Gamma(p))(\Delta(p))}{\Sigma(\varphi \vee \psi) \vdash^I \chi} \vee L^I$
By IH, we have $\Gamma(\varphi) \vdash \chi$ and $\Delta(\psi) \vdash \chi$
Since we have $\Delta(p) \sqsubseteq \Sigma(p)$ and $\Gamma(p) \sqsubseteq \Sigma(p)$ we know $\Sigma(\varphi) \vdash \chi$ and $\Sigma(\psi) \vdash \chi$ so we can use rule $\vee L$ to get $\Sigma(\varphi \vee \psi) \vdash \chi$

case : Last rule is $\dfrac{\Gamma(\varphi_1) \vdash^I \chi}{\Gamma(\varphi_1 \wedge \varphi_2) \vdash^I \chi} \wedge L_1^I$
By IH, we have $\Gamma(\varphi_1) \vdash \chi$.
We can use rule W to get $\Gamma(\varphi_1; \varphi_2) \vdash \chi$ then rule $\wedge L$ to get $\Gamma(\varphi_1 \wedge \varphi_2) \vdash \chi$

We conclude the proof by observing that $\wedge L_2$ is parallel to $\wedge L_1$ and the rest of the rules are identical to the corresponding backward sequent calculus rules (E^I, $*$, and $-\!*$ rules)

Because our completeness proof will say that if $\Gamma \vdash \varphi$ then $\Gamma' \vdash^I \varphi$ such that $\Gamma' \sqsubseteq \Gamma$, we need a lemma about bunches that weaken to a split bunch (i.e. we need to be able to say something about the form of Γ when we know $\Gamma \sqsubseteq \Sigma(\Delta)$).

Lemma 1 (Weakening Split). *If $\Gamma \sqsubseteq \Sigma(\Delta)$ then either $\Gamma \sqsubseteq \Sigma(p)$ or else $\Gamma \equiv \Sigma'(\Delta')$ such that, $\Sigma'(p) \sqsubseteq \Sigma(p)$ and $\Delta' \sqsubseteq \Delta$ (where p is a new parameter).*

Proof (By Structural induction).

We will do induction on the derivation of $\Sigma(\Delta) \vdash \varphi$ from $\Gamma \vdash \varphi$. We may assume WLOG that the first rule is E. In the base case, $\Gamma \equiv \Sigma(\Delta)$ so the second case of the lemma holds.

If the last rule is rule E, then for any $\Sigma'(\Delta') \equiv \Sigma(\Delta)$ either case obviously carries through.

If the last rule is rule W, then we must consider the location of the use of rule W. The bunch weakened on (or removed, if we look at the reverse direction) must be either entirely within $\Sigma(p)$ and disjoint from Δ or else it must entirely contain Δ or be entirely contained in Δ (this can easily be seen by considering the tree structure of bunches). In the first case, either case of the IH carries through. In the second case, the entirety of Δ was simply weakened on and we could have just as easily weakened on p in its place, so the first case of the lemma holds. In the last case, the final step looks like:

$$\frac{\Sigma(\Sigma''(\Delta'')) \vdash \varphi}{\Sigma(\Delta) = \Sigma(\Sigma''(\Delta''; \Delta''')) \vdash \varphi} W$$

and since $\Sigma''(\Delta'') \sqsubseteq \Delta$, either case of the IH carries through.

Now we can prove the completeness of our calculus. We use a fairly straightforward structural induction on the derivation, the main complication is that we have to distinguish cases for the possible forms of $\Gamma \sqsubseteq \Sigma(\Delta)$ as given in the previous lemma.

Theorem 2 (Completeness). *If $\Gamma \vdash \varphi$ then $\Gamma^\circ \vdash^I \varphi$ such that, $\Gamma^\circ \sqsubseteq \Gamma$.*

Intuitively we think of Γ° as a bunch that we can weaken to get Γ (these are the types of sequents our inverse method will prove).

Proof (By structural induction).

case . *Derivation is* $\dfrac{}{\varphi \mid \varphi}$ INIT

We have immediately $\varphi \vdash^I \varphi$ $INIT^I$.

case : *Last rule is* $\dfrac{\Gamma(\Delta) \vdash \varphi}{\Gamma(\Delta; \Delta') \vdash \varphi}$ W

By IH, have $(\Gamma(\Delta))° \vdash^I \varphi$ with $(\Gamma(\Delta))° \sqsubseteq \Gamma(\Delta)$ and since $\Delta \sqsubseteq \Delta; \Delta'$, $(\Gamma(\Delta))° \sqsubseteq \Gamma(\Delta; \Delta')$ as required.

case : *Last rule is* $\dfrac{\Gamma(\Delta; \Delta) \vdash \varphi}{\Gamma(\Delta) \vdash \varphi}$ C

By IH, we have $(\Gamma(\Delta; \Delta))° \vdash^I \varphi$
Either $(\Gamma(\Delta; \Delta))° \sqsubseteq \Gamma(p)$ or $(\Gamma(\Delta; \Delta))° \equiv \Gamma°((\Delta; \Delta)°)$ with $(\Delta; \Delta)° \sqsubseteq \Delta; \Delta$ by previous lemma.
In the first case, clearly if $(\Gamma(\Delta; \Delta))° \sqsubseteq \Gamma(p)$ then $(\Gamma(\Delta; \Delta))° \sqsubseteq \Gamma(\Delta)$, so we are done.
In the second case, either $(\Delta; \Delta)° \sqsubseteq \Delta$ or $(\Delta; \Delta)° \equiv \Delta_1; \Delta_2$ such that $\Delta_i \sqsubseteq \Delta(i = 1, 2)$.
In the first case we are done.
In the second case we have $\Delta_i \sqsubseteq \Delta(i = 1, 2)$ so we have some $\Sigma \in lubs_\sqsubseteq (\Delta_1) (\Delta_2)$ such that $\Sigma \sqsubseteq \Delta$, so we use rule C^I to get $\Gamma°(\Sigma) \vdash^I \varphi$.

case : *Last rule is* $\dfrac{\Gamma \vdash \varphi}{\Delta \vdash \varphi}$ $(\Delta \equiv \Gamma)E$

Again, this is immediate from IH because $\Delta \equiv \Gamma$.

case : *Last rule is* $\dfrac{\Gamma \vdash \varphi \quad \Delta(\Delta'; \psi) \vdash \chi}{\Delta(\Gamma; \Delta'; \varphi \supset \psi) \vdash \chi}$ $\supset L$

By IH have $\Gamma° \vdash^I \varphi$ and $(\Delta(\Delta'; \psi))° \vdash^I \chi$
Either $(\Delta(\Delta'; \psi))° \sqsubseteq \Delta(p)$ or $(\Delta(\Delta'; \psi))° \equiv \Delta°((\Delta'; \psi)°)$ such that $\Delta°(p) \sqsubseteq \Delta(p)$ and $(\Delta'; \psi)° \sqsubseteq \Delta'; \psi$.
In the first case we are done.
In the second case, either $(\Delta'; \psi)° \sqsubseteq \Delta'$ or $(\Delta'; \psi)° \equiv \Delta'°; \psi$ such that $\Delta'° \sqsubseteq \Delta'$.
In the first case we are done.
In the second case we can apply rule $\supset L^I$ to get $\Delta°(\Gamma°; \Delta'°; \varphi \supset \psi) \vdash^I \chi$.

case : *Last rule is* $\dfrac{\Gamma; \varphi \vdash \psi}{\Gamma \vdash \varphi \supset \psi}$ $\supset R$

By IH have $(\Gamma; \varphi)° \vdash \psi$.
Either $(\Gamma; \varphi)° \equiv \Gamma° \sqsubseteq \Gamma$ or $(\Gamma; \varphi)° \equiv \Gamma°; \varphi$ such that $\Gamma° \sqsubseteq \Gamma$.
In the first case we use rule $\supset R_2^I$ and in the second $\supset R_1^I$ to get $\Gamma° \vdash^I \varphi \supset \psi$

case : *Last rule is* $\dfrac{\Gamma(\varphi) \vdash \chi \quad \Gamma(\psi) \vdash \chi}{\Gamma(\varphi \vee \psi) \vdash \chi}$ $\vee L$

By IH have $(\Gamma(\varphi))° \vdash \chi$ and $(\Gamma(\psi))°) \vdash \chi$.
Either $(\Gamma(\varphi))° \sqsubseteq \Gamma(p)$ or $(\Gamma(\varphi))° \equiv \Gamma_1°(\varphi)$ such that $\Gamma_1°(p) \sqsubseteq \Gamma(p)$.

In the first case we are done.
In the second case, either $(\Gamma(\psi))^\circ \sqsubseteq \Gamma(p)$ *or* $(\Gamma(\psi))^\circ \equiv \Gamma_2^\circ(\psi)$ *such that* $\Gamma_2^\circ(p) \sqsubseteq \Gamma(p)$.
In the first case we are done.
In the second case, since $\Gamma_i^\circ(p) \sqsubseteq \Gamma(p)(i = 1,2)$, *we have* $\Sigma^\circ(p) \in \text{lubs}_\sqsubseteq$ $(\Gamma_1^\circ(p))(\Gamma_2^\circ(p))$ *such that* $\Sigma^\circ(\varphi \vee \psi) \sqsubseteq \Gamma(\varphi \vee \psi)$. *So we apply rule* $\vee L^I$ *and we are done.*

case : *Last rule is* $\dfrac{\Gamma(\varphi; \psi) \vdash \chi}{\Gamma(\varphi \wedge \psi) \vdash \chi} \wedge L$

By IH, we have $(\Gamma(\varphi; \psi))^\circ \vdash^I \chi$ *such that* $(\Gamma(\varphi; \psi))^\circ \sqsubseteq \Gamma(\varphi; \psi)$.
By the lemma, either $(\Gamma(\varphi; \psi))^\circ \sqsubseteq \Gamma(p)$ *or* $(\Gamma(\varphi; \psi))^\circ \equiv \Gamma^\circ((\varphi; \psi)^\circ)$ *with* $\Gamma^\circ(p) \sqsubseteq \Gamma(p)$ *and* $(\varphi; \psi)^\circ \sqsubseteq (\varphi; \psi)$.
In the first case we are done.
In the second case we need to consider $(\varphi; \psi)^\circ$. *It cannot be empty or we would be in the first case.*
If $(\varphi; \psi)^\circ \equiv \varphi$ *then we use rule* $\wedge L_1^I$ *to get* $\Gamma^\circ(\varphi \wedge \psi) \vdash^I \chi$.
If $(\varphi; \psi)^\circ \equiv \psi$ *then we use rule* $\wedge L_2^I$ *to get* $\Gamma^\circ(\varphi \wedge \psi) \vdash^I \chi$.
If $(\varphi; \psi)^\circ \equiv (\varphi; \psi)$ *then we use rule* $\wedge L_1^I$ *to get* $\Gamma^\circ(\varphi \wedge \psi; \psi) \vdash^I \chi$ *then rule* $\wedge L_2^I$ *to get* $\Gamma^\circ(\varphi \wedge \psi; \varphi \wedge \psi) \vdash^I \chi$ *then rule* C^I *to get* $\Gamma^\circ(\varphi \wedge \psi) \vdash^I \chi$.

note : *The remaining cases are similar.*

3.2 An Example

Inverse method theorem proving in **BI** proceeds in the same way as in intuitionistic logic. Consider the (true) goal sequent $\emptyset_m \vdash^I (p * (q \wedge r)) \twoheadrightarrow ((p \wedge q) * (p \wedge r))$. We start by enumerating the signed subformulas and identifying the initial sequents.

$+ (p * (q \wedge r)) \twoheadrightarrow ((p \wedge q) * (p \wedge r))$	$+ (p \wedge r)$
$- (p * (q \wedge r))$	$- q$
$+ ((p \wedge q) * (p \wedge r))$	$- r$
$- (q \wedge r)$	$+ p$
$- p$	$+ q$
$+ (p \wedge q)$	$+ r$

From this we can see that the initial sequents we need are $p \vdash^I p$, $q \vdash^I q$ and $r \vdash^I r$. Theorem proving proceeds in rounds as follows (some unnecessary sequents are omitted).

1. $p \vdash^{\mathcal{I}} p$ init
2. $q \vdash^{\mathcal{I}} q$ init
3. $r \vdash^{\mathcal{I}} r$ init
4. $p, q \vdash^{\mathcal{I}} p * q$ $*R^{\mathcal{I}}$ 1 2
5. $p, r \vdash^{\mathcal{I}} p * r$ $*R^{\mathcal{I}}$ 1 3
6. $q \wedge r \vdash^{\mathcal{I}} q$ $\wedge L_1^{\mathcal{I}}$ 2
7. $q \wedge r \vdash^{\mathcal{I}} r$ $\wedge L_2^{\mathcal{I}}$ 3
8. $(p, q); (p, r) \vdash^{\mathcal{I}} (p * q) \wedge (p * r)$ $\wedge R^{\mathcal{I}}$ 4 5
9. $p, (q \wedge r) \vdash^{\mathcal{I}} p * q$ $*R^{\mathcal{I}}$ 1 6
10. $p, (q; r) \vdash^{\mathcal{I}} (p * q) \wedge (p * r)$ $C^{\mathcal{I}}$ 8
11. $p, (q \wedge r) \vdash^{\mathcal{I}} (p * q) \wedge (p * r)$ $\wedge L^{\mathcal{I}}$ 10
12. $p * (q \wedge r) \vdash^{\mathcal{I}} (p * q) \wedge (p * r)$ $*R^{\mathcal{I}}$ 11
13. $\emptyset_m, (p * (q \wedge r)) \vdash^{\mathcal{I}} (p * q) \wedge (p * r)$ $E^{\mathcal{I}}$ 12
14. $\emptyset_m \vdash^{\mathcal{I}} (p * (q \wedge r)) \twoheadrightarrow ((p * q) \wedge (p * r))$ $\twoheadrightarrow R^{\mathcal{I}}$ 13

3.3 An $\equiv$ Canonical Form for Bunches

While there is no canonical form which equates bunches modulo $\equiv$, weakening and contraction, there is a canonical form modulo $\equiv$ alone. Although this is fairly obvious, we have not seen it published anywhere. In [2], Armelín gives a similar canonical form which does not equate bunches modulo units as ours does. Use of this canonical form during proof-search lets us drop rule $E^{\mathcal{I}}$ altogether.

It is helpful, both in guiding an actual implementation and in understanding the structure of bunches, to have a canonical representative of $[\Gamma]_{\equiv}$ for any bunch Γ. To do so we define the following grammar.

$$\text{Bunches } \Gamma ::= \varphi \mid \Pi \mid \Sigma$$
$$\text{Multiplicative Bunches } \Pi ::= \varphi \mid \{\Sigma^*\}_m$$
$$\text{Additive Bunches } \Sigma ::= \varphi \mid \{\Pi^*\}_a$$

where $\{A^*\}$ denotes a multiset with elements from A.

We maintain the invariant that the multisets $\{A^*\}$ are never singletons (empty sets are fine, they are the units). If a subbunch which is supposed to be a multiset is a singleton, then we simply promote it in the tree and union it on to its parent. It is easy to see that φ's can always be promoted. Since the levels of the tree alternate between $\{\Sigma^*\}_m$ and $\{\Pi^*\}_a$, if e.g. $\{\Sigma^*\}_m = \{\Sigma\}_m$ and $\Sigma \neq \varphi$ then $\Sigma = \{\Pi^*\}_a$ so we can union that into the context of which $\{\Sigma^*\}_m$ was a member. We also maintain the invariant that a subbunch only appears once in any additive context, so we treat $\{\Pi^*\}_a$ as a set rather than a multiset.

This gives us an $\equiv$-canonical form. To see if two bunches are equivalent we convert to canonical form by these steps: first, flatten binary connectives into n-ary connectives (justified by associativity of , and ;), then forget about ordering by making them multiset operators (justified by commutativity of , and ;) then eliminate singletons by propagating them upwards. This last step is justified by the unit laws (we think of $\{\Sigma\}$ as $\Sigma, \emptyset_m$) which let us promote and the associativity and commutativity laws which let us fold in (union) multisets that we promote. Lastly, we forget about the number of occurrences in the additive levels of the tree (justified by contraction for additive conjunction).

3.4 Implementation

We have implemented our inverse method for propositional **BI** without units in SML. We use the above canonical form for our bunches and generate proof-terms which are checked at the end.

Proof-terms for **BI** are terms of the $\alpha\lambda$-calculus [15]. We store proof-terms with each derived sequent in the database, so when we finish with a positive answer we have also a proof that the theorem is in fact true. We then check the proof in a straightforward way. This gives us a *certifying* theorem prover. Since the proof-checking code is much shorter and simpler than the proof-search code, we can have much higher confidence in a certified result than one that lacks proof-terms and checking.

In order to accommodate proof-terms in the inverse method, it is helpful to define a new intermediate proof-term `let` $x = e_1$ `in` e_2 which we convert to $[e_1/x]e_2$ before type-checking. This is used in elimination rules so we do not have to do proof substitution on-line.

At present, we only have a very simple prototype implementation without any of the customary optimizations applied in the inverse method. Nonetheless, we have found it useful for validating our ideas. In the conclusion we mention some planned improvements.

4 Related Work and Conclusions

Separation Logic [16] is a logic for reasoning about programs similar to Hoare Logic. Instead of standard intuitionistic logic, Separation Logic uses the connectives of **BI**, along with some other primitives, to express properties about data structures with shared mutable state. Therefore, automated theorem provers for **BI** are likely to eventually have practical uses in reasoning about programs. In particular, it is quite tedious to write out proofs of each inference step in Separation Logic and a good theorem prover for **BI** could go a long way towards automating the process of checking Separation Logic assertions.

There has been some work on a semantic tableau proof-search by Galmiche and Méry in **BI** [9,5] which has so far produced the BILL theorem prover for propositional **BI** without $\bot$, a later paper [8] extends this work to include $\bot$. Our work presents an alternative method for theorem proving in **BI**. We believe it is useful to investigate thoroughly both backward and forward search procedures for **BI** as work in other logics has shown that these methods have different properties and find different theorems easily.

There is also work on the inverse method in intuitionistic logic [18] and linear logic [17] which have resulted in inverse method provers for full first-order intuitionistic and linear logics. Most of the improved strategies and optimizations used in these works (some described in the previous section) would most probably be applicable to inverse method theorem proving in **BI**.

Work by Armelín and Pym [3] develops a logic programming language, BLP, based on the hereditary Harrop fragment of **BI** with additive predication. Their work devlops a bottom-up proof search as its basis. By extending our inverse method to this fragment, it should be possible to develop an alternative, top-down basis for bunched logic programming.

In this paper, we have demonstrated that the inverse method is applicable to the core of propositional **BI**. Standard efficiency improvements [7] and the addition of units [6] should be relatively straightforward and lead to a theorem prover for full propositional **BI**. Additionally, formulation of a full first-order focusing prover for **BI** is likely to be fruitful for a number of reasons. Firstly, many investigations in proof-search, particularly an analysis of focusing [1] in **BI**, may lead to deeper understandings of its proof theory. And secondly, efficient provers for **BI** will likely become practically useful for program analysis as this is the logic that underlies Separation Logic.

5 Acknowledgments

We are grateful to Frank Pfenning for teaching us about the inverse method, offering some insightful suggestions and providing helpful feedback, and also to the anonymous reviewers for their comments.

References

1. Jean-Marc Andreoli. Logic programming with focusing proofs in linear logic. *Journal of Logic and Computation*, 2(3):197–347, 1992.
2. Pablo Armelín. *Logic programming with bunched logic*. PhD thesis, University of London, 2002.
3. Pablo A. Armelín and David J. Pym. Bunched logic programming. In *IJCAR '01: Proceedings of the First International Joint Conference on Automated Reasoning*, pages 289–304. Springer-Verlag, 2001.
4. L. Bachmair and H. Ganzinger. Resolution theorem proving. In A. Robinson and A. Voronkov, editors, *Handbook of Automated Reasoning*, volume 1, chapter 2, pages 19–100. North Holland, 2001.
5. Frederic Beal, Daniel Méry, and Didier Galmiche. Bill: A theorem prover for propositional bi logic.
6. Kaustuv Chaudhuri and Frank Pfenning. Resource management for the inverse method in linear logic. Carnegie Mellon University, Unpublished Maniscript, January 2003.
7. Anatoli Degtyarev and Andrei Voronkov. The inverse method. In A. Robinson and A. Voronkov, editors, *Handbook of Automated Reasoning*, volume 1, pages 179–272. Elsevier Science and MIT Press, 2001.
8. Didier Galmiche, Daniel Méry, and David J. Pym. Resource tableaux. In *CSL '02: Proceedings of the 16th International Workshop and 11th Annual Conference of the EACSL on Computer Science Logic*, pages 183–199. Springer-Verlag, 2002.

9. Didier Galmiche and Daniel Méry. Semantic labelled tableaux for propositional bi (without bottom). *Journal of Logic and Computation*, 13(5), October 2003.
10. Jean-Yves Girard. Linear logic. *Theoretical Computer Science*, 50:1–102, 1987.
11. James Harland and David Pym. Resource-distribution via boolean constraints. *ACM Trans. Comput. Logic*, 4(1):56–90, 2003.
12. S. Maslov. The inverse method of establishing deducibility in classical predicate calculus. *Soviet Mathematical Doklady*, 5:1420–1424, 1964.
13. P.W. O'Hearn and D. J. Pym. The logic of bunched implications. *Bulletin of Symbolic Logic*, 5(2):215–244, June 1999.
14. Frank Pfenning. The inverse method. Carnegie Mellon University, Lecture Notes, Ch. 5, February 2004.
15. D.J. Pym. *The Semantics and Proof Theory of the Logic of the Logic of Bunched Implications*, volume 26 of *Applied Logic Series*. Kluwer Academic Publishers, 2002. Errata and Remarks maintained at:
    http://www.cs.bath.ac.uk/~pym/BI-monograph-errata.pdf.
16. John C. Reynolds. Separation logic: A logic for shared mutable data structures. In *Proceedings of the 17th Annual IEEE Symposium on Logic in Computer Science*, pages 55–74. IEEE Computer Society, 2002.
17. T. Tammet. Proof strategies in linear logic. *Journal of Automated Reasoning*, 12(3):273–304, 1994.
18. Tanel Tammet. A resolution theorem prover for intuitionistic logic. In M. A. McRobbie and J. K. Slaney, editors, *Proceedings 13th Intl. Conf. on Automated Deduction, CADE'96, New Brunswick, NJ, USA, 30 July – 3 Aug 1996*, volume 1104, pages 2–16. Springer-Verlag, Berlin, 1996.

Cut-Elimination: Experiments with CERES*

Matthias Baaz[1], Stefan Hetzl[2], Alexander Leitsch[2], Clemens Richter[2], and Hendrik Spohr[2]

[1] Institute of Discrete Mathematics and Geometry (E104),
Vienna University of Technology, Wiedner Hauptstraße 8-10,
1040 Vienna, Austria
baaz@logic.at
[2] Institute of Computer Languages (E185),
Vienna University of Technology, Favoritenstraße 9,
1040 Vienna, Austria
{hetzl|leitsch|richter|spohr}@logic.at

Abstract. Cut-elimination is the most prominent form of proof transformation in logic. The elimination of cuts in formal proofs corresponds to the removal of intermediate statements (lemmas) in mathematical proofs. The cut-elimination method CERES (cut-elimination by resolution) works by constructing a set of clauses from a proof with cuts. Any resolution refutation of this set can then serve as a skeleton of a proof with only atomic cuts.

In this paper we present a systematic experiment with the implementation of CERES on a proof of reasonable size and complexity. It turns out that the proof with cuts can be transformed into two *mathematically different* proofs of the theorem. In particular, the application of positive and negative hyperresolution yield different mathematical arguments. As an unexpected side-effect the derived clauses of the resolution refutation proved particularly interesting as they can be considered as meaningful universal lemmas.

Though the proof under investigation is intuitively simple, the experiment demonstrates that new (and relevant) mathematical information on proofs can be obtained by computational methods. It can be considered as a first step in the development of an experimental culture of *computer-aided proof analysis* in mathematics.

1 Introduction

Proof analysis is a central mathematical activity which proved crucial to the development of mathematics. Indeed many mathematical concepts such as the notion of group or the notion of probability were introduced by analyzing existing arguments. In some sense the analysis and synthesis of proofs form the very core of mathematical progress[7,8].

Cut-elimination introduced by Gentzen [4] is the most prominent form of proof transformation in logic and plays an important role in automatizing the

---
* supported by the Austrian Science Fund (project no. P16264-N05)

analysis of mathematical proofs. The removal of cuts corresponds to the elimination of intermediate statements (lemmas) from proofs resulting in a proof which is analytic in the sense, that all statements in the proof are subformulas of the result. Therefore, the proof of a combinatorial statement is converted into a purely combinatorial proof. Cut-elimination is therefore an essential tool for the analysis of proofs, especially to make implicit parameters explicit. Cut free derivations allow for

- the extraction of Herbrand disjunctions, which can be used to establish bounds on existential quantifiers (e.g. Luckhardt's analysis of the Theorem of Roth [6]).
- the construction of interpolants, which allow for the replacement of implicit definitions by explicit definitions according to Beth's Theorem.
- the calculation of generalized variants of the end formula.

In a formal sense Girard's analysis of van der Waerden's proof [5] is the application of cut-elimination to the proof of Fürstenberg/Weiss with the "perspective" of obtaining van der Waerden's proof. Indeed an application of a complex proof transformation like cut-elimination by humans requires a goal oriented strategy. In contrast, as we demonstrate in this paper, the application of purely computational methods on existing proofs may produce new interesting proofs. Note that cut-elimination is *non-unique*, i.e. there is no single cut-free proof which represents *the* analytic version of a proof with lemmas. Indeed, it is non-uniqueness which makes computational experiments with cut-elimination interesting. The experiments can be considered as a source for a base of proofs in formal format which provide different mathematical and computational information.

CERES [2] is a cut-elimination method that is based on resolution. The method roughly works as follows: The structure of the proof containing cuts is mapped to a clause term which evaluates to an unsatisfiable set of clauses C (the *characteristic clause set*). A resolution refutation of C, which is obtained using a first-order theorem prover, serves as a skeleton for the new proof which contains only atomic cuts. In a final step also these atomic cuts can be eliminated, provided the (atomic) axioms are valid sequents; but this step is of minor mathematical interest only. In the system CERES[3] this method of cut-elimination has been implemented. The system is capable of dealing with formal proofs in **LK**, among them also very large ones.

In this paper we present a systematic experiment with CERES on a proof defined in [9]. It turns out that the proof with cuts is transformed into two *mathematically* different proofs of the theorem. In particular, the application of positive and negative hyperresolution yield different mathematical arguments. As the core of the method is resolution, which works on the characteristic clause set, it is worthwhile to investigate also the resolution proof itself. In fact the derived clauses of the proof can be considered as universal lemmas, which are eventually instantiated in the procedure. As an unexpected side-effect also these

---

[3] available at http://www.logic.at/ceres/

lemmas proved particularly interesting in the experiment. Though the proof under investigation is intuitively simple, the experiment demonstrates that new (and relevant) mathematical information on proofs can be obtained by computational methods. It can be considered as a first step in the development of an experimental culture of *computer-aided proof analysis* in mathematics.

2 The System CERES

The system CERES is an implementation of the cut-elimination method CERES which will be roughly explained below. Also a short description of the behavior of the system will be given including some implementational details.

2.1 Short Description of the Method via an Example

The cut-elimination method by resolution (CERES) is demonstrated in this paper by the following example. You can find an in-depth explanation of the method itself and the underlying **LK** in [3], [2] and on the CERES web page[4].

To simplify the understanding of the method all the premises (the auxiliary formulas of the inferences) are put in bold face, the conclusions are underlined and the ancestors of cut-formulas are marked with an asterisk in the following input proof.

Now, let φ be the proof

$$\frac{\varphi_l \quad \varphi_r}{(\forall x)(\forall y)(P(x,y) \supset Q(x,y)) \vdash (\exists x)(\exists y)(\neg Q(x,y) \supset \neg P(x,y))} \text{ cut}$$

where φ_l is

$$\frac{\dfrac{\boldsymbol{P(z,a)^*} \vdash P(z,a)}{\vdash \boldsymbol{\neg P(z,a)^*}, P(z,a)} \neg : \text{r}}{\vdash \underline{\neg P(z,a) \vee Q(z,a)^*}, \boldsymbol{P(z,a)}} \vee : \text{r}_1 \quad \dfrac{Q(z,a) \vdash \boldsymbol{Q(z,a)^*}}{Q(z,a) \vdash \underline{\neg P(z,a) \vee Q(z,a)^*}} \vee : \text{r}_2$$

$$\dfrac{\boldsymbol{P(z,a) \supset Q(z,a)} \vdash \underline{\neg P(z,a) \vee Q(z,a)^*}}{\dfrac{\boldsymbol{(\forall y)(P(z,y) \supset Q(z,y))} \vdash \underline{\neg P(z,a) \vee Q(z,a)^*}}{\dfrac{\boldsymbol{(\forall x)(\forall y)(P(x,y) \supset Q(x,y))} \vdash \underline{\neg P(z,a) \vee Q(z,a)^*}}{\dfrac{(\forall x)(\forall y)(P(x,y) \supset Q(x,y)) \vdash \underline{(\exists y)(\neg P(z,y) \vee Q(z,y))^*}}{(\forall x)(\forall y)(P(x,y) \supset Q(x,y)) \vdash \underline{(\forall x)(\exists y)(\neg P(x,y) \vee Q(x,y))^*}} \forall : \text{r}} \exists : \text{r}} \forall : \text{l}} \forall : \text{l}} \supset : \text{l}$$

---

[4] The documentation and an online version of the system CERES are available at http://www.logic.at/ceres/.

and φ_r is

$$
\cfrac{
\cfrac{
\cfrac{
\cfrac{
\cfrac{
\cfrac{
\cfrac{
\cfrac{
\cfrac{P(b,v) \vdash \boldsymbol{P(b,v)}^*}{\neg P(b,v)^*, \boldsymbol{P(b,v)} \vdash} \neg : l
}{\neg \boldsymbol{P(b,v)}^* \vdash \neg P(b,v)} \neg : r \quad \cfrac{\cfrac{Q(b,v)^* \vdash \boldsymbol{Q(b,v)}}{\neg Q(b,v), \boldsymbol{Q(b,v)}^* \vdash} \neg : l}{}
}{\neg Q(b,v), \neg \boldsymbol{P(b,v)} \vee Q(b,v)^* \vdash \neg P(b,v)} \vee : l'
}{\neg \boldsymbol{P(b,v)} \vee Q(b,v)^* \vdash \neg Q(b,v) \supset \neg P(b,v)} \supset : r
}{\neg \boldsymbol{P(b,v)} \vee Q(b,v)^* \vdash (\exists y)(\neg Q(b,y) \supset \neg P(b,y))} \exists : r
}{\neg \boldsymbol{P(b,v)} \vee Q(b,v)^* \vdash (\exists x)(\exists y)(\neg Q(x,y) \supset \neg P(x,y))} \exists : r
}{\boldsymbol{(\exists y)(\neg P(b,y) \vee Q(b,y))}^* \vdash (\exists x)(\exists y)(\neg Q(x,y) \supset \neg P(x,y))} \exists : l
}{\boldsymbol{(\forall x)(\exists y)(\neg P(x,y) \vee Q(x,y))}^* \vdash (\exists x)(\exists y)(\neg Q(x,y) \supset \neg P(x,y))} \forall : l
$$

The extraction of the characteristic clause term happens top down starting with those parts of the initial sequents that are marked as ancestors of cut formulas which are now interpreted as sets. At every occurrence of a binary rule the two clause terms resulting from the premises are connected by a binary operator. Depending whether the auxiliary formulas of the inference were ancestors of cut formulas or not the operator will either be $\oplus$ or $\otimes$. All unary inference rules have no influence on the clause term and hence it remains unchanged.

For the example this yields the following characteristic clause term

$$\Theta(\varphi) = ((\{P(z,a) \vdash\} \otimes \{\vdash Q(z,a)\}) \oplus (\{\vdash P(b,v)\} \oplus \{Q(b,v) \vdash\}))$$

which characterizes those parts of the axiom sequents which have been used to derive the cut formula (on both sides).

The operator $\oplus$ of the clause term is interpreted as union and the operator $\otimes$ as merge, i.e. the antecedens and consequent parts of different sequents are exchanged such that only one part is exchanged at once.

Hence by evaluation of $\Theta(\varphi)$ for the characteristic clause set $|\Theta(\varphi)|$ of φ we obtain

$$
\begin{align}
|\Theta(\varphi)| = \{P(z,a) \vdash Q(z,a), & \quad (C_2) \\
\vdash P(b,v), & \quad (C_1) \\
Q(b,v) \vdash \}. & \quad (C_3)
\end{align}
$$

The characteristic clause set of an **LK** derivation is always unsatisfiable. Therefore one can always find a resolution refutation of the characteristic clause set.

In particular, we define a resolution refutation δ of $|\Theta(\varphi)|$:

$$\cfrac{Q(b,v) \vdash \quad \cfrac{\vdash P(b,v) \quad P(z,a) \vdash Q(z,a)}{\vdash Q(b,a)}}{\vdash}$$

and a corresponding ground refutation γ of δ, i. e. $\gamma = \delta\sigma$:

$$\cfrac{Q(b,a) \vdash \quad \cfrac{\vdash P(b,a) \quad P(b,a) \vdash Q(b,a)}{\vdash Q(b,a)}}{\vdash}$$

with the ground substitution $\sigma = \{v \mapsto a, z \mapsto b\}$.

Now we have to reduce φ to projections of the clauses used as initial clauses in the resolution refutation of $|\Theta(\varphi)|$. A projection of φ w.r.t. a clause in $|\Theta(\varphi)|$ is defined by skipping all inferences going into cuts, which leads to cut-free proof of (a subsequent of) the end sequent extended by C. Projections may be understood as projection schemes of the clauses in question modulo a corresponding ground substitution.

Again, we start at the initial sequents (without those parts marked as ancestors of cut formulas and not necessary for the creation of the clause in question) and apply all inference rules not operating on ancestors of cut formulas until all such binary rules have been applied and at least one formula also occurring in the end sequent has been composed.

The projection scheme of φ corresponding to the clause C_1 is:

$\varphi(C_1) =$

$$\cfrac{\cfrac{\cfrac{\cfrac{\cfrac{\cfrac{P(b,v) \vdash P(b,v)}{\vdash P(b,v), \neg P(b,v)} \neg : r}{\neg Q(b,v) \vdash P(b,v), \neg P(b,v)} w : l}{\vdash \neg Q(b,v) \supset \neg P(b,v), P(b,v)} \supset : r}{\vdash (\exists y)(\neg Q(b,y) \supset \neg P(b,y)), P(b,v)} \exists : r}{\vdash (\exists x)(\exists y)(\neg Q(x,y) \supset \neg P(x,y)), P(b,v)} \exists : r}$$

and let the ground projection $\chi_1 = \varphi(C_1)\sigma$.

The projection scheme of φ corresponding to the clause C_2 is:

$\varphi(C_2) =$

$$\cfrac{\cfrac{\cfrac{\cfrac{P(z,a) \vdash P(z,a) \quad Q(z,a) \vdash Q(z,a)}{P(z,a) \supset Q(z,a), P(z,a) \vdash Q(z,a)} \supset : l}{(\forall y)(P(z,y) \supset Q(z,y)), P(z,a) \vdash Q(z,a)} \forall : l}{(\forall x)(\forall y)(P(x,y) \supset Q(x,y)), P(z,a) \vdash Q(z,a)} \forall : l}$$

and let the ground projection $\chi_2 = \varphi(C_2)\sigma$.

The projection scheme of φ corresponding to the clause C_3 is:

$\varphi(C_3) =$

$$\dfrac{\dfrac{\dfrac{\dfrac{\dfrac{\dfrac{Q(b,v) \vdash Q(b,v)}{\neg Q(b,v) Q(b,v) \vdash} \neg : l}{\neg Q(b,v) Q(b,v) \vdash \neg P(b,v)} w : r}{Q(b,v) \vdash \neg Q(b,v) \supset \neg P(b,v)} \supset : r}{Q(b,v) \vdash (\exists y)(\neg Q(b,y) \supset \neg P(b,y))} \exists : r}{Q(b,v) \vdash (\exists x)(\exists y)(\neg Q(x,y) \supset \neg P(x,y))} \exists : r$$

and let the ground projection $\chi_3 = \varphi(C_3)\sigma$.

Finally the ground projections can be composed to a cut-free proof of φ, i.e. a proof of φ containing only atomic cuts, using its resolution refutation as a skeleton.

$$\dfrac{\dfrac{\overset{(\chi_1)}{\vdash Y, P(b,a)} \quad \overset{(\chi_2)}{P(b,a), X \vdash Q(b,a)}}{X \vdash Y, Q(b,a)} \text{cut} \quad \overset{(\chi_3)}{Q(b,a) \vdash Y}}{X \vdash Y} \text{cut}$$

where $X = (\forall x)(\forall y)(P(x,y) \supset Q(x,y))$ and $Y = (\exists x)(\exists y)(\neg Q(x,y) \supset \neg P(x,y))$.

2.2 Description of the Program

The cut-elimination program CERES is written in ANSI-C++[5]. There are two main tasks. On the one hand to compute an unsatisfiable set of clauses $\mathcal{C}$ characterising the cut formulas. This is done by automatically extracting the characteristic clause term and computation of the resulting characteristic clause set. On the other hand to evaluate the resolution refutation gained from an external theorem prover[6] and to compute the necessary projection schemes which are properly instantiated and concatenated using the resolution refutation as a skeleton of the cut-free proof, i.e. a proof without non-atomic cuts.

The input format and the output format are following the *proof* style[7] of LaTeX with some extensions, and are translatable by any LaTeX compiler. This feature allows an easier input of proofs and reading of the output. Nevertheless new approaches are planned (see section 4 for details).

---

[5] The C++ Programming Language following the International Standard 14882:1998 approved as an American National Standard (see http://www.ansi.org).

[6] The current version of CERES uses the automated theorem prover Otter (see http://www-unix.mcs.anl.gov/AR/otter/), but any refutational theorem prover may be used.

[7] see http://research.nii.ac.jp/~tatsuta/proof-sty.html

3 Experiments with Resolution Refinements

The use of the resolution refutation of the characteristic clause set as a skeleton for the cut-free proof makes it possible to change the mathematical character of the resulting proof via different resolution refutations, e.g. using different resolution refinements. Within these refutations *universal lemmas*, i.e. clauses containing variables representing universal formulas, appear which do neither occur in the original proof nor in the cut-eliminated proofs, where they are already instantiated.

Now we are doing exactly such an interesting experiment using an input proof already analyzed and defined as an **LK**-derivation in [9] with the program CERES.

The proof deals with the following situation: We are given an infinite tape where each cell contains either '0' or '1'. We prove that on this tape there are two cells with the same value. The contents of a cell of the tape is denoted by f, s is the sucessor function and $m^{x,y}$ is the maximum of x and y.

Within this section the following formula abbreviations are used:

$$M_1 = (\forall y)(\forall x) x \leq m^{x,y}$$
$$M_2 = (\forall y)(\forall x) y \leq m^{x,y}$$
$$S = (\forall x)(\forall y)(s(x) \leq y \supset x < y)$$
$$T = (\forall i)(\forall x)(\forall y)((f(x) = i \wedge f(y) = i) \supset f(x) = f(y))$$
$$A = (\forall x)(f(x) = 0 \vee f(x) = 1)$$
$$P = (\exists p)(\exists q)(p < q \wedge f(p) = f(q))$$
$$\infty_0 = (\forall n)(\exists k)(n \leq k \wedge f(k) = 0)$$
$$\infty_1 = (\forall m)(\exists l)(m \leq l \wedge f(l) = 1)$$

moreover 1 is an abbreviation for $s(0)$.

Then, let the proof φ be defined as follows.

$\varphi =$

$$\cfrac{\cfrac{(\tau)}{M_1, M_2, A \vdash \infty_0, \infty_1} \quad \cfrac{(\epsilon_1)}{\infty_1, S, T \vdash P}}{\cfrac{M_1, M_2, S, T, A \vdash P, \infty_0}{M_1, M_2, S, T, A \vdash P} \text{ cut} \quad \cfrac{(\epsilon_0)}{\infty_0, S, T \vdash P}} \text{ cut}$$

For the subproofs of τ, ϵ_0 and ϵ_1 please see [9] and the appendix.

The characteristic clause term $\Theta(\varphi)$ extracted from φ is

$$\Theta(\varphi) = (((\{\vdash v \leq m^{u,v}\} \oplus (\{\vdash u \leq m^{u,v}\} \oplus (\{\vdash f(m^{u,v}) = 0\} \otimes \{\vdash f(m^{u,v}) = 1\})))$$
$$\oplus ((\{s(u) \leq v \vdash\} \otimes \{\vdash\}) \otimes ((\{f(u) = 1 \vdash\} \otimes \{f(v) = 1 \vdash\}) \otimes \{\vdash\})))$$
$$\oplus ((\{s(u) \leq v \vdash\} \otimes \{\vdash\}) \otimes ((\{f(u) = 0 \vdash\} \otimes \{f(v) = 0 \vdash\}) \otimes \{\vdash\})))$$

and the corresponding characteristic clause set $|\Theta(\varphi)|$ obtained from $\Theta(\varphi)$ is

$$|\Theta(\varphi)| = \{ \vdash v \leq m^{u,v}, \qquad (C_1)$$
$$\vdash u \leq m^{u,v}, \qquad (C_2)$$
$$\vdash f(m^{u,v}) = 0, f(m^{u,v}) = 1, \qquad (C_3)$$
$$s(u) \leq v, f(u) = 1, f(v) = 1 \vdash, \qquad (C_4)$$
$$s(u) \leq v, f(u) = 0, f(v) = 0 \vdash \} \qquad (C_5)$$

The projection schemes obtained from φ for the five clauses above are the following:

$\varphi(C_1) =$

$$\cfrac{\cfrac{\cfrac{v \leq m^{u,v} \vdash v \leq m^{u,v}}{(\forall x)v \leq m^{x,v} \vdash v \leq m^{u,v}} \; \forall : l}{(\forall y)(\forall x)y \leq m^{x,y} \vdash v \leq m^{u,v}} \; \forall : l}$$

$\varphi(C_2) =$

$$\cfrac{\cfrac{\cfrac{u \leq m^{u,v} \vdash u \leq m^{u,v}}{(\forall x)x \leq m^{x,v} \vdash u \leq m^{u,v}} \; \forall : l}{(\forall y)(\forall x)x \leq m^{x,y} \vdash u \leq m^{u,v}} \; \forall : l}$$

$\varphi(C_3) =$

$$\cfrac{\cfrac{\cfrac{f(m^{u,v}) = 0 \vdash f(m^{u,v}) = 0 \quad f(m^{u,v}) = 1 \vdash f(m^{u,v}) = 1}{f(m^{u,v}) = 0 \vee f(m^{u,v}) = 1 \vdash f(m^{u,v}) = 0, f(m^{u,v}) = 1} \; \vee : l}{(\forall x)(f(x) = 0 \vee f(x) = 1) \vdash f(m^{u,v}) = 0, f(m^{u,v}) = 1} \; \forall : l}$$

$\varphi(C_4) = \psi_1$
$\varphi(C_5) = \psi_0$

where ψ_j is defined:

$\psi_j =$

$$\cfrac{\cfrac{\cfrac{\cfrac{\cfrac{\cfrac{\cfrac{\cfrac{s(u) \leq v \vdash s(u) \leq v \quad u < v \vdash u < v}{s(u) \leq v \supset u < v, s(u) \leq v \vdash u < v} \; \supset : l}{(\forall y)(s(u) \leq y \supset u < y), s(u) \leq v \vdash u < v} \; \forall : l}{(\forall x)(\forall y)(s(x) \leq y \supset x < y), s(u) \leq v \vdash u < v} \; \forall : l \quad \psi'_j}{S, s(u) \leq v, T, f(u) = j, f(v) = j \vdash u < v \wedge f(u) = f(v)} \; \wedge : r}{S, s(u) \leq v, T, f(u) = j, f(v) = j \vdash (\exists q)(u < q \wedge f(u) = f(q))} \; \exists : r}{S, s(u) \leq v, T, f(u) = j, f(v) = j \vdash (\exists p)(\exists q)(p < q \wedge f(p) = f(q))} \; \exists : r}$$

$\psi'_j =$

$$\cfrac{\cfrac{\cfrac{\cfrac{\cfrac{\cfrac{f(u) = j \vdash f(u) = j \quad f(v) = j \vdash f(v) = j}{f(u) = j, f(v) = j \vdash f(u) = j \wedge f(v) = j} \; \wedge : r \quad \cfrac{f(u) = f(v) \vdash f(u) = f(v)}{(f(u) = j \wedge f(v) = j) \supset f(u) = f(v), f(u) = j, f(v) = j \vdash f(u) = f(v)} \; \supset : l}{(\forall y)((f(u) = j \wedge f(y) = j) \supset f(u) = f(y)), f(u) = j, f(v) = j \vdash f(u) = f(v)} \; \forall : l}{(\forall x)(\forall y)((f(x) = j \wedge f(y) = j) \supset f(x) = f(y)), f(u) = j, f(v) = j \vdash f(u) = f(v)} \; \forall : l}{(\forall i)(\forall x)(\forall y)((f(x) = i \wedge f(y) = i) \supset f(x) = f(y)), f(u) = j, f(v) = j \vdash f(u) = f(v)} \; \forall : l}$$

The resolution refutations yielding two mathematically different proofs of φ are demonstrated in the following two subsections. The resulting cut-free proofs have been ommited because of their sizes.

3.1 Positive Hyperresolution

Derivation of C_6:

$$\underbrace{\cfrac{\cfrac{(C_4\sigma_1)}{s(u') \leq v', f(u') = 1, f(v') = 1 \vdash} \quad \cfrac{(C_2\sigma_2)}{\vdash u \leq m^{u,w}}}{\cfrac{f(u') = 1, f(m^{s(u'),w}) = 1 \vdash}{f(m^{s(m^{u,v}),w}) = 1 \vdash f(m^{u,v}) = 0}} \sigma_3 \quad \cfrac{(C_3)}{\vdash f(m^{u,v}) = 0, f(m^{u,v}) = 1}}_{C_X} \sigma_4$$

$$\cfrac{\cfrac{(C_3\sigma_5)}{C_X \quad \vdash f(m^{u',v'}) = 0, f(m^{u',v'}) = 1}}{\vdash f(m^{u,v}) = 0, f(m^{s(m^{u,v}),w}) = 0} \sigma_6 \qquad (C_6)$$

where $\sigma_1 = \{u \mapsto u', v \mapsto v'\}$, $\sigma_2 = \{v \mapsto w\}$, $\sigma_3 = \{u \mapsto s(u'), v' \mapsto m^{s(u'),w}\}$, $\sigma_4 = \{u' \mapsto m^{u,v}\}$, $\sigma_5 = \{u \mapsto u', v \mapsto v'\}$ and $\sigma_6 = \{u' \mapsto s(m^{u,v}), v' \mapsto w\}$.

> For arbitrary u, v and w either the cell with index $i = m^{u,v}$ is labelled '0' or the cell with index $m^{i+1,w}$.

Derivation of C_7:

$$\underbrace{\cfrac{\cfrac{(C_5\sigma_7)}{s(u') \leq v', f(u') = 0, f(v') = 0 \vdash} \quad \cfrac{(C_1\sigma_8)}{\vdash v \leq m^{u'',v}}}{\cfrac{f(u') = 0, f(m^{u'',s(u')}) = 0 \vdash}{f(m^{u'',s(m^{s(m^{u,v}),w})}) = 0 \vdash f(m^{u,v}) = 0}} \sigma_9 \quad \cfrac{(C_6)}{\vdash f(m^{u,v}) = 0, f(m^{s(m^{u,v}),w}) = 0}}_{C_Y} \sigma_{10}$$

$$\cfrac{\cfrac{(C_6\sigma_{11})}{C_Y \quad \vdash f(m^{u',v'}) = 0, f(m^{s(m^{u',v'}),w'}) = 0}}{\cfrac{\vdash f(m^{u,v}) = 0, f(m^{u',v'}) = 0}{\vdash f(m^{u,v}) = 0} \sigma_{13}} \sigma_{12} \qquad (C_7)$$

where $\sigma_7 = \{u \mapsto u', v \mapsto v'\}$, $\sigma_8 = \{u \mapsto u''\}$, $\sigma_9 = \{v \mapsto s(u'), v' \mapsto m^{u'',s(u')}\}$, $\sigma_{10} = \{u' \mapsto m^{s(m^{u,v}),w}\}$, $\sigma_{11} = \{u \mapsto u', v \mapsto v', w \mapsto w'\}$, $\sigma_{12} = \{u'' \mapsto s(m^{u',v'}), w' \mapsto s(m^{s(m^{u,v}),w})\}$ and $\sigma_{13} = \{u' \mapsto u, v' \mapsto v\}$.

> For arbitrary u and v the cell with index $i = m^{u,v}$ is labelled '0'.

$$\dfrac{\dfrac{(C_5)}{s(u) \leq v, f(u) = 0, f(v) = 0 \vdash} \quad \dfrac{(C_2\sigma_{14})}{\vdash u' \leq m^{u',v'}}}{\dfrac{f(u) = 0, f(m^{s(u),v'}) = 0 \vdash}{f(m^{s(m^{u',v}),v'}) = 0 \vdash}} \sigma_{15} \quad \dfrac{(C_7\sigma_{16})}{\vdash f(m^{u',v}) = 0} \sigma_{17} \quad \dfrac{(C_7\sigma_{18})}{\vdash f(m^{u,v''}) = 0} \sigma_{19}$$

where $\sigma_{14} = \{u \mapsto u', v \mapsto v'\}$, $\sigma_{15} = \{u' \mapsto s(u), v \mapsto m^{s(u),v'}\}$, $\sigma_{16} = \{u \mapsto u'\}$, $\sigma_{17} = \{u \mapsto m^{u',v}\}$, $\sigma_{18} = \{v \mapsto v''\}$ and $\sigma_{19} = \{u \mapsto s(m^{u',v}), v'' \mapsto v'\}$.

> For arbitrary u and v where $u < v$ at least one of the cells with index u or v should be labelled '1' but again for arbitrary u' and v' the cell with index $i = m^{u',v'}$ is labelled '0'. Hence choosing one time u as u' and one time v as v' leads to a contradiction.

3.2 Negative Hyperresolution

Derivation of C_6':

$$\dfrac{\dfrac{(C_1\sigma_1)}{\vdash v' \leq m^{u,v'}} \quad \dfrac{(C_4\sigma_2)}{s(v) \leq u', f(v) = 1, f(u') = 1 \vdash}}{f(v) = 1, f(m^{u,s(v)}) = 1 \vdash} \sigma_3 \qquad (C_6')$$

where $\sigma_1 = \{v \mapsto v'\}$, $\sigma_2 = \{u \mapsto v, v \mapsto u'\}$ and $\sigma_3 = \{u' \mapsto m^{u,s(v)}, v' \mapsto s(v)\}$.

> If a cell with index v is labelled '1' then no cell with an index bigger than v is labelled '1'.

Derivation of C_7':

$$\dfrac{\dfrac{(C_2\sigma_4)}{\vdash u' \leq m^{u',v}} \quad \dfrac{(C_5\sigma_5)}{s(u) \leq v', f(u) = 0, f(v') = 0 \vdash}}{f(u) = 0, f(m^{s(u),v}) = 0 \vdash} \sigma_6 \qquad (C_7')$$

where $\sigma_4 = \{u \mapsto u'\}$, $\sigma_5 = \{v \mapsto v'\}$ and $\sigma_6 = \{u' \mapsto s(u), v' \mapsto m^{s(u),v}\}$.

> If a cell with index u is labelled '0' then no cell with an index bigger than u is labelled '0'.

Derivation of C'_0:

$$\frac{\overset{(C_3\sigma_7)}{\vdash f(m^{u',v'}) = 0, f(m^{u',v'}) = 1} \quad \overset{(C'_7)}{f(u) = 0, f(m^{s(u),v}) = 0 \vdash}}{\underbrace{f(u) = 0 \vdash f(m^{s(u),v'}) = 1}_{C'_X}} \sigma_8$$

$$\frac{C'_X \quad \overset{(C'_6\sigma_9)}{f(v) = 1, f(m^{u',s(v)}) = 1 \vdash}}{f(v) = 1, f(u) = 0 \vdash} \sigma_{10} \qquad (C'_8)$$

where $\sigma_7 = \{u \mapsto u', v \mapsto v'\}$, $\sigma_8 = \{u' \mapsto s(u), v \mapsto v'\}$, $\sigma_9 = \{u \mapsto u'\}$ and $\sigma_{10} = \{u' \mapsto s(u), v' \mapsto s(v)\}$.

> If a cell with index v is labelled '1' then there is no cell with index u labelled '0', i.e. all cells are either only labelled '0' or only labelled '1'.

Derivation of C'_9:

$$\frac{\overset{(C_3\sigma_{11})}{\vdash f(m^{u',v'}) = 0, f(m^{u',v'}) = 1} \quad \overset{(C'_7)}{f(u) = 0, f(m^{s(u),v}) = 0 \vdash}}{\underbrace{f(u) = 0 \vdash f(m^{s(u),v}) = 1}_{C'_Y}} \sigma_{12}$$

$$\frac{\dfrac{C'_Y \quad \overset{(C'_8\sigma_{13})}{f(v') = 1, f(u') = 0 \vdash}}{f(u) = 0, f(u') = 0 \vdash} \sigma_{14}}{f(u) = 0 \vdash} \sigma_{15} \qquad (C'_9)$$

where $\sigma_{11} = \{u \mapsto u', v \mapsto v'\}$, $\sigma_{12} = \{v' \mapsto v, u' \mapsto s(u)\}$, $\sigma_{13} = \{u \mapsto u', v \mapsto v'\}$, $\sigma_{14} = \{v' \mapsto m^{s(u),v}\}$ and $\sigma_{15} = \{u' \mapsto u\}$.

> No cell is labelled '0'.

Derivation of C'_{10}:

$$\frac{\overset{(C_3\sigma_{16})}{\vdash f(m^{u',v'}) = 0, f(m^{u',v'}) = 1} \quad \overset{(C'_8)}{f(v) = 1, f(u) = 0 \vdash}}{\underbrace{f(v) = 1 \vdash f(m^{u',v'}) = 1}_{C'_Z}} \sigma_{17}$$

$$\frac{\dfrac{C'_Z \quad \overset{(C'_6\sigma_{18})}{f(v'') = 1, f(m^{u,s(v'')}) = 1 \vdash}}{f(v) = 1, f(v'') = 1 \vdash} \sigma_{19}}{f(v) = 1 \vdash} \sigma_{20} \qquad (C'_{10})$$

where $\sigma_{16} = \{u \mapsto u', v \mapsto v'\}$, $\sigma_{17} = \{u \mapsto m^{u',v'}\}$, $\sigma_{18} = \{v \mapsto v''\}$, $\sigma_{19} = \{u' \mapsto u, v' \mapsto s(v'')\}$ and $\sigma_{20} = \{v'' \mapsto v\}$.

No cell is labelled '1'.

$$\cfrac{\cfrac{(C_3)}{\vdash f(m^{u,v}) = 0, f(m^{u,v}) = 1 \quad \cfrac{(C_9'\sigma_{21})}{f(u') = 0 \vdash}}{\vdash f(m^{u,v}) = 1} \sigma_{22} \quad \cfrac{(C_{10}'\sigma_{23})}{f(v') = 1 \vdash}}{\vdash} \sigma_{24}$$

where $\sigma_{21} = \{u \mapsto u'\}$, $\sigma_{22} = \{u' \mapsto m^{u,v}\}$, $\sigma_{23} = \{v \mapsto v'\}$ and $\sigma_{24} = \{v' \mapsto m^{u,v}\}$.

The contradiction follows from the axiom that for arbitrary u and v the cell with the index $m^{u,v}$ is either labelled with '0' or with '1' in combination with the facts that no cell is labelled '0' and no cell is labelled '1'.

4 Possible Extensions

We plan to develop the following extensions of CERES:

- Due to the central importance of equality in mathematical proofs an investigation of cut-elimination in proofs with equality is very important to the application of cut-elimination. We intend to use the Gentzen calculus **LK** with the paramodulation rule (we refer to [10]) and to extend CERES to equality.

- As the cut-free proofs are often very large and difficult to interpret, we intend to provide the possibility to analyse certain characteristics of the cut-free proof (which are simpler than the proof itself). An important example are Herbrand sequents which may serve to extract bounds from proofs (see e.g. [6]). We plan to develop algorithms for extracting Herbrand sequents (also from proofs of nonprenex sequents as indicated in [1]) and for computing interpolants.

- A great challenge in the formal analysis of mathematical proofs lies in providing a suitable format for the input and output of proofs. We plan to develop an intermediary proof language connecting the language of mathematical proofs with **LK**. Furthermore we will implement a proof editor with a graphical user interface that allows for convenient input and analysis of the output of CERES.

- In the present version CERES eliminates all cuts at once. But - for the application to real mathematical proofs - only interesting cuts (i.e. lemmas) deserve to be eliminated, others should be integrated as additional axioms.

5 Conclusion

The computer experiments with CERES described in this paper lead to the following main consequences:

- even in the simple proof under consideration numerous formal variants of cut free proofs condense to relatively few mathematically distinguishable variants.

- On the other hand, the number of mathematically distinguishable variants is *greater than one*. This demonstrates, that the non-confluence of CERES is not just a formality within **LK**.

- CERES does not eliminate the mathematical activity of cut-elimination, it just supports it. In fact it is essential to interpret the resources and results mathematically.

- New features of CERES, concerning the relation of resolution refutations of the characteristic clause set and the proof projections, evolved in the course of the computer experiments.

References

1. M. Baaz, A. Leitsch: On skolemization and proof complexity, *Fundamenta Informaticae*, 20(4), pp. 353–379, 1994.
2. M. Baaz, A. Leitsch: Cut-Elimination and Redundancy-Elimination by Resolution, *Journal of Symbolic Computation*, 29, pp. 149-176, 2000.
3. M. Baaz, A. Leitsch: Towards a Clausal Analysis of Cut-Elimination, *Journal of Symbolic Computation* to appear.
4. G. Gentzen: Untersuchungen über das logische Schließen, *Mathematische Zeitschrift*, 39, pp. 405–431, 1934–1935.
5. J.Y. Girard: Proof Theory and Logical Complexity, in *Studies in Proof Theory*, Bibliopolis, Napoli, 1987.
6. H. Luckhardt: Herbrand-Analysen zweier Beweise des Satzes von Roth: polynomiale Anzahlschranken. *The Journal of Symbolic Logic*, 54, pp. 234–263, 1989.
7. G. Polya: Mathematics and plausible reasoning, Volume I: Induction and Analogy in Mathematics. Princeton University Press, Princeton, New Jersey, 1954.
8. G. Polya: Mathematics and plausible reasoning, Volume II: Patterns of Plausible Inference. Princeton University Press, Princeton, New Jersey, 1954.
9. C. Urban: Classical Logic and Computation. Ph.D. Thesis, University of Cambridge Computer Laboratory, 2000.
10. A. Degtyarev, A. Voronkov: Equality Reasoning in Sequent-Based Calculi, *Handbook of Automated Reasoning*, vol. I, ed. by A. Robinson and A. Voronkov, chapter 10, pp. 611-706, Elsevier Science, 2001.

APPENDIX

Input Proof

This is the proof[8] used for the experiments in section 3. Again all the premises (the auxiliary formulas of the inferences) are put in bold face, the conclusions are underlined and the same formula abbreviations are used.

$p =$

$$\cfrac{\cfrac{(\tau) \qquad (\epsilon_1)}{M_1, M_2, A \vdash \infty_0, \infty_1 \quad \infty_1, S, T \vdash P}}{\cfrac{M_1, M_2, S, T, A \vdash P, \infty_0}{M_1, M_2, S, T, A \vdash P}} \text{cut} \quad \cfrac{(\epsilon_0)}{\infty_0, S, T \vdash P} \quad \text{cut}$$

$\tau =$

$$\cfrac{\cfrac{\cfrac{v \leq m^{u,v} \vdash v \leq m^{u,v}}{(\forall x) v \leq m^{x,v} \vdash v \leq m^{u,v}} \forall : l}{(\forall y)(\forall x) y \leq m^{x,y} \vdash v \leq m^{u,v}} \forall : l \quad \cfrac{\cfrac{\cfrac{u \leq m^{u,v} \vdash u \leq m^{u,v}}{(\forall x) x \leq m^{x,v} \vdash u \leq m^{u,v}} \forall : l}{(\forall y)(\forall x) x \leq m^{x,y} \vdash u \leq m^{u,v}} \forall : l \quad (\tau')}{M_1, A \vdash u \leq m^{u,v} \wedge f(m^{u,v}) = 0, f(m^{u,v}) = 1} \wedge : r}{\cfrac{M_1, M_2, A \vdash u \leq m^{u,v} \wedge f(m^{u,v}) = 0, v \leq m^{u,v} \wedge f(m^{u,v}) = 1}{\cfrac{M_1, M_2, A \vdash (\exists k)(u \leq k \wedge f(k) = 0), v \leq m^{u,v} \wedge f(m^{u,v}) = 1}{\cfrac{M_1, M_2, A \vdash (\exists k)(u \leq k \wedge f(k) = 0), (\exists l)(v \leq l \wedge f(l) = 1)}{\cfrac{M_1, M_2, A \vdash (\forall n)(\exists k)(n \leq k \wedge f(k) = 0), (\exists l)(v \leq l \wedge f(l) = 1)}{M_1, M_2, A \vdash \infty_0, (\forall m)(\exists l)(m \leq l \wedge f(l) = 1)} \forall : r} \exists : r} \exists : r}$$

$\tau' =$

$$\cfrac{\cfrac{f(m^{u,v}) = 0 \vdash f(m^{u,v}) = 0 \quad f(m^{u,v}) = 1 \vdash f(m^{u,v}) = 1}{f(m^{u,v}) = 0 \vee f(m^{u,v}) = 1 \vdash f(m^{u,v}) = 0, f(m^{u,v}) = 1} \vee : l}{(\forall x)(f(x) = 0 \vee f(x) = 1) \vdash f(m^{u,v}) = 0, f(m^{u,v}) = 1} \forall : l$$

$\epsilon_0 =$

$$\cfrac{\cfrac{\cfrac{\cfrac{\cfrac{(\epsilon'_0)}{0 \leq u \wedge f(u) = 0, s(u) \leq v \wedge f(v) = 0, S, T \vdash P}}{0 \leq u \wedge f(u) = 0, (\exists k)(s(u) \leq k \wedge f(k) = 0), S, T \vdash P} \exists : l}{0 \leq u \wedge f(u) = 0, (\forall n)(\exists k)(n \leq k \wedge f(k) = 0), S, T \vdash P} \forall : l}{(\exists k)(0 \leq k \wedge f(k) = 0), (\forall n)(\exists k)(n \leq k \wedge f(k) = 0), S, T \vdash P} \exists : l}{\cfrac{(\forall n)(\exists k)(n \leq k \wedge f(k) = 0), (\forall n)(\exists k)(n \leq k \wedge f(k) = 0), S, T \vdash P}{(\forall n)(\exists k)(n \leq k \wedge f(k) = 0), S, T \vdash P} c : l} \forall : l$$

---

[8] specified and analyzed by Urban[9]

ς_1 –

$$\frac{\frac{\frac{\frac{\frac{(\epsilon'_1)}{1 \leq u \wedge f(u) = 1, s(u) \leq v \wedge f(v) = 1, S, T \vdash P}}{1 \leq u \wedge f(u) = 1, (\exists l)(s(u) \leq l \wedge f(l) = 1), S, T \vdash P} \exists : l}{1 \leq u \wedge f(u) = 1, (\forall m)(\exists l)(m \leq l \wedge f(l) = 1), S, T \vdash P} \forall : l}{(\exists l)(1 \leq l \wedge f(l) = 1), (\forall m)(\exists l)(m \leq l \wedge f(l) = 1), S, T \vdash P} \exists : l}{\frac{(\forall m)(\exists l)(m \leq l \wedge f(l) = 1), (\forall m)(\exists l)(m \leq l \wedge f(l) = 1), S, T \vdash P}{(\forall m)(\exists l)(m \leq l \wedge f(l) = 1), S, T \vdash P} c : l} \forall : l$$

$\epsilon'_j =$

$$\frac{\frac{\frac{\frac{\frac{\frac{\frac{\frac{\frac{s(u) \leq v \vdash s(u) \leq v \quad u < v \vdash u < v}{s(u) \leq v, s(u) \leq v \supset u < v \vdash u < v} \supset : l}{s(u) \leq v, (\forall y)(s(u) \leq y \supset u < y) \vdash u < v} \forall : l}{s(u) \leq v, (\forall x)(\forall y)(s(x) \leq y \supset x < y) \vdash u < v} \forall : l \quad (\epsilon''_j)}{f(u) = j, s(u) \leq v, f(v) = j, S, T \vdash u < v \wedge f(u) = f(v)} \wedge : r}{f(u) = j, s(u) \leq v \wedge f(v) = j, S, T \vdash u < v \wedge f(u) = f(v)} \wedge : l}{j \leq u \wedge f(u) = j, s(u) \leq v \wedge f(v) = j, S, T \vdash u < v \wedge f(u) = f(v)} \wedge : l}{j \leq u \wedge f(u) = j, s(u) \leq v \wedge f(v) = j, S, T \vdash (\exists q)(u < q \wedge f(u) = f(q))} \exists : r}{j \leq u \wedge f(u) = j, s(u) \leq v \wedge f(v) = j, S, T \vdash (\exists p)(\exists q)(p < q \wedge f(p) = f(q))} \exists : r$$

$\epsilon''_j =$

$$\frac{\frac{\frac{\frac{\frac{\frac{f(u) = j \vdash f(u) = j \quad f(v) = j \vdash f(v) = j}{f(u) = j, f(v) = j \vdash f(u) = j \wedge f(v) = j} \wedge : r \quad f(u) = f(v) \vdash f(u) = f(v)}{f(u) = j, f(v) = j, ((f(u) = j \wedge f(v) = j) \supset f(u) = f(v)) \vdash f(u) = f(v)} \supset : l}{f(u) = j, f(v) = j, (\forall y)((f(u) = j \wedge f(y) = j) \supset f(u) = f(y)) \vdash f(u) = f(v)} \forall : l}{f(u) = j, f(v) = j, (\forall x)(\forall y)((f(x) = j \wedge f(y) = j) \supset f(x) = f(y)) \vdash f(u) = f(v)} \forall : l}{f(u) = j, f(v) = j, (\forall i)(\forall x)(\forall y)((f(x) = i \wedge f(y) = i) \supset f(x) = f(y)) \vdash f(u) = f(v)} \forall : l$$

Uniform Rules and Dialogue Games for Fuzzy Logics*

Agata Ciabattoni, Christian G. Fermüller, and George Metcalfe

Technische Universität Wien, A-1040 Vienna, Austria
{agata,chrisf,metcalfe}@logic.at

Abstract. We provide uniform and invertible logical rules in a framework of relational hypersequents for the three fundamental t-norm based fuzzy logics i.e., Łukasiewicz logic, Gödel logic, and Product logic. Relational hypersequents generalize both hypersequents and sequents-of-relations. Such a framework can be interpreted via a particular class of dialogue games combined with bets, where the rules reflect possible moves in the game. The problem of determining the validity of atomic relational hypersequents is shown to be polynomial for each logic, allowing us to develop Co-NP calculi. We also present calculi with very simple initial relational hypersequents that vary only in the structural rules for the logics.

1 Introduction

Fuzzy logics based on t-norms and their residua are formal systems providing a foundation for reasoning under vagueness. Following e.g., [10], conjunction and implication are interpreted on the real unit interval $[0, 1]$ by a continuous t-norm and its residuum, respectively. The most important of these logics are Łukasiewicz logic **Ł**, Gödel logic **G**, and Product logic **Π**. These three are viewed as fundamental since *all* continuous t-norms can be constructed from their respective t-norms.

A variety of proof methods have been proposed for **Ł**, **G**, and **Π**. In particular, calculi for many fuzzy logics have been presented in a framework of *hypersequents*, a generalization of Gentzen sequents to multisets of sequents (see e.g., [2]). A very attractive calculus has been defined for **G** in [2] by embedding Gentzen's **LJ** for intuitionistic logic into a hypersequent calculus without modifying the rules for connectives. Elegant hypersequent calculi have also been defined for **Ł** [16] and **Π** [14], but using different rules for connectives. A further calculus for **G**, which unlike the respective hypersequent calculus has *invertible* rules, has been introduced in a framework of *sequents-of-relations* [5]. More proof search oriented calculi include a tableaux calculus for **Ł** [9], decomposition proof systems for **G** [3], and goal-directed systems for **Ł** [15] and **G** [13]. Finally, a general approach is presented in [1] where a calculus for any logic based on a continuous t-norm is obtained via reductions to suitable finite-valued logics.

In this paper we introduce a generalization of both hypersequents and sequents-of-relations, that we call *relational hypersequents*. A relational hypersequent, or, for short, r-hypersequent, is a multiset of two different types of sequents, where Gentzen's sequent arrow is replaced in one by $<$ and in the other by $\leq$. Intuitively we may think

---

* Research supported by C. Bühler-Habilitations-Stipendium H191-N04, FWF Project Nr. P16539-N04, and Marie Curie Fellowship 501043.

of an r-hypersequent as a meta-level (classical) disjunction of negated and non-negated sequents. Within this framework, we are able to give logical rules for Ł, G, and Π, that are *uniform* i.e., identical for all three logics. Since these rules are also *invertible*, we thus obtain uniform proof search procedures where the validity problem for r-hypersequents in Ł, G, or Π can be reduced to the validity problem in the respective logic for r-hypersequents containing only atomic formulas.[1] Moreover, we show that this latter problem is *polynomial* for each logic. Simple modifications then allow us to use these rules to present Co-NP decision procedures for Ł, G, and Π, matching the complexity class of the logics (see e.g., [10]). Furthermore, purely syntactic calculi with very simple initial relational hypersequents are obtained by introducing structural rules reflecting the characteristic properties of the particular logic.

We also present an interpretation of the uniform logical rules in terms of *dialogue games combined with bets*, that stems from Giles's game-theoretic characterization of Ł in the seventies [7,8]. Giles defined a Lorenzen-style game for which the existence of winning strategies for a formula corresponds to the validity of that formula in Ł. Here we reveal a deep connection between the search for winning strategies in Giles's game and the r-hypersequent rules for Ł, and extend this connection to G and Π.

2 t-Norm Based Fuzzy Logics

Continuous t-norms and their residua are defined as follows:

Definition 1. *A continuous t-norm is a continuous, commutative, associative, monotonically increasing function $* : [0,1]^2 \to [0,1]$ where $1 * x = x$ for all $x \in [0,1]$. The residuum of $*$ is a function $\Rightarrow_* : [0,1]^2 \to [0,1]$ where $x \Rightarrow_* y = max\{z \mid x * z \leq y\}$.*

The most important examples of continuous t-norms and their residua are:

	t-Norm	Residuum
Łukasiewicz	$x *_Ł y = max(0, x+y-1)$	$x \Rightarrow_Ł y = min(1, 1-x+y)$
Gödel	$x *_G y = min(x,y)$	$x \Rightarrow_G y = \begin{cases} 1 & \text{if } x \leq y \\ y & \text{otherwise} \end{cases}$
Product	$x *_Π y = x \cdot y$	$x \Rightarrow_Π y = \begin{cases} 1 & \text{if } x \leq y \\ y/x & \text{otherwise} \end{cases}$

Any continuous t-norm is an ordinal sum construction of these three, see e.g., [10] for details. Observe also that the functions min and max can be expressed in terms of $*$ and $\Rightarrow_*$, i.e., $min(x,y) = x * (x \Rightarrow_* y)$ and $max(x,y) = min((x \Rightarrow_* y) \Rightarrow_* y, (y \Rightarrow_* x) \Rightarrow_* x)$. Each continuous t-norm determines a *propositional logic* as follows:

Definition 2. *For a continuous t-norm $*$ with residuum $\Rightarrow_*$, we define a logic $\mathbf{L}_*$ based on a language with binary connectives $\to$, $\odot$, constant $\bot$, and defined connectives $\neg A =_{def} A \to \bot$, $A \land B =_{def} A \odot (A \to B)$, $A \lor B =_{def} ((A \to B) \to B) \land ((B \to$*

---
[1] These may also be viewed as providing a uniform *normal form* for Ł, G, and Π.

$A) \to A)$. *A valuation for $\mathbf{L}_*$ is a function v assigning to each propositional variable a truth value from the real unit interval $[0, 1]$, uniquely extended to formulas by:*

$$v(A \odot B) = v(A) * v(B) \qquad v(A \to B) = v(A) \Rightarrow_* v(B) \qquad v(\bot) = 0$$

A formula A is valid in $\mathbf{L}_*$, written $\models_{\mathbf{L}_*} A$, iff $v(A) = 1$ for all valuations v for $\mathbf{L}_*$.

We call the logics $\mathbf{L}_{*_\mathrm{L}}$, $\mathbf{L}_{*_\mathrm{G}}$, and $\mathbf{L}_{*_\Pi}$, Łukasiewicz logic Ł, Gödel logic $\mathbf{G}$, and Product logic Π, respectively.

3 Uniform Rules

We give uniform and invertible logical rules for Ł, $\mathbf{G}$, and Π in a framework of *relational hypersequents*, which are defined as follows:

Definition 3. *A relational hypersequent (r-hypersequent) is a finite multiset of the form:*

$$G = \Gamma_1 \triangleleft_1 \Delta_1 \mid \ldots \mid \Gamma_n \triangleleft_n \Delta_n$$

where $\triangleleft_i \in \{<, \leq\}$ and Γ_i and Δ_i are finite multisets of formulas for $i = 1, \ldots, n$. G is atomic if all formulas occurring in G are atomic. The size of G is the total number of symbols occurring in formulas of G.

The use of *multisets* in this definition means that the multiplicity but not the order of elements is important. Hence all set notation will refer to multisets, denoted by the symbols Γ and Δ. Also, we take advantage of standard conventions such as allowing Γ, A and Γ, Δ to stand for $\Gamma \cup \{A\}$ and $\Gamma \cup \Delta$ respectively, $\lambda \Gamma$ for $\Gamma, \ldots, \Gamma$ (λ times), and the empty space for the empty multiset $\emptyset$. Note moreover, that the use of inequality symbols $<$ and $\leq$ in the definition is purely syntactic (although of course also suggestive of the intended meaning). Finally, we remark that a *hypersequent* (see e.g., [2]) may be viewed as an r-hypersequent with just one relation symbol, while a *sequent-of-relations* (see e.g., [5]) may be viewed as an r-hypersequent where all multisets contain exactly one formula.

Below, we define validity for r-hypersequents in each of the three logics, informally understanding $\mid$ as a meta-level "or" and $<$ and $\leq$ as denoting inequalities between combinations (different for each logic) of truth values of formulas. Note that here (and throughout this paper) the symbols $<$ and $\leq$ have *two* uses: a syntactic one as part of an r-hypersequent, and a semantic one as inequalities holding between two mathematical expressions. We rely on context to make clear which use is intended.

Definition 4. *An r-hypersequent $G = \Gamma_1 \triangleleft_1 \Delta_1 \mid \ldots \mid \Gamma_n \triangleleft_n \Delta_n$ is valid for $L \in \{\text{Ł}, \mathbf{G}, \Pi\}$, written $\models_L G$, iff for all valuations v for L,*

$$\#_L^v \Gamma_i \triangleleft_i \#_L^v \Delta_i \text{ for some } i, 1 \leq i \leq n,$$

where $\#_L^v \emptyset = 1$ for $L \in \{\text{Ł}, \mathbf{G}, \Pi\}$ and

$$\#_\text{Ł}^v(\Gamma) = 1 + \sum_{A \in \Gamma}\{v(A) - 1\} \qquad \#_\mathbf{G}^v(\Gamma) = \min_{A \in \Gamma}\{v(A)\} \qquad \#_\Pi^v(\Gamma) = \prod_{A \in \Gamma}\{v(A)\}$$

Observe that for all formulas A, $\models_L \leq A$ iff $\models_L A$ for $I_i \in \{Ł, G, \Pi\}$. Below we present uniform logical rules in this framework, using G and H as metavariables to denote (possibly empty) r-hypersequents called *side r-hypersequents*.

Definition 5. *We define the following* uniform logical rules *for* $\triangleleft \in \{<, \leq\}$:

$$(\rightarrow, \triangleleft, l) \quad \frac{G \mid \Gamma \triangleleft \Delta \mid \Gamma, B \triangleleft A, \Delta \quad G \mid \Gamma \triangleleft \Delta \mid B < A}{G \mid \Gamma, A \rightarrow B \triangleleft \Delta}$$

$$(\rightarrow, \triangleleft, r) \quad \frac{G \mid \Gamma \triangleleft \Delta \quad G \mid \Gamma, A \triangleleft B, \Delta \mid A \leq B}{G \mid \Gamma \triangleleft A \rightarrow B, \Delta}$$

$$(\odot, \triangleleft, l) \frac{G \mid \Gamma, A, B \triangleleft \Delta \quad G \mid \Gamma, \bot \triangleleft \Delta}{G \mid \Gamma, A \odot B \triangleleft \Delta} \quad (\odot, \triangleleft, r) \frac{G \mid \Gamma \triangleleft \bot, \Delta \mid \Gamma \triangleleft A, B, \Delta}{G \mid \Gamma \triangleleft A \odot B, \Delta}$$

Note that uniform rules for $\wedge$ and $\vee$ are derivable using Definition 2. However we can also give more streamlined versions, i.e., for $\triangleleft \in \{<, \leq\}$:

$$(\wedge, \triangleleft, l) \quad \frac{G \mid \Gamma, A \triangleleft \Delta \mid \Gamma, B \triangleleft \Delta}{G \mid \Gamma, A \wedge B \triangleleft \Delta} \qquad (\wedge, \triangleleft, r) \frac{G \mid \Gamma \triangleleft A, \Delta \quad G \mid \Gamma \triangleleft B, \Delta}{G \mid \Gamma \triangleleft A \wedge B, \Delta}$$

$$(\vee, \triangleleft, l) \frac{G \mid \Gamma, A \triangleleft \Delta \quad G \mid \Gamma, B \triangleleft \Delta}{G \mid \Gamma, A \vee B \triangleleft \Delta} \qquad (\vee, \triangleleft, r) \quad \frac{G \mid \Gamma \triangleleft A, \Delta \mid \Gamma \triangleleft B, \Delta}{G \mid \Gamma \triangleleft A \vee B, \Delta}$$

Observe that the rules for $\rightarrow$, $\wedge$ and $\vee$ have the *subformula property*, i.e., all formulas occurring in the premises of a rule occur as subformulas of formulas in the conclusion. The rules for $\odot$ do not have this property, since $\bot$ appears in the premises and possibly not the conclusion. Nevertheless, the right premise in $(\odot, \triangleleft, l)$, and $\Gamma \triangleleft \bot, \Delta$ in the premise of $(\odot, \triangleleft, r)$ may be removed with no loss of soundness for **G** and **Π**. Moreover, since **Ł** can be based on a language without $\odot$, non-uniform rules with the subformula property can be given for all three logics.

Definition 6. *A rule* $\frac{G_1 \ldots G_n}{G}$ *is* sound *for a logic L if whenever* $\models_L G_i$ *for* $i = 1, \ldots, n$, *then* $\models_L G$, *and* invertible *if whenever* $\models_L G$, *then* $\models_L G_i$ *for* $i = 1, \ldots, n$.

Lemma 1. *If* $\frac{G_1 \ldots G_n}{G}$ *is sound (invertible) for L, then so is* $\frac{H \mid G_1 \ldots H \mid G_n}{H \mid G}$.

Proof. Follows directly from Definition 4. □

Theorem 1. *The uniform logical rules are sound and invertible for* **Ł**, **G**, *and* **Π**.

Proof. We consider only the rules for $\rightarrow$ (the cases for $\odot$ being similar), using Lemma 1 to disregard side r-hypersequents. Let v be a valuation for **Ł**, **G**, or **Π**. If $v(A) \leq v(B)$, then $v(A \rightarrow B) = 1$, and clearly for both $(\rightarrow, \triangleleft, l)$ and $(\rightarrow, \triangleleft, r)$, the premises hold iff the conclusion holds. Now suppose that $v(A) > v(B)$. We consider each rule in turn:

- $(\rightarrow, \triangleleft, l)$. The right premise clearly holds. For **Ł** and **Π**, by simple arithmetic, the conclusion holds iff the left premise holds. For **G**, $v(A \rightarrow B) = v(B)$ and $min(\#^v_{\mathbf{G}}(\Gamma), v(B)) \triangleleft min(v(A), \#^v_{\mathbf{G}}(\Delta))$ iff $min(\#^v_{\mathbf{G}}(\Gamma), v(B)) \triangleleft v(A)$ and $min(\#^v_{\mathbf{G}}(\Gamma), v(B)) \triangleleft \#^v_{\mathbf{G}}(\Delta)$. However, $min(\#^v_{\mathbf{G}}(\Gamma), v(B)) \triangleleft v(A)$ since $v(A) > v(B)$, so we have that the left premise holds iff the conclusion holds.

- $(\to, \triangleleft, r)$. If the conclusion holds, then the left premise, and (by simple arithmetic) the right premise hold. For **Ł** and **Π**, by simple arithmetic, the conclusion holds iff the right premise holds. For **G**, if $min(\#_{\mathbf{G}}^v(\Gamma), v(A)) \triangleleft min(v(B), \#_{\mathbf{G}}^v(\Delta))$ then $min(\#_{\mathbf{G}}^v(\Gamma), v(A)) \triangleleft v(B)$ holds, and, since $v(A) > v(B)$, $min(\#_{\mathbf{G}}^v(\Gamma), v(A)) = \#_{\mathbf{G}}^v(\Gamma)$. Hence the right premise holds iff the conclusion holds. □

Example 1. The uniform logical rules may be applied upwards exhaustively to reduce r-hypersequents to atomic r-hypersequents, e.g.,

$$\dfrac{\dfrac{p \leq q \mid p, q \leq p, q \quad p \leq q \mid q < p}{p, p \to q \leq q} \,(\to, \leq, 1) \quad \bot \leq q}{p \odot (p \to q) \leq q} \,(\odot, \leq, 1)$$

Proposition 1. *Applying the uniform logical rules upwards to r-hypersequents terminates with atomic r-hypersequents.*

Proof. We define the following measures and well-orderings:

$c(q) = 1$ for q atomic, $c(A \odot B) = c(A \to B) = c(A) + c(B) + 1$ for formulas A, B.
$mc(\Gamma \triangleleft \Delta) = \{c(A) \mid A \in \Gamma \cup \Delta\}$ for multisets Γ, Δ, and $\triangleleft \in \{<, \leq\}$.
$mmc(G) = \{mc(\Gamma \triangleleft \Delta) \mid \Gamma \triangleleft \Delta \in G\}$ for an r-hypersequent G.

For multisets α, β of integers: $\alpha <_m \beta$ iff (1) $\alpha \subset \beta$, or (2) $\alpha <_m \gamma$ where $\gamma = (\beta - \{j\}) \cup \{i, \ldots, i\}$, and $i < j$.

For multisets ϕ, ψ of multisets of integers, $\phi <_{mm} \psi$ iff (1) $\phi \subset \psi$, or (2) $\phi <_{mm} \chi$ where $\chi = (\psi - \{\alpha\}) \cup \{\beta, \ldots, \beta\}$ and $\beta <_m \alpha$.

For each uniform logical rule $\dfrac{G_1 \ldots G_n}{G}$ it is easy to check that $mmc(G_i) <_{mm} mmc(G)$ for $i = 1, \ldots, n$. Hence, since there is always a rule for any non-atomic formula, the rules applied upwards terminate with atomic r-hypersequents. □

4 Evaluating Atomic Relational Hypersequents

Let us take stock of what we have achieved so far. By providing uniform rules for **Ł**, **G**, and **Π**, that are sound and invertible, we are able to reduce the validity problem (i.e., checking the validity of a formula) in these logics to checking the validity of atomic r-hypersequents. We might also view the atomic r-hypersequents thus obtained as a sort of "uniform normal form" for these logics. This is a pleasant enough achievement in itself but it is only really useful *computationally* if we can show that checking the validity of atomic r-hypersequents is less complex than deciding the validity problem for each logic. In fact, while it is well-known that the validity problem for all these logics is Co-NP complete (see e.g., [10] for proofs and references), we show here that checking validity for atomic r-hypersequents is in each case *polynomial*.

We begin with a useful translation of atomic r-hypersequents into a set of inequations, where an atomic r-hypersequent is valid in a logic iff the associated set is inconsistent over $[0, 1]$.

Definition 7. *For atomic* $G = \Gamma_1 \vartriangleleft_1 \Lambda_1 \mid \ldots \mid \Gamma_n \vartriangleleft_n \Lambda_n$ *and* $L \in \{\mathbf{Ł}, \mathbf{G}, \mathbf{\Pi}\}$.

$$S_G = \{\circ_L \Gamma_1 \not\vartriangleleft_1 \circ_L \Delta_1, \ldots, \circ_L \Gamma_n \not\vartriangleleft_n \circ_L \Delta_n\}$$

where $\not\leq$ *is* $>$ *and* $\not<$ *is* $\geq$, $\circ_L \emptyset = 1$, *and*

$$\circ_{\mathbf{Ł}}(\Gamma) = 1 + \sum_{q \in \Gamma}\{x_q - 1\} \quad \circ_{\mathbf{G}}(\Gamma) = \min_{q \in \Gamma}\{x_q\} \quad \circ_{\mathbf{\Pi}}(\Gamma) = \prod_{q \in \Gamma}\{x_q\}$$

where x_q *is a real-valued variable for all propositional variables* q, *and* $x_\perp = 0$.

Lemma 2. *For atomic* G *and* $L \in \{\mathbf{Ł}, \mathbf{G}, \mathbf{\Pi}\}$, $\models_L G$ *iff* S_G *is inconsistent over* $[0, 1]$.

Proof. Immediate from Definition 4. □

For **Ł** we obtain the desired result using linear programming methods.

Theorem 2. *Checking* $\models_\mathbf{Ł} G$ *for an atomic r-hypersequent* G *is polynomial.*

Proof. By Lemma 2, since linear programming is polynomial, see e.g., [17]. □

To show that checking the validity of atomic r-hypersequents for **G** is polynomial, we use a result of Jeavons et al. [11] concerning relations over a finite domain.

Definition 8. *Let R be an n-ary relation over a domain D and $\otimes : D^2 \to D$ be an ACI operation, i.e., a binary idempotent, associative, and commutative operation. We say that R is closed under $\otimes$ if $(t_1, \ldots t_n), (t'_1, \ldots t'_n) \in R$ implies $(t_1 \otimes t'_1, \ldots, t_n \otimes t'_n) \in R$. A set of relations S is closed under $\otimes$ iff R is closed under $\otimes$ for all $R \in S$.*

Theorem 3 ([11]). *If a set of relations Γ over a finite domain D is closed under some ACI operation, then its constraint satisfaction problem is solvable in polynomial time.*

Theorem 4. *Checking* $\models_\mathbf{G} G$ *for an atomic r-hypersequent G is polynomial.*

Proof. Let $x_1, \ldots, x_n$ be the distinct variables occurring in S_G. It can be shown that S_G is inconsistent over $[0, 1]$ iff S_G is inconsistent over the set $D_n = \{0, \frac{1}{n}, \ldots, \frac{n-1}{n}, 1\}$. Associate with each $\circ_\mathbf{G} \Gamma \not\vartriangleleft_\mathbf{G} \Delta \in S_G$ a relation $R(x_1, \ldots, x_n)$ such that $R(a_1, \ldots, a_n)$ for $a_i \in D_n$, $i = 1, \ldots, n$, holds iff $\circ_\mathbf{G} \Gamma \not\vartriangleleft \circ_\mathbf{G} \Delta$ holds when x_i is replaced by a_i. Moreover, if $R(a_1, \ldots, a_n)$ and $R(b_1, \ldots, b_n)$ hold for $a_i, b_i \in D_n$, $i = 1, \ldots, n$, then also $R(min(a_1, b_1), \ldots, min(a_n, b_n))$ holds. Hence the set of relations associated with S_G is closed under the ACI operation $min : D_n^2 \to D_n$, and, by Theorem 3, its constraint satisfaction problem is solvable in polynomial time. However, this problem is equivalent to checking the inconsistency of S_G which, by Lemma 2, is equivalent to checking the validity of G. □

For **Π** we again use linear programming methods, dealing separately with the cases where propositional variables are assigned the value 0.

Definition 9. *Let G be an atomic r-hypersequent. An atomic formula q is:*

- *0-zero-ok for G if $\Gamma, q \leq \Delta \in G$.*

- n-zero-ok *for* G *if* $\Gamma, q < \Delta \in G$, *and for all* $p \in \Delta$, p *is* m-zero-ok for G for some $m \in \mathbb{N}$, $m < n$, where $n = 1 + \sum_{p \in \Delta} min\{k \mid p \text{ is } k\text{-zero-ok for } G\}$.
- zero-ok *for* G *if* q *is* n-zero-ok for G for some $n \in \mathbb{N}$.

Lemma 3. *Let* $H = G \mid \Gamma < \Delta$ *be an atomic r-hypersequent, and* $p \in \Gamma \cup \Delta$ *where* p *is not zero-ok for* H. *If* $\models_\Pi H$, *then* $\models_\Pi G$.

Proof. Note first that if $p \in \Gamma$ is not zero-ok, then there must be $q \in \Delta$ such that q is not zero-ok for H. Hence we can assume that $p \in \Delta$. Suppose $\not\models_\Pi G$, i.e., there is a valuation v for Π such that for all $\Gamma' \triangleleft \Delta' \in G$, $\#_\Pi^v \Gamma' \not\triangleleft \#_\Pi^v \Delta'$. We define a valuation v' such that $v'(q) = 0$ if q is not zero-ok, $v'(q) = v(q)$ otherwise. Clearly, $\#_\Pi^{v'} \Gamma \not< \#_\Pi^{v'} \Delta = 0$. Consider $\Gamma' \triangleleft \Delta' \in G$. If all $q \in \Gamma'$ are zero-ok, then $\#_\Pi^{v'} \Gamma' = \#_\Pi^v \Gamma'$. If $q \in \Gamma'$ is not zero-ok, then $\triangleleft$ is $<$, and for some not zero-ok $q' \in \Delta'$, $v'(q') = 0$. In both cases $\#_\Pi^{v'} \Gamma' \not\triangleleft \#_\Pi^v \Delta' \geq \#_\Pi^v \Delta'$. Hence $\not\models_\Pi H$ as required. □

Lemma 4. *Let* G *be an atomic r-hypersequent where* p *is zero-ok for* G. *For all valuations* v *for* Π, *if* $v(p) = 0$, *then* $\#_\Pi^v(\Gamma) \triangleleft \#_\Pi^v(\Delta)$ *for some* $\Gamma \triangleleft \Delta \in G$.

Proof. A simple induction on n where p is n-zero-ok. □

Theorem 5. *Checking* $\models_\Pi G$ *for an atomic r-hypersequent* G *is polynomial.*

Proof. It is straightforward to show that finding the zero-ok atomic formulas of G is polynomial in the size of G. Moreover, by repeated applications of Lemma 3, $\models_\Pi G$ iff $\models_\Pi G'$ for some $G' \subseteq G$ containing only zero-ok atomic formulas. If $\bot$ occurs in G' (which can be checked in polynomial time) then by Lemma 4, G' is valid. If $\bot$ does not occur in G', by Lemma 2, $\models_\Pi G'$ iff $S_{G'}$ is inconsistent over $[0,1]$ iff, by Lemma 4, $S_{G'}$ is inconsistent over $(0,1]$. However this latter problem is isomorphic to a linear programming problem over the positive reals, known to be polynomial. □

5 Co-NP Calculi

Despite having invertible rules and polynomially decidable atomic r-hypersequents, we do not yet have Co-NP calculi for **Ł**, **Π**, and **G**, since the rules applied upwards may increase the size of r-hypersequents exponentially. This problem is overcome by giving rules that make use of new propositional variables.

Definition 10. *We define the following revised logical rules for* $\triangleleft \in \{<, \leq\}$, *where* p *and* q *are propositional variables not occurring in the conclusions of the rules:*

$$(\rightarrow, \triangleleft, l)' \quad \frac{G \mid \Gamma, q \triangleleft \Delta \mid B < q, A}{G \mid \Gamma, A \rightarrow B \triangleleft \Delta}$$

$$(\rightarrow, \triangleleft, r)' \quad \frac{G \mid \Gamma \triangleleft \Delta \quad G \mid \Gamma, p \triangleleft q, \Delta \mid p \leq q \mid A < p \mid q < B}{G \mid \Gamma \triangleleft A \rightarrow B, \Delta}$$

$$(\odot, \triangleleft, l) \quad \frac{G \mid \Gamma, A, B \triangleleft \Delta \quad G \mid \Gamma, \bot \triangleleft \Delta}{G \mid \Gamma, A \odot B \triangleleft \Delta} \quad (\odot, \triangleleft, r)' \quad \frac{G \mid \Gamma \triangleleft q, \Delta \mid q < A, B \mid q < \bot}{G \mid \Gamma \triangleleft A \odot B, \Delta}$$

Theorem 6. *The revised logical rules are sound and invertible for* Ł, **G**, *and* Π.

Proof. We consider just the rules for $\to$ (the cases for $\odot$ being similar), using Lemma 1 to disregard side r-hypersequents. Let $L \in \{Ł, \mathbf{G}, \Pi\}$.

- $(\to, \triangleleft, l)'$. For soundness, given a valuation v, we can assume (since q does not occur in the conclusion) that $v(q) = v(A \to B)$. From $v(B) \geq \#^v_L(q, A)$ we get $\#^v_L(\Gamma, A \to B) \triangleleft \#^v_L(\Delta)$ as required. For invertibility, given a valuation v, if $v(B) < \#^v_L(q, A)$ then we are done, otherwise we must have $v(q) \leq v(A \to B)$ and hence, $\#^v_L(\Gamma, q) \triangleleft \#^v_L(\Delta)$ as required.
- $(\to, \triangleleft, r)'$. For soundness, consider a valuation v. If $v(A) \leq v(B)$, then $v(A \to B) = 1$ and we are done by the first premise. If $v(A) > v(B)$, then we can assume (since p and q do not occur in the conclusion) that $v(p) = v(A)$ and $v(q) = v(B)$. Hence, $\#^v_L(\Gamma, p) \triangleleft \#^v_L(q, \Delta)$ and, similarly to the case of $(\to, \triangleleft, r)$ in Theorem 1, $\#^v_L(\Gamma) \triangleleft \#^v_L(A \to B, \Delta)$ as required. For invertibility, the left premise is obvious, for the right premise consider a valuation v. If $v(A) < v(p)$, $v(q) < v(B)$, or $v(p) \leq v(q)$, then we are done. Otherwise, $\#^v_L(\Gamma, A) \triangleleft \#^v_L(B, \Delta)$ and, similarly to the case of $(\to, \triangleleft, r)$ in Theorem 1, $\#^v_L(\Gamma, p) \triangleleft \#^v_L(q, \Delta)$ as required. □

Proposition 2. *Applying the revised logical rules upwards to an r-hypersequent G terminates with atomic r-hypersequents of size polynomial in the size of G.*

Proof. Similar to the proof of Proposition 1, except that also each upward application of a rule gives only a constant increase in the size of the r-hypersequent. □

Theorem 7. *The revised logical rules provide Co-NP decision procedures for the validity problems for* Ł, **G**, *and* Π.

Proof. To show that a formula is not valid we apply the revised logical rules upwards exhaustively, making a non-deterministic choice of two branches where necessary. The result follows from Proposition 2, and Theorems 2, 4, and 5. □

6 Structural Rules

The aim of this section is to use the uniform logical rules to give purely syntactic calculi for Ł, **G**, and Π with very simple axioms and structural rules.

Definition 11. *We define the following uniform axioms and structural rules:*

$$(ID) \ A \leq A \qquad (\bot) \ \bot \leq A \qquad (\Lambda) \ \leq \qquad (<) \ \bot <$$

$$(EW) \ \frac{G}{G \mid \Gamma \triangleleft \Delta} \qquad (EC) \ \frac{G \mid \Gamma \triangleleft \Delta \mid \Gamma \triangleleft \Delta}{G \mid \Gamma \triangleleft \Delta} \qquad (WL) \ \frac{G \mid \Gamma \triangleleft \Delta}{G \mid \Gamma, A \triangleleft \Delta}$$

$$(S_\leq) \ \frac{G \mid \Gamma_1, \Gamma_2 \leq \Delta_1, \Delta_2}{G \mid \Gamma_1 \leq \Delta_1 \mid \Gamma_2 \leq \Delta_2} \qquad (M) \ \frac{G \mid \Gamma_1 \triangleleft \Delta_1 \quad G \mid \Gamma_2 \triangleleft \Delta_2}{G \mid \Gamma_1, \Gamma_2 \triangleleft \Delta_1, \Delta_2}$$

Lemma 5. *The uniform axioms and rules are sound for* Ł, **G**, *and* Π.

Proof. Straightforward using Definition 4. □

We now define calculi for **Ł**, **G**, and **Π** by extending the core uniform axioms and rules with further structural rules reflecting the characteristic properties of each logic.

Definition 12. **rHŁ** *consists of the uniform axioms and rules together with:*

$$(S_{\text{Ł}}) \ \frac{G \mid \Gamma_1, \Gamma_2 \leq \Delta_1, \Delta_2}{G \mid \Gamma_1 \leq \Delta_1 \mid \Gamma_2 < \Delta_2} \qquad (W\bot) \ \frac{G \mid \Gamma \leq \Delta}{G \mid \Gamma, \bot < \Delta}$$

Theorem 8. *An r-hypersequent G is derivable in* **rHŁ** *iff* $\models_{\text{Ł}} G$.

Proof. For soundness it is enough and easy to show that $(S_{\text{Ł}})$ and $(W\bot)$ are sound. For completeness we apply the invertible logical rules to G upwards to obtain valid atomic r-hypersequents. For each atomic r-hypersequent $H = \Gamma_1 \triangleleft_1 \Delta_1 \mid \ldots \mid \Gamma_n \triangleleft_n \Delta_n$, $\models_{\text{Ł}} H$ iff S_H is inconsistent over $[0,1]$. By linear programming methods [17], this holds iff there exist $\lambda, \lambda_1, \ldots, \lambda_n \in \mathbb{N}$ where either $\lambda > 0$, or $\lambda_i > 0$ and $\triangleleft_i$ is $\leq$ for some i, $1 \leq i \leq n$, and:

$$\lambda \bot \cup \bigcup_{i=1}^{n} \lambda_i \Delta_i \subseteq^* \bigcup_{i=1}^{n} \lambda_i \Gamma_i$$

where (1) $\Delta \subseteq^* \Gamma$ if $\Delta \subseteq \Gamma$, and (2) $\Delta \cup \{A\} \subseteq^* \Gamma \cup \{\bot\}$ if $\Delta \subseteq^* \Gamma$. If $\lambda > 0$, then we choose any i such that $\bot \in \Gamma_i$ and apply $(W\bot)$ upwards to get an r-hypersequent H' where $S_{H'}$ meets the conditions of the second case. If $\lambda_i > 0$ and $\triangleleft_i$ is $\leq$ for some i, $1 \leq i \leq n$, then we apply (EW) and (EC) upwards to get λ_i copies of $\Gamma_i \triangleleft_i \Delta_i$. Applying $(S_{\text{Ł}})$ and $(S_{\leq})$ upwards we have that H is derivable if $H' = \lambda_1 \Gamma_1, \ldots, \lambda_n \Gamma_n \leq \lambda_1 \Delta_1, \ldots, \lambda_n \Delta_n$ is derivable. However, H' is derivable by repeated applications of (M), (WL), (ID), $(\bot)$, and (Λ). □

Definition 13. **rHG** *consists of the uniform rules and axioms together with:*

$$(S_{\mathbf{G}}, \triangleleft) \ \frac{G \mid \Gamma_1, \Gamma_2 \triangleleft \Delta_1 \quad G \mid \Gamma_1 \leq \Delta_2}{G \mid \Gamma_1 \triangleleft \Delta_1 \mid \Gamma_2 < \Delta_2} \qquad (CL) \ \frac{G \mid \Gamma, A, A \triangleleft \Delta}{G \mid \Gamma, A \triangleleft \Delta}$$

Lemma 6. *The following rules are invertible for* **G**, *and derivable in* **rHG**:

$$(M, \triangleleft, l) \ \frac{G \mid \Gamma_1 \triangleleft \Delta \mid \Gamma_2 \triangleleft \Delta}{G \mid \Gamma_1, \Gamma_2 \triangleleft \Delta} \qquad (M, \triangleleft, r) \ \frac{G \mid \Gamma \triangleleft \Delta_1 \quad G \mid \Gamma \triangleleft \Delta_2}{G \mid \Gamma \triangleleft \Delta_1, \Delta_2}$$

Proof. It is straightforward to show that $(M, \triangleleft, l)$ and $(M, \triangleleft, r)$ are invertible for **G**. They are derivable in **rHG** as follows, where we write $(WL)^*$ and $(CL)^*$ for multiple applications of (WL) and (CL) respectively:

$$\frac{\dfrac{G \mid \Gamma_1 \triangleleft \Delta \mid \Gamma_2 \triangleleft \Delta}{G \mid \Gamma_1, \Gamma_2 \triangleleft \Delta \mid \Gamma_1, \Gamma_2 \triangleleft \Delta} \ (WL)^*}{G \mid \Gamma_1, \Gamma_2 \triangleleft \Delta} \ (EC) \qquad \frac{\dfrac{G \mid \Gamma \triangleleft \Delta_1 \quad G \mid \Gamma \triangleleft \Delta_2}{G \mid \Gamma, \Gamma \triangleleft \Delta_1, \Delta_2} \ (M)}{G \mid \Gamma \triangleleft \Delta_1, \Delta_2} \ (CL)^* \quad \square$$

Theorem 9. *An r-hypersequent G is derivable in* **rHG** *iff* $\models_{\mathbf{G}} G$.

Proof. For soundness, it suffices and is easy to show that (CL) and $(S_\lhd, \lhd)$ are sound for **G**. For completeness, we first apply the invertible logical rules to G upwards to obtain valid atomic r-hypersequents. By Lemma 6, applying $(M, \lhd, l)$ and $(M, \lhd, r)$ upwards, atomic r-hypersequents are derivable if valid r-hypersequents in which all multisets contain at most one atomic formula are derivable. Such an r-hypersequent H is valid iff the sequent of relations obtained by replacing the empty set by $\top$ is valid, and hence, using a result of [4] for sequents-of-relations, we get that H must have one of the following forms, where $\lhd_i \in \{<, \leq\}$ for $i = 1, \ldots, n$, and we allow $C, C_1, \ldots, C_n$ to stand for multisets containing at most one formula.

1. *(cycles)* $G' \mid C \leq C$ or $G' \mid C_1 \lhd_1 C_2 \mid \ldots \mid C_{n-1} \lhd_{n-1} C_n \mid C_n \leq C_1$.
2. *(1-chains)* $G' \mid C \leq$ or $G' \mid C_1 \leq C_2 \mid C_2 < C_3 \mid \ldots \mid C_{n-1} < C_n \mid C_n <$
3. *(0-chains)* $G' \mid \bot \leq C$ or $G' \mid \bot < C_1 \mid C_1 < C_2 \mid \ldots \mid C_{n-1} < C_n \mid C_n \leq C$.
4. *(0-1-chains)* $G' \mid \bot <$ or $G' \mid \bot < C_1 \mid C_1 < C_2 \mid \ldots \mid C_n <$.

It is straightforward to show that the above r-hypersequents are derivable in **rHG**. □

Definition 14. **rHΠ** *consists of the uniform rules together with:*

$$(S_\Pi) \frac{G \mid \Gamma_1, \Gamma_2 \leq \Delta_1, \Delta_2 \quad G \mid \Gamma_3 \leq \Delta_2}{G \mid \Gamma_1 \leq \Delta_1 \mid \Gamma_2 < \Delta_2 \mid \Gamma_3 \leq \Delta_3} \qquad (RCL) \frac{G \mid \Gamma, \bot, \bot \lhd \Delta}{G \mid \Gamma, \bot \lhd \Delta}$$

Lemma 7. *If $G \mid \Gamma_1, \Gamma_2 \leq \Delta_1, \Delta_2$ is atomic and derivable in **rHΠ** and p is zero-ok for all $p \in \Delta_2$, then $G \mid \Gamma_1 \leq \Delta_1 \mid \Gamma_2 < \Delta_2$ is derivable in **rHΠ**.*

Proof. We proceed by induction on $n = 1 + \sum_{p \in \Delta_2} \min\{m \mid p \text{ is } m\text{-zero-ok for } G\}$ For each $p \in \Delta_2$, we have two cases. If p is 0-zero-ok, then $\Gamma', p \leq \Delta' \in G$. If p is m-zero-ok for some $m > 0$, then $\Gamma', p < \Delta' \in G$ where all $q \in \Delta'$ are zero-ok. Repeatedly applying $(S_\leq)$ upwards in the former case, and the induction hypothesis in the latter, plus repeated applications of (EC) and (EW) upwards, we get that $G \mid \Gamma_1 \leq \Delta_1 \mid \Gamma_2 < \Delta_2$ is derivable if $H = G \mid \Gamma_1 \leq \Delta_1 \mid \Gamma_2 < \Delta_2 \mid \Gamma_3 \leq \Delta_3$ is derivable where $\Delta_2 \subseteq \Gamma_3$. Now applying (S_Π) upwards, since $G \mid \Gamma_3 \leq \Delta_2$ is derivable, we get that H is derivable if $G \mid \Gamma_1, \Gamma_2 \leq \Delta_1, \Delta_2$ is derivable. □

Theorem 10. *An r-hypersequent G is derivable in **rHΠ** iff $\models_\Pi G$.*

Proof. It is easy to show that (RCL) is sound for **Π**. For (S_Π), if v is a valuation for **Π** in which the conclusion does not hold, and $\#_\Pi^v(\Gamma_1) \cdot \#_\Pi^v(\Gamma_2) \leq \#_\Pi^v(\Delta_1) \cdot \#_\Pi^v(\Delta_2)$, then, since $\#_\Pi^v(\Gamma_1) > \#_\Pi^v(\Delta_1)$ and $\#_\Pi^v(\Gamma_2) \geq \#_\Pi^v(\Delta_2)$, we must have $\#_\Pi^v(\Delta_2) = 0$. Hence, since $\#_\Pi^v(\Gamma_3) > \#_\Pi^v(\Delta_3) \geq 0$, the right premise cannot hold. For completeness, we apply the invertible logical rules to G upwards to obtain valid atomic r-hypersequents. By Lemma 3, for each valid atomic r-hypersequent H, $\models_\Pi H$ implies $\models_\Pi H'$ for some $H' \subseteq H$ such that H' contains only zero-ok atomic formulae. If H' contains $\bot$ then it is easy to prove that H' is derivable as required. Otherwise $S_{H'}$ is inconsistent over $(0,1]$ and by linear programming methods there exist $\lambda_1, \ldots, \lambda_n \in \mathbb{N}$ with $\lambda_i > 0$, where $\lhd_i$ is $\leq$ for some i, $1 \leq i \leq n$, and

$$\bigcup_{i=1}^{n} \lambda_i \Delta_i \subseteq \bigcup_{i=1}^{n} \lambda_i \Gamma_i$$

By (EC) applied upwards to obtain λ_i copies of $\Gamma_i \lhd_i \Delta_i$, then multiple applications of Lemma 7 and $(S_\leq)$, and (EW) applied upwards, H is derivable if $\lambda_1\Gamma_1, \ldots, \lambda_n\Gamma_n \leq \lambda_1\Delta_1, \ldots, \lambda_n\Delta_n$ is derivable. But this r-hypersequent is derivable using (M), (WL), (ID) and (Λ). □

It is important to note that for each logic there may be considerable redundancy in the rules presented. For example, for Ł we can drop the right premise of $(\rightarrow, l)$ and maintain soundness; we are then able to drop all rules and axioms referring to $<$. What we obtain is essentially the hypersequent calculus presented in [16]. For Π our pruning leads to a calculus that, unlike the sequent or hypersequent calculi of [14], has the subformula property, albeit with more complicated structures. For G simplifications lead to a calculus very similar to the sequent-of-relations calculus presented in [5].

7 Game Interpretation

In the 1970s [7,8] Robin Giles presented a characterization of Ł in terms of a dialogue game combined with bets. In this section we review (very briefly) Giles's game and generalize it with the aim of revealing a deep connection between our uniform r-hypersequent rules and the search for winning strategies in versions of the game for Ł, Π, and G.[2] Giles's game consists of two largely independent building blocks:

1. Betting for positive results of experiments. There are two players — say, me and you — who agree to pay 1\$ to the opponent player for every false statement that they assert.[3] By $[p_1, \ldots, p_m \| q_1, \ldots, q_n]$ we denote an *elementary state* in the game, where I assert each of the q_i in the multiset $\{q_1, \ldots, q_n\}$ of statements (atomic formulas), and you assert each $p_i \in \{p_1, \ldots, p_m\}$.

Each statement q refers to an experiment E_q with a binary (yes/no) result: q can be read as 'E_q yields a positive result'. The same experiment may yield different results when repeated. However, for every run of the game, a certain *risk value* $\langle q \rangle^* \in [0, 1]$ is associated with q, denoting the probability that E_q yields a negative result. For the special atomic formula $\bot$ (*falsum*) we define $\langle \bot \rangle^* = 1$. The risk associated with a multiset $\{p_1, \ldots, p_m\}$ of atomic formulas is defined as $\langle p_1, \ldots, p_m \rangle^* = \sum_{i=1}^{m} \langle p_i \rangle^*$. The risk $\langle \rangle^*$ associated with $\emptyset$ is defined as 0. The risk associated with an elementary state $[p_1, \ldots, p_m \| q_1, \ldots, q_n]$ is calculated from my point of view. Therefore the condition $\langle p_1, \ldots, p_m \rangle^* \geq \langle q_1, \ldots, q_n \rangle^*$ expresses that I do not expect any loss (but possibly some gain) when betting as explained above.

2. A Lorenzen-style dialogue game for compound formulas. Giles follows Paul Lorenzen (see e.g., [12]) in implicitly defining the meaning of logical connectives by reference to rules of a dialogue game that proceeds by systematically reducing arguments about compound formulas to arguments about their subformulas.

---

[2] We also generalize the results of [6] that relate a dialogue game for G to the sequents-of-relations calculus of [5].

[3] For a detailed motivation and explanation of the game we refer to [8].

To assist a concise presentation, we will only consider implication ($\rightarrow$), noting that in Ł all other connectives can be defined from $\rightarrow$ and $\bot$. The central dialogue rule can be stated as follows:

(R) If I assert $A \rightarrow B$, then whenever you choose to attack this assertion by asserting A, I have to assert also B. (And *vice versa*, i.e., for the roles of me and you switched.)

No special regulations on the succession of moves in the dialogue game are required. However, each assertion is attacked at most once: this is reflected by the removal of $A \rightarrow B$ from the multiset of all formulas asserted by a player during a run of the game, as soon as the other player has either attacked by asserting A, or indicated that she will not attack $A \rightarrow B$ at all. Observe that these stipulations ensure that every run of the dialogue game ends in an elementary state $[p_1, \ldots, p_m \| q_1, \ldots, q_n]$. Given an assignment $\langle \cdot \rangle^*$ of risk values to the p_is and q_is we say that I *win* the game if I do not expect any loss, i.e., if $\langle p_1, \ldots, p_m \rangle^* \geq \langle q_1, \ldots, q_n \rangle^*$.

As an almost trivial example consider the game with intial state $[\| p \rightarrow q]$; i.e., I initially assert $p \rightarrow q$, for some atomic formulas p and q. In response, you can either assert p in order to force me to assert q, or explicitly refuse to attack $p \rightarrow q$. In the first case the game ends in the elementary state $[p\|q]$; in the second case it ends in $[\|]$. If an assignment $\langle \cdot \rangle^*$ of risk values gives $\langle p \rangle^* \geq \langle q \rangle^*$, then I win the game, whatever move you choose to make. In other words: I have a winning strategy associated with $p \rightarrow q$ for assignments of risk values such that $\langle p \rangle^* \geq \langle q \rangle^*$.

Theorem 11 (R. Giles [7,8]). *A formula A is valid in Ł iff for all assignments of risk values to atomic formulas occurring in A, I have a winning strategy.*

Giles proved the theorem without formalizing the concept of strategies. However, to reveal the connection to analytic proof systems we need to define structures that register possible choices for both players. These structures, called *disjunctive strategies* or, for short, *d-strategies*, appear at a different level of abstraction to strategies. The latter are only defined with respect to given assignments of risk values (and may be different for different assignments), whereas d-strategies abstract away from particular assignments.

Definition 15. *A d-strategy (for me) is a tree whose nodes are disjunctions of states:*

$$[A_1^1, \ldots, A_{m_1}^1 \| B_1^1, \ldots, B_{n_1}^1] \bigvee \ldots \bigvee [A_1^k, \ldots, A_{m_k}^k \| B_1^k, \ldots, B_{n_k}^k]$$

which fulfill the following conditions:

1. *All leaf nodes of a d-strategy denote disjunctions of elementary states.*
2. *Internal nodes are partitioned into I-nodes and you-nodes.*
3. *Any I-node is of the form $\mathcal{G} \bigvee [A \rightarrow B, \Gamma \| \Delta]$ and has exactly one successor node of the form $\mathcal{G} \bigvee [\Gamma, B \| A, \Delta] \bigvee [\Gamma \| \Delta]$, where $\mathcal{G}$ denotes a (possibly empty) disjunction of states, and Γ, Δ denote (possibly empty) multisets of formulas.*
4. *For every state $[\Gamma \| \Delta]$ of a you-node and every occurrence of $A \rightarrow B$ in Δ, the you-node has a successor node of the form $\mathcal{G} \bigvee [\Gamma, A \| B, \Delta]$ as well as a successor node of the form $\mathcal{G} \bigvee [\Gamma \| \Delta]$. Moreover, there is at least one occurrence of an implication on the right hand side of some disjunct (i.e., state) of a you-node.*[4]

---

[4] If there is a total of n occurrences of compound formulas on the right hand sides of states in a you-node, then it has $2n$ successor nodes, i.e., corresponding to $2n$ possible moves for you.

We call a d-strategy winning *(for me)* if, for all leaf nodes ν and for all possible assignments $\langle \cdot \rangle^*$ of risk values to atomic formulas, there is a disjunct $[p_1, \ldots, p_m \| q_1, \ldots, q_n]$ in ν, such that $\langle p_1, \ldots, p_m \rangle^* \geq \langle q_1, \ldots, q_n \rangle^*$.

In game theory a winning strategy (for me) is usually defined as a function from all possible states where I have a choice, into the set of my possible moves. Note that winning strategies in the latter sense exist for all assignments of risk values if and only if a winning d-strategy exists.

Strictly speaking we have only defined d-strategies (and therefore, implicitly, also strategies) with respect to some given regulation that, for each possible state, determines who is to move next. Each consistent partition of internal nodes into I-nodes and you-nodes corresponds to such a regulation. However, it has been (implicitly) proved by Giles that the order of moves is irrelevant. Therefore no loss of generality is involved.

The defining conditions for I-nodes and you-nodes not only correspond to possible moves in the dialogue game, but also to the introduction rules for implication in the hypersequent calculus for Ł defined in [16]. In fact, every winning d-strategy corresponds to a family of proofs in that hypersequent calculus. In order to establish a similar relation between our uniform r-hypersequent rules and game based characterizations of Ł, Π, and G, we start by observing that the phrase 'betting for a positive result of (a multiset of) experiments' is ambiguous. As we have seen, Giles identified the combined risk associated with such a bet with the *sum* of risks associated with the single experiments. However, other ways of interpreting the combined risk are worth exploring. In particular, we are interested in a second version of the game, where an elementary state $[p_1, \ldots, p_m \| q_1, \ldots, q_n]$ corresponds to my single bet that *all* experiments associated with the q_is ($1 \leq i \leq n$) show a positive result, against your single bet that *all* experiments associated with the p_is ($1 \leq i \leq m$) show a positive result. A third form of the game arises if one decides to perform only *one* experiment for each of the two players, where the relevant experiment is chosen by the opponent.

To achieve a direct correspondence between the three versions of the game and the standard t-norm based semantics for Ł, Π, and G, respectively, we invert risk values into probabilites of *positive* results of associated experiments. More formally, the value of an atomic formula q is defined as $\langle q \rangle = 1 - \langle q \rangle^*$; in particular, $\langle \bot \rangle = 0$.

My expected gain in the elementary state $[p_1, \ldots, p_m \| q_1, \ldots, q_n]$ in Giles's game for Ł is the sum of money that I expect you to have pay me minus the sum that I expect to have to pay you. This amounts to $\sum_{i=1}^{m}(1 - \langle p_i \rangle) - \sum_{i=1}^{n}(1 - \langle q_i \rangle)$ \$. Therefore my expected gain is greater or equal to zero if and only if the condition $1 + \sum_{i=1}^{m}(\langle p_i \rangle - 1) \leq 1 + \sum_{i=1}^{n}(\langle q_i \rangle - 1)$ holds.

In the second version of the game, you have to pay me 1\$ unless all experiments associated with the p_is test positively, and I have to pay you 1\$ unless all experiments associated with the q_is test positively. My expected gain is therefore $1 - \prod_{i=1}^{m}\langle p_i \rangle - (1 - \prod_{i=1}^{n}\langle q_i \rangle)$ \$. The corresponding winning condition is $\prod_{i=1}^{m}\langle p_i \rangle \leq \prod_{i=1}^{n}\langle q_i \rangle$.

To maximize the expected gain in the third version of the game I will choose a $p_i \in \{p_1, \ldots, p_m\}$ where the probability of a positive result of the associated experiment is least; and you will do the same for the q_is that I have asserted. Therefore my expected gain is $(1 - \min_{1 \leq i \leq m}\langle p_i \rangle) - (1 - \min_{1 \leq i \leq n}\langle q_i \rangle)$ \$. Hence the corresponding winning condition is $\min_{1 \leq i \leq m}\langle p_i \rangle \leq \min_{1 \leq i \leq n}\langle q_i \rangle$.

We thus arrive at the following definitions for the value of a multiset $\{p_1, \ldots, p_n\}$ of atomic formulas, according to the three versions of the game:

$$\langle p_1, \ldots, p_n \rangle_{\text{Ł}} = 1 + \sum_{i=1}^{n}(\langle p_i \rangle - 1) \quad \langle p_1, \ldots, p_n \rangle_{\Pi} = \prod_{i=1}^{n} \langle p_i \rangle \quad \langle p_1, \ldots, p_n \rangle_{\mathbf{G}} = \min_{1 \leq i \leq n} \langle p_i \rangle$$

For the empty multiset we define $\langle \rangle_{\text{Ł}} = \langle \rangle_{\Pi} = \langle \rangle_{\mathbf{G}} = 1$.

A disjunction of elementary states ν is now called *winning according to logic* $L \in \{\text{Ł}, \Pi, \mathbf{G}\}$ if for every assignment $\langle \cdot \rangle$ of values there is a state $[p_1, \ldots, p_m \| q_1, \ldots, q_n]$ in ν where $\langle p_1, \ldots, p_m \rangle_L \leq \langle q_1, \ldots, q_n \rangle_L$.

It turns out that, in order to characterize Π and $\mathbf{G}$, the dialogue game rule (R) has to be augmented[5] by the following additional rule:

(Q) If I have a strategy for winning the game starting in the state $[A \| B]$, then I am not allowed to attack your assertion of $A \to B$. (And *vice versa*.)[6]

The trees of disjunctive states as presented in Definition 15 do not yet contain all the information that is needed to formulate winning d-strategies for the new versions of the game. To see what kind of information is missing, observe that rule (Q), at the meta-level, corresponds to

- if $v(A) \leq v(B)$, then I have to quit on your assertions of $A \to B$, and you have to quit on my assertions of $A \to B$,

where v is the valuation extending the relevant assignment $\langle \cdot \rangle$ from atomic formulas to arbitrary formulas. Incorporating this fact into the definition of d-strategies seems, at first glance, to require additional notation for *conditions* of the form 'if $A \leq B$'. However, we can use the fact that 'if X then Y' (at the classical meta-level) is equivalent to 'not X or Y'. Thus we remain within the notation for *disjunctive* states, as long as we are willing to use also the strict inequality $<$, in order to be able to express 'not $A \leq B$' as '$B < A$'. Consequently, states $[\Gamma \| \Delta]$ now come in two different forms: $[\Gamma < \Delta]$ and $[\Gamma \leq \Delta]$.

Taking into account these modifications, condition 3 of Definition 15 is replaced by

3'. Any I-node is of the form $\mathcal{G} \bigvee [A \to B, \Gamma \triangleleft \Delta]$, where $\triangleleft$ is either $\leq$ or $\leq$. It has exactly two successor nodes: one of the form $\mathcal{G} \bigvee [\Gamma, B \triangleleft A, \Delta] \bigvee [\Gamma \triangleleft \Delta]$ and one of the form $\mathcal{G} \bigvee [B < A] \bigvee [\Gamma \triangleleft \Delta]$.

Note that this new condition corresponds directly to the uniform logical rules $(\to, \triangleleft, l)$ for r-hypersequents.

In Definition 15 conditions 3 and 4 are dual. In fact, the availabilty of both inequality relations allows us to express the dual to conjunctions of disjunctive states as conjunctions of disjunctive states, by pushing negations inside and finally expressing 'not $\Gamma \leq \Delta$' as '$\Delta < \Gamma$'. After removing some redundancies, the result of this purely mechanical dualization of condition 3' results in a version 4' that corresponds to rule $(\to, \triangleleft, r)$.

---

[5] We could have used rule (Q) already in Giles's original game. However, in contrast to the game for Π and $\mathbf{G}$, (Q) does not affect the existence of winning strategies for formulas valid in Ł.

[6] Recall that the strategies mentioned in (Q) refer to a given assignment $\langle \cdot \rangle$ of values.

Concluding Remark. We have presented invertible uniform logical rules for the fundamental t-norm based fuzzy logics Ł, **G**, and Π, that both provide the basis for Co-NP decision procedures, and may be interpreted within a framework of dialogue games with bets. However, these rules are also sound and invertible for a number of related logics. This raises the interesting question as to which other logics can be characterized in an analogous way. In particular we hope to find a first natural calculus for Hájek's Basic logic **BL** [10], the logic characterizing all logics based on continuous t-norms.

References

1. S. Aguzzoli. Uniform description of calculi for all t-norm logics. In L. Henkin et al., editors, *Proceedings of 34th IEEE International Symposium on Multiple-Valued Logic (ISMVL'04)*, pages 38–43, 2004.
2. A. Avron. Hypersequents, logical consequence and intermediate logics for concurrency. *Annals of Mathematics and Artificial Intelligence*, 4(3–4):225–248, 1991.
3. A. Avron and B. Konikowska. Decomposition Proof Systems for Gödel-Dummett Logics. *Studia Logica*, 69(2):197–219, 2001.
4. M. Baaz, A. Ciabattoni, and C. Fermüller. Cut-elimination in a sequents-of-relations calculus for Gödel logic. In *International Symposium on Multiple Valued Logic (ISMVL'2001)*, pages 181–186. IEEE, 2001.
5. M. Baaz and C. Fermüller. Analytic calculi for projective logics. In *Proc. TABLEAUX '99*, volume 1617 of *LNAI*, pages 36–50, 1999.
6. C. Fermüller and N. Preining. A dialogue game for intuitionistic fuzzy logic based on comparison of degrees of truth. In *Proceedings of InTech'03*, 2003.
7. R. Giles. A non-classical logic for physics. *Studia Logica*, 4(33):399–417, 1974.
8. R. Giles. A non-classical logic for physics. In R. Wojcicki and G. Malinkowski, editors, *Selected Papers on Łukasiewicz Sentential Calculi*, pages 13–51. Polish Academy of Sciences, 1977.
9. R. Hähnle. *Automated Deduction in Multiple-Valued Logics*. Oxford University Press, 1993.
10. P. Hájek. *Metamathematics of Fuzzy Logic*. Kluwer, Dordrecht, 1998.
11. P. G. Jeavons, D. A. Cohen, and M. Gyssens. Closure properties of constraints. *The Journal of the ACM*, 44:527–548, 1997.
12. P. Lorenzen. Logik und Agon. In *Atti Congr. Internaz. di Filosofia*, pages 187–194. Sansoni, 1960.
13. G. Metcalfe, N. Olivetti, and D. Gabbay. Goal-directed calculi for Gödel-Dummett logics. In M. Baaz and J. A. Makowsky, editors, *Proceedings of CSL 2003*, volume 2803 of *LNCS*, pages 413–426. Springer, 2003.
14. G. Metcalfe, N. Olivetti, and D. Gabbay. Analytic proof calculi for product logics. *Archive for Mathematical Logic*, 43(7):859–889, 2004.
15. G. Metcalfe, N. Olivetti, and D. Gabbay. Goal-directed methods for Łukasiewicz logics. In J. Marcinkowski and A. Tarlecki, editors, *Proceedings of CSL 2004*, volume 3210 of *LNCS*, pages 85–99. Springer, 2004.
16. G. Metcalfe, N. Olivetti, and D. Gabbay. Sequent and hypersequent calculi for abelian and Łukasiewicz logics. To appear in ACM TOCL, 2005.
17. A. Schrijver. *Theory of Linear and Integer Programming*. John Wiley and Sons, 1987.

Nonmonotonic Description Logic Programs: Implementation and Experiments *

Thomas Eiter, Giovambattista Ianni, Roman Schindlauer, and Hans Tompits

Institut für Informationssysteme, Technische Universität Wien
Favoritenstraße 9-11, A-1040 Vienna, Austria
{eiter, ianni, roman, tompits}@kr.tuwien.ac.at

Abstract. The coupling of description logic reasoning systems with other reasoning formalisms (possibly over the Web) is becoming an important research issue and calls for advanced methods and algorithms. Recently, several notions of *description logic programs* have been introduced, combining rule-based semantics with description logics. Among them are *nonmonotonic description logic programs* (or *dl-programs* for short) which combine nonmonotonic logic programs with description logics under a generalized version of the answer-set and the well-founded semantics, respectively, which are the predominant semantics for nonmonotonic logic programs. In this paper, we consider some technical issues regarding an efficient implementation for both semantics, which has been realized in a working prototype exploiting the two state-of-art tools DLV and RACER. A major issue in this respect is efficient interfacing between the two reasoning systems at hand, for which we devised special methods. Such methods may fruitfully be used for the implementation of systems of similar nature. Reported experimentation activities with our prototype show that the methods we have developed are effective and are a key for highly optimized nonmonotonic dl-program engines.

1 Introduction

Description logics are well-known formalisms for describing ontological knowledge, and play an important role for building the *Semantic Web* [3,4,9]. The latter is conceived as a hierarchy of different layers, of which the *Ontology Layer* is currently the highest layer of sufficient maturity, as evidenced by the W3C recommended *Web Ontology Language* (*OWL*) [21,13]. OWL has three increasingly expressive sublanguages, namely *OWL Lite*, *OWL DL*, and *OWL Full*. As shown in [12], the logical underpinnings of the former two is provided by the description logics $\mathcal{SHIF}(\mathbf{D})$ and $\mathcal{SHOIN}(\mathbf{D})$, respectively.

The further steps in the development of the Semantic Web are realizing the *Rules*, *Logic*, and *Proof Layers* on top of the Ontology layer, which should offer sophisticated representation and reasoning capabilities. This requests, in particular, the need to integrate the Rules and the Ontology layer.

Towards this goal, several approaches for combining description logics with rule-based languages have been proposed recently [5,16,17,1,6,7,22]. Among them are *description logic programs*, or *dl-programs* for short, presented in [6,7] as a novel method

---
* This work was partially supported by the Austrian Science Fund under grant P17212-N04, and by the European Commission through the IST REWERSE Network of Excellence (IST-506779) and the IST Working Group in Answer Set Programming (IST 2001-37004 WASP).

to couple description logics with nonmonotonic logic programs. Roughly speaking, a dl-program consists of a knowledge base L in a description logic and a finite set P of generalized logic-program rules, called *dl-rules*. These are similar to usual rules in logic programs with negation as failure, but they may also contain *queries to L* in their bodies. Importantly, such queries also allow for specifying an input from P to L, and thus for a *bidirectional flow of information between P and L*. Consequently, dl-programs allow for building rules on top of ontologies, but also, to some extent, building ontologies on top of rules.

By virtue of their design, dl-programs fully support encapsulation and privacy of the description logic knowledge base, in the sense that logic programming and description logic inference are technically separated and only interfacing details need to be known. The description-logic knowledge bases in dl-programs are theories in the description logics $\mathcal{SHIF}(\mathbf{D})$ and $\mathcal{SHOIN}(\mathbf{D})$. However, the framework can be easily extended to other description logics as well.

Two basic types of semantics have been defined for dl-programs: in [6], a generalization of the answer-set semantics [10] for ordinary logic programs is given, and in [7], a generalization of the well-founded semantics [19,2]. In fact, two versions of the answer-set semantics for dl-programs are introduced in [6], namely the *weak answer-set semantics* and the *strong answer-set semantics*. Every strong answer set is also a weak answer set, but not vice versa. The two notions differ in the way they deal with *nonmonotonic dl-queries*. We recall that the answer-set semantics and the well-founded semantics are the two predominant semantics for nonmonotonic logic programs.

In this paper, we consider technical issues regarding an efficient implementation of the answer-set and the well-founded semantics for dl-programs, which has been realized in a working prototype exploiting the two state-of-the-art solvers DLV [15] and RACER [11]. A major issue in this respect is an efficient interfacing between the two reasoning systems at hand, for which we devised special methods.

The main contributions of this paper can be summarized as follows:

- We give novel methods and algorithms for computing answer sets and the well-founded semantics of dl-programs. Starting from a simple guess-and-check algorithm for weak answer sets, we devise more efficient techniques which prune the number of guesses and reduce the effort for dl-query evaluation.
- As a first improvement over the naive guess-and-check method, we discuss the case of *stratified dl-programs*, which, as follows from one of our results, can be evaluated without explicitly using or even knowing some stratification, at the ground or non-ground level, with a standard answer-set solver.
- We devise special optimization techniques in order to avoid redundant computations. To wit, we discuss a method to avoid multiple ground program generation, as well as special methods to reduce the number of calls to the description logic engine. The latter techniques involve, on the one hand, an exploitation of function calls to the description logic reasoner using non-ground queries, and, on the other hand, special caching data structures tailored for fast access to previous query calls. Also, hierarchic structures of the dependency graph can be taken into account for evaluating unstratified dl-programs.
- The well-founded semantics is computed through an iterative procedure in terms of the greatest and the least fixpoint of a monotonic operator. Techniques devised for the answer-set semantics can be fruitfully applied here as well for improving

the evaluation. Moreover, the computation of answer sets can be optimized with the help of a prior computation of the well-founded semantics, by introducing suitable constraints.
– We implemented the above algorithms and optimization techniques in a working prototype, both for computing the answer-set semantics as well as the well-founded semantics, and performed experiments on a suite of benchmark problems. Our experimental results show that the optimization techniques can drastically improve the performance of dl-programs over incremental grades of optimization.

Note that most of our methods and results are at an abstract level, and thus may also be exploited for implementing similar computational-logic systems based on coupling.

2 Background

In this section, we recall syntax and semantics of description logic programs, introduced in [6,7]. In what follows, we assume a function-free first-order vocabulary, Φ, with nonempty finite sets of constant and predicate symbols, and a set $\mathcal{X}$ of variables. As usual, a *classical literal* (or *literal*), l, is an atom a or a negated atom $\neg a$.

2.1 $\mathcal{SHIF}(\mathbf{D})$ and $\mathcal{SHOIN}(\mathbf{D})$

Intuitively, description logics allow for expressing knowledge about concepts, roles, and individuals in a (possibly extended) first-order logic (with concepts and roles being unary and binary predicates $C(a)$ and $R(a,b)$, respectively) using a special syntax. Since for the purpose of this paper we mainly interface description logics through queries, we omit definitions of $\mathcal{SHIF}(\mathbf{D})$ and $\mathcal{SHOIN}(\mathbf{D})$ at this point and refer to Appendix A (or, alternatively, to [12,6]) for more details.

A ($\mathcal{SHIF}(\mathbf{D})$ resp. $\mathcal{SHOIN}(\mathbf{D})$) description logic *knowledge base* L is a finite set of axioms in the respective description logic. We denote logical consequence of an axiom α from L, which is defined as usual, by $L \models \alpha$.

2.2 Description Logic Programs

Informally, a description logic program consists of a description logic knowledge base L and a generalized normal program P which may contain queries to L. Roughly, in such a query, it is asked whether a certain description logic axiom or its negation logically follows from L or not. For details, we refer to [6,7].

Syntax. We first define dl-queries and dl-atoms, which are used to access the description logic knowledge base. A *dl-query*, $Q(\mathbf{t})$, is either (a) a concept inclusion axiom $C \sqsubseteq D$ or its negation $\neg(C \sqsubseteq D)$, or (b) of the form $C(t)$ or $\neg C(t)$, where C is a concept and t is a term, or (c) of the form $R(t_1, t_2)$ or $\neg R(t_1, t_2)$, where R is a role and t_1, t_2 are terms.[1]

---
[1] Note that $\mathcal{SHOIN}(\mathbf{D})$ does not provide terminological role negation; we use the expression $\neg(\exists R.\{b\})(a)$ in order to add and query $\neg R(a, b)$ for a specific pair of individuals.

A *dl-atom* has the form

$$DL[S_1 op_1 p_1, \ldots, S_m op_m p_m; Q](\mathbf{t}), \qquad m \geq 0, \tag{1}$$

where each S_i is either a concept or a role, $op_i \in \{⊎, ⋓, ⋒\}$, p_i is a unary resp. binary predicate symbol, and $Q(\mathbf{t})$ is a dl-query. We call $p_1, \ldots, p_m$ its *input predicate symbols*. Intuitively, $op_i = ⊎$ (resp., $op_i = ⋓$) increases S_i (resp., $\neg S_i$) by the extension of p_i, while $op_i = ⋒$ constrains S_i to p_i.

Example 21 The dl-atom $DL[buying ⊎ buy\_cand, buying ⊎ contract; Discount](V)$ queries for all individuals of the concept $Discount$ after adding the extensions of both buy_cand and $contract$ to the role $buying$.

A *dl-rule*, r, is an expression of the form,

$$a \leftarrow b_1, \ldots, b_k, \text{not } b_{k+1}, \ldots, \text{not } b_m, \quad m \geq k \geq 0, \tag{2}$$

where a is a literal and $b_1, \ldots, b_m$ are either literals or dl-atoms. The symbol "*not*" stands for *weak negation*, also called *negation as failure* (NAF). We refer to a as the *head* of r, denoted $H(r)$, and to the part right of "$\leftarrow$" as the *body* of r. Its *positive part* is $b_1, \ldots, b_k$, and its *negative part* is $\text{not } b_{k+1}, \ldots, \text{not } b_m$. Furthermore, we define $B(r) = B^+(r) \cup B^-(r)$, where $B^+(r) = \{b_1, \ldots, b_k\}$ and $B^-(r) = \{b_{k+1}, \ldots, b_m\}$.

A dl-rule is *ordinary*, if it contains no dl-atom. An ordinary program is a finite set of ordinary rules. A *description logic program*, or *dl-program*, $KB = (L, P)$, consists of a description logic knowledge base L and a finite set of dl-rules P.

Semantics. We first recapitulate the strong and weak answer-set semantics for dl-programs [6], and then the well-founded semantics for dl-programs [7]. They generalize the familiar answer-set semantics [10] and well-founded semantics [19] for ordinary programs, respectively, which are the predominant semantics for nonmonotonic logic programs.

We need some auxiliary notions. In what follows, let $KB = (L, P)$ be a dl-program. The *Herbrand base* of P, denoted HB_P, is the set of all ground literals with a standard predicate symbol that occurs in P and constant symbols in Φ, where Φ is assumed to contain (a subset of) the constant symbols from L. An *interpretation* I relative to P is a consistent subset of HB_P. Such an I is a *model* of $l \in HB_P$ under L, denoted $I \models_L l$, iff $l \in I$, and a *model* of a ground dl-atom $a = DL[S_1 op_1 p_1, \ldots, S_m op_m p_m; Q](\mathbf{c})$ under L, denoted $I \models_L a$, iff $L \cup \bigcup_{i=1}^m A_i(I) \models Q(\mathbf{c})$, where

- $A_i(I) = \{S_i(\mathbf{e}) \mid p_i(\mathbf{e}) \in I\}$, for $op_i = ⊎$,
- $A_i(I) = \{\neg S_i(\mathbf{e}) \mid p_i(\mathbf{e}) \in I\}$, for $op_i = ⋓$, and
- $A_i(I) = \{\neg S_i(\mathbf{e}) \mid p_i(\mathbf{e}) \in I \text{ does not hold}\}$, for $op_i = ⋒$.

I is a *model* of a ground dl-rule r iff $I \models_L H(r)$ whenever both $I \models_L l$ for all $l \in B^+(r)$ and $I \not\models_L l$ for all $l \in B^-(r)$. I is a model of a dl-program $KB = (L, P)$, or I *satisfies* KB, denoted $I \models KB$, iff $I \models_L r$ for all r in the grounding, $grd(P)$, of P. We say that KB is *satisfiable* if it has some model, otherwise KB is *unsatisfiable*.

A ground dl-atom a is *monotonic* relative to $KB = (L, P)$, providing $I \models_L a$ implies $I' \models_L a$, for $I \subseteq I' \subseteq HB_P$. A dl-program $KB = (L, P)$ is *positive*, if (i) P is *not*-free and (ii) every ground dl-atom occurring in $grd(P)$ is monotonic relative to KB.

Observe that while dl-atoms containing only $\uplus$ and $\cup$ are always monotonic, a dl-atom containing $\cap$ may fail to be monotonic, since an increasing set of $p_i(\mathbf{e})$ in P results in a reduction of $\neg S_i(\mathbf{e})$ in L.

We are now in the position to define the answer-set semantics for dl-programs. For any dl-program $KB = (L, P)$, we denote by DL_P the set of all ground dl-atoms that occur in $ground(P)$. We assume in the following that KB has an associated set $DL_P^+ \subseteq DL_P$ of ground dl-atoms which are known to be monotonic, and we denote by $DL_P^? = DL_P - DL_P^+$ the set of all other dl-atoms. An *input literal* of $a \in DL_P$ is a ground literal with an input predicate of a and constant symbols in Φ.

Strong answer sets. The *strong dl-transform* of P relative to L and an interpretation $I \subseteq HB_P$, denoted sP_L^I, is the set of all dl-rules obtained from its grounding $grd(P)$ with respect to Φ by (i) deleting every dl-rule r such that either $I \not\models_L a$ for some $a \in B^+(r) \cap DL_P^?$, or $I \models_L l$ for some $l \in B^-(r)$, and (ii) deleting from each remaining dl-rule r all literals in $B^-(r) \cup (B^+(r) \cap DL_P^?)$.

Notice that (L, sP_L^I) is a positive dl-program, which, as shown in [6], has a least model if it is satisfiable. We call $I \subseteq HB_P$ a *strong answer set* of KB iff it is the least model of (L, sP_L^I).

Weak answer sets. Weak answer sets are like strong answer sets if monotonicity of all dl-atoms is unknown resp. ignored (i.e., technically, if $DL_P^? = DL_P$). In the respective *weak dl-transform*, wP_L^I, of P relative to L and $I \subseteq HB_P$, all dl-atoms are removed from $grd(P)$. A *weak answer set* of KB, then, is an interpretation $I \subseteq HB_P$ such that I is the least model of the ordinary positive program wP_L^I. Note that strong answer sets of KB are weak answer sets of KB, but not vice versa in general.

For any *not*-free dl-program P, both the strong reduct as well as the weak reduct coincide with the usual Gelfond-Lifschitz reduct [10], and thus the strong and weak answer sets of $KB = (L, P)$ coincide with the standard answer sets of P.

Well-founded Semantics (WFS). The WFS is defined in [7] for dl-programs KB without classical negation and where all dl-atoms are monotonic. The former is no real restriction but the latter a technical necessity. In practice, most dl-atoms are monotonic.

The WFS in [7] generalizes the classical WFS [19] by suitably generalizing the notion of an *unfounded set* as in [19] to the setting of dl-atoms as follows. Let, for any set S of literals, $\neg.S$ be the set of the opposite literals of S. A set $U \subseteq HB_P$ is an *unfounded set* of $KB = (L, P)$ relative to a consistent set I of ground literals, if for every $a \in U$ and every $r \in grd(P)$ with $H(r) = a$, either (i) $\neg b \in I \cup \neg.U$ for some ordinary atom $b \in B^+(r)$, or (ii) $b \in I$ for some ordinary atom $b \in B^-(r)$, or (iii) for some dl-atom $b \in B^+(r)$, $S^+ \not\models_L b$ for every consistent set S of ground literals with $I \cup \neg.U \subseteq S$, or (iv) $I^+ \models_L b$ for some dl-atom $b \in B^-(r)$.

Compared to [19], Conditions (iii) and (iv) are novel. The WFS is then defined in [7] like in [19] as the least fixpoint of a monotonic operator $W_{KB}(I)$ (this is feasible since the greatest unfounded set of I always exists); for computation purposes, an alternative characterization, discussed in Section 3.6, is more advantageous.

If P does not contain any dl-atoms, then the well-founded semantics for $KB = (L, P)$ coincides with the well-founded semantics for P in the sense of [19].

Stratified Semantics. The notion of *stratification* for dl-programs [6] is similar as for ordinary programs. Roughly speaking, stratified dl-programs are composed of hierarchic layers of positive dl-programs that are linked via default negation (for a formal definition, we refer the reader to [6]). As discussed in [7], if $KB = (L, P)$ is positive or stratified, then it has a single strong answer set, which coincides with $WFS(KB) \cap HB_P$.

Example 22 A computer shop obtains its hardware from several vendors. It uses a knowledge base L_1 (see Appendix B), which contains information about the product range that is provided by each vendor (property *provides*) and about possible rebate conditions (concept *Discount*, depending on property *buying*; here we assume that buying two or more parts from the same seller causes a discount). To evaluate possible combinations of purchases, the following program P_1 is specified:

(1) $vendor(s_1); \; vendor(s_5); \; vendor(s_9);$
(2) $needed(cpu); \; needed(harddisk); \; needed(case);$
(3) $contract(s_9, case);$
(4) $avoid(V) \leftarrow vendor(V), not\, rebate(V);$
(5) $rebate(V) \leftarrow vendor(V), DL[buying \uplus buy\_cand, buying \uplus contract; Discount](V);$
(6) $buy\_cand(V, P) \leftarrow vendor(V), not\, avoid(V), DL[provides](V, P), needed(P),$
      $not\, exclude(P)$
(7) $exclude(P) \leftarrow buy\_cand(V_1, P), buy\_cand(V_2, P), V_1 \neq V_2;$
(8) $exclude(P) \leftarrow contract(V, P), needed(P);$
(9) $supplied(V, P) \leftarrow DL[buying \uplus buy\_cand, buying \uplus contract; buying](V, P),$
      $needed(P).$

Rules (1)–(3) state the considered vendors as well as the needed parts; for some parts, a vendor may already be contracted as supplier. Rules (4)–(6) choose a possible vendor (*buy_cand*) for each needed part, taking into account that the selection might affect the rebate condition (by feeding the possible vendor back to L_1, where the discount is determined). Rules (7) and (8) assure that each hardware part is bought only once, considering that for some parts a supplier might already be chosen. Rule (9) eventually summarizes all purchasing results. Evaluating this program under the strong answer-set semantics yields the following answer sets (quoting only the relevant atoms):

$\{supplied(s_9, case); supplied(s_5, cpu); supplied(s_5, harddisk); rebate(s_5); \ldots\};$
$\{supplied(s_9, case); supplied(s_9, harddisk); rebate(s_9); \ldots\};$
$\{supplied(s_9, case); \ldots\}.$

For more details, discussion, and examples, see [6,7].

3 Implementing dl-Programs

In this section, we consider methods for computing dl-programs by using an answer-set solver on the one hand and a description logic (DL) engine on the other. We start with a simple method, and then present progressively methods to increase the efficiency.

3.1 Naive Computation of Weak Answer Sets

The computation of the weak answer sets of a given dl-program $KB = (L, P)$ can be encoded by ordinary logic programs under the answer-set semantics, following a generate and test approach, as follows:

1. Let P_d be the ordinary logic program having each dl-atom $a(\mathbf{t})$ occurring in Γ replaced by the atom $d_a(\mathbf{t})$ (we call this kind of atoms *replacement atoms*), where d_a is a fresh predicate symbol.
2. Add to P_d from Step 1 for each replacement atom $d_a(\mathbf{t})$ all rules

$$d_a(\mathbf{c}) \leftarrow not \, \neg d_a(\mathbf{c}) \quad \text{and} \quad \neg d_a(\mathbf{c}) \leftarrow not \, d_a(\mathbf{c}) \tag{3}$$

such that $a(\mathbf{c})$ is a ground instance of dl-atom $a(\mathbf{t})$. Intuitively, the rules (3) "guess" the truth values of the dl-atoms of P.[2] Denote the resulting program by P_{guess}.
3. Compute the answer sets $Ans = \{M_1, \ldots, M_n\}$ of P_{guess}.
4. For each answer set $M \in Ans$ of P_{guess}, test whether the original "guess" of the value of $d_a(\mathbf{c})$ is compliant with L. That is, for each dl-atom a of form (1), check whether $d_a(\mathbf{c}) \in M$ iff $M \models_L a$, i.e., $L \cup \bigcup_{i=1}^{m} A_i(M) \models Q(\mathbf{c})$. If this condition holds (and only if), then $M \cap HB_P$ is a weak answer set of P.

If only one answer set is desired, the algorithm may stop after the first one is found.
While simple and elegant, this method becomes quickly infeasible. If the number of ground dl-atoms grows, the number of candidate answer sets generated may become very large, and Ans may occupy a lot of space. It is more efficient to interleave Steps 3 and 4 and to test each candidate answer set M_i immediately upon its generation. Still, a lot of effort may be spent for evaluating dl-atoms. Efficient implementations try to prune the number of guesses, and to reduce the effort for dl-atom evaluation.

3.2 Stratified dl-Programs

In case of a stratified dl-program $KB = (L, P)$, the guessing of the outcome of dl-atoms can be avoided entirely. In the presence of monotonic dl-atoms only, a simple method for computing the (unique) strong answer set of KB is given by a fixpoint iteration of the operator $\Lambda_{KB} : 2^{HB_P} \to 2^{HB_P}$, defined by $\Lambda_{KB}(I) = M(P_d \cup D_P(I)) \cap HB_P$, where:

- P_d is as in Step 1 of the naive computation above;
- $D_P(I)$ is the set of all facts $d_a(\mathbf{c}) \leftarrow$ such that $I \models_L a(\mathbf{c})$; and
- $M(P_d \cup D_P(I))$ is the single answer set of $P_d \cup D_P(I)$; since P_d is stratified, this answer set is guaranteed to exist and to be unique.

For the sequence of powers $I_{KB}^0 = \emptyset$, $I_{KB}^{i+1} = \Lambda_{KB}^{i+1}(\emptyset) = \Lambda_{KB}(I_{KB}^i)$, $i \geq 0$, we then have:

Lemma 1. *For each stratified KB, the sequence I_{KB}^i, $i \geq 0$, converges, and its limit I_{KB}^∞ coincides with the strong answer set of KB.*

---

[2] Note that, when using the system DLV, rules (3) can equivalently be replaced by the disjunctive facts $d_a(\mathbf{c}) \vee \neg d_a(\mathbf{c}) \leftarrow$.

Notice that Λ_{KB} is neither monotonic nor anti-monotonic, and that the sequence I_{KB}^i, $i \geq 0$, is not a chain. The proof of convergence is along a stratification.

In view of this lemma, we can evaluate a stratified dl-program very easily *without explicitly using or even knowing some stratification, at the ground or non-ground level*, with a standard answer-set solver (which is used to compute $M(P_d \cup D_P(I))$) and multiple calls to a DL reasoner (for deciding $I \models_L a(\mathbf{c})$ when it is needed to add facts $d_a(\mathbf{c})$ to $D_P(I)$), in a simple loop.

In fact, the above method is applicable beyond stratified dl-programs. Let us call a program P *dl-stratified*, if in the usual dependency graph G of $grd(P_d \cup DLI(P))$, where $DLI(P)$ consists of all rules $d_a(\mathbf{X}) \leftarrow p_i(\mathbf{Y})$, $i \in \{1, \ldots, m\}$, for each dl-atom a of form (1) occurring in P, no replacement atom $d_a(\mathbf{c})$ is reachable from a cycle having negative arcs.

The class of dl-stratified dl-programs is still rich in the sense that it features nondeterminism for problem solving, where ontologies can be accessed in portions of the program that computes information in a stratified layer (possibly through positive recursion, e.g., by taking transitive closure).

Let us call an answer-set solver *deterministic*, if it returns for any input program P on each call always the same result; i.e., if multiple answer sets exist, a "canonical" answer set $can(P)$ will be output. Then the following holds:

Proposition 1. *Given a deterministic answer-set solver, for each dl-stratified KB, the sequence I_{KB}^i, $i \geq 0$, (where $can(P_d(I))$ replaces $M(P_d(I))$ in Λ_{KB}) converges, and its limit I_{KB}^∞ is a strong answer set of KB.*

Since in dl-stratified programs terminological knowledge is involved only in a stratified portion of the program, it can be dealt with a quick preprocessing (cf. Section 3.5) by easy means. We thus can solve a very relevant class of unstratified dl-programs through the above technique.

Intuitively, assuming the given program has a stratification $\lambda = \{KB_0, \ldots, KB_n\}$, a disadvantage of this simple method is the effort spent for evaluating dl-atoms in higher levels KB_i of the stratification in the early stages of the fixpoint iteration, where the input from lower levels has not converged yet. This effort can be saved by proceeding along λ and computing $\Lambda_{KB_0}, \ldots, \Lambda_{KB_n}$, for the associated strata $KB_0, \ldots KB_n$, at the cost of pre-computing λ. This may pay off in general, given that the entailment to dl-atoms is costly.

Furthermore, it turns out that both the answer-set solver and the DL engine are invoked repeatedly, so that it is very important to avoid redundant computations. Thus, two more additional optimization techniques are fruitful, namely ground program re-using, and dl-atom caching and intelligent evaluation, discussed next.

3.3 Avoiding Multiple Ground Program Generation

The above method relies on the evaluation of a collection of ordinary logic programs $P_d \cup D(I_{KB}^j)$ starting from $I_{KB}^0 = \emptyset$. The programs of this sequence are very similar: indeed, for any I_{KB}^j and $I_{KB}^{j'}$, the programs $P_d \cup D(I_{KB}^j)$ and $P_d \cup D(I_{KB}^{j'})$ differ only in the set of facts $d_a(\mathbf{c})$ such that $I_{KB}^j \models_L a(\mathbf{c})$ is different from $I_{KB}^{j'} \models_L a(\mathbf{c})$, and so, their ground versions are very similar.

Indeed, it is possible to compute and store $grd(P_d)$ only once, and then, for any interpretation I, compute $M(grd(P_d) \cup D(I))$ whenever necessary.

This method can be enhanced by considering that answer-set programming systems, like DLV, allow to obtain significantly smaller versions of ground programs, where only meaningful rules are kept; in particular, such grounding systems compute only those ground rules which can be grounded not with respect to the whole Herbrand base HB_P but with respect to a notion of "active" domain of the rules (for more technical details, see [8]). Let $ogrd(P)$ denote the optimized ground version of a program P. For space reasons, we cannot describe this operator in detail, but we observe that, in general, for a given I, $ogrd(P_d \cup D(I)) \neq ogrd(P_d) \cup ogrd(D(I))$, whereas for the usual grounding of $P_d \cup D(I)$ with respect to Φ it holds that $grd(P_d \cup D(I)) = grd(P_d) \cup grd(D(I))$.

This latter property prevents, in principle, to have any benefit in computing and storing $ogrd(P_d)$ instead of $grd(P_d)$. Nonetheless, we can prove that there exists an optimized version $ogrd^*(P_d)$ of $grd(P_d)$, such that it holds that $M(ogrd^*(P_d) \cup D(I)) = M(grd(P_d) \cup D(I))$, for each I, and $ogrd^*(P_d) \subseteq grd(P_d)$. Details of this optimization technique are somehow intricate, so we give only an intuition on how it is carried out for not-free programs.

Given a rule $r \in P_d$, we consider a replacement atom $d_a(\mathbf{t})$ *safe*, if each variable $X \in \mathbf{t}$ appears at least once in some non-replacement atom in the body of r. The program $ogrd^*(P_d)$ is obtained as follows:

1. Build a program P'_d from P_d by removing from every rule $r \in P_d$ each replacement atom $d_a(\mathbf{t})$. In case this atom is not safe, we add in the body of r a predicate $dom(X)$ for each variable $X \in \mathbf{t}$ witnessing unsafety. Furthermore, we add to P'_d a rule r' with head $d_a(\mathbf{t})$ and body consisting of the ordinary body atoms of r, plus an atom $dom(X)$ for each variable $X \in \mathbf{t}$.
2. Add to P'_d a fact $dom(a) \leftarrow$ for each $a \in HB_P$.
3. Let $\bar{D}$ be the set $\{d_a(\mathbf{c}) \leftarrow \mid d_a(\mathbf{c}) \in M(P'_d)\}$.[3]
4. Define $ogrd^*(P_d) = ogrd(P_d \cup \bar{D}) - \bar{D}$.

Intuitively, in Step 1, we create an envelope for the least model of $P_d \cup D(I)$ on the original predicates, which then allows to limit the set of ground dl-atoms $a(\mathbf{c})$, potentially relevant for evaluating P, to those such that $d_a(\mathbf{c})$ is true in the least model of P'_d. For programs with not, we can proceed similarly discarding in Step 1 all not literals.

3.4 Efficient dl-Atom Evaluation and Caching

Since the calls to the DL reasoner are a bottleneck in the coupling of an ASP solver with a DL engine, special methods need to be devised in order to save on the number of calls to the DL engine. To this end, we use complementary techniques.

DL-Function Calls. One of the features of DL reasoners which may be fruitfully exploited for speed up are non-ground queries. RACER provides the possibility to retrieve in a function call all instances of a concept C (resp., of a role R) that are provable in the DL knowledge base. Given that the cost for accessing the DL reasoner is high, in

---
[3] In order to prevent DLV from optimized unfolding cancelling out significant rules, some other specialized rules are added.

the case when several different ground instances $a(\mathbf{c}_1), a(\mathbf{c}_2), \ldots, a(\mathbf{c}_k)$ of the dl-atom $a(\mathbf{t})$ have be evaluated, it is a reasonable strategy to retrieve at once, using the apposite function call feature from the DL reasoner, all instances of the concept C (resp., a role R) in $a(\mathbf{t}) = DL[S_1 op_1 p_1, \ldots; C](\mathbf{t})$. This allows to avoid issuing k separate calls for the single ground atoms $a(\mathbf{c}_1), \ldots, a(\mathbf{c}_k)$.

If the retrieval set has presumably many more than k elements, we can filter it with respect to $\mathbf{c}_1, \ldots, \mathbf{c}_k$, by pushing these instances to a DL engine as follows. For the query concept C, we add in L axioms to the effect that $C'' = C \sqcap C'$, where C' and C'' are fresh concept names, and axioms $C'(\mathbf{c}_1), \ldots, C'(\mathbf{c}_k)$; then we ask for all instances of C''. For roles, a similar yet more involved approximation method is introduced, given that $\mathcal{SHIF}(\mathbf{D})$ and $\mathcal{SHOIN}(\mathbf{D})$ do not offer role intersection.

With the above techniques, the number of calls to the DL reasoner can be greatly reduced. Another very useful technique to achieve this goal is caching.

DL-Caching. Whatever semantics is considered, a number of calls will be made to the DL engine. Therefore, it is is very important to avoid an unnecessary flow of data between the two engines, and to save time when a redundant DL query has to be made. In order to achieve these objectives, it is important to introduce some special caching data structures tailored for fast access to previous query calls. Such a caching system needs to deal with the case of Boolean as well as non-Boolean DL-calls.

For any dl-atom $DL[\lambda; Q](\mathbf{t})$, where λ is a list $S_1 op_1 p_1, \ldots, S_n op_n p_n$, and interpretation I, let us denote by I^λ the projection of I on $p_1, \ldots, p_n$.

Boolean DL-calls. In this case, an external call must be issued in order to verify whether a given ground dl-atom b fulfills $I \models_L b$, where I is the current interpretation and L is the DL knowledge base hosted by the DL engine. In this setting, the caching system exploits properties of monotonic dl-atoms $a = DL[\lambda; Q](\mathbf{c})$.

Given two interpretations I_1 and I_2 such that $I_1 \subseteq I_2$, monotonicity of a implies that (i) if $I_1 \models_L a$ then $I_2 \models_L a$, and (ii) if $I_2 \not\models_L a$ then $I_1 \not\models_L a$. This property allows to set up a caching machinery where only the outcome for ground dl-atoms with minimal/maximal input is stored.

Roughly speaking, for each monotonic ground dl-atom a we store a set $cache(a)$ of pairs $\langle I^\lambda, o \rangle$, where $o \in \{true, undefined\}$. If $\langle I^\lambda, true \rangle \in cache(a)$, then we can conclude that $J \models_L a$ for each J such that $I^\lambda \subseteq J^\lambda$. Dually, if $\langle I^\lambda, undefined \rangle \in cache(a)$, we can conclude that $J \not\models_L a$ for each J such that $I^\lambda \supseteq J^\lambda$.

We sketch the maintenance strategy for $cache(a)$ in the following. The rationale is to cache minimal (resp., maximal) input sets I^λ for which a is evaluated to $true$ (resp., $undefined$) in past external calls.

Suppose a ground dl-atom $a = DL[\lambda; Q](\mathbf{c})$, an interpretation I, and a cache set $cache(a)$ are given. With a small abuse of notation, let $I(a)$ be a function whose value is $true$ iff $I \models_L a$ and $undefined$ otherwise. In order to check whether $I \models_L a$, $cache(a)$ is consulted and updated as follows:

1. Check whether $cache(a)$ contains some $\langle J, o \rangle$ such that $J \subseteq I^\lambda$ if $o = true$, or $J \supseteq I^\lambda$ if $o = undefined$. If such J exists, conclude that $I(a) = o$.
2. If no such J exists, then decide $I \models_L a$ through the external DL engine. If $I \models_L a$, then add $\langle I^\lambda, true \rangle$ to $cache(a)$, and remove from it each pair $\langle J, true \rangle$ such that

$I^\lambda \subset J$. Otherwise (i.e., if $I \not\models_L a$) add $\langle I^\lambda, \mathit{undefined}\rangle$ to $\mathit{cache}(a)$ and remove from it each pair $\langle J, \mathit{undefined}\rangle$ such that $I^\lambda \supset J$.

Some other implementational issues are worth mentioning. First of all, since the subsumption test between sets of atoms is a critical task, some optimization is made in order to improve cache look-up. For instance, an element count is stored for each atom set, in order to prove early that $I \not\subseteq J$ whenever $|I| > |J|$. More intelligent strategies could be envisaged in this respect. Furthermore, a standard *least recently used* (LRU) algorithm has been introduced in order to keep a fixed cache size.

Non-Boolean DL-calls. In most cases, a single non-ground query for retrieving all instances of a concept or role might be employed. Caching of such queries is also possible, but cache look-up cannot take advantage of monotonicity as in the Boolean case. For each non-ground dl-atom $a = DL[\lambda; Q](\mathbf{c})$, a set $\mathit{cache}(a)$ of pairs $\langle I^\lambda, a\!\downarrow\!(I^\lambda)\rangle$ is maintained, where $a\!\downarrow\!(I)$ is the set of all ground instances a' of a such that $I \models_L a'$. Whenever for some interpretation I, $a\!\downarrow\!(I)$ is needed, then $\mathit{cache}(a)$ is looked up for some pair $\langle J, a\!\downarrow\!(J)\rangle$ such that $I^\lambda = J$.

3.5 Unstratified dl-Programs

When looking at the corresponding dependency graph, it often occurs in practice that answer-set programs are structured in three separate and hierarchic layers:

- a first, stratified layer at the bottom which performs some preprocessing on the input data;
- a second, strongly connected and unstratified layer, usually aimed at encoding some nondeterministic choice, and, eventually,
- a third "checking" layer on top, where values computed through the other layers are filtered with respect to some constraint criteria.

Following this common setting, we conceived an evaluation strategy where each component is evaluated sequentially and results are fed from one layer to another. This way, the bottom layer is computed exploiting techniques from Subsection 3.2. General techniques are strictly limited to situations in which this cannot be avoided, as in non-stratified layers.

3.6 Implementing the Well-Founded Semantics

An implementation of WFS for KB by fixpoint iteration of the defining monotonic operator $W_{KB}(I)$ as in [7] is not attractive, since a polynomial-time algorithm for computing the greatest unfounded set of KB with respect to I, due to Condition (iii) of an unfounded set, is not evident (even if deciding $I \models_L l$ is polynomial).

As shown in [7], the WFS for KB, denoted $WFS(KB)$, is alternatively given by

$$WFS(KB) = \mathit{lfp}(\gamma^2_{KB}) \cup \{\neg a \mid a \in HB_P - \mathit{gfp}(\gamma^2_{KB})\},$$

where the operator $\gamma_{KB}(I)$ assigns each interpretation $I \subseteq HB_P$ the least model M_{KB^I} of the strong reduct $KB^I = (L, sP^I_L)$. Since γ_{KB} is anti-monotonic, γ^2_{KB} is monotonic and thus has a least and greatest fixpoint, $\mathit{lfp}(\gamma^2_{KB})$ and $\mathit{gfp}(\gamma^2_{KB})$, respectively.

This way, $WFS(KB)$ is computable through a fixpoint iteration which computes and outputs the greatest and the least fixpoint of the γ_{KB}^2 operator, starting from $\emptyset$ resp. HB_P (which may be represented by its complement). Since KB^I is a positive dl-program, machinery developed in Section 3.2 for computing M_{KB^I} is very helpful in this respect. Caching also proves to be very fruitful.

3.7 Enhancing Answer-Set Generation with Well-Founded Semantics

Another interesting result from [7] allows to speed up the computation of the answer sets of a given $KB = (P, L)$ by means of a pre-evaluation of $WFS(KB)$:

Theorem 31 *Every strong answer set of a dl-program $KB = (L, P)$ includes $lfp(\gamma_{KB}^2)$ and no atom $a \in HB_P - gfp(\gamma_{KB}^2)$.*

For computing answer sets, we can exploit the possibility to introduce *constraints* to a DLV program [15]. Constraints allow to filter out models which do not fulfill prescribed requirements. An intermediate ordinary program P' obtained from P can be then enriched with the constraint $\leftarrow not\ a$ for any atom a such that $a \in WFS(KB)$, and with a constraint $\leftarrow a$ for any atom a such that $\neg a \in WFS(KB)$. Notice that such constraints may also be added only for a subset of $WFS(KB)$ (e.g., the one obtained after some steps in the least resp. greatest fixpoint iteration of γ_{KB}^2). This technique proves to be useful for helping the answer-set programming solver to converge to solutions faster.

4 System Prototype

The architecture of our system prototype is depicted in Figure 1. The system comprises six modules: the two external engines DLV and RACER, the latter embedded into a caching module, a WFS module, an answer-set semantics module, as well as a preprocessing and a postprocessing module. Each internal module is coded in the PHP scripting language; the overhead is insignificant, provided that most of the computing power is devoted to the execution of the two external reasoners.

Our prototypical implementation is capable of evaluating a dl-program in three different modes: (1) under answer-set semantics, (2) under WFS, and (3) under answer-set semantics with preliminary computation of the WFS.

In Mode (1), the answer-set semantics is computed through a preprocessing step, aimed at computing all those dl-atoms which do not depend from the program P itself. Then, an ordinary program P_d is generated whose models $M_1, \ldots, M_n$ are checked and filtered through several consistency checks performed by querying the RACER engine in an interleaved fashion. The stratified bottom portion of P_d is evaluated iteratively as in Subsection 3.2. Eventually, the system outputs a list of answer sets $M_{k_1}, \ldots, M_{k_m}$.

In Mode (2), we compute the well-founded semantics of a program P by generating a corresponding ordinary program P_d which is grounded using the grounding module of the DLV system. This instantiation $grd(P_d)$ is fed back to the well-founded semantics module, where an iterative algorithm, calling the RACER engine several times, is carried out in order to compute the well-founded semantics of P.

In Mode (3), the answer-set semantics is computed by taking advantage of the WFS which is combined with P_d in order to get a better constrained program, as described in Section 3.7.

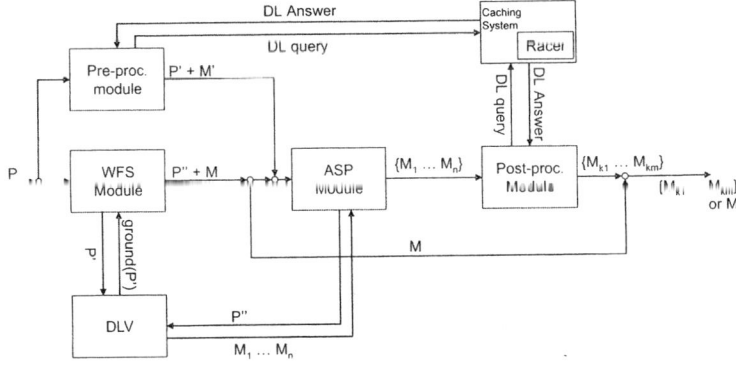

Fig. 1. System architecture of the dl-program evaluation prototype

5 Experiments

As mentioned in the previous section, we decided to exploit the scripting language PHP. Clearly, the speed and grade of optimization of PHP applications cannot be compared to ones natively compiled in a high-level programming language; however, during the development of our prototype, we realized that the major bottlenecks are the external reasoning applications. Thus, our benchmarks already show significant results with respect to different methods of integrating the external reasoners.

RACER's restriction of not allowing reasoning with nominals in concept definitions as well as its slow performance on large knowledge bases seriously limited the ability of performing realistic assertional knowledge reasoning tests with existing ontologies (e.g., the OWL wine ontology from [20]). For this reason, we decided to carry out the benchmarks with abstract, but well-scalable graph examples in addition to the already presented computer shop application.

The benchmarks were carried out on an AMD Athlon 1.2GHz CPU with 256MB RAM. We used the official DLV version of May 23th, 2004, and RACER version 1.7.23.

Positive Programs. In order to assess our evaluation strategy for positive dl-programs, we considered the computation of the transitive closure of a graph. We evaluated five graphs (taken from [18]) of different size with two different dl-programs, $KB_{LP} = (L_2, P_2)$ and $KB_{ONT} = (L_3, P_3)$, where:

$L_2 = \{arc(1, 2);\ arc(1, 4);\ \ldots\};$
$P_2 = \{tc(X, Y) \leftarrow DL[arc \uplus tc;\ arc](X, Y);\ tc(X, Y) \leftarrow DL[arc](X, Z), tc(Z, Y)\};$
$L_3 = L_2 \cup \text{Trans}(arc);$
$P_3 = \{tc(X, Y) \leftarrow DL[arc](X, Y)\}.$

Here, $\text{Trans}(arc)$ denotes the DL transitivity axiom. Figure 2 shows the results against a logarithmic time scale. We display total evaluation times for KB_{ONT} and KB_{LP} as well as the respective time needed for querying the DL engine. The logarithmic scale shows very clearly that although KB_{ONT} scales as good as KB_{LP}, it is always two orders of magnitude slower than KB_{LP}. In both cases, a significant percentage of the overall execution time is spent by RACER calls.

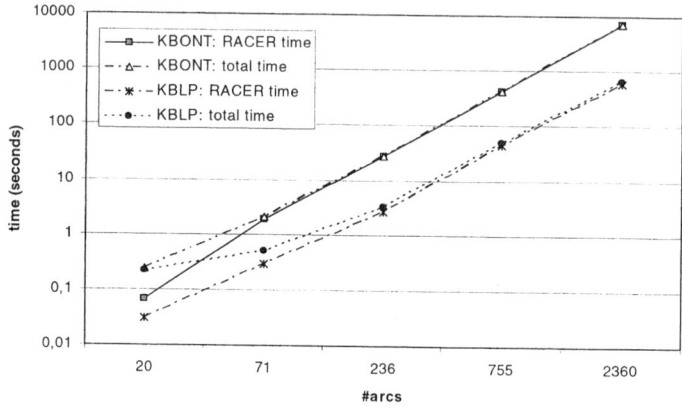

Fig. 2. Graph experiment benchmark results

The reason of feeding the extension of tc back to the DL knowledge base in L_2 is not obvious here at first sight. However, we wanted to simulate a situation where the terminological information enlarges the extension of the relation. We illustrate this with the following dl-program $KB = (L_4, P_4)$:

$L_4 = \{\exists R.\{c\} \sqsubseteq \exists R^-.\{d\};\ R(a,b);\ R(b,c)\};$
$P_4 = \{r(X,Y) \leftarrow DL[R \uplus r; R](X,Y);\ r(X,Y) \leftarrow r(X,Z), r(Z,Y)\}.$

The task of this program is to compute the transitive closure of R. In contrast to the graph example, here it is not possible to query the entire relation and compute the closure solely by rules, since the given subsumption axiom creates new tuples from existing ones, which makes it necessary to feed the inferred facts back to the DL reasoner. Unfortunately, we were not able to conduct experiments with such a scenario because RACER is not able to handle individuals in concept expressions.

Unstratified dl-Programs. Unstratified dl-programs have been assessed exploiting Example 22. The data set at hand is constituted of about 20 individuals.

The computation of this example involves evaluating the least model of the stratified part, then the answer-set validation of the entire program. Figure 3 shows the result for three different evaluation scenarios.

In the first setting, we switched off the DL engine caching module: the number of DL calls is in this case very high, and stems from the fact that (almost) each query is preceded by calls that clone and extend the knowledge base at hand with facts coming from the logic program. Since RACER does not provide other ad-hoc features, this technique proves to be effective in order to quickly augment and restore a given knowledge base.

In the second case, we switched caching on, and this saved a lot of calls to RACER. The remaining computation time, apart from DLV and RACER external calls, is consumed mainly by a loop that examines answer sets for validity with respect to the DL

	total time	DLV time	RACER time	#cache hits	#DL calls
cache off	23.83	0.82	13.65	0	11535
cache on	9.65	0.81	0.26	3786	179
cache on, WFS first	6.57	1.02	4.50	152	137
cache on, $lfp(\gamma_{KB}^2)$ first	5.82	0.61	0.11	2283	131

Fig. 3. Shop example results (time expressed in seconds)

knowledge base and also by initializing RACER. These two experiments involved the validation of 1280 answer sets, generated by the guessing mechanism for unstratified dl-atoms.

In the third setting, we did a pre-computation of the WFS of the program before the answer-set generation. The pre-evaluation of this model limits the number of possible answer sets to 24, which narrows the execution time mainly to DL-calls.

An interesting variation of this method is to calculate only the positive facts of $WFS(KB)$, i.e., $lfp(\gamma_{KB}^2)$. When this method is applied on the current example, some time-consuming calls to RACER that are involved in computing $gfp(\gamma_{KB}^2)$ are avoided. However, the overall time is only slightly less, since this subset of $WFS(KB)$ reduces the number of answer sets to be checked only to 768.

In this last experiment with the unstratified dl-program, we considered to compute only a subset of the well-founded semantics prior to the answer-set generation. Although this resulted in a reduced overall execution time, this might not apply to other programs. As we pointed out, the advantage of having less calls to the DL reasoner by omitting $gfp(\gamma_{KB}^2)$ is compensated by an increase of the answer sets that have to be checked for compliance with L. This tradeoff very much depends on the size of the assertional facts in the DL knowledge base as well as on the number of answer sets, i.e., on the specific design of the program and its stratification.

6 Conclusion

We have presented methods and algorithms for implementing nonmonotonic description logic programs. The issue of efficient interfacing between a description logic reasoner and an answer-set solver has been solved by means of several methods which can be fruitfully exploited for the implementation of systems of similar nature.

We assumed in most cases to deal with monotonic dl-atoms only. It is worth pointing out that this confinement benefits of useful nonmonotonic features in this setting as well. Our semantics provides a safe coupling between rule-based languages and description logics, since decidability is preserved. Furthermore, extending our semantics for dealing with many of the special features of answer-set programming systems (e.g., weak and integrity constraints, or aggregates) is quite straightforward.

Experimental results proved that description logics systems would benefit from this kind of coupling, since relieving a reasoner like RACER from some reasoning tasks, which such kind of systems are not aimed at, proved to be effective, also from a performance perspective. It turned out also that our system heavily relies on both reasoning systems, and would benefit from any performance improvement on both sides.

Our experimental prototype implementation, using DLV [15] and RACER [11], is available at

http://www.kr.tuwien.ac.at/staff/roman/semweblp/.

A $\mathcal{SHIF}(\mathbf{D})$ and $\mathcal{SHOIN}(\mathbf{D})$ Syntax

We briefly recall the elements of the description logics $\mathcal{SHIF}(\mathbf{D})$ and $\mathcal{SHOIN}(\mathbf{D})$, starting with the latter. We assume a set $\mathbf{D}$ of *elementary datatypes*. Every $d \in \mathbf{D}$ has a set of *data values*, called the *domain* of d, denoted $\mathrm{dom}(d)$. We use $\mathrm{dom}(\mathbf{D})$ to denote $\bigcup_{d \in \mathbf{D}} \mathrm{dom}(d)$. A *datatype* is either an element of $\mathbf{D}$ or a subset of $\mathrm{dom}(\mathbf{D})$ (called *datatype oneOf*). Let $\mathbf{A}$, $\mathbf{R}_A$, $\mathbf{R}_D$, and $\mathbf{I}$ be nonempty finite and pairwise disjoint sets of *atomic concepts*, *abstract roles*, *datatype roles*, and *individuals*, respectively. We use $\mathbf{R}_A^-$ to denote the set of all inverses R^- of abstract roles $R \in \mathbf{R}_A$.

A *role* is an element of $\mathbf{R}_A \cup \mathbf{R}_A^- \cup \mathbf{R}_D$. *Concepts* are inductively defined as follows. Every $C \in \mathbf{A}$ is a concept, and if $o_1, o_2, \ldots \in \mathbf{I}$, then $\{o_1, o_2, \ldots\}$ is a concept (called *oneOf*). If C and D are concepts and $R \in \mathbf{R}_A \cup \mathbf{R}_A^-$, then $(C \sqcap D)$, $(C \sqcup D)$, and $\neg C$ are concepts (called *conjunction*, *disjunction*, and *negation*, respectively), as well as $\exists R.C$, $\forall R.C$, $\geq nR$, and $\leq nR$ (called *exists*, *value*, *atleast*, and *atmost restriction*, respectively) for an integer $n \geq 0$. If $d \in \mathbf{D}$ and $U \in \mathbf{R}_D$, then $\exists U.d$, $\forall U.d$, $\geq nU$, and $\leq nU$ are concepts (called *datatype exists*, *value*, *atleast*, and *atmost restriction*, respectively) for an integer $n \geq 0$. We write $\top$ and $\bot$ to abbreviate $C \sqcup \neg C$ and $C \sqcap \neg C$, respectively, and we eliminate parentheses as usual.

An *axiom* is of one of the following forms: (1) $C \sqsubseteq D$, where C and D are concepts (*concept inclusion*); (2) $R \sqsubseteq S$, where either $R, S \in \mathbf{R}_A$ or $R, S \in \mathbf{R}_D$ (*role inclusion*); (3) $\mathrm{Trans}(R)$, where $R \in \mathbf{R}_A$ (*transitivity*); (4) $C(a)$, where C is a concept and $a \in \mathbf{I}$ (*concept membership*); (5) $R(a, b)$ (resp., $U(a, v)$), where $R \in \mathbf{R}_A$ (resp., $U \in \mathbf{R}_D$) and $a, b \in \mathbf{I}$ (resp., $a \in \mathbf{I}$ and $v \in \mathrm{dom}(\mathbf{D})$) (*role membership*); and (6) $a = b$ (resp., $a \neq b$), where $a, b \in \mathbf{I}$ (*equality* (resp., *inequality*)).

A *knowledge base* L is a finite set of axioms. (For decidability, number restrictions in L are restricted to simple $R \in \mathbf{R}_A$ [14]).

$\mathcal{SHIF}(\mathbf{D})$ is the restriction of $\mathcal{SHOIN}(\mathbf{D})$ which excludes the *oneOf* constructor and limits the *atleast* and *atmost* constructors to 0 and 1.

For the semantics of $\mathcal{SHIF}(\mathbf{D})$ and $\mathcal{SHOIN}(\mathbf{D})$, we refer to [12] or [6].

B Example Ontology L_1

$\geq 1\ buying \sqsubseteq Shop$; $\top \sqsubseteq \forall buying.Part$; $\geq 2\ buying \sqsubseteq Discount$;
$Part(graphiccard)$; $Part(memory)$; $Part(fan)$;
$Part(harddisk)$; $Part(cdrom)$; $Part(dvdrom)$;
$Part(soundcard)$; $Part(cpu)$; $Part(wlan)$; $Part(case)$;
$provides(s_1, case)$; $provides(s_1, cpu)$;
$provides(s_2, dvdrom)$;
$provides(s_3, cpu)$; $provides(s_3, fan)$; $provides(s_3, wlan)$;
$provides(s_4, case)$; $provides(s_4, cdrom)$; $provides(s_4, harddisk)$;
$provides(s_5, cpu)$; $provides(s_5, harddisk)$;
$provides(s_6, graphiccard)$; $provides(s_6, soundcard)$; $provides(s_6, harddisk)$;
$provides(s_7, graphiccard)$; $provides(s_7, memory)$;
$provides(s_8, wlan)$;
$provides(s_9, case)$; $provides(s_9, harddisk)$.

References

1. G. Antoniou. Nonmonotonic Rule Systems on Top of Ontology Layers. In *Proc. ISWC 2002*, volume 2342 of *LNCS*, pages 394–398, 2002.
2. C. Baral and V. S. Subrahmanian. Dualities Between Alternative Semantics for Logic Programming and Nonmonotonic Reasoning. *J. Automated Reasoning*, 10(3):399–420, 1993.
3. T. Berners-Lee. *Weaving the Web*. Harper, San Francisco, CA, 1999.
4. T. Berners-Lee, J. Hendler, and O. Lassila. The Semantic Web. *Scientific American*, 284(5):34–43, 2001.
5. F. M. Donini, M. Lenzerini, D. Nardi, and A. Schaerf. $\mathcal{AL}$-log: Integrating Datalog and Description Logics. *Journal of Intelligent Information Systems*, 10(3):227–252, 1998.
6. T. Eiter, T. Lukasiewicz, R. Schindlauer, and H. Tompits. Combining Answer Set Programming with Description Logics for the Semantic Web. In *Proc. KR 2004*, pages 141–151, 2004. Extended Report RR-1843-03-13, Institut für Informationssysteme, TU Wien, 2003.
7. T. Eiter, T. Lukasiewicz, R. Schindlauer, and H. Tompits. Well-founded Semantics for Description Logic Programs in the Semantic Web. In *Proc. RuleML 2004*, number 3323 in LNCS, pages 81–97. Springer, 2004.
8. W. Faber, N. Leone, C. Mateis, and G. Pfeifer. Using Database Optimization Techniques for Nonmonotonic Reasoning. In *Proc. DDLP-99*, pages 135–139. Prolog Association of Japan, September 1999.
9. D. Fensel, W. Wahlster, H. Lieberman, and J. Hendler, editors. *Spinning the Semantic Web: Bringing the World Wide Web to Its Full Potential*. MIT Press, 2002.
10. M. Gelfond and V. Lifschitz. Classical Negation in Logic Programs and Deductive Databases. *New Generation Computing*, 17:365–387, 1991.
11. V. Haarslev and R. Möller. RACER System Description. In *Proc. IJCAR 2001*, volume 2083 of *LNCS*, pages 701–705, 2001.
12. I. Horrocks and P. F. Patel-Schneider. Reducing OWL Entailment to Description Logic Satisfiability. In *Proc. ISWC 2003*, volume 2870 of *LNCS*, pages 17–29, 2003.
13. I. Horrocks, P. F. Patel-Schneider, and F. van Harmelen. From $\mathcal{SHIQ}$ and RDF to OWL: The Making of a Web Ontology Language. *Journal of Web Semantics*, 1(1):7–26, 2003.
14. I. Horrocks, U. Sattler, and S. Tobies. Practical Reasoning for Expressive Description Logics. In *Proc. LPAR 1999*, volume 1705 of *LNCS*, pages 161–180, 1999.
15. N. Leone, G. Pfeifer, W. Faber, T. Eiter, G. Gottlob, S. Perri, and F. Scarcello. The DLV System for Knowledge Representation and Reasoning. *ACM Transactions on Computational Logic*, 2004. To appear.
16. A. Y. Levy and M.-C. Rousset. Combining Horn Rules and Description Logics in CARIN. *Artif. Intell.*, 104(1-2):165–209, 1998.
17. R. Rosati. Towards Expressive KR Systems Integrating Datalog and Description Logics: Preliminary Report. In *Proc. DL-99*, pages 160–164, 1999.
18. M. Trick. Graph Coloring Instances, 1994.
    http://mat.gsia.cmu.edu/COLOR/instances.html.
19. A. Van Gelder, K. A. Ross, and J. S. Schlipf. The Well-Founded Semantics for General Logic Programs. *Journal of the ACM*, 38(3):620–650, 1991.
20. W3C. OWL Web Ontology Language Guide, 2003. W3C Proposed Recommendation 15 December 2003. http://www.w3.org/TR/2003/PR-owl-guide-20031215/.
21. W3C. OWL Web Ontology Language Overview, 2004. W3C Recommendation 10 February 2004. www.w3.org/TR/2004/REC-owl-features-20040210/.
22. K. Wang, D. Billington, J. Blee, and G. Antoniou. Combining Description Logic and Defeasible Logic for the Semantic Web. In *Proc. RuleML 2004*, number 3323 in LNCS, pages 170–181. Springer, 2004.

Implementing Efficient Resource Management for Linear Logic Programming

Pablo López[1] and Jeff Polakow[2]

[1] Universidad de Málaga
lopez@lcc.uma.es
[2] National Institute of Advanced Industrial Science and Technology (AIST),
Research Center for Verification and Semantics (CVS), CREST, Japan Science and Technology Agency (JST)
j-polakow@aist.go.jp[*]

Abstract. The Tag-Frame system of resource management [1] reunited two divergent threads of linear logic programming research by achieving the efficient proof search behaviour of abstract systems, such as [2], while using a low-level tag-based approach, as in [3], suitable for specifying an abstract machine. However, Tag-Frame relies on set operations which are linear in the size of the sets, and is not as efficient, in general, as it could be. We present a new tag-based derivation system which relies solely on low-level concepts to implement efficient resource management, where most linear time operations have been replaced by constant time ones. Though motivated and informed by the Tag-Frame system, we derive our system directly from, and prove its correctness with respect to the system of Cervesato et al. [2]. An abstract machine based on the new system has been implemented by Tamura and Banbara, and its performance compared to their previous machine.

1 Introduction

In the early nineties, work by Andreoli [4], Harland and Pym [5], and Hodas and Miller [6] showed that *goal-directed, focussed* proof search is complete for a fragment of linear logic [7]. Although this result qualified linear logic as an *abstract logic programming language* [8], the enormous amount of nondeterminism in goal-directed proof search, due to the need to split resources (linear hypotheses) between premises, rendered a naive implementation useless. Hodas and Miller [6] also introduced the I/O system, which Hodas further refined to the $I/O_\top$ system [9] to implement the first feasible method of managing resources; this work gave birth to Lolli, a linear logic programming language which conservatively extends λProlog [10].

Subsequent work on improving the implementation of Lolli[1] split into two general categories: refining resource management strategies to further remove

---

[*] Work carried out while a JSPS Fellow at Kobe University.
[1] For this paper we only consider pure Lolli, i.e. no extra-logical operations.

nondeterminism from proof search [2,11]; and investigating low-level implementation techniques suitable for extending the WAM [3,12,13]. The work on resource management largely succeeded in removing unnecessary nondeterminism, at least that related to linearity, from proof search. However, the proposed systems rely upon high-level operations such as context intersection and union which are linear in the size of the contexts. On the other hand, the work on compilation associates tags with each resource and then maintains linearity constraints by manipulating individual formula tags, rather than whole contexts. This approach produced very fast implementations, as evidenced by the Lolli-Cop theorem prover [14], but did not manage to capture the more ideal proof search behavior of the abstract systems– in particular, these systems lack the notion of strict resources and thus may diverge where the more abstract systems will simply fail.

These divergent research paths were reunited with the Tag-Frame system of Hodas et al. [1] which captures the behavior of the resource management systems using the low-level techniques of compiled implementations. Specifically, the system abstracts the linear context into a set of tags, each representing some portion of the context. Linearity constraints are then enforced by carefully keeping track of which tags may and must be consumed at any point in the proof. However, as argued by Polakow in [15], the machinery for managing tags presented in [1] both requires more work than necessary and obfuscates the proof search algorithm.

This paper presents a new proof search system for Lolli which improves upon the Tag-Frame system in efficiency. Although informed by our experience with the Tag-Frame system, we derive our new system, which we call $\mathcal{TF}_4$, directly from RM_3, the efficient resource management system of Cervesato et al. [2].

The rest of this paper is organized as follows. Section 2 formally introduces the formula language of Lolli. Section 3 reviews developments in resource management up to the Tag-Frame system. Section 4 presents an inefficient, tag-based version of RM_3 which illustrates the main intuition behind $\mathcal{TF}_4$ and serves as an intermediate system in our proof of correctness. Sections 5 refines our intermediate system to a new, very efficient system based on the intuition that tags are pointers. Section 6 presents one further refinement which results in $\mathcal{TF}_4$, our final system. Section 7 presents LLP-TF, an abstract machine based on $\mathcal{TF}_4$ and discusses its performance. Finally, section 8 offers some conclusions and further work.

2 Formulas and Residuation

We now formally introduce our formula language. Due to space limitations, we limit ourselves to a fragment of Lolli sufficient to illustrate all the features of our system; our system easily extends to the full formula language of Lolli including quantifiers, and intuitionistic implication and bang. We divide our formulas into *goal* formulas, G, which may appear as goals, and *definite clause* formulas, D, which may appear as hypotheses. The grammars for goal and clause formulas are as follows:

$$G ::= A \mid D \multimap G \mid G_1 \& G_2 \mid \top \mid G_1 \otimes G_2 \mid \mathbf{1}$$
$$D ::= A \mid G \multimap D \mid \top$$

where A represents atomic predicates. Note that D is restricted to asynchronous [4] formulas which allows goal-directed proof search to be complete.

In the usual presentation of sequent systems, there are right rules which act on the goal formula, and left rules which act upon hypotheses. In goal-directed proof search, we only use right rules when the goal is non-atomic. When solving an atomic goal, we choose a hypothesis, whose head matches (unifies with) our goal, to focus on, i.e. to apply left rules generating new goals.

As shown by Cervesato [16], the new goals which will be generated by focussing on a hypothesis may be eagerly generated by *residuating*, or "logically compiling," the hypothesis into one new goal formula. We note that this basic idea underlies the earlier notion of a *backchaining* rule present in the original presentation of Lolli [6]. For our presentation, we opt to dispense with left rules in favor of residuation.

We make use of the following judgement to residuate a clause formula, D, whose head matches a given atom, A, into a goal formula, G:

$$D \gg A \backslash G$$

The rules for residuation are as follows (where $\doteq$ signifies unification.):

$$\frac{A' \doteq A}{A' \gg A \backslash \mathbf{1}} \qquad \frac{D \gg A \backslash G}{G' \multimap D \gg A \backslash G \otimes G'} \qquad \text{(no rule for } \top\text{)}$$

3 A Review of Resource Management

The chief source of nondeterminism in linear logic programming (after restricting to goal-directed, focussed proof search) arises from the need to distribute resources among the premises of multiplicative rules. When designing Lolli, Hodas and Miller realized that resources may be lazily distributed during proof search; when solving a goal with two premises, *all* currently available resources can be given to the first premise and those left-over can be further passed to the second premise. The I/O system [6] follows this intuition and its sequents have the form:

$$\Delta_I \backslash \Delta_O \Longrightarrow G$$

where Δ_I contains the input linear hypotheses while Δ_O contains the output linear hypotheses, G is the goal to be proved.

In the I/O system, the actual linear context consumed by the derivation corresponds to $\Delta_I - \Delta_O$. Thus we can write the $\otimes$ rule as:

$$\frac{\Delta_I \backslash \Delta_M \Longrightarrow G_1 \qquad \Delta_M \backslash \Delta_O \Longrightarrow G_2}{\Delta_I \backslash \Delta_O \Longrightarrow G_1 \otimes G_2} \otimes R$$

$$\frac{}{\Delta_I\backslash\Delta_I \Rightarrow_1 \top}\top \quad \frac{}{\Delta_I\backslash\Delta_I \Rightarrow_0 1} 1$$

$$\frac{(\Delta_I \cup \{D\})\backslash\Delta_O \Rightarrow_0 G \quad D \notin \Delta_O}{\Delta_I\backslash\Delta_O \Rightarrow_0 D\multimap G}\multimap_0 \quad \frac{(\Delta_I \cup \{D\})\backslash\Delta_O \Rightarrow_1 G}{\Delta_I\backslash(\Delta_O - \{D\}) \Rightarrow_1 D\multimap G}\multimap_1$$

$$\frac{\Delta_I\backslash\Delta_M \Rightarrow_{v_1} G_1 \quad \Delta_M\backslash\Delta_O \Rightarrow_{v_2} G_2}{\Delta_I\backslash\Delta_O \Rightarrow_{v_1\vee v_2} G_1 \otimes G_2}\otimes$$

$$\frac{\Delta_I\backslash\Delta_O \Rightarrow_0 G_1 \quad \Delta_I\backslash\Delta_O \Rightarrow_0 G_2}{\Delta_I\backslash\Delta_O \Rightarrow_0 G_1 \& G_2}\&_{00} \quad \frac{\Delta_I\backslash\Delta_O \Rightarrow_0 G_1 \quad \Delta_I\backslash(\Delta_O \cup \Delta) \Rightarrow_1 G_2}{\Delta_I\backslash\Delta_O \Rightarrow_0 G_1 \& G_2}\&_{01}$$

$$\frac{\Delta_I\backslash(\Delta_O \cup \Delta) \Rightarrow_1 G_1 \quad \Delta_I\backslash\Delta_O \Rightarrow_0 G_2}{\Delta_I\backslash\Delta_O \Rightarrow_0 G_1 \& G_2}\&_{10} \quad \frac{\Delta_I\backslash\Delta_{O1} \Rightarrow_1 G_1 \quad \Delta_I\backslash\Delta_{O2} \Rightarrow_1 G_2}{\Delta_I\backslash(\Delta_{O1} \cap \Delta_{O2}) \Rightarrow_v G_1 \& G_2}\&_{11}$$

$$\frac{D \gg A\backslash G \quad (\Delta_I - \{D\})\backslash\Delta_O \Rightarrow_v G}{\Delta_I\backslash\Delta_O \Rightarrow_v A}\text{Pick} (D \in \Delta_I)$$

Fig. 1. The I/O$_\top$ system

Linearity constraints are maintained by checking that the output context does not contain a formula which must be consumed, i.e.:

$$\frac{(\Delta_I \cup \{D\})\backslash\Delta_O \Rightarrow G \quad D \notin \Delta_O}{\Delta_I\backslash\Delta_O \Rightarrow D\multimap G}\multimap_R$$

However, rather than remove the nondeterminism, the idea of lazy splitting only pushes it into the ⊤ (additive unit) rule which can, in this setting, consume an arbitrary subset of the input:

$$\frac{\Delta_I \supseteq \Delta_O}{\Delta_I\backslash\Delta_O \Rightarrow \top}\top_R$$

3.1 The I/O$_\top$ System

Hodas removed nondeterminism from the ⊤ rule by creating the I/O$_\top$ system [9]. This system decorates sequents with a boolean flag indicating whether a ⊤ was encountered which could implicitly consume extra resources. Thus I/O$_\top$ sequents have the form:

$$\Delta_I\backslash\Delta_O \Rightarrow_v G$$

where v is a boolean, the ⊤ flag, and everything else is the same as in I/O.

In the I/O$_\top$ system, the ⊤ rule becomes lazy; rather than consume any of its input, it simply sets the ⊤ flag. When the ⊤ flag is set, linearity constraints may be relaxed since any unconsumed resources could have been consumed by the ⊤. Figure 1 presents the derivation rules for I/O$_\top$ adapted to use residuation and our syntax.

While the I/O$_\top$ system removes much of the nondeterminism of resource distribution, its direct implementation as a logic programming interpreter allows needless backtracking due to the inefficient treatment of & (additive conjunction). Since both premises of & must consume exactly the same resources, giving the same input context to both premises potentially creates useless choice points in the derivation of the second premise.

$$\overline{\Xi;\Delta\backslash\Delta \Longrightarrow_1 \top}\ \top_{RM_3} \qquad \overline{\emptyset;\Delta\backslash\Delta \Longrightarrow_0 1}\ \mathbf{1}_{RM_3} \qquad \frac{\Xi \cup \{D\}; \Delta_I\backslash\Delta_O \Longrightarrow_v G}{\Xi; \Delta_I\backslash\Delta_O \Longrightarrow_v D \multimap G}\ \multimap_{RM_3}$$

$$\frac{\emptyset; \Xi \cup \Delta_I\backslash\Delta_M \Longrightarrow_0 G_1 \quad \Xi \cap \Delta_M; \Delta_I \cap \Delta_M \backslash \Delta_O \Longrightarrow_v G_2}{\Xi; \Delta_I \backslash \Delta_O \Longrightarrow_v G_1 \otimes G_2}\ \otimes_{0\,RM_3}$$

$$\frac{\emptyset; \Xi \cup \Delta_I \backslash \Delta_M \Longrightarrow_1 G_1 \quad \emptyset; \Delta_M \backslash \Delta_O \Longrightarrow_v G_2}{\Xi; \Delta_I \backslash \Delta_I \cap \Delta_O \Longrightarrow_1 G_1 \otimes G_2}\ \otimes_{1\,RM_3}$$

$$\frac{\Xi; \Delta_I \backslash \Delta_O \Longrightarrow_0 G_1 \quad \Xi \cup (\Delta_I - \Delta_O); \emptyset \backslash \emptyset \Longrightarrow_v G_2}{\Xi; \Delta_I \backslash \Delta_O \Longrightarrow_0 G_1\ \&\ G_2}\ \&_{0\,RM_3}$$

$$\frac{\Xi; \Delta_I \backslash \Delta_M \Longrightarrow_1 G_1 \quad \Xi \cup (\Delta_I - \Delta_M); \Delta_M \backslash \Delta_O \Longrightarrow_v G_2}{\Xi; \Delta_I \backslash \Delta_O \Longrightarrow_v G_1\ \&\ G_2}\ \&_{1\,RM_3}$$

$$\frac{D \gg A \backslash G \quad \Xi; \Delta_I \backslash \Delta_O \Longrightarrow_v G}{\Xi \cup \{D\}; \Delta_I \backslash \Delta_O \Longrightarrow_v A}\ \text{pick}\ \Xi_{RM_3} \qquad \frac{D \gg A \backslash G \quad \Xi; \Delta_I \backslash \Delta_O \Longrightarrow_v G}{\Xi; \Delta_I \cup \{D\} \backslash \Delta_O \Longrightarrow_v A}\ \text{pick}\ \Delta_{RM_3}$$

Fig. 2. The RM_3 system

3.2 The RM_3 System

The RM_3 system of Cervesato et al. [2] extends I/O$_\top$ with the ability to keep track of exactly which resources must be consumed at any point in the proof. RM_3 is characterized by the following judgement

$$\Xi; \Delta_I \backslash \Delta_O \Longrightarrow_v G$$

where: Ξ is a set of *strict* linear clause formulas; Δ_I, Δ_O are sets of *lax* linear clause formulas, the input and output contexts respectively; v is the $\top$ flag; and G is the goal formula being derived. All linear hypotheses, i.e. the contents of Ξ, Δ_I, Δ_O, are implicitly uniquely labelled so that we can distinguish different occurrences of the same formula in a set. We assume new labels are tacitly generated as formulas are added to Ξ. Figure 2 gives a version of the derivation rules for RM_3 slightly modified to use residuation.

The basic idea behind RM_3 is that strict resources *must* be consumed while lax resources *may* be consumed. Because we have a lazy $\top_R$ rule, resources can either be explicitly consumed in the **pick** rules, or implicitly consumed in the $\top_R$ rule. Thus Ξ is required to be empty in the $\mathbf{1}_R$ rule which also sets the $\top$ flag to 0. Furthermore, by adding new resources to Ξ in the $\multimap_R$ rule, we guarantee they will be consumed and have no need to check the output context regardless of the $\top$ flag's value. The formulation of the remaining rules serves to insure accurate bookeeping of strict resources.

The RM_3 system specifies a proof search behavior which is very appropriate for linear logic programming– at least for goal-directed, left-to-right proof search. However, the context intersections in the $\otimes$ rules, and context differences in the $\&$ rules, render a direct implementation of the system extremely slow. A more concrete, lower-level specification is needed for efficient implementation. In sections 4 through 6 we successively refine RM_3 into such a system. However, we first discuss two earlier refinements of RM_3 which inform our work.

3.3 Frames and Tag-Frames

Upon closer analysis, the strict formulas of RM_3 can be seen to follow a stack-like behavior. The Frame system, $\mathcal{F}$, of López and Pimentel [11], exposes and exploits this behavior to improve upon RM_3's efficiency. In $\mathcal{F}$, the linear contexts, Δ_I and Δ_O, are actually stacks of strict contexts, called frames. This representation alleviates the need for context intersection, in the $\otimes$ rules, to disentangle strict and lax resources.

Although significantly more concrete, and efficient, than RM_3, the $\mathcal{F}$ system remains too abstract for direct implementation as a logic programming language. In addition to relying upon context-wide comparisons, i.e. context difference, the system does not maintain the order of linear hypotheses. Such information is necessary to implement the depth first search operational semantics of Prolog-style languages.

To improve the treatment of &, and maintain context order, Hodas et al. created the $\mathcal{TF}$ system [1] which employs low-level implementation techniques of [3] to capture the proof search behavior of $\mathcal{F}$ (and RM_3). Specifically, $\mathcal{TF}$ assigns tags to each resource and then keeps track of exactly which tags must be consumed, i.e. are strict, in the current sub-proof. This requires new delete tags to be generated in the & rules to identify resources consumed in the first premise. Consumption of a resource amounts to changing the resource's tag, rather than explicitly removing the formula from the linear context. The use of individual formula tags allows strict resources to be identified while maintaining the order of linear hypotheses.

Although the $\mathcal{TF}$ could be used as the basis of an abstract machine for Lolli, it is not the ideal candidate. The system still relies upon set membership and set union to manage linearity constraints and requires scanning the linear context[2] in the **1** rule as well as scanning the list of available tags in the **pick** rule. These operations are not only linear in time, but the machinery for managing tags is heavier than need be; see [15] for an alternative formulation.

4 Naive Tag-Based System

We start our development of a low-level and efficient resource management specification with a simple and inefficient tag-based system which captures the same proof search behavior of RM_3. This system, $\mathcal{TFN}$, which maintains context order, ensures that every strict input formula is marked as consumed in the output. The system will use lists of tagged clause formulas to represent linear contexts. We respectively use nil, :: and @ for the empty list, list constructor, and list append function. We also assume each linear hypothesis is implicitly uniquely labelled so that we may distinguish between different occurrences of the same formula. We assume that new labels are generated as the linear context expands.

---

[2] This could be optimized to just scanning the strict frame if tags are implemented as pointers to counters.

$$\frac{}{\Delta\setminus M(s,d,\Delta) \xrightarrow{s::\pi \ \ d}_1 \top} \top_{\mathcal{TFM}} \qquad \frac{[\Delta]_s = \emptyset}{\Delta\setminus\Delta \xrightarrow{s::\pi \ \ d}_0 1} 1_{\mathcal{TFM}}$$

$$\frac{D^s :: \Delta_I \setminus D^d :: \Delta_O \xrightarrow{s::\pi \ \ d}_v G}{\Delta_I \setminus \Delta_O \xrightarrow{s::\pi \ \ d}_v D \multimap G} \multimap_{\mathcal{TFM}}$$

$$\frac{\Delta_I\setminus\Delta_M \xrightarrow{t::s::\pi \ \ d}_0 G_1 \qquad \Delta_M\setminus\Delta_O \xrightarrow{s::\pi \ \ d}_v G_2}{\Delta_I\setminus\Delta_O \xrightarrow{s::\pi \ \ d}_v G_1 \otimes G_2} \otimes_{0\mathcal{TFM}} \quad (t \text{ not in conclusion})$$

$$\frac{\Delta_I\setminus\Delta_M \xrightarrow{t::s::\pi \ \ d}_1 G_1 \qquad \Delta_M\setminus\Delta_O \xrightarrow{t::s::\pi \ \ d}_v G_2}{\Delta_I\setminus M(s,d,\Delta_O) \xrightarrow{s::\pi \ \ d}_1 G_1 \otimes G_2} \otimes_{1\mathcal{TFM}} \quad (t \text{ not in conclusion})$$

$$\frac{\Delta_I\setminus\Delta_M \xrightarrow{s::\pi \ \ d'}_0 G_1 \qquad \Delta_M\setminus\Delta_O \xrightarrow{d'::\mathrm{nil} \ \ d}_v G_2}{\Delta_I\setminus\Delta_O \xrightarrow{s::\pi \ \ d}_0 G_1 \& G_2} \&_{0\mathcal{TFM}} \quad (d' \text{ not in conclusion})$$

$$\frac{\Delta_I\setminus\Delta_M \xrightarrow{s::\pi \ \ d'}_1 G_1 \qquad \Delta_M\setminus\Delta_O \xrightarrow{d'::\pi \ \ d}_v G_2}{\Delta_I\setminus\Delta_O \xrightarrow{s::\pi \ \ d}_v G_1 \& G_2} \&_{1\mathcal{TFM}} \quad (d' \text{ not in conclusion})$$

$$\frac{D \gg A\setminus G \qquad \Delta_L @(D^d :: \Delta_R)\setminus\Delta_O \xrightarrow{s::\pi \ \ d}_v G}{\Delta_L @(D^t :: \Delta_R)\setminus\Delta_O \xrightarrow{s::\pi \ \ d}_v A} \mathrm{pick}_{\Delta \mathcal{TFM}} \quad (t \in s :: \pi)$$

Fig. 3. The $\mathcal{TFM}$ system

We make use of the following two functions on lists of tagged formulas:

$$\begin{array}{llll}
[\mathrm{nil}]_t & = & \emptyset & \qquad M(s,t,\mathrm{nil}) = \mathrm{nil} \\
[D^t :: \Delta]_t & = & \{D\} \cup [\Delta]_t & \qquad M(s,t,(D^s :: \Delta)) = D^t :: M(s,t,\Delta) \\
[D^s :: \Delta]_t & = & [\Delta]_t \quad (\text{if } s \neq t) & \qquad M(s,t,(D^{s'} :: \Delta)) = D^{s'} :: M(s,t,\Delta) \quad (\text{if } s \neq s')
\end{array}$$

$[\Delta]_t$ returns the set of all formulas in Δ tagged with t. $M(s,t,\Delta)$ explicitly changes all occurrences in Δ of tag s to t.

$\mathcal{TFM}$ sequents have the form

$$\Delta_I\setminus\Delta_O \xrightarrow{s::\pi \ \ d}_v G$$

where: Δ_I, Δ_O are lists containing tagged clause formulas, the input and output contexts; s is the strict tag; π is a list of available tags; d is the delete tag; v is the $\top$ flag; and G is the goal formula being derived. Note that list $s :: \pi$ is manipulated as a stack. The basic intuition is that input formulas tagged with s are strict, those tagged with $t \in \pi$ are lax[3], and those with other tags are not available for consumption; furthermore, all formulas consumed in the derivation will be tagged with d in the output. Figure 3 presents the derivation rules for $\mathcal{TFM}$.

---

[3] We overload $\in$ to mean list membership as well as set membership.

4.1 Correctness of $\mathcal{TFM}$

We now prove $\mathcal{TFM}$ sound and complete with respect to RM_3. In the following statements, we assume that all variables are universally quantified at the outermost level, unless explicitly noted otherwise.

We make use of the following function:

$$[\![\Delta]\!]_{\text{nil}} = \emptyset$$
$$[\![\Delta]\!]_{t::\pi} = [\Delta]_t \cup [\![\Delta]\!]_\pi$$

$[\![\Delta]\!]_\pi$ returns the set of all formulas in Δ whose tag is in π.

We begin with a lemma that relates the input and output contexts of a $\mathcal{TFM}$ provable sequent.

Lemma 1 (Properties of $\mathcal{TFM}$).
$\Delta_I \backslash \Delta_O \xrightarrow{s::\pi \quad d}_v G$ implies

1. $[\Delta_O]_s = \emptyset$
2. $[\![\Delta_I]\!]_\pi \supseteq [\![\Delta_O]\!]_\pi$
3. $[\Delta_O]_d = [\Delta_I]_s \cup [\Delta_I]_d \cup ([\![\Delta_I]\!]_\pi - [\![\Delta_O]\!]_\pi)$

whenever $s \neq d$, $s \notin \pi$, $d \notin \pi$ and all tags in π are unique.

Proof. By induction on the structure of the given derivation.

Part 1 states that there are no strict resources in the output. Part 2 states that the optional output is a subset of the optional input. Finally, part 3 states what resources are marked as consumed in the output.

The proof of correctnes is divided into two parts, a soundness result and a completeness result.

Theorem 1 (Soundness with respect to RM_3).
$\Delta_I \backslash \Delta_O \xrightarrow{s::\pi \quad d}_v G$ implies
$[\Delta_I]_s ; [\![\Delta_I]\!]_\pi \backslash [\![\Delta_O]\!]_\pi \Longrightarrow_v G$
whenever $s \neq d$, $s \notin \pi$, $d \notin \pi$ and all tags in π are unique.

Proof. By induction on the structure of the given derivation, making use of lemma 1.

Theorem 2 (Completeness with respect to RM_3).
$\Xi; \Delta_I \backslash \Delta_O \Longrightarrow_v G$ and $[\Delta_I']_s = \Xi$ and $[\![\Delta_I']\!]_\pi = \Delta_I$ implies
$\exists \Delta_O'. \; \Delta_I' \backslash \Delta_O' \xrightarrow{s::\pi \quad d}_v G$ and $[\![\Delta_O']\!]_\pi = \Delta_O$
whenever $s \neq d$, $s \notin \pi$, $d \notin \pi$ and all tags in π are unique.

Proof. By induction on the structure of the given derivation, making use of lemma 1.

4.2 Tags as Counters

Exactly four rules of $\mathcal{TFM}$ require (non-constant time) work to manage linearity constraints. The **1** rule requires scanning the context for tag s. The ⊤ rule must traverse the context and explicitly change all the strict tags to delete tags. Likewise, since s is not strict in either premise, the $\otimes_1$ rule must explicitly consume any resources tagged with s leftover from the derivations of its premises. Finally, since consumed formulas remain in the context, the **pick** rule must check that the chosen formula is available for consumption, i.e. that t occurs in $s :: \pi$.

By implementing tags as counters, we can turn the strictness check in the **1** rule to a constant time memory lookup operation. In such an implementation, each tag would be a reference to a memory location containing the number of formulas marked with that tag. The implementations of the $\multimap$ and **pick** rules, as well as the $\mathcal{M}(s, t, \Delta)$ function, would manipulate the counters appropriately to maintain the representation.

5 Indirect Tag-Based System

Suppose we have three tags, s, t and d, and a context $\Delta = D_1^s, D_2^s, D_3^t, D_4^d$ which we want to change to $\Delta' = D_1^d, D_2^d, D_3^t, D_4^d$. Then, letting the tags be memory addresses, we wish to make the following transformation:

d	1
s	2
t	1

$D_1^s, D_2^s, D_3^t, D_4^d$

$\longmapsto$

d	3
s	0
t	1

$D_1^d, D_2^d, D_3^t, D_4^d$

By building on the intuition that tags are memory locations, it is possible to effectively accomplish the preceding transformation in constant time by using indirection and considering tags as memory locations which contain either a natural number or another memory location:

d	1
s	2
t	1

$D_1^s, D_2^s, D_3^t, D_4^d$

$\longmapsto$

d	3
s	d
t	1

$D_1^s, D_2^s, D_3^t, D_4^d$

If we modify memory lookup to chase down alias chains, s and d will effectively represent the same tag.

In other words, we would like to maintain equivalence classes of tags. The machinery we subsequently add to our derivation rules may be seen as the implementation of a union-find structure.

5.1 Memory and Partial Functions

In order to formalize and prove correct the previous ideas, we will model memory as a partial function from a countably infinite set of locations, $\mathcal{L}$, to the disjoint union of all possible value types. For our purposes, we will only consider value types to be natural numbers, $\mathbb{N}$, locations, and pairs.

We understand a partial function, σ, from $\mathcal{A}$ to $\mathcal{B}$ to be a set of pairs, (x, y) where $x \in \mathcal{A}$ and $y \in \mathcal{B}$, for which there is *at most one* $b \in \mathcal{B}$ for every $a \in \mathcal{A}$ such that $(a, b) \in \sigma$. We use the following functional notations:

$$\sigma(a) = \begin{cases} b & \text{if } \exists b.\, (a, b) \in \sigma \\ \text{undefined} & \text{otherwise} \end{cases}$$

$$\sigma[a := b] = \begin{cases} (\sigma - (a, b')) \cup (a, b) & \text{if } \exists b'.\, \sigma(a) = b' \\ \sigma \cup (a, b) & \text{otherwise} \end{cases}$$

$$\sigma \smallsetminus a = \begin{cases} \sigma - (a, b') & \text{if } \exists b'.\, \sigma(a) = b' \\ \sigma & \text{otherwise} \end{cases}$$

which correspond to memory lookup, memory modification (and allocation), and memory deallocation. Note that our presentation is purely declarative. $\sigma[a := b]$ does not change σ but rather stands for the modified partial function; thus $\sigma[a := \sigma(b)][b := \sigma(a)] = \sigma[b := \sigma(a)][a := \sigma(b)]$

We make use of the following syntax to denote the domain and codomain of a partial function from $\mathcal{A}$ to $\mathcal{B}$:

$$\mathrm{dom}(\sigma) = \{a \in \mathcal{A} \mid \exists b \in \mathcal{B}.\, \sigma(a) = b\} \qquad \mathrm{cod}(\sigma) = \{b \in \mathcal{B} \mid \exists a \in \mathcal{A}.\, \sigma(a) = b\}$$

5.2 Aliasing and Memory Lookup

For $\mathcal{TF}+$, formula tags will be locations $l \in \mathcal{L}$. Intuitively, these locations are memory addresses which store natural numbers. However, since we want to be able to alias one tag to another, we will model memory as a partial function Σ from $\mathcal{L}$ to $\mathbb{N} \uplus \mathcal{L}$ where $\Sigma(l) \in \mathcal{L}$ implies l is aliased to some other memory location.

We use an explicit lookup judgement to find the current alias of a given tag. In order to improve overall efficiency, we will update the Σ function to point to the current (i.e. last in the chain) alias whenever we have to lookup the value of a location. Our lookup judgement has the following form

$$\Sigma_I \backslash \Sigma_O \models l \leadsto l'$$

where: Σ_x are partial functions of type $\mathcal{L} \to \mathbb{N} \uplus \mathcal{L}$; and l, l' are elements of $\mathcal{L}$. The derivation rules for the judgement are as follows:

$$\frac{\Sigma(l) \in \mathbb{N}}{\Sigma \backslash \Sigma \models l \leadsto l} \text{ value} \qquad \frac{\Sigma_I(l) \in \mathcal{L} \quad \Sigma_I \backslash \Sigma_O \models \Sigma_I(l) \leadsto l'}{\Sigma_I \backslash \Sigma_O[l := l'] \models l \leadsto l'} \text{ alias}$$

We use the following notational conveniences, where $l \in \mathcal{L}$ and $n \in \mathbb{N}$, for common memory operations:

$$\Sigma[l + n] = \begin{cases} \Sigma[l := n' + n] & \text{if } \exists n' \in \mathbb{N}.\, \Sigma(l) = n' \\ \text{undefined} & \text{otherwise} \end{cases}$$

$$\Sigma[l - n] = \begin{cases} \Sigma[l := n' - n] & \text{if } \exists n' \in \mathbb{N}.\, \Sigma(l) = n' \text{ and } n' \geq n \\ \text{undefined} & \text{otherwise} \end{cases}$$

$$\cfrac{}{\Sigma \backslash \Sigma[s := d][d + \Sigma(s)] \, ; \, \Delta \backslash \Delta \xrightarrow{s::\pi \ \ d}_1 \top} \top_{\mathcal{TF}+} \qquad \cfrac{\Sigma(s) = 0}{\Sigma \backslash \Sigma \, ; \, \Delta \backslash \Delta \xrightarrow{s::\pi \ \ d}_0 1} \mathbf{1}_{\mathcal{TF}+}$$

$$\cfrac{\Sigma_I[s+1]\backslash \Sigma_O \, ; \, D^s :: \Delta_I \setminus D^- :: \Delta_O \xrightarrow{s::\pi \ \ d}_v G}{\Sigma_I \backslash \Sigma_O[d-1] \, ; \, \Delta_I \backslash \Delta_O \xrightarrow{s::\pi \ \ d}_v D \multimap G} \multimap_{\mathcal{TF}+}$$

$$\cfrac{\Sigma_I[l := 0]\backslash \Sigma_M \, ; \, \Delta_I \backslash \Delta_M \xrightarrow{l::s::\pi \ \ d}_0 G_1 \qquad (\Sigma_M \setminus l)\backslash \Sigma_O \, ; \, \Delta_M \backslash \Delta_O \xrightarrow{s::\pi \ \ d}_v G_2}{\Sigma_I \backslash \Sigma_O \, ; \, \Delta_I \backslash \Delta_O \xrightarrow{s::\pi \ \ d}_v G_1 \otimes G_2} \otimes_{0\mathcal{TF}+}$$
where l not in conclusion

$$\cfrac{\Sigma_I[l := 0]\backslash \Sigma_M \, ; \, \Delta_I \backslash \Delta_M \xrightarrow{l::s::\pi \ \ d}_1 G_1 \qquad \Sigma_M[l := 0]\backslash \Sigma_O \, ; \, \Delta_M \backslash \Delta_O \xrightarrow{l::s::\pi \ \ d}_v G_2}{\Sigma_I \backslash (\Sigma_O[s := d][d + \Sigma_O(s)] \setminus l) \, ; \, \Delta_I \backslash \Delta_O \xrightarrow{s::\pi \ \ d}_1 G_1 \otimes G_2} \otimes_{1\mathcal{TF}+}$$
where l not in conclusion

$$\cfrac{\Sigma_I[l := 0]\backslash \Sigma_M \, ; \, \Delta_I \backslash \Delta_M \xrightarrow{s::\pi \ \ l}_0 G_1 \qquad \Sigma_M \backslash \Sigma_O \, ; \, \Delta_M \backslash \Delta_O \xrightarrow{l::nil \ \ d}_v G_2}{\Sigma_I \backslash \Sigma_O \, ; \, \Delta_I \backslash \Delta_O \xrightarrow{s::\pi \ \ d}_0 G_1 \& G_2} \&_{0\mathcal{TF}+}$$
where $l \notin (\mathrm{dom}(\Sigma_I) \cup \mathrm{cod}(\Sigma_I))$ and $[\Delta_I]_l = \emptyset$

$$\cfrac{\Sigma_I[l := 0]\backslash \Sigma_M \, ; \, \Delta_I \backslash \Delta_M \xrightarrow{s::\pi \ \ l}_1 G_1 \qquad \Sigma_M \backslash \Sigma_O \, ; \, \Delta_M \backslash \Delta_O \xrightarrow{l::\pi \ \ d}_v G_2}{\Sigma_I \backslash \Sigma_O \, ; \, \Delta_I \backslash \Delta_O \xrightarrow{s::\pi \ \ d}_v G_1 \& G_2} \&_{1\mathcal{TF}+}$$
where $l \notin (\mathrm{dom}(\Sigma_I) \cup \mathrm{cod}(\Sigma_I))$ and $[\Delta_I]_l = \emptyset$

$$\cfrac{\Sigma_I \backslash \Sigma_M \models t \leadsto l \qquad D \gg A \backslash G \qquad \Sigma_M[l-1][d+1]\backslash \Sigma_O \, ; \, \Delta_L @(D^d :: \Delta_R)\backslash \Delta_O \xrightarrow{s::\pi \ \ d}_v G}{\Sigma_I \backslash \Sigma_O \, ; \, \Delta_L @(D^t :: \Delta_R)\backslash \Delta_O \xrightarrow{s::\pi \ \ d}_v A} \mathrm{pick}\,\Delta_{\mathcal{TF}+}$$
where $l \in s :: \pi$

Fig. 4. The $\mathcal{TF}+$ system

5.3 $\mathcal{TF}+$ Sequents

$\mathcal{TF}+$ sequents are of the form

$$\Sigma_I \backslash \Sigma_O \, ; \, \Delta_I \backslash \Delta_O \xrightarrow{s::\pi \ \ d}_v G$$

where: Σ_I, Σ_O are partial functions of type $\mathcal{L} \to \mathbb{N} \uplus \mathcal{L}$, representing the state of memory before and after the derivation; and everything else remains unchanged from $\mathcal{TFM}$, unique labelling included. It is assumed that $s \neq d$, $s \notin \pi$, and $d \notin \pi$. Figure 4 contains the derivation rules for $\mathcal{TF}+$.

5.4 Correctness of $\mathcal{TF}+$

We now prove $\mathcal{TF}+$ correct with respect to $\mathcal{TFM}$. In all logical statements, all variables are implicitly universally bound at the outermost level unless explicitly stated otherwise. We introduce the following notation:

$$\begin{aligned} \Sigma(\mathrm{nil}) &= \mathrm{nil} \\ \Sigma(D^t :: \Delta) &= D^l :: \Sigma(\Delta) \qquad \text{where } \Sigma \backslash_- \models t \leadsto l \end{aligned}$$

to apply all aliases to a contex; and:

$$\begin{aligned} \mathrm{nil} - \mathrm{nil} &= \emptyset \\ (D^t :: \Delta) - (D^t :: \Delta') &= \Delta - \Delta' \\ (D^t :: \Delta) - (D^{t'} :: \Delta') &= \{t'\} \cup (\Delta - \Delta') \qquad \text{where } t \neq t' \end{aligned}$$

Implementing Efficient Resource Management for Linear Logic Programming   539

for the tag difference of two contexts. Additionally, $\#(\mathcal{S})$ denotes the cardinality of a (multi)set $\mathcal{S}$.

For a $\mathcal{TF}+$ sequent to be provable, Σ_I must map every tag to an appropriate counter, possibly through a chain of aliases. We formalize this as follows:

Definition 1 (Well-Formedness).
$\Sigma_I \backslash \Sigma_O \, ; \, \Delta_I \backslash \Delta_O \xrightarrow{s::\pi \quad d}_v G$ is **well-formed** iff

1. $\forall t \in \mathrm{dom}(\Sigma_I). \exists l \in \mathrm{dom}(\Sigma_I). \Sigma_I\backslash_- \models t \leadsto l$ and $\Sigma_I(l) = \#([\Sigma_I(\Delta_I)]_l)$
2. $\forall t \in d :: s :: \pi. \Sigma_I\backslash_- \models t \leadsto t$

A derivation is well-formed iff every sequent is well-formed. We now state some fundamental properties of well-formed derivations.

Lemma 2 (Properties of $\mathcal{TF}+$).
A well-formed derivation of $\Sigma_I \backslash \Sigma_O \, ; \, \Delta_I \backslash \Delta_O \xrightarrow{s::\pi \quad d}_v G$ implies all of the following:

1. $\forall t \in \mathrm{dom}(\Sigma_O). \exists l \in \mathrm{dom}(\Sigma_O). \Sigma_O\backslash_- \models t \leadsto l$ and $\Sigma_O(l) = \#([\Sigma_O(\Delta_O)]_l)$
2. $[\Sigma_O(\Delta_O)]_s = \emptyset$
3. $(\Sigma_I(\Delta_I) - \Sigma_O(\Delta_O)) \subseteq \{d\}$

Proof. By structural induction on the given derivation.

Part 1 states that well-formedness is preserved. Part 2 states that the output contains no strict resources. Part 3 states that a tag in the input can only be changed to denote consumption.

We are now in a position to prove $\mathcal{TF}+$ correct. We break the proof into soundness and completeness results.

Theorem 3 (Soundness with respect to $\mathcal{TF}\mathord{/\!\!\!\backslash}$).
A well-formed derivation $\Sigma_I \backslash \Sigma_O \, ; \, \Delta_I \backslash \Delta_O \xrightarrow{s::\pi \quad d}_v G$ implies
$\Sigma_I(\Delta_I) \backslash \Sigma_O(\Delta_O) \xrightarrow{s::\pi \quad d}_v G$

Proof. By structural induction on the given derivation, making use of lemma 2.

Theorem 4 (Completeness with respect to $\mathcal{TF}\mathord{/\!\!\!\backslash}$).
$\Delta_I \backslash \Delta_O \xrightarrow{s::\pi \quad d}_v G$ *implies*
$\exists \Sigma'_O, \Delta'_O. \; \Sigma'_O(\Delta'_O) = \Delta_O$ and $\Sigma'_I \backslash \Sigma'_O \, ; \, \Delta'_I \backslash \Delta'_O \xrightarrow{s::\pi \quad d}_v G$
whenever
$\Sigma'_I(\Delta'_I) = \Delta_I$ and
$(\forall t \in \mathrm{dom}(\Sigma'_I). \exists l \in \mathrm{dom}(\Sigma'_I). \Sigma'_I\backslash_- \models t \leadsto l$ and $\Sigma'_I(l) = \#([\Sigma'_I(\Delta'_I)]_l))$ and
$\forall t \in d :: s :: \pi. \Sigma'_I\backslash_- \models t \leadsto t$

Proof. By induction on the structure of the given derivation making use of lemma 2. Note that given Δ_I, s, π, d, it is always possible to construct Σ'_I and Δ'_I such that the resulting $\mathcal{TF}+$ sequent is well-formed.

$$\frac{}{\Lambda; \Sigma\backslash\Sigma[s := d][d + \Sigma(s)] \; ; \; \Delta\backslash\Delta \xrightarrow{s \ d}_1 \top} \top_{\mathcal{TF}\natural} \qquad \frac{\Sigma(s) = 0}{\Lambda; \Sigma\backslash\Sigma \; ; \; \Delta\backslash\Delta \xrightarrow{s \ d}_0 1} 1_{\mathcal{TF}\natural}$$

$$\frac{\Lambda; \Sigma_I[s+1]\backslash\Sigma_O \; ; \; D^s :: \Delta_I \backslash D^- :: \Delta_O \xrightarrow{s \ d}_v G}{\Lambda; \Sigma_I\backslash\Sigma_O[d-1] \; ; \; \Delta_I\backslash\Delta_O \xrightarrow{s \ d}_v D \multimap G} \multimap_{\mathcal{TF}\natural}$$

$$\frac{\Lambda[l := \Lambda(s)]; \Sigma_I[l := 0]\backslash\Sigma_M \; ; \; \Delta_I\backslash\Delta_M \xrightarrow{l \ d}_0 G_1 \qquad \Lambda; (\Sigma_M \backslash l)\backslash\Sigma_O \; ; \; \Delta_M\backslash\Delta_O \xrightarrow{s \ d}_v G_2}{\Lambda; \Sigma_I\backslash\Sigma_O \; ; \; \Delta_I\backslash\Delta_O \xrightarrow{s \ d}_v G_1 \otimes G_2} \otimes_{0\mathcal{TF}\natural}$$
where l not in conclusion

$$\frac{\Lambda[l := \Lambda(s)]; \Sigma_I[l := 0]\backslash\Sigma_M \; ; \; \Delta_I\backslash\Delta_M \xrightarrow{l \ d}_1 G_1 \qquad \Lambda[l := \Lambda(s)]; \Sigma_M[l := 0]\backslash\Sigma_O \; ; \; \Delta_M\backslash\Delta_O \xrightarrow{l \ d}_v G_2}{\Lambda; \Sigma_I\backslash(\Sigma_O[s := d][d + \Sigma_O(s)] \backslash l) \; ; \; \Delta_I\backslash\Delta_O \xrightarrow{s \ d}_v G_1 \otimes G_2} \otimes_{1\mathcal{TF}\natural}$$
where l not in conclusion

$$\frac{\Lambda; \Sigma_I[l := 0]\backslash\Sigma_M \; ; \; \Delta_I\backslash\Delta_M \xrightarrow{s \ l}_0 G_1 \qquad \Lambda[l := n]; \Sigma_M\backslash\Sigma_O \; ; \; \Delta_M\backslash\Delta_O \xrightarrow{l \ d}_v G_2}{\Lambda; \Sigma_I\backslash\Sigma_O \; ; \; \Delta_I\backslash\Delta_O \xrightarrow{s \ d}_0 G_1 \& G_2} \&_{0\mathcal{TF}\natural}$$
where $[\Delta_I]_l = \emptyset$, $l \notin \mathrm{dom}(\Lambda) \cup \mathrm{dom}(\Sigma_I) \cup \mathrm{cod}(\Sigma_I)$, and $n \notin \mathrm{cod}(\Lambda)$

$$\frac{\Lambda; \Sigma_I[l := 0]\backslash\Sigma_M \; ; \; \Delta_I\backslash\Delta_M \xrightarrow{s \ l}_1 G_1 \qquad \Lambda[l := \Lambda(s)]; \Sigma_M\backslash\Sigma_O \; ; \; \Delta_M\backslash\Delta_O \xrightarrow{l \ d}_v G_2}{\Lambda; \Sigma_I\backslash\Sigma_O \; ; \; \Delta_I\backslash\Delta_O \xrightarrow{s \ d}_v G_1 \& G_2} \&_{1\mathcal{TF}\natural}$$
where $[\Delta_I]_l = \emptyset$, $l \notin \mathrm{dom}(\Lambda) \cup \mathrm{dom}(\Sigma_I) \cup \mathrm{cod}(\Sigma_I)$, and $n \notin \mathrm{cod}(\Lambda)$

$$\frac{\Sigma_I\backslash\Sigma_M \models t \rightsquigarrow l \qquad D \gg A\backslash G \qquad \Lambda; \Sigma_M[l-1][d+1]\backslash\Sigma_O \; ; \; \Delta_L@(D^d :: \Delta_R)\backslash\Delta_O \xrightarrow{s \ d}_v G}{\Lambda; \Sigma_I\backslash\Sigma_O \; ; \; \Delta_L@(D^t :: \Delta_R)\backslash\Delta_O \xrightarrow{s \ d}_v A} \mathrm{pick}\,\Delta_{\mathcal{TF}\natural}$$
where $\Lambda(l) = \Lambda(s)$

Fig. 5. The $\mathcal{TF}\natural$ system

6 The $\mathcal{TF}\natural$ System

Our final refinement concerns the role of π which serves only to denote available tags. By carrying around a complete stack of available tags, we are forced to search through that stack to determine if a given formula may be focussed upon. We can abstract this stack, or more precisely membership in this stack, by associating an availability value with each tag and then ensuring that all available tags have the same availability value, and all unavailable tags do not have that value.

To carry out this idea, the $\mathcal{TF}\natural$ associates with each tag (location) another value which will be used to determine that tag's availability. $\mathcal{TF}\natural$ sequents are of the form

$$\Lambda; \Sigma_I\backslash\Sigma_O \; ; \; \Delta_I\backslash\Delta_O \xrightarrow{s \ d}_v G$$

where: Λ is a partial function of type $\mathcal{L} \to \mathbb{N}$ which tracks each tag's availability; and everything else remains the same as in $\mathcal{TF}+$ sequents. The extension of $\mathcal{TF}+$ rules to $\mathcal{TF}\natural$ rules is based on the observation that the strict tag is always available. Figure 5 contains the $\mathcal{TF}\natural$ derivation rules. Note that the second premise of the $\&_0$ rule assigns the new strict tag l a new availability number, thus making l the only available tag; in contrast, the $\&_1$ rule assigns l the same availability number as s, thus allowing all tags available in the first premise to also be in consumed the second premise.

The systems $\mathcal{TF}\natural$ and $\mathcal{TF}+$ are essentially isomorphic. The following theorem states the logical equivalence of both proof systems.

Theorem 5 (Equivalence of $\mathcal{TF}_\ell^\natural$ and $\mathcal{TF}+$).
$\Lambda; \Sigma_I \backslash \Sigma_O ; \Delta_I \backslash \Delta_O \xrightarrow{u\ d}_v G$ iff $\Sigma_I \backslash \Sigma_O ; \Delta_I \backslash \Delta_O \xrightarrow{s''\pi\ d}_v G$
whenever $s \in \mathrm{dom}(\Lambda)$ and $\forall t \in \Sigma_I(\Delta_I). t \in \mathrm{dom}(\Lambda)$ and $(t \in \pi$ iff $\Lambda(t) = \Lambda(s))$

Proof. By induction on the structure of the given derivation.

7 Implementation and Benchmarks

The first and only published abstract machine for Lolli, LLP, comes from a low-level tag-based resource management system [3,12]. While this approach yields a fast implementation, as evidenced by its performance on LolliCop [14]– a lean connection method theorem prover for Lolli– it fails to preserve the ideal proof search behavior of the more abstract systems. The main design goal for $\mathcal{TF}_\ell^\natural$ was to provide a basis for an efficient low-level implementation while retaining the ideal behavior of more abstract systems.

Tamura and Banbara have recently developed and implemented LLP-TF [17], an abstract machine for Lolli directly based on $\mathcal{TF}_\ell^\natural$. They have also executed a series of benchmarks to compare the performance of LLP-TF to that of LLP. The results of these experiments are summarized in Fig. 6. The with-test, which

		LLP-TF	LLP
with-test	time	0.006	0.506
	speedup	84.33	1.00
LolliCoP	time	1.920	1.794
	speedup	1.00	1.07
12-Queens	time	5.110	3.372
	speedup	1.00	1.51

Fig. 6. LLP-TF benchmarks (CPU time in seconds)

tests the performance of & (additive conjunction), shows that, as expected, LLP-TF outperforms LLP for &-intensive tasks. The LolliCoP benchmark exhibits similar performance in both systems, though LLP is slightly faster in general. For the N-Queens program, LLP is still faster than LLP-TF.

The loss of efficiency in LLP-TF is attributed to the treatment of the multiplicative conjunction. Though the tensor rule is in fact constant time, it requires the creation of a new tag and a check of the ⊤ flag, both of which are absent in LLP. However, LLP checks linear constraints in the linear implication rule, thus eager failure is not available and LLP is less complete than LLP-TF[4]. Additionally, LLP relies on a linear time rule for the additive conjunction while LLP-TF's rule is constant time. As a result, it is possible to write programs that are faster in LLP than in LLP-TF, and vice-versa.

---
[4] LLP will sometimes diverge where LLP-TF will simply fail, but not the converse.

In order to improve the performance of LLP-TF, the code generation for tensor goals $G_1 \otimes G_2$ must be optimized. Whenever G_1, G_2 or both are intuitionistic, optimized code can be generated to avoid the extra cost incurred by the general case. In fact, the current implementation generates optimized code for built-in predicates. For other predicates, static analysis using abstract interpretation seems the most promising technique. It should be noted that this is a compiler optimization independent of both the $\mathcal{TF}\!\!\!/$ proof system and its abstract machine. From that point of view, we believe that $\mathcal{TF}\!\!\!/$ fulfills its original goal.

8 Conclusions and Further Work

We have presented $\mathcal{TF}\!\!\!/$, a new tag-based resource management system for linear logic. This system is based on the intuition that tags are memory locations which store a counter or a reference to another memory location. By using a memory lookup scheme supporting indirections, most linear time operations of previous proposals can be replaced by constant time operations without sacrificing proof search behavior. In particular, the scan of the linear context necessary in the **1** rule of $\mathcal{TF}$[1], has been replaced by a constant-time memory lookup in $\mathcal{TF}\!\!\!/$.

The only non-constant time work for managing linearity constraints in the $\mathcal{TF}\!\!\!/$ system occurs in the **pick** rule which requires looking up the current alias of a given tag. Since the lookup derivation short circuits the alias chains it follows, only the first attempt to lookup a given tag's alias will require a non-constant amount of work.

The implementation of LLP-TF, an abstract machine based on $\mathcal{TF}\!\!\!/$, shows that the proof system is detailed enough to allow a direct, low-level implementation which preserves the ideal proof search behavior of more abstract systems. The performance benchmarks show that LLP-TF is competitive with LLP, though some optimization work remains to be done. In particular, given the pervasive use of tensor in linear logic programming, it is essential to optimize the code generation of tensor goals. We plan to extend the compiler with a static analysis phase to detect intuitionistic predicates.

9 Acknowledgements

The authors are indebted to Professors Naoyuki Tamura and Mutsunori Banbara of Kobe University for implementing an abstract machine based on $\mathcal{TF}\!\!\!/$ and measuring its performance.

References

1. Hodas, J., López, P., Polakow, J., Stoilova, L., Pimentel, E.: A tag-frame system of resource management for proof search in linear-logic programming. In Bradfield, J.C., ed.: CSL'02, Edinburgh, Scotland (2002) 167–182

2. Cervesato, I., Hodas, J.S., Pfenning, F.: Efficient resource management for linear logic proof search. Theoretical Computer Science **232** (2000) 133–163
3. Hodas, J.S., Watkins, K., Tamura, N., Kang, K.S.: Efficient implementation of a linear logic programming language. In: JICSLP'98, IEEE Computer Society Press (1998) 145–149
4. Andreoli, J.M.: Logic programming with focusing proofs in linear logic. Journal of Logic and Computation **2** (1992) 297–347
5. Pym, D., Harland, J.: A uniform proof-theoretic investigation of linear logic programming. Journal of Logic and Computation **4** (1994) 175–207
6. Hodas, J.S., Miller, D.: Logic programming in a fragment of intuitionistic linear logic. Information and Computation **110** (1994) 327–365
7. Girard, J.Y.: Linear logic. Theoretical Computer Science **50** (1987) 1–102
8. Miller, D., Nadathur, G., Pfenning, F., Scedrov, A.: Uniform proofs as a foundation for logic programming. Annals of Pure and Applied Logic **51** (1991) 125–157
9. Hodas, J.S.: Logic Programming in Intuitionistic Linear Logic: Theory, Design and Implementation. PhD thesis, University of Pennsylvania, Department of Computer and Information Science (1994)
10. Miller, D., Nadathur, G.: Higher-order logic programming. In Shapiro, E., ed.: Proceedings of the Third International Logic Programming Conference, London (1986) 448–462
11. López, P., Pimentel, E.: Resource management in linear logic proof search revisited. In Ganzinger, H., McAllester, D., Voronkov, A., eds.: LPAR'99, Tbilisi, Republic of Georgia, Springer-Verlag LNAI 1705 (1999) 304–319
12. Banbara, M., Tamura, N.: Compiling resources in a linear logic programming language. In Sagonas, K., ed.: JICSLP'98 Post Conference Workshop on Implementation Technologies for Programming Languages based on Logic. (1998) 32–45
13. Tamura, N., Kaneda, Y.: Extension of wam for a linear-logic programming language. In Ida, T., Ohori, A., Takeichi, M., eds.: Second Fuji International Workshop on Functional and Logic Programming, World Scientific (1996) 33–50
14. Hodas, J.S., Tamura, N.: lolliCOP - a linear logic encoding of a lean connection-method theorem prover for first-order classical logic. In: IJCAR'01, Siena, Italy (2001) 670–684
15. Polakow, J.: Linearity constraints as bounded intervals in linear logic programming. In: Proceedings of LRPP'04, Turku, Finland (2004)
16. Cervesato, I.: Proof-theoretic foundation of compilation in logic programming languages. In Jaffar, J., ed.: JICSLP'98, Manchester, UK, MIT Press (1998) 115–129
17. Tamura, N., Banbara, M.: Llp-tf: an abstract machine for lolli based on tag-frame-fast. http://bach.istc.kobe-u.ac.jp/llp/tf.html (2004)

Layered Clausal Resolution in the Multi-modal Logic of Beliefs and Goals

Jamshid Bagherzadeh* and S. Arun-Kumar **

Indian Institute of Technology Delhi, 110016, New Delhi, India
jamshid@cse.iitd.ernet.in, sak@cse.iitd.ernet.in

Abstract. In this paper a proof technique for reasoning about the multi-modal logic of beliefs and goals is defined based on resolution at different levels of a tree of clauses. We have considered belief and goal as normal modal logic operators. The technique is inspired by that in [6,7] and allows for a locality property to be satisfied. The main motivation for this work arises not as much from theorem-proving as from the notion of belief and goal revision under an assumption of consistency of the beliefs and goals of an agent. We also present proofs of soundness and completeness of the logic.

Keywords: multi-modal logic, multi-agent systems, resolution, proof method, belief revision.

1 Introduction

Modal logics are widely used for different purposes in computer science and mathematics. This class of logics extends classical logic with two main operators, necessity ($\Box$) and possibility ($\Diamond$) [4]. The semantics of these logics are usually defined in terms of Kripke structures [15]. Modal logics are used in the representation of knowledge, belief, goals and other mental attitudes of agents. Agents usually have three aspects:

- Informational aspects like Knowledge and Beliefs. The modal logics of S5, and KD45 are used usually for these aspects.
- Motivational aspects like Goals, Desires and Intentions. Modal logics of KD are used commonly for these aspects.
- Dynamic or temporal aspects. Linear time or branching time temporal logics are used for modeling these aspects.

In this paper we don't consider the dynamic aspects of agents and we only assume the informational and motivational issues. We use *Belief*, *Goal* and *Intention* for informational and motivational aspects respectively.

In some of the recent literature on agents, the mental state of an agent (in a system of many communicating agents each with incomplete knowledge of the global state of the system) is usually represented by data structures representing

---

* Supported by the ministry of science, research and technology, I.R. Iran.
** Partly supported by research grant F.26-1/2002-TS.V from MHRD, Govt. of India.

the beliefs, goals and intentions of the agents [21]. Two important issues arise in the context of execution of agent programs:

1. How does the mental state of an agent get revised when a new input arrives?
2. How does one reason about the mental state of an agent assuming that it has a finite base of beliefs, goals and intentions, even though their logical consequences may be infinite?

The two issues are closely linked since it is necessary to be able to reason about the mental state to ensure that its revision does not create any logical inconsistency. We will discuss these issues in this paper.

Assume Ψ_i is the mental state of agent i. Alchourron et.al. in [1] have proposed some postulates for belief expansion, contraction and revision which are well known as AGM postulates. The idea is to satisfy the AGM postulates when a new belief ϕ is observed and intended to be added to the belief state of the agent. For example one of the important issues in the revision is the consistency issue, i.e. if Ψ_i is consistent before addition of ϕ, then it should remain consistent after the addition also. This may result in the removal of some of the existing formulas from Ψ_i which contradict ϕ. There are different ways of defining functions for expansion, contraction and revision which satisfy AGM postulates (perhaps not all) in the belief sets[1]. We are not going to define these methods in detail.

We assume each agent has a belief base and a goal base consisting of a set of formulas. The structure of the formulas will be discussed in section 3. Although not common, we assume AGM postulates should hold for the goal base too. The consistency of the set of formulas is checked using the resolution method which will be discussed later. For the sake of completeness we define a simple procedure of revision (using expansion and contraction according to Levi [16]).

Function Revise(S, ϕ)   S is belief or goal base and ϕ is a new formula.
    S= S ∪ {ϕ};   expansion
    return (Contraction(S));   contraction of $\neg\phi$
End Revise.

Function Contraction(S)
    $S_0 = S$; i=0;
    while ($S_i \models$ **false**) do
        Find minimum $F_i \subseteq S_i$ s.t. $F_i \models$ **false**;
        $g_i = \gamma(F_i)$; g_i is one of the formulas of F_i
        $S_{i+1} = S_i - \{g_i\}$;   remove g_i from S_i
        $i = i + 1$;
    end while;
    return S_i;
End Contraction.

---

[1] A belief set is closed under logical consequence and so it is infinite but belief base is not closed under logical consequence and so it is finite

where γ is a function to select a formula from F_i (according to some criteria). In the function Contraction, F_i is one of the minimal subsets of S_i which implies **false**. To find F_i we start from the rule which has implied **false** and by backtracking the route which has resulted in **false**, we may find the subset of formulas which have implied it. If there are more subsets of formulas which imply **false**, they will be found in the next iterations.

Our contraction function is similar to *kernel base contraction* method. It has been shown in the literature [13] that kernel base contraction method satisfies the postulates of AGM (except recovery postulate for contraction[2]).

2 Beliefs and Goals

In this framework we consider n agents each of which has a belief base and a goal base for representing his mental state. We assume the modal operators B and G which stand for belief and goal respectively, satisfy the axioms of **KD45** and **KD**.

A crucial question is that how we can corporate the *intention* modality in such a framework since intentions are also an important part of any agent's mental state. Various authors [5,20,14] have given sound reasons that intention should be treated as non-normal modal operator. Therefor we assume intention is a derived operator in the spirit of [5], which may be defined as $I_i \phi \equiv G_i \phi \wedge B_i \neg \phi$.

Suppose $Ag = \{1, \ldots, n\}$ is a set of agents, and B_i and G_i (Belief and Goal respectively) for any $i \in Ag$, are called the *mental attitudes* for agent i. Let $\mathcal{O} = \{B, G\}$ be a set of symbols. Let **V** be the set $(\mathcal{O} \times Ag)^*$, i.e., the set of finite strings of the form $o_{1_{i_1}} \ldots o_{n_{i_n}}$ with $o_k \in \mathcal{O}$ and $i_k \in Ag$. We call any $v \in$ **V**, a view. Intuitively, each view in **V** represents a possible nesting of mental attitudes. We may imagine the information store as a collection of n trees, such that the tree rooted at Ag_i consists of the information of agent i. Figure 1 shows a schematic information store of the multi-agent system and particularly that of agent i. Considering this structure, we assume any agent has a set of beliefs called the **belief base** and a set of goals called the **goal base**. We assume beliefs of an agent should be consistent. We also suppose the goals of an agent are consistent (set of goals is a subset of desires which are themselves consistent). These two sets are represented by Ψ_{B_i} and Ψ_{G_i} respectively. Each of these sets, contains formulas of a multi-modal logic called BG_n, which will be discussed below. Each formula of BG_n will be transformed to clauses, and clauses will be stored in different nodes (or views) of the tree. Then for reasoning about the system we use resolution inside any view or between two adjacent views.

The remaining part of this paper is organized as follows. In section 3 we define the syntax and semantics of the logic BG_n. Section 4 discusses the normal form NF_{BG} and the transformation of BG_n formulas to NF_{BG} clauses with a small example. Section 5 defines the resolution rules. Then we prove the soundness

---

[2] If we want to remove $p \vee q$ then we must remove p and q consequently, but after re-addition of $p \vee q$ it will imply neither p nor q.

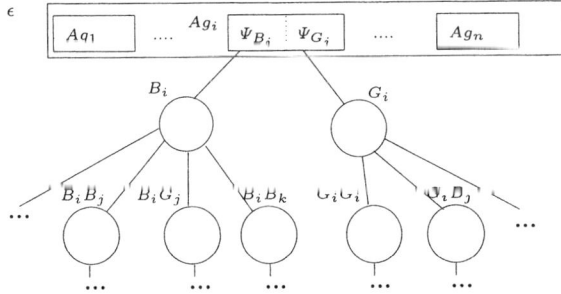

Fig. 1. Information store as a tree, with nodes representing views

and completeness of the resolution system in section 6 and finally section 7 is the conclusion.

3 Syntax and Semantics of BG_n

As we said, any agent has two sets of BG_n formulas representing its beliefs, and goals. Formulas of BG_n are constructed from a set $\mathcal{P} = \{p, q, r, ...\}$ of atomic propositions, and the constants **true** and **false**. The language contains the standard propositional connectives $\neg$, $\wedge$, $\vee$, and unary modal connectives B_i and G_i ($i \in Ag$). Formally the set WFF_{BG} of well-formed formulas of BG_n, is defined as the smallest set such that

- any element of $\mathcal{P}$ is in WFF_{BG};
- **true** and **false** are in WFF_{BG};
- if F and G are in WFF_{BG} then so are
  $\neg F$, $F \vee G$, $F \wedge G$, $B_i F$, $G_i F$ where $i \in Ag$.

We use another binary operator $F \Rightarrow G$ which is an abbreviation of $\neg F \vee G$. We define some particular classes of formulas that will be useful later.

Definition 1. A **literal** l is either p or $\neg p$ where $p \in \mathcal{P}$. A **simple modal literal** is either $O_i l$, or $\neg O_i l$, where l is a literal, $i \in Ag$ and $O \in \{B, G\}$. A **modal literal** is a literal l or its negation $\neg l$ and if F is a modal literal then $O_i F$ and $\neg O_i F$ also are modal literals, where $O \in \{B, G\}$.

Definition 2. A Model M is a structure $M = \langle S, L, S_0, B_1, ..., B_n, G_1, ..., G_n \rangle$, where S is a set of states ranged over by s and t and $\{\} \neq S_0 \subseteq S$ is a set of initial states. L is a state labeling function, i.e., $L : S \to 2^{\mathcal{P}}$. B_i, for all $i \in Ag$ is the agent belief accessibility relation over states, i.e., $B_i \subseteq S \times S$, where each B_i is transitive ($\forall s, s', s'' \in S$: if $(s, s') \in B_i$ and $(s', s'') \in B_i$ then $(s, s'') \in B_i$), serial ($\forall s \in S, \exists s' \in S$ s.t. $(s, s') \in B_i$), and euclidean ($\forall s, s', s'' \in S$, if $(s, s') \in B_i$ and $(s, s'') \in B_i$ then $(s', s'') \in B_i$). Finally G_i, for all $i \in Ag$ is the agent goal accessibility relation over states, i.e., $G_i \subseteq S \times S$, where each G_i is serial.

In Fig. 2 the semantics of the language is defined as the satisfaction relation $\models$ between the states of a model and BG_n formulas by induction on the structure of formulas. We note here that B_i satisfies the axioms of the modal logic **KD45** and

$(M,s) \models \mathbf{true}$	for any state s.
$(M,s) \models p$	iff $p \in L(s)$ (where $p \in \mathcal{P}$).
$(M,s) \models \neg F$	iff $(M,s) \not\models F$
$(M,s) \models F \wedge H$	iff $(M,s) \models F$ and $(M,s) \models H$
$(M,s) \models F \vee H$	iff $(M,s) \models F$ or $(M,s) \models H$
$(M,s) \models O_i F$	iff $\forall t \in S$, if $(s,t) \in O_i$ then $(M,t) \models F$

Fig. 2. Semantics of BG_n

G_i satisfies the axioms of the modal logic **KD**. These axioms for $O \in \{B, G\}$ are:

K: $\vdash O_i(F \Rightarrow H) \Rightarrow (O_i F \Rightarrow O_i H)$ **4**: $\vdash B_i F \Rightarrow B_i B_i F$
D: $\vdash O_i F \Rightarrow \neg O_i \neg F$ **5**: $\vdash \neg B_i F \Rightarrow B_i \neg B_i F$

4 A Normal Form for Formulas of BG_n

We first transform formulas of BG_n to a normal form called NF_{BG}. For this purpose we introduce a symbol **start** such that $(M, s_0) \models \mathbf{start}$ for any initial state s_0. Formulas in NF_{BG} are of the general form

$$\bigwedge_i v_i : C_i$$

where $v_i \in \mathbf{V}$ is a view and C_i is a *clause*. Clauses are of the following form:

start $\Rightarrow \bigvee_{a=1}^{r} l_a$ (an initial clause) , **true** $\Rightarrow \bigvee_{a=1}^{r} m_{Bi_a}$ (a B_i clause)
true $\Rightarrow \bigvee_{a=1}^{r} l_a$ (a literal clause) , **true** $\Rightarrow \bigvee_{a=1}^{r} m_{Gi_a}$ (a G_i clause)

Here l_a are literals, m_{Bi_a} are either literals or simple modal literals involving the B_i modality, and m_{Gi_a} are either literals or simple modal literals involving the G_i modality. For convenience the conjunction is dropped and we consider just the set of clauses of the form $v_i : C_i$.

4.1 Translation to Normal Form

Before the translation to normal form we replace formulas of the form $B_i B_i F$ and $B_i \neg B_i F$ by $B_i F$ and $\neg B_i F$ respectively. The translation to normal form requires a number of propositional variables $x, y, \ldots$ proportional to the number of modal operators and propositional connectives in the formula. In this section we define the process of translation of arbitrary BG_n formulas to the set of clauses in normal form. Consider a formula F of BG_n. The translation will be done in two steps by applying transformations τ_0 and τ_1 as described below (f is a new propositional variable).

$$\tau_0[F] \longrightarrow (\ \epsilon : \textbf{start} \Rightarrow f\ ) \land \tau_1[\ \epsilon :\ f \Rightarrow F\ ]. \tag{1}$$

ϵ denotes the initial view in the tree of clauses. Next, we define τ_1 as follows, assuming x is a proposition. If the main operator on the right side of the implication is either $\land$ or $\neg$ we remove it as follows.

$$\tau_1[v : x \Rightarrow (F \land H)] \longrightarrow \tau_1[v : x \Rightarrow F] \land \tau_1[v : x \Rightarrow H]$$
$$\tau_1[v : x \Rightarrow \neg(F \land H)] \longrightarrow \tau_1[v : x \Rightarrow (\neg F \lor \neg H)]$$
$$\tau_1[v : x \Rightarrow \neg(F \lor H)] \longrightarrow \tau_1[v : x \Rightarrow \neg F] \land \tau_1[v : x \Rightarrow \neg H]$$
$$\tau_1[v : x \Rightarrow \neg\neg F] \longrightarrow \tau_1[v : x \Rightarrow F].$$

Complex sub-formulas that appear within the scope of any modal operator, are transformed as follows (where y is a new proposition, $O_i \in \{B_i, G_i\}$, and F is not a literal).

$$\tau_1[v : x \Rightarrow O_i F] \longrightarrow \tau_1[v : x \Rightarrow O_i y] \land \tau_1[vO_i : y \Rightarrow F]$$
$$\tau_1[v : x \Rightarrow \neg O_i F] \longrightarrow \tau_1[v : x \Rightarrow \neg O_i \neg y] \land \tau_1[vO_i : y \Rightarrow \neg F]$$

Next, we use renaming on formulas whose right hand side has disjunction as its main operator but may not be in the correct form (y is a new proposition and D is a disjunction of formulas which are not necessarily in the normal form).

$\tau_1[v : x \Rightarrow D \lor F] \longrightarrow \tau_1[v : x \Rightarrow D \lor y] \land \tau_1[v : y \Rightarrow F]$
   where F is neither a literal nor a simple modal literal, nor a disjunction of literals and simple modal literals. (For example F could be a conjunction of formulas)
$\tau_1[v : x \Rightarrow D \lor O_i F] \longrightarrow \tau_1[v : x \Rightarrow D \lor y] \land \tau_1[v : y \Rightarrow O_i F]$,
   where D contains a disjunct of the form O'_j or $\neg O'_j$ and $O \neq O'$ or $i \neq j$.
$\tau_1[v : x \Rightarrow D \lor \neg O_i F] \longrightarrow \tau_1[v : x \Rightarrow D \lor y] \land \tau_1[v : y \Rightarrow \neg O_i F]$,
   where D contains a disjunct of the form O'_j or $\neg O'_j$ and $O \neq O'$ or $i \neq j$.
$\tau_1[v : x \Rightarrow D \lor O_i F] \longrightarrow \tau_1[v : x \Rightarrow D \lor O_i y] \land \tau_1[vO_i : y \Rightarrow F]$,
   where F is not a literal and D contains only the modality O_i.
$\tau_1[v : x \Rightarrow D \lor \neg O_i F] \longrightarrow \tau_1[v : x \Rightarrow D \lor \neg O_i \neg y] \land \tau_1[vO_i : y \Rightarrow \neg F]$,
   where F is not a literal and D contains only the modality O_i.

According to the definition of NF_{BG}, each modal clause may contain simple modal literals involving only one modal operator. Thus clause $\textbf{true} \Rightarrow B_1 x \lor y \lor \neg B_1 z$ is allowed, but $\textbf{true} \Rightarrow B_1 x \lor y \lor B_2 z$ and $\textbf{true} \Rightarrow B_1 x \lor y \lor G_1 z$ are not allowed, as they contain more than one modality. The above transformations will make sure that each modal clause contains only one modal operator on the right hand side. Finally we transform the formulas whose right hand side is a disjunction of literals or simple modal literals of the same type: (D is a disjunction of literals and simple modal literals only involving one modal operator.)

$$\tau_1[v : x \Rightarrow D] \longrightarrow v : \textbf{true} \Rightarrow \neg x \lor D$$

$\tau_0[B_i(p \vee \neg B_j(q \vee \neg t))] = (\epsilon : \textbf{start} \Rightarrow f) \wedge \tau_1[\epsilon : f \Rightarrow B_i(p \vee \neg B_j(q \vee \neg t))]$

$\downarrow$

$\tau_1[\epsilon : f \Rightarrow B_i x_1] \wedge \tau_1[B_i : x_1 \Rightarrow p \vee \neg B_j(q \vee \neg t))]$

$\downarrow \qquad\qquad \downarrow$

$\epsilon : \textbf{true} \Rightarrow \neg f \vee B_i x_1 \qquad \tau_1[B_i : x_1 \Rightarrow p \vee \neg B_j \neg x_2] \wedge \tau_1[B_i B_j : x_2 \Rightarrow \neg(q \vee \neg t)]$

$\downarrow \qquad\qquad \downarrow$

$B_i : \textbf{true} \Rightarrow \neg x_1 \vee p \vee \neg B_j \neg x_2 \qquad \tau_1[B_i B_j : x_2 \Rightarrow \neg q \wedge t]$

$\downarrow$

$\tau_1[B_i B_j : x_2 \Rightarrow \neg q] \wedge \tau_1[B_i B_j : x_2 \Rightarrow t]$

$\downarrow \qquad\qquad \downarrow$

$B_i B_j : \textbf{true} \Rightarrow \neg x_2 \vee \neg q \qquad B_i B_j : \textbf{true} \Rightarrow \neg x_2 \vee t$

Fig. 3. Transformation of $F = B_i(p \vee \neg B_j(q \vee \neg t))$ into normal form

After the above transformations we will have a set of clauses in NF_{BG} normal form. Figure 3 shows the different steps in the transformation of the formula $F = B_i(p \vee \neg B_j(q \vee \neg t))$ into normal form.

Proposition 1. *τ_0 transforms every $\varphi \in WFF_{BG}$ into normal form in $O(m+p)$ steps with an extra $O(m+p)$ new propositional variables, where m is the number of modal operators and p is the number of propositional connectives.*

5 Resolution for NF_{BG} Normal Form Formulas

In this section we define the resolution rules for inferring a formula from the information store. Assuming F and H are disjunctions of literals, the initial rules are:

$$[\text{IRES1}] \quad \frac{\epsilon : \textbf{true} \Rightarrow (F \vee l)}{\epsilon : \textbf{start} \Rightarrow (H \vee \neg l)} \qquad [\text{IRES2}] \quad \frac{\epsilon : \textbf{start} \Rightarrow (F \vee l)}{\epsilon : \textbf{start} \Rightarrow (H \vee \neg l)}$$
$$\frac{}{\epsilon : \textbf{start} \Rightarrow (F \vee H)} \qquad\qquad \frac{}{\epsilon : \textbf{start} \Rightarrow (F \vee H)}$$

Next we define modal resolution rules which are used to resolve two simple modal literals in the same view (MRES1, MRES2), or to resolve two clauses in adjacent views (MRES3, MRES4).

$$[\text{MRES1}] \quad \frac{v : \textbf{true} \Rightarrow D \vee m}{v : \textbf{true} \Rightarrow D' \vee \neg m} \qquad [\text{MRES3}] \quad \frac{v : \textbf{true} \Rightarrow D \vee \neg O_i l}{vO_i : \textbf{true} \Rightarrow D' \vee l}$$
$$\frac{}{v : \textbf{true} \Rightarrow D \vee D'} \qquad\qquad \frac{}{v : \textbf{true} \Rightarrow D \vee mod_{O_i}(D')}$$

$$[\text{MRES2}] \quad \frac{v : \textbf{true} \Rightarrow D \vee O_i l}{v : \textbf{true} \Rightarrow D' \vee O_i \neg l} \qquad [\text{MRES4}] \quad \frac{v : \textbf{true} \Rightarrow D \vee O_i l}{vO_i : \textbf{true} \Rightarrow D' \vee \neg l}$$
$$\frac{}{v : \textbf{true} \Rightarrow D \vee D'} \qquad\qquad \frac{}{v : \textbf{true} \Rightarrow D \vee mod_{O_i}(D')}$$

where $mod_{O_i}(D')$ is defined below. In MRES1 and MRES2, D and D' have the same kind of modal operators, i.e. if D has a simple modal literal $O_i l$ then all other simple modal literals of D and all simple modal literals of D' must involve O_i only. In MRES3 and MRES4 if D has belief modality operator, say B_i, then D' must not have any simple modal literals involving O_j such that $O_j \neq B_i$, i.e. all the simple modal literals of D and D' must have B_i only, otherwise we may obtain a resolvent containing a modal literal which has a nesting of two modal operators like $B_i O_j l'$ which is not in the normal form. In this case, if D' has a simple modal literal $O_j l'$ ($O_j \neq B_i$), it must be resolved with another clause already. In MRES3 and MRES4 if $O_i = G_i$, then D' must be a disjunction of literals only, to avoid the problem of nested modal operators.

Definition 3. The function $mod_{O_i}(D)$, is defined on the disjunction of literals or simple modal literals as follows: ($O_i \in \{B_i, G_i\}$)

$mod_{O_i}(l) = \neg O_i \neg l$, $mod_{B_i}(B_i l) = B_i l$
$mod_{O_i}(F \vee H) = mod_{O_i}(F) \vee mod_{O_i}(H)$, $mod_{B_i}(\neg B_i l) = \neg B_i l$

Note that $mod_{B_i}(O_j l)$ where $O_j \neq B_i$ and $mod_{G_i}(O_j l)$ are not defined, as these cases will not occur in the resolution process. Let us justify MRES3, assuming $O_i = B_i$; the same argument holds for G_i. The first clause $v : \mathbf{true} \Rightarrow D \vee \neg B_i l$ is from view v, and the second clause $vB_i : \mathbf{true} \Rightarrow D' \vee l$ is from view vB_i. In resolution rule MRES3, the second clause can be written as $vB_i : \neg D' \Rightarrow l$ and after distributing B_i it will be $v : B_i(\neg D' \Rightarrow l)$, which implies $v : B_i \neg D' \Rightarrow B_i l$. As D' is a disjunction of simple modal literals involving only B_i, i.e., $D' = m_1 \vee \dots \vee m_k$ then $\neg D' = \neg m_1 \wedge \dots \wedge \neg m_k$, and so $B_i \neg D' = B_i \neg m_1 \wedge \dots \wedge B_i \neg m_k$. Finally we obtain the clause $v : \mathbf{true} \Rightarrow \neg B_i \neg m_1 \vee \dots \vee \neg B_i \neg m_k \vee B_i l$. Now we can resolve two clauses $v : \mathbf{true} \Rightarrow D \vee \neg B_i l$ and $v : \mathbf{true} \Rightarrow \neg B_i \neg m_1 \vee \dots \neg B_i \neg m_k \vee B_i l$, which will yield a new clause $v : \mathbf{true} \Rightarrow D \vee \neg B_i \neg m_1 \vee \dots \neg B_i \neg m_k$. If m_i is a simple modal literal then according to a theorem of the logic KD45 [6] which says $\neg B_i \neg B_i \neg F \Leftrightarrow B_i \neg F$, we can remove $\neg B_i \neg$ from the simple modal literals and if $m_i = l'$ it will remain in the form $\neg B_i \neg l'$. In the case of goals, D' is just a disjunction of literals, that is because we don't have the equivalence $\neg G_i \neg G_i \neg F \Leftrightarrow G_i \neg F$ in the logic KD.

Example. Suppose agent i has the **belief base:** $B_i(\neg p \vee B_j q)$, $B_i B_j \neg q$. The question is, whether $B_i \neg p$ is implied by the belief base. We add $\neg B_i \neg p$ to the belief base and check if the resolution process results in the clause $\epsilon : \mathbf{start} \Rightarrow$ **false** (see Fig. 4).

6 Soundness and Completeness

We will prove that the transformation into NF_{BG} preserves satisfiability. Assume $M = \langle S, L, S_0, B_1, \dots, B_n, G_1, \dots, G_n \rangle$ is a Kripke structure. We say s' is accessible from s via relation O_i if $(s, s') \in O_i$. Moreover if s'' is accessible from s' via v' and s' is accessible from s via v, then s'' is accessible from s via vv' where vv' is concatenation of v and v'. If state s is accessible from an initial state

Clauses :

$$\frac{B_i(\neg p \vee B_j q)}{\begin{array}{l} 1.\ \epsilon : \textbf{start} \Rightarrow f \\ 2.\ \epsilon : \textbf{true} \Rightarrow \neg f \vee B_i x_1 \\ 3.\ B_i : \textbf{true} \Rightarrow \neg x_1 \vee \neg p \vee B_j q \end{array}} \qquad \frac{B_i B_j \neg q}{\begin{array}{l} 4.\ \epsilon : \textbf{start} \Rightarrow f \\ 5.\ \epsilon : \textbf{true} \Rightarrow \neg f \vee B_i y_1 \\ 6.\ B_i : \textbf{true} \Rightarrow \neg y_1 \vee B_j \neg q \end{array}} \qquad \frac{\neg B_i \neg p}{\begin{array}{l} 7.\ \epsilon : \textbf{start} \Rightarrow f \\ 8.\ \epsilon : \textbf{true} \Rightarrow \neg f \vee \neg B_i \neg p \end{array}}$$

Resolution :

$\begin{array}{c} 3 \\ 6 \end{array} \xrightarrow{\text{MRES2}}$ 9. $B_i : \textbf{true} \Rightarrow \neg x_1 \vee \neg p \vee \neg y_1 \xrightarrow{8 \quad \text{MRES3}}$ 10. $\epsilon : \textbf{true} \Rightarrow \neg f \vee \neg B_i x_1 \vee \neg B_i y_1$

$\begin{array}{c} 2 \\ 10 \end{array} \xrightarrow{\text{MRES1}}$ 11. $\epsilon : \textbf{true} \Rightarrow \neg f \vee \neg B_i y_1 \xrightarrow{5 \quad \text{MRES1}}$ 12. $\epsilon : \textbf{true} \Rightarrow \neg f \xrightarrow{1 \quad \text{IRES1}} \epsilon : \textbf{start} \Rightarrow \textbf{false}$

Fig. 4. Clausal form and resolution process of belief base of the example

s_0 via v, we say s is at **level** v of the Kripke structure M. We say $M, s \models v : F$ iff for any state s' accessible from s via v, $M, s' \models F$. The following proposition shows that the transformation τ_0 preserves satisfiability and unsatisfiability.

Proposition 2. *Assume M is a Kripke structure and s_0 is an initial state,*
1. $(M, s_0) \models \tau_1[v : x \Rightarrow F]$ *implies* $(M, s_0) \models (v : x \Rightarrow F)$.
2. $(M, s_0) \models \tau_0[F]$ *implies* $(M, s_0) \models F$.
3. *If there is a model M, such that $(M, s_0) \models \epsilon : x \Rightarrow F$, then there is a model M' s.t. $(M', s'_0) \models \tau_1[\epsilon : x \Rightarrow F]$.*
4. *For any model M of F, there exists a model M_0 of $\tau_0[F]$.*

From the above proposition we have:

Theorem 1. *A BG_n formula A is satisfiable if and only if $\tau_0[A]$ is satisfiable.*

Theorem 2 (Soundness). *Let T be a set of NF_{BG} clauses. Let the clause set R be obtained from T by applying one of the resolution rules. Then T is satisfiable if and only if R is satisfiable.*

Sketch of the proof. We prove the above theorem by considering any rule and assuming its premises are satisfiable, then we prove its conclusion (or resolvent) is also satisfiable. For reverse direction, if T is unsatisfiable then after adding the new clause to obtain R, still R is unsatisfiable. □

Theorem 3 (Termination). *The resolution process (repeated applications of the rules in section 5) in a set of NF_{BG} clauses always terminates.*

Sketch of the proof. As the resolution rules don't create new views, so the resolution process terminates after some steps, because there are a finite number of propositions, views and modal operators. □

The completeness proof is based on the construction of a behavior graph [7,6]. We construct a graph of NF_{BG} clauses which has belief and goal relations for any agent i. We will show that the set of resolution rules presented here is complete, and there is a refutation by resolution if the set of clauses is unsatisfiable. Note that we use the word 'view' when we refer to a subset of clauses (we say clauses of view v) and we use the word 'level' when we refer to some subset of states in the graph (we say states of level v).

Definition 4. The depth of a modal literal F is the number of modal operators applied to a literal. Depth of literal l or its negation $\neg l$ is 0. Depth of $O_i F$ or $\neg O_i F$ is $1 + depth(F)$.

Definition 5. Given a set of NF_{BG} clauses, the view $v = O_{i_1} \ldots O_{i_k}$ is called a *deepest view* if there are clauses in view v, but no clause in view $vO_{i_{k+1}}$ for any $O \in \{B, G\}$ and $i_1, \ldots, i_{k+1} \in Ag$.

It is possible to have more than one deepest view in a set of clauses.

Definition 6. Let $C = v : \textbf{true} \Rightarrow \phi$ be a NF_{BG} clause, we define $lset(C) = \{l, \neg l \mid l \text{ is an atomic proposition in } \phi\}$ and $mset(C) = \{m, \neg m \mid m \text{ is a simple modal literal in } \phi\}$. If v is a view and $C_1, \ldots, C_n$ are all of the clauses of the form $v : \textbf{true} \Rightarrow \phi$ then we define $cl(v) = \{C_1, \ldots, C_n\}$ which is the set of clauses contained in view v. Moreover we define $lset(v) = lset(C_1) \cup \cdots \cup lset(C_n)$ and $mset(v) = mset(C_1) \cup \cdots \cup mset(C_n)$.

For example if $C_1 \equiv B_j : \textbf{true} \Rightarrow \neg x \vee B_i p \vee q$ and $C_2 \equiv B_j : \textbf{true} \Rightarrow y \vee B_k t \vee p$ then $lset(C_1) = \{x, p, q, \neg x, \neg p, \neg q\}$ and $mset(C) = \{B_i p, \neg B_i p\}$. If view B_j contains only clauses C_1 and C_2, then $lset(B_j) = \{x, p, q, y, t, \neg x, \neg p, \neg q, \neg y, \neg t\}$, and $mset(B_j) = \{B_i p, B_k t, \neg B_i p, \neg B_k t\}$.

Graph Construction Assume as before $Ag = \{1, \ldots, n\}$ is a set of agents and T is a set of clauses. For any set $S = \{f_1, \ldots, f_n\}$ of modal literals (cf. Def. 1), $i \in Ag$ and $O \in \{B, G\}$ **Application** of O_i to S is represented as $O_i.S$ and defined as $O_i.S = \{O_i f_1, \ldots, O_i f_n\}$. We start with the clauses in the deepest views. Assume $v = O_1 \ldots O_k$ is a deepest view. Let $\Delta_k = lset(v) \cup mset(v)$. We take $\Delta_{k-1} = lset(O_1 \ldots O_{k-1}) \cup mset(O_1 \ldots O_{k-1}) \cup O_k.\Delta_k \cup \{\neg f \mid f \in O_k.\Delta_k\}$. Now we will do the same process for obtaining elements of Δ_{k-2} ($\Delta_{k-2} = lset(O_1 \ldots O_{k-2}) \cup mset(O_1 \ldots O_{k-2}) \cup O_{k-1}.\Delta_{k-1} \cup \{\neg f \mid f \in O_{k-1}.\Delta_{k-1}\}$). We repeat the same process till we get the set Δ_0. We define $\Delta_v = \Delta_0 \cup \cdots \cup \Delta_k$.[3] Now consider all other deepest views v' and do the same for v' to obtain other sets $\Delta_{v'}$. Finally we define $\Delta = \bigcup_v \Delta_v$ where v is a deepest view.

Definition 7. Let F and H be modal literals. We define the relation $\mathbf{F \Rightarrow H}$ as: $F \Rightarrow F$, $O_i F \Rightarrow O_i H$ iff $F \Rightarrow H$, $O_i F \Rightarrow \neg O_i \neg H$ iff $F \Rightarrow H$. Moreover a pair of formulas is **complementary** if they are of one of the following forms (assume $F \Rightarrow H$): F and $\neg F$, $O_i F$ and $\neg O_i H$, $O_i F$ and $O_i \neg H$.

For example $B_i p$ and $B_i \neg p$, $G_i G_j p$ and $G_i \neg G_j p$, $B_i G_j B_k p$ and $\neg B_i \neg G_j \neg B_k p$ are all complementary pairs.

Graph $G = (S, B_1, \ldots B_n, G_1, \ldots, G_n)$ is constructed as follows. The set of states S is constructed by considering all possible maximal subsets of Δ (which

---
[3] Note that Δ_v has modal literals of depth at most $k + 1$.

is defined earlier as $\bigcup_v \Delta_v$) which are consistent. δ is a maximal consistent subset of Δ if we can not add any more element from Δ to δ, otherwise it will be inconsistent. δ is consistent if it doesn't have a complementary pair.

Definition 8. For each maximal consistent subset δ of Δ, we will have a corresponding state $s \in S$ and will say δ is the **label** of s, and we write $label(s) = \delta$.

Let us consider a simple example. Consider only one clause B_j : **true** $\Rightarrow p$. Then Δ includes $\{p, \neg p, B_j p, B_j \neg p, \neg B_j p, \neg B_j \neg p\}$ and it has six maximal subsets:

$$S = \{\ \{p, B_j p, \neg B_j \neg p\},\ \{p, B_j \neg p, \neg B_j p\},\ \{p, \neg B_j p, \neg B_j \neg p\},$$
$$\{\neg p, B_j p, \neg B_j \neg p\},\ \{\neg p, B_j \neg p, \neg B_j p\},\ \{\neg p, \neg B_j p, \neg B_j \neg p\}\ \}$$

(Note that there are exactly some clauses in the view ϵ but we haven't considered them in this example.) So far we have considered all the possible states of a Kripke structure. We must check which states satisfy the clauses in different views. Let $C = vO_i$: **true** $\Rightarrow F$ be a clause, where $F = f_1 \vee \cdots \vee f_n$ and each f_i is a modal literal.

1. We move all but one of the disjuncts of F to the left of $\Rightarrow$ in clause C. Without loss of generality assume f_1 remains in the right hand side. Thus: $C = vO_i : \neg f_2 \wedge \cdots \wedge \neg f_n \Rightarrow f_1$.
2. We apply O_i to the clause and we obtain $C = v : O_i(\neg f_2 \wedge \cdots \wedge \neg f_n \Rightarrow f_1)$
3. Based on axiom **K** we have $v : O_i(\neg f_2 \wedge \cdots \wedge \neg f_n) \Rightarrow O_i f_1$
4. This in turn implies $v : O_i \neg f_2 \wedge \cdots \wedge O_i \neg f_n \Rightarrow O_i f_1$.
5. We again move formulas from left of $\Rightarrow$ to its right side,
v : **true** $\Rightarrow O_i f_1 \vee \neg O_i \neg f_2 \vee \cdots \vee \neg O_i \neg f_n$.

The clause of step 5 is called a **pushed** clause (we have pushed O_i into clause) and it is a pushed clause in the view v. If $O_i = B_i$ and $f_j = B_i g_j$, with $j \neq 1$, then from the equivalence $\neg B_i \neg B_i f \Leftrightarrow B_i f$ of the logic KD45 we obtain $\neg B_i \neg B_i g_j = B_i g_j = f_j$ (so $\neg B_i \neg f_j = f_j$). But if $f_j = l$ is a literal, then it will remain $\neg B_i \neg f_j$. Similarly for $B_i f_1$. The reader can see that if in step 1 we keep f_j, $j \neq 1$, on the right side we obtain another pushed clause. In summary we have the following definition.

Definition 9. Let $C = vO_i$: **true** $\Rightarrow F$ be a clause of view vO_i. We define $C^{\rightarrow} = \{v : \textbf{true} \Rightarrow F'\}$ to be a set of clauses obtained after **pushing** O_i to clause C. F' is obtained from O_i and F using the above algorithm. If vO_i is a view such that $S = cl(vO_i) = \{C_1, \ldots, C_n\}$, then $S^{\rightarrow} = C_1^{\rightarrow} \cup \cdots \cup C_n^{\rightarrow}$ is the set of pushed clauses (in the view v) after pushing O_i.

For example suppose $C = vO_k$: **true** $\Rightarrow l$. Then $C^{\rightarrow} = \{v : \textbf{true} \Rightarrow O_k l\}$ has only one element. If $C = vO_k$: **true** $\Rightarrow l_1 \vee l_2$. Then $C^{\rightarrow} = \{v : \textbf{true} \Rightarrow O_k l_1 \vee \neg O_k \neg l_2, v : \textbf{true} \Rightarrow \neg O_k \neg l_1 \vee O_k l_2\}$. Consider $C = vB_i$: **true** $\Rightarrow l_1 \vee l_2 \vee B_i l_3$, then $C^{\rightarrow} = \{v : \textbf{true} \Rightarrow B_i l_1 \vee \neg B_i \neg l_2 \vee B_i l_3, v : \textbf{true} \Rightarrow \neg B_i \neg l_1 \vee B_i l_2 \vee B_i l_3\}$. Here v : **true** $\Rightarrow \neg B_i \neg l_1 \vee \neg B_i \neg l_2 \vee B_i l_3$ is a pushed clause also, but we may ignore it as it is implied by the first and second clauses. As a final example suppose $C = vG_i$: **true** $\Rightarrow l_1 \vee B_i l_2$, then $C^{\rightarrow} = \{v : \textbf{true} \Rightarrow G_i l_1 \vee \neg G_i \neg B_i l_2, v : \textbf{true} \Rightarrow \neg G_i \neg l_1 \vee G_i B_i l_2\}$.

Definition 10. Let $w_n = O_1 \ldots O_n$ be a sequence of n modal operators ($|w_n| = n$). Let vw_n be a view with the set of clauses $S = cl(vw_n)$ then $S^{\rightarrow n} = S^{\rightarrow}(\ldots(S^{\rightarrow}))$ where $\rightarrow$ is applied n times, is a set of pushed clauses of the form $v : \mathbf{true} \Rightarrow \phi$. This intuitively means all modal operators of w_n consecutively are pushed to clauses of S. Generally if $\lambda_v = \{vw \mid vw \text{ is a view with a nonempty set of clauses}\}$ is a set of all nonempty views which include subview v, then we define the **entire set of pushed clauses of** v as $pcl(v) = \bigcup_{vw \in \lambda_v} cl(vw)^{\rightarrow |w|}$. Intuitively $pcl(v)$ contains all pushed clauses which are in view v.

Now we go back to the graph and find the states which satisfy clauses of view v for any v. We assign v to state $s \in S$ if $label(s) \models cl(v) \wedge pcl(v)$, i.e. s can be in level v (it is accessible from one of the initial states via relation v) of the graph if it satisfies the clauses and pushed clauses of v. If state s is assigned more than one level (for example s is assigned v and v') then we make one copy of s for each combination of these levels and we assign that combination to the labeling of the corresponding copy of s. For example suppose s is assigned v and v', then we consider four copies of s as: s^1, s^2, s^3, s^4, which are assigned by $\{v\}$, $\{v'\}$, $\{v, v'\}$, and $\{\}$ respectively. The reason for this will become clear in the proof of theorem 4. For a sketch intuition behind this, assume $s \in S$ belongs to levels v_1 and v_2. Assume there is a state $t \in S$ which belongs to level $v_1 B_i$ but is not a member of level $v_2 B_i$. As we will discuss below this means we can not make a B_i transition from s to t as t is not in level $v_2 B_i$, although t is in level $v_1 B_i$. For solving this problem we make various copies of s with different levels assigned to them. For example the copy of s which is assigned only by v_1 has a transition to t. Finally we define level(v) to be the set of all states assigned v as $\mathbf{level(v)} = \{s \in S \mid s \text{ is assigned } v\}$.

Definition 11. For any agent i and set of modal literals X, $O_i\_set(X) = \{F \mid O_i F \in X\}$.

Now the set S of states is ready. The initial states are $\{s \in S \mid s \in level(\epsilon) \text{ and } label(s) \models f\}$ where f is defined in the transformation process. We will find the accessibility relations B_i and G_i for any agent i. In the behavior graph we show each relation by edges between states labeled by the name of the relation. We add an edge from s to s' labeled by B_i iff the three following conditions hold:

a. If $V = \{v_1, \ldots, v_k\}$ is the set of levels assigned to s, then $VB = \{v_1 B_i, \ldots, v_k B_i\}$ is the set of levels assigned to s' s.t. if vB_i is a view with an empty set of clauses, then vB_i is omitted from VB. Also $v_j B_i B_i = v_j B_i$.
b. $label(s') \models B_i\_set(label(s))$ which means if $label(s) \models B_i F$ then $label(s') \models F$ for any F.
c. $B_i F \in label(s)$ iff $B_i F \in label(s')$ and $\neg B_i F \in label(s)$ iff $\neg B_i F \in label(s')$, which means s and s' have the same set of beliefs involving B_i. This rule guarantees B_i to be euclidean and transitive.

To find G_i relations for state s we will find all states s' which satisfy only conditions **a.** and **b.** replacing B_i with G_i. Now we will delete those states which can not be a state in any model. If v is a view with a nonempty set of clauses, but $level(v)$ is empty, i.e. $\neg \exists s \in S : label(s) \models cl(v) \wedge pcl(v)$, then the set of clauses does not have any model. In this case we will delete all the states of graph, and we say graph is **empty**. Otherwise for any v with a nonempty set of clauses, $level(v) \neq \emptyset$. Now the graph is constructed. We can show the relations B_i are *serial, transitive, and euclidean* and the relations G_i are *serial*.

Proposition 3. *1. The relations G_i in the behavior graph are serial.*
2. The relations B_i in the behavior graph are serial, transitive and euclidean.

We could also prove the following lemma to ensure consistency between adjacent levels.

Lemma 1. Let T be a set of NF_{BG} clauses, and G be the behavior graph constructed by the above process. For any node s of the graph, if $\neg O_i f \in label(s)$ then there is a node s', s.t. $(s, s') \in O_i$ and $\neg f \in label(s')$.

The Above lemma and proposition show that the constructed graph is a Kripke structure for the set of clauses. But there is a point which must be cleared here. In the construction process of the graph, for each state of the graph in level v, we checked if it satisfies clauses of view v ($cl(v)$) and pushed clauses of view v ($pcl(v)$). The following lemma shows it is not possible that the set of original normal form clauses to be satisfiable while the set of clauses obtained after pushing the modalities is unsatisfiable.

Lemma 2. Let T be a set of clauses including a clause C in view vO_i. Let $R = T \cup C^{\rightharpoonup}$ be the set of clauses of T and the pushed clauses obtained from C. T is satisfiable if and only if R is satisfiable.

This lemma shows that pushing modalities into clauses preserves satisfiability. Finally we can prove that, for an unsatisfiable set of clauses, the constructed graph is empty, and thus there is no model.

Theorem 4. *The set of clauses T is unsatisfiable iff its behavior graph G is empty.*

Now we can prove the completeness of the method. The resolution rules are complete if they can detect the emptiness of the graph. The graph is empty if some level v (with nonempty set of clauses in view v) is empty. A level v is empty if the clauses and pushed clauses of view v imply **false**. In the following we will prove that our resolution calculus is complete.

Before proving the next theorem we will define two new resolution rules and later we will prove that they can be eliminated. Assume F and H are modal literals then resolution rules MRESC1 and MRESC2 are defined as:

$$[\text{MRESC1}] \quad \frac{v : \textbf{true} \Rightarrow D \vee O_i F \qquad v : \textbf{true} \Rightarrow D' \vee O_i H}{v : \textbf{true} \Rightarrow D \vee D'} \qquad [\text{MRESC2}] \quad \frac{v : \textbf{true} \Rightarrow D \vee O_i F \qquad v : \textbf{true} \Rightarrow D' \vee \neg O_i H}{v : \textbf{true} \Rightarrow D \vee D'}$$

where in MRESC1, F and H are complementary, and in MRESC2, $F \Rightarrow H$

Theorem 5 (Completeness). Let T be a set of clauses and their pushed clauses. Then T is unsatisfiable iff there is a refutation by resolution rules IRES1, IRES2, MRES1, MRES2, MRESC1 and MRESC2.

Next we will prove that rules MRESC1 and MRESC2 are not necessary.

Definition 12. If F, F_1 and F_2 are modal literals and $O_i \in \{B_i, G_i\}$ then Rev is defined as:

1. $Rev(\neg O_i F) = \neg F$ 2. $Rev(O_i F) = F$ 3. $Rev(B_i l) = B_i l$
4. $Rev(\neg B_i l) = \neg B_i l$ 5. $Rev(F_1 \vee F_2) = Rev(F_1) \vee Rev(F_2)$.

Relation $Rev(F)$ is the reverse of pushing modal operators $(C^{\rightarrow})$ into clauses. Any pushed clause P in view v has a corresponding original clause C in view $v\omega$ s.t. P is obtained by pushing modalities of ω into C. Relation Rev takes P and computes C. Note that for modal literals $B_i l$ and $\neg B_i l$ there might be two reverses (depending on the other disjunct). For example, if we have clause $v: B_i B_j p \vee \neg B_i q$ then its reverse can be either $vB_i: B_j p \vee \neg B_i q$ or $vB_i: B_j p \vee \neg q$, but the first one is not possible as it has two different modal operators and second one is the correct reverse. Using the relation Rev, we can prove the following lemma which completes the proof of completeness.

Lemma 3. If two clauses of view v can be resolved with resolution rules MRESC1 and MRESC2, then their corresponding original clauses can be resolved with resolution rules MRES1, MRES2, MRES3 and MRES4.

7 Conclusion and Future Work

In this paper we have defined a framework for belief and goal bases and a resolution based proof method for reasoning about them. We have also proved the soundness, termination and completeness of the method.

There do exist tableau based methods for various modal logics in the literature (notably [12,17,3]). For certain modal logics such as S4, S5 and T resolution methods exist [8]. Our method closely follows that of [6,7]. However we have advanced their work to include an additional **KD** modality while dropping the temporal operators.

Our motivation however is not just to provide a proof system but instead to tackle the problem of revision of an information store organized hierarchically. The main feature of our method is the "locality" property enjoyed by our rules. We have shown that it is necessary to consider complementary pairs of clauses only at the same or between adjacent levels. This we believe considerably simplifies the tasks of belief and goal revision in order to keep the information store consistent on fresh inputs. Secondly, it is no longer necessary to translate the formulas into classical logic as is recommended by some authors [18,22,19,9]. However, even though we have combined the logics of **KD45** and **KD**, we have not defined any interactions between them as it gets complicated to manage using resolution rules. This is a subject of future research.

The idea of hierarchical structure for information store is taken (in some sense) from Benerecetti et.al. [2]. More details of hierarchical structures and the proposed logic can be found in [11,10].

Acknowledgment We thank the anonymous referees for some very insightful comments.

References

1. C. Alchourron, P. Gardenfors, and D. Makinson. On the logic of theory change: Partial meet contraction and revision functions. *The Journal of Symbolic Logic*, 50(2):510–530, 1985.
2. M. Benerecetti, F. Giunchiglia, and L. Serafini. Model checking multi-agent systems. *Journal of Logic and Computation*, 8(3):401–424, 1998.
3. B. Bennett, C. Dixon, M. Fisher, U. Hustadt, E. Franconi, I. Horrocks, and M. De Rijke. Combinations of modal logics. *Artif. Intell. Rev.*, 17(1):1–20, 2002.
4. Brian F. Chellas. *Modal Logic: An Introduction*. Cambridge University Press, 1980.
5. P. R. Cohen and H. J. Levesque. Intention is choice with commitment. *Artificial Intelligence*, 42(2-3):213–261, 1990.
6. Clare Dixon, Michael Fisher, and Alexander Bolotov. Clausal resolution in a logic of rational agency. *Artif. Intell.*, 139(1):47–89, 2002.
7. M. Fisher, C. Dixon, and M. Peim. Clausal temporal resolution. *ACM Trans. Coput. Logic*, 2(1):12–56, 2001.
8. M. Fitting. Proof methods for modal and intuitionistic logics. In *volume 169 of Synthese Library*. D. Reidel, Dordrecht. 1983.
9. A. M. Frisch and R. B. Scherl. A general framework for modal deduction. In *proccedings of KR*, pages 196–207. Morgan Kaufmann, 1991.
10. C. Ghidini and F. Giunchiglia. Local models semantics, or contextual reasoning = locality+compatibility. *Artificial Intelligence*, 127(2):221–259, 2001.
11. F. Giunchiglia and L. Serafini. Multilanguage hierarchical logics or: How we can do without modal logics. *Artificial Intelligence*, 65(1):29–70, 1994.
12. R. Gore. Tableau methods for modal and temporal logics. In M. D'Agostino, D. Gabbay, R. Haehnle, and J. Posegga, editors, *Handbook of Tableau Methods*, pages 297–396. Kluwer Academic Publishers, 1999.
13. Sven Ove Hansson. *A Textbook of Belief Dynamics*. Kluwer Academic Press, 1999.
14. A. Herzig and D. Longin. A logic of intention with cooperation principles and with assertive speech acts as communication primitives. In *Proc. first Int. joint Conf. on Autonomous agents and multiagent systems*, pages 920–927. ACM Press, 2002.
15. S. A. Kripke. Semantical considerations on modal logic. In *A Colloquium on Modal and Many-Valued Logics*, Helsinki, 1962.
16. I. Levi. Subjunctive, dispositions and chances. *Synthese*, 34:423–455, 1977.
17. F. Massacci. Single step tableaux for modal logics. *Journal of Automated Reasoning*, 24(3):319–364, 2000.
18. Robert C. Moore. A formal theory of knowledge and action. In J. R. Hobbs and R. C. Moore, editors, *Formal Theories of the Commonsense World*, pages 319–358, Ablex, Norwood NJ, 1985.
19. H. J. Ohlbach. Semantics-based translation methods for modal logics. *Journal of Logic and Computation*, 1(5):691746, 1991.

20. M. D. Sadek. A study in the logic of intention. In B. Nebel, C. Rich, and W. Swartout, editors, *Proc. Third Int. Conf. on Principles of knowledge Representation and Reasoning (KR'92)*, pages 462–473. Morgan Kaufmann Publisher, 1992.
21. Y. Shoham. Agent-oriented programming. *Artificial Intelligence*, 60(1):51–92, March 1993.
22. R. M. Smullyan. A generalization of intuitionistic and modal logics. In H. Leblanc, editor, *Truth, Syntax and Modality*, pages 274–293, Amsterdam, 1973.

Author Index

Abadi, Martín, 110
Albert, Elvira, 380
Aminof, Benjamin, 194
Areces, Carlos, 125
Arun-Kumar, S., 544
Ayala-Rincón, Mauricio, 433

Baaz, Matthias, 1, 481
Bagherzadeh, Jamshid, 544
Ball, Thomas, 194
Benedetti, Marco, 285
Benzmüller, Christoph, 415
Beringer, Lennart, 347
Berwanger, Dietmar, 209
Bickford, Mark, 449
Bordeaux, Lucas, 270

Cadoli, Marco, 270
Ciabattoni, Agata, 496
Constable, Robert C., 449

Dahllöf, Vilhelm, 95
de Moura, Flávio L.C., 433
Di Cosmo, Roberto, 240
Donnelly, Kevin, 466
Drielsma, Paul Hankes, 363
Dufour, Thomas, 240

Eiter, Thomas, 511

Fermüller, Christian G., 496
Fontaine, Pascal, 51

Gibson, Tyler, 466
Giesl, Jürgen, 301
Gorín, Daniel, 125
Grädel, Erich, 209

Halpern, Joseph Y., 449
Hardin, Chris, 224
Hasegawa, Ryuzo, 67
Hermenegildo, Manuel, 380
Hetzl, Stefan, 481
Heymans, Stijn, 169
Hofmann, Martin, 347
Hustadt, Ullrich, 21

Ianni, Giovambattista, 511

Jamnik, Mateja, 415

Kamareddine, Fairouz, 433
Kerber, Manfred, 415
Koshimura, Miyuki, 67
Krishnaswami, Neel, 466
Kupferman, Orna, 194

López, Pablo, 528
Leitsch, Alexander, 1, 481
Linke, Thomas, 154

Mödersheim, Sebastian, 363
Müller-Olm, Markus, 432
Magill, Stephen, 466
Mancini, Toni, 270
Marcinkowski, Jerzy, 142
Metcalfe, George, 496
Momigliano, Alberto, 347
Motik, Boris, 21

Nieuwenhuis, Robert, 36
Nordh, Gustav, 257

Oliveras, Albert, 36
Otop, Jan, 142

Park, Sungwoo, 466
Petride, Sabina, 449
Polakow, Jeff, 528
Puebla, Germán, 380

Ranise, Silvio, 51
Richter, Clemens, 481

Sarsakov, Vladimir, 154
Sattler, Ulrike, 21
Schindlauer, Roman, 511
Schirmer, Norbert, 398
Schneider-Kamp, Peter, 301
Schweitzer, Stephan, 332
Seidl, Helmut, 79, 432
Shkaravska, Olha, 347
Sorge, Volker, 415
Spohr, Hendrik, 481
Stelmaszek, Grzegorz, 142

Thiemann, René, 301
Tinelli, Cesare, 36
Tompits, Hans, 511

Umeda, Mayumi, 67

Van Nieuwenborgh, Davy, 169
Verma, Kumar Neeraj, 79

Vermeir, Dirk, 169
Viganò, Luca, 363

Walther, Christoph, 332
Walukiewicz, Igor, 184
Whitehead, Nathan, 110

Zarba, Calogero G., 51

Lecture Notes in Artificial Intelligence (LNAI)

Vol. 3452: F. Baader, A. Voronkov (Eds.), Logic Programming, Artificial Intelligence, and Reasoning. XII, 562 pages. 2005.

Vol. 3416: M. Böhlen, J. Gamper, W. Polasek, M.A. Wimmer (Eds.), E-Government: Towards Electronic Democracy. XIII, 311 pages. 2005.

Vol. 3403: B. Ganter, R. Godin (Eds.), Formal Concept Analysis. XI, 419 pages. 2005.

Vol. 3398: D.-K. Baik (Ed.), Systems Modeling and Simulation: Theory and Applications. XIV, 733 pages. 2005.

Vol. 3397: T.G. Kim (Ed.), Artificial Intelligence and Simulation. XV, 711 pages. 2005.

Vol. 3396: R.M. van Eijk, M.-P. Huget, F. Dignum (Eds.), Agent Communication. X, 261 pages. 2005.

Vol. 3374: D. Weyns, H.V.D. Parunak, F. Michel (Eds.), Environments for Multi-Agent Systems. X, 279 pages. 2005.

Vol. 3369: V.R. Benjamins, P. Casanovas, J. Breuker, A. Gangemi (Eds.), Law and the Semantic Web. XII, 249 pages. 2005.

Vol. 3366: I. Rahwan, P. Moraitis, C. Reed (Eds.), Argumentation in Multi-Agent Systems. XII, 263 pages. 2005.

Vol. 3359: G. Grieser, Y. Tanaka (Eds.), Intuitive Human Interfaces for Organizing and Accessing Intellectual Assets. XIV, 257 pages. 2005.

Vol. 3346: R.H. Bordini, M. Dastani, J. Dix, A.E.F. Seghrouchni (Eds.), Programming Multi-Agent Systems. XIV, 249 pages. 2005.

Vol. 3345: Y. Cai (Ed.), Ambient Intelligence for Scientific Discovery. XII, 311 pages. 2005.

Vol. 3343: C. Freksa, M. Knauff, B. Krieg-Brückner, B. Nebel, T. Barkowsky (Eds.), Spatial Cognition IV. Reasoning, Action, and Interaction. XIII, 519 pages. 2005.

Vol. 3339: G.I. Webb, X. Yu (Eds.), AI 2004: Advances in Artificial Intelligence. XXII, 1272 pages. 2004.

Vol. 3336: D. Karagiannis, U. Reimer (Eds.), Practical Aspects of Knowledge Management. X, 523 pages. 2004.

Vol. 3327: Y. Shi, W. Xu, Z. Chen (Eds.), Data Mining and Knowledge Management. XIII, 263 pages. 2005.

Vol. 3315: C. Lemaître, C.A. Reyes, J.A. González (Eds.), Advances in Artificial Intelligence – IBERAMIA 2004. XX, 987 pages. 2004.

Vol. 3303: J.A. López, E. Benfenati, W. Dubitzky (Eds.), Knowledge Exploration in Life Science Informatics. X, 249 pages. 2004.

Vol. 3275: P. Perner (Ed.), Advances in Data Mining. VIII, 173 pages. 2004.

Vol. 3265: R.E. Frederking, K.B. Taylor (Eds.), Machine Translation: From Real Users to Research. XI, 392 pages. 2004.

Vol. 3264: G. Paliouras, Y. Sakakibara (Eds.), Grammatical Inference: Algorithms and Applications. XI, 291 pages. 2004.

Vol. 3259: J. Dix, J. Leite (Eds.), Computational Logic in Multi-Agent Systems. XII, 251 pages. 2004.

Vol. 3257: E. Motta, N.R. Shadbolt, A. Stutt, N. Gibbins (Eds.), Engineering Knowledge in the Age of the Semantic Web. XVII, 517 pages. 2004.

Vol. 3249: B. Buchberger, J.A. Campbell (Eds.), Artificial Intelligence and Symbolic Computation. X, 285 pages. 2004.

Vol. 3248: K.-Y. Su, J. Tsujii, J.-H. Lee, O.Y. Kwong (Eds.), Natural Language Processing – IJCNLP 2004. XVIII, 817 pages. 2005.

Vol. 3245: E. Suzuki, S. Arikawa (Eds.), Discovery Science. XIV, 430 pages. 2004.

Vol. 3244: S. Ben-David, J. Case, A. Maruoka (Eds.), Algorithmic Learning Theory. XIV, 505 pages. 2004.

Vol. 3238: S. Biundo, T. Frühwirth, G. Palm (Eds.), KI 2004: Advances in Artificial Intelligence. XI, 467 pages. 2004.

Vol. 3230: J.L. Vicedo, P. Martínez-Barco, R. Muñoz, M. Saiz Noeda (Eds.), Advances in Natural Language Processing. XII, 488 pages. 2004.

Vol. 3229: J.J. Alferes, J. Leite (Eds.), Logics in Artificial Intelligence. XIV, 744 pages. 2004.

Vol. 3228: M.G. Hinchey, J.L. Rash, W.F. Truszkowski, C.A. Rouff (Eds.), Formal Approaches to Agent-Based Systems. VIII, 290 pages. 2004.

Vol. 3215: M.G. Negoita, R.J. Howlett, L.C. Jain (Eds.), Knowledge-Based Intelligent Information and Engineering Systems, Part III. LVII, 906 pages. 2004.

Vol. 3214: M.G.. Negoita, R.J. Howlett, L.C. Jain (Eds.), Knowledge-Based Intelligent Information and Engineering Systems, Part II. LVIII, 1302 pages. 2004.

Vol. 3213: M.G.. Negoita, R.J. Howlett, L.C. Jain (Eds.), Knowledge-Based Intelligent Information and Engineering Systems, Part I. LVIII, 1280 pages. 2004.

Vol. 3209: B. Berendt, A. Hotho, D. Mladenic, M. van Someren, M. Spiliopoulou, G. Stumme (Eds.), Web Mining: From Web to Semantic Web. IX, 201 pages. 2004.

Vol. 3206: P. Sojka, I. Kopecek, K. Pala (Eds.), Text, Speech and Dialogue. XIII, 667 pages. 2004.

Vol. 3202: J.-F. Boulicaut, F. Esposito, F. Giannotti, D. Pedreschi (Eds.), Knowledge Discovery in Databases: PKDD 2004. XIX, 560 pages. 2004.

Vol. 3201: J.-F. Boulicaut, F. Esposito, F. Giannotti, D. Pedreschi (Eds.), Machine Learning: ECML 2004. XVIII, 580 pages. 2004.

Vol. 3194: R. Camacho, R. King, A. Srinivasan (Eds.), Inductive Logic Programming. XI, 361 pages. 2004.

Vol. 3192: C. Bussler, D. Fensel (Eds.), Artificial Intelligence: Methodology, Systems, and Applications. XIII, 522 pages. 2004.

Vol. 3191: M. Klusch, S. Ossowski, V. Kashyap, R. Unland (Eds.), Cooperative Information Agents VIII. XI, 303 pages. 2004.

Vol. 3187: G. Lindemann, J. Denzinger, I.J. Timm, R. Unland (Eds.), Multiagent System Technologies. XIII, 341 pages. 2004.

Vol. 3176: O. Bousquet, U. von Luxburg, G. Rätsch (Eds.), Advanced Lectures on Machine Learning. IX, 241 pages. 2004.

Vol. 3171: A.L.C. Bazzan, S. Labidi (Eds.), Advances in Artificial Intelligence – SBIA 2004. XVII, 548 pages. 2004.

Vol. 3159: U. Visser, Intelligent Information Integration for the Semantic Web. XIV, 150 pages. 2004.

Vol. 3157: C. Zhang, H. W. Guesgen, W.K. Yeap (Eds.), PRICAI 2004: Trends in Artificial Intelligence. XX, 1023 pages. 2004.

Vol. 3155: P. Funk, P.A. González Calero (Eds.), Advances in Case-Based Reasoning. XIII, 822 pages. 2004.

Vol. 3139: F. Iida, R. Pfeifer, L. Steels, Y. Kuniyoshi (Eds.), Embodied Artificial Intelligence. IX, 331 pages. 2004.

Vol. 3131: V. Torra, Y. Narukawa (Eds.), Modeling Decisions for Artificial Intelligence. XI, 327 pages. 2004.

Vol. 3127: K.E. Wolff, H.D. Pfeiffer, H.S. Delugach (Eds.), Conceptual Structures at Work. XI, 403 pages. 2004.

Vol. 3123: A. Belz, R. Evans, P. Piwek (Eds.), Natural Language Generation. X, 219 pages. 2004.

Vol. 3120: J. Shawe-Taylor, Y. Singer (Eds.), Learning Theory. X, 648 pages. 2004.

Vol. 3097: D. Basin, M. Rusinowitch (Eds.), Automated Reasoning. XII, 493 pages. 2004.

Vol. 3071: A. Omicini, P. Petta, J. Pitt (Eds.), Engineering Societies in the Agents World. XIII, 409 pages. 2004.

Vol. 3070: L. Rutkowski, J. Siekmann, R. Tadeusiewicz, L.A. Zadeh (Eds.), Artificial Intelligence and Soft Computing - ICAISC 2004. XXV, 1208 pages. 2004.

Vol. 3068: E. André, L. Dybkjær, W. Minker, P. Heisterkamp (Eds.), Affective Dialogue Systems. XII, 324 pages. 2004.

Vol. 3067: M. Dastani, J. Dix, A. El Fallah-Seghrouchni (Eds.), Programming Multi-Agent Systems. X, 221 pages. 2004.

Vol. 3066: S. Tsumoto, R. Słowiński, J. Komorowski, J.W. Grzymała-Busse (Eds.), Rough Sets and Current Trends in Computing. XX, 853 pages. 2004.

Vol. 3065: A. Lomuscio, D. Nute (Eds.), Deontic Logic in Computer Science. X, 275 pages. 2004.

Vol. 3060: A.Y. Tawfik, S.D. Goodwin (Eds.), Advances in Artificial Intelligence. XIII, 582 pages. 2004.

Vol. 3056: H. Dai, R. Srikant, C. Zhang (Eds.), Advances in Knowledge Discovery and Data Mining. XIX, 713 pages. 2004.

Vol. 3055: H. Christiansen, M.-S. Hacid, T. Andreasen, H.L. Larsen (Eds.), Flexible Query Answering Systems. X, 500 pages. 2004.

Vol. 3048: P. Faratin, D.C. Parkes, J.A. Rodríguez-Aguilar, W.E. Walsh (Eds.), Agent-Mediated Electronic Commerce V. XI, 155 pages. 2004.

Vol. 3040: R. Conejo, M. Urretavizcaya, J.-L. Pérez-dela-Cruz (Eds.), Current Topics in Artificial Intelligence. XIV, 689 pages. 2004.

Vol. 3035: M.A. Wimmer (Ed.), Knowledge Management in Electronic Government. XII, 326 pages. 2004.

Vol. 3034: J. Favela, E. Menasalvas, E. Chávez (Eds.), Advances in Web Intelligence. XIII, 227 pages. 2004.

Vol. 3030: P. Giorgini, B. Henderson-Sellers, M. Winikoff (Eds.), Agent-Oriented Information Systems. XIV, 207 pages. 2004.

Vol. 3029: B. Orchard, C. Yang, M. Ali (Eds.), Innovations in Applied Artificial Intelligence. XXI, 1272 pages. 2004.

Vol. 3025: G.A. Vouros, T. Panayiotopoulos (Eds.), Methods and Applications of Artificial Intelligence. XV, 546 pages. 2004.

Vol. 3020: D. Polani, B. Browning, A. Bonarini, K. Yoshida (Eds.), RoboCup 2003: Robot Soccer World Cup VII. XVI, 767 pages. 2004.

Vol. 3012: K. Kurumatani, S.-H. Chen, A. Ohuchi (Eds.), Multi-Agents for Mass User Support. X, 217 pages. 2004.

Vol. 3010: K.R. Apt, F. Fages, F. Rossi, P. Szeredi, J. Váncza (Eds.), Recent Advances in Constraints. VIII, 285 pages. 2004.

Vol. 2990: J. Leite, A. Omicini, L. Sterling, P. Torroni (Eds.), Declarative Agent Languages and Technologies. XII, 281 pages. 2004.

Vol. 2980: A. Blackwell, K. Marriott, A. Shimojima (Eds.), Diagrammatic Representation and Inference. XV, 448 pages. 2004.

Vol. 2977: G. Di Marzo Serugendo, A. Karageorgos, O.F. Rana, F. Zambonelli (Eds.), Engineering Self-Organising Systems. X, 299 pages. 2004.

Vol. 2972: R. Monroy, G. Arroyo-Figueroa, L.E. Sucar, H. Sossa (Eds.), MICAI 2004: Advances in Artificial Intelligence. XVII, 923 pages. 2004.

Vol. 2969: M. Nickles, M. Rovatsos, G. Weiss (Eds.), Agents and Computational Autonomy. X, 275 pages. 2004.

Vol. 2961: P. Eklund (Ed.), Concept Lattices. IX, 411 pages. 2004.

Vol. 2953: K. Konrad, Model Generation for Natural Language Interpretation and Analysis. XIII, 166 pages. 2004.

Vol. 2934: G. Lindemann, D. Moldt, M. Paolucci (Eds.), Regulated Agent-Based Social Systems. X, 301 pages. 2004.

Vol. 2930: F. Winkler (Ed.), Automated Deduction in Geometry. VII, 231 pages. 2004.

Vol. 2926: L. van Elst, V. Dignum, A. Abecker (Eds.), Agent-Mediated Knowledge Management. XI, 428 pages. 2004.